India

a travel survival kit

Geoff Crowther

Hugh Finlay

Prakash A Raj

Tony Wheeler

India - a travel survival kit
  4th edition

Published by
  Lonely Planet Publications
  Head Office: PO Box 617, Hawthorn, Victoria 3122, Australia
  US Office: PO Box 2001A, Berkeley, CA 94702, USA

Printed by
  Colorcraft Ltd, Hong Kong

Photographs by
  Geoff Crowther (GC), Richard Everist, Hugh Finlay (HF), Linda Henderson,
  Susan Mitra (SM), Paul Slaughter (PS), Tony Wheeler (TW)
  Front cover: Safdarjang's Tomb, New Delhi (PS), The Image Bank
  Back cover: The ghats, Varanasi (HF)

Cartoons by
  Tony Jenkins

First published
  October 1981

This edition
  June 1990

Although the author and publisher have tried to make the information as
accurate as possible, they accept no responsibility for any loss, injury or
inconvenience sustained by any person using this book.

National Library of Australia Cataloguing in Publication Data

Crowther, Geoff, 1944– .
  India, a travel survival kit.

  4th ed.
  Includes index.
  ISBN 0 86442 081 1.

  1. India – Description and travel – 1981 – –
  Guide-books. I. Raj, Prakash A., 1943– . II. Wheeler,
  Tony, 1946– . III. Title.

915.40452

text © Geoff Crowther, Prakash A Raj, Tony Wheeler, 1990
maps © Lonely Planet 1990
photos © photographers as indicated 1990

The Authors

Geoff Crowther Born in Yorkshire, England, Geoff started his travelling days as a teenage hitchhiker in search of the miraculous. After many short trips around Europe and two years in Asia and Africa, Geoff became involved with the London alternative information centre BIT in the late '60s. With Lonely Planet, Geoff has also written or collaborated on guides to Africa, South America, Malaysia, Korea and Taiwan, East Africa, Morocco, Algeria and Tunisia.

Geoff, Hyung Pun and their son Ashley have moved out of the banana shed into the house that Geoff (et al) built somewhere in the wilds of northern New South Wales. Geoff continues to pursue noxious weeds and brew mango wine.

Hugh Finlay After a failed career in engineering, Hugh set off around Australia in the mid '70s, working at everything from parking cars to diamond prospecting in outback South Australia. He spent three years travelling on three continents, all financed by Arab petrobucks earned working on an irrigation project in Saudi Arabia. He finally descended from the ozone in 1985 and joined Lonely Planet soon after.

Hugh has also written Lonely Planet's guide to *Jordan & Syria* and with Geoff has written guides to North Africa and Kenya.

Prakash A Raj Prakash was born in Nepal and studied for two years in Varanasi where he learnt to speak fluent Hindi. He spent five years at university in the USA and a year in the Netherlands. He travelled extensively in Europe and returned to Nepal where he worked on the Kathmandu English-language daily as a journalist and also for the Nepalese government's planning agency. Prakash has also worked for the OECD in Paris, the UN secretariat in New York and is now working for the UNHCR in Asia. Prakash has written several books about Nepal and his life there in both English and Nepali.

Tony Wheeler Tony was born in England but spent most of his younger years overseas including a lengthy spell in Pakistan, a shorter period in the West Indies and all his high school years in the USA. He then did an engineering degree in the UK, worked briefly as an automotive design engineer and went back to university and completed an MBA. He then got a bad case of the travel bug while on the Asian trail with his wife Maureen; they've been travelling, writing and publishing guidebooks ever since they set up Lonely Planet Publications in the mid-70s.

This Book

When the first edition of this book emerged in 1981 it was the biggest, most complicated and most expensive project we'd tackled at Lonely Planet. It began with an exploratory trip to south India by Tony and Maureen to see what information would be needed, how long it would take to gather and how big the book would be. The actual process took longer than estimated and the book turned out bigger.

The following year Geoff, Prakash, Tony and Maureen - all of whom had visited India on numerous occasions - returned to India and spent a combined total of about a year more-or-less nonstop travel. Back in Australia much additional work went into desk research and producing maps and illustrations. The end result exceeded all our hopes and expectations: it instantly became our best-selling guide, in Britain it won the Thomas Cook 'Guidebook of the Year' award and in India it became the most popular guide to the country; a book used even by Indians to explore their own country.

This Edition

For this fourth edition of *India - a travel survival kit* we once again returned to comprehensively update our work. This time around Tony took a break from India to work on other projects and Hugh Finlay stepped in to replace him. Hugh also handled the final integration of the three writers' contributions and completed much of the additional desk research back at Lonely Planet. The Jammu & Kashmir chapters were updated from Englishman Neil Tilbury's recent work for our *Kashmir, Ladakh & Zanskar* guidebook.

Apart from the writers, thanks must also go to a number of additional contributors including Australian Roman Wowk who wrote the motorcycling in India section, American Ann Sorrel who wrote the bicycle section and Englishman (but Australian resident) Mark Carter who wrote the 'gricing' section about India's wonderful railway steam engines. The cartoon is by Canadian Tony Jenkins and the original Garwhal Himal trek reports were written by Davindra Garbyal.

Last, but far from least, thanks to the many, many travellers who took the time to tell us where we went wrong or what additional items we should have mentioned. At Lonely Planet Sue Tan and Richard Nebesky face the monumental task of sorting through this constantly mounting pile of letters. There is a list of names at the back of the book.

Acknowledgements

Hugh would like to thank Abhijeet and Smita Roy in Bombay for their outstanding hospitality, and to Ramu and Laxmi Venkatraman who gave him the red carpet treatment in Madras.

Thanks to Richard Ellis in New Delhi for providing additional material on Punjab, and to Vyvyan Cayley for her account of an audience with His Holiness the Dalai Lama. David Bradley from Melbourne provided us with update material on Darjeeling, and Jon Murray, former LP editor, faxed us update information on the costs of cycling in India.

Lonely Planet Credits

Editors	Susan Mitra
	Diana Saad
	Alan Tiller
Cover design, design & illustrations	Valerie Tellini
Maps	Fiona Boyes
	Chris Lee-Ack
	Ralph Roob
	David Windle
Typesetting & illustrations	Ann Jeffree

Thanks also to Allison White, Chris Andrews and Mark Ellis for copy editing; Sharan Kaur for proofreading; David Windle for the copious map corrections; Margaret Jung for illustrations; and Sharon Wertheim for the index.

A Warning & a Request

Things change, prices go up, schedules change, good places go bad and bad ones go bankrupt - nothing stays the same. So if you find things better or worse, recently opened or long since closed, please write and tell us about it.

Between editions, when it is possible, we'll publish the most interesting letters and important information in a Stop Press section at the back of the book.

All information is greatly appreciated, and the best letters will receive a free copy of the next edition, or any other Lonely Planet book of your choice.

Contents

Introduction

India, it is often said, is not a country but a continent. From north to south and east to west, the people are different, the languages are different, the customs are different, the country is different. There are few countries on earth with the enormous variety that India has to offer. It's a place that somehow gets into your blood. Love it or hate it you can never ignore India. It's not an easy country to handle, and more than a few visitors are only too happy to finally get on an aircraft and fly away. Yet a year later they'll be hankering to get back.

It all comes back to that amazing variety – India is as vast as it is crowded, as luxurious as it is squalid. The plains are as flat and featureless as the Himalaya are high and spectacular, the food as terrible as it can be magnificent, the transport as exhilarating as it can be boring and uncomfortable. Nothing is ever quite the way you expect it to be.

India is far from the easiest country in the world to travel around. It can be hard going, the poverty will get you down, Indian bureaucracy would try the patience of even a Hindu saint, and the most experienced travellers find themselves at the end of their tempers at some point in India. Yet it's all worth it.

Very briefly, India is a triangle with the top formed by the mighty Himalayan mountain chain. Here you will find the intriguing Tibetan region of Ladakh and the astonishingly beautiful Himalayan areas of Kashmir, Himachal Pradesh, the Garwhal of Uttar Pradesh and the Darjeeling and Sikkim regions. South of this is the flat Ganges basin with the colourful and comparatively affluent Punjab to the north-west, the capital city, New Delhi, and important tourist attractions like Agra (with the Taj Mahal), Khajuraho, Varanasi and the holy Ganges. This plain reaches the sea at the northern end of the Bay of Bengal where you find teeming Calcutta, a city which seems to sum up all of India's enormous problems.

South of this northern plain the Deccan plateau rises. Here you will find cities that mirror the rise and fall of the Hindu and Muslim kingdoms, and the modern metropolis that their successors, the British, built at Bombay. India's story is one of many different kingdoms competing with each other, and this is never more clear than in places like Bijapur, Mandu, Golconda and other centres in central India. Finally, there is the steamy south where Muslim influence reached only fleetingly. Here Hinduism was least altered by outside influences and is at its most exuberant. The temple towns of the south are quite unlike those of the north and are superbly colourful.

Basically India is what you make of it and what you want it to be. If you want to see temples, there are temples in profusion with enough styles and types to confuse anybody. If it's history you want India has plenty of it; the forts, abandoned cities, ruins, battlefields and monuments all have their tales to tell. If you simply want to lie on the beach there are enough of those to satisfy the most avid sun worshipper. If walking and the open air is your thing then head for the trekking routes of the Himalaya, some of which are as wild and deserted as you could ask for. If you simply want to meet the real India you'll come face to face with it all the time – a trip on Indian trains and buses may not always be fun, but it certainly is an experience. India is not a place you simply and clinically 'see'; it's a total experience, an assault on the senses, a place you'll never forget.

Facts about the Country

HISTORY

India is the home of one of the world's 'great' civilisations – its social structure as it exists today can be traced back thousands of years. Empires of great size and complexity existed here far earlier than anything comparable in Europe. Yet India as an entity is a comparatively recent invention put together by the British. Even the mightiest of India's ancient civilisations did not encompass all of modern India, and today it is still as much a country of diversities as of unities. Few people in the Tamil-speaking south speak Hindi, the national language, for example. Beyond India's own history and development, its role as the birthplace of two of the world's great religions is enough to ensure its historical importance.

Indus Valley Civilisation

India's first major civilisation flourished for 1000 years from around 2500 BC along the Indus River valley in what is now Pakistan. Its great cities were Mohenjodaro and Harappa, where a civilisation of great complexity developed. The major city sites were only discovered during this century but other, lesser cities have been subsequently unearthed at sites like Lothal, near Ahmedabad in India.

The Indus Valley cities were ruled by a religious group rather than by kings, but the most interesting thing about them was their highly developed engineering. Four thousand years ago they already had a sophisticated drainage system and even an organised garbage collection! Despite the extensive excavations conducted at the sites, comparatively little is known about the development and eventual demise of this civilisation. Their script has still not been deciphered, nor is it known why such an advanced civilisation collapsed so quickly with the invasion of the Aryans.

Early Invasions

The early Aryan invasions were vague and disjointed, although the people of north India today are defined as Aryans and those of the south as Dravidians. The Aryans entered India from the north around 1500 BC and gradually spread across India from the Punjab and Sind (now in Pakistan) and along the Ganges towards Bengal. Under Darius (521-486 BC) the Punjab and Sind became part of the Persian Empire, but this was still peripheral to India itself.

Alexander the Great reached India in his epic march from Greece during 326 BC, but his troops refused to march further than the Beas River, the easternmost extent of the Persian Empire he had conquered, and he turned back without extending his power into India itself. The most lasting reminder of his appearance in the east was the development of Gandharan art, that strange mixture of Grecian artistic ideals with the new religious beliefs of Buddhism.

The Rise of Religions

Two great religions had their birth on the subcontinent – Buddhism and Hinduism. The Hindu religion is one of the oldest in the world. Even the priest-dominated Indus Valley civilisation bears many similarities to Hinduism. The great Hindu books are all thought to refer to actual historical events. The Vedas, written around 1500-1200 BC, tell of the victory of Brahma over Indra, the god of thunder and battle. This probably refers to the revival of Brahmanism (the predecessor of Hinduism) following the Aryan invasions.

Hinduism has had a series of declines and revivals, most recently during the past century, but the greatest challenge it has faced came from India's other great religion, Buddhism. First formulated

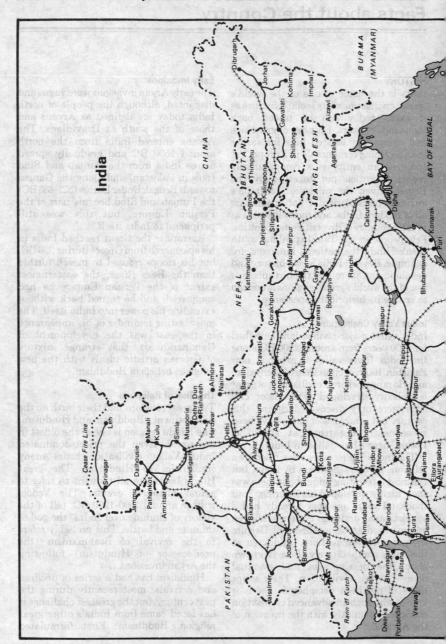

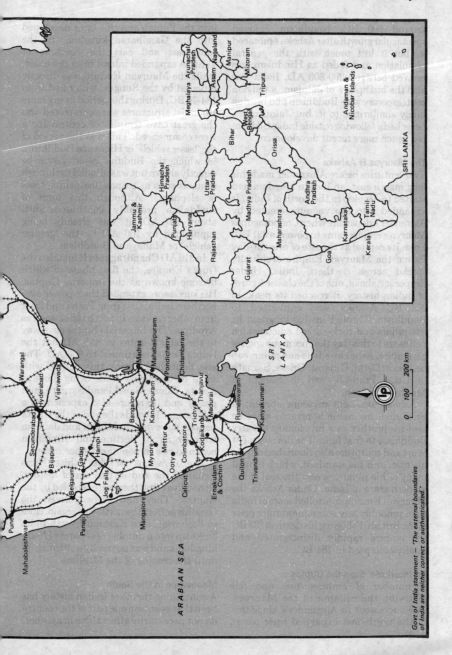

0 100 200 km

ARABIAN SEA

SRI LANKA

around 500 BC, Buddhism enjoyed spectacular growth after Ashoka embraced it, but it lost touch with the general population and faded as Hinduism was revived between 200-800 AD. India was also the birthplace of Jainism, a religion contemporary with Buddhism and bearing many similarities to it, but Jainism has never had a following outside India. Sikhism is a much more recent development.

The Mauryas & Ashoka

Two centuries before Alexander made his long march east, an Indian kingdom had started to develop in the north of India. It expanded into the vacuum created by Alexander's departure when Chandragupta Maurya's empire came to power in 321 BC. From its capital at the site of present-day Patna, the Mauryan Empire eventually spread across northern India. Under Emperor Ashoka, one of the classic figures of Indian history, it reached its peak. In 262 BC Ashoka was converted to Buddhism. Throughout his kingdom he left pillars and rock-carved edicts which delineate to this day the enormous span of his empire. Ashokan edicts and pillars can be seen in Delhi, Gujarat, Orissa, Sarnath in Uttar Pradesh, and at Sanchi in Madhya Pradesh.

Ashoka also sent missions abroad; in Sri Lanka his name is revered since he sent his brother as a missionary to carry Buddhism to that land. The development of art and sculpture also flourished during his rule, and his standard, which topped many of his pillars, is now the seal of the modern state of India. Under Ashoka the Mauryan Empire controlled more of India than probably any subsequent ruler prior to the British. Following his death in 232 BC the empire rapidly disintegrated and finally collapsed in 184 BC.

An Interlude, then the Guptas

A number of empires rose and fell following the collapse of the Mauryas. The successors to Alexander's kingdoms in the north-east expanded their power into the Punjab and this later developed into the Gandharan kingdom. In the south-east and east the Andhras or Telugus expanded inland from the coast, while the Mauryan Empire was directly replaced by the Sungas, who ruled from 184-70 BC. During this period many more Buddhist structures were completed and the great cave temples of central India were commenced. This was the period of the 'lesser vehicle' or Hinayana Buddhism, in which the Buddha could never be directly shown but was alluded to through symbols such as stupas, footprints, trees or elephants. Although this form of Buddhism probably continued until about 400 AD, it was already being supplanted by 100 AD by the 'greater vehicle' or Mahayana Buddhism.

In 319 AD Chandragupta II founded the Gupta Empire, the first phase of which became known as the Imperial Guptas. His successors extended their power over northern India, first from Patna and later from other capitals in north India, such as Ayodhya. The Imperial Guptas gave way to the later Guptas in 455 AD but the Gupta period continued to 606 AD. The arts flourished during this period, with some of the finest work being done at Ajanta, Ellora, Sanchi and Sarnath, and poetry and literature also experienced a golden age. Towards the end of the Gupta period, however, Buddhism and Jainism both began to decline and Hinduism began to rise in popularity once more.

The invasions of the White Huns signalled the end of this era of history, although at first they were repelled by the Guptas. They had earlier driven the Gandharas from the north-east region, close to Peshawar, into Kashmir. North India broke up into a number of separate Hindu kingdoms and was not really unified again until the coming of the Muslims.

Meanwhile in the South

A continuing theme of Indian history has been that events in one part of the country do not necessarily affect those in another.

The kingdoms that rose and fell in the north of the country generally had no influence or connection with those in the south. While Buddhism, and to a lesser extent Jainism, was displacing Hinduism in the centre and north of India, Hinduism continued to flourish in the south.

The south's prosperity was based upon its long-established trading links with other civilisations. The Egyptians and later the Romans both traded by sea with the south of India and, later still, strong links were formed with South-East Asia. For a time Buddhism and later Hinduism flourished in the Indonesian islands and the people of the region looked towards India as their cultural mentor. The *Ramayana*, that most famous of Hindu epics, is today told and retold in various forms in many South-East Asian countries. Outside influences also came to the south of India. In 52 AD St Thomas the Apostle is said to have arrived in Kerala and to this day there is a strong Christian influence in this region.

Great empires that rose in the south included the Cholas, Pandyas, Cheras, Chalukyas and Pallavas. The Chalukyas ruled mainly over the Deccan region of central India, although at times their power extended further north. With a capital at Badami in Karnataka, they ruled from 550-753 AD before falling to the Rashtrakutas – only to rise again in 972 and continue their rule through to 1190. Further south, the Pallavas pioneered Dravidian architecture with its exuberant, almost baroque style. They also carried Indian culture to Java in Indonesia, Thailand and Cambodia.

In 850 AD the Cholas rose to power and gradually superseded the Pallavas. They too were great builders, as their temple at Thanjavur indicates. They also carried their power overseas with raids into Ceylon and a long-running war with the Sumatran-based Srivijaya Empire. At times they actually controlled part of Sumatra and the Malay peninsula.

The First Muslim Invasions

While the Hindu kingdoms ruled in the south and Buddhism was rising and falling in the north, Muslim power was creeping towards India from the Middle East. In 622 AD Mohammed fled from Mecca and in 630 AD marched back in to start Islam's period of rapid expansion. Less than a century later there were raids to the Sind and even to Gujarat by Arabs carrying, as Mohammed had recommended, the Koran and the sword.

Muslim power first made itself strongly felt on the subcontinent with the raids of Mahmud of Ghazni. Today Ghazni is just a grubby little town between Kabul and Kandahar in Afghanistan, but from 1001 Mahmud conducted raids on virtually an annual basis. His army would descend upon India destroying infidel temples and carrying off everything of value that could be moved. In 1033, after his death, one of his successors actually took Varanasi; but in 1038 the Seljuk Turks, also expanding eastwards, took Ghazni and the raids into India soon ceased.

These early visits were no more than banditry and it was not until 1192 that Muslim power arrived on a permanent basis. In that year Mohammed of Ghori, who had been expanding his powers across the Punjab, broke into India and took Ajmer. The following year his general Qutb-ud-din took Varanasi and then Delhi and, after Mohammed of Ghori was killed in 1206, he became the first of the Sultans of Delhi. Within 20 years they had brought the whole of the Ganges basin under their control, but the Sultans of Delhi were never consistent in their powers. With each new ruler the kingdom grew or shrank depending on personal abilities.

In 1297, Ala-ud-din Khilji pushed the borders south into Gujarat; his general subsequently moved further south, but could not maintain the boundaries. In 1338, Mohammed Tughlaq decided to move his capital south from Delhi to Daulatabad, near Aurangabad in Maharashtra, but having marched most of Delhi's population south eventually had to return north. Soon after, the Bahmani kingdom arose here and the Delhi Sultanate began to retreat north, only to be further weakened when Timur made a devastating raid from Samarkand into India in 1398. From then on the power of this Muslim kingdom steadily contracted, until it was supplanted by another Muslim kingdom, the mighty Moghuls.

Meanwhile in the South (again)

Once again events in the south of India took a different path than in the north. Just as the Aryan invasions never reached the south, so the Muslim invasions failed to permanently affect events there. Between 1000-1300 AD, the Hoysala Empire, with centres at Belur, Halebid and Somnathpur, was at its peak but fell to a predatory raid by Mohammed Tughlaq in 1328, and then to the combined opposition of other Hindu kingdoms.

Two other great kingdoms developed in the north of modern-day Karnataka – one Muslim and one Hindu. With its beautiful capital at Hampi, the Hindu kingdom of Vijayanagar was founded in 1336. It was probably the strongest Hindu kingdom in India during the time the Muslim Sultans of Delhi were dominating the north of the country. Meanwhile, the Bahmani Muslim kingdom also developed, but in 1489 it split into five separate kingdoms at Berar, Ahmednagar, Bijapur, Golconda and Ahmedabad. In 1520 Vijayanagar took Bijapur, but in 1565 the kingdom's Muslim opponents combined to destroy Vijayanagar in the epic battle of Talikota. Later the Bahmani kingdoms were to fall to the Moghuls.

The Moghuls

Only Ashoka is as giant a figure in Indian history as the Moghul emperors. These larger-than-life individuals ushered in another Indian golden age and spread their control over India to an extent

rivalled only by Ashoka and the British. Their rise to power was rapid but the decline was equally quick; there were only six great Moghuls. After Aurangzeb the rest were emperors in name only.

The Moghuls did more than simply rule, they had a passion for building which resulted in some of the great buildings in India – Shah Jahan's magnificent Taj Mahal ranks as one of the greatest buildings in the world. Art and literature also flourished under the Moghuls and the magnificence of their court stunned early European visitors.

The six great Moghuls were:

Babur	1527-1530
Humayun	1530-1556
Akbar	1556-1605
Jehangir	1605-1627
Shah Jahan	1627-1658
Aurangzeb	1658-1707

Babur, a descendant of both Timur and Genghis Khan, marched into the Punjab from his capital at Kabul in Afghanistan and defeated the Sultan of Delhi at Panipat. This initial success did not totally destroy opposition to the Moghuls, and in 1540 the Moghul Empire came to an abrupt end when Sher Shah defeated Humayun, the second great Moghul. For 15 years Humayun lived in exile until he was able to return and regain his throne. By 1560 Akbar, his son and successor, who had come to the throne aged only 14, was able to claim effective and complete control of his empire.

Akbar was probably the greatest of the Moghuls, for he not only had the military ability required of a ruler in that time, but he was also a man of culture and wisdom with a sense of fairness. He saw, as previous Muslim rulers had not, that the number of Hindus in India was too great to simply subjugate them. Instead he integrated them into his empire and made use of many Hindu advisers, generals and administrators. Akbar also had a deep interest in religions and spent many hours in discussion with religious experts of all persuasions, including Christians. He eventually formulated a religion which combined the best points of all those he had studied.

Jehangir followed Akbar but devoted much of his reign to expressing his love for Kashmir and eventually died while en route there. His tomb is at Lahore in Pakistan. Shah Jahan, however, stuck much more to Agra and Delhi, and during his reign some of the most vivid and permanent reminders of the Moghuls' glory were constructed. Best known, of course, is the Taj Mahal, but that was only one of Shah Jahan's many magnificent buildings. Indeed some say that it was his passion for building that led to his downfall and that his son, Aurangzeb, deposed his father in part to put a halt to his architectural extravagances.

Aurangzeb was the last of the great Moghuls, and although he extended the empire's boundaries to their furthest he also ensured its downfall by failing to follow the ground rules Akbar had so successfully established. Akbar had combined his flair for magnificence and grandeur with a sense of fairness. He had kept his Hindu subjects 'on side' by including them in the governing process and respecting their beliefs.

In contrast, Aurangzeb was a penny pincher and a religious zealot. His belief in Islam was deep, austere and puritanical, with the result that he soon lost the trust and respect of his subjects and had to cope with revolts on all sides. In many parts of India stand mosques built by Aurangzeb on the foundations of temples destroyed due to his fanatical beliefs. With his death in 1707 the Moghul Empire rapidly disintegrated. Although there were 'Moghul emperors' right up to the time of the mutiny, when the British exiled the last one and executed his sons, they were emperors in name only. In sharp contrast to the magnificent tombs of his Moghul predecessors, Aurangzeb's tomb is a simple affair at Rauza, near Aurangabad.

The smaller states which followed on from the Moghul Empire did in some cases continue for a while. In the south, the viceroyalty in Hyderabad became one of the British-tolerated princely states and survived right through to independence.

Babur leading his Moghul army into battle

The nawabs of Oudh in north India ruled eccentrically, flamboyantly and badly until 1854 when the British 'retired' the last nawab. In Bengal, the Moghuls unwisely clashed with the British far earlier, and their rule was terminated by the Battle of Plassey in 1757.

The Marathas

Moghul power was not simply supplanted by another, greater power. It fell through a series of factors and to a number of other rulers. Not least of these were the Marathas. Throughout the Muslim period in the north of India there were still strong Hindu powers, most notably the Rajputs. Centred in Rajasthan, the Rajputs were a warrior caste with a strong and almost fanatical belief in the dictates of chivalry both in battle and in the conduct of state affairs. Their place in Indian history is much like that of the knights of medieval Europe. The Rajputs opposed every foreign incursion into their territory, but were never united or sufficiently organised to be able to deal with superior forces on a long-term basis. Not only that, but when not battling foreign oppression they squandered their energies fighting each other. This eventually led to them becoming vassal states of the Moghul Empire, but their prowess in battle was well recognised, and some of the best military men in the emperors' army were Rajputs.

The Marathas first rose to prominence with Shivaji, who took over his father's kingdom and between 1646 and 1680 performed feats of arms and heroism all over central India. Tales of his larger-than-life exploits are popular with wandering storytellers in small villages. He is a particular hero in Maharashtra, where many of his wildest exploits took place, but is also revered for two other things: as a lower-caste Sudra he showed that great leaders do not have to be Brahmins, and he demonstrated great abilities in confronting the Moghuls. At one time Shivaji was even captured by the

Emperor Shah Jahan

Moghuls and taken back to Agra but, naturally, he managed to escape and continue his adventures.

Shivaji's son was captured, blinded and executed by Aurangzeb. His grandson was not made of the same sturdy stuff, but the Maratha Empire continued under the Peshwas, hereditary government ministers who became the real rulers. They gradually took over more and more of the weakening Moghul Empire's powers, first by supplying troops and then by actually taking control of Moghul land.

When Nadir Shah from Persia sacked Delhi in 1739, the declining Moghuls were even further weakened, but the expansion of Maratha power came to an abrupt halt in 1761 at Panipat. There, where Babur had won the battle that established the Moghul Empire over 200 years earlier, the Marathas were defeated by Ahmad Shah Durani from Afghanistan. Their expansion to the west halted, they nevertheless consolidated their control over central India and their region known as Malwa. Soon, however, they were to fall to India's final great imperial power, the British.

Expansion of British Power

The British were not the first European power to arrive in India, nor were they the last to leave – both those honours go to the Portuguese. In 1498, Vasco da Gama arrived on the coast of modern-day Kerala, having sailed around the African Cape of Good Hope. Pioneering this route gave the Portuguese a century of uninterrupted monopoly over Indian trade with Europe. In 1510 they captured Goa, the Indian enclave they controlled right through to 1961, 14 years after the British had left.

In 1612, the British made their first permanent inroad into India when they established a trading post at Surat in Gujarat. In 1600, Queen Elizabeth I had granted a charter to a London trading company giving them a monopoly on British trade with India. For 250 years British power was exercised in India not by the government but by the East India Company which developed from this initial charter. British trading posts were established on the other coast at Madras in 1640, at Bombay in 1668 and at Calcutta in 1690. The British and Portuguese were not the only Europeans in India. The Dutch also had trading posts, and in 1672 the French established themselves at Pondicherry, an enclave they, like the Portuguese in Goa, would hold even after the British had finally departed.

Naturally Anglo-French enmity spread to India, and in 1746 the French took Madras only to hand it back in 1749. In subsequent years there was to be much intrigue between the imperial powers. If the British were involved in a struggle with one local ruler they could be certain the French would be backing him with arms, men or expertise. In 1756 Suraj-ud-daula, the Nawab of Bengal, attacked Calcutta and outraged Britain with the 'black hole of Calcutta' incident. A year later Robert Clive retook Calcutta and in the Battle of Plassey defeated Suraj-ud-daula and his French supporters, thus not only extending British power but also curtailing French influence.

India at this time was in a state of flux due to the power vacuum created by the disintegration of the Moghul Empire. The Marathas were the only real Indian power to step into this gap and they were more a group of local kingdoms who sometimes cooperated, sometimes did not, than a power in their own right. In the south, where Moghul influence had never been so great, the picture was confused by the strong British-French rivalries with one ruler consistently played off against another.

This was never clearer than in the series of Mysore Wars with that irritation to British power, Tipu Sultan. In the 4th Mysore War in 1789-99, Tipu was killed at Srirangapatnam and British power took another step forward, French influence another step back. The long-running British struggle with the Marathas was finally concluded in 1803, which left only the Punjab outside British control; that, too, came under British control in 1849 after the two Sikh Wars. Britain also took on the Nepalese, whom they defeated but did not annexe, and the Burmese, whom they did.

Rise & Fall of British India

By the early 19th century India was effectively under British control. In part this takeover had come about because of the vacuum left by the demise of the Moghuls, but the British also followed the rules Akbar had laid down so successfully. To them India was principally a place to make money, and the Indians' culture, beliefs and religions were left strictly alone. Indeed it was said the British didn't give a damn what religious beliefs a person held so long as they made a good cup of tea. Furthermore, the British had a disciplined, efficient army and astute political advisers. They followed the policy of divide and rule with great success and negotiated distinctly one-sided treaties giving them the right to intervene in local states if they were inefficiently run; 'inefficient' could be and was defined as the British saw fit.

Even under the British, India remained a patchwork of states, many of them nominally independent but actually under strong British influence. This policy of maintaining 'princely states' governed by maharajas, nawabs or whatever, continued right through to independence and was to cause a number of problems at that time. The British interest in trade and profit resulted in the expansion of iron and coal mining; the development of tea, coffee and cotton growing; the construction of the basis of today's vast Indian railways network; the commencement of irrigation projects which have today revolutionised agriculture; and other important and worthwhile developments.

In the sphere of government and law, Britain gave India a well-developed and smoothly functioning government and civil service structure. The fearsome love of bureaucracy which India also inherited from Britain may be a down side of that, but overall the country reached independence with a better organised, more efficient and less corrupt administrative system than most ex-colonial countries.

Britain also made some less helpful moves in India. Cheap textiles from the new manufacturing industry of Britain flooded into India, virtually crippling the local cottage industries. On one hand the British outlawed *sati*, the Hindu custom of burning the wife on her husband's funeral pyre, but on the other hand they encouraged the system of *zamindars*. These absentee landlords eased the burden of administrative and tax collection for the British, but contributed to an impoverished and landless peasantry in parts of India – a problem which in Bihar

and West Bengal is still chronic today. The British also instituted English as the local language of administration; in a country with so many different languages it still partially fulfils that function of nationwide communication today. Nevertheless many British kept themselves to some extent at 'arms length' from the Indians.

In 1857, less than a half century after Britain had taken firm control of India, they had their first serious setback. To this day the causes of the 'Indian Mutiny' are hard to unravel – it's even hard to define if it really was the 'War of Independence' by which it is referred to in India, or merely a mutiny. The causes were an administration which had been run down and other more specific cases. The dismissal of local rulers, inefficient and unpopular as they might have been, proved to be a flashpoint in certain areas but the main single cause was, believe it or not, bullets. A rumour, quite possibly true, leaked out that a new type of bullet issued to the troops, many of whom were Muslim, was greased with pig fat. A similar rumour developed that the bullets were actually greased with cow fat. Pigs, of course, are unclean to Muslims, and cows are holy to Hindus.

The British were slow to deny these rumours and even slower to prove that either they were incorrect or that changes had been made. The result was a loosely coordinated mutiny of the Indian battalions of the Bengal Army. Of the 74 battalions, seven (one of them Gurkhas) remained loyal, 20 were disarmed and the other 47 mutinied. The mutiny first broke out at Meerut, close to Delhi, and soon spread across north India. There were massacres and acts of senseless cruelty on both sides, long sieges, decisive victories and protracted struggles, but in the end the mutiny died out rather than coming to a conclusive finish. It never spread beyond the north of India, and although there were brilliant self-made leaders on the Indian side, there was never any real coordination or common aim.

The British made two moves with the conclusion of the mutiny. First, they wisely decided not to look for scapegoats or to exact official revenge, although revenge and looting had certainly taken place on an unofficial level. Second, the East India Company was wound up and administration of the country was belatedly handed over to the British government. The remainder of the century was the peak period for the empire on which 'the sun never set' and in which India was one of its brightest stars. Two parallel developments during the latter part of the 19th century gradually paved the way for the independent India of today. First, the British slowly began to hand over power and bring more people into the decision-making processes. Democratic systems began to be implemented in India although the British government retained overall control. In the civil service higher and higher posts were opened up for Indians and not simply retained for colonial administrators.

At the same time Hinduism began to go through another wholesale resurgence and adjustment. The Hindu religion is one of the world's oldest religions but once before, when it shrank before the growth of Buddhism, it had failed to keep in touch with its mass support. Once again it was realised that Hinduism had lost touch with the masses and required a complete shake-up to turn it away from its role as a religion for the priests and high-caste Brahmins. Reformers like Ram Mohan Roy, Ramakrishna and Swami Vivekananda pushed through sweeping changes in Hindu society and paved the way for the Hindu beliefs of today, beliefs which have enormous appeal to modern western society.

With the turn of the century, opposition to British rule began to take on a new light. The 'Congress' which had been established to give India a degree of self-rule now began to push for the real thing. Outside of the Congress more hot-blooded individuals pressed for independence by more violent means. Eventually the British mapped out a path towards independence similar to that pursued in Canada and Australia. However, WW I shelved these plans; the events in Turkey, a Muslim country, alienated many Indian

Anyone for tea?

Muslims. After the war the struggle was on in earnest and its leader was Mahatma Gandhi.

Gandhi & Passive Resistance

In 1915, Mohandas Gandhi returned from South Africa, where he had practised as a lawyer and devoted himself to righting the wrongs the country's many Indian settlers had to face. In India he soon turned his abilities to the question of independence, particularly after the massacre at Amritsar in 1919 when a British army contingent opened fire on an unarmed crowd of protesters. Gandhi, who subsequently became known as Mahatma, the 'great soul', adopted a policy of passive resistance or *satyagraha* to British rule. His central achievement was to change the level of the independence struggle from the middle class to the village. He led movements against the iniquitous salt tax and boycotts of British textiles, and for his efforts made a number of visits to British prisons.

Others involved in the struggle did not follow Gandhi's policy of noncooperation and nonviolence, and at times the battle was bitter and bloody. Nevertheless the Congress Party and Mahatma Gandhi were in the forefront, although it was not until after WW II that a conclusion was finally reached. By then independence was inevitable, as the war had dealt a death blow to colonialism and the myth of European superiority. Britain no longer had the power or the desire to maintain a vast empire, but within India a major problem had developed. The large Muslim minority had realised that an independent India would also be a Hindu-dominated India, and that despite Gandhi's fair-minded and even-handed approach others in the Congress Party would not be so willing to share power.

Independence

With the close of WW II it was clear that the European colonial era was over and that independence for India would have to

come soon, but how? Congress' refusal to deal with the Muslim League had rebounded on them with the Muslim demand for an independent Pakistan, to be carved out of India. The abrupt end of the war with the atomic bombing of Japan and the July 1945 Labour party victory in the British election made the search for a solution to the Indian problem imperative.

Elections within India revealed the obvious – the country was split on purely religious grounds with the Muslim League, led by Muhammad Ali Jinnah, speaking for the overwhelming majority of Muslims, and the Congress Party, led by Jawaharlal Nehru, commanding the Hindu population. Mahatma Gandhi remained the father figure for Congress but without an official role and, as events were to prove, his political influence was slipping.

'I will have India divided, or India destroyed', were Jinnah's words. This direct conflict with Congress' desire for an independent greater-India was the biggest stumbling block to the British grant of independence, but with each passing day the prospects for intercommunal strife and bloodshed increased. In early 1946, a British mission failed to bring the two sides together and the country slid increasingly towards civil war. A 'Direct Action Day', called by the Muslim League in August 1946, led to a slaughter of Hindus in Calcutta followed by reprisals against Muslims. Attempts to make the two sides see reason had no effect and in February 1947 the British government made a momentous decision. The current viceroy, Lord Wavell, would be replaced by Lord Louis Mountbatten and independence would come by June 1948.

Already the Punjab region of northern India was in a state of chaos and the Bengal region in the east was close to it. The new viceroy made a last-ditch attempt to convince the rival factions that a united India was a more sensible proposition, but they – Jinnah in particular – remained intransigent and the reluctant decision was made to divide the country. Only Gandhi stood firmly against the division, preferring the possibility of a civil war to the chaos he so rightly expected.

As in so many other parts of the world, neatly slicing the country in two proved to be an impossible task. Although some areas were clearly Hindu or Muslim, others had very evenly mixed populations, and still others remained isolated 'islands' of Muslims surrounded by Hindu regions no matter how the country was divided. The complete impossibility of dividing all the Muslims from all the Hindus is illustrated by the fact that after partition India was still the third largest Muslim country in the world - only Indonesia and Pakistan had greater populations of Muslims. Even today India has a greater Muslim population than any of the Arab countries, or Turkey, or Iran.

Worse, the two overwhelmingly Muslim regions were on the exact opposite sides of the country - Pakistan would inevitably have an eastern and western half divided by a hostile India. The instability of this arrangement was self-evident, but it took 25 years before the predestined split came and East Pakistan became Bangladesh.

Other problems showed up only after independence was achieved. Pakistan was painfully short of the administrators and clerical workers with which India is so well endowed; these were occupations simply not followed by many Muslims. Many other occupations, such as money lenders, were purely Hindu callings and the unfortunate untouchables did the dirty work not only for higher-caste Hindus but also for the Muslims.

Mountbatten decided to follow a breakneck pace to independence and announced that it would come on 14 August 1947. Historians have wondered ever since if much bloodshed might not have been averted if the impetuous and egotistical Mountbatten had not decided on such a hasty process.

Once the decision had been made to divide the country there were countless administrative decisions to be made, the most important being the actual location of the dividing line. Since a locally adjudicated dividing line was certain to bring recriminations from either side, an independent British referee was given the odious task of drawing the line, knowing that its effects would be disastrous for countless people. The most difficult decisions had to be made in Bengal and the Punjab. In Bengal, Calcutta, with its Hindu majority, port facilities and jute mills, was divided from East Bengal, with a Muslim majority, jute production as its major industry, yet not a single jute mill for its processing, or a suitable port for its export.

The problem was far worse in the Punjab, where intercommunal antagonisms were already running at a fever pitch. Here one of the most fertile and affluent regions of the country had large percentages of Muslims (55%) and Hindus (30%), and a substantial number of India's Sikhs. The Punjab contained all the ingredients for an epic disaster, and with the announcement of the dividing line, only days after independence, the resulting bloodshed was even worse than expected. Huge exchanges of population took place as Muslims moved to Pakistan and Hindus to India. The dividing line cut neatly between the Punjab's two major cities - Lahore and Amritsar. Prior to independence Lahore's population of 1.2 million included approximately 500,000 Hindus and 100,000 Sikhs. When the dust had finally settled Lahore had a Hindu and Sikh population of only 1000.

For months the greatest exodus in human history took place east and west across the Punjab. Trainloads of Muslims, fleeing westward, would be held up and slaughtered by Hindu and Sikh mobs. Hindus and Sikhs fleeing to the east would suffer the same fate. The army force sent to maintain order proved totally inadequate and at times all too ready to join the partisan carnage. By the time the

Punjab chaos had run its course, over 10 million people had changed sides and even the most conservative estimates calculate that 250,000 people had lost their lives. The figure may well have been over half a million. An additional million people changed sides in Bengal, mainly Hindus since few Muslims migrated from West Bengal to East Pakistan.

The outright division of the Punjab was not to be the only excuse for carnage. Throughout the British era India had retained many 'princely states', and incorporating these into independent India and Pakistan proved to be a considerable headache. Guarantees of a substantial measure of independence convinced most of them to opt for inclusion into the new countries, but at the time of independence there were still three holdouts.

One was Kashmir, predominantly Muslim but with a Hindu maharaja. In October the Maharaja had still not opted for India or Pakistan and a ragtag Pathan army crossed the border from Pakistan, intent on racing to Srinagar and annexing Kashmir without provoking a real India-Pakistan conflict. Unfortunately for the Pakistanis, the Pathans had been inspired to this little invasion by the promise of plunder, and they did so much plundering on the way that India had time to rush troops to Srinagar and prevent the town's capture. The indecisive Maharaja finally opted for India, a brief India-Pakistan war took place, the UN eventually stepped in and Kashmir has remained a central cause for disagreement between the two countries ever since. With its overwhelming Muslim majority and its geographic links to Pakistan, many people are inclined to support Pakistan's claims to the region. But Kashmir is Kashmir and India has consistently evaded a promised plebiscite. India and Pakistan are divided in this region by a demarcation line, and to this day neither side agrees on an official border.

The final stages of independence had one last tragedy to be played out. On 30 January 1948 Gandhi, deeply disheartened by partition and the subsequent bloodshed, was assassinated by a Hindu fanatic.

Independent India

Since independence, India has made enormous strides but faced enormous problems. The mere fact that India has not, like so many third world countries, bowed to dictatorships, military rule or foreign invasion is a testament to the basic strength of the country's government and institutions. Economically it has made major steps forward in improving agricultural output, and its industries have expanded to the stage where India is one of the world's top 10 industrial powers.

Jawaharlal Nehru, India's first prime minister, tried to follow a strict policy of nonalignment, although India has maintained generally excellent relations with its former coloniser – a fact which has caused some little annoyance to the critics of imperialism. Despite this nonaligned policy India has moved towards the USSR – partially because of conflicts with China and partially because of US support for archenemy Pakistan. Since independence, Gandhi's belief in peaceful neutrality has on a number of occasions been thrown out of the window. Three times India has clashed with Pakistan (1948, 1965 and 1971) over bitter disputes concerning Kashmir and Bangladesh. Border wars have been fought with China, and India still disputes the area of Aksai Chin, Ladakh, which China seized in 1962.

These outside events have taken the attention from India's often serious internal problems. As in any third world country, population growth holds the potential for ultimate disaster. India weathered the first energy crisis of the early '70s remarkably well and no better advertisement could be found for the green revolution.

Indira's India

Politically India's major problem since independence has been the personality cult that has developed with its leaders. There have been three main prime ministers – Nehru, his daughter Indira Gandhi (no relation to the Mahatma) and her son Rajiv Gandhi. Having won election in 1966, Indira Gandhi faced serious opposition and unrest in 1975 which she countered by declaring a state of emergency, a situation which in many other countries might quickly have become a dictatorship.

During the 'emergency' a mixed bag of good and bad policies were followed. Freed of many parliamentary constraints, Indira was able to control inflation remarkably well, boost the economy and decisively increase efficiency. On the negative side political opponents often found themselves behind bars, India's judicial system was turned into a puppet theatre, the press was fettered and there was more than a hint of personal aggrandisement, as in the disastrous Sanjay Gandhi 'people's car' plan. An equally disastrous programme of virtually forced sterilisations, also masterminded by her son Sanjay, caused much anger. Despite murmurings of discontent Indira decided that the people were behind her and in 1977 called a general election to give credence to her emergency powers. Sanjay had counselled against holding the election and his opinion proved to be a wise one, because Indira and her Congress Party were bundled out of power in favour of the hastily assembled Janata Peoples' Party.

Janata, however, was a device with only one function, defeating Indira. Once it had won, it had no other cohesive function and its leader, Moraji Desai, seemed more interested in protecting cows, banning alcohol and getting his daily glass of urine than coming to grips with the country's problems. With inflation soaring, unrest rising and the economy stumbling, nobody was surprised when Janata fell apart in late 1979 and the 1980 election brought Indira back to power with a larger majority than ever.

India in the 80s

Mrs Gandhi's political touch seemed to have faded as she grappled unsuccessfully with communal unrest in several areas, violent attacks on untouchables, numerous cases of police brutality and corruption, and the upheavals in the north-east and the Punjab. Then her son and political heir, the none-too-popular Sanjay, was killed in a light aircraft accident, and in 1984 Mrs Gandhi was assassinated by her Sikh bodyguards. Her son Rajiv, an Indian Airlines pilot until his younger brother's death, had quickly become the next heir to the throne, and he was soon swept into power with an overwhelming majority and enormous popular support.

The Nehru family has supplied prime ministers to India for three generations and the latest, Rajiv Gandhi, brought new and pragmatic policies to the country. Foreign investment and modern technology were encouraged, import restrictions eased and many new industries set up. The rise of the Indian middle class under Rajiv was also very noticeable – the number of cars in India has grown enormously in the last few years. Whether these policies were necessarily in the best interests of India is, however, an open question. Furthermore, the unrest in the Punjab continued to burn and at the other end of the country the turmoil in neighbouring Sri Lanka caused further difficulties. Rajiv was unable to stop Tamil support for the Sri Lankan Tamils because he needed the support of the state government of Tamil Nadu, home for most of India's Tamils. Nor could he tell the Sri Lankan government how to clean up their mess when the Punjab was in a similar mess.

Despite all these problems, it's worth remembering that of all the people in the world who live in what we know as democratic societies, nearly 50% of them are

Indians; as 1977 indicated, it's a democratic society with teeth. Furthermore, India, despite its population problems and vast poverty, manages to do something neither the USSR or China can manage: feed its own people without importing food. Unfortunately the food surplus isn't always where it should be (it stacks up in the Punjab while other areas go hungry) but those old tales of famine and starvation are, hopefully, a thing of the past – at least at the present population levels.

India Today

After the November 1989 elections, Rajiv Gandhi's Congress Party, although the largest single party in Parliament, was unable to form a government in its own right. The new National Front Government, made up of five parties including the Hindu fundamentalists' Bharatiya Janata Party, is headed by Prime Minister V P Singh, a former cabinet minister under Rajiv Gandhi. This minority coalition focused their election campaign on corruption and Rajiv Gandhi's inept leadership. Conflicts between the National Front's extreme right and left supporting parties is the biggest threat to its survival.

GEOGRAPHY

India has a total area of 3,287,782 square km. The north of the country is decisively bordered by the long sweep of the Himalaya, the highest mountains on earth. They run in a south-east to north-west direction, separating India from China. Bhutan in the east and Nepal in the centre actually lie along the Himalaya, as does Darjeeling, the northern part of Uttar Pradesh, Himachal Pradesh and Jammu & Kashmir.

The Himalaya are not a single mountain range but a series of ranges with beautiful valleys wedged between them. The Kulu Valley in Himachal Pradesh and the Vale of Kashmir in Jammu & Kashmir are both Himalayan valleys, as is the Kathmandu Valley in Nepal. Kanchenjunga (8598 metres) is the

highest mountain in India although until Sikkim (and Kanchenjunga) were absorbed into India that honour went to Nanda Devi (7818 metres). Beyond the Himalaya stretches the high, dry and barren Tibetan plateau; in Ladakh a small part of this plateau actually lies within India's boundaries.

The final range of the Himalaya, the Siwalik Hills, ends abruptly in the great northern plains of India. In complete contrast to the soaring mountain peaks, the northern plain is oppressively flat and slopes so gradually that all the way from Delhi to the Bay of Bengal it drops only 200 metres. The mighty Ganges River, which has its source in the Himalaya, drains a large part of the northern plain and is the major river of India. The Brahmaputra, flowing down from the north-east of the country, is the other major river of the north. In the north-west the Indus River starts out flowing through Ladakh in India but soon dives off into Pakistani territory and is the most important river of that nation.

South of the northern plains the land rises up into the high plateau known as the Deccan. The Deccan Plateau is bordered on both sides by ranges of hills which parallel the coast to the east and west. The Western Ghats are higher and have a wider coastal strip than the Eastern Ghats. The two ranges meet in the extreme south in the Nilgiri Hills. The southern hill stations are in these hills – Matheran and Mahabaleshwar near Bombay in the Western Ghats, Ooty in the extreme south in the Nilgiri Hills. The major rivers of the south are the Godavari and the Krishna. Both rise on the eastern slope of the Western Ghats and flow across the Deccan into the sea on the east coast.

The eastern boundary of India is also defined by ranges of hills, foothills of the Himalaya, which separate the country from Burma (Myanmar). In this north-eastern region India bends right around Bangladesh, a low-lying country at the

delta of the Ganges, and almost meets the sea to totally surround it.

On the western side, India is separated from Pakistan by three distinct regions. In the north, in the disputed area of Kashmir, the Himalaya forms the boundary between the two countries. The Himalaya drops down to the plains of the Punjab, which then merge into the Great Indian Thar Desert. In the western part of Rajasthan this is an area of great natural beauty and extreme barrenness. Finally, the Indian state of Gujarat is separated from the Sind in Pakistan by the unusual marshland known as the Rann of Kutch. In the dry season the Rann dries out, leaving isolated salt islands on an expansive plain; in the wet season it floods over to become a vast inland sea.

CLIMATE

India is so vast that the climatic conditions in the far north have little relation to that of the extreme south. While the heat is building up to breaking point on the plains, the people of Ladakh will still be waiting for the snow to melt on the high passes. Basically India has a three-season year – the hot, the wet and the cool.

The Hot

The heat starts to build up on the plains of India from around February, and by April or May it becomes unbearable. In central India temperatures of 45°C and above are commonplace. It's dry and dusty and everything is seen through a haze. From the air the country looks parched and barren, but usually all you can see below is a blanket of hazy brown from all the dust in the atmosphere. Later in May the first signs of the monsoon are seen – short sharp rainstorms, violent electric storms, dust storms that turn day into night and cover everything with a film of dust. The heat towards the end of the hot season is like a hammer blow; you feel listless and tired and tempers are short. It's said to be the time of year when murders and suicides take place!

The hot season is the time to leave the plains, which are at their worst, and retreat to the hills. Kashmir comes into its own and all the Himalayan hill stations are at their best. The hill stations further south – Mt Abu in Rajasthan, Matheran in Maharashtra, Ooty and Kodaikanal in Tamil Nadu – are generally not high enough to be really cool but they are better than being down at sea level. By early June the snow on the passes into Ladakh should be melted and the road will be open. You can also get into Keylong from Manali in Himachal Pradesh. This is the best trekking season in Kashmir and Ladakh.

The Wet

When the monsoon finally arrives it's a great relief. As the chart (page 26) indicates it doesn't arrive in one day. After a period of advance warning the rain comes in steadily, starting around 1 June in the extreme south and sweeping north to cover the whole country by early July. The monsoon doesn't really cool things off; at first you simply trade the hot, dry, dusty

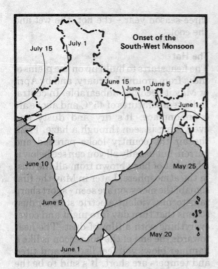

weather for hot, humid, muddy conditions. Even so it's a great relief, not least for farmers who now have the busiest time of year ahead of them as they prepare their fields for the rice planting. During the monsoon it doesn't simply rain solidly all day every day; it certainly rains every day but the water tends to come down in buckets for a while and then the sun comes out and it's quite pleasant.

Some places are at their best during the monsoon - like Rajasthan with its many palaces on lakes. In Nepal, the monsoon is a very bad time to trek, yet in the north-west Indian Himalayan regions it is a good time to trek. In Nepal, the trekking season commences when the monsoon finishes, but the regions of Himachal Pradesh, Kashmir and Ladakh in India are further north and the weather is too cold for trekking.

Although the monsoon brings life to India it also brings its share of death. Every year there are many destructive floods and thousands of people are made homeless. Rivers rise and sweep away road and railway lines and many flight schedules are disrupted. Travel can

definitely be more difficult during the monsoon.

The Cool

Finally around October the monsoon ends, and this is probably the best time of year in India. Everything is still green and lush but you don't get rained on daily. The temperatures are delightful, not too hot and not too cool. The air is clear in the Himalaya, and the mountains are clearly visible, at least early in the day. As the cool rolls on it actually becomes cold at night in the north. Delhi and other northern cities become quite crisp at night in December and January.

In the far north it's more than just a little chilly, it's downright cold. The passes into Ladakh are once more snowed in and few people want to be staying on a houseboat on Dal Lake in Kashmir when the lake is frozen over. Snow does bring India's small skiing industry into its own, however, so Kashmir has a winter season too. In the far south, where it never really gets less than hot, the temperatures do become comfortably warm rather than hot. Then around February the temperatures

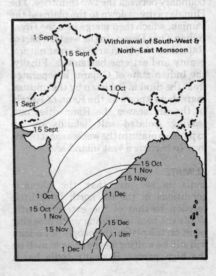

		Jan	Feb	Mar	Apr	May	June	July	Aug	Sept	Oct	Nov	Dec
Agra	min °C	7	10	16	22	27	30	27	26	24	19	12	8
	max °C	22	26	32	38	42	41	35	33	33	33	30	24
	rain mm	16	9	11	5	10	60	210	263	152	24	2	4
Bangalore	min °C	15	17	19	21	21	20	19	19	19	19	17	15
	max °C	27	30	32	32	33	29	27	27	28	28	26	26
	rain mm	3	10	6	46	117	80	117	147	143	185	54	16
Bombay	min °C	19	20	23	25	27	26	25	25	25	25	23	21
	max °C	29	30	31	32	33	32	30	30	30	32	32	31
	rain mm	2	1	–	3	16	520	710	439	297	88	21	2
Calcutta	min °C	14	17	22	25	27	27	26	26	26	24	18	14
	max °C	27	30	34	36	36	34	32	32	32	32	30	27
	rain mm	14	24	27	43	121	259	301	306	290	160	35	3
Cochin	min °C	23	24	26	26	26	24	24	24	24	24	24	24
	max °C	31	31	31	31	31	29	28	28	28	29	30	30
	rain mm	10	34	50	140	364	756	572	386	235	333	184	37
Darjeeling	min °C	3	4	8	11	13	15	15	15	15	12	7	4
	max °C	9	11	15	18	19	19	20	20	20	19	15	12
	rain mm	22	27	52	109	187	522	713	573	419	116	14	5
Delhi	min °C	7	10	15	21	27	29	27	26	25	19	12	8
	max °C	21	24	30	36	41	40	35	34	34	33	30	23
	rain mm	25	22	17	7	8	65	211	173	150	31	1	5
Goa	min °C	19	20	23	25	27	25	24	24	24	23	22	21
	max °C	31	32	32	33	33	31	29	29	29	31	33	33
	rain mm	2	–	4	17	18	500	892	341	277	122	20	37
Jaisalmer	min °C	8	11	17	21	26	27	27	26	25	20	13	9
	max °C	24	28	32	38	42	41	38	36	36	36	31	26
	rain mm	2	1	3	2	5	7	90	86	14	1	5	2
Leh	min °C	-14	-12	-6	-1	3	7	10	10	5	-1	-7	-11
	max °C	-3	1	6	12	17	21	25	24	21	14	8	2
	rain mm	12	9	12	7	7	4	16	20	12	7	3	8
Madras	min °C	20	21	24	26	28	28	26	26	25	25	23	21
	max °C	29	31	33	35	38	37	35	35	34	32	29	28
	rain mm	24	7	15	25	52	53	84	124	118	267	309	139
Mysore	min °C	16	18	20	21	21	20	20	20	19	20	18	17
	max °C	28	31	34	34	33	29	27	28	29	28	27	27
	rain mm	3	6	12	68	156	61	72	80	116	180	67	15
Ooty	min °C	5	6	8	10	11	11	11	11	10	10	8	6
	max °C	20	21	22	22	22	18	10	17	18	19	19	20
	rain mm	26	12	30	109	173	139	177	128	110	213	127	59
Srinagar	min °C	-2	-1	4	7	11	14	18	18	13	6	0	-2
	max °C	4	8	13	19	25	29	31	30	28	23	16	9
	rain mm	73	72	–	–	63	1	61	63	32	29	18	36
Trivandrum	min °C	22	23	24	25	25	24	23	23	23	23	23	22
	max °C	31	32	33	32	32	29	29	29	30	30	30	31
	rain mm	20	20	44	122	249	331	215	164	123	271	207	73

start to climb again and before you know it you're back in the hot weather.

Some Regional Variations

As in Sri Lanka, the south-east coast is also affected by the short north-east monsoon which brings rain from mid-October to the end of December. The usual monsoon is the south-west since it comes from that direction. It can get surprisingly wet during the north-east monsoon.

It's easy to forget just how cold it can get in the far north. Even along the Ganges you'll need a sweater or jacket at night, and in Kashmir the snow will be up to your neck. Basically the best time to visit India is November through February, except for the northern Himalayan region where April through July is the best time.

The table (page 27) shows average minimum and maximum temperatures (in °C) and rainfall (in mm).

FLORA & FAUNA

The following description of India's flora and fauna and its national parks and wildlife sanctuaries was written by Murray D Bruce & Constance S Leap Bruce.

The concept of forest and wildlife conservation is not new to India. Here, since time immemorial, wildlife has enjoyed a privileged position of protection through religious ideals and sentiment. Early Indian literature, including the Hindu epics, the Buddhist Jatakas, the Panchatantra and the Jain strictures, teach nonviolence and respect for even lowly animal forms. Many of the gods are associated with certain animals: Brahma with the deer, Vishnu the lion; and Ganesh, the eternal symbol of wisdom, is half man and half elephant. The earliest known conservation laws come from India in the 3rd century BC, when Emperor Ashoka wrote the Fifth Pillar Edict, forbidding the slaughter of certain wildlife and the burning of forests.

Unfortunately, during the recent turbulent history of India, much of this tradition has been lost. Extensive hunting by the British and Indian rajas, the large-scale clearing of forests for agriculture, the availability of guns, strong pesticides and the ever-increasing population have had disastrous effects on India's environment. However, in the past few decades the government has taken serious steps toward environmental management and has established over 100 parks, sanctuaries and reserves.

A visit to one or more of these wildlife refuges is a must on any traveller's itinerary. Protected areas have been established throughout India, and many, such as the Bharatpur Bird Sanctuary near Agra, are readily accessible. Parks such as Corbett and Manas offer the best opportunity to experience India's outstanding natural scenic beauty and, for abundance and visibility of a variety of wildlife, parks such as Kaziranga compare with the best in East Africa.

Many of the wildlife sanctuaries, and some national parks, are established in the former private hunting reserves of the British and Indian aristocracy. Often the parks offer a speciality, such as the Asian lion in Gir, Indian rhinoceros in Kaziranga, elephant in Periyar, and tiger in Kanha and Corbett; other areas have been established to preserve unique habitats such as lowland tropical rainforest or the mangrove forest of the Sunderbans.

Some parks offer modern-style guest houses with electricity, while in others only Dak-style bungalows are available. Facilities usually include van and jeep rides, and at some you can take an elephant ride or boat trip to approach wildlife more discreetly. In addition, watchtowers and hides are often available and provide good opportunities to observe and photograph wildlife at close range.

National parks and other protected areas in India are administered at the state level and are often promoted as part of each state's tourist attractions. To encourage more visitors, road systems, transport, accommodation and other facilities continue to be developed and upgraded. Whenever possible, book in advance for transport and accommodation through the local tourist offices or state departments, and check if a permit is required, particularly in border areas. Various fees are charged for your visit (entrance, photography, etc) and these are usually included with advance arrangements. Meals may also be arranged when you book, but in some cases you must take your food and have it prepared for you.

The diversity of India's climate and topography, varying from arid desert and tropical rainforest to some of the world's highest mountains, is reflected in its rich flora and fauna, with many species found only in India. More than 500 species of mammals, the tiger, elephant and rhinoceros still exist in India and many conservation projects have been established to preserve them. For some species the protection came too late; the Indian cheetah was last recorded in 1948.

A variety of deer and antelope species can be seen. However, these are now virtually confined to the protected areas as a result of competition with domestic animals and the effects of their diseases. They include the graceful Indian gazelle (chinkara); the Indian antelope (black-buck); the diminutive four-horned antelope (chowsingha); the large and ungainly looking blue bull (nilgai), capable of great speed; the rare swamp deer (barasingha); the sambar, India's largest deer; the beautiful spotted deer (chital), usually seen in herds; the larger barking deer (muntjac); and the tiny mouse deer (chevrotain).

Also seen are wild buffalo, massive Indian bison (gaur), shaggy sloth bear, striped hyena, wild pig, jackal, Indian fox, wolf (although much more local in range now), and Indian wild dog (dhole), resembling a giant fox but found in packs in forests. Amongst the smaller mammals

are the mongooses, renowned as snake killers, and giant squirrels.

Cats include leopard or panther, the short-tailed jungle cat, and the beautiful leopard cat. Various monkeys can be seen, with the rhesus macaque, bonnet macaque (south only), and long-tailed common langur as the most likely.

With over 2000 species and varieties of birds, few countries outside of tropical America can compete with India. The diverse birdlife of the forests includes large hornbills, serpent eagles and fishing owls, as well as the elegant national bird, the peacock. Waterbirds, such as herons, ibises, storks, cranes, pelicans and others, are seen not only in parks but at numerous special waterbird sanctuaries. These sanctuaries contain large breeding colonies, and are also of great importance for the countless numbers of migrating birds which visit India annually.

Among the other wildlife are over 500

30 Facts about the Country

species of reptiles and amphibians, including the infamous cobra, other large snakes such as pythons, crocodiles, large freshwater tortoises and monitor lizards (goannas). Then there are the 30,000 insect species, including large and colourful butterflies.

The vegetation, from dry desert scrub to alpine meadow, comprise some 15,000 species of plant recorded to date.

Geographically, India is divided into three main regions, each with many subregions and distinctive altitudinal climatic variations. From these regions, 24 national parks, wildlife sanctuaries and reserves are listed.

Northern India
This is a region of extremes ranging from the snow-bound peaks and deep valleys of the Himalaya to flat plains and tropical lowlands.

Dachigam Wildlife Sanctuary (Kashmir)
A very scenic valley with a large meandering river. The surrounding mountainsides contain the rare Kashmir stag (hangul), also black and brown bears. A trek to the upper reaches, where you can camp, offers spectacular vistas. There you may also see the musk deer, a small species widely hunted for the male's musk gland, considered valuable in treating impotence and a major export to Europe's perfumeries. The sanctuary is 22 km by road from Srinagar and certainly worth a visit. The best time is from June to July.

Flower Valley National Park (Uttar Pradesh)
This 'garden on top of the world' is in the north of Uttar Pradesh near Badrinath, at an elevation of 3500 metres. The famous Valley of Flowers is now a national park and, when in bloom, an unforgettable experience. The best time is from June to July.

The Gangetic Plain
Some of the most famous parks in Asia are in this region. It contains the flat, alluvial

plains of the Indus, Ganges and Brahmaputra rivers – an immense tract of level land stretching from sea to sea and separating the Himalayan region from the southern peninsula proper. Climate varies greatly, from the arid, sandy deserts of Rajasthan and Gujarat, with temperatures up to 50°C, to the cool highlands of Assam, where annual rainfall can exceed 15 metres, perhaps the wettest place on earth.

Corbett National Park (Uttar Pradesh)
The most famous park for the tiger, now rare throughout India but saved from extinction by India's successful Project Tiger. Other wildlife includes chital and hog deer, elephant, leopard, sloth bear and muntjac. There are numerous watchtowers, but only daylight photography is allowed. The park has magnificent scenery, from sal forest (giant, teak-like hardwood trees) to extensive river plains. The Ramganga River offers tranquil settings and good fishing. A bit touristy, but worth a visit. The best time is from November to May.

Hazaribagh Wildlife Sanctuary (Bihar)
An area of rolling, forested hills with large herds of deer, notably sambar but also nilgai and chital, as well as tiger and leopard. The best time is from February to March.

Palamau Game Preserve (Bihar)
Smaller than Hazaribagh, but with good concentrations of wildlife including tiger, leopard, elephant, gaur, sambar, chital, nilgai, and muntjac; also rhesus macaque, common langur and (rarely) wolf. It is 150 km south of Ranchi, with bungalows at Betla. The best time is from February to March.

Sunderbans Tiger Reserve (West Bengal)
These extensive mangrove forests of the Ganges Delta are an important haven for tiger. The reserve is south-east of Calcutta, bordering Bangladesh. The area protects the largest area of mangroves in India and

offers an exceptional chance to see tiger and other wildlife, such as the fishing cat, looking for fish at the water's edge. The only access is by chartered boat (Sunderbans Launch Association, Calcutta). The best time is from February to March.

Jaldhapara Wildlife Sanctuary (West Bengal)

The tropical forests extending from South-East Asia end around here, and if you don't go further east, this is your chance to see the Indian rhinoceros, elephant and other wildlife. The area protects 100 square km of lush forest and grasslands, cut by the wide Torsa River. It is 224 km from Darjeeling, via Siliguri and Jalpaiguri (nearest railhead, Hashimara). There is a rest house at Jaldhapara. The best time is from March to May.

Manas Wildlife Sanctuary (Assam)

This lovely area is formed from the watershed of the Manas, Hakua and Beki rivers and borders with Bhutan. The bungalows at Mothanguri, on the banks of the Manas,

offer views of jungle-clad hills. Established trails enter nearby forests and follow the riverbanks. Try to arrange a boat cruise. Besides tiger, the grassland is home to wild buffalo, elephant, sambar, swamp deer and other wildlife; the rare and beautiful golden langur may be seen on the Bhutan side of the Manas. The best time is from January to March.

Kaziranga National Park (Assam)

The most famous place to see the one-horned Indian rhinoceros, hunted almost to extinction for its prize as big game and for the Chinese apothecary trade. The park is dominated by tall (up to six metres) grasslands and swampy areas (jheels). Travelling is best done by elephant, which can be arranged at the park. The first sighting of a rhinoceros is always impressive and awesome, as they can reach a height of over two metres and weigh more than two tonnes. Despite the prehistoric appearance, rhinos are incredibly agile and fast. Spotting them in the tall grass may be difficult. Watch for egrets and other birds who use the rhino's armoured back as a perch, and also listen for the 'churring' sound of a large animal moving through the grass. Best viewing may be by the jheels, where they bathe. The best time is from February to March.

Sariska Wildlife Sanctuary & Sawai Madhopur Wildlife Sanctuary (Rajasthan)

Both areas provide good opportunities to see the wildlife of the Indian plains. Sariska is notable for night viewing and its nilgai herds. Sawai Madhopur (or Ranthambore) is smaller, which can make seeing animals easier, and has a lake with crocodiles. It is on the Delhi to Bombay railway line, and 160 km south of Jaipur by road. You can stay at the Sawai Madhopur railway retiring rooms. The best time is from February to June (Sariska), and November to May (Sawai Madhopur).

Keoladeo Ghana Bird Sanctuary (Rajasthan)

The best known and most touristy bird

sanctuary (usually just called Bharatpur). It features large numbers of breeding waterbirds and thousands of migrating birds from Siberia and China, including herons, storks, cranes and geese. The network of crossroads and tracks through the sanctuary can increase opportunities to see the birds, deer and other wildlife. It is also on the Delhi to Bombay railway line. The best time is from September to February.

Gir National Park (Gujarat) Famous for the last surviving Asian lions (under 200), Gir also supports a large variety of other wildlife, notably the chowsingha. This forested oasis in the desert contains Lake Kamaleshwar, complete with crocodiles. The lake and other watering holes are good places to spot animals. The best time is from January to May.

Velavadar National Park (Gujarat) This park, 65 km north of Bhavnagar, protects the rich grasslands in the delta region on the west side of the Gulf of Khambhat (Cambay). The main attraction is a large concentration of the beautiful blackbuck.

There is a park lodge available for visitors. The best time is from October to June.

Little Rann of Kutch Wildlife Sanctuary (Gujarat) A sanctuary designated for the protection of the desert region of north-west Gujarat, especially the outer rim and a narrow belt of adjacent land. A variety of desert life can be found here, notably the surviving herds of the Indian wild ass (khur); also wolf and caracal (a large, pale cat with tufted ears). Access can be arranged at Bhuj. The best time is from October to June.

Shivpuri National Park (Madhya Pradesh) A picturesque park with open forests surrounding a lake. Good for photographing various deer, including chinkara, chowsingha and nilgai; also tiger and leopard. It is close to Gwalior. The best time is from February to May.

Kanha National Park (Madhya Pradesh) One of India's most spectacular and exciting parks for both variety and numbers of wildlife and well worth a visit. Originally proposed to protect a unique type of swamp deer (barasingha), it is also important area for tiger. There are large herds of chital, plus blackbuck, gaur, leopard and hyena. The best time is from November to March.

Similipal Tiger Reserve (Orissa) A vast and beautiful area protecting India's largest region of sal forest, with magnificent scenery and a variety of wildlife, including tiger, elephant, leopard, sambar, chital, muntjac and chevrotain. The best time is from November to June.

Southern India

Here is the Deccan Peninsula, which takes the form of a triangular plateau, ranging in altitude from 300 to 900 metres, intersected with rivers, scattered peaks and hill ranges, including the Western and Eastern ghats. The ghats form a natural barrier to the monsoons and have created areas of great humidity and rainfall, as on the Malabar coast where lush lowland tropical rainforest still occur with drier regions on the mountains' leeward sides.

Krishnagiri Upavan National Park (Maharashtra) This park, formerly known as Borivilli, protects an important and scenic area close to Bombay and other attractions. Amongst the smaller types of wildlife to be seen are a variety of waterbirds. The best time is from October to June.

Taroba National Park (Maharashtra) A large park featuring mixed teak forests and a lake, with night viewing available to see its large wildlife populations. These include tiger, leopard, gaur, nilgai, sambar and chital. It is 45 km from Chandrapur, south-west from Kanha National Park. You can arrange to stay in the park. The best time is from March to May.

Periyar Wildlife Sanctuary (Kerala) A large and scenic park formed by the watershed of a reservoir developed around a large, artificial lake. It is famous for the large elephant population which can easily be seen as you travel by boat on the lake.

Other wildlife sometimes seen from the boat are the gaur, Indian wild dog and nilgiri langur, as well as otters, large tortoises, and a rich birdlife, including flights of hornbills. Along the water's edge you may see the flashing, brilliant hues of several kinds of kingfisher, perhaps even a fishing owl. The best time is from February to May.

Jawahar National Park There was a recent proposal to cover Bandipur National Park (Karnataka), Nagarhole National Park (Karnataka), Mudumulai Wildlife Sanctuary (Tamil Nadu), and Wynaad Wildlife Sanctuary (Kerala).

Situated at the junction of the Western Ghats, the Nilgiri Hills and the Deccan Plateau, the merging of these contiguous areas protects the largest elephant population in India, as well as one of the most extensive forested areas in the south. The mixed, diverse forests and their terrain also protect a large variety of other wildlife, including many rare species such as leopard, gaur, sambar, chital, muntjac, chevrotain, bonnet macaque and giant squirrels. The very rich birdlife includes many spectacular species such as hornbills, barbets, trogons, parakeets, racquet-tailed drongos and streamer-tailed Asian paradise flycatchers. The two most popular areas are Bandipur and Mudumulai. Not to be missed if you visit the south. The best time is from January to June.

Murray D Bruce
Constance S Leap Bruce

Know your Monkey

Rats apart, the monkey is the most commonly seen wild mammal in India. The common or sacred langur is probably seen most often. This is a large monkey of slender build with pale grey fur and black face, hands and feet. It is often seen in large troops in woods, ruins and even in towns (like Pushkar). Because of its association with the monkey-god, Hanuman, it is venerated by Hindus.

The rhesus macaque is the other common monkey of northern India. The stocky monkey has a pink face, short tail and grey-brown fur tending to reddish on the rump. Again it is found in woods and sometimes towns (as at the Durga Temple in Varanasi). The related bonnet macaque is similar with a longer tail and takes the place of the rhesus in southern India.

Another commonly seen animal is the striped palm squirrel – that cute little fellow with the white back stripes often seen scampering on and about trees.

Lloyd Jones, New Zealand

GOVERNMENT

India has a parliamentary system of government with certain similarities to the US government. There are two houses – a lower house known as the Lok Sabha (House of the People) and an upper house known as the Rajya Sabha (Council of States). The lower house has up to 500 members elected on a population basis while the upper has up to 250 members. As in the British House of Commons or the Australian House of Representatives, the lower house can be dissolved but the upper house, unlike Britain's or Australia's, cannot. There are also state governments with legislative assemblies known as Vidhan Sabha. The two national houses and the various state houses elect the Indian president who is a figurehead – the prime minister wields the real power.

There is a strict division between the activities handled by the states and by the national government. The police force, education, agriculture and industry are reserved for the state governments. Certain other areas are jointly administered by the two levels of government. All adult Indians have the vote, and the constitution provides for special facilities and assistance for India's Harijans and for the tribal groups still found in various parts of the country.

ECONOMY

India is a predominantly agricultural country. It is also one of the world's major industrial powers with important iron and steel works and a growing manufacturing industry. Textiles are still the backbone of India's industrial exports.

Recently major efforts have been made to launch Indian industry into modern 'high tech' areas, away from the traditional heavy engineering areas. Nevertheless a recent Japanese study indicated that India's policy of protecting local industry from imports rather than promoting exports, even when it meant importing foreign technology, has been far less successful than the opposite policy followed in countries like Japan or South Korea.

The central planning policies and mountains of red tape and paperwork have also held economic development back. It's interesting that China, which followed similar protectionist and isolationist policies under Mao, made an abrupt about-turn, and India also seems to have become intent upon updating key industries, even if that necessitates importing modern technology.

Despite these industrial and manufacturing activities, 70% of India's population is engaged in work on the land – much of it inefficient and unproductive. Small landholdings, poor methods and lack of investment all contribute to this record, although since independence the agricultural production levels have actually increased at a faster rate than the population. The green revolution in India, involving new strains and improved use of fertilisers, has resulted in a food surplus for several years now.

India also has nearly 200 million cattle which in the rural economy are vitally important – pulling the farmer's cart to market or ploughing the fields. Their religious protection probably first developed as a means of protecting them during droughts or famine when the cows might have been killed off and subsequently been hard to replace. There is also some dairy production. In the cities cows are an involuntary arm of the garbage disposal department and, when not roaming the streets munching on cardboard, can be seen rummaging through the concrete bins where waste vegetable matter is tipped.

POPULATION & PEOPLE

India is second only to China in having the world's largest population. In 1961 it had 439 million; in 1971 it had 547 million. By 1981 the figure had increased to 687 million and is now estimated to be over 800 million. Despite extensive birth control programmes it is still growing far too rapidly for comfort.

Despite India's many large cities the country is still overwhelmingly rural. It is estimated that only about 100 million of the total population live in cities or towns, but with increasing industrialisation the shift from village to city continues to grow.

The Indian people are not a homogeneous group. It is quite easy to tell the difference between the shorter Bengalis of the east, the taller and lighter-skinned people of the centre and north, the Kashmiris with their distinctly central Asian appearance, the Tibetan people of Ladakh and the north of Himachal Pradesh, and the dark-skinned Tamils of the south. Despite these regional variations, the government has managed to successfully establish an 'Indian' ethos and nationalistic feeling.

Although India is overwhelmingly Hindu, there are large minorities of other religions. These include 76 million Muslims, making India one of the largest Muslim countries in the world, much larger than any of the Arab Middle East nations. Christians number about 19 million, Sikhs 13 million, Buddhists five million and Jains three million. About 7% of the population is classified as 'tribal'. They are found scattered throughout the country although there are concentrations of them in the north-east corner of the country as well as in Orissa and a number of other states.

The average per capita income is Rs 3184 annually, or less than Rs 9 per day. By comparison, teachers earn about Rs 18,000, bank clerks Rs 25,000, engineers Rs 35,000, and the head of a small government department about Rs 50,000.

Birth Control

India's attempts at birth control have been varied, but although there has been some success at slowing the rate of increase the picture is far from happy. Today many international experts feel that the solution to the population increase problem in the third world is not to slow the birth rate, which will then bring prosperity in its wake, but to establish a degree of prosperity which will then bring a desire for fewer children. So long as children are a source of security in old age and so long as male heirs are so avidly desired, it will be difficult to successfully bring population pressures under control.

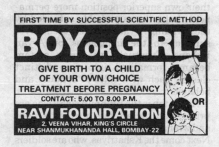

In the early '70s India had a birth control blitz with slogans and posters appearing all over the country, and the famous 'transistor radio in exchange for sterilisation' campaign. More sinister was the brief campaign of the emergency era when squads of sterilisers terrorised half the country and people were afraid to go out after dark. That over-kill campaign probably put the birth control programme in India back by years, and it currently enjoys a very low priority in the government's platform, although billboards showing the happy two-child family are a familiar sight all over India.

Castes

The caste system is one of India's more confusing mysteries – how it came about, how it has managed to survive for so long, how much harm it causes, are all topics of discussion for visitors to India. Its origins are lost in the mists of time but basically it seems to have been developed by the Brahmins or priest class in order to make their own superior position more permanent. Later it was probably extended by the invading Aryans who felt themselves superior to the indigenous pre-Aryan Indians. Eventually the caste system became formalised into four distinct classes, each with rules of conduct and behaviour.

At the top is the Brahmin class, who are priests and the arbiters of what is right and wrong in matters of religion and caste. Next come the Kshatriyas, who are soldiers and administrators. The Vaisyas are the artisan and commercial class, and finally the Sudras are the farmers and the peasant class. These four castes are said to have come from Brahma's mouth (Brahmins), arms (Kshatriyas), thighs (Vaisyas) and feet (Sudras). Beneath these four castes is a fifth group, the untouchables, who literally have no caste. They perform the most menial and degrading jobs. At one time, if a high-caste Hindu used the same temple as an untouchable, was touched by one, or even had an untouchable's shadow

cast across them, they were polluted and had to go through a rigorous series of rituals to be cleansed.

Today the caste system has been much weakened but it still has considerable power, particularly amongst the less educated people. Gandhi put great effort into bringing the untouchables into society, including renaming them the 'Harijans' or 'children of god'. But an untouchable by any other name.... It must be remembered that being born into a certain caste does not limit you strictly to one occupation or position in life, just as being black in the USA does not mean you are poverty stricken and live in Harlem. Many Brahmins are poor peasants, for example, and hundreds of years ago the great Maratha leader Shivaji was a Sudra. None of the later Marathas, who controlled much of India after the demise of the Moghuls, were Brahmins. Nevertheless you can generalise that the better-off Indians will be higher caste and that the 'sweeper' you see desultorily cleaning the toilet in your hotel will be a Harijan. In fact when Indian Airlines appointed their first untouchable flight attendant it was front-page news in Indian newspapers.

How can you tell which caste a Hindu belongs to? Well, if you know that their job is a menial one such as cleaning streets or in some way defiling, such as working with leather, they are a Harijan. But for most Hindus you can't really tell which caste they belong to. However, if you see a man with his shirt off and he has the sacred thread looped round one shoulder he is a Brahmin, but then Parsis also wear a sacred thread. Of course the Sikhs, Muslims and Christians do not have caste.

In many ways the caste system also functions as an enormous unofficial trade union with strict rules to avoid demarcation disputes. Each caste has many subdivisions so that the servant who polishes the brass cannot, due to their caste, also polish silver. Many of the old caste rules have been considerably relaxed, although less educated or more isolated Hindus may still avoid having a lower-caste person prepare their food for fears of becoming polluted. Better-educated people probably are not too worried about shaking hands with a caste-less westerner though! Nor does the thought of going overseas, and thus losing caste completely, carry too much weight these days.

The caste system still produces enormous burdens for India, however. During the last few years there have been frequent outbreaks of violence towards lower-caste Hindus. In some rural communities higher-caste Hindus have lynched Harijans whom they felt were getting 'uppity', and there are often latent tensions between the castes which can easily spill over into violence. In 1980, a number of Harijans were killed at one village after a riot broke out because a bridegroom didn't dismount from his wedding horse when passing a group of higher-caste men! In 1981, there was a whole series of violent riots in Ahmedabad, Gujarat due to the practice of reserving university places for Harijans, whether or not there were sufficient Harijan applicants for the places. Higher-caste Hindus who could not obtain

Looking for a partner?

university places despite having good qualifications prompted these outbreaks.

It's debatable, however, whether it is always caste as such which prompts these riots. Studies done on the problem point to poverty, economic deprivation and opportunism by religious zealots as the root causes.

It's interesting to compare these problems with the situation in the US where, during the desegregation era, many blacks experienced great difficulties in being allowed into 'all-white' schools and restaurants. Similarly in the US today there is a degree of protest about the reservation of college positions for disadvantaged minorities. Going far back into western history, it's interesting that the medieval ideal of heaven was developed in part to keep the peasants in their place – behave yourself, work hard, put up with your lot and you'll go to heaven. Probably caste developed in a similar fashion – your life may be pretty miserable but that's your caste, behave yourself and you may be born into a better one next time around.

Tribals

For most people it comes as a surprise to learn that more than 40 million Indians belong to tribal communities as distinct from the great mass of Hindu caste society. These Adivasi, as they are known in India, have origins which precede the Vedic Aryans and even the Dravidians of the south. For thousands of years they have lived undisturbed in the hills and densely wooded regions which were regarded as unattractive by the peasantry of more dynamic populations. Many still speak tribal languages not understood by the politically dominant people, and they follow archaic customs foreign to both Hindus and Muslims alike.

Although there was obviously some contact between the tribals and the Hindu villagers of the open plains in some areas, this rarely led to friction since there was little or no competition for resources and land. All this changed dramatically when improved communications opened up previously inaccessible tribal areas and rapid growth of the Indian population led to pressure on the land's resources. In the space of just 40 years the vast majority of tribals have been dispossessed of their ancestral land and turned into impoverished labourers exploited by all and sundry. The only region where this has not taken place and where tribals continue to manage their own affairs is in Arunachal Pradesh, in the extreme north-east of India. Only here can it be said that the tribes have benefited from contact with modern civilisation and are managing to hold their own.

Elsewhere in India, and especially in Andhra Pradesh, a shocking tale of exploitation, dispossession and widespread hunger has unfolded with the connivance and even encouragement of officialdom. It's a record which the government would prefer to forget about and which it vehemently denies exists. Instead, it points to the millions of rupees which it says have been sunk into schemes to improve the condition of the aboriginals. Undoubtedly some of this has actually got through but much of it has disappeared in various corruption scams.

It's unlikely that any genuine effort will be made to improve the lot of the tribals in peninsula India, given the pressure for land. What is far more likely is that the erosion of their cultures and traditions will continue until they eventually 'disappear' as distinct tribes.

CULTURE
Painting, Sculpture & Architecture
Indian art and sculpture is basically religious in its themes and developments, and appreciation requires at least some knowledge of its religious background. The earliest Indian artefacts are found in the Indus Valley cities in modern-day Pakistan. Pieces are mainly small items of sculpture and it was not until the Mauryan period that India's first major

artistic period flowered. This classical school of Buddhist art reached its peak during the reign of Ashoka. The superb sculpture of this period can be seen at its best at Sanchi. The Sungas, who followed the Mauryas, continued their artistic traditions.

When this empire ended the Gandharan period came into its own in the north-west. Close to Peshawar, in today's Pakistan, the Gandharan period combined Buddhism with a strong Greek influence from the descendants of Alexander the Great's invading army. During this period the Buddha began to be represented directly in human form rather than by symbols such as the footprint or the stupa. Meanwhile, in India proper another school began to develop at Mathura, between Agra and Delhi. Here the religious influence was also Buddhist but was beginning to be altered by the revival of Brahmanism, the forerunner of Hinduism. It was in this school that the tradition of sculpturing *yakshis*, those well-endowed heavenly damsels, began.

During the Gupta period from 320-600 AD, Indian art went through a golden age, and the Buddha images developed their present-day form – even today in Buddhist countries the attitudes, clothing and hand positions have scarcely altered. This was, however, also the end of Buddhist art in India, for Hinduism began to reassert itself. At the same time as the Guptas were bringing Buddhist art to its final zenith in the north, a strongly Hindu tradition was developing in the south. Both schools of art produced metal cast sculptures by the lost wax method, as well as larger sculptures in stone.

The following 1000 years saw a slow but steady development through to the exuberant medieval period of Indian Hindu art. This development can be studied at the caves of Ajanta and Ellora, where there are some of the oldest wall paintings in India and the sculpture can be traced from the older, stiff and unmoving Buddhist sculptures through to the dynamic and dramatic Hindu figures.

These reached their culmination in the period when sculpture became an integral part of architecture; it is impossible to tell where building ends and sculpture begins. Some of the finest examples of this era can be seen in the Hoysala temples of Karnataka, the elaborate Sun Temple at Konarak and the Chandelas' temples at Khajuraho. In all of these the architecture competes valiantly with the artwork, which manages to combine high quality with quite awesome quantity. An interesting common element is the highly detailed erotic scenes. The heavenly maidens of an earlier period have blossomed into scenes, positions and possibilities that leave little to the imagination. Art of this period was not purely a representation of gods and goddesses. Every aspect of human life appeared in the sculptures and obviously in India sex was considered a fairly important aspect!

The arrival of the Muslims with their hatred of other religions and 'idols' caused enormous damage to India's artistic relics. The early invaders' art was chiefly confined to paintings, but with the Moghuls, Indian art went through yet another golden period. Best known of the art forms they encouraged was the miniature painting. These delightfully detailed and brightly coloured paintings showed the events and activities of the Moghuls in their magnificent palaces. Other paintings included portraits, or studies of wildlife and plants.

At the same time there was a massive revival of folk art; some of these developments embraced the Moghul miniature concepts but combined them with Indian religious arts. The popular Rajasthan or Mewar schools often included scenes from Krishna's life and escapades – Krishna is always painted blue. Interestingly, this school followed the Persian-influenced Moghul school in its miniaturised and highly detailed

Ladies worshipping Lord Shiva

approach but made no use of the Persian developed sense of perspective, and works are generally almost two dimensional.

In the north of India – at Jammu, Basohli and Kangra – the Pahari miniatures followed the Moghul school in having a definite sense of perspective, but in their often religious themes were closer to the Rajasthan school. The Basohli paintings are very dark and use much gold colouring, while the Pahari paintings are often pale and delicate.

The Moghuls' greatest achievements were, however, in the architectural field; it is chiefly for their magnificent buildings that they are remembered. After the Moghuls there has not been another major artistic period of purely Indian background. During the British period art became imitative of western trends and ideals. Although there is much British painting in India it is interesting primarily as an historical record rather than as art itself.

Music

Indian music is most unlike the concept of music in the west. It is very difficult for a westerner to appreciate it without a lengthy introduction and much time spent in listening. The two main forms of Indian music are the southern Carnatic and the northern Hindustani traditions. The basic difficulty is that harmony, so important to western music, has no place in Indian music. The music has two basic elements, the *tala* and the *raga*. Tala is the rhythm and is characterised by the number of beats. *Teental* is a tala of 16 beats. The audience follows the tala by clapping at the appropriate beat which in teental is at one, five and 13. There is no clap at the beat of nine since that is the *khali* or 'empty section' indicated by a wave of the hand.

Just as tala is the rhythm, so is raga the melody; just as there are a number of basic talas so there are many set ragas. The classical Indian music group consists of three musicians who provide the drone, the melody and the rhythm – in other words a background drone, a tala and a raga. The musicians are basically soloists – the concept of an orchestra of Indian musicians is impossible since there is not the harmony that a western orchestra provides – each musician selects their own tala and raga. The players then zoom off in their chosen directions, as dictated by the tala and the raga selected, and, to the audience's delight, meet every once in a while before again diverging.

Yehudi Menuhin, who has devoted much time and energy to understanding Indian music, suggests that it is much like Indian society: a group of individuals not working together but every once in a while meeting at some common point. Western music is analogous to western democratic societies, a group of individuals (the orchestra) who each surrender part of their freedom to the harmony of the whole. Although Indian classical music has one of the longest continuous histories of any musical form, the music has never,

until quite recently, been recorded in any written notation. Furthermore, within the basic framework set by the tala and the raga, the musicians improvise – providing variations on the basic melody and rhythm.

Best known of the Indian instruments are the sitar and the tabla. The sitar is the large stringed instrument popularised by Ravi Shankar in the west – and which more than a few westerners have discovered is more than just slightly difficult to tune. This is the instrument with which the soloist plays the raga. Other stringed instruments are the sarod (which is plucked) or the sarangi (which is played with a bow). The tabla, a twin drum rather like a western bongo, provides the tala. The drone, which runs on two basic notes, is provided by the oboe-like shehnai or the tampura.

Dance

Indian dancing relates back to Shiva's role as Nataraj, Lord of the Dance. Lord Shiva's first wife was Sati and when her father, who disliked Shiva, insulted him Sati committed suicide in a sacrifice by fire that later took her name. Outraged, Shiva killed his father-in-law and danced the Tandava – the Dance of Destruction. Later Sati reincarnated as Parvati, married Shiva again and danced the Lasya. Thus the Tandava became the male form of dance, the Lasya the female form. Dancing was a part of the religious temple rituals and the dancers were known as *devadasis*. Their dances retold stories from the *Ramayana* or the *Mahabharata*.

Temple dancing is no longer practised but classical Indian dancing is still based on its religious background. Indian dance is divided into *nritta* – the rhythmic elements, *nritya* – the combination of rhythm with expression, and *natya* – the dramatic element. Nritya is usually expressed through eye, hand and facial movements and with nritta makes up the usual dance programmes. To appreciate natya, dance drama, you have to understand and appreciate Indian legends and mythology.

Dance is divided into four basic forms known as Bharat Natyam, Kathakali, Kathak and Manipuri. Bharat Natyam is further subdivided into three other classical forms. One of the most popular, it originated in the great temples of the south and usually tells of events in Krishna's life. Bharat Natyam dancers are usually women and, like the sculptures they take their positions from, always dance bent-kneed, never standing upright, and use a huge repertoire of hand movements. Orissi, Mohini Attam and Kuchipudi are variations of Bharat Natyam which take their names from the places where they originated.

Kathakali, the second major dance form, originated in Kerala and is exclusively danced by men. It tells of epic battles of gods and demons and is as dynamic and dramatic as Bharat Natyam is austere and expressive. Kathakali dancing is noted for the elaborate make-up and painted masks which the dancers wear. Eyedrops even turn their eyes a bloodshot red!

Manipuri dances come, as the name indicates, from the Manipur region in the north-east. These are folk dances and the message is made through body and arm movements. The women dancers wear hooped skirts and conical caps which are extremely picturesque.

The final classical dance type is Kathak, which originated in the north and at first was very similar to the Bharat Natyam school. Persian and Muslim influences later altered the dance from a temple ritual to a courtly entertainment. The dances are performed straight-legged and there are intricately choreographed foot movements to be followed. The ankle bells which dancers wear must be adeptly controlled and the costumes and themes are often similar to those in Moghul miniature paintings.

There are many opportunities to see classical Indian dancing while you are in India. The major hotels often put on performances to which outsiders as well as hotel guests are welcome.

RELIGION

India has a positive kaleidoscope of religions. There is probably more diversity of religions and sects in India than anywhere else on earth. Apart from having nearly all the world's great religions represented here, India was also the birthplace of two of the world's greatest (Hinduism and Buddhism), an important home to one of the world's oldest (Zoroastrianism), and home to an ancient religion unique to India (Jainism).

Hindus

India's major religion, Hinduism, is practised by approximately 80% of the population, over 500 million people. Only in Nepal, the Indonesian island of Bali, the Indian Ocean island of Mauritius and possibly Fiji, do Hindus also predominate, but it is the largest religion in Asia in terms of number of adherents. Despite its colourful appearance it is actually one of the oldest extant religions with firm roots extending back to beyond 1000 BC.

The Indus Valley civilisation developed a religion which shows a close relationship to Hinduism in many ways. Later, it further developed through the combined religious practices of the southern Dravidians and the Aryan invaders who arrived in the north of India around 1500 BC. Around 1000 BC, the Vedic scriptures were introduced and gave the first loose framework to the religion.

Hinduism today has a number of holy books, the most important being the four *Vedas* 'divine knowledge' which are the foundation of Hindu philosophy. The *Upanishads* are contained within the Vedas and delve into the metaphysical nature of the universe and soul. The *Mahabharata* 'Great War of the Bharatas' is an epic poem containing over 220,000 lines. It describes the battles between the

Kauravas and Pandavas, who were descendants of the Lunar race. In it is the story of Rama, and it is probable that the most famous Hindu epic, the *Ramayana*, was based on this. The *Ramayana* is highly revered by Hindus, perhaps because a verse in the introduction says 'He who reads and repeats this holy life-giving *Ramayana* is liberated from all his sins and exalted with all his posterity to the highest heaven'. The *Bhagavad Gita* is a famous episode of the *Mahabharata* where Krishna relates his philosophies to Arjuna.

Basically the religion postulates that we will all go through a series of rebirths or reincarnations that eventually lead to *moksha*, the spiritual salvation which frees one from the cycle of rebirths. With each rebirth you can move closer to or further from eventual moksha; the deciding factor is your *karma*, which is literally a law of cause and effect. Bad actions during your life result in bad karma, which ends in a lower reincarnation. Conversely, if your deeds and actions have been good you will reincarnate on a higher level and be a step closer to eventual freedom from rebirth.

Dharma or the natural law defines the total social, ethical and spiritual harmony of your life. There are three categories of dharma, the first being the eternal harmony which involves the whole universe. The second category is the dharma that controls castes and the relations between castes. The third dharma is the moral code which an individual should follow.

The Hindu religion has three basic practices. They are *puja* or worship, the cremation of the dead, and the rules and regulations of the caste system. There are four main castes: the Brahmin, or priest caste; the Kshatriyas, or soldiers and governors; the Vaisyas, or tradespeople and farmers; and the Sudras or menial workers and craftspeople. These basic castes are then subdivided into a great number of lesser divisions. Beneath all the castes are the Harijans, or untouchables, the lowest caste-less class for whom all the most menial and degrading tasks are reserved.

Westerners have trouble understanding Hinduism principally because of its vast pantheon of gods. In fact you can look upon all these different gods simply as pictorial representations of the many attributes of a god. The one omnipresent god usually has three physical representations. Brahma is the creator, Vishnu is the preserver and Shiva is the destroyer and reproducer. All three gods are usually shown with four arms, but Brahma has the added advantage of four heads to represent his all-seeing presence. The four *Vedas* are supposed to have emanated from his mouths.

Each god has an associated animal known as the 'vehicle' on which they ride, as well as a consort with certain attributes and abilities. Generally each god also holds a symbol; you can often pick out which god is represented by the vehicle or symbol. Brahma's consort is Sarasvati, the goddess of learning. She rides upon a white swan and holds the stringed musical instrument known as a *veena*.

Vishnu, the preserver, is usually shown in one of the physical forms in which he has visited earth. In all, Vishnu has paid nine visits and on his 10th he is expected as a Kalki, riding a horse. On earlier visits he appeared in animal form, as in his boar or man-lion (Narsingh) incarnations, but on visit seven he appeared as Rama, regarded as the personification of the ideal man and the hero of the *Ramayana*. Rama also managed to provide a number of secondary gods including his helpful ally Hanuman, the monkey god. Hanuman's faithful nature is illustrated by the representation of him often found guarding fort or palace entrances. Naturally incarnations can also have consorts and Rama's lady was Sita.

On visit eight Vishnu came as Krishna, who was brought up with peasants and thus became a great favourite of the working classes. Krishna is renowned for his exploits with the *gopis* or shepherdesses and his consorts are Radha the head of the gopis, Rukmani and Satyabhama. Krishna is often blue in colour and plays a flute. Vishnu's last incarnation was on visit nine, as the Buddha. This was probably a ploy to bring the Buddhist splinter group back into the Hindu fold.

When Vishnu appears as Vishnu, rather than one of his incarnations, he sits on a couch made from the coils of a serpent and in his hands he holds two symbols, the conch shell and the discus. Vishnu's vehicle is the half-man half-eagle known as the Garuda. The Garuda is a firm do-gooder and has a deep dislike of snakes – Indonesia's national airline is named after the Garuda. His consort is the beautiful Lakshmi (Laxmi) who came from the sea and is the goddess of wealth and prosperity.

Shiva's creative role is phallically symbolised by his representation as the frequently worshipped lingam. Shiva rides on the bull Nandi and his matted hair is said to have Ganga, the goddess of the river Ganges in it. He is supposed to live in the Himalaya and devote much time to smoking dope. He has the third eye in the middle of his forehead and carries a trident. Shiva is also known as Nataraja, the cosmic dancer whose dance shook the cosmos and created the world. Shiva's consort is Parvati, the beautiful. She, however, has a dark side when she appears as Durga, the terrible. In this role she holds weapons in her 10 hands and rides a tiger. As Kali, the fiercest of the gods, she demands sacrifices and wears a garland of skulls. Kali usually handles the destructive side of Shiva's personality.

Shiva and Parvati have two children. Ganesh is the elephant-headed god of prosperity and wisdom, and is probably the most popular of all the gods. Ganesh obtained his elephant head due to his father's notorious temper. Coming back from a long trip, Shiva discovered Parvati in her room with a young man. Not pausing to think that their son might have grown up a little during his absence, Shiva lopped his head off! He was then forced by Parvati to bring his son back to life but could only do so by giving him the head of the first living thing he saw – which happened to be an elephant. Ganesh's vehicle is a rat! Shiva and Parvati's other son is Kartikkaya, the god of war.

Ganesh

A variety of lesser gods and goddesses also crowd the scene. Most temples are dedicated to one or other of the gods, but curiously there are very few Brahma temples – perhaps just two or three in all of India. Most Hindus profess to be either Vaishnavites (followers of Vishnu) or Shaivites (followers of Shiva). The cow is, of course, the holy animal of Hinduism.

Hinduism is not a proselytising religion since you cannot be converted. You're either born a Hindu or you are not; you can never become one. Similarly, once you are a Hindu you cannot change your caste –

you're born into it and are stuck with it for the rest of that lifetime. Nevertheless Hinduism has a great attraction to many westerners and India's 'export gurus' are many and successful.

A *guru* is not so much a teacher as a spiritual guide, somebody who by example or simply by their presence indicates what path you should follow. In a spiritual search one always needs a guru. A *sadhu* is an individual on a spiritual search. They're an easily recognised group, usually wandering around half-naked, smeared in dust with their hair and beard matted. Sadhus following Shiva will sometimes carry his symbol, the trident. A sadhu is often someone who has decided that his business and family life have reached their natural conclusions and that it is time to throw everything aside and go out on a spiritual search. He may previously have been the village postman, or a businessman. Sadhus perform various feats of self-mortification and wander all over India, occasionally coming together in great pilgrimages and other religious gatherings. Many sadhus are, of course, simply beggars following a more sophisticated approach to gathering in the paise, but others are completely genuine in their search.

Entry Prohibited

One clear contrast to the general Indian mood of tolerance is the way westerners are not allowed into some Hindu temples. This chiefly applies to the temples in Orissa and Varanasi, and to some temples in the south, particularly in Kerala. It's in complete contrast to Jain and Buddhist temples or Muslim mosques, where you are almost always allowed to wander at will. These regulations have been relaxed over the years and today there are far fewer places where an outright ban applies. It's worth noting that it took Mahatma Gandhi to open many temples, even to some Hindus. Untouchables were banned from entering temples earlier this century.

An irritation is that in many cases the national or state tourist boards expound at length about the glories of these temples, and yet never mention, even in the smallest print,

that if you're a westerner you may not be allowed into various parts of the temples and sometimes not at all. The Orissa publicists are particularly guilty of this. In Tamil Nadu, where there are many wonderful temples, attitudes are fairly relaxed and you can explore all but the inner sanctum at almost any temple; if you're appropriately dressed and sufficiently respectful you may even be invited in there.

Buddhists

Although there are only about five million Buddhists in India, the religion is of great importance because it had its birth here and there are many reminders of its historic role. Strictly speaking Buddhism is not a religion, since it is not centred on a god, but a system of philosophy and a code of morality.

Buddhism was founded in northern India about 500 BC when Siddhartha Gautama, born a prince, achieved enlightenment. Gautama Buddha was not the first Buddha but the fourth, and is not expected to be the last 'enlightened one'. Buddhists believe that the achievement of enlightenment is the goal of every being so eventually we will all reach Buddhahood.

The Buddha never wrote down his dharma or teachings, and a schism later developed so that today there are two major Buddhist schools. The Theravada, Hinayana, 'doctrine of the elders' or 'small vehicle' holds that the path to *nirvana*, the eventual aim of all Buddhists, is an individual pursuit. In contrast, the Mahayana or 'large vehicle' school holds that the combined belief of its followers will eventually be great enough to encompass all of humanity and bear it to salvation. To some the less austere and ascetic Mahayana school is a 'soft option'. Today it is chiefly practised in Vietnam, Japan and China, while the Hinayana school is followed in Sri Lanka, Burma (Myanmar) and Thailand. There are other, sometimes more esoteric, divisions of Buddhism such as the Hindu-Tantric Buddhism of Tibet which you can see in Ladakh and other parts of north India.

The Buddha renounced his material life to search for enlightenment but, unlike other prophets, found that starvation did not lead to discovery. Therefore he developed his rule of the 'middle way', moderation in everything. The Buddha taught that all life is suffering but that suffering comes from our sensual desires and the illusion that they are important. By following the 'eight-fold path' these desires will be extinguished and a state of nirvana, where they are extinct and we are free from their delusions, will be reached. Following this process requires going through a series of rebirths until the goal is eventually reached and no more rebirths into the world of suffering are necessary. The path that takes you through this cycle of births is karma, but this is not simply fate. Karma is a law of cause and effect; your actions in one life determine the role you will play and what you will have to go through in your next life.

In India Buddhism developed rapidly when it was embraced by the great emperor Ashoka. As his empire extended over much of India, so was Buddhism

carried forth. He also sent out missions to other lands to preach the Buddha's word, and his own son is said to have carried Buddhism to Sri Lanka. Later, however, Buddhism began to contract in India because it had never really taken a hold on the great mass of people. As Hinduism revived, Buddhism in India was gradually reabsorbed into the older religion.

Today Buddha, to Hindus, is another incarnation of Vishnu. At its peak, however, Buddhism was responsible for magnificent structures erected wherever it held sway. The earlier Theravada form of Buddhism did not believe in the representation of the Buddha in human form. His presence was always alluded to in Buddhist art or architecture through symbols such as the bo tree, under which he was sitting when he attained enlightenment, the elephant, which his mother dreamed of before he was born, or the wheel of life. Today, however, even Theravada Buddhists produce Buddha images.

Muslims

Muslims, followers of the Islamic religion, are India's largest religious minority. They number about 75 million in all, over 10% of the country's population. This makes India one of the largest Islamic nations in the world. India has had two Muslim presidents, several cabinet ministers and state chief ministers since independence. Islam is the most recent and most widespread of the Asian religions; it predominates from the Mediterranean across to India and is the major religion east of India in Bangladesh, Malaysia and Indonesia.

The religion's founder, the prophet Mohammed, was born in 570 AD at Mecca, now part of Saudi Arabia. He had his first revelation from Allah, God, in 610 and this and later visions were compiled into the Muslim holy book, the Koran. As his purpose in life was revealed to him, Mohammed began to preach against the idolatry for which Mecca was then the centre. Muslims are strictly monotheistic and believe that to search for God through images is a sin. Muslim teachings correspond closely with the Old Testament of the Bible, and Moses and Jesus are both accepted as Muslim prophets, although Jesus is not the son of God.

Eventually Mohammed's attacks on local business caused him and his followers to be run out of town in 622. They fled to Medina, the 'city of the prophet', and by 630 were strong enough to march back into Mecca and take over. Although Mohammed died in 632, most of Arabia had been converted to Islam within two decades.

The Muslim faith was more than a religion; it called on its followers to spread the word – if necessary by the sword. In succeeding centuries Islam was to expand over three continents. The Arabs, who first propagated the faith, developed a reputation as being ruthless opponents but reasonable masters, so people often found it advisable to surrender to them. In this way the Muslims swept aside the crumbling Byzantine Empire, whose people felt no desire to support their distant Christian emperor.

Islam only travelled west for 100 years before being pushed back at Poitiers, France, in 732, but it continued east for centuries. It regenerated the Persian Empire, which was then declining from its protracted struggles with Byzantium, and in 711, the same year the Arabs landed in Spain, they sent dhows up the Indus River into India. This was more a casual raid than a full-scale invasion, but in the 12th century all of north India fell into Muslim hands. Eventually the Moghul Empire controlled most of the subcontinent. From here it was spread by Indian traders into South-East Asia.

At an early stage Islam suffered a fundamental split that remains to this day. The third Caliph, successor to Mohammed, was murdered and followed by Ali, the prophet's son-in-law, in 656.

Ali was assassinated in 661 by the governor of Syria, who set himself up as Caliph in preference to the descendants of Ali. Most Muslims today are Sunnites, followers of the succession from the Caliph, while the others are Shias or Shi'ites who follow the descendants of Ali.

Despite its initial vigour, Islam eventually became inertial and unchanging though it remains to be seen what effect the fanatical fundamentalism of Shi'ite Iran will have on the religion world-wide. In India itself, despite Islam's long period of control over the centuries, it never managed to make great inroads into Hindu society and religion. Converts to Islam were principally made from the lowest castes, with the result that at partition Pakistan found itself with a shortage of the educated clerical workers and government officials with which India is so liberally endowed. Although it did not make great numbers of converts, the visible effects of Muslim influence in India are strong in architecture, art and food.

Converts to Islam have only to announce that 'There is no God but Allah

and Mohammed is his prophet' and they become Muslims. Friday is the Muslim holy day and the main mosque in each town is known as the Jami Masjid or Friday Mosque. One of the aims of every Muslim is to make the pilgrimage to Mecca and become a *hajji*.

Sikhs

The Sikhs number 13 million and are particularly found in the Punjab, although they are all over India. They are the most visible of the Indian religious groups because of the five symbols introduced by Guru Gobind Singh so that Sikh men could easily recognise each other. They are known as the five *kakkars* and are: *kesh* – uncut hair; *kangha* – the wooden or ivory comb; *kachha* – shorts; *kara* – the steel bracelet; and *kirpan* – the sword. Because of their kesha, Sikh men wear their hair tied up in a bun and hidden by a long turban. Wearing kachha and carrying a kirtipan came about because of the Sikhs' military tradition – they didn't want to be tripping over a long *dhoti* or caught without a weapon. Normally the sword is simply represented by a tiny image set in the comb. The steel bracelet has the useful secondary function of making a good bottle opener. With his beard, turban and upright, military bearing, the 'noble' Sikh is hard to miss!

The Sikh religion was founded by Guru Nanak, who was born in 1469. It was originally intended to bring together the best of the Hindu and Islamic religions. Its basic tenets are similar to those of Hinduism with the important modification that the Sikhs are opposed to caste distinctions and pilgrimages to rivers. They are not, however, opposed to pilgrimages to holy sites. They worship at temples known as *gurdwaras*, baptise their children, when they are old enough to understand the religion, in a ceremony known as *pahul*, and cremate their dead. The holy book of the Sikhs is the *Granth Sahib* which contains the works of the 10 Sikh gurus

together with Hindu and Muslim writings. The last guru died in 1708.

In the 16th century, Guru Gobind Singh introduced military overtones into the religion in an attempt to halt the persecution the Sikhs were then suffering. From that time all Sikhs have borne the surname Singh which means 'lion'. Sikhs believe in one god and are opposed to idol worship. They practise tolerance and love of others, and their belief in hospitality extends to offering shelter to anyone who comes to their gurdwaras. Because of their get-on-with-it attitude to life they are one of the better-off groups in Indian society. They have a well-known reputation for mechanical aptitude and specialise in handling machinery of every type, from auto-rickshaws to jumbo jets.

At present, the Punjab region of India is torn by strife due to a minority of Sikhs demanding greater autonomy for the Punjab, or even an independent state to be called Khalistan. A solution to these problems is still not in sight and the Punjab is presently under martial law. Although foreigners are now allowed into the Punjab without permits, the situation is volatile and may change.

Jains

The Jain religion is contemporaneous with Buddhism and bears many similarities to it. It was founded around 500 BC by Mahavira, the 24th and last of the Jain prophets, known as *tirthankars* or 'finders of the path'. The Jains now number only about 3½ million and are found all over India, but predominantly in the west and south-west. They believe that the universe is infinite and was not created by a deity. They also believe in reincarnation and eventual spiritual salvation, or moksha, through following the path of the tirthankars. One factor in the search for salvation is *ahimsa*, or reverence for all life and the avoidance of injury to all living things. Due to this belief Jains are strict vegetarians and some monks actually cover their mouths with a piece of cloth in order to avoid the risk of accidentally swallowing an insect.

The Jains are divided into two sects, the Shvetambara and the Digambara. The Digambaras are the more austere sect and their name literally means 'sky clad' since as a sign of their contempt for material possessions, they do not even wear clothes. Not surprisingly Digambaras are generally monks who confine their nudity to the monasteries! The famous Sravanabelagola shrine in Karnataka state, south India is a Digambara temple. Jain temples are noted for the large number of similar buildings which are often erected at one place. Their temples also have many columns, no two of which are ever identical. The Jains tend to be commercially successful and have an influence disproportionate to their actual numbers. Their temples are often extremely well kept. There are many Jains in Rajasthan, Gujarat and Bombay.

Parsis

This is one of the oldest religions on earth and was founded in Persia by the prophet Zarathustra in the 6th or 7th century BC. He was born in Mazar-i-Sharif in what is now Afghanistan. At one time Zoroastrianism stretched all the way from India to the Mediterranean but today is found only around Shiraz in Iran, Karachi in Pakistan, and Bombay in India. The followers of Zoroastrianism are known as Parsis since they originally fled to India to escape persecution in Persia.

Zoroastrianism was one of the first religions to postulate an omnipotent and invisible god. Their scripture is the *Zend-Avesta*, which describes the continual conflict between the forces of good and evil. Their god is Ahura Mazda, the god of light, who is symbolised by fire. Humanity ensures the victory of good over evil by following the principles of *humata* or good thoughts, *hukta* or good words and *huvarshta* or good deeds.

Parsis worship in fire temples and wear a *sadra* or sacred shirt and a *kasti* or sacred thread. Children first wear these sacred items in a ceremony known as Navjote. Flames burn eternally in their fire temples but fire is worshipped as a symbol of God, not for itself. Because Parsis believe in the purity of elements they will not cremate or bury their dead since it would pollute the fire, earth, air or water. Instead they leave the bodies in 'Towers of Silence' where they are soon cleaned off by vultures.

Although there are only about 85,000 Parsis, concentrated in Bombay, they are very successful in commerce and industry. and have become notable philanthropists. Parsis have influence far greater than their numbers would indicate and often acted as a channel of communication between India and Pakistan when the two countries were at loggerheads. Because of the strict requirements that a Parsi must only marry another Parsi and children must have two Parsi parents to be Parsis, their numbers are gradually declining.

Christians & Jews

India has around 18 million Christians. There have been Christian communities in Kerala as long as Christianity has been in Europe, for St Thomas the Apostle is supposed to have arrived here in 54 AD.

The Portuguese, who unlike the English were as enthusiastic about spreading their brand of Christianity as making money from trade, left a large Christian community in Goa. Generally though, Christianity has not had great success in India, if success is counted in number of converts. The first round of Indian converts to Christianity were generally those from the ruling classes and after that the converts were mainly from the lower castes.

There are, however, two small states (Mizoram and Nagaland) where Christians form a majority of the population. A quarter of the population of Kerala and a third of Goa are also Christian. There are small Jewish communities in a number of cities, but the Jews of Cochin in Kerala are of interest because a group claims to have arrived here in 587 BC.

HOLIDAYS & FESTIVALS

Due to its religious and regional variations India has a great number of holidays and festivals. Most of them follow the lunar calendar, which differs from the Gregorian (western) calendar; thus they fall on a different date each year. Apart from the holidays and festivals celebrated nationally there are many local and regional occasions. PH – public holiday.

January

Sankranti Celebrated predominantly in Andhra Pradesh and amongst the Tamil people of the south in Tamil Nadu. This is a Hindu festival marking the change of season when the sun is supposed to move to its northern home, and the days get longer and the nights get shorter. It falls sometime in the middle of January.

Pongal This is a Tamil festival to mark the end of the harvest season. It is observed on the first day of the Tamil month of Thai, which is in the middle of January. The festivities last four days and include such activities as the boiling-over of a pot of *pongal* (a mixture of rice, sugar, dahl and milk), symbolic of a prosperity and abundance.

26 January

Republic Day Celebrates the anniversary of India's establishment as a republic in 1950; there are activities in all the state capitals but most spectacularly in New Delhi, where there is an enormously colourful military parade. (PH)

January-February

Vasant Panchami This festival to honour the goddess of learning, Saraswati, is celebrated on the 5th of Magha. Books, musical instruments and other objects related to the arts are placed in front of the goddess to receive her blessing.

February-March

Shivaratri This day of fasting is dedicated to Lord Shiva. Processions to the temples are followed by the chanting of mantras and anointing of lingams.

Holi This is one of the most exuberant Hindu festivals, with people marking the end of winter by throwing coloured water or powder at one another – don't wear good clothes on this day!

On the night before Holi bonfires are built to symbolise the destruction of the evil demon Holika. It's mainly a northern festival; in the south, where there is no real winter to end, it only takes place in Bangalore. In Maharashtra it is known as *Rangapanchami* and is celebrated with dancing and singing. (PH)

March-April

Mahavir Jayanti This major Jain festival marks the birth of Mahavira, the 24th and last Jain tirthankar. (PH)

Ramanavami In temples all over India the birth of Rama, an incarnation of Vishnu, is celebrated on this day. (PH)

Good Friday This Christian holiday is also celebrated in India. (PH)

May-June

Buddha Jayanti The Buddha's birth, enlightenment and reaching of nirvana are all celebrated on this day. The Buddha is supposed to have gone through each of these experiences on the same day but in different years. (PH)

June-July

Rath Yatra (Car Festival) Lord Jagannath's great temple chariot makes its stately journey from his temple in Puri, Orissa. Similar, but far less grandiose, festivals take place in other locations.

Lord Jagannath is one of Krishna's names, who is the eighth incarnation of Vishnu. The main procession in Puri celebrates Krishna's journey to Mathura to visit his aunt for a week! The images of his brother (Balarama) and sister (Subhadra) are paraded with him.

July-August

Naga Panchami This festival is dedicated to Ananta, the serpent upon whose coils Vishnu rested between universes. Offerings are made to snake images and snake charmers do a roaring trade. Snakes are supposed to have power over the monsoon rainfall and keep evil from homes.

15 August

Independence Day The anniversary of India's independence from Britain in 1947. The prime minister delivers an address from the ramparts of Delhi's Red Fort. (PH)

August-September

Nariel Purnima A celebration of the official end of the monsoon. Observed by sailors and fishermen.

Shravan Purnima After a day-long fast, high-caste Hindus replace the sacred thread which they always wear looped over their left shoulder.

Raksha Bandhan On the full-moon day of the Hindu month of Shravan, girls fix amulets known as *rakhis* to their brothers' wrists to protect them in the coming year. The brothers give their sisters gifts.

Pateti Parsis celebrate their new year. A week later *Khordad Sal* celebrates the birth of Zarathustra.

Janmastami The anniversary of Krishna's birth is celebrated with happy abandon – in tune with Krishna's own mischievous moods. Although it is a national holiday, Agra, Bombay and Mathura (his birthplace) are the main centres. Devotees fast all day until midnight. (PH)

September

Ganesh Chaturthi This festival, held on the fourth day of the Hindu month Bhadon, is dedicated to the popular elephant-headed god Ganesh. It is widely celebrated all over India, but with particular enthusiasm in Maharashtra.

In every village, shrines are erected and a clay Ganesh idol is installed. Firecrackers are let off at all hours. Each family also buys a clay idol, and on the day of the festival it is brought into the house where it is kept and worshipped for a specified period before being ceremoniously immersed in a river, tank or the sea.

As Ganesh is the god of wisdom and prosperity, Ganesh Chaturthi is considered to be the most auspicious day of the year. It is considered unlucky to look at the moon on this day.

Onam Harvest Festival This is a Keralan harvest festival. During it the famous snake boat races are held.

September-October

Dussehra This is the most popular of all the Indian festivals and takes place over 10 days, beginning on the first day of the Hindu month of Ashwin. It celebrates Rama's victory over the demon king Ravana and in many places culminates with the burning of huge images of Ravana and his accomplices.

In Delhi it is known as *Ram Lila* ('life-story of Rama') and there are re-enactments of the *Ramayana* and fireworks. In Mysore and Ahmedabad there are great processions. In West Bengal the festival is known as *Durga Puja* since Durga aided Rama in his defeat of Ravana. In Gujarat as *Navaratra* ('festival of nine nights'). In Kulu, in the north, the festival takes place a little later than elsewhere, and it is a delightful time when the Kulu Valley shows why it is known as the 'Valley of the Gods'. (PH – two days)

2 October

Gandhi Jayanti A solemn celebration of Gandhi's birthday with prayer meetings at the Raj Ghat in Delhi where he was cremated. (PH)

October-November

Diwali (or *Deepavali*) This is the happiest festival of the Hindu calendar, celebrated on the 15th day of Kartik. At night countless oil lamps are lit to show Rama the way home from his period of exile. Today the festival is also dedicated to Lakshmi (particularly in Bombay) and to Kali in Calcutta. In all, the festival lasts five days. On the first day, houses are thoroughly cleaned and doorsteps are decorated with intricate *rangolis* (chalk designs). Day two is dedicated to Krishna's victory over Narakasura, a legendary tyrant. In the south, new clothes are worn on this day following a pre-dawn oil bath. Day three is spent in worshipping Lakshmi, the goddess of fortune. Traditionally, this is the beginning of the new financial year for companies. Day four commemorates the visit of the friendly (but uppity) demon Bali whom Vishnu put in his place. On the fifth day men visit their sisters to have a tikka put on their forehead.

Diwali has also become the 'festival of sweets' and families give and receive sweets. This has become as much a part of

Ganesh festival, Badami, Karnataka

the traditon as the lighting of oil lamps and firecrackers.

Diwali is also celebrated by the Jains as their New Year's Day. (PH)

November

Govardhana Puja A Hindu festival dedicated to that holiest of animals, the cow. (PH)

Pushkar Camel Fair This incredibly colourful camel and cattle fair in Rajasthan includes camel races amongst other events.

Nanak Jayanti The birthday of Guru Nanak, the founder of the Sikh religion, is celebrated with prayer readings and processions, particularly in Amritsar and Patna. (PH)

December

Feast of St Francis Xavier On 3 December this festival and the feast of Our Lady of the Immaculate Conception are two of the most important festivals in Goa.

25 December

Christmas Day A holiday in India. (PH)

Muslim Holidays

Muslim festivals are not fixed as they fall about 11 days earlier each year.

Ramadan The most important Muslim festival is a 30-day dawn-to-dusk fast. It was during this month that the prophet Mohammed had the Koran revealed to him in Mecca. In Muslim countries this can be a difficult time for travellers since restaurants are closed and tempers tend to run short. Fortunately, despite India's large Muslim minority, it causes few difficulties for visitors.

Id-ul-Fitr This day celebrates the end of Ramadan. (PH)

Id-ul-Zuhara A Muslim festival commemorating Abraham's attempt to sacrifice his son. It is celebrated with prayers and feasts. (PH)

Muharram A 10-day festival commemorating the martyrdom of Mohammed's grandson, Imam Hussain. (PH)

Festival Calendar

festival	place	1990	1991	1992
Pongal	Tamil Nadu	15-16 Jan	15-16 Jan	15-16 Jan
Republic Day	New Delhi	26 Jan	26 Jan	26 Jan
Basant Panchami		31 Jan	21 Jan	9 Feb
Shivaratri		24 Feb	13 Feb	3 Mar
Holi		10 Mar	28 Feb	18 Mar
Good Friday		13 Apr		
Ramanavami		3 Apr	24 Mar	11 Apr
Mahavir Jayanthi		7 Apr		
Buddha's Birthday		9 May	28 Apr	16 May
Car Festival	Puri	24 Jun	13 Jul	2 Jul
Janmastami		13 Aug	2 Sep	21 Aug
Teej	Jaipur	23 Aug	11 Sep	30 Aug
Ganesh Chaturthi		29 Oct		
Diwali		18 Oct	5 Nov	25 Oct
Camel Fair	Pushkar	1-2 Nov	19-21 Nov	8-10 Nov

Seasons

English	Hindi	English	Hindi
Spring	Vasanta	March-April	Chaitra
		April-May	Baisakh
Hot Season	Grishma	May-June	Jeth
		June-July	Asarh
Rains	Varsha	July-August	Shrawan
		August-September	Bhadon
Autumn	Sharada	September-October	Ashwin
		October-November	Kartik
Winter	Hemanta	November-December	Aghan
		December-January	Pous
Cold Season	Shishira	January-February	Magh
		February-March	Phalgun

LANGUAGE

There is no 'Indian' language, which is part of the reason why English is still widely spoken 40 years after the British left India. The country is divided into a great number of local languages and in many cases the state boundaries have been drawn on linguistic lines. In all there are 14 major languages in India and probably over 200 minor languages and dialects. The scope for misunderstanding can be easily appreciated!

The most important Indian language is Hindi, although it is only spoken by about 20% of the population. In recent years major efforts have been made to promote Hindi as the national language of India and to gradually phase out English. A stumbling block to this plan is that while Hindi is the predominant language in the north – and also related to other northern languages such as Urdu (4%), Punjabi (2%), Gujarati (3%), Oriya (2%) and Bengali (5%) – it bears little relation to the Dravidian languages of the south; and in the south very few people speak Hindi. Tamil is the most important Dravidian language (spoken by about 5%), while others include Telugu (5%), Kannada (3%) and Malayalam (3%). It is from the south, particularly the state of Tamil Nadu, that the most vocal opposition to the adoption of Hindi comes, along with the strongest support for the retention of English.

For many educated Indians, English is virtually their first language, and for a great number of Indians who speak more than one language it will be their second language. Thus it is very easy to get around India with English – after all, many Indians have to speak English to each other if they wish to communicate. Nevertheless it's always nice to know at least a little of the local language.

Hindi

The following words and phrases are in Hindi:

Where is a hotel (tourist office)?
hotal (turist afis) kahan hai?
How far is. . .?
. . .kitne dur hai?
How do I get to. . .?
. . .kojane ke liye kaise jana parega?

hello, goodbye	*namaste*
yes/no	*han/nahin*
please	*meharbani se*
thank you	*shukriya,*
	dhanyawad
How much?	*kitne paise?*
This is expensive.	*yeh bahut*
	mehnga hai

What is your name?	*apka shubh nam kya hai?*
What is the time?	*kitne baje hain?*
Come here.	*idhar aaiyee*
Show me the menu.	*mujhe minu dikhayee*
The bill please.	*bill de dijiyee*
big	*bara*
small	*chota*
today	*aaj*
day	*din*
night	*rat*
week	*saptah*
month	*mahina*
year	*sal*
medicine	*dawa*
ice	*baraf*
egg	*anda*
fruit	*phal*
vegetables	*sabzi*
water	*pani*
rice	*chawal*
tea	*chai*
coffee	*kafi*
milk	*dudh*
sugar	*chini*
butter	*makkhan*

Beware of *acha*, that all-purpose word for 'OK'. It can also mean 'OK, I understand what you mean, but it isn't OK'. As in 'Have you got a room available?' to which the answer *acha* means 'I understand you want a room but I haven't got one'.

Tamil

Although Hindi is being promoted as the 'official' language of India, it won't get you very far in the south, where Tamil reigns supreme. Tamil is a much more difficult language to master and the pronunciation is not easy. The following words and phrases are in Tamil:

I want to go to. . . .
  naan. . . kku poga-vendum
How do I get there?
  naan anke eppadi povathu

Where is. . . .?	
. . . . yenge irukkirathu	
good morning/ good night	*vanakkam*
good bye	*poi varukiren*
good bye (to you)	*poi varungal*
How do you do?	*nalama?*
yes/no	*aam/illai*
thank you	*nandri*
How much?	*ennavillai?*
too expensive	*athikavillai*
big	*perithu*
small	*siriyathu*
good	*nallathu*
bad	*kettathu*
today	*indru*
day*	*naal*
day**	*pahal neram*
night	*iravu neram*
week	*vaaram*
month	*maatham*
year	*varudam*
time	*kalam*
eat	*sappidu*
drink	*kudi*

* as a period of time
** as opposed to night

Numbers

A peculiarity of Indian numbers is that whereas we count in tens, hundreds, thousands, millions, billions, the Indian numbering system goes tens, hundreds, thousands, hundred thousands, ten millions. A hundred thousand is a *lakh* and 10 million is a *crore*.

These two words are almost always used in place of their English equivalent. Thus you will see 10 lakh rather than one million and one crore rather than 10 million. Furthermore, the numerals are generally written that way too – thus 3,00,000 (three lakh) not 300,000 (three hundred thousand) or 1,05,00,000 (one crore, five lakh) not 10,500,000 (ten million, five hundred thousand). If you say something costs five crore or someone is worth 10 lakh it always means 'of rupees'.

	Hindi	Tamil
1	ek	onru
2	do	irandu
3	tin	moonru
4	char	naangu
5	panch	ainthu
6	chhe	aaru
7	sat	ezhu
8	ath	ettu
9	nau	onpathu
10	das	pathu
100	sau	nooru
1000	hazar	aayiram
100,000	lakh	
10,000,000	crore	

Phrasebooks

Once again, Lonely Planet has the subcontinent well covered with phrasebooks for Hindi/Urdu, Nepali and Sinhala.

There are also many phrasebooks and teach-yourself books available in India for Hindi and the other major languages, if you want to learn more of the language. Some of them are typically and amusingly Indian. A section on a visit to the doctor in one phrasebook included the following useful series of phrases, the first of which is quite unlikely in India:

I suffer from severe constipation.
I am feeling a bit out of sorts today.
The patient is sinking fast.
He has much run down.
The patient is in a precarious condition.
Cholera has broken out in the city.
He is dying by inches.

Facts for the Visitor

VISAS

These days virtually everybody needs a visa to visit India and, if you intend to stay longer than 90 days, you will also have to go through the paperwork and red tape involved in extending a visa. In fact, getting your visa will probably be your first encounter with the morass of Indian bureaucracy and, although generally your application will go through smoothly, we consistently receive more complaints about problems, delays, extra costs and unfair actions over visas for India than for any other country.

Indian visas are available from Indian consular offices and usually cost around US$5 or equivalent. Make sure you know what the price is, though. We've had several complaints from people who sent in the visa fee requested on the form only to discover much later that the fee had been changed and their visa request was on hold until they sent the correct amount. As a result of what the Indian Government sees as racist legislation passed through the British Parliament, UK citizens have to pay a much higher visa fee (£23), and many British residents of Australia have been tripped up by this as there is no indication on the form that different fees apply. We've also had a couple of letters from people who, when they enquired why their visa was taking so long to issue, were told it could be rushed through for an additional fee! Corruption in high places!

Where you apply for a visa also seems to make a difference. Numerous travellers have written to complain that Athens is an absolutely terrible place to get an Indian visa but Ankara, capital of neighbouring Turkey, is no problem at all. In Karachi they are loathe to give out double and triple-entry visas. In South-East Asia some people say Bangkok is fine, others say that it's chaotic but

Chiang Mai in the north of Thailand is a breeze. In some countries (Malaysia and Nepal for example) the Indian consular office insists that British passport holders supply a letter from the British consular office confirming that they really are British! This costs the unfortunate Brits another US$5 or so!

Make sure your visa is a multiple-entry one if you intend to depart and return. Some people unwittingly end up with single-entry visas which do not permit you to return to India. Also, some offices will not allow you to renew your visa until it is less than 14 days from expiry. The visa renewal hassles are not due to reluctance to let people stay longer, but to the usual Indian red tape and bureaucracy.

Embassies

Some of the major Indian consular offices overseas include:

Australia
   3-5 Moonah Place, Yarralumla, ACT 2600 (tel (062) 733 999)
Bangladesh
   120 Road 2, Dhanmodi Residential Area H No 129, Dhaka (tel 507 670)
Burma (Myanmar)
   545-547 Merchant St, Rangoon (tel 15933, 16381)

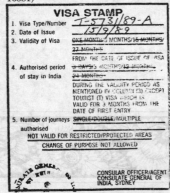

VISA STAMP
1. Visa Type/Number   I-573/89-A
2. Date of Issue   15/9/89
3. Validity of Visa   ONE MONTH/3 MONTHS/15 MONTHS/22 MONTHS
   FROM THE DATE OF ISSUE OF VISA
4. Authorised period   3 DAYS/3 MONTHS/12 MONTHS/
   of stay in India   24 MONTHS
   DURING THE VALIDITY PERIOD AS
   MENTIONED IN COLUMN (3) EXCEPT
   TOURIST (T) VISA WHICH IS
   VALID FOR 3 MONTHS FROM THE
   DATE OF FIRST ENTRY
5. Number of journeys   SINGLE/DOUBLE/MULTIPLE
   authorised
   NOT VALID FOR RESTRICTED/PROTECTED AREAS
   CHANGE OF PURPOSE NOT ALLOWED
   CONSULAR OFFICER/AGENT
   CONSULATE GENERAL OF
   INDIA, SYDNEY

Canada
    10 Springfield Rd, Ottawa K1M 1C9 (tel 744 3751)
France
    15 Rue Alfred Dehodencq, 75016 Paris (tel 4520 3930)
Japan
    2-11 Kudan Minami 2-Chome, Chiyoda-ku, Tokyo (tel 262 2391)
Kenya
    Jeevan Bharati Building, Harambee Ave (tel 22566)
Malaysia
    United Asian Bank Building, 19 Malacca St, Kuala Lumpur (tel 221766)
Nepal
    Lainchaur, GPO Box 292, Kathmandu (tel 211300)
Netherlands
    Buitenrustwg 2, The Hague (tel (070) 469771)
New Zealand
    180 Molesworth St, Princess Towers, Wellington (tel 736 390)
Pakistan
    482-F Sector G-6/4, Islamabad (tel 821049)
Singapore
    India House, 31 Grange Rd (tel 737 6777)
Sri Lanka
    3rd floor, State Bank of India Building, 18-3/1 Sir Baron Jayatilaka Mawatha, Colombo 1 (tel 21604, 22788)
Switzerland
    Weltportstr 17, 3015 Berne (tel (031) 440193)
Thailand
    46 Soi Prasarmitr, Sukhumvit 23, Bangkok (tel 258 0300)
UK
    India House, Aldwych, London WC2B 4NA (tel 836 8484)
USA
    2107 Massachusetts Ave NW, Washington DC 20008 (tel 939 7000)
West Germany
    Adenaverallee 262, 5300 Bonn (tel 54050)

Visa Extensions

If your stay in India is going to be more than 90 days, you have to extend your visa and need to have a few days to spare while you wait for it to come through. The time taken varies from one hour (Bangalore) to 10 days (Cochin). At present, visa extensions cannot be obtained in Goa. You would have to go to either Bombay or

Bangalore to do this. Officially there is no charge for visa extensions although public servants fishing for baksheesh are not unheard of. Four identical passport photos are needed.

If you leave the country and pop across the border to Nepal after 60 days, for example, when you return you will only have until the original 90 days runs out. In other words, you do not have 30 days left, nor do you start the 90 days again. A 90-day visa is just that; it lasts for 90 days from the date of the first entry into India, regardless of the number of days you actually spend in India.

If you stay beyond 90 days you are also supposed to get an income tax clearance before you leave. See section further on for details.

There is reportedly a regulation which allows you to stay three days after your visa has expired without incurring the wrath of the authorities, although this is unsubstantiated at present.

Foreigners' Registration Offices

Visa renewals and also permits for Darjeeling and the Andaman Islands are issued by the Foreigners' Registration offices. The main offices include:

Bombay
    Special Branch II, Annexe 2, Office of the Commissioner of Police (Greater Bombay), Dadabhoy Naroji Rd (tel 268111)
Calcutta
    237 Acharya Jagdish Bose Rd (tel 443301)
New Delhi
    1st floor, Hans Bhavan, Tilak Bridge (tel 272790)
Madras
    9 Village Rd (tel 478210)

Visas can also be renewed in all state and district capitals at the District Police Commissioner's office.

Tax Clearance Certificates

If you stay in India for more than 90 days you need a 'tax clearance certificate' to leave the country. This supposedly proves that your time in India was financed by your own money, not by working in India or by selling things or playing the black market. A few years ago getting a tax clearance certificate was a major operation requiring all sorts of forms and lots of time. Today it is much simpler and more straightforward.

Basically all you have to do is find the Foreign Section of the Income Tax Department in Delhi, Calcutta, Madras or Bombay and turn up with your passport, visa extension form, any other similar paperwork and a handful of bank exchange receipts (to show you really have been changing foreign currency into rupees). You fill in a form and wait for 'only 10 minutes' (say the best-case people) to 'only a couple of hours' (say the worst). You're then given your tax clearance certificate and away you go. Nearly everybody reports that when you depart the country, nobody even asks for it.

Special Permits
Even with a visa you are not allowed everywhere in India. Certain places require special additional permits. These are covered in the appropriate sections in the main text, but briefly they are:

Darjeeling Permits can be obtained from consular offices abroad or from the main Foreigners' Registration offices in Bombay, Calcutta, Delhi or Madras. They cannot be obtained while en route to Darjeeling from Calcutta or at the border if you are coming through Nepal from Kathmandu. The permits are generally valid for an initial stay of 15 days and are easy to obtain. Kalimpong is generally included on a Darjeeling permit but not always, so make sure you specify this on your application form. The only exception from the permit system is if you fly to and from Bagdogra, the airport for Darjeeling.
North-East Frontier You must have a permit for these remote north-east states

and where you may go is restricted. The permits can be obtained (with difficulty) at the offices in Calcutta.
Andaman Islands If you are arriving at these islands by ship, you need a permit in advance. For those arriving by plane, permits are issued on arrival in Port Blair. The permits are obtainable from an embassy or consulate abroad or from the Ministry of Home Affairs in New Delhi. The application to these places must be made at least six weeks in advance although they recommend you allow 12 weeks. In Madras, however, you can get a permit in just three days.
Sikkim You must apply for a permit at least six weeks in advance at a diplomatic office abroad or the Ministry of Home Affairs in New Delhi. To be sure of getting one, however, it's best to apply three months in advance. Your initial permit allows a stay of only four days but this is easily extended once in Sikkim. You are restricted as to where you may go in Sikkim.
Bhutan Although Bhutan is an independent country, India has firm control over foreign policy and most other things. Applications to visit Bhutan must be made through the Director of Tourism, Ministry of Finance, Tachichho Dzong, Thimpu, Bhutan; or through the Bhutan Foreign Mission (tel 74075), Chandragupta Marg, New Delhi 110021, India; or through the Bhutanese mission in New York. Before applying, you must have the relevant permits for the restricted areas of India you must pass through in order to reach Bhutan. And don't hold your breath – unless you have high-up Indian connections or a personal friend in the Bhutanese aristocracy, you needn't expect to get a permit. At present permits appear to be issued only to groups, and then generally only for tours which cost over US$100 per day.
Punjab Permits for the Punjab were no longer required when this book went to print – check before you travel.

Other Visas

If you're heading to other places around India the visa stories are as follows:

Afghanistan There is an embassy in Delhi although it may be easier and cheaper to get a visa in Pakistan. Any visit to Afghanistan is still likely to be a fly-in fly-out operation and completely restricted to Kabul.

Burma (Myanmar) The embassy in New Delhi is fast and efficient and issues two-week visas. There is *no* Burmese consulate in Calcutta although there is one in Kathmandu.

Nepal The Nepalese Embassy in New Delhi is on Barakhamba Rd, quite close to Connaught Place, not out at Chanakyapuri like most other embassies. There is also a consulate in Calcutta. Visas take 24 hours and cost Rs 150. A 14-day visa is available on arrival in Nepal and can be extended, but doing so involves rather a lot of form filling and queueing – better to have a visa in advance if possible.

Sri Lanka Most western nationalities do not need a visa to visit Sri Lanka, but there are diplomatic offices in New Delhi, Bombay and Madras.

Thailand There are Thai embassies in New Delhi and Calcutta. The visa costs about US$10 and is issued in 24 hours. If you are flying in and out of Thailand within 15 days, a visa is not required but the 15 days cannot be extended.

CUSTOMS

The usual duty-free regulations apply for India, that is, one bottle of whiskey and 200 cigarettes. If you bring in more than US$1000 in cash and/or travellers' cheques you are supposed to fill in a currency declaration form. This is another totally useless bit of red tape because once you have filled in the form at the airport, it is never checked or asked for again.

You're allowed to bring in all sorts of western technological wonders, but big items, such as video cameras, are likely to be entered on a 'Tourist Baggage Re-Export' form to ensure you take them out with you when you go.

DOCUMENTS

You must have a passport; it's the most basic travel document. In fact it appears you should have your passport with you all the time. We had a letter from two Australians who spent four days in jail during the Pushkar cattle fair because they'd left their passports for safekeeping in Jaipur. Two of the four days were after a friend had returned to Jaipur and collected the passports for them! Another traveller who was comprehensively ripped off on a day trip to Gwalior had fortunately left his passport in Agra. The police, however, were more upset about the passport left behind than the theft! The fact that if he had had it with him he would now not have it made no difference!

A health certificate, while not necessary in India, may well be required for onward travel. Student cards are virtually useless these days – many student concessions have either been eliminated or replaced by 'youth fares' or similar age concessions. Similarly, a Youth Hostel card is not generally required for India's many hostels but you do pay slightly less with one.

There is not much opportunity to get behind the wheel in India, but if you do intend to drive then get an International Driving Permit from your local national motoring organisation. These days motorcycles are more readily available for hire, particularly in Goa, and an International Permit is useful if you rent one. An International Permit can also be used for other identification purposes, such as plain old bicycle hire. It's worth having a batch of passport photos for visa applications and other uses. If you run out, Indian photo studios will do excellent portraits at pleasantly low prices.

MONEY

A$ 1 = Rs 13
US$ 1 = Rs 16.8
UK£1 = Rs 26

The rupee (Rs) is divided into 100 paise (p). There are coins of 5, 10, 20, 25 and 50 paise and Rs 1, and notes of Rs 1, 2, 5, 10, 20, 50 and 100.

Currency Exchange Forms

You are not allowed to bring Indian currency into the country or take it out of the country. You are allowed to bring in unlimited amounts of foreign currency or travellers' cheques but you are supposed to declare anything over US$1000 on arrival. All money is supposed to be changed at official banks or money-changers, and you are supposed to be given a currency exchange form for each transaction. In actual practice you can surreptitiously bring rupees into the country with you – they can be bought at a useful discount price in places like Singapore or Bangkok. Indian rupees can be brought in fairly openly from Nepal and again you can get a slightly better rate there.

Banks will usually give you a currency exchange form but occasionally they don't bother. It is worth getting them for several reasons: firstly, you will need one for any re-exchange when you depart India; secondly, certain official purchases, such as airline tickets, must be paid for either with foreign currency or with rupees accompanied by sufficient exchange forms to account for the ticket price. This is actually a complete waste of time since some little note will be scrawled on the form to the effect that it was sighted when you bought a ticket from A to B. When you buy a ticket from B to C somebody else can quite easily scrawl a similar little note on another corner of the same form! The third reason for saving exchange forms is that if you stay in India longer than 90 days then you have to get an income tax clearance and this requires production of a handful of exchange forms to prove you've been changing money all along and not earning money locally.

Which Currency or TC?

In major cities you can change most foreign currencies or travellers' cheques – Australian dollars, Deutschmarks, yen or whatever – but out of town it's best to stick to US dollars or pounds sterling. The pound still has a sentimental appeal in India. Thomas Cook and American Express are both popular travellers' cheques and have a number of branches in India. Due to problems of fraudulent use, some banks, principally the State Bank of India, will not accept American Express travellers' cheques. The Bank of Baroda and the Canara Bank both accept them. In some towns you may find it impossible to cash them at all, so although most of the time they are OK, it's probably wise to bring at least a few other travellers' cheques just in case.

Many people make the mistake of bringing too many small-denomination cheques. Although many middle-range hotels now demand payment in foreign currency, unless you are moving rapidly from country to country you only need a handful of small denominations for end-of-stay conversions. In between, change as much as you feel happy carrying. This applies particularly in India where changing money can take time. You can also spend a lot of time finding a bank which will change money. The answer is to change money as infrequently as possible and to change it only in big banks in big cities.

Most branches of the State Bank of India and the Bank of Baroda now have special foreign exchange counters (often called Foreign Exchange Cell!) which are usually very efficient and sometimes stay open longer than normal bank hours. When changing money at a State Bank of India you must go to the main branch in any particular city. Smaller branches won't change travellers' cheques. Large hotels often offer exchange facilities but sometimes at a poorer rate than the banks.

Money Problems

In the major cities there is a black market for foreign currencies in cash. The best rate is paid for large denomination US dollar bills. In the four big cities, expect about 15% over the bank rate, 10% to 12% in other large places. If you have no qualms about dealing with the black market, it's quite accessible, with a little caution it's quite safe, and it does make the money go further. It is, of course, illegal.

Airline tickets (both domestic and international) must be paid for with a specific bank exchange form so wait until you actually book the ticket before exchanging.

Credit Cards

Credit cards are now widely accepted in India, particularly Diners Club, American Express and Visa. Card acceptability can vary depending on how fast the credit card company is paying their bills.

With American Express you can use your card to obtain dollar or sterling travellers' cheques locally from an Amex office. Similarly, you can obtain rupees on a Visa card at any Andhra Bank branch. With their love of forms and carbon paper Indians delight in credit cards. You'll be delighted too when you get back; those bills eventually turn up and you find that the superb splash-out meal at the Ritz actually cost $12 or something equally ridiculous. Avoid paying for airline tickets with a credit card unless you have no alternative. It's considerably cheaper to pay for them with hard currency or travellers' cheques.

Transferring Money

Finally, don't run out of money in India. Getting money transferred to India is often a time-consuming, boring, tricky and unpleasant operation. Even transferred by cable it can take weeks and weeks; and by mail it can take forever. Banks have a reputation for not telling people when money has arrived - better in their balance than your pocket seems to be the mood.

If you must have money sent to you in India, specify the bank, the branch and the address you want it sent to; get it sent by telex or cable rather than by mail; and keep your fingers crossed. Preferably send it to a foreign bank since they are much more efficient when it comes to overseas transactions than Indian banks. Overseas banks with branches in India include Bank of America, Chartered Bank and, particularly, Grindlays which has many branches in smaller cities as well as in the major cities where Amex also operate. Grindlays is a subsidiary of the Australian ANZ bank. Thomas Cook has also been recommended as a good organisation to transfer money through; a New Zealander who was robbed had money transferred through Thomas Cook in less than 24 hours. Other time periods we have had quoted include Citibank - less than one week by cable from the US; State Bank of India - a month by cable; Bank of Baroda - don't even consider it. American Express won't transfer money but will issue dollar travellers' cheques over the counter if you have a card. You have to give them a personal cheque to cover the amount but, if you don't have a cheque book, then ask for a counter cheque.

Indian money has its own special angles and curiosities. For a start there is never any change. The restaurant may have been crowded all day but when you give them Rs 5 for a Rs 2 drink they won't have any change. Actually the shortage of change is not quite as bad as they'd like to make out. Often they do have change but are trying to bluff you into parting with yours rather than vice versa. The solution is to always insist that you haven't got any change, then with luck when you meet up with someone who really doesn't have any you will.

Bus conductors never start trips with change. You pay for a Rs 6.60 fare with a Rs 10 note and your ticket is marked to indicate you're owed Rs 3.40. Don't lose it and don't forget to demand your change at the end of the trip.

Giving you change is also open to game playing. Change is never counted out as it is in the west; you're simply handed a handful. Very often if you stand there looking blank you'll be handed some more. Then some more. Post office staff are particularly good at this. You ask for a couple of aerograms, a couple of stamps to America, one for a card to England. Total amount, who knows? Everybody behind you in the queue is jostling to get to the front. You can be certain that first handful of change isn't the total due. Wait. This isn't, so I have subsequently been told, necessarily a way of jipping you out of what you're due, it's just the way change is given!

The quality of change is also important. Notes circulate far longer than they do in the west and the small notes in particular become very tatty. A note can have holes right through it and be quite acceptable but if it's torn at the top or bottom on the crease line then it's no good and you'll have trouble spending it. Even a missing corner makes a bill unacceptable. The answer to this is to simply accept it philosophically or think of clever uses. Use it for tips or for official purposes. I'd love to pay the Rs 300 departure tax with 300 totally disreputable Rs 1 notes – although someone who did just that wrote to say he had some trouble getting them to accept it! Of course you could just take it to a bank, but who wants to visit Indian banks more than necessary?

COSTS

It is virtually impossible to say what travelling around India will cost you. It depends on where you stay, what you eat, how you travel and how fast you travel. Two people travelling at exactly the same standard can spend vastly different amounts on a daily basis if one travels twice as fast as the other. A week lying on the beach at Goa watching the waves roll in brings daily costs down very rapidly.

From top to bottom: if you stay in luxury hotels, fly everywhere, and see a lot of India in a very short trip, you can spend a lot of money. India has plenty of hotels at US$50 or more a day and some where a room can cost US$100 plus – more than

what most Indians earn in a year. At the other extreme, if you scrimp and save, stay in dormitories or the cheapest hotels, always travel 2nd class on trains, and learn to exist on dhal and rice, you can see India on less than US$5 a day.

Most travellers will probably be looking for something between those extremes. If so, you'll stay in reasonable hotels with the sort of standard provided by the tourist bungalows in many states – a clean but straightforward room with fan cooling and bathroom. You'll eat in regular restaurants but occasionally splash out on a fancy meal when you're in a big town. If you mix your travel, you'll try 2nd class sometimes for short trips, and opt for 1st class if you're travelling on a long overnight trip. You'll take auto-rickshaws occasionally rather than always looking for a bus. In that case India could cost you something like US$15 to US$25 a day on average. It totally depends on what you're looking for.

As everywhere in Asia, you get pretty much what you pay for, and many times it's worth paying a little more for the experience. That old-fashioned Raj-style luxury is part of India's charm and sometimes it's foolish not to lay out the money and enjoy it.

TIPPING

In most Asian countries tipping is virtually unknown but India is an exception to that rule – although tipping has a rather different role in India than in the west. The term baksheesh, which encompasses tipping and a lot more besides, aptly describes the concept in India. You 'tip' not so much for good service but to get things done. A 'tip' to a station porter will ensure you a seat when the train is packed out to the very limit.

Judicious baksheesh will open closed doors, find missing letters and perform other small miracles. Tipping is not necessary for taxis nor for cheaper restaurants, but if you're going to be using something repeatedly an initial tip will ensure the standards are kept up – this may explain why the service is slower every time in your hotel restaurant for example. Keep things in perspective though. Demands for baksheesh can quickly become never-ending. Ask yourself if it's really necessary or desirable before shelling it out.

In tourist restaurants or hotels, where service is usually tacked on in any case, the normal 10% figure usually applies. In smaller places, where tipping is optional, you need only tip a couple of rupees, not a percentage of the bill. Hotel porters usually get about Rs 1 per bag; other possible tipping levels are Rs 1 to Rs 2 for bike watching, Rs 10 for train conductors or station porters performing miracles for you, and Rs 5 to Rs 15 for extra services from hotel staff.

TOURIST INFORMATION
Local Tourist Offices

Within India the tourist office story is somewhat blurred by the overlap between the national and state tourist offices. As well as the national tourist office, each state maintains its own tourist office and this can lead to some confusion. In some cities the national office is much larger than the state one or the state one is virtually nonexistent. Government of India tourist offices include:

Agra
   191 The Mall (tel 72377)
Aurangabad
   Krishna Vilas, Station Rd (tel 4817)
Bangalore
   KFC Building, 48 Church St (tel 579517)
Bombay
   123 M Karve Rd, Churchgate (tel 293144)
Calcutta
   4 Shakespeare Sarani (tel 441402)
Cochin
   Willingdon Island (tel 6045)
New Delhi
   88 Janpath (tel 320005)
Gawahati
   B K Kakati Rd, Ulubari (tel 31381)
Jaipur
   Khasa Kothi Hotel (tel 72200)

Khajuraho
   Near Western Group Temples (tel 47)
Madras
   154 Mount Rd (tel 869685)
Panaji (Goa)
   Communidade Building, Church Square (tel 3412)
Patna
   Tourist Bhavan, Beer Chand Patel Marg (tel 26721)
Shillong
   Directorate of Tourism, GS Rd, Police Bazaar (tel 25632)
Varanasi
   15B The Mall (tel 43189)

The state tourist offices vary widely in their efficiency and usefulness. Some of them are very good, some completely hopeless. In many states the tourist offices also run a chain of tourist bungalows which generally offer good accommodation at very reasonable prices. State tourist offices will usually be in the tourist bungalows.

The confusion and overlap between the national and state tourist offices often causes wasteful duplication. Both offices produce a brochure on place A, neither produces anything on place B. More confusion arises with the division between the Government of India Tourist Office and the Indian Tourism Development Corporation (ITDC). The latter is more an actual 'doing' organisation than a 'telling' one. The ITDC will actually operate the tour bus on the tour for which the tourist office sells tickets. The ITDC also runs a series of hotels and Travellers' Lodges around the country under the Ashok name. States may also have a tourist transport operation equivalent to the national ITDC, so in some cities you can have a national and a state tourist operator as well as a national and a state tourist office!

Overseas Reps

The Government of India Department of Tourism maintains a string of tourist offices overseas where you can get brochures, leaflets and some information about India. The tourist office leaflets and brochures are often very high in their informational quality and worth getting hold of. On the other hand, some of the overseas offices are not always as useful for obtaining information as those within the country. There are also smaller 'promotion offices' in Osaka (Japan) and in Dallas, Miami, San Francisco and Washington DC (USA).

Australia
  Carlton Centre, 55 Elizabeth St, Sydney NSW 2000 (tel (02) 232 1600)
  8 Parliament Court, 1076 Hay St, West Perth WA 6005 (tel (06) 321 6932)
Austria
  Opernring 1/E/II, 1010 Vienna (tel 5871462)
Belgium
  60 Rue Ravenstein, Boite 15, 1000 Brussels (tel (02) 511 1796)
Canada
  60 Bloor St, West Suite No 1003, Toronto, Ontario M4W 3B8 (tel (416) 962 3787)
France
  8 Boulevard de la Madeleine, 75009 Paris (tel 4265 8386)
Italy
  Via Albricci 9, 20122 Milan (tel 804952)
Japan
  Pearl Building, 9-18 Ginza, 7 Chome, Chuo ku, Tokyo 104 (tel 571 5062/3)
Malaysia
  Wisma HLA, Lot 203 Jalan Raja Chulan, 50200 Kuala Lumpur (tel 242 5301)
Singapore
  Podium Block, 4th floor, Ming Court Hotel, Tanglin Rd, Singapore 1024 (tel 235 5737)
Sweden
  Sveavagen 9-11 (Box 40016), S-III-57 Stockholm (tel (08) 215081)
Switzerland
  1-3 Rue de Chantepoulet, 1201 Geneva (tel (022) 321813)
Thailand
  Singapore Airlines Building, 3rd floor, 62/5 Thaniya Rd, Bangkok (tel 235 2585)
UK
  7 Cork St, London WIX QAB (tel (01) 437 3677/8)
USA
  30 Rockefeller Plaza, 15 North Mezzanine, New York NY 10020 (tel (212) 586 4901)

  230 North Michigan Ave, Chicago IL 60601 (tel (312) 236 6899)
  3550 Wilshire Blvd, Suite 204, Los Angeles CA 90010 (tel (213) 380 8855)
West Germany
  Kaiserstrasse 77-III, 6000 Frankfurt Main-1 (tel 235423)

Foreign Embassies

Countries with diplomatic relations with India generally have their consular offices in New Delhi, the capital, although many also have offices in Bombay and/or Madras or Calcutta. See the relevant sections for addresses.

GENERAL INFORMATION
Post

The Indian postal and poste restante services are generally excellent. Expected letters almost always are there and letters you send almost invariably get there, although they take up to three weeks. American Express, in its major city

locations, offers an alternative to the poste restante system.

Have letters addressed to you with your surname in capitals and underlined, the poste restante, GPO, and the city in question. Many 'lost' letters are simply misfiled under given names, so always check under both your names.

You can often buy stamps at good hotels, saving a lot of queueing in crowded post offices.

Posting Parcels Most people discover how to do this the hard way, in which case it demands all morning or all afternoon. If you're not that keen to reach a peak of hitherto unknown frustration, then go about it this way:

(1) Take the parcel to a tailor and tell him you'd like it stitched up in cheap linen and the seams sealed with sealing wax. The wax has to be pressed with a seal which cannot be duplicated (if all else fails a non-Indian coin will serve). At some larger post offices this stitching service is offered outside. For a small parcel it should cost Rs 7 to Rs 10.
(2) Go to the post office with your parcel and ask for two customs declaration forms. Fill them in and glue one to the parcel. The other will be stitched onto it. Write your passport number (or any likely looking number) somewhere on the forms together with 'bona fide tourist'. To avoid excise duty at the delivery end it's best to specify that the contents are a 'gift'.
(3) Have the parcel weighed and ask how much it's going to cost.
(4) Buy the stamps (usually not sold at the parcel counter) and stick them on.
(5) Hand the parcel in at the parcel counter and get a receipt for it.

Even if you do it this way it can still take up to two hours. Any other way and you say goodbye to the whole day. That is, if you don't take the easy way out and pay somebody else to do the whole thing! Be cautious with places which offer to mail

things to your home address after you have bought them. Government emporiums are usually OK, but although most people who buy things from other places get them eventually, some items never turn up (were they ever sent?) or what turns up isn't what they bought.

Sending parcels in the other direction (to you in India) is an extremely hit-and-miss affair. Don't count on anything bigger than a letter getting to you. Don't count on a letter getting to you if there's anything worthwhile inside it.

Telephone

The telephone system in India is hit and miss. Local calls sometimes work, sometimes don't. Trunk calls are even more a matter of chance. Many calls can be dialled direct but if you get through it feels like a pure fluke. It's probably even more flukey if you can actually hear anything. It's more time-consuming but more positive putting trunk calls through the operator, but again there's no guarantee you'll have a clear line.

For long-distance calls within India you can use the operator, or direct dial by STD (Standard Trunk Dialling), or make a Demand Call or Lightning Call. A Demand Call is made faster than a regular call and costs more too. A Lightning Call is supposed to go through (more or less) immediately and costs eight times the regular rate. It's often possible to make phone calls from big hotels far more quickly than from the crowded phone centres.

International calls, however, have improved dramatically in the past few years. You can now generally (but not always) get through quite quickly and the lines are usually remarkably clear. At phone centres in the major towns you can book a call for a couple of hours hence, go away and just turn up a few minutes before your call is due to go through but you have to leave a deposit (returnable if you don't get a connection) which is typically Rs 200. At major airports you can make international calls from the post office almost instantly – sometimes you can even dial the call yourself. Big hotels will put through international calls for you and these days a few small ones will too. Hotels will charge you extra for this service (about 25% is normal). If they appear to be making no effort to get you through then have a word with the telephonist and remember that baksheesh oils the cogs. A typical three-minute overseas call costs about US$10.

Telex

Domestic and international telex services in India are good, reasonably priced and not heavily used like the telephone services. Telex is a good way to reconfirm flights, as you have evidence of having done so. The bigger hotels will sometimes let you use their telex.

Electricity

The electric current is 230-240 volts AC, 50 cycles. Electricity is widely available in India but breakdowns and blackouts are not uncommon.

You can buy small immersion elements, perfect for boiling water for tea or coffee, for Rs 30. For about Rs 70 you can buy electric mosquito zappers. These are the type that take chemical tablets which melt and give off deadly vapours (deadly for the mosquito, that is). There are many different brands and they are widely available – they come with quaint names such as Good Knight.

Time

India is 5½ hours ahead of GMT, 4½ hours behind Australian Eastern Standard Time and 10½ hours ahead of American Eastern Standard Time.

Business Hours

Indian shops, offices and post offices are not early starters. Generally shops are open from 10 am to 5 pm Monday to Saturday. Some government offices open on alternate Saturdays and some commercial offices are open Saturday mornings. Post offices are open 10 am to 5 pm weekdays and Saturday mornings. Main city offices may be open longer hours, such as 8 am to 6 pm in Delhi.

Banks are open for business between 10 am and 2 pm on weekdays and 10 am and 12 noon on Saturdays. Sunday is the general closing day.

Dhobi-Wallahs

Your clothes will undoubtedly become involved at some point in your travels with the Indian ability to make systems of amazing complexity function smoothly. When you travel in India there's hardly any need for more than one change of clothes. Every day there will be a knock on your door and the laundry boy will collect all those dusty, sweaty clothes you wore yesterday, and every evening those same clothes will reappear – washed and ironed with more loving care than any washing-powder-ad mum ever lavished upon anything. And all for a few rupees per item. But what happened to your clothes between their departure and their like-new return?

Well, they certainly did not get anywhere near a washing machine. First of all they're collected and taken to the *dhobi ghat*. A ghat is a place with water, a dhobi is a washerperson, so the dhobi ghat is where the dhobis ply their trade and wash clothes. In big cities, dhobi ghats will be huge places with hundreds of dhobis doing their thing with thousands of articles of clothing.

Then the clothes are separated – all the white shirts are washed together, all the grey trousers, all the red skirts, all the blue jeans. By now, if this was the west, your clothes would either be hopelessly lost or you'd need a computer to keep track of them all. Your clothes are soaked in soapy water for a few hours, following which the dirt is literally beaten out of them. No multiprogrammed miracle of technology can wash as clean as a determined dhobi, although admittedly after a few visits to the Indian laundry your clothes do begin to look distinctly thinner. Buttons also tend to get shattered, so bring some spares. Zips sometimes fare likewise.

Once clean, the clothes are strung out on miles of clothesline to quickly dry in the Indian sun. They're then taken to the ironing sheds where hundreds of ironers wielding primitive irons press your jeans like they've never been pressed before. Not just your jeans – your socks, your T-shirts, even your underwear will come back with knife-edge creases. Then the Indian miracle takes place. Out of the thousands upon thousands of items washed that day, somehow your very own brown socks, blue jeans, yellow T-shirt and red underwear all find their way back together and head for your hotel room. A system of marking clothes, known only to the dhobis, is the real reason behind this feat. They say criminals have been tracked down simply by those tell-tale 'dhobi marks'.

MEDIA
Newspapers & Magazines
There are a number of daily English-language newspapers in India. All of them are of the heavy news variety; there are no tabloids on the subcontinent. The *Times of India*, the *Hindu* and the *Indian Express* are the best papers; many feel the *Express* is now the best of the bunch. The *Times* has its headquarters in Bombay and the *Statesman* in Calcutta but there are many regional editions in both cases.

The *Illustrated Weekly of India* makes good reading on long train rides and is readily available at train and bus station newsstands. The same applies to the fortnightly *India Today*, a news magazine very *Time*-like in its size, format, approach and layout. Also good reading is the magazine *Sunday*, a weekly which appears on the day of its name. The problem with all these Indian publications is that they are so inward looking that you soon become starved for outside news. *India Today*, in particular, is stuffed full of dull stories about state government politics. The strangely named magazine *Gentleman* also makes good reading.

Time and *Newsweek* are only available in the main cities, and anyway, once you've become used to Indian prices they seem very expensive! There are all sorts of other Indian magazines written in English although many are of very limited interest to western visitors – it takes a long time to build up an interest in Indian movie stars

and their fanzines. Indian women's magazines, so alike yet so unlike their western counterparts, are definitely worth looking at. There's even an Indian 'male interest' (we all know what that is) magazine called *Debonair* with photographs of nice ladies discreetly dropping their saris.

In keeping with the Indian preoccupation with sport, there is an incredible proliferation of sports magazines, but apart from tennis and cricket, there is little about what's happening on the international scene.

Radio & Television
India has a wide network of radio stations, and TV stations are becoming increasingly widespread. The TV programmes are very much intended to be educational rather than entertainment, however, and the sheer dreadfulness of Indian TV is a subject of continual discussion in the newspapers and other media. There are, however, some delightful exceptions though they're regrettably short in duration. The main one runs from 6.30 or 6.45 to 7 pm and features one or another variety of Indian classical music. Some of the performances are pure magic and watching this programme will give you an excellent idea of which ensembles are worth pursuing in the cassette shops.

SPORTS
Indians follow a variety of sports including field hockey, soccer and cricket. In hockey they are one of the world's leaders with several Olympic golds to their credit. Soccer has a keen following in a number of big cities, particularly Calcutta, where it is a major sport.

India's national sport (obsession almost) has to be cricket. There's something about a game with as many idiosyncrasies and peculiarities as cricket which simply has to appeal to the Indian temperament. During the cricket season, if an international side is touring India and there is a test match on, you'll see crowds at every street corner in the big cities clamouring to hear what the latest score is from someone who is listening to the radio. Test matches with Pakistan, one sign of the thaw in relations between the countries, have a particularly strong following as the rivalry is intense. One thing you can count on is that most Indians will know the names of the entire cricket touring team and, if you come from the same country but don't know their names, then you may well be regarded as mentally retarded.

HEALTH
Vaccinations
Smallpox has now been totally eradicated worldwide, so apart from yellow fever vaccinations for people coming from infected areas, there are no vaccination requirements for visitors to India. Nevertheless, you may consider protection against the diseases listed worthwhile.

Cholera is a disease of insanitation and usually occurs in epidemics. Protection against cholera is recommended for India and the vaccination is good for six months. A very useful vaccination, although not required by health authorities, is TABT. This provides protection against typhoid, paratyphoid A and B and tetanus. Typhoid and paratyphoid are both diseases of insanitation, spread by contaminated food. Tetanus is usually caused by a cut or skin puncture. All three are prevalent in hot climates. There are a number of medical centres in India where it is possible to get free or cheap cholera vaccinations and other vaccinations.

Polio is also a disease spread by insanitation and is more common in hot climates. A booster every five years is recommended by many doctors. The other vaccination you may wish to consider having is against infectious hepatitis. This disease is, once again, spread by infected water or food and the gamma globulin injection prescribed against it is now thought to give good protection for up to six months.

AIDS is perhaps less widespread in India than anywhere in Asia and likely to remain so. One of the main reasons is that sex doesn't enjoy a high profile and that prostitution is largely confined to areas and networks where foreigners wouldn't be welcome or wouldn't dream of going.

Travel Insurance
Don't travel without it! Hopefully you'll never need it but if you do, you'll be glad you've got it. There are many policies around and any good travel agency can put you on the right track. Most insurance packages include baggage and life insurance. Make sure it also covers flying you home in an emergency. Read the fine print and find one that suits your needs.

Medical Kit
It's wise to carry at least a basic medical kit. Items worth carrying include: bandaids, sterile gauze bandage, antiseptic cream or liquid, cotton wool, thermometer, tweezers, scissors, antibiotic cream, a mild pain killer (for toothaches, etc), a course of a broad-spectrum antibiotic (check with your doctor), insect repellent, antimalarial tablets, water purifying tablets and perhaps multivitamins.

Hospitals
Although India does have a few excellent hospitals such as the Mission Hospital in Vellore, Tamil Nadu, the Jaslok Hospital in Bombay and the All India Medical Institute in Delhi, most Indian cities do not have the quality of medical care available in the west. Usually hospitals run by western missionaries have better facilities than government hospitals where long waiting lines are common. Unless you have something very unusual, these Christian-run hospitals are the best places to head for in an emergency.

India also has many qualified doctors with their own private clinics which can be quite good and, in some cases, as good as anything available anywhere in the world. The usual fee for a clinic visit is about Rs 25; Rs 40 for a specialist. Home calls usually cost Rs 50.

Malaria

It is not (yet) possible to be vaccinated against malaria but it is absolutely necessary to take precautions against it while you are in India. Malaria is spread by mosquitoes and the disease has a nasty habit of coming back in later years even if you are cured at the time – and it can be fatal. Protection is simple – a daily or weekly tablet depending on which one your doctor recommends.

Chloroquine is quite safe for general use, side effects are minimal and it can be taken by pregnant women. Maloprim can have rare but serious side effects if the weekly dose is exceeded and some doctors recommend a check-up after six months continuous use. Fansidar, once used as a Chloroquine alternative, is no longer recommended as a prophylactic, as it can have dangerous side effects, but it may still be recommended as a treatment for malaria. Chloroquine is also used for malaria treatment but in larger doses than for prophylaxis. Doxycycline is another antimalarial for use where chloroquine resistance is reported; it causes hypersensitivity to sunlight, so sunburn can be a problem.

When travelling with very small children try to avoid using daily tablets – getting a tablet into a small child every day of the week is not a pleasant task. A syrup form of antimalarial is available for children. A final quirk of antimalarials is that they are absurdly expensive in the USA. A course of antimalarial tablets which might cost US$1 over the shelf in Asia or US$10 in Australia or Europe can set you back US$100 from a US drugstore! In many parts of Asia you can get antimalarials without even a prescription; if you're an American this can save you a lot of money.

Rabies

Rabies is widespread in India – don't be friendly to India's numerous stray dogs and beware of those picturesque monkeys.

The monkeys (particularly macaques) can be very aggressive if you are carrying food. If you are bitten by a possibly rabid animal you should wash the wound thoroughly and then embark on a series of injections which will prevent the disease from developing. Rabies, once developed, is almost always fatal.

New rabies vaccines have been developed which have fewer side effects than the older animal-derived serums and vaccines, but head for one of the big cities to get this treatment. There is also a rabies pre-exposure vaccination which requires just two shots, but you still need to have follow-up jabs if bitten. If you're going to a very isolated part of India and are worried about rabid animals, this might be worth considering.

Stomach Problems

The usual health problem afflicting visitors to India is far more mundane than rabies, hepatitis or malaria. It's simply Delhi belly, the old upset stomach. Often this can be due to a change of diet or a system unused to spicy food. Many times, however, contaminated food or water is the problem.

The primary answer to the upset stomach problem is to avoid getting it in the first place by taking care in what you eat and drink. Uncooked foods are always more likely to harbour germs, but so are cooked foods once they have been allowed to cool. Try to eat only freshly cooked foods and beware of places where food is left sitting around for long periods, particularly if exposed to flies.

The main cause of upset stomachs is probably drinking water – see the section on nonalcoholic drinks later in this chapter. If you do get a stomach bug, the first thing to do is nothing. If you can simply get back to health by yourself you'll probably build up some immunity against a recurrence. Stick to hot tea and try not to eat too much. People who take antibiotics at the first sign of an upset stomach are only asking for trouble. Not only does it make another assault more difficult to repel, it also kills off the useful organisms in your digestive tract just as efficiently as it kills off the harmful ones. People whose travels in India are one long series of stomach problems are often the people who overdid the modern medicines. India is also a good place to catch the stomach upset known as giardiasis. Tinidazole, a milder sister antibiotic to Flagyl, has been recommended as a cure for this problem.

If you do have a bad dose of diarrhoea and are finding it hard to keep yourself hydrated, Electral powder is a mixture of glucose and electrolytic salts designed specifically for rehydration. It is available from 'medical shops' and costs Rs 6 for a packet.

Some advice from two doctors in Nepal on diarrhoea and dysentery:

Diarrhoea is very different from dysentery, and it might be a good idea to define dysentery, which will require drugs to treat it. Dysentery is diarrhoea with blood, pus or fever. Diarrhoea with blood or pus but without fever is usually amoebic dysentery and requires an antiamoebic drug like Metronidazole or Flagyl.

Diarrhoea with blood or pus and fever is usually bacillary dysentery and requires antibiotics like tetracycline, or a sulfa drug. None of these drugs need to be given under the supervision of a doctor if a traveller has dysentery, and they can all be obtained in India or from a family doctor before leaving home. Most over-the-counter proprietary stomach-upset cures in India are worthless or dangerous, and if travellers save the drugs suggested for true dysentery they will avoid one long series of stomach problems.

Most of the diarrhoea that travellers pick up is named appropriately 'travellers' diarrhoea' and is without pus, blood or fever. Here the most important advice is to keep drinking to avoid dehydration. Lomotil is neither a heavy gun nor a general cure; it doesn't cure anything but just slows down the guts so that the cramps go away and you don't have to run to the toilet all the time. Lomotil is available over the counter in India but plain codeine is cheaper and works as well.

Hot-Season Health

During the hot season there are some additional precautions to take to ensure good health. First of all, protect yourself from the sun as much as possible. When the air is hazy due to dust you are less likely to get burnt by the sun but it certainly does you no good. Secondly, keep your liquid intake up. If you find you are urinating very infrequently or your urine turns a deep yellow or orange, you're becoming dehydrated. It's very easy to become dehydrated in the hot season.

At times like this you have to balance the dangers of drinking untreated water against the dangers of dehydration. The first is possible, the second is definite, so if necessary throw caution to the winds and drink more water. If you can't find purified water, can't face more tea or soft drinks and don't want to risk the water, green coconuts and oranges make good thirst quenchers too.

When the sun is shining through loud and clear you can easily get sunburnt, and suntan lotion and sun screen are not widely available in India. Bring some.

General Thoughts

Finally some miscellaneous thoughts: make sure your teeth are in good shape before departing – dentists' equipment is not always what we've got used to in the west. It's wise to clean your teeth with 'safe' water as well. Always carry a spare pair of glasses or your prescription in case of loss or breakage, although it's relatively easy to get glasses made in an emergency. Don't walk around in bare feet; that is how you get hookworms or worse. Thongs are useful protectors in hotel showers against athlete's foot or other fungal infections. Treat any simple scratch or cut with care – clean it thoroughly with antiseptic and keep it clean. In India's tropical climate it's very easy for the simplest scratch to get infected. 'Wet Ones' or similar premoistened towelettes are a convenient aid to keeping things clean and can be bought in the bigger cities.

Take extra care with medicines if you're travelling with children. You rarely need a prescription to buy medicines in India – if it's available at all it will be available over the counter. Be aware of possible differences in names, however. If you're after a specific drug it's worthwhile knowing the scientific as well as the trade name. Remember that drugs may not be of the same strength as in other countries or may have deteriorated due to age or poor storage conditions. They most probably will, however, be far cheaper than in the west. Prices for common drugs in Europe or the USA are often 10 or more times the retail price in India.

If a simple stomach upset turns out to be real down-to-earth dysentery, the most important thing is to not become dehydrated. Get plenty of liquids. If you get the dreaded hep, rest, good food, no alcohol and generally taking it easy is the cure. If you do need a doctor or other medical help, your embassy or consulate or a good hotel should be able to recommend someone.

It's probably wise to carry your health certificate with you just like your passport. One traveller wrote of having his bus stopped at a 'Cholera Inoculation Checkpoint'. All those who couldn't produce proof of immunisation got a jab on the spot, without benefit of sterilising the needle between goes! The concise and usable *Staying Healthy in Asia* (Volunteers in Asia Publications) or *The Traveller's Health Guide* by Dr Anthony Turner (Roger Lascelles, London) have some good basic advice on staying healthy while travelling. A traveller recommended *In Search of the Masters*, a book about ashrams in India, for its résumé on health problems in India.

It hardly needs saying, but street-corner acupuncturists or ear cleaners (!) are not to be trusted in India. Amazingly, some people do let these folk have a go at them and regret it afterwards!

Most important of all, don't get overly concerned about your health. Most people survive India with very few problems. During the course of researching the first edition of this book Tony and Maureen spent three months in India in one stretch, during the hot season, while Maureen was pregnant, with nothing more than a couple of mild stomach upsets between them.

WOMEN TRAVELLERS

India doesn't present the problems for solo women travellers that some Asian countries can – Pakistan in particular – but some care can help. Since the first edition several women travellers have written with their thoughts and suggestions.

One woman suggested that 'you should keep your upper arms, chest and back covered because these areas are, for some reason, considered erotic. A big shawl of light cloth will provide some privacy. Don't return male stares', she continued, 'it is considered a come-on. Turning away haughtily and draping your shawl over your head will have the desired effect. Getting involved in inane conversations with men is also considered a turn-on. Keep discussions down to a necessary minimum unless you're interested in getting hassled. If you get the uncomfortable feeling he's encroaching on your space, the chances are that he is. A firm request to keep away – use your best memsahib tone – may help. Firmly return any errant limbs, put some item of luggage in between you and if all else fails find a new spot, with offended dignity. You're also within your rights to tell him to push off!'

A couple of women wrote in some anger over the way they were treated in India. It came down, they decided, to a belief that if you're not married there's something wrong with you and if you are married then what are you doing here all alone!

Being a woman also has some advantages. There is often a special ladies' queue for train tickets or even a ladies' quota and ladies' carriages! One woman wrote that these ladies' carriages were often nearly empty – another said that they were full of screaming children. Special ladies' facilities are also sometimes found in cinemas and other places.

Close attention to standards of dress will go a long way to minimising problems for female travellers. The light cotton draw-string skirts that many western women pick up in India are really sari petticoats and to wear them in the street is rather like going out half dressed. Other ways of blending into the Indian background include avoiding sleeveless blouses, skirts that are too short and, of course, the bra-less look. Remember that lungis are only acceptable wear for women in the state of Kerala.

DANGERS & ANNOYANCES
Theft

Having things stolen is a problem in India, not so much because it's a theft-prone country – it isn't – but because you can become involved in a lot of hassles getting the items replaced. If your passport is stolen you may have a long trip back to an embassy to replace it. Travellers' cheques may be replaceable if stolen, but first of all avoid theft. Always lock your room, preferably with your own padlock in cheaper hotels. Lock it at night as well; countless people have had things stolen from their rooms when they've actually been in them.

Never leave those most important valuables (passport, tickets, health certificates, money, travellers' cheques) in your room; they should be with you at all times. Either have a stout leather passport wallet on your belt, or a passport pouch under your shirt, or simply extra internal pockets in your clothing. On trains at night keep your gear near you; padlocking a bag to a luggage rack can be useful. Never walk around with valuables casually slung over your shoulder. Take extra care in crowded public transport. In Bombay, for example, pickpockets are adept at the 'razor on the back pocket or shoulder bag' technique.

Thieves are particularly prevalent on train routes where there are lots of tourists. The Delhi to Agra express service is notorious; and Delhi to Jammu Tawi, Delhi to Calcutta, Delhi to Bombay and Agra to Varanasi are other routes to take care on. Train departure time, when the confusion and crowds are at their worst, is the time to be most careful. Just as the train is about to leave, your bags suddenly fly out the window to a waiting accomplice. On the Delhi to Jammu service the 'instant crowd' technique is the usual method. Young men work in teams so that you suddenly find yourself surrounded by jostling people and your bags disappear in an instant. Airports are another place to be careful, especially for international arrivals which often take place in the middle of the night, when you are unlikely to be at your most alert.

A few years ago there was a spate of drugging episodes, but we haven't heard of any happening for quite some time. Travellers would meet somebody on a train or bus or in a town, start talking and then be offered a cup of tea or something similar. Hours later they'd wake up with a headache and all their gear gone. The tea was full of sleeping pills. Don't accept drinks or food from strangers no matter how friendly they seem, particularly if you're on your own.

Beware also of your fellow travellers. Unhappily there are more than a few backpackers who make the money go further by helping themselves to other peoples'. At places like Goa be very careful with things on the beach – while you're in the water your camera or money can walk away very fast.

Remember that backpacks are very easy to rifle through. Don't leave valuables in them, especially for flights. Remember also that something may be of little or no value to a thief, but to lose it would be a real heartbreak to you – like film. Finally, a good travel insurance policy helps.

Stolen Travellers' Cheques If you're unlucky enough to have things stolen, some precautions can ease the pain. All travellers' cheques are replaceable but this does you little immediate good if you have to go home and apply to your bank. What you want is instant replacement. Furthermore, what do you do if you lose your cheques and money and have a day or more to travel to the replacement office? The answer is to keep an emergency cash-stash in a totally separate place. In that same place you should keep a record of the cheque serial numbers and your passport number.

American Express make considerable noise about 'instant replacement' of their cheques but a lot of people find out, to their cost, that without a number of precautions it isn't necessarily so. For a start, 'no bank will give an instant refund if the amount stolen is over US$1000', reported one unhappy traveller – a good reason for carrying more than one brand of cheque. The same person said that it is necessary to get a receipt to prove that you phoned the nearest American Express office after the theft. The receipt should indicate the number you called and the date. 'Keep the original receipt from when you bought the cheques separate from the cheques themselves', he continued. 'Without that, you won't even get a single dollar for weeks and weeks'. However, I met one Briton who had his stolen travellers' cheques (American Express) replaced within 48 hours; according to him he was dressed like a businessman when he reported the theft. He felt the refund would have taken much longer if he had been dressed as a 'hippie'.

Another traveller wrote that his travellers' cheques were stolen and he didn't discover the loss for a month. They had been left in his hotel room and the thief (presumably from the hotel) had neatly removed a few cheques from the centre of the book. Explaining that sort of theft is really difficult and, of course, the thief has had plenty of time to dispose of them.

We've had a number of letters concerning theft in India, including one from a woman who was so upset when her camera was stolen soon after arrival that she left on the next available flight. Other writers' belongings were ripped off from a beach hut at Goa, on various trains, from the top of the bus to Darjeeling, on internal flights and from their hotel rooms. One man had his camera stolen at knife point by a rickshaw rider who was supposedly about to buy it, and Geoff even had stuff stolen while researching the second edition. What can we say – be careful.

But, of course, there's a reverse side. In many years of travel I (Tony speaking here) have had various things stolen in France, Italy, Thailand (more than once), Malaysia, Indonesia, Peru, the USA and even Australia. On all my visits to India (touch wood) I've never once lost anything. India has no world-exclusive on thieves; it's just a matter of luck.

I'll leave the final word to an elderly visitor (he and two friends who visited India and told us about it had a combined age of 200 years!): 'I have never had anything stolen while in transit or in hotels. I am not a particularly careful person and can only conclude that the risk is exaggerated. We found it only too easy to be suspicious and were frequently humbled by realising that people we thought were trying to con us were only trying to be helpful. Every time we misplaced some item of luggage our first thought was that it had been stolen; but we lost absolutely nothing in that way. On the other hand we were several times followed with things we had inadvertently left in teashops or buses'.

FILM & PHOTOGRAPHY

Colour print film is readily available in India, and developing and printing facilities are not hard to find in the major cities. They're usually cheap and the quality is usually (but not always) good. Kodak 100 colour print film costs around Rs 90 for a roll of 36. Developing costs are around Rs 15, plus Rs 2 per photo for printing.

If you're taking slides bring the film with you, and bring plenty – India is a photogenic country. Colour slide film can really only be found in the major cities, although colour slides can be developed and the quality is usually good. Fujichrome slide film costs around Rs 115 for 36 exposures. Developing costs about Rs 50.

Kodachrome or other 'includes developing' film will have to be sent overseas, however. It's up to you whether you send it straight back or carry it back with you at the end of your trip. Film manufacturers warn that once exposed, film should be developed as quickly as possible; in practice the film seems to last, even in India's summer heat, without deterioration for months.

There are plenty of camera shops which should be able to make minor repairs should you have any mechanical problems. Photography itself presents some special problems in India. In the dry season the hazy atmosphere makes it difficult to get sharp shots or to get much contrast between what you are photographing and the background. Everything looks washed out and flat even with a polarising filter. In the mountains you should allow for the extreme clarity of the air and light intensity, and take care not to overexpose your shots.

Be careful what you photograph. India is touchy about places of military importance – this can include train stations, bridges, airports and any military installations. If in doubt ask. In general most people are happy to be photographed, but care should be taken in pointing cameras at Muslim women. Again, if in doubt, ask.

ACCOMMODATION

India has a very wide range of accommodation possibilities apart from straightforward hotels. Some of them include:

Cheap Hotels

There are hotels all over India with conditions ranging from extremely drab and dismal (but prices at rock bottom) up to quite reasonable in both standards and prices. Lazily swishing ceiling fans, mosquito nets on the beds, private toilets and bathrooms are all possibilities even in rooms which cost Rs 60 or less per night for a double.

Throughout India hotels are defined as 'western' or 'Indian'. The differentiation is basically meaningless, although expensive hotels are always western, cheap ones Indian. 'Indian' hotels will be more simply and economically furnished but the acid test is the toilet. 'Western' hotels have a sit-up-style toilet; 'Indian' ones usually (but not always) have the traditional Asian squat style. You can find modern, well-equipped, clean places with Indian toilets and dirty, dismal dumps with western toilets, so don't be put off them.

Although prices are generally quoted in this book for singles and doubles, most hotels will put an extra bed in a room to make a triple for about an extra 25%. This is a considerable saving if there are more than two of you. In some smaller hotels it's often possible to bargain a little if you really want to. On the other hand these places will often put their prices up if there's a shortage of accommodation.

Many hotels, and not only the cheap ones, operate on a 24-hour system. This can be convenient if you check in at 8 pm, as it gives you until 8 pm the following day to check out. Conversely, if you arrive at 8 am one day it can be a nuisance to have to be on the streets again by 8 am the next day.

Expensive Hotels

You won't find 'international standard' hotels throughout India. The big, air-conditioned, swimming-pool places are generally confined to the major tourist centres and the large cities. There are a number of big hotel chains in India. The Taj Group has some of India's flashiest hotels, including the luxurious Taj Mahal Inter-Continental in Bombay, the romantic Rambagh Palace in Jaipur and the Lake Palace in Udaipur. Other interesting hotels are the Taj Coromandel in Madras and the Fort Aguada Resort in Goa. The Oberoi chain is, of course, well known outside India as well as within. Clarks are a small chain with popular hotels in Varanasi and Agra, amongst other places. The Welcomgroup and the Air-India-associated Centaur hotels are other chains.

The chains include the government-operated ITDC group who usually append the name 'Ashok' to their hotels. There's an Ashok hotel in virtually every town in India, so that test isn't foolproof, but the ITDC places include a number of smaller (but higher-standard) units in places like Sanchi or Konarak where accommodation possibilities are limited. The ITDC has been getting a lot of complaints in India recently for its inefficiency and large financial losses. We've also been getting numerous reports from travellers on badly maintained and poorly run ITDC hotels.

Beware of extra taxes and charges in the more expensive hotels. There will almost always be a 10% service charge, and in addition there will often be a 'luxury tax'. This tax, which is usually either 5% or 10%, depends on the room cost and other factors like air-conditioning. It also varies from state to state. In some places, where there are different off-season and high-season rates, you may find the luxury tax is higher in the high season – presumably because the higher room rate in season moves it from one bracket to another. Sometimes a room rate will be broken down into individual charges, thereby keeping the basic room rate low enough to avoid luxury tax. Thus you might find the total price is Rs x for the room plus Rs y for the phone (which you never used). On x alone there is no tax but on x plus y there would be. Rates quoted in this book are generally the basic rate only – taxes and charges are additional.

Government Accommodation

Back in the days of the Raj, a whole string of government-run accommodation units were set up with labels like Rest Houses, Dak Bungalows, Circuit Houses, PWD (Public Works Department) Bungalows, Forest Rest Houses and so on. Today most of these are reserved for government officials, although in some places they may still be available for tourists, if there is room. In an approximate pecking order the dak bungalows are the most basic; they often have no electricity and only essential equipment in out-of-the-way places. Rest houses are next up and then come the circuit houses, which are strictly for travelling VIPs.

Tourist Bungalows

Usually run by the state government, these often serve as replacements for the older government-run accommodation units. Tourist bungalows are generally excellent value, although in the last few years prices have risen dramatically in some states. They often have dorm beds as well as rooms – typical prices are around Rs 15 to Rs 25 for a dorm bed or Rs 60 to Rs 100 for a double room. The rooms are well kept and have a fan, two beds and bathroom; there are often more expensive air-conditioned rooms. Generally there's a restaurant or 'dining hall' and often a bar. There are particularly good tourist bungalows in Tamil Nadu (where they are known as Hotel Tamil Nadu) and in Karnataka (Hotel Mayura), although almost every state has some towns where the tourist bungalow is definitely the best place to stay.

In tourist bungalows, as in many other government-run institutions such as the railways in India, you will find a curiously Indian institution, the 'complaints book'. In this you can write your complaints and periodically someone higher up the chain of command comes along, reads the terrible tales and the tourist bungalow manager gets his knuckles rapped. In disputes or other arguments, calling for the complaints book is the angry customer's final weapon. In many places the complaints book can provide interesting and amusing reading.

Railway Retiring Rooms

These are just like regular hotels or dormitories except they are at the railway stations. To stay here you are generally supposed to have a railway ticket or Indrail Pass. The rooms are, of course, extremely convenient if you have an early train departure, although they can be noisy if it is a busy station. They are often very cheap and in some places they are also excellent value. Some stations have retiring rooms of definite Raj pretensions, with huge rooms and enough furniture to do up a flat or apartment back home.

Railway Waiting Rooms
Emergency accommodation when all else fails or when you just need a few hours' shut-eye before your train departs at 2 am. These are a free place to rest your weary head. The trick is to rest it in the comfortable 1st-class waiting room and not the crowded 2nd-class one. Officially you need a 1st-class ticket to be allowed to use the 1st-class room and its superior facilities. In practice, luck, a 2nd-class Indrail Pass or simply your foreign appearance may work.

Youth Hostels
Indian youth hostels are generally very cheap and sometimes in excellent condition with superb facilities. They are, however, often some distance from the town centres. You are not usually required to be a YHA member (as in other countries) to use the hostels, although your YHA card will generally get you a lower rate. The charge is typically Rs 5 for members, Rs 8 for nonmembers. Nor do the usual rules about arrival and departure times, lights-out or not using the hostel during the day apply. A list of Government of India hostels includes:

Andhra Pradesh
    Youth Hostel, near Secunderabad Sailing Club, Secunderabad
Goa
    Youth Hostel, Panaji (tel 2433)
Gujarat
    Youth Hostel, Sector 16, Gandhinagar (tel 2364)

Haryana
    Panchkula Youth Hostel, Haryana Tourist Complex, Panchkula, Ambala
Himachal Pradesh
    Youth Hostel, bus stand, Dalhousie (tel 89)
Jammu & Kashmir
    Patni Top Youth Hostel, c/o Tourist Office, Kud (tel 7)
Madhya Pradesh
    Youth Hostel, North TT Nagar, Bhopal (tel 63671)
Maharashtra
    Youth Hostel, Padampura, Station Rd, Aurangabad (tel 3801)
Orissa
    Youth Hostel, Sea Beach, Puri (tel 424)
Punjab
    Youth Hostel, Mal Mandi, GT Rd, Amritsar (tel 48165)
Rajasthan
    Youth Hostel, SMS Stadium, Bhagwandas Rd, Jaipur (tel 69084)
Tamil Nadu
    Youth Hostel, Indira Nagar, Madras (tel 412882)
    Youth Hostel, Solaithandam Kuppam, Pondicherry
Uttar Pradesh
    Youth Hostel, Malli Tal near Ardwell Camp, The Mall, Naini Tal (tel 513)
West Bengal
    Darjeeling Youth Hostel, 16 Dr Zakir Hussain Rd, Darjeeling (tel 2290)

There are some state government-operated youth hostels. In Tamil Nadu, for example, there are state hostels in Mahabalipuram, Madras, Rameswaram, Kanyakumari, Kodaikanal, Mudumalai and Ooty.

Other Possibilities
There are YMCAs and YWCAs in many of the big cities – some of these are modern, well equipped and more expensive (but still good value). There are also a few Salvation Army Hostels – in particular in Bombay and Calcutta. There are a few camping places around India, but travellers with their own vehicles can almost always find hotels with gardens where they can park and camp.

    Free accommodation is available at

some Sikh temples where there is a tradition of hospitality to visitors. It can be interesting to try one, but please don't abuse this hospitality and spoil it for other travellers. At many pilgrimage sites there are dharamsalas and choultries offering accommodation to pilgrims, and travellers are often welcome to use these. This particularly applies at isolated sites like Ranakpur in Rajasthan. The drawback here (especially with Jain choultries) is that no leather articles are allowed inside.

Staying with an Indian family can be a real education. It's a change from dealing strictly with tourist-oriented people, and the differences and curiosities of everyday Indian life can be very interesting.

Touts

Hordes of accommodation touts operate in many towns in India – Jaipur and Varanasi in particular and at any international airport terminal. Very often they are the rickshaw-wallahs who meet you at the bus or train station. The technique is simple – they take you to hotel A and rake off a commission for bringing you there rather than to hotel B. The problem with this procedure is that you may well end up not at the place you want to go to but at the place that pays the best commission. Some very good cheap hotels simply refuse to pay the touts and you'll then hear lots of stories about the hotel you want being 'full up', 'closed for repairs' or 'no good anymore'. Nine chances out of 10 they will be just that – stories.

Touts do have a use though – if you arrive in a town when some big festival is on (or a cricket test match against England or Australia!), finding a place to stay can be very difficult. Hop in a rickshaw, tell him in what price range you want a hotel, and off you go. He'll know which places have rooms available and unless the search is a long one you shouldn't have to pay him too much. Remember that he'll be getting a commission from the hotel too!

FOOD

Despite the very fine meals that can be prepared in India, you'll often find food a great disappointment. In many smaller centres there is not a wide choice and you'll get bored with rice and dhal. When you're in larger cities where the food can be excellent, take advantage of it.

Contrary to popular belief, not all Hindus are officially vegetarians. Strict vegetarianism is confined more to the south, which has not had the meat-eating influence of the Aryan and later Muslim invasions, and also to the Gujarati community. For those who do eat meat, it is not always a pleasure to do so in India – the quality tends to be low (most chickens give the impression that they died from starvation) and the hygiene is not all that it might be. Beef, from the holy cow, is strictly taboo of course – and leads to interesting Indian dishes like the mutton-burger. Where steak is available, it's usually buffalo. Pork is equally taboo to the Muslims. If you're a non-vegetarian you'll end up eating a lot more vegetarian food in India.

Railway station restaurants in the main cities are always a good bet. Food is generally safe and, if one more curry will kill you, they often have a western menu – at higher prices. Of course no culinary achievement awards are ever going to be made to station restaurants, but in general they're not bad.

Indian interpretations of western cuisine can be pretty horrific; it's usually best to let them stick to preparing Indian food. Meals served on trains are usually palatable and reasonably cheap. At most stops you will be besieged by food and drink sellers. Even in the middle of the night that raucous cry of 'Chai! Chai!' or 'Ah, coffeecoffeecoffee!' will inevitably break into your sleep. The sheer bedlam of an Indian station when a train is in is a part of India you never forget.

If, after some time in India, you do find the food is getting you down physically or psychologically, there are a couple of escapes. It is very easy for budget travellers to lose weight in India and feel lethargic and drained of energy. The answer is to increase your protein intake – eat more eggs, which are readily available. It also helps to eat more fruit and nuts, so buy bananas, mandarin oranges or peanuts, all easily found at stations or in the markets. Many travellers carry multi-vitamins with them. Another answer, if you're travelling on a budget, is to occasionally splash out on a meal in a fancy hotel or restaurant – compared to what you have been paying it may seem amazingly expensive, but try translating the price into what it would cost at home.

There are considerable regional variations from north to south, partly because of climatic conditions and partly because of historical influences. In the north, as already mentioned, much more meat is eaten and the cooking is often 'Moghul style', which bears a closer relationship to food of the Middle East and central Asia. The emphasis is more on spices and less on chilli. In the north far more grains and breads are eaten and less rice.

In the south more rice is eaten, there is more vegetarian food, and the curries tend to be hotter. Sometimes very hot. Another feature of southern vegetarian food is that you do not use eating utensils; food is always eaten with fingers (of the right hand only). Scooping up food that way takes a little practice but you soon become quite adept at it. It is said that eating this way allows you to get the 'feel' of the food, as important to south Indian cuisine as the aroma or arrangement are to other cooking styles. It also offers the added protection that you never need worry if the eating utensils have been properly washed.

In the most basic Indian restaurants and eating places, the cooking is usually done right out front so you can see exactly what is going on and how it is done. Vegetables will be on the simmer all day and tend to be over cooked and mushy to western tastes. In these basic places *dhal* is usually free but you pay for *chapattis, parathas, puris* or rice. *Sabzi* (vegetable preparations), dhal and a few chapattis make a passable meal for around Rs 10. If you order half-plates of the various dishes brewing out front you get half the quantity at half the price and get a little more variety. With chutneys and a small plate of onions, which come free, you can put together a reasonable vegetarian meal for Rs 15, or non-vegetarian for Rs 20. In railway station restaurants and other cheaper restaurants always check the prices and add up your bill. If it's incorrect query it.

At the other end of the price scale there are many restaurants in India's five-star hotels that border on the luxurious and by western standards are absurdly cheap. Paying US$10 to US$15 for a meal in India seems exorbitant after you've been there for a while, but check what a meal in your friendly local Hilton would cost you. As one traveller put it:

If not on a starvation budget the occasional splurge on a really good meal is very worthwhile in India. Best value are the unlimited 'buffet lunches' which are available at a number of the larger hotels. The *Taj Mahal Inter-Continental* in Bombay is one of the best. A large, opulent dining room complete with orchestra and an astonishing array of every kind of food imaginable.

The *Oberoi Grand* in Calcutta comes a close second – a much smaller dining room here and perhaps not quite so much variety, but the quality is even higher. Where else can you find a tray of steaks to help yourself from? It's slightly more expensive than the Taj, but in Madras the *Connemara* is rather cheaper. The food here is not in quite such abundant variety but you can still eat yourself silly. Extras like soft drinks are very expensive in these hotels – drink water or make yourself a milk shake from the ice cream!

Many other international standard hotels, like the *Oberoi Palace* in Srinagar and the *Malabar Hotel* in Cochin, offer similar deals. One place to which *every* traveller goes for a splurge is the *Lake Palace* in

Udaipur where, for US$10, you can treat yourself to the most amazing range of dishes in one of India's most luxurious settings – and that includes the boat fare. For budget travellers it makes a very pleasant change from dhal and rice.

Finally, a couple of hints on how to cope with curry. After a while in India you'll get used to even the fiercest curries and will find western food surprisingly bland. If, however, you do find your mouth is on fire don't reach for water. In emergencies that hardly helps at all. Curd (yoghurt) or fruit do the job much more efficiently.

Curry & Spice

Believe it or not, there is no such thing as 'curry' in India. It's an English invention, an all-purpose term to cover the whole range of Indian food spicing. *Carhi*, incidentally, is a Gujarati dish, but never ask for it in Kumaon where it's a very rude word!

Although all Indian food is certainly not curry, this is the basis of Indian cuisine. Curry doesn't have to be hot enough to blow your head off, although it can do that if it's made that way. Curry most definitely is not something found in a packet of curry powder. Indian cooks have about 25 spices on their regular list and it is from these that they produce the curry flavour. Normally the spices are freshly ground in a mortar and pestle known as a *sil-vatta*. Spices are usually blended in certain combinations to produce *masalas*. *Garam masala*, for example, is a combination of cloves, cinnamon, cardamom, coriander seeds and peppercorns.

Popular spices include saffron, an expensive flavouring produced from flowers. This is used to give rice that yellow colouring and delicate fragrance. Tumeric also has a colouring property, acts as a preservative and has a distinctive smell and taste. Chillies are ground, dried or added whole to supply that curry heat. They come in red and green varieties but

Indian food market

the green ones are the hottest. Ginger is supposed to be good for the digestion, while many masalas contain coriander because it is said to cool the body. Strong and sweet cardamom is used in many desserts and in rich meat dishes. Other popular spices and flavourings include nutmeg, cinnamon, poppy seeds, caraway seeds, cumin, fenugreek, mace, garlic, cloves, bay leaves and curry leaves.

Breads & Grains

Rice is, of course, the basic Indian staple, but although it is eaten throughout the country, it's all-important only in the south. The best Indian rice, it is generally agreed, is found in the north where Basmati rice grows in the Dehra Dun Valley. It has long grains, is yellowish and has a slightly sweetish or 'bas' smell. In the north (where wheat is the staple) rice is supplemented by a whole range of breads known as *rotis* or *chapattis*. In the Punjab a roti is called *phulka*. You can also find western-style sliced bread (*double roti*) in India but it is almost always horrible, sickly sweet and nearly inedible.

Indian breads are varied but always delicious. Simplest is the chapatti/roti, which is simply a mixture of flour and water cooked on a hot plate known as a *tawa*. Direct heat blows them up but how well that works depends on the gluten content of the wheat. A *paratha* is also cooked on the hot plate but ghee is used and the bread is rolled in a different way. There are also parathas that have been stuffed with peas or potato. Deep-fried bread which puffs up is known as a *puri* in the north and a *luchi* in the east. Found all over India but originating from the south are *dosas*. These are made from lentil flour. Curried vegetables wrapped inside a dosa makes it a *masala dosa* – a terrific snack meal. Bake the bread in a clay oven and you have *nan*. However you make them, Indian bread tastes great.

Use your chapatti or paratha to mop or scoop up your curry. An *idli* is a kind of rice dumpling, often served with a spicy curd sauce (*dahi idli*) or with spiced lentils and chutney. *Papadums* are crispy deep-fried lentil-flour wafers often served with thalis or other meals.

Outside the Delhi Jami Masjid you may see 'big' chapattis known as *rumali roti* (handkerchiefs). Note that Hindus use their tawa concavely, Muslims convexly! In some hill stations (like Naini Tal or Mussoorie) you can get quite good western-style bread.

Chapatti tin

Basic Dishes

Curries can be vegetable, meat (usually chicken or lamb) or fish, but they are always fried in ghee (clarified butter) or vegetable oil. North or south they will be accompanied by rice, but in the north you can also choose from the range of breads. There are a number of dishes which aren't really curries but are close enough to them for western tastes. *Vindaloos* have a vinegar marinade and tend to be hotter than most curries. *Pork vindaloo* is a favourite dish in Goa. *Kormas*, on the other hand, are rich, substantial dishes prepared by braising. There are both meat and vegetable kormas. *Dopiaza* literally means 'two onions' and is a type of korma which uses onions at two stages in its preparation.

Probably the most basic of Indian dishes is *dhal*, rather like a lentil soup. Dhal is almost always there, whether as an accompaniment to a curry or as a very basic meal in itself with chapattis or rice. In many places dhal and rice is just about all there is on the menu so you'll get heartily sick of it before you leave! The favourite dhal of Bengal and Gujarat is yellow *arhar*; whereas in Punjab it is *black urad*; *rajma* is the Heinz 57 varieties of dhal!

Other basic dishes include *mattar panir* – peas and cheese in gravy; *saag gosht* – spinach and meat; *alu dum* – potato curry; *palak panir* – spinach and cheese; *alu chhole* – diced potatoes and spicy-sour chickpeas. Some other vegetables include *gobi* (cauliflower), *brinjal* (eggplant) and *mattar* (peas).

Tandoori & Biryani

Tandoori food is a northern speciality and refers to the clay oven in which the food is cooked after first being marinated in a complex mix of herbs and yoghurt. Tandoori chicken is a favourite. This food is not as hot as curry dishes and usually tastes terrific.

Biryani (again chicken is a popular biryani dish) is another northern Moghul dish. The meat is mixed with a deliciously flavoured, orange-coloured rice which is sometimes spiced with nuts or dried fruit.

A *pulao* is flavoured rice usually without meat and you will also find it in other Asian countries further west. Those who have the idea that Indian food is always curry and always fiery hot will be surprised by tandoori and biryani dishes.

Regional Specialities

Rogan josh is straightforward lamb curry always popular in the north and in Kashmir where it originated. *Gushtaba*, pounded and spiced meat balls cooked in a yoghurt sauce, is another Kashmiri speciality. Still in the north, *chicken makhanwala* is a rich dish cooked in a butter sauce.

Many coastal areas have excellent seafood, including Bombay where the *pomfret*, a flounder-like fish, is popular;

so is Bombay duck, which is not a duck at all but another fish dish. *Dhansaak* is a Parsi speciality found in Bombay – lamb or chicken cooked with curried lentils and steamed rice. Further south, Goa has excellent fish and prawns; in Kerala, Cochin is famous for its prawns.

Another indication of the influence of central Asian cooking styles on north Indian food is the popularity of *kababs*. You'll find them all across north India with a number of local variations and specialities. The two basic forms are *sikh* (skewered) or *shami* (wrapped). In Calcutta *kati kababs* are a local favourite. Another Bengali dish is *dahi maach* – curried fish in yoghurt sauce, flavoured with ginger and tumeric. Further south in Hyderabad you could try *haleen*, pounded wheat with a lightly spiced mutton gravy.

Side Dishes

Indian food generally has a number of side dishes to go with the main meal. Probably the most popular is *dahi* – curd or yoghurt. It has the useful ability of instantly cooling a fiery curry – either blend it into the curry or, if it's too late, you can administer it straight to your mouth. Curd is often used in the cooking or as a dessert and appears in the popular drink *lassi*. *Raita* is another popular side dish consisting of curd mixed with cooked or raw vegetables, particularly cucumber (similar to Greek zatziki) or tomato.

Sabzi is curried vegetables, *began bharta* is pureed eggplant curry, *bhujias* or *pakoras* are vegetables deep fried in chickpea flour. *Mulligatawny* is a soup-like dish which is really just a milder, more liquid curry. It's a dish adopted into the English menu by the Raj. *Chutney* is pickled fruit or vegetables and is the standard relish for a curry.

Thalis

A *thali* is the all-purpose Indian vegetarian dish. Although it is basically a product of south India, you will find restaurants serving thalis or 'vegetarian plate meals' all over India. Often the sign will simply announce 'Meals'. In addition, there are regional variations like the particularly sumptuous Gujarati thalis.

The name is taken from the 'thali' dish in which it is served. This consists of a metal plate with a number of small metal bowls known as *katoris* on it. Sometimes the small bowls will be replaced by simple indentations in the plate; in more basic places the 'plate' will be a big, fresh banana leaf. A thali consists of a variety of curry vegetable dishes, relishes, a couple of papadams, puris or dosas and a mountain of rice. A fancy thali may have a *pata*, a rolled leaf stuffed with fruit and nuts. There'll probably be a bowl of curd and possibly even a small dessert.

Thalis are consistently tasty and good food value, but they have two other unbeatable plus points for the budget traveller - they're cheap and they're usually 100% filling. Thalis can be as little as Rs 4 or Rs 5 and will rarely cost much more than Rs 15 at the very most though Gujarati thalis are the exception and you'll consistently be paying Rs 15 to Rs 18 for these at reasonable restaurants. Most are 100% filling because they're normally 'all you can eat'. When your plate starts to look empty they come round, add another mountain of rice and refill the katoris. Thalis are eaten with fingers, although you may get a spoon for the curd or dhal. Always wash your hands before you eat one - a sink or other place to wash your hands is provided in a thali restaurant.

One enthusiast's findings from four weeks of thalis in the south:

I tried a total of 35 different thalis. The tastiest was probably at the *Mathura Restaurant* in Madras, closely followed by the *Laxmi Vilas* in Bombay and the one in the dining hall at Ranakpur. The best for your money is in the downstairs restaurant at *New College House* in Madurai - very good service and a record 13 side dishes. Second best was the 'special thali' in the back part of *Mamalla Bhavan* in Mahabalipuram. The *worst* was at a small beachfront restaurant in Kovalam; I was in withdrawal and a desperate man. This was closely followed by every thali in Ernakulam.

Ivor McMahen, Canada

Snacks

Samosas are curried vegetables fried in a pastry triangle. They are very tasty and are found all over India. *Bhelpuri* is a popular Bombay snack peddled across the city. *Channa* is spiced chickpeas (*gram*) served with puris. *Sambhar* is a soup-like lentil and vegetable dish with a sour tamarind flavour. *Chat* is the general term for snacks and nibbles.

Western Food

Sometimes Indian food simply becomes too much and you want to escape to something familiar and reassuring. It's not always easy, but railway station restaurants often have something palatable and close to the food 'back home'. The Indian-food blues are particularly prone to hit at breakfast time - somehow idlis never really feel like a breakfast. Fortunately that's the meal where you'll find an approximation to the west most easily obtained. All those wonderful Indian varieties of eggs can be had - half-fried, omelettes, you name it.

Toast and jam can almost always be found, and very often you can get cornflakes and hot milk, although Indian cornflakes would definitely be rejects from Mr Kellogg's production line. The Scots must have visited India too, because porridge is often on the breakfast menu and is usually good.

That peculiar Raj-era term for a mid-morning snack still lives - tiffin. Today tiffin means any sort of light meal or snack. One western dish which Indians seem to have come 100% to terms with is chips (French fries). It's quite amazing how, if they are available, they will almost always be excellent. To be safe, ask for 'finger chips' or you may end up with what the English know as 'potato crisps' although to Americans they'll be 'potato chips'! Some Indian cooks call French fries 'Chinese potatoes'.

Other Asian foods, apart from Indian, are often available. There's still a small Chinese population in India, particularly in Calcutta and Bombay. You can find Chinese food in the larger cities, and Bombay in particular has excellent Chinese food. In the north, where many Tibetans settled following the Chinese invasion of Tibet, you'll find Tibetan restaurants in places like Dharamsala, Manali or Srinagar.

Desserts & Sweets

Indians have quite a sweet tooth and an amazing selection of desserts and sweets to satisfy it. The desserts are basically rice or milk based, and consist of various interesting things in sweet syrup or else sweet pastries.

Kulfi is pistachio flavoured ice cream and is widely available. You can, of course, also get western-style ice cream all over India. The major brands are healthy and very good. *Ras gullas* are another very popular Indian dessert, sweet little balls of cream cheese flavoured with rose water.

Gulub jamuns are a typical example of the small 'things' in syrup – they're fried and made from thickened boiled-down milk (known as *khoya*) and flavoured with cardamon and rosewater. *Jalebi* are made of flour and yoghurt and are the orange-coloured squiggles in syrup.

Barfi is also made from khoya and is available in flavours like coconut, chocolate or almond. *Sandesh* is another kind of milk dish, a particular favourite in Calcutta. *Payasam* is a southern sweet made from milk simmered with crushed cashews, cereals and sugar, topped with raisins. *Firnee* is a rice-pudding dessert with almonds, raisins and pistachios.

Many of the Indian sweets are covered in a thin layer of silver, as are some of the desserts. It's just that, silver beaten paper

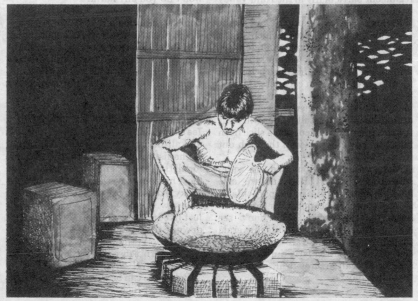
Bengali sweet maker

thin. Don't peel it off, it's quite edible. There are countless sweet shops with their goodies all lined up in glass showcases. Prices vary from Rs 40 to Rs 60 for a kg but you can order 50 or 100 grams at a time or simply ask for a couple of pieces. These shops often sell curd, as well as sweet curd which makes a very pleasant dessert. Sweets include all sorts of unidentifiable goodies; try them and see. *Gajar ka halwa* is a translucent, vividly coloured sweet made from carrot, sweet spices and milk.

Fruit

If your sweet tooth simply isn't sweet enough to cope with too many Indian desserts, you'll be able to fall back on India's wide variety of fruit. It varies all the way from tropical delights in the south to apples, apricots and other temperate-region fruits in the north. Some local specialities include cherries and strawberries in Kashmir, and apricots in Ladakh and Himachal Pradesh. Apples are found all over this north-western region but particularly in the Kulu Valley of Himachal Pradesh.

Melons are widespread in India, particularly watermelons, which are a fine thirst quencher when you're unsure about the water and fed up with soft drinks. Try to get the first slice before the flies discover it. Green coconuts are even better and there are coconut stalls on many city street corners. When you've drunk the milk the stall holder will split the coconut open and cut you a slice from the outer covering to scoop the flesh out with.

Mangoes are delicious and are widespread in summer. Bananas are also found in many parts of India, particularly in the south; pineapples are found in Assam and elsewhere. You don't see oranges all over the place (lots in Kerala though), but tangerines are widespread in central India, particularly during the hot season. You can go through an awful lot of them in a day.

Pan

An Indian meal should properly be finished with *pan* – the name given to the collection of spices and condiments chewed with betel nut. Found throughout eastern Asia, betel is a mildly intoxicating and addictive nut, but by itself it is quite inedible. After a meal you chew a pan as a mild digestive.

Pan sellers have a whole collection of little trays, boxes and containers in which they mix either *sadha* 'plain' or *mitha* 'sweet' pans. The ingredients may include, apart from the betel nut itself, lime paste (the chemical not the fruit), the powder known as *catachu*, various spices and even a dash of opium in a pricey pan. The whole concoction is folded up in a piece of edible leaf which you pop in your mouth and chew. When finished you spit the left-overs out and add another red blotch to the sidewalk. Over a long period of time, indulgence in pan will turn your teeth red-black and even addict you to the betel nut. But trying one occasionally won't do you any harm.

Cooking back Home

There are all sorts of books about Indian cooking should you want to continue the experiment after you leave India. *Indian Cookery* by Dharamjit Singh (Penguin, London, 1970) is a useful paperback introduction to the art.

Drinks – nonalcoholic

Tea Surprisingly, tea is not the all-purpose and all-important drink it is in Iran and Afghanistan. What's worse, the Indians, for all the tea they grow, make some of the most hideously over-sweetened, murkily-milky excuses for that fine beverage you ever saw. It may go by the name of *chai*, just like in the rest of Asia, but what a let down. Still, some people like it and it is cheap. 'Don't think of bazaar tea as tea in the western sense', was the advice one traveller gave!

Better tea can be obtained if you ask for 'tray tea', which gives you the tea, the milk and the sugar separately and allows you to combine them as you see fit. Usually tea is 'mixed tea' or 'milk tea', which means it has been made by putting cold water, milk, sugar and tea into one pot and bringing the whole concoction to the boil, then letting it stew for a long time. The result can be imagined.

Tea is more popular in the north, while in the south coffee, which is generally good, is the number one drink. There are Indian Coffee Houses all over the country.

Water In the big cities, the water is chlorinated and safe to drink, although if you've just arrived in India, the change from what you are used to drinking is in itself enough to bring on a mild dose of the shits.

Outside of the cities you're on your own. Some travellers drink the water everywhere and never get sick, others are more careful and still get hit with a bug. Basically, you should not drink the water in small towns unless you know it has been boiled, and definitely avoid the street vendors' carts everywhere – not only is the water of questionable quality but the glasses are given only a perfunctory rinse. Even in the better class of hotel and restaurant, the water is usually only filtered and not boiled. The local water filters remove solids and do nothing towards removing any bacteria. Water is generally safer in the dry season than in the monsoon when it really can be dangerous.

Most travellers use purifying tablets or filters, or avoid the water altogether by drinking bottled soda, Bisleri and soft drinks. Water purifying tablets are available from pharmacies and camping shops in the west, but not in India. Most tablets, such as Puritabs, do not remove amoebic cysts (hepatitis, giardia, amoebic dysentery) but are sufficient to make tap water safe. Iodine solution or, more conveniently, tablets such as those made by Coghlans in the USA, do remove these amoebas and are necessary if you are trekking and will be drinking stream water. Either way, the purified water tastes pretty much like swimming pool water!

One-litre plastic bottles of Bisleri mineral water can be bought in most places. Despite the name this is an Indian company. These bottles cost around Rs 10 but we've had a lot of reports recently of unscrupulous vendors refilling these bottles with plain old tap water as the seals are easily removed without breaking them. Although recycling should be encouraged wherever possible, this is one case where you should destroy the bottle after use.

Soft Drinks Soft drinks are a safe substitute for water although they tend to have a high sugar content. Coca-Cola got the boot from India a few years back for not cooperating with the government, but both they and Pepsi Cola are presently close to an agreement under which they will be able to operate again in India. There are many similar indigenous brands with names like Campa Cola, Thums Up, Limca, Gold Spot or Double Seven. By Asian standards they are pretty expensive at around Rs 3 to Rs 4 for a 190-ml bottle (more in restaurants). They're also sickly sweet if you drink too many of them, as you're virtually forced to in the hot season.

Juices & Other Drinks One very pleasant escape from the sickly sweet soft drinks is the Kashmiri apple juice drink Apco, but unfortunately it's only available in Kashmir. Apple juice drinks are also available in Himachal Pradesh and from Bhutan. Another recent arrival on the scene is the small Fruti cardboard boxes of mango, lemon and apple juice. For Rs 3.50 these are excellent, if a little sweet.

Coconut milk, straight from the young green coconut, is a popular drink, especially in the south. Another alternative to soft drinks is soda water – Bisleri, Spencer's and other brands are widely available. Not only does it come in a larger bottle, but it is also cheaper – generally around Rs 2.50. With soda water you can get excellent, and safe, lemon squash sodas.

Finally there's *lassi*, that oh so cool, refreshing and delicious iced curd (yoghurt) drink.

Drinks – alcoholic
Alcohol is expensive – a bottle of Indian beer can cost anything from Rs 12 up to Rs 65 or more in a flashy hotel; Rs 12 to Rs 25 is the usual price range. In some states (like Goa) it is very cheap, some (like Tamil Nadu) very expensive. Indian beers have delightful names like Golden Eagle, Rosy Pelican, Cannon Extra Strong, Bullet, Black Label, Knock Out, Kingfisher, Guru or Punjab. They're not too bad if you can find them cold, but all tend to be gassy.

Beer and other Indian interpretations of western alcoholic drinks are known as IMFL – Indian Made Foreign Liquor. Local drinks are known as Country Liquor and include *toddy*, a mildly alcoholic extract from the coconut palm flower, and *feni*, a distilled liquor produced from fermented cashew nuts or from coconuts. The two varieties taste quite different.

The only state in India which is 'dry' is Gujarat. You cannot buy beer or any other liquor here for love nor money except at the most expensive hotels and even then you'll have to consume it in your room. Bars don't exist. The only way of satisfying that desperate, desert-like thirst is to visit one or both of the tiny enclaves of Daman or Diu where it flows freely. Gujaratis have discovered the same thing and flock there in the thousands at weekends.

Beer Tasting
Travelling English beer enthusiast John Lia sent us his rating of 39 brands of Indian beer ranging from PALS ('the pits, like dog food') to Rosy Pelican ('good and refreshing'). I wasn't totally in agreement with his tastes (good old Kingfisher – 'very weak' he reported – can't be that bad) and a knowledgeable bartender in Bhubaneswar thought his preferences were slanted towards strong or (as he put it) 'kicking' beers. Certainly he couldn't knock Black Label (a Bengali beer). I managed to try about 10 different varieties but surprisingly four of them weren't on John's lengthy tasting list! There are a hell of a lot of beer brands in India.

Indian Menus
One of the delights of Indian menus is their amazing English. Start the morning, for example, with corn flaks, also useful for shooting down enemy aircraft. Or perhaps corn flex – Indian corn flakes are often so soggy they'll do just that.

Even before your corn-whatever you should have some tea, and what a variety of types of tea India can offer. You can try bed tea, milk tea, light tea, mixed tea, tray tea, plain tea, half set tea and even (of course) full set tea. Eggs also offer unlimited possibilities: half-fried eggs, pouch eggs (or egg pooch), bolid eggs, scimbled eggs, sliced omelettes, skerem boil eggs (interesting combination there) or simply aggs. Finally, you could finish off breakfast with that popular Scottish dish – pordge.

Soup before a meal – how about French onion soup? Or Scotch brath, mughutoni or perhaps start with a parn coactale. Follow that up with some amazing interpretations of western dishes, like the restaurant that not only had Napoleon spaghetti but also Stalin spaghetti! Perhaps a seezling plator sounds more like it? Or simply bum chicken, or perhaps chicken cripes? A light meal – well, why not have a sandwitch or a vegetable pup? Feeling strong – then try a carate salad. And if you want a drink how about orange squish or that popular Indian soft drink Thumps Up.

Chinese dishes offer a whole new range of possibilities, including mashrooms and bamboo sooghts, spring rolos, American chopsy, Chinies snakes, vegetable chop off, vegetable

nuddles, plane fried rice and park fried rice. Finally for dessert you could try apple pai or banana panecake, or treat yourself to leeches & cream!

Travellers have sent in lots more menu suggestions since the first edition of this book. Like tired fruit juice (tinned you know), plane tost (the stuff they serve on Indian Airlines?), omlet & began, two eggs any shape, loose curds, curds bath, tomatoe stuff, scram bled eggs, chicken poodle soup, screambled eggs, banana frilters, pain-apple cream and chocolet padding. Or something even Colonel Sanders hasn't thought of yet – fried children.

BOOKS

India is a great place for reading – there's plenty to read about, there's plenty of time to read on those never-ending bus or train trips, and when you get to the big cities you'll find plenty of bookshops to get the reading matter from.

India is one of the world's largest publishers of books in English. After the USA and the UK, it's up there with Canada or Australia as a major English-language publisher. You'll find a great number of interesting books on India by Indian publishers, books which are generally not available in the west.

At the other extreme, Indian publishers do cheap reprints of western bestsellers at prices far below western levels. A meaty Leon Uris or Arthur Hailey novel, ideal for an interminable train ride, will often cost less than US$2. Compare that with your local bookshop prices. The favourite western author is probably P G Wodehouse – 'Jeeves must be considered another incarnation of Vishnu', was one explanation.

Recently published British and American books also reach Indian bookshops remarkably fast and with very low markups. If a bestseller in Europe or America has major appeal for India they'll often rush out a paperback in India to forestall possible pirates. The novel *City of Joy* (a European bestseller about Calcutta) was out in paperback in India before the hardback had even reached Australia.

The suggested books that follow are only a few interesting ones that should be readily available. Of course there are far more now long out of print. In addition there are many beautiful coffee-table books on India – ideal for whetting the appetite or for conjuring up the magic of India after your return. India has spawned an equally large number of cookery books – if you want to get into curry and all those spices you'll have no trouble finding plenty of instructions. Indian art has also generated a great number of interesting books of all types.

Novels

Plenty of authors have taken the opportunity of setting their novels in a country as colourful as India. Rudyard Kipling, with books like *Kim* and *Plain Tales from the Hills*, is the Victorian English interpreter of India par excellence. In *A Passage to India*, E M Forster perfectly captures that collision of incomprehension in India between the English and the Indians. A very readable book.

Much more recent but again following that curious question of why the English and Indians, so dissimilar in many ways, were so similar in others, is Ruth Prawer Jhabwala's *The Heat & The Dust*. The contemporary narrator of the tale also describes the backpacker's India in a flawless fashion.

Probably the most widely acclaimed Indian novel since the war was Salman Rushdie's *Midnight's Children*, which won the Booker Prize. It tells of the children who were born, like modern India itself, at the stroke of midnight on that August night in 1947 and how the life of one particular 'midnight's child' is inextricably intertwined with events in India itself. Rushdie's follow-up, *Shame*, was set in modern Pakistan. His sardonic treatment of the post-independence rulers of India and Pakistan in these two novels upset quite a few over-inflated egos. Paul Scott's *The Raj Quartet* and

Staying On are other important novels set in India. The big 'bestseller' Indian novel of recent years was the monster tome *Far Pavilions* by M M Kaye. Women's magazine romance in some ways, but some interesting angles on India. *Nectar in a Sieve* by Kamala Markandaya has been recommended as an interesting account of a woman's life in rural India. See the Calcutta chapter for more on *City of Joy*, the 1986 bestseller in Europe and India.

General Interest

John Keay's *Into India* (John Murray, London, 1973) is a fine general introduction to travelling in India. One traveller's observations and perceptions of life in India today provide an illuminating idea of what it's really like.

Paul Theroux's best-selling railway odyssey *The Great Railway Bazaar* takes you up and down India by train (and across most of the rest of Asia) and turns the whole world into a railway carriage. Engrossing, like most such books, as much for insights into the author as into the people he meets. *Slow Boats to China* by Gavin Young follows much the same path but this time by boat. *Slowly Down the Ganges* by Eric Newby is another boat-trip tale; this one borders, at times, on sheer masochism!

Karma Kola by Gita Mehta is accurately subtitled 'the marketing of the mystic east'. It amusingly and cynically describes the unavoidable and hilarious collision between India looking to the west for technology and modern methods, and the west descending upon India in search of ancient wisdom.

India File by Trevor Fishlock (Indian paperback by Rupa, New Delhi, 1984) is a very readable collection of articles on India by the *Times* correspondent. The chapter on sex in India is often hilarious.

Ved Mehta has written a number of interesting personal views of India. *Walking the Indian Streets* (Penguin paperback) is a slim and highly readable account of the culture shock he went through on returning to India after a long period abroad. *Portrait of India* is by the same author. Ronald Segal's *The Crisis of India* (Penguin, London, 1965) is written by a South African Indian on the theme that spirituality is not always more important than a full stomach – a counter-argument to all the praise of Hinduism and its spirituality. *An Indian Summer* (Penguin, 1987) by James Cameron is worth reading.

Third Class Ticket by Hilary Ward is an interesting account of the culture shock experienced by a group of Bengali villagers as they explore the country for the first time. *Unveiling India* (Penguin) by Anees Jung is a contemporary documentary on women in India.

Finally, no survey of personal insights into India can ignore V S Naipaul's two controversial books *An Area of Darkness* and *India – A Wounded Civilisation*. Born in Trinidad but of Indian descent, Naipaul tells in the first book of how India, unseen and unvisited, haunted him and the impact upon him when he made the pilgrimage to the motherland. You may well find that much of this book rings very true with your own experiences while in India. In the second book he writes of India's unsuccessful search for a new purpose and meaning for its civilisation.

History

If you want a thorough introduction to Indian history then look for the Pelican two-volume *A History of India*. In volume one Romila Thapar follows Indian history from 1000 BC to the coming of the Moghuls in the 16th century AD. Volume two by Percival Spear follows the rise and fall of the Moghuls through to India since independence. At times both volumes are a little dry, but if you want a reasonably detailed history in a handy paperback format they're worth having.

The Wonder that was India by A L Basham gives detailed descriptions of the Indian civilisations, origins of the caste system and social customs, and detailed information on Hinduism, Buddhism and other religions in India. It is also very informative about art and architecture. It has a wealth of background material on ancient India without being overly academic.

Christopher Hibbert's *The Great Mutiny - India 1857* (Penguin, London, 1980) is a recently published single-volume description of the often lurid events of the mutiny. This readable paperback is illustrated with contemporary photographs.

Plain Tales from the Raj, edited by Charles Allen (Futura paperback, London, 1976), is the delightful book derived from the equally delightful series of radio programmes of the same name. It consists of a series of interviews with people who took part in British India on both sides of the table. Extremely readable and full of fascinating little insights into life during the Raj era.

The Nehrus & the Gandhis (Picador, 1988) by Tariq Ali is a very readable account of the history of these families and hence of India this century.

Freedom at Midnight is India's best-selling book of the past decade. Its authors Larry Collins and Dominique Lapierre have written other equally popular modern histories, but you could hardly ask for a more enthralling series of events than those that led to India's independence in 1947. In India you can find *Freedom at Midnight* in a cheap Bell Books paperback (Vikas Publishing, Delhi, 1976).

Highness - the Maharajas of India by Ann Morrow (Grafton Books, 1986) provides an illuminating, if at times sycophantic, insight into the rarefied and extravagant lives of these Indian rulers during the days of the Raj and since independence.

For a good insight on the country since independence there is *From Raj to Rajiv - 40 Years of Indian Independence* (BBC Books UK, Universal Book Stall, Delhi, 1988). It is written by old India hand and BBC correspondent Mark Tully and Zareer Masani.

Two current affairs books which are well worth reading are *Bhopal - the Lessons of a Tragedy* by Sanjoy Hazarika and *Riot after Riot - Reports on Caste & Communal Violence in India* by M J Akbar. Both are published by Penguin.

Finally, for those interested in the continuing and often shocking and sad story of India's treatment of its tribals, there is the scholarly *Tribes of India - the Struggle for Survival* by Christoph von Fürer-Haimendorf (Oxford University Press, 1982)

Religion

If you want a better understanding of India's religions there are plenty of books available in India. The English series of Penguin paperbacks are amongst the best and are generally available in India. In particular, *Hinduism* by K M Sen (Penguin, London, 1961) is brief and to the point. If you want to read the Hindu holy books these are available in translations: *The Upanishads* (Penguin, London, 1965) and *The Bhagavad Gita* (Penguin, London, 1962). *Hindu Mythology*, edited by Wendy O'Flaherty (Penguin, London), is an interesting annotated collection of extracts from the Hindu holy books. Convenient if you don't want the whole thing.

A Classical Dictionary of Hindu Mythology & Religion by John Dowson (Rupa, New Delhi, 1987) is an Indian paperback reprint of an old English hardback. As the name suggests, it is in dictionary form and is one of the best sources for unravelling who's who in Hinduism.

Penguin also has a translation of the Koran. If you want to know more about Buddhism, *Buddhism* by Christmas Humphreys (Penguin, London, 1949) is an excellent introduction. *A Handbook of Living Religions* edited by John R Hinnewls (Pelican, London, 1985) provides a succinct and readable summary of all the various religions you will find in India, including Christianity and Judaism.

Guides

First published in 1859, the 22nd edition of *A Handbook for Travellers in India, Pakistan, Nepal, Bangladesh & Sri Lanka* (John Murray, London, 1975) is that rarest of animals, a Victorian travel guide. If you've got a deep interest in Indian architecture and can afford the somewhat hefty price, then take along a copy of this immensely detailed guidebook. Unfortunately its system of following 'routes', in the manner of all good Victorian guidebooks, makes it somewhat difficult to locate things but the effort is worth it. Along the way you'll find a lot of places where the British army made gallant stands, and more than a few statues of Queen Victoria – most of which have been replaced by statues of Mahatma Gandhi.

For relatively cheap but excellently produced photo-essays of the subcontinent try the Insight Guides, *Rajasthan* and *India* by APA Productions. They're both done by a team of experienced writers, many of them Indian, and while the text and photographs are generally excellent, the 'Guide in Brief' section at the back is of extremely limited use.

There are a great number of regional and local guidebooks published in India. Many of them are excellent value and describe certain sites (the Ajanta and Ellora Caves or Sanchi for example) in much greater detail than is possible in this book. The guides produced by the Archaeological Survey of India are particularly good. Many of the other guides have a most amusing way with English. Another good guide, this time on the art of Rajasthan, is *The Guide to Painted Towns of Shekhawati* by Ilay Cooper which comes complete with street maps. It's available in the bookshops of Jaipur.

Books on wildlife are difficult to get, but bird-watchers may find the *Collins* *Handguide to the Birds of the Indian Subcontinent* useful. It doesn't cover all the birds by any means but it does have the best illustrations and text, and if you're not a very serious bird-watcher you will probably find it useful. Visitors to Kashmir can use *Birds of Nepal*, which includes notes on Kashmir and Sikkim. The Insight *Indian Wildlife* guide (APA, 1988) is available from major bookshops in India and is valuable if you're keenly interested in visiting national parks.

Other Lonely Planet Regional Guides

It's pleasant to be able to claim that for more information on India's neighbours and for travel beyond India most of the best guides come from Lonely Planet! If you're heading north to Nepal then look for *Kathmandu & the Kingdom of Nepal* for complete information on the mountain nation. If you're planning on trekking in Nepal or simply want more information on trekking in general, then look for *Trekking in the Nepal Himalaya* and *Trekking in the Indian Himalaya*. Or you can cross right over the Himalaya with our *Tibet – a travel survival kit* and *Karakoram Highway – a travel survival kit*.

For other Indian neighbours there are other Lonely Planet guides. *Pakistan – a travel survival kit* is our guide to the 'unknown land of the Indus'. We also have a guide to India's other Muslim neighbour – *Bangladesh – a travel survival kit*. *Burma – a travel survival kit* covers that thoroughly delightful and totally eccentric country. If it's possible to travel to Sri Lanka then you need *Sri Lanka – a travel survival kit*. If you are making a visit to the Maldives there is also Lonely Planet's *Maldives & Islands of the East Indian Ocean*. Finally, if you want more information on the north-west of India then look for our comprehensive guide to *Kashmir, Ladakh & Zanskar*.

If you're travelling further than India across Asia to Europe (Iran permitting), then our book is *West Asia on a*

Shoestring. If it's further east you want then look for *South-East Asia on a Shoestring*.

Also Recommended

Readers have recommended numerous other books such as *Eating the Indian Air* by John Morris; *The Gorgeous East* by Rupert Croft-Cooke; *Delhi is Far Away* and *The Grand Trunk Road* by John Wiles; and books by Jan & Rumer Godden. *A Princess Remembers* by Gayatri Devi is useful if you're going to Jaipur. *Train to Pakistan* by Kushwant Singh is an excellent novel on the traumas of partition. Irish wanderer Dervla Murphy heads south in her book *On a Shoestring to Coorg*. There are some wonderful Indian comic books dealing with Hindu mythology and Indian history. *An Indian Summer* by James Cameron (Penguin) is an autobiographical account of independence and south India.

FILMS

Once you've read all you can about India, keep your eyes open for a showing of Louis Malle's two-part film *Phantom India*. Running about seven hours in all, this is a fascinating in-depth look at India today. At times it's very self-indulgent, but as an overall view it can't be beaten – it has been banned in India. The Australian ABC TV channel has produced two excellent documentary series on India, one titled *Journey into India*, the other *Journey into the Himalayas*. Both of them, but particularly the former, are worth seeing if you get a chance.

Of course the epic *Gandhi* was a major film, spawning a host of new and reprinted books on the Mahatma. *Heat & Dust* has also been made into an excellent film, as has *A Passage to India* and *The Far Pavilions*. Filmed on the streets of Bombay is the excellent film *Salaam Bombay*. It concentrates on the plight of the street children in Bombay.

MAPS

Bartholomew's map of *India, Pakistan, Nepal, Bangladesh & Sri Lanka* is probably the most useful general map of India. It gives you plenty of detail of small towns and villages to help speed along those long bus or train trips. If it has any fault for the traveller, it is that it does not always include places of great interest but small population. The map is widely available in India as well as overseas.

Locally, the Government Map Office produces a series of maps covering all of India. In Delhi their office is opposite the tourist office on Janpath. It's upstairs, above the cafeteria beside the Central Cottage Industries Emporium. The maps are not all that useful since they will not allow production of anything at a reasonable scale which shows India's sea or land borders. It is illegal to take any Survey of India map of larger than 1:250,000 scale out of the country.

The Government of India tourist office has a number of excellent give-away city maps and also a reasonable all-India map. State tourist offices do not have much by the way of maps, but the Himachal Pradesh office has three excellent trekking maps which cover the trekking routes in that state.

Although they are not available in India, the APA Press series of Indian maps are some of the most detailed and comprehensive available. They are distributed in Asia by APA Press of Singapore.

THINGS TO BUY

India is packed with beautiful things to buy – you could easily load yourself up to the eyeballs with goodies you pick up around the country. The cardinal rule of purchasing handicrafts is to bargain and bargain hard. You can get a good idea of what is reasonable in quality and in price by visiting the various state emporiums, particularly in New Delhi, and the Central Cottage Industries Emporium. Here you can inspect items from all over the country at fixed prices which indicate fairly well what you can knock the regular dealers down below.

As with handicrafts in any country, don't buy until you have developed a little understanding and appreciation. Rushing in and buying the first thing you see will inevitably lead to later disappointment. In touristy places, particularly places like Varanasi, take extreme care with the commission merchants – these guys hang around waiting to pick you up and cart you off to their favourite dealers where whatever you pay will have a hefty margin built into it to pay their commission. Stories about 'my family's place', 'my brother's shop', 'special deal at my friend's place', are just stories and nothing more.

Carpets

It may not surprise you that India produces and exports more hand-crafted carpets than Iran, but it probably is more of a surprise that some of them are of virtually equal quality. In Kashmir, where India's best carpets are produced, the carpet-making techniques and styles were brought from Persia even before the Moghul era. The art flourished under the Moghuls and today Kashmir is packed with small carpet producers. There are many carpet dealers in Delhi as well as in Kashmir. Persian motifs have been much embellished on Kashmiri carpets, which come in a variety of sizes – three by five feet, four by six feet and so on. They are either made of pure wool, wool with a small percentage of silk to give a sheen (known as silk touch) or pure silk. The latter are more for decoration than hard wear. Expect to pay from Rs 5000 for a good-quality four-by-six carpet and don't be surprised if the price is more than twice as high.

Other carpet-making areas include Badhoi and Mirzapur in Uttar Pradesh or Warangal and Eluru in Andhra Pradesh. In Kashmir and Rajasthan the coarsely woven woollen *numdas* are made. These are more primitive and folksy than the fine carpets. Around the Himalaya and Uttar Pradesh *durries*, flat-weave cotton warp and weft rugs, are woven. In Kashmir *gabbas* are appliqué-like rugs. The many Tibetan refugees in India have brought their craft of making superbly colourful Tibetan rugs with them. A three-by-five Tibetan rug will be less than Rs 1000.

Unless you're an expert it is best to have expert advice or buy from a reputable dealer if you're spending large amounts of money on carpets. Check prices back home too; many western carpet dealers sell at prices you would have difficulty matching even at the source.

Papier Mâché

This is probably the most characteristic Kashmiri craft. The basic papier-mâché article is made in a mould, then painted and polished in successive layers until the final intricate design is produced. Prices depend upon the complexity and quality of the painted design and the amount of gold leaf used. Items include bowls, cups, containers, jewel boxes, letter holders, tables, lamps, coasters, trays and so on. A cheap bowl might cost only Rs 15, a large, well-made item might approach Rs 1000.

Pottery

In Rajasthan interesting white-glazed pottery is made with hand-painted blue-flower designs – attractively simple. Terracotta images of the gods and children's toys are made in Bihar.

Metalwork

Copper and brass items are popular throughout India. Candle holders, trays, bowls, tankards and ashtrays are made in Bombay and other centres. In Rajasthan and Uttar Pradesh the brass is inlaid with exquisite designs in red, green and blue enamel. Bidhri is a craft of Andhra Pradesh and particularly Hyderabad, where silver is inlaid into gunmetal. Hookah pipes, lamp bases and jewellery boxes are made in this manner.

Jewellery

Many Indian women put most of their wealth into jewellery, so it is no wonder that so much of it is available. For western tastes the heavy folk-art jewellery of Rajasthan has particular appeal. You'll find it all over the country, but particularly in Rajasthan. In the north you'll also find Tibetan jewellery, even chunkier and more folk-like than the Rajasthan variety.

Leatherwork

Of course Indian leatherwork is not made from cow-hide but from buffalo-hide or some other substitute. *Chappals*, those basic sandals found all over India, are the most popular purchase. In craft shops in Delhi you can find well-made leather bags, handbags and other items. In Kashmir leather shoes and boots, often of quite good quality, are made, along with coats and jackets of often abysmally low quality.

Textiles

This is still India's major industry and 40% of the total production is at the village level where it is known as *khadi*. Bedspreads, table cloths, cushion covers or material for clothes are all popular purchases. There is an amazing variety of styles, types and techniques around the country. In Gujarat and Rajasthan heavy material is embroidered with tiny mirrors and beads to produce the mirror-work used in everything from dresses to stuffed toys to wall hangings. Tie-dye work is also popular in Rajasthan.

In Kashmir embroidered materials are made into shirts and dresses. Fine shawls of pashmina goats' wool also come from Kashmir. Phulkari bedspreads or wall hangings come from the Punjab. Another place which is famous for its stunning embroidery work is Barmer close to the Pakistani border and south-west of Jaisalmer in Rajasthan. Batik is a recent introduction from Indonesia but already

Sari borders & bangles

widespread; kalamkari cloth from Andhra Pradesh and Gujarat is an associated but far older craft.

Bronze Figures

In the south delightful small images of the gods are made by the age-old lost-wax process. A wax figure is made, a mould is formed around it and the wax is melted and poured out. The molten metal is poured in and when it's solidified the mould is broken open. Figures of Shiva as dancing Nataraj are amongst the most popular.

Woodcarving

In the south, images of the gods are also carved out of sandalwood. Rosewood is used to carve animals – elephants in particular. Carved wooden furniture and other household items, either in natural finish or lacquered, are also made in various locations. In Kashmir intricately carved wooden screens, tables, jewellery boxes, trays and the like are carved from Indian walnut. They follow a similar pattern to that seen on the decorative trim of houseboats. Old temple carvings can be delightful.

Clothes & Saris

In Bombay and Delhi in particular you can find many readymades exactly like those you'll find from India in western boutiques. Indeed they're most probably the rejects from some export order or other. The prices are so low you need hardly worry, but as usual it's wise to check the quality. Saris, the most Indian of women's outfits, are made in various styles and types of material around the country. Varanasi is famous for its silk saris which often have gold edging.

Paintings

Reproductions of the beautiful old miniatures are painted in many places, but beware of paintings claimed to be antique – it's highly unlikely that they are. Also note that quality can vary widely; low prices often mean low quality and if you buy before you've had a chance to look at a lot of miniatures and develop some appreciation you'll inevitably find you bought unwisely. Udaipur (Rajasthan) has some good shops specialising in modern reproductions.

Other

Marble inlay pieces from Agra are pleasant reminders of the beauty of the Taj. They come as either simple little pieces or larger items like jewellery boxes. Appliqué work is popular in many places such as Orissa. In the Kutch region of Gujarat interesting stuffed toys are made.

Indian musical instruments always have an attraction for travellers, although you don't see nearly as many backpackers lugging sitars around as you did 15 years ago. A more sensible Indian music buy might be records or tapes. You can always take back Indian tea, packs of bidis, and food products like mango pickles or papadams.

At the many Bata shoe shops in India, western-style shoes are cheap and reasonably well made. Their best-quality men's shoes are about US$20 to US$25, far less than shoes of similar quality in London or New York.

A Warning!

Lots of people want to buy things in India but aren't keen on carting them all around the country with them and then back home. *No problem* say the shops. We'll mail it for you. We've been doing it for years, never had a problem, *trust us*. People trust them and nine times out of 10 there is no problem, the goods turn up *eventually* and everyone is happy. But that one time out of 10, you never see the goodies again. Maybe they were lost in the post, maybe they never were sent in the first place, maybe they never had any intention of sending them, who knows?

Since the first edition of this book we've had lots of letters from unhappy people who have paid for crafts that have never turned up and want us to do something about it. There is no room in this book to list all the names of shops that were going to send something but didn't. The message? Take it with you, send it yourself, or don't tell us about it!

Antiques

Articles over 100 years are not allowed to be exported from India. If you have doubts about any item and think it could be defined as an antique, you can check with:

Bombay
   Superintending Archaeologist, Antiquities, Archaeological Survey of India, Sion Fort
Calcutta
   Superintending Archaeologist, Eastern Circle, Archaeological Survey of India, Narayani Building, Brabourne Rd
New Delhi
   Director, Antiquities, Archaeological Survey of India, Janpath
Madras
   Superintending Archaeologist, Southern Circle, Archaeological Survey of India, Fort St George
Srinagar
   Superintending Archaeologist, Frontier Circle, Archaeological Survey of India, Minto Bridge

THINGS TO SELL

All sorts of western technological items are good things to sell in India, but cameras, tape recorders and the like are as dead as a dodo in terms of making profit. The market is flooded with them and, anyway, they might well be entered into your passport to ensure they leave the country with you. Video cassette recorders are a better bet but Bombay, at least, is flooded with them. Particularly in Calcutta, Delhi and Madras there is a good market for your bottle of duty-free whisky (say Rs 250). The same applies in Patna if you fly down from Nepal. It has been suggested that prices are even better in smaller towns.

Pocket calculators and watches are

popular things to sell and are less likely to be recorded in your passport. The best market is for high-quality watches, not cheap digital things. Don't try and bring several of the same items through customs – it's a bit obvious. Make sure they have 'Made in. . .' prominently marked on them. Japan or West Germany are preferable to Taiwan, Korea, etc. Your selling price will be much better if you can supply original boxes, instruction manuals and the lot. It's necessary to bargain hard. In Delhi the underground market is a good place to sell, in Bombay along D Naoragi Rd between Victoria Terminus and Flora Fountain, in Calcutta the New Market.

Be very wary of the buying-to-sell-later game – most people buying things in India to sell elsewhere know what they are about and have spent a lot of time testing the market and establishing good relations with suppliers. Buying precious stones in Agra and Jaipur to sell in Nepal is a favourite game which is unlikely to return the average traveller any profit. We regularly get letters from unfortunate travellers who have been talked into buying precious stones which they are assured can be sold in the west for several times the purchase price. Inevitably it turns out to be a small proportion of the purchase price!

WHAT TO TAKE & HOW TO TAKE IT

The usual travellers' rule applies – bring as little as possible. It's much better to have to get something you've left behind than find you have too much and need to get rid of it. In the south of India you can count on shortsleeve weather year round, but in the north it can get cool enough to require a sweater or light jacket in the evenings during the winter. In the far north it will get down to freezing and you will need all the warm-weather gear you can muster.

Remember that clothes are easily and cheaply purchased in India. You can buy things off the peg or have clothes made to measure in the small tailor shops found everywhere in India. In the big cities there are plenty of the Indian fashions so popular in the west, and the prices often approximate in rupees what they cost in dollars in the west! One item of clothing to have made as soon as possible is a pair of lightweight pyjama-style trousers. You'll find them far cooler and more comfortable than jeans and they'll only cost a few rupees.

Modesty rates highly in India, as in most Asian countries. Although men wearing shorts is accepted as a western eccentricity, women should dress more discreetly. Even for men, however, wearing shorts or going shirtless in a more formal situation is not very polite. A reasonable clothes list would include:

– underwear & swimming gear
– one pair of cotton trousers, one pair of shorts
– a few T-shirts or short-sleeved shirts
– sweater for cold nights
– one pair of sneakers or shoes
– sandals and/or thongs
– lightweight jacket or raincoat
– a 'dress up' set of clothes

Other useful items include washing gear, medical & sewing kit, sunglasses and a padlock. A number of travellers have suggested taking small gifts such as biros (very popular), combs, sweets, etc for people, especially children, who have been friendly or helpful. Another item to consider is an umbrella, invaluable in the monsoon.

Sleeping Bag
A sleeping bag can be a hassle to carry but can serve as something to sleep in (and avoid unsavoury-looking hotel bedding), a cushion on hard train seats, a seat for long waits on railway platforms or a bed top-cover (since cheaper hotels rarely give you one). If you're trekking in the north then a sleeping bag will be an absolute necessity. Unlike Nepal, it is not so easy to hire trekking gear in India. A sheet sleeping bag, like those required by youth

hostels in the west, can be very useful, particularly if you don't trust the hotel's sheets. Mosquito nets are also rare so your own sheet or sheet sleeping bag will also help to keep mosquitoes at bay.

Some travellers find that a plastic sheet is useful for a number of reasons, including to bedbug-proof unhealthy looking beds. Others have recommended an inflatable pillow as a useful accessory.

Toilet Paper
Toilet paper is a necessity if you can't adapt to the Indian method of a jug of water and your left hand. Gone are the days when you needed to bring rolls of the stuff to India. It is now widely available throughout the country in all but the smallest towns. Quality varies enormously, and it's generally not that cheap, so if you find some good stuff it might be worth stocking up with a spare or two.

Toiletries
Soap, toothpaste and other toiletries are readily available. A sink plug is worth having since few cheaper hotels have plugs. A nail brush can be very useful. For women, tampons are not that easy to find in India. Except in 'strange, varied, toxic-shock-inducing forms', wrote one woman.

Men, don't bother taking shaving stuff to India. Every few days pop into one of the barber shops you find in every town. An ordinary shave is quite an experience. First comes the lathering, then the first shave with an ordinary razor blade (which is unwrapped in front of you) fitted into a handle device. Next comes relathering and reshaving followed by an assortment of oils and lotions, some of which sting like hell. Finally, there's the hot, damp towel (and once, some lavender talcum powder!). The total cost of all this, plus interesting advice on where to stay and eat and what to see in town, is Rs 3 to Rs 3.50.

Patrick Hosking, UK

How to Carry It
Where to put all this gear? Well, for budget travellers the backpack is still the best carrying container. You can make it a

bit more thief proof by sewing on tabs so you can padlock it shut. A modern variation on the backpack is the travel pack – a backpack with a flap which zips over the shoulder straps to turn it into a soft bag. It looks more presentable that way and is also less prone to damage – the major problem with backpacks. Some airlines will no longer accept responsibility for damage or theft from backpacks.

An alternative is a large, soft, zip bag with a wide shoulder strap. It's not so easy to carry for distances but it is rather more thief proof and less damage prone. Suitcases are only for jet-setters! Lots of plastic bags will keep your gear in some sort of order and will also be invaluable for keeping things dry during the wet season.

Miscellaneous Useful Things

It's amazing how many things you wish you had with you when you're in India. One of the most useful for budget travellers is a padlock. In fact a padlock is a virtual necessity. Many cheaper hotels, in fact most of them, have doors locked by a latch and padlock. You'll find having your own sturdy lock on the door instead of the flimsy thing the hotel supplies does wonders for your peace of mind. Other uses are legion. You can lock a pack onto a railway luggage rack at night, for example. It may not make it thief proof but it helps. You can buy a reasonable lock in India for Rs 15 to Rs 30.

A universal sink plug is useful as sinks never have them. Ever tried to wash your underwear in a sink without a plug? A knife (Swiss Army for preference) finds a whole field of uses, in particular for peeling fruit. Some travellers rhapsodise about the usefulness of a miniature electric element to boil water in a cup. I carry my Balinese sarong with me everywhere – it's a bed sheet, an item of clothing, an emergency towel, something to lie on at the beach, a pillow on trains!

Insect repellent can also be extremely useful. A 10-metre length of nylon cord makes an excellent clothesline. Power cuts are common in India ('load shedding' as it is euphemistically known) and there's little street lighting at night so a torch (flashlight) and candles can be useful. A small rubber wedge door-stop was one suggestion. It helps keep doors both open and closed. Bring along your spectacle prescription if you're short-sighted. Should you lose or damage your glasses a new pair can be made very cheaply, although the quality may be suspect. Earplugs are useful for light sleepers, and even heavier sleepers can have difficulty shutting out the din in some hotels.

Hot-weather survival requires another book of rules in India. First of all a sun hat is essential. Stepping out into the sun in the hot season is like using your head as a blacksmith's anvil. You don't just feel the sun, it reaches out and hits you. Secondly, a water bottle should always be by your side; and thirdly, have water purification tablets. In the heat you need water – cups of tea, fruit and soft drinks are just not going to do the job. Purification tabs are not 100% effective but when it gets really hot you're not going to care how effective they are! You'll also need something with long sleeves, particularly if you're going to ride a bicycle very far. High-factor sun block cream is not available anywhere in India.

INDIAN CLOTHING

Many travellers start wearing Indian clothes while in India – after all, much of it is a lot more appropriate to India's climate than jeans and T-shirts. The best known Indian clothing is the *sari*. It is also the one piece of clothing which is very difficult for western women to carry off properly. This supremely graceful attire is simply one length of material, a bit over a metre in width and five to nine metres long (usually around six metres long). It's worn without any pins, buttons or fastenings to hold it in place so in part its graceful appearance is a necessity. The tightly fitted, short blouse worn under a sari is a *choli*. The final length of the sari, which is draped over the wearer's shoulder, is known as the *pallav* or *palloo*.

There are a number of variations in types of saris and styles of wearing them, but there are also other styles of women's costume in India. Sikh women wear pyjama-like trousers drawn tightly in at the waist and the ankles. Over these trousers, known as *salwars*, they wear a long, loose tunic known as a *kameez*. This attire is comfortable and 'respectable'. A *churidhar* is similar to the salwar but tighter fitting at the hips. Over this goes a collar-less or mandarin-collar *kurta* – an item of clothing just as popular in the west, where it is worn by men as much as women, as in India.

Although the overwhelming majority of Indian women wear traditional costume, many Indian men wear quite conventional western clothing. Indeed a large proportion of India's consumer advertising appears to be devoted to 'suitings & shirtings' – the material made for tailor-made western-style business suits and shirts.

The traditional *lungi* originated in the south and today is worn by women as well as men. It's simply a short length of material worn around the thighs rather like a sarong. The lungi can be rolled up but should be lowered when sitting down or when entering someone's home or a temple. A *dhoti* is like a longer lungi but with a length of material pulled up between the legs, effective but a long way from elegant! A dhoti is a more formal piece of attire than a lungi, however. Pyjama-like trousers, worn by countryfolk, are known as *lenga*. Regular striped pyjamas are casual and comfortable but they're looked upon as a labourer's outfit; not something to wear to a fancy restaurant or to somebody's home.

There are many religious and regional variations, such as the brightly mirrored Rajasthani skirts and their equally colourful tie-dye materials. In Ladakh the women wear superbly picturesque Tibetan costumes with high 'top hats'. Their men

wear long dressing-gown-like coats. Muslim women, of course, wear much more staid and all-covering attire than their Hindu sisters. More traditional Muslim women wear the all-enveloping tent-like *burkha*.

WHERE TO FIND WHAT
India can offer almost anything you want, whether it's beaches, forts, amazing travel experiences, fantastic spectacles or a search for yourself. Listed here are just a few of those possibilities and where to start looking.

Beaches
People generally don't come all the way to India to laze on a beach – but there are some superb beaches if you're in that mood. On the west coast, at the southern end of Kerala, there's Kovalam; further north, Goa has a whole collection of beautiful beaches complete with the soft white sand, gentle lapping waves and swaying palms. If you find it a little overcommercialised these days then head for the tiny ex-Portuguese island of Diu off the southern coast of Saurashtra (Gujarat).

Over on the east coast you could try the beach at Mahabalipuram in Tamil Nadu. From the Shore Temple the beaches stretch north towards Madras and there are some fine places to stay. In Orissa the great temple of Konarak is only a couple of km away from another superb, and virtually deserted, beach.

beach	state	page
Kovalam	Kerala	810
Goa		690
Diu	Gujarat	513
Mahabalipuram	Tamil Nadu	840
Konarak	Orissa	602
Puri	Orissa	596

Faded Touches of the Raj
Although the British left India over 40 years ago, there are many places where you'd hardly know it. Of course much of India's government system, bureaucracy, communications, sports (the Indians are

crazy over cricket) and media are British to the core, but you'll also find the British touch in more unusual, enjoyable and amusing ways. For example, the Fairlawn Hotel in Calcutta where the Raj definitely lives in totally unfaded glory. The imposing Victoria Memorial, also in Calcutta, where they tried to build an imitation British Taj Mahal. The Maharajah's Palace in Mysore, rebuilt after it burned down earlier this century.

Could anything be more British than the Dal Lake houseboats, all chintz, over-stuffed armchairs and understatement? Or the Residency at Lucknow where with stiff upper lip the British held out against those pesky mutineers in 1857. Or relax in true British style for afternoon tea at Glenary's Tea Rooms in Darjeeling and later retire to your room at the Windamere Hotel; come to think of it, all of Darjeeling is a touch of the Raj.

Freak Centres

India has been the ultimate goal of the on-the-road hippy dream for years and somehow the '60s still continues in India's kind climate. From the clothes, the attitude and the music, Woodstock lives and the Beatles haven't even broken up yet. Goa has always been a great freak centre, the beaches are an attraction at any time of the year and every full moon is the occasion for a great gathering of the clans – but Christmas is its peak period when half the freaks in India seem to flock to its beaches. There are occasional 'purges' of the Goan beaches which shouldn't worry most people but the purist die-hards have decided this is too uncool and have moved to more remote locations such as Arambol (in the far north of Goa) and even over the border into northern Karnataka.

In Rajasthan the holy lake of Pushkar has a smaller, but semipermanent, freak population. Further south at Kovalam the fine beaches attract a steady clientele. The technicolour Tibetan outlook on life (they've got a way with hotels and restaurants too) works well in Kathmandu so why not in India – you'll find Dharamsala and Manali, both in Himachal Pradesh, also have longer-term populations of visitors. Hampi, capital of the Vijayanagar Kingdom, is very small in terms of number of visitors but definitely on the circuit. Finally, Puri in Orissa and Mahabalipuram in Tamil Nadu both have temples and beaches, a sure-fire combination.

Great Places to Stay

India has some superb hotels – it's also got a large number of bug-infested filthy dumps and a fair number of 'international class' hotels which are mediocre in standards and service but decidedly first class in price. But it's hard to think of a more enchanting hotel than the *Lake Palace* in Udaipur – it's far more than merely a palace; elegant, whimsical and romantic are all labels that can be applied to it. Or in Kashmir, staying on a houseboat is half the fun of going there; they come in all price ranges, from the rock-bottom 'doonga boats' to 'five-star' luxury complete with television.

The *Fairlawn Hotel* in Calcutta is Raj-style elegance totally untarnished by time – a shame if this one ever fades. In Bombay the elegant *Taj Mahal Inter-Continental Hotel* is probably the best in India – even if you don't stay there its air-conditioned lounge and strategic location are a magnet for everyone from backpackers on up. There are some very fine tourist bungalows, run by the state government tourist offices, scattered around India. They're often in fine locations and usually great value.

Backpackers' favourites include the wonderful old *Broadlands* in Madras and the equally well-kept *Z Hotel* in Puri. In Cochin the *Bolghatty Palace Hotel* is an old Dutch Palace built in 1744 and later a British residency – now a cheap hotel. Or try the *Bikaner Palace Hotel* with its quite amazing suites. The *Naggar Castle*, high up on the valley side between Kulu and Manali, is a fairy-tale eagle's nest and so romantic it's ridiculous! But most romantic of all, especially for castle and desert lovers, is the *Jaisal Palace Hotel* in Jaisalmer.

hotel	place	page
Lake Palace Hotel	Udaipur, Rajasthan	449
houseboats	Dal Lake, Kashmir	232
Fairlawn Hotel	Calcutta, West Bengal	344
Taj Mahal Inter-Continental	Bombay, Maharashtra	622
Broadlands Hotel	Madras, Tamil Nadu	825
Z Hotel	Puri, Orissa	599
Bolghatty Palace Hotel	Cochin, Kerala	792
Bikaner Palace Hotel	Mt Abu, Rajasthan	458
Naggar Castle	Naggar, Himachel Pradesh	208
Jaisal Castle Hotel	Jaisalmer, Rajasthan	473

Getting There is Half the Fun

A lot of travel in India can be indescribably dull, boring and uncomfortable. Trains take forever, buses fall apart and shake your fillings loose, even Indian Airlines sometimes manages to make your delay time far longer than your flying time. Despite the hassles there are a fair number of trips where getting there is definitely half the fun. Trains, of course, are the key to Indian travel and elsewhere in this book you'll find a section on India's unique and wonderful old steam trains. The Darjeeling Toy Train, which winds back and forth on its long climb up to the hill station, is half the fun of visiting Darjeeling. Other 'toy trains' include the run up to Matheran, just a couple of hours outside of Bombay, and the 'rack train' which makes the climb to Ooty from Mettupalayam in Tamil Nadu.

Then there is the delightful backwater trip through the waterways between Quilon and Alleppey – not only is the trip fascinating, it's absurdly cheap. Indian buses are generally a refined form of torture but the two-day trip between Srinagar in Kashmir and Leh in Ladakh is too good to miss. Finally, there could hardly be a more spectacular flight in the world than the Srinagar/Leh route which crosses the full width (and height) of the Himalaya.

trip	state	page
Siliguri to Darjeeling (toy train)	West Bengal	373
Neral to Matheran (toy train)	Maharashtra	636
Mettupalayam to Ooty (rack train)	Tamil Nadu	874
Alleppey to Quilon (back-water trip)	Kerala	804
Srinagar to Leh (bus or jeep)	Jammu & Kashmir	250
Srinagar to Leh (Indian Airlines)	Jammu & Kashmir	250

Places to Be & When to be There

India is a country of festivals and there are a number of places and times that are not to be missed. They start with the Independence Day festival in New Delhi each January – elephants, procession and military might with Indian princely splendour.

In June-July the great Car Festival in Puri is another superb spectacle as the gigantic temple car of Lord Jagannath makes its annual journey, pulled by thousands of eager devotees.

September-October is the time to head for the hills to see the delightful Festival of the Gods in Kulu. That is part of the Dussehra Festival which in the south is known as Dassehra and is at its most spectacular in Mysore. November is the time for the huge and colourful Camel Festival at Pushkar in Rajasthan. Finally, at Christmas where else is there to be in India than Goa?

festival	place	page
Republic Day Parade	New Delhi	49/140
Car Festival	Puri, Orissa	50/597
Festival of the Gods	Kulu, Himachal Pradesh	51/204
Dussehra	Mysore, Karnataka	50/723
Camel Fair	Pushkar, Rajasthan	52/425
Christmas	Goa	52/671

Deserted Cities

There are a number of places in crowded India where great cities of the past have been deserted and left. Fatehpur Sikri, near Agra, is the most famous since Akbar founded, built and left this impressive centre in less than 20 years. Hampi, the centre of the Vijayanagar Empire, is equally impressive. Not too far from there are the ancient centres of Aihole and Badami. Some of the great forts that follow are also really deserted cities.

site	state	page
Fatehpur Sikri	Uttar Pradesh	268
Hampi	Karnataka	745
Aihole & Badami	Karnataka	753

Great Forts

India has more than its share of great forts – many of them now deserted – to tell of its tumultuous history. The Red Fort in Delhi is one of the most impressive but Agra Fort is an equally massive reminder of Moghul power at its height. A short distance south is the huge, impregnable-looking Gwalior Fort. The Rajputs in Rajasthan could build forts like nobody else and they've got them in all shapes and sizes and with every imaginable tale to tell. Chittorgarh Fort is tragic, Bundi and Kota forts whimsical, Jodhpur Fort huge and high, Amber Fort simply beautiful, and Jaisalmer the essence of romance.

Further south there's Mandu, another fort impressive in its size and architecture but with a tragic tale to tell. Further south again at Daulatabad it's a tale of power, ambition and not all that much sense with another immense fort (they went in for large size) which was built and soon deserted. Important forts in the south include Bijapur and Golconda.

Naturally the European invaders had their forts too. You can see Portuguese forts in Goa, Daman and Diu. The British also built their share: Fort William in Calcutta is, unfortunately, not open to the public, but Fort St George in Madras certainly is and has a fascinating museum.

fort	state	page
Red Fort	Delhi	148
Agra	Uttar Pradesh	260
Chittorgarh	Rajasthan	438
Bundi	Rajasthan	435
Kota	Rajasthan	432
Jodhpur	Rajasthan	461
Amber	Rajasthan	415
Jaisalmer	Rajasthan	471
Mandu	Madhya Pradesh	576
Gwalior	Madhya Pradesh	540
Daulatabad	Maharashtra	656
Bijapur	Karnataka	756
Golconda, Hyderabad	Andhra Pradesh	766
Warangal	Andhra Pradesh	773
Chapora	Goa	704
Daman	Gujarat	503
Diu	Gujarat	512
Fort William, Calcutta	West Bengal	338
Fort St George, Madras	Tamil Nadu	821

Where Gandhi Went

Following the success of the film *Gandhi* you might be interested in making a Gandhi trek round India, starting at Porbandar where he was born and Rajkot where he spent the early years of his life. After his period in South Africa he returned to India and stayed in Bombay, a city he visited on numerous occasions. The massacre of 2000 peaceful protesters, one of the seminal events in the march to independence, took place in Amritsar. For many years Gandhi had his ashram at Sabarmati, across the river from Ahmedabad. The British interned him in the Aga Khan's Palace in Pune. Finally he was assassinated in the garden of the wealthy Birla family in New Delhi and his cremation took place at Raj Ghat.

event	place	page
Kirti Mandir	Porbandar, Gujarat	529
Kaba Gandhi	Rajkot, Gujarat	530
Mani Bhuvan	Bombay, Maharashtra	616
Jalianwala Bagh	Amritsar, Punjab	179
Sabarmati	Ahmedabad, Gujarat	492
Sevagram	Wardha, Maharashtra	665
Aga Khan's Palace	Pune, Maharashtra	643
Raj Ghat	New Delhi	150

Gurus & Religion

With India's great importance as a religious centre it's no wonder that so many people embark on some sort of spiritual quest here. There are all sorts of places and all sorts of gurus.

Rishikesh has been a guru centre ever since the Beatles went there with the Maharishi Mahesh Yogi; it's still popular today. Vrindaban near Mathura, which is between Delhi and Agra, is the centre for the Hare Krishna movement. Muktananda had his ashram at Ganeshpuri but since his death there has been a bitter battle for the succession. The Theosophical Society and the Krishnamurty Foundation have their headquarters in Madras. The Ramakrishna Mission has centres all over India although Calcutta is its headquarters.

Sai Baba is at Puttaparthi near Bangalore while Brahma Kumaris' Raja Yoga (Prajapita Brahma) is based in Mt Abu. Raja Yoga followers wear all white. There are plenty of other centres but one guru you won't find in India is the Divine Light Mission's Guru Maharaji; when he's there he stays in a hotel, his followers report.

And finally, with the Dalai Lama living in Dharamsala, where better to study Tibetan Buddhism.

movement	place	page
various	Rishikesh, Uttar Pradesh	306
Krishna Consciousness	Brindavan, Uttar Pradesh	272
Theosophical Society	Madras, Tamil Nadu	816
Krishnamurty Foundation	Madras, Tamil Nadu	816
Ramakrishna	Calcutta, West Bengal	342
Sri Aurobindo	Pondicherry, Tamil Nadu	850
Sai Baba	Puttaparthi, Andhra Pradesh	771
Raja Yoga	Mt Abu, Rajasthan	455
Rajneesh	Pune, Maharashtra	642
Tibetan Buddhism	Dharamsala, Himachal Pradesh	196

Holy Cities

Though India has plenty of holy cities, seven of them are of particular holiness. Some of them, like Varanasi, are obvious while some, like Dwarka, are relatively unknown outside of India. Three of them are dedicated to Shiva, three to Vishnu; Kanchipuram covers both gods. India's richest temple, however, is the Tirumala temple in Andhra Pradesh.

Other particularly holy cities include Rameswaram and Kanyakumari in Tamil Nadu, Puri in Orissa and Badrinath in

Uttar Pradesh. A pilgrimage to Badrinath, Puri, Rameswaram and Dwarka covers the four corners (north, east, south and west) of India.

Travellers' Notebook

Keeping Your Cool

Sometimes India can simply be too much for anyone to take. This has been called culture shock enough times, and in a way that is what it is. Remember that habits and practices which annoy or even revolt you – the continuous hawking and spitting, the practice of making every wall a public urinal – are probably matched by some western habits that an Asian would find just as incomprehensible. Westerners blithely walk into houses without pausing to take their shoes off, they sit on toilet seats, they carry dirty handkerchiefs in their pockets.

The habit of fixedly staring at you is one you just have to get used to. It's simply unembarrassed interest and there is nothing you can do about it. Staring right back is not going to change anything.

Summon up as much understanding as you can, but sometimes pushing and shoving, cutting into queues, continuously trying to get you to do something you don't want to, the inevitable rip-offs, all become too much and even the most easygoing travellers lose their temper. Treat these things as part of life, practise staying more relaxed next time, but if they start to happen too often perhaps it's time you took a break from India. After all, that's what Nepal and Sri Lanka are there for, aren't they?

Tony Wheeler

Some Facts on India

Every day 11,000,000 people take trains in India (this increases by 25% during holidays).

Blind people and people with cancer pay 10% less with Air India.

The world record for eating chilli powder (without drinking water) is 50 grams, set in June 1989 at Coimbatore, Tamil Nadu.

Dr J Lobstein

Getting There

ROUND-THE-WORLD FARES

Round-the-world (RTW) fares have become all the rage in the past few years; basically there are two types – airline tickets and agent tickets. An airline RTW ticket usually means two airlines have joined together to market a ticket which takes you round the world on their combined routes. Within certain limitations of time and number of stopovers you can fly pretty well anywhere you choose using their combined routes so long as you keep moving in the same direction. Compared to the full-fare tickets, which permit you to go anywhere you choose on any IATA airline so long as you do not exceed the 'maximum permitted mileage', these tickets are much less flexible. But they are also much cheaper.

Quite a few of these combined-airline RTW tickets go through India, including ones in combination with Air India which will allow you to make several stopovers within India. RTW tickets typically cost around A$2000 to A$3000, £1000 to £1750 and US$1250 to US$2500; tickets restricted to the northern hemisphere are cheaper

The other type of RTW ticket, the agent ticket, is a combination of cheap fares strung together by an enterprising travel agent. These can be cheaper than an airline RTW ticket but the choice of routes may not be so wide.

TO/FROM AFRICA

There are plenty of flights between East Africa and Bombay due to the large Indian population in Kenya. Typical fares from Bombay to Nairobi are around US$440 return with either Ethiopian Airlines, Kenya Airways or PIA (via Karachi).

Aeroflot flies Delhi/Cairo (via Moscow) for around US$280 one way.

The shipping services between Africa and India only carry freight (including vehicles), not passengers.

FROM AUSTRALIA & NEW ZEALAND

Advance-purchase return fares from the east coast of Australia to India range from A$900 to A$1200 depending on the season and the destination in India. Fares are slightly cheaper to Madras and Calcutta than to Bombay or Delhi. From Australia fares are cheaper from Darwin or Perth than from the east coast. The low travel period is from March to September; peak is from October to February.

Tickets from Australia to London or other European capitals with an Indian stopover are around A$1700 return.

Return advance-purchase fares from New Zealand to India range from NZ$1450 to NZ$1700 depending on the season.

TO/FROM BURMA (MYANMAR)

There are no land crossing points between Burma and India, or between Burma and any other country for that matter. If you want to visit Burma your only choice is to fly there. Burma (Myanmar) Airways Corporation flies Calcutta/Rangoon; Bangladesh Biman flies Dhaka/Rangoon.

TO/FROM MALAYSIA

Not many travellers fly between Malaysia and India because it is so much cheaper from Thailand, but there are flights between Penang and Madras. You can generally pick up tickets for the Malaysian Airlines Systems flight from Penang travel agents for around M$500 to M$600, rather cheaper than the regular fare.

The MV *Chidambaram*, which used to operate a shipping service between Penang and Madras, caught fire some years ago and has not yet been replaced. The Shipping Corporation of India has indicated it intends to restart the service, but it's unknown when that will happen, if at all.

TO/FROM THE MALDIVES

Trivandrum/Male costs US$63, Madras/Male US$124. The Trivandrum flight is cheaper than flying to the Maldives from Colombo in Sri Lanka.

TO/FROM THE MIDDLE EAST

There are many flights between Bombay and the Gulf states. There may still be ships operating between Bombay and Kuwait – the route would probably be Bombay/Karachi/Port Qaboos/Dubai/Doha/Bahrain/Kuwait. The trip takes about six days from Bombay to Kuwait but about 13 days in the opposite direction – for fares check with the shipping agents in Bombay. Boats between Karachi and the gulf are more reliable. There are services roughly twice a month, although these go mostly to and from Saudi Arabia ferrying expatriate Pakistanis back and forth.

TO/FROM SINGAPORE

Singapore is a great cheap-ticket centre and you can pick up Singapore/Bombay tickets for about S$700, and Singapore/Madras tickets for about S$600.

TO/FROM THAILAND

Bangkok is the most popular departure point from South-East Asia into Asia proper because of the cheap flights from there to Calcutta, Rangoon in Burma, Dhaka in Bangladesh or Kathmandu in Nepal. The popular Bangkok/Kathmandu flight is about US$250. You can make a stopover in Burma on this route and do a circuit of that fascinating country. Bangkok/Calcutta is about US$180, Bangkok/Delhi about US$250.

FROM THE UK

Various excursion fares are available from London to India, but you can get better prices through London's many cheap-ticket specialists or 'bucket shops'. Check the travel page ads in the *Times, Business Traveller* and the weekly 'what's on' magazine *Time Out*; or check giveaway papers like the *Australasian Express* and *LAW*. Two reliable London bucket shops are Trailfinders at 46 Earls Court Rd, London W8; and STA Travel at 74 Old Brompton Rd, London SW7 or 117 Euston Rd, London NW1.

Fares range from around £225 one way or £325 to £440 return, and depend very much on the carrier. The cheapest fares are usually with Middle Eastern or Eastern European airlines. You'll also find very competitive air fares to the subcontinent with Bangladesh Biman or Air Lanka. Thai International always seems to have competitive fares despite their high standards.

Some travel companies offer packages to Goa at competitive rates which include accommodation, breakfast, transfers and an Indrail Pass – check with travel agents and travel page ads in newspapers and magazines.

If you want to stop in India en route to Australia expect to pay around £500 to £600. You might find fares via Karachi (Pakistan) or Colombo (Sri Lanka) slightly cheaper than fares via India.

FROM THE USA & CANADA

The cheapest return air fares from the USA west coast to India are around US$1200. Another way of getting there is to fly to Hong Kong and get a ticket from there. Tickets to Hong Kong costs about US$500 one way and just under US$800 return from San Francisco or Los Angeles; in Hong Kong you can find one-way tickets to Bombay for US$300 depending on the carrier. Alternatively, you can fly to Singapore for around US$535 one way, US$835 return or to Bangkok for US$535 one way, US$865 return.

From the east coast you can find return tickets to Bombay or Delhi for around US$1100. The cheapest one-way tickets will be around US$550 to US$600. An alternative way of getting to India from

New York is to fly to London and buy a cheap fare from there.

Check the Sunday travel sections of papers like the *New York Times, San Francisco Chronicle/Examiner* or *Los Angeles Times* for cheap fares. Good budget travel agents include the student travel chains STA or CIEE.

Fares from Canada are similar to the USA fares. From Vancouver the route is like that from the USA west coast, with the option of going via Hong Kong. From Toronto it is easier to travel via London.

TO/FROM BANGLADESH

You can travel to or from Bangladesh by land and air. Unfortunately most land entry and exit points are closed, so the choice is much more limited than a glance at the map would indicate. You do not need an exit permit to leave Bangladesh on the Calcutta route; you may need one on the Darjeeling route.

Air

Bangladesh Biman and Indian Airlines fly from Calcutta to Dhaka (US$39) and Chittagong (US$49) in Bangladesh. Many people use Biman from Calcutta through to Bangkok – partly because they're cheap and partly because they fly through Rangoon in Burma. Biman should put you up overnight in Dhaka on this route but be careful – it appears they will only do so if your ticket is specifically endorsed that you are entitled to a room. If not, tough luck – you can either camp out overnight in the hot transit lounge or make your way into Dhaka on your own, pay for transport and accommodation, and get hit for departure tax the next day.

Land

Calcutta to Dhaka The Calcutta to Dhaka route is the one used by the majority of land travellers. Stage one is a train from Sealdah station (Calcutta) to Bongaon, the end of the line. The trip takes about 2¼ hours and the fare is Rs 10; the train is all 2nd class. From Bongaon station it's

about 10 km by rickshaw to the border at Haridaspur on the Indian side. A seat in an auto-rickshaw will cost about Rs 10, the whole vehicle Rs 50. Remember that in Bangladesh auto-rickshaws are called 'baby taxis'. It's possible to change money at the border.

Crossing the border takes an hour or two with the usual form filling and stamping. From the border it's about 10 minutes by rickshaw to Benapole on the Bangladesh side. Standard fare seems to be Tk 7 per person either two to a rickshaw or three to a 'van', a sort of freight rickshaw.

It's then an eight or nine-hour bus trip from Benapole to Dhaka, a distance of 291 km which costs Tk 95. The first leg of the trip, to Jessore, takes about 1½ hours; then it's an hour to a small ferry crossing. It's only about 10 minutes across the river but the waiting, loading and unloading will occupy an hour or two. Another 1½ hours takes you to a larger ferry crossing at Aricha. Getting across the river takes a couple of hours; going to Dhaka this ferry takes about half an hour longer as the crossing is upstream. Finally it's another 1½ hours to Dhaka. Coming from Dhaka it's wise to book your seat on the bus at least a day in advance.

The buses that operate overnight between Dhaka and the border are direct. Coming from Dhaka you can take a bus from 8 to 11 pm and arrive in Benapole at dawn. From Calcutta, if you leave in the early afternoon you should be in Benapole in time for the bus departures between 6 and 8.30 pm. During the day there are no direct buses so you have to take a 'coaster' between the border and Jessore (Tk 13) and a Jessore to Dhaka bus (Tk 72). The last 'direct' buses from Jessore leave around 1 to 2 pm.

Darjeeling From New Jalpaiguri it's about 2½ hours and costs Rs 4 by train to Haldibari, the Indian border checkpoint, but you have a little travelling yet before you reach Bangladesh. It's a seven-km walk along the disused railway line from

Haldibari to the Bangladesh border point at Chiliharti! 'It's here you discover how much excess baggage you're carrying', wrote one traveller. You should be able to find someone to carry your pack for you. There's a train station at Chiliharti from where you can set off into Bangladesh. Bring some takkas into Bangladesh with you. This is officially illegal but changing money in Chiliharti is virtually impossible. You should be able to change some at Haldibari.

TO/FROM NEPAL

There are a number of land crossings and air links between Nepal and India. In 1989, however, a dispute over the terms of a new border treaty led India to close all but the three most popular land crossings to travellers. When and if the situation returns to normal there will be other options. Flights are not affected.

Air

You can fly to Kathmandu, the capital of Nepal, from Delhi (US$142), Calcutta (US$96), Varanasi (US$71) or Patna (US$41). Note that flying Delhi/Patna and Patna/Kathmandu is much cheaper than flying Delhi/Kathmandu direct. Both Royal Nepal Airlines and Indian Airlines have a 25% discount on the fares shown for those under 30.

Land

Travelling by land is, of course, by far the cheapest option. At times a direct bus has run from Delhi to Kathmandu but the 1989 border dispute had temporarily halted this. Normally people catch trains as far as they can go, then take an Indian bus to the border and, finally, a Nepalese bus from the border to Kathmandu or Pokhara. Travel agents can handle all these bookings, but it's easy enough to handle it yourself as you go. An agent will of course charge a fee, and you will need to book at least a week in advance.

For more details of the land routes into Nepal see the Uttar Pradesh, Bihar and

West Bengal sections in this book. The most popular routes are from Raxaul (near Muzaffarpur), Sunauli (near Gorakhpur), and Kakarbhitta (near Siliguri) and these were not affected by the border dispute. If you are heading straight to Nepal from Delhi or elsewhere in western India then the Gorakhpur to Sunauli route is the most convenient. From Calcutta, Patna or most of eastern India, Raxaul to Birganj is the best entry point. From Darjeeling it's easiest to go to Kakarbhitta.

To give an idea of costs, a 2nd-class rail ticket from Delhi to Gorakhpur costs US$15 and buses from Gorakhpur to the border and then on to Kathmandu cost another US$6.

There are other roads into Nepal from northern Bihar to the east of Birganj but they are rarely used by travellers and they were closed in late 1989. One that would be worth considering, once the border dispute is resolved, is the crossing from Jogbani (near Purnia) to Biratnagar, which is convenient if you are coming from Calcutta. There's also a narrow gauge railway that runs across the border from Jaynagar (near Darbhanga) to Janakpur, an attractive Nepalese city famous as the birthplace of Sita.

TO/FROM PAKISTAN

Relations between India and Pakistan have certainly improved if travel between the two countries is anything to go by. After the Bangladesh war, border crossings were limited to one road which was open for one morning each week. Today there are a variety of direct flights and there are daily trains across the border.

Air

Pakistan International Airlines and Indian Airlines operate flights from Karachi to Bombay for approximately US$106 (depending on exchange rates), Karachi/Delhi for about US$127 and Lahore/Delhi for about US$60.

Land

Amritsar to Lahore Due to the unrest in the Punjab the situation at this border crossing changes regularly. Presently, foreigners do not need permits to travel in the Punjab and the crossing at Attari has been opened daily to all traffic. It may be worth checking the situation in the Punjab with the Home Ministry in New Delhi or the Indian Embassy in Islamabad, Pakistan, before you travel.

For the Lahore (Pakistan) to Amritsar (India) train you have to buy one ticket from Lahore to Attari, the border town, and another from Attari to Amritsar, but the total fare is only about Rs 12. The train departs Lahore daily at 2 pm and arrives in Amritsar around 6 pm after a couple of hours at the border passing through immigration and customs. Going the other way, you leave Amritsar at 9.30 am and arrive in Lahore at 2 pm. Pakistan immigration and customs are handled at Lahore station. Sometimes, however, border delays can make the trip much longer.

From Amritsar you cannot buy a ticket until the morning of departure and there are no seat reservations; so arrive early and push. Moneychangers offer good rates for Pakistan rupees on the platform, but you cannot get Indian rupees coming the opposite way. Travellers have reported that whichever direction you're travelling, the exchange rate between Indian and Pakistan rupees is more advantageous to you on the Pakistan side of the border, but you can change Indian rupees to Pakistani rupees or vice versa at Wagah and in Amritsar – no matter what the Pakistanis may tell you!

Since the rail route opened far fewer travellers use the road. It's mainly of interest to people with vehicles or those on overland buses. By public transport the trip from Lahore entails taking a bus to the border at Wagah between Lahore and Amritsar, walking across the border and then taking another bus or taxi into Amritsar.

From Lahore buses and minibuses depart from near the general bus station on Badami Bagh. The border opens at 9.15 am and closes at 3.30 pm. If you're stuck on the Pakistan side you can stay at the *PTDC Motel*, where there are dorm beds and double rooms.

Other Routes Prior to partition there were, of course, many more routes across the border, but the roads have been cut and the railway lines torn up. The old road connecting Rawalpindi in Pakistan to Srinagar in Kashmir used to be the main route to Kashmir and was much more heavily used than the Jammu to Srinagar route. There was also a route into Kashmir and Ladakh from Skardu, Pakistan, to Kargil on the Srinagar to Leh road.

TO/FROM SRI LANKA

Far fewer travellers are continuing onto Sri Lanka from India due to the level of unrest and violence in that unhappy country, and also because the ferry service is out of operation so flying is now the only way to get there.

Air

There are flights to and from Colombo (the capital of Sri Lanka) and Bombay, Madras, Tiruchirapalli or Trivandrum. Flights are most frequent on the Madras/Colombo route.

Sea

The ferry service from Rameswaram, southern India, to Talaimannar in Sri Lanka is currently suspended due to the unrest in Sri Lanka. This was a favourite route for shipping arms and equipment to the Tamil guerrilla forces in the north of the country.

OVERLAND – FROM EUROPE

The classic way of getting to India has always been overland. Sadly the events in Iran and Afghanistan have turned the cross-Asian flow into a trickle, although these days more travellers are coming this way. Before these regional conflicts you travelled through Europe to Greece, crossed from Europe into Asia at Istanbul in Turkey, and crossed Turkey by a number of routes to Iran. You then continued to Tehran and, possibly with a detour to see Isfahan and Shiraz, went on to Mashed and finally Afghanistan. In that magical country you followed the well-beaten track through Herat, Kandahar and Kabul with possibly an excursion further north to the Bamiyan Valley and then Mazar-i-Sharif. From Kabul you crossed the Khyber Pass into Pakistan, then followed the Grand Trunk Road through Peshawar to Lahore and eventually into India near Amritsar in the Punjab.

Today, Afghanistan is still off limits and Iran is certainly difficult, although it's only really impossible for Americans. Despite the tensions and uncertainties, many overlanders did continue to travel through Iran during the year of the US hostage drama, and even Iraq has not stopped intrepid travellers. With the cessation of the Gulf War, hopefully things will improve rapidly in this part of the world.

The Asia overland trip is certainly not the breeze it once was, but people continue to do it. Many travellers combine travel to the subcontinent with the Middle East by flying from India or Pakistan to Amman in Jordan or one of the Gulf states. A number of the London-based overland companies still operate their bus or truck trips across Asia on a regular basis. Check with Exodus, Encounter Overland, Top Deck or Hann Overland for more information.

For more detail on the Asian overland route see the Lonely Planet guide *West Asia on a Shoestring*.

OVERLAND - THROUGH SOUTH-EAST ASIA

In contrast to the difficulties in central Asia, the South-East Asian overland trip is still wide open and as popular as ever. From Australia the first step is to Indonesia – either Bali or Jakarta.

Although most people fly from an east coast city or from Perth to Bali, there are also flights from Darwin and from Port Hedland in the north of Western Australia. The shortest route is the flight between Darwin and Kupang on the Indonesian island of Timor. From Bali you head north through Java to Jakarta, from where you either travel by ship or fly to Singapore or continue north through Sumatra and then cross to Penang in Malaysia. After travelling around Malaysia you can fly from Penang to Madras in India or, more popularly, continue north to Thailand and eventually fly out from Bangkok to India.

An interesting alternative route is to travel from Australia to Papua New Guinea and from there cross to Irian Jaya; then to Sulawesi in Indonesia. There are all sorts of travel variations possible in South-East Asia; the region is a delight to travel through; it's good value for money; the food is generally excellent and healthy; and all in all it's an area of the world not to be missed. For full details see the Lonely Planet guide *South-East Asia on a Shoestring*.

CHEAP TICKETS IN INDIA

Although you can get cheap tickets in Bombay and Calcutta, it is in Delhi that the real wheeling and dealing goes on. There are countless 'bucket shops' around Connaught Place, but enquire with other travellers about their current trust-worthiness! With most cheap tickets you will have to pay the full official fare through a bank – the agent gets you a bank form stating what the official fare is, you pay the bank and the bank pays the agent. You then receive a refund from the agent, but in rupees. Therefore, it is wise either to buy your ticket far enough ahead that you can use those rupees up, or have plenty of bank exchange certificates in hand to change the rupees back. This also applies to credit card purchases.

Fares from Delhi to various European capitals cost between Rs 5000 to Rs 7000, a bit less from Bombay. The cheapest flights to Europe are with airlines like Aeroflot, LOT, Kuwait Airways, Syrian Arab Airways or Iraqi Airways. Officially Aeroflot is not allowed to sell tickets in India but they do, and the tickets are stamped as having been issued in Moscow or Singapore. You can fly with good airlines like Thai International for around Rs 5500. Delhi/Hong Kong/San Francisco costs around US$520.

Although Delhi is the best place for cheap tickets, most flights between Europe and South-East Asia or Australia pass through Bombay; it's also the place for flights to East Africa. Furthermore, if you're heading east from India to Bangladesh, Burma or Thailand you'll probably find much better prices in Calcutta than in Delhi, even though there are fewer agents.

AIRPORT TAX

India now has one of the higher airport taxes in the world for international flights; for flights to neighbouring countries (Pakistan, Sri Lanka, Bangladesh, Nepal) it's Rs 100, but to other countries it's a hefty Rs 300.

This airport tax applies to everybody, even to babies who do not occupy a seat –

in most countries airport tax applies only to seat occupants or adults. The method of collecting the tax varies but generally you have to pay it before you check in, so look out for an airport tax counter as you enter the check-in area.

Warning

This chapter is particularly vulnerable to change – prices for international travel are volatile, routes are introduced and cancelled, schedules change, rules are amended, special deals come and go, and borders open and close. Airlines and governments seem to take a perverse pleasure in making price structures and regulations as complicated as possible. You should check directly with the airline or a travel agent to make sure you understand how a fare (and ticket you may buy) works. In addition, the travel industry is highly competitive and there are many lurks and perks. The upshot of this is that you should get opinions, quotes and advice from as many airlines and travel agents as possible before you part with your hard-earned cash. The details given in this chapter should be regarded as pointers and are not a substitute for careful, up-to-date research.

Travellers' Notebook

Runaway Luggage

I was taking the Jaipur to Jodhpur express, minding my own business in a 1st-class compartment occupied by a very pleasant Indian family. My backpack was padlocked and chained to the compartment's parcel shelf; for the first (and last!) time I'd taken my moneybelt off and put it in the locked pack because I was feeling rather hot and sweaty wearing it across the desert (the number of times I pulled out damp Rs 100 notes!). In true Indian fashion, the train stopped from time to time for anything from two to 20 minutes, to be besieged by hordes of chai, cold drink and snack sellers.

Halfway into the journey, I found my stocks of mineral water were low. Concerned about dehydration, I decided to replenish my supply at the next station. The Indian family assured me that it was to be a five to 10-minute stop, so I hopped off the train in search of mineral water. There was nothing for sale on the platform so I ran out of the station and tried a few stalls. I was greeted with blank stares which, I guess, meant: 'There's a tap over there – why do you want to pay for water in a bottle?' Little English was spoken and in the end, I settled for two cartons of mango fruit drink.

I'd been gone for about four minutes when I sprinted back to the station to find – you guessed it – only a stretch of empty track where my train should have been. I don't think I will ever forget the overwhelming sense of blind panic and desperation that came over me. This would have been bad enough in England. . .but in India! It was my worst nightmare realised, almost everything I had was on that train: backpack, clothes, camera, film, medical supplies, most of my money, and my moneybelt which had my passport and travellers' cheques. I was left with only the clothes I wore and around Rs 100 in change. . .oh, and two cartons of mango juice.

I raced madly up the platform, shouting at people and asking them where the train had gone. There was no sign of it along the track, and the vague wave one guy gave in the direction of the empty stretch of line confirmed that it had left without me.

After sprinting back to the stationmaster's office, I breathlessly tried to explain what had happened, only to find that he too spoke very little English and insisted that I write down whatever I wanted to say. It was the most frustrating half-hour of my life – playing with a pen and paper as my luggage steamed ever further into the dry, distant desert.

By this time I was really starting to lose my cool, and in true Indian fashion, the station staff seemed unperturbed by the whole scenario. I wandered around the office muttering a stream of invectives, thumping the walls and kicking the furniture in an effort not to go totally bananas – much to the amusement of a band of locals pressing at the door. In the middle of this desperate situation, the line that came flooding into my head was one from an English TV comedy, spoken by a hotel proprietor trying frantically to communicate with his spanish waiter: 'Please try and understand before one of us dies!'

Several pieces of paper later, it became apparent that all I could hope for was that my luggage would be unloaded at Degana (a name eternally etched in my memory!), the next station about 45 km away and the last stop before Jodhpur. A hesitant call was duly put through to Degana, but it was hardly a confidence-inspiring effort. The line appeared to keep going dead and the phone was one of those 'wind-up' affairs! After an agonising half-hour wait, Degana replied confirming that my luggage was there.

Still not convinced that the luggage was safe, I decided to head off to Degana by road to collect my luggage rather than wait for it to return on the next train. There then followed a couple of sprints between the jeep taxi rank and the station in an effort to arrange the trip as quickly as possible; in the end I was stung Rs 250 for the two-hour journey. They're not daft, they know when there's a panic on.

By this time I had my fan club, a group of 30 or so locals, following my every move, anxious to see what this eccentric westerner would do next – more running around, more shouting and waving or more furniture thumping. They weren't disappointed as I made my way back to the mango juice stall and tried to explain I wanted 20 cartons to last me across the desert. The stallkeeper was amazed, and the locals loved the finale to the saga as the western visitor leaped into a taxi jeep with two bulging carrier bags full of mango juice cartons. (I've gone off mango juice now.)

The ride seemed like an eternity, yet when I reached Degana all my luggage was there – intact! Not only had they removed it from the train (cutting the chain that secured the pack to the train in the process) but they'd taken all the contents out of the unlocked side and top pockets of the pack and put them into bags sealed with wax, to ensure that nobody could interfere with them. Everything had been carefully logged and held secure in a locked cupboard till I arrived – it was an amazing feat of organisation. I was given something to eat and drink – the station superintendent had a meal brought from his own home. I was given a chit stating what had happened and that I was to be allowed to continue my journey to Jodhpur on a different train but using the same ticket. I was safely deposited on the night train which arrived in Jodhpur at 5 am the next day. Was it all a dream I wondered when I woke up.

I offered the Degana crew some money for their trouble but they refused and insisted that all I should do is take some group photos and send them copies. I reckon they deserve medals – well done India!

Two important lessons I learnt from this experience were: never let go of the most important possessions – passport and money; and never lose sight of the train you are travelling in when stopped at a station. Both are painfully obvious 'golden rules' but it took my escapade to hammer them home to me. I'm left in no doubt that I was extraordinarily fortunate to get away with it all.

François Baker, UK

Getting Around

AIR

India's major domestic airline, Indian Airlines, flies extensively throughout the nation and into neighbouring countries. Air India also operates domestic services, principally on the Bombay/Delhi, Bombay/Calcutta and Bombay/Madras routes. Indian Airlines is the largest regional carrier in South Asia, with a fleet of A300 Airbuses and Boeing 737s. The recent expansion of the fleet and some hefty fare increases have made getting a seat on Indian Airlines flights much easier.

Vayudoot is India's second domestic airline, operating the twin-engined Dornier, Fokker F27 and Avro aircraft. Vayudoot flies to many small centres not covered by Indian Airlines, opening new possibilities for visitors with limited time – or whose patience has run out. Vayudoot has taken over Indian Airlines' turboprop services as well, leaving the larger airline with the more important jet aircraft routes. One advantage of Vayudoot is that its flights are less crowded so it is often possible to get a booking only one day in advance.

This small airline, only introduced in the last few years, is so successful that it now wants authorisation to compete with Indian Airlines on some of the major routes.

Booking Flights

Indian Airlines has computerised booking at all the larger and many of the smaller offices, making air travel in India much simpler. The airline once operated multimillion dollar wide-body jets with a booking system more suited to a Victorian era railway service. Computers have even considerably shortened the waiting list, or 'chance list' as it is more appropriately known in India.

If you want to know what precomputer air travel was like, however, Vayudoot can show you. Getting a seat on a Vayudoot flight is still a fraught and problematical affair, hampered by some of their agents.

Tickets

All Indian Airline tickets must be paid for with foreign currency, travellers' cheques or currency exchange forms. Infants up to two years old travel at 10% fare, but only one infant per adult. Children two to 12 years old travel at 50% fare. There is no student reduction for overseas visitors but there is a youth fare for people 12 to 30 years old. This allows a 25% reduction, but on the dollar tariff. Since the dollar tariff is much higher than the rupee tariff converted into dollars, youth fares are not such a bargain – in fact 25% off the dollar fare is likely to be more than the full fare in rupees! Neat trick, huh? If you book Indian Airlines tickets overseas you have to pay the more expensive dollar tariff fares.

There are heavy penalties for cancellations or no-shows on Indian Airlines flights. If you cancel more than 48 hours ahead the charge is Rs 30; from 24 to 48 hours it's 10%; from one hour to 24 hours it's 25%; and if you change your mind in the last hour or fail to show up you can throw the ticket away. These penalties do not apply, however, if you've bought your tickets overseas on the more expensive dollar tariff. Unlike almost every other

Indian Airlines logo

112

airline in the world, Indian Airlines accepts no responsibility if you lose your tickets. They absolutely will not replace lost tickets, so treat them like cash, not travellers' cheques.

Fares

The accompanying chart details the main Indian Airlines domestic routes and fares. Indian Airlines also have a 21-day 'Discover India' fare which costs US$400 and a 14-day version called 'Tour India' which costs US$300, or US$200 for seven days. These allow unlimited travel on their domestic routes and can be reasonable value if you have limited time.

Indian Airlines have a number of excursion-fare circuit trips providing a 20% or 30% discount on the normal fare. These usually link domestic travel with an Air India overseas route.

In Flight

Indian Airlines flights usually have a choice of vegetarian or non-vegetarian meals; unless you request otherwise, westerners will always be assumed to be non-veg. The food is usually not very good in either case and Indian Airlines' flight attendants can be grumpy. Other minor Indian Airlines irritations are the complete lack of effort to keep you informed of delays, check-in counters are rarely open as far ahead as the requested reporting times, and luggage is often unloaded at a snail's pace.

Offices

The Indian Airlines' office addresses are listed here with the distance from the office to the airport:

Agartala (12 km)
    Khosh Mahal Building, Central Rd (tel 60)
Agra (7 km)
    Hotel Clarks-Shiraz, 54 Taj Rd (tel 73434, 72421)

Ahmedabad (10 km)
    Airlines House, Lal Darwaja (tel 391736, 391797, 391619)
Allahabad (12 km)
    18 Tashkant Marg, Tata Auto Sales Building (tel 42607, 61633)
Amritsar (11 km)
    48 The Mall (tel 42607)
Aurangabad (10 km)
    Anvikar Building, Adalat Rd (tel 4864)
Bagdogra (14 km)
    Hotel Sinclairs, Mallaguri PO Pradhanagar, Siliguri (tel 20692)
Bangalore (13 km)
    Housing Board Building, Kempe Gowda Rd (tel 76851)
Belgaum (14 km)
    Hotel Sanman Deluxe, College Rd (tel 20801, 25898)
Bhavnagar (8 km)
    Diwanpara Rd (tel 27144, 23214)
Bhopal (11 km)
    Bhadbhada Rd, TT Nagar (tel 61633, 61155)
Bhubaneswar (4 km)
    V11-C/8 Raj Path, Bapuji Nagar (tel 50533, 50544)
Bhuj (6 km)
    Outside Waniawad Gate, Station Rd (tel 34)
Bombay (26 km)
    Air India Building, 1st floor, Madam Cama Rd, Nariman Point (tel 2023031, 2023521, 2023154)
Calcutta (16 km)
    Airlines House, 39 Chittaranjan Ave (tel 263135, 250730/1, 263390, 262954)
Calicut
    Eroth Centre, Bank Rd (tel 65482)
Chandigarh (11 km)
    SCO-186-187-188 Sector 17C (tel 28721, 26443)
Chittagong
    Hotel Agrabad (tel 838542)
Cochin (6 km)
    Durbar Hall Rd, Ernakulam (tel 352465)
Coimbatore (11 km)
    503 Trichy Rd (tel 22743, 22208)
Colombo (18 km)
    95 Sir Baron Jayatilaka Mawatha (tel 23136)
Dabolim (37 km)
    Dempo House, Campal, Panaji (tel 3826, 4190)

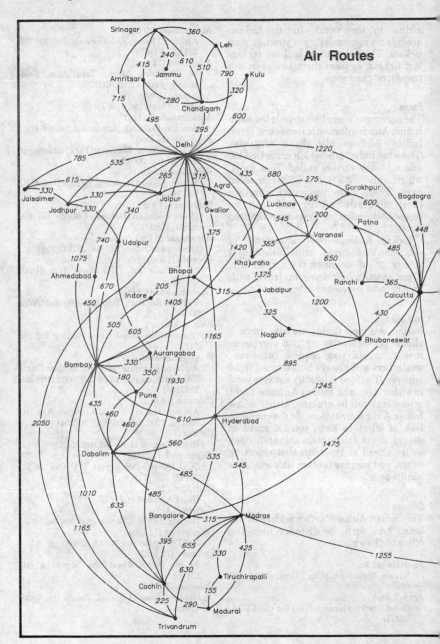

Air Routes

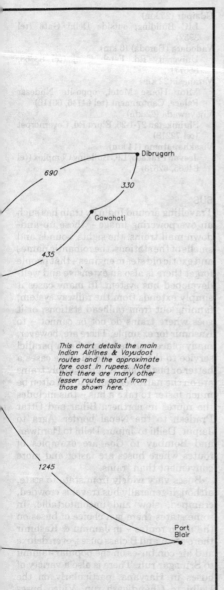

This chart details the main Indian Airlines & Vayudoot routes and the approximate fare cost in rupees. Note that there are many other lesser routes apart from those shown here.

690

330

435

1245

Dibrugarh

Gawahati

Port Blair

Delhi (13 km)
Malhotra Building, Connaught Place (tel 3310646, 3310454)

Dhaka (7 km)
Hotel International (tel 231687)

Dibrugarh (26 km)
CIWTC Bungalow, Assam Medical College Rd (tel 114)

Dimapur (5 km)
Dimapur-Imphal Rd (tel 2375)

Gawahati (22 km)
Paltan Bazar (tel 23128, 26655, 23734)

Gorakhpur (7 km)
Park Rd (tel 3940)

Gwalior (12 km)
Tansen Marg, Barrar (tel 21773)

Hyderabad (9 km)
Saifabad, near Legislative Assembly Building (tel 72051)

Imphal (7 km)
Mahatma Gandhi Rd (tel 28/1377)

Indore (9 km)
164/1 Rabindranath Tagore Marg (tel 7069)

Jabalpur (15 km)
Chadha Travels, Jackson Hotel, Civil Lines (tel 21324, 22178, 21320)

Jaipur (15 km)
Mundhara Bhawan, Ajmer Rd (tel 72940, 74500)

Jammu (7 km)
Tourist Reception Centre, Veer Marg (tel 42735, 47577)

Jamnagar (10 km)
Indra Mahal, near Bhind Bhanjan Temple (tel 4285)

Jodhpur (5 km)
Rupali Tourist Bungalow, High Court Rd (tel 20909)

Jorhat (6 km)
Garhali (tel 11)

Kabul (7 km)
Chanrahi Malick, Asghar Desh (tel 31469, 32920)

Kanpur (13 km)
15/69 Civil Lines (tel 63356, 65042)

Karachi (15 km)
Hotel Inter-Continental (c/o PIA) (tel 511577, 515021, 522034)

Kathmandu (8 km)
Durbar Marg (tel 11198, 13053)

Keshod (3 km)
Rajmahal Plot, New Railway Station (tel 344)

Khajuraho (5 km)
Khajuraho Hotel (tel 35)

Lahore (10 km)
  33 Falletis Hotel, Eagerton Rd (tel 305712)
Leh (8 km)
  Ibex Guest House (tel 76)
Lucknow (15 km)
  Clarks Avadh, 5 Mahatma Gandhi Marg (tel 48081)
Madras (16 km)
  19 Marshalls Rd, Egmore (tel 477977, 478333)
Madurai (12 km)
  Pandyan House, 7A West Veli St (tel 26795, 415987, 26707)
Male (3 km)
  Beach Hotel (tel 2106, 3003/4)
Mangalore (20 km)
  Poonja International Hotel, KS Rao Rd (tel 21300)
Mysore
  Hotel Mayura Hoysala, Jhansi Lakshmi Bair Rd (tel 21486)
Nagpur (10 km)
  242A Manohar Niwar, Rabindranath Tagore Rd, Civil Lines (tel 23186, 25057)
Patna (8 km)
  South Gandhi Maidan (tel 54984, 25936)
Porbandar (5 km)
  Harish Mansion, opposite Indian Oil petrol pump (tel 18)
Port Blair (4 km)
  Middle Point G-55 (tel 208)
Pune (8 km)
  Connaught Rd (tel 64189)
Raipur (19 km)
  Natraj Hotel, GE Rd (tel 26460)
Rajkot (4 km)
  Angel Chamber, Jhabar Rd (tel 23306, 24857, 34122)
Ranchi (7 km)
  Nataya Flat 4, Kedru, B/258 Sector 3 (tel 23350, 21841)
Silchar (25 km)
  Red Cross Rd (tel 72)
Srinagar (13 km)
  Tourist Reception Centre (tel 73538, 73270/1)
Tezpur (18 km)
  Jankin Rd (tel 83, 162)
Tiruchirapalli (8 km)
  Southern Railway Employees Co-op Credit Society Building, Dindigul Rd (tel 23116)
Tirupati (15 km)
  Hotel Vishnupriya, opposite State Bus Stand (tel 2369)
Trivandrum (7 km)
  Muscat Junction, Museum Rd (tel 66940)

Udaipur (25 km)
  LIC Building, outside Delhi Gate (tel 3952)
Vadodara (Baroda) (6 km)
  University Rd, Fateh Ganj (tel 63868, 65677)
Varanasi (22 km)
  Mint House Motel, opposite Nadesar Palace, Cantonment (tel 64146, 66116)
Vijayawada (22 km)
  Shriniketan 27-1-26, Eluru Rd, Covernorpet (tel 72218)
Visakhapatnam (14 km)
  Jeevan Prakash, LIC Building Complex (tel 64665, 62673)

BUS

Travelling around India by train has such an overpowering image – those up-and-down mail trains, the sights, sounds and smells of the stations, the romantic names and exotic old steam engines – that people forget there is also an extensive and well-developed bus system. In many cases it simply extends from the railway system, fanning out from railhead stations, or it goes where trains do not or cannot – to Kashmir for example. There are, however, many places where buses offer a parallel service to the trains and in some cases a better or faster one. Where the only trains are on the narrower gauges it will often be much faster to take a bus – this includes the routes in northern Bihar and Uttar Pradesh to the Nepal border. Agra to Jaipur, Delhi to Jaipur, Delhi to Hardwar, and Bombay to Goa are examples of routes where buses are faster and more convenient than trains.

Buses vary widely from state to state, although generally bus travel is crowded, cramped, slow and uncomfortable. In some states there is a choice of buses on the main routes – in Jammu & Kashmir there are A and B class buses, even deluxe and air-con buses on the popular Jammu to Srinagar run. There is also a variety of buses in Haryana, particularly on the Delhi to Chandigarh run. Video buses have become the rage on some routes where there is a variety of buses, but in most cases there is no choice – they will all be bad.

There is generally a state-operated bus company in each state, but in some (Orissa, Jammu & Kashmir for example) this is backed up by privately operated buses – although they may only operate on certain routes. Despite the extra speed buses often offer (and lesser safety), they become uncomfortable sooner than trains. If it's a long trip, particularly overnight, it's better opting for a train. On many private buses a constant barrage of loud and discordant Hindi pop music is another disadvantage – 'as if the roads aren't rough enough'.

If there are two of you, work out a bus-boarding plan where one of you can guard the gear while the other storms the bus in search of a seat. The big advantage of buses over trains is that they go more frequently and getting one involves comparatively little pre-departure hassle. You can, however, often make advance reservations for an additional fee, usually

Rs 0.50 or Rs 1. Waving that magic ticket in front of you can sometimes get you on board when space is at a premium or can get you a better seat: not at the back, not over a wheel, on the scenic side. On some routes the booking system (so long as you start at the beginning of the route) is efficient and works well although you may find your seating space disappearing as the trip wears on.

At many bus stations there is a separate women's queue. You may not notice this because the relevant sign will not be in English and there may not be any women queueing. Usually the same ticket window will handle the male and the female queue, taking turn about. What this means is that women can usually go straight up to the front of the queue (ie straight up beside the front of the male queue) and get almost immediate service.

Baggage is generally carried on the roof so it's an idea to take a few precautions. Make sure it's tied on properly and that nobody dumps a tin trunk on top of your

(relatively) fragile backpack. At times a tarpaulin will be tied across the baggage – make sure it covers your gear adequately. Theft is sometimes a problem so keep an eye on your bags at chai stops. Having a large, heavy-duty bag into which your pack will fit can be a good idea, not only for bus travel but also for air travel. On long-distance bus trips chai stops can be far too frequent or, conversely, agonisingly infrequent. They can be a real hassle for women travellers – toilet facilities are generally inadequate to say the least.

There are extensive local bus routes in all the major cities. These vary from city to city – in Bombay and Madras they're surprisingly good, in Delhi they're surprisingly crowded, in Calcutta they are also very crowded but supported by a more expensive and marginally less crowded minibus service.

TRAIN

The Indian Railways system is the world's fourth largest with a route length of over 60,000 km and 11 million passengers daily. The first step in coming to grips with Indian Railways is to get a timetable. *Trains at a Glance* (Rs 6) is a handy, 100-page guide covering all the main routes and trains. It is usually available at major railway stations, and sometimes on newsstands in the larger cities. If you can't find it, a regional timetable provides much the same information, including the more local train services and a pink section with timetables for the major mail and express trains (the fast ones) throughout the country. There is an *Indian Bradshaw* which covers every train service throughout the country. It's more detailed than most people need but for serious exploring it's invaluable. Published monthly, it's not widely available but you can usually find it at major city train stations. Thomas Cook's *Overseas Timetable* has good train timetables for India.

The timetables indicate the km distance between major stations and a table in front shows the fares for distances from one km to 5000 km for the various train types. With this information it is very easy to calculate the fare between any two stations. The fares quoted in this guide are approximations of the fares on the faster trains. Travel times vary widely between trains and the times indicated are usually for the faster mail or express services. In any case Indian trains often suffer delays.

A factor to consider with Indian trains is that getting there may not always be half the fun but it is certainly 90% of the experience. Indian rail travel is unlike any other sort of travel in any other place on earth. At times it can be uncomfortable or incredibly frustrating (since the trains are not exactly fast) but an experience it certainly is. Money aside, if you simply want to get from A to B, fly. If getting from A to B is as much a part of India as what you see at both ends, then take the train.

During and shortly after the monsoon, rail services can be drastically affected by floods and high rivers, particularly in low-lying areas along the Ganges basin or where major rivers reach the sea, such as the coastal region of Andhra Pradesh.

Classes

There are generally two classes – 1st and 2nd – but there are a number of subtle variations on this basic distinction. For a start there is 1st class and 1st-class air-con. The air-con carriages only operate on the major trains and routes. The fare for 1st class air-con is more than double normal 1st class. A slightly cheaper air-con alternative is the air-con two tier sleeper (AC-2 tier) which costs about 30% more than 1st class. These carriages are a lot more common than 1st-class air-con, but are still only found on the major routes.

Between 1st and 2nd class there is another air-con option, the air-con chair car. As the name suggests, these are carriages with aircraft-type layback seats.

Once again, these carriages are only found on the major routes, and only on day trains. The cost is about double the 2nd-class fare, and 60% of the 1st-class fare. With a 1st-class Indrail Pass you can make use of air-con chair cars, which are often a better alternative.

Types

What you want is a mail or express train. What you do not want is a passenger train. No Indian train travels very fast, but at least the mail and express trains do keep travelling more of the time. Passenger trains spend a lot of time at a lot of stations, which quickly becomes very boring unless you have a keen interest in small-town stations. Passenger trains are usually 2nd class only; 2nd-class fares on passenger trains are less than on a mail or express train over the same route. Recently, Superfast Express services have been introduced on certain main routes, and because of tighter scheduling and fewer stops they are much faster.

Gauge

There are three gauge types in India: broad, metre and narrow, and what you want nearly as much as a mail or express train is broad gauge. In broad gauge the rails are 1.676 metres apart; metre gauge is, as it says, one metre wide; narrow gauge is either 0.762 metres (two feet six inches) or 0.610 metres (two feet).

Broad gauge has a major advantage – it is much faster. The carriages are much the same between broad gauge and metre gauge, but on narrow gauge they are narrower and the accommodation less comfortable. In areas where there are no broad-gauge lines it may be worth taking a bus, which will often be faster. These areas include Rajasthan and the northern Bihar and Uttar Pradesh areas towards the Nepal border.

Life on Board

It's India for real on board the trains. In 2nd class, unreserved travel can be a nightmare since the trains are often hopelessly crowded, and not only with people – Indians seem unable to travel without the kitchen sink and everything that goes with it. There's an ongoing campaign to educate people not to carry so much junk but it doesn't seem to have much effect.

Combined with the crowds, the noise and the confusion there's the discomfort. Fans and lights have a habit of failing at prolonged stops when there's no air moving through the carriage. Toilets are often so dirty as to be unusable, and in any case there'll be somebody asleep in it. Worst of all are the stops. Trains seem to stop often, interminably and for no apparent reason. Often it's because somebody has pulled the emergency stop cable because they are close to home – well, so it's said; some people deny this. Still, it's all part of life on the rails.

Costs

Fares operate on a distance basis. The timetables indicate the distance in km between the stations and from this it is simple to calculate the cost between any two stations. If you have a ticket for at least 400 km you can break your journey at the rate of one day per 200 km so long as you travel at least 300 km on the first sector. This can save a lot of hassle buying tickets and also, of course, results in a small saving.

Costs and distances listed here are for mail and express trains; passenger trains are cheaper.

km	air-con	1st class	air-con chair	2nd class
50	Rs 85	Rs 38	Rs 26	Rs 8
100	Rs 136	Rs 59	Rs 36	Rs 14
200	Rs 206	Rs 95	Rs 58	Rs 28
300	Rs 290	Rs 134	Rs 82	Rs 37
400	Rs 371	Rs 171	Rs 100	Rs 47
500	Rs 439	Rs 201	Rs 119	Rs 55
1000	Rs 750	Rs 344	Rs 190	Rs 91
2000	Rs 1262	Rs 575	Rs 310	Rs 141

Reservations.

The cost of reservations is nominal – it's the time it takes which hurts, although even this is becoming easier as computerised reservation becomes more widespread. At the moment it is limited to the major cities only. Reservations can be made up to six months in advance and the longer in advance you make them the better. Your reservation ticket will indicate which carriage and berth you have, and when the train arrives you will find a sheet of paper fixed to each carriage listing passenger names beside their appropriate berth number. Usually this information is also posted on notice boards on the platform. It's Indian rail efficiency at its best.

As at many bus stations, there are separate women's queues, usually with a sign saying Ladies' Queue. Usually the same ticket window handles the male and female queue, taking one at a time. This means that women can go to the front of the queue, next to the first male at the window, and get almost immediate service.

Reservation costs are Rs 12 in air-con class, Rs 6 in 1st class, Rs 5 in air-con chair class and 2nd-class sleeper, and Rs 2 in 2nd-class sitting. There are very rarely any 2nd-class sitting compartments with reservations. There are also some Superfast Express trains that require a supplementary charge.

If you've not had time to get a reservation or been unable to get one, it's worth just getting on the train in any reserved carriage. If there are spare seats the ticket inspector will come round and charge you an extra reservation fee. If they are already reserved you'll simply be banished to the crush and confusion in the unreserved carriages. This trick only works for day travel. At night sleepers are generally booked out well in advance so if you can't get one then sitting up in 2nd class is your only choice.

If you plan your trip well ahead, you can avoid all the hassles by booking in advance from abroad. A good Indian travel agent will book and obtain tickets in advance and have them ready at your hotel when you arrive.

Sleepers

There are 2nd-class and 1st-class sleepers, although by western standards even 1st class is not luxurious and you usually don't get bedding. First-class sleepers are generally private compartments with two or four sleepers in them, sometimes with a toilet as well. Usually the sleeping berths fold up to make a sitting compartment during the day. First-class air-con sleepers are more luxurious, and more expensive, than regular 1st-class sleepers. Sleeping berths are only available between 9 pm and 6 am. On some 1st-class sleepers, two-tier sleepers and a very few major 2nd-class sleepers, it is possible to hire a 'bed roll' for Rs 5 per night. These are well worth it but need to be booked with your ticket.

There is no additional sleeper charge in 1st class but there is one in 2nd class. The Rs 10 charge (or Rs 15, depending on the distance) is on top of the sleeper reservation charge and is a once-only charge irrespective of the number of nights the trip lasts. For any sleeper reservation you must book at least several days ahead. At busy times, such as the Delhi to Jammu route for Kashmir during the hot season, you need to plan weeks ahead.

There is usually a board in each station indicating what is available or how long before the next free sleeper comes up on the various routes. You have to fill in a sleeper reservation form, so save time by doing this before you get to the front of the queue. The forms are usually found in boxes around the reservation hall. The demand for 1st-class sleepers is generally far less than for 2nd class.

Two-Tier vs Three-Tier

Second-class sleepers are of two sorts: two-tier and three-tier. Superficially the padded two-tier sleepers seem more comfortable than the hard wooden three-tier ones, although on many broad-gauge routes three-tier sleepers are also padded. During the day the three-tier sleepers are folded up to make seats for six or eight. At night they are folded down, everybody has to bed down at the same time, and a guard ensures that nobody without a reservation gets into the carriage.

In the two-tier compartments there are still regular unreserved seats below the padded bunks, so people get on and off and it's noisier and more difficult to sleep. In any case the racket and noise from the chai-wallahs and other merchants operating at every station can make sleeping on Indian trains a hit-and-miss affair.

Getting a Space Despite Everything

If you want a sleeper and there are none left then it's time to try and break into the quotas. Ask at the tourist office if there is a tourist quota on that train. Ask the stationmaster, often a helpful man who speaks English, if he has a station quota or if there is a VIP quota. The latter is often a good last bet because VIPs rarely turn up to use their quotas.

If all that fails then you're going to be travelling unreserved and that can be no fun at all. To ease the pain get yourself some expert help. For, say, Rs 10 baksheesh you can get a porter, or the tourist officer may find one for you, who will absolutely ensure you get a seat. If it's a train starting from your station, the key to success is to be on the train before it arrives at the station. Your porter will do just that so when it rolls in you simply stroll on board and take the seat he has warmed for you. If it's a through train then it can be real free-for-all, and you can be certain he'll be better at it than you are – he'll also not be encumbered with baggage or backpacks.

Women can ask about the Ladies' Compartments which many trains seem to have and are often a refuge from the crowds in other compartments.

Left Luggage

Most stations have a left-luggage facility, quaintly called a Cloak Room, where backpacks can be left for Rs 1 per day. This is a very useful facility if you're visiting (but not staying in) a town, or if you want to find a place to stay, unencumbered by gear. The regulations state that any luggage left in a Cloak Room must be locked, so suggesting to one of the clerks that he break the rules because your bag isn't locked is like suggesting that he go and slay a cow – it's sacrilege. You can usually get away with it if you just attach a padlock to the outside of your pack somewhere, although many packs these days are lockable anyway.

Special Trains

A special 'Palace on Wheels' makes a regular circuit around Rajasthan – you not only travel by train, you stay in the 'fit for a maharaja' carriages. See the Rajasthan section for more details.

The English organisation Butterfield's Indian Railway Tours operates regular train tours of India using a special carriage in which you travel, eat and sleep. The carriage is hooked on to regular trains and left on the sidings of various towns you visit. The accommodation facilities are basic but you cover a lot of India. Tours from 18 to 29 days are available. For more information contact Butterfield's Railway Tours (tel 026 287230) Burton Fleming, Driffield, East Yorkshire, England or Madras Hotel, Connaught Circus, New Delhi, 110001.

Indrail Passes

The very popular Indrail Passes permit unlimited travel on Indian trains for the period of their validity. The cost of the passes in US$ is as follows:

days	air-con	1st class	2nd class
7	190	95	45
15	230	115	55
21	280	140	65
30	350	175	75
60	520	260	115
90	690	345	150

Children aged five to 12 years pay half these fares. Indrail tickets can be bought overseas through travel agents or in India at certain major railway offices. Payment in India must be made in either US dollars or pounds sterling, cash or travellers' cheques. Indrail Passes cover all reservation and berth costs at night. They can be extended if you wish to keep on travelling. The main offices in India which handle Indrail Passes are:

New Delhi
    Railway Tourist Guide, New Delhi Railway Station
    Central Reservation Office, Northern Railway, Connaught Place
Bombay
    Railway Tourist Guide, Western Railway, Churchgate
    Railway Tourist Guide, Central Railway, Victoria Terminal
Calcutta
    Railway Tourist Guide, Eastern Railway, Fairlie Place
    Central Reservation Office, South-Eastern Railway, Esplanade Mansion
Madras
    Central Reservation Office, Southern Railway, Madras Central

They are also available from central reservation offices at Secunderabad-Hyderabad, Rameswaram, Bangalore, Vasco da Gama, Jaipur and Trivandrum, as well as at certain 'recognised tourist agencies'.

Is the Indrail Pass worth having? Well, yes and no. In purely financial terms it's probably not. Unless you're travelling very heavily, on the go nearly every day, it's virtually impossible to cover enough distance to make the pass worthwhile *if* you're looking at it on a purely cost basis. The shorter the length of the pass the less sense it makes cost-wise. The 1st-class passes are also far better value than the 2nd-class ones. Although there is an air-con Indrail Pass as well as a 1st-class one, you only find air-con carriages on certain main routes. You might find it disappointing to

invest in an air-con pass and then find you travel by regular 1st class anyway.

That's the downside of Indrail Passes, but pure cost isn't all there is to it. First of all you never need to join the interminable queues to buy tickets. You already have your ticket, so if you're travelling unreserved you simply hop aboard. If you are travelling reserved then you still have to get a reservation, and that's where the second advantage comes in. There is always a tourist quota, a VIP quota, a stationmaster's quota and so on. Indrail Pass users report that when the train is 'full', production of their pass often results in another quota making a miraculous appearance.

One traveller reported that 'I always went round the back to the Chief Reservations office instead of queueing up; he usually shook my hand and came back in five minutes with the reservations. Only in Bombay did this method not succeed'. Another traveller reported this series of steps for breaking into the tourist quota:

If the train is fully booked go directly to the area officer or station superintendent and ask for 'special permission' to get a berth on the train. You will have to fill out a form and then be given a note to take to the reservation counter where your berth is allocated. Sometimes you're told that your berth is booked and there is nothing further to do. Always insist that they write the berth number on your ticket (especially if you have a tourist quota berth) because your name may not appear on the train listings. If you do not have proof of your bookings you have no recourse with the conductor.

Your Indrail Pass also allows you use of the station waiting rooms, often a peaceful haven in the 1st-class variety, and makes it easier to get into the retiring rooms. The retiring room dormitories are often used by Indian travelling salespeople who speak English and know all the best local places to eat. The main virtue of the Indrail Pass, however, is its ability to produce a seat or a sleeper when there isn't one. That can be worth far more than mere money, so overall, yes an Indrail Pass can be a good buy, but convenience and simplicity (both very important features in India) are the plus points, not cost saving. In particular, short-term passes are not so worthwhile, especially the 2nd-class ones. If you're going to travel by Indrail then go the whole hog and get a 1st-class pass.

Other Considerations

In New Delhi, Bombay and Madras there are special tourist booking offices at the main stations. These are for any foreign tourists, not just Indrail Pass holders, and they make life much easier. The people at these offices are generally very knowledge-able but you will be surprised how often you find railway booking clerks who really know their stuff. They will often give you excellent advice and suggest connections and routes which can save you a lot of time and effort.

As an alternative to an Indrail Pass or buying tickets as you go along, it's possible to buy a ticket from A to Z with all the stops along the way prebooked. It might take a bit of time sitting down and working it out at the start, but if your time is limited and you can fix your schedule fairly rigidly this can be a good way of going.

If you arrive too late to get a ticket for a train or the queues are too horrendous, don't despair. Get a ticket, any ticket – even a platform ticket will do – and get on board. When the conductor comes around you can then pay the additional cost plus a small extra charge. If you get on without any ticket at all the fine is high, though not as high as for riding without a ticket with the intention of not paying at all!

Gricing

For some travellers, India's rail system is more than just public transport:

Just what gricing is should become apparent over the next few pages, though don't go rushing to find the word in the Oxford Dictionary. Used loosely, it identifies the antics of that strangest of breeds, the railway enthusiast – or gricer! Amongst the temples, villages, gurus and instant karma of India is found the world's second largest treasure trove of steam locomotives. Over 6000 of them still at work at chores long given over to the infernal combustion engine in the western world. Only in China, and only in the last few years, have these numbers been exceeded.

Three gricers, including myself, spent five months travelling the length and breadth of India tracking down the rarest and most obscure of these steel behemoths. The stations and locomotive sheds became our temples, the locomotives the gods we worshipped and our tributes were not measured in gold or silver, but in the profits of Kodak and Agfa. It's unlikely you will be able to match this enthusiasm for steam, but many of the locomotives are real museum pieces and definitely worth checking out. Some of you have probably never even seen a steam locomotive, or travelled on a train for that matter. A passing interest in India's railways will also give you some idea of what helped hold the Raj together for so long, and continues to play a major role in India's development.

Gricing does not include just locomotives. There's also the 40-year-old Bengal & Nagpur Railway teacups in the refreshment rooms at Kharagpur; the magnificent station architecture of Lucknow, Bombay and Madras; the mass of humanity that keeps Calcutta's Howrah terminus buzzing 24 hours a day; or the stationmaster's clock at Kalabagh in Pakistan – built in Croydon, England in 1911 and still ticking today!

The first railways in India appeared during the mid-19th century, usually financed by London-based companies that raised funds with a return on invested capital guaranteed by the Indian government. All lines were initially built to the somewhat arbitrary width of five feet six inches – or broad gauge. Remarkably, this gauge was adhered to for all the early, major routes. Unlike Australia, for example, where separate development of major railway routes by individual colonies caused break of gauge problems that still hinder rail operations in Australia. In India it was not until railway building costs became too great for the government that an alternative gauge was sought. A track width of one metre was chosen, obviously cheaper and quicker to construct

A Swiss-built X class locomotive on the narrow gauge 'rack' line to Ootacamund.

Built in 1906 in Glasgow this CC class locomotive is on the narrow gauge line from Rupsa to Bangriposi.

An American-built broad gauge WP class passenger locomotive.

'Tweed', probably the oldest regularly working engine in the world.

than broad gauge. It was used on many secondary routes, except in Assam and what is today Bangladesh, where it predominates. India's burgeoning 20th-century population means there is a continuous programme of converting heavily trafficked metre-gauge lines to broad gauge. A number of narrow-gauge lines (two feet, and two feet six inches) were also built as short feeder routes to the main lines.

India's railways are now divided into nine zonal systems, a result of amalgamations and nationalisations over the years of the various London-based and state concerns. The old romantic company names such as The Great Indian Peninsular Railway and The Oudh & Rohilkhand have long faded into obscurity.

The uniformity of gauge adopted by this patchwork of companies was not mirrored in their steam locomotive designs, leading to problems in operation and with the locomotive builders back in Britain. An attempt was made, starting in 1903, by the British Engineering Standards Association (BESA) to achieve some degree of standardisation. This was only partially successful and a further list of standard designs was drawn up in the 1920s, known as the Indian Railway Standard (IRS). Nearly all the BESA and IRS designs were of British construction and when locomotives had to be ordered from foreign manufacturers because of full order books in Britain, angry questions were asked in parliament.

During WW II large numbers of American locomotives were brought in to cope with increased traffic and these had a profound influence on the post-war designs. These were of a highly standardised nature, incorporating many interchangeable parts. Although Britain was involved in the design and manufacture of the post-war locomotives, well over half of those now remaining are home-grown, while builders from America, Germany, Japan, Eastern Europe and Canada are also represented. Recent upheavals within the Ministry of Railways have produced a more youthful management structure. The first casualties of these moves were the ageing BESA and IRS designs, which apart from a few isolated examples had completely disappeared by the early 1980s.

Fortunately representatives of most major designs have been preserved in the Rail Transport Museum at Shantipath, New Delhi, near the Chanakyapuri diplomatic enclave. Locomotives from all three gauges have been beautifully restored, many in their original railway company colours. Amongst those on show is the oldest surviving engine in India, built in 1855, and a diminutive two-foot-gauge loco from Darjeeling, making a stark contrast beside a 234-ton Beyer Garratt locomotive.

With the withdrawal of the older nonstandard classes, the remaining 3000 broad-gauge steam locomotives are of only two basic and rather austere designs. The more attractive of the two is the distinctive semi-streamlined WP class introduced in 1947. Although similar in appearance to the American streamliners of the '30s and '40s, these bullet-nosed passenger locomotives never attain speeds they look capable of, and rarely exceed 80 km/h. All require a crew of four – driver, two firemen and a workman – to break up the large lumps of coal. Around 700 remain and while their use on express trains is now limited they are used on stopping passenger trains all over the country, except in the south, which is too far away from the coalfields. The 2350 members of the WG class were originally built for heavy freight traffic, but as most of these duties are now worked by diesel and electric traction, the WGs have been allotted such menial tasks as shunting, local freight and slow passenger trains. There's plenty of room on the footplate of these broad-gauge giants and many of the crew are not averse to having you aboard; it's always worth asking.

Although the older BESA designs are no longer seen in India, a few hundred remain in secondary duties in Pakistan. They are usually away from the main travel corridors, but if you pass through Quetta, Peshawar or Lahore there should be a few of these veterans puffing around.

The metre-gauge system has been built up since 1873. The system is not as extensive as broad gauge although it is still possible to travel from the east of Assam to within 80 km of Cape Comorin by metre gauge. The locomotives are generally cleaner than their broad-gauge counterparts, though once again variety has suffered with the withdrawal of older locomotives. The mainstays of the metre gauge are the postwar YP (passenger) and YG (freight) designs which are found everywhere. A large number were built in India, the last YG not appearing until 1972. A handful of the attractive IRS classes YD and YB have managed to survive. The YDs still slog their way up the ghats east of Goa on local passenger trains, while the last few YBs are found on the Western Railway in Gujarat.

The star metre-gauge attraction is the rack railway from Mettupalayam to the hill resort of Ootacamund in the Nilgiri Hills. Smart blue engines, built in Switzerland to a 1914 design, push their trains of blue and white coaches through quite spectacular scenery. This was graphically highlighted by the acrobatics of Dr Aziz when the railway featured in the film *Passage to India*. When the gradient becomes too steep a second pair of cylinders activates a mechanism beneath the locomotive which engages a toothed rail in the middle of the track, providing that extra 'push'. Wellington is a good place to watch the train climbing both sides of the valley, and opposite the station at Coonor they serve some of the best masala dosas in India.

It is on the narrow-gauge lines that the real adventure is found; nothing can compete with the Darjeeling Himalayan Railway, arguably the most famous and most spectacular steam railway in the world. The line was opened in 1880 and the oldest engine, 779 *Mountaineer*, was built in 1892, others of the same design following until 1927. The bus from Siliguri to Darjeeling takes 3½ hours, the train may take all day but you'd never know what you're missing. There are loops and spirals, Z reverses, and sheer drops where you can look down to see where you were half an hour ago. Batasia loop between Darjeeling and Ghoom is a popular morning viewpoint, and you may be lucky enough to photograph the morning school train from Kurseong with snow-capped Kanchenjunga as a backdrop!

Two other spectacular hill railways run from Kalka to Simla and from Neral (near Bombay) to Matheran, although both are unfortunately worked by diesels. The first narrow-gauge railways in India were built by the Gaekwar of Baroda in 1873 and these lines still exist south of Baroda. The network is centred on Dhaboi, which still runs 44 steam trains a day, though with the arrival of the first of a new generation of narrow-gauge diesels this situation will change rapidly.

Two lines on the east coast appealed to me. The first runs from seemingly nowhere to nowhere, from Naupada on the main line to Gunupur. Originally known as the Parlakimedi Light Railway, the diminutive locomotives were built in Stoke on Trent, England between 1903 and 1931. Further north runs the line from

Rupsa to Bangriposi through the land of the Sontal tribe. Immaculate red and black engines, decorated with paintings of peacocks, run on this line. All were built between 1906 and 1908 by the famous North British Company of Glasgow. The majority of narrow-gauge lines are found on the Western, Central and South Eastern Railways.

Finally, India boasts perhaps the greatest steam gem of all – *Tweed*, a metre-gauge relic built by Dubs of Glasgow in 1873. It is still at work at the Saraya Sugar Mills near Gorakhpur and is probably the oldest steam engine in the world still in regular use. Two other centenarians are used occasionally at the mill and until recently *Mersey*, a sister engine to *Tweed*, was at work at Hathua sugar mill.

Although steam locomotives will be around in India well past the year 2000, the variety and colour that remain, especially on the narrow gauge, will certainly have disappeared before then. But before you point that camera, a word of warning. Indian authorities can go overboard when it comes to railway security, so try and ensure that no police or other officials are around. Better still, get a permit from the Indian consular office before you leave home. If it sounds silly the joke's on you when you face a railway police officer threatening to burn your film and smash your camera. Luckily I talked my way out of it – Happy Gricing!

Mark Carter

DRIVING

There are no car rental systems like those in the west, but it is possible to hire chauffeur-driven cars quite easily. This tends to be a little expensive, not because of the chauffeur but because of the cost of the cars, fuel and upkeep – all very expensive in India by western standards. Basically a chauffeur-driven car is just a long-distance taxi. In some places they run fairly regularly such as Chandigarh to Manali or Jammu to Srinagar in the north-west. It is also possible to hire jeeps for the two-day run from Srinagar to Leh in Ladakh. Typically, hiring a car and driver might cost around Rs 400 a day depending on the length of hire and the distance covered.

Fewer people bring their own vehicles to India since the overland trip became so curtailed because of the problems in Afghanistan and the Gulf War between Iraq and Iran. If you do decide to bring a car or motorcycle to India it must be brought in under a carnet, a customs document guaranteeing its removal at the end of your stay. Failing to do so will be very expensive.

Driving in India is a matter of low speeds and great caution. Indian roads are narrow and crowded. At night there are unlit cars and ox carts, and in daytime there are fearless bicycle riders and hordes of pedestrians. Day and night there are the crazy truck drivers to contend with. A loud horn definitely helps since the normal driving technique is to put your hand firmly on the horn, close your eyes and plough through regardless. Vehicles always have the right of way over pedestrians and bigger vehicles always have the right of way over smaller ones. On the Indian roads might is right.

Because of the extreme congestion in the cities and the narrow bumpy roads in the country, driving is often a slow, stop-start process – hard on you, the car, and fuel economy. Service is so-so in India, parts and tyres are hard to obtain. All in all driving is no great pleasure.

People driving across India on the overland trip will most likely start either from Calcutta, Madras or Bombay. The route from Madras crosses the country to Bombay, then heads north to Delhi and out to Pakistan.

From Madras & Bombay

Route A47	sector km	total km
Madras to Chittoor	157	157
Chittoor to Bangalore	174	331
Bangalore to Chitradurga	202	533
Chitradurga to Hubli	206	739
Hubli to Belgaum	94	833
Belgaum to Kolhapur	103	936
Kolhapur to Pune	234	1170
Pune to Bombay	185	1355
Bombay to Nasik	197	1552
Nasik to Malegan	106	1658
Malegan to Indore	310	1968

Indore to Shivpuri	376	2344
Shivpuri to Gwalior	113	2457
Gwalior to Agra	117	2574

Route A1

Agra to Delhi	204	2778
Delhi to Ambala	294	3072
Ambala to Jullundur	174	3246
Jullundur to Amritsar	77	3323
Amritsar to Wagah (border)	26	3349

From Madras the road crosses a plain, then climbs up to Bangalore. Karnataka, between Bangalore and Belgaum, is heavily cultivated and part of the Deccan Plateau. From Belgaum the road leaves the hilly Deccan area and runs down to the coast at Bombay. Leaving Bombay it climbs over the hill range known as the Western Ghats, then traverses a number of hill ranges through Dhulia, Indore and Shivpuri; at times the road is very winding. At Shivpuri you can diverge east and visit Khajuraho, then rejoin the route at Gwalior, adding 422 km to the trip. At Agra the route meets the busy Grand Trunk Road and continues to Delhi, then crosses the flat Punjab region to Amritsar and the border with Pakistan.

From Calcutta

	sector	total
Route A1	*km*	*km*
Calcutta to Asansol	222	222
Asansol to Varanasi	454	676
Varanasi to Allahabad	128	804
Allahabad to Kanpur	192	996
Kanpur to Agra	288	1284
Agra to Wagah (border)	775	2059

From Calcutta the road crosses the heavily populated and fertile West Bengal plain. Traffic all the way is heavy and slow as this route traverses the most densely populated part of India. From Agra the route is the same as from Madras or Bombay.

Road Safety

In India there are almost 100 road deaths daily – 35,000 or so a year – an astonishing total in relation to the number of vehicles on the road. In the USA, for instance, there are 43,000 road fatalities per year, but they also have more than 20 times the number of vehicles that India does.

The reasons for the high death rate in India are numerous and many of them fairly obvious – starting with the congestion on the roads and the equal congestion in vehicles. When a bus runs off the road there are plenty of people stuffed inside to get injured, and it's unlikely too many of them will be able to escape in a hurry. One newspaper article recently stated that 'most accidents are caused by brake failure or the steering wheel getting free'!

Many of those killed are pedestrians involved in hit-and-run accidents. The propensity to disappear after the incident is not wholly surprising – lynch mobs can assemble remarkably quickly, even when the driver is not at fault! Most accidents are caused by trucks, for on Indian roads might is right and trucks are the biggest, heaviest and mightiest. You either get out of their way or get run down. As with so many Indian vehicles they're likely to be grossly overloaded and not in the best of condition. Trucks are actually licensed and taxed to carry a load 25% more than the maximum recommended by the manufacturer.

The karma theory of driving also helps to push up the statistics – it's not so much the vehicle which collides with you as the events of your previous life which caused the accident.

Indian Vehicles

The Indian vehicle manufacturing industry has gone through an explosion in the last few years, and the number of cars and motorcycles on the road has increased dramatically. The old totally Indian, Hindustan Ambassador, a copy of an early '50s British Morris Oxford, is still the everyday vehicle on the Indian roads but there are now several more modern ones. These include licence-manufactured Rover 2000s (for the Indian executive),

Datsun-engined Fiat 124s and a version of the British Vauxhall – but the big story is the Maruti.

The Maruti is a locally assembled Japanese Suzuki minicar, put together in the abortive Sanjay Gandhi 'people's car' factory near New Delhi. They've swept the country and you now see them everywhere in surprisingly large numbers. Whether they will have the endurance of the old rock-solid (and rock-heavy), fuel guzzling Ambassador is a different question. Whether abandoning the old 'All Indian' policy in favour of assembly operations is a good idea is another moot point.

India's truck and bus industry was always a more important business, with companies like Tata and Ashok Leyland turning out sturdy trucks which you see all over India. Here too there has been a Japanese onslaught; modern Japanese trucks are starting to appear and the tiny Maruti-Suzuki minivans are very popular. All Japanese vehicle builders in India must have at least 50% Indian ownership, and so the name becomes an Indo-Japanese hybrid, so you get Maruti-Suzuki, Hindustan-Isuzu, Allwyn-Nissan, Swaraj-Mazda and Kinetic-Honda.

The active motorcycle and motor scooter industry has also experienced rapid growth. The motorcycles include the splendid Enfield India – a replica of the old British single-cylinder 350 cc Royal Enfield Bullet of the '50s. Enthusiasts for the old British singles will be delighted to see these modern-day vintage bikes still being made. Motor-scooters include Indian versions of both the Italian Lambretta and the Vespa. When production ceased in Italy, India bought the manufacturing plant from them lock, stock and barrel.

There is a variety of mopeds but the assembly of small Honda, Suzuki and Yamaha motorcycles is widespread and they are becoming as familiar a sight on the roads of India as in South-East Asia. The arrival of Japanese manufacturing companies in India has provided some insightful culture clashes. A recent *Time* magazine article noted that Honda had found it impossible to instill the Japanese-style team spirit at the Hero-Honda plant near New Delhi. Workers didn't mind rubbing shoulders with the management – but not with the untouchables, please. And despite having quality inspectors, unknown in Japanese plants where everybody is a quality inspector, the rejection rate at the end of the assembly line was 30% against 3% in Japan.

TWO-WHEELED EXPERIENCES

The following descriptions of two different ways of travelling independently in India were contributed by Roman Wowk and Ann Sorrel. Motorcycling around India has become more feasible and popular in the past few years and Roman's comments have been updated accordingly, particularly the 'Which Motorcycle?' section.

INDIA ON AN ENFIELD

The possibility of touring India on an Indian motorcycle started as a wild brainstorm with three friends. We jetted into India from Europe via Karachi and first made our way by bus, train and taxi to the snow-covered slopes of Gulmarg in Kashmir. We met our long-lost Scottish companion who had spent six months getting there from Europe via Turkey, Iran and Pakistan on a custom-built touring bicycle. From Kashmir we headed back across the mountain passes to Amritsar on the plains. For a change I relieved my friend of the bicycle and chased the others back south.

We had decided that the Enfield Bullet (350 cc, single-cylinder, four-stroke, vintage British design) was the only feasible machine for our trip and started looking for suitable machines to buy at the army depots in Jammu and Pathankot. New ones, at around Rs 15,000 (including insurance, taxes and fees) were out of the question as this would have left us with no money to pay for the petrol and running costs. So for three weeks we resided at the Golden Temple in Amritsar, courtesy of the ever-hospitable Mr Singh, while we surveyed the used-motorcycle scene.

Having tried and tested what felt like every Enfield Bullet for sale in the city and stretching the patience of many an Indian, we finally purchased two 1971 models and took them on a trial run over the plains and up the mountains to Dharamsala and back. After some incredibly cheap major repairs and adjustments to the machines by a befriended mechanic we were finally ready to go. We grabbed our packed lunch and compass, adjusted our goggles, pointed the bikes in the general direction of east (bearing north-east to south!), kicked them over and took off.

Some 8000 km and 16 weeks later, after innumerable adventures, misadventures, pleasures, trials, punctures, repairs, rip-offs and arguments we had traversed India, visited Nepal and ended up in Calcutta, the end of the road and of our money. Here our patience and the Indians' was tested once again as we bartered the Enfields for a healthy bundle of rupees and departed in different directions.

Perhaps the only better and less obtrusive way to enjoy the kaleidoscopic activity of India would have been by bicycle. But for this you must be willing to expend a much greater amount of physical energy and have much more time, although you would also need much less money. We found that the feeling of participation offered by this method of travel was much preferable to crowded buses.

Costs

It's possible to fully recover your initial expenditure on a motorcycle if you have the time, patience and some knowledge of prices. We purchased two 1971 models for Rs 6000 and Rs 6500 and managed to sell them for the same price, having spent around Rs 6500 in running and repair costs over four months and 8000 km. Divided by four people, this came to around Rs 1600 each over the period, much less than Rs 1 a km. Of course the costs are double if you ride solo. As a second example another couple we met in Calcutta paid Rs 14,000 for their almost new Bullet, sold it three months later for Rs 10,500 but spent almost nothing on repairs.

Which Motorcycle?

There are far more motorcycles available in India than a few years ago. Perhaps because of this, seeing western visitors exploring India by motorcycle is becoming reasonably common. The new locally assembled Japanese 100 cc motorcycles (Suzukis, Yamahas and Hondas) are available for virtually immediate delivery if you pay in foreign currency. They cost around Rs 15,000. Otherwise there are various scooters,

several single-cylinder two-strokes of around 175 or 200 cc, the 250 cc Yezdi, and the fastest two-wheeler in India – the 350 cc twin-cylinder Rajdoot-Yamaha. Of course true enthusiasts still turn to the wonderful old Enfield India Bullet, which is also possibly the best motorcycle for long-distance touring.

Price New Bullets cost about Rs 30,000. One under three years old and in as-new condition should cost around Rs 20,000. Older bikes up to around six years old in original condition will be in the Rs 13,000 to Rs 15,000 range. The price of older models depends more on condition than age. If it's very good expect to pay Rs 8000 to Rs 10,000; if it's just good Rs 7000 to Rs 8000. A reasonably well-kept bike should cost Rs 6000 to Rs 7000 while a very scrappy example will be Rs 5000 to Rs 6000.

For the smaller two-stroke motorcycles and scooters you can expect to pay Rs 2000 or Rs 3000 less for older models. The price will also depend on availability. For example, in Amritsar, where the majority of the traffic is two-wheeled because of the narrow streets, the prices may be lower than in other cities.

Where & How to Purchase

India does not have used-vehicle dealers, motorcycle magazines or weekend newspapers with pages of motorcycle classified advertisements. To purchase a second-hand machine one simply needs to enquire. A good place to start is with mechanics. They are likely to know somebody who is selling a bike. Also there are a number of commission agents who act as go-betweens to bring buyers and sellers together. They will usually be able to show you a number of machines to suit your price bracket. These agents can be found by enquiring or may sometimes advertise on their shop fronts.

The commission to these agents is usually Rs 100 each from buyer and seller. For an additional fee, which usually covers a bribe to officials, they will assist you in transferring the ownership papers through the bureaucracy. Without their help this could take a couple of weeks. If you intend buying a new machine this can be done directly through the dealer in the capital city of any state.

Ownership Papers A needless hint perhaps, but do not part with your money until you have the ownership papers, receipt and affidavit signed by a magistrate authorising the owner (as recorded in the ownership papers) to sell the machine. Not to mention the keys to the bike and the bike itself!

Each state has a different set of ownership transfer formalities. Get assistance from the agent you're buying the machine through or from one of the many 'attorneys' hanging around under tin roofs by the Motor Vehicles Office. They will charge you a fee of up to Rs 100, which will consist largely of a bribe to expedite matters.

Alternatively you could go to one of the many typing clerk services and request them to type out the necessary forms, handling the matter cheaply yourself – but with no guarantee of a quick result. Remember to dress very neatly as Indian officials have a great contempt for dirty foreigners, and inversely great respect for a well-dressed, well-spoken one. If you are female or there is a female in your party send her to do it, especially if she is blonde!

Check that your name has been recorded in the ownership book and stamped and signed by the department head. If you intend to sell your motorcycle in another state then you will need a 'No Objections Certificate'. This confirms your ownership and is issued by the Motor Vehicles Department in the state of purchase, so get it immediately when transferring ownership papers to your name. The standard form can be typed up for about Rs 10 or more speedily and expensively through one of the many attorneys. We were unaware of the need for this certificate and discovered that nobody was willing to risk buying our machines without it. I had the pleasure of the Calcutta to Amritsar return train trip (2000 km each way) to collect these pieces of paper!

Other Formalities You can get an Indian licence on application, but it is more convenient if you have an International Driving Permit or a licence from home, even if it is out of date or does not cover riding a motorcycle. It is sufficient if it has 'driver's licence' written on it, and your name. In some states (for example the Punjab) women are forbidden to ride a motorcycle (chauvinists!); they can only ride pillion. Also in the Punjab it is illegal for two men to ride on one motorcycle. This is to reduce the number of armed hold-ups as motorcycles are the fastest things on the road and used as getaway vehicles. Being a foreigner, however, this law will not necessarily apply.

As in most countries it is compulsory to have third-party insurance. The New India Assurance Company or the National Insurance Company are just two of a number of companies who can provide it. The cost will be approximately Rs 60 for a year or Rs 45 for six months. Road tax must also be paid and costs around Rs 16 per quarter. Delhi is the only place in India where crash helmet use is enforced.

Repairs & Maintenance
Anyone who can handle a screwdriver and spanner in India can be called a mechanic or *mistri*, so be careful. If you have any mechanical knowledge it may be better to buy your own tools and learn how to do your own repairs. This will save a lot of arguments over prices. If, however, you are in need of a mechanic, try to find a Mr Singh (look for the tell-tale turban, beard and steel bangle). He may charge a little more but you can be assured of proud work at a fair price.

Original Enfield parts bought from an 'Authorised Enfield Dealer' can be rather expensive compared to the copies available from your spare parts wallah. Again a Mr Singh can be trusted and is not impartial to a little bargaining. Some typical spare parts or labour costs include: air filter elements – around Rs 5; batteries – Rs 50 on exchange, Rs 400 new and a recharge for Rs 2; cables – Rs 7; clutch plates – Rs 65, and Rs 10 to fit them; front and rear chains – Rs 75; new carburetor –Rs 700 but a Japanese one will cost Rs 350; front fork oil seals – Rs 6, and Rs 4 to fit; complete engine overhaul – Rs 450; points – Rs 20; piston rings – Rs 25 (Rs 40 for genuine Enfield); head gasket – Rs 8; wheel bearings – Rs 70; and a rear-wheel sprocket – Rs 25.

These prices are only approximate, and as a foreigner you're an obvious target for a quick rupee for a dishonest mechanic. Beware of 15-minute jobs, which should cost about Rs 10 for labour, taking three hours and costing nearly Rs 100. A good mechanic makes about Rs 50 per day, so calculate your labour costs on this.

If you buy an older machine you would do well to check and tighten all nuts and bolts every few days. Indian roads and engine vibration tend to work things loose and constant checking could save you rupees and trouble. Check the engine and gearbox oil level regularly. With the quality of oil it is advisable to change it and clean the oil filter every couple of thousand km.

Punctures Either you're lucky or you're not. One of our bikes did not have a single puncture the whole trip. The other had innumerable punctures, including three in one day! In some places I even suspected (paranoia?) nails being scattered on the road to boost business. Pushing a loaded motorcycle is hard enough; with a flat tyre it's like pushing a tractor. Puncture-wallahs are quite frequent (you'll be surprised where you find them), but it's advisable to at least have tools sufficient to remove your own wheel and take it to the puncture-wallah (*punkucha wallah* in Hindi).

To remove the rear wheel a pair of adjustable multigrips is the only tool necessary, although spanners may be easier. First remove the brake adjusting nut, then the brake cover plate anchor nut. Loosen but do not remove the hub spindle nuts on either side, disconnect the chain at the spring link and disconnect the speedo cable (in the unlikely event that it's connected!). Finally loosen the exhaust and silencer nuts if necessary, and off comes the wheel.

A puncture repair will cost Rs 5 for one hole while a new tube will cost Rs 15. Tyres are Rs 100 to Rs 150 retread, or Rs 400 new. When replacing the rear wheel ensure that the chain connecting link fastener has its split end pointing in the opposite direction to that in which the chain travels. Adjust the chain with the cam-shaped adjusters so that the chain tension allows about three cm of up-and-down movement. Check that each cam plate is set on the same number of notches. Finally adjust the foot brake.

Fuel
Petrol is expensive relative to the west and when compared to the cost of living in India. An Enfield Bullet petrol tank holds 14.5 litres (good for 300 to 400 km), so when the pump reading shows 18 litres you can safely assume the meter has been fixed!

Petrol is usually readily available in all larger towns and along the main roads so there is no need to carry spare fuel. Should you run out, try flagging down a passing car (not a truck or bus

since they use diesel) and beg for some. Most Indians are willing to let you have some if you have a hose or syphon and a container. Alternatively, hitch a truck ride to the nearest petrol station.

Maps

Bartholomew's *Indian Subcontinent* is probably the best road map, although it's not really detailed enough and not readily available outside the larger cities. Alternatively, tourist maps of each state, available from tourist offices, are quite good. If you have no maps then ask the locals. Tell them in which direction you're heading and they will probably give you a list of every town, together with distances between each one. Then again, you can work out your general direction from the sun and head off that way. We found this the most adventurous.

Truck or Train Transport

If you break down well away from a mechanic and spare parts wallah, it is possible to catch a ride with a truck for around Rs 5 per 10 km. For the price the driver will drop you off at the doorstep of the nearest mechanic. It's also possible to transport a motorcycle by train over longer distances. As an example, a trip of nearly 2000 km costs about Rs 140 for a passenger in 2nd class, Rs 70 for a bicycle or Rs 220 for a motorcycle.

Going Abroad

No special permission is needed to take your motorcycle into Nepal so long as you have your normal visa and you are the registered owner. The motorcycle is declared at customs at the border on entry and is free for the first 15 days, then it costs Nepalese Rs 15 per day. Before you can take a motorcycle on to the ferry to Sri Lanka (assuming the ferry is running) you have to obtain special permission in Madras.

Selling It

Selling is really a matter of waiting. The more patience and the more time you have the better the price you will get, or rather the closer you will get to the market value. You will undoubtedly be offered ridiculous prices; the first counter-offer is likely to be half what you ask, so when questioned for the selling price ask the prospective buyer whether they want the 'Indian price' or the 'English price'. The Indian price being twice the English!

If you have time it is well worth dressing the machine up, particularly if it looks scrappy. A paint job for Rs 120 to Rs 500 (depending on the number of coats) will more than likely recover its cost. You can get new mudguards for Rs 45, mirrors for Rs 20, a seat cover for Rs 25. Word spreads quickly that you have a machine to sell and if the bike 'looks nice' you'll soon get offers.

Roman Wowk

AND INDIA ON A BICYCLE

Every day millions of Indians pedal along the country's roads. If they can do it so can you. India offers an immense array of challenges for a long-distance bike tourer – there are high-altitude passes and rocky dirt tracks; smooth-surfaced, well-graded highways with roadside restaurants and lodges; coastal routes through coconut palms; and winding country roads through coffee plantations. Not to mention city streets with all manner of animal and human-powered carts and vehicles as well as the spectacle of the Asian bazaar. Hills, plains, plateaus, deserts – you name it, India's got it!

As elsewhere in the world, long-distance cycling is not for the faint of heart or weak of knee. You'll need physical endurance to cope with the roads and the climate, plus you'll face cultural challenges which I called 'the people factor'.

Books to Read

Before you set out, read some books on bicycle touring like *Bike Touring* by Raymond Bridge (Sierra Club, 1979), *Bike Tripping* by Tom Cuthbertson (10 Speed Press, 1972) or *The Bicycle Touring Book* by Tom & Glenda Wilhelm (Rodale Press, 1980). Cycling magazines in your own country will provide useful information and addresses of spare-parts suppliers which may be vital if you have to send for a part. They're also good places to look for a riding companion. For a real feel of the adventure of bike touring in strange places there's Dervla Murphy's classic *Full Tilt – From Ireland to India on a Bike* now available in paperback, or Lloyd Summer's *The Long Ride*. Look for *Riding the Mountains Down* for a more recent 'biking through India' adventure.

Bring your own Bike

Bringing your own lightweight touring bicycle will give you lots of mechanical advantages and make mountainous areas much more approachable, but it does have disadvantages.

Your machine is likely to be a real curiosity and subject to much pushing, pulling and probing. If you can't tolerate people touching your quality bicycle don't bring it to India!

There are also technical problems, so have a working knowledge of your machine and bring any special tools with you. Bring a compact bike manual with lots of diagrams and pictures in case the worst happens and you need to get your rear derailleur or another strategic part remade – the right Indian mechanic/tinkerer can do wonders and illustrations help break down language barriers.

Either bring a good quality bicycle equipped with top-line touring components or a no-name 10-speed that you won't regret parting with when damaged, stolen or sold. Make sure it's a machine that you're comfortable with.

Spare Parts If you bring a bicycle to India, apart from all the normal tools and spares (plenty of spokes) bring a good wire cutter to cleanly cut brake and gear cables. Finding a suitable tool or chisel always seems difficult. Long, thin cables for derailleurs aren't available outside major cities so bring enough spares. Bike or moped brake cables bought in India (Rs 30) have to be modified to fit brake levers correctly – I found a spoke nipple threaded through the cable is perfect. Be ready to make do and improvise. Roads don't have paved shoulders and are very dusty so take care to keep your chain lubricated.

Although India is theoretically metricated, tools and bike parts are 'standard' or 'English' measurement. Don't expect to find tyres for 700c rims, although 27 x 1¼ tyres are produced in India by Dunlop and Sawney. Indian cycle pumps cater to a tube valve different from the Presta and Schraeder valves common on bikes in the west. If you're travelling with Presta valves (most high-pressure 27 x 1¼ tubes) bring a Schraeder (car type) adapter. In India you can get the Indian pump adapter, which means you'll have an adapter on your adapter! But bring your own pump as well; most Indian pumps require two or three people to get air down the leaky cable.

In big cities Japanese tyres and parts (derailleurs, freewheels, chains) are available and pricey – but then so are postage costs, and transit time can be considerable. If you receive bike parts from abroad beware of exorbitant customs charges. Say you want the goods as 'in transit' to avoid these charges. They may list the parts in your passport!

There are a number of shops where you may locate parts. Try Metre Cycle, Kalba Devi Rd, Bombay or their branch in Trivandrum; the cycle bazaar in the old city around Esplanade Rd, Delhi; Popular Cycle Importing Company on Popham's Broadway, Madras; Nundy & Company, Bentinck St, Calcutta. Or locate the cycle market and ask around with your bike – someone will know which shop is likely to have things for your 'special' cycle. Beware of Taiwanese imitations and do watch out for old rubber on tyres which may have been sitting collecting dust for years.

Luggage Your cycle luggage should be as strong, durable and waterproof as possible. I don't recommend a set with lots of zippers, as it makes pilfering of contents easier. As you'll be frequently removing luggage when taking your bike to your room (*never* leave your cycle in the lobby or outside – take it to bed with you!), a set designed for easy removal from racks is a must and the fewer items the better. Think about a large-capacity handlebar bag and a rear pannier set. Front bags mean two more items to haul about. Richard Jones, PO Box 919, Fort Collins, Colorado 80522, USA makes a set of bike luggage that can be easily reassembled into a backpack. Just the thing when you want to park your bike and go by train or on a trek.

Theft If you're on an imported bike try to avoid losing your pump (and the water bottle from your frame) – they're popular items for theft because of their novelty, and their loss is very inconvenient. Don't leave anything on your bike that can be easily removed when it's unattended. Don't be paranoid about theft – outside of the four big cities it would be well-nigh impossible for a thief to resell your bike as it'll stick out too much. And not many folk understand quick-release levers on wheels. Your bike is probably safer in India than in western cities.

Buying a Bike in India
Finding an Indian bike is no problem, every Indian town will have at least a couple of cycle shops. Shop around for prices and remember to bargain. Try to get a few extras – bell, stand, spare tube – thrown in. There are many

different brands of Indian clunkers – Hero, Atlas, BSA, Raleigh, Bajaj, Avon – but they all follow the same basic, sturdy design. Raleigh is considered the finest quality, followed by BSA which has a big line of models including some sporty jobs. Hero and Atlas both claim to be the biggest seller but basically look for the cheapest or the one with the snazziest plate label.

Once you've decided on the bike you have a choice of luggage carriers – mostly the rat-trap type varying in size, price and strength. There's a wide range of saddles available but all are equally bum-breaking. A stand is certainly a useful addition and a bell or airhorn is a necessity in India. An advantage of buying a new bike is that the brakes actually work. Centre-pull and side-pull brakes are also available but at extra cost and may actually make the bike more difficult to sell. The average Indian will prefer the standard model.

Spare Parts As there are so many repair 'shops' (some consist of a pump, box of tools, tube of rubber solution and water pan under a tree) there is no need to carry spare parts, especially as you'll only own the bike for a few weeks or months. Just take a roll of tube-patch rubber, a tube of Dunlop patch glue, two tyre irons and a wonderful 'universal' bike spanner for Indian bikes which will fit all the nuts. There are plenty of puncture-wallahs in all towns and villages who will patch tubes for Rs 1, so chances are you won't have to fix a puncture yourself anyway. Besides, Indian tyres are pretty heavy duty so with luck you won't get a flat.

Luggage It's easiest to get a rack modified to suit your pack or travel bags. You may want to have special canvas pannier bags or adopt the popular green canvas school bags for the job.

Selling It Reselling the bike is no problem. Ask the proprietor of your lodge if they know anyone who is interested in buying a bike. Negotiate a price and do the deal personally or through the hotel. Most people will be only too willing to help you. Count on losing Rs 50 to Rs 100 depending on local prices. Retail bike stores are not usually interested in buying or selling second-hand bikes. A better bet would be a bike-hire shop, which may be interested in expanding its fleet.

On the Road

The 'people factor' makes a bike ride in India both rewarding and frustrating. It is greatly reduced for those with Indian bikes and can be decisive in opting not to bring a 10-speed sports bike. Mob scenes are likely to occur. A tea stop can cause a crowd of 50 men and boys to encircle you and your machine, who comment to one another about its operation – one points to the water-bottle saying 'petrol', another twists the shifter lever saying 'clutch', another squeezes a tyre saying 'tubeless' or 'airless', yet others nod knowingly as 'gear system', 'automatic' and 'racing bike' are mouthed. In some areas you'll even get 'disco bike'!

The worst scenario is stopping on a city street for a banana, looking up as you are pushing off to find rickshaws, cyclists and pedestrians all blocking your way! At times the crowd may be unruly – schoolboys especially. If the mob is too big just request a lathi-wielding policeman to come. The boys scatter pronto! Sometimes hostile boys may throw rocks. Best advice is to keep pedalling, don't turn around or stop, don't leave your bike and chase them as this will only incite them further. Appeal to adults to discipline them. Children, especially boys seven to 13 years old, aren't disciplined and are dangerous in crowds. Avoid riding by a boys' school at recess.

Routes You can go anywhere on a bike that you would on trains and buses with the added pleasure of seeing all the places in between. Those in great shape and with good cycles may want to ride the Jammu to Srinagar and Leh road, which appears to have become the ride 'to do' if you're a long-distance cyclist in India.

Try to avoid the major highways up north like NH1 through Haryana and NH2 – the Grand Trunk (GT) between Delhi and Calcutta. They're plagued by speeding buses and trucks. Other national highways can be pleasant – often lonely country roads well marked with a stone every km. Learn Hindi to translate signs, although at least one marker in five will be in English.

Distances If you've never cycled distances before, start with 20 to 40 km per day and build up as you gain stamina and confidence. Cycling long distances is 80% determination and 20% perspiration. Don't be ashamed to push up steep hills either. For an eight-hour pedal a serious cyclist and interested tourist will average 125 to 150 km a day on undulating plains or 80 to 100 km in mountainous areas.

Accommodation There's no need to bring a tent, as cheap lodges are available almost everywhere and a tent pitched by the road would draw crowds. There's also no need to bring a stove and cooking kit (unless you cannot tolerate Indian food), as there are plenty of tea stalls and restaurants (called 'hotels'). When you want to eat ask for a 'hotel', when you want a room ask for a 'lodge'. On big highways stop at *dhabhas*, the Indian version of a truck stop. The one with the most trucks parked in front has the best food (or serves alcohol). Dhabhas have *charpois* (string beds) to serve as tables and seats or as beds for weary cyclists. They're not recommended for single women riders and you should keep your cycle next to you throughout the night. There will be no bathroom or toilet facilities and plenty of road noise.

This is the best part of travelling on a bike – finding places to stay between the cities or important tourist places. You get to meet Indians in places like Iglas, Hunsur, Santoli, Ramdeora, Cuddalore or Nandyal – places that may only be whistle stops or small hamlets which the buses speed straight through. First, to make it understood that you're seeking a place to stay, use the expression 'night halt'. Then go down the following list: dak bungalow, PWD rest house, inspection bungalow, travellers bungalow, municipal or panchayat guest house. These are all government accommodation, and are often dirt cheap.

Circuit houses are more expensive while dharamsalas (pilgrim lodges) offer primitive conditions in unfurnished rooms – some can be pleasant, and for just Rs 3 to Rs 5 or free they can't be beaten. Ashrams and meditation centres are good bets for lodging and a meal for wandering cyclists. In a village off the road you may end up with a teacher or bank clerk (the most likely people to speak English). They may put you in the school building or simply invite you home to stay with their families. Accommodation will always turn up in some manner or form.

Towns will have lodges and real hotels – start looking near the bus and train stations.

Directions Asking directions can be a real frustration. Approach people who look like they can speak English and aren't in a hurry. Always ask three or four different people just to be certain, using traffic police only as a last resort. Try to be patient; be careful about 'left' and 'right' and be prepared for instructions like 'go straight and turn here and there'!

Maps The most detailed maps are the Travel & Tourism plates of the *National Atlas* prepared by the National Atlas Organisation, 1 Acharya Jagadish Bose Rd, Calcutta 20, available at most major Automobile Association offices. The AA has other road maps too. The plates mark places of historic and architectural interest, indicating road types, temples, mosques and dak bungalows. India is mapped in 15 plates costing approximately Rs 4 to Rs 5 each; their weight and bulk is the major disadvantage.

The small and light book, *The Maps Road Atlas of India*, costs Rs 12 and is highly recommended. It's published by Tamilnad Printers & Traders, Chrompet, Madras 600044. It includes street maps of major cities, distance charts and an excellent concise guide to the states. The Government of India tourist information booklets not only have fairly good road maps of each state but also road distances to places of tourist interest and break-up distances. They issue certain road route maps specifically for tourists with vehicles.

Bartholomew's *Indian Subcontinent* map includes roads and can be useful in some areas because it includes small town maps and gives an idea of geographic features. It's best to have two or three different maps of the same region.

Transporting your Bike Sometimes you may want to quit pedalling – for sports bikes, air travel is easy. With luck airline staff may not be familiar with procedures, so use this to your advantage. Tell them it doesn't need to be dismantled and you've never had to pay for it. Remove all luggage and accessories and let the tyres down a bit.

Bus travel with a bike varies from state to state. Generally it goes for free on the roof. If it's a sports bike stress that it's lightweight. Secure it well to the roof rack, check it's in a place where it won't get damaged and take all your luggage inside.

Train travel is more complex – pedal up to the railway station, buy a ticket and explain you want to book a cycle for the journey. You'll be directed to the luggage offices or officer where a triplicate form is prepared. Fill out and note down your bike's serial number and a good description of it. Again only the bike, not luggage or accessories. Your bike gets decorated with one copy of the form, usually pasted on the seat, you get another, and God only knows what happens to the third. The minimum rate is Rs 8 but overall it's not too expensive. Produce your copy of the form to claim the bicycle from the luggage van at your destination. If you change trains en route, *personally* ensure the cycle changes too!

Final Words
Just how unusual is a cycle tourist in India? I'd venture to guess about 500 foreign cyclists each year go on a month-long or more ride somewhere on the subcontinent. And the number's growing rapidly. Perhaps 5000 Indians do tours too – mostly young men and college students. 'Kashmir to Kanyakumari' or a pilgrimage to holy places are their most common goals. For your ego, newspaper attention is there for the asking.

If you're a serious cyclist or amateur racer and want to contact counterparts while in India there's the Cycle Federation of India; contact the Secretary, Yamun Velodrome, New Delhi. Last words of advice – make sure your rubber solution is gooey, all your winds are tailwinds and that you go straight and turn here and there.

Ann Sorrel

BOAT
Apart from ferries across rivers – of which there are many – there are few boat trips to be made in India, although a couple are really good. One is the popular Bombay to Goa trip; since rail connections between the two places are not particularly good this shipping service is very popular. It is suspended during the monsoon, however, and at other times if the boats are commandeered by the army to ferry troops and supplies to Sri Lanka, for example. Further south the backwater trip in Kerala is an excellent way of not only getting from A to B but also experiencing Kerala as you travel – a trip not to be missed.

HITCHHIKING
Possible but not always easy. There are not that many private cars streaking across India so you are likely to be on board trucks. You are then stuck with the old quandaries of: 'do they understand what I am doing?'; 'should I be paying for this?'; 'will the driver expect to be paid?'; 'will they be unhappy if I don't offer to pay?'; 'will they be unhappy if I do offer or simply want too much?'. But it is possible. However, it is a very bad idea for women to hitch. Remember it is a third world country with a patriarchal society far less sympathetic to rape victims than the west, and that's saying something. A woman in the cabin of a truck on a lonely road is perhaps tempting fate.

LOCAL TRANSPORT
Although there are comprehensive local bus networks in most major towns, unless you have time to familiarise yourself with the routes you're better off sticking to taxis, auto-rickshaws and cycle-rickshaws. Apart from in a few cities, the buses are usually so hopelessly overcrowded that you can only really use them if you get on

at the starting point – and get off at the terminus!

A basic ground rule applies to any form of transport where the fare is not ticketed or fixed (unlike a bus or train), or metered – agree on the fare beforehand. If you fail to do that you can expect enormous arguments and hassles when you get to your destination. And agree on the fare clearly – if there is more than one of you make sure it covers both of you. One writer suggested an alternative plan of attack with drivers who will not use the meter – jump aboard without agreeing on any fare and at the end of the trip pay what you think it should be. If he doesn't agree then suggest he calls the police to settle the matter. In that traveller's experience agreement usually quickly resulted! If you have baggage make sure there are no extra charges, or you will certainly have to pay more at the end of the trip.

In India's chaotic traffic conditions most forms of powered transport, from taxis and auto-rickshaws to jet aircraft, are operated by a disproportionate number of Sikhs.

Airport Transport

There are official buses, either operated by the government, Indian Airlines or a local cooperative, to most airports in India. Where there isn't one there will be taxis or auto-rickshaws. There are even some airports close enough to town to get to by cycle-rickshaw! The bus services keep other operators reasonably honest so it is not difficult to get to or from any of India's airports.

Taxi

There are taxis in most towns in India, most of them (certainly in the major cities) metered. Getting a metered fare is rather a different situation. First of all the meter may be 'broken'. Threatening to get another taxi will usually fix it immediately, except during rush hours.

Secondly the meter will certainly be out of date. Fares are adjusted upwards so

much faster and more frequently than meters are recalibrated that drivers almost always have 'fare adjustment cards' indicating what you should pay compared to what the meter indicates. This is, of course, wide open to abuse. You have no idea if you're being shown the right card or if the taxi's meter has actually been recalibrated and you're being shown the card anyway. The only answer is to try and get an idea of what the fare should be before departure (ask information desks at the airport or your hotel). You'll soon begin to develop a feel for what the meter says, what the cards say and what the two together should indicate.

Auto-Rickshaw

An auto-rickshaw is a noisy three-wheel device powered by a two-stroke motorcycle engine with a driver up front and seats for two passengers behind. They're generally about half the price of a taxi, usually metered and follow the same ground rules as taxis. Because of their size they are often faster than taxis for short trips and their drivers are decidedly nuttier – glancing-blow collisions are not infrequent. Also known as scooters or motor trishaws.

Tempo

Somewhat like a large auto-rickshaw, these ungainly looking devices operate rather like minibuses or share-taxis along fixed routes. In Delhi there are three-wheeler vehicles pulled by old Harley Davidson motorcycles which perform the same function.

Cycle-Rickshaw

Also known as a trishaw or a pedicab, this is effectively a three-wheeler bicycle with a seat for two passengers behind the rider. Although they no longer operate in the big cities, you will find them in all the smaller towns where they're the basic means of transport. Fares must always be agreed on in advance. In places like Agra, where there are a lot of them, the riders are as talkative and opinionated as any New

A TEMPO

York cabby. Once upon a time there used to be the old people-drawn rickshaws but today these only exist in Calcutta.

It's quite feasible to hire a rickshaw-wallah by time, not just for a straight trip. Hiring one for a day or even several days can make good sense. One traveller commented how, when taking on a rickshaw for several days, the rider insisted his passenger should 'pay as you like, I just want to please' but, the traveller continued, 'no matter where we went, no matter how generous we were, we were always told at leaving that we had not given them enough'. Settle the price beforehand, no matter how much they insist they don't want to.

Hassling over the fares is the biggest difficulty of cycle-rickshaw travel. They'll often go all-out for a fare higher than it would cost you by taxi or auto-rickshaw. Nor does actually agreeing on a fare always make a difference; there is a greater possibility of a post-travel fare disagreement when you travel by cycle-rickshaw than by taxi or auto-rickshaw – metered or not.

Other Transport

In some places, tongas (horse-drawn two-wheelers) and victorias (horse-drawn carriages) still operate. Calcutta has an extensive tramway network and India's first underground railway. Bombay and Madras have suburban trains.

Bicycle

India is a country of bicycles – an ideal way of getting around the sights in a city or even of making longer trips – see the section on touring India by bicycle. Even in the smallest of towns there will be a shop which rents bicycles. They charge from around Rs 0.50 an hour or Rs 4 or Rs 6 per day. In tourist areas (such as hill stations) and places where foreigners are common (like Pondicherry) you'll pay about double the normal rate. In some places they may be unwilling to hire to you since you are a stranger, but you can generally get around this by offering some sort of ID card as security. Check the time they put in the log book before you pedal off.

If you should be so unfortunate as to get a puncture, you'll soon spot men sitting under trees with puncture-repair outfits at the ready – less than Rs 1 to fix it. If you're asking distances you'll often be told in furlongs – eight to a mile, five to a km.

If you're travelling with small children and would like to use bikes a lot, consider getting a bicycle seat made. If you find a shop making cane furniture they'll quickly make up a child's bicycle seat from a sketch. Get it made to fit on a standard-size rear carrier and it can be securely attached with a few lengths of cord. Tony's two children, Tashi and Kieran, have both done a bit of travelling on the back of Indian bicycles.

TOURS

At almost any place of tourist interest in India, and quite a few places where there's not much tourist interest, there will be tours operated either by the Government of India tourist office, the state tourist office or the local transport company – sometimes by all three. These tours are usually excellent value, particularly in cities or places where the tourist sights are widespread. You probably could not even get around the sights in New Delhi on public transport as cheaply as you could on a half-or full-day tour.

These tours are not strictly for western tourists; you will almost always find yourself far outnumbered by local tourists, and in many places just a little off the beaten track you will often be the only westerner on the bus. Despite this the tours are usually conducted in English – which is possibly the only common language for the middle-class Indian tourists in any case. These tours are an excellent place to meet Indians.

The big drawback is that many of them try to cram far too much into too short a period of time. A one-day tour which whisks you from Madras to Kanchipuram, Tirukalikundram, Mahabalipuram and back to Madras is not going to give you time for more than the most fleeting glimpse. If a tour looks too hectic, you're better off doing it yourself at a more appropriate pace or taking the tour simply to find out what places you want to devote more time to.

Travellers' Notebook

Noise

In one way, bus travel in India has taken a terrible step backwards in the past few years. The reason? Video buses. This horrible invention combines VCRs, TV sets, Hindi movies and Indian buses into a form of purgatory even Dante couldn't have dreamed up. It doesn't take long in India to realise that popular music is the Indian equivalent of Chinese water torture or having the soles of

your feet beaten by the police in South America. It isn't that the music is bad (bad to western ears, but not that bad), it's the unalterable practice of always playing it at top volume, at levels way beyond the capacity of the speakers, at levels that result in nothing but ear-shattering, nerve-twisting distortion. Get the picture? Now put that noise inside a bus, put yourself into the bus, shut the doors, turn the volume up and suffer!

Tony Wheeler

New Delhi

Population: 6.8 million
Area: 1485 square km
Main languages: Hindi, Urdu & Punjabi

New Delhi is the capital of India and its third largest city. The city actually consists of two parts. Delhi or 'old' Delhi was the capital of Muslim India between the 12th and 19th centuries. In old Delhi you will find many mosques, monuments and forts relating to India's Muslim history. The other Delhi is New Delhi, the imperial city created as a capital of India by the British. It is a spacious, open city and contains many embassies and government buildings. In addition to its historic interest and role as the government centre, New Delhi is a major travel gateway. It is one of India's busiest entrance points for overseas airlines, the hub of the north Indian travel network and is on the overland route across Asia.

History

Delhi has not always been the capital of India but it has played an important role in Indian history ever since the epic *Mahabharata*, 5000 years ago. Over 2000 years ago, Pataliputra (near modern-day Patna) was the capital of the emperor Ashoka's kingdom. More recently, the Moghul emperors made Agra the capital through the 16th and 17th centuries. Under the British, Calcutta was the capital until the construction of New Delhi in 1911. Of course, it is only comparatively recently that India as we know it has been unified as one country. Even at the height of their power the Moghuls did not control the south of India, for example. But Delhi has always been an important city or a capital of the northern region of the subcontinent.

There have been at least eight cities around modern Delhi. The first four were to the south around the area where the

Qutab Minar stands. The earliest known Delhi was called Indraprastha and was centred near present-day Purana Qila. At the beginning of the 12th century AD the last Hindu kingdom of Delhi was ruled by the Tomar and Chauthan dynasties and was also near the Qutab Minar and Suran Kund, now in Haryana.

This city was followed by Siri, constructed by Ala-ud-din near present-day Hauz Khas in the 12th century. The third Delhi was Tughlaqabad, now entirely in ruins, which stood 10 km south-east of the Qutab Minar. The fourth Delhi dates from the 14th century and was also a creation of the Tughlaqs. Known as Jahanpanah, it also stood near the Qutab Minar.

The fifth Delhi, Ferozabad, was sited at Feroz Shah Kotla in present-day old Delhi. Its ruins contain an Ashoka pillar, moved here from elsewhere, and traces of a mosque in which Tamerlane prayed during his attack on India.

Emperor Sher Shah created the sixth Delhi at Purana Qila, near India Gate in New Delhi today. Sher Shah was an Afghan ruler who defeated the Moghul

Humayun and took control of Delhi. The Moghul emperor Shah Jahan constructed the seventh Delhi in the 17th century; his Shahjahanabad roughly corresponds to old Delhi today and is largely preserved. His Delhi included the Red Fort and the majestic Jami Masjid. Finally the eighth Delhi, New Delhi, was constructed by the British – the move from Calcutta was announced in 1911 but construction was not completed and the city officially inaugurated until 1931.

Delhi has seen many invaders through the ages. Tamerlane plundered it in the 14th century, and in 1739 the Persian emperor Nadir Shah sacked the city and carted the Kohinoor Diamond and the famous Peacock Throne off to Iran. The British captured Delhi in 1803, but during the Indian mutiny in 1857 it was a centre of resistance against the British. Prior to partition Delhi had a very large Muslim population and Urdu was the main language. Now Hindu Punjabis have replaced many of the Muslims, and Hindi predominates.

Orientation

Delhi is a relatively easy city to find your way around although it is very spread out. The section of interest to visitors is on the west bank of the Yamuna River and is divided basically into two parts – old Delhi and New Delhi. Desh Bandhu Gupta Rd and Asaf Ali Rd mark the boundary between the tightly packed streets of the old city and the spaciously planned areas of the new capital.

Old Delhi is the 17th-century walled city with city gates, narrow alleys, the enormous Red Fort and Jami Masjid of Shah Jahan, temples, mosques, bazaars and the famous street known as Chandni Chowk. Here you will find the Delhi railway station and, a little further north, the Interstate bus terminal near Kashmir Gate. Near New Delhi railway station, and acting as a sort of 'buffer zone' between the old and new cities, is Paharganj. There are several popular cheap hotels and restaurants in this area.

The hub of New Delhi is the great circle of Connaught Place and the streets that radiate from it. Here you will find most of the airline offices, banks, travel agents, the various state tourist offices and the national one, more budget accommodation and several of the big hotels. The Regal Cinema, at the south side of the circle, and the Plaza Cinema, at the north, are two important Connaught Place landmarks and are very useful for telling taxi or auto-rickshaw drivers where you want to go.

Janpath, running off Connaught Place to the south, is one of the most important streets with the Government of India tourist office, the Student Travel Information Centre in the Imperial Hotel and a number of other useful addresses. New Delhi is a planned city of wide, tree-lined streets, parks and fountains. It can be further subdivided into the business and residential areas around Connaught Place and the government areas around Raj Path to the south. At one end of Raj Path is the India Gate memorial and at the other end is the Indian parliament building.

South of the New Delhi government areas are Delhi's more expensive residential areas with names like Defence Colony, Lodi Colony, Greater Kailash and Basant Vihar. Delhi airport is to the south-west of the city, and about halfway between the airport and Connaught Place is Chanakyapuri, the diplomatic enclave. Most of Delhi's embassies are concentrated in this modern area and there are several major hotels here.

Information

Tourist Offices The Government of India tourist office (tel 3320005) at 88 Janpath is open from 9 am to 6 pm Monday to Friday, 9 am to 1 pm Saturday; closed Sunday. The office has a lot of information and brochures on destinations all over India, but none of it is on display – you have to know what you want and ask for it. They

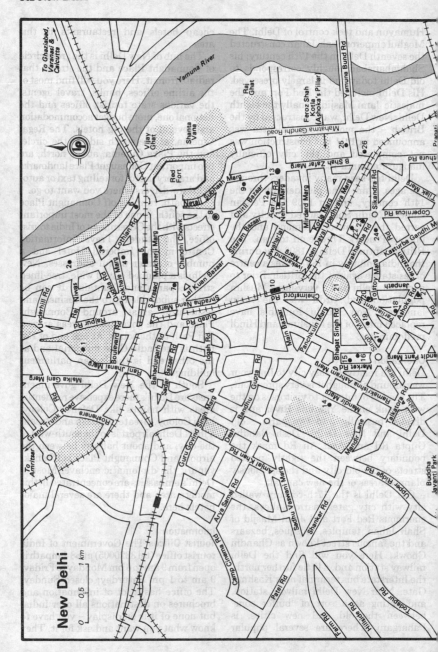

New Delhi

0   0.5   1 km

1	Ashoka Pillar
2	Qudsia Gardens Tourist Camp
3	Interstate Bus Terminal
4	Kashmir Gate
5	Delhi Station
6	Old Delhi GPO
7	Fatehpuri Mosque
8	Jami Masjid
9	Moti Mahal Restaurant
10	New Delhi Railway Station
11	Tourist Camp
12	President Hotel
13	Delhi Gate
14	Lakshmi Narayan Temple
15	Poste Restante
16	Overseas Communications Service
17	YWCA Blue Triangle Hostel
18	YWCA International Guest House
19	YMCA Tourist Hotel
20	Jantar Mantar
21	Connaught Place
22	Bengali Market
23	Natural History Museum
24	Nepalese Embassy
25	Gandhi Memorial
26	Foreigners' Registration & Income Tax Office
27	Ashok Yatri Niwas
28	Parliament Building
29	National Museum
30	Taj Mahal Hotel
31	Bikaner House – Jaipur Buses
32	Ashok Hotel
33	Lodi Tombs
34	Tibet House
35	Hotel Oberoi New Delhi
36	Nizam-ud-din Railway Station
37	Humayun's Tomb
38	Rail Transport Museum

have a good giveaway map of Delhi and New Delhi, and can also assist you in finding accommodation.

At the airport there is a tourist counter open around the clock for domestic and international arrivals. Here, too, they can help you find accommodation although, like many other Indian tourist offices, they may tell you the hotel you choose is 'full' and steer you somewhere else when actually your selected hotel is not full at all.

There is also a Delhi Tourism Corporation office (tel 3313637) in N Block, Connaught Place. Most of the state governments have information centres in New Delhi, and the offices for Assam, Bihar, Gujarat, Karnataka, Maharashtra, Orissa and West Bengal are all on Baba Kharak Singh Marg. The offices for Haryana and Himachal Pradesh are in the Chandralok Building at 36 Janpath. Jammu & Kashmir, Punjab, Kerala and Madhya Pradesh have their offices in the Kanishka Shopping Centre between the Yatri Niwas and Kanishka hotels.

A publication called *Delhi Diary*, available for Rs 2 from many hotels and bookshops, gives information on what's happening in Delhi each week.

Post & Telephone There is a post office at 9A Connaught Place but New Delhi's efficient poste restante is on Market St (officially renamed Bhai Vir Singh Marg), a short distance from Connaught Place. Poste restante mail addressed simply to 'Delhi' will end up at the inconveniently situated old Delhi post office. Some people also send mail to the tourist office on Janpath or the Student Travel Information Centre. Of course American Express have their clients' mail service.

The Overseas Communications Service (OCS) office is on Bangla Shahib Rd, more or less directly behind the poste restante which is on Market Rd. You can make overseas phone calls here fairly quickly and efficiently – if you book the call ahead of time you can usually return just before it's due to go through and not have to hang around. You can also make international calls from the telephone office on Janpath, opposite the Janpath Hotel.

Banks In New Delhi, there are major offices of all the Indian and foreign banks operating in India. As usual, some branches will change travellers' cheques, some won't. If you need to change money outside regular banking hours, the Ashok

Hotel has an efficient 24-hour service but it means trekking out to Chanakyapuri.

American Express American Express have their office in A Block, Connaught Place, and although they are usually crowded their service is very fast. If you want to replace stolen or lost American Express travellers' cheques, you need a photocopy of the police report and one photo as well as the proof-of-purchase slip and the numbers of the missing cheques. If you don't have the latter they will insist on telexing the place where you bought them before re-issuing. If you've had the lot stolen they are empowered to give you up to US$200 while all this is going on.

Visa Extensions & Other Permits Hans Bhawan, near the Tilak Bridge railway station, is where you'll find the Foreigners' Registration Office (tel 3319489). Come here to get visa extensions or permits for restricted areas such as Darjeeling. It's chaotic and confused as ever with no organisation or plan, but surprisingly, with a little push and shove, you can get visas renewed or permits issued remarkably quickly. Four photos are required for visa extensions; a photographer outside the building will do them on the spot for Rs 20. The office is closed from 1 to 1.30 pm.

If you need a tax clearance certificate before departure, the Foreign Section of the Income Tax Department (tel 3317826) is around the corner from Hans Bhawan in the Central Revenue Building. Bring exchange certificates with you, though it's quite likely nobody will ask for your clearance certificate when you leave the country. The office is closed from 1 to 2 pm.

Permits to visit the Punjab (if needed) are issued by the Home Ministry, Lok Nayak Bhawan near Khan Market in New Delhi. It's open Monday to Friday from 2 to 4 pm.

Travel Agencies Tripsout Travel at 72/7 Tolstoy Lane behind the Government of India tourist office on Janpath is popular, appears to be trustworthy and offers discounts which match (or beat) the many Connaught Place agencies. Lots of travellers use the place. Magic Travel, behind British Airways, have also been recommended.

In the Imperial Hotel the Student Travel Information Centre (tel 344789) is also used by many travellers and is the place to renew or obtain student cards, although their tickets are not usually as cheap as elsewhere. Some of the ticket discounters around Connaught Place are real fly-by-night operations so take care.

There are all sorts of stories about the best deals on offer, but Aeroflot, various Eastern European airlines (such as LOT) and the less popular Middle Eastern airlines still seem to offer the best deals to Europe. The cheapest tickets usually entail hassles like overbooking and long waits for flights.

Bookshops There are a number of excellent bookshops around Connaught Place – a good place to look for interesting Indian books or stock up with hefty paperbacks to while away those long train rides. Some of the better shops include the New Book Depot at 18 B Block, Connaught Place; the English Book Depot; the Piccadilly Book Store; the Oxford Book Shop in N Block, Connaught Place; and the Cottage Goods Emporium bookshop just off Janpath.

Book World has shops in Palika Bazaar (the underground bazaar on Connaught Place) and at the Ashok Hotel. There are lots of books for sale near the Regal Cinema. The Soviet Bookshop on Connaught Place sells Russian classics and illustrated children's books (fairy tales, etc) at knock-down prices.

Libraries & Organisations The US Information Service is at 24 Kasturba Gandhi Marg and is open from 11 am to 6 pm, but their range of books is very limited. The British Council Library (tel 381401) is open from 10 am to 7 pm and is in the

AIFACS Building, Rafi Marg. It's much better than its US equivalent but you officially have to join to get in. There are also cultural centres from France, Bulgaria, Italy, Japan and the USSR.

Sapru House on Barakhamba Rd is an institution devoted to the study of people of the world and has a good library. The India International Centre, beside the Lodi Tombs, has lectures each week on art, economics and other contemporary issues by Indian and foreign experts.

Airlines Addresses of airlines that fly to Delhi include:

Aeroflot
 BMC House, 1st floor, N-1 Connaught Place (tel 3312843)
Air France
 Ashok Hotel, Chanakyapuri (tel 604691)
Air India
 Jeevan Bharati, 124 Connaught Circus (tel 3311225)
Air Lanka
 Hotel Imperial. Janpath (tel 3324789)
Alitalia
 19 Kasturba Gandhi Marg (tel 3311019)
British Airways
 1A Connaught Place (tel 3317428)
Indian Airlines
 Kanchenjunga Building, Barakhamba Rd (tel 3310052)
Japan Airlines
 Chandralok Building, 36 Janpath (tel 3324922)
KLM
 Tolstoy Marg (tel 3315841)
Lot Polish Airlines
 G-55 Connaught Place (tel 3324308)
Lufthansa
 56 Janpath (tel 3323206)
Pan Am
 Chandralok Building, 36 Janpath (tel 3325222)
PIA
 Kailash Building, 26 Kasturba Gandhi Marg (tel 3313161)
Royal Nepal Airlines
 44 Janpath (tel 321572)
SAS
 12A Connaught Place (tel 392526)
Thai International
 12A Connaught Place (tel 3323638)

Vayudoot
 Malotra Building, F-Block, Janpath (tel 3328129)

Embassies Addresses of some of the foreign missions in Delhi include:

Australia
 1/50G Shantipath, Chanakyapuri (tel 601336)
Bangladesh
 56 Ring Rd (tel 6834688)
Bhutan
 Chandra Gupta Marg, Chanakyapuri (tel 609217)
Burma (Myanmar)
 3/50F Nyaya Marg, Chanakyapuri (tel 600251)
Canada
 7/8 Shantipath, Chanakyapuri (tel 608161)
China
 50D Shantipath, Chanakyapuri (tel 600328)
Denmark
 2 Golf Links (tel 616273)
Finland
 25 Golf Links (tel 616006)
Germany (West)
 6/60G Shantipath, Chanakyapuri (tel 604861)
Indonesia
 50A Chanakyapuri (tel 602352)
Iran
 5 Barakhamba Rd (tel 385491)
Ireland
 13 Jor Bagh (tel 617435)
Italy
 13 Golf Links (tel 618311)
Japan
 4/50G Chanakyapuri (tel 604071)
Malaysia
 50M Satya Marg, Chanakyapuri (tel 601291)
Nepal
 Barakhamba Rd (tel 3811484)
Netherlands
 6/50F Shantipath, Chanakyapuri (tel 609571)
New Zealand
 25 Golf Links (tel 697296)
Norway
 50C Kautilya Marg, Chanakyapuri (tel 605982)
Pakistan
 2/50G Shantipath, Chanakyapuri (tel 600604)

Singapore
    E6 Chandra Gupta Marg, Chanakyapuri
    (tel 604162)
Sri Lanka
    27 Kautilya Marg, Chanakyapuri (tel
    3010201)
Sweden
    Nyaya Marg, Chanakyapuri (tel 604961)
Thailand
    56N Nyaya Marg, Chanakyapuri (tel
    605679)
UK
    Shantipath, Chanakyapuri (tel 601371)
USA
    Shantipath, Chanakyapuri (tel 600651)
USSR
    Shantipath, Chanakyapuri (tel 606026)
UN
    56 Lodi Estate (tel 690410)

New Delhi is a good place for getting visas. Thai visas are issued with less fuss here than in Kathmandu.

Hospital If you need medical attention in Delhi, the East West Medical Centre (tel 699229, 623738), 38 Golf Links Rd, has been recommended by many travellers, diplomats and other expatriates. It's well equipped and the staff know what they're doing. Charges are high by Indian standards, but if you want good treatment. . .

Swimming Pools If Delhi's summer heat (night temperatures in June average 37°C after days in the 41 to 45°C bracket) gets too much, hotel pools are a good retreat and several international hotels will let you use theirs for around Rs 30 a day.

Delhi Architecture
The various periods of Delhi's history can be traced in the many historic buildings around the city. These can be roughly divided into early, middle and late-Pathan periods followed by early, middle and late-Moghul periods.

Early Pathan (1193-1320) The Qutab Minar complex dates from this period, which was characterised by a combination

of Hindu designs with those of the Muslim invaders. Domes and arches were the chief imported elements.

Middle Pathan (1320-1414) The Tughlaqabad buildings date from the beginning of this period. Later buildings include the Feroz Shah Kotla Mosque, the Hauz Khas Tomb, the Nizam-ud-din Mosque and the Khirki Mosque. At first, local stone and red sandstone were used, later giving way to stone and mortar walls with plaster facing. Characteristic design elements include sloping walls and high platforms for the mosques.

Late Pathan (1414-1556) The Sayyid and Lodi tombs and the Purana Qila date from this period. The impressive domes and coloured marble or tile decorations are characteristic of this time.

Moghul (1556-1754) During the early Moghul period, buildings were of red sandstone with marble details; Humayun's and Azam Khan's tombs are typical examples. During the middle period, much more use of marble was made and buildings had bulbous domes and towering minarets. The Red Fort, the Jami Masjid and the Fatehpuri Mosque are all good examples, but the supreme building from this period is, of course, the Taj Mahal in Agra. In the later Moghul period the style became overelaborate; good examples of this decadent period are the Sunehri Mosque on Chandni Chowk in old Delhi and the Safdarjang Tomb, probably the last notable Moghul building.

Old Delhi
The old walled city of Shahjahanabad stands to the west of the Red Fort and was at one time surrounded by a sturdy defensive wall, only fragments of which now exist. The Kashmir Gate, at the northern end of the walled city, was the scene for desperate fighting when the British retook Delhi during the Mutiny. West of here, near Sabzi Mandi, is the

British-erected Mutiny Memorial to the soldiers who lost their lives during the uprising. Near the monument is another Ashoka pillar, and like the one in Feroz Kotla, it was brought here by Feroz Shah Tughlaq.

The main street of old Delhi is the colourful shopping bazaar known as Chandni Chowk. It's hopelessly congested day and night, a very sharp contrast to the open, spacious streets of New Delhi. At the east (Red Fort) end of Chandni Chowk, and north of the Jami Masjid, there is a Jain temple with a small marble courtyard surrounded by a colonnade. Next to the Kotwali (police station) is the Sunehri Masjid. In 1739 Nadir Shah, the Persian invader who carried off the Peacock Throne when he sacked Delhi, stood on the roof of the mosque and watched while his soldiers conducted a bloody massacre of the Delhi inhabitants.

The west end of Chandni Chowk is marked by the Fatehpuri Mosque which was erected in 1650 by one of Shah Jahan's wives.

Red Fort

The red sandstone walls of Lal Qila, the Red Fort, extend for two km and vary in height from 18 metres on the river side to 33 metres on the city side. Shah Jahan started construction of the massive fort in 1638 and it was completed in 1648. He never completely moved his capital from Agra to his new city of Shahjahanabad in Delhi because his son Aurangzeb deposed him and imprisoned him in Agra Fort.

The Red Fort dates from the very peak of Moghul power. When the emperor rode out on elephant back into the streets of old Delhi it was a display of pomp and power at its most magnificent. The Moghul reign was a short one, however. Aurangzeb was the first and last great Moghul emperor to rule from here.

Today, the fort is typically Indian with would-be guides leaping forth to offer their services as soon as you enter. It's still a calm haven of peace if you've just left the

frantic streets of old Delhi. The city noise and confusion are light years away from the fort gardens and pavilions. If you look out over the fort wall towards the Yamuna River there will probably be assorted musicians, contortionists, rope climbers, magicians, dancing bears and rope climbers down below. Entry to the fort is Rs 0.50, free on Fridays.

Lahore Gate The main gate to the fort takes its name from the fact that it faces towards Lahore, now in Pakistan. You enter the fort here and immediately find yourself in a vaulted arcade, now given over to small shops. This was once the Meena Bazaar – the shopping centre for ladies of the court. The arcade of shops leads into the Naubat Khana, which used to be a gallery for musicians but is now just an open courtyard.

Diwan-i-Am The 'Hall of Public Audiences' was where the emperor would sit to hear complaints or disputes from his subjects. His alcove in the wall was marble-panelled and set with precious stones, many of which were looted following the Mutiny. This elegant hall was restored by Lord Curzon.

Diwan-i-Khas The 'Hall of Private Audiences' was the luxurious chamber where the emperor would hold private meetings. Centrepiece of the hall, until Nadir Shah carted it off to Iran in 1739, was the magnificent Peacock Throne. The solid gold throne had figures of peacocks standing behind it, their beautiful colours coming from countless inlaid precious stones. Between them was the figure of a parrot carved out of a single emerald. This masterpiece in precious metals, sapphires, rubies, emeralds and pearls was broken up, and the so-called Peacock Throne displayed in Tehran simply utilises various bits of the original.

In 1760, the Marathas also removed the silver ceiling from the hall so today it is a pale shadow of its former glory. Inscribed

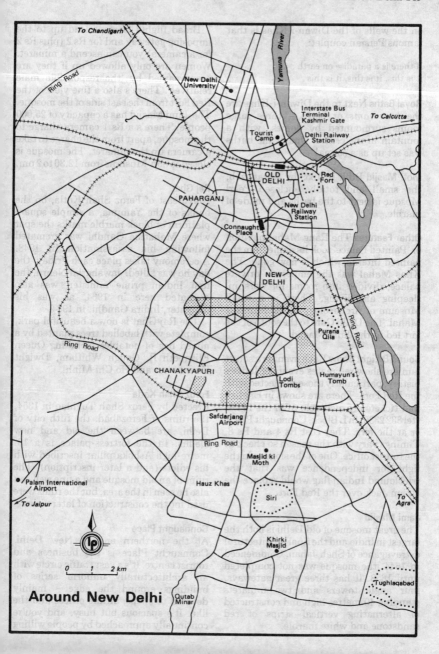

Around New Delhi

on the walls of the Diwan-i-Khas is that famous Persian couplet:

If there is a paradise on earth
it is this, it is this, it is this

Royal Baths Next to the Diwan-i-Khas are the *hammams* or baths – three large rooms surmounted by domes, with a fountain in the centre. One of the baths was set up as a sauna!

Moti Masjid Built in 1659 by Aurangzeb, the small and totally enclosed Pearl Mosque is next to the baths and made of marble.

Other Features The Rang Mahal pavilion or 'Painted Palace' took its name from the painted interior which is now gone. The Khas Mahal was the emperor's private palace, divided into rooms for worship, sleeping and living. There is a small Museum of Archaeology in the Mumtaz Mahal. The Delhi Gate to the south of the fort led to the Jami Masjid.

Sound & Light Show Each evening a son et lumière show re-creates events of India's history, particularly those connected with the Red Fort. There are shows in English and tickets are available from the ITDC (tel 332 2336) in L Block, Connaught Place, or at the fort. They cost Rs 4 and Rs 8. Timings vary with the season so check at the tourist office. One of the slogans in the fight for independence was that the tricoloured Indian flag would replace the Union Jack over the Red Fort.

Jami Masjid
The great mosque of old Delhi is both the largest in India and the final architectural extravagance of Shah Jahan. Commenced in 1644, the mosque was not completed until 1658. It has three great gateways, four angle towers and two minarets standing 40 metres high and constructed of alternating vertical strips of red sandstone and white marble.

Broad flights of steps lead up to the imposing gateway and for Rs 2 (plus Rs 2 for a camera) you can ascend a minaret. Women are only allowed up if they are accompanied by 'the responsible male relatives'. There's also a fine view of the Red Fort from the east side of the mosque. The Jami Masjid has a capacity of 25,000 people. There's a Rs 1 camera charge to the mosque, apart from the charge to take a camera up the minaret. The mosque is closed to non-Muslims from 12.30 to 2 pm.

Raj Ghat
North-east of Feroz Shah Kotla, on the banks of the Yamuna, a simple square platform of black marble marks the spot where Mahatma Gandhi was cremated following his assassination in 1948. A ceremony takes place each Friday, the day he was killed. Jawaharlal Nehru, the first Indian prime minister, was also cremated here in 1964, as was his daughter, Indira Gandhi, in 1984.

The Raj Ghat is now a beautiful park, complete with labelled trees planted by a mixed bag of notables including Queen Elizabeth II, Gough Whitlam, Dwight Eisenhower and Ho Chi Minh!

Feroz Shah Kotla
Erected by Feroz Shah Tughlaq in 1354, the ruins of Ferozabad, the fifth city of Delhi, are between the old and new Delhis. In the fortress-palace is a 13-metre-high Ashoka pillar inscribed with his edicts (and a later inscription). The ruins of an old mosque and a fine well can also be seen in the area, but the ruins were used for the construction of later cities.

Connaught Place
At the northern end of New Delhi, Connaught Place is the business and tourist centre. It's a vast traffic circle with an architecturally uniform series of buildings around the edge – mainly devoted to shops, airline offices and the like. It's spacious but busy, and you're continually approached by people willing

to provide you with every imaginable necessity from an airline ticket for Timbuktu to having your fortune read.

Jantar Mantar
Only a short stroll down Parliament St from Connaught Place, this strange collection of salmon-coloured structures is another of Maharaja Jai Singh II's observatories. The ruler from Jaipur constructed this observatory in 1725 and it is dominated by a huge sundial known as the 'Prince of Dials'. Other instruments plot the course of heavenly bodies and predict eclipses.

Lakshmi Narayan Temple
Due west of Connaught Place, this garish modern temple was erected by the industrialist Birla in 1938. It's dedicated to Vishnu and his consort Laxmi, the goddess of wealth.

India Gate
The 42-metre-high stone arch of triumph stands at the eastern end of the Raj Path. It bears the name of 90,000 Indian Army soldiers who died in the campaigns of WW I, the North-West Frontier operations of the same time and the 1919 Afghan fiasco.

Rashtrapati Bhavan
The official residence of the president of India stands on Raisini Hill, at the opposite end of the Raj Path from India Gate. Completed in 1929, the palace-like building has an elegant Moghul garden and occupies 130 hectares. Prior to independence this was the Viceroy's House, the residence of the viceroy of India. At the time of Mountbatten, India's last viceroy, the number of servants needed to maintain the 340 rooms and its extensive gardens was enormous. There were 418 gardeners alone, 50 of them boys whose sole job was to chase away birds!

Parliament House
Sansad Bhavan, the Indian parliament building, stands at the end of Sansad Marg, or Parliament St, just north of the Raj Path. This is one of the key elements in the design of New Delhi. A straight line, drawn from the parliament building down Parliament St, passes through the centre of Connaught Place and intersects the Jami Masjid beyond. The building is a circular colonnaded structure 171 metres in diameter.

National Museum
On Janpath just south of Raj Path, the National Museum has a good collection of Indian bronzes, terracotta and wood sculptures dating back to the Mauryan period (2nd-3rd century BC), exhibits from the Vijayanagar period in south India, miniature and mural paintings, and costumes of the various tribal peoples. The museum is definitely worth visiting and is open from 10 am to 5 pm daily, closed on Mondays. The small entry fee varies through the week; it's free on Saturday and Sunday. There are film shows most days of the week.

Right next door is the Archaeological Survey of India office. Their publications cover all the main sites in India and are available here, although many of them are not available at the particular sites themselves.

Nehru Museum
On Teen Murti Rd near Chanakyapuri, the residence of the first Indian prime minister has been converted into a museum and has fascinating but badly organised items and documents related to his life. During the tourist season there is a sound & light show about his life and the independence movement. The museum is open from 10 am to 5 pm daily, closed on Mondays. Admission is free.

Rail Transport Museum
This museum at Chanakyapuri will be of great interest to anyone who becomes

fascinated by India's exotic collection of railway engines. The collection includes an 1855 steam engine, still in working order, and a large number of oddities such as the skull of an elephant that charged a mail train in 1894, and lost. See the Gricing section in the Getting Around chapter for details. Recent reports suggest that this museum is poorly maintained and the locos are just rotting away – a great pity.

The museum is open from 9.30 am to 1 pm, 1.30 to 5 pm, closed on Mondays. Admission is Rs 2 and an additional Rs 5 for taking photographs.

Tibet House

This small museum has a fascinating collection of ceremonial items brought out of Tibet when the Dalai Lama fled the Chinese. Downstairs is a shop selling a wide range of Tibetan handicrafts. There are often lecture/discussion sessions and there's also a nice little museum. It's at 16 Jorbagh, near the Oberoi New Delhi Hotel. Hours are from 9.30 am to 1 pm and 2.30 to 6 pm, April to September; 9 am to 1 pm and 2 to 5 pm the rest of the year. It's closed Sundays and admission is free.

International Dolls Museum

In Nehru House on Bahadur Shah Zafar Marg, the museum displays 6000 dolls from 85 different countries. Over a third of them are from India and one exhibit comprises 500 dolls in the costumes worn all over India. The museum is open from 10 am to 6 pm daily, closed Mondays. Admission is Rs 0.50, half price for children.

Crafts Museum

In the Aditi Pavilion at the Exhibition Grounds, Mathura Rd, this museum contains a collection of traditional Indian crafts in textiles, metal, wood and ceramics. The museum is part of a 'village life' complex where you can visit rural India without ever leaving Delhi. Opening hours are from 9.30 am to 4.30 pm, closed Sundays. Admission is free.

Other Museums

The Museum of Natural History is opposite the Nepalese Embassy on Barakhamba Rd. Fronted by a large dinosaur model, it has a collection of fossils, stuffed animals and birds, and a 'hands on' discovery room for children. It's open from 10 am to 5 pm, closed Mondays. The Gandhi Balidan Sthal in Tees January Marg is where Gandhi was killed and there's a display on his life.

The former residence of Indira Gandhi at 1 Safjardung Rd has also been converted into a museum. On show are some of her personal effects, including the sari (complete with blood stains) she was wearing at the time of her assassination.

There is a National Philatelic Museum at Dak Tar Bhavan, Sardar Patel Square on Parliament St. It's closed on Saturdays and Sundays. At Indira Gandhi International airport there is an Air Force Museum open from 10 am to 1.30 pm, closed Tuesdays. Admission is free.

Purana Qila

Just south-east of India Gate and north of Humayun's Tomb and the Nizam-ud-din railway station is the old fort, Purana Qila. This is the supposed site of Indraprastha, the original city of Delhi. The fort has massive walls and three large gateways. Sher Shah, who briefly interrupted the Moghul empire by defeating Humayun, built the fort during his reign from 1538-1545 before Humayun regained control of India.

Entering from the south gate you'll see the small octagonal red sandstone tower, the Sher Manzil, later used by Humayun as a library. It was in this tower that he slipped, fell and received injuries from which he died. Just beyond it is the Qila-i-Kuhran Mosque or Mosque of Sher Shah.

Humayun's Tomb

Built in the mid-16th century by Haji Begum, wife of Humayan, the second Moghul emperor, this is an early example of Moghul architecture. The elements in

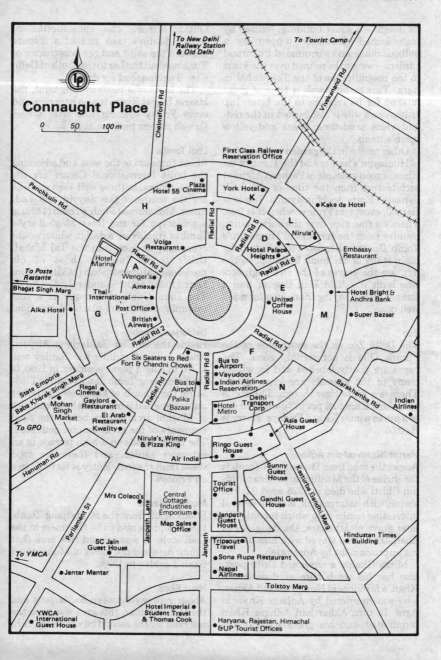

its design – a squat building, lighted by high arched entrances, topped by a bulbous dome and surrounded by formal gardens – were to be refined over the years to the magnificence of the Taj Mahal in Agra. This earlier tomb is thus of great interest for its relation to the later Taj. Humayun's wife is also buried in the red-and-white sandstone, black-and-yellow marble tomb.

Other tombs in the garden include that of Humayun's barber and the Tomb of Isa Khan, a good example of Pathan (Afghan) architecture from the time of the Lodi dynasty. Entry to Humayun's Tomb is Rs 0.50, except on Fridays when it is free. There's a fine view over the surrounding country from the terraces of Humayun's Tomb. One traveller noted that just up the main stairs of the tomb building, to the left, are the graves of the five engineers who built it – 'Old Haji Begum had a strange way of saying thank you for a job well done'.

Zoo

The Delhi Zoo on the south side of the Purana Qila is not terribly good. The cages are poorly labelled and in winter many of the animals are kept inside. There is a white tiger though. The zoo is open from 8 am to 6 pm in summer, 9 am to 5 pm in winter; closed Fridays. Entry is Rs 0.50.

Hazrat Nizam-ud-din Aulia

Across the road from Humayun's Tomb is the shrine of the Muslim saint Nizam-ud-din Chisti who died in 1325 aged 92. His shrine, with its large tank, is one of several interesting tombs here which include the later grave of Jahanara, the daughter of Shah Jahan who stayed with him during his imprisonment by Aurangzeb.

Mirza Ghalib, a renowned Urdu poet, also has his tomb here as does Azam Khan, a favourite of Humayun and Akbar, who was murdered by Adham Khan in Agra. In turn Akbar had Adham Khan terminated and his grave is near the Qutab Minar. The construction of Nizam-ud-din's tank caused a dispute between the saint and the constructor of Tughlaqabad further to the south of Delhi – see Tughlaqabad for details.

The tomb of a modern Sufi saint, the Hazrat Inayat Khan, is also near here and every Friday evening just after sunset Qawali singers perform at it.

Lodi Tombs

About three km to the west and adjoining the India International Centre are the Lodi Gardens. In these well-kept gardens are the tombs of the Sayyid and Lodi rulers. Mohammed Shah's Tomb (1450) is a prototype for the later Moghul-style Tomb of Humayun, a design which would eventually develop into the Taj Mahal. Other tombs include those of his predecessor Mubarak Shah (1433), Ibrahim Lodi (1526) and Sikander Lodi (1517). The Bara Gumbad Mosque is a fine example of its type of plaster decoration.

Safdarjang Tomb

Beside the smaller Safdarjang Airport, where Indira Gandhi's son Sanjay was killed in a light plane accident in 1980, is the Safdarjang Tomb. It was built in 1753-54 by the Nawab of Oudh for his father Safdarjang and is one of the last examples of Moghul architecture before the final remnants of the great empire collapsed. The tomb stands on a high terrace in an extensive garden, and there are good views from the roof. Entry is Rs 0.50; free on Fridays.

Moth ki Masjid

South again from the Safdarjang Tomb, this mosque is said to be the finest in the Lodi style. It was around this area that Timur defeated the forces of Mohammed Shah Tughlaq in 1398.

Hauz Khas

About midway between Safdarjang and the Qutab Minar, this area was once the reservoir for the second city of Delhi, Siri,

SAFDAR JANG TOMB — DELHI

which lies slightly to the east. Interesting sights here include Feroz Shah's Tomb (1398) and the remains of an ancient college.

Khirki Masjid & Jahanpanah

This interesting mosque with its four open courts dates from 1380. The nearby village of Khirki also takes its name from the mosque.

Close to the mosque are remains of the fourth city of Delhi, Jahanpanah, including the high Bijai Mandal platform and the Begumpur Mosque with its multiplicity of domes.

Tughlaqabad

The massively strong walls of Tughlaqabad, the third city of Delhi, are east of the Qutab Minar. The walled city and fort with its 13 gateways was built by Ghiyas-ud-din Tughlaq and its construction involved a legendary quarrel with the saint Nizam-ud-din. When the Tughlaq ruler took the workers whom Nizam-ud-din wanted for work on his shrine, the saint cursed the king with the warning that his city would be inhabited only by Gujars

(shepherds). Today that is indeed the situation.

The dispute between king and saint did not end with curse and countercurse. When the king prepared to take vengeance on the saint, Nizam-ud-din calmly told his followers, in a saying that is still current in India today, 'Delhi is a long way off'. Indeed it was, for the king was murdered on his way from Delhi in 1325.

The fort walls are constructed of massive blocks and outside the south wall of the city is an artificial lake with the king's tomb in its centre. A long causeway connects the tomb to the fort, both of which have walls that slope inward.

Qutab Minar Complex

The buildings in this complex, 15 km south of New Delhi, date from the onset of Muslim rule in India and are fine examples of early-Afghan architecture. The Qutab Minar itself is a soaring tower of victory which was started in 1193, immediately after the defeat of the last Hindu kingdom in Delhi. It is 73 metres high and tapers from a 15-metre-diameter base to just 2½ metres at the top.

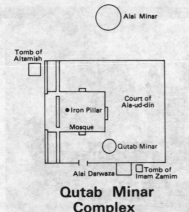

Qutab Minar Complex

The tower has five distinct storeys, each marked by a projecting balcony. The first three storeys are made of red sandstone, the fourth and fifth of marble and sandstone. Although Qutab-ud-din began construction of the tower, he only got to the first storey. His successors completed it and, in 1368, Feroz Shah Tughlaq rebuilt the top storeys and added a cupola. An earthquake brought the cupola down in 1803 and it was replaced and modified in 1829.

Today, this impressively ornate tower has a slight tilt, but otherwise has worn the centuries remarkably well. The tower was closed to visitors for some time after a stampede during a school trip led to a number of deaths.

Quwwat-ul-Islam Mosque At the foot of the Qutab Minar stands the first mosque to be built in India, the 'Might of Islam' mosque. Qutab-ud-din began construction of the mosque in 1193, but it has had a number of additions and extensions over the centuries. The original mosque was built on the foundations of a Hindu temple, and an inscription over the east gate states that it was built with materials obtained from demolishing '27 idolatrous temples'. Many of the elements in the mosque's construction indicate their Hindu or Jain origins.

Altamish surrounded the original small mosque with a cloistered court in 1210-20. Ala-ud-din added a court to the east and the magnificent Alai Darwaza gateway in 1300. Points of interest in and around the mosque include:

The Iron Pillar This seven-metre-high pillar stands in the courtyard of the mosque and has been there since long before the mosque's construction. It was originally erected in the 5th century AD by the Hindu king Chandra Varman, but a six-line Sanskrit inscription indicates that it was probably brought from elsewhere. It is thought to date from the Gupta period and may once have been crowned by a Garuda figure, indicating that it may have been in a temple to Vishnu.

What those lines of poetry do not tell is how it was made, for the iron in the pillar is of quite exceptional purity. Scientists have never discovered how iron of such purity that it has not rusted after 2000 years could be cast with the technology of the time. It is said that if you can encircle the pillar with your hands with your back to the pillar, your wish will be fulfilled.

Alai Minar At the same time Ala-ud-din made his additions to the mosque, he also conceived a far more ambitious construction programme. He would build a second tower of victory, exactly like the Qutab Minar, except it would be twice as high! When he died the tower had reached 27 metres and no-one was willing to continue his overambitious project. The uncompleted tower stands to the north of the Qutab Minar and the mosque.

Other Features Ala-ud-din's Alai Darwaza gateway is the main entrance to the whole complex. It was built of red sandstone in 1310 and stands just south-east of the Qutab Minar. The tomb of Imam Zamin stands beside the gateway, while the tomb of Altamish, who died in 1235, is by the north-west corner of the mosque.

Getting There & Away You can get out to the Qutab Minar by a No 505 bus from in front of the Delhi Transport Corporation office in Connaught Place, or by minibus from in front of the Super Bazaar. The cost is about Rs 1 in either case.

Around the Qutab

There are a number of other points of interest around this complex. West of the enclosure is the Tomb of Adham Khan who, amongst other things, drove Rupmati to suicide following the capture of Mandu (see Mandu). When Akbar became displeased with him he ended up being heaved off a terrace in the Agra Fort.

There are some summer palaces in the area and also the tombs of the last kings of Delhi, who succeeded the last Moghuls. An empty space between two of the tombs was intended for the last king of Delhi, who died in exile in Rangoon, Burma (Myanmar), in 1862, following his implication in the 1857 Indian Mutiny.

Bahai House of Worship

In the same area, this new building shaped like a lotus flower is set amongst pools and gardens. Adherents of any faith are free to visit the temple and pray or meditate silently according to their own religion. It looks particularly spectacular at dusk when it is floodlit.

Tours

Delhi is very spread out, so taking a city tour makes a lot of sense. Even by public transport getting from, say, the Red Fort to the Qutab Minar is comparatively expensive.

Three major organisations arrange Delhi tours – beware of agents offering cut-price (and sometimes inferior) tours. The ITDC (tel 3322336) have tours which include guides and a luxury coach. Their office is in L Block, Connaught Place, but their tours also start from the major hotels. Delhi Tourism, a branch of the city government, arrange similar tours and their office is in N Block. Finally, the

Delhi Transport Corporation tours do not always include guides but are cheaper than the others and are exceptionally good value.

A four-hour morning tour costs Rs 30 (or Rs 40 air-con) with ITDC, Rs 15 with Delhi Tourism. Starting at 9 am, the morning tour includes the Qutab Minar, Humayun's Tomb, India Gate, the Jantar Mantar and the Lakhsmi Narayan Temple. The similarly priced afternoon tour covers the Red Fort, Jami Masjid, Raj Ghat, Shantiban and Feroz Shah Kotla. If you take both tours on the same day it costs Rs 50 (Rs 70 air-con) with ITDC, Rs 30 with Delhi Tourism.

'Delhi by Evening' is a Rs 40 tour which takes in a number of sights, including the sound & light show at the Red Fort.

Tours further afield include Delhi Tourism day tours to Agra for Rs 150 or weekend tours to Hardwar and Rishikesh for Rs 150.

There are various cultural performances in Delhi at night. 'Dances of India' takes place from 7 to 8 pm every night at Parsi Anjuman Hall (tel 275978) on Bahadurshah Zafar Marg at Delhi Gate. It's well worth the entry charge.

Places to Stay – bottom end

Delhi is certainly no bargain when it comes to cheap hotels. You can easily pay Rs 60 for the most basic single room – a price that elsewhere in India will generally get you a reasonable double room with bath.

There are basically two areas for cheap accommodation in Delhi. The first is around Janpath at the southern side of Connaught Place in New Delhi. The second is Paharganj near New Delhi railway station – this is about midway between old and New Delhi.

There are also a number of rock-bottom hotels in old Delhi itself. They're colourful but too far away from New Delhi's agents, offices, airlines and other facilities for most travellers; especially given Delhi's difficult public transport situation. Other possibilities are scattered around Delhi, such as the two popular tourist camps and the youth hostel in the Chanakyapuri diplomatic quarter.

Janpath Area There are several cheaper lodges or guest houses near the Government of India tourist office. They're often small and cramped but you meet lots of fellow travellers; they're also conveniently central and there are often dormitories for shoestring travellers. Since many of these places are so popular you may find that your specific choice is full. If that's the case simply stay at one of the others until a room becomes available – it's unlikely you'll have to wait more than a day. For accommodation information in the Janpath area check with the tourist office at 88 Janpath, or try the helpful Student Travel Information Centre at the Imperial Hotel.

One of the most well known places to stay is the *Ringo Guest House* (tel 3310605) at 17 Scindia House, round Scindia House behind Air India. This place is in the same league as the Rex and Stiffles in Bombay and the Malaysia Lodge in Madras and, in common with these other places, it has its fair share of detractors. Nevertheless, it is still popular. Dorm beds cost Rs 35, doubles with common bath are Rs 60 and doubles with private bath are Rs 85 to Rs 160. The rooms are very small but the management are friendly; it's clean and the showers and toilets are well maintained. Meals are available in the rooftop courtyard, although at a higher price than in the nearby restaurants, and there are always interesting people to talk to.

Another place with similar prices is the nearby *Sunny Guest House* (tel 46033) at 152 Scindia House with singles at Rs 50 to Rs 60, doubles at Rs 85 to Rs 100. Dorm beds cost Rs 30. The somewhat spartan *Asia Guest House* (tel 43393), 14 Scindia House, has singles/doubles with bath for Rs 91/143 as well as a number of more expensive air-con rooms. The *Gandhi*

Guest House at 80 Tolstoy Lane is in this same area and has similar prices – basic but OK.

Still on the east side of Janpath, the *Royal Guest House* (tel 353485) is up four flights of gloomy steps at 44 Janpath, near Nepal Airlines. The rooms are reasonable and cost Rs 104 or Rs 156 with bath. *R C Mehta* on the 3rd floor at 52 Janpath, next to the Lufthansa office, is inconspicuously signposted and reasonably cheap.

On the west side of Janpath along Janpath Lane are several places which have been minor legends among travellers for well over a decade now. *Mrs Colaco's* (tel 3328758) at No 3 is the first one you'll come to. The dormitory costs Rs 35 and there are singles/doubles for Rs 70/95 with common bath. There's a safe deposit for valuables, a laundry service and baggage storage for Rs 2 per day. Unfortunately the famed Mrs Colaco died a few years ago but her son has taken over. It's basic, crowded and rather hard on the nerves.

Round the corner, *Mr S C Jain's Guest House*, at 7 Pratap Singh Building also on Janpath Lane, is yet another legend. Extremely plain rooms with common bath cost less than Rs 100. The *Soni Guest House* on Janpath Lane has similar prices.

Across the other side of Connaught Place is the *Hotel Bright* (tel 350444), M-85 Connaught Circus, opposite the Super Bazaar. It's not that bright but rooms cost Rs 80 to Rs 120 depending on whether they have bathrooms. Air-con and air cooling is available at additional cost.

Paharganj Area Directly opposite New Delhi railway station is the start of Main Bazaar, which stretches due west for about a km. In the last few years it has become a bustling market selling locally made clothes and saris. There are any number of cheap hotels along this road, offering varying degrees of quality. Many are very popular with budget travellers.

As you walk up Main Bazaar from the station some of the better places include the *Hotel Kiran* (tel 526104) at 4473 Main Bazaar. It's friendly and clean with double rooms at Rs 80. The rooms on the street are best as they have windows. Continuing up Main Bazaar the larger *Hotel Vivek* (tel 521948) at 1541-50 has rooms at Rs 52, Rs 78 and Rs 156. More expensive rooms have bathrooms and there's an additional 10% charge if you use the lift. Beware of other extra charges. It's a clean, friendly, rambling rabbit warren of a place.

The *Hotel Vishal* (tel 527629) is similar to the Vivek but has its own restaurant. There are dorm beds, and singles/doubles with common bath are Rs 45/58, doubles with private bath are Rs 97. At 5153 Main Bazaar, near the Metropolis Restaurant, the similarly priced *Hotel Sapna* (tel 528273) has small but clean rooms with bath. The *Princes Palace Guest House* is clean, comfortable and charges Rs 45 for singles.

Turn right immediately before the Metropolis and walk down past the Imperial Theatre (on your right) to the *Hotel Chanakya* at 1634 on your left.

Rooms are Rs 75 and there is a dormitory. It's clean, has iced-water dispensers on each floor and is run by pleasant people. There are many other places along Main Bazaar or on the small roads leading off it. The *Venus Hotel* (tel 526256) at 1566 Main Bazaar has rooms which are quite clean and cost Rs 39 to Rs 45 or Rs 52 to Rs 78 with bath.

Still in Paharganj, Desh Bandhu Gupta Rd is a major road parallel to Main Bazaar and a block to the north. Continue north to the smaller Arakashan Rd, which again runs parallel. Along it you'll find a number of slightly more expensive places like the *White House Tourist Lodge* at 8177 which has, according to one visitor, 'really good, clean and comfortable rooms' for Rs 70/80, although another traveller reported it was already becoming run-down. The *Apsara Tourist Lodge* next door at 8501/1 charges Rs 95 and offers similar standards although the people are not so friendly. At 8126 Arakashan Rd there's the slightly more expensive *Hotel Crystal* run by the same people. The old-fashioned and rather

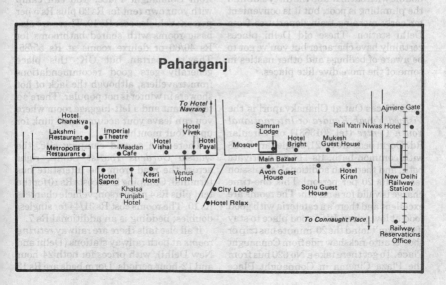

drab *Hotel Airlines* (tel 517571/3) is in this same area, directly opposite the New Delhi railway station, and has rooms at Rs 117/175.

Between Main Bazaar and Desh Bandhu Gupta Rd, at the station end, the *Hotel Little Star* (tel 777819) at 2721 Chowk Sangtrashan is another relatively new cheapie with rooms from Rs 52. A good cheapie is the *Mohit Guest House* at 647 Mohatta Bowali, Main Bazaar. Rooms cost Rs 25/35, and it's not far from the railway station. Just off Main Bazaar and past the mosque is the friendly *Hotel Navrang* with singles/doubles for Rs 35/55.

The new *Rail Yatri Niwas* near New Delhi railway station has expensive rooms but also has dorm beds for Rs 30 to Rs 35. To stay there you have to arrive in Delhi by train and have the ticket to prove it.

Old Delhi The *Khushdil* and *Crown* hotels are at the west end of Chandni Chowk near the Fatehpuri Mosque, an easy walk from old Delhi station. The Crown has better facilities than the rather more spartan Khushdil and charges Rs 75 for a double with bath. It's on the dirty side and the plumbing is poor, but it is convenient for early morning train departures from Delhi station. These old Delhi places certainly have character but you've got to be aware of bedbugs and other nasties in some of the more dive-like places.

Other Places Out at Chanakyapuri is the *Vishwa Yuvak Kendra* or *International Youth Centre* (tel 3013631) on Circular Rd. Dorm beds are Rs 21, singles are Rs 88 with common bath, Rs 114 with private bath, and there's an additional 'admission fee' of Rs 20 per person! This one-time charge is valid for a month. The rooms are excellent and there's a cafeteria with good food at low prices. It's a good place to stay if you don't mind the 20-minute bus trip or shorter auto-rickshaw ride from Connaught Place. To get there take a No 620 bus from the Plaza Cinema in Connaught Place

and get off near the Indonesian Embassy, or take a No 662 from old Delhi station and get off at the Ashok Hotel. It's right behind the Chinese Embassy and near the Chanakyapuri police station.

Also in Chanakyapuri is a *Youth Hostel* (tel 376285) at 5 Nyaya Marg where there are dorm beds at Rs 19 for members. Membership costs Rs 17, and you need your own padlock. There's a bank and a travel agency which will arrange trips to Agra, Jaipur, Delhi and other destinations. The location is quiet, peaceful and, of course, close to the embassies.

If you want to camp there are several possibilities in Delhi. The *Tourist Camp* (tel 278929) is one of the cheapest places to stay and very popular. It's some distance from Connaught Place but is well served by six-seaters. Most of the overland operators stay here and it's also the starting point for the overland buses through west Asia. Run by retired Indian Army officers, the camp is actually in old Delhi, near Delhi Gate on Jawaharlal Nehru Marg, across from the J P Narayan Hospital (Irwin Hospital), only two km from Connaught Place. You can camp with your own tent for Rs 20 plus Rs 5 per person; vehicles cost Rs 10. There are also basic rooms with shared bathrooms for Rs 40/60 or deluxe rooms at Rs 55/85. They're spartan but OK; this place generally gets good recommendations from travellers, although the lack of hot showers in winter is not popular. There's a restaurant and a left-luggage room where you can leave your accumulated junk for up to four months.

There is a second camping site, the *Qudsia Gardens Tourist Camp*, right across the road from the Interstate bus terminal. Camping here costs Rs 10 for the tent plus Rs 4 per person; vehicle charge is Rs 10. The rooms cost Rs 31/44 for singles/doubles; bedding is an additional Rs 7.

If all else fails there are railway *retiring rooms* at both railway stations (Delhi and New Delhi), with prices for both 24-hour and 12-hour periods. Dorm beds are Rs 13

New Delhi Top: View of Delhi from the Jami Masjid (SM)
Left: Fruit vendor (TW)
Right: The Moti Masjid or 'Pearl Mosque' taken from the Diwan-i-Khas in the Red Fort (TW)

New Delhi Top: Lodi Tombs, Delhi (TW)
Left: Jami Masjid, Delhi (TW)
Right: Jami Masjid, Delhi (TW)

(Rs 8 for 12 hours). Deluxe dorm beds are Rs 26 (Rs 16). At New Delhi station there are rooms without air-con for Rs 65 (Rs 39), but both stations have air-con rooms for Rs 97 (Rs 58) and deluxe air-con rooms for Rs 208 (Rs 130). There are also *retiring rooms* at the airport, and you can use them if you have a confirmed departure within 24 hours. They're booked through the airport manager (tel 391351), cost Rs 140 for a double and are in the International Terminal building.

Places to Stay – middle

There are several middle-bracket hotels around Janpath and Connaught Place, including the popular ITDC *Ashok Yatri Niwas* (tel 3324511) just 10 minutes walk from Connaught Place on Ashoka Rd at the intersection with Janpath. This huge hotel (556 rooms) has been something of a political football, but prices have been pushed up sufficiently that it's no longer the astounding bargain it was when it first opened and, therefore, it's no longer always full. The rooms are very plain and spartan, and singles/doubles with bath are Rs 120/160. Four-bed rooms are Rs 185. Rooms above the 8th floor seem to be better maintained, but then the lifts are neither fast nor reliable. In fact they're so unreliable and so slow that people report walking up to the 14th floor rather than waiting! Foreigners must pay their bills in foreign currency. There's a good restaurant, a bad cafeteria and a TV lounge. The airport hotel booking desk and the airport bus are both reluctant to book you in or to take you there – probably a question of commissions! This is another of those many Indian hotels which upon completion start a rapid downhill run due to miserable upkeep and maintenance.

The *Janpath Guest House* (tel 321935) is a few doors down from the tourist office at 82-84 Janpath. It's popular with travellers, reasonably well kept and clean, and the staff are friendly; the rooms, though, are claustrophobically small and most don't have a window to talk of. Singles/doubles cost Rs 110/156, more if you want air-con.

There are lots of places around Connaught Place. The *Hotel 55* (tel 321244) at H-55 Connaught Circus, near the Nirula restaurants, is well designed with air-con throughout. Rooms with balcony and bath are Rs 350/425.

The *Hotel Palace Heights* (tel 351361) in D Block, Connaught Place is a moderately priced place close to Nirula's. It's on the 3rd floor of an office building and has a huge verandah overlooking Connaught Place – great for breakfast or afternoon tea. Rooms cost from Rs 72 without bath, Rs 150 for a double with air-con. It's a bit scruffy and indifferently kept but the location is great and the prices reasonable.

The *Alka Hotel* (tel 344328) is also centrally located at 16/90 Connaught Circus and has air-con singles/doubles for Rs 292/546. The *Hotel Metro* (tel 48905) on N Block is better than initial impressions might indicate, with rooms for Rs 136/214, Rs 260/325 with air-con.

Moving away from Connaught Place, the small but popular *Roshan Villa Guest House* (tel 3311770) is at 7 Babar Lane, close to the Bengali Market. To get there go down Barakhamba Rd from Connaught Place, turn left on Tolstoy Marg and go under the flyover to find Babar Rd. It's very clean and well kept, the owners are friendly and hospitable, and it's quiet. There's a Rs 39 dorm and rooms at Rs 180 and Rs 200. Middle-priced rooms share a bath with one other room; the top-priced ones have their own bathrooms. Meals are available and there's hot water in the bathrooms. You can also sleep in the lounge if you arrive late and there are no spare rooms.

The *Hotel Shangri-La* (tel 522629), at 8694-A Desh Bandhu Gupta Rd, behind the Ashwini Hotel, is a new place with good air-cooled rooms from Rs 105/145. It's five minutes walk from New Delhi railway station.

The *Puri Yatri Paying Guest House* (tel 525463) is at Yatri House, 3/4 Rani Jhansi Rd (at the junction of Panchkuin Rd and Mandir Marg, near Connaught Place). It's calm, secure and moderately priced.

A number of expensive guest houses have opened in the Sundar Nagar area which is a Rs 10 taxi ride from Connaught Place. The best known is the *Maharani Guest House* (tel 693128) where singles/doubles cost Rs 375/500. In the same area, *La Sangrita* (tel 694541) and *Kailash* (tel 617401) are good value and slightly less expensive. The *Gaiety Palace Hotel* (tel 3321362) at 9 Kasturba Gandhi Marg has singles/doubles for Rs 350/450.

There are several YMCA and YWCA places, all of which take either sex. The *YMCA Tourist Hotel* (tel 311915) is very central, near the Regal Cinema on Jai Singh Rd and opposite the Jantar Mantar. It's excellent value with rooms having hot and cold water, and there are gardens, lounges and a restaurant with western, Indian and Mughlai cuisine. Including breakfast, double rooms with common bath are Rs 265; with private bath and air-con, Rs 365. There's a 5% service charge and a transient membership fee of Rs 5 valid for 30 days. There is also a left-luggage facility for Rs 1 per day.

The *YWCA International Guest House* (tel 311561) at 10 Parliament St (Sansad Marg) has singles/doubles for Rs 140/230 (plus 10% service charge), and all rooms have bath and air-con. It's convenient for Connaught Place and has a restaurant. There's a second, lesser known YWCA, the *YWCA Blue Triangle Family Hostel* (tel 310133, 310875) on Ashoka Rd just off Parliament Rd (Sansad Marg). It's clean, well run and has a restaurant. Rates, including breakfast, range from Rs 135 to Rs 240 for singles, Rs 175 to Rs 260 for doubles, all with bathrooms. There are rooms with and without air-con and an expensive dormitory for Rs 60. There's also a Rs 5 temporary membership fee and a 5% service charge. The newer Blue Triangle Y is run by the Delhi YWCA; the

International Y is run by the national organisation.

An excellent place for a longer stay is the *India International Centre* (tel 619431) beside the Lodi tombs in the south of New Delhi. It is a good place to meet people involved with international aid agencies and each week there are lectures on art, economics and other contemporary issues by Indian and foreign experts. The centre, which is near the UN offices in Delhi, has air-con rooms, but you must be a centre member or a guest of a member before you can stay here, and there is a 10-day limit. Members pay Rs 230/365, nonmembers Rs 325/475.

Places to Stay – top end

Many of the 'tourist class' hotels are at Chanakyapuri, the main location of the foreign embassies. This is about midway between the airport and the New Delhi city centre. There are, however, more places around the centre as well. In these international hotels there is often a 10% to 15% 'luxury tax' and 5% to 10% 'service charge'.

More moderately priced top-end hotels include *Nirula's Hotel* (tel 3322012) on L Block, Connaught Place, right beside the Nirula restaurants and snack bars. Singles/doubles range from Rs 390/635 in this small but good standard hotel.

The *Hotel Marina* (tel 344658) on the outer circle of Connaught Place in G Block is surprisingly good inside; the outside is drab. Rooms are Rs 525/625. The *Lodhi Hotel* (tel 362422) is in south Delhi on Lala Rajput Rai Marg, rather a long way from Connaught Place, and has air-con rooms at Rs 500/625.

Other top-end hotels include:

Ambassador Hotel (tel 690391) is a small hotel at Sujan Singh Park. There are just 73 rooms costing Rs 655/875 and a noted vegetarian restaurant.

Ashok Hotel (tel 600121), 50B Chanakyapuri, is the 589-room flagship of the ITDC hotel fleet. It offers everything from restaurants, coffee shops, bars, discos, conference rooms and swimming pool to full air-conditioning. Singles/doubles cost Rs 1250/1400.

Centaur Hotel (tel 5452223) is on Gurgaon Rd at the airport. It's a big modern hotel with rooms from Rs 950/1050.

Claridges Hotel (tel 3010211), 12 Aurangzeb Rd, is south of the Raj Path in New Delhi. Singles/doubles cost from Rs 940/1040 in this older hotel.

Holiday Inn (tel 3320101), Barakhamba Rd, charges Rs 1450/1600 for singles/doubles.

Hotel Hans Plaza (tel 3316861), 19 Barakhamba Rd, is conveniently central but otherwise not very good value. Rooms are Rs 650/770.

Hyatt Regency (tel 609911), another big new hotel with 535 rooms is on Bhikaji Cama Place and costs from Rs 1400/1525.

Hotel Imperial (tel 3325332), conveniently situated on Janpath near the centre of the city is an old-fashioned hotel with a very pleasant shopping arcade and gardens. Singles/doubles cost Rs 1000/1100.

Hotel Janpath (tel 3320070), beside the Imperial, run by the ITDC. Rooms cost from Rs 925/1050.

Hotel Kanishka (tel 3324422), next to the Hotel Janpath, an ITDC hotel with rooms at Rs 925/1050.

Hotel Maurya Sheraton (tel 3010101), on Sardar Patel Marg at Chanakyapuri, has 500 rooms costing from Rs 1450/1600. The Bukhara is one of the best restaurants in Delhi.

Hotel Meredin (tel 383960), on Janpath, charges Rs 1650/1750 for singles/doubles.

Hotel Oberoi New Delhi (tel 699571) is south of New Delhi near the Purana Qila. This is perhaps the best value among the luxury places and there are 350 rooms costing Rs 1600/1750.

Taj Mahal Hotel (tel 3016162), 1 Man Singh Rd is a luxurious hotel that is fairly central but quiet. Singles/doubles cost from Rs 1500/1700.

Places to Eat

Like its places to stay, Delhi's many restaurants and snack bars can be divided by price range and location.

Janpath & Connaught Place There are many Indian-style fast-food places in this area. Their plus point is that they have good food at reasonable prices and are clean and healthy. A minus point for some of them is they have no place to sit – it's

stand, eat and run. They serve Indian food (from samosas to dosas) and western food (burgers to sandwiches). Ice-cream parlours have also hit Delhi with a vengeance.

Nirula's is probably the most popular and long running of these fast-food places and does a wide variety of excellent light snacks, both Indian and western. They've also got good cold drinks, milk shakes and ice cream, or they will pack you a lunch box, ideal to take on train trips. The main Nirula's is on L Block on the outer circle, and there's a second snack bar on N Block where Janpath runs into the circle.

Next door to Nirula's L Block snack bar is an ice-cream parlour on one side and pizzas on the other. Above the ice-cream bar there's the fourth part of Nirula's, a sit-down restaurant called *Pot Pourri* with appetising food including a Rs 35 eat-all-you-like salad smorgasbord. They've also got pizzas, chilli con carne and a good range of soups and sweets. It's a good place for breakfast from 7.30 am; you can have an all-American breakfast of pancakes, eggs and bacon. It's a very pleasant place to eat and the service is good; all in all it's probably the number one place for a minor splurge.

Opposite the main Nirula's is the *National Restaurant*, which is clean and has excellent non-vegetarian food and somewhat lower prices than Nirula's. The *Embassy* restaurant on D Block has excellent veg and non-veg food including korma and biryani. It's not too expensive and is popular among office workers. The *Hotel Imperial* has excellent steaks for Rs 55.

On Janpath at N Block, opposite the underground bazaar, there is a small string of fast-food places including Nirula's. At the outer end is a branch (believe it or not) of the British *Wimpy* hamburger chain. This is the closest you're going to get to a Big Mac (100% lamb!) in India. The 'lamburgers' are fair imitations costing Rs 8 to Rs 16, French fries are Rs 4. It even operates like a western fast-food place – somehow they've resisted the urge to have people writing out chits in quadruplicate.

Don't Pass Me By is right by Ringo's Guest House. The Chinese dishes are good, and this is also a popular meeting place. Other places around Connaught Place include *Sona Rupa* on Janpath with very good south Indian vegetarian food – Rs 15 for thali or Rs 22 for an all-you-can-eat lunch buffet with dessert and coffee. The *United Coffee House* on Connaught Place is pleasantly relaxed and popular.

There's a good collection of cheap restaurants and food markets in Mohan Singh Place, on the same block as the Regal Cinema in Connaught Place. Look for fresh and dried fruits, curd, sweets and so on.

The fresh milk is excellent at *Keventers*, the small milk bar at the corner of Connaught Place and Radial Rd No 3, round the corner from American Express. If you just want a cheap soft drink and somewhere cool to drink it, descend into the air-conditioned underground market between Janpath and Parliament St (Sansad Marg) at Connaught Place.

Moving up a price category, there are several restaurants worth considering on Parliament St and by the Regal Cinema. The *Kwality Restaurant* on Parliament St is spotlessly clean and very efficient but the food is only average. The menu is the almost standard non-vegetarian menu you'll find at restaurants all over India. Main courses are mainly in the Rs 23 to Rs 29 range. This is also a good place for non-Indian food if you want a break; you can have breakfast here for Rs 26.

El Arab, right on the corner of Parliament St and the outer circle of Connaught Place, has an interesting Middle Eastern menu with most dishes in the Rs 35 to Rs 60 bracket and there's a buffet lunch or dinner. Underneath El Arab is *The Cellar*, where breakfast costs Rs 18 to Rs 23 or main courses cost Rs 23 to Rs 32. Round the corner is the more expensive *Gaylord* with big mirrors, chandeliers and excellent Indian food.

Also on Connaught Place you can find good vegetarian food at the *Volga*; it's a little expensive but it's air-conditioned, and the food and service are excellent.

Right across the street from Nirula's on the outer circle are a string of popular small dhaba places. The famous *Kake da Hotel* doesn't seem to have been discovered by westerners at all. Despite having no atmosphere whatsoever, it is crowded most of the time. Try the excellent butter chicken, but note the warning sign that there will be 'no extra gravy'! A good place for an early breakfast in this area is the *Hotel Marina*. There are also 24-hour restaurants in the *Yatri Niwas* and *Hotel Janpath*.

Finally there's one Delhi food place that should not be forgotten. *Wenger's* on Connaught Place is a cake shop with an awesome range of little cakes (Rs 4 to Rs 7 each) which they'll put in a cardboard box and tie up with a bow so you can self-consciously carry them back to your hotel room for private consumption. Take care, reported one hungry traveller – 'In great anticipation as about to devour a famous Wenger's cake, this bloody hawk deftly lifted my cake out of my hands and near gave me a heart attack in the process'.

Paharganj Towards the end of Main Bazaar, in the Paharganj area near New Delhi station, is the long-running and ever-popular *Metropolis Restaurant*. The food is mainly Chinese and western and a little expensive, but it has been a travellers' hangout for years and the food is not bad.

Underneath the Hotel Sapna is the considerably cheaper *Restaurant Light* where you can get very good vegetarian food for just a few rupees per dish. It's popular with budget travellers in the evenings. The *Khalsa Punjabi Hotel*, on Main Bazaar Rd towards the station beyond the Vishal and Venus hotels, also has good food, and their milk shakes are only Rs 3.

Gobind is a narrow-fronted place on the

opposite side towards the Metropolis and is good for lassi or espresso coffee. Breakfast places and stalls offer cheap and tasty food just off Main Bazaar towards the Chanakya Hotel. The popular *Lakshmi Restaurant* in this area has a cheap breakfast including fantastic porridge.

Old Delhi In old Delhi there are many places to eat at the west end of Chandni Chowk. The *Inderpuri Restaurant* has a good selection of vegetarian dishes, and *Giani* has good masala dosas. *Ghantewala*, near the Siganj Gurdwara on Chandni Chowk, is reputed to have some of the best Indian sweets in Delhi. An extremely cheap and good place to eat is *Sonis* in Chandni Chowk. It's upstairs in Nai Sarak. They have a very good thali for Rs 10.

The stalls along the road in front of the Jami Masjid are very cheap. In the Interstate bus terminal the *ISBT Workers' Canteen* has good food at low prices, and Delhi Tourism's *Nagrik Restaurant* is also here.

At the other end of the price scale there are two well-known tandoori restaurants in old Delhi. The *Tandoor* at the Hotel

President on Asaf Ali Rd near the tourist camp is an excellent place with the usual two waiters-per-diner service and a sitar playing in the background. The tandoor kitchen can be seen through a glass panel.

Round the corner on Netaji Subhash Marg in Darayaganj, the famous old *Moti Mahal* is noted for its tandoori dishes including murga musalam, but it seems to live more on reputation than actual ability these days. Quantities are large, however.

Other Places The *YWCA International Guest House* has a restaurant with good food, or, if you are out at Chanakyapuri (waiting for a visa perhaps), the *International Youth Centre* near the Indonesian Embassy has good and inexpensive Indian food.

Not far from Connaught Place the *Ashok Yatri Niwas* has a not-very-good cafeteria (thalis for Rs 20) but also a restaurant. Near the Bengali Market at the traffic circle where Tan Sen Marg meets Babar Rd, the neat and clean *Bengali Sweet House* is a good place for

JAMA MASJID INTERIOR VIEW

DELHI

sweets or for a meal of the snacks known as chat. You could try *cholaphatura* (puffed rotis with a lentil dip), *tikkas* (fried stuffed potatoes), *papri chat* (sweet/hot wafers), or *golguppas* (hollow puffs you break open and use as a scoop for a peppery liquid accompaniment). They also do good masala dosas.

International Hotels Many Delhi residents reckon that the best food to be found in the capital is at the large five-star hotels. At the Maurya Sheraton the *Bukhara* has many central Asian specialities, including tandoori cooking and dishes from the Peshawar region in north-west Pakistan. This is a place for big meat eaters and you can expect to pay around Rs 104 to Rs 130 per person. Main courses are generally around Rs 65, some Rs 97 to Rs 104; the rotis are excellent. It's so successful it's even got a branch in New York.

The *Haveli* at the Taj Mahal Hotel is also popular. Here the food is more mainstream Indian but the quality is high and there is Indian music and dancing as entertainment. Prices are similar to the Bukhara's. Other popular restaurants at the large hotels include the *Peacock* at the Ashok Hotel, the *Mughal Room* at the Oberoi and the *Machan* at the Hotel Taj.

Several cheaper hotels have noted vegetarian restaurants. Thalis at *Dasaprakash* in the Hotel Ambassador are good value. The Lodhi Hotel is noted for the thalis at its *Woodlands Restaurant*. The old *Imperial Hotel* is great for an alfresco breakfast in the pleasant garden.

Things to Buy

Good buys include silk products, precious stones, leather and woodwork, but the most important thing about Delhi is that you can find almost anything from anywhere in India. If this is your first stop in India, and you intend to buy something while you are here, then it's a chance to compare what is available from all over India. If this is your last stop and there was something you missed elsewhere in the country, Delhi provides a chance to find it.

Two good places to start are in New Delhi, near Connaught Place. The Central Cottage Industries Emporium is on Janpath, opposite the tourist office. In this large building you will find items from all over India, generally of good quality and reasonably priced. Whether it's wood-carvings, brasswork, paintings, clothes, textiles or furniture, you'll find it here. Along Baba Kharak Singh Marg, two streets round from Janpath, are the various State Emporiums run by the state governments. Each displays and sells handicrafts from their state. There are many other shops around Connaught Place and Janpath. By the nearby Imperial Hotel there are a number of stalls and small shops run by Tibetan refugees selling carpets, jewellery and many (often instant) antiques.

In old Delhi, Chandni Chowk is the famous shopping street. Here you will find carpets and jewellery but you have to search the convoluted back alleys. In the narrow street called Cariba Kalan, perfumes are made as well. You can find an interesting variety of perfumes, oils and soaps at Chhabra Perfumery at 1573 Main Bazaar, Paharganj, near the Vivek Hotel. More than a hundred oils are available in small bottles. The cheap Karol Bagh market has become even more popular than Connaught Place or Chandni Chowk.

Just south of the Purana Qila, beside Dr Zakir Hussain Rd and across from the Oberoi New Delhi Hotel, is the Sunder Nagar market, a collection of shops selling antiques and brassware. The prices may be high but you'll find fascinating and high-quality artefacts. Shops in the major international hotels often have very high-quality items, at equally high prices.

Getting There & Away

Delhi is a major international gateway to India; for details on arriving from overseas see the introductory Getting There chapter. At certain times of the year international flights out of Delhi can be heavily booked so it's wise to make reservations as early as possible. This particularly applies to some of the heavily discounted airlines out of Europe – double-check your reservations and make sure you reconfirm.

Delhi is also a major centre for domestic travel, with extensive bus, rail and air connections.

Air Indian Airlines flights depart from Delhi to all the major Indian centres. Some important connections include Bombay (Rs 1075, around eight flights daily), Madras (Rs 1520), Calcutta (Rs 1220, two daily), Srinagar (Rs 715), Jaipur (Rs 285), Agra (Rs 230), Hyderabad, Bangalore, Pune (Rs 1207) and Varanasi (Rs 690).

India is not a great place for air-fare bargains on domestic flights – Indian Airlines fly too close to 100% capacity to worry about the hard sell. The Indian Airlines office in Delhi is in the Kanchenjunga Building on Barakhamba Rd. The office occupies a large open area upstairs around the back of the building – you wouldn't know it was there! Reservations can be made for flights all over India and, with the computer system, you can make them quickly and reliably.

Bus The large Interstate bus terminal is at Kashmir Gate, north of the Delhi railway station in old Delhi. Buses depart from here to locations all around Delhi – ring 229083 for details. State government bus companies operating from here are:

Haryana Government Roadways (tel 221292), bookings 6 am to 12 noon and 1.30 to 9 pm.
Jammu & Kashmir Government Roadways (tel 224559), bookings 10 am to 5 pm but only on air-con buses.
Rajasthan Roadways (tel 222276), bookings 6 am to 8 pm.
Uttar Pradesh Roadways (tel 226175, 273379), bookings 8 am to 4 pm.

Popular buses include the approximately

hourly buses to Agra which cost Rs 28. There is also a frequent and fast service to Jaipur for Rs 40. For Chandigarh, from where you can take a bus or the narrow-gauge train up to Simla, the regular buses cost Rs 40. There are deluxe video buses for Rs 65 and even an air-con video bus. You can also get buses direct to Simla (10 hours) for Rs 53; Dharamsala, Rs 71; and Kulu, Rs 57. To northern Uttar Pradesh buses cost Rs 32 for Hardwar or Rs 35 for Dehra Dun.

The large Dhaula Kuan bus stop is south of the city near the airport. Catching buses here can save you the trip to the station in old Delhi and then the long journey through the city centre.

In the popular travellers' hangouts there are adverts for a four-times-weekly bus service to Kathmandu which takes about 36 hours and costs Rs 375. There are also super-deluxe buses to Simla for Rs 130, Srinagar for Rs 220 and other destinations. The Europe-bound overland bus service operates two or three times a month from the tourist camp in New Delhi and charge about US\$350 to London.

Train Delhi is an important rail centre and an excellent place to make bookings. There is a special foreign tourist booking office in New Delhi station. It is a calm, quiet and efficient place where you can buy tickets and make 1st and 2nd-class reservations all in one go. They also sell Indrail passes and can give advice on all classes of rail travel.

Remember that there are two main stations in Delhi – Delhi station in old Delhi, and New Delhi station at the northern end of New Delhi, more or less on the old Delhi border. The latter is much closer to Connaught Place, and if you're departing from Delhi station you should allow adequate time to wind your way through the traffic snarls of old Delhi. Between the Delhi and New Delhi stations you can take the No 6 bus for just Rs 1. There's also the Nizam-ud-din station south of the New Delhi area where some trains start or finish. It's worth getting off here if you are staying in Chanakyapuri or elsewhere south of Connaught Place.

There are several special tourist trains operating from Delhi. The Taj Express is ideal for day-trips to Agra, 199 km south. The train departs and returns to the New Delhi station and takes three hours each way. The fare is Rs 95 in 1st class, Rs 28 in 2nd. The new one-class Shatabdi express is faster, leaves earlier and costs Rs 115, which includes meals.

The Pink City Express is a direct train from Delhi station to Jaipur, departing at 6 am and arriving five hours later. Fare for the 308-km trip is Rs 137 in 1st class, Rs 40 in 2nd.

Some other important connections by mail or express train include:

		1st class	2nd class
Amritsar	from 7 hours	Rs 185	Rs 52
Bangalore	from 42 hours	Rs 687	Rs 163
Bombay	from 17 hours	Rs 428	Rs 97
Calcutta	from 17 hours	Rs 453	Rs 115
Hyderabad (AP)	from 26 hours	Rs 500	Rs 125
Jammu Tawi	from 15 hours	Rs 245	Rs 59
Madras	from 40 hours	Rs 620	Rs 150
Trivandrum	from 52 hours	Rs 822	Rs 195
Varanasi	from 13 hours	Rs 283	Rs 77

Getting Around

Distances around Delhi are large and the buses are generally hopelessly crowded, although there is a more expensive deluxe bus service. The alternative is a taxi or auto-rickshaw.

Airport Transport Delhi's somewhat chaotic, confusing and tatty Palam airport is now officially the Indira Gandhi International airport. The domestic and international

terminals are nine km apart, and Delhi Transport Corporation buses connect the two for Rs 5. There is a counter at the international terminal for making domestic reservations but it's often closed. The one counter at the domestic terminal is open 24 hours but is pure chaos.

Fortunately, airport-to-city and vice-versa transport is relatively simple. EATS (the Ex-Servicemen's Air Link Transport Service) have a regular bus service between the airport and their office in Connaught Place. The fare is Rs 13 and they will drop you off or pick you up at most of the major hotels en route if you ask. Departures, from opposite the underground bazaar, begin around 5 am and run through to nearly midnight. Departures from the airport to the centre are timed according to aircraft arrivals. There is also a regular Delhi Transport Corporation bus service that runs from the airport to New Delhi and Delhi railway stations and the Interstate bus terminal; it costs Rs 10 and there is a Rs 5 charge for luggage.

Taxis cost about Rs 60 to Rs 80 from the airport to Connaught Place, although they frequently ask for considerably more. Auto-rickshaws will run out to the airport too, although your teeth will be shaking by the time you get there! If you can find a driver willing to use the meter it should cost about Rs 26 to Rs 32. There is a public bus service to the airport (No 780) from the Super Bazaar at Connaught Place but it can get very crowded.

If you're arriving at New Delhi airport from overseas, the State Bank foreign exchange counter is in the arrivals hall, after you've gone through customs and immigration. Once you've left the arrivals hall you won't be allowed back in. The service is fast and efficient, although quite a few travellers have complained about being short-changed here, so count what they give you.

Many international flights to Delhi arrive and depart at terrible hours in the early morning. Take special care if this is your first foray into India and you arrive exhausted and jet-lagged. If you're leaving Delhi in the early hours of the morning, book a taxi the afternoon before. They'll be hard to find in the night. See the accommodation section for information about the retiring rooms at the airport.

Bus Avoid buses during the rush hours as the situation is hopeless. Whenever possible try to board (and leave) at a starting or finishing point as there is more chance of a seat and less chance of being trampled; the Regal and Plaza cinemas in Connaught Place are such places. There are some seats reserved for women on the left side of the bus. The Delhi Transport Corporation run the buses and you can get a route guide from their office in Scindia House.

Useful buses include bus No 504 to the Qutab Minar from the Super Bazaar, and bus No 502 from the Red Fort. Bus No 101 runs between the Interstate bus terminal and Connaught Place. Bus No 620 or 630 will take you between Connaught Place and Chanakyapuri. Bus Nos 101, 104 and 139 run between the Regal Cinema bus stand and the Red Fort. A short bus ride (like Connaught Place to Red Fort) is only about Rs 1. Buses to New Delhi railway station from Connaught Place (Regal Cinema) include bus No 157 and the No R40.

Taxi & Auto-Rickshaw All taxis and auto-rickshaws are metered but the meters are invariably out of date, allegedly 'not working' or the drivers will simply refuse to use them. It matters not a jot that they are legally required to do so. A threat to report them to the police results in little more than considerable mirth, so you will often have to negotiate a price before you set out. Naturally, this will always be more than it should be. There are exceptions; occasionally a driver will reset the meter without even a word from you.

At places like New Delhi station or the airport, where there are always plenty of police hanging around, you can generally rely on the meter being used because it's too easy to report a driver. Trips during the rush hour or middle-of-the-night journeys to the airport are the times when meters are least likely to be used.

At the end of a journey you will have to pay according to a scale of revised charges or simply a flat percentage increase. Some drivers display these cards in the cab, others consign them to the oily-rag compartment, still others feed them to the cows. So if you do come across a legible copy it's worth noting down a few of the conversions, paying what you think is the right price and leaving it at that. You may rest assured that no-one is going to be out of pocket, except yourself, despite hurt or angry protestations to the contrary.

Flag fall is Rs 3 in taxis and Rs 2.30 in auto-rickshaws. Connaught Place to the Red Fort should cost around Rs 25 by taxi or Rs 12 by auto-rickshaw, depending on the traffic. From 11 pm to 5 am there is a 25% surcharge in taxis. There are also old Harley Davidson 'four-seater' or 'six-seater' auto-rickshaws running fixed routes at fixed prices. From Connaught Place their starting point is Palika Bazaar in the centre of Connaught Place and your Sikh driver will chop his way through the traffic as far as the fountain in Chandni Chowk via the Red Fort in old Delhi. They cost less than Rs 2 each and are good value, especially during rush hours.

Bicycle & Cycle-Rickshaw Unlike many Indian cities, New Delhi is not a good place for bicycles – too much high-speed motorised traffic and large distances. Nevertheless, you can hire bicycles for Rs 8 a day near the Bengali Market. Cycle-rickshaws are banned from New Delhi but you still find them in the more crowded and slower-moving streets of old Delhi.

Punjab & Haryana

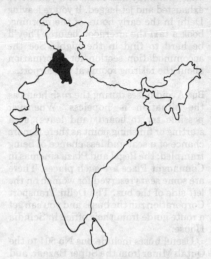

Haryana
Population: 15 million
Area: 44,222 square km
Capital: Chandigarh
Main language: Hindi

Punjab
Population: 20 million
Area: 50,362 square km
Capital: Chandigarh
Main language: Punjabi

The Punjab was probably the part of India which suffered the most destruction and damage at the time of partition, yet today it is far and away the most affluent state in India. No natural resource or advantage gave the Punjabis this enviable position; it was sheer hard work.

Prior to partition the Punjab extended across both sides of what is now the Pakistan-India border, and its capital Lahore is now the capital of the Pakistani state of Punjab. The population of the Punjab was split into a Muslim region and a Sikh and Hindu region by the grim logic of partition that sliced the region in two. As millions of Sikhs and Hindus fled eastward and equal numbers of Muslims fled west, there were innumerable atrocities and killings on both sides. More recently Sikh political demands have wracked the state, particularly Amritsar, with violence; in 1990 the situation looks as insoluble as ever. The demands are somewhat vague and difficult for outsiders to understand, and the escalating violence between Sikh and Hindu factions has made the Punjab an uncomfortable place.

The major city in the Punjab is Amritsar, the holy city of the Sikhs, but it is so close to the Pakistani border that it was thought wise to build a safer capital further within the borders of India. At first Simla, the old imperial summer capital,

served as capital but Chandigarh, a new planned city, was conceived and built to serve as the capital of the new Punjab.

In 1966, however, the Punjab was to undergo another split. This time it was divided into the predominantly Sikh and Punjabi-speaking state of Punjab and the state of Haryana. At the same time some of the northern parts of the Punjab were hived off to Himachal Pradesh. Chandigarh, on the border of Punjab and Haryana, remained the capital of both states until 1986 when it was announced that it would be handed over to Punjab as an attempt to placate the Sikhs. However, with the continued violence in Punjab it seems unlikely that this will happen.

At the time of partition the Punjab was devastated but the Sikhs' no-nonsense approach to life has won for it a position that statistics sum up admirably. The Punjab's per capita income is 50% higher than the all-India average (in second place is Haryana). Although Punjabis comprise less than 2½% of India's population, they provide 22% of India's wheat and 10% of its rice. The Punjab provides a third of all the milk produced in

India. Punjabis have 5% of India's total bank deposits, and their life expectancy is 65 years against the all-India average of 50 years.

Although the Punjab is predominantly an agricultural state, it also has thriving industries including Hero Bicycles at Ludhiana, India's biggest bicycle manufacturer. The Punjabis also have the highest consumption of alcohol in India – the iron bangle (kara), which all Sikh men must wear, is an ideal instrument for taking the caps off beer bottles!

From the traveller's point of view, neither Punjab nor Haryana has an enormous amount to offer and with the present uncertainty there are few visitors. Major attractions are the Le Corbusier-planned city of Chandigarh and the Sikhs' golden city of Amritsar. Those cities apart, the two states are mainly places of transit, and since they're on the way to the hill stations of Himachal Pradesh and the delights of Kashmir, a lot of people do pass through them.

The Sikhs

The Sikhs are the reason for the Punjab's success story and they're amongst the most interesting people in India. See the introductory Facts about the Country chapter for a description of their religion and customs.

Apart from anything else, the Sikhs are the most instantly recognisable people in India. The requirement that they do not cut their hair (kesha) ensures that all Sikh men are bearded and turbaned. For some reason they all seem to be big, bulky men too – you never see a weedy-looking Sikh. Sikh women also have a unique costume, the salwar-kameez: wide pyjama-style trousers fastened at the ankles, topped by a long shirt which almost reaches the knees. All Sikhs have the surname Singh, meaning 'lion'.

Curiously, despite their undoubted success the Sikhs have a reputation in India, rather like the Irish in the west. The Indians have as many Sikh jokes as the west has Irish jokes. Not many translate very well but they basically follow the same line, which is strange since the stereotyped Sikh is quite unlike the stereotyped Irishman. The Irish-joke Irishman is supposed to be all thumbs; the Sikhs have a reputation for great dexterity and mechanical ability. Sikhs have always been at home with machines, and in India any activity with machines, from driving an auto-rickshaw to piloting a 747, will employ a disproportionate number of Sikhs. Despite this, other Indians mock Sikhs as being blunt and straightforward to the point of stupidity!

Punjab Permits

Despite the fact that the Sikh homeland problems persist, permits are no longer required for visits to the Punjab, so you're free to wander (and take your chances) at will. This does not include the 35 km

Punjab & Haryana

security zone at the border with Pakistan which remains off limits to everyone. In 1989 more people were killed in the Punjab than in Beirut.

Haryana

The state of Haryana has one of the most successful tourist departments in India, which is very interesting when you consider how few tourist attractions the state has. What the clever Haryanans have done is take advantage of their geographical location. If you're going from Delhi to almost any major attraction in the north – Jaipur, Agra, Kashmir, Amritsar – you go through Haryana. So they've built a series of 'service centres' along the main roads – the sort of motel-restaurant-service station complexes which in the west are quite common, but in India are all too rare. They are all named after birds found in Haryana and are clean, well kept and, if you're after a place to stay, make travelling through Haryana a pleasure. Typically the complexes may have a camping site, camper huts (usually Rs 75 to Rs 175) and rooms (usually in the Rs 100 to Rs 225 range if they have air-con, cheaper without). Some places also have dormitories. The main Haryana complexes with their distance from Delhi include:

Badkhal Lake (tel 26900/4, 32 km) restaurants, swimming pool, boating, fishing, air-con rooms, camper huts.

Rajhans, Surajkund (tel 6830766, 8 km) swimming pool, boating, air-con rooms, camper huts, fishing.

Magpie, Faridabad (tel 23473, 30 km) air-con rooms, restaurant.

Dabchick, Hodal (tel 91, 92 km) elephant rides, boating, children's playgrounds, air-con rooms, camper huts with and without air-con.

Barbet, Sohna (tel 56, 56 km) restaurant, cafe, bath complex, swimming pool, air-con rooms, camper huts.

Jangle Babbleng, Dharuhera (tel 25, Rewari, 70 km) restaurant, cafe, camel riding, rooms with and without air-con.

Rosy Pelican, Sultanpur (46 km) restaurant, bird-watching facilities, camping site, air-con rooms, camper huts.

Shama Restaurant (tel 2683, 32 km) restaurant, rooms without air-con.

Mor Pankh (70 km) restaurant, rooms without air-con.

Ulchana, Karnal (tel 2179, 124 km) restaurant, cafe, kebab corner, boating, air-con rooms, camper huts.

Parakeet, Pipli (tel 250, 152 km) restaurant, cafe, camping facilities, air-con rooms, camper huts.

Blue Jay, Samalkha (tel 10, 60 km) restaurant, rooms with and without air-con, camper huts.

Yadavindra Gardens, Pinjore (tel 155, 281 km) at the Moghul gardens, restaurant, open-air cafe, dosa shop, mini-zoo, children's games, air-con rooms, camper huts.

Kingfisher, Ambala (tel 58352, 55 km from Chandigarh), motel, restaurant, bar, health club, swimming pool.

Skylark, Panipat (tel 3579, 90 km) restaurant, air-con rooms.

Tilyar, Rohtak (tel 3966, 70 km) restaurant, boating, rooms with and without air-con.

Myna, Rohtak (tel 4594, 72 km) restaurant, camper huts.

Flamingo, Hissar (tel 2602, 160 km) restaurant, air-con rooms.

Bulbul, Jind (127 km) restaurant, camper huts.

Kala Teetar, Abubshehr (325 km) restaurant, boating, air-con rooms.

Sohna, (56 km), sulphur springs, steam bath, restaurant.

Surajkund and Badkhal Lake are on the Delhi to Agra road. Skylark, Parakeet and Kingfisher are on the Delhi to Chandigarh road.

SULTANPUR

There are many birds, including flamingos, at the bird sanctuary here. September to March is the best time to visit, and you can stay at the Rosy Pelican complex. To get there take a blue Haryana bus to Gurgaon (buses every 10 minutes from Dhaula Kuan), and then take a Chandu bus (three or four times a day) to Sultanpur, 46 km from Delhi.

DELHI TO CHANDIGARH

There are many places of interest along the 260-km route from Delhi to Chandigarh. The road, part of the Grand Trunk Road, is one of the busiest in India with a lot of different types of traffic.

Panipat

Panipat, 92 km north of Delhi, is reputed to be one of the most fly-infested places in India – due, it is said, to a Muslim saint buried here. He is supposed to have totally rid Panipat of flies, but when the people complained that he had done too good a job he gave them all the flies back, multiplied by a thousand.

It is also the site of three great battles, although there is nothing much to be seen of these today. In 1526, Babur defeated Ibrahim Lodi, King of Delhi, at Panipat and thus founded the Moghul Empire in India. In 1556, Akbar defeated the Pathans at this same site. Finally in 1761, the Marathas, who had succeeded the Moghuls, were defeated here by the Afghan forces of Ahmad Shah Durani.

Gharaunda

The gateways of an old Moghul *serai* (rest house) stand to the west of this village, 102 km north of Delhi. Shah Jahan built *kos minars*, 'milestones', along the road from Delhi to Lahore and serais at longer intervals. Most of the kos minars still stand but there is little left of the various serais.

Karnal & Kurukshetra

Events in the *Mahabharata* are supposed to have occurred in Karnal, 118 km from Delhi, and also at the tank of Kurukshetra, a little further north. It was at Karnal that Nadir Shah, the Persian who took the Peacock Throne from Delhi, defeated the Moghul emperor Mohammed Shah in 1739. The Kurukshetra tank has attracted as many as half a million pilgrims during

eclipses, as at these times the water in the tank is said to contain water from every other sacred tank in India. Thus its cleansing ability, during the eclipse, is unsurpassed. Kurukshetra also has an interesting small mosque, the Lal Masjid, and a finely designed tomb.

Places to Stay There is a Haryana government *Krishnadham Yatri Niwas* where doubles cost Rs 100 and dorm beds Rs 25.

CHANDIGARH (population 500,000)

Construction of Chandigarh from a plan by the French architect, Le Corbusier, began in the 1950s. Although to many western visitors it appears to be a rather sterile and hopelessly sprawling city, Indians are very proud of it and Chandigarh's residents feel that it is a good place to live.

Chandigarh is a truly dreadful piece of town planning. It's a car city in a country where the general population don't own cars. It's as if Le Corbusier sat down and laid the city out having never visited India and without giving a second's thought to what India was like. The end result is a city where walking is a near impossibility, where bicycle rickshaws look lost and spend half their time taking shortcuts the wrong way around sweeping traffic circles, and where the huge expanses of road space in the shopping centre would be fine as car parks in the west but here are simply empty. Between the city's scattered buildings are long, ugly, barren stretches of wasteland. In Le Corbusier's home environment they might be parks or gardens, but in India empty ground is obviously doomed.

Information & Orientation

Chandigarh is on the edge of the Siwalik Hills, the outermost edge of the Himalaya. It is divided into 47 numbered sectors, separated by broad avenues. The bus station and modern shopping centre are in Sector 17. The railway station is a long

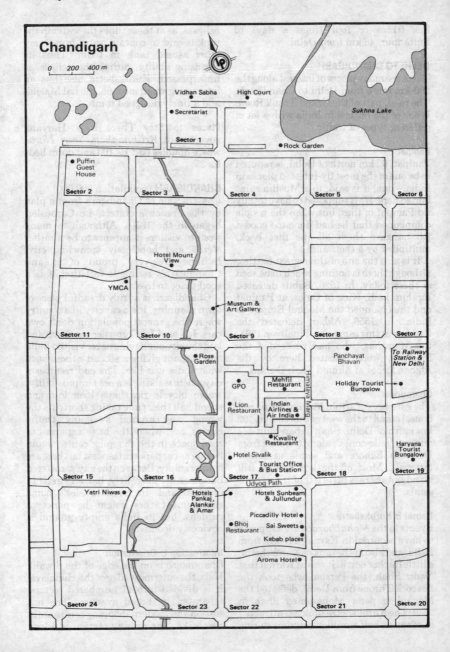

Chandigarh

0   200   400 m

Vidhan Sabha   High Court

Secretariat

Sector 1

Sukhna Lake

Rock Garden

Puffin
Guest
House

Sector 2   Sector 3   Sector 4   Sector 5   Sector 6

Hotel Mount
View

YMCA

Museum &
Art Gallery

Sector 11   Sector 10   Sector 9   Sector 8   Sector 7

Rose
Garden

Panchayat
Bhavan

To Railway
Station &
New Delhi

GPO

Mehfil
Restaurant

Holiday Tourist
Bungalow

Lion
Restaurant

Indian
Airlines &
Air India

Himalaya Marg

Kwality
Restaurant

Hotel Sivalik

Tourist Office
& Bus Station

Haryana
Tourist
Bungalow

Sector 15   Sector 16   Sector 17   Sector 18   Sector 19

Udyog Path

Yatri Niwas

Hotels
Pankaj,
Alankar
& Amar

Hotels Sunbeam
& Jullundur

Piccadilly Hotel

Sai Sweets

Bhoj
Restaurant

Kebab places

Aroma Hotel

Sector 24   Sector 23   Sector 22   Sector 21   Sector 20

way out of Chandigarh so buses are much more convenient than trains, but you can make rail bookings from the office above the central bus terminus.

The Secretariat and other important government buildings are in Sector 1, to the north. The museum is in Sector 10 and the Rose Garden in Sector 16, next to the bus station. The shopping centre has restaurants, ice-cream parlours, book shops and a wide variety of other retail outlets. The tourist office is upstairs in the bus station.

Government Buildings
The Secretariat and the Legislative Assembly buildings are in Sector 1. Between 10 am and 12 noon you can go to the top of the Secretariat, from where there is an excellent view over Chandigarh. Eventually the huge hand here will revolve. It is supposed to be the centrepiece of the government sector and the symbol of Chandigarh.

Rock Garden
Close to the government buildings is a not-to-be-missed attraction, the bizarre Rock Garden – a sort of concrete maze with a lot of rocks and very little garden. This strange and whimsical fantasy has grown and grown over the years and is now very extensive. It's open from 9 am to 1 pm and 3 to 7 pm from 1 April to 30 September. The rest of the year it opens and closes an hour earlier in the afternoons. Entry is Rs 0.70.

Close by is the artificial Sukhna Lake, where you can rent rowboats or just stroll round its two-km perimeter.

Museum & Art Gallery
The art gallery in Sector 10 is open daily except Mondays and contains a modest collection of Indian stone sculptures dating back to the Gandhara period, together with some miniature paintings and modern art. The adjacent museum has fossils and implements of prehistoric man found in India. Opening hours are 10 am to 5 pm Wednesday to Sunday.

Rose Garden
The Rose Garden in Sector 16 is claimed to be the biggest in Asia and contains more than a thousand varieties of roses.

Places to Stay – bottom end
There are no great bottom-end bargains in Chandigarh. The *Youth Hostel* is at Panchkula, between Chandigarh and the Pinjore Gardens. It's a little way out of town, but there are frequent buses and the hostel is good value.

Much more central is the *Chandigarh Yatri Niwas* at the corner of Sectors 15 and 24 on the roundabout nearest the bus station. It's rather anonymously hidden behind a block of flats and is a Rs 4 rickshaw ride from the bus station. It's a bit hostel-like and the rooms only have common bathrooms, although there seems to be one bathroom for every two rooms. There's hot water and a cafeteria (vegetarian dinner for Rs 9) with hopelessly slow service. Although fairly new, it's already suffering from that Indian instant decay – wiring tumbling out of the walls and so on – but it's clean and at Rs 75/100 for singles/doubles is the best value in town. It is, however, away from the main market and restaurants.

There are two *Tourist Bungalows* in Sector 19, both somewhat inconspicuous although the bus station rickshaw-wallahs certainly know how to find them. Unlike other states, the tourist bungalows in Chandigarh are privately owned and are not good value; Rs 95 only gets you a room with common bath. The *YMCA* (tel 26532) is in Sector 11 but only takes weekly guests. *Panchayat Bhavan* in Sector 18 has doubles for Rs 48 and dorm beds for Rs 12.

Opposite the bus station towards the Sector 21 roundabout is the *Hotel Jullundur* with rooms from Rs 70/110.

Places to Stay – middle
Opposite the bus station on Udyog Path in Sector 22 there are three bottom to middle-range hotels side by side at the roundabout

towards Sector 23. The *Hotel Pankaj* (tel 41906) has comfortable rooms at Rs 170/185 or deluxe rooms at Rs 210/230. The *Alankar* (tel 21303) is cheaper at Rs 100 for singles and Rs 150 to Rs 200 for doubles. The *Amar* (tel 26608) is cheaper still with rooms from Rs 100 to Rs 130.

The *Hotel Divyadeep* on Himalaya Marg has rooms at Rs 90/120, or Rs 130/156 with air-cooling and Rs 182/208 with air-con. Just past the traffic lights, about 10 minutes walking distance from the bus station, is the long-running *Aroma Hotel* (tel 23359). Rooms with bath cost Rs 117/143 and it's clean and well kept.

Places to Stay – top end

Several modern top-end hotels have been built in the last few years. Opposite the bus station in Sector 22, by the Sector 21 roundabout, is the *Hotel Sunbeam* (tel 41335) with air-con rooms costing Rs 310/400. There are several hotels along Himalaya Marg in Sector 22, including the *Hotel Piccadily* (tel 32223) which charges Rs 280/375 for singles/doubles and is centrally located. The *Hotel President* (tel 40840) in Sector 26 is one of the best in Chandigarh and charges Rs 395/595 for singles/doubles.

The *Mount View* (tel 41773) in Sector 10 is Chandigarh's top hotel. It's less central than the other main hotels but has pleasant gardens and costs Rs 500/600 for singles/doubles. The *Puffin Guest House* (tel 27653) run by Haryana Tourism is in Sector 2 and has doubles with air-con for Rs 275.

Places to Eat

Chandigarh has plenty of places to eat, including a proliferation of fast-food outlets. Beside the Sunbeam Hotel in Sector 22 is the neon-lit *Traffic Jam* with masala dosas, pizzas, ice creams and even 'Donald Burgers'.

South along Himalaya Marg from the Sunbeam Hotel in Sector 22 are a number of places to eat. The *Bhoj Restaurant* at the Hotel Divyadeep serves slightly expensive vegetarian food in glossy surroundings. Further south at 1102 Himalaya Marg is *Sai Sweets* which serve the snacks known as chat, dosas and, of course, a wide variety of excellent Indian sweets. Continuing along Himalaya Marg there is a group of open-air kebab places, all called *Singh* something or other. Strictly for meat eaters but good value.

There is another bunch of fast-food places in the Sector 17 shopping centre. They include *Piccad's, Hot Millions* and the engagingly named *Food Fight* – it conjures up images of your stomach in turmoil. The menu includes not only the inevitable muttonburgers but also a 'brahmin burger' – held together with a sacred thread, perhaps. There's also an *Indian Coffee House* in the shopping centre.

Finally, still in the Sector 17 shopping centre, there's a street with a cluster of top-end restaurants, including the *Mehfil Restaurant*. This tandoori specialist looks flashy – white tablecloths, soft music, etc – but it is not too extravagantly priced. The menu is the standard mix of continental, Chinese and Indian dishes, and main courses are Rs 16 to Rs 25, desserts Rs 8 to Rs 10. Close by are the *Ghazal* and the *Mughal Mahal* restaurants, and there is a *Kwality* restaurant in the shopping centre. The *Shagun Restaurant* next to the Hotel Piccadily has a Rs 10 thali which is good value.

Things to Buy

Woollen sweaters and shawls from the Punjab are good buys, especially in the Government Emporium. The Chandigarh shopping centre is probably the most extensive in India.

Getting There & Away

Air There are daily Indian Airlines flights between Delhi and Chandigarh for Rs 315, and five days a week the flight continues to Jammu (Rs 455) and Srinagar (Rs 610). Twice a week there are flights to Leh for Rs 510. Three times a week Vayudoot fly

Delhi/Chandigarh/Kulu, and the Chandigarh/Kulu fare is Rs 310.

Bus Buses depart regularly from the Interstate bus terminal in Delhi (near Kashmir Gate) for the five-hour trip to Chandigarh. Regular buses cost Rs 36, and there are also deluxe video buses (Rs 71) and even air-con deluxe video buses (Rs 125).

There are regular and deluxe buses to other places such as Simla (Rs 22 regular, Rs 40 deluxe), Dharamsala (Rs 40 to 45 regular), Manali (Rs 65 regular) and Jaipur (Rs 127 deluxe). It takes about 14 hours to Manali by bus, only nine by taxi. Buses take five hours to Simla, 12 hours to Kulu, six hours to Amritsar, 10 hours to Dharamsala and seven hours to Pathankot.

Train Buses are more convenient than trains to or from Chandigarh, but reservations can be made at the booking agency in Sector 22 (tel 29117) or at the office above the Central bus station. Enquiries can be made by phoning 27605. Delhi to Chandigarh is 245 km and costs Rs 32 in 2nd class, Rs 115 in 1st.

Getting Around
Airport Transport The airport is 12 km from Sector 17 and it's Rs 60 by taxi or Rs 25 by auto-rickshaw.

Local Transport Chandigarh is much too spread out to get around on foot, but a day is certainly sufficient to see all it has to offer. The extensive bus network is the cheapest way of getting around. Bus No 1 runs by the Aroma Hotel as far as the government buildings in Sector 1, and bus Nos 6, 6A and 6B all run to the railway station.

Cycle-rickshaws operate on the normal bargaining basis but Chandigarh is a bit big even for them. If you're planning a longer trip across the city consider an auto-rickshaw, of which there aren't so many. They're metered but drivers positively refuse to use them. If you do

want to try walking, start off at Sector 1 and stroll back through Sector 10 (Museum & Art Gallery) and 16 (Rose Garden) to the bus station and shopping centre in Sector 17.

AROUND CHANDIGARH
Pinjore
The Moghul gardens at Pinjore were designed by Fidai Khan, Aurangzeb's foster brother, who also designed the Badshahi Mosque in Lahore, Pakistan. Situated 20 km from Chandigarh, the gardens include the Rajasthani-Moghul-style Shish Mahal palace. Below it is the Rang Mahal and the cubical Jal Mahal. There is an otter house and other animals can be seen in the mini-zoo near the gardens. The fountains only operate on weekends.

Places to Stay The *Rest House* at Yadabindra Garden (tel 455959) has air-con rooms from Rs 200 to Rs 350.

Getting There & Away There are hourly buses from Chandigarh which stop at Pinjore Gardens gate. They take 45 minutes and cost Rs 3.

Punjab

AMRITSAR (population 700,000)
Until a second India-Pakistan border crossing is open, travellers heading overland have to go through Amritsar, close to the only land crossing open to Pakistan.

Founded in 1577 by Ram Das, the fourth guru of the Sikhs, Amritsar is both the centre of the Sikh religion and the major city of Punjab state – where the majority of Sikhs live. Amritsar or 'pool of nectar' is the name of the sacred pool by which the Sikhs' golden temple is built.

The original site for the city was granted by the Moghul emperor Akbar, but in 1761 Ahmad Shah Durani sacked

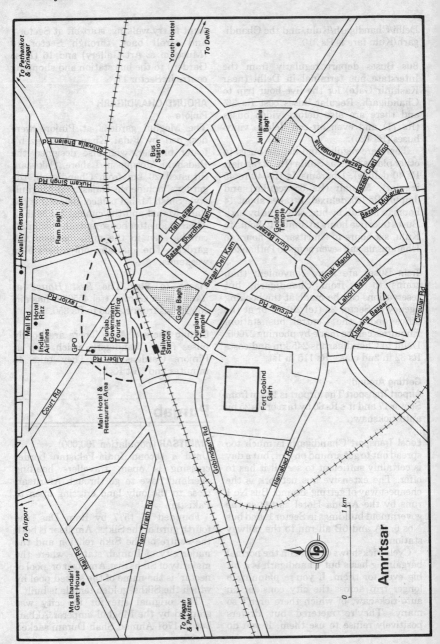

Amritsar

To Pathankot & Srinagar

Youth Hostel

To Delhi

Bus Station

Shiwala Bhajan Rd

Hukam Singh Rd

Jallianwala Bagh

Bazaar Hanuman

Bazaar CharI Wind

Bazaar Mukerian

Kwality Restaurant

Ram Bagh

Hall Bazaar

Bazaar Shardha Nand

Bazaar Deri Kem

Guru Bazaar

Golden Temple

Nimak Mand

Lahori Bazaar

Khazana Bazaar

Circular Rd

Mall Rd

Hotel Ritz

Taylor Rd

Indian Airlines

GPO

Punjab Government Tourist Office

Albert Rd

Gole Bagh

Circular Rd

Durgiana Temple

Railway Station

Court Rd

Main Hotel & Restaurant Area

Fort Gobind Garh

To Airport

Ram Tirath Rd

Mall Rd

Mrs Bhandari's Guest House

Gobindgarh Rd

Islamabad Rd

To Wagah & Pakistan

0   1 km

the town and destroyed the temple. The temple was rebuilt in 1764, and in 1802 it was roofed over with copper-gilded plates by Ranjit Singh and became known as 'the golden temple'. During the turmoil of the partition of India in 1948, Amritsar was a flashpoint for the terrible events that shook the Punjab. The region's recovery has been remarkable and today Amritsar even looks better off than other parts of India; you see few beggars in the streets.

Although the whole state is wracked by political violence, travellers have commented on the friendliness and helpfulness of the Sikhs.

Information & Orientation

The old city is south-east of the main railway station and is surrounded by a circular road which used to contain the massive city walls. There are 18 gates still in existence but only the north gate, facing the Ram Bagh gardens, is original. The Golden Temple and the narrow alleys of the bazaar area are in the old city.

The more modern part of Amritsar is north-east of the railway station, where you will also find the beautiful gardens known as Ram Bagh, The Mall and 'posh' Lawrence St. The bus station is two km east of the railway station on the road to Delhi, and the tourist office is opposite the railway station.

The Golden Temple

The holiest shrine of the Sikh religion is in the centre of the old part of town. The temple itself is surrounded by the pool which gave the town its name, and is reached by a causeway. A loudspeaker broadcasts a continuous reading of the *Granth Sahib* in Punjabi. The high priest who reads from the Sikh's holy book sits on the east side of the temple. The original copy of the *Granth Sahib* is kept in the Golden Temple and is occasionally taken out on procession. To the south of the temple enclosure is a garden in which stands the Baba Atal Tower. The tall

Ramgarhia Minars stand outside the temple enclosure.

Earlier in the Punjab unrest the Golden Temple was occupied by Sikh extremists who were only evicted by the Indian Army in 1984 with much bloodshed. This action was a contributing factor to Indira Gandhi's subsequent assassination. The temple was again occupied by extremists in 1986.

Nowadays, the Golden Temple is again under the control of the central government. The temple has been cleaned and a great deal of restoration has been completed (bullet holes are still visible). A wide swath has been cleared around the complex to prevent infiltration by militants and a park area is planned.

The small rooms around the tank and those in the basement have been sealed along with other hiding places favoured by the Kalistanis. Everyone who enters the temple must be body searched.

Pilgrims and visitors to the Golden Temple must remove their shoes and cover their heads before entering the precincts. An English-speaking guide is available at the clock tower which marks the temple entrance. The Central Sikh Museum is upstairs in the clock tower.

The Old City

A 15-minute walk from the Golden Temple through the narrow alleys of the old city brings you to the Hindu Durgiana temple. This small temple, dedicated to the goddess Durga, dates back to the 16th century. A larger temple, built like the Golden Temple in the centre of a lake, is dedicated to the Hindu deities Laxmi and Narayan.

There are a number of mosques in the old city, including the mosque of Mohammed Jan with three white domes and slender minarets.

Jallianwala Bagh

This park is just five minutes walk from

the Golden Temple and commemorates the 2000 Indians who were killed or wounded at this site, shot indiscriminately by the British in 1919. This was one of the major events in India's struggles for independence and was movingly re-created in the film *Gandhi*. Bullet marks and the well into which some people jumped to escape can still be seen. Officially, over 300 were killed.

Ram Bagh

This beautiful garden is in the new part of town and has a museum in the small palace built there by the Sikh Maharaja Ranjit Singh. The museum contains weapons dating back to Moghul times and some portraits of the ruling houses of the Punjab. It's closed on Wednesdays.

Other Attractions

The Fort Gobind Garh is south-west of the city centre. It was built in 1805-09 by Ranjit Singh, who was also responsible for constructing the city walls. Tarn Taran is an important Sikh tank about 25 km south of Amritsar. There's a temple, which predates Amritsar, and tower on the east side of the tank, also constructed by Ranjit Singh. It's said that any leper who can swim across the tank will be miraculously cured.

Places to Stay – bottom end

The *Tourist Guest House*, across from the railway station and near the Airlines Hotel, has rooms from Rs 40 and is popular with shoestring travellers. The *Hotel Temple View* has rooms at Rs 35 a double – 'clean, real Sikh friendliness and one of the best views of the Golden Temple in town'.

Station Links Rd, opposite the railway station, has three moderately priced hotels. The *Hotel Skylark* (tel 46738) and *Hotel Chinar* (tel 33455) have rooms from Rs 75, and the *Hotel Palace*, which also houses the state tourist information office, has some cheaper rooms.

If you're on a really tight budget, the

The Golden Temple

state government *Youth Hostel* (tel 48165) is three km out of town on the Delhi road. There are dorm beds for Rs 10 (cheaper for YHA members) and doubles (doorless!) for Rs 26. The hostel has hot showers and good, albeit expensive, food. It's one of the better youth hostels in India and has camping facilities.

There are many cheap hotels around the temple such as the *Vikas Guest House* or the slightly cheaper *Amritsar Majestic Hotel*.

Places to Stay - middle

On Mall Rd, in the new area of the city and about one km from the railway station, you'll find the pleasant *Hotel Blue Moon* (tel 33416) with rooms at Rs 90/135 or Rs 130/170 with air-con. In the same area the *Hotel Odeon* (tel 43474) is somewhat cheaper. This is also the area for a number of restaurants, including a Kwality restaurant opposite the Ram Bagh.

The *Grand Hotel* (tel 33821) on Queens Rd opposite the railway station has rooms at Rs 80/115 and Rs 140/170 with air-con. Other more expensive hotels include the *Airlines Hotel* (tel 44545), on Cooper Rd near the railway station, where air-cooled rooms are Rs 100/150 or Rs 150/190 with air-con. The *Astoria* (tel 48479) on Queens Rd has rooms at Rs 85/135 or with air-con at Rs 155/190.

Places to Stay - top end

Built by the Punjab state government, the centrally air-conditioned *Amritsar International Hotel* (tel 31991) is a modern building near the bus station. Rooms cost from Rs 250/300. The smaller *Mohan International Hotel* (tel 34146) on Albert Rd has rooms at Rs 350/450; it is centrally air-conditioned and has a swimming pool.

The *Hotel Ritz* (tel 44199), at 45 Mall Rd near the railway station, has singles/ doubles, all air-con, for Rs 355/425; there's also a swimming pool.

Places to Eat

There are a number of more expensive restaurants in the new part of town such as *Napoli, Kwality* and *Crystal*. There's an ice-cream parlour near the Kwality restaurant.

Amritsar also has a number of cheaper and locally popular places such as *Kasar de Dhawa* near the Durgiana Temple and the telephone exchange in the old town. Parathas and other vegetarian dishes are the speciality here, and you can eat well for around Rs 15. *Kundan di Dhawa* near the railway station and *Mangal de Dhawa* are other popular cheapies, and *Sharma Vaishna Dhaba*, near the temple, has good vegetarian food too. Also near the temple entrance, the *Losy Restaurant* has 'superb, real Punjabi food'.

Things to Buy

Woollen blankets and sweaters are supposed to be cheaper in Amritsar than in other places in India, as they are locally manufactured. Katra Jaimal Singh, near the telephone exchange in the old city, is a good shopping area.

Getting There & Away

Air There's a daily flight from Delhi to Amritsar that continues on to Srinagar, twice a week via Jammu. The fares to or from Amritsar are: Delhi Rs 506, Jammu Rs 253 and Srinagar Rs 429.

Train & Bus Amritsar is 447 km from Delhi and it takes seven hours by mail or express train (Rs 52 in 2nd class, Rs 185 in 1st). It's rather less comfortable by bus, which takes 10 hours.

Amritsar is a departure point to other places in north-west India. Pathankot (on the way to Kashmir) is three hours away by bus and Chandigarh is four. Jammu takes five hours (which is fast for the 215-km trip) and costs Rs 28. The bus to Dharamsala takes 6½ hours (250 km) for Rs 36.

See the introductory Getting There chapter for details on the Amritsar/Attari/ Lahore trip by rail or Amritsar/Wagah/ Lahore road route. It's only 30 km from

Amritsar to Wagah, on the Pakistani border.

PATHANKOT

The town of Pathankot in the extreme north of the Punjab, 107 km from Amritsar, is important to travellers purely as a crossroad. It's the gateway to Jammu in the state of Jammu & Kashmir, which in turn is the starting point for the bus trip up to Srinagar.

Pathankot is also the bus centre for departures to the Himachal Pradesh hill stations, particularly Dalhousie and Dharamsala. Otherwise it's a dull little place, although there's the picturesque Shahpur Kandi Fort about 13 km north of the town on the River Ravi.

Places to Stay & Eat

The *Gulmohar Tourist Bungalow* (tel 292) has rooms for Rs 45/80 or Rs 145/180 with air-con, and there's a dormitory for Rs 12 (Rs 20 with bedding). Pathankot also has a *Rest House* and cheap hotels like the *Green Hotel* and the *Imperial Hotel*.

There's reasonable food in the railway station restaurant.

Getting There & Away

The dusty bus station and the railway station are only a hundred or so metres apart. Buses from Pathankot to Jammu take about three hours and cost Rs 15. The trip to Dalhousie costs Rs 18 and takes about four hours, to Dharamsala Rs 20 and five hours. You can also get taxis for these longer trips next to the railway station.

PATIALA (population 190,000)

A little south of the road and rail lines from Delhi to Amritsar, Patiala was once the capital of an independent Sikh state. There is a museum in the Moti Bagh and the palaces of the maharaja in the Baradari Gardens.

SIRHIND

This was once a very important town and

the capital of the Pathan Sur dynasty. In 1555, Humayun defeated Sikander Shah here and a year later his son, Akbar, completed the destruction of the Sur dynasty at Panipat. From then until 1709 Sirhind was a rich Moghul city, but clashes between the declining Moghul and rising Sikh powers led to the city's sacking in 1709 and complete destruction in 1763.

The Pathan-style Tomb of Mir Miran and the later Moghul Tomb of Pirbandi Nakshwala, both ornamented with blue tiles, are worth seeing. The mansion or *haveli* of Salabat Beg is probably the largest private home remaining from the Moghul period. South-east of the city is an important Moghul serai.

LUDHIANA (population 700,000)

An important textile centre, Ludhiana was the site of a great battle in the First Sikh War. Hero bicycles are manufactured here.

JULLUNDUR (population 400,000)

Only 80 km south-east of Amritsar, this was once the capital of an ancient Hindu kingdom. It survived a sacking by Mahmud of Ghazni nearly a thousand years ago and later became an important Moghul city. The town has a large serai built in 1857 and is a good place to get out and see some Sikh farming villages.

Places to Stay

Not far from the bus stand, the *Skylark Hotel* (tel 75891) has fine food and good rooms at Rs 95/140 or Rs 180/300 with air-con. Other places to stay include the *Plaza Hotel* and the *Hotel Ramji Dass*.

Getting There & Away

Trains take about six hours from Delhi to Jullundur, and there's also a bus stand where frequent services run to other northern centres.

DELHI TO FEROZEPORE

This route takes you through Haryana and the Punjab, further south than the

Delhi to Chandigarh and Delhi to Amritsar routes. From Delhi the railway line runs through Rohtak, 70 km north-west of Delhi, which was once a border town between the Sikhs and Marathas regions and the subject of frequent clashes.

Bhatinda, 296 km north-west of Delhi, was an important town of the Pathan Sur dynasty. Sirsa, to the south of Bhatinda,

is an ancient city but little remains apart from the city walls. Hansi, south-east of Sirsa, was where Colonel Skinner (of the legendary regiment 'Skinner's Horse') died. Faridkot, 350 km north-west of Delhi, was once the capital of a Sikh state of the same name and has a 700-year-old fort. Ferozepore is 382 km north-west of Delhi; the railway line continued to Lahore from here until partition.

Travellers' Notebook

Patient Punjabis
Visiting the Punjab for the first time, I was struck by how orderly people were compared with most other parts of India. Bus stations are well organised; unseemly rushes when a bus appears do not seem normal practice, and the art of queuing is respected. An attempted piece of queue jumping by a nonlocal soldier at Jullundur city station stirred up righteous indignation in the patient souls waiting their turn; the offender was given a sharp lecture on the evils of 'double lining' and was sent to the back of the queue. Good for the Punjabis

John King, England

Himachal Pradesh

Population: 5 million
Area: 55,673 square km
Capital: Simla
Main languages: Hindi, Pahari

The state of Himachal Pradesh came into being in its present form with the partition of the Punjab into Punjab and Haryana in 1966. Himachal Pradesh is essentially a mountain state – it takes in the transition zone from the plains to the high Himalaya, and in the trans-Himalayan region of Lahaul & Spiti actually crosses that mighty barrier to the Tibetan plateau. It's a delightful state for visitors, particularly during the hot season when people flock to its hill stations to escape the searing heat of the plains.

High points for the visitor include Simla, the 'summer capital' of British India and still one of India's most important hill stations. The Kulu Valley is simply one of the most beautiful areas on earth – a lush, green valley with the sparkling Beas River running through it and the snow-capped Himalayan peaks forming the background. Then there's Dharamsala, home-in-exile for the Dalai Lama, and a host of other hill stations, lakes, walks and mountains. In the far north of the state the winter snow melts, permitting visitors to explore for a few brief summer months the Tibetan culture of Keylong in Lahaul & Spiti.

Trekking & Mountaineering

See Lonely Planet's *Trekking in the Indian Himalaya* for more information on trekking in this region. The Himachal Pradesh tourist office has a brochure on trekking which briefly details a number of treks in the state. They also have three excellent large-scale maps of Himachal Pradesh, invaluable for trekkers.

The trekking season in Himachal Pradesh runs from mid-May to mid-

October. In Manali there is a Department of Mountaineering & Allied Sports (tel 42) which can advise you on trekking possibilities in the state and also on the numerous unscaled peaks. Unlike in Nepal, no trekking permits are necessary in Himachal Pradesh and this helps to make trekking here relatively cheap.

Equipment and provisions will depend very much on where you trek. In the lower country in the Kulu or Kangra valleys, or around Simla, there are many rest houses and villages. On the other hand, in Lahaul & Spiti the population is much less dense and conditions are more severe. You will need to be better equipped in terms of cold-weather gear, food and provisions. Some of the better-known treks are detailed in the appropriate sections. There are many forest rest houses, PWD rest houses and other semiofficial accommodation possibilities along the Himachal Pradesh trekking routes. Enquire at local tourist offices about using these places before setting off.

The *Trekking Guide* published by the HPTDC (Himachal Pradesh Tourism Development Corporation) lists 136

mountains over 5000 metres high. The majority of them are unclimbed, most not even named. It's virgin territory for mountaineers.

Wildlife

There are fishing possibilities in many places in Himachal Pradesh and a number of trout hatcheries have been established. The various local tourist offices can advise you on where to fish and how to obtain fishing licences. These are much cheaper than in Kashmir.

Some of the state's deer, antelope, mountain goats and sheep are now rather rare. Himalayan black bears and brown bears are found in many parts of the state; the black bear is fairly common but the brown bear is usually found only at higher elevations. Wild boar are found at lower elevations in certain districts.

Snow leopards are now very rare and only found at high elevations in the most remote parts of the state. Panthers and leopards are, however, still found in many forested regions. Himachal Pradesh has numerous kinds of pheasants and partridges and many mountain birds.

Temples

Although Himachal Pradesh does not have any particularly renowned temples, it does have many interesting and architecturally very diverse ones. In the Kangra and Chamba valleys there are several 8th to 10th-century temples in the Indo-Aryan sikhara style. Pagoda-style temples with multitiered roofs are found in the Kulu Valley. There are many temples of purely local design, often with interesting woodcarvings, particularly in the Chamba region.

In the south of the state there are numerous temples with elements of Moghul and Sikh design, while in several locations there are cave temples. Finally the Tibetans, who came to the state following the Chinese invasion of their country, have built colourful *gompas* (monasteries) and temples. The people of Lahaul & Spiti in the north of the state are also of Tibetan extraction and have many interesting gompas.

Things to Buy

The Kulu Valley is full of spinners and weavers, mostly men, and their fine shawls are very popular. These are made from the fleece shed in the summer by mountain goats. The shawls made from the hair of the pashmina goat are the finest. Chamba is well known for its leather chappals (sandals). In the high Himalaya soft, fleecy blankets known as *gudmas* are woven, as well as traditional rugs and numdas. In the bazaars you can find locally made jewellery and metalwork. Tibetan handicrafts include coral jewellery, carpets and religious paraphernalia.

Getting Around

Apart from two railway lines which are both narrow gauge and hence rather more 'fun' than 'transport', getting around Himachal Pradesh means taking a bus – unless you can afford a taxi. The two trains run from Kalka (just north of Chandigarh) to Simla, and from Pathankot along the Kangra Valley to Jogindarnagar.

Himachal Pradesh buses are generally the Indian norm – slow, crowded, uncomfortable and tiring. Things are made a little worse by the mountainous terrain. If you can manage to average 20 kph on a bus trip, you're doing well. Taxis are readily available but rather expensive. One way you can make a saving is to find a taxi on a return trip – in that case you can often knock the price down a bit. Ask the people running your hotel; they're sometimes in the know as to who is going where and when.

The HPTDC has a number of deluxe tourist bus services. They often operate overnight but usually only in the high seasons or on demand. Typical fares are Delhi to Manali 16 hours, Rs 250; Simla to Manali 10 hours, Rs 100; Chandigarh to Manali 11 hours, Rs 125.

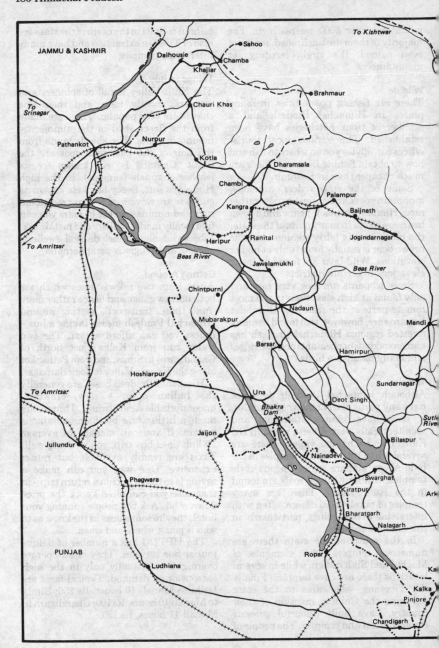

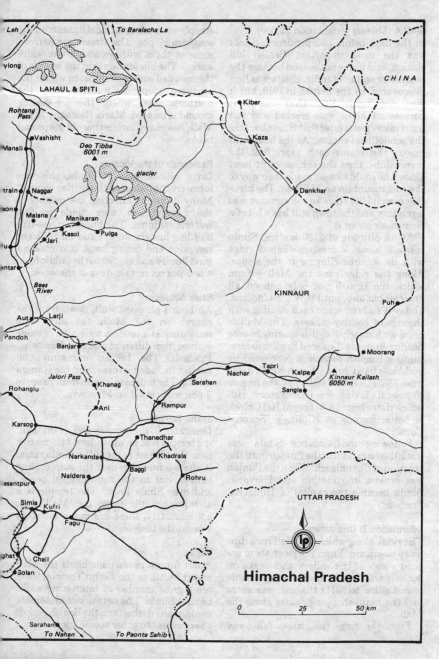

Himachal Pradesh

0   25   50 km

SIMLA (Shimla) (population 72,000)
In the days before independence, Simla was the most important British hill station, and in the hot season became the 'summer capital' of India. Simla was first 'discovered' by the British in 1819, but it was not until 1822 that the first permanent house was erected and not until many years later that Simla became the semiofficial capital. As the heat built up on the plains each year, first the memsahibs, then the sahibs, or at least those who could escape, made their way to the cool mountain air of Simla. The high-flown social life there in the summer was legendary and the town still has a bit of a British air about it.

At an altitude of 2130 metres, Simla sprawls along a crescent-shaped ridge with its suburbs clinging to the slopes. Along the ridge runs the Mall – from which the British not only banned all vehicles but also, until WW I, all Indians. Today it's a busy scene each evening with throngs of holiday-makers. The Mall is lined with stately English-looking houses bearing strangely displaced English names. Simla's English flavour is continued by buildings like Christ Church which dates from 1857, Gorton Castle, and the former Viceroyal Lodge on Observatory Hill which dates from 1888. Lajpat Rai Chowk is better known as Kipling's 'Scandal Corner'.

Following independence Simla was initially the capital of the Punjab until the creation of Chandigarh. When the Punjab was broken into Punjab and Haryana, Simla became the capital of Himachal Pradesh.

Information & Orientation
The ridge along which the Mall runs dips away westward. From the ridge there are good views of the valleys and peaks on both sides. You'll find the miserable tourist office (tel 3311), the best restaurants and the main shopping centre along the Mall.

From the ridge the streets fall away steeply with colourful local bazaars on the southern slopes. The streets are narrow, some of them with verandah-like 'sidewalks'. The bus station is in the middle of the crowded southern slope. In winter the southern slope is warmer than the northern side, where the ice-skating ground is located. Maria Brothers, 78 the Mall, has many interesting old maps and books.

Residence of the Viceroy
On a hillock west of Simla, this was formerly the palace of the British viceroy. Many decisions affecting the destiny of the subcontinent were made in this historic building. The huge, fortress-like building has six storeys and magnificent reception and dining halls. It contains a good library and is open to the public from 4 to 5 pm on certain days of the week.

State Museum
An hour's pleasant walk down from the church on the Mall, the nice little museum has a modest collection of stone statues from different places in Himachal Pradesh. The Indian miniatures on exhibit include pictures from the Kangra school. The museum is open from 10 am to 5 pm, and closed on Mondays.

Jakhu Temple
Dedicated to the monkey god, Hanuman, the temple is at an altitude of 2455 metres near the highest point of the Simla ridge. It offers a fine view over the surrounding valleys, out to the snow-capped peaks, and over Simla itself. The temple is a 45-minute walk from the Mall and, appropriately, there are many monkeys around the temple.

Walks
Apart from a promenade along the Mall and the walk to the Jakhu Temple, there are a great number of interesting walks around Simla. The network of motorable roads, many dating from the British period, offers access to other scenic spots.

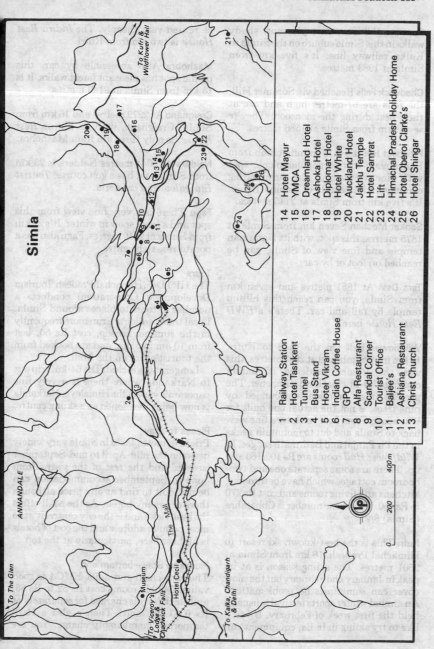

Simla

To The Glen

To Kufri & Wildflower Hall

ANNANDALE

The Mall

To Kalka, Chandigarh & Delhi

Museum

Hotel Cecil

To Viceroy's Lodge & Chadwick Falls

1 Railway Station
2 Hotel Tashkent
3 Tunnel
4 Bus Stand
5 Hotel Vikram
6 Indian Coffee House
7 GPO
8 Alfa Restaurant
9 Scandal Corner
10 Tourist Office
11 Baljee's
12 Ashiana Restaurant
13 Christ Church
14 Hotel Mayur
15 YMCA
16 Dreamland Hotel
17 Ashoka Hotel
18 Diplomat Hotel
19 Hotel White
20 Auckland Hotel
21 Jakhu Temple
22 Hotel Samrat
23 Lift
24 Himachal Pradesh Holiday Home
25 Hotel Oberoi Clarke's
26 Hotel Shingar

0   200   400m

Summer Hill There are pleasant, shady walks in this Simla suburb on the Simla to Kalka railway line. It's five km from Simla at 1983 metres.

Chadwick Falls Reached via Summer Hill, the falls are 67-metres high and are at their best during the monsoon. They're seven km from Simla at 1586 metres.

Prospect Hill It's a 15-minute climb from Boileauganj to this popular picnic spot with fine views over the surrounding country and a temple of Kamna Devia. It's five km from Simla at 2145 metres.

Sankat Mochan Seven km from Simla at 1875 metres, this spot, with its Hanuman temple and fine view of Simla, can be reached on foot or by car.

Tara Devi At 1851 metres and seven km from Simla, you can reach this hilltop temple by rail and car. There's a *PWD Rest House* here.

Wildflower Hall On the road to Kufri, 13 km from Simla and at 2593 metres, this was the former residence of Indian commander-in-chief Lord Kitchener. The present huge mansion, surrounded by pine trees, is not the actual one built for Kitchener. From here you have a fine view back to Simla and out to mountain peaks in the Pir Panjal and Badrinath ranges. In *Wildflower Hall* rooms are Rs 100/160 and up. There are some separate one and two-bedroom cottages which have bathrooms, kitchens and living rooms and cost Rs 270 to Rs 450. The phone number is Chharabra (Simla) 8/212.

Kufri This is the best-known ski resort in Himachal Pradesh, 16 km from Simla at 2501 metres. The skiing season is at its peak in January and February but the snow cover can sometimes be problematical. An annual winter sports festival is usually held the first week of February. If you'd like to try skiing in India, equipment can be rented very cheaply. The *Indira Rest House* is two km from Kufri.

Mashobra Also accessible by car, this picnic spot has pleasant forest walks. It is 13 km from Simla at 2149 metres.

Craignano At 2279 metres and 16 km from Simla, Craignano, with its hilltop *Rest House*, is only three km from Mashobra.

Naldera At 2044 metres Naldera is 23 km from Simla and has a golf course, *Tourist Bungalow* and cafeteria.

Fagu There is a very fine view from this spot and a lot of snow in winter. It's 22 km from Simla at 2510 metres. Fagu also has a potato research centre.

Tours
The HPTDC (Himachal Pradesh Tourism Development Corporation) conducts a number of tours to places around Simla. Local tours, which are run more frequently in the summer season, cost Rs 50, last from 10 am to 5 pm, and are booked from the tourist office on the Mall.

Longer tours include the 64-km trip out to Narkanda where there is a very fine panoramic view of the Himalaya. Narkanda is now being developed as a skiing centre.

Places to Stay
Prices in most places in Simla vary widely between the mid-April to mid-September 'season' and the rest of the year. From June to September accommodation can be difficult to find at any price although there are many hotels. As the Mall offers the best views and is the city centre, it's the most popular address and the cost of hotels is highest here, particularly at the top.

Places to Stay – bottom end
The very clean and quiet *YMCA* is good value. Double rooms cost Rs 52 to Rs 65, and electricity is charged for separately at Rs 0.80 per unit! There's also a Rs 5 temporary membership charge. You are

provided with a bath and an immersion heater which, according to one cold guest, 'takes at least six hours to heat the water to a temperature which gives you a chance of surviving'. Meals are also available although they don't get rave reviews. The YMCA is above Christ Church behind the big Hotel Mayur.

The *Hotel Tashkent*, just down the north side from The Mall and virtually above the Victory Tunnel, has rather primitive rooms with bath for Rs 27/40. On the south side of the ridge there are a number of cheap hotels around the bus stand, including the very basic but clean enough *Hotel Vikram*, where windowless and bathless singles cost Rs 45, singles with a window are Rs 50 and there's an extra Rs 5 charge for bedding. Doubles are Rs 80 to Rs 130.

Up from the the Mall the *Ashoka Hotel* is good value with reasonable rooms with bath from Rs 90. Not to mention monkeys clattering around on the corrugated iron roof at 6 am! On the way up to the Ashoka from the Mall you pass *Dreamland Hotel*, which is a bit cheaper with rooms from Rs 60 – good value for Simla.

Places to Stay - top end
Just beyond the 'lift' and Hotel Oberoi Clarke's at the eastern end of the Mall is the *Hotel Shingar* (tel 2881) with rooms from Rs 190 to Rs 210. It's of reasonable middle-price standard. Just beyond the Shingar is the *Hotel Samrat* where rooms cost Rs 130 to Rs 200.

If you take the road off to the north-east from the open area in front of Christ Church on the Mall, you'll soon come to the *Diplomat Hotel* (tel 3033). It's a relatively modern building but already showing serious signs of Indian decline. The rooms start from around Rs 180 but that's for a windowless little box. Better rooms with a view are Rs 240 and go up to Rs 300 to Rs 400, even more for suites. There's hot water in the bathrooms.

Just beyond the Diplomat, the *Hotel White* (tel 6136) is similar in standard but

a bit cheaper. Prices start from around Rs 130 for rooms with balcony and bathroom. It's reasonably well kept, bright and airy, and has good views from the rooms looking out from the hill. Down the hill on the Circular Rd is *Auckland Hotel* (tel 6315), a modern place a notch up-market from the Diplomat and the Hotel White. Rooms in this hotel are Rs 200/240.

You can't miss the sign for the big *Hotel Mayur* (tel 6047/9), which is just above Christ Church. Rooms cost Rs 200 to Rs 260 depending on their size and the view. It's a good standard middle-range Indian hotel. On Circular Rd down below the Mall ridge on the north side is *Lord's Grey Hotel* (tel 5146) where rooms are Rs 145 to Rs 215.

Simla's top hotel is the *Hotel Oberoi Clarke's* (tel 6091/5) on the Mall at the eastern end. Rooms are Rs 650/850 including meals. The other Oberoi hotel, the Cecil along the Mall to the west, seems to be permanently closed.

On Cart Rd on the south-eastern side of the slope, down below Oberoi Clarke's, is the state government's *Holiday Home* (tel 6031/8) where doubles are Rs 185 to Rs 400, deluxe doubles Rs 250 to Rs 450. Beyond here is the *Himland Hotel* (tel 3595) on Circular Rd. Rooms cost from Rs 235/350, but it's so far round the road you'd need a car to stay there.

Places to Eat
Curiously Simla is not as well endowed with restaurants as other hill stations – it's a long way behind Darjeeling for example. All the better-known restaurants are along the Mall. *Baljee's* is often crowded in the evening – it has the standard Indian non-vegetarian menu, zero decor and reasonable food. Upstairs there is an associated restaurant known as *Fascination*. Count on around Rs 60 for a meal.

A little further down the Mall the *Alfa Restaurant* also has the standard non-vegetarian menu. Just beyond the Alfa there are two *Indian Coffee Houses* with south Indian food and snacks at reasonable prices. There are various small restaurants in the bazaar area on the southern slopes. The *Sher-e-Punjab* on the Mall near the lift is pretty good. Just beyond the Indian Coffee House is *Ajays* which serves excellent set meals for Rs 16 to Rs 24.

The state tourism department has two restaurants at the main square on the ridge, close to the tourist office. The *Ashiana* upstairs is much brighter than the gloomy *Goofa* down below. Prices are much the same in both restaurants. The ritzier Ashiana is supposed to be a cut above the cafe-like Goofa, although the latter does have good pizzas. The food is fairly mediocre; Simla is not going to be anybody's culinary highlight.

The *Golden Dragon*, in the Holiday Home, has reasonable, if slightly expensive, Chinese food.

Getting There & Away

Air There is a daily Delhi to Simla Vayudoot flight which costs Rs 485. Vayudoot also flies to Kulu for Rs 160.

Bus A bus from Chandigarh is the easiest way to get to Simla. The 117-km trip takes four hours and costs Rs 22 in an ordinary bus or Rs 40 in a deluxe bus. You can reach Chandigarh from Delhi by a variety of buses and by air. The bus trip straight from Delhi takes around 10 hours and costs Rs 104 in a deluxe bus.

There are buses north from Simla to other hill stations in Himachal Pradesh such as Dharamsala or the Kulu Valley. From Simla to Manali costs Rs 50 and takes 11 hours. To Dharamsala costs Rs 57 and takes 10 to 12 hours. To Mandi it's about six hours for Rs 25. Dehra Dun is a weary nine-hour trip for Rs 45. A taxi to Manali would cost about Rs 1000.

Train The journey to Simla by rail involves a change from broad gauge to narrow gauge at Kalka, a little north of Chandigarh. The narrow-gauge trip to Simla takes nearly six hours. Add on two or more hours to change trains at Kalka

plus the trip from Delhi, and you'll find it much faster by bus. On the other hand the rail trip is great fun! The total distance is 364 km from Delhi and the fare is Rs 45 in 2nd class, Rs 159 in 1st.

Getting Around

Local bus services operate from the Cart Rd bus stand. A bus runs from the stand to Boileauganj in the west. Apart from that the best way around Simla is to walk. A little east of the bus stand a two-part 'tourist lift' takes you up to the Mall for Rs 1. It saves a long and tedious climb and it's the only lift I've ever seen with a fire to keep the operator warm!

AROUND SIMLA
Kalka

The narrow-gauge railway line from Kalka to Simla was built in 1903-04. Although going by road is cheaper and quicker, the rail trip is fun.

Pinjore, 21 km south-east of Kalka near Chandigarh, has a Moghul summerhouse and garden, built by Fidai Khan, who also built the Badshahi Mosque in Lahore, Pakistan.

Chail

This was once the summer capital of the princely state of Patalia. Today the old palace is a luxurious hotel. Chail is 45 km from Simla via Kufri, or you can reach it via Kandaghat on the Simla to Kalka road or narrow-gauge rail line.

Chail, at an altitude of 2250 metres, is built on three hills, one of which is topped by the Chail Palace, and one by the ancient Sidh temple. Chail also boasts a temple of quite another religion – cricket. Here you will find the highest cricket pitch in the world!

Places to Stay In the *Chail Palace Hotel* (tel Chail 43/7) rooms are Rs 240 to Rs 550 but the Maharaja and Maharani suites are Rs 800 and Rs 1000. Chail also has a number of HPTDC cottages and log huts from Rs 300 to Rs 475, and the *Himneel*

Himachal Pradesh Top: Children in Malana, Kulu Valley (HF)
Left: Hotel signs at McLeod Ganj, Dharamsala (HF)
Right: Bringing the crops in, Kulu Valley (HF)

Jammu & Kashmir Top: Kashmiri children on the Pahalgam to Aru walk (TW)
Bottom: A 'supermarket' shikara on Dal Lake, Kashmir (TW)

Hotel with rooms from Rs 45 to Rs 105. There are also a number of local hotels.

Getting There & Away There are direct buses to Chail from Kalka and Simla.

Kasauli

This pleasant little hill station at 1927 metres is only a short distance north of Kalka. It's an interesting 15-km trek from Kalka to Kasauli, or you can get there from Dharampur, which is on the Kalka to Simla railway line.

Only four km from Kasauli is Monkey Point, a picnic spot and lookout with a very fine view over the plains to the south and to the mountains in the north. Sabathu, 38 km from Kasauli, has a 19th-century Gurkha-built fortress.

Places to Stay & Eat There is a *PWD Rest House* and a number of private guest houses such as the *Alasia, Morris* and *Kalyan*. The *Hotel Ros Common* has rooms from Rs 300. In Dharampur the simple *Mazdoor Dhaba* restaurant near the station has good (and cheap) vegetarian meals and a dormitory upstairs.

Solan

This town is between Kalka and Simla, on both the railway line and the road. It's named after the Soloni Devi Temple on the southern side of the town. There are pleasant picnic spots and streams around this 1350-metre hill station.

Places to Stay & Eat The HPTDC *Tourist Bungalow* has rooms from Rs 65 to Rs 165 and dorm beds as well. It's a noisy place as it is on the main road.

Narkanda

At 2700 metres, 64 km from Simla, this is a popular spot for viewing the Himalaya, particularly from the 3300-metre Hattu Peak. Narkanda has recently been developed as a skiing centre. The season lasts from late December to early March

and you can take 10-day courses which include your room and board.

From Narkanda you can make trips to Baggi and Khadrala, which are on the Hindustan to Tibet road leading to the Tibetan border. Or you can visit the apple-growing area around Kotgarh or continue to the Kulu Valley via Luhri.

Places to Stay The HPTDC *Hotel Himview* has doubles at Rs 90 and dorm beds for Rs 15. Reservations are made through the tourist office in Simla. There's also a *PWD Rest House*.

Tattapani

There's a direct bus to these popular sulphur hot springs, 51 km from Simla and at only 655 metres. Doubles in the *Tourist Bungalow* are Rs 60.

Chabba

This *Rest House*, 35 km from Simla, is a pleasant five-km walk from Basantpur, on the road to Tattapani.

Thanedhar

This is a centre for apple growing, 82 km from Simla on the route past Narkanda.

Baggi & Khadrala

Also past Narkanda there are *Rest Houses* in both these places. Baggi is 82 km from Simla at 2648 metres, Khadrala is 11 km further on at 2987 metres.

Rohru

Situated 129 km from Simla, this is the site for the Rohru Fair which takes place during two days each April. The temple of Devta Shikri is the centre for this colourful fair. The Pabar River, which runs through Rohru, is noted for its trout; there's a trout hatchery 13 km upstream at Chirgaon. Haktoti, a little before Rohru, has an interesting ancient Hindu temple dedicated to the goddess Durga. The temple contains a metre-high image of the eight-armed goddess, made of copper and bronze.

Places to Stay There's a *Rest House* in Rohru, a small *Forest Rest House* (booked in Rohru) at Chirgaon and log cabins at Seema, eight km upstream towards Chirgaon.

OTHER PLACES IN THE SOUTH

There are a number of other places of interest in the south of the state, where Himachal Pradesh borders Uttar Pradesh and Haryana. This district is known as Sirmur.

Paonta Sahib

Situated on the Yamuna River, on the border with Uttar Pradesh, Paonta Sahib is a transit point for travellers from the hill stations of northern Uttar Pradesh to Simla and other hill stations in Himachal Pradesh.

Paonta Sahib is linked with Gobind Singh, the 10th of the Sikhs' gurus who lived here. At Bhangani, 23 km away, he achieved a great military victory when his forces defeated the combined might of 22 hill-country kingdoms. His weapons are displayed in the town and his gurdwara still overlooks the river.

Places to Stay There's the HPTDC *Hotel Yamuna* with doubles from Rs 120 to Rs 270. There are also local hotels.

Renuka

North-west of Paonta Sahib a major festival is held each November at this lake. There's a small zoo and a wildlife sanctuary with deer and many water birds.

Places to Stay The HPTDC have a *Tourist Inn* at the lake with rooms for Rs 70, and the *Hotel Renuka* with rooms from Rs 105 to Rs 200.

Nahan

At 932 metres, Nahan is in the Shivalik hills, where the climb to the Himalayan heights commences. There are a number of interesting walks around the town, including the trek to Choordhar (3647

metres) from where there are fine views of the plains to the south and the Sutlej River. Saketi, 14 km south of Nahan, has a fossil park with life-sized fibreglass models of prehistoric animals whose fossilised skeletons were unearthed here.

Places to Stay There are a number of rest houses and local hotels.

THE SOUTH-WEST
Bhakra-Nangal

The giant Bhakra Dam, one of the largest in the world, provides irrigation water for a vast area of the Punjab and also produces hydroelectric power. The public relations office at the dam arranges permits to inspect this major project.

Bilaspur & Naina Devi

In Bilaspur, on the route from Chandigarh to Mandi, and on the shore of the Gobindsagar Lake, are the interesting Vyas Gufa, Lakshmi Narayan and Radhashyam temples. There are fine views over the lake from Naina Devi.

MANDI

The town of Mandi, on the Beas River, is the gateway to the Kulu Valley. From here you climb up the narrow, spectacular gorge of the river and emerge from this grey and barren stretch into the green and inviting Kulu Valley. At an altitude of only 760 metres temperatures are higher here and Mandi mainly serves as a travel crossroads, as its name, which means 'market', might suggest.

Mandi is 202 km north of Chandigarh and 110 km south of Manali. Dharamsala is 150 km to the north-west on the road to Pathankot.

Rewalsar Lake

The Rewalsar Lake, a pilgrimage centre for Hindus, Buddhists and Sikhs, is 24 km south-east of Mandi. There is a mountain cave-refuge for many foreign Buddhists near here. You can stay in the Tibetan

Buddhist monastery for Rs 2 and there's also a hotel.

Sivarati Festival

This is one of the most interesting festivals in Himachal Pradesh. It lasts for a week and deities from all over Mandi district are brought here, and large numbers of people have darshan at the Bhutnath Temple.

Places to Stay & Eat

Mandi has a *Tourist Bungalow* with a variety of rooms from Rs 90 to Rs 250. There are also dorm beds at Rs 20. It is a steep 10-minute walk up from the bus stand, and is reportedly not that great.

For real maharaja standards try the *Raj Mahal*, a wonderful old palace-hotel. It's run down, but at Rs 40/110 for singles/doubles who cares. There's a pleasant garden, strange old rooms and large, ancient bathrooms.

There are also a number of extremely basic, cheap hotels in the town. The *Adarsh Hotel*, just across the bridge in the old town, is a rock-bottom place. The *Cafe Shiraz* is run by the state tourist office and serves snacks.

KANGRA VALLEY

The beautiful Kangra Valley starts near Mandi, runs north, then bends west and extends to Shahpur near Pathankot. To the north the valley is flanked by the Dhauladhar mountain range, to the side of which Dharamsala clings. There are a number of places of interest along the valley, including the popular hill station Dharamsala.

The main Pathankot to Mandi road runs through the Kangra Valley and there is a narrow-gauge railway line from Pathankot as far as Jogindarnagar. The Kangra school of painting developed in this valley.

Baijnath

Only 16 km from Palampur, the small town of Baijnath is an important

pilgrimage place due to its very old Shiva temple. The temple is said to date from 804 AD. There is a *PWD Rest House* in Baijnath.

Palampur

A pleasant little town surrounded by tea plantations, Palampur is 35 km from Dharamsala and stands at 1260 metres. The main road runs right through Palampur and there are some pleasant walks around the town.

Places to Stay & Eat The HPTDC *Hotel T-Bud* is about a km from the bus station and has rooms for Rs 150 and Rs 200, and dorm beds for Rs 20. Meals are available.

The new *Silver Oaks Motel*, 2½ km from the bus station, has great views. Double rooms cost Rs 150. For something cheaper, try the *Hotel Sawney*, near the bus station. Rooms in this basic place cost Rs 45.

The HPTDC *Neugal Cafe* is 1½ km from the Hotel T-Bud.

Kangra

There is little to see in this ancient town, 18 km almost directly south of Dharamsala, but at one time it was a place of considerable importance. The famous temple of Bajreshwari Devi was of such legendary wealth that every invader worth their salt took time to sack it. Mahmud of Ghazni carted off a fabulous fortune in gold, silver and jewels in 1009. In 1360 it was plundered once again by Tughlaq but it was still able to recover and, in Jehangir's reign, was paved in plates of pure silver.

The disastrous earthquake which shook the valley in 1905 destroyed the temple, which has since been rebuilt. Kangra also has a much-ruined fort on a ridge overlooking the Baner and Manjhi rivers. It too was sacked by Mahmud, captured by Jehangir in 1620 and severely damaged in the 1905 quake.

Kangra has a *PWD Rest House*.

Jawalamukhi

In the Beas Valley, 34 km south of Kangra, the temple of Jawalamukhi is famous for its eternally burning flame. It's the most popular pilgrimage site in Himachal Pradesh.

Places to Stay The HPTDC *Hotel Jwalaji* (tel 81) has rooms from Rs 125 to Rs 175, and Rs 200 with air-con; and there's a Rs 20 dorm. There's also a *PWD Rest House*.

Nadaun, south of Jawalamukhi on the Beas River, has another *Rest House*.

Chintpurni

Near Bharwain, 80 km south of Dharamsala and across the Beas, this town has an important temple.

Masrur

Three km from Haripur, about 15 km south of Kangra, Masrur has 15 richly carved rock-cut temples in the Indo-Aryan style. They are partly ruined but still show their relationship to the better-known and much larger temples at Ellora in Maharashtra.

Nurpur

Only 24 km from Pathankot on the Mandi to Pathankot road, this town acquired its name in 1622 when Jehangir named it after his wife, Nurjahan. Nurpur fort is now in ruins but still has some finely carved reliefs. A ruined Krishna temple, also finely carved, stands within the fort. Nurpur has a *PWD Rest House*.

TREKS FROM KANGRA VALLEY

From Baijnath you can make an interesting trek to Dharamsala, Chamba or Manali. The first day's trek to Bir Khas can be done by bus. At Bara Bhangal, reached on Day 6, you can choose to go east to Manali or west to Dharamsala or Chamba.

Day 1	Baijnath to Bir Khas	1600 m	26 km
Day 2	Bir Khas to Rajgaunda	2500 m	13 km
Day 3	Rajgaunda to Palachak Deota	2750 m	8 km
Day 4	Palachak Deota to Panardu Got	3700 m	8 km
Day 5	Panardu Got to Thamsar Jot	4750 m	6 km
Day 6	Thamsar Jot to Bara Bhangal	2541 m	14 km

From here you can turn west and in four days reach Chanota which is on the Chamba to Dharamsala trek – see Treks from Chamba for details. The days' walks are:

Day 7	Bara Dhangal to Dhardi	21 km
Day 8	Dhardi to Naya Graun	24 km
Day 9	Naya Graun to Holi	16 km
Day 10	Holi to Chanota	13 km

Alternatively you can turn east, and a day's trek will bring you to the Manali Pass treks described in the 'Treks from Manali' section. There are a number of possible routes down to Manali.

DHARAMSALA (population 16,000)

The hill station of Dharamsala is actually split into two totally separate parts. Close to the snow line, the town is built along a spur of the Dhauladhar range and varies in height from 1250 metres at the Civil and Depot Bazaar up through Kotwali Bazaar and Forsyth Ganj to nearly 1800 metres at McLeod Ganj. There's quite a temperature variation between the top and bottom.

As in other hill stations there is a wide variety of short and long walks, but Dharamsala has the additional attraction of its strong Tibetan influence. It was here that the Dalai Lama and his followers fled after the Chinese invasion of Tibet.

The Dalai Lama is the recipient of the 1989 Nobel Peace Prize, awarded to him not only for his spiritual activities but for 'his struggle for the liberation of Tibet'. It can also be seen as a reproach to the

Chinese government in the wake of the Tiananmen Square massacre. Throughout his 30 years of exile, for religious as well as practical reasons the Dalai Lama has worked for a peaceful settlement with China, which is in line with his pacifist approach to all personal and political conflicts in the world. Tibetans in exile view the award not only as well-deserved recognition for their leader but as acknowledgement of the long struggle for peaceful negotiation in the face of extreme provocation. As the Dalai Lama said in his acceptance speech: 'I hope this prize will provide courage to the six million people of Tibet...(it) is a profound recognition of their faith and perseverance'.

For the serious student of Tibetan culture there's the monastery up at McLeod Ganj and the school of Tibetan studies and its library, one of the best in the world for studying Tibet and its culture, about midway between McLeod Ganj and the lower town.

For the not so serious, McLeod Ganj is a small freak centre with lots of Tibetan-run hotels and restaurants, all the menu favourites, low prices, crowds of western travellers – almost another Kathmandu in fact. McLeod Ganj is full of colour and energy: those little Tibetan terriers (yappy but spry) scoot around everywhere; in the middle of the main street there's a small temple with a giant prayer wheel; and you may even catch a glimpse of the Dalai Lama cruising by in his Mercedes.

Of course Dharamsala was originally a British hill resort and one of the most poignant memorials of that era is the pretty Church of St John in the Wilderness. It is only a short distance below McLeod Ganj and has beautiful stained-glass windows. Here Lord Elgin, Viceroy of India, was buried after his death in 1863. There are many fine walks and even finer views around Dharamsala. The sheer rock wall of Dhauladhar rises behind McLeod Ganj. From the road up from the lower town it seems just an arm's length away.

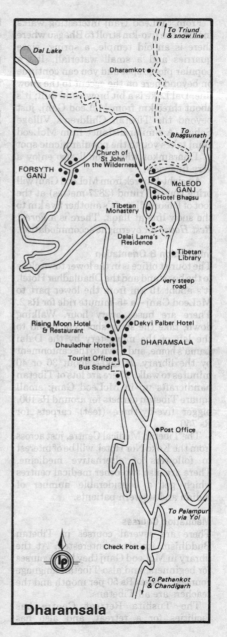

Dharamsala

From McLeod Ganj interesting walks include the two-km stroll to Bhagsu where there is an old temple, a spring, slate quarries and a small waterfall. It's a popular picnic spot and you can continue on beyond here on the ascent to the snow line. Dal Lake is a bit brown and dull; it's about three km from McLeod Ganj, just beyond the Tibetan Children's Village School. A similar distance from McLeod Ganj takes you to the popular picnic spot at Dharamkot where you'll also enjoy a very fine view.

An eight-km trek from McLeod Ganj will bring you to Triund (2827 metres) at the foot of Dhauladhar. It's another five km to the snow line at Ilaqa. There is a *Forest Rest House* for overnight accommodation.

Information & Orientation

The tourist office is in the lower town close to the bus stand and the Dhauladhar Hotel. It's about 10 km from the lower part to McLeod Ganj – a 45-minute ride for Rs 2. There are buses every hour. Walking down, take the steep short cut round to the left of the monastery by the Dalai Lama's home, and down to the cantonment by the library. It takes about 30 or 40 minutes to walk. There are lots of Tibetan handicrafts up in McLeod Ganj: small square Tibetan carpets for around Rs 100, bigger five-by-three (feet) carpets for Rs 750.

The Tibetan Medical Centre, just across from the Koko Nor Hotel, will be of interest to followers of alternative medicine. There are also two other medical centres which get a considerable number of Indian and western patients.

Meditation Courses

There are several courses in Tibetan Buddhism for those interested. At the library in McLeod Ganj they have courses for beginners, and also Tibetan language courses. It costs Rs 50 per month and the teachers are all Tibetans.

The Tushita Retreat Centre has facilities for a retreat, and also has Buddhism courses. The monks here are either Tibetan or western. Even if you don't stay at the Retreat Centre it is possible to attend some of the courses.

There are also many courses offered by individual monks who live in monasteries.

Meeting His Holiness the Dalai Lama

Travellers may request an audience with His Holiness the Dalai Lama of Tibet at his residence in Dharamsala. However, you need to do so at least one month in advance (by contacting his Private Office in McLeod Ganj) because he is so much in demand by Tibetans, Indians and westerners alike.

Meeting this 14th incarnation of Chenresig, Tibetan Buddhism's deity of Universal Compassion, is no ordinary event. Not so much because of his title, nor even because of the high degree of reverence in which he is held by the Tibetan people; but more because of how it feels to be in his company. As an American friend put it: 'When you look at him, he is the size of a normal human being; but when you look away; you realise that his presence is filling the whole room'.

After waiting, strangely nervous, in the anteroom, we were ushered into his reception room for our audience with His Holiness, which seemed to speed by in a flash. However, several strong impressions remain, including the way in which he gives his whole attention to questions. He really listens, and pauses before replying, to give consideration to the subject matter. He responds rather than reacts to the issue under discussion. There is a wisdom in his thinking which comes through clearly in his words, filled as they are with common sense and realism.

I remember his direct and friendly gaze, his firm handshake, and a sense of compassion almost palpable. He also has a superb sense of humour, often remarked upon by those who meet him. He laughs often and easily – and what a laugh! He throws back his head to release a deep, thorough chuckle which rises from his abdomen and expresses pure mirth. It is kind laughter, and highly infectious.

As our audience came to a close, he accompanied us to the door. With each of us in turn, he took one of our hands in both of his. Bowing slightly over the joined hands, he looked up into our faces and beamed. Following this farewell, we seemed to be walking inches above the streets of McLeod Ganj. And we just couldn't stop smiling.

Vyvyan Cayley

Places to Stay

Dharamsala Dharamsala has two accommodation areas – the lower part of town and the upper part known as McLeod Ganj. In the lower part Dharamsala's deluxe hotel is the HPTDC *Dhauladhar Hotel* (tel 2107) with a Rs 20 dorm or doubles from Rs 125 to Rs 250. Prices are reduced 25% for single occupancy. There's a restaurant and a pleasant garden patio – ideal for sipping a sunset beer while you look out over the plains below.

As in McLeod Ganj, the pick of the cheapies are all Tibetan. There's the extremely laid-back and rather basic *Rising Moon Hotel & Restaurant* with dorm beds and rooms for around Rs 20, some with bathroom. Behind it is the *Tibet United Association Hotel* with rooms at similar prices.

Just left from the fountain you'll find the *Dekyi Palber Hotel*. Finally there's the *Hotel Simla* opposite the tourist office, which has good rooms with bath for Rs 65, and downhill beyond the bus stand is the *Sun & Snow*.

McLeod Ganj Most western visitors to Dharamsala stay not in the main part of town but 500 metres (and 10 km by road) higher up the hill at McLeod Ganj. Here the Tibetan community who followed the Dalai Lama into exile have set up a whole series of hotels and restaurants. The accent is very much on cheapness but the hotels are clean and the restaurants are surprisingly good. For those heartily sick of dhal and rice they offer a wide range of Tibetan-Chinese dishes plus western travellers' favourites such as banana pancakes.

McLeod Ganj is very popular and so many places are permanently full, but a quick wander will soon turn something up. The Bhagsu road from the bus stop is the best bet. The *Hotel Tibet* (tel 2587) is simple and straightforward but also about the most luxurious of the Tibetan hotels. Rooms with common bath cost Rs 40, and Rs 100 with bath. They also have more expensive deluxe rooms, and there's a popular restaurant here.

Further up the Bhagsu road, the *Koko Nor Hotel* has rooms for Rs 25 to Rs 35. The *Green Hotel* is a popular cheapie and has doubles for Rs 25 with common bath, and Rs 50 with bath. The *Kalsang Guest*

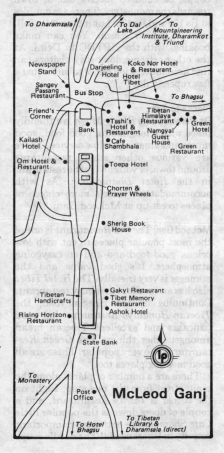

McLeod Ganj

House up the hill from the Green Guest House has singles/doubles for Rs 20/30 with common bath. The *Tibetan Himalaya Restaurant* has rooms a few rupees cheaper. At the *Namgyal Guest House* there are rooms for Rs 25, Rs 30 and Rs 35.

Away from the Bhagsu road, just below the main street, is the very popular *Om Hotel*, with prices around Rs 25. On the main street the *Toepa Hotel* is also in the standard Rs 25 price range.

For those determined to spend more, the HPTDC has the *Hotel Bhagsu*, a couple of hundred metres out of town towards the monastery. There are doubles at Rs 150 and Rs 175, but it is usually full, even in the off season. You can make bookings with the HPTDC in Delhi. At the other extreme, long-stay visitors can find accommodation out of town for just a few rupees a day.

Places to Eat
Dharamsala The *Rising Moon* is a friendly place with a long menu, good food, good music and amazingly slow service. There are various other small restaurants around town, or you can try the restaurant in the *Hotel Dhauladhar*. As with accommodation, there's more choice of places to eat up at McLeod Ganj.

McLeod Ganj The *Om Restaurant* is one of the most popular places to eat with low prices, good food and and an easygoing atmosphere. It's good value and the manager is very friendly. The *Hotel Tibet* also has an excellent and busy restaurant. Continuing up the Bhagsu road, the *Tibetan Himalaya Restaurant* has good pancakes and excellent Tibetan bread amongst other things. The *Green Restaurant* is also very popular. These are all good meeting places too.

There are a number of places along the main street from the bus stop. Right on the corner is *Tashi's Restaurant*, and a couple of doors down is the popular little *Cafe Shambhala* – eating is an important activity in Dharamsala! The noodle soups

in the *Darjeeling Hotel* rate as some of the best, and the *Rising Horizon Restaurant* has received good raves from a number of travellers.

Other places include the *Tibet Memory Restaurant* and *Friend's Corner*, which is good for a drink either downstairs or up on the roof. Overall, food in McLeod Ganj is a pleasant change from the Indian norm.

Getting There & Away
If you're taking an early morning bus, it's probably an idea to spend the night down in the lower town – all the buses start from there. You can also make train reservations at the railway booking office, although they have a quota of only two reservations per day per train.

There are about four buses a day to Simla and Delhi, just one or two to other destinations. Approximate distances, times (in hours) and fares from Dharamsala are:

	distance	time	fare
Manali	253 km	12½	Rs 53-65
Kulu	214 km	10	Rs 50-61
Simla	317 km	10	Rs 67
Chandigarh	248 km	9	Rs 47
Pathankot	90 km	3½	Rs 17
Delhi	526 km	14	Rs 72
Jullundur	197 km	8	Rs 25

DALHOUSIE (population 5000)
Sprawling over and around five hills, Dalhousie was, in the British era, a sort of 'second string' hill station. A place where those who could not aspire to Simla went. The town was founded by Lord Dalhousie, and has some pleasant walks.

Today Dalhousie also has a busy population of Tibetan refugees – if you take the footpath from Subhash Chowk to Gandhi (GPO) Chowk, you'll pass brightly painted low-relief pictures the Tibetans have carved into the rocks. There is a nice little Tibetan refugee handicrafts shop with carpets whose unusual designs feature rabbits and elephants. It's by GPO Chowk. With its dense forest, old English houses and colourful Tibetans, Dalhousie can be a good place to spend some time.

About two km from GPO Chowk along Ajit Singh Rd, Panch Pulla 'five bridges' could be quite a pleasant spot, but it's disfigured by the series of horrible concrete steps and seats built over the stream. Along the way there's a small, and easily missed, freshwater spring known as Satdhana. Kalatope is 8½ km from the GPO and offers a fine view over the surrounding country. There's a *Forest Rest House* here. Lakhi Mandi, 15 km out and at around 3000 metres, has stupendous mountain views.

Information & Orientation

The tourist office (tel 36) is by the bus stand, but Dalhousie is very scattered. Most of the shops are clustered around GPO Chowk, while the 'town' – if Dalhousie can be spoken of as such a thing – is crowded down the hillside close to

Subhash Chowk, a steep uphill climb from the bus stand. The houses almost stand on top of one another.

Places to Stay

Dalhousie has plenty of hotels, although a fair number of them have a run-down, left-by-the-Raj feel to them.

Prices fluctuate with the season. In the off season hotels discount by up to 50% and even top-end hotels shouldn't cost more than Rs 100.

Places to Stay – bottom end

The tourist bungalow known as the *Hotel Geetanjali* (tel 55), is on the hill just above the bus stand and has doubles ranging from Rs 90 to Rs 140. The rooms are extraordinarily large and even contain separate living rooms.

The *Youth Hostel* near the bus stand has dorm beds for Rs 20, or Rs 6 if you are a member.

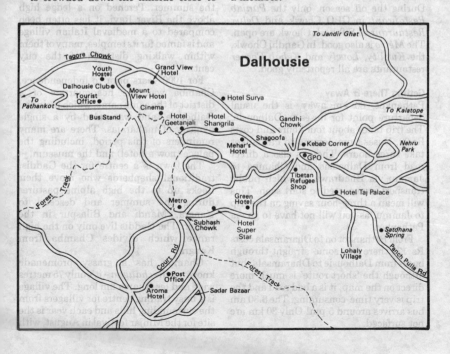

Places to Stay - middle

The *Hotel Shangrila* is an old house which has been converted. It is within walking distance of GPO Chowk and has very good views. Doubles cost between Rs 125 and Rs 250.

The new *Hotel Surya* (tel 58) in the Mall also has rooms for Rs 125 to Rs 250. The *Grand View Hotel* (tel 23) has good views of the surrounding area and charges Rs 110 to Rs 225 for doubles.

The *Mount View Hotel* has been completely rebuilt after a fire some years ago and charges Rs 150/400 for singles/ doubles.

Places to Stay - top end

The *Aroma Hotel* on Court Rd near the Mall has rooms with a touch of the Raj for Rs 200 to Rs 400. Some rooms have refrigerators as well as TV.

Places to Eat

During the off season, only the *Punjab Restaurant* in GPO Chowk and *Delux Restaurant* in Subhash Chowk are open. The *Metro* is also good. In Gandhi Chowk, the *Kwality, Lovely* and *Kebab Corner* restaurants are all reportedly good.

Getting There & Away

Pathankot, 80 km away, is the usual departure point for buses to Dalhousie. The trip takes about four hours and costs Rs 22. Buses from Jammu to Pathankot take three hours. There is also a direct road from Dalhousie and Chamba to Jammu via Bhadrawa on which public transport is expected to start soon. This will mean a three-hour saving on the trip to Jammu, as you will not have to go via Pathankot.

From Pathankot on to Dharamsala costs Rs 17; there are some straight-through buses from Dalhousie to Dharamsala, but although the 'short route' is much more direct on the map, it is a bad road and the trip is very time-consuming. The 8.30 am bus arrives around 5 pm! Only 30 km are not surfaced.

KHAJIAR

This grassy 'marg' is 22 km from Dalhousie. Over a km long and nearly a km wide, it is ringed by pine trees with a lake in the middle. There's a golf course here and a golden-domed temple. The wood carvings in the temple are very impressive and date back to the 14th century.

Places to Stay

The tourist bungalow, *Hotel Devdar*, has dorm beds at Rs 20 and doubles at Rs 75 to Rs 125. Other alternatives are the *Youth Hostel* with dorm beds at Rs 10 and the *PWD Rest House*.

Getting There & Away

You can walk there in a day, or go by bus.

CHAMBA

Situated 56 km from Dalhousie, beyond Khajiar, Chamba is at 926 metres – quite a bit lower than Dalhousie, so it's warmer in the summer. Perched on a ledge high above the River Ravi, it has often been compared to a medieval Italian village and is famed for its temples, many of them within walking distance of the city centre.

For 1000 years prior to independence, Chamba was the headquarters of a district of the same name, which included Dalhousie, and was ruled by a single dynasty of maharajas. There are many reminders of this period, including the palace (now a hotel) and the museum.

The town is a centre for the Gaddis, traditional shepherds who move their flocks up to the high alpine pastures during the summer and descend to Kangra, Mandi and Bilaspur in the winter. The Gaddis live only on the high range which divides Chamba from Kangra.

Chamba has a grassy promenade known as the *chaugan* – it's only 75 metres wide and less than a km long. The village is a busy trading centre for villagers from the surrounding hills and each year is the site for the Minjar festival in August, with a colourful procession and busy crowds of Gaddi, Churachi, Bhatti and Gujjar people. An image of Lord Raghuvira leads the procession and other gods and goddesses follow in palanquins.

Chamba's Temples

The Chamundra Temple on top of a hill gives an excellent view of Chamba with its slate-roof houses (some of them up to 300 years old), the River Ravi and the surrounding countryside. It's a steep half-hour climb.

Next to the maharaja's palace is the temple complex of Laxmi Naryan which contains six temples, three dedicated to Shiva and three to Vishnu, the oldest dating back to the 10th century, the newest to 1828. The Hariraya Temple is also dedicated to Vishnu and is in the Sikhara style of architecture.

Bhuri Singh Museum

Chamba also has the Bhuri Singh Museum with an interesting collection relating to the art and culture of this region – particularly the miniature paintings of the Basohli and Kangra schools. It is open from 10 am to 5 pm daily except Sunday. The Rang Mahal palace in the upper part of town was badly fire-damaged, but some of its murals are now in the museum.

Places to Stay & Eat

The HPTDC has two tourist bungalows: the *Hotel Champak* with doubles from Rs 40 to Rs 50, dorm beds at Rs 15; and the *Hotel Iravati* with rooms at Rs 100 and Rs 150 for doubles.

The *Hotel Akhand Chandi* (tel 2371) on College Rd has rooms at Rs 50 to Rs 60 for singles and Rs 75 for doubles. The *Janta Hotel* is fairly cheap.

Meals are available in the *Ravi View Cafe* and the *Hotel Iravati*. Despite its grotty appearance, the *Gupta Dhaba*, opposite RK Tailors near the GPO, has excellent food; and at the *Khalsa Tea Stall* you can get butter toast with real Chamba butter.

Getting There & Away

Taxis and jeeps can be hired in Dalhousie but they're expensive. The local bus is Rs 12 and takes two hours, or you can walk there in two days, resting overnight in Khajiar. Buses from Pathankot take five hours and leave every two hours.

From Chamba trekkers can make an interesting, but hard-going, trek through Bharmour and Triund to Dharamsala. Or via Tisa you can trek all the way into Lahaul or Kashmir.

TREKS FROM CHAMBA

There are a number of interesting treks from Chamba, both short out-and-back treks and longer treks to places like Dharamsala. The shorter ones include the eight-km walk to Sarol, 24 km to Bandal and the 40-km trek to Chhatrari. In Chhatrari, on the route to Brahmaur, the temple of Devi Adi Shakti is dedicated to the goddess of primeval energy.

Brahmaur (Brahmpura)

Vehicles can cover the whole 65 km from Chamba to Brahmaur, although the last 16 km from Kharamukh require 4WD. Buses run up to Kharamukh.

Also known as Shivbhumi, this is the heart of the Gaddi's land. There are some very old temples grouped in a compound known as the *chaurasi* in Brahmaur, and accommodation is available in a *Forest Rest House*.

From Brahmaur it is about 80 km to Dharamsala and takes about six days to walk:

Day 1	Brahmaur to Chanota	22 km
Day 2	Chanota to Kuarsi	13 km
Day 3	Kuarsi to Chatta	13 km
Day 4	Chatta to Lakagot	10 km
Day 5	Lakagot to Triund	6 km
Day 6	Triund to Dharamsala	13 km

The Chatta to Lakagot sector crosses the 4300-metre Indrahas Pass with fine views over the Kangra Valley.

From Brahmaur you can make the 35-km trek to Manimahesh Lake at 3950 metres. This important pilgrimage spot is at the base of the 5575-metre Manimahesh Kailash. Thousands flock here on the 15th day after Janamashtami, which falls in August or September each year.

Pangi Valley

Kilar, 167 km north-east of Chamba, is in the deep and narrow gorge of the Chenab River. Here you are in the high Himalaya, in the scenic but lightly populated Pangi Valley, between the Pangi and Zanskar ranges. From Kilar you can trek north-west to Kishtwar in Jammu & Kashmir, or turn east about halfway to Kishtwar and cross the Umasi La Pass into the Zanskar Valley, or trek south-east to Keylong and Manali.

The Kulu Valley

The fertile Kulu Valley rises northward from Mandi at 760 metres to the Rohtang Pass at 3915 metres, the gateway to Lahaul & Spiti. In the south the valley is little more than a narrow, precipitous gorge, with the Beas River (pronounced bee-ahs) sometimes a sheer 300 metres below the narrow road. Further up, the valley widens and its main part is 80 km long, though rarely more than a couple of km wide. Here there are stone-fruit and apple orchards, rice paddies and wheat fields along the valley floor and lower slopes, and deodar forests higher up the slopes, with snow-crowned rocky peaks towering behind. The main towns, Kulu and Manali, are in this fertile section of the valley.

The light-skinned people are friendly, devout, hard working and relatively prosperous. The men wear the distinctive Kulu cap, a pillbox with a flap around the

back in which they may stick flowers. The women wear lots of silver jewellery and long garments of homespun wool secured with great silver pins; they are rarely without a large conical basket on their backs, filled with fodder, firewood or even a goat kid.

The other people of the valley are the nomads (Gaddis) who take their flocks of black sheep and white goats up to the mountain pastures in the early summer and retreat before the winter snows. You don't really know what wool smells like until you've travelled in a bus overcrowded with rain-soaked villagers. The valley also has many Tibetan refugees, some running restaurants and hotels in Manali, but many others in camps near the rivers, prayer flags fluttering. The Tibetans are great traders – you'll find them in all the bazaars – but many work in road gangs, whole families toiling together.

KULU (population 12,000)

At an altitude of 1200 metres, Kulu is the district headquarters but it is not the main tourist centre; that honour goes to Manali. Nevertheless there are a number of interesting things to see around Kulu, and some fine walks.

The town, which sprawls on the western bank of the Beas, is dominated by the grassy maidans on the southern side of town. They're the site for Kulu's fairs and festivals, in particular the colourful Dussehra festival, from which the Kulu Valley gained the name 'valley of the gods'.

The Shyamananda Meditation Centre holds meditation courses, although students must make their own accommodation arrangements.

Dussehra Festival

The Dussehra Festival, in October after the monsoons, is celebrated all over India but most particularly in Kulu. The festival starts on the 10th day of the rising moon, known as Vijay Dashmi, and continues for seven days. Dussehra celebrates Rama's victory over the demon king Ravana but in Kulu the festival does not include the burning of Ravana and his brothers, as it does in other places around India.

Kulu's festival is a great gathering of the gods from temples all around the valley. Approximately 200 gods are brought from their temples down to Kulu to pay homage to Raghunathji from the temple in Raghunathpura in Kulu. The festival cannot commence until the powerful goddess Hadimba, tutelary deity of the Kulu rajas, arrives from Manali. Like the other gods she is pulled in her own temple car, or *rath*, and Hadimba likes speed so she has to be pulled as fast as possible. She not only arrives before all the other gods but also leaves before them. Another curiosity is that the Jamlu god from Manali comes to the festival but does not take part – this god stays on the opposite side of the river from the Dhalpur maidan.

The Raghunathji rath is brought down, decked with garlands and surrounded by the other important gods. Priests and the descendants of Kulu's rajas circle the rath before it is pulled to the other side of the maidan. There is great competition to aid in pulling the car since this is a very auspicious thing to do.

The procession with the cars and bands takes place on the evening of the first day of the festival. During the following days and nights of the festival there are dances, music, a market and festivities far into the night. On the penultimate day the gods assemble for the 'Devta darbar' with Raghunathji, and on the final day the temple car is taken to the river bank where a small heap of grass is burnt to symbolise Ravana's destruction. Raghunathji is carried back to his main temple in a wooden palanquin.

Information & Orientation

The tourist office (tel 7) is by the maidan on the southern side of town. There's a bus and taxi stand here, and all the HPTDC accommodation units and several of the

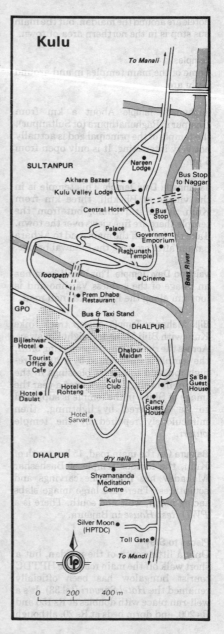

hotels are around the maidan, but the main bus stop is in the northern area of town.

Temples
Some of the main temples in and around Kulu are:

Raghunath Temple About a km from Dhalpur in Raghunathpura (or Sultanpur), the temple of the principal god is actually not very interesting. It is only open from 5 pm.

Jagannathi Devi Temple This temple is in the village of Bhekhli, three km from Kulu. It's a stiff climb, but from the temple there are fine views over the town. Take the path off the main road to Akhara bazaar after crossing the Sarawai bridge.

Vaishno Devi Temple This small cave has an image of the goddess Vaishno and is four km along the Kulu to Manali road.

Bijli Mahadev Temple A jeep track links Kulu with Bijli Mahadev, eight km away. Across the river, high on a projecting bluff, the temple is surmounted by a 20-metre-high rod said to attract blessings in the form of lightning. At least once a year the image of Shiva in the temple is supposed to be shattered by lightning, then miraculously repaired by the temple *pujari*.

Bajaura On the main road, 15 km south of Kulu, the famous temple of Basheshar Mahadev has fine stone carvings and sculptures. There are large image slabs facing north, west and south. There is a *PWD Rest House* in Bajaura.

Places to Stay
Only a little south of the maidan, but a short walk off the main road, the HPTDC tourist bungalow has been officially renamed the *Hotel Sarvari* (tel 33). It's a well-run place with doubles at Rs 150 and Rs 200, and dorm beds at Rs 20, although

they don't seem very keen on people using the dorm beds.

Right beside the maidan is the *Hotel Rohtang* which is good value at Rs 60/165. Behind the tourist office is the *Bijleshwar Hotel* where doubles range from Rs 45 to Rs 75. Hot water is available for Rs 3 per bucket. Up the road behind the Maidan, the *Hotel Daulat* (tel 358) has very plain rooms.

Across the other side of the maidan, towards the river, are the cheap and basic *Sa Ba Guest House* and *Fancy Guest House*. There are other rock-bottom places at the Manali end of town, by the main bus stop, such as the *Kulu Valley Lodge* or the *Central Hotel*.

Finally, the HPTDC *Silver Moon* is to the left of the road just as you enter town from the south. It has six rooms, with singles at Rs 325, doubles at Rs 400. There is a 25% off-season discount.

Places to Eat
The *Hotel Sarvari* has the usual sort of dining hall. By the tourist office there's the HPTDC's *Monal Cafe* with good light meals and snacks, but sometimes painfully slow service. Just downhill from the main street is the *Prem Dhaba*.

Getting There & Away
Air There is an airport at Bhuntar, 10 km south of Kulu, and Vayudoot fly Delhi/Chandigarh/Kulu twice weekly. The fare is Rs 600 from Delhi, Rs 320 from Chandigarh. Vayudoot also flies to Simla for Rs 160.

Bus & Taxi There are direct buses to Kulu from Dharamsala, Simla (235 km), Chandigarh (270 km) or Delhi (512 km). The Kulu to Chandigarh buses do not go via Simla. All these direct buses continue to Manali, 42 km further north.

A direct bus from Delhi is supposed to take 15 hours but probably takes a good bit more. Regular express buses cost Rs 98, but there are various classes right up to

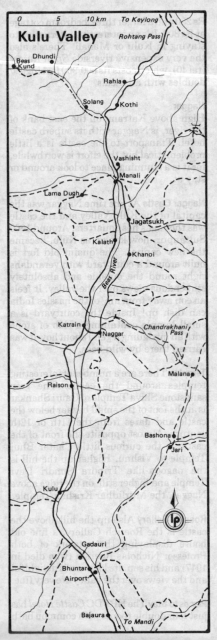

Kulu Valley

the HPTDC super-deluxe bus which costs nearly Rs 150. Chandigarh to Kulu takes about 12 hours and costs Rs 50.

Plenty of taxis make the trip up from the plains, but count on around Rs 1400 or more for Simla or Chandigarh to Kulu or Manali. A taxi from Kulu to Manali costs about Rs 225; it's Rs 8 by bus.

AROUND KULU

You can make some interesting excursions from Kulu to the adjoining valleys which run into the Kulu Valley. See also the 'Treks from Manali' section.

Parvati Valley

The Parvati Valley runs off north-east from Bhuntar, which is south of Kulu. You can travel up the valley by bus. Manikaran is built near sulphur hot springs and it's interesting to watch the locals cook their food in the pools of hot water at the Sikh temple. There are also hot baths, separate for men and women, at the temple and, of course, free accommodation. Hot water is nice to have in Manikaran because the valley is so steep-sided that not much sun gets in.

There are a lot of French and Italian freaks in the area; they've been in Manikaran so long 'it's hard to tell them from the locals. Unfortunately there is much friction between freaks and locals although the locals are friendly and helpful'. There's great trekking and wonderful scenery here.

Places to Stay Rooms in shops or houses are easily available if you ask around. The *Padha Family House*, near the bridge, is an excellent place where quite a few travellers stay. There are big, clean rooms with rope beds for Rs 25. And there's a private sulphur rock-bath indoors. You can get food and expensive, but beautiful, wild bee honey.

In the local chai shops try *kihr*, a delicious rice dessert made with milk, sugar, fresh coconut and sultanas. It's said that Shiva sat and meditated for 2000 years at Kihr Ganga, a 30-km walk from Manikaran.

Getting There & Away Buses from Kulu to Bhuntar take 1½ hours and cost about Rs 4. Bhuntar to Manikaran is another 1½ hours for about the same price.

Sainj Valley

The area from Aut to Sainj is not as beautiful as the other valleys but it has a charm of its own. It's also very rarely visited by travellers so the locals are friendly. There is no accommodation as such, but rooms are easily available if you ask around.

Getting There & Away A bus from Bhuntar to Aut takes an hour and costs Rs 3.

KULU TO MANALI

There are a number of interesting things to see along the 42-km road between Kulu and Manali. There are actually two Kulu to Manali roads; the direct road runs along the west bank of the Beas, while the much rougher and more winding east bank road is not so regularly used, but does take you via Naggar with its delightful Forest Rest House.

Raison

Only eight km from Kulu there's a camping place on the grassy meadow beside the river. It's a good base for treks in the vicinity. There are 12 *Tourist Huts* at the site with doubles at Rs 60, which can be booked through the Kulu tourist office.

Katrain

At about the midpoint on the Kulu to Manali road, this is the widest point in the Kulu Valley and is overlooked by the 3325-metre Baragarh peak. Two km up the road on the left side is a trout hatchery.

Places to Stay There's a small *Rest House* and a pleasant HPTDC tourist bungalow known as the *Hotel Apple Blossom* with doubles at Rs 100, cottages from Rs 200 to

Rs 250 and a larger three-bedroom cottage at Rs 300. It's an interesting alternative to staying in Kulu or Manali. There's also the very expensive riverside *Span Resort* (tel 40), which costs Rs 600/900 for singles/doubles with all meals.

Naggar

High above Katrain, on the east bank of the river, is Naggar with its superb castle hotel. Transport to the castle is a little problematical but the effort is worthwhile, for it is a stunning place to look around or stay at.

Naggar Castle At one time Naggar was the capital of the Kulu Valley and the castle was the raja's headquarters. Around 1660 Sultanpur, now known as Kulu, became the new capital. The quaint old fort is built around a courtyard with verandahs right round the outside and absolutely stupendous views over the valley. It feels an eon away from any of the hassles India can dish up! Inside the courtyard is a small temple containing a slab of stone with an intriguing legend about how it was carried there by wild bees.

Temples There are a number of interesting temples around the castle. The grey sandstone Shiva Temple of Gauri Shankar is at the foot of the small bazaar below the castle and dates from the 11th or 12th century. Almost opposite the front of the castle is the curious little Chatar Bhuj Temple to Vishnu. Higher up the hill is the pagoda-like Tripura Sundri Devi Temple and higher still, on the ridge above Naggar, the Murlidhar Krishna Temple.

Roerich Gallery Also up the hill above the castle is the Roerich Gallery, a fine old house displaying the artwork of both Professor Nicholas Roerich (who died in 1947) and his son. Its location is delightful and the views over the valley are very fine.

Places to Stay The HPTDC *Castle Hotel* has just four double rooms with common bath for Rs 75 and six with bath at Rs 200, plus a larger family suite for Rs 350. There's also a five-bed dorm. This place is deservedly popular and often booked out; the Kulu tourist office can make reservations, but plan ahead. There's a *Forest Rest House* in Naggar. Travellers recommend the *Poonam Mountain Lodge & Restaurant*, opposite Naggar Castle near the post office. The owner is extremely helpful. There are two doubles with common bath at Rs 80 and 12 dorm beds at Rs 10; the bathrooms have hot water. The restaurant is open for breakfast, lunch and dinner, and serves excellent Indian, Chinese and western food. Picnic lunches are also available.

Kulu to Manali Transport

Buses run regularly along the main road for Rs 8; the trip takes under two hours. There are only one or two buses daily on the east side of the river and the trip can take a long time, up to two hours from Manali to Naggar alone. Add another 1½ hours from Naggar to Kulu. The combined fare is not much different from the direct one.

Cars can get to Naggar by crossing the river at Patlikuhl near Katrain – the bridge is very narrow. Or you can get off the Kulu to Manali bus there and walk up. It's six km up to the castle by road but much less on foot, although the path is very steep.

MANALI (population 2500)

Manali, at the top end of the Kulu Valley, is the main resort in the valley. It's beautifully situated and there are many pleasant walks around the town, as well as a large number of hotels and restaurants. It's also very much a 'scene' – at the height of the tourist season it's packed out with Indian and western tourists. Smaller villages around Manali have semi-permanent 'hippie' populations. The nearby country and villages are truly beautiful and not to be missed.

Information & Orientation

Manali has one main street where you'll find the bus stop and most of the restaurants. The tourist office (tel 25) is further down the street towards the river and opposite the taxi stand. It's a very well organised office and has a list of hotels and tariffs, and of taxi routes and fares.

Hotels are scattered all over town, some of them within easy walking distance of the bus stop, some of them, like the Tourist Bungalow (Hotel Manalsu), a good long stretch uphill. It stays cold in Manali until surprisingly late in the season; there may still be snow on the ground in late March.

Warning Manali is famous for its marijuana, which is not only esteemed by connoisseurs, but also grows wild all around. However, there have been a number of police busts on the more popular cheap hotels so smokers should beware. We've also had reports of local dope sellers turning in the people they just sold stuff to. Take care.

Hadimba Temple

The temple of the goddess Hadimba, who plays such a major part in Kulu's annual festival, is a sombre wooden temple in a clearing in the dense forest about 2½ km from the tourist office.

Hadimba is supposed to be the wife of Bhima in the epic *Mahabharata*. It's a pleasant stroll up to the temple, which was built in 1553. Also known as the Dhungri Temple, it's the site of a major festival in May of each year, and non-Hindus are allowed to enter.

Old Manali Village

The current town of Manali is actually a new creation which has superseded the old village, a couple of km away. Follow the trail off the road out of town, cross a very picturesque bridge over the cascading Manalsu stream, and then climb up to this interesting little village.

Around the Town

Manali is basically a place to get out and walk around, but there are a few sites of interest in the town itself. The colourful, pleasant new Tibetan Monastery has a carpet-making operation; you can buy carpets and other Tibetan handicrafts here.

The tourist office will arrange a fishing licence if you want to try your luck with the Beas River trout – you'll need your own gear though.

Tours

In season there are daily bus tours to the Rohtang Pass (Rs 65) which last the whole day. There are also tours to Manikaran (Sikh temple and hot springs) for Rs 70 and to Naggar Castle for Rs 55.

Places to Stay

Prices in Manali are very variable. In May-June they go sky high, in July-August they drop down a bit and again in September-October. From December to February, when there are no tourists at all, the prices are very low. At that time people come down from the hills and can get rooms for Rs 200 to Rs 300 a month which, at the height of the season, can cost that much for a few days! Those same rooms go up to Rs 25 a day in March-April, then Rs 60 at peak times, even Rs 80 at peak-peaks. When the costs go up Manali's resident traveller population tends to head out to the villages around Manali.

Even at the height of the season it's possible to rent a house for Rs 300 a month, but conditions are likely to be a little primitive. There may be a stove but you'll need your own cooking utensils, and you may have a long walk to get water. In the pits of the off season many places close completely.

The *Youth Hostel* is just outside the town, across the river on the road to Vashisht and the Rohtang Pass. Dorm beds are Rs 5.

Back in town are a number of places run by the HPTDC. They can all be reserved through the tourism development officer (tel 25). During the off season, nongovernment hotels give discounts of up to 50% and so are often better value than the HPTDC hotels at that time. The *Manalsu Hotel*, formerly the tourist bungalow, is up the hill a little from the town; it's totally covered with ivy and quite a picture. Doubles cost Rs 125 to Rs 200. There are also *Tourist Cottages* and *Log Huts* – these are self-contained, with their own kitchens and living rooms and modern facilities. Nightly costs are through the roof at Rs 1000 to Rs 1200 for the flashier log huts.

The riverside *Tourist Lodge* is much simpler, with bare rooms with four beds costing Rs 80 plus additional charges for bedding. There's also the *Beas Hotel*, right beside the Beas River, with singles at Rs 40, doubles from Rs 90 to Rs 150. All this HPTDC accommodation tends to be fairly heavily booked, so plan ahead.

The ITDC have an *Ashok Travellers' Lodge* (tel 31) in Manali, a little out of town on the Naggar road. There are just 10 rooms, with singles at Rs 200 (Rs 100 off season) and doubles from Rs 250 to Rs 300 (Rs 150 to Rs 200). The season starts on 1 April. The doubles are really suites with a sitting room and fine views of the snow-capped peaks around Manali.

In the private-hotel sector your best bet is simply to wander around and have a look at a few, bearing in mind that prices are likely to be variable, depending on when you're there and how many rooms happen to be vacant. Some names to start with include the *Skylark Guest House* (rooms Rs 100 to Rs 150), *Mt View Guest House*, *John Banon Guest House* (Rs 250 to Rs 500) and *Pinewood Hotel* (Rs 200 to Rs 250). Travellers have also recommended the *Siwalik Hotel* (Rs 75 to Rs 90), just behind the Civil Hospital. The *Mayflower Hotel* (tel 104) is popular and charges Rs 200 to Rs 525 including all meals.

In Old Manali, the *Manalsu Hotel* has excellent views, and rooms from Rs 25.

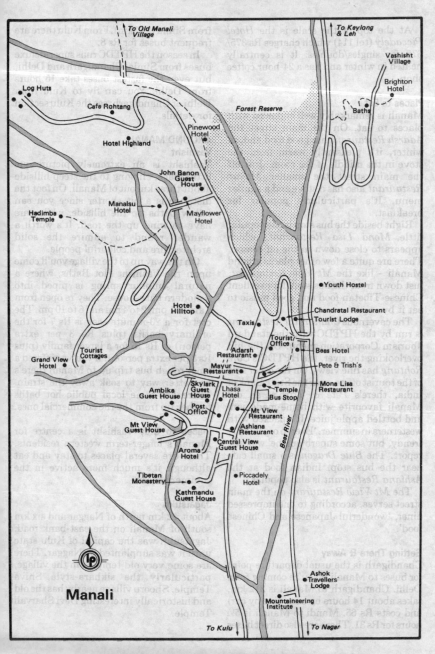

To Old Manali Village

Log Huts

Cafe Rohtang

Hotel Highland

Pinewood Hotel

Forest Reserve

John Banon Guest House

Manalsu Hotel

Hadimba Temple

Mayflower Hotel

Hotel Hilltop

Taxis

Tourist Cottages

Grand View Hotel

Chandratal Restaurant
Tourist Lodge

Adarsh Restaurant

Tourist Office

Beas Hotel

Mayur Restaurant

Pete & Trish's

Ambika Guest House

Skylark Guest House

Lhasa Hotel

Temple Bus Stop

Mona Lisa Restaurant

Post Office

Mt View Guest House

Mt View Restaurant

Aroma Hotel

Ashiana Restaurant

Central View Guest House

Beas River

Tibetan Monastery

Kathmandu Guest House

Piccadely Hotel

Manali

To Kulu

To Nagar

Vashisht Village

Brighton Hotel

Baths

Youth Hostel

Ashok Travellers' Lodge

Mountaineering Institute

To Keylong & Leh

At the top of the scale is the *Hotel Piccadely* (tel 114) which charges Rs 375/675 for singles/doubles. It is centrally heated in winter and has a 24-hour coffee shop.

Places to Eat

Manali is remarkably well endowed with places to eat. On the main street the *Adarsh Restaurant* has good food and, in winter, it's pleasantly warm from the stove in the middle of the room. Just off the main street the smaller *Mayur Restaurant* also has a stove and a similar menu. It's particularly popular for breakfast.

Right beside the bus stop is the popular little *Mona Lisa Restaurant*, which appears to close down in the off season. There are quite a few other places around Manali – like the *Mt View Restaurant*, just down from the bus stop, for excellent Chinese-Tibetan food and good music to eat it by.

The cavernous *Chandratal Restaurant* is run by the HPTDC with the standard Tourism Corporation menu. Up the hill overlooking the river, the HPTDC's *Cafe Rohtang* has fine views. On the other side of the tourist office, near the State Bank of India, there's *Pete & Trish's*, an old Manali favourite with home-made jam and bottled apple juice. It's packed with westerners in summer. 'Ever so organically trendy, but some superb quiche' was one report. The *Blue Dragon* is a small cafe near the bus stop. Indian food at the *Ashiana Restaurant* is also popular.

The *Mt View Restaurant* on the main street serves, according to one impressed diner, 'wonderful Japanese and Chinese food'.

Getting There & Away

Chandigarh is the usual departure point for buses to Manali if you're coming from Delhi. Chandigarh to Manali is 312 km, takes about 14 hours by bus (nine by car) and costs Rs 65. Mandi to Manali is 5½ hours for Rs 31. There are also direct buses from Simla (247 km). From Kulu there are frequent buses for Rs 8.

In season the HPTDC runs super-deluxe buses from Simla, Chandigarh and Delhi, but even the fastest buses take 15 hours from Delhi. You can fly to Kulu from Delhi or Chandigarh; see the Kulu section for details.

AROUND MANALI
Vashisht

Vashisht is an extremely picturesque little place, clinging to the steep hillside about three km out of Manali. On foot the distance is a bit shorter since you can follow paths up the hillside, while cars have to wind up the road. It's worth a wander round to admire the solid architecture and colourful people.

On the way up to the village you'll come upon the Vashisht Hot Baths, where a natural sulphur spring is piped into a modern bath-house. They're open from 7 am to 1 pm, 2 to 4 pm and 6 to 10 pm. The cost for a 20-minute soak is Rs 7 for the ordinary baths (plus Rs 3 per extra person) or Rs 15 for a larger family (plus Rs 3 per extra person). If you've suffered a long, rough bus trip up to Manali there's no better way to soak away the strain. There are some local public hot baths further up from the the commercial ones.

Places to Stay Vashisht is a centre for Manali's longer-term western residents. There are several places to stay and eat although it's much more active in the summer season.

Jagatsukh

About 12 km north of Naggar and six km south of Manali on the east-bank road, Jagatsukh was the capital of Kulu state until it was supplanted by Naggar. There are some very old temples in the village, particularly the sikhara-style Shiva Temple. Shooru village nearby has the old and historically interesting Devi Sharvali Temple.

Kothi

Kothi is a pretty little village, 12 km from Manali on the Keylong road.

There are very fine views from Kothi, and the Beas River flows through a very deep and narrow gorge at this point. The trip to Rahla Falls, 16 km away, is another popular excursion.

Places to Stay The *Rest House* is a popular resting place for trekkers heading for the Rohtang Pass. It's surrounded by glaciers and mountains, two old tea stalls and nothing else. Doubles have bathroom, two big beds, carpets and a balcony. The food is good and it's quiet.

Other Places

Arjun Gufa, with a legendary cave, is near the village of Prini, five km from Manali. A cold-water spring, named the Nehru Kund after former prime minister Nehru, is six km from Manali on the Keylong road. The Solang Valley is north-west of Manali, before Kothi. The glacier nearest Manali is here, only 13 km from town. You can get here by taking a bus to Palchan village, and then following the jeep track.

TREKS FROM MANALI

There are many treks from Manali, both round trips and journeys further afield.

Malana Valley

It is less than 30 km from Katrain, on the Kulu to Manali road, across the Chandrakhani Pass to the interesting Malana Valley. The pass is at less than 3600 metres and is open from March to December. Malana can also be reached from the Parvati Valley – either from Manikaran over the 3150-metre Rashol Pass or from Jari. Jari is connected with the Kulu Valley by a jeep track and is only 12 km from Malana.

There are about 500 people in Malana and they speak a peculiar dialect with strong Tibetan elements. It's an isolated village with its own system of government.

When visiting the village it is important not to touch *anything*, as local customs are very strict about this.

The 6001-metre peak of Deo Tibba overlooks Malana and from the top of the Chandrakhani Pass you can see snow-capped peaks on the border of Spiti to the east. Starting from Naggar, it is possible to climb up to the pass summit and return to Naggar in the same day – but it is fairly hard going.

Local legends relate that when Jamlu, the main deity of Malana, first came there, he bore a casket containing all the other Kulu gods. At the top of the pass he opened the casket and the breeze carried the gods to their present homes, all over the valley.

At the time of the Dussehra festival in Kulu, Jamlu plays a special part. He is a very powerful god with something of the demon in him. He does not have a temple image so, unlike the other Kulu gods, has no temple car to be carried in. Nor does he openly show his allegiance to Raghunathji, the paramount Kulu god, like the other Kulu gods. At the time of the festival Jamlu goes down to Kulu but stays on the east side of the river, from where he watches the proceedings. Every few years a major festival is held for Jamlu in the month of Bhadon. In the temple at Malana there is a silver elephant with a gold figure on its back which is said to have been a gift from Emperor Akbar.

It takes three days to trek from Naggar to Malana, spend a day there, then return to Naggar or continue to Jari. A seven-day trek from Manali to Malana could be:

Day 1	Manali to Rumsu	2060 m	24 km
Day 2	Rumsu to Chandrakhani	3650 m	8 km
Day 3	Chandrakhani to Malana	2100 m	7 km
Day 4	Malana to Kasol	1580 m	8 km
Day 5	Kasol to Jari	1560 m	15 km
Day 6	Jari to Bhuntar	900 m	12 km
Day 7	Bhuntar to Manali	by bus	

The trek can be extended by continuing

from Jari along the east bank of the Beas via Bijli Mahadev, with its famous temple, and Naggar to Manali.

Deo Tibba Trek

This is an easy trek east of Manali to the base of 6000-metre Deo Tibba. The trek offers fine views and pleasant walking through forests and alpine meadows. From Manali you start via Jagatsukh to Khanol and Chhika (not the Chhika north-east of Manali on the way to the Hamta Pass). Seri is at the base of Deo Tibba and from here you can make an excursion to Lake Chandratal.

Day 1	Manali to Khanol	8 km
Day 2	Khanol to Chhika	6 km
Day 3	Chhika to Seri	5 km
Day 4	Seri to Bhanara	14 km
Day 5	Bhanara to Manali	

Chandratal

This circular trek from Manali over the Hamta, Chandratal and Baralacha La passes is one of the finest in Himachal Pradesh and takes 11 days to complete. From Manali you start at Jagatsukh, on the east bank road to Kulu. At the village of Prini you turn north-east and climb up to Chhika – a steep climb at first but later it becomes easier over grassy downs and pleasant meadows.

The next day involves a long and wearisome climb over the 4270-metre Hamta Pass, then a quick descent to Chhatru on the Chandra River. The pass is generally open from June to September, although it may be open longer. There are fine views of Deo Tibba (6001 metres) and Indrasan (6221 metres) from the pass. Two days' walk takes you through Chhota Dara to Batal, where the route branches off north-east to Spiti through the Kunzam Pass. There are magnificent views of the Bara Shigri glacier from here.

Succeeding days take you north over the Chandratal 'lake of the moon' Pass, the Likhim Gongma (upper) and Likhim Yongma (lower), and the Topko Yongma

before you reach the Keylong to Leh road at the Baralacha La Pass. Three more days of walking bring you to Keylong, from where you can bus back to Manali. It may be possible to get a bus earlier and shorten the time to Keylong.

Day 1	Manali to Chhika	2960 m	21 km
Day 2	Chhika to Chhatru	3360 m	16 km
Day 3	Chhatru to Chhota Dara	3740 m	16 km
Day 4	Chhota Dara to Batal	3960 m	16 km
Day 5	Batal to Chandratal	4270 m	18 km
Day 6	Chandratal to Likhim Yongma	4320 m	12 km
Day 7	Likhim Yongma to Topko Gongma	4640 m	11 km
Day 8	Topko Gongma to Baralacha La	4885 m	10 km
Day 9	Baralacha La to Patsio	3820 m	19 km
Day 10	Patsio to Jispa	3320 m	14 km
Day 11	Jispa to Keylong	3340 m	21 km

Parvati Valley

The Parvati Valley is now accessible by bus from Kulu or Bhuntar (Rs 8 from Kulu). The last part of the Malana Valley trek descends the Parvati Valley to its junction with the Kulu Valley. An interesting alternative is to ascend the Parvati Valley to its upper reaches; it is much wilder and more rugged than the Kulu Valley. From Bhuntar, near the junction of the Beas and Parvati rivers, you can visit the Adibrahma Temple in Khokhan, about a km away, or the pagoda-shaped temple of Triyugi Narain in Diar village. The first day's walk takes you to Jari, on a hillside high above the Parvati River and near where the Malana River joins the Parvati.

It's a short trek to Kasol with its pleasantly sited *Tourist Hut* (doubles Rs 25) and *Forest Rest House*. There is good trout fishing here. Manikaran is a very short walk away and the river is wild at this point. Manikaran's famous hot spring, almost at boiling temperature, is near the river as you enter the village. There are several guest houses in

Manikaran. Be sure not to miss the evening worship accompanied by harmonium, tablas and singing.

It's a long walk, rough and stony at first, to Pulga, where again there is a very pleasant *Forest Rest House*. The pretty little village is 300 metres above the river and is the usual end point of this trek, although hardy and well-equipped trekkers could continue further up the Parvati River and cross the Pin Parvati Pass into Spiti. Khirganga, just 10 km upstream from Pulga, has more hot springs. Or you could explore the Tos Nullah, which joins the Parvati River from the north-east, just upstream from Pulga.

Day 1	Bhuntar to Jari	15 km
Day 2	Jari to Kasol	8 km
Day 3	Kasol to Manikaran	3 km
Day 4	Manikaran to Pulga	16 km

Seraj Valley to Narkanda
The Seraj Valley branches off south-east from the southern end of the Kulu Valley and makes an interesting alternative route between the Kulu Valley and Simla. Aut, on the main road between Kulu and Manali, is the starting point; and Larji, at the junction of the Sainj and Tirthan rivers, is the first stop. There's a *PWD Rest House* here and good fishing is available during March, April and October – when the Sainj River runs clear.

In the lower reaches of the Tirthan Valley is Banjar, with an interesting group of temples. Continuing south you reach Shoja, where there is another *PWD Rest House* with a scenic setting. From here you can make excursions to the old ruined fort of Raghupur Gahr where there is a beautiful view; even Simla can be seen on a clear day. Another interesting day trip from Shoja is to the beautiful flower-strewn meadow of Dughu Thatch.

From Shoja you cross the 3135-metre Jalori Pass. The view of the surrounding mountains from the pass crest is stunning. Khanag, at 2500 metres, is on the other

side of the pass and has a *PWD Rest House*. Ani, again with a *PWD Rest House*, is the next stop, and from here you can either continue straight on to the main highway where buses run to Narkanda and Simla, or turn east to Nirmand with its temple of Devi Ambika. There is a bus service between Ani and Luhri, on the north side of the Sutlej River.

Day 1	Aut to Larji	5 km
Day 2	Larji to Banjar	20 km
Day 3	Banjar to Shoja	13 km
Day 4	Shoja to Khanag	10 km
Day 5	Khanag to Ani	20 km
Day 6	Ani to Luhri	15 km

As an alternative to this route, you can branch off at Banjar and follow the Tirthan River to Narkanda. The first day's walk takes you from Banjar to Goshaini, but you can get that far by bus. It's then a gentle climb to Bathad where there is a *PWD Rest House*, followed by a very hard climb to the Bashleo Pass at 3250 metres, 13 km on. A steep descent takes you to Sarahan, only three km further.

There is another beautifully situated *Rest House* here. From here it is an easy, pleasant walk to Arsu (another *PWD Rest House*) and then to Rampur on the main road.

Day 3	Banjar to Goshaini	13 km
Day 4	Goshaini to Bathad	16 km
Day 5	Bathad to Sarahan	16 km
Day 6	Sarahan to Arsu	13 km
Day 7	Arsu to Rampur	13 km

Solang Valley
There are a number of treks from Manali to the Solang Valley looping back to Manali, either from the north or the south. A seven-day trek takes you to Beas Kund, the source of the Beas River, and across the remains of dying glaciers. The first day takes you to Solang Nullah, where there is a mountain hut with rooms for 80 people. There are ski-runs here in the winter.

The second day's trek continues to

Dhundi, on an alpine plateau, where you can see Deo Tibba and Indrasan, and admire the many alpine flowers. The third day takes you to Beas Kund and back, and the next day continues to Shagara Dugh, with a good chance of seeing red bears along the way. On the fifth day you reach Marrhi over a small 4000-metre pass with views to the Kulu Valley and Rohtang Pass. Finally, on Day 6 you continue down the Keylong to Manali road to Kothi, via the Rahla waterfall. On the last day you return to Manali.

Day 1	Manali to Solang Nullah	2480 m	11 km
Day 2	Solang Nullah to Dhundi	2840 m	8 km
Day 3	Dhundi to Beas Kund & back	3540 m	10 km
Day 4	Dhundi to Shagara Dugh	3600 m	8 km
Day 5	Shagara Dugh to Marrhi	3380 m	10 km
Day 6	Marrhi to Kothi	2500 m	6 km
Day 7	Kothi to Manali		13 km

Manali Pass Treks

These two treks continue on from the Solang Valley trek but loop back to Manali from the south. They are both difficult treks involving long, hard ascents over rugged terrain. The first alternative continues from Beas Kund over the Tentu Pass (an arduous and tiring climb) to Phulangot through an uninhabited region. You then cross the Manali Pass to Rani Sui and go via Bhogi Thatch to Kalath, a little south of Manali on the Kulu to Manali road.

Day 3	Dhundi to Beas Kund	3540 m	6 km
Day 4	Beas Kund to Tentu Pass	4996 m	4 km
Day 5	Tentu Pass to camping ground	3856 m	10 km
Day 6	camping ground to Phulangot	4000 m	6 km
Day 7	Phulangot to Manali Pass	4988 m	6 km

Day 8	Manali Pass to Rani Sui	4200 m	8 km
Day 9	Rani Sui to Bhogi Thatch	2800 m	6 km
Day 10	Bhogi Thatch to Kalath	1800 m	12 km

The second alternative is to join the Manalsu Nullah from the Manali Pass and follow this straight back to Manali – up to Day 8 this trek is the same as the first alternative.

An easy trek, which includes the last two days of the first alternative, involves going to Rani Sui via Lama Dugh. You leave Manali via the Hadimba Temple and climb through pleasant country to the camp site at Lama Dugh. On the second day you cross the Thanpri Tibba ridge to Rani Sui, and then Day 3 and Day 4 are as Day 9 and Day 10 of the first Manali Pass trek.

| Day 1 | Manali to Lama Dugh | 3380 m | 6 km |
| Day 2 | Lama Dugh to Rani Sui | 4200 m | 5 km |

LAHAUL & SPITI

Only since 1977 have visitors been permitted to cross the Rohtang Pass to Keylong in Lahaul. Just 117 km from Manali, this is a Tibetan region, quite unlike the Kulu Valley. The Rohtang Pass has the same 'gateway' nature as the Zoji La Pass between Kashmir and Ladakh. The region is bounded by Ladakh to the north, Kulu to the south and Tibet to the east.

A large chunk of Lahaul (and all of Spiti) are off limits to visitors without special permission. As of July 1989, only groups in jeeps with a police escort can use the jeep road from Keylong to Leh in Ladakh, but independently you can make the long and difficult trek from Keylong to Padum in the Zanskar Valley and from there into Ladakh.

See the Lonely Planet guides *Kashmir, Ladakh & Zanskar* and *Trekking in the*

Indian Himalaya for more information on treks in this region.

Climate

As in Ladakh, little rain gets over the high Himalayan barrier so Lahaul & Spiti are dry and, for the most part, barren. The air is sharp and clear and the warm summer days are followed by cold, crisp nights. Beware of the burning power of the sun in this region - you can get burnt very quickly even on cool days. The heavy winter snow from September to May closes the passes except for a few months of each year.

Culture

The people of Lahaul & Spiti follow a Tibetan form of Tantric Buddhism with a panoply of demons, saints and followers. The monasteries, known as gompas, are colourful places where the monks or lamas lead lives ordered by complicated regulations and rituals. There are many similarities between these people and the Ladakhis, further north. The people of Spiti are almost all Buddhists of Tibetan stock, but Lahaul is split roughly 50:50 between Buddhists and Hindus.

Rohtang Pass

The 3915-metre Rohtang Pass is the only access into Lahaul and is open only from June to September each year, although trekkers can cross the pass a little before it opens for vehicles. During the short season it's open, there are regular buses from Manali to Keylong. The tourist office operates a daily Rs 60 bus up to the pass, mainly for tourists to 'see the snow'. It's a very spectacular trip over the pass.

Keylong

Keylong is the main town in the Lahaul & Spiti region; there are a number of interesting monasteries within easy reach of this oasis-like town. The old Kharding Monastery, formerly the capital of Lahaul, overlooks Keylong, only 3½ km

away. Other monasteries include Shashur (three km), Tayal (six km) and Guru Ghantal (11 km).

A ten-minute walk from the bus stand past the Tibetan village, the Tibetan Centre for Performing Arts presents a video on Tibet several times a week in season.

Places to Stay & Eat The HPTDC *Tourist Bungalow* has just three doubles at Rs 50, but during the summer season they set up tents which cost Rs 30. There is also a *PWD Rest House*. The *Lamayuru* serves up good food and music in a pleasant atmosphere, although the Rs 25 rooms are dark and dirty.

The *A-Ha Tibetan Restaurant* is gloomy but has good cheap food.

Other Places

Gondhla, with its eight-storey castle of the Thakur of Gondhla and the historically significant gompa, is a short distance before Keylong on the Manali to Keylong road. You can trek back to Gondhla from Keylong, cutting across the loop the road makes. Between Gondhla and Keylong is Tandi, where the Chandrabagha or Chenab River meets the road.

Following the Chenab Valley to the north-west towards Kilar (see treks from Chamba) will bring you to Triloknath with its six-armed white-marble image of Avalokitesvara. Close by is the village of Udaipur, with a finely carved wooden temple from the 10th or 11th century which is dedicated to Mrikula Devi.

SPITI

The 4500-metre Kunzam Pass connects the Lahaul and Spiti valleys. Eventually a road will be completed from Kaza, the principal Spiti village, south-east through Samdoh to meet the Hindustan to Tibet road (see Kinnaur).

There are few settlements in this barren, high region. Kaza (or Kaja) is the main village. Slightly north-west of it is Kibar (or Kyipur), which at 4205 metres is reputed to be the highest village in the world. Tabo Kye and Dhankhar are two of the most important gompas.

Getting There & Away

Although the pass may be open by mid-May, a safer date is mid-June. The bus trip takes eight hours and costs Rs 30. It's 475 km from Manali to Leh via Keylong, but you need to be in a group and have a police escort to use this road.

KINNAUR

Most of this region, in the valley of the Sutlej River extending up towards the Tibetan border, is off limits unless you have permission from the Ministry of Home Affairs in New Delhi. Without a permit you can only go as far as the Wangtu Bridge just beyond Nachar.

Rampur

Rampur, 140 km from Simla, beyond Narkanda, is the gateway to the region. It's the site for a major trade fair in the second week of November each year, and was once a major centre for trade between India and Tibet. There are direct buses from Simla to Rampur, which has a *PWD Rest House*.

Sarahan

The last village in the district before entering Kinnaur, Sarahan is a beautiful little place with the interesting Bhimkali Temple which shows a curious blend of Hindu and Buddhist architecture.

Nachar

This picturesque village on the Hindustan to Tibet road is four km from the Wangtu Bridge, beyond which you need a permit to continue. Like Sarahan, Nachar is on the old road, which has been replaced by the new Hindustan to Tibet road nearby. There's a *Rest House* in the orchards.

Tapri & Choltu

Only 15 km further up the valley from Nachar, three roads meet at this scenic spot. One is the main road continuing up the valley to Kalpa. The second is the old road, also continuing to Kalpa via Rogi. The third is a small road which crosses the river and passes through Choltu and Kilba to the Sangla Valley. Choltu has a pleasant *Rest House*.

Sangla

The main village in the Sangla Valley is 18 km from Karcham, on the new Hindustan to Tibet road, and can be reached by jeep or on foot. It's a good base for trekking and there's a *Rest House*.

Kalpa

The main town in Kinnaur is close to the foot of 6050-metre-high Kinnaur Khailash. This is the legendary winter home of Lord Shiva; during the winter the god is said to retire to his Himalayan home here and indulge his passion for hashish. In the month of Magha (January-February) the gods of Kinnaur supposedly meet here for an annual conference with Lord Shiva.

Kalpa has a *Rest House* and from here you can continue on the northern side of the river to Puh and Namgia, close to the Tibetan border. Only 14 km from Kalpa, the tiny village of Pangli has a small *Rest House* and a fine view of Kinnaur Khailash. Rarang, eight km further on, is another centre for trade to Tibet.

Jammu & Kashmir

Population: 7.2 million
Area: 222,236 square km
Capital: Srinagar
Main languages: Kashmiri, Dogri

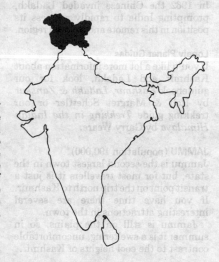

The state of Jammu & Kashmir, J&K for short, is a region of widely varying people and geography. In the south, Jammu is a transition zone from the Indian plains to the Himalaya. Correctly the rest of the state is Kashmir but in practice this title is reserved for the beautiful Vale of Kashmir, a large Himalayan valley in the north of the state. Here the people are predominantly Muslim and in many ways look towards Pakistan and central Asia rather than towards India.

Finally, to the north-east is the remote Tibetan plateau region known as Ladakh, primarily Buddhist and Tibetan in its culture and a very clear contrast to the rest of Kashmir, indeed to the rest of India. Sandwiched between the Kashmir and Ladakh regions is a long narrow valley known as Zanskar. This valley is even more isolated than Ladakh although, with the improvement of the road into the valley, the number of visitors has soared in recent years and things are changing rapidly.

For visitors J&K is one of India's most popular states. Kashmir is simply beautiful and a spell on a houseboat on Dal Lake is one of India's real treats. Kashmir also offers some delightful trekking opportunities and unsurpassed scenery. Ladakh, on the other hand, offers a chance to study a region which, in today's world, is probably even more Tibetan than Tibet. It's one of the most other-worldly parts of India.

No special permits are required to visit Kashmir or Ladakh today, but your movements are restricted in that you are not allowed to approach within a certain distance of the border. In Ladakh this means you are not allowed more than 1.6 km north of the Srinagar to Leh road.

History

Jammu & Kashmir has always been a centre of conflict for independent India. When India and Pakistan became independent, there was much controversy over which country the region should go to. The population was predominantly Muslim but J&K was not a part of 'British India', it was a 'princely state' and as such the ruler had to decide which way his state would move – to Muslim Pakistan or Hindu India. As *Freedom at Midnight* by Larry Collins and Dominique Lapierre relates, the indecisive maharaja only made his decision when a Pakistani-prompted invasion was already crossing his borders and the inevitable result was the first Indo-Pakistani conflict.

Since that first battle Kashmir has remained a flashpoint for relations between the two countries. Two-thirds of the region is now Indian and one-third is Pakistani; both countries claim all of it. Furthermore, Kashmir's role as a sensitive border zone applies not only to Pakistan. In 1962 the Chinese invaded Ladakh, prompting India to rapidly reassess its position in this remote and isolated region.

Lonely Planet Guides

If you'd like a lot more information about Kashmir and Ladakh, look for our guidebook *Kashmir, Ladakh & Zanskar* by Rolf & Margret Schettler or our trekking guide *Trekking in the Indian Himalaya* by Garry Weare.

JAMMU (population 190,000)

Jammu is the second largest town in the state, but for most travellers it is just a transit point on the trip north to Kashmir. If you have time there are several interesting attractions in the town.

Jammu is still on the plains, so in summer it is a sweltering, uncomfortable contrast to the cool heights of Kashmir.

Orientation

Jammu is actually two towns – the old town sits on a hilltop overlooking the river. Here you'll find most of the hotels, the Tourist Reception Centre and the tourist office, from where deluxe buses depart for Kashmir. Down beside the hill is the station for buses to other parts of north India and for the standard buses to Srinagar.

Several km away across the river is the new town of Jammu Tawi and the railway station where you'll find a second Tourist Reception Centre.

If you're en route to Srinagar and arrive in Jammu by train (as most people do), then you have two choices: you can keep going straight through to Srinagar or stay overnight in Jammu.

If you choose the first option you have to take one of the buses which wait at the railway station for the arrival of the trains.

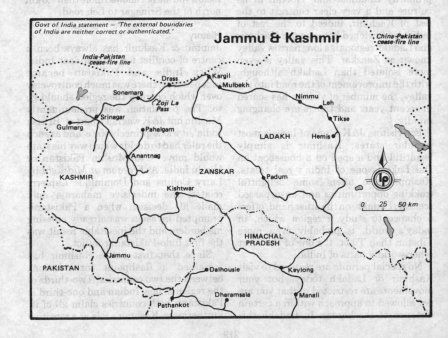

Govt of India statement – 'The external boundaries of India are neither correct or authenticated.'

Jammu & Kashmir

If these buses don't leave Jammu early enough they usually stop for the night at Banihal, just below the Banihal Tunnel, and continue on to Srinagar the following day. Accommodation in Banihal is usually in the *Tourist Lodge* and is very basic.

The second choice is to stay overnight in Jammu and take a bus to Srinagar the first thing next day. These early buses complete the journey to Srinagar in one day.

If you decide to stay overnight then it's important first to find yourself a room and then book a ticket on the bus. Don't hang about as competition for both can be fierce during the tourist season. If you're coming down from Srinagar it's even more necessary to quickly find a room, as you arrive late in the day when spare rooms may be at a premium.

Information

The Government of India tourist office (tel 5121) on Gulab Bhavan and the J&K Tourist Reception Centre (tel 5324) on Vir Marg are the standard reference centres. Neither is great, and the information they have is limited; both offices are open from 9 am to 5 pm. The Indian Airlines office (tel 5935, 3088) is also at the Tourist Reception Centre.

Raghunath Temple

The Raghunath Temple is in the centre of the city, only a short stroll from the Tourist Reception Centre. This large temple complex was built in 1835 but is not especially interesting, although it makes a good sunset silhouette. The Rambireswar Temple, also centrally located, is dedicated to Lord Shiva and dates from 1883.

Dogra Art Gallery

The Dogra Art Gallery, in the Gandhi Bhavan near the New Secretariat, has an important collection of miniature paintings including many from the locally renowned Basohli and Kangra schools. The gallery

is open from 7.30 am to 1 pm in summer and from 11 am to 5 pm in winter but is closed on Mondays; admission is free.

Amar Mahal Palace

On the northern outskirts of town, just off the Srinagar road, is the Amar Mahal Palace, a curious example of French architecture. The palace museum has a family portrait gallery and another important collection of paintings.

Places to Stay – bottom end

At the bottom end of the market, the popular *Tawi View Hotel* (tel 47301), Maheshi Gate, is the best of the bunch at Rs 45 for doubles with bath. Another simple but clean place is the *Hotel Kashmir*, Vir Marg, with bathless doubles at a similar price. The *Tourist Home Hotel* opposite the Tourist Reception Centre is of a similar standard and price, and is convenient although noisy.

There are many other budget hotels but there's not much to choose between them; it's usually a question of which ones have rooms available. Reasonable places include the *Hotel Aroma*, Gumat Bazaar, which charges Rs 35 for doubles with bath; the *Hotel Raj*, Rs 22 for bathless doubles; or the overpriced and grubby *Hotel Aryabhat*, Rs 45 for doubles with bath. The *Hotel Broadway* (tel 43636) on Gumat Chowk has a wide variety of rooms with and without bath from around Rs 35 to Rs 100.

At the railway station there's Jammu's second *Tourist Reception Centre* (tel 8803) with doubles from Rs 25 and beds in a dismal dorm. The station also has *retiring rooms* at Rs 50 (more with aircon) and dorm beds at Rs 12. Remember that the railway station is across the Tawi River, several km from the centre of Jammu. The bus station is close to the city centre and has rather decrepit *retiring rooms* with doubles for Rs 30 and dorm beds for Rs 5.

At the top of this range, one of the best places is the *Hotel Jagan* (tel 42402),

Raghunath Bazaar, which also has an air-con restaurant. It's spotlessly clean, pleasantly decorated and has singles/doubles for Rs 45/60, or doubles with air-con from Rs 100 to Rs 125.

Another popular place in this end of the market is the 128-room *Tourist Reception Centre* (tel 5421) on Vir Marg. Doubles range from Rs 50 to Rs 60. The dormitory is grim and should be avoided. In an alley close by, the *Sartaj Hotel* has clean double rooms with bath for Rs 44.

Places to Stay – middle

Across Vir Marg from the Tourist Reception Centre the much improved *Premier Hotel* is one of the best places around the centre with rooms at Rs 97/130 or Rs 175/225 with air-con. Also on Vir Marg the *Natraj Hotel* (tel 7450) has rooms with bath at Rs 40/90. Down the road from the Raghunath Temple are a

number of bottom and middle-range hotels. Other middle-bracket hotels include the *Gagan, Amar* and *City View* (tel 46120), all in Gumat Bazaar.

The *Hotel Cosmo* (tel 47561) is also on Vir Marg and has singles from Rs 60 to Rs 100, doubles from Rs 100 to Rs 150 or Rs 200 with air-con.

At the top end of the market is the *Hotel Jammu Ashok* (tel 46154, 42084) on the northern outskirts of town, close to the Amar Mahal Palace. Rooms are Rs 156/225 or Rs 345/455 with air-con. The *Hotel Asia* (tel 6373/5), similarly priced, is in Nehru Market close to the Jammu Tawi railway station and the airport, but a long way from the city centre. Both these upper-bracket hotels have a bar and restaurant.

Places to Eat

The usual government tourist centre menu is available at the *Tourist Reception*

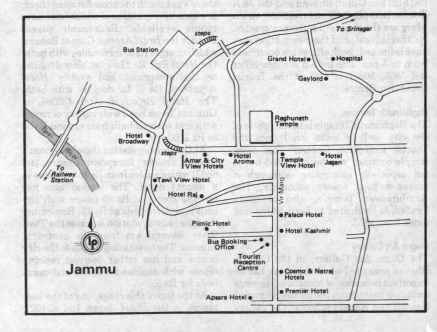

Centre and the food is reasonable. The air-conditioned restaurant at the *Cosmo Hotel* is better than the hotel – good for a cold beer and a pleasant meal in cool surroundings. A few doors down the *Premier* has Chinese and Kashmiri food but is rather expensive. There is a collection of little kebab stalls between the two.

The bus and railway stations have the usual restaurant facilities.

Getting There & Away

Air The airport is seven km out of town. There are flights to Srinagar (Rs 224), Chandigarh and Delhi.

Bus Srinagar buses depart from various locations: A class and deluxe go from the Tourist Reception Centre; B class from the bus station; and private buses from various parts of the city. Buses also run from the railway station where they meet arriving trains – thus you can take the overnight 145 Shalimar Express from Delhi and catch a bus as soon as you arrive at around 7 am. Buses normally depart between 6 and 7 am in order to reach Srinagar by nightfall. It is vital to book your bus ticket as soon as you arrive. Jammu to Srinagar bus fares are Rs 43 B class, Rs 53 A class, Rs 75 deluxe and Rs 100 video.

Southbound, there are frequent buses from Jammu to Amritsar, Pathankot (three hours) and other cities. Pathankot is the departure point for Dharamsala, Dalhousie and the other Himachal Pradesh hill stations.

Train The 145 Shalimar Express leaves Delhi at 4 pm and arrives in Jammu at 7 am. This is the only train that arrives early enough to link up with the early buses to Srinagar. The fare for the 535-km trip from Delhi is Rs 59 in 2nd class, Rs 215 in 1st.

Getting Around

Jammu has metered taxis, auto-rickshaws, a minibus service and a tempo service between a number of points. From the railway station to the bus station it costs Rs 1 by minibus. The same trip by auto-rickshaw is about Rs 7. It's only a short distance from the Tourist Reception Centre in the town centre to the bus station, say Rs 4 by auto-rickshaw.

JAMMU TO SRINAGAR

Although most people simply head straight through from Jammu to Srinagar, there are a few places of interest between the two centres. Some can also be reached using Jammu as a base. Prior to the completion of the Jawarhar Tunnel into the Kashmir Valley, the trip from Jammu took two days with an overnight stop at Batote.

Akhnoor

The Chenab River meets the plains here, 32 km north-west of Jammu. This used to be the route to Srinagar in the Moghul era. Jehangir, who died en route to Kashmir, was temporarily buried at Chingas.

Jammu to Srinagar

Basohli

Situated fairly close to Dalhousie, which is across the border in Himachal Pradesh, this is the birthplace of the Pahari miniature painting style.

Billawar, Sukrala, Babor & Permandal

All these places have ruined and uncompleted temples of some interest.

Surinsar & Mansar Lakes

East of Jammu, these lakes are picturesque and the scene for an annual festival at Mansar.

Vaishno Devi

This important cave temple is dedicated to the three mother goddesses of Hinduism. Thousands of pilgrims visit the cave each year after making a steep 12-km climb from the roadhead at Katra or taking a shorter and easier climb from a new road.

Riasi

Near this town, 80 km beyond Katra, is the ruined fort of General Zorawar Singh, renowned for his clashes with the Chinese over Ladakh. Nearby is a gurdwara with some interesting old frescoes and another important cave temple.

Ramnagar

The 'palace of colours' has many beautiful Pahari-style wall paintings. Buses run here from Jammu or Udhampur. Krimchi, 10 km from Udhampur, has Hindu temples with fine carvings and sculptures.

Kud

This is a popular lunch stop on the Jammu to Srinagar route at 1738 metres. It's also popular in its own right as a hill resort and has a *Tourist Bungalow*. There's a well-known mountain spring, Swamai Ki Bauli, 1½ km from the road.

Batote

Only 12 km further on, and connected to Patnitop and Kud by a number of footpaths, this hill resort at 1560 metres

was the overnight stop between Jammu and Srinagar before the tunnel was opened. There is a *Tourist Bungalow*, tourist huts and several private hotels. As in Kud, there is a spring close to the village – Amrit Chasma is only 2½ km away.

Patnitop

At 2024 metres this popular hill station has many pleasant walks. Patnitop is intended to be the nucleus of tourist developments in this area, and there are tourist huts, a *Rest House* and a *Youth Hostel*.

Sudh Mahadev

Many pilgrims visit the Shiva temple here during the annual July-August Asad Purnima festival which features three days of music, singing and dancing.

Five km from Sudh Mahadev is Man Talai, where some archaeological discoveries have been made. An eight-km walking or jeep track leads to Sudh Mahadev from Kud or Patnitop.

Sanasar

At 2079 metres, this beautiful valley is a centre for the Gujjar shepherds each summer. There is a *Tourist Bungalow*, tourist huts and several private hotels.

Bhadarwah

Every two years a procession of pilgrims walks from this beautiful high-altitude valley to the 4400-metre-high Kaplash Lake. A week later the three-day Mela Patt festival takes place in Bhadarwah. There is a *Rest House* in this scenic location.

Kishtwar

Well off the Jammu to Srinagar road there is a trekking route from Kishtwar to Srinagar. You can also trek from Kishtwar into Zanskar. There are many waterfalls around Kishtwar, and 19 km from the town is the pilgrimage site of Sarthal Devi.

Jawarhar Tunnel

During the winter months Srinagar was often completely cut off from the rest of India before this tunnel was completed. The 2500-metre-long tunnel is 200 km from Jammu and 93 km from Srinagar and has two separate passages. It's extremely rough and damp inside.

From Banihal, 17 km before the tunnel, you are already entering the Kashmiri region and people speak Kashmiri as well as Dogri. As soon as you emerge from the tunnel you are in the green, lush Vale of Kashmir.

Kashmir

This is one of the most beautiful regions of India. The Moghul rulers of India were always happy to retreat from the heat of the plains to the cool green heights of Kashmir, and indeed Jehangir's last words, when he died en route to the 'happy valley', was a simple request for 'only Kashmir'. The Moghuls developed their formal garden-style art to its greatest heights in Kashmir, and some of their gardens are beautifully kept even to this day.

One of Kashmir's greatest attractions is undoubtedly the Dal Lake houseboats. During the Raj period Kashmir's ruler would not permit the British (who were as fond of Kashmir's cool climate as the Moghuls) to own land here. So they adopted the superbly British solution of building houseboats – each one a little bit of England, afloat on Dal Lake. A visit to Kashmir, it is often said, is not complete until you have stayed on a houseboat.

Of course Srinagar, Dal Lake and houseboats are not all there is to Kashmir. Around the edges of the valley are Kashmir's delightful hill stations. Places like Pahalgam and Gulmarg are pleasant in their own right and also good bases for trekking trips.

SRINAGAR (population 700,000)

The capital of Kashmir stands on Dal Lake and the Jhelum River, and is the transport hub for the valley as well as the departure point for trips to Ladakh.

Srinagar is a crowded, colourful city with a distinctly central-Asian flavour. Indeed the people look different from those in the rest of India; and when you head south from Srinagar it is always referred to as 'returning to India'.

Orientation

Srinagar is initially a little confusing because Dal Lake, so much a part of the city, is such a strange lake. It's actually three lakes, separated by dykes or 'floating gardens', and at times it's hard to tell where lake ends and land begins.

On the lake there are houseboats that are firmly attached to the bottom, and houses that look like they could float away. Most of the houseboats are at the southern end of the lake, although you will also find them on the Jhelum River and north on Nagin Lake. The Jhelum River makes a loop around the main part of town, and a canal connecting the river with Dal Lake converts that part of town into an island. Along the south of this 'island' is the Bund, a popular walk where you will find the GPO and the handicrafts centre. The large Tourist Reception Centre is just north of the Bund.

There are many restaurants, shops, travel agents and hotels in the island part of town. The more modern part of Srinagar stretches away south of the Jhelum River while the older parts of town are north and north-west of here.

The Boulevard, running alongside Dal Lake, is an important address in Srinagar with the shikara ghats providing access to the houseboats, hotels, restaurants and shops along the way. Other main roads are Residency Rd, linking the Tourist Reception Centre with the downtown area, and Polo View Rd, lined with handicraft shops and travel agencies.

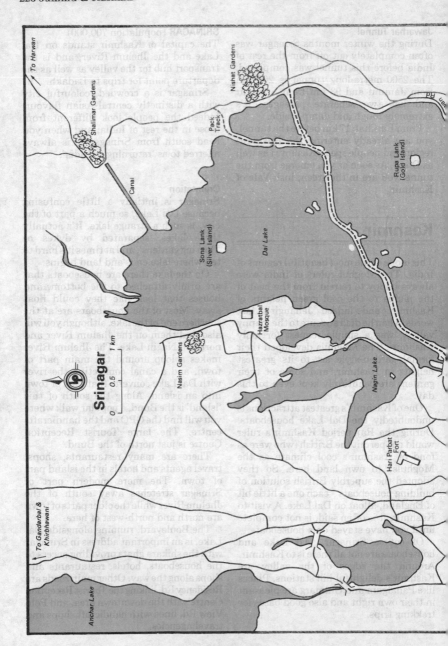

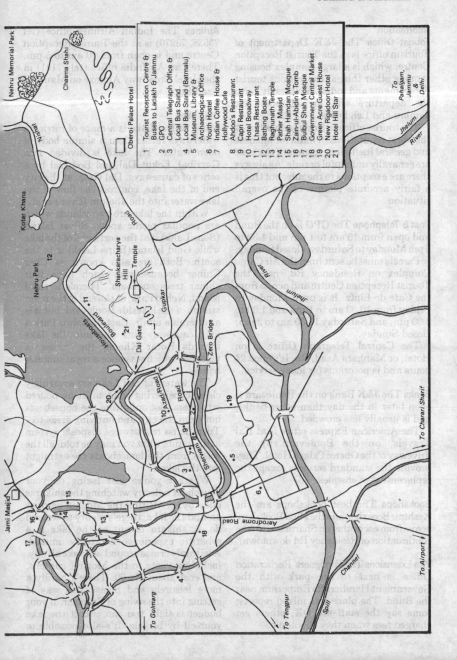

1 Tourist Reception Centre &
   Buses to Ladakh & Jammu
2 GPO
3 Central Telegraph Office &
   Local Bus Stand
4 Local Bus Stand (Batmalu)
5 Museum, Library &
   Archaeological Office
6 Youth Hostel
7 Indian Coffee House &
   Hollywood Cafe
8 Ahdoo's Restaurant
9 Capri Restaurant
10 Hotel Broadway
11 Lhasa Restaurant
12 Bathing Boats
13 Raghunath Temple
14 Pather Masjid
15 Shah Hamdan Mosque
16 Zain-ul-Abidin's Tomb
17 Bulbul Shah Mosque
18 Government Central Market
19 Green Acre Guest House
20 New Rigadoon Hotel
21 Hotel Hill Star

Information

Tourist Office The J&K Department of Tourism office is at the Tourist Reception Centre, which is a large complex housing (among other things) the various tourist departments and Indian Airlines. It's also the departure and arrival point for Jammu and Leh buses.

The tourist office in Srinagar has one of the worst reputations in India for idleness and general inefficiency; some of the staff are genarally unhelpful or rude. As always there are exceptions to the rule, but this is a fairly accurate picture of the overall situation.

Post & Telephone The GPO is on the Bund and open from 10 am to 1 pm and 1.30 to 6 pm Monday to Saturday, closed Sunday.

Parcels must be sent from the Air Cargo Complex on Residency Rd, near the Tourist Reception Centre and across from the Cafe de Lintz. It is open Monday to Friday from 10.30 am to 1 pm and 1.30 to 3.30 pm, and Saturday 10.30 am to 2 pm; closed Sunday.

The Central Telegraph Office is on Hotel, or Manhara Azad, Rd. It's open 24 hours and is notorious for lousy service.

Banks The J&K Bank on the Boulevard is open later in the day than other banks, and is usually less crowded.

The American Express office is at Kai Travels, on the Boulevard by the driveway of the Oberoi Palace Hotel. They provide the standard services except the replacement of cheques.

Bookshops The best bookshops are the Kashmir Bookshop and the Hind Bookshop, across from each other on Sharmani Rd (the continuation of Residency Rd downtown).

Visa Extensions The Foreigners' Registration Office is next to the park with the Government Handicrafts Emporium near the Bund. The place gets mixed reports; some say the staff are OK, others get charged fees when they shouldn't.

Airlines The Indian Airlines office (tel 73538, 73270) is at the Tourist Reception Centre and is open from 10 am to 5 pm. There's an Air India office (tel 77141) in the Hotel Broadway Annexe on Maulana Azad Rd.

Dal Lake

Much of Dal Lake is a maze of intricate waterways rather than a simple body of open water. The lake is divided into Gagribal, Lokut Dal and Bod Dal by a series of causeways. Dal Gate, at the city end of the lake, controls the flow of the lake water into the Jhelum River canal.

Within the lake are two islands which are popular picnic spots. Silver Island (Sona Lank) is at the north end of the lake while Gold Island (Rupa Lank) is to the south. Both are also known as Char Chinar because they each have four chinar trees on them. There's a third island, Nehru Park, at the end of the main stretch of the lakeside Boulevard, but it is a miserable affair. East of Nehru Park a long causeway juts out into the lake towards Kotar Khana, the 'house of pigeons', which was once a royal summer house.

The waters of Dal Lake are amazingly clear, considering what must be poured into them, not only from the houseboats but from the city and outlying areas too. There is no real sewage disposal system and, despite what you may be told, all the waste from the houseboats goes straight into the lake.

Whether you're just lazing on your houseboat balcony watching the shikaras glide by, or visiting the Moghul gardens around the lake, there's plenty to see and do. A shikara circuit of the lake is a sybaritic experience not to be missed. A leisurely cruise around will take all day, including visits to the Moghul gardens, and cost about Rs 60. There's hardly a more leisurely and pleasurable way of getting into the swing of Srinagar. If your budget is tight you can circuit the lake yourself by bicycle. It's also possible to ride right across the lake on the central causeway – see the Getting Around section.

Jhelum River & Bridges

The Jhelum flows from Verinag, 80 km south of Srinagar, to the Wular Lake to the north. This wide, swift-flowing, muddy and picturesque river sweeps through Srinagar, and is famed for its nine old bridges, but new bridges have popped up between them. There are a number of interesting mosques and other buildings near it, and a leisurely stroll or bicycle ride through the narrow lanes that run close to the river is very rewarding.

Museum

The Shri Pratap Singh Museum is in Lal Mandi, just south of the Jhelum River between Zero Bridge and Amira Kadal, the first 'old' bridge. It has an interesting collection of exhibits relevant to Kashmir, including illustrated tiles from Harwan. It's open every day from 10.30 am to 4.30 pm,

closed all day Mondays and on Fridays between 1 and 2.30 pm; admission is free.

Shah Hamdan Mosque

Originally built in 1395, the all-wooden mosque was destroyed by fire in 1479 and 1731. The present mosque is shaped like a cube with a pyramidal roof rising to a spire. Non-Muslims are not allowed inside.

Pather Masjid

On the opposite bank of the Jhelum River is the unused and run-down Pather Masjid. This fine stone mosque was built by Nur Jahan in 1623.

Tomb of Zain-ul-Abidin

Back on the east bank between the Zaina Kadal and Ali Kadal bridges is the slightly decrepit tomb of King Zain-ul-Abidin, the highly regarded son of Sultan Sikander. Built on the foundations of an earlier temple, the tomb shows a clear Persian influence in its domed construction and glazed tiles.

Houseboats on Dal Lake

Jami Masjid

This impressive wooden mosque is notable for the 300-plus pillars supporting the roof, each made of a single deodar tree trunk. The present mosque, with its green and peaceful inner courtyard, was rebuilt to the original design after a fire in 1674.

The mosque has had a chequered history: first built in 1385 by Sultan Sikander, it was enlarged by Zain-ul-Abidin in 1402 and then destroyed by fire in 1479. Rebuilt in 1503, it was destroyed by another fire during Jehangir's reign. Again it was rebuilt only to burn down once more before its most recent rebuilding.

Shankaracharya Hill

Rising up behind the Boulevard beside Dal Lake, the hill was once known as Takht-i-Sulaiman, the 'Throne of Solomon'. A temple is said to have first been built here by Ashoka's son around 200 BC, but the present Hindu temple dates from Jehangir's time. It's a pleasant stroll to the top, from where you have a fine view over Dal Lake – the Srinagar TV tower is also here. Alternatively there's a road right to the top.

Moghul Gardens

Chasma Shahi (9 km from Srinagar) Smallest of the Moghul gardens at Srinagar, the Chasma Shahi are well up the hillside, above the Nehru Memorial Park. The gardens were laid out in 1632 but have been recently extended. These are the only gardens with an admission charge.

Pari Mahal (10 km) Just above the Chasma Shahi is this fine old Sufi college. The ruined, arched terraces have recently been turned into a very pleasant and well-kept garden with fine views over Dal Lake. From the Pari Mahal you can descend straight down the hill to the road that runs back to the Oberoi Palace Hotel.

Nishat Bagh (11 km) Sandwiched between the lake and the mountains, the Nishat gardens have a superb view across the lake

to the Pir Panjal mountains. Designed in 1633 by Nur Jahan's brother Asaf Khan, this is the largest of the Moghul gardens and follows the traditional pattern of a central channel running down a series of terraces.

Shalimar Bagh (15 km) Set some distance back from the lake but reached by a small canal, the Shalimar gardens were built for Nur Jahan, 'light of the world', by her husband Jehangir in 1616.

During the Moghul period the topmost of the four terraces was reserved for the emperor and the ladies of the court. During the May to October tourist season a nightly son et lumiére (sound and light show) is put on in these beautiful gardens. The English performance is at 9 pm and tickets cost Rs 10 or Rs 15.

Nasim Bagh (8 km) Just beyond the Hazratbal Mosque, these gardens were built by Akbar in 1586 and are the oldest of Kashmir's Moghul gardens. Today, they are used by an engineering college and not maintained as a garden. It's possible to camp in this garden if you get prior permission from the Tourist Reception Centre.

Hazratbal Mosque

This shiny new mosque is on the northwest shore of Dal Lake. The mosque enshrines a hair of the prophet, but to nonbelievers it is most interesting for its stunningly beautiful setting on the shores of the lake with the snow-capped peaks as a backdrop.

Nagin Lake

The 'jewel in the ring' is held to be the most beautiful of the Dal lakes and is ringed by trees. There are a number of houseboats on this quieter, cleaner lake – ideal if you want to get away from it all.

Hari Parbat Fort

Clearly visible on top of the Sharika hill, to the west of Dal Lake, this fort was originally built between 1592 and 1598 during the rule of Akbar but most of the present construction dates from the 18th century. Visits are only possible with written permission from the Archaeology Department, so for most visitors the fort will remain just a pleasant backdrop. At the southern gate there is a shrine to the sixth Sikh Guru.

Pandrethan Temple

This small but beautifully proportioned Shiva temple dates from 900 AD and is in the military cantonment area on the Jammu road out of Srinagar.

Harwan

At the northern end of Dal Lake, archaeologists have discovered unusual ornamented tiles near Harwan. The tiles are believed to have been from a 3rd-century Buddhist monastery which was built on the site, and examples of them can be seen in the Srinagar museum. The water supply for Srinagar is pumped from here and piped along the causeway across the lake.

Tours

The J&K Road Transport Corporation operates a number of daily tours from the Tourist Reception Centre in Srinagar. Private bus companies, particularly the KMDA (Kashmir Motor Drivers' Association) also have several tours. The one-way/return fares for J&KRTC tours are:

Pahalgam	daily	Rs 33/56
Daksum	daily	Rs 33/56
Gulmarg	daily	Rs 33/56
Aharbal	Tues, Thur, Sun	Rs 33
Verinag	Wed, Sun	Rs 30
Wular Lake	Mon, Wed, Fri	Rs 30
Yusmarg	Tues, Thur, Sun	Rs 30/48
Sonamarg	daily	Rs 30/48
Moghul Gardens	twice daily	Rs 33

Places to Stay

Although houseboats are a prime attraction of a stay in Srinagar, there are also plenty of hotels in all price categories. The tourist centre would like to handle all the houseboat bookings, but there is no reason why you shouldn't just go out to the lake and look around for yourself. Booking through the tourist centre only means you get less choice in the matter and pay a higher price.

Srinagar is, however, notorious for its houseboat touts. They'll grab you at the airport, hassle you as you walk through town, and even try to snare you in Jammu! Even at the height of the season it's wise to treat tales of 'every houseboat is full, better take mine right now' with healthy scepticism. Don't consider any houseboat until you've actually been out and looked at it for yourself. It may sound terrific on paper but turn out to be a miserable dump overdue for downgrading to a lower category, or it might be a fine place in a terrible location. Despite this advice, it's amazing the number of letters we get from people who do commit themselves to a particular boat without seeing it and end up regretting it.

Dal Lake shikara

Houseboats There is no greater escape from the noise and hassle of Srinagar, a typically noisy Asian city, than the superbly relaxing houseboats. As soon as you get out on the lake traffic, pollution and hassles fade away. Basically most houseboats are the same. There's a small verandah at one end where you can sit and watch the world pass by, and behind this is a living room, usually furnished in British '30s style. Then there is a dining room and beyond that two or three bedrooms, each with a bathroom. Officially houseboats come in five categories, each with an officially approved price for singles/doubles with and without meals.

	full board	lodging only
Deluxe or five-star	Rs 275/405	Rs 190/270
A class	Rs 172/253	Rs 120/175
B class	Rs 120/204	Rs 80/140
C class	Rs 78/138	Rs 30/60
D class*	Rs 54/72	Rs 20/40

*doonga boats

There are different charges for children or for renting an entire boat.

In practice these 'official prices' are a bit meaningless. For a start there is a wide variance between boats – some are five-star and others FIVE-STAR! A good C-class boat can be better than a poor A-class boat. Also, most houseboats are managed in groups of three or more. You can be sure the food is not going to differ much from the best boat in the group to the worst. Plus, of course, there is competition. With so many houseboats (there are hundreds of them) a little negotiation is inevitable.

To find a houseboat, go down to the shikara ghats along the lakeside and announce that you want one. Either there will be somebody there with a boat available or you can hire a kid with a shikara to paddle you around the boats to ask. Generally you can get away with paying the price level for the category below each boat – for an A class boat pay

B class prices. If you decide to miss a meal (eg lunch) each day, then that can generally be negotiated into a lower price. Check if shikara trips to shore are included; they should be. This is Kashmir so pin down as many details as possible. Check what breakfast is going to be, for example – exactly how many eggs? Check if they'll supply a bucket of hot water for washing each morning – Kashmir can be chilly.

With the number of touts around these days, most travellers find it more convenient to check into a hotel for the first night, dump their gear and take a shikara to look at some boats without appearing obvious as new arrivals.

It's virtually impossible to recommend a particular boat; there are so many, they all only have a few rooms and there are so many variable factors. A pleasant shikara man, who runs you back and forth between boat and shore, makes tea, supplies hot water and so on, can make a nondescript boat into a pleasant one. A pleasant boat can be ruined by a poor cook. Or simply having some pleasant fellow houseboaters to chat with in the evening can make all the difference. Even on the best boats the food can get rather monotonous but there are plenty of 'supermarket' boats cruising by if you need soft drinks, chocolate, toilet paper, hashish or any other of life's necessities.

A peaceful life out on the lake depends, to some extent, on avoiding the attentions of the salesmen who continually paddle by. If you don't want to spend your whole time going through everything from woodcarvings to carpets and embroidery to papier mâché, it's necessary to be very firm and decisive with these people. You can always retreat from the houseboat verandah to the more secluded roof, but why should you have to? Equally important is the attitude of the houseboat owners who rake off a handy little commission from everything that gets sold on their houseboat. On some houseboats you may actually find that the service, food or general attitude take a disastrous dip if you don't spend, spend, spend. The only answer to this policy is to move to a better houseboat, where the owners have more respect for their guests' comfort.

Although it's impractical to recommend good houseboats, there are some which get consistently bad reports from travellers. They have earned themselves a reputation for dubious and dishonest practices. Use them at your peril. They include: the *Lake Placid* group of houseboats (Nagin Lake), HB *Lagoo Palace* and *Top Erin* (Dal Lake), HB *New Montral* (Dal Lake), and HB *Young Bombay* (Dal Lake).

Places to Stay – bottom end

There are cheap hotels scattered all around Srinagar, although those in the Lal Chowk area tend to be noisy. The best of the cheapies are in three main areas: amongst the houseboats around Dal Gate; along Buchwara Chowk, which runs parallel with the Boulevard; and in the Raj Bagh area across the Jhelum River.

There are several hotels, surrounded by houseboats, on small Dal Lake islands. Most are pretty spartan and cater mainly to Indian tourists. Two places popular with budget travellers are the *Hotel Sundowna* and, next door, the *Hotel Savoy*. They cost Rs 10 for a dorm bed and Rs 30/40 for singles/doubles. Take a shikara from the first ghat by Dal Gate.

The *New Hotel Rigadoon* is a real step up. Clean and pleasant, its comfortable singles/doubles cost Rs 70/100, but it also has dorm beds for Rs 15. To find it cross over Dal Gate and it's on the right after the bridge.

The *Hotel Hill Star* in Buchwara Rd has a lovely garden, pleasant management and staff, is fairly clean and does a good breakfast. Rooms cost Rs 40/80. Head east from Dal Gate along the Boulevard, turn south (right) by the John Trading Corp sign, and at the end of the block is Buchwara Rd.

Follow the signs to the nearby *Rubina Guest House, Hotel Sultan, Hotel Raj*

and *Hotel Heeven*. Owned and operated by Bengalis, these are also above average by local standards. The Rubina has double rooms for Rs 40. Continue east along Buchwara Rd and you come to the *Tibetan Guest House* on the left. Another favourite, it's hidden behind a high wall and gate, so look out for it.

Raj Bagh, a quiet residential area, is on the south bank of the Jhelum River, opposite the Bund. The *Bhat Guest House*, one of the cheapest places in Srinagar, is surprisingly clean and comfortable with rooms for Rs 26/30. There are several other places in this area.

There are rooms at the *Tourist Reception Centre*, although these will almost certainly be full in the high season. The rooms range from Rs 80 for doubles to Rs 100 for deluxe doubles, and there are dorm beds for Rs 20.

Across the river from the city centre on Wazir Bagh, the Srinagar *Youth Hostel* is rather out of the way. Foreigners need to be YHA members, but it is very cheap at Rs 3 for a dorm bed and Rs 15 for double rooms.

Places to Stay – middle

The *Green Acre Guest House* (tel 73349), a large private house in Raj Bagh, is a delightful haven from Srinagar's hustle and bustle. The management staff are pleasant, there's a delightful garden, a wide choice of rooms and consistently good food. It's understandably very popular; singles cost Rs 120 and doubles range from Rs 150 to Rs 400. To find it, cross Zero Bridge, turn right, then left by the Snow Hut Cafe, and it's on the left at the foot of the slope. Take an auto-rickshaw from the Tourist Reception Centre if you're arriving with baggage.

On Buchwara Rd adjacent to the Lhasa Restaurant, the fairly new *Pinegrove Hotel* (tel 72405) has rooms for Rs 130/210 including breakfast. It's a good deal compared to what else is on offer.

On the Boulevard facing Dal Lake, the

Hotel Mazda (tel 72842) stands out as good value with rooms for Rs 95/145. The best rooms are in the main building at the rear. The *Lake Isle Resort* (tel 78446) is beautifully located on an island in the middle of Dal Lake. Singles/doubles cost Rs 175/200 with breakfast.

Places to Stay – top end

The *Oberoi Palace Hotel* (tel 75641) is the ex-palace of the Maharaja of Kashmir and is Srinagar's top establishment. It's several km around the Boulevard from Dal Gate and singles/doubles are Rs 625/725, Rs 900/2500 for suites. The actual building is rather uninspired, particularly if you've seen the sumptuous palace hotels of Rajasthan, but the gardens in front provide superb views over the lake.

The *Hotel Broadway* (tel 79001) is a good modern alternative to the Oberoi Palace and is more conveniently located, on Mandana Azad Rd across from the polo field. Singles/doubles cost Rs 500/680 and there's a good restaurant and swimming pool.

There are a number of hotels along the Boulevard, the best of which is probably the *Welcome*, with rooms for Rs 250/350, and the *Asia Brown Palace*, which charges Rs 200 for singles and Rs 290 to Rs 390 for doubles.

The only hotel by Nagin Lake is the elegant *Hotel Dar-es-Salan* (tel 77803). It is reasonably priced with rooms for Rs 225/350 and has good food and a good location.

Places to Eat

Probably because so many people eat on board their houseboats, Srinagar is not a very exciting place for eating out.

The Rs 90 buffet dinner at the *Oberoi Palace Hotel* is a great splurge, although you do have the problem of getting there and back. The *Broadway* has a cheaper buffet on some nights, and the food on nonbuffet nights is good and priced at around Rs 35 to Rs 45 per dish.

The tiny *Alka Salka* on Residency Rd across from Polo View Rd serves very good

Chinese and Indian food for around Rs 20 per dish. *Ahdoo's*, in new premises on Residency Rd, has long been one of Srinagar's best places for Kashmiri food and Indian specialties.

The *Mughal Darbar* is another of Srinagar's better places for Kashmiri and Indian food. This is despite its often filthy appearance, its scruffy and inefficient waiters and the loud and overbearing locals. It's adjacent to the Suffering Moses store and across from the polo field on Residency Rd.

The *Lhasa Restaurant* serves good Chinese-Tibetan style food and is popular with travellers. It's near Dal Lake, just off the Boulevard.

The *Tao Cafe* on Residency Rd, by the turn-off to the GPO, has a lovely garden which makes a nice place to chat or write postcards while you wait for your order. Further downtown, the dingy *Indian Coffee House* is the place where the local literary set hang out. The menu is limited to coffee and snacks. The *Hollywood Cafe* opposite looks unimpressive but the food is not bad by local standards.

The bakeries near Dal Gate do a roaring trade with travellers. *Sultan Bakery* has excellent gingernut biscuits, apple pie and cheesecake. The *Glocken Bakery* has tables and also serves hot and cold drinks. Stock up with goodies before heading to Leh.

For cheap south Indian food try the *Ramble Restaurant* near Dal Gate. The roast chicken here is also good, as are the breakfasts.

Things to Buy

Kashmir is famous for its many handicrafts, and selling them is an activity pursued with amazing energy. You can visit workshops to see many of them being made. Popular buys include carpets, papier mâché articles, leather and furs, woodcarvings, shawls and embroidery, honey, tailor-made clothing, pleasantly coarse-knitted sweaters and cardigans, that expensive spice saffron and many other items.

There is a whole string of government handicraft emporiums scattered around Srinagar, but the main one is housed in the fine old British Residency building by the Bund. The flashiest shops are along the Boulevard by Dal Lake. The Bund also has some interesting shops, including Suffering Moses with high-quality goods. Shikaras patrol Dal Lake like sharks, loaded down with goodies.

Getting There & Away
Air Indian Airlines fly to Srinagar from New Delhi (Rs 715), Chandigarh (Rs 610), Amritsar (Rs 415), Jammu (Rs 240) and Leh (Rs 360). Flights are more frequent during the summer tourist season. Flight time from Delhi on the direct flights is about 70 minutes. As usual in India, you should book your flights as early as possible.

Bus See the Jammu and Leh sections for details about bus services from those places to Srinagar.

The Jammu & Kashmir Road Transport Corporation buses go from the Tourist Reception Centre, while private buses operate from a variety of stands in Srinagar. Certain major long-distance routes are reserved for the J&K buses (Jammu, Leh, etc), but others are open for competition and there will be a great number of buses operating.

When planning to leave, it is best to book a seat as soon as possible as buses are often fully booked the day before. Nearly all buses arrive at and depart from the Tourist Reception Centre bus compound, although some B-class buses stop at Lal Chowk.

Train There's a railway booking office at the Tourist Reception Centre for train departures to Jammu.

Taxi For those with thick wallets, taxis are available for long-distance trips such as Jammu (Rs 800 for the whole vehicle) and Leh (Rs 2000).

Getting Around
There is a wide choice of transport available either on or around the lake, plus a variety of tours. The tour buses are generally much more comfortable than the usual run of overcrowded local buses and, since many of them offer one-way fares, they can be used for getting out to hill stations in the valley.

Airport Transport From Srinagar airport, which is about 13 km out of the city, there's an airport bus to the Tourist Reception Centre in Srinagar that costs Rs 12.50.

Shikara These are the graceful, long boats which crowd the Srinagar lakes. They're used for getting back and forth from the houseboats or for longer tours. Officially there is a standard fare for every trip around the lake and these are prominently posted at the main landings (ghats); in practice the fares can be quite variable. To be shuttled across to your houseboat should cost Rs 2 in a covered ('full spring seats') shikara, but the kids who are always out for a little money will happily paddle you across for Rs 0.50 or less in a basic, open shikara. Of course, late at night, particularly if it is raining, the tables are turned and getting back to your houseboat at a reasonable price may require a little ingenuity!

Try paddling a shikara yourself sometime – it's nowhere near as easy as it looks. You'll spend lots of time going round in circles.

Bus Take a No 12 bus to Nagin Lake or the Hazratbal Mosque.

Taxi & Auto-Rickshaw There are stands for these at the Tourist Reception Centre and other strategic locations in town. Srinagar's taxi-wallahs are extremely reluctant to use their meters so you'll have to bargain hard. Count on about Rs 10 to Rs 15 for a taxi from the Tourist Reception Centre to Dal Gate, Rs 5 to Rs 10 by auto-rickshaw. For longer trips the official fares are all posted by the stands.

Bicycle Cycling is an extremely pleasant way of getting around, especially as the valley is fairly flat. You can hire bikes for Rs 10 per day and there are several stores along the Boulevard close to Dal Gate. Following are some suggested trips.

Around Dal Lake – an all-day trip going by the Moghul gardens. It's particularly pleasant around the north of the lake where the villages are still relatively untouched. Across the lake – you can ride across the lake on the causeway, a nice trip since there are no traffic problems and there is plenty of opportunity to observe lake life without being in a boat. Nagin Lake – you can ride out to the Hazratbal Mosque via Nagin Lake and then make a complete loop around the lake on the way back. This trip can easily be combined with a trip along the Jhelum, taking in the various mosques close to the river. The streets here are very narrow so vehicles keep away and bike riding is pleasant.

KASHMIR VALLEY

When lazing around on your houseboat begins to pall, it's time to head off around the valley. There are a number of interesting places in the Kashmir Valley for day trips from Srinagar and several popular hill stations which serve as good bases for short or long treks into the surrounding mountains. Pahalgam and Gulmarg are the two main Kashmiri hill resorts.

SRINAGAR TO PAHALGAM

The route to Pahalgam passes through some interesting places including, if you take the bus tour to Pahalgam, enough Moghul gardens to leave you thoroughly saturated. Only 16 km south-west of Srinagar is Pampore, centre of Kashmir's saffron industry. Saffron is highly prized for its flavouring and colouring properties and is consequently rather expensive.

At Avantipur are two ruined Hindu temples built between 855 and 883 AD. The Avantiswami Temple, the larger of the two, is dedicated to Vishnu and still has some fine relief sculptures and columns of an almost Grecian appearance. The smaller temple, dedicated to Shiva, is about one km before the main temple and close to the main road. At Anantnag the road forks, and the Pahalgam road turns north from here.

Just beyond the Pahalgam turn-off is Achabal, a Moghul garden laid out in 1620 by Shah Jahan's daughter, Jahanara. This carefully designed garden was said to be a favourite retreat of Nur Jahan. Kokarnag, further on, is certain to give you garden overload but is famous for its rose gardens. Back on the Pahalgam route Mattan has a fish-filled spring which is an important pilgrimage spot. Above Mattan on a plateau is the huge ruined temple of Martland.

Not actually on or even close to the Pahalgam route is Verinag in the extreme south of the Kashmir Valley. The spring here is said to be the actual source of the Jhelum River. Jehangir built an octagonal stone basin at the spring in 1612 and Shah Jahan laid out a garden around it in 1620.

Sangam, 35 km north-east of Srinagar, is a centre for production of (would you believe) cricket bats. They're lined up by the road in their thousands.

PAHALGAM

Pahalgam is about 95 km from Srinagar and at 2130 metres the night-time temperatures here are warmer than in Gulmarg, which is higher up.

The beautiful Lidder River flows right through the town, which is at the junction of the Sheshnag and Lidder rivers and is surrounded by soaring, fir-covered mountains with snow-capped peaks rising behind them.

There are many short walks from Pahalgam and it is an ideal base for longer treks to Kolahoi Glacier or Amarnath Cave – see Treks in Kashmir later in this chapter, or the Lonely Planet guide *Trekking in the Indian Himalaya*. Pahalgam is also famous for its many shepherds. They're a common sight, driving their flocks of sheep along the paths all around town.

Information
The rather useless tourist office (tel 24) is just around the corner from the bus stop. There is a bank and a post office open in the tourist season.

Fishing permits have to be obtained in Srinagar but trekking supplies can be bought here, although they are cheaper in Srinagar.

Pahalgam Walks
Mamaleswara Only a km or so downstream and on the opposite bank of the Lidder, this small Shiva temple with its square stone tank is thought to date back to the 12th century.

Baisaran There are excellent views over the town and the Lidder Valley from this meadow, five km from Pahalgam. A further 11 km takes you to the Tulian Lake at 3353 metres. It is covered with ice for much of the year.

Aru The pleasant little village of Aru makes a very interesting day walk, following the Lidder River for 11 km upstream. Unfortunately, the main track on the left bank also takes cars, although there is a less used (and more difficult) track on the right bank. This is actually the first stage of the Kolahoi Glacier trek.

Places to Stay – bottom end
There are many hotels along the main street of Pahalgam, and these cater mainly to Indian tourists. Most travellers head across the river to one of the lodges on the western bank. The *Aksa Lodge* (tel 59) is the most popular, although the rooms can be a bit basic. It's generally well

run, and rooms cost Rs 30 to Rs 120 for singles, and Rs 50 to Rs 200 for doubles. Hot water is always available and the food is good.

The other lodges are not as good. The best among them is probably the *Brown Palace*, although it is a long way from town. The trekking agency, Pahalgam Guided Treks, which has its office in this hotel, has been recommended as a reliable operator. Another option is the *Windrush House*. To get there continue past the path leading up to Aksa Lodge and go down to the right, on the riverbank.

The *Hotel Kolahoi Kabin*, between the two rivers, could also be worth checking out; double rooms cost Rs 80. The other places are a lot more decrepit. These include the *White House*, *Woodlands*, *Bentes Lodge* and *Highland Palace*.

The government *Tourist Bungalow* has doubles for Rs 35 while the adjacent *Tourist Huts* has rooms for Rs 90/150.

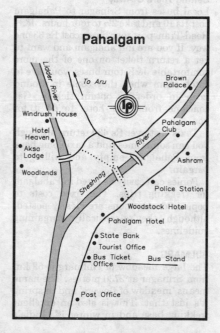

Just outside of Pahalgam on the Amarnath route the *Yog Niketan* ashram is an interesting place to stay and take yoga and meditation courses.

Places to Stay – top end

The *Pahalgam Hotel* (tel 26) is the top place to stay and has singles/doubles for Rs 525/700 with meals. It has all the facilities you'd expect in this price range, including heated swimming pool, sauna and massage. The *Woodstock Hotel* (tel 27) next door has singles/doubles for Rs 350/400 without the extras.

Places to Eat

If you're staying on the west bank area it's convenient to eat there as well. In the main street on the west bank, the *Lhasa Restaurant* is not as good as its namesake in Srinagar. The *Pahalgam Hotel* does a pretty good set-meal for Rs 65.

Getting There & Away

Local buses from Srinagar to Pahalgam cost Rs 10 and take 2½ to four hours. J&K Road Transport tour buses cost Rs 33 one way. If you are in Pahalgam and want to get a return ticket on one of the more comfortable J&K tour buses, you have to catch them when they come in around noon in order to obtain tickets. Get someone from your hotel to do it for you.

Taxis cost over Rs 430 return although you can sometimes find a taxi going back from Pahalgam empty and willing to bargain.

Ponies can easily be hired in Pahalgam for trekking trips. The fixed costs to popular destinations are clearly posted, although they're basically bargaining guidelines.

GULMARG

The large meadow of Gulmarg is 52 km from Srinagar at 2730 metres. The name means 'meadow of flowers' and in spring it's just that. This is also an excellent trekking base and in winter it's India's premier skiing resort. The skiing equipment available is fairly good and the costs are very low. The area is also wonderful for ski-touring although very little cross-country equipment is available.

Gulmarg can get pretty cold at times, even compared to Pahalgam, so come prepared with plenty of warm clothes.

Information

The tourist office, in the valley bottom about half a km beyond the golf course, is the green-blue building complex with three patches of new wooden roof.

Skiing

There is one chair lift, one T-bar and four pomas. The slopes vary from beginner to intermediate and are usually deserted. Equipment hire is about Rs 50, lessons are Rs 40, and lift passes are Rs 30 for the pomas, Rs 80 for the chair lift – all on daily basis. All lifts operate from 10 am to 5 pm; they're closed for one hour at lunch. Limited amounts of cross-country equipment is available. Contact S D Singh, Hut 209A for more information.

A new cable car has been constructed to the top of Mt Apharwat, and this has opened up some superb new areas above the tree line.

Gulmarg Walks

Outer Circular Walk A circular road, 11 km in length, runs right round Gulmarg through pleasant pine forests with excellent views over the Kashmir Valley. Nanga Parbat is visible to the north, and Haramukh and Sunset Peak are visible to the south-east.

Khilanmarg This smaller valley is about a six-km walk from the Gulmarg bus stop and car park. The meadow, carpeted with flowers in the spring, is the site for Gulmarg's winter ski runs and offers a fine view of the surrounding peaks and the Kashmir Valley. During the early spring, as the snow melts, it can be a very muddy hour's climb up the hill.

Alpather Beyond Khilanmarg, 13 km from Gulmarg at the foot of the 4511-metre Apharwat peak, this lake is frozen until mid-June, and even later in the year you can see lumps of ice floating in its cold waters. The walk from Gulmarg follows a well-graded pony track over the 3810-metre Apharwat Ridge, separating the lake from Khilanmarg, and proceeds up the valley to the lake at 3843 metres.

Ningle Nallah Flowing from the melting snow and ice on Apharwat Peak and Alpather Lake, this pretty mountain stream is 10 km from Gulmarg. The stream continues down into the valley below and joins the Jhelum River near Sopore. The walking path crosses the Ningle Nallah by a bridge and continues on to the Lienmarg, another grassy meadow and a good spot for camping.

Ferozpore Nallah Reached from the Tangmarg road, or from the outer circular walk, this mountain stream meets the Bahan River at a popular picnic spot known as 'waters meet'. The stream is reputed to be particularly good for trout fishing; it's about five km from Gulmarg. You can continue on from here to Tosamaidan, a three-day, 50-km walk to one of Kashmir's most beautiful meadows.

Ziarat of Baba Reshi This Muslim shrine is on the slopes below Gulmarg and can be reached from either Gulmarg or Tangmarg. The *ziarat*, or tomb, is of a well-known Muslim saint who died here in 1480. Before renouncing worldly ways he was a courtier of the Kashmir king Zain-ul-Abidin.

Places to Stay – bottom end
Budget accommodation is in short supply, as is hot water. The *Tourists Hotel* (tel 53), opposite the bus stand, is a remarkably baroque and weathered fantasy in wood, like something out of *Lord of the Rings* although it's rather dirty and grubby inside. Rooms cost Rs 30 to Rs 50.

The *City View* has superb views, a friendly manager and fine food; the basic rooms costs around Rs 30. The nearby *Tourist Bungalow* is probably the most comfortable place with rooms at Rs 45.

The shabby *Kingsley Hotel* (tel 55) costs a ridiculous Rs 150, while the old *New Punjab* is Rs 30. The pleasant *Green View* is a nice contrast at Rs 120.

Places to Stay – top end
The *Hotel Highlands Park* (tel 7, 30) is Gulmarg's overrated topnotch hotel, and single/double rooms cost Rs 525/725 with all meals. The rooms are OK but the food is poor considering the high price. The pleasant bar is the hotel's saving grace. *Nedou's Hotel* (tel 23) charges Rs 400/500.

Places to Eat
Limited and not very good sums up the situation. For cheap meals there are the south Indian cafes by the bus stand. Elsewhere, prices are considerably higher. *Ahdoo's* next to the bus stand is probably the best in Gulmarg.

Getting There & Away
There are a variety of buses running from Srinagar to Gulmarg, many of them on day tours. On a day tour you have only a few hours at the hill resort, just long enough for one of the shorter day walks. J&K tour buses cost Rs 33 one way, ordinary buses are around Rs 10 one way or Rs 15 return.

At one time the road from Srinagar only ran to Tangmarg, seven km in distance and 500 metres in altitude below Gulmarg. The last stretch then had to be completed on foot or by pony. Although the road now runs to Gulmarg, some buses still terminate at Tangmarg. The winding road from Tangmarg is 13 km in length, nearly twice as far as the more direct pony track.

SOUTH OF SRINAGAR
Interesting places in the south-west of the Kashmir valley include Yusmarg, reputed to have the best spring flowers in

Kashmir, and a good base for treks further afield. Chari Sharif is on the road to Yusmarg and has the shrine, or ziarat, of Kashmir's patron saint. Aharbal was a popular resting place for the Moghul emperors when they made the long trip north from Delhi.

SINDH VALLEY

This is a scenic area north of Srinagar through which the road to Ladakh passes. The Zoji La pass marks the boundary from the Sindh Valley into Ladakh. From Srinagar you pass the Dachigam wildlife reserve, once a royal game park; you need a signed permit (Rs 20) from the Srinagar tourist office to enter the reserve.

Anchar Lake, rarely visited, is close to Srinagar and has a wide variety of water birds. There is a Moghul garden built by Nur Jahan at Manasbal Lake. Wular Lake is possibly the largest freshwater lake in India and the Jhelum River flows into it.

Sonamarg, at 2740 metres, is the last major town before Ladakh and an excellent base for trekking. Its name means 'meadow of gold', which could derive from the spring flowers or from the strategic trading position it once enjoyed. There are *Tourist Huts*, a *Rest House* and some small hotels here.

The tiny village of Baltal is the last place in Kashmir, right at the foot of the Zoji La. When conditions are favourable you can walk to the Amarnath Cave from here. The Zoji La is the watershed between Kashmir and Ladakh – on one side you have the green, lush scenery of Kashmir while on the other side everything is barren and dry.

TREKS IN KASHMIR

There are various treks both within Kashmir and from Kashmir to Ladakh or Zanskar. The short Pahalgam to Kolahoi Glacier trek is particularly popular and the Pahalgam to Amarnath Cave trek is well known not only for the natural scenery, but for the great religious festival that takes place here.

Porters in Kashmir are used less frequently than they are in Nepal; ponies carry the gear. Although trekking companies are not as widespread as in Nepal they are starting to pop up. Summit Treks and Choomti Trekkers, both in Srinagar, have been recommended.

Pahalgam to Kolahoi Glacier

This short and very popular trek takes only four days from Pahalgam to Pahalgam, but it can be extended before returning to Pahalgam or continued up into the Sindh Valley. The first day from Pahalgam takes you to Aru along the bank of the Lidder River. This is also a very popular day trek from Pahalgam since Aru is a pretty little village.

The second day's walk takes you to Lidderwat which has a *Government Rest House* and a very pleasant campsite, and where the stream from the glacier meets the stream from Tarsar Lake. There is also the friendly *Paradise Guest House* here. There are double rooms for Rs 30 or you can sleep on the 'dormitory' floor. The people who run it cope admirably with large groups of hungry trekkers – their Paradise Rice Pie is excellent.

On the third day you trek up to the lake and back to Lidderwat. The glacier, climbing from 3400 metres to 4000 metres, descends from the 5485-metre Kolahoi mountain. On Day 4 you can either walk straight back to Pahalgam in one day or the trek can be extended another day by walking from Lidderwat to Tarsar Lake and back. You can shorten the trek by going straight from Pahalgam to Lidderwat in one day, quite an easy walk.

Instead of returning to Pahalgam, three days' further trek will take you to Kulan near Sonamarg in the Sindh Valley. It's only 16 km from Kulan to Sonamarg, which you can walk or travel by bus.

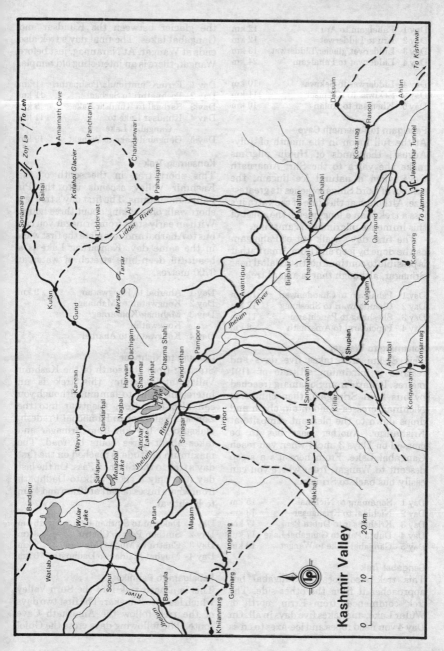

Kashmir Valley

To Leh
Zoji La
Sonamarg
Baltal
Kulan
Gund
Wayul
Karcan
Gandarbal
Safapur
Bandipur
Wular Lake
Watlab
Sopur
Baramula
Khilanmarg
Gulmarg
Tangmarg
Magam
Patan
Manasbal Lake
Nagbal
Harwan
Dachigam
Shalimar
Nishat
Chasma Shahi
Dal Lake
Srinagar
Anchar Lake
Airport
Jhelum River
Pandrethan
Pandrethan
Pampore
Avantipur
Jhelum River
Hakhal
Yus
Sangarwani
Killa
Shupian
Aharbal
Kongwatam
Konsarnag
Kulgam
Bijbihar
Khanabal
Anantnag
Achabal
Oazigund
Kotamarg
Maitan
Akhtan
Achabal
Kokarnag
Rasool
Daksum
Ahlan
To Jammu
Jawarhar Tunnel
To Kishtwar
Amarnath Cave
Panchtarni
Chandanwari
Pahalgam
Aru
Lidderwat
Liddar River
Tarsar
Marsar
Kolahoi Glacier

0   10   20 km

Day 1	Pahalgam to Aru	12 km
Day 2	Aru to Lidderwat	12 km
Day 3	Lidderwat/glacier/Lidderwat	13 km
Day 4	Lidderwat to Pahalgam	24 km
or		
Day 4	Lidderwat to Sekiwas	10 km
Day 5	Sekiwas to Khemsar	11 km
Day 6	Khemsar to Kulan	10 km

Pahalgam to Amarnath Cave

At the full moon in the month of July-August, thousands of Hindu pilgrims make the yatra to the Shri Amarnath Cave when a natural ice lingam, the symbol of Lord Shiva, reaches its greatest size. Although at the time of the yatra it's less a trek than a long queue, the spirit of this immense pilgrimage is amazing.

The first day's walk out of Pahalgam can be done by jeep and from Amarnath it is possible to continue north to Baltal near Srinagar, although that is a hard trek.

Day 1	Pahalgam to Chandanwari	13 km
Day 2	Chandanwari to Sheshnag	12 km
Day 3	Sheshnag to Panchtarni	11 km
Day 4	Panchtarni to Amarnath	8 km

Sonamarg to Wangat

This 81-km trek takes five days and reaches a maximum altitude of 4191 metres. It starts from Sonamarg (reached by bus from Srinagar), then climbs to Nichinai, crosses a mountain chain and drops down to the pleasant campsite at Krishansar. Another pass has to be crossed on Days 3 and 4 when you reach Gangabal Lake. From here it's a steep descent to Wangat, from where you can easily bus back to Srinagar.

Day 1	Sonamarg to Nichinai	15 km
Day 2	Nichinai to Krishansar	13 km
Day 3	Krishansar to Dubta Pani	17 km
Day 4	Dubta Pani to Gangabal Lake	17 km
Day 5	Gangabal Lake to Wangat	19 km

Gangabal Trek

This trek also goes to Gangabal but approaches it from the other side. The trek commences from Errin, north of Wular Lake, and takes five days in all. On Day 4 you need ropes and ice-axes to cross the glacier between the Kundsar and Gangabal lakes. The final day's trek also ends at Wangat. At Narannag, just before Wangat, there is an interesting old temple.

Day 1	Errin/Chuntimula/Poshpathri	11 km
Day 2	Poshpathri to Sarbaal	11 km
Day 3	Sarbaal to Kundsar Lake	9 km
Day 4	Kundsar Lake to Gangabal Lake	11 km
Day 5	Gangabal Lake to Wangat	19 km

Konsarnag Trek

This short trek in the south of the Kashmir Valley ascends into the Pir Panjal mountains. The first day's trek is a short walk only taking about three hours. With an early start from Srinagar you can bus to Aharbal and complete the first walk in the same day. Konsarnag Lake is a beautiful deep-blue stretch of water at 3700 metres.

Day 1	Aharbal to Kongwatan	9 km
Day 2	Kongwatan to Mahinag	
Day 3	Mahinag/Konsarnag/Kongwatan	
Day 4	Kongwatan to Aharbal	

Daksum to Kishtwar

Starting from the south of the Kashmir Valley at Daksum, this trek is an interesting route to Jammu, although you can also trek from Kishtwar into the Zanskar Valley or to Himachal Pradesh. Daksum is 100 km from Srinagar and takes about three hours by road. The maximum altitude is reached on the first day's trek to the Sinthan Pass. On the last day it is only a short walk to Dadhpath from where buses depart at 10 am and 4 pm to Kishtwar.

Day 1	Daksum to Sinthan Pass	16 km
Day 2	Sinthan Pass to Chatru	8 km
Day 3	Chatru to Mughal Maidan	9 km
Day 4	Mughal Maidan to Dadhpath	8 km

Pahalgam to Pannikar

This is a hard trek into the Suru Valley which leads to Zanskar. The first two days of the trek follow the Amarnath Cave route. The following days cross the Gulol

Gali Pass, climb to the Lonvilad Gali, go over the Chalong Glacier and continue down to Pannikar. From Pannikar you can take the road north to Kargil or east into the Zanskar Valley.

Day 1 & 2	Amarnath Cave	
Day 3	Sheshnag to Rangmarg	8 km
Day 4	Rangmarg to Hampet	6 km
Day 5 & 6	Hampet to Lonvilad Gali	22 km
Day 7	Lonvilad Gali	
Day 8	Chalong Glacier to Pannikar	15 km

Ladakh

'Little Tibet', 'the moonland' and 'the last Shangri La' are names that have been applied to Ladakh, all with a bit of truth. Ladakh is a high-altitude plateau north of the Himalaya situated geographically in Tibet. It is a miniature version of Tibet, the people are Tibetan in their culture and religion, and there are many Tibetan refugees.

The Himalaya are a very effective barrier to rain – few clouds creep across their awesome height and as a result Ladakh is barren beyond belief. Only where rivers, running from faraway glaciers or melting snow, carry water to habitation do you find plant life – hence the moonland label, since Ladakh is as dry as the Sahara.

Finally, Ladakh could well be a last Shangri La. Only in the mid-70s was it opened to outside visitors. Its strategic isolation is matched by its physical isolation – only from June to September is the road into Ladakh from Kashmir not covered by snow and only since 1979 has there been airline flights into Ladakh. That flight is one of the most spectacular in the world.

If you're in Kashmir don't fail to make the trip to Ladakh. It's an other-worldly place – strange gompas perched on soaring hilltops, shattered-looking landscapes splashed with small but brilliant patches of green, and ancient palaces clinging to sheer rock walls. But most of all there are the delightful Ladakhis, friendly as only Tibetan people can be and immensely colourful.

General Advice

A sleeping bag is very useful in Ladakh even if you're not trekking or camping. The nights can get very cold and visiting many of the gompas by public transport will require an overnight stop. Be prepared for dramatic temperature changes and for the extreme burning power of the sun in Ladakh's thin air (Leh is at 3500 metres). A cloud across the sun will change the air temperature from T-shirt to sweater level in seconds. Without a hat and/or sunscreen you'll have sunburn and a peeling nose in hours.

Acclimatise to Ladakh's altitude slowly – don't go scrambling up mountainsides as soon as you arrive. A spell in Kashmir is a good halfway acclimatisation, but people who fly straight from Delhi to Ladakh may feel very uncomfortable for a few days.

Outside Leh it is not easy to change money and in the tourist season there is often a severe shortage of small change. One very important word to learn for Ladakh is the all-purpose and frequently used greeting 'Jullay'. Finally, remember that this is a sensitive border region disputed by India, Pakistan and China. You are not allowed more than a mile north of the Srinagar to Leh road.

Religion

At Kargil, on the Srinagar to Leh road, the Islamic influence dies out and you are in a Buddhist region. The people follow Tibetan Tantric Buddhism which has much emphasis on magic and demons. All around Ladakh are gompas, the Buddhist monasteries. They're fascinating to visit, although they have become very commercially minded since Ladakh's tourist boom commenced. There's a good side to this though. Prior to tourism the gompas were gradually becoming more and more neglected. Today many of them are being refurbished and repaired with the profits from visiting westerners! The monks are happy to have visitors wander around the gompas, sit in on the ceremonies, try the appalling taste of butter tea (bring your own cup) and take photographs.

SRINAGAR TO LEH

It's 434 km from the Vale of Kashmir to Ladakh and the road is surfaced most of the way. It follows the Indus River for much of the distance. Buses run along this road daily during the summer season (see Getting There for Leh) and take two days with an overnight stop at Kargil. Sonamarg is the last major town in Kashmir, shortly before you climb up over the Zoji La pass (3529 metres) and enter the Ladakh region.

Zoji La

This is one of the few unsurfaced stretches on the route. It's also the first pass to snow over in winter and the last to be cleared in summer. It is not, however, the highest pass along the route. The other passes get less snow because they are across the Himalaya and in the mountain rain shadow.

The road up the pass is breathtaking and there are times when you'll wonder if you were sane to make this trip.

Drass

This is the first village after the pass and the place from where road crews clear the road up to the pass for the start of the summer season. In winter, Drass is noted for its heavy snowfalls and extreme cold.

The buses stop here and tourists have to register their names and passport numbers.

Kargil

Once an important trading post, Kargil is now simply an overnight halt on the way to Leh or the point where you turn south

for the Zanskar Valley. The people of Kargil are chiefly Muslim and noted for their extreme orthodoxy. Already you are in a region where irrigation is vitally important.

Information There is a tourist officer stationed at the new J&K Tourist Reception Centre next to the taxi stand.

There is also a post office and bank in Kargil.

Places to Stay On the main street, the *Popular Chacha, De Lux, New Light, Puril, Pujab Janta* and *Argalia* provide the rock-bottom accommodation at around Rs 20 a bed. The *Naktul View*, between the main street and the truck park, and the *Crown* and *International*, on the other side of the truck park, are all of a better standard.

The best deal is at the *Tourist Bungalow*, where clean doubles go for Rs 35 and Rs 50, and buckets of hot water are available on request. Next up the scale are the *Greenland Hotel* with running water and rooms at Rs 115/150, and the *Marjina Tourist Home* which charges Rs 80/130 up to Rs 120/175.

The *Caravan Serai, Siachen, Broadway Suru View* and the *D'Zojila* all charge around Rs 220/350.

There is also accommodation of some form or other at Drass, Mulbekh, Bodh Kharbu, Lamayuru, Khalsi, Nurla, Saspul and Nimmu.

Places to Eat The food is little better than the accommodation. The *Naktul* is easily the best in town and provides Chinese dishes. Otherwise the *Marjina Tourist Home* leads the pack, with the *Babu* and *New Light* taking the overflow and those fooled by the rash promises of French, Italian, German, Chinese and Tibetan cuisine.

Getting There & Away As well as the daily buses to Leh and Srinagar, there are daily services to Mulbekh, Drass, Pannikar and

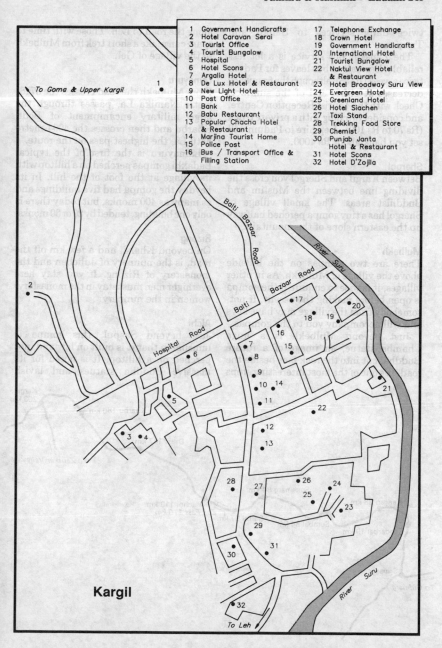

1 Government Handicrafts
2 Hotel Caravan Serai
3 Tourist Office
4 Tourist Bungalow
5 Hospital
6 Hotel Scons
7 Argalia Hotel
8 De Lux Hotel & Restaurant
9 New Light Hotel
10 Post Office
11 Bank
12 Babu Restaurant
13 Popular Chacha Hotel
& Restaurant
14 Marjina Tourist Home
15 Police Post
16 Bus / Transport Office &
Filling Station

17 Telephone Exchange
18 Crown Hotel
19 Government Handicrafts
20 International Hotel
21 Tourist Bungalow
22 Naktul View Hotel
& Restaurant
23 Hotel Broadway Suru View
24 Evergreen Hotel
25 Greenland Hotel
26 Hotel Siachen
27 Taxi Stand
28 Trekking Food Store
29 Chemist
30 Punjab Janta
Hotel & Restaurant
31 Hotel Scons
32 Hotel D'Zojila

To Goma & Upper Kargil

Balti Bazaar Road

River Suru

Balti Bazaar Road

Balti

Hospital Road

Kargil

River Suru

To Leh

twice daily services to Sauku and Trespone.

The Zanskar bus service is a lot less reliable. Basically a bus leaves for Padum twice a week (Rs 56), although the frequency decreases at either end of the summer. Check with the Tourist Reception Centre, and consider hitching with a private truck (Rs 70 to Rs 100). Jeep hire to Padum will set you back about Rs 4000.

Shergol

Between Kargil and Shergol you cross the dividing line between the Muslim and Buddhist areas. The small village of Shergol has a tiny gompa perched halfway up the eastern slope of the mountain.

Mulbekh

There are two gompas on the hillside above the village of Mulbekh. As in other villages, it is wise to enquire if the gompa is open before making the ascent. If not, somebody from the village may have keys and will accompany you to the gompas.

Just beyond Mulbekh is a huge Chamba statue, an image of a future Buddha, cut into the rock face beside the road. It's one of the most interesting stops along the road to Leh. Those with time to spare can make a short trek from Mulbekh to the village of Gel.

Lamayuru

From Mulbekh the road crosses the 3718-metre Namika La, passes through the large military encampment of Bodh Kharbu and then crosses the 4094-metre Fatu La, the highest pass on the route.

Lamayuru is the first of the typical Ladakhi gompas perched on a hilltop with its village at the foot of the hill. In its heyday the gompa had five buildings and as many as 400 monks, but today there is only one building, tended by 20 or 30 monks.

Rizong

On beyond Khalsi, and a few km off the road, is the nunnery of Julichen and the monastery of Rizong. If you stay here overnight men must stay in the monastery, women in the nunnery.

Alchi

Just beyond Saspul, this gompa is unusual in that it is built on lowland, not perched on a hilltop. It is noted for its massive Buddha statues and lavish

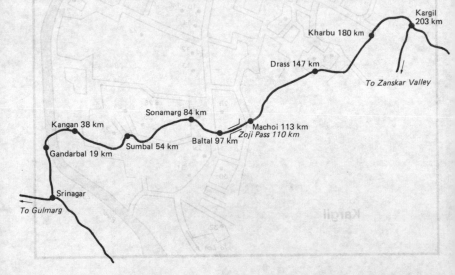

woodcarvings and artwork. There are many chortens around the village.

A hotel here has basic rooms and a small dorm. There's also a pleasant little hotel in Saspul; it makes a good base for visiting Rizong, Alchi and Lekir.

Lekir & Basgo

Shortly after Saspul a steep road turns off to the Lekir Gompa, which also has a monastery school. Closer to Leh there is a badly damaged fort at Basgo and the Basgo Gompa with interesting Buddha figures, although its wall paintings have suffered much water damage.

LEH (population 20,000)

Centuries ago this was an important stop on the old caravan silk route from China. Today it's merely a military base and tourist centre, but wandering the winding back streets of the town is still fascinating. It's about 10 km north-east of the Indus River in a fertile side valley.

Orientation

Leh is small enough to make finding your way around very easy. There's one main street with the Leh Palace rising up at the end of it. The bus station and jeep halt is on the southern or airport side of town. The airport, with its steeply sloping

runway, is several km out of town near the Spitok Gompa.

Information

There's a tourist office and Indian Airlines office and a noisy power generator in the middle of town; fortunately it shuts down at 11 pm. The Ecological Development Group has a solar demonstration house and a good library on Ladakh.

Leh Palace

Looking for all the world like a miniature version of the Potala in Lhasa, Tibet, the palace was built in the 16th century. It is now deserted and badly damaged, a legacy of Ladakh's wars with Kashmir in the last century.

The main reason for making the climb up to the palace is for the superb views from the roof. The Zanskar mountains, across the Indus River, look close enough to touch. The palace is still the property of the Ladakhi royal family, although they now reside at nearby Stok. Try to get a monk to unlock the preserved, but now unused, central prayer room; its dusty, spooky, with huge faces looming out of the dark.

Leh & Tsemo Gompas

The Leh Gompa stands high above the

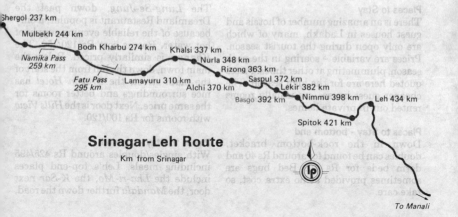

Srinagar-Leh Route

Km from Srinagar

Shergol 237 km
Mulbekh 244 km
Bodh Kharbu 274 km
Namika Pass 259 km
Khalsi 337 km
Fatu Pass 295 km
Nurla 348 km
Lamayuru 310 km
Rizong 363 km
Alchi 370 km
Saspul 372 km
Lekir 382 km
Basgo 392 km
Nimmu 398 km
Leh 434 km
Spitok 421 km

To Manali

palace and houses manuscripts and paintings. The Red (Tsemo) Gompa, built in 1430, contains a fine three-storey-high seated Buddha image. It's open from 7 to 9 am. The gompa above the Leh and Tsemo gompas is in a very ruined condition but the views down on Leh are superb.

Sankar Gompa
It's an easy stroll to the Sankar Gompa, a couple of km north of the town centre. This interesting little gompa is only open from 7 to 10 am and from 5 to 7 pm, and there's a Rs 10 entry fee. The gompa has electric lighting so an evening visit is worthwhile. Upstairs is an impressive representation of Avalokitesvara complete with 1000 arms and 1000 heads.

Centre for Ecological Development
Next door to the Tsemo-La Hotel is the HQ of the Ladakh Ecological Development Group (LEDeG), which initiates and promotes 'a development strategy for Ladakh that is carefully tailored to its environment, available resources and culture'. This includes solar energy, environmental and health education, strengthening the traditional system of organic farming and publishing books in the local language. Visitors are welcome to hear what LEDeG is all about, and to use the library and the restaurant.

Places to Stay
There is an amazing number of hotels and guest houses in Ladakh, many of which are only open during the tourist season. Prices are variable – soaring in the peak season, plummeting at other times. Prices quoted here are for the high season. The cheaper guest houses are usually rooms rented out in private homes.

Places to Stay – bottom end
Down in the rock-bottom bracket, doubles can be found for around Rs 40 and dorm beds for Rs 10. Bed bugs are sometimes provided at no extra cost, so take care.

The *Old Ladakh Guest House* and the *Tak Guest House* are both basic and popular bottom-end places. The larger *Palace View Kiddar* is much the same. More central and better is the friendly *Khan Manzil Guest House*.

West of the stream past the Dreamland Restaurant is a group of popular places off to the right which have lovely gardens and great views. The friendly *Bimla* is at the top of this bracket and charges from Rs 75 for a double. The *Indus* is similarly priced, while the *Delux* is a French favourite. Last in the row is the *Ti-sei* with singles/doubles for Rs 15/35. The new *Jorchung Guest House* is also good.

Up past the Tsemo-La Hotel, the *Two Star Guest House* is another favourite with singles/doubles from Rs 20/30. The *Tsaro* is very basic but is an authentic Ladakhi home and has rooms from Rs 10/20. Further on out of town are the *Otsal, Asia* and *Larchang*, about 20 minutes walk.

Changspa village is about 10 minutes walk from Leh and is a good place to escape the noise. The *Eagle Guest House* has double rooms for Rs 35. The *Renchens Guest House* here has beautiful clean rooms for Rs 30 a double, and you can eat with the family. A further 10 minutes walk away is the *Oriental Guest House* which has doubles for Rs 30.

Places to Stay – middle
The *Lung-Se-Jung*, down past the Dreamland Restaurant is popular, if only because of the reliable evening supply of hot water. Rooms cost Rs 120/150. The *Khangri* is similarly priced. Below the main town, down the hill from the start of the main street, the *Dragon Hotel* has nice surroundings and better rooms for the same price. Next door is the *Hills View* with rooms for Rs 100/120.

Places to Stay – top end
With singles/doubles around Rs 425/495 including meals, Leh's top-end places include the *Lha-ri-Mo*, the *K-Sar* next door, the *Mandala* further down the road,

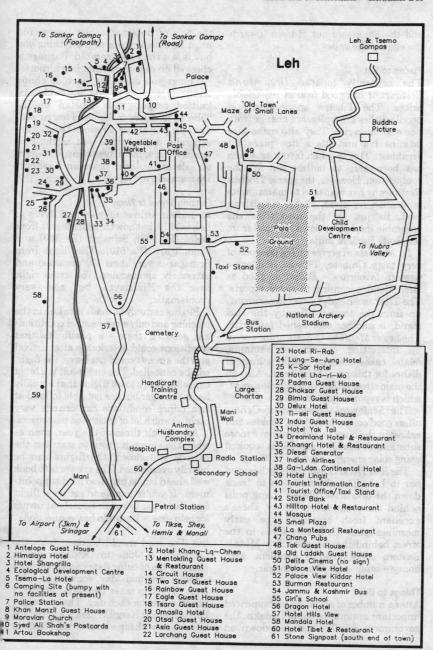

Leh

To Sankar Gompa (Footpath)

To Sankar Gompa (Road)

Leh & Tsemo Gompas

Palace

'Old Town' Maze of Small Lanes

Buddha Picture

Vegetable Market

Post Office

Polo Ground

Child Development Centre

To Nubra Valley

Taxi Stand

National Archery Stadium

Cemetery

Bus Station

Handicraft Training Centre

Large Chortan

Mani Wall

Animal Husbandry Complex

Hospital

Radio Station

Mani

Secondary School

Petrol Station

To Airport (3km) & Srinagar

To Tikse, Shey, Hemis & Manali

1 Antelope Guest House
2 Himalaya Hotel
3 Hotel Shangrilla
4 Ecological Development Centre
5 Tsemo–La Hotel
6 Camping Site (bumpy with no facilities at present)
7 Police Station
8 Khan Manzil Guest House
9 Moravian Church
10 Syed Ali Shah's Postcards
11 Artou Bookshop

12 Hotel Khang–Lq–Chhen
13 Mentokling Guest House & Restaurant
14 Circuit House
15 Two Star Guest House
16 Rainbow Guest House
17 Eagle Guest House
18 Tsaro Guest House
19 Omasila Hotel
20 Otsal Guest House
21 Asia Guest House
22 Larchang Guest House

23 Hotel Ri–Rab
24 Lung–Se–Jung Hotel
25 K–Sar Hotel
26 Hotel Lha–ri–Mo
27 Padma Guest House
28 Choksar Guest House
29 Bimla Guest House
30 Delux Hotel
31 Ti–sei Guest House
32 Indus Guest House
33 Hotel Yak Tail
34 Dreamland Hotel & Restaurant
35 Khangri Hotel & Restaurant
36 Diesel Generator
37 Indian Airlines
38 Ga–Ldan Continental Hotel
39 Hotel Lingzi
40 Tourist Information Centre
41 Tourist Office/Taxi Stand
42 State Bank
43 Hilltop Hotel & Restaurant
44 Mosque
45 Small Plaza
46 La Montessori Restaurant
47 Chang Pubs
48 Tak Guest House
49 Old Ladakh Guest House
50 Delite Cinema (no sign)
51 Palace View Hotel
52 Palace View Kiddar Hotel
53 Burman Restaurant
54 Jammu & Kashmir Bus
55 Girl's School
56 Dragon Hotel
57 Hotel Hills View
58 Mandala Hotel
60 Hotel Tibet & Restaurant
61 Stone Signpost (south end of town)

and the *Shambala* out of town towards the edge of the valley.

Places to Eat

The centrally located *Dreamland Restaurant* has good food at reasonable prices. The Tibetan specialities and noodle dishes are a pleasant change from rice and more rice. They also make nice jasmine tea and it's a fine place for breakfast. This is a Leh favourite which has been able to outlast any of the competition. However, the sparse *Tibetan Restaurant* has managed to maintain its reputation for great, cheap, nourishing food. Its just up the road from the vegetable market, or down the road from the State Bank of India.

La Montessori serves up big portions of very tasty Chinese, Tibetan and some western favourites – almost as good as Dreamland according to some reports. The *Tibetan Friends Corner Restaurant*, up from the tourist office by the taxi stand, is another established favourite. The newer *Mentokling Restaurant* serves up interesting versions of hummus, felafel, cakes, pies and generally unusual dishes for this part of the world. Also on the main street is the *Tripicks Restaurant*, which is reportedly good.

The *Ecological Development Centre* offers good coffee, herbal tea, cookies and cakes. In the busy season they have more substantial health food meals cooked using solar energy.

The *Ibex Hotel* boasts the only licensed bar in Leh. The alternative is to track down the unofficial (illegal) chang pubs behind the main street. Lastly, there's excellent fresh bread in the early mornings from the bakery stalls in the street behind the mosque. This Middle Eastern style bread is excellent with honey – bring some from Srinagar.

Things to Buy

After a number of greedy tourists spirited important antiquities out of Ladakh, the government sensibly clamped down on the sale of important older items. You must be able to prove that anything you buy is less than 100 years old. Baggage is checked on departure from Leh airport.

Things you might buy include chang and tea vessels, cups and butter churns, knitted carpets with Tibetan motifs, Tibetan jewellery or, for just a few rupees, a simple prayer flag. Prices in Ladakh are generally quite high – you might find exactly the same Tibetan-inspired item on sale at far lower prices in Kashmir, Dharamsala or Nepal.

Getting There & Away

Air Indian Airlines only started flying to Leh in 1979, but now there are flights from Delhi (Rs 790), Srinagar (Rs 360) and Chandigarh (Rs 510). The flight from Srinagar is very short (30 minutes) and extremely spectacular (you cross right over the Himalaya), but also very problematic.

Flights can only be made into Leh in the morning and only when weather conditions are good. If there's a possibility that conditions could deteriorate after arrival and the aircraft could not leave, the flight will be cancelled. The end result is a lot of cancellations, a lot of flights that actually leave Srinagar but are not able to land at Leh (since conditions can change very rapidly) and a lot of frustrated passengers.

At difficult times of the year, such as when the season is about to start but the road is still closed, the flights can be heavily overbooked. The answer is to book well ahead but be prepared for disappointment. If you're unable to get on a flight from Srinagar ask your houseboat owner for help – every Kashmiri has 'connections'.

Bus The road should be open from the beginning of June to October, but in practice the opening date can be variable – sometimes mid-May, sometimes mid-June. The trip takes two days, about 12 hours' travel on each day. The overnight halt is made at Kargil. There is a variety of bus classes with fares from around Rs 60 to

Rs 150. Jeeps, which take up to six passengers, will cost something like Rs 2000 but will permit additional stops and diversions along the interesting route.

A complication on the return trip to Srinagar is that you may not be able to buy tickets until the evening before departure, because buses may not turn up from Srinagar. Thus you can't be certain you will be leaving until the last moment. The buses are very heavily booked in both directions at the height of the season (August). You have to book days ahead.

Before the road officially opens it is possible to cross the Zoji La on foot or by pony, although if there is still a lot of snow the Beacon Patrol will only let you through if you're properly equipped. The pass is cleared of snow before the road is repaired and ready for vehicles, and there is usually transport running along the roads on both sides of the pass before the through buses start to operate. Locals cross the pass regularly on foot in the preseason so it is easy to tag along with a larger group or find a guide. But it can be hard work!

Leh to Manali Road The Leh to Manali jeep road was only opened to foreigners in 1989. It is open for three months each year (July-September) and then only to groups, who must also have a police escort. Check with the tourist office for details.

Getting Around

Airport Transport The bus service from Leh to the airport costs Rs 3; a jeep or taxi costs about Rs 25.

Bus There is a reasonably extensive bus network around Leh, although the buses are decidedly ramshackle and extremely crowded. The main services from Leh are:

to	distance	buses daily	fare
Choglamsar	8 km	4	Rs 1.20
Chushot	25 km	3	Rs 3.30
Hemis	45 km	1	Rs 6.00
Khalsi	98 km	1	Rs 12.95
Matho	27 km	2	Rs 3.75
Phyang	22 km	3	Rs 3.10
Sabu	9 km	2	Rs 1.35
Sakti	51 km	1	Rs 6.95
Saspul	62 km	1	Rs 7.90
Shey	16 km	2	Rs 2.10
Spitok	8 km	2	Rs 1.20
Stok	17 km	2	Rs 2.85
Tikse	20 km	3	Rs 3.00

There are also buses to further afield. The tourist office has the full details. Services are much less frequent in winter.

Jeep & Taxi Jeeps can also be hired and, although not cheap, for a group of people they can be a good alternative to the crowds and delays of the buses. Taxis charge Rs 4 per km and, on out-and-back trips, Rs 3 per km on the return leg. About 30% is added for longer trips. Overnight stays are charged at the rate of Rs 96. Basically it works out to between Rs 400 and Rs 600 per day.

AROUND LEH
Spitok Gompa
On a hilltop above the Indus and beside the end of the airport runway, the Spitok Gompa is 10 km from Leh. The temple (Gonkhang) is about 1000 years old. There are fine views over the Indus from the gompa.

Phyang
About 24 km from Leh, on the road back towards Srinagar, the gompa has 50 monks and the entry fee is Rs 10. There is an interesting little village below the gompa.

Beacon Highway
You are not allowed to visit the Nubra Valley without special permission, but if you could, it would involve taking what is probably the highest road in the world. It crosses a pass at 5606 metres! The road is only open in September and October – it takes the whole summer for the snow and ice to melt for that brief time.

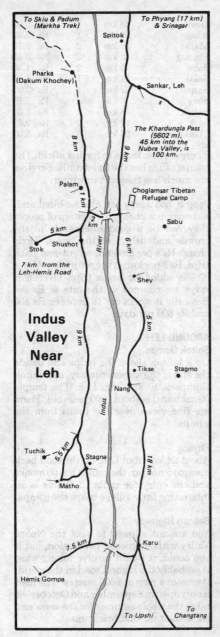

To Skiu & Padum (Markha Trek)

Spitok

To Phyang (17 km) & Srinagar

Pharka (Dakum Khochey)

Sankar, Leh

The Khardungla Pass (5602 m), 45 km into the Nubra Valley, is 100 km.

8 km

9 km

Palam

Choglamsar Tibetan Refugee Camp

1 km

Sabu

2 km

5 km

Shushot

6 km

Stok

River

7 km from the Leh-Hemis Road

Indus Valley Near Leh

9 km

Shey

Indus

5 km

Tikse

Stagmo

Nang

Tuchik

5.5 km

Stagna

Matho

18 km

Karu

7.5 km

Hemis Gompa

To Upshi

To Changtang

Tibetan Refugee Camp

The refugee camp at Choglamsar has become an important centre for the study of Tibetan literature and history, and Buddhist philosophy. Don't indulge the kids who demand 'bon-bons' – it turns them into beggars. Nearby, a bridge crosses the Indus to Stok and a rougher road to Hemis.

Shey

This was the old summer palace of the kings of Ladakh and was built about 560 years ago. It's now in ruins but the palace gompa has a 12-metre-high seated Buddha image. Entry fee is Rs 5 and the gompa is open from 7 to 9 am and 5 to 6 pm. At other times ask for the monk, Tashi, in the village below; he will know where to find the key.

Tikse Gompa

The Tikse Gompa, 17 km from Leh, is visible from Shey. Its new-found tourist wealth is being put to good use in extensive restoration work. The monastery is very picturesque and superbly sited on a hilltop overlooking the village and the Indus. Beside the car park is the small Zan-La Temple.

The gompa has an important collection of Tibetan-style books in its library and some excellent artwork. This is a good place to watch the religious ceremonies either around 6.30 am or noon. They are preceded by long mournful sounds from horns on the roof. Entry fee is Rs 10.

Places to Stay You can get good doubles at the *Shalzang Chamba Hotel*. There are no dorm beds or singles here.

Hemis Gompa

Hemis Gompa, one of the largest and most important gompas in Ladakh, is 45 km from Leh on the western side of the Indus. It's easy to get there by car or jeep, but on public transport you will have to spend the night at the monastery as it is not easy to bus out there, walk the six km up from the river to the gompa, see it, walk back down and get back to Leh in one day.

The Hemis Gompa is famous for its Hemis Festival, which usually falls in the second half of June or in early July. This is one of the largest and most spectacular of the gompa festivals and at one time was virtually the only one which took place in the summer tourist season. The business-minded monks at some other gompas are now switching their festivals to more lucrative dates. The festival takes two days and features elaborate mask dances and crowds of eager spectators.

The gompa has an excellent library, well-preserved wall paintings and good Buddha figures. Entry is Rs 10.

If instead of turning right at Karu to climb up to Hemis you had turned left, you would have reached the Chemre Gompa, five km off the road, and the Trak Tok Gompa, 10 km further on. Both lie in the restricted zone but tourists are allowed to visit them.

Places to Stay There's a *rest house/ restaurant* with rather dirty dorm beds for Rs 10. You'll find cheaper and much cleaner rooms in local homes. The *Parachute Restaurant*, next to the bus stand, has good food.

Matho Gompa

The west-bank road on the Indus is not in as good condition as the more used east-bank road, but you can return from Hemis on it and there are several interesting places to visit. Matho is in a side valley five km from Stagna, and in an important festival the monks are possessed by spirits and go into a trance. Stagna, on the west-bank road, has a gompa too.

Stok Palace

Close to the Choglamsar bridge, a road turns off the west-bank road to the palace of Stok. The last king of Ladakh died in 1974 but his widow, the Rani of Stok, still lives in this 200-year-old palace. It is expected that her eldest son will become

king when he reaches an auspicious age. You can only enter the museum here, which costs Rs 20.

Pharka Gompa

This small cave gompa is almost directly opposite the Spitok Gompa on the Stok side of the Indus. You can reach it by crossing the Choglamsar bridge, but the last few km must be made on foot.

Zanskar

The long, narrow Zanskar Valley was opened even more recently than Ladakh. A jeep road has now reached all the way from Kargil to Padum, the capital, and although it is not open all the time, it has opened the area up to more outside influence.

For the moment at least, it remains an area for trekkers, and some of the treks are definitely hard going. You can make a number of interesting ones either down the valley or out of it to Ladakh, Kashmir or Himachal Pradesh.

PADUM

The 'capital' of Zanskar has a population of less than 1000, of whom about 300 are Sunnite Muslims. It's on the southern part of a wide fertile plain where two rivers join to form the Zanskar River.

There is a tourist bureau where you can arrange accommodation and the hire of horses. On arrival in Padum you must register with the Tourism Department.

Places to Stay

There's a limited choice of a few basic hotels, and rooms in private houses. The *Haftal View* and *Ibex* hotels have doubles for Rs 30 to Rs 50. The *Shapodok-la*, in the centre of town, has dorm beds for Rs 5 and Rs 10, and the *Chora-la* opposite has doubles from Rs 35 to Rs 50.

The *Tourist Bungalow* is the best deal at Rs 35 for doubles with bath.

AROUND PADUM
Zangla & Karsha Gompa
This is an interesting four-day trek around Padum. The first day takes you to Thonde on the riverbank with a monastery high above it. Since horses cannot cross the rope bridge from Padum, this is the first place on this side of the river where they can be hired for treks further afield to places like Lamayuru.

The second day takes you from Thonde to Zangla, where the King of Zanskar has his castle. On day three you backtrack towards Thonde, cross the river and continue to Karsha, the most important gompa in Zanskar. On the final day you can cross the river directly by ferry or continue down to the wooden Tungri Bridge and double back to Padum.

Tungri-Zongkhul Gompa Round Trip
This four-day trek around Padum takes you to the Sani and Zongkhul gompas by following the route up towards the Muni La, then cutting across to the base of the Umasi La.

TREKS IN LADAKH & ZANSKAR
Trekking in Ladakh and Zanskar can be hard going and you should be equipped for every eventuality. Srinagar is the best place to purchase supplies, but you will not find trekking gear like you do in Kathmandu, Nepal.

Treks into Zanskar are principally down the valley from the north (from Kargil) or up the valley from the south (from Manali in Himachal Pradesh). Remember to take your garbage out with you; many areas are already becoming fouled with trekkers' rubbish.

Drass to Sanku
This is a short three-day trek into the Suru Valley joining the Kargil to Padum road at Sanku. It's simply an alternative route to the road down from Kargil.

Kargil to Padum
Although there is a road all the way to Padum, it is not always open all the way and is rough going at the best of times. The seven-day trek from Kargil on the Srinagar to Ladakh road can be shortened by four days if you can get a ride all the way from Kargil to the Pensi La. When all bridges are open the route is accessible from early June to late October.

The first day's travel is mainly on a surfaced road by bus to Sanku. Beyond Parkutse you pass close to Kun and Nun. The Rangdum Gompa is the first gompa reached in Zanskar; the road is still reasonably good to this point. Beyond the gompa you have to cross the 4401-metre Pensi La into Zanskar proper. On the last day's walk from Phe to Padum you cross the river and pass by the Sani Gompa, one of the most important in Zanskar.

Day 1	Kargil to Namsuru
Day 2	Namsuru/Pannikar/Parkutse
Day 3	Parkutse/Parkachik/Yuldo/ Rangdum Gompa
Day 4	Rangdum Gompa to Pensi La
Day 5	Pensi La to Abran
Day 6	Abran to Phe
Day 7	Phe to Padum

Manali to Padum
This 10-day trek can be very hard going at its southern end. Firstly, take a bus across the Rothang Pass from Manali to Keylong and on to Darcha where the trek starts. On the second day you cross the Baralacha La, a double pass where even the lower side is higher than Europe's highest mountain and twice the height of Australia's highest.

At the end of Day 6 continue north to Padum or turn back south and cross the Shingo La back to Darcha in two days. You are not, however, allowed to take the alternative route if you're heading north. On Day 7 you make a detour to the spectacular Phuctal Gompa. Continuing north to Kargil on this route would take, with a few days for shorter treks around Padum, something like 20 days.

Day 1 Darcha to Mane Bar
Day 2 Mane Bar to Sarai Kilang
Day 3 Sarai Kilang to Debni
Day 4 Debni to Chumik Marpo
Day 5 Chumik Marpo to Shingsan
Day 6 Shingsan/Kargiakh/Purni
Day 7 Purni to Phuctal Gompa
Day 8 Phuctal Gompa to Katge Lato
Day 9 Katge Lato to Reru
Day 10 Reru to Padum

Padum to Lamayuru

There are a number of alternatives for this trek from Padum into Ladakh, intersecting the road at Lamayuru, about halfway from Kargil to Leh. The trek starts from Padum to Thonde, as on the short trek to the Zangla and Karsha gompas. On Day 3 the difficult ascent to the 4500-metre Shing La pass has to be made, but on Day 4 the Nerag La, at 4900 metres, is even more difficult and a local guide is a necessity. From Photosar, a small village, it is only two days' walk to Lamayuru. There is an alternative route from Photosar that takes a day longer. The alternative route from Padum starts out on the opposite side of the Zanskar River and takes you to the Linghsot Gompa before joining up with the first route at Day 5.

Day 1 Padum to Thonde
Day 2 Thonde to Honia
Day 3 Honia/Shing La/Kharmapu
Day 4 Kharmapu to Nerag La
Day 5 Nerag La to Nerag
Day 6 Nerag/Yulching/Singi La/Photosar
Day 7 Photosar/Shirshi La/Hanupatta
Day 8 Hanupatta/Wanla/Shill/
         Prikiti La/Lamayuru

or
Day 1 Padum to Pishu
Day 2-4 Pishu to Linghsot Gompa
Day 5 Linghsot Gompa to Yulching

Padum to Kishtwar

This trek into the southern part of Kashmir is not especially difficult although it crosses the 5234-metre Umasi La, which can only be done in fine weather. You cannot use horses on this route but must take porters.

On the second day you reach the Zongkhul Gompa, which can also be visited on a short trek from Padum. Day 3 is a long climb and long descent over the snow-covered Umasi La. On Day 4 your Zanskari porters will not continue further and you must hire local porters or a pony.

The last few days are hard work with many ascents and descents but the road from Kishtwar, already extending to Galar, is gradually being lengthened.

Day 1 Padum to Ating
Day 2 Ating to Ratrat
Day 3 Ratrat/Umasi La/Bhuswas
Day 4 Bhuswas to Matsel
Day 5 Matsel to Atholi
Day 6 Atholi to Shasho
Day 7 Shasho/Galar/Kishtwar

Other Treks

Padum to Nimmu follows the Padum to Lamayuru route for most of its length, then turns off eastwards to join the Srinagar to Leh road at Nimmu.

Padum to Leh by the Markha Valley is a hard but rewarding trek which goes via Zangla before turning east over the Charcha La and the Ruberung La to the Markha Gompa, and eventually reaching Hemis near Leh. This trek can only be made in late August. Earlier than that the rivers which must be crossed are too high from melting snow and after that it's too cold.

You can trek from Padum to the Phuctal Gompa by an alternative route to that described in Manali to Padum, but the trail is poor and little used.

Uttar Pradesh

Population: 130 million
Area: 294,413 square km
Capital: Lucknow
Main language: Hindi

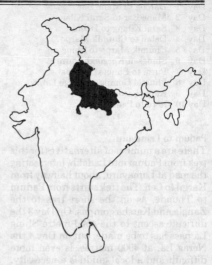

In terms of population Uttar Pradesh is the largest state in India. In terms of variety and problems, it's also India larger than life. This is one of the great historical and religious centres of India. The Ganges River, which forms the backbone of Uttar Pradesh, is the holy river of Hinduism, and there are several important pilgrimage towns along it. The main ones are Rishikesh and Hardwar, where the river emerges from the Himalaya and starts across the plains, but there's also Varanasi, the most holy city of all. Buddhism also has its great shrine in the state, for it was at Sarnath, just outside Varanasi, that the Buddha first preached his message of the middle way.

Geographically and socially the state varies greatly. Most of it consists of the vast Ganges plain, an area of awesome flatness which suffers dramatic floods during the monsoon. The people of this region are predominantly backward farming peasants who scratch a bare existence from the overcrowded land. The north-west corner of the state is a part of the soaring Himalaya, with excellent treks, beautiful scenery and some of India's highest mountains. It's a state of strong contrasts.

History

Over 2000 years ago the state was part of Ashoka's great Buddhist Empire. More recently it was part of the Moghul Empire, and for some years Agra was its capital. Today, of course, Agra is famed for that most perfect of Moghul masterpieces, the Taj Mahal. More recently still, it was in Uttar Pradesh that the Mutiny broke out in 1857 (at Meerut) and some of its most

dramatic (Lucknow) and unfortunate (Kanpur) events took place. The state was first known as United Province when Agra was merged with Oudh after the British took over, but was renamed Uttar Pradesh 'northern state' after Independence. Uttar Pradesh has produced five of the six prime ministers since independence in 1947 – Nehru, Indira Gandhi, Rajiv Gandhi, Lal Bahadur Shastri and Charan Singh.

Agra

Population: one million

At the time of the Moghuls, in the 16th and 17th centuries, Agra was the capital of India, and its superb monuments date from that era. Agra has a magnificent fort and the building which many people come to India solely to see – the Taj Mahal.

Situated on the banks of the Yamuna River with its crowded alleys and predatory rickshaw riders, Agra is much like any other north Indian city, once you're away from its imposing Moghul monuments. It's possible to day-trip to Agra from Delhi (there's an excellent train service making this eminently practicable), but Agra is worth more than a day, particularly if you intend to visit, as you certainly should, the deserted city of Fatehpur Sikri. In any case, the Taj deserves more than a single visit if you're going to appreciate how its appearance changes under different lights.

History

Agra became the capital of Sikandar Lodi in 1501 but was soon passed on to the Moghuls, and both Babur and Humayun made some early Moghul constructions here. It was under Akbar that Agra first aspired to its heights of magnificence. From 1570 to 1585 he ruled from nearby Fatehpur Sikri. When he abandoned that city he moved to Lahore (now in Pakistan) but returned to Agra in 1599 and remained there until his death in 1605.

Jehangir, with his passion for Kashmir,

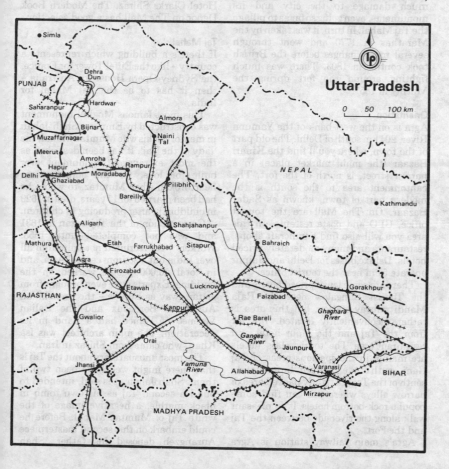

Uttar Pradesh

0   50   100 km

did not spend a great deal of time in the city; Shah Jahan is the name inevitably connected with Agra. He built the Jami Masjid, most of the palace buildings inside the Agra Fort and, of course, the Taj Mahal. Between 1638 and 1650 he built the Red Fort and Jami Masjid in Delhi and would probably have moved the capital there had he not been deposed and imprisoned by his son, Aurangzeb, in 1658. Aurangzeb did transfer the capital there.

In 1761, Agra fell to the Jats who did much damage to the city and its monuments, even going so far as to pillage the Taj Mahal. In turn, it was taken by the Marathas in 1770 and went through several more changes before the British took control in 1803. There was much fighting around the fort during the Mutiny in 1857.

Orientation

Agra is on the west bank of the Yamuna River, 204 km south of Delhi. The old part of the town, where you'll find the Kinari Bazaar (the main market place) in a narrow street, is north of the fort. The cantonment area to the south is the modern part of town, known as Sadar Bazaar. On The Mall are the tourist office, GPO and poste restante. In this area you will also find handicraft shops, restaurants and many moderately priced hotels. Deluxe buses for Delhi and Jaipur operate from near the tourist office.

There are some lower priced hotels and the Tourist Bungalow near the Raja Mandi railway station, but this area is rather inconveniently located. It's far from the Taj and the main hotel and restaurant area. The 'tourist class' hotels are mainly in the spacious areas of Taj Ganj, south of the Taj itself. Immediately south of the Taj is a tightly packed area of narrow alleys where you can find some popular rock-bottom hotels. It's a pleasant walk along the riverside between the Taj and the Fort. :

Agra's main railway station is Agra Cantonment; trains from New Delhi arrive here. The main bus station for cities in Rajasthan, Delhi and for Fatehpur Sikri is Idgah. Buses going to Mathura leave from the Fort bus station. Agra airport is seven km out of town.

Information

The Government of India tourist office (tel 72377) is at 191 The Mall. It's open from 9 am to 5 pm weekdays and 9 am to 1 pm Saturday; closed Sunday.

Indian Airlines (tel 73434) is in the Hotel Clarks Shiraz. The Modern Book Depot on The Mall has a good selection.

Taj Mahal

If there's a building which represents a country – like the Eiffel Tower for France, the Sydney Opera House for Australia – then it has to be the Taj Mahal for India.

This most famous Moghul monument was constructed by Emperor Shah Jahan in memory of his wife Mumtaz Mahal, the 'lady of the Taj'. It has been described as the most extravagant monument ever built for love, for the emperor was heartbroken when Mumtaz, to whom he had been married for 17 years, died in 1629 in childbirth, after producing 14 children.

Construction of the Taj began in 1631 and was not completed until 1653. Workers were recruited not only from all over India but also from central Asia, and in total 20,000 people worked on the building. Experts were even brought from as far away as Europe – the Frenchman Austin of Bordeaux and the Italian Veroneo of Venice had a hand in its decoration. The main architect was Isa Khan, who came from Shiraz in Iran.

The most unusual story about the Taj is that there might well have been two of them. Shah Jahan, it is said, intended to build a second Taj as his own tomb in black marble, a negative image of the white Taj of Mumtaz Mahal. Before he could embark on this second masterpiece Aurangzeb deposed his father. Shah

Taj Mahal

Jahan spent the rest of his life in the Agra Fort, looking out along the river to the final resting place of his wife.

The Taj Mahal stands on a raised marble platform with tall white minarets at each corner of the platform. They are just for decoration; nobody is called to prayer from them. The central structure has four small domes surrounding the huge, bulbous, central dome. The tombs of Mumtaz Mahal and Shah Jahan are in a basement room. Above them in the main chamber are false tombs, a common practice in Indian mausoleums of this type. Light is admitted into the central chamber by finely cut marble screens. The echo in this high chamber, under the soaring marble dome, is superb and there is always somebody there to demonstrate it.

Although the Taj is amazingly graceful from almost any angle, it's the close-up detail which is really astounding. Semiprecious stones are inlaid into the marble in beautiful patterns and with superb craft in a process known as *pietra dura*. The precision and care which went into the Taj Mahal's design and construction is just as impressive whether you view it from across the river or from arm's length.

The building, which stands beside the Yamuna River, is in a large formal garden. Twin red sandstone mosques frame the building when viewed from the river. You enter the Taj grounds through a high red sandstone gateway inscribed with verses from the Koran in Arabic. Paths leading to the Taj are divided by a long watercourse in which the Taj is beautifully reflected – if it's filled with water! The Taj is worth more than a single visit as it's one building under the light of dawn, another at sunset, and still another under moonlight. Full moons bring people flocking to Agra in their thousands.

Admission is Rs 2 except on Fridays when it is free. Fridays also tend to be impossibly crowded and noisy, not very conducive to calm enjoyment of this most serene of buildings. Opening hours are normally from sunrise to 6 pm. Under normal circumstances, on full-moon nights and the four nights around the full moon, it stays open until midnight. These days it closes at 6 pm due to the unrest in the Punjab and the consequent fear of extremist activities. Hopefully it's only a temporary situation. A bus from Sadar to the Taj is less than Rs 1.

A final sad note about the Taj – scientists fear that after centuries of undiminished glory the modern world may finally be shortening its life. Industrial pollution, particularly a proposed chemical plant, could cause irreparable damage to the marble before the turn of the century. Not that people haven't damaged it in the past – in 1764 silver doors at the entrance were ripped off and carted away, and raiders have also made off with the gold sheets that once lined the subterranean vault.

Agra Fort

Construction of the massive Agra Fort was begun by Emperor Akbar in 1565, and additions were made until the time of his grandson, Shah Jahan. While in Akbar's time the fort was principally a military structure, by Shah Jahan's time the fort had become partially a palace. A visit to the fort is an Agra 'must' since so many of the events which led to the construction of the Taj took place here.

There are many fascinating buildings inside the massive 20-metre-thick walls which stretch for 2½ km, surrounded by a moat over 10 metres wide. The fort is on the banks of the Yamuna River and only the Amar Singh Gate to the south is open. Inside, the fort is really a city within the city. It is open from sunrise to sunset and admission is Rs 2 except on Fridays when it is free. Some of the important buildings within the fort include:

Moti Masjid The 'Pearl Mosque' was built by Shah Jahan between 1646 and 1653. The marble mosque is considered to be perfectly proportioned and a Persian inscription inside the building compares it to a perfect pearl. The mosque's courtyard is surrounded by arcaded cloisters and a marble tank stands in the centre.

Diwan-i-Am The 'Hall of Public Audiences' was also built by Shah Jahan and replaced an earlier wooden structure. Shah Jahan's predecessors had a hand in the hall's construction, but the throne room, with its typical inlaid marble work, is indisputably from Shah Jahan. Here he sat to meet officials or listen to petitioners. Beside the Diwan-i-Am is the small Nagina Masjid or 'Gem Mosque' and the 'ladies' bazaar' where merchants came to display and sell goods to the ladies of the Moghul court.

Diwan-i-Khas The 'Hall of Private Audiences' was also built by Shah Jahan in 1636-37. Here the emperor would meet important dignitaries or foreign ambassadors. The hall consists of two rooms connected by three arches. The famous 'peacock throne' was kept here before being moved to Delhi by Aurangzeb. It was later carted off to Iran and its remains are now in Tehran.

Octagonal Tower The Musamman Burj, or Octagonal Tower, stands close to the Diwan-i-Khas and the small, private Mina Masjid. Also known as the Saman Burj, this tower was built by Shah Jahan for Mumtaz Mahal and is another of his finely designed buildings. It was here, with its views along the Yamuna to the Taj, that Shah Jahan died in 1666, after seven years' imprisonment. Unfortunately the tower has been much damaged over the years.

Jehangir's Palace Akbar is believed to have built this palace, the largest private residence in the fort, for his son. This was one of the first constructions demonstrating the fort's changing emphasis from military to luxurious living quarters. The palace is also interesting for its blend of

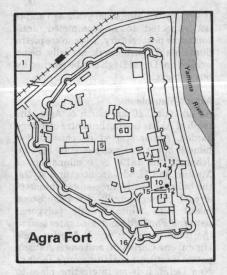

Agra Fort

1	Jami Masjid
2	Northern Tower
3	Delhi Gate
4	Elephant Gate
5	Ladies' Bazaar
6	Moti Masjid
7	Nagina Masjid
8	Diwan-i-Am
9	Mina Mosque
10	Grape Garden
11	Octagonal Tower
12	Khas Mahal
13	Jehangir's Palace
14	Diwan-i-Khas
15	Shish Mahal
16	Amar Singh's Gate

Hindu and central Asian architectural styles – a contrast to the unique Moghul style which had developed by the time of Shah Jahan.

Other Buildings Shah Jahan's Khas Mahal is a beautiful white marble structure used as a private palace. The rooms underneath it were intended as a cool retreat from the summer heat. The Shish Mahal or 'Mirror Palace' was supposed to have been the harem dressing room and its walls are inlaid with tiny mirrors. The Anguri Bagh or 'Grape Garden' probably never had any grapevines but was simply a small, formal Moghul garden. It stood in front of the Khas Mahal. The Delhi Gate and Hathi Pol, or 'Elephant Gate', are now closed.

In front of the Jehangir Palace is the Hauz-i-Jehangri, a huge 'bath' carved out of a single block of stone – by whom and for what purpose is a subject of conjecture. The Amar Singh Gate takes its name from a maharaja of Jodhpur who was killed beside the gate, along with his followers, after a brawl in the Diwan-i-Am in 1644! Justice tended to be summary in those days; there is a shaft leading down to the river into which those who made themselves unpopular with the great Moghuls could be hurled without further to-do.

Itimad-ud-daulah

There are several interesting sights on the opposite bank of the Yamuna and north of the fort. You cross the river on a narrow two-level bridge carrying pedestrians, bicycles, rickshaws and bullock carts. The first place of interest is the Itimad-ud-daulah – the tomb of Mirza Ghiyas Beg. This Persian gentleman's beautiful daughter married Emperor Jehangir and became known as Nur Jahan, the 'light of the world'. In turn her daughter was Mumtaz Mahal, the lady of the Taj. The tomb was constructed by Nur Jahan between 1622 and 1628 and is very similar to the tomb she constructed for her husband, Jehangir, near Lahore in Pakistan.

The tomb is of particular interest since many of its design elements foreshadow the Taj, construction of which started only a few years later. The Itimad-ud-daulah was the first Moghul structure totally constructed of marble and the first to make extensive use of pietra dura, the inlay work of marble so much a part of the Taj. The mausoleum is small and squat compared to the soaring Taj, but the smaller, more human scale somehow makes it attractive, and the beautifully patterned surface of the tomb is superb. Extremely fine marble lattice-work passages admit light to the interior. It's well worth a visit. The Itimad-ud-daulah is open from sunrise to sunset and admission is Rs 2, free on Fridays.

Chini Ka Rauza

The 'china tomb' is one km north of the Itimad-ud-daulah. The squat, square tomb, surmounted by a single huge dome, was constructed by Afzal Khan, who died at Lahore in 1639. He was a high official in the court of Shah Jahan. The exterior was covered in brightly coloured enamelled tiles and the whole building clearly displayed its Persian influence. Today it is much decayed and neglected, and the remaining tilework only hints at the building's former glory.

Ram Bagh

Laid out in 1528 by Babur, first of the Moghul emperors, this is the earliest Moghul garden. It is said that Babur was temporarily buried here before being permanently interred at Kabul in Afghanistan. The Ram Bagh is two to three km further north of the Chini Ka Rauza on the riverside and is open from sunrise to sunset; admission is free. It's rather overgrown and neglected.

Jami Masjid

Across the railway tracks from the Delhi Gate of Agra Fort, the Jami Masjid was built by Shah Jahan in 1648. An inscription over the main gate indicates that it was built in the name of Jahanara, Shah Jahan's daughter, who was imprisoned with Shah Jahan by Aurangzeb. Large though it is, the mosque is not as impressive as Shah Jahan's Jami Masjid in Delhi.

Dayal Bagh Temple

In Dayal Bagh, 10 km north of Agra, the white marble temple of the Radah Soami Hindu sect is currently under construction.

It was started almost 90 years ago and is not expected to be completed until sometime next century. You can see pietra dura inlaid marblework actually being worked on. Dayal Bagh can be reached by bus or bicycle.

Akbar's Mausoleum

At Sikandra, 10 km north of Agra, the tomb of Akbar lies in the centre of a large garden. Akbar started its construction himself but it was completed by his son, Jehangir, in 1613. A combination of Muslim and Hindu architectural styles, the building, with three-storey minarets at each corner, is built of red sandstone inlaid with white marble polygonal patterns. Four red sandstone gates lead to the tomb complex: one is Muslim, one Hindu, one Christian, and one is Akbar's patent mixture. Like Humayun's Tomb in New Delhi, it is an interesting place to study the gradual evolution in design that culminated in the Taj Mahal. Akbar's mausoleum is open from sunrise to sunset and entry is Rs 2, except on Fridays when it is free.

Sikandra is named after Sultan Sikandar Lodi, the Delhi ruler who was in power from 1488 to 1517, immediately preceding the rise of Moghul power on the subcontinent. The Baradi Palace, in the mausoleum gardens, was built by Sikandar Lodi. Across the road from the mausoleum is the Delhi Gate. Between Sikandra and Agra are several tombs and two kos minars, or 'milestones'.

It's a fair way out to Sikandra; count on Rs 25 to Rs 40 for the return trip in an auto-rickshaw.

Other Attractions

The Kinari Bazaar, or old market place, is a fascinating area to wander around. It's in the old part of Agra, near the fort, and the narrow alleys of the market start near the Jami Masjid. There are several market areas, or *mandis*, in Agra with names left over from the Moghul days, although they have no relation to what is sold there today. The Loha Mandi (iron market) and Sabji Mandi (vegetable market) are still used, but the Barber's Mandi (nai ki mandi) is now famous for textiles. In the Malka Bazaar, you'll see women beckon to single men from upstairs balconies.

Tours

If you're just day-tripping from Delhi, tours commence from Agra railway station and tickets are sold on the Taj Express or Shatabdi Express. The tours start when the trains arrive (9.30 am for the Taj Express, 8.30 am for the Shatabdi). They last all day and include visits to the Taj, the Fort and Fatehpur Sikri. Tickets cost Rs 40 or Rs 50.

In Agra itself, you can book for the tours (and get picked up) from the tourist office near The Mall. At the Cantonment railway station tickets are sold at the enquiry window near platform 1.

There are also tours just to Fatehpur Sikri. These start at 10.30 am and cost Rs 30.

Places to Stay – bottom end

The Sadar area, close to the Cantonment railway station, the tourist office and the GPO and only a Rs 4 rickshaw ride from the Taj, is a good place for reasonably cheap accommodation. There are also many good restaurants in this same vicinity. Taj Rd is the hub of the Sadar area and is parallel to The Mall. Next to Sadar is an area called Baluganj which has some popular budget hotels. If you're after rock-bottom prices then head for the maze of small streets immediately to the south of the Taj. Hotel touts and rickshaw-wallahs are heavily into commissions in Agra, so go to the hotel of your choice rather than theirs because commission (up to 40%) will be built into the price you pay at any hotel they take you to.

The very popular *Tourist Rest House* (tel 64961) is opposite the office of the District Board and is conveniently close to the GPO and the tourist office. It is run by two helpful brothers who will even make train reservations for you. This pleasant though slightly dog-eared hotel has a

Maintaining the lawns of the Taj

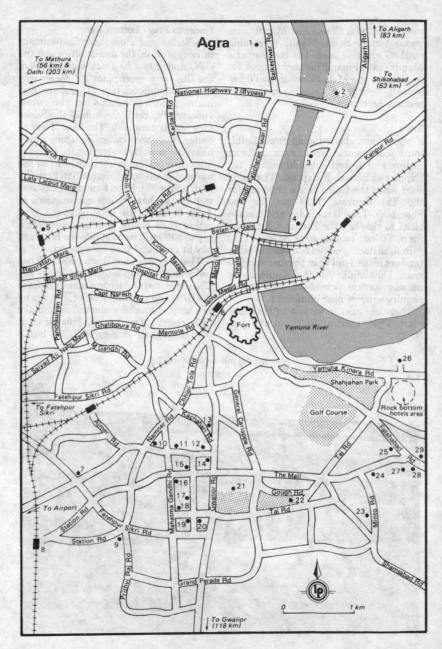

1	Dayal Bagh Temple
2	Ram Bagh
3	Chini Ka Rauza
4	Itimad-ud-daulah's Tomb
5	Tourist Bungalow
6	Agra Fort Railway Station
7	Idgah Bus Station
8	Agra Cantonment Railway Station
9	Grand Hotel
10	Lauries Hotel
11	Major Bakshi's Guest House
12	Khanna Hotel
13	Tourist Rest House
14	Agra Ashok Hotel
15	GPO
16	Tourist Office
17	Zorba the Buddha
18	Prakash Restaurant
19	Kwality Restaurant
20	Jai Hind Hotel
21	Telegraph Office
22	Hotel Clarks Shiraz & Indian Airlines
23	Highway Inn
24	Mumtaz Hotel
25	Taj View Hotel
26	Taj Mahal
27	Holiday Inn
28	Mayur Tourist Complex
29	Mughal Sheraton Hotel

variety of rooms with and without bath. Singles/doubles with bath are about Rs 30/40 and there are dorm beds for Rs 7. Rooms with hot water are Rs 70. The rooms are around a small garden area; the verandah is a good place to meet others. Rickshaws are unwilling to take you there as they don't get a commission; beware of the much inferior 'New Tourist Rest House' just a stone's throw away. It's very small and is purely a rip-off from the original.

Close to the Tourist Rest House, the basic *Hotel Ajay* costs around Rs 60/80. The *Hotel Sarang* (tel 63894) is a new place in the Baluganj area and although more expensive is still good value at Rs 80 for singles.

Another good place in the Sadar area is the *Jai Hind Hotel* (tel 73502) on

Naulakha Rd, a small side street off Taj Rd. The *Major Bakshi's Guest House* (tel 76828) at 33/83 Ajmer Rd is still operating and has rooms with bath for Rs 80/100 and a couple of bathless doubles for Rs 50. *Colonel Duggal's Guest House* at 155 Pratapura (near the GPO and tourist office) has doubles for Rs 80. The rooms are somewhat basic but are clean, and the place is run by a friendly Sikh family.

The *India Guest House* is a good family-run place. Spartan but clean, doubles cost Rs 30. As commission is not paid to rickshaws, they'll probably tell you it's full of hippies, etc. The *Akbar International Hotel* (tel 65749) on Fatehabad Rd has also been recommended.

The *Agra Hotel* (tel 72330) on General Cariappa Rd has views of the Taj as well as airy and spacious rooms for Rs 50/70.

Other hotels offering good value in this price range include the *Seetal Tourist Home* and the *Rose Hotel*, both near the Idgah bus station. The *Hotel Tajkhema* (tel 65383) near the eastern gate of the Taj is run by the Uttar Pradesh government and has dorm beds for Rs 15 as well as more expensive rooms. The *Deepak Lodge* at 178 Ajmer Rd has rooms for Rs 60.

Agra's *Tourist Bungalow* is in Raja Mandi area, a long way from anywhere. Rooms range from Rs 75 to Rs 125, and dorm beds cost Rs 15. At the top of this range is the new *Paradise Guest House*, on Fatehabad Rd not far from the Taj. Rooms cost Rs 80/120 and you can dine on the roof with views of the Taj.

There are camping facilities at the *Grand Hotel*, *Lauries Hotel* and the *Mayur Tourist Complex*. There are *retiring rooms* at both the Cantonment and Agra Fort railway stations.

Places to Stay – middle

Near the Cantonment railway station, the fairly modern *Grand Hotel* (tel 74014) charges Rs 140/190 and is a good place in this price range. Doubles with air-con are Rs 300. In the same area as the more expensive hotels is the *Mayur Tourist*

Complex (tel 67582) on Fatehabad Rd. Rooms in cottages range from Rs 155/195 to Rs 260 depending on facilities. This place also has a pleasant garden and good restaurant.

Also on Fatehabad Rd, the *Hotel Amar* (tel 65696) has rooms ranging from Rs 200/270 to Rs 340 with air-con and is quite a good place. Close by is the friendly and good *Hotel Rantandeep*.

The government-run *Hotel Tajkhema* (tel 65383) by the eastern gate of the Taj has rooms from Rs 75 to Rs 150. The *Colonel Bakshi's Guest House* (tel 61292) by the airport is at 5 Lakshman Nagar. The owner is the son of the late Major Bakshi whose guest house is in the Sadar area. Very pleasant rooms in this well-equipped and clean place are Rs 175/225. The food is good and they can also arrange to pick you up from the station or airport.

Although the *Hotel Jaiwal* (tel 64171) is in the Sadar area, most of the rooms are windowless and are not great value at Rs 200. The *Lauries Hotel* is used by overland groups and has a 'disgusting looking but surprisingly pleasant' mineral water pool.

The *Upadhyaya Tourist Guest House* (tel 74837) is in Vibhav Nagar, one km from the Taj. Rooms cost Rs 120/150 and the whole place is clean and the staff friendly.

Places to Stay – top end

Agra's tourist-class hotels are generally in the open area south of the Taj. The *Mughal Sheraton Hotel* (tel 64701, 64729) on Fatehabad Rd has elegant, fort-like architecture and offers everything from camel or elephant rides to an in-house astrologer who will tell your fortune for Rs 50. There are 200 rooms with doubles ranging from Rs 975 to Rs 1025.

The older *Hotel Clarks Shiraz* (tel 72421) is a long-standing Agra landmark. It too is fully air-conditioned and has a swimming pool; the Indian Airlines office is here. Singles/doubles cost Rs 750/830, and it is one of the better expensive Agra hotels.

South-east of the Taj, the *Mumtaz Hotel* (tel 64771) on Fatehabad Rd is a smaller hotel with 40 rooms, all air-con; singles/doubles are Rs 290/390. On the same road the *Taj View Hotel* (tel 64171) has rooms for Rs 825/925. The ITDC *Agra Ashok Hotel* (tel 76223) in The Mall charges Rs 850/975.

Places to Eat

The deluxe hotels have excellent food – for a major splurge *Clarks Shiraz* is worth considering; their lunchtime buffet is good value, as is the one at the *Mughal Sheraton*, although it is expensive at Rs 200.

In the Sadar area the *Kwality Restaurant* on Taj Rd is air-conditioned and excellent. The *Prakash Restaurant* across the street can also be good, and they have a good thali for Rs 20. The *Hotel Gaylord* also serves good food. Opposite the Kwality in a modern shopping block, the *Brijwasi Sweet House* is very clean and helpful and all the sweets are named and priced. Further along from the Kwality is the Chinese *Chung Wah*.

For those on a tighter budget, the *Hotel Jai Hind* and the *Hotel Jaiwal* are good places to eat. *Laxmi Vilas* is a fine place for south Indian food in this same area. On M G Rd the *Mahesh Veshnu* has excellent thalis.

At E/13 Shopping Arcade, off Gopi Chand Shivhare Rd which runs between The Mall and Taj Rd in Sadar, is *Zorba the Buddha*, another Rajneesh restaurant. The food is excellent and the desserts delicious.

In the rock-bottom hotel area immediately south of the Taj is *Joney's Place*. It's as basic as you could ask for, but is a good meeting place and the drinks are cold. The all-in breakfast for Rs 7 is good value, as are the banana lassis. The ITDC *Cafeteria & Restaurant* just outside the Taj entrance has fine Indian and western food. At the east gate the *Relax Restaurant* does excellent real coffee and desserts. The *Nice Point Restaurant* at the west gate has also been recommended.

A three-course meal for two here costs around Rs 30.

Agra has a local speciality, the ultrasweet candied melon called *petha*.

Activities

When you tire of the Taj there are various nonsightseeing possibilities in Agra. Nonresidents can use the swimming pool at the *Clarks Shiraz* for a mere Rs 55 or the pool at *Lauries* for a more reasonable Rs 15. The pool at the *Taj View Hotel* can also be used by nonguests for a fee. There is a cinema in the Baluganj area of the city which shows English-language movies every evening.

Things to Buy

Agra is well known for leather goods, jewellery and marble items inlaid like the pietra dura work on the Taj. The Sadar and Taj areas are the main tourist shopping centres, although the prices here are likely to be more expensive. Around Pratapur there are many jewellery shops, but precious stones are cheaper in Jaipur.

Beware of rickshaw-wallahs taking you to shops – they'll inevitably be raking off a commission at your expense. Beware too of 'marble' that turns out to be alabaster. Alabaster will scratch, marble will not. Agra's shopkeepers are unbelievably smooth talking and persuasive. There are *no* government craft shops apart from the state government emporiums. Don't believe people who tell you otherwise.

Agra, along with Jaipur and Varanasi, is one of the truly notorious places in India for buy-and-sell scams. If you believe any stories about buying here to sell at a profit there, you'll simply be proving (once again) that old adage about separating fools from their money! Precious stones are a favourite for this game. They'll tell you that you can sell stones in Australia, Europe or the US for several times the purchase price, and will even give you the (often imaginary!) addresses of dealers who will buy them. The stones you buy,

however, will be worth only a fraction of what you pay. Credit card fraud is also practised, so take care if you're purchasing that way.

Getting There & Away

Air Agra is on the popular daily tourist route Delhi/Agra/Khajuraho/Varanasi and return. It's only a 30-minute flight from Delhi to Agra. Fares from Agra are: Delhi Rs 230, Khajuraho Rs 355, Varanasi Rs 545. There are also Vayudoot flights from Agra to Khajuraho and Varanasi (Rs 545), Jaipur (Rs 255) and Delhi (Rs 230).

Bus Most buses leave from the Idgah bus station. Buses between Delhi and Agra operate about every hour and cost Rs 37; the trip takes about five hours. There's a daily ITDC deluxe bus between Agra and Jaipur which leaves at 7 am, takes five hours and costs Rs 52. There's an early morning bus to Khajuraho, but it's better to take the fastest express train to Jhansi, from where it's only three hours by bus to Khajuraho.

Train Agra is on the main Delhi to Bombay broad-gauge railway line, so there are plenty of trains coming through. Agra is 200 km from Delhi and 1344 km from Bombay. There is the daily Taj Express to and from Delhi which costs Rs 28 in 2nd class, Rs 95 in 1st. There is also a new superfast train, the Shatabdi Express, connecting Agra and Delhi. Like the Taj Express, it leaves Delhi in the morning and returns the same evening. It is also more expensive at Rs 110, but it does give you a bit more time at Agra, and the fare includes meals. Avoid the slow passenger trains at all costs. Take great care at New Delhi station; pickpockets, muggers and others are very aware that this is a popular tourist train and they work overtime at parting unwary visitors from their goods.

To Bombay the journey takes 27 hours at a cost of Rs 110 in 2nd class and Rs 429 in 1st. There are also direct trains to Madras and Trivandrum.

If you're heading north towards the Himalaya there are trains through Agra which continue straight through Delhi, saving you stopping and getting more tickets.

Getting Around

Agra is very spread out so walking is really not on – even if you could. It's virtually impossible to walk because Agra's hordes of rickshaw-wallahs pursue would-be pedestrians with unbelievable energy and persuasive ability. Beware of rickshaw-wallahs who take you from A to B via a few marble shops, jewellery shops and so on. Just great when you want to catch a train, and it can also work out very expensive!

A simple solution to Agra's transport problem is to hire a rickshaw for the day. You can easily negotiate an all-in daily rate (Rs 35 to Rs 40) for which your rickshaw-wallah will not only take you everywhere, he'll wait outside while you sightsee or even have a meal. Agra is so touristy that many of them speak fine English and, like western cabbies, are great sources of amusing information – like how much they can screw out of fat-cat tourists for a little pedal down to the Taj and back to the hotel's air-conditioning. Otherwise Rs 5 to Rs 10 will take you from pretty well anywhere in Agra to anywhere else.

If, however, you really don't want to be pedalled around, Agra is sufficiently traffic-free to make pedalling yourself an easy proposition. There are plenty of bicycle hire places around, such as the petrol station near the Tourist Rest House. They can be rented for Rs 5 a day.

FATEHPUR SIKRI

Between 1570 and 1586, during the reign of Emperor Akbar, the capital of the Moghul Empire was situated here, 40 km west of Agra. Then, as suddenly and dramatically as this new city had been built, it was abandoned. Today it's a perfectly preserved example of a Moghul city at the height of the empire's splendour; an attraction no visitor to Agra should miss.

Legend says that Akbar was without a male heir and made a pilgrimage to this spot to see the saint Shaikh Salim Chisti. The saint foretold the birth of Akbar's son, the future Emperor Jehangir, and in gratitude Akbar named his son Salim. Furthermore, Akbar transferred his capital to Sikri and built a new and splendid city. Later, however, the city was abandoned due, it is said, to difficulties with the water supply.

Although a Muslim, Akbar was known to be very tolerant towards other religions, and he spent much time discussing and studying them in Fatehpur Sikri. He also developed a new religion called 'Deen Ilahi' which attempted to synthesise elements from all the major religions. Akbar's famous courtiers, such as Bibal, Raja Todarmal and Abu Fazal, had their houses near his palace in the city.

Information & Orientation

The deserted city lies along the top of a ridge while the modern village, with its bus stand and railway station, is down the ridge's southern side. Fatehpur Sikri is open from sunrise to sunset and entry is Rs 1, free on Fridays. The Jami Masjid is outside the city enclosure.

As Fatehpur Sikri is one of the most perfectly preserved 'ghost towns' imaginable, you may well decide it is worthwhile spending a few rupees to hire a guide. When you arrive, look for 'Shahi Darwaza', not 'Buland Darwaza'. Shahi Darwaza is the official entrance to the fort where licensed guides are available. At the Buland Darwaza, the gateway to the mosque and shrine, unlicensed guides will try to lure you into hiring them. The mosque and shrine are not inside the city walls; you have to go there separately.

Jami Masjid or Dargah Mosque

Fatehpur Sikri's mosque is said to be a

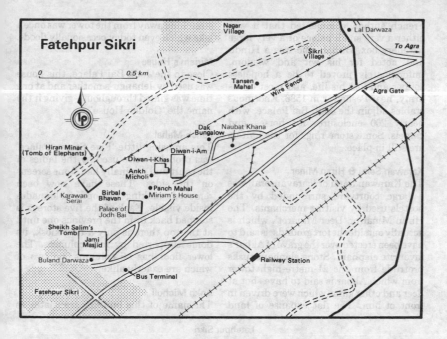

Fatehpur Sikri

copy of the mosque at Mecca and is a
beautiful building containing elements of
Persian and Hindu design. The main
entrance is through the 54-metre-high
Buland Darwaza, the 'Gate of Victory',
constructed to commemorate Akbar's
victory in south India. The impressive
gateway is reached by an equally
impressive flight of steps. An inscription
inside the archway includes the useful
thought: 'The world is a bridge, pass over
it but build no house upon it. He who
hopes for an hour may hope for eternity'.
Just outside the gateway is a deep well
and, when there is a sufficient number of
tourists assembled, local daredevils leap
from the top of the entrance into the
water.

Inside the mosque is the tomb, or dargah,
of Shaikh Salim Chisti, surrounded by
marble lattice screens. Just as Akbar
came to the saint four centuries ago
looking for a son, so do childless women

visit his tomb today. The saint's grandson,
Islam Khan, also has his tomb within the
mosque. Abul Fazl and Faizi, adviser and
poet to Akbar, had their homes just
outside the mosque.

Palace of Jodh Bai
North-east of the mosque is this palace
named after Jehangir's wife, although it
was probably used more by Akbar's wife,
who was a Hindu. Here again the
architecture is a blend of styles with
Hindu columns and Muslim cupolas. The
'Palace of the Winds' is a projecting room
with walls made entirely of stone lattice-
work. The ladies of the court probably sat
in here to keep a quiet eye on events below.

Birbal Bhavan
Built either by or for Raja Birbal, Akbar's
favourite courtier, this small palace is
extremely elegant in its design and
execution. Victor Hugo, the 19th-century

French author, commented that it was either a very small palace or a very large jewellery box. Birbal, who was a Hindu and noted for his wit and wisdom, unfortunately proved to be a hopeless soldier and lost his life, and most of his army, near Peshawar in 1586. Enormous stables adjoin the Jodh Bai Palace, with nearly 200 enclosures for horses and camels. Some stone rings for the halters are still in place.

Karawan Serai & Hiran Minar

The Karawan Serai or 'caravanserai' was a large courtyard surrounded by the hostels used by visiting merchants. The Hiran Minar or 'Deer Minaret', which is actually outside the fort grounds, is said to have been erected over the grave of Akbar's favourite elephant. Stone elephant tusks protrude from the 21-metre-high tower from which Akbar is said to have shot at deer and other game which were driven in front of him. The flat expanse of land stretching away from the tower was once a lake which even today occasionally floods.

Miriam's House

Close to the Jodh Bai Palace, this house was used by Jehangir's mother and at one time was gilded throughout – giving it the name the 'Golden House'.

Panch Mahal

This amusing little 'Five Storey Palace' was probably once used by the ladies of the court and originally had stone screens on the sides. These have now been removed, making the open colonnades inside visible. Each of the five storeys is stepped back from the previous one until at the top there is only a tiny kiosk, its dome supported by four columns. The lower floor has 56 columns, no two of which are exactly alike.

Ankh Micholi

The name of this building translates as

Fatehpur Sikri

something like 'hide and seek', and the emperor is supposed to have amused himself by playing that game with ladies of the harem! The building was more probably used for storing records, although it has some curious struts with stone monsters carved into them. By one corner is a small canopied enclosure where Akbar's Hindu guru may have sat to instruct him.

Diwan-i-Khas

The Hall of Private Audiences' exterior is plain but its interior design is unique. A stone column in the centre of the building supports a flat-topped 'throne'. From the four corners of the room stone bridges lead across to this throne, and it is thought that Akbar sat in the middle while his four principal ministers sat at the four corners.

Diwan-i-Am

Just inside the gates at the north-east end of the deserted city is the Hall of Public Audiences. This consists of a large open courtyard surrounded by cloisters. Beside the Diwan-i-Am is the Pachchisi courtyard, set out like a gigantic gameboard. It is said that Akbar played chess here, using slave girls as the pieces.

Other Monuments

Musicians would play from the Naubat Khana, at one time the main entrance to the city, as processions passed by beneath. The entrance road then ran between the mint and the treasury before reaching the Diwan-i-Am. The Khwabgah, in front of the Daftar Khana, or record office, was Akbar's own sleeping quarters. Beside the Khwabgah is the tiny but elaborately carved Rumi Sultana or 'Turkish Queen's House'.

Near the Karawan Serai, badly defaced elephants still guard the Hathi Pol, or 'Elephant Gate'. There is also a Hakim, or 'doctor's house', and a fine hammam, or 'Turkish bath', beside it. Outside Dargah Mosque are the remains of the small stone-cutters' mosque. Shaikh Salim Chisti's cave was supposedly at this site and the mosque predates Akbar's imperial city.

Places to Stay

Although most people day trip from Agra, you can stay at the *Archaeological Survey Rest House* for only about Rs 25. It's great value; book it at the Archaeological Survey of India, 22 The Mall, Agra. You can get great value food in the hotel across the road from the bus station.

The *DAK Bungalow* has huge doubles for just Rs 9.

Getting There & Away

The tour buses only stop for an hour or so at Fatehpur Sikri. If you want to spend longer it is worth taking a bus from the Idgah bus station for about Rs 5; the trip takes a bit over an hour. Along the way you pass milestones, known as kos minars, about every three km. There's a train service but it's very slow. Along the road you'll often see dancing bears – the villagers dance their trained bears out into the road to block your way while they demand money!

You can spend a day in Fatehpur Sikri and continue on to Bharatpur in the evening. The bus station restaurant will let you lock up your bags in their garage, but firmly agree on the price beforehand or they may try overcharging you when you return.

MATHURA (population 180,000)

On the Delhi to Agra road 57 km north of Agra, Mathura is an ancient site. According to legends this is where Lord Krishna was born 3500 years ago. Today the town is an important pilgrimage place for followers of this popular incarnation of Vishnu. There are many places in and around Mathura connected with the Krishna legend.

History

Mathura, or Muttra as it has also been known, is mentioned by Ptolemy and by the Chinese visitors Fa Hian (in India 401-410 AD) and the later Hiuen Tsang (634 AD). By then the population of the 20 Buddhist monasteries (for this was a great Buddhist centre) had dropped from 3000 to 2000. By the time Mahmud of Ghazni arrived on his rape, burn and pillage trip from Afghanistan in 1017, Buddhism had totally disappeared.

Sikandar Lodi did further damage to the shrines of Mathura in 1500, but the town rebounded during the tolerant reigns of Akbar and Jehangir, only for fanatical Aurangzeb to do another demolition job. He destroyed the Kesava Deo Temple, which had been built on the site of one of the most important Buddhist monasteries, and built a mosque in its place.

Along the Yamuna River
The 300-metre-wide Yamuna River, which flows through Mathura, is lined with bathing ghats and is full of large turtles. The Sati Burj, on the banks of the Yamuna River, is a four-storey tower built in 1570 to commemorate the sati of the builder's mother. Aurangzeb knocked down the upper storeys, but they have since been rebuilt.

The ruined Kans Qila fort on the riverbank was built by Raja Man Singh of Amber; Jai Singh of Jaipur built one of his observatories here, but it has since disappeared. Vishram Ghat is the most important bathing ghat where Lord Krishna is said to have rested after killing a tyrant king.

Mathura is full of Krishna reminders (even the Hare Krishnas have their Indian HQ near here); you can even see the Potara-Kund, near the Katra Kesava, where baby Krishna's nappies (diapers to Americans) are supposed to have been washed.

Museum
The Government Museum in Dampier Nagar has sculptures, terracotta work, coins and bronze objects dating from the 5th century AD. The standing Buddha image, found in excavations at Mathura,

is particularly renowned. The museum is open daily, except Mondays, from 10.30 am to 4.30 pm from 1 July to 15 April, and 7.30 am to 12.30 pm the rest of the year. Admission is free.

Places to Stay & Eat
For somewhere close to Krishna's birth place, try the *International Rest House* (tel 588) where doubles with bath cost Rs 40. They also have a Rs 6 'all you can eat' thali which is good value. The *Hotel Nepal* (tel 430) near the bus station has singles ranging from Rs 50 to Rs 75, and doubles from Rs 60 to Rs 115.

The *Hare Krishna Guest House* is a very nice three-star hotel with rooms for Rs 40/60 but it's often full.

Getting There & Away
Mathura is on the Delhi to Agra road and railway routes. It's 57 km north of Agra, 141 km south of Delhi. By rail the fare from Delhi is Rs 22 in 2nd class, Rs 75 in 1st. There are also hourly buses from Agra.

AROUND MATHURA
Brindavan
Brindavan, 10 km north of Mathura, is the place where Krishna sported with his milkmaids and stole their clothes while they were bathing in the river. No wonder he's so popular.

The large Red Temple, or Radha Govind ('Divine Cowherd' - in other words Krishna), was built in 1590 and is one of the most advanced Hindu temples in the north of India. It has a vaulted ceiling in contrast to the utilitarian ceilings found in most temples. Other temples in Brindavan include Gopi Nath, Jugal Kishor (1027), Radha Ballabh (1626) and Madan Mohan.

Places to Stay & Eat The *ISKON Guest House* (tel 82478) has single/double rooms for Rs 40/70. The food at the restaurant is not that great.

Jammu & Kashmir Top: Crossing the Himalaya on the Srinagar to Leh flight (TW)
Left: Shy monks Tikse Monastery, Ladakh (TW)
Right: Tikse Monastery, Ladakh (TW)

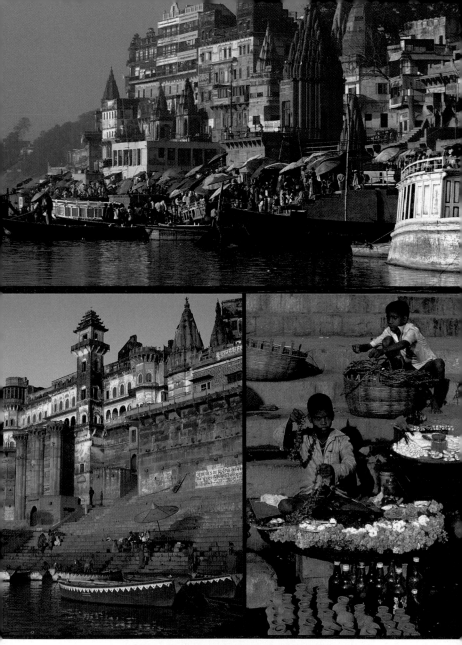

Uttar Pradesh Top: Morning on the Ganges, Varanasi (TW)
Left: Bathing Ghat, Varanasi (TW)
Right: Flower vendor at the ghats, Varanasi (HF)

Mahaban

Mahaban, 11 km south-east of Mathura, is another place from the Krishna legend. The Palace of Nanda, Krishna's foster father, is said to contain his actual cradle. Gokul, a few km away, is where Krishna was secretly raised. Hordes of pilgrims flock here during his birthday festival each July-August.

Goverdhan

At Goverdhan, 26 km from Mathura, Lord Krishna is said to have protected the inhabitants from Indra's wrath (rain) by holding the hilltops, neatly balanced on top of his finger, over the town for seven days. Krishna's favourite gopi (milkmaid) is said to have come from Barsana, 47 km from Mathura.

Terauli

One traveller wrote to suggest an interesting day trip to the village of Terauli, about 20 km away, where you will find two local child-gurus – 'a bloody fascinating day'. You could hire a bike in Mathura or Brindavan and ride there, he suggested.

Central Uttar Pradesh

DELHI TO KANPUR

Aligarh (population 335,000)

Formerly known as Koil, this was the site of an important fort as far back as 1194. During the upheavals following the death of Aurangzeb and the collapse of the Moghul Empire, the region was fought for by the Afghans, Jats, Marathas and Rohillas – first one coming out on top, then another. In 1776, the fort's name was changed to Aligarh (the high fort) but in 1803, despite French support for the then-ruler Scindia, it fell to the British. The fort is three km north of the town, and its present form dates from 1524. The ancient City of Koil has traces of Buddhist and Hindu temples of great antiquity.

Aligarh is best known today for the Aligarh Muslim University where the 'seeds of Pakistan were sown'. Muslim students come here not only from all over India but from all over the Islamic world.

Sankasya

Sankasya is reached via Farrukhabad and Pakhna, 11 km away. There is an Ashokan elephant capital here. A mound topped by a ruined stupa marks the spot where Buddha descended from heaven to earth after preaching to his mother.

Kanauj

Only a few dismal ruins indicate that this was once a mighty Hindu city, which quickly fell into disrepair after Mahmud of Ghazni's raids. This was where Humayun was defeated by Sher Shah in 1540, forcing him to temporarily flee India.

Etawah

This town rose to some importance during the Moghul period, only to go through the usual series of rapid changes during the turmoil that followed the Moghuls. The Jami Masjid shows similarities to the mosques of Jaunpur, and there are bathing ghats on the riverbank, below the ruined fort.

KANPUR (population 1,900,000)

Sometimes called 'the Manchester of India', this important industrial town attracts very few tourists, although it is not a great distance south of Lucknow. During the 1857 Mutiny, some of the more tragic events took place here. At that time the city was known as Cawnpore. Sir Hugh Wheeler defended a part of the Cantonment for most of the month of June but, with supplies virtually exhausted and having suffered considerable losses, he surrendered, only to have his party massacred. All Souls Memorial Church, built in 1875, has some rather moving reminders of the tragic events. It's two km from the station. Kanpur has a large and modern zoo.

The main shopping centre, Navin

Market, is famous for its locally produced cotton goods. The main leather market is on Matson Rd and articles such as bags and shoes are very cheap. The JK Temple is made of white marble and has some unusual glass statues.

Places to Stay

The best hotel in town is the *Hotel Meghdoot* (tel 51141) on The Mall. It's also the most expensive at Rs 500/700. The *Hotel Suarabh* (tel 61725) on Vidhana Rd is slightly less expensive. Cheaper hotels include the *Vaishali Hotel* on Matson Rd, the *Mira Inn* on The Mall, and the *Grand Trunk Hotel* on Grand Trunk Rd.

Getting There & Away

Kanpur can be reached daily by air from Delhi (Rs 425). It's on the main Delhi to Calcutta railway line; some express trains take as little as five hours from Delhi to Kanpur. From Delhi the fare is Rs 52 in 2nd class, Rs 185 in 1st for the 435-km trip. From Calcutta it's 1007 km costing Rs 93 in 2nd class, Rs 350 in 1st. Kanpur to Bombay is 1348 km and costs Rs 110 in 2nd class, Rs 439 in 1st.

LUCKNOW (population 1,200,000)

The capital of Uttar Pradesh, Lucknow rose to prominence as the capital of the nawabs of Oudh. These rulers controlled a region of north-central India for about a century after the decline of the Mogul Empire, and most of the interesting monuments in Lucknow date from this period. The nawabs were:

Sa'adat Khan Burhan-ul-mulk	1724-1739
Safdar Jang	1739-1753
Shuja-ud-daula	1753-1775
Asaf-ud-daula	1775-1797
Sa'adat Ali Khan	1798-1814
Ghazi-ud-din Haidar	1814-1827
Nasir-ud-din Haidar	1827-1837
Mohammad Ali Shah	1837-1842
Amjad Ali Shah	1842-1847
Wajid Ali Shah	1847-1856

It was not until Asaf-ud-daula that the capital of Oudh was moved to Lucknow from Faizabad. Safdar Jang lived and ruled from Delhi and his tomb is a familiar landmark near the Safdarjung Airport After Sa'adat Ali Khan the rest of the Oudh nawabs were a uniformly hopeless lot. Wajid Ali Shah was so extravagant and indolent that to this day his name is regarded by many in India as synonymous with lavishness. In 1856 the British, as was their wont, pensioned him off for incompetence and exiled him to Calcutta for the rest of his life. This was one of the sparks that lit the Indian Mutiny. Lucknow became the scene for some of the most dramatic events of the Mutiny as the British residents held out in the Residency for 87 harrowing days, only to be besieged again for a further two months after being relieved.

The nawabs were Shi'ite Muslims, and Lucknow remains the principal Indian Shi'ite city – unlike other major Muslim cities in India like Delhi and Agra, where

1	Residency
2	Kaiserbagh Bus Station
3	Hotel Gulmarg
4	Kaiserbagh
5	Hotel Clarks Avadh
6	Shah Najaf Imambara
7	Botanical Gardens
8	Carlton Hotel
9	Hotel Gomti (Tourist Bungalow) & State Tourist Office
10	Hotel Elora
11	Kwality Restaurant
12	Royal Cafe
13	Hotel Capoor's
14	Tourist Office
15	Janpath Market
16	Jone Hing Restaurant
17	Chaudhary's Place
18	GPO
19	Zoo & Museum
20	La Martiniere School
21	Hotel Kohinoor
22	Charbagh Bus Station
23	Railway Station

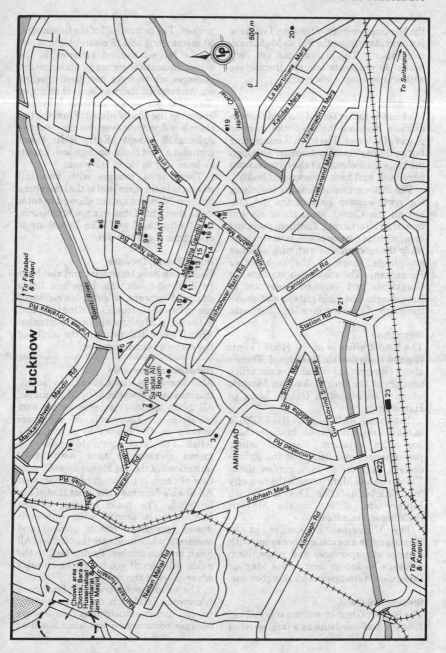

Lucknow

To Sultanpur

La Martiniere Marg
Kalidas Marg
Vikramaditya Marg
Vivekanand Marg

Haider Canal

20

19

HAZRATGANJ

Ram Tirth Marg
Sapru Marg
Shah Najaf Rd
Mahatma Gandhi Rd
Bishesbwar Nath Rd

Sapna Marg

7
6
8
9

18
17
16
15
14
13
12
11
10

Gomti River

To Faizabad & Aliganj

Vidhan

Cantonment Rd

Station Rd

21

Manikarneshwar Mandir Rd

Vishwa Vidyalaya Rd

Tomb of Saadat Ali & Begum
2

5

4

1

J Narain Hospital Rd
J Narain Rd
Nilab Rd

AMINABAD

Aminabad Rd

Shruti Marg
Guru Govind Singh Marg
Biddpra Rd

23

22

Subhash Marg

Nadan Mahal Rd
Murtaza Hussain Marg
Aishbagh Rd
Maghegh Rd

Chowk area -
Chotta, Bara &
Hussainabad
Imambaras &
Jami Masjid

To Airport & Kanpur

500 m
0

the Muslims are mainly Sunnite. Lucknow is a good place to see the Shi'ite Muharram celebrations. The activity can get very hectic as penitents scourge themselves with whips; keep a low profile.

Orientation

Lucknow is rather spread out and there is quite a distance between the various places of interest. The town is interesting but sadly neglected by tourists, although the huge mausoleums of the nawabs were jerry-built and have deteriorated badly.

The historic monuments are mainly in the north-eastern part of the old city around the Chowk area, about six km from the Hotel Gomti. The main shopping area, with its narrow alleys, is Aminabad, while the modern area with wide avenues and large shops is the fashionable Hazratganj. The major bus stations for Gorakhpur and Varanasi buses are in Kaiserbagh. The main railway station, in the south of the city, is called Charbagh.

Information

The tourist office is at the Hotel Gomti (Tourist Bungalow) in Hazratganj. There's also a Government of India tourist office upstairs at the back of Janpath Market, which is on Mahatma Gandhi Marg in Hazratganj.

The Indian Airlines office (tel 44030) is at the Hotel Clarks Avadh. In winter there are often excellent classical music performances and dances at the Rabindralaya auditorium in a garden down Vidhan Sabha Marg towards the new city from Charbagh station. There is a British Library (tel 42144) in the Mayfair Building in Hazratganj.

The Universal Bookseller at 82 Hazratganj is an excellent bookshop with a range of paperbacks and maps. Ram Advani's bookshop, next to the Mayfair Cinema on Hazratganj, is another good one.

Great Imambara

The Bara or Great Imambara was built in 1784 by Asaf-ud-daula as a famine-relief project. The central hall of the Imambara, 50 metres long and 15 metres high, is one of the largest vaulted galleries in the world. Beneath it are many underground passages which have now been blocked up. An external stairway leads to an upper floor laid out as an amazing labyrinth known as the *bhulbhulaiya*. From the top there's a fine view over the city and the Aurangzeb Mosque. Entry is Rs 4 and includes a visit to the ancient well known as *baoli* and to Rumi Darwaza.

There is a mosque with two tall minarets in the courtyard of the Imambara but non-Muslims are not allowed to enter it. To the right of this, in a row of cloisters, is a 'bottomless' well. The Imambara is open from 6 am to 5 pm.

Rumi (Roomi) Darwaza

Beside the Bara Imambara and also built by Asaf-ud-daula, this huge and finely designed darwaza, or 'gate', is a replica of one in Istanbul. 'Rumi' (relating to Rome) is the term Muslims applied to Istanbul when it was still Byzantium, the capital of the eastern Roman Empire.

Hussainabad Imambara

Also known as the Chhota, or 'small' Imambara, this was built by Muhammad Ali Shah in 1837 to serve as his own mausoleum. Thousands of labourers worked on the project to gain famine relief. The large courtyard encloses a raised rectangular tank with small imitations of the Taj Mahal on each side. One of them is the tomb of Muhammad Ali Shah's daughter, the other that of her husband. The main building of the Imambara is topped with numerous domes (the main one is golden) and minarets, while inside are the tombs of Ali Shah and his mother. Paying Rs 2 to the guide will permit you to see the nawab's silver-covered throne.

The watchtower opposite the Imambara is known as Satkhanda, or the 'seven-storey tower', but it actually has four storeys because construction was abandoned at that level when Ali Shah died in 1840. The Imambara is open from 6 am to 5 pm and is a little beyond the Great Imambara and the Rumi Darwaza.

Clock Tower
Opposite the Hussainabad Imambara is the 67-metre-high clock tower and the Hussainabad Tank. The clock tower was built between 1880 and 1887.

Picture Gallery
Also facing the Hussainabad Tank is a *baradari* or summer house, built by Ali Shah. Now restored, it houses portraits of the various nawabs of Oudh. It is open from 8 am to 5 pm and admission is Rs 1.

Jami Masjid
West of the Hussainabad Imambara is the great Jami Masjid mosque with its two minarets and three domes. Construction was started by Muhammad Ali Shah but completed after his death. This is one of the few mosques in India not open to non-Muslims.

Residency
Built in 1800 for the British Resident, this extensive building became the stage for the most dramatic events of the 1857 Mutiny (or War of Independence in India) – the Sieges of Lucknow. The British inhabitants of Lucknow all took refuge in the Residency with the outbreak of the Mutiny. The commander, Sir Henry Lawrence, expected to be able to hold out for as long as 15 days before relief arrived. It was 87 days later that a small force under Sir Henry Havelock broke through the besiegers to the remaining half-starved defenders. The story was still not over, for once Havelock and his troops were within the Residency the siege recommenced and continued from 25 September to 17 November, when Sir Colin Campbell broke through to the Residency for the second time.

Today, the Residency is maintained exactly as it was at the time of the final relief. The shattered walls are still scarred by cannon shots and the cemetery at the nearby ruined church has the graves of

Great Imambara

2000 men, women and children, including that of Sir Henry Lawrence, who died during the first siege. The area around the Residency is now well-kept lawns and gardens, but at the time of the siege the surrounding buildings were only separated from the Residency by narrow streets and lanes. The besiegers frequently attempted to dig tunnels into the Residency.

From 1857 right up to the day India became independent in 1947, a Union Jack was flown night and day from one of the Residency's towers. Times have changed: today there is a Martyr's Memorial to the martyrs of India's independence struggle directly opposite the Residency. It was opened in 1957, the 100th anniversary of the Mutiny. There are no set opening hours for the Residency, but the 'model room', where a very tatty model of the positions during the siege is on display, is only open from 9 am to 5.30 pm. Admission is Rs 0.50 to the garden, Rs 1 to the model room, except on Fridays when it is free.

Lakshman Tila

This high ground on the right bank of the River Gomti was the original site of the town which became known as Lucknow in the 15th century. Aurangzeb's Mosque now stands on this site.

Shah Najaf Imambara

Close to the Hotel Gomti, this mausoleum takes its name from Najaf, the town 190 km south-west of Baghdad in Iraq where Hazrat Ali, the Shi'ite Muslim leader, is buried. The Imambara is the tomb of Ghazi-ud-din Haidar Khan, who died in 1827. His wives are also buried here. This was the scene for desperate fighting in November 1857 during the second relief of Lucknow. The domed exterior is comparatively plain, but inside are chandeliers and it's said that at one time the dome was covered with gold. The building is used to store *tazia*, elaborate creations of wood, bamboo and silver paper which are carried through the streets at Muharram. They are usually models of the Kerbala in Iraq. Many precious items from the mausoleum were looted following the mutiny. The Imambara is open from 6 am to 5 pm.

Martiniere School

Outside the town is this strange school built by the Frenchman Major-General Claude Martin. Taken prisoner at Pondicherry in 1761, he joined the East India Company's army, then in 1776 entered service with the Nawab of Oudh, while at the same time maintaining his East India Company connections. He quickly made a substantial fortune from his dual occupations of soldier and businessman, and started to build a palatial home which he named Constantia.

Martin designed much of the building himself, and his architectural abilities were, to say the least, a little mixed – Gothic gargoyles were piled merrily atop Corinthian columns to produce a finished product which a British Marquess sarcastically pronounced took its ideas from a wedding cake. Martin died in 1800 before his stately home could be completed, but left the money and directions that it should become a school. The building could definitely do with a coat of paint, and Martin keeps watch from his tomb in the basement.

'Kim', the boy hero of Kipling's story of the same name, went to this school and there are similar establishments, also financed from Martin's fortune, in Calcutta and Lyon, France. The building is two km from the Hotel Gomti and is fronted by an artificial lake (now dried up) with a 38-metre-high column in its centre. The school is still run like a very British private school – the boys sing hymns in chapel every morning even though, a teacher reported with almost a tinge of regret, 'very few of them are Christians'.

Other Attractions

Near the Hotel Clarks Avadh and the Kaiserbagh are the stone tombs of Sa'adat

Ali and his wife. There is also a summer house in the well-kept garden. There are two museums, both closed on Mondays, and a children's museum. The Archaeological Museum is on the Kaiserbagh. The State Museum (open 10.30 am to 4.30 pm) is in the Banarsi Bagh. The zoo, founded in 1921, is also here and has a large collection of snakes. It is open from 5 am to 7 pm.

Sikandarbagh, scene of pitched battles in November 1857, is now the home of the National Botanical Research Institute. The gardens are open from 6 am to 5 pm. General Havelock, who led the first relief of Lucknow, has his grave and memorial in the Almbagh. Nadan Mahal is the tomb of the first governor of Oudh appointed by Akbar, and it is one of the earliest buildings in Lucknow, dating from around 1600. Other buildings nearby include the small Sola Khamba pavilion and the tomb of Ibrahim Chisti.

Places to Stay – bottom end

The popular *Hotel Capoor's* (tel 43958) is on Mahatma Gandhi Marg in Hazratganj and costs from Rs 70/100. Rooms with air-con and TV are more expensive. The *Hotel Elora* (tel 31307) is at 3 Lalbagh, about midway between the Kaiserbagh bus station and the Hotel Gomti. Rooms start from Rs 75/180 and there are extra costs for air-cooling or air-con. The rooms are tiny but the hotel is clean, friendly and does excellent food.

Another cheaper hotel is the *Avadh Lodge* (tel 43821) at 1 Ram Mohan Rai Marg near the botanical gardens. It looks worn out and charges Rs 60/100. The *Hotel Amber* (tel 43075) near the railway station charges Rs 90 for large double rooms. Other cheapies include the *Deep Hotel* at Bidhan Sabha Marg and the *Ramakrishna Lodge* next to the Hotel Gomti. This latter place has double rooms for Rs 60. A good cheap place near the railway station is the friendly *Bengali Hotel*, where rooms cost Rs 60 with bath.

The *Naresh Hotel*, on Ram Tirth Marg

in a pleasant market area, is clean and has singles/doubles for Rs 40/60. There are railway *retiring rooms* at Charbagh station with rooms from Rs 50 and dorms.

Places to Stay – middle & top end

The big state government *Hotel Gomti* (tel 34708) is at 6 Sapru Marg in Hazratganj. Rooms, all doubles with bath, cost from Rs 100 up to Rs 325 for the newer ones with air-con. The rooms are well furnished, if slightly run-down, and there's also a Rs 15 dorm. The Gomti is 4½ km from the railway station; get there on a No 4 bus, or take a cycle-rickshaw for about Rs 6. There is a tourist office here also, although the main one is opposite the Hotel Kohinoor.

The *Hotel Varuna* at 22 Gulab Bagh has clean and spacious rooms with balcony for Rs 150. The *Hotel Clarks Avadh* (tel 40130/1) at 8 Mahatma Gandhi Marg is Lucknow's best hotel – its only real 'international' standard hotel in fact, but service and facilities don't match the prices. It has everything from central air-conditioning to restaurants and a 24-hour coffee shop. Singles/doubles cost Rs 750/800.

In the Hazratganj area near the Hotel Gomti is the old-fashioned-looking *Carlton Hotel* (tel 44021/4) on Shah Najaf Rd. There are wonderful gardens around the hotel, and rooms cost Rs 225/300 with air-con. The *Hotel Kohinoor* (tel 33849, 43892), at 6 Station Rd about one km from the railway station, charges Rs 220 to Rs 300, or Rs 300 to Rs 400 with air-con.

Places to Eat

For good non-veg food try the *Royal Cafe* in the Hotel Capoor's, or the *Seema Restaurant* in Hazratganj. The *Ritz*, near the Hotel Gomti, is a popular place serving snacks, masala dosa and sweets. There are four Chinese restaurants in Hazratganj which serve similar food. The *Hong Kong Restaurant* is the best of them.

The *Indian Coffee House* near the Sahu

Cinema is a good place to meet Indian intellectuals spending hours over a coffee but the food is nothing special. The *Basant Restaurant* has excellent masala dosa and snacks known as chat. The *Marksman Cafe* on Mahatma Gandhi Rd is a good place for cappuccino coffee.

Next to Clarks are a number of new eating places which offer reasonable Chinese, Indian and European food. The *Safina Restaurant* is reportedly good for traditional Lucknow food.

The *Spicy Bite* in the Tulsi Theatre Building on Rani Laxmi Bai Marg has good Indian and Chinese food.

Lucknow has some fine Mughlai food specialities. *Kulfi faluda*, ice cream with cornflour noodles, is a popular dessert, and there are several places in Aminabad that serve it. The sweet orange-coloured rice dish *zarda* is also popular. The huge paper-thin chapattis *rumali roti* are served in many small Muslim restaurants in the old city. They arrive folded up and should be eaten with a goat or lamb curry like *bhuna ghosht* or *roghan josh*. In the hot months of May and June, Lucknow has some of the world's finest mangoes, particularly the wonderful *dashhari* mangoes grown in the village of Malihabad, west of the city.

Things to Buy
Lucknow is famed for its hand-woven embroidery known as *chikan*. It's made into saris for women and kurtas for men. The Gangotri government emporium in Hazratganj is a good place for this and other handicrafts. Prices are lower in Aminabad, but you have to bargain.

The traditional north Indian perfume known as *itar* has been made and sold by the firm of Muhammad Ali-Ashraf Ali since the time of the nawabs; you can buy it in Aminabad. It's a very powerful perfume.

Getting There & Away
Air There are many air connections to Lucknow: two daily Delhi/Lucknow flights, a daily Delhi/Lucknow/Allahabad/ Varanasi flight or a Delhi/Lucknow/ Gorakhpur connection, a daily Delhi/

Lucknow/Patna/Ranchi/Calcutta flight and a four-times-weekly Bombay/Varanasi/ Lucknow flight. Some fares include Delhi Rs 435, Patna Rs 485 and Bombay Rs 1420.

Bus Charbagh bus station, by the railway station, can be phoned on 50988. The Kaiserbagh bus station number is 42503. Buses to Delhi, Agra, Allahabad, Varanasi, Kanpur (Rs 19) and Gorakhpur (six hours, Rs 45) all operate from Kaiserbagh.

Train By express train, Lucknow is six hours from Varanasi and only eight hours from Delhi if you travel on the Gomti Express, which runs daily except Tuesdays. The Varanasi to Lucknow fare is Rs 40 in 2nd class, Rs 137 in 1st for the 301-km trip. Delhi to Lucknow costs Rs 55 in 2nd class, Rs 201 in 1st for the 487-km trip.

There is only a metre-gauge line between Lucknow and Gorakhpur, for the Nepal border, so this trip takes five hours and costs Rs 41 in 2nd class, Rs 141 in 1st. Both the metre-gauge North-Eastern Railway lines and the broad-gauge Northern Railway lines run through the main railway station.

For Northern Railway enquiries ring 51234 or 51333. First-class bookings are made on 51833, 2nd class on 51488. For North-Eastern Railway enquiries call 51433 and for all reservations call 51383.

To/from Nepal From the border at Sunauli, where you enter Nepal, it is a 12-hour, Rs 51 bus ride to Lucknow.

Getting Around
Airport Transport Amausi airport is 15 km out of Lucknow and taxis charge Rs 80.

Local Transport Local transport is not very frequent but a tempo will take you from the GPO to Chowk, near the Great Imambara, for about Rs 1. There are also buses from Chowk to the railway station, or you could take a rickshaw from Hazratganj to Aminabad and then a bus to Chowk. The two Imambaras and the

Jami Masjid are all around the Chowk area, while Shah Najaf is in Hazratganj and the Residency is about midway between the two. A cycle-rickshaw for a day's sightseeing costs Rs 30 to Rs 40. A tonga tour of the historic areas of Lucknow is a quintessential Lucknow experience.

Most locals take the six-seaters which run between the station, Hazratgnaj and Chowk for Rs 1.

ALLAHABAD (population 780,000)

The city of Allahabad is 135 km west of Varanasi at the confluence of two of India's most important rivers – the Ganges and the Yamuna (Jumna). This meeting point of the rivers, the *sangam*, is belived to have great soul-cleansing powers and is an important pilgrimage site. It is even more holy because the invisible Saraswati River is supposed to join the Ganges and the Yamuna at this point.

Allahabad also has an historic fort built by Akbar which overlooks the confluence of the rivers and contains an Ashoka pillar. The Nehru family home, Anand Bhawan, is in Allahabad and is open for inspection. Not many western visitors pause in this city, but it can be an interesting and worthwhile stop. Built on a very ancient site, it was known in Aryan times as Prayag, and Brahma himself is said to have performed a sacrifice here.

History

The Chinese pilgrim Hiuen Tsang described visiting the city in 634 AD, and it acquired its present name in 1584, under Akbar. Later Allahabad was taken by the Marathas, sacked by the Pathans and finally ceded to the British in 1801 by the Nawab of Oudh. It was in Allahabad that the East India Company officially handed over control of India to the British government in 1858, following the Mutiny.

Information & Orientation

Allahabad is less congested and more modern than its sister city, touristy Varanasi. Civil Lines, with its modern shopping centre, has broad, tree-lined avenues and the main bus station. The older part of town is near the Yamuna River. The hub of the older part of the city is known as Chowk, and this is also the location of the main produce market, known as Loknath.

The tourist office (tel 52722) is at the Tourist Bungalow on Mahatma Gandhi Rd.

Sangam

At the confluence, the Ganges is about two km wide – it's a shallower, muddier river than the clearer, deeper, green Yamuna. Boats out on to the river are a bit of a tourist trap – right by the confluence you should be able to get a boat for about Rs 5; from Saraswati Ghat further upriver you might pay, say, Rs 20.

The confluence of the rivers is the scene for a great annual bathing festival which takes place between mid-January and mid-February of each year. The festival, known as Magh Mela, lasts from 15 days to a month and attracts thousands of pilgrims who come for a dip in the holy rivers. Every 12th year the Magh Mela is known as the Kumbh Mela and the thousands increase to over a million pilgrims!

A huge temporary township springs up on the vacant land on the Allahabad side of the river and elaborate precautions have to be taken for the pilgrims' safety – in the early '50s, 350 people were killed in a stampede to the water. The Kumbh Mela alternates between Nasik, Ujjain and Hardwar every three years and will next return to Allahabad in 2001.

The Fort

Built by Akbar in 1583, the fort, which stands at the confluence on the Yamuna side, has massive walls and pillars and three magnificent gateways flanked by high towers. It is made from huge bricks and is at its most impressive when viewed from the river. Apart from one Moghul building there are no old constructions remaining within the fort – which is just as well, since foreigners aren't allowed inside. Officially, passes can be obtained from the Security Officer (tel 51370), but it appears you're simply told 'No'. However, you can enter part of the fort complex if you visit the Patalpuri Temple which is open to non-Hindus but is not particularly interesting.

Ashoka Pillar Unfortunately you're not allowed to see the Ashoka pillar in front of the gateway inside the fort. The 10.6-metre-high polished sandstone shaft dates from 232 BC; it was found lying on the ground in the fort in 1837 and was set up at its present location. Inscribed on the column are Ashoka's edicts and a later inscription eulogising the victories of Samudragupta (326-375 AD). This is the only record of the events in this Gupta ruler's life. There is also a later inscription by Jehangir.

The Undying Tree A small door in the east wall of the fort near the river, leads to the 'undying banyan tree' – one place in the fort you are allowed to visit. This tree is mentioned by Hiuen Tsang, who tells of pilgrims sacrificing their lives by leaping to their deaths from it in order to seek salvation. Also known as Akshai Veta, the tree is actually in a curious basement and the only sign of it is the bunches of leaves tied haphazardly in place.

Hanuman Temple This popular temple, open to non-Hindus, is interesting because of the reclining position of Hanuman, in contrast to the usual standing position. It is said that every year during the floods the Ganges rises high enough to touch the feet of the sleeping Hanuman and then starts receding.

Anand Bhawan
The Nehru family home was donated to the Indian government by Indira Gandhi

in 1970; it's in the eastern part of town, near the Ganges. The exhibits in the house show how this well-off family became involved in the struggle for Indian independence and later produced four generations of astute politicians – Motilal Nehru, Jawaharlal Nehru, Indira Gandhi and Rajiv Gandhi.

The two-storey mansion has a large garden and contains many personal items connected with the life of three generations of the Nehru family. Opening hours are from 9.30 am to 5 pm, closed Mondays; there's a Rs 2 charge for going upstairs. Two points of interest are a room where Mahatma Gandhi used to stay during his visits to the Nehrus and the room where Indira was born.

Khusru Bagh
This peaceful garden, close to the railway station, contains the tomb of Prince Khusru, son of Jehangir, who was executed by his own father. Nearby is the unoccupied tomb intended for his sister and the tomb of his Rajput mother who was said to have poisoned herself in despair at Khusru's opposition to his father.

1	Presidency Hotel
2	YMCA
3	Indian Airlines
4	Hotel Yatrik
5	Allahabad Regency Hotel
6	All Saints' Cathedral
7	GPO
8	Hotel Harsh
9	Tipso Hotel
10	Kwality Restaurant
11	Tandoor Restaurant
12	Lucky Sweet Mart
13	El Chico Restaurant
14	Samrat Hotel
15	Royal Hotel
16	Tourist Office & Tourist Bungalow
17	Bus Stand
18	Museum
19	Anand Bhawan
20	Fort

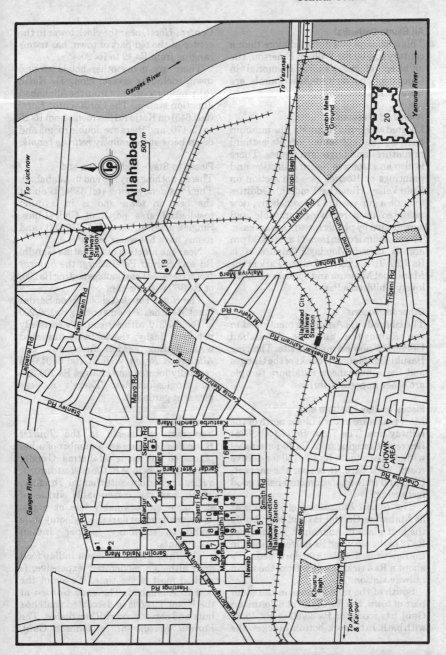

All Saints Cathedral

This cathedral was designed more than a century ago by Sir William Emerson, the architect of the Victoria Memorial in Calcutta. The stained-glass murals are beautiful.

Allahabad Museum

Located on Kamla Nehru Rd, the museum has a fine collection of Rajasthani miniatures and terracotta figures. There is also an extensive Nehru collection and paintings by Roerich (see the section on Kulu Valley, Himachal Pradesh). Oddities include a gun used to kill somebody, now mounted on a revolving turntable and surrounded by plastic roses in a glass case. The museum is open from 11 am to 4.30 pm and is closed Mondays; admission is Rs 0.20. To the north of Alfred Park is the Municipal Museum and opposite that is a lovely Children's Park.

Other Attractions

The Bharadwaja Ashram is mentioned in the *Ramayana* and the Allahabad University now occupies its site. The Nag Basuki Temple on the banks of the Ganges and the subterranean Patalpuri Temple are other important shrines.

Places to Stay – bottom end

Most hotels are in Civil Lines, north of the railway line. The *Tipso Hotel* (tel 3635) has rooms ranging from Rs 40 for singles without bath up to Rs 125/150 for deluxe rooms with bath. It is near the market, GPO and railway station, and has a good restaurant.

The *Tourist Bungalow* (tel 53640) is at 35 Mahatma Gandhi Rd and is probably the best place in Allahabad. Rooms cost Rs 72 in the old wing, Rs 100 for doubles in the new wing, and Rs 15 for dorm beds. It's about a Rs 4 rickshaw ride from the main railway station.

South of the railway lines in the older part of town, the *Raj Hotel* at 6 Johnston Ganj has rooms at Rs 35/60 or Rs 45/65 with bath. In the rock-bottom bracket, the *Central Hotel*, near the clock tower in the centre of the old part of town, has rooms ranging from Rs 12 to Rs 20.

There are many other hotels around town, including several along Dr Katiu Rd, running south-east from the Allahabad Junction station. The *Continental Hotel* (tel 5643) on Katju Rd has rooms from Rs 25 to Rs 170, and there are double rooms and dorm beds at the railway *retiring rooms*.

Places to Stay – middle & top end

There's nothing very top end in Allahabad. The *Presidency Hotel* (tel 3394) is about the best in town and is in a quiet residential area north of Civil Lines. Singles/doubles cost Rs 210/260 and rooms have hot water and TV.

Near the junction of Mahatma Gandhi Rd and Sardar Patel Marg, the *Samrat Hotel* (tel 4854) has doubles costing Rs 200, or Rs 360 with air-con.

The *Hotel Yatrik* (tel 56920) on Sardar Patel Marg has 38 rooms costing Rs 150/200 or Rs 270/310 with air-con. It's certainly not very flashy; the lobby is furnished with folding garden furniture! The *Allahabad Regency Hotel* (tel 56043) is centrally located and charges Rs 295/325 for singles/doubles. There's a very pleasant garden.

Places to Eat

You can get meals in the *Tourist Bungalow*, or there are a number of other places to eat along Mahatma Gandhi Marg. They include *El Chico Restaurant*, a *Kwality* and opposite that the *Tandoor*, which has the considerable virtue of staying open reasonably late at night. They're all in that darkened, gloomy style found in so many 'proper' Indian restaurants.

The *Tandoor* has excellent Indian food and, although moderately expensive, is packed most of the time. It's about the best in Allahabad. The *Jade Garden* at the Hotel Tipso is in decorated thatched huts and serves good chicken dishes. The *Purohit Restaurant* in Johnson Ganj, between Civil Lines and Chowk, has good Indian food at reasonable prices, including a Rs 15 thali. The *Umesha* on Mahatma Gandhi Rd has good sweets.

There are also many restaurants in the crowded streets of the old town on the southern side of the railway tracks, plus many small dhaba places close to the station along Dr Katiu Rd. The *Ginza Restaurant*, next to the Raj Hotel in the older part of town, has a typical non-vegetarian menu but the food is said to be very good.

Getting There & Away

Allahabad is a good place from which to travel to Khajuraho. If you spend the night in Allahabad you can catch a morning train to Satna, from where buses go to Khajuraho. Alternatively you can take a bus to Satna (eight hours) and another from there to Khajuraho (three hours).

Air Allahabad is connected to Delhi (Rs 600) by daily Indian Airlines and Vayudoot flights. Indian Airlines also operates flights twice weekly to Gorakhpur (Rs 275) and five times weekly to Varanasi and Patna (Rs 375).

Train There are two railway stations – the main one is Allahabad Junction in the central part of the city. Most trains to Varanasi, however, go from the Allahabad City station, about three km away on the metre-gauge line.

Allahabad is on the main Delhi to Calcutta line. It takes about nine hours from Delhi to cover the 627 km at a cost of Rs 67 in 2nd class, Rs 242 in 1st. From Varanasi it takes about three hours to cover the 137 km to Allahabad and costs Rs 20 in 2nd class, Rs 72 in 1st.

Getting Around

If you arrive at Allahabad Junction station, the main entrance to the station faces towards the old city; you have to cross over the railway lines at the back

entrance for Civil Lines. Allahabad has plenty of cycle and auto-rickshaws.

AROUND ALLAHABAD
Bhita

On the opposite side of the Yamuna River, 18 km south-west of Allahabad, are the excavated remains of this fortified city. Archaeological digs in 1910-11 revealed successive layers dating from the Gupta period (320-455 AD) back to the Mauryan period (321-184 BC) and even earlier. There is a museum with stone and metal seals, coins from various kingdoms of the time, terracotta statues, figures and various utensils, and personal possessions.

Garwha

The ruined temples in this walled enclosure are about 50 km from Allahabad. Garwha is eight km from Shankargarh and the last three km have to be completed on foot. The major temple has 16 beautifully carved stone pillars, and inscriptions reveal that the temples date back to the Gupta period at the very least. Some of the better sculptures from Garwha are now shown in the State Museum in Lucknow.

Kausambi

This ancient Buddhist centre, once known as Kosam, is 63 km from Allahabad. At one time it was the capital of King Udaya, a contemporary of the Buddha. There's a huge fortress near the village, and the broken remains of an Ashoka pillar, minus any pre-Gupta period inscriptions, can be seen inside the fort. A bus runs from Allahabad to the fort at Kausambi.

LUCKNOW TO VARANASI
Bahraich & Saheth-Maheth

The nephew of that scourge of India, Mahmud of Ghazni, was killed in Bahraich in 1033. There is a shrine to him about three km from the town. At Saheth-Maheth the Buddha performed the miracle of sitting on a 1000-petalled lotus and multiplying himself a million times. The town is also known as Sravasti and can be reached from Gorakhpur on the Naugarh-Gonda loop line. Gainjohwa is the nearest station and there are extensive ruins and a few modern Buddhist temples.

Faizabad (population 120,000)

Faizabad was once the capital of Oudh but rapidly declined after the death of Bahu Begum. Her mausoleum is said to be the finest of its type in Uttar Pradesh. Her husband, Nawab Shujaddaula, who preceded her as ruler, also has a fine mausoleum. There are pleasant gardens in Guptar Park, where the temple from which Rama is supposed to have disappeared stands.

There are three large mosques in the market (chowk) area. The green one and the big one to the north are Shia Imambaras, the third is a Sunni Muslim mosque.

Places to Stay The *Hotel Abha* (tel 2550) has singles/doubles for Rs 40/50 with bath. The *Hotel Priya* (tel 3540) in the same area is cheaper. For something a bit better, the *Hotel Shan-e-Awadh* (tel 2104) in Rikabganj charges Rs 60/80 for singles/doubles, Rs 125/150 with air-con.

The railway *retiring rooms* cost Rs 25 for a double, Rs 10 for a dorm bed.

Getting There & Away Faizabad is three hours by train from either Varanasi or Lucknow. Buses to Allahabad take four hours and cost Rs 25. There are buses to Gorakhpur near the Nepalese border for Rs 20.

Ayodhya

Only six km from Faizabad, Ayodhya is a popular pilgrimage place as it was the birthplace of Rama. Many of the sites in the town are supposed to be linked with events in the *Ramayana*.

There are numerous picturesque temples (many open to non-Hindus) and a ghat; the town is on the Gogra (Ghaghara) River. In recent times the town has become the focus of a 'temple-mosque' dispute. A mosque was originally constructed on the site of Rama's birth by a Moghul emperor in the 15th century, but it was taken over by Hindus after 400 or so years. Today the matter rests with the courts and armed guards help keep the two communities from each others' throats.

This was also a great Buddhist centre at one time and, as usual, Hiuen Tsang dropped by to list how many monasteries there were and how many monks were in residence.

Other temples worth visiting include the Hanumangadhi (dedicated to Hanuman) and the Kanak Mandir (built by the Maharaja of Tikamgadh last century).

Places to Stay Faizabad makes a better base. The *Pathik Niwas Tourist Bungalow* is next to the railway station and double rooms cost Rs 60 to Rs 100. Dorm beds cost Rs 15.

Getting There & Away There are regular buses from Faizabad for Rs 1.50.

Varanasi

Population: one million

Varanasi, the 'eternal city', is one of the most important pilgrimage sites in India and also a major tourist attraction. Situated on the banks of the sacred Ganges, Varanasi has been a centre of learning and civilisation for over 2000 years. It was at Sarnath only 10 km away that the Buddha first preached his message of enlightenment, 25 centuries ago. Later the city became a great Hindu centre, but was looted a number of times by Muslim invaders from the 11th century on. These destructive visits climaxed with that of the Moghul emperor Aurangzeb, who destroyed almost all of the temples and converted the most famous one into a mosque.

Varanasi has also been known as Kashi and Benares, but its present name is a restoration of an ancient name meaning the city between two rivers – the Varauana and Asi. For the pious Hindu the city has always had a special place. Besides being a pilgrimage centre, it is considered an auspicious place to die, ensuring an instant route to heaven. To this day Varanasi is a centre of learning, especially for Sanskrit scholars, and students flock here from all over India. Ironically it is in the centre of one of the most backward areas of India – a largely agrarian, rural and overpopulated area that has developed little since independence.

On the other hand Varanasi has become a symbol of the Hindu renaissance and has a special role in the development of Hindi – the national language of India. The well-known novelist Prem Chand and the literary figure Bharatendu Harischand have played their parts in this development. Tulsi Das, the famous poet who wrote the Hindi version of the *Ramayana* known as the *Ram Charit Manas*, also lived in this city for many years.

Orientation

The old city of Varanasi is situated along the west bank of the Ganges and extends back from the riverbank ghats in a winding collection of narrow alleys. They're too narrow for anything but walking, and tall houses overhang the picturesque, though hardly clean, lanes. It's a fascinating area to wander around. The town extends from Raj Ghat, near the bridge, to Asi Ghat, near the university. Areas known as Chowk, Lahurabir and Godaulia are just outside the old city area along the river.

One of the best ways to get oriented in Varanasi is to remember the positions of the ghats, particularly important ones like Dasaswamedh Ghat. The big 'international hotels' and the national tourist office are in the Cantonment area north of the Varanasi

Junction railway station. The broad, tree-lined avenues of the Cantonment are a great contrast to the crowds of people, bicycles and rickshaws in the old part of town.

Information

The state tourist office is in the Tourist Bungalow and there's a helpful smaller office in the railway station. The Government of India tourist office (tel 43189) is at 15B The Mall in the Cantonment.

The Varanasi GPO is a good place to send parcels from, as there are tailors' stalls for wrapping and sealing right outside.

The Indian Airlines office (tel 64146, 66116) is in the Mint House Motel, opposite Nadesar Palace in the Cantonment. Railway reservations at the Varanasi Junction (Cantonment) station are made by phoning 64920. The bus station is also close to the Cantonment.

If you're staying in one of Varanasi's cheaper hotels and could do with a swim, several of the hotels in the Cantonment area permit the use of their pools for a charge of Rs 35 to Rs 40. They include the Clark's Varanasi Hotel, Varanasi Ashok Hotel and the Taj Ganges Hotel.

If you're interested in studying yoga, pay a visit to the Malaviya Bhawan at the university. They offer courses in yoga and also in Hindu philosophy. There are also many private teachers and organisations offering courses which cost from virtually nothing up to very expensive.

The *Pioneer* is an informative local English-language newspaper. *Benares: City of Light* by Diana Eck (Princeton University Press) is a good guide to the city, with information on each ghat and temple and a good introduction to Hinduism.

The Ghats

Varanasi's principal attraction is the long string of bathing ghats which line the west bank of the Ganges. Ghats are the steps which lead down to the river where

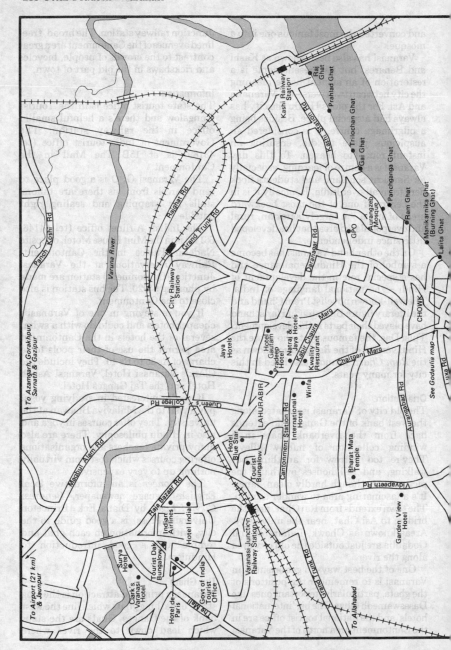

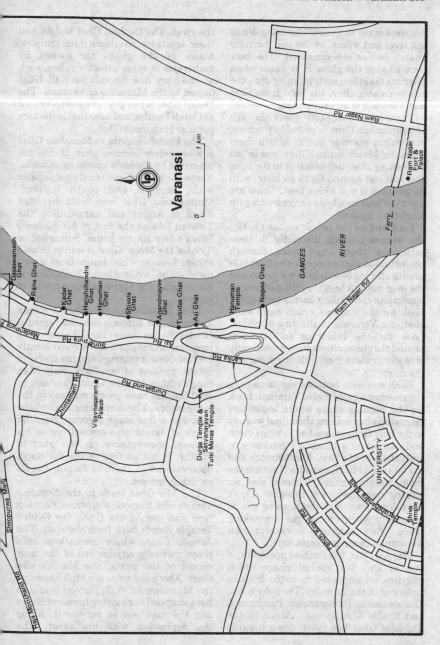

Varanasi

0   1 km

pilgrims make their soul-cleansing dip in the river and where, at the two 'burning ghats', bodies are cremated. The best time to visit the ghats is at dawn when pilgrims take their early morning dip – the city is coming alive, the light is magical and Varanasi is an exotic place.

There are over 100 ghats in all; Dasaswamedh Ghat is probably the most convenient starting point. A trip from there to Manikarnika Ghat makes an interesting short introduction to the river and will cost around Rs 15 an hour (with bargaining) if you hire a boat. There are plenty of boatmen by the river waiting for tourists to appear.

Look out for the people on the ghats – the women bathing discreetly in their saris, the young men going through contortionist yoga exercises, the Brahmin priests offering blessings (for a price) and the ever-present beggars giving others an opportunity to do their karma some good. Look for the lingams which mark each ghat, for Varanasi is the city of Shiva. Look for the buildings and temples around the ghats, often tilting precariously or in some cases actually sliding down into the river.

Each monsoon causes great damage to the riverbank buildings of Varanasi. Look for the burning ghats where bodies are cremated after making their final journey to the holy Ganges swathed in white cloth and carried on a bamboo stretcher – or even the roof of a taxi. Manikarnika and the less used Harishchandra Ghat are the main burning ghats. There's also an electric crematorium at this ghat. Don't try taking photos at the burning ghats, especially when cremations are taking place. Just carrying a camera can sometimes cause problems here.

The Asi Ghat, the furthest upstream, is one of the five special ghats which pilgrims are supposed to bathe from in order and on the same day. The order is Asi, Dasaswamedh, Barnasangam, Panchganga and finally Manikarnika. Much of the Tulsidas Ghat has fallen down towards the river. The Bachraj Ghat is Jain and there are three riverbank Jain temples. Many of the ghats are owned by maharajas or other princely rulers, such as the very fine Shivala or Kali Ghat owned by the Maharaja of Varanasi. The Dandi Ghat is the ghat of ascetics known as Dandi Panths, and near that is the very popular Hanuman Ghat.

The Harishchandra or Smashan Ghat is a secondary burning ghat. Bodies are cremated by outcasts known as *chandal*. Above the Kedar Ghat is a shrine popular with Bengalis and south Indians. Mansarowar Ghat was built by Man Singh of Amber and named after the Tibetan lake at the foot of Mt Kailash, Shiva's Himalayan home. Someswar or 'Lord of the Moon' Ghat is said to be able to heal diseases. The Munshi Ghat is very picturesque, while Ahalya Bai's Ghat is named after the Maratha woman ruler of Indore.

The Dasaswamedh Ghat's name indicates that Brahma sacrificed (medh) 10 (das) horses (aswa) here. It's one of the most important ghats and is conveniently central. Note its statues and the shrine of Sitala, goddess of smallpox. Raja Man Singh's Man Mandir Ghat was built in 1600 but has been poorly restored in the last century. The northern corner of the ghat has a fine stone balcony. Raja Jai Singh of Jaipur also erected one of his unusual observatories on this ghat in 1710. It is not as fine as the Jai Singh observatories in Delhi or Jaipur, but its setting is unique.

The Mir Ghat leads to the Nepalese Temple with its erotic sculptures. Between here and the Jalsain Ghat, the Golden Temple stands back from the river. The Jalsain Ghat, where cremations take place, virtually adjoins one of the most sacred of the ghats, the Manikarnika Ghat. Above the steps is a tank known as the Manikarnika Well; Parvati is said to have dropped her earring here and Shiva dug the tank out to recover it, filling the depression with his sweat! The

Bathing ghats, Varanasi

Charandpaduka, a slab of stone between the well and the ghat, bears footprints made by Vishnu. Privileged VIPs are allowed to be cremated at the Charandpaduka. There is also a temple to Ganesh on the ghat.

Dattatreya Ghat bears the footprint of the Brahmin saint of that name in a small temple nearby. Scindia's Ghat was originally built in 1830 but was so huge and magnificent that it collapsed into the river and had to be rebuilt. The Ram Ghat was built by the Raja of Jaipur. The Panchganga Ghat, as its name indicates, is were five rivers are supposed to meet. Above the ghat is Aurangzeb's smaller mosque, also known as the Alamgir Mosque, built over a Vishnu temple. The Gai Ghat has a figure of a cow made of stone upon it. The Trilochan Ghat has two turrets emerging from the river, and water between them is especially holy. Raj Ghat was the ferry pier until the road and rail bridge were completed here.

Golden Temple

Dedicated to Vishveswara (Vishwanath), Shiva as Lord of the Universe, the Golden Temple is across the road from its original position. Aurangzeb destroyed the original temple and built a mosque over it – traces of the earlier 1600 temple can be seen behind his mosque. The present temple was built in 1776 by Ahalya Bai of Indore, and the gold plating (three-quarters of a ton of it!) on the towers was provided by Maharaja Ranjit Singh of Lahore. Next to the temple is the Gyan Kupor well, the 'well of knowledge'. Much esteemed by the faithful, this well is said to contain the Shiva lingam removed from the original temple and hidden to protect it from Aurangzeb. Non-Hindus are not allowed into the temple but can view it from upstairs in a house across the street – soldiers sit downstairs. Near the temple, which is interesting to visit in the evening, are narrow alleys filled with many shops.

Great Mosque of Aurangzeb

Constructed using columns from the Biseswar Temple razed by Aurangzeb, this great mosque has minarets towering 71 metres above the Ganges. Armed guards protect the mosque as the Indian government wants to ensure there are no problems between Hindus and Muslims.

Durga Temple

The Durga Temple is commonly known as the Monkey Temple due to the many monkeys that have made it their home. It was built in the 18th century by a Bengali maharani and is stained red with ochre. The small temple is built in north Indian Nagara style with a multi-tiered shikara. Durga is the 'terrible' form of Shiva's consort Parvati, so at festivals there are often sacrifices of goats. Although this is one of the best known temples in Varanasi, it is, like some other Hindu temples, closed to nonbelievers. However, you can look down inside the temple from a walkway at the top. Beware of the monkeys here who are daring and vicious – they'll snatch glasses off your face, even scratch or bite if you get too close.

Next to the temple is a tank with stagnant water where, as usual, pilgrims bathe.

Tulsi Manas Temple

Next to the Durga Temple is this modern marble shikara-style temple. Built in 1964, the walls of the temple are engraved with verses and scenes from the *Ram Charit Manas*, the Hindi version of the *Ramayana*. This tells of the history and deeds of Lord Rama, an incarnation of Vishnu. Its medieval author, Tulsi Das, lived here while writing it and died in 1623. On the 2nd floor you can watch the production of moving and performing statues and scenes from Hindu mythology. If you are at all familiar with figures from the *Ramayana* or *Mahabharata*, you will find a visit here very enjoyable. Non-Hindus are allowed into this temple.

Benares Hindu University

A further 20-minute walk from the Durga Temple, or a Rs 1 rickshaw ride, is the Benares Hindu University, constructed at the beginning of the century. The large university covers an area of five square km, and you can get there by bus from Godaulia or by a rickshaw for about Rs 3.

The university was founded by Pandit Malaviya as a centre of education in Indian art, culture and music, and for the study of Sanskrit. The Bharat Kala Bhawan at the university has a fine collection of miniature paintings and also sculptures from the 1st to 15th centuries. In a room upstairs there are some old photographs and a map of Varanasi. It's open from 11 am to 4 pm (8 am to 12.30 pm in May and June) and is closed on Sundays.

New Vishwanath Temple

It's about a 30-minute walk from the gates of the university to the new Vishwanath Temple which was planned by Pandit Malaviya and built by the wealthy Birla family of industrialists. A great nationalist, Pandit Malaviya wished to see Hinduism revived without its caste distinctions and prejudices – accordingly this temple, unlike so many in Varanasi, is open to all, irrespective of caste or religion. The interior has a Shiva lingam and verses from Hindu scriptures inscribed on the walls. The temple is supposed to be a replica of the original Vishwanath Temple, destroyed by Aurangzeb.

Alamgir Mosque

Locally known as Beni Madhav Ka Darera, this was originally a Vishnu temple erected by the Maratha chieftain Beni Madhav Rao Scindia. Aurangzeb destroyed it and erected the mosque in its place, but it is a curious Hindu-Muslim mixture with the bottom part entirely Hindu.

Bharat Mata Temple

Dedicated to 'Mother India', this temple has a marble relief map of India instead of the usual images of gods and goddesses. It gives an excellent impression of the high isolation of the Tibetan plateau. The temple was opened by Mahatma Gandhi, and non-Hindus are allowed inside. It's away from the crowded riverside area, about 1½ km south of the Varanasi Junction station.

Ram Nagar Fort

On the other side of the river, this 17th-century fort is the home of the Maharaja of Benares. There are tours to the fort or you can catch a ferry across the river to get to it. The interesting fort museum contains old silver and brocade palanquins for the ladies of the court, elephant howdahs made of silver, old brocades, a replica of the royal bed and an armoury of swords and old guns. The fort is open from 10 am to 12 noon and 1 to 5 pm; entry to the museum costs Rs 1.

Tours

Varanasi tours cost Rs 30 each for morning or afternoon tours. They start from the Tourist Bungalow or the major hotels in the Cantonment area in the morning and from the Government of India tourist office on The Mall in the afternoon. Telephone 63233 for booking details.

The morning tour leaves at 6 am and takes you down the Ganges by the ghats, around the various temples and out to the university. The morning tour finishes at 12.15 pm and the afternoon tour commences at 2 pm and runs to 5.55 pm – definitely a full day. The afternoon tour takes you out to Sarnath and to the Ram Nagar Fort – if there's time! In summer all times are half an hour earlier.

The Varanasi tours don't get unquestioned recommendations:

The bus arrived late and there were more people than could fit in. . .We couldn't all get on the boat so had to take a second boat, for which they tried to charge extra. . .We were marched through various temples without any explanation. . . arrived at the university to see the miniature paintings an hour before it opened. . .The breakfast stop never happened. . .We abandoned

the afternoon tour and did it ourselves. As we were leaving the museum at the Ram Nagar Fort the tour bus turned up, just before closing time!

Places to Stay – bottom end

For shoestring travellers there are three important areas for accommodation – the spacious Cantonment area with open spaces and broad avenues north of the railway tracks, the newer part of the city south of the railway tracks, and the crowded, confused but colourful old city area by the river. The old city places are the cheapest you'll find, and staying close to the river has the advantage of being cooler during the hot season, and you can go down to the ghats at any time.

Wherever you stay in Varanasi, remember that rickshaw-wallahs are often reluctant to take you to places where they won't get a commission – be wary of tales that a lodge is 'closed up', 'full up' or 'burnt down'. Places by the river may even be 'flooded'!

Bathing ghats at Varanasi

Railway & Bus Station Area The *Tourist Bungalow* (tel 43413) is only a five-minute walk from the Varanasi Junction station and has dorm beds at Rs 15, singles at Rs 45 and doubles at Rs 103. The more expensive rooms have a bath, and in summer there's an extra Rs 10 charge for air-cooling. There's a pleasant grassy garden but the staff have a well-earned reputation for being less than helpful. Food in the restaurant is nothing special and the service can be very slow.

There are several hotels around the Tourist Bungalow. The *Hotel Amar* (tel 64044), *Hotel Relax* and *Hotel Diwan* all charge between Rs 50 and Rs 100 for double rooms. They all do good business when the Tourist Bungalow is full. Another good one, but more expensive, is the new *Hotel Malti* (tel 56844). Rooms here cost Rs 120/150, or Rs 200/250 with air-con.

Halfway between the Varanasi Junction station and the ghats, the *Venus Hotel* and the *Garden View Hotel* (tel 63026) on Vidyapeth Rd are both cheap and have been recommended by travellers. The Garden View has singles at Rs 45 to Rs 50, doubles at Rs 60 to Rs 80. Beware of booking things through this hotel, however. They're very keen on big commissions, tours that go via the silk factories and so on. There are *retiring rooms* at the Varanasi Junction station.

Cantonment Area In the Cantonment area, on the north side of the Varanasi Junction station, hotels are mainly at the top of the price scale but the *Hotel India* (tel 42161) is a good, comfortable and reasonably clean place. It's at 59 Patel Nagar, just behind the station and close to the Indian Airlines office. There's a garden, and rooms cost Rs 75/125, but this is another place not popular with touts and commission-seeking rickshaw-wallahs.

A couple of places next to the Hotel India have become popular. The new *Hotel Temple Town* (tel 43750) charges Rs 50/100 for singles/doubles or if this one is full, there's the *Hotel Rudra* and *Hotel Pervez* in the same area. The *Surya Hotel* (tel 43014), just behind the big Clark's

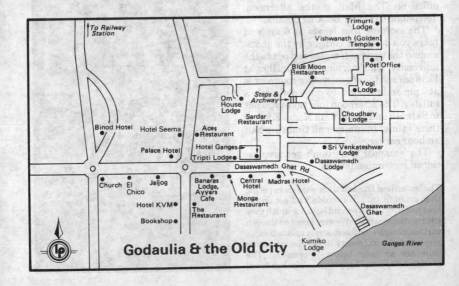

Godaulia & the Old City

Varanasi Hotel, is good value at Rs 55/80 for good rooms with bath. It also has a pleasant garden and fine restaurant – recommended.

The *Tourist Dak Bungalow* (tel 56461) on The Mall is very popular with over-landers; singles/doubles cost Rs 75/150 and there's also a dorm. They also have camping facilities and classical Indian dancing at 7.30 pm each day. There's a beautiful garden here which is ideal for relaxing, and the food is not bad.

City Centre – Godaulia & Lahurabir Area
Godaulia is the place near the Dasas-wamedh Ghat where auto-rickshaws, cycle-rickshaws and tempos stop. On the north side of the street between Godaulia and the ghats is the *Hotel Ganges*, a big place with rooms at Rs 45/75.

In Godaulia itself the *Hotel KVM* (tel 63749) is now overpriced and nothing special. It's certainly not a travellers' place. Also in Godaulia is the new *Hotel Seema* which is a moderately expensive place near the river, but it's in a noisy and crowded area of the city; double rooms cost Rs 150. Hotels in Lahurabir, between the station and Godaulia, are mainly in the middle-price bracket. The *Pradeep Hotel* (tel 44963) at Jagatganj near Lahurabir is good value as singles/doubles cost Rs 60/100. The *Hotel Gautam* in the same area is also reasonable.

Old City & Ghats Area This is the place to look for rock-bottom hotels. The streets here are very narrow; you even have to abandon cycle-rickshaws and make your way down the convoluted alleys on foot. There are three popular lodges near the river and the Golden Temple in Godaulia which are good value and put you right in the thick of the action. Rickshaw drivers are unlikely to take you to any of them as they don't give commissions. The *Yogi Lodge* (tel 53986) has long been a favourite with budget travellers and is actually an old house converted to a lodge. Dorm beds cost Rs 12 and doubles Rs 30 to Rs 45. As

it's so popular it fills up early. *Trimurti Lodge* (tel 56084) is also good value and has almost identical prices. The third place is the *Sri Venkateshwar Lodge* (tel 66820) which is run by friendly people and charges Rs 20/25 for singles/doubles.

In the same area, *Kumiko Lodge* is popular with Japanese tourists and costs Rs 15 for dorm beds and Rs 30/40 for single/double rooms. The *Shanti Lodge* in the narrow alley behind Yogi Lodge has dorms for Rs 10 and singles for Rs 20. It also has the luxury of hot water in winter and has great views from the roof. The *Vishnu Guest House* is also popular among travellers.

Further back from the river, *Om House Lodge*, in the Bansphatak area of the old city, is extremely cheap with dorm beds at Rs 8 and rooms for Rs 20/30. It's popular with travellers and the owner gives yoga lessons. You have to wander down a maze of winding lanes to find it, but it's pleasantly quiet.

Tandon House Lodge, right on the river at Gai Ghat, is close to the GPO from Maidagin and is difficult to find. There are excellent views of the river from the courtyard, and dorm beds cost Rs 10 and singles Rs 30. The *Hotel Maharaja* near Dasaswamedh Rd is good value and reasonably clean and quiet. On the other side of the main road *Krishna Lodge* is above a sitar and tabla shop. Rooms cost from around Rs 20 and there are good views from the roof.

The *New Imperial Hotel* on Luxa Rd, a few minutes walk from the ghats, has also received good raves from travellers. Another recommended place is the *Vaibhov Lodge*.

Places to Stay – top end
Varanasi's major 'tourist class' hotels are all in the new Cantonment area near the Varanasi Junction railway station. The somewhat Victorian *Clark's Varanasi Hotel* (tel 42401) is the oldest, dating back to the British era. Air-conditioned singles/doubles cost Rs 650/720, and there is a

swimming pool, shops and other facilities. It is definitely the best place in town.

The *Hotel de Paris* is also on The Mall and has singles/doubles for Rs 375/450, but is overpriced for what it offers. The newer *Hotel Ganges* (tel 42485) costs Rs 700/800.

Places to Eat

Tourist Bungalow & Lahurabir Areas

Food at the *Tourist Bungalow* is overpriced but there are excellent places to eat close by. The *Chinese Mandarin Restaurant*, right outside it, does very reasonable Chinese food and the owner is friendly. Around the corner, the small *Most Welcome* prepares excellent food and the manager is a real salesman, although the place is somewhat overpriced.

The *Winfa Restaurant* in Lahurabir, behind the cinema, is possibly Varanasi's best Chinese restaurant, with dishes at around Rs 20. In the Pradeep Hotel in Lahurabir, the *Poonam Restaurant* does excellent Indian and Chinese food. The *Basant Bihar* has good sweets.

Cantonment Area

The *Tourist Dak Bungalow* is noted for its western breakfast, which includes porridge, eggs and toast with butter. Varanasi's railway station restaurant also has a good reputation for all types of food. Their breakfasts are particularly good as is their 'pot tea'. If you want to dine in style in the Cantonment, *Clark's Varanasi Hotel* does continental breakfasts for Rs 35.

Godaulia & the Old City

The *Aces Restaurant* is a good place for breakfast and is still popular, although recent reports suggest that it is on the way down. The 'pleasant courtyard' mentioned in the previous edition of this book is now better described as a filthy farmyard. The *Tulasi Restaurant* has excellent Indian food. *The Restaurant*, a drab-looking place, is reputed to be the local meeting place for politicians. It's about 200 metres south of the main square, opposite the

KVM Hotel, and has excellent Bengali food and a 'racy Bengali intellectual atmosphere'.

There are several places to eat along the road from Godaulia to the ghats. On the south side of the street, under the Benares Lodge, is *Ayyars Cafe* with good masala dosa and other light meals. The *Sardar Restaurant*, on the north side, is also popular with budget travellers looking for good vegetarian food. Try *Jaljog*, by the main square in Godaulia, for an Indian-style breakfast of puris and vegetables known as *kachauri*.

El Chico, an underground restaurant in Godaulia which serves both Indian and western food, is moderately expensive. There are many small restaurants with good thalis in the alleys between Godaulia and the Dasaswamedh Ghat. Varanasi is well known for its excellent sweets, and *Madhur Jalpan Grih*, on the same side of the street as the cinema in Godaulia, is an excellent place to try them. Varanasi is also supposed to have very high quality pan.

In Bhelupura, near the Lalita Cinema, the *Sindhi Restaurant* does excellent vegetarian food.

Things to Buy

Varanasi is famous all over India for silk brocades and beautiful Benares saris. However, there are lots of rip-off merchants and commission people at work. Invitations to 'come to my home for tea' will inevitably mean to somebody's silk showroom, where you will be pressured into buying things. Beware of anyone in your hotel (including the manager) who offers to take you to a cheap place. You'll be quoted at least 30% more for goods as commission has to be paid.

There is a market near the GPO called Golghar where the makers of silk brocades sell directly to the shops in the area. You can get cheaper silk brocade in this area than in the big stores, but you must be careful about the quality. The big shops selling silk brocades are all in the Chowk area of the old city.

The same care is necessary with sitars – yes, Ravi Shankar does live here (or nearby), but don't believe that every sitar maker is his personal friend!

Getting There & Away

Air Varanasi is on several Indian Airlines routes, including the popular daily tourist service Delhi/Agra/Khajuraho/Varanasi. There are also flights to Patna, Bhubaneswar, Gorakhpur and Calcutta. Fares are: Delhi Rs 690, Agra Rs 545, Khajuraho Rs 365, Bhubaneswar Rs 650, Gorakhpur Rs 200 and Lucknow Rs 305. The daily flight to Kathmandu costs US$71.

Vayudoot has flights to Kanpur (Rs 335), Agra (Rs 545) and Delhi (Rs 690).

Bus The bus station is next to the main railway station. If you are heading for Nepal the bus may be better than the metre-gauge trains from here to the border. Buses leave almost hourly to Gorakhpur, five hours away. A tourist bus operates from there to Sunauli on the Nepal border; it takes three hours. There are also direct Varanasi to Sunauli buses for about Rs 40 or deluxe buses for Rs 60.

Private companies operate buses to the Nepalese border and Kathmandu. They charge about Rs 200 to Kathmandu which includes spartan accommodation at the border. Alternatively, you can simply travel to the border for Rs 60 and take another bus from the border to Kathmandu for the Nepalese equivalent of about Indian Rs 30. This is not only much cheaper but you get a much better choice of bus within Nepal.

Train There are not many trains running directly between Delhi and Varanasi or between Calcutta and Varanasi, although most Delhi to Calcutta trains do pass through Moghulserai, 10 km south of Varanasi, about 20 minutes by bus. Express trains between Delhi and Varanasi take 13 to 16 hours for the 764-km trip and cost Rs 77 in 2nd class, Rs 283 in 1st. From Calcutta the 678-km trip takes about 12

hours and costs Rs 69 in 2nd class, Rs 257 in 1st. The Rajdhani Express takes only nine hours from Delhi and costs Rs 255; from Calcutta it takes eight hours at a cost of Rs 230.

The fare for the five-hour 228-km journey to Patna is Rs 31 in 2nd class, Rs 107 in 1st, and for the three-hour 137-km run to Allahabad it is Rs 20 in 2nd class, Rs 73 in 1st.

If you're travelling from Varanasi to Kashmir or Himachal Pradesh, you can avoid going through Delhi by taking the three-times-weekly overnight Himgiri Express. This originates at Howrah (Calcutta), runs through Lucknow and terminates at Jammu Tawi, so you can be well on your way to Srinagar by the evening. If you want to get to the Himachal Pradesh hill stations the Himgiri Express also stops at Chakki Bank, Pathankot's little-known alternative station, a couple of hours before Jammu Tawi. From there it's a Rs 4 rickshaw ride to the main Pathankot train and bus stations.

The 1509-km trip from Mughalserai to Bombay takes 27½ hours on the Bombay Mail and costs Rs 118 in 2nd class, Rs 468 in 1st. To Madras, the twice-weekly Ganga Kaveri Express takes 41 hours to cover the 2147 km at a cost of Rs 148 in 2nd class, Rs 609 in 1st.

Varanasi has two railway stations – Kashi and Varanasi Junction. The Varanasi Junction station used to be known as the Cantonment station.

Getting Around

Airport Transport Babatpur Airport is a lengthy 22 km out of the city. The airline bus costs Rs 20 for the trip between the airport and the airline office in the Cantonment area. Taxis are expensive at around Rs 100.

Bus Godaulia (also spelt Godowlia and Gadaulia), a useful city landmark, is the midtown bus stop, just an easy walk from the ghats. Lanka is the bus stop closest to

Benares Hindu University. Between the railway station and Godaulia a bus costs less than a rupee, but unless you can get on at the starting point Varanasi buses tend to be very crowded.

Cycle-Rickshaw & Bicycle Cycle-rickshaws are still comparatively cheap in Varanasi, and a trip between the railway station and Godaulia, near Dasaswamedh Ghat, is about Rs 4. An auto-rickshaw is about double that. You can hire a cycle-rickshaw for Rs 26 per day. There are several places to rent bicycles around Lanka; all-day rates are about Rs 5, although the Aces Restaurant in Godaulia rents bikes for Rs 12 a day.

There are also six-seaters which run on set routes (such as Godaulia to the station) and charge Rs 2.

SARNATH

Only 10 km from Varanasi, the most holy of Hindu cities, is Sarnath, one of the major Buddhist centres. Having achieved enlightenment at Bodhgaya, the Buddha came to Sarnath to preach his message of the middle way to final nirvana. Later Ashoka, the great Buddhist emperor, erected magnificent stupas and other buildings here. Sarnath was at its peak when those indefatigable Chinese travellers Fa Hian and Hiuen Tsang visited the site. In 640 AD, when the latter made his call, Sarnath had 1500 priests, a stupa nearly 100 metres high, Ashoka's mighty stone pillar and many other wonders.

Soon after, Buddhism went into decline and after the Muslim invaders destroyed and desecrated the cities buildings, Sarnath was little more than a shell. It was not until 1836 when British archaeologists started excavations that Sarnath regained some of its past glory. The city was known as the 'deer park'.

Dhamekh Stupa

Believed to date from around 500 AD, this stupa was probably rebuilt a number of times. The geometrical and floral patterns on the stupa are typical of the Gupta period, but excavations have revealed brickwork from the Mauryan period around 200 BC.

Dharmarajika Stupa

This large stupa has been comprehensively excavated by 19th-century treasure seekers. Near it is the building known as the 'main shrine' where Ashoka is said to have meditated.

Ashoka Pillar

Standing in front of the main shrine are the remains of Ashoka's Pillar. At one time this stood over 20 metres high, but today the capital has been removed and can be seen in the Sarnath museum. An edict issued by Ashoka is engraved on the remaining portion of the column. The capital is the Ashokan symbol of four back-to-back lions which has now been adopted as the state symbol of modern India. On the lower portion of the column are representations of a lion, elephant, horse and bull. The lion is supposed to represent bravery, the elephant symbolises the dream Buddha's mother had before

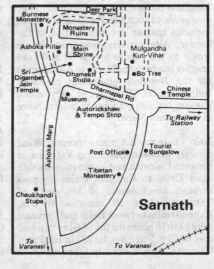

his birth, and the horse recalls that Buddha left his home on horseback in search of enlightenment.

Museum

Sarnath's excellent Archaeological Museum has the capital from the Ashokan pillar together with many other relics found on the site. These include many figures and sculptures from the various periods of Sarnath – Mauryan, Kushana, Gupta and later. Among them is the earliest Buddha image found at Sarnath, Buddha figures in various positions dating back to the 5th and 6th centuries, and many images of Hindu gods such as Saraswati, Ganesh and Vishnu from the 9th to 12th centuries. The museum is open from 10 am to 5 pm daily, except Fridays when it is closed. Entry is Rs 0.50, and there is a booklet available for Rs 2 at the counter.

Other Attractions

The modern Maha Bodhi Society temple known as the Mulgandha Kuti-Vihar has a series of frescoes by a Japanese artist in the interior. A bo tree growing here is a transplant from the tree in Anuradhapura, Sri Lanka, which in turn is said to be an offspring of the original tree under which the Buddha attained enlightenment. The brick remnants of the monastery or *vihara* can still be seen, and amongst the mango trees you can see a deer park off to one side.

Places to Stay

Sarnath has a *Tourist Bungalow* (tel 8485) with rooms at Rs 75 or dorm beds at Rs 15.

Getting There & Away

You can visit Sarnath on a tour from Varanasi or get there by bus from Varanasi station for Rs 1.50. Six-seater tempos run to and from Godaulia and cost Rs 4 per person. An auto-rickshaw from Varanasi costs about Rs 20 one way or Rs 40 return, with a reasonable waiting period at Sarnath.

Eastern Uttar Pradesh

JAUNPUR (population 100,000)

Founded by Feroz Shah Tughlaq in 1360, this town later became the capital of the independent Muslim Sharqui Kingdom. Eventually it fell to Sikandar Lodi and then the Moghuls. Prior to the arrival of the Muslims it had a great number of Hindu, Buddhist and Jain temples, shrines and monasteries. Many of these have been utilised by the Muslims to construct Jaunpur's architecturally unique mosques.

The more important mosques include the Atala Masjid, built in 1408 on the site of a Hindu temple dedicated to Atala Devi. The large Jami Masjid was built between 1438 and 1478 during the Sharqui period. There are half a dozen other interesting mosques – the Jaunpur mosques are notable for their use of Jain and Hindu building materials, for their two-storey arcades and large gateways, and for their unusual minarets. The tombs of the Sharqui sultans are north of the Jami Masjid. Other important constructions include Feroz Shah's fort built in 1360 and the stone Akbari Bridge built between 1564 and 1568.

Places to Stay Jaunpur has some cheap hotels, and at the *Marwari Dharamsala*, near the fort, you can get a private room for just a few rupees.

Getting There & Away Buses and taxis are available from Varanasi, 58 km away.

CHUNAR

The fort here overlooks the Ganges and was captured by Humayun in 1537, but was captured by Sher Shah soon after and not recovered by the Moghuls until 1575, when Akbar took it. Chunar is 37 km from Varanasi and can be reached by bus.

GORAKHPUR (population 400,000)

This is a town which travellers on their way

to Kathmandu or Pokhara from Delhi or Varanasi usually pass through. Gorakhpur is in the centre of a rich agricultural area which has nevertheless remained very backward. The famous temple of Gorakhnath is here, as is the Geeta Press which specialises in publishing Hindu religious literature. In April, noted one visitor, 'Gorakhpur is covered solidly in flies'.

There are tourist offices at the railway station and in Park Rd on the way to the city centre. If you have just come from Nepal, Indrail passes can be bought (with foreign currency) at the railway station.

Places to Stay

The *Hotel Standard* in the railway station area charges Rs 40/75, and it's OK for an overnight stay. In the same area, the spartan but clean *Hotel Raj* is much better and charges Rs 30/40 for singles/doubles; buckets of hot water are supplied on request. The *Gupta Tourist Lodge*, also close to the station, is not a bad place.

Moving up the scale, the *Hotel Upvan* (tel 8003), one km from the railway station, has rooms for Rs 90/125. Next door is the *Hotel Bobina* (tel 6563) which is more expensive at Rs 100/150 but has a bar and restaurant. This is about the best Gorakhpur has to offer.

For a place in the city centre (Golghar), the *Hotel Marina* is good value at Rs 60 up to Rs 210 and rooms have TV and hot water. A cheaper place in the same area is the *Hotel Amber* which charges Rs 40/60 for singles/doubles.

Places to Eat

The *Ganesh Restaurant* is the best place for masala dosa and sweets. The *Hotel Marina* has good vegetarian thalis for Rs 15.

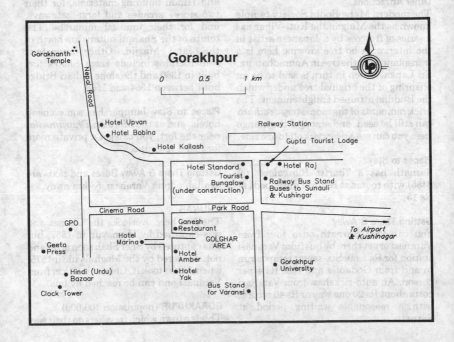

Getting There & Away

Air There are regular flights to Delhi (Rs 680), Calcutta (Rs 600) and Lucknow, and three flights a week from Varanasi (but not vice versa) for Rs 200.

Bus The best way to get to the Nepalese border is by bus, which takes three hours and costs Rs 15.

Buses to Varanasi depart from a bus station which is a Rs 2 rickshaw ride from the city centre. Varanasi is five or six hours away and the fare is Rs 27.

Train It is 778 km and 14½ hours from Delhi to Gorakhpur and costs Rs 79 in 2nd class, Rs 286 in 1st. Gorakhpur to Varanasi is 231 km, takes six hours and costs Rs 32 in 2nd class, Rs 109 in 1st. The 276-km metre-gauge journey to Lucknow takes five hours and costs Rs 36 in 2nd class, Rs 126 in 1st.

Getting Around

Airport Transport The airport is nine km from the city centre and airline buses charge a hefty Rs 25.

KUSHINAGAR

The town of Kasia, near Kushinagar and 55 km east of Gorakhpur, is supposed to be the site of Buddha's death and cremation. There are a number of Buddhist buildings of various ages, large seated and reclining Buddha figures, and Burmese, Japanese and Chinese monasteries. A local bus to Kasia from the Gorakhpur bus stand near the railway station takes 1½ hours and costs Rs 8.

Places to Stay

There's a small ITDC *Traveller's Lodge* (tel 38) in Kushinagar. The *Tourist Bungalow* has singles/doubles for Rs 75/100, and it's also possible to stay in some of the monasteries.

LUMBINI

Lumbini, the birthplace of Buddha, is also close to the 'backdoor' entrance into

Nepal for Pokhara. All those going to Lumbini, even pilgrims just crossing the border for a few hours, require a Nepalese visa. This can be obtained at the border checkpoint for US$10. It is not possible to go to Lumbini via Naugadh anymore because there is no longer an official border crossing on this route. The only practical way to visit Lumbini now is to cross the border into Nepal at Sunauli and take a bus or taxi from Bhairawa.

Northern Uttar Pradesh

The northern part of Uttar Pradesh, a rough rectangle bordered by Himachal Pradesh to the north-west and China to the north-east, is an area of hills, mountains and lakes. There are several popular hill stations, such as Naini Tal and Almora, and many trekking routes – most of them little known and even less used. Important pilgrimage centres include Hardwar and Rishikesh, where the holy Ganges leaves its Himalayan birthplace and joins the plains for its long trip to the sea. The area is known as Uttarakhand, or 'land of the north', and there is some local agitation to make it a separate state.

Toll Taxes

If you're travelling up to the Uttar Pradesh hill stations (Naini Tal, Almora, Ranikhet, Mussoorie), somebody will jump on the bus just as you approach the towns to charge you a Rs 1 or Rs 2 toll tax. In Himachal Pradesh these toll taxes are included in the bus fare.

MEERUT (population 1,000,000)

Only 67 km north-east of Delhi, this was the place where the 1857 Mutiny first broke out. There's little to remember that event today, although the cemetery near St John's Church has the grave of Sir Ochterlony, whose monument dominates the Maidan in Calcutta. The Suraj

Khund is the most interesting Hindu temple in Meerut and there's a Moghul mausoleum, the Shahpir, near the old Shahpir Gate.

Meerut is a green revolution boom town and the new-found wealth, indicated by the many well-stocked stores, has led to intercommunal tensions which sometimes turn into violence. The Nauchandi Mela is a huge month-long fair which takes place in the south-east of the city before the Hindu new year, which usually falls in April. Traditional *nautanki* dramas are a feature.

Meerut has some adequate hotels and restaurants. *Gajak*, a sweet made from crude sugar and sesame, is a local treat.

SAHARANPUR (population 500,000)
Situated 178 km north of Delhi, the large botanical gardens here, known as the Company Bagh, are over 150 years old.

DEHRA DUN (population 372,000)
Also spelt Dehra Doon, this is the gateway to places in the Garwhal Himal such as Badrinath and Joshimath. Dehra Dun is in the centre of a forest area and has a Forest Research Institute, the Indian Military Academy and is well known for its basmati rice.

The town is situated in an intermontane valley in the Siwaliks, the southernmost and lowest of the Himalayan ranges. The high mountain range just to the north of Dehra Dun contains the hill station Mussoorie, 22 km away.

Information & Orientation
The tourist office (tel 3217) is in the Hotel Drona close to the bus stands and the railway station. The clock tower is the hub of the town and most of the budget hotels are on the road from the railway station to the tower. The main market is known as Paltan Bazaar.

Things to See
Dehra Dun is of very little interest in itself, although the Forest Research

Institute is the biggest of its kind in India and has a botanical garden. The institute's library was rather chaotic reported a visitor: 'A far better source of information is a small publisher/bookshop on the road back to town; he had all the Research Institute's publications, along with a weird and wonderful collection that included all eight volumes of *The Fish in the British Museum*'. To get there take a six-seater from the clock tower to the institute. It's one km from the main Forestry building.

Dehra Dun is also the site for the 'Doon School', India's most exclusive private school (Rajiv Gandhi went there). It is also the headquarters of the Survey of India which sells maps of many Indian cities.

Popular picnic spots, with their distance from the town, include: Sahastradhara (14 km) with natural sulphur springs; Tapkeshwar Temple (six km), a Shiva temple; the 'robbers cave' just beyond Anarwala village (seven km); Laxman Sidh, another temple, on the Dehra Dun to Rishikesh road; and Tapovan (six km) is two km off the Dehra Dun to Rajpur road and has an ashram.

There is a mountain flight once a week, similar to the one in Nepal. Among the peaks flown over are Nandadevi and Kedarnath. It costs Rs 400 for the one-hour flight, the main drawback (apart from the price) being that you have to fly to Dehra Dun to be eligible to take it.

Places to Stay
Dehra Dun is not a great place for hotels, which are generally overpriced for what they offer. The new state run *Drona Hotel* is the best place for the money; singles/doubles cost Rs 70/90 and there are dorm beds for Rs 20. All rooms have a bath and there is hot water in winter. The *President Hotel* charges Rs 170 and has a good restaurant. The friendly *Relax Hotel* near the railway station is noisy and rooms cost Rs 60/100.

At the top of the scale, the *Meedo's*

Grand Hotel charges Rs 380/450 for singles/doubles. The *Madhuban Hotel* (tel 24094/7), much further out at 97 Rajpur Rd, has rooms with air-con for Rs 525/625 plus service and taxes. They've also got separate cottages with kitchens.

Places to Eat
The *Vaishno Restaurant*, opposite the Jain dharamsala near the station, has a bargain thali which includes the dessert known as kihr. There are good Indian dishes at the *Motimahal Restaurant* on Rajpur Rd, just behind the local bus stand. It is moderately expensive and is good for non-veg food. The *Sind-Hyderabad Restaurant* next door is cheaper and has good food. The *Yeti Restaurant* near the Hotel Madhuban serves excellent Chinese dishes.

Right by the clock tower, the *Bengali Sweet Shop* has a wide selection of Indian sweets. Nearby, the *Kumar Sweet Shop* has an excellent selection including their speciality *kesar ka halwa*. There are some good small restaurants on Paltan Bazaar near the Mussoorie bus stand.

Getting There & Away
Air Vayudoot have daily (twice daily on some days) flights between Dehra Dun and Delhi; the fare is Rs 415.

Bus There are two main bus stations – the one nearer the railway station is for buses to the hills, and the one nearer the clock tower is for other destinations. A deluxe bus service operates between Delhi and Dehra Dun for between Rs 42 and Rs 65 (deluxe). The trip takes six hours.

Dehra Dun to Hardwar is 54 km and takes about 1½ hours. It's a similar distance and time from Rishikesh at a fare of Rs 9.50. Continuing on to Simla is a

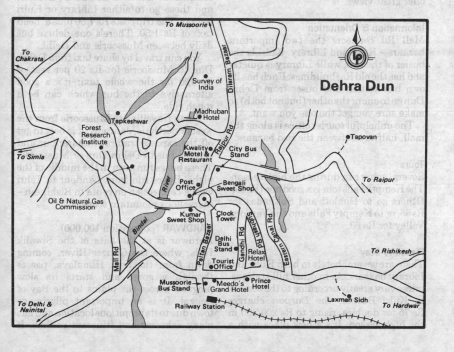

long, weary all-day trip costing Rs 70 on a deluxe bus.

Train Dehra Dun is also connected with major north Indian cities by rail. The Delhi/Hardwar/Dehra Dun 320-km train trip costs Rs 41 in 2nd class, Rs 141 in 1st. At 11 hours it is almost twice as long as the bus trip. The overnight service departs Delhi at 10.30 pm and arrives in Dehra Dun at 8.30 am.

MUSSOORIE (population 24,000)
At an altitude of 2000 metres and 22 km beyond Dehra Dun, Mussoorie is a popular hill resort in the hot weather. It's on a horseshoe-shaped hill where much fruit is grown. There is a ropeway (Rs 6, enjoyable in the early morning) up to Gun Hill and Municipal Gardens to the west of the town.

Many of the walks around Mussoorie offer great views.

Information & Orientation
Mall Rd connects the two important bazaars – Kulri and Library. Kulri is the busier of the two, while Library is quieter and has the old Raj buildings. Each has its own bus station and buses from Dehra Dun go to one or the other (but not both) so make sure you get the one you want.

The unhelpful tourist office is along the mall, halfway between the two bazaars.

Tours
Several tours run during the high season. The Kempty Falls tour is a good one (Rs 35). Others go to Dhaloti and Sukhadas for Rs 35, or to Kempty Falls and the Yamuna Valley for Rs 60.

Places to Stay
There are several hotels in both Kulri and Library bazaars. As in other hill stations, prices vary greatly according to the season. In Kulri Bazaar, the *Darpan* charges Rs 75 for doubles, rising to Rs 200/300 in the high season. It's a new place with a

pleasant terrace. In winter you have to pay extra for hot water and blankets.

The *Hotel Apsara* is more basic and charges Rs 75 in the off season. Other hotels in Kulri include the *Sipra* and the *Samrat*. In Library Bazaar, the *Roselyn* and the *Halmands Grand* hotels are OK.

The *Tourist Bungalow* on Mall Rd charges Rs 103 for doubles.

Places to Eat
The *Greens Vegetarian Restaurant* on The Mall has very good vegetarian food at moderately expensive prices. For non-veg food, popular places include the *Tavern* and *Neelam*, both in the Kulri area.

Le Suisse is a very Americanised pastry shop which offers delicious pizzas, toasted sandwiches and various cakes.

Getting There & Away
There are hourly buses between the railhead at Dehra Dun and Mussoorie, and these go to either Library or Kulri bazaar. The trip costs Rs 7.50 plus a 'head tax' of Rs 1.50. There's one deluxe bus daily between Mussoorie and Delhi.

You can travel by share taxi from Dehra Dun to Mussoorie for Rs 20 per seat or Rs 120 for the whole taxi; it's a good alternative to the bus which can be a rough ride.

When travelling to Mussoorie from the west or north (ie, Jammu), it is best to get off the express train at Saharanpur and catch a bus to Dehra Dun or Mussoorie. These buses run even in the middle of the night. Buses run from Landour to Tehri with a connection en route to Rishikesh – marvellous mountain scenery.

HARDWAR (population 100,000)
Hardwar is at the base of the Siwalik Hills, where the Ganges River, coming down from the high Himalaya, passes through a gorge and starts its slow progress across the plains to the Bay of Bengal. It is an important pilgrimage town due to its propitious location and has many ashrams and itinerant sadhus. If

Uttar Pradesh Top: Varanasi (HF)
            Left: Taj Mahal, Agra (TW)
            Right: Children in Varanasi (TW)

Bihar Top: Buddhist monk under the bo tree, Bodhgaya (TW)
Bottom: Spiral staircase up the Golgumbaz, Patna (TW)

you wish to study Hinduism you may find Rishikesh, 24 km further north, a more pleasant place. Despite its religious sanctity Hardwar is really just another noisy north Indian city.

Every 12 years the Kumbh Mela comes to Hardwar and attracts millions of pilgrims. It takes place every three years, consecutively at Allahabad, Nasik, Ujjain and then here. It's next due in 1998. At the 1986 Kumbh Mela, despite extensive safety precautions, 50 people were killed in one stampede to the river, and dozens were drowned when they lost their footing in the swift-flowing river.

Information & Orientation

The main street of Hardwar is narrow and long, although the suburban area is spread out. There is a delightful narrow street of small shops leading south from Har Ki Pairi Ghat. The bus stand and railway station are side by side; the tourist office (tel 19) is a little north of them. A copy of *The Gateway to the Gods, Hardwar, Rishikesh & Kankhal* provides Rs 5 of guaranteed amusement.

Things to See

Although Hardwar is a very old town mentioned by the Chinese scholar-traveller Hiuen Tsang, its many temples are comparatively recent and of little architectural interest. They do have many idols and illustrated scenes from the Hindu epics. Har ki Pairi is the most important bathing ghat, as it is supposed to be at the precise spot where the Ganges leaves the mountains and enters the plains. Consequently the river's power to wash away sins at this spot is superlative. There is a footprint of Vishnu in a stone at this ghat. It is also interesting to watch the Arati, or river worship, ceremony each evening at sunset. If you are non-Hindu, you can only watch from the bridge or the other side of the river.

The Daksha Mahadev Temple, four km downstream, is Hardwar's most important temple. According to legend, Daksha was the father of Sati, Shiva's first wife. Daksha performed a sacrifice here but neglected to invite Shiva, and Sati was so angry at this disrespect to her husband that she managed to spontaneously self-immolate! There are some fine but decaying old townhouses on the way to the temple – look for the coloured paintings on the outside.

Other temples and buildings of lesser interest include the Sapt Rishi Ashram, where the Ganges divides into several

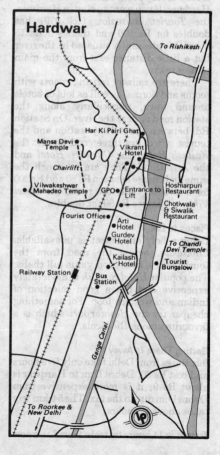

Hardwar

To Rishikesh

Har Ki Pairi Ghat

Mansa Devi Temple

Vikrant Hotel

Chairlift

Hoshiarpuri Restaurant

Vilwakeshwar Mahadeo Temple

GPO

Entrance to Lift

Chotiwala & Siwalik Restaurant

Tourist Office

Arti Hotel

Gurdev Hotel

To Chandi Devi Temple

Kailash Hotel

Railway Station

Bus Station

Tourist Bungalow

Ganga Canal

To Roorkee & New Delhi

smaller streams; and the Parmath Ashram, six km towards Rishikesh, with fine images of the goddess Durga. The Mansa Devi Temple overlooks the tourist office and can be reached by a chairlift (Rs 6), while Beauty Point, in the same direction, offers fine views over the town. Chandi Devi and a number of other temples are reached by a three-km walk to the east.

Places to Stay

Hardwar and Rishikesh are so close that it is easy to stay in the latter and day trip to Hardwar. If you want to stay in Hardwar, the *Tourist Bungalow* (tel 379) has doubles for Rs 100 and there's a Rs 15 dorm. It's pleasantly situated by the river but a little distance east from the main part of town.

There are railway *retiring rooms* with rooms and dorms, as well as lots of hotels around town, particularly along the station road or near the river. On Station Rd, between the railway station and the tourist office, are three good hotels: the *Kailash Hotel*, the *Gurudev Hotel* and the *Arti Hotel*. They are all much the same and charge between Rs 80 and Rs 200 for a double. Near the river, the *Hotel Vikrant* charges Rs 80 for doubles.

Places to Eat

Being a holy city, meat is unavailable. *Chotiwala*, across the road from the tourist office, does good-value full thalis. The popular *Hotel Siwalik* is moderately expensive and has a good selection of Indian and western food. For something cheaper try the *Hoshiarpuri* which is a favourite among the locals.

Getting There & Away

Bus Buses from Delhi take only five hours and cost Rs 30. Dehra Dun to Hardwar is about Rs 9; it is more expensive from Dehra Dun due to the tax. The 54-km trip takes about 1½ hours.

Train It is 14 hours by train from Lucknow to Hardwar or seven hours from Delhi. There's an overnight train service from Delhi, leaving at 10.30 pm, arriving at Hardwar at 6.30 am and continuing on to Dehra Dun. It's an excellent, hassle-free and comfortable train service. Fare for the 268-km trip is Rs 34 in 2nd class, Rs 123 in 1st.

RISHIKESH (population 26,000)

Surrounded by hills on three sides, Rishikesh is a quieter and more easygoing place than Hardwar, although at 356 metres it is only 63 metres higher than Hardwar. Like Hardwar, there are many ashrams and sadhus and this is an excellent place to study Hinduism.

Back in the '60s Rishikesh gained instant – and fleeting – fame as the place where the Beatles came to be with their guru, the Maharishi Mahesh Yogi. Rishikesh is also the starting point for treks to Himalayan pilgrimage centres like Badrinath, Kedarnath and Gangotri.

Information

The tourist office (tel 209) is on Railway Station Rd. The bus stand is close by on Agarwal Rd.

Things to See

The most interesting ghats and temples in Rishikesh are across the river on the left (east) bank but are connected by a free launch system. The Lakshman Jhula suspension bridge is further upstream. Interesting temples include the Parmarth Temple with many images from Hindu mythology. The Lakshman Temple is by the bridge, three km from the town centre. Neel Khanth Mahadev is 12 km further on; there are fine views on the way up to the temple at 1700 metres.

Meditation

Studying Hinduism has, naturally, become somewhat commercialised at Rishikesh. The Divine Life Society, founded by Swami Shivanand, is an authentic place, and it's on the tourist

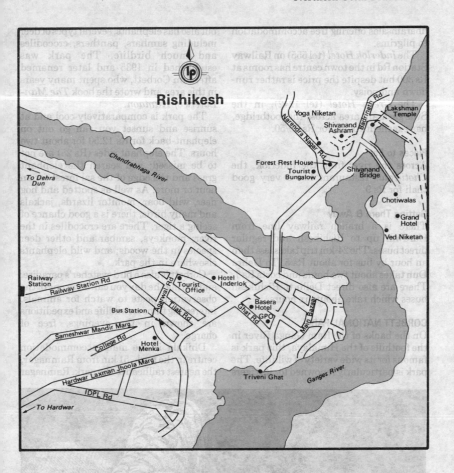

Rishikesh

To Dehra Dun

Chandrabhaga River

Railway Station

Railway Station Rd

Tourist Office

Hotel Inderlok

Agarwal Rd

Tilak Rd

Bus Station

Sameshwar Mandir Marg

College Rd

Hotel Menka

Hardwar Laxman Jhoola Marg

IDPL Rd

To Hardwar

Basera Hotel

GPO

Main Bazaar

Ghat Rd

Triveni Ghat

Ganges River

Yoga Niketan

Shivanand Ashram

Narendra Nagar Rd

Badrinath Rd

Lakshman Temple

Forest Rest House

Tourist Bungalow

Shivanand Bridge

Chotiwalas

Grand Hotel

Ved Niketan

bungalow side of the river. You can stay there for short-term study or for longer three-month courses, although to do this you need to write one month in advance. Or simply drop by for the evening lecture at 'Satsanga'. At Ved Niketan, an Indian sadhu gives lectures in English to those interested, and there are rooms for Rs 20 although you must stay for a minimum of 15 days. And, of course, there's the Maharishi Mahesh Yogi's Transcendental Meditation Centre.

Places to Stay

The popular and pleasantly situated *Tourist Bungalow* (tel 372) is about three km from the bus and railway stations and has rooms at Rs 60 or deluxe rooms at Rs 80. It has a dining hall and a pleasant garden to relax in, and is usually crowded in summer.

Other hotels include the *Hotel Menka* (tel 285), right across from the bus stand, and the *Janta Tourist Lodge* on Dehra Dun Rd. There are various other hotels around town and, as at Hardwar, many dharamsalas offering free accommodation to pilgrims.

The *Inderlok Hotel* (tel 555) on Railway Station Rd in the town centre has rooms at Rs 300 but despite the price is rather run-down and noisy.

The *Green Hotel* (tel 1242), in the Swargashram area across the footbridge, has excellent rooms for Rs 30/50.

Places to Eat
Across the river from the Inderlok, the *Chotiwalas* restaurant has a very good thali for Rs 9.

Getting There & Away
There is a branch railway line from Hardwar up to Rishikesh and regular direct buses. The 24-km trip takes less than an hour by bus for about Rs 5. To Dehra Dun takes about two hours and costs Rs 7. There are also direct Delhi to Rishikesh buses which take about six hours.

CORBETT NATIONAL PARK
On the banks of the Ram Ganga River in the foothills of the Himalaya, this park is famous for its wide variety of wildlife. The park is particularly renowned for its tigers but also has elephants, several types of deer including sambars, panthers, crocodiles and much birdlife. The park was established in 1935 and later renamed after Jim Corbett, who spent many years in this area and wrote the book *The Man-Eaters of Kumaon*.

The park is comparatively cool and at sunrise and sunset you can go out on elephant-back for Rs 12.50 for about two hours. The elephant rides (Rs 25) are not to be missed; you search the elephant grass and the edge of the sal forest for an hour or more. As well as spotted and hog deer, wild boar, monitor lizards, jackals and many birds, there is a good chance of seeing a tiger. There are crocodiles in the river; monkeys, sambar and other deer species in the woods; and wild elephants elsewhere in the park.

Corbett is also a bird-watcher's paradise, and during the day you can sit in one of the observation posts to watch for animals. Interesting films on wildlife and expeditions are shown in the evenings, free of charge.

Dhikala is the main accommodation centre in the park, 51 km from Ramnagar, the nearest railhead to the park. Ramnagar

is connected by train with Moradabad and by bus with Delhi and Lucknow. Most tours into the park are operated from Dhikala, although there are also three-day package tours operated from New Delhi. Entry to the park costs Rs 35 (Rs 2 for students) for three days, then Rs 12 per day. Permits for an overnight stay have to be obtained from the Director of Project Tiger at Ramnagar. The park is open from December to May but avoid the crowded weekends. As it's not possible to get around the park on foot ('walking can be suicidal' according to one sign), you must come by car, or hitch a ride with other guests.

Places to Stay
At Dhikala there are cabins, *Forest Rest Houses* at Rs 100 per day, *Tourist Huts* (Rs 40), *Swiss Cottage Tents* (Rs 10), *Log Huts* (Rs 6 per person) and camping facilities (Rs 3 per person). One large restaurant caters for all the accommodation facilities. The meals are set price (Rs 10) but the food is good and it's 'all you can eat'. There are also forest rest houses at Sarapduli, Bijrani, Gairal, Kanda and Sultan. The park is closed at sunset, so make sure you arrive there before then.

Ramnagar, which is a crossroad between the plains and the hills, has a few overpriced hotels and many restaurants with beds in the back rooms – grotty but cheap. The dumpy *Benwari* has doubles for Rs 60. A better bet is the *Tourist Bungalow*, next to the Project Tiger office, which has doubles for Rs 50 and dormitory beds for a hefty Rs 30. This place is good but heavily booked. The new *Govind Restaurant & Hotel* has good doubles for Rs 40 with common bath, and a good clean restaurant.

Getting There & Away
Ramnagar is the nearest railhead to the park, and there is a daily bus from Naini Tal via Ramnagar to Dhikala. The bus leaves Ramnagar at 3.30 pm and the return trip departs from Dhikala at 9 am. The trip should take about five hours from

Ramnagar. There are also buses just from Ramnagar to Dhikala or to the Dhangadri park entrance, where you can take an afternoon bus into the park HQ at Dhikala or try and hitch a lift.

ALMORA (population 26,000)
This picturesque hill station was taken from Nepal following the 1815 Gurkha War. It's at an altitude of 1650 metres and many travellers live in cottages in the hills around the town. There is a good walk from Almora up to the Kasar Devi Temple, which has excellent views. Some of the walks out of town take you to isolated woods full of monkeys, if you walk far enough.

Places to Stay
There are several hotels including the popular *Tourist Cottage* (tel 12) with rooms from Rs 15 to Rs 25. The *Neelkanth Hotel* (tel 32) has rooms from Rs 20 to Rs 40. At the state government *Tourist Bungalow* (tel 250) doubles are Rs 50, deluxe doubles Rs 75, and there's a Rs 20 dorm.

The *Kailash Hotel* is close to the Tourist Cottage but, according to one traveller, 'Mr Shah is so busy revealing to you his deep insights in human life that he forgets all about the bedbugs and other creatures in his freaky little place'.

Getting There & Away
The nearest railhead to Almora and all the eastern Garwhal hill stations is Kathgodam, where buses connect with arriving trains.

KAUSANI
Situated 53 km north of Almora, this small village is on a ridge looking out to 300 km of mountains!

Places to Stay
The *Tourist Bungalow* (tel 26) has rooms at Rs 50. It is a two-km walk from town but is well worth it – good views, balconies, hot water and clean sheets. The *Pine View Hotel* has rooms from Rs 10 to Rs 25. There are excellent views from the similarly priced *Hotel Prashant*, about 10 minutes

up the road from the bus stand. Or there's the *Gandhi Ashram* and various other private hotels.

Getting There & Away

Buses to Ramnagar via Ranikhet pass Kausani. Kathgodam is the nearest railhead.

NAINI TAL (population 32,000)

In this lake-dotted area of the Kumaon Hills the pretty hill town of Naini Tal was once the summer capital of Uttar Pradesh. There are many interesting walks and lakes around the town – which itself is divided into two parts, upper and lower lake (tal).

Climb up to China Peak in the early morning for fine views over Naini Tal and the snow-clad Himalaya off in the distance. In the middle of the summer season Naini Tal is packed full of local tourists and spoilt children and the prices go up.

The ropeway is open from 10.30 am to 4.45 pm and costs Rs 16. Boats can be rented from the St Joseph's College Boat House on the lake shore.

Tours

There are local tours arranged by the Kumaon Division Development Corporation. These includes visits to Naukuchia Lake (Rs 20), Ranikhet (Rs 50) and several other places.

Places to Stay

The *Youth Hostel* has dorm beds for Rs 6, but it's at the west end of the town, about three km from the bus stand. It's a 40-minute uphill walk to a lovely, peaceful location; they also have double rooms.

The *Hotel Coronation* (tel 2649), opposite the Naini Tal Club in the old colonial part of town, is very basic with rooms from Rs 25. On the other side of town, which is less 'rich tourist', *Saidar Bhawan* and the *Punjab Hotel* (tel 2545) are two fairly basic hotels which overlook the lake; rooms are Rs 20 to Rs 40. The

Prashant is a pleasant hotel with good food in its restaurant and doubles at Rs 50.

The *Evelyn Hotel* (tel 2457) has spacious doubles with bath, hot water and a separate sitting room for Rs 125 even at the height of the season. There are terrific views from the top-floor rooms, a good restaurant and friendly management.

The *Tourist Bungalow* has dorm beds for Rs 20, and deluxe doubles for Rs 150, more in season.

There are a many other hotels, including expensive places on The Mall like the *Grand Hotel* (tel 2406) with doubles at Rs 170, or the *Royal Hotel* (tel 2007) with doubles at Rs 300, and the similarly priced *Swiss Hotel* (tel 2603).

Places to Eat

The *Capri Restaurant*, across from the Naini Tal Boat Club House, has good food for around Rs 30 per meal. *Sakley's Restaurant*, on The Mall, is another good place, and it has great pastries as well.

The *Sharma Vaishnow Restaurant* in the Malli Tal Bazaar offers all-you-can-eat vegetarian meals for around Rs 5.

The *Shivalik Restaurant* has, according to one impressed traveller, 'the best food in India'. The *Merino Restaurant* on The Mall has also been well received.

Getting There & Away

The nearest airport is at Pantanagar, 71 km away. There are Vayudoot flights four times a week to Delhi for Rs 340.

Kathgodam is the nearest railway station, 35 km to the south. Almora is 68 km away by road, Ranikhet 59 km and there are bus services to these and other northern Uttar Pradesh towns.

RANIKHET

North of Naini Tal and only a short distance west of Almora, this hill station offers excellent views of the snow-capped Himalaya. Only eight km away, Chaubattia is famous for its fruits. There's a tourist office by the bus stand in Ranikhet.

Places to Stay

The *Moon Hotel & Restaurant* (tel 58) has rooms at Rs 50/75. There are many other hotels both cheaper and more expensive, including the *Tourist Bungalow* (tel 97) with rooms at Rs 75 and dorm beds at Rs 20.

Getting There & Away

As with the other northern hill stations, Kathgodam is the nearest railhead.

OTHER PLACES IN THE NORTH

Bareilly (population 430,000)

Former capital of the region known as Rohilkand, Bareilly came under British control when the Rohillas, an Afghan tribe, became too involved with the Marathas and the Nawab of Oudh.

Rampur (population 215,000)

In this former Rohilla state capital, the State Library has an important collection of old manuscripts and is housed in a fine building in the old fort. The library also contains a good collection of old miniatures, some of great importance, but these are normally only on view for scholars. There is a large Jami Masjid nearby and interesting bazaars around the walls of the palace.

TREKKING IN THE GARWHAL HIMAL

Although the Garwhal Himal is little known as a trekking region, it boasts a number of famous peaks, including Trisul and India's highest mountain, Nanda Devi – or at least it was the highest until Sikkim (and thus Kanchenjunga) was absorbed into India. There are also many important pilgrimage sites, such as Badrinath and Kedarnath or Gaumukh, the actual source of the Ganges. The trekking routes pass through rich, green forests and cross beautiful meadows carpeted with flowers in summer. Glistening glaciers complement the soaring Himalayan peaks and there are many excellent state government tourist bungalows along the routes to simplify the question of shelter.

The best times to trek in the Garwhal Himal are May-June and September-October. Some places, like the Valley of Flowers and the high-altitude *bugyals* (meadows), are at their best during the July-August rainy period. The Mountaineering Division at the Tourist Bungalow in Rishikesh can provide more information on trekking in the Garwhal Himal; or check the Lonely Planet guide *Trekking in the Indian Himalaya*. Although high-altitude trekking is difficult in the winter due to snow, the hill country itself is still very pleasant.

Actually the term Garwhal Himal is something of a misnomer. There is only Garwhal (the Himal is an incorrect addition). Garwhal and Kumaon are neighbouring cultural provinces known under the combined name of Uttarakhand.

Kedarnath

Like Badrinath, this is an important Hindu pilgrimage centre. The temple of Lord Kedar (Shiva) is surrounded by snow-capped peaks, but although the shrine is said to date back to the 8th century, very little is known about it.

To get to Kedarnath you can either make the short, direct trek from Sonprayag, 205 km from Rishikesh, or you can follow the longer and more arduous yatra route from Gangotri. Along the way you pass through beautiful scenery and see many colourful mountain villages. The trek starts from Mala, 20 km beyond Uttarkashi towards Lanka and Gangotri.

Day 1	Mala to Belak Khal	15 km
Day 2	Belak Khal to Budakedar	14 km
Day 3	Budakedar to Ghuttu	16 km
Day 4	Ghuttu to Panwali Khanta	12 km
Day 5	Panwali Khanta to Maggu	8 km
Day 6	Maggu to Sonprayag	9 km
Day 7	Sonprayag to Kedarnath	20 km*
Day 8	Kedarnath to Sonprayag	20 km*

*the first six km of Sonprayag to Kedarnath can be made by taxi.

Gangotri & Gaumukh

This trek to the source of the holy Ganges can be made from either Mussoorie or Rishikesh. Lanka, reached via Uttarkashi/Bukhi/Dabrani, is the end of the vehicle road. It's 212 km from Mussoorie to Lanka, 247 km from Rishikesh. The tiny village of Gangotri stands at 3140 metres. The temple of the goddess Ganga is on the right bank of the Bhagirathi River, which eventually becomes the holy Ganges. Gaumukh, the actual source of the river, is at the base of the Bhagirathi peaks.

At 4225 metres, the Gangotri Glacier is nearly 24 km long and two to four km wide. The glacier ends at Gaumukh, where the Bhagirathi River finally appears. The glacier has gradually retreated over the centuries, but during the Vedic era it is supposed to have reached down to Gangotri. Beyond Gaumukh places like Nandanvan and Tapovan are great pilgrimage centres where sadhus often retreat to meditate in remote caves.

Day 1	Lanka to Gangotri	11 km
Day 2	Gangotri to Chirbasa	12 km
Day 3	Chirbasa to Gaumukh	7 km
Day 4	Gaumukh to Chirbasa	7 km
Day 5	Chirbasa to Gangotri	12 km
Day 6	Gangotri to Lanka	11 km

Nanda Devi Sanctuary

Some of the most outstanding peaks in the central Himalaya are clustered between the glaciers of Gangotri and Milan. Nanda Devi with its camel-humped summit is the most important peak at 7818 metres. The Nanda Devi Sanctuary is surrounded by almost 70 white peaks which form a sort of natural fortress. The sanctuary has a perimeter of nearly 120 km and an area of 640 square km. It's dotted with meadows and waterfalls and is the base camp and starting point for mountaineering assaults on Nanda Devi.

The seven-day trek from Lata, the roadhead 15 km from Joshimath, to Tilchaunni is at times difficult and tedious but the scenic grandeur you walk through will often compensate for weary bodies and frayed nerves. The first six km from Lata to Lata Kharak is a tiring uphill struggle of 1524 metres, but one is well rewarded by glorious views of Ronti, Nanda Ghunti and Bethartoli across the Rishi Ganga.

The broad open grassy ridge of Lata Kharak is covered with flowers in the summer but is always windy and cold. From here there are fine views of the northern face of Bethartoli Himal and the Trisul massif to the south. Another long uphill trek crosses the 4253-metre Dharansi Pass taking you to Dharansi. On approaching the pass you get your first glimpse of Dunagiri (7068 metres), and immediately after crossing it Nanda Devi can be seen.

From Dharansi the trail winds its way across the Malatuni Pass (4238 metres), where the western face of Hanuman (6076 metres) can be seen; it then descends almost 750 metres through grass and snow slopes and dense forest to a stream. After crossing the stream you finally arrive at the hospitable meadows of Dibrugheta, where a camp can be made by the river. In summer the grass is carpeted with flowers. From here to Deodi the track rises steeply at first, then makes a long traverse across several ridges before you cross a bridge over the Rishi Ganga and arrive at Deodi. From Deodi it is an eight-km trek through juniper and rhododendron forests to Ramani.

Nanda Devi comes ever closer as you approach Tilchaunni 'slate quarry'. It's a delightful birch clearing, the last on the Rishi gorge, but it means climbing *down* from the Bhujgara trail. Hence all porters prefer to climb up to Patalkhan, about a km above, where there is a cave and water. Most people would prefer to camp at Dibrugheta, four km below Dharansi, where wood is available.

There are three other routes in the sanctuary: Dunagiri and Changabang base (the ultimate mountain); Trisul base (with a new route into the inner south

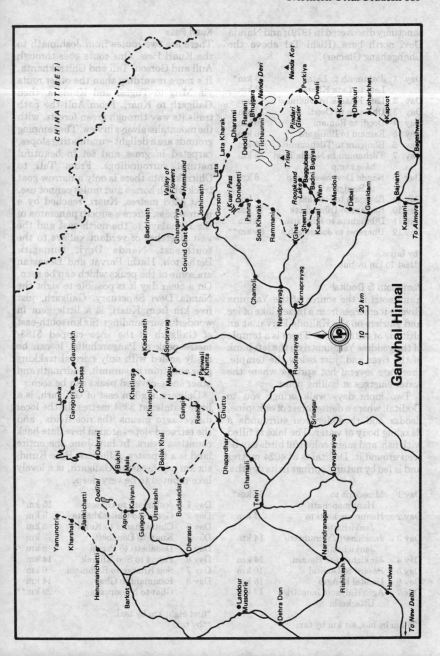

Garwhal Himal

sanctuary discovered in 1979); and Nanda Devi north base (Rishi Tal above the Changabang Glacier).

Day 1	Joshimath to Lata	25 km*
	Lata to Lata Kharak	6 km
Day 2	Lata Kharak to Dharansi	10 km
Day 3	Dharansi to Deodi	13 km
Day 4	Deodi to Ramani	8 km
Day 5	Ramani to Bhujgara	6 km
Day 6	Bhujgara to Tilchaunni	8 km
Day 7	Tilchaunni to Nanda Devi base camp	5 km
Day 8	Nanda Devi base camp to Bhujgara	6 km
Day 9	Bhujgara to Ramani	6 km
Day 10	Ramani to Dibrugheta	17 km
Day 11	Dibrugheta to Dharansi	4 km
Day 12	Dharansi to Joshimath	31 km**

*by bus
**last 15 km by bus

Yamunotri & Dodital

Yamunotri is the source of the Yamuna River – it emerges from a frozen lake of ice and glaciers on the Kalinda Parvat at an altitude of 4421 metres. There is a temple of the goddess Yamunotri on the left bank of the river and, just below the temple, there are several hot springs where the water emerges at boiling point.

Two more days walk brings you to Dodital, where a dense forest of oak, pine, deodar and rhododendron surrounds a dazzling body of water. The lake is filled with fish, and many colourful birds can be seen around it. Dodital is at 4024 metres and is fed by natural springs in its depths.

Day 1	Mussoorie to Hanumanchatti	81 km*
Day 2	Hanumanchatti to Jankichatti	7 km
Day 3	Jankichatti/Yamunotri/ Jankichatti	14 km
Day 4	Jankichatti to Basard	14 km
Day 5	Basard to Dodital	16 km
Day 6	Dodital to Agro	15 km
Day 7	Agro/Kalyani/Gangotri/ Uttarkashi	17 km

*75 km by bus, six km by taxi

Kuari Pass

There are two routes from Joshimath to the Kuari Pass. One route goes through Auli and Gorson, Tali and Chitrakhanta. It's more rewarding than the other route via Mrig to Tugasi and Khulara, then Gailgarh to Kuari. From Auli the path trails its way through green forests, with the mountains always in view. The camping grounds are a delight – undulating slopes, carpeted in grass and set in beautiful natural surroundings. From Tali to Chitrakhanta there is only a narrow goat track which horses and mules cannot use.

At 4268 metres, Kuari, reached by a narrow pass, offers a superb panorama of the Himalaya to the north-east and the vast stretches of verdant valleys to the south-east. Nanda Devi, Dunagiri, Bethartoli, Hathi Parvat and Devastan are some of the peaks which can be seen. On a clear day it is possible to sight the Nanda Devi Sanctuary. Gailgarh, just five km from Kuari, is a little gem in wonderful surroundings. Six km south-east of Gailgarh is the snow-capped 5183-metre peak of Pangarchulia. It can be easily scaled with only normal trekking gear and, from its summit, Badrinath and other snow-covered peaks can be seen.

Delisera, six km east of Gailgarh, is a little hamlet at 3354 metres. In the local dialect *sera* means 'the rice fields', and the terraced slopes around here date back countless years. In late June the entire land is a tapestry of flowers. Bore Kund, six km north-east of Gailgarh, is a lovely lake reputed to be very deep.

Day 1	Joshimath to Gorson	15 km*
Day 2	Gorson to Chitrakhanta	9 km
Day 3	Chitrakhanta to Kuari	8 km
Day 4	Kuari to Donabetti	7 km
Day 5	Donabetti to Panna	8 km
Day 6	Panna to Son Kharak	14 km
Day 7	Son Kharak to Rammani	6 km
Day 8	Rammani to Ghat	14 km
	Ghat to Nandprayag	29 km**

*first eight km by taxi
**by taxi

Khatling Glacier

The first four days of this trek follow the yatra route to Kedarnath before the trail branches off north-east to the glacier. It then retraces the route to Ghuttu and continues south-west to Ghamsali, where buses run to Tehri and Rishikesh. The Khatling Glacier is a lateral glacier from the centre of which the Bhilangana River emerges. The rich pasturelands here make ideal camping sites – the summer rains make the flat land on the glacial moraines into excellent pastures. The glaciers are associated with the giant hanging glaciers of Ratangian, Jogin and Phating. Around Katling Glacier are the snow-capped peaks of the Jogin ground (6466 metres), spectacular Sphetic Prishtwan (6905 metres), Kirti Stambh (6402 metres) and Barte Kanta (6579 metres).

The yatra route is tiring with its constant ascents and descents, but colourful. There are many rippling streams to be crossed by improvised log bridges. Gangi, the last village before the glacier, is still very much cut off from the outside world. The people here are so isolated that they have been forced to frequently intermarry within their own community and as a result many are sterile.

Day 1-3	as Kedarnath Trek	
Day 4	Ghuttu to Reeh	10 km
Day 5	Reeh to Gangi	10 km
Day 6	Gangi to Khansoli	15 km
Day 7	Khansoli to Khatling	11 km
Day 8	Khatling to Naumuthi	9 km
Day 9	Naumuthi to Kalyani	12 km
Day 10	Kalyani to Reeh	15 km
Day 11	Reeh to Dhapardhar	15 km
Day 12	Dhapardhar to Ghamsali	25 km
	Gamsali to Tehri	31 km*
Day 13	Tehri to Rishikesh	72 km*

*by bus

The Khatling Glacier trek can also be made from the Kedarnath side. In that case the first three days of the trek are like Days 6, 5 and 4 of the Kedarnath Trek. On Day 3 you reach Ghuttu and then the route is the same as from the Gangotri side.

Valley of Flowers & Hemkund

The beautiful 'Valley of Flowers' and the holy Hemkund lake can be reached in one short trek from Govind Ghat. In addition, you can visit the pilgrimage centre of Badrinath, now accessible by road, on the same trip. From Rishikesh it is 252 km by bus to Joshimath and a further 44 km to Badrinath. You then have to backtrack 30 km to Govind Ghat for the start of the trek. From June to September the trail up to Hemkund Sahib is crowded with Sikh pilgrims.

Badrinath Surrounded by snow-capped peaks, Badrinath has been a Hindu pilgrimage centre since time immemorial. There are many temples, ashrams and dharamsalas here. The most important temple, on the left bank of the Alakananda, shows clear Buddhist influence in its architecture, indicating that in an earlier period this must also have been a Buddhist centre.

The mountaineer Frank Smythe is believed to be the discoverer of the Valley of Flowers. Between mid-June and mid-September the valley is an enchanting sight with a bewildering variety of flowers fluttering in the gentle breezes. As a backdrop, snow-clad mountains stand in bold relief against the skyline. The valley is nearly 10 km long and two km wide, and is divided by the Pushpawati stream, into which several tiny streams and waterfalls merge. The huge Ghoradhungi mountain blocks one end of the valley.

From the valley you can backtrack to Ghangariya, then follow the Laxma Ganga to the lake of Hemkund. In the Sikh holy book, the *Garanth Sahib*, the Sikh Guru Govind Singh recounts that in a previous life he had meditated on the shores of a lake surrounded by seven snow-capped mountains. Hemkund Sahib, Sikh pilgrims have decided, is that holy lake. From Govind Ghat it is a gentle incline to the Valley of Flowers, but the trek from the pretty hamlet of Ghangariya to Hemkund is rather steep.

Day 1	Govind Ghat to Ghangariya	14 km
Day 2	Ghangariya to Valley of Flowers	6 km
Day 3	Valley of Flowers to Ghangariya	
	Hemkund to Ghangariya	16 km

Roopkund Lake

At an altitude of 4778 metres, below the 7122-metre-high Trisul massif, Roopkund Lake is sometimes referred to as the 'mystery lake' because of skeletons of humans and horses found here. Every 12 years thousands of devout pilgrims make an arduous trek when following the Raj Jay Yatra from Nauti village, near Karnaprayag. The pilgrims are said to be led by a mysterious four-horned ram which takes them from there through Roopkund to the Shrine of Nanda Devi, where it disappears. A golden idol of the goddess Nanda Devi is carried by the pilgrims in a silver palanquin.

The trek starts at Gwaldam, accessible by bus from Rishikesh, where there's a *Tourist Rest House*. It passes through delightful alpine pastures and snow fields and offers magnificent views of Trisul and Nanda Ghunti peaks in the Garwhal Himal.

Day 1	Rishikesh to Gwaldam	240 km*
Day 2	Gwaldam to Debal	10 km
Day 3	Debal to Mandoli	15 km
Day 4	Mandoli to Wan	14 km
Day 5	Wan to Badni Bugyal	8 km
Day 6	Badni Bugyal to Baggubasa	8 km
Day 7	Baggubasa/Roopkund/ Baggubasa	8 km
Day 8	Baggubasa to Wan	16 km
Day 9	Wan to Kannual	9 km
Day 10	Kannual to Sheetal	9 km
Day 11	Sheetal to Ghat	14 km
	Ghat to Nandprayag	30 km**
Day 12	Nandprayag to Rishikesh	192 km*

*by bus
**by taxi

Pindari Glacier

The magnificent Pindari Glacier is the most easily accessible in the region. It owes its existence to the snow sliding down from Nanda Kot and other lofty peaks. The glacier, three km long and nearly half a km wide, is at an altitude of 3353 metres. Close to it is an undulating meadow, and to the east a moraine projects into the glacier.

The trek offers views of the soaring peaks all the way and passes through pine forests, glades of ferns and wildflowers and tumbling waterfalls. From mid-May to mid-June there are many wildflowers, while from mid-September to mid-October the air is exceptionally clear and it has not yet got too cold.

From Rishikesh buses now go to Song, only a km or so before Loharkhet. You can stay in Bharari, between Kapkot and Loharkhet, and catch the one daily bus (around 2 pm) for the hair-raising ride to Song. Or, if you can manage to get a jeep you can leave Bharari earlier in the day. It's also possible to stay in the excellent *Tourist Bungalow* in Bageshwar and catch one of the several daily buses to Song.

The first couple of days from Song through Loharkhet and up to the Dhakuri Pass is a long, hard uphill slog. A km or two over the pass is the *Dhakuri Dak Bungalow*. Nevertheless this is a fine walk with wonderful scenery. There is an excellent view of the glacier from Purkiya, where some trekkers stop. On the return trek you can travel by road from Bajnath to Almora and Naini Tal rather than return to Rishikesh.

There are excellent *PWD Bungalows* at Kapkot, Loharkhet, Dhakuri, Khati, Dwali and Purkiya. Foreigners are charged around Rs 40 for a huge suite but they tend to fill up relatively early in the day. Khati is the only place which has supplies after Bharari. The small *Himalayan Hotel* (with a restaurant) is also here.

Day 1	Rishikesh to Gwaldam	240 km*
Day 2	Gwaldam/Kapkot/Bharari	80 km*
Day 3	Bharari/Song/Loharkhet	12 km**
Day 4	Loharkhet to Khati	18 km
Day 5	Khati to Purkiya	16 km
Day 6	Purkiya to Pindari	7 km
Day 7	Pindari to Khati	21 km
Day 8	Khati to Loharkhet	18 km
Day 9	Loharkhet to Bajnath	47 km*
Day 10	Bajnath/Kausani/Almora	71 km*

*by bus
**mostly by bus

Travellers' Notebook

Weird Scenes

India is full of weird scenes, I'm on my way from Varanasi station in a rickshaw when we pass a guy walking along wearing an orange sarong, bare-chested with bangles on his arms and ankles and barefoot. He looks a bit like an Indian version of George Harrison when the Beatles just started, but obviously he's on some sort of yagna. He carries a long whip. Behind him walks a woman (his wife) clutching a drum in one arm, a small baby and drumstick in the other.

They stop, she beats the drum and he whirls the whip and flogs himself. The whip cracks and he turns, to his audience, to show more blood streaming down his already bloody chest and arm. He repeats the process twice more and then walks away to repeat it again a little further down the road. His wife passes the offering bowl around and then hurries after him. Why he was engaged in this particularly gruesome yagna I have no idea but it was sufficiently unusual for my rickshaw-wallah to stop and gawp. Nobody had so much as given a second glance to the dead body I saw floating by the bathing ghats that morning.

Tony Wheeler

SKIING IN THE GARWHAL HIMAL
Auli

A new resort has been opened at Auli, 16 km from Joshimath. There are daily buses from Rishikesh which go via Joshimath. A nine-km trek is then necessary to get to the resort. It's reportedly the best equipped in the country.

Advanced and beginners ski courses are offered, and there is an Institute of Mountaineering nearby (at Uttarkashi) if you'd like to get into that.

Accommodation is in two and four-bed dormitories.

Beware of Cows

You walk by cows a dozen times a day in India. In Varanasi you can make that 100 times a day. Once I'd got used to their presence in places where cows would hardly be expected in the west, I hardly gave them a second thought. Until one day in Varanasi one of them suddenly wheeled its head round and jabbed me in the ribs with its horn. I couldn't get out of the way, as I was wedged in by a rickshaw wallah doing a hard-sell job. For a second I got a flash of what it must be like to be a bullfighter on the losing end, and I think I actually did crack a rib because it hurt to laugh, sneeze or lie down for the next week. I give cows a wider berth now; it must be very inauspicious to get attacked by a holy cow in Varanasi.

Tony Wheeler

Bihar

Population: 84 million
Area: 173,876 square km
Capital: Patna
Main language: Hindi

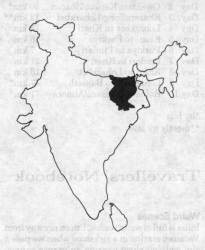

The northern state of Bihar is one of the most backward and depressed in India. Its dense population scratches a bare living from rice growing. For visitors, Bihar is usually little more than a place to pass through, perhaps with a pause in Patna if you are heading for Nepal by land. Yet 25 centuries ago, this was the capital of the greatest empire in India when Ashoka ruled his kingdom from Pataliputra, where Patna is today.

Furthermore, Bihar was a great religious centre for Jains, Hindus and, most importantly, Buddhists. It was at Bodhgaya that the Buddha sat under the Bo tree and attained enlightenment, and a descendant of that original tree still flourishes there today. Nearby Nalanda was a world famous university for the study of Buddhism in the 5th century AD, while Rajgir was associated with both the Buddha and the Jain apostle Mahavira.

The state has a very low literacy rate and Patna is the only city with more than 500,000 inhabitants. Bihar is also the state considered by many Indians to have the most widespread corruption.

PATNA (population 775,000)

For many centuries, Patna was the capital of a huge empire spanning a large part of ancient India. Then, it was called Pataliputra. Today, this surprisingly pleasant city is the capital of Bihar. Patna sprawls along the southern bank of the Ganges, which at this point is very wide; between Varanasi and Patna, three major tributaries join the Ganges and the river triples in width.

Orientation

The city stretches for 15 km along the south bank of the Ganges. The airport, airline offices and main railway station are all at the western end of town, while the older and more traditional parts of Patna are to the east. The 'hub' of the new Patna is at Gandhi Maidan. The main market area is Ashok Raj Path, which starts from Gandhi Maidan.

Two important roads near the railway station, Frazer Rd and Exhibition Rd, have officially had their names changed to M Haque Path and Braj Kishore Path respectively but, in reality, there is absolutely no indication of a change. On the other hand, Gardiner Rd does appear to have been renamed Beer Chand Patel Marg.

Information

Tourist Office The state tourist office is on Frazer Rd but is of little use. The small counter on the railway station platform is much more helpful. There's also a Government of India tourist office at the Tourist Bungalow (Tourist Bhavan) on Beer Chand Patel Marg.

Bookshops & Libraries There are a couple of reasonable small bookshops on Frazer Rd, including Tricel near the Hotel Saktar. This bookshop stocks *Time* and *Newsweek*.

There is a British Library (tel 24198) on Bank Rd near Gandhi Maidan. It is on a side street near the Bishuram Bhavan building and is open from 11 am to 6 pm Tuesday to Saturday.

Golghar

Overlooking the maidan, the huge, beehive-shaped Golghar was constructed in 1786 as a granary to store surpluses against possible famines. It was built by Captain John Garstin at the instigation of the British administrator, Warren Hastings, following a terrible famine in 1770, but has scarcely been used since that time. The Golghar stands about 25 metres high with steps winding around the outside to the top, and provides a fine view over the town and the Ganges. Inside there is a superb echo.

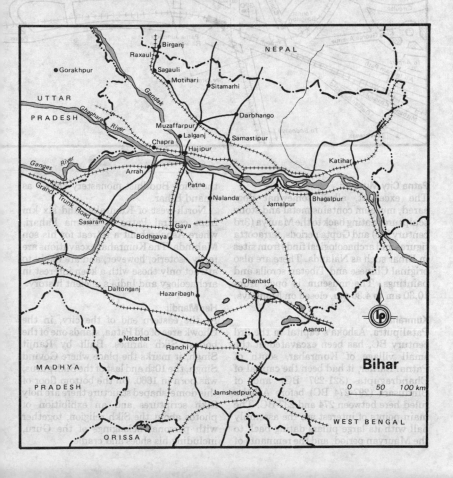

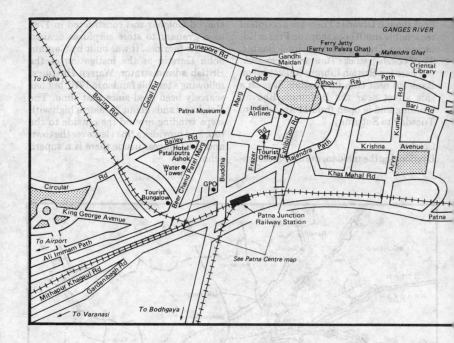

Patna City Museum

The excellent, albeit somewhat dog-eared, museum contains metal and stone sculptures dating back to the Maurya (3rd century BC) and Gupta periods, terracotta figures and archaeological finds from sites in Bihar such as Nalanda. There are also original Chinese and Tibetan scrolls and paintings. The museum is open from 10.30 am to 4.30 pm, closed on Mondays.

Kumrahar

Pataliputra, Ashoka's capital in the 3rd century BC, has been excavated at the small village of Kumrahar, south of Patna. Earlier, it had been the capital of Chandragupta (321-297 BC) and of Bindusara (297-274 BC) before Ashoka ruled here between 274 and 237 BC. The main points of interest are the assembly hall with its large pillars dating back to the Mauryan period, and the remnants of

the brick Buddhist monastery known as Anand Bihar.

North-west of Kumrahar and six km from central Patna is Bhikna Pahari, where Ashoka built a retreat for his son Mahinda. The Kumrahar excavations are fairly esoteric, however, and are likely to attract only those with a keen interest in archaeology and India's ancient history.

Har Mandir

At the eastern end of the city, in the Chowk area of old Patna, stands one of the holiest Sikh shrines. Built by Ranjit Singh, it marks the place where Govind Singh, the 10th and last of the Sikh gurus, was born in 1660. On the bottom floor of this dome-shaped structure there are holy Sikh scriptures and an exhibition of photos about the Sikh religion, together with personal belongings of the Guru, including his shoes and cradle.

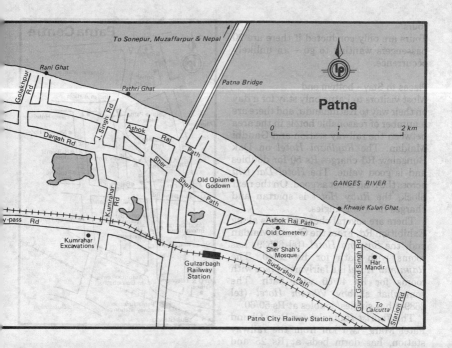

To Sonepur, Muzaffarpur & Nepal

Patna

0   1   2 km

GANGES RIVER

Rani Ghat

Pathri Ghat

Patna Bridge

Golakhpur Rd

J. Singh Rd

Dargah Rd

Ashok Raj Path

Sher Shah Path

Old Opium Godown

Kumrahar Rd

y-pass Rd

Kumrahar Excavations

Gulzarbagh Railway Station

Sudarshan Path

Ashok Raj Path

Old Cemetery

Sher Shah's Mosque

Guru Govind Singh Rd

Station Rd

Har Mandir

Khwaje Kalan Ghat

To Calcutta

Patna City Railway Station

Not only must you go barefoot within the temple precincts, but your head must be covered. They lend cloths for this purpose at the entrance. Celebrations to mark the Guru's birthday are held here each year in December-January. Shops near the Har Mandir sell attractive painted wooden toys. A tempo from Gandhi Maidan to the Chowk area costs only a few rupees.

Khudabaksh Oriental Library

Founded in 1900, this library has a renowned collection of rare Arabic and Persian manuscripts, Moghul and Rajput paintings, and oddities like the Koran inscribed in a book only an inch wide. The library also contains the only books which survived the sacking of the Moorish University of Cordoba in Spain.

Other Attractions

Gulzarbagh, to the east of the city, was the site of the East India Company's opium warehouse. Today, the building houses a Bihar government printing works. Ask for the Barkipor bus stand from the Patna City railway station.

The heavy, domed Sher Shahi, built by the Afghan ruler Sher Shah in 1545, is the oldest mosque in Patna. Other mosques include the squat Pathar ki Masjid and the riverbank Madrassa. Jalan's Quila houses a collection of antiques. One km west of the Har Mandir, the old cemetery is an overgrown and decaying reminder of the days of the British Raj. On Beer Chand Patel Marg, a little north of the Tourist Bungalow, stands a wonderful old water tower with brick walls two metres thick. It withstood the major 1934 earthquake and is still in use today.

Tours
Tours are only conducted if there are 20 passengers wanting to go – an unlikely occurrence.

Places to Stay – bottom end
Most visitors to Patna only stay for a day on their way to Kathmandu, and there are a number of reasonable hotels in the area between the railway station and Gandhi Maidan. The *Rajdhani Hotel* on Dak Bungalow Rd charges Rs 50 for doubles and is good value. The *Hotel Dai Ichi* across the road is not as good. On the next block, the *Ruby Hotel* is spartan and charges Rs 35 for singles.

There are several cheaper hotels along Exhibition Rd. From the Gandhi Maidan end, the *Shyama Hotel* (tel 32539) has rooms with bath for Rs 25/40. The *Rajkumar Hotel* is a fairly new place with rooms for Rs 40/60 with bath. The somewhat shabby *Vikram Hotel* (tel 26894) has singles/doubles at Rs 50/60.

The *Tourist Bungalow* on Beer Chand Patel Marg, two km from the railway station, has dorm beds at Rs 25 and doubles with bath at Rs 95. The tourist office is in the same building. There are some cheaper hotels in alleys off Frazer Rd. At the station there are *retiring rooms* at Rs 45, or Rs 100 with air-con.

Places to Stay – middle
Rooms are variable at the *Rajasthan Hotel* (tel 25102) on Frazer Rd, so look before you say OK. Rooms, all with bathroom and TV, range from Rs 90 to Rs 140. The hotel is pretty good value and has a good restaurant.

There are several newish medium-priced hotels along Frazer Rd from the station. The *Samrat International* (tel 31841) has rooms at Rs 160/225. Across the road is the sadly neglected *Satkar International* (tel 25771-8) with rooms at Rs 185/200. The *Hotel Chanakya* (tel 23141) on Beer Chand Patel Marg charges Rs 325/425 for singles/doubles.

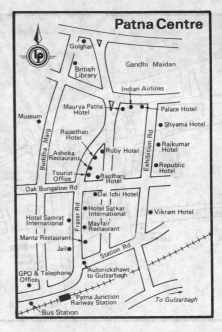

Places to Stay – top end
Overlooking Gandhi Maidan, the *Welcomgroup Maurya Patna* (tel 22061-65) is Patna's top hotel. All rooms have air-con, and the usual mod cons are available, including a pool. Singles cost Rs 610 to Rs 950, doubles Rs 710 to Rs 1050. The *Hotel Pataliputra Ashok* (tel 26270) on Beer Chand Patel Marg has air-con rooms at Rs 395/595.

Places to Eat
Patna has plenty of places to eat, many of which are along Frazer Rd from the station. The *Mayfair Restaurant* is a clean, straightforward and brightly lit place with good masala dosas for Rs 5.50 and other snacks, as well as 16-odd ice-cream flavours.

Close by, the *Manta Restaurant* is good and often packed. Its fare includes Chinese dishes. Further up Frazer Rd, the *Ashoka Restaurant* is extremely dark –

you need to strike a match to read the menu – but the non-vegetarian food is excellent. Beers are Rs 18. Further along again, the *Rajasthan Hotel* has a good vegetarian restaurant, with a separate 'family room'.

Other restaurants include the *Hsin Long Chinese Restaurant* and the *Udipi Coffee House*.

Getting There & Away

See the following Patna to Nepal section for details of transport to Nepal.

Air There is a daily flight from Calcutta to Delhi via Patna, and a daily flight to Lucknow. Delhi/Patna is Rs 810, Calcutta/Patna Rs 485, and Lucknow/Patna Rs 495. There are three flights a week to and from Ahmedabad and Bombay, and five flights a week to Varanasi.

Bus The main bus station is just west of the Patna Junction railway station, opposite the GPO and Hardinge Park. Buses leave here for Muzaffarpur, and for Raxaul on the Nepalese border. A bus to Siliguri for Darjeeling costs Rs 62 and the trip takes at least 12 hours, even on the fastest night bus. Some buses on this trip are very overcrowded – Ranjit Travel is one to be wary of.

Train There are several express and mail trains daily between Delhi and Patna taking 14½ to 24 hours. The distance is almost exactly 1000 km. The Delhi to Patna fare is Rs 91 in 2nd class, Rs 344 in 1st. The 533-km trip from Calcutta to Patna takes about eight to 10 hours and costs Rs 59 in 2nd class, Rs 215 in 1st. You can also catch trains for Bhubaneswar in Orissa from here.

If you're heading to Darjeeling or the north-east region, the fast NE Express from Delhi leaves Patna at 9.20 pm, arriving in New Jalpaiguri at 10 am.

There are also direct trains to Madras, Bombay and Dehra Dun.

Getting Around

Airport Transport The Indian Airlines bus is Rs 10 and you have to get to the Indian Airlines office to start with. The airport is so close to town that you can get there on a cycle-rickshaw for Rs 8 to Rs 10.

Local Transport Shared auto-rickshaws shuttle back and forth between the main Patna Junction railway station and Gulzarbagh for Rs 2 per person. They pass right by the Kumrahar excavations and you can ask to be dropped there.

PATNA TO NEPAL

Patna is very popular as a departure point for Nepal, whether you are travelling by land or by air. The twice-weekly Indian Airlines flight to Kathmandu costs US$41, less 25% for those under 30. On the way to Raxaul (on the Indian side of the Nepal border), you can pause in a number of towns.

Sonepur

Just across the river from Patna is Sonepur. A month-long cattle fair is held here each October-November, culminating on the full moon night of Kartika Purnima. Even elephants are still occasionally bought and sold at this fair – Rs 10,000 will get you a decent specimen.

Vaisali

Only 44 km north of Patna, Vaisali is the birthplace of Mahavira, one of the Jain tirthankars. Over 2000 years ago, it was the capital of a republic. Very few of the remains thought to lie here have been excavated although an Ashoka pillar, topped by his lion symbol, has been unearthed. It was one of a series of Ashoka pillars erected along the route between Pataliputra (Patna) and Nepal.

Vaisali is not on the direct Patna to Muzaffarpur route, but you can easily divert to make the journey Patna/Hajipur/Lalganj/Vaisali/Muzaffarpur, all by bus.

Places to Stay There is a *Youth Hostel* and a *Tourist Rest House* here. A dorm bed costs about Rs 5. The local speciality in Vaisali is *chura*, a mixture of rice and curd.

Muzaffarpur (population 170,000)

Apart from being a bus changing point on the way to the Nepal border, Muzaffarpur is of limited interest. This is a poverty-stricken, agriculturally backward area. North of Muzaffarpur, the area becomes even poorer. Motihari, where George Orwell was born, is a small provincial town which is also the district headquarters.

Places to Stay & Eat The *Hotel Deepak* has reasonable food and very spartan rooms. The *Hotel Elite*, only a couple of hundred metres from the railway station on Saraiya Gunj, is more expensive.

Raxaul & Birganj

Raxaul is right on the border and is virtually a twin town with Birganj in Nepal. Both towns are dirty, unattractive transit points strung along the highway and full of heavy traffic. There's a long line of Dickensian-looking factories on the Nepalese side. The border is open at night and it takes about 30 minutes and Rs 10 to get from the border itself to the bus station in Birganj by cycle-rickshaw.

Places to Stay Single rooms at the *Hotel Kaveri* in Raxaul cost Rs 20. The slightly more expensive *Hotel Taj* is also a reasonable place to stay on the Indian side of the border. Alternatively, you can cross the border and stay in Birganj. There are several cheap and grotty hotels around the bus station. The best of the cheapies is the *Maha Lakshmi* with doubles with attached bathrooms for around Rs 20. Also overlooking the bus station, the up-market *Hotel Diyalo* is a clean, decent place with a restaurant and a roof garden. Doubles with bathrooms start at around Rs 70 and go up to Rs 220 if you want air-conditioning.

Patna to Nepal Routes

Air Indian Airlines has a twice-weekly Patna/Kathmandu flight which costs US$41. Compared to flying directly from Delhi to Kathmandu, you can make a considerable saving by travelling from Delhi to Patna by land, then flying Patna/Kathmandu. Even flying Delhi/Patna and Patna/Kathmandu is somewhat cheaper than flying direct.

Bus It makes little sense to take a train to the Nepal border – the buses are much faster. From the main Patna bus station, buses cost Rs 30 for the three-hour trip to Raxaul. From there, it costs about Rs 10 for a rickshaw across the border and Rs 45 on to Kathmandu, an 11 hour journey. You can get tickets all the way through to Kathmandu for Rs 145, including the border rickshaw, accommodation and breakfast before a 7 am departure for Kathmandu the next day. There are also night buses to Kathmandu which go straight through from Patna and arrive at 5 am.

Train Some trains from Delhi go right through to Muzaffarpur via Patna. All the trains take a long time to reach Muzaffarpur, so it's better to get off in Patna and take a bus from there to the Nepal border.

PATNA TO VARANASI
Sasaram

Sasaram is at the junction of the Grand Trunk Road and the road to Patna. There are some fine Muslim tombs in this town, particularly that of the Afghan ruler Sher Shah who died in 1545. The dome of his tomb, visible from the railway line, rises 46 metres above the water level of the surrounding tank. The tomb of his father and the unfinished tomb of his son are also in Sasaram.

There are more Muslim tombs at Maner. At Dehri, 17 km from Sasaram, the railway and the Grand Trunk Road cross the River Son on a three-km bridge. The hill fort of Rohtas is 38 km from here.

PATNA TO GAYA
Nalanda

This was a great Buddhist centre over 1000 years ago until the monastery, school and library were sacked and burnt by Muslims. When Hieun Tsang, the Chinese scholar and traveller, stayed here for five years in the early 7th century AD, there were 10,000 monks and students in residence.

The remains are extensive and include the Great Stupa, with steps, terraces and a few intact votive stupas around it. An archaeological museum houses sculpture and other remains found on the site, and an international centre for the study of Buddhism was established here in 1951. There are Burmese, Japanese and Jain rest houses at Nalanda. Buses connect Nalanda with Rajgir, Gaya, and with Patna 90 km away.

Rajgir

Little remains of the Buddhist ruins at Rajgir, 19 km south of Nalanda towards Gaya. The first Buddhist council was held here after the Buddha attained nirvana. Rajgir was the capital of this part of India during the Buddha's lifetime and he spent 12 years here. Buy one of the local guidebooks to the sites – they're only about Rs 3. There is a Japanese stupa on a nearby hill, and three km away are hot sulphur springs, which are overpopulated. There's a tourist information office at Rajgir Kund.

Places to Stay & Eat The *Tourist Bungalow Number 2* (tel 39) is convenient and has a Rs 10 dormitory. The *Tourist Bungalow Number 1* (tel 26) has Rs 40 doubles as well as a dorm. There's also a *Rest House* and *Youth Hostel* in Rajgir. The Burmese Temple has a coffee house within the grounds specialising in south Indian food and is also a good place to stay. It's clean, popular and conveniently close to the Tourist Bungalow.

Triptee's Hotel has rooms from Rs 40. There are a number of cheaper hotels such as the *Anand Hotel* or the *Hill View Hotel*.

Pawapuri

The Jain tirthankar, Mahavira, attained nirvana here, 25 km from Nalanda. It is an important Jain pilgrimage spot.

GAYA (population 240,000)

Gaya is about 100 km south of Patna. Just as nearby Bodhgaya is a major centre for Buddhist pilgrims, so Gaya is a centre for Hindu pilgrims, second only to Varanasi in its sanctity. Pilgrims believe that offering *pindas* (funeral cakes) here, and performing a lengthy circuit of the holy places around Gaya, will free their ancestors from bondage to the earth.

Vishnupad Temple

In the crowded central part of the old town, this sikhara-style temple was constructed in 1787 by Queen Ahalya Bai of Indore on the banks of the Falgu River.

Although you can view its exterior and the picturesque bathing ghats, non-Hindus are not allowed inside the temple. During the monsoon the river carries a great deal of water but it dries up completely during the winter. You can see cremations taking place on the river banks.

A 30-metre-high octagonal tower surmounts the temple. Inside, the 40-cm-long 'footprint' of Vishnu is imprinted in solid rock and surrounded by a silver-plated basin.

Other Attractions

A temple of the Sun God stands north of the Vishnupad Temple. A flight of 1000 stone steps leads to the top of the Brahmajuni Hill, one km south-west. There is a good view over Gaya from the top of the hill. At the base of the hill is the Akshyabat, or immortal banyan tree, which pilgrims visit to complete the cycle of rituals for their ancestors commenced in Varanasi. Gaya has a museum but it is usually closed.

Twenty km north of Gaya are the ancient Barabar Caves, dating back to 200 BC. Two of the caves contain inscriptions from Ashoka himself. These are the 'Marabar' caves of E M Forster's *A Passage to India.*

Places to Stay & Eat

There are railway *retiring rooms* at Gaya station with a Rs 20 dorm and singles/doubles at Rs 90/125. There are a few other places to stay around the station, most of them spartan but OK for a short pause. The *Ajatsatu Hotel* (tel 1514) is on Station Rd, just across the street from the station. It is about the best place near the railway station and has good singles/doubles at Rs 45/60. The hotel's *Sujata Restaurant* is pretty good.

The *Pal Rest House* has doubles with bathroom for Rs 25. The station tourist office may try to steer you into the *Sri Kailash Rest House* (tel 383) on Fateh Bahadur Siwala Rd. It's pretty basic with rooms from Rs 30. Further from the station, the *Samrat Hotel* is OK although

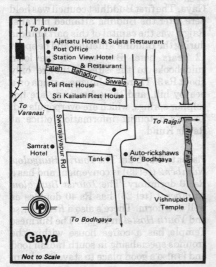

To Patna
• Ajatsatu Hotel & Sujata Restaurant
• Post Office
Station View Hotel
& Restaurant
Fateh Bahadur Siwala Rd
• Pal Rest House
Sri Kailash Rest House

To Varanasi

To Rajgir

River Falgu

Swarajayapur Rd

Samrat Hotel
Tank •
• Auto-rickshaws for Bodhgaya

Vishnupad Temple

To Bodhgaya

Gaya

Not to Scale

rather isolated. Rooms are Rs 40/50 with bath. A rickshaw from the station is about Rs 3 and you can walk from the hotel to the Bodhgaya auto-rickshaw stand.

Getting There & Away
It takes eight to 10 hours by train for the 458-km trip from Calcutta (Rs 53 in 2nd class, Rs 189 in 1st) or 3½ to six hours for the 220-km trip from Varanasi (Rs 31 in 2nd class, Rs 104 in 1st). Patna to Gaya takes two to three hours on the faster express, but trains tend to run late on this relatively short trip. It is 589 km and 14 hours from Gaya to Puri on the Neelachal Express. The fare is Rs 61 in 2nd class, Rs 230 in 1st.

Getting Around
A rickshaw from the station through the narrow alleys to the Vishnupad Temple costs about Rs 5.

BODHGAYA
There are four holy places associated with the Buddha – Lumbini, in Nepal, where he was born; Sarnath, near Varanasi, where he first preached his message; Kushinagar, near Gorakhpur, where he died; and Bodhgaya, where he attained enlightenment. A bo tree growing at Bodhgaya is said to be a direct descendant of the original tree under which the Buddha sat, meditated and achieved enlightenment.

Buddhists from all over the world flock to Bodhgaya, along with many westerners who come here to learn about Buddhism or meditation. Bodhgaya is small and quiet and, if you are not planning a longer study stay, a day is quite sufficient to see everything. Apart from the stupa and various monasteries, Bodhgaya doesn't have a great deal to offer travellers, except for those interested in Buddhism.

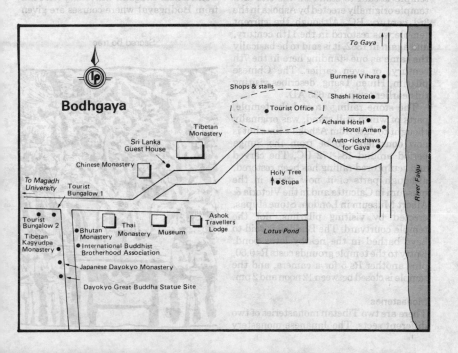

Bodhi Tree

The sacred Bo tree growing here is said to be a direct descendant of the original tree under which the Buddha sat. Although that tree has died, a sapling from the original tree was carried to Sri Lanka by Sanghamitta (the Emperor Ashoka's daughter) when he brought Buddhism to that island. That tree now flourishes at Anuradhapura in Sri Lanka and, in turn, a sapling from that tree was carried back to Bodhgaya where it grows today. A red sandstone slab under the tree is said to be the Vajrasan, or diamond throne, on which the Buddha sat.

Mahabodhi Temple

A pyramidal spire 50 metres high tops the Mahabodhi Temple, inside which is a large gilded image of the Buddha. You enter the temple courtyard by the east gate through a typical Buddhist torana gateway. The temple is said to stand on the site of a temple originally erected by Ashoka in the 3rd century BC. Although the current temple was restored in the 11th century, and again in 1882, it is said to be basically the same as one standing here in the 7th century, or even earlier. The Chinese pilgrim, Hiuen Tsang, describes visiting this earlier temple in 635 AD.

The stone railing around the temple, parts of which still stand, was originally thought to date from Ashoka's time but is now considered to be from the Sunga period around 184-172 BC. The carved and sculptured railing has been restored, although parts of it now stand in the museum in Calcutta and in the Victoria & Albert Museum in London. Stone stupas, erected by visiting pilgrims, dot the temple courtyard. The Buddha is said to have bathed in the nearby lotus pond. Entry to the temple grounds costs Rs 0.50, plus another Rs 5 for a camera, and the temple is closed between 12 noon and 2 pm.

Monasteries

There are two Tibetan monasteries of two different sects. The Japanese monastery has a very beautiful image of the Buddha brought from Japan. There is also a Burmese monastery; the Burmese attempted a restoration of the Mahabodhi in 1306-09. The Thai monastery looks very much like the colourful *wats* you see throughout Thailand. There is a Chinese monastery and the latest addition is a Bhutanese monastery.

Museum

The Archaeological Survey of India maintains a museum with an interesting collection of stone idols and other art from the area. It is open from 10 am to 5 pm daily except Fridays.

Meditation Courses

There are meditation courses offered by Burmese, Tibetan and Thai monasteries in the winter (December-January). There is also an International Meditation Centre near Magadh University (five km from Bodhgaya) where courses are given

Sacred bo tree

on a regular basis by a Bengali monk. Courses are free; food and board costs Rs 25 a day.

Places to Stay - bottom end

There are two *Tourist Bungalows* (No 1 and No 2), each with rooms and a hostel-style dormitory. Double rooms cost Rs 125 and dorm beds Rs 25. One of the best value places is the *Sri Lanka Guest House* run by the Mahabodhi Society which charges Rs 50 to Rs 60 – recommended. On the Gaya side of town there are some basic little hotels like the *Aman* and the *Shashi*.

If you're planning a longer stay and/or don't mind roughing it a little, it is possible to stay at the monasteries. The Burmese monastery is particularly popular for its study courses. There are often numerous western visitors here although most of the rooms are extremely basic.

The monastery has a garden which is very restful. If you do stay here, remember that dignified conduct is expected of the guests. There is no charge for staying but you should, of course, make a donation. Unfortunately, some western visitors have abused the monastery's hospitality by smoking or in other ways breaking the rules.

The Japanese monastery is also clean and comfortable, but during the tourist season, it can be packed with Japanese tour groups and it may be very difficult to find a place. Your stay there is limited to three days and, unhappily, some western visitors have made themselves unpopular here too.

Another good place is the Bhutanese monastery where rooms without bath cost between Rs 30 and Rs 60. The Tibetan monastery is somewhat more spartan and charges Rs 15. The second Tibetan monastery may also take visitors.

Places to Stay - top end

The ITDC *Ashok Travellers Lodge* (tel 25) has singles/doubles at Rs 350/450 including breakfast. Prices and charges are lower in the April to September off-season. It's the best place available and all rooms have bathrooms.

Places to Eat

There is a shortage of good eating places. The *Sri Lanka Guest House* has a fairly good restaurant which serves western food. There are also several restaurants run by Tibetans behind the Tibetan monastery. These restaurants operate in tents and only during the season. They also serve good pies. There is a similar place opposite the Burmese monastery, run by a person who used to work in the Pumpernickel Bakery in Kathmandu. The *Kalyan Restaurant* has basic thalis for Rs 3. For a splurge, visit the *Ashok Travellers Lodge*.

Getting There & Away

Bodhgaya is 13 km from Gaya and auto-rickshaws shuttle back and forth, starting from the Kacheri in the city centre at Gaya, a Rs 3 rickshaw ride from the station. The auto-rickshaws between Bodhgaya and Gaya are phenomenally overloaded. They carry three passengers on each side on benches in the back, one squeezed between them at the front, and another standing up at the very back. Then the driver up front sits on a plank with two people see-sawing on each side of him. A total of 13 people (plus children, goods, etc) travel on a vehicle intended for three! The fare is Rs 3 and rickshaws depart as soon as they're full. To rent the whole auto-rickshaw costs Rs 35.

Buses depart less frequently. If you arrive in Gaya after dark, you're advised to spend the night there rather than try to get to Bodhgaya.

SOUTHERN BIHAR

Parasnath

Just inside the Bihar state boundary from West Bengal, and only a little north of the Grand Trunk Road, Parasnath is the major Jain pilgrimage centre in the east of India. Like so many other pilgrimage centres, it's perched on top of a steep hill and is reached by a stiff climb on foot.

The 24 temples, representing the Jain tirthankars, stand at an altitude of 1366 metres. Parasnath, the 23rd tirthankar, achieved nirvana at this spot 100 years after his birth in Varanasi.

Hazaribagh

South of Gaya, the quiet little hill resort of Hazaribagh is in the Damodar Valley, 67 km from the railway junction at Hazaribagh Rd. There's a wildlife sanctuary here and accommodation is available in a *Tourist Lodge* or a *Forest Rest House*.

Ranchi

At the other end of the Damodar Valley, 93 km away, is Bihar's other hill resort. Ranchi is nearly as quiet as smaller Hazaribagh. At the foot of Ranchi Hill two temples flank an artificial lake. The town is particularly noted for its mental asylum, probably the best-known on the subcontinent.

Jagannathpur village, 10 km south-west, has the Jagannath Temple, a smaller copy of the great Jagannath Temple at Puri, and celebrates its own, smaller festival of the cars. See the Orissa section for more details of this great festival.

The high Hundru Falls are 43 km north-east of Ranchi, and there are other falls in the area. The isolated but beautiful resort of Netarhat is 150 km away, close to the border with Madhya Pradesh.

Places to Stay & Eat The *Hotel Yuvraj* (tel 23430) in Doranda has rooms from Rs 80 to Rs 160, or with air-con from Rs 180 to Rs 350. Other hotels include the new *Monarch Hotel* (tel 20440) which has good doubles with bath at Rs 100 and a good restaurant. Cheaper hotels include the *Hotel Akashdeep* and the *Palace Hotel* in Kadru.

Getting There & Away There are through buses to Ranchi from Raxaul, Patna and Gaya. A through bus to Puri takes 15 hours. Ranchi also has good rail connections.

Calcutta

Population: 12 million
Main language: Bengali

Calcutta is the capital of West Bengal

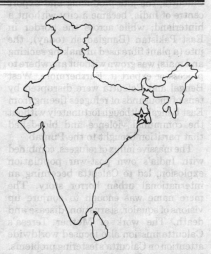

Calcutta, India's largest city, is probably ahead of London as the largest city in the Commonwealth. It's often an ugly and desperate place that to many people sums up the worst of India, yet it's also one of the country's more fascinating centres and has some scenes of rare beauty. Certainly the people are a friendly bunch and Bengali humour is renowned throughout India. Don't let the squalor of first impressions put you off this city. There are a lot of jewels to be discovered and they're not far from the surface.

Calcutta isn't an ancient city like Delhi with its impressive relics of the past. In fact, it's largely a British creation which dates back only some 300 years and was the capital of British India until the beginning of this century.

In 1686, the British abandoned Hooghly, their trading post 38 km up the Hooghly River from present-day Calcutta, and moved downriver to three small villages – Sutanati, Govindpur and Kalikata. Calcutta takes its name from the last of those three tiny settlements. Job Charnock, an English merchant who later married a Brahmin's widow whom he dissuaded from becoming a sati, was the leader of the British merchants who made this move. At first the post was not a great success and was abandoned on a number of occasions, but in 1696 a fort was laid out near present-day BBD Bagh (Dalhousie Square) and in 1698 Aurangzeb's grandson gave the British official permission to occupy the villages.

Calcutta then grew steadily until 1756, when Suraj-ud-daula, the Nawab of Murshidabad, attacked the town. Most of the British inhabitants escaped, but those captured were packed into an underground cellar where, during the night, most of them suffocated in what became known as 'the black hole of Calcutta'.

Early in 1757, the British, under Clive of India, retook Calcutta and made peace with the nawab. Later the same year, however, Suraj-ud-daula sided with the French and was killed in the Battle of Plassey, a turning point in British-Indian history. A much stronger fort was built in Calcutta and the town became the capital of British India.

Much of Calcutta's most enduring development took place between 1780 and 1820. Later in the 19th century, Bengal became an important centre in the struggle for Indian independence, and this was a major reason for the decision to transfer the capital to New Delhi in 1911. Loss of political power did not alter Calcutta's economic control, and the city continued to prosper until after WW II.

Partition affected Calcutta more than any other major Indian city. Bengal and the Punjab were the two areas of India with mixed Hindu and Muslim populations and the dividing line was drawn through them. The result in Bengal was that

Calcutta, the jute-producing and export centre of India, became a city without a hinterland; while across the border in East Pakistan (Bangladesh today), the jute (a plant fibre used in making sacking and mats) was grown without anywhere to process or export it. Furthermore, West Bengal and Calcutta were disrupted by tens of thousands of refugees fleeing from East Bengal, although fortunately without the communal violence and bloodshed that partition brought to the Punjab.

The massive influx of refugees, combined with India's own post-war population explosion, led to Calcutta becoming an international urban horror story. The mere name was enough to conjure up visions of squalor, starvation, disease and death. The work of Mother Teresa's Calcutta mission also focused worldwide attention on Calcutta's festering problems. In 1971, the India-Pakistan conflict and the creation of Bangladesh led to another flood of refugees, and Calcutta's already chaotic condition further deteriorated.

Economically it is still suffering further setbacks; the port has been silting up, making navigation from Calcutta down to the sea steadily more difficult and limiting the size of ships which can use the port. The Farakka Barrage (250 km north of Calcutta), designed to improve the river flow through Calcutta, has been the subject of considerable dispute between India and Bangladesh because it will also affect the flow of the Ganges through Bangladesh.

Furthermore, Calcutta has been plagued by chronic labour unrest resulting in a decline of its productive capacity. The situation is summed up in the city's hopeless power-generation system. Electrical power in Calcutta has become so on-again off-again that virtually every hotel, restaurant, shop or small business has to have some sort of stand-by power generator or battery lighting system. The workers are blamed, the technicians are blamed, the power plants are blamed, the coal miners are blamed, even Indian railways are blamed for not delivering the coal on time, but it's widely pointed out that Bombay certainly doesn't suffer the frequency and extent of power cuts that are a way of life in Calcutta.

The Marxist government of West Bengal has come in for much criticism over the chaos currently existing in Calcutta but, as it is also pointed out, their apparent neglect and mismanagement of the city is combined with a considerable improvement in the rural environment. Threats of flood or famine in the countryside no longer send hordes of refugees streaming into the city as in the past.

Despite all these problems Calcutta is a city with a soul, and one which many residents are inordinately fond of. The Bengalis, so ready to raise arms against the British in the struggle for independence, are also the poets and artists of India. The contrast between the Bombay and Calcutta movie industries more or less sums it up. While Bombay, the Hollywood of India, churns out movies of amazing tinsel banality, the smaller number of movie makers in Calcutta make noncommercial gems that stand up to anything produced for sophisticated western audiences. The city's soul shows in other ways too, and amongst the squalor and confusion Calcutta has places of sheer magic: flower sellers beside the misty, ethereal Hooghly River; the majestic sweep of the Maidan; the arrogant bulk of the Victoria Memorial; the superb collection of archaeological treasures exhibited in the Indian Museum. They're all part of this amazing city, as are massive Marxist and trade union rallies which can block traffic in the city centre for hours at a time. There's never a dull moment!

Orientation

Calcutta sprawls north-south along the east bank of the Hooghly River, which divides it from Howrah on the west bank. If you arrive from anywhere west of Calcutta by rail, you'll come into the immense Howrah station and have to cross the Howrah Bridge into Calcutta proper. Some of Calcutta's worst slums sprawl behind the station on the Howrah side.

For visitors, the more relevant parts of Calcutta are south of the bridge in the areas around BBD Bagh and Chowringhee. BBD Bagh, formerly Dalhousie Square, is the site of the GPO, the international telephone office, the West Bengal tourist office, and is close to the American Express office and various railway booking offices.

South of BBD Bagh is the open expanse of the Maidan along the river, and west from here is the area known as Chowringhee. Most of the cheap and middle-range hotels (and many of the upper-bracket ones) are concentrated in Chowringhee together with many of the airline offices, restaurants, travel agencies and the Indian Museum. At the southern end of Chowringhee you'll find the Government of India tourist office on Shakespeare Sarani, and, nearby, the Birla Planetarium and Victoria Memorial.

There are a number of landmarks in Calcutta and a couple of important streets to remember. The Ochterlony Monument at the northern end of the Maidan is one of the most visible landmarks – it's a tall column rising from the flat expanse of the Maidan. Sudder St runs off Chowringhee Rd and is the core of the Calcutta travellers' scene. Most of the popular cheap hotels are along Sudder St so it is well known to any taxi or rickshaw-wallah, and the airport bus runs right by it. Furthermore, the Indian Museum is on the corner of Sudder St and Chowringhee Rd. Further south down Chowringhee Rd, which runs alongside the eastern edge of the Maidan, is Park St with a great number of more expensive restaurants and the Thai International Airlines office – an important address for people heading on to South-East Asia.

Street Names As in many Indian cities, getting around Calcutta is slightly confused by the habit of renaming city streets, particularly those with Raj-era connotations. As usual this renaming has been done in a half-hearted fashion, and many street signs still display the old names, while some maps show old names and others show new ones; taxi-wallahs inevitably only know the old names. It's going to be a long time before Chowringhee Rd becomes Jawaharlal Nehru Rd!

Other renamed roads include Ballyganj Store Rd (now Gurusday Rd), Bowbazar St (Bepin Behary Ganguly), Buckland Rd (Bankim Ch Rd), Harrington St (Ho Chi Minh Sarani!), Harrison Rd (Mahatma Gandhi Rd), Kyd St (Dr M Ishaque Rd), Lansdowne Rd (Sarat Bose Rd), Lower Chitpur Rd (Rabindra Sarani), Lower Circular Rd (Acharya Jagadish Chandra Bose Rd), Machuabazar St (Madan Mohan St & Keshab Sen St), Mirzapore St (Suryya Sen St), Theatre Rd (Shakespeare Sarani), Wellesley St (Rafi Ahmed Kidwai Rd) and Wellington St (Nirmal Chunder St). There's a certain irony that the street the US consulate is on was renamed Ho Chi Minh Sarani!

Information

Tourist Offices The Government of India tourist office (tel 441402, 443521) is at 4 Shakespeare Sarani. The West Bengal tourist bureau (tel 238271) is at 3/2 BBD Bagh – the opposite side to the post office. Both the state and national tourist offices have counters at the airport.

To find out exactly what's happening on the cultural front, get hold of a copy of *Calcutta this Fortnight* from either the state or national tourist offices. It's free.

Post & Telephone The large Calcutta GPO is on BBD Bagh and has an efficient poste restante and a philatelic bureau for stamp collectors. The Telephone Bhawan is also on BBD Bagh, while the Central Telegraph Office is at 8 Red Cross Place. International phone calls can often be made with amazing ease from here.

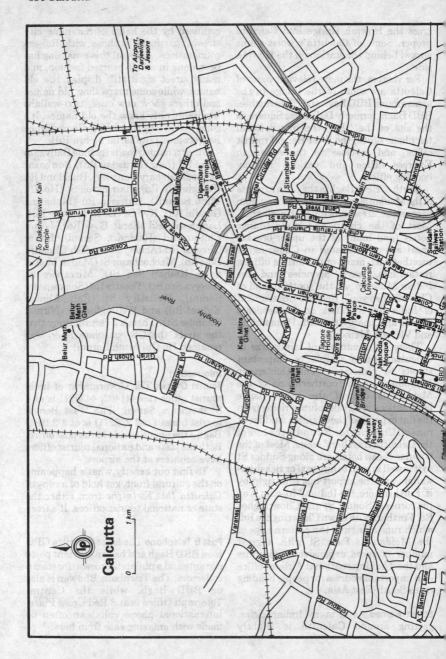

Calcutta

0   1 km

1 Dum Dum Station
2 Belgachia Station
3 Shyam Bazaar Station
4 Shoba Bazaar Station
5 Girish Park Station
6 MG Rd Station
7 Central Station
8 Chandni Chowk Station
9 Esplanade Station
10 Park St Station
11 Maidan Station
12 Rabindra Sadan Station
13 Bhawanipore Station
14 Jatindas Park Station
15 Kalighat Station
16 Rabindra Sarobar Station
17 Tollygunge Station

Banks American Express is at 21 Old Court House St (tel 236281).

Visa Extensions & Permits The Foreigners' Registration Office (tel 44301) is at 237 Acharya J C Bose Rd. Visa extensions and permits for the Andaman Islands are issued here. Tax clearance certificates are available from Room 11, 4th floor, Income Tax Building, Bentinck St.

Books & Bookshops Geoffrey Moorhouse's classic 1971 study *Calcutta* is available as a Penguin paperback. More recently Dominique Lapierre's *City of Joy* has become *de rigeur* reading among travellers to Calcutta and is available in paperback at almost every bookstore (pirated or otherwise). It's dangerous to criticise this book given the guru-like status that many readers accord him, but I found many parts of the book a little fanciful though otherwise interesting. What it certainly has done is to put the Anand Nagar slums in Howrah onto the tourist circuit, but I have a nagging feeling that this is pure voyeurism.

The Cambridge Book & Stationery Company at 20D Park St is a good small bookshop. Further down Park St towards Chowringhee Rd the Oxford Book Shop is larger, but much of their stock is either very specialised or very old. The Bookmark, upstairs at 56D Mirza Ghalib St (Free School St), has a good general selection of books. Classic Books at 10 Middleton Row has a wide variety of both Indian and western books, and the owner, Bharat, is also a mine of information.

There are quite a few secondhand bookshops along Mirza Ghalib St, and Booklands at that end of Sudder St. All of them have an excellent range of titles.

Airlines Most airline offices are around Chowringhee. Notable exceptions are Indian Airlines on Chittaranjan Ave and Burma (Myanmar) Airways which now only has an office at the airport.

Aeroflot
    58 Chowringhee (tel 449831)
Air France
    41 Chowringhee (tel 296161)
Air India
    50 Chowringhee (tel 442356)
Bangladesh Biman
    1 Park St (tel 292832)
British Airways
    41 Chowringhee (tel 293430)
Burma (Myanmar) Airways
    Dum Dum Airport (tel 572611)
Cathay Pacific/KLM
    1 Middleton St (tel 293211)
JAL
    35A Chowringhee (tel 248371)
Indian Airlines
    39 Chittaranjan Ave (tel 260731)
Royal Nepal Airlines
    41 Chowringhee (tel 298534)
Singapore Airlines
    Park St (tel 291525)
Thai International
    18G Park St (tel 299846)
Vayudoot
    Dum Dum Airport (tel 576582)

If you're looking for cheap airline tickets, various places advertise their services around Sudder St. Pan Asian Tours, a tiny office on the 2nd floor at 20 Mirza Ghalib St (Free School St), seem to know what they're on about. One traveller wrote to commend their 'friendly and efficient service'. The managers of both the Salvation Army Red Shield Guest House and the Modern Lodge are also mines of reliable information about where to go for discounted tickets.

Consulates Some of the useful addresses in Calcutta include:

Bangladesh
    9 Circus Ave (tel 445208)
Bhutan
    48 Tivoli Court, Pramothesh Barua Sarani (tel 441301)
Denmark
    18G Park St (tel 249696)
France
    26 Park St (tel 298314), inside the courtyard on the right-hand side of Alliance Francaise

Calcutta Top: Howrah Bridge, Calcutta (TW)
        Bottom: Rickshaw-wallahs in the early morning,
            Calcutta (SM)

West Bengal Top: Darjeeling (GC)
         Bottom: The Bhutan Gompa in Kalimpong (TW)

West Germany
  1 Hastings Park Rd (tel 459141)
Italy
  3 Raja Santosh Rd (tel 451411)
Japan
  12 Pretoria St (tel 442241)
Nepal
  19 Sterndale Rd (tel 452024)
Netherlands
  18A Brabourne Rd (tel 262160)
Thailand
  18B Mandeville Gardens (tel 460836)
UK
  1 Ho Chi Minh Sarani (tel 445171)
USA
  5/1 Ho Chi Minh Sarani (tel 442335)
USSR
  50/12 Rowland Rd (tel 483656)
  31 Shakespeare Sarani (tel 442006)

There is a Burmese consulate listed in the current telephone book at 67 Park St (tel 213200) but it doesn't exist. The nearest Burmese consulates are in Dhaka, Kathmandu and Delhi. Burma (Myanmar) Airways cannot issue visas. For visas to Bangladesh travellers have to go to Delhi.

Those requiring Thai visas also have a problem as the Thai consulate is hard to find. It's probably best to take a taxi though the No 102 bus will get you close to it. The consulate closes at 12 noon.

Botanical Gardens
On the west bank of the Hooghly River, south of Howrah, are the extensive Botanical Gardens. They stretch for over a km along the riverfront and occupy 109 hectares. The gardens were originally founded in 1786 and initially administered by Colonel Kyd. It was from these gardens that the tea now grown in Assam and Darjeeling was first developed. The gardens' prime attraction is the 200-year-old banyan tree, claimed to be the largest in the world. It covers an area of ground nearly 400 metres in circumference and continues to flourish despite having its central trunk removed in 1925, due to fungus damage. The cool and tropical

tall-palm house in the centre of the gardens is also well worth a visit.

The gardens are at Sibpur over the Howrah Bridge and 19 km from Chowringhee. More directly, you may be able to get a ferry across the river from Chandpal or Takta Ghat, or from the Matia Bruz Ghat further south. Ferries shuttle across the river regularly for just Rs 0.50 a round trip! The gardens are open from sunrise to sunset, and although they tend to be very crowded on Sundays, on other days they are peaceful and make a pleasant escape from the hassles and crowds of Calcutta. A No 55 or 56 bus will take you to the gardens in about an hour.

Indian Museum
The Indian Museum, on the corner of Sudder St and Chowringhee Rd, was built in 1875 and is probably the best museum in India and one of the best in Asia. Unfortunately, it appears to have been starved of funds in recent years and many of the exhibits are literally falling apart. Its widely varied collection includes oddities such as a whole roomful of meteorites. Other exhibits include the usual fossils, stuffed animals, skeletons and so on. There are a number of unique fossil skeletons of prehistoric animals, among them giant crocodiles and an amazingly big tortoise.

The art collection has many fine pieces from Orissan and other temples, and superb examples of Buddhist Gandharan art – an interesting meeting point between Greek artistry and Buddhist ideals centred around the North-West Frontier Province, now in Pakistan, that produced Buddha images and other sculptures of extreme beauty.

The museum is open from 10 am to 5 pm daily except Mondays. Between December and February it closes half an hour earlier. Entry fee is Rs 2 except on Fridays when it is free.

Ochterlony Monument
Now officially renamed the Shahid

(Martyr's) Minar, this 48-metre-high column towers over the northern end of the Maidan. It was erected in 1828 and named after Sir David Ochterlony, credited with winning the Nepal War (1814-16). The column is a curious combination of Turkish, Egyptian and Syrian architectural elements.

There's a fine view from the top of the column, but permission to ascend it must be obtained from the Deputy Commissioner of Police, Police HQ, Lal Bazaar St. It's only open Monday to Friday and you should simply ask for a 'monument pass' at the Assistant Commissioner's office on the 2nd floor.

Rabindra Sarobar & Ramakrishna Mission

Rabindra Sarobar, in the south of the city, is a park and picnic spot with a central lake. Beside the park is the Ramakrishna Mission Institute of Culture with a library, reading rooms and lecture halls.

Maidan & Fort William

After the events of 1756, the British decided there would be no repetition of the attack on the city and set out to replace the original Fort William, in the Maidan, with a massive and impregnable new fort. First they cleared out the inhabitants of the village of Govindpur and in 1758 laid the foundations of a fort which, when completed in 1781, would cost them the awesome total, for those days, of £2 million. Around the fort a huge expanse of jungle was cut down to give the cannons a clear line of fire but, as usual, the fort has never fired a shot in anger. You can walk around the fort's massive walls, which have deep fortifications and trenches fronting them, but visitors are only allowed inside with special permission because the fort is still in use today.

The area cleared around Fort William became the Maidan, the 'lungs' of modern Calcutta. This huge green expanse stretches three km north to south and is over a km wide. It is bounded by Strand Rd along the river to the west and by Chowringhee Rd, lined with shops, offices, hotels and eating places, to the east. The stream known as Tolly's Nalla forms its southern boundary, and here you will find a racecourse and the Victoria Memorial. In the north-west corner of the Maidan is Eden Gardens, while Raj Bhavan overlooks it from the north.

Within the gardens are cricket and football fields, tennis courts, ponds and trees. Cows graze, political discussions are held, people stroll across the grounds or come for early morning yoga sessions. And of course the place is used, like any area of open land in India, as a public toilet.

Eden Gardens

In the north-west corner of the Maidan are the small and pleasantly laid-out Eden Gardens. A tiny Burmese pagoda was brought here from Prome, Burma (Myanmar) in 1856; it's set in a small lake and is extraordinarily picturesque. The gardens were named after the sister of Lord Auckland, the former governor general. The Calcutta Cricket Ground, where international test matches are held, is also within the gardens.

Near the gardens is a pleasant walk along the banks of the Hooghly River. Ferries run across the river from several ghats and there are plenty of boatmen around offering to take you out on the water for half an hour.

Victoria Memorial

At the southern end of the Maidan stands the Victoria Memorial, the most solid reminder of British Calcutta, in fact probably the most solid reminder of the Raj to be found in India. The Victoria Memorial is a huge white-marble museum, a strange combination of classical European architecture with Moghul influences or, as some have put it, an unhappy British attempt to build a better Taj Mahal.

The idea behind the memorial was conceived by Lord Curzon, and the money for its construction was raised from 'voluntary contributions by the princes and peoples of India'. The Prince of Wales (later King George V) laid the foundation stone in 1906 and it was opened by another Prince of Wales (later the Duke of Windsor) in 1921.

Whether you're interested in the British Raj period or not, the memorial is an attraction not to be missed. It tells the story of the British Empire in India at its peak, just when it was about to begin its downhill slide. The imposing statue of Queen Victoria, at her bulky and least amused best, fronts the memorial and sets the mood for all the displays inside.

Inside you'll find portraits, statues and busts of almost all the main participants in British-Indian history. Scenes from military conflicts and events of the mutiny are illustrated. There are some superb watercolours of Indian landscapes and buildings made by travelling Victorian artists. A Calcutta exhibit includes many early pictures of the city and a model of Fort William. Of course there are many

fine Indian and Persian miniatures and rare manuscripts and books. Queen Victoria appears again inside, much younger and slimmer than her statue outside. There's also a piano she played as a young girl and other memorabilia. A huge painting depicts King Edward VII entering Jaipur in a regal procession in 1876. French guns captured at the Battle of Plassey are on exhibit along with the black stone throne of the nawab whom Clive defeated. To top it all off, there is a good view over the Maidan from the balcony above the entrance.

The booklet *A Brief Guide to the Victoria Memorial* is available in the building. The memorial is open from 10 am to 3.30 pm in winter, an hour later in summer. It is closed on Mondays, and entry costs Rs 1.

St Paul's Cathedral
Built between 1839 and 1847, St Paul's Cathedral is one of the most important

Victoria Memorial, Calcutta

churches in India. It stands just to the east of the Victoria Memorial at the southern end of the Maidan. The steeple fell during an earthquake in 1897, and following further damage in a 1934 quake was redesigned and rebuilt.

Birla Planetarium

This planetarium, near the Government of India tourist office, is one of the largest in the world and well worth the Rs 5 admission. There are daily programmes in Hindi, Bengali and English (two per day in English but times vary), and the shows start at 12.30 pm, except on Sunday when they start at 10 am; the last show is at 6.30 pm.

Kali Temple

This temple, also known as Kalighat, is believed to be about 500 years old and the actual temple from which Kalikata (anglicised to Calcutta) takes its name.

According to legend, when Shiva's wife's corpse was cut up, one of her fingers fell here. Since then it has been an important pilgrimage site. The temple is about two km directly south of St Paul's Cathedral.

Zoo

South of the Maidan, Calcutta's 16-hectare zoo was opened in 1876. Some of the animals are displayed in near natural conditions, and the zoo is open from sunrise to sunset; admission is Rs 1.

Just south of the zoo on Alipore Rd are the pleasant and quiet horticultural gardens. They're open 6 to 10 am and 2 to 5 pm except on Mondays; admission is Rs 0.50.

Howrah Bridge

Until 1943, the Hooghly River was crossed by a pontoon bridge which had to be opened to let river traffic through. There was considerable opposition to construction of a bridge due to fears that it would affect the river currents and cause silting problems. This problem was eventually avoided by building a bridge that crosses the river in a single 450-metre span with no piers at all within the river.

The cantilevered bridge is similar in size to the Sydney Harbour Bridge but carries a flow of traffic which Sydney could never dream of – it's intriguing to stand at one end of the bridge at morning rush hour and watch the procession of double-decker buses come across. They heel over like yachts due to the weight of passengers hanging onto the sides. In between are countless rickshaws, lumbering bullock carts, hordes of bicycles and even the odd car. The bridge is also known as Rabindra Setu.

The bridge is usually horribly congested and some years ago an additional bridge was planned a couple of km downriver. Construction was commenced but the funds ran out at a very early stage, and the site remained untouched for a number of years. In the early '80s the plans were revived and construction recommenced, but once again funds have dried up. It can take up to 45 minutes to cross the Howrah Bridge.

BBD Bagh (Dalhousie Square)

When Calcutta was the administrative centre for British India, BBD Bagh was the centre of power. On the north side of the square stands the huge Writers' Building which dates from 1880. In those days clerical workers were known as 'writers' and the East India Company's 'writers' have been replaced by modern-day ones employed by the West Bengal state government. That's where all the quintuplicate forms, carbon copies and red ink come from. Also on Dalhousie Square is a rather more useful place, the Calcutta GPO, and on the eastern side of the square is the West Bengal Tourist Development Corporation's office.

Until it was abandoned in 1757, the original Fort William used to stand where the post office now does. It stretched from there down to the river, which has also changed its course since that time. Brass markers by the post office indicate where the fort walls used to be. Calcutta's famous black hole actually stood at the north-east corner of the post office, but since independence all indications of its position have been removed. The black hole was actually a tiny guardroom in the fort and 146 people were forced into it on that fateful night when the city fell to Suraj-ud-daula. Next morning only 23 were still alive.

St John's Church
A little south of Dalhousie Square is the Church of St John, which dates from 1787. The graveyard here has a number of interesting monuments, including the octagonal mausoleum of Job Charnock, founder of Calcutta, who died in 1692. Admiral Watson, who supported Clive in retaking Calcutta from Suraj-ud-daula, is also buried here.

Other British Buildings
The Victoria Memorial is the most imposing reminder of the British presence in Calcutta, but the city's commercial wealth resulted in quite a few other interesting buildings. Raj Bhavan, the old British Government house, is now occupied by the governor of West Bengal and entry is restricted. The Marquess Wellesley built it between 1799 and 1805, modelling it on Lord Curzon's home, Kedleston Hall, Derbyshire, England which was only completed a couple of years before. Raj Bhavan stands at the north end of the Maidan and contains many rare works of art and other interesting items, including Tipu Sultan's throne.

Next to Raj Bhavan is the Doric-style Town Hall, and next to that the High Court, which was copied from the Staadhaus at Ypres, Belgium, and completed in 1872. It has a tower 55 metres high. Just south of the zoo in Alipur is the National Library, the biggest in India, which is housed in Belvedere House, the former residence of the Lieutenant-Governor of Bengal.

South Park St Cemetery is being restored and shows the high price paid by the early settlers from England. There are marvellous tombs and inscriptions at this peaceful site.

Other Museums
Calcutta has a number of other interesting museums apart from the magnificent Indian Museum and the Victoria Memorial. The Asutosh Museum at Calcutta University has a collection of art objects with emphasis on Bengali folk art. Admission is free and it is open from 10.30 am to 4.30 pm on weekdays, and 10.30 am to 3 pm on Saturdays.

At 19A Gurusday Rd is the Birla Industrial & Technological Museum, open from 10 am to 5 pm daily. Admission is free except on Sundays. Those philanthropic (and very wealthy) Birlas have also provided the Birla Academy of Art & Culture at 109 Southern Ave, open from 4.30 to 7 pm daily except Mondays; admission is Rs 0.50. It has a good collection of sculptures and modern art. They are also building a huge new Birla temple, just around the corner from the Industrial & Technological Museum.

The Academy of Fine Arts, on Cathedral Rd beside the cathedral, has a permanent exhibition and is open from 3 to 8 pm daily except Mondays. Entry is free. The Nehru Children's Museum at 94/1 Chowringhee Rd (Jawaharlal Nehru Rd) is open from 1 to 8 pm daily except Mondays. Tales from the Hindu epics are depicted with beautiful miniature clay figures.

On Muktaram Babu St, a narrow lane in north Calcutta, is the Marble Palace, an incongruous one-man collection of statues and paintings, including works of Rubens and Sir Joshua Reynolds. It's open from 10 am to 4.30 pm except on Mondays and Thursdays, and entry is free with a permit from the Government of India tourist office. Nearby is the rambling old Tagore House, a centre for

Indian dance, drama, music and other arts. This is the birthplace of Rabindranath Tagore, India's greatest modern poet, and his final resting place. It's just off Rabindra Sarani.

Culture

Calcutta is famous for its culture – film, poetry, music, art and dance all have their devotees here. There are dances on at the Oberoi Grand Hotel on Chowringhee Rd every night at 7 pm, Rs 15 or Rs 12 with a student card. Sometimes the audience is extremely small. A dance-drama performance, Bengali poetry reading or similar event takes place on most nights at the Rabindra Sadan (tel 449936) on Cathedral Rd.

Sitambara Jain Temple

This temple, in the north-east of the city, was built in 1867 and dedicated to Sheetalnathji, the 10th of the 24 Jain tirthankars. The temple is an ornate mass of mirrors, coloured stones and glass mosaics. It overlooks a garden, and is open from 6 am to 12 noon and 3 to 7 pm daily.

Dakshineshwar Kali Temple

Nakhoda Mosque

North of BBD Bagh is Calcutta's principal Muslim place of worship. The huge Nakhoda Mosque is said to accommodate 10,000 people and was modelled on Akbar's tomb at Sikandra near Agra. The red sandstone mosque has two 46-metre-high minarets and a brightly painted onion-shaped dome.

Anand Nagar

Since Dominique Lapierre wrote his book, *City of Joy*, about these Howrah slums, he has almost become a cult figure and the slums themselves are well on the way to becoming a 'tourist attraction'.

Belur Math

North of the city on the west bank of the Hooghly River is the headquarters of the Ramakrishna Mission, Belur Math. Ramakrishna, an Indian philosopher, preached the unity of all religions and, following his death in 1886, his follower Swami Vivekananda founded the Ramakrishna Mission in 1897. There are now branches all over India. Belur Math, the movement's international headquarters, was founded in 1899. It is supposed to represent a church, a mosque and a temple, depending on how you look at it. Belur Math is open from 6.30 am to 12 noon and from 3.30 to 7.30 pm daily, and admission is free.

Dakshineshwar Kali Temple

Across the river from Belur Math is this Kali temple where Ramakrishna was a priest, and where he reached his spiritual vision of the unity of all religions. The temple was built in 1847.

Barrackpore

There is a memorial to Gandhi called Gandhi Ghat at Barrackpore, 25 km north of Calcutta on the banks of the Hooghly.

Serampore

Across the river from Barrackpore, 25 km from Calcutta, this was a Danish centre until their holdings in India were transferred to the East India Company in 1845. The old Danish Church and cemetery still stand. The missionaries Ward, Marshman and Carey operated from here in the early 1800s.

Mahesh, three km from Serampore, has a large and very old Jagannath temple. In June-July of each year the Mahesh Yatra car festival takes place here, it is second in size only to the great car festival of Jagannath at Puri, Orissa.

Tours

The Government of India tourist office (tel 441402, 443521) at 4 Shakespeare Sarani and the West Bengal tourist bureau (tel 238271) at 3/2 BBD Bagh both have daily tours of Calcutta except on Sundays. The morning tour from 8 am to 12.30 pm costs Rs 25 and takes in the area around BBD Bagh, including Eden Gardens, Raj Bhavan, the Jain temple plus the sights further out like Belur Math, the Dakshineshwar Temple and the Botanical Gardens.

The afternoon tour operates from 1.30 to 5.15 pm and also costs Rs 25, but covers the Indian Museum, Victoria Memorial and the zoo.

The morning tour is better value since it covers the sights further out. Instead of taking the afternoon tour you could easily get around yourself and have more time. Bus tours are also conducted for the various festivals and pujas around the state – consult Calcutta this Fortnight or a tourist office for details.

Lastly, there are also two-day bus-launch tours twice a month to the Sunderbans which cost Rs 325 including food.

Places to Stay – bottom end

Sudder St, running off Chowringhee beside the Indian Museum, is a lively street and Calcutta's cheap accommodation centre. At 2 Sudder St the popular Salvation Army Red Shield Guest House (tel 242895) has dorm beds at Rs 16 and private rooms at Rs 35/60/80. The more

expensive rooms have a bath. The place is clean and well kept although the water supply is decidedly erratic; it's a real drag to arrive after a hot, sweaty train trip to find there'll be no water available for hours to come.

East down Sudder St a bit, Stuart Lane turns off to the right, and here you'll find two of Calcutta's most popular budget establishments. The Modern Lodge (tel 244960) is at No 1, and the very popular Hotel Paragon is at No 2. The Paragon has dorm beds at Rs 15 (downstairs) and Rs 20 (upstairs), singles with common bath for Rs 35 and singles/doubles with bath for Rs 60/80. There's a pleasant courtyard upstairs but the ground-floor rooms are rather gloomy. Baggage lockers (Rs 1 per day) and meals are available.

The Modern Lodge is very similar but marginally better, and it was repainted not long ago. Dorm beds cost from Rs 10 to Rs 25 depending on the number of beds to a room. Singles/doubles with common bath cost Rs 30/40 and doubles with bath are Rs 80 and Rs 100. There's also a four-bed room with bath for Rs 150. All the rooms have a fan, the toilets are clean and the food is reasonable. The rooftop area is a popular meeting place in the evening, and tea and soft drinks are available. The manager, Mr Roy, is very friendly and helpful, and is a good person to see about airline tickets.

Two other hotels in this bracket on Sudder St are the Shilton Hotel and the Hilston Hotel. The Shilton has singles with common bath for Rs 65 and singles/doubles/triples with bath for Rs 80/120/150. The staff are friendly. The Hilston at 4 Sudder St has clean singles with common bath for Rs 45 to Rs 50 and doubles with bath for Rs 100.

Also on Sudder St are the Tourist Inn (tel 243732) at No 4/1 and the Hotel Diplomat at No 10, opposite the Shilton. Both are cheapies but they are essentially private houses with a few rooms for guests. They're OK for a night if everywhere else is full but not as good as the Modern or the

Paragon. A better choice is either the *Capital Guest House* (tel 213844) at 11B Chowringhee Lane, or the *Timestar Hotel* on the next lane over.

South of Sudder St, there are two excellent hotels right opposite each other along Dr M Ishaque Rd. The first is the *East End Hotel* (tel 298921), an old place but well maintained and run by friendly people. It has singles/doubles with common bath for Rs 50/140. The other is the *Neelam Hotel* which has singles/doubles for Rs 55/90. Nearby is the *Classic Hotel*, down an alley off Mirza Ghalib St (Free School St), which has singles with common bath for Rs 55 and singles/doubles with bath for Rs 75/110. The showers have only cold water but bucket hot water is available at no extra charge.

The Ys Calcutta has a collection of Ys. The *YMCA* (tel 233504), 25 Chowringhee Rd, is a big, gloomy building but a good place to stay. All rooms have a bath and cost Rs 180/230 for singles/doubles including breakfast and dinner, and there's a Rs 10 temporary membership fee. The breakfast features two eggs, porridge or cornflakes, toast and butter, tea and a banana. They also have dorm beds for Rs 85 (three to five beds per room) including meals. They've got some excellent full-size snooker and billiard tables in the lounge! If you're discreet it's possible to use them without being a resident. There is a second, similarly priced *YMCA* (tel 240260) at 42 Surendra Nath Banerjee Rd.

The *YWCA* (tel 297033), 1 Middleton Row, is also similarly priced but is for women only. It's a grand old place, airy, spotless and with a beautiful tennis court. Unfortunately, they won't take overnight guests any longer – minimum stay is one week – but it's excellent value at Rs 700 per week or Rs 2000 per month including all meals. One resident I spoke to, however, commented that 'only the breakfast is edible'. There's a 1 am curfew except by prior arrangement in writing!

Other Places The *Youth Hostel* (tel 672869) is at 10 Dr J B Ananda Dutta Lane in Howrah. It's small and homely; take a No 52 or 58 bus from Howrah railway station to Shamasri Cinema, or a No 63 bus to Khirertala. Dorm beds are Rs 10 and breakfast costs Rs 5.

Dum Dum Airport (tel 572611) has *rest rooms* if you're in transit. Check at the reservations desk in the terminal. Finally, Howrah and Sealdah railway stations both have *retiring rooms* with single and double rooms. Howrah also has dorm beds and Sealdah has air-con doubles.

Places to Stay – middle

At one time, the *Carlton Hotel* (tel 233009), 2 Chowringhee Place, was a very popular place to stay. It was obviously a fine old building in its heyday but sadly it has been allowed to deteriorate, though it's certainly no worse in this respect than many other budget hotels and it still exudes a degree of charm. It's also a bargain at Rs 150/225 for singles/doubles including all meals.

Up a notch is the *Astoria Hotel* (tel 241359), 6/2/3 Sudder St. This used to be a budget hotel but has been considerably upgraded and now costs Rs 80 for a single without air-con and Rs 275 to Rs 450 for an air-con double. All the rooms have a bath, colour TV and telephone, and breakfast is available (but no other meals) for Rs 14.

Places to Stay – top end

It's said often enough that 'getting there is half the fun'. Well, at the *Fairlawn Hotel* (tel 244460), 13A Sudder St, staying there is half the fun. It's a piece of Calcutta that should not be missed because here the Raj doesn't just live, it simply never ended. The terribly English couple who still run the hotel more than 40 years after independence look like they've been time-warped from Brighton in the '50s, and their establishment is spotless, packed with memorabilia and a positive delight.

The bearer carries your gear upstairs on his head, meal times are announced with

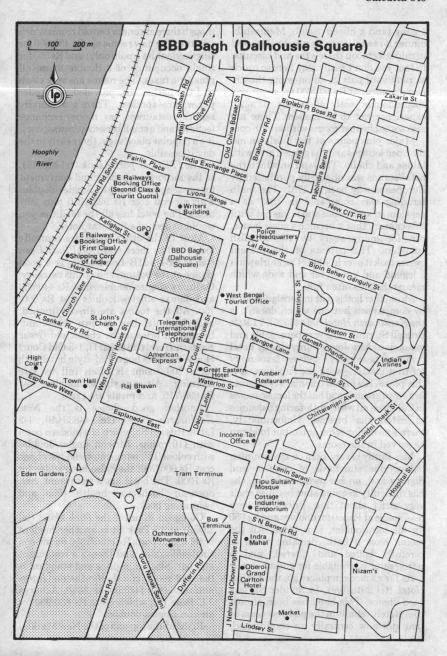

0   100   200 m

BBD Bagh (Dalhousie Square)

Zakaria St

Hooghly River

Clive Row

Netaji Subhash Rd

Old China Bazaar St

Biplabi R Bose Rd

Brabourne Rd

Ezra St

Rabindra Sarani

Fairlie Place

India Exchange Place

Strand Rd South

Strand Rd

E Railways Booking Office (Second Class & Tourist Quota)

Lyons Range

New CIT Rd

Writers Building

Kalighat St

GPO

Police Headquarters

BBD Bagh (Dalhousie Square)

Lal Bazaar St

E Railways Booking Office (First Class) / Shipping Corp of India

Hare St

Bipin Behari Ganguly St

Bentinck St

West Bengal Tourist Office

Church Lane

St John's Church

Telegraph & International Telephone Office

Church Lane

K Sankar Roy Rd

West Council House St

Old Court House St

Mangoe Lane

Weston St

Ganesh Chandra Ave

American Express

High Court

Great Eastern Hotel

Amber Restaurant

Princep St

Indian Airlines

Esplanade West

Town Hall

Raj Bhavan

Waterloo St

Dacres Lane

Chittaranjan Ave

Chandni Chauk St

Esplanade East

Income Tax Office

Eden Gardens

Tram Terminus

Lenin Sarani

Tipu Sultan's Mosque

Hospital St

Cottage Industries Emporium

Bus Terminus

S N Banerji Rd

Ochterlony Monument

Indra Mahal

Nizam's

Red Rd

Guru Nanak Sarani

Dufferin Rd

J Nehru Rd (Chowringhee Rd)

Oberoi Grand Carlton Hotel

Market

Lindsay St

a gong (and a hissed 'Sahib, Memsahib, dinner is ready' if you dare to be late) and in mid-afternoon there's tea and biscuits. In fact you don't really stay here so much as play your part in an on-going theatre performance. At Rs 480/600 for an air-con single/double with all meals, it's an experience not to be missed. There are also some cheaper rooms without air-con.

Major plus points at the Fairlawn are the open lounges and the garden area with tables and chairs. The land on which the hotel stands was originally purchased by Europeans way back in 1781. The main building was completed in 1803 as a gentleman's residence and it was not until this century that it became a guest house, run for many years by two English spinsters. The parents of the present owner took it over in 1936. The Fairlawn is a legend and known far and wide which means that it's often full.

Most other hotels pale into insignificance by comparison but one which doesn't is the *Kenilworth Hotel* (tel 445325), 7 Little Russell St, run by the very personable and loquacious Mrs Joyce Purdy. If any hotel compares favourably – and very favourably for that matter – with the Fairlawn, it is this place. It's an old colonial-style house in its own grounds and has the largest rooms in Calcutta, all with south-facing balconies to catch the breezes. Unfortunately, there's no dining room or bar but food can be served in the rooms.

Mrs Purdy is very keen on maintaining olde-worlde standards of comfort and dignity and, on her own admission, she has difficulty keeping staff because she's very strict about this. Prices are very reasonable at Rs 550 for doubles and Rs 650 for air-con doubles, plus taxes. All the rooms have a bath, drinking water is carefully boiled and filtered, and a refrigerator is available for guests' use.

As far as modern places go, the *Lytton Hotel* (tel 291875/9), 14 Sudder St, is a good choice. This hotel has been almost completely rebuilt in the past few years so that it's now centrally air-conditioned, though there are one or two old rooms which remain. The new rooms are Rs 450/600 for singles/doubles (room only) and Rs 550 for single occupancy of a double room, all plus 10% taxes. The rooms are very clean and the bathrooms, provided with toilet paper, are spotless. There's a laundry service, restaurant, bar, money exchange facilities and a small bookshop/newsagency. It's a popular place so get there early in the day if possible.

The *ITDC Airport Ashok* (tel 575111), at the airport, is modern and convenient for passengers in transit. Singles/doubles with air-con cost Rs 925/1050 plus 20% taxes. The hotel has all the facilities you would expect of a five-star hotel.

Most of the other hotels are centrally located. The three-star *Hotel Rutt Deen* (tel 443884), 21B Loudon St, is a good choice at the bottom end of this category. Ordinary singles/doubles cost Rs 440/600 and deluxe singles/doubles cost Rs 600/750. All the rooms are air-conditioned, and the hotel has its own restaurant. Similar in price is the classic old *Great Eastern Hotel* (tel 232311), 1-3 Old Court House St. This huge, Raj-style hotel with some 200 rooms is often full by late morning. Air-con singles/doubles cost Rs 630/715, and meals are extra.

Another good choice is the *New Kenilworth Hotel* (tel 448394/9), 1-2 Little Russell St, which is a modern hotel with 110 rooms. Air-con singles/doubles with colour TV, refrigerator and telephone cost Rs 600/700; they also have suites for Rs 1000. The hotel has a restaurant, bar, open-air barbecue, health club and swimming pool.

Going up in price, the *Park Hotel* (tel 29733) at 17 Park St is another modern hotel which costs Rs 1250/1350 for air-con singles/doubles, and there's a restaurant and bar. Similar in price and standard is the 212-room *Hotel Hindustan International* (tel 442394) at 235/1 Acharya J C Bose Rd, which costs Rs 830/930 for air-con singles/doubles.

Right at the top end of the New Market,

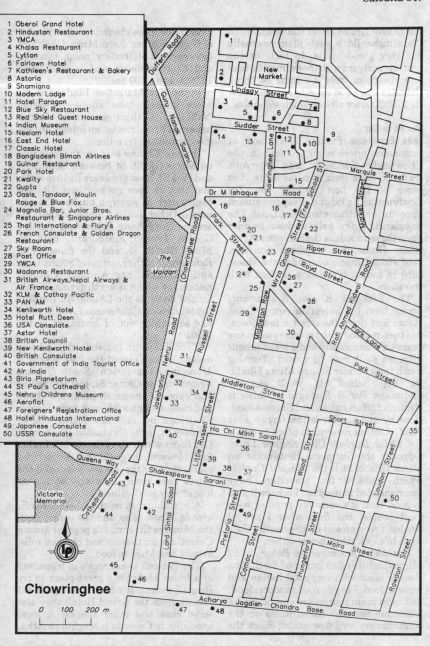

1 Oberoi Grand Hotel
2 Hindustan Restaurant
3 YMCA
4 Khalsa Restaurant
5 Lytton
6 Fairlawn Hotel
7 Kathleen's Restaurant & Bakery
8 Astoria
9 Shamiana
10 Modern Lodge
11 Hotel Paragon
12 Blue Sky Restaurant
13 Red Shield Guest House
14 Indian Museum
15 Neelam Hotel
16 East End Hotel
17 Classic Hotel
18 Bangladesh Biman Airlines
19 Gulnar Restaurant
20 Park Hotel
21 Kwality
22 Gupta
23 Oasis, Tandoor, Moulin
   Rouge & Blue Fox
24 Magnolia Bar, Junior Bros.
   Restaurant & Singapore Airlines
25 Thai International & Flury's
26 French Consulate & Golden Dragon
   Restaurant
27 Sky Room
28 Post Office
29 YWCA
30 Madonna Restaurant
31 British Airways, Nepal Airways &
   Air France
32 KLM & Cathay Pacific
33 PAN AM
34 Kenilworth Hotel
35 Hotel Rutt Deen
36 USA Consulate
37 Astor Hotel
38 British Council
39 New Kenilworth Hotel
40 British Consulate
41 Government of India Tourist Office
42 Air India
43 Birla Planetarium
44 St Paul's Cathedral
45 Nehru Childrens Museum
46 Aeroflot
47 Foreigners' Registration Office
48 Hotel Hindustan International
49 Japanese Consulate
50 USSR Consulate

Chowringhee

0   100   200 m

the *Oberoi Grand Hotel* (tel 292323), 15 Chowringhee Rd, is pretty plain externally but very grand inside. In fact, in the central courtyard with the swimming pool and the palm trees it's hard to think Calcutta can be so close by! Rooms cost Rs 1750/2000 for air-con singles/doubles.

Places to Eat

Less Expensive Finding good food at reasonable prices is no problem in the Chowringhee/Sudder St area. Everyone seems to have their own favourite, but some of the best include the *Taj Continental*, a good and cheap restaurant opposite the entrance to Stuart Lane. The popular *Blue Sky*, halfway down Sudder St on the same side as the Salvation Army Guest House, has excellent porridge, sandwiches, fruit juices and 'the finest curd in India'. It's always packed with travellers.

The Sikh-run *Khalsa Restaurant*, across from the Salvation Army Guest House and down the street a few doors, has been popular with travellers for many years but has recently had a lot of labour disputes so it may be closed. Turning south from Sudder St onto Mirza Ghalib St (Free School St), you'll see the *Shamiana Bar & Restaurant* which is clean and offers Indian and Chinese food; close by and similar is the *Gypsy Fast Food*. Another reasonable place to eat is the *Delhi Durbar*, Chowringhee Lane. Opposite the Shamiana Restaurant on Mirza Ghalib St is the *Moghul Durbar* which quite a few travellers have recommended in the past. Perhaps it still is good (and it's certainly popular with local people) but from what I saw, I wouldn't recommend it. The nearby *Cafe 48* didn't look much better either.

Kathleen's Restaurant & Bakery at 12 Mirza Ghalib St (left from Sudder St) is a classier place with very good Indian and western food. They do good tandoori food, and most main courses are around Rs 20. There are fantastic baked items on the confectionery level downstairs; check the amazing children's birthday cakes. Similar is *Gupta* further down Mirza Ghalib St towards Park St. It offers Indian, tandoori and Chinese dishes and is open from 10.30 am to 10.30 pm.

In the New Market on Lindsay St are some superb cake shops including *Nahoum*, a third-generation Jewish bakery in F row, run by 'an interesting old guy', wrote one traveller.

For good Chinese food, try the *How Hua* on Mirza Ghalib St between Sudder St and Park St. Most dishes are Rs 10 to Rs 15, and they've even got northern Chinese dishes such as *jiaozi*, a bit like Tibetan momo. Other similar Chinese restaurants are the *Hong Kong Restaurant* and the *Golden Dragon Restaurant*, both on Mirza Ghalib St, and the *Lung Fung Restaurant* at the junction of Stuart Lane and Marquis St. Another Chinese restaurant which is worth trying, if only for the decor, is the *Chung Wa Chinese Restaurant* on Chitteranjan Ave. It looks like something out of Shanghai in the 1930s!

If you like south Indian food – and who doesn't – then one of the best places is *Madonna Vegetarian South Indian Restaurant* on Camac St, just off Park St and opposite the small park. It's cheap and clean though a fair walk from Sudder St. Closer by, on Chowringhee end of Lindsay St, is the *Hindustan Restaurant* (1st floor) which also offers south Indian food. However, the quality has deteriorated markedly over the last few years and the prices have risen alarmingly so it's no longer very good value.

Also within easy reach of the Sudder St area is *Nizam's*, around the corner from the Minerva Cinema. It's popular among Calcuttans for mutton and chicken rolls, kebabs and Muslim food.

The Bengali sweet tooth is legendary and *Indra Mahal* is a great place to try Bengali sweets. It's on Chowringhee Rd just up from the Grand Hotel; they also serve chat and other snacks. A local speciality in Calcutta is Moghul paratha, but curiously it's all but impossible to find real Bengali food in Calcutta unless you dine at a Bengali's home.

More Expensive Park St is the place to go for a splurge though there are one or two cheap places in amongst the more expensive restaurants. There are a whole stack of restaurants to choose from, some with very un-Calcutta names like *Blue Fox* and *Moulin Rouge*! Whichever you decide to eat at, remember that any restaurant or bar which has live music will attract a surcharge of between 30% and 100% depending on the establishment. Make sure you ask about this before sitting down to eat.

One of the cheapest of the restaurants on this street is the *Kwality* at 17 Park St, beside the Park Hotel. It has virtually the same menu as any other Kwality restaurant you'll find in India. The *Tandoor*, on the same side of the street, appears to pay more attention to its decor than it does to the quality of the food which it serves. It isn't cheap and the food is only average. Better is the *Sky Room*, over the junction with Mirza Ghalib St, which offers Indian and European food but isn't licenced. Expect to pay around Rs 45 plus taxes for a meal. The *Magnolia Bar* on Park St is recommended for ice cream.

One of the best restaurants on Park St is the *Gulnar Restaurant* next to the Park Hotel. The food is excellent but quite expensive and you'll have to pay a surcharge if, as is usual, there's a band playing. It's very popular with relatively affluent local people. The restaurant is open from 5.30 to 11.30 pm and is licenced (last drinks 11 pm).

The *New Kenilworth Hotel*, Little Russell St, may be worth checking out if you'd like to eat barbecued food out in the open air.

Right in the centre of town at 11 Waterloo St (the narrow street that runs by the Great Eastern Hotel) is the *Amber Hotel & Restaurant*. The food is excellent and the place is highly regarded by residents of Calcutta – so highly regarded, in fact, that you may have to reserve a table in advance or be prepared to wait. Despite it's name, there is no hotel here.

At the *Fairlawn Hotel* on Sudder St food is English style, but surprisingly good. If you're staying here all meals are included in the room tariff. If you're not, and would like to experience that old-style service, meals can be arranged.

Entertainment

Quite a few of the larger hotels have discos which go on until early morning. The best of them is probably the *Pink Panther* at the Oberoi Grand Hotel but it's going to cost you Rs 55 to get in as a nonresident, and all the drinks cost around double their normal price. The waiters also have a habit of 'forgetting' to bring your change, so make sure you examine the bill closely and point out 'lapses of memory' quickly.

Much less expensive drinks can be found at the *Sun Set Bar* at the Lytton Hotel, Sudder St. This bar is surprisingly popular with travellers, young expatriate workers and local young people involved on the fringes of the tourist trade. It's a friendly place and they have a good music system. Similar is the open-air bar in the forecourt of the *Fairlawn Hotel* where there's always an interesting crowd.

There are plenty of other, much more basic bars, some with bizarre names like *Off cum On Rambo Bar*! (Mirza Ghalib St).

Thursday is a 'dry' day in Calcutta and the only places where you can get alcoholic drinks are in the four and five-star hotels plus one other place which we'll leave you to discover for yourself but it's not hard to find.

Things to Buy

Calcutta has the usual government emporiums and quite a good Central Cottage Industries Emporium at 7 Chowringhee. There are numerous interesting shops along Chowringhee selling everything from carpets to handicrafts. The shops along the entrance arcade to the Oberoi Grand Hotel are particularly interesting. There's also an amazing variety of pavement vendors selling everything imaginable.

Amid this melee are many runners from other shops, particularly the New Market, looking for customers. Naturally, 'their' shop is only 'just round the corner', yet rarely is this true. If you follow them, it's going to take up quite a bit of your time and the prices of the goods which you're invited to examine will be relatively high. After all, it's a long way back and a lot of wasted time for them to find another punter.

New Market, formerly Hogg Market, is Calcutta's premier place for bargain shopping despite part of it being burnt out in late '85. Here you can find a little of almost everything, and it is always worth an hour or so wandering around. A particular bargain, if you're flying straight home

from Calcutta, is caneware. This is ridiculously cheap compared to prices in the west and, of course, very light if rather bulky.

The market is the place to buy and sell, as long as those 'Singapore goodies' are not recorded in your passport. Whisky, cigarettes, watches, Walkmans and cameras are in great demand but the prices offered for optical and electronic goods are nothing to write home about. The market is also a very popular place to change money (at a small premium over the bank rate). If nobody approaches you, the uniformed porters will know where to find what you want. The rate for US dollars here is as good as in Delhi.

There's another good street market (mainly clothes) along Lenin Sarani in the evenings.

Down Sudder St or in the lanes off there, those in search of highs derived from the plant kingdom can expect to be offered a tola (about 12 grams) of the best

Lindsay Street, Calcutta

resin for less than Rs 100. Don't smoke openly; Uncle Sam doesn't like it and neither do the Indian authorities.

Getting There & Away

Air Calcutta is a good place for competitive air fares to South-East Asia, and there are also flights to Kathmandu. You can expect to pick up tickets to Bangkok for around US$100 and to Kathmandu for around US$75 – payable in Indian rupees with bank certificates. Flights are usually with Indian Airlines, Thai International, Royal Nepal Airlines or Bangladesh Biman.

On internal routes, Calcutta is connected by air with all the major centres and is the departure point for flights to the north-east region, Darjeeling and Port Blair in the Andaman Islands. Other destinations served from Calcutta include Delhi, Bombay, Madras, Patna, Hyderabad, Bangalore and Lucknow.

Calcutta's Indian Airlines office is fully computerised and it's a breeze buying tickets. There's a tourist counter which rarely has anyone in front of it so it's very quick. Even refunds or a change of flight date are no hassle. Credit cards are also accepted but using them attracts a surcharge so it's better to pay in travellers' cheques.

Vayudoot fly from Calcutta to Patna (Rs 485), Shillong (Rs 475) and many other places in the north-east.

Bus The bus services from Calcutta are not as good an alternative as they are from a number of other Indian cities. It's generally better to travel from Calcutta by train, although there are several useful bus routes to other towns in West Bengal.

Buses generally depart from the bus stand area at the north end of the Maidan, near Chowringhee, but there are a number of private companies which have their own terminals.

The only buses which travellers use with any regularity are those from Calcutta to Siliguri and New Jalpaiguri (for Darjeeling). The fare for this trip is Rs 82 and the journey takes 10 to 12 hours but it's much rougher than going by train.

Train Calcutta has two major railway stations. Howrah, on the west bank of the Hooghly River, handles most trains into the city, but if you're going north to Darjeeling or the north-east region then the trains leave from Sealdah station on the east side of the Hooghly. Beware of pickpockets and people of similar inclination at Howrah railway station.

The railway booking office for 2nd-class and tourist-quota bookings is on the 1st floor at 6 Fairlie Place. It's fully computerised and a breeze buying a ticket – they'll tell you instantly the state of the booking in any class on any day and make a reservation for you on the spot. This office is open daily from 9 am to 4 pm except between 1 and 1.30 pm. The 1st-class bookings office is at 14 Strand Rd.

Trains to Delhi take around 17 hours for the 1441-km trip and cost Rs 453/115 in 1st/2nd class. The 678-km trip to Varanasi takes from 12 hours and costs Rs 257/69 in 1st/2nd class. For Darjeeling, the 566-km trip takes about 12 hours from Calcutta (Sealdah station) to New Jalpaiguri or Siliguri, where you take a bus or the toy train (if running) up to the hill station. The fares from Calcutta to New Jalpaiguri are Rs 215/59 in 1st/2nd class.

It's a long way from Calcutta to Bombay, the 1968-km trip takes 36 hours even on the fast mail train. Fares are Rs 553/137 in 1st/2nd class. The trip to Madras is nearly as long – 33 hours to cover 1662 km at a cost of Rs 484/121 in 1st/2nd class. During and soon after the monsoon season, the railway line can be cut off by the Godavari or Krishna rivers in north Andhra Pradesh. If this is the case the Calcutta to Madras service will make a loop inland and the trip takes a good deal longer. The normal service to Madras runs down the coast all the way, passing through Bhubaneswar in Orissa en route.

Ship See the Andaman & Nicobar Islands section for details on the shipping services from Calcutta.

Getting Around

Airport Transport An airport bus costing Rs 15 runs by the Indian Airlines office and down Chowringhee Rd past Sudder St on its way in from the airport. On the way out to the airport it only departs from the Indian Airlines office. A taxi costs Rs 50 from the airport to the centre of the city so long as you pay for it at the prepaid taxi kiosk at the airport. In the opposite direction expect to pay Rs 60 and often more. All the same, shared between four people, that's about as cheap as the bus.

There is a public minibus from BBD Bagh to the airport for about Rs 2. If your endurance knows no limits you can get to the airport from Howrah station on a No 11A and then a No 30B bus, or from the Esplanade bus terminal on a No S10 bus for just Rs 1.

Incidentally, Calcutta's airport takes its name, Dum Dum Airport, from the fact that this was the site of the Dum Dum Barracks, where the explosive dumdum bullet, banned after the Boer War, was once made.

Bus Calcutta's bus system is hopelessly crowded. It's an edifying sight to watch the double-decker buses come across Howrah Bridge during the rush hour. Fares are Rs 0.50 to Rs 1.30. Take a No 5 or 6 bus between Howrah station and Sudder St; ask for the Indian Museum. There is a secondary private minibus service, rather faster and slightly more expensive, with fares from Rs 0.75 to Rs 2. You need to be a midget to ride in these buses though. Beware of pickpockets in any of Calcutta's public transport.

Tram Calcutta has a public tram service but the trams are like sardine tins. Take a

No 12A from Howrah to the Indian Museum. Standard fares are Rs 0.35 in the front, Rs 0.30 in the back. On Sunday it is possible to buy a day-trip ticket from the terminus for Rs 1. They're quiet – well, quiet by Calcutta standards – on that day.

Underground Calcutta's underground railway system is being built at minimum cost and in maximum time almost totally by hand. The soggy soil makes digging holes by hand no fun at all, and after each monsoon it takes half the time to the next monsoon simply to drain out what has already been dug. Nevertheless, after many delays the first stretch along Chowringhee Rd is now open, but only Monday to Friday from 9 to 11 am and 3 to 8 pm. The standard fare is Rs 1. Eventually the Metro Railway will run from Tollygunge station in the south to Dum Dum station in the north.

Taxi Calcutta's taxi drivers are renowned not only for their passion for strikes, which in turn causes the buses to be even worse than usual, but also for their belligerent refusal to use the meter. Officially, the fare starts at Rs 8 and goes up by Rs 0.25 increments, but that's all in theory. In practice you have to agree on a price before setting off and that will always be more than it should cost. If there's a group of up to four of you then perhaps it doesn't matter since you share the cost. On your own, however, it's an expensive form of transport.

Rickshaw Calcutta is the last bastion of the human-powered rickshaw. The rickshaw-wallahs would not accept the new-fangled cycle-rickshaws when they were introduced elsewhere in India. After all, who could afford a bicycle? Most can't even afford their rickshaw and have to rent it from someone who takes the lion's share of the fares.

You may find it morally unacceptable to have a man pulling you around in a carriage – and these men are usually very thin, unhealthy and die early – but Calcutta's citizens are quite happy to use them. The only compensation is that they wouldn't have a job if people didn't use them and, as a tourist, you naturally pay more than local people. These sort of rickshaws only exist in central Calcutta,

though. Across the river in Howrah or in other Calcutta suburbs cycle-rickshaws are available.

Bicycle The Blue Sky restaurant on Sudder St rents bicycles at Rs 2 an hour or Rs 10 per day.

Travellers' Notebook _____

Off to the Races
Tired of temples? Had it with handicrafts? Sick of souvenirs? Well, if you're in Calcutta during the monsoons the place to head for is the racetrack.

As befits the sport of kings, the raj racecourse is regally resplendent and although it's seen better days, like most things in India, it still retains a slight air of grandeur. From the top of the main grandstand there's a magnificent vista across the course to the Victoria Memorial and the skyscrapers at Chowringhee. On a bright afternoon with the grass still lush from the rain and the horses pounding up the straight, the squalor of the city becomes just a faint memory.

It's Rs 14 to get into the main grandstand area which also gives you access to the parade ring. There are foodstalls, infinitely better than the garbage they serve at British racetracks, a bar, where you can sit and watch an instant video replay of the action and a win/place totalisator where for Rs 10 you can back your selection. For the more serious punter there's the betting ring where the Indian bookmakers, one of whom goes under the wonderful name of T U Shark, are ready to part you with your cash.

The monsoon season has 15 meetings stretching from 1 July until 9 October. If you can't make it to Calcutta there are also racetracks at Mysore, Hyderabad and Pune where the Indian Derby is run on 14 October, and the season goes to the end of the month.

So, even if racing isn't your great interest, it's always pleasant to have a different day out and meet Indians who aren't trying to sell you something. And finally, where else in the world would you get to pick the winner of the Prawn Curry Handicap over 1100 metres – Rattan at 11/10 favourite.

Michael Bowman, England

The Rats of Calcutta
A special tourist attraction in Calcutta has to be the resident rat population at the Maidan, near the corner of West Council House St and Esplanade East and West. Literally thousands of these huge rodents have made the corner of the park their home. It's quite a sight to see, especially the reaction of the local businessmen at lunch.

Paul O'Brien, Australia

West Bengal

Population: 66 million
Area: 87,853 square km
Capital: Calcutta
Main language: Bengali

At the time of partition Bengal was split into East and West Bengal. East Bengal became the eastern wing of Pakistan and later, with the disintegration of that country, Bangladesh. West Bengal became a state of India with its largest city, Calcutta, the capital. The state is long and narrow, running from the delta of the Ganges River system at the Bay of Bengal in the south to the heights of the Himalaya at Darjeeling in the north.

There is not a great deal of interest in the state apart from these two extremes – Calcutta, with its bewildering miasma of noise, culture, confusion and squalor at one end; and Darjeeling, serene and peaceful, at the other. At least, this was true until the Gurkhas began agitating for a separate state. Nevertheless the intrepid traveller will find a number of places to consider visiting, either south of Calcutta on the Bay of Bengal or north along the route to Darjeeling.

The agitation of the past three years in the Darjeeling District has virtually stopped, with the agreement between the central government and Gheising, head of the Gorkhaland National Liberation Front, for Darjeeling to be a Nepali-language administrative unit within West Bengal. The Marxist West Bengal government is not too overjoyed about this, but at least the burnings and riots have stopped, and the massive Central Reserve Police presence has decreased. Because of the unrest Darjeeling has been relatively empty of Indian tourists, and is now even more peaceful than usual.

David Bradley, Australia

Permits

Before you can visit Darjeeling, Kalimpong or Sikkim, special permits are required.

Only in the case of Darjeeling are certain exceptions made to this rule. All these places are in what the Indian government refers to as 'sensitive border regions' and the rationale behind the permit requirements is to keep track of who goes there. Anyone having the slightest familiarity with Indian bureaucracy will know what a farce this is. As far as Darjeeling and Kalimpong are concerned it's merely a formality, but it keeps plenty of people employed pushing pens and wielding rubber stamps. With Sikkim, obtaining a permit is more involved and you must plan ahead.

Darjeeling The only exception to the permit rule is if you travel by air from Calcutta to Bagdogra (the nearest airport to Darjeeling), return the same way, and do not stay in Darjeeling more than 15 days from the date of arrival at Bagdogra. If you do this you can have your passport endorsed at Bagdogra airport for a visit to Darjeeling.

If you intend to go there by bus or train then you must obtain a permit. You can get these from any of the following places:

Indian embassies, consulates and high commissions outside India.

Ministry of Home Affairs, Government of India, North Block, New Delhi.

Home Political Department, 1st floor, Block 2, Writers' Building, BBD Bag, Calcutta.

Any Foreigners' Registration Office in India. In Delhi the office is in Hans Bhavan; in Calcutta it's at 237 Acharya J C Bose Rd.

There is one form to complete, no photographs are required and the permit is issued free of charge within 24 hours in India. If you apply outside India then three photographs are needed. Permits allow for a stay of 15 days, which *may* be extendable in Darjeeling at the Foreigners' Registration Office (tel 2261), Laden La Rd. If extensions are being granted no photographs are required, no fee is charged and they are issued while you wait. On first application you are given what you ask for, so always ask for the maximum number of days (15) and, if you want to visit Kalimpong, then write that on the application form too.

If you're planning on trekking to Sandakphu and/or Phalut, a separate special permit is required – again obtainable from the Foreigners' Registration Office in Darjeeling. If you flew into Bagdogra airport then you are exempt from this requirement on condition that you report your intentions to the Darjeeling office 24 hours before leaving.

Don't expect to get through to Darjeeling without a permit. Inspectors at New Jalpaiguri/Siliguri wait for every train arriving from Calcutta and want to see foreigners' permits. It's a long way to go only to be refused. On the other hand, permits for Kalimpong can be obtained while you wait as a rule once you've got as far as Darjeeling.

Kalimpong A permit for Darjeeling does not automatically entitle you to visit Kalimpong. To go there you must obtain a separate endorsement on your Darjeeling permit. Ask for it at the same time you apply for the Darjeeling permit, or get one

from the Foreigners' Registration Office in Darjeeling. A three-day visit is normally allowed. If you want longer, get authorisation before you go.

Sikkim There are no exceptions to the permit requirements for Sikkim regardless of your mode of transport. You need to apply at least three months in advance of your proposed visit, either to an Indian embassy/consulate/high commission outside India or to the Deputy Secretary, Ministry of Home Affairs (F-l), North

West Bengal

Block, New Delhi 110001. You won't get this permit any faster by applying in person at the New Delhi office. There are three forms to complete, three photographs are required and you have to state the exact days on which you want to visit. No fee is charged for the permit.

If you apply via an embassy/consulate/high commission, what you will receive is a letter which states that 'the Government of India has no objection to your visit' and that you can pick up your permit from the Deputy Commissioner's Office, Darjeeling (at the junction of Cutchery Rd and Cart Rd next to the Loreto Convent). The initial permitted length of stay varies between two and four days but is extendable in Gangtok at the Foreigners' Regional Registration Office. Extensions are a mere formality and issued on the spot – just tell them where you want to go and how much time you require. No photographs are required and no fee charged for extensions. Your permit will be collected on leaving Sikkim at the Rangpo checkpost.

Permits allow foreigners to go to Gangtok, Rumtek and Phodang. If you want to go to Pemayangtse you can only do this if you are travelling in a group with a liaison officer. The same applies if you want to go on a trek to Dzongri.

SOUTH OF CALCUTTA
Down the Hooghly
The Hooghly River is a very difficult river to navigate due to the constantly shifting shoals and sandbanks. Hooghly River pilots have to continuously stay in touch with the river to keep track of the frequent changes in its course. When the Hooghly Bridge was constructed it was feared that it would cause severe alterations to the river's flow patterns. The tide rises and falls 3½ metres at Calcutta and there is a bore, which reaches two metres in height, at the time of the rising tide. Because of the navigational difficulties and the silting up of the Hooghly, Calcutta is losing its importance as a port.

Falta, 43 km downriver, was the site of a Dutch factory. The British retreated here in 1756 when Calcutta was captured by Suraj-ud-daula. It was also from here that Clive recaptured Calcutta. Just below Falta the Damodar joins the Hooghly.

Bengali children's poem

শিব সদাগর

এপার গঙ্গা ওপার গঙ্গা মধ্যিখানে চর।
তারি মধ্যে বসে আছেন শিব সদাগর॥
শিব গেলেন শ্বশুরবাড়ি বসতে দিল পিঁড়ে;
জলপান করতে দিল শালিধানের চিঁড়ে।
শালিধানের চিঁড়ে নয় রে বিন্নিধানের খই—
মোটা মোটা সবরি কলা কাগমারি দই॥

The Rupnarain also joins the Hooghly and a little up this river is Tamluk, an important Buddhist centre over 1000 years ago. The James & Mary Shoal, the most dangerous on the Hooghly, is just above the point where the Rupnarain River enters. It takes its name from a ship which was wrecked here in 1694.

Diamond Harbour

A resort 51 km south of Calcutta by road, Diamond Harbour is at the point where the Hooghly turns south and flows into the open sea. Launches run from here to Sagar Island.

Places to Stay Accommodation in the *Sagarika Tourist Lodge* can be booked through the West Bengal Tourism Corporation in Calcutta.

Haldia

The new port of Haldia is 96 km south of Calcutta, on the west bank of the Hooghly. The port was constructed to try to regain the shipping lost from Calcutta's silting problems. There are regular buses between Calcutta and Haldia.

Sagar Island

At the mouth of the Hooghly, this island is considered the point where the Ganges joins the sea, and a great three-day bathing festival takes place here early each January. A lighthouse marks the south-west tip of the island but navigation is still difficult for a further 65 km south.

Digha

Close to the border with Orissa, 185 km south-east of Calcutta on the Bay of Bengal, Digha is a beach resort with a six-km-long beach. There are daily buses between Calcutta and Digha operated by the CSTC. The trip takes about six hours and buses depart from 7 am. The Chandaneshwar Shiva temple is just across the border in Orissa, eight km from Digha.

Places to Stay There is a *Tourist Lodge* (tel Digha 54/5) with rooms and meals at reasonable prices. Digha has a wide range of other accommodation, including new and old *Tourist Cottages* and a *Youth Hostel* with dorm beds at Rs 10 (Rs 6 for members). The *Hotel Sea Hawk* (tel Digha 35) has a range of rooms, with or without air-con, from Rs 25 and dorm beds for Rs 15 per bed. All these places can be booked through the West Bengal Tourist Development Corporation in Calcutta (tel 288271). Digha also has a number of private hotels and boarding houses.

Bakkhali

Also known as Fraserganj, this is another beach resort, 132 km from Calcutta and on the east side of the Hooghly. Accommodation here can again be reserved through the West Bengal Tourist Corporation. From here you can get boats to the small island of Jambu Dwip to the south-west.

Sunderbans

Spreading across the border into Bangladesh, the Sunderbans is the forest at the delta where the Ganges meets the sea. Royal Bengal tigers can still be seen here, particularly on Lothian Island and Chamta Block. Over 2500 square km of this estuarine forest has been declared a tiger sanctuary but there are many other animals including deer, wild boar, monkeys, snakes and crocodiles. The best time to visit is from September to May. Short bus/launch tours can be arranged with the West Bengal Tourist Corporation, otherwise access is fairly difficult.

NORTH OF CALCUTTA
Chandernagore

Also known as Chandarnagar, this was one of the French enclaves in India which were handed over at the same time as Pondicherry in 1951. On the banks of the Hooghly, 39 km north of Calcutta, are several buildings dating from the French era. The first French settlers arrived here in 1673 and the place later became an important trading post, although it was taken by the British during conflicts with the French.

Hooghly

This historic town is 41 km north of Calcutta and very close to two other interesting sites – Chinsura and Bandel. Hooghly was an important trading port long before Calcutta rose to prominence. In 1537 the Portuguese set up a factory here; before that time Satgaon, 10 km further north, had been the main port of Bengal but was abandoned because of the river silting up. There are still a few traces of Satgaon's former grandeur, including a ruined mosque.

The Portuguese were kicked out of Hooghly in 1632 by Shah Jahan, after a lengthy siege, but were allowed to return a year later. The British East India Company also established a factory here in 1651. The Imambara, built in 1836, with its gateway flanked by lofty minarets, is the main sight. Across the road is an older Imambara, dating from 1776-77.

Chinsura

Only a km or so south of Hooghly, Chinsura was exchanged by the Dutch for the British-held Indonesian island of Sumatra in 1825. The Dutch Church is octagonal and dates from 1678. There is a Dutch cemetery with many old tombs a km to the west.

Bandel

A couple of km north of Hooghly, Bandel is 43 km north of Calcutta. A Portuguese church and monastery was built here in 1599 but destroyed by Shah Jahan in 1640. It was later rebuilt.

Getting There & Away Get off the train at Naihati and take the hourly shuttle service across the river.

Bansberia

A further four km north of Bandel,

Bansberia has the Vasudev Temple with interesting terracotta wall carvings and the Hanseswari Temple.

Jairambati & Kamarpukur

Ramakrishna was born in Kamarpukur, 143 km north-west of Calcutta, and there is a Ramakrishna Mission Ashram here. Ramakrishna was a 19th-century Hindu saint who did much to rejuvenate Hinduism when it was going through a period of decline during the British rule. Jairambati, five km away, is another important point for Ramakrishna devotees.

Shantiniketan

Near Bolpur, the Visvabharati University is here. The brilliant and prolific poet, writer and nationalist Rabindranath Tagore (1861-1941) founded a school here in 1901. It later developed into a university with emphasis on humanity's relation with nature – many classes are conducted in the open air. Tagore went on to win the Nobel Prize in 1913 and is credited with introducing India's historical and cultural greatness to the modern world. In 1915, Tagore was awarded a knighthood by the British but he surrendered it in 1919 as a protest against the Amritsar Massacre.

Places to Stay There is a small *University Guest House* as well as railway *retiring rooms* at Bolpur station.

Nabadwip & Mayapur

Nabadwip is an ancient centre of Sanskrit culture, 114 km north of Calcutta. There are many temples here and across the river at Mayapur; both are important pilgrimage centres and Mayapur is a centre for the Iskon (Hare Krishna) movement.

Plassey

In 1757 Clive defeated Suraj-ud-daula and his French supporters here, a turning point in British influence in India. Plassey is 172 km north of Calcutta.

Murshidabad (population 20,000)

This was once an important trading town between inland India and the port of Calcutta, 221 km south. Today it's a quiet town in central Bengal, a chance to see typical rural Bengali life. This was also once the home of Suraj-ud-daula, the local sultan who put Calcutta's British residents into that infamous 'black hole'. A year later the British defeated his forces at Plassey and nominated a more reliable successor.

They built him a large Italian-style palace, the Nizamat Kila, which was

Rabindranath Tagore

completed in 1837 and still stands beside the Bhagirathi River (closed Fridays). Cross the river in a small boat to see Suraj's tomb at Khusbagh, the 'Garden of Happiness', where the nawabs are buried. Opposite it is the Moti Jhil, or 'Pearl Lake', a fine place to view the sunsets. There are a number of other interesting buildings and ruins, and this is a notable silk-producing area.

Places to Stay Near the palace in Murshidabad is the cheap *Hotel Historical*. If it's full you can sleep on the roof. Meals are also cheap. The *Tourist Lodge* in Berhampore is cleaner and more reliable, but it's 12 km away by bus. Rooms can be booked through the West Bengal Tourism Corporation in Calcutta and there is also a dorm.

Getting There & Away There are half a dozen trains daily from Sealdah station in Calcutta and the trip takes six hours.

English Bazaar

North of the Ganges on the route to Darjeeling, this town has a population of 85,000. Nearby are the interesting remains of several ancient Bengali capital cities.

This is a restricted area, but permits are easily obtainable in Calcutta.

Places to Stay The *Malda Tourist Lodge* charges Rs 32 for a double room. The railway *retiring rooms* cost Rs 36.

Gaur

Seven km south of English Bazaar, this was the capital of Bengal in the pre-Muslim days. The large city stood at the junction of the Ganges and Mahananda rivers and was once extensively fortified. There are still many remains of the fortifications, mosques and towers and, as legend has it, a footprint of Mohammed. Oh well, there's another legend that Jesus' 40 days in the wilderness were spent attaining enlightenment in India.

Old Malda

At the junction of the Kalindri and Mahananda rivers, this was once an important port for the former Muslim capital of Pandua. An English factory was established here in 1656 but moved to English Bazaar in 1771.

Pandua

Gaur once alternated with Pandua as the seat of power. Many of Pandua's now ruined buildings were constructed from material taken from Gaur, which accounts for its strange blend of architectural styles. Pandua is 11 km from Old Malda and 18 km from English Bazaar.

SILIGURI & NEW JALPAIGURI

This crowded, sprawling, noisy place is the departure point for visits to Darjeeling, Kalimpong or Sikkim. Siliguri is a real boom town as the major trade centre for the north-east, Darjeeling, Sikkim and the east of Nepal, so it's packed with trucks and buses and not a pleasant place to stay for a moment more than necessary. New Jalpaiguri, the main railway junction, is a couple of km south of Siliguri though there's effectively no break in the urban sprawl between the two places.

Information & Orientation

Siliguri is very confusing at first, especially if you arrive at night. New Jalpaiguri is the main railway junction, nothing more. The distance is about five km from there to Siliguri Town station and another three or four km on to Siliguri Junction station. You can catch the toy train (if it is running) to Darjeeling from any of these three stations. The bus stand is about halfway between Siliguri Town railway and Siliguri Junction railway station opposite the Airview Hotel.

Siliguri is essentially just one north-south main road. There's a tourist information counter at the New Jalpaiguri station.

Places to Stay

If you arrive in Siliguri too late to continue straight on to Darjeeling, there are numerous places to stay. There are good *retiring rooms* at Rs 24 a double at New Jalpaiguri station but they're often full. Dorm beds are Rs 12.

Just past the Siliguri Town station and to the left is the *Rajasthan Guest House* (tel 21815), singles/doubles with bathroom cost Rs 65/120 including bed tea. There are some bathless doubles for Rs 100. It's a fairly modern hotel and fine for staying overnight.

Continuing along Hill Cart Rd, there is a string of places including, just before the river and opposite the bus stand, the *Airview Hotel*. It's a typical big Indian hotel with lots of rooms – most of them very grubby and dirty. Singles cost from Rs 22, doubles Rs 45 or Rs 55.

Just north of the Airview you cross a river, and the old *Tourist Lodge* is on the right, just before the Siliguri Junction station. Here dorm beds cost Rs 24, and doubles are from Rs 45. Further along is the larger and newer *Mainak Tourist Lodge* (tel 20986), also run by the West Bengal Tourism Development Corporation. Rooms are Rs 105/140 and Rs 170/240 with air-con. Similar in price is the *Hotel Gateway* (tel 23539), Sevoke Rd about one km from Siliguri Junction station. It's a large hotel with 60 rooms, all with bathrooms. Singles/doubles cost Rs 110/180 and Rs 200/290 with air-con.

The best hotel in Siliguri is *Sinclair's Hotel* (tel 22674/5) which is a three-star hotel but quite a distance from the railway station. Singles/doubles cost Rs 155/225, with air-con they cost Rs 360/500 plus 15% taxes. All rooms have a bath with hot water and the hotel has its own restaurant, bar, swimming pool and foreign exchange facilities.

Places to Eat

There are several places to eat along Hill Cart Rd, including the *Amber* and *Saluja* restaurants. For Punjabi food, there's the *Shere Punjab Hotel & Restaurant*. You can get a beer at all of these places as well. The *Airview* has a restaurant and there's a good vegetarian restaurant at the *Rajasthan Guest House*.

Getting There & Away

Air Bagdogra is the airport near Siliguri with flights to Patna, Delhi, Calcutta and towns in the north-east. See the Darjeeling section for details.

There is also a daily helicopter service between Bagdogra and Gangtok (Rs 375) which connects with the flights to and from Calcutta. See the Sikkim section for details.

Bus There are several private bus companies as well as the State Transport Corporation which operate overnight bus services between Calcutta and Siliguri at a cost of Rs 82. Buses can be booked in Darjeeling, in Calcutta at the North Bengal State Transport Corporation (tel 231854) at the Esplanade bus stand, or in

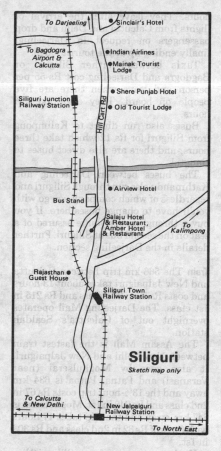

Siliguri at the bus stand (tel 20531). These buses are faster than the train (10 to 12 hours) but choose your company carefully as the buses vary in quality.

Some companies also run buses from Siliguri to Patna and vice versa.

Buses to Darjeeling are much faster than the toy train either from Siliguri or from Bagdogra. From Siliguri there are buses all day which cost Rs 16 and take 3½ hours. From Bagdogra airport there are West Bengal Tourist Corporation buses which do the run for Rs 35 and take 3½ hours. They leave after the arrival of flights from Calcutta and Delhi and drop passengers on request in Darjeeling, finally ending up at the tourist lodge.

Taxis between either Siliguri or Bagdogra and Darjeeling cost Rs 55 per person and leave when there are five people on board. They also take 3½ hours.

Buses also run direct to Kalimpong from Siliguri for Rs 12 which take three hours, and there are also direct buses to Gangtok.

The buses between Darjeeling and Kathmandu also run through Siliguri and regardless of which company you go with you'll have to change buses here. If you buy a through ticket you're assured of a seat on the second bus at Siliguri. Further details in the Darjeeling section.

Train The 566-km trip between Calcutta and New Jalpaiguri takes about 13 hours and costs Rs 59 in 2nd class and Rs 215 in 1st class. The Darjeeling Mail operates overnight out of Calcutta's Sealdah station.

The Assam Mail is the fastest train between New Delhi and New Jalpaiguri. It also goes by Moghulserai (near Varanasi) and Patna. Patna is 634 km away and the 13½-hour trip costs Rs 67 in 2nd class and Rs 242 in 1st. Moghulserai is 847 km away and the trip takes 17 hours with fares of Rs 82 in 2nd class and Rs 303 in 1st.

If the toy train from Siliguri/New Jalpaiguri to Darjeeling is running, it's possible to buy through tickets to Darjeeling all the way from your point of origin. For details on the toy train see the Darjeeling section.

Getting Around

A cycle-rickshaw from New Jalpaiguri station to Siliguri Town costs about Rs 5; to Siliguri Junction the fare is about Rs 10.

DARJEELING (population 60,000)

Straddling a ridge at 2123 metres and surrounded by tea plantations on all sides, Darjeeling has been a very popular hill station since the British established it as an R&R centre for its troops in the mid-1800s. These days people come here to escape from the heat, humidity and hassle of the north Indian plain. You get an indication of how popular Darjeeling is from the 60 or so hotels recognised by the West Bengal Tourist Development Corporation and the scores of others which don't come up to its requirements. Here you will find yourself surrounded by mountain people from all over the eastern Himalaya who have come here to work, to trade or – in the case of the Tibetans – as refugees.

Outside of the monsoon season (June to September) the views over the mountains to the snowy peaks of Kanchenjunga and down to the swollen rivers in the valley bottoms are magnificent. Darjeeling is a fascinating place where you can see Buddhist monasteries, visit a tea plantation and see how the tea is processed, go for a ride on the chairlift (if it's operating), spend days hunting for bargains in colourful markets and handicraft shops, or go trekking to high-altitude spots near the border with Sikkim.

Like many places in the Himalaya, half the fun is in getting there and Darjeeling has the unique attraction of the famous toy train. This miniature train loops and switchbacks its way up the steep mountainsides from New Jalpaiguri to Darjeeling.

History

Until the beginning of the 18th century the whole of the area between the present borders of Sikkim and the plains of Bengal, including Darjeeling and Kalimpong, belonged to the rajas of Sikkim. In 1706 they lost Kalimpong to the Bhutanese, and control of the remainder was wrested from them by the Gurkhas who invaded Sikkim in 1780, following consolidation of the latter's rule in Nepal.

These annexations by the Gurkhas, however, brought them into conflict with the British East India Company. A series of wars were fought between the two parties, eventually leading to the defeat of the Gurkhas and the ceding of all the land they had taken from the Sikkimese to the East India Company. Part of this territory was restored to the rajas of Sikkim and the country's sovereignty guaranteed by the British in return for British control over any disputes which arose with neighbouring states.

One such dispute in 1828 led to the dispatch of two British officers to this area, and it was during their fact-finding tour that they spent some time at Darjeeling (then called Dorje Ling – 'Place of Thunderbolts'). The officers were quick to appreciate Darjeeling's value as a site for a sanatorium and hill station and as the key to a pass into Nepal and Tibet. The officers' observations were reported to the authorities in Calcutta and a pretext was eventually found to pressure the raja into granting the site to the British in return for an annual stipend of Rs 3000 (raised to Rs 6000 in 1846).

This transfer, however, rankled with the Tibetans who regarded Sikkim as a vassal state. Darjeeling's rapid development as a trading centre and tea-growing area in a key position along the trade route leading from Sikkim to the plains of India began to make a considerable impact on the fortunes of the lamas and leading merchants of Sikkim. Tensions arose and in 1849 two British travellers, Sir Joseph Hooker and Dr Campbell, who were visiting Sikkim with the permission of the raja and the British government, were arrested. Various demands were made as a condition of their release, but the Sikkimese eventually released both prisoners unconditionally about a month later.

In reprisal for the arrests, however, the British annexed the whole of the land between the present borders of Sikkim and the Bengal plains and withdrew the annual Rs 6000 stipend from the raja. The latter was restored to his son, raised to

Rs 9000 in 1868 and raised again to Rs 12,000 in 1874.

The annexations brought about a significant change in Darjeeling's status. Previously it had been an enclave within Sikkimese territory and to reach it the British had to pass through a country ruled by an independent raja. After the takeover, Darjeeling became contiguous with British territory further south and Sikkim was cut off from access to the plains except through British territory. This was eventually to lead to the invasion of Sikkim by the Tibetans and the British military expedition to Lhasa.

When the British first arrived in Darjeeling it was almost completely forested and virtually uninhabited, though it had once been a sizeable village before the wars with Bhutan and Nepal. Development was rapid and by 1840 a road had been constructed, numerous houses and a sanatorium built and a hotel opened. By 1857 Darjeeling had a population of some 10,000.

Most of the increase in the population was accounted for by the recruitment of labourers from Nepal, who were brought in to work the tea plantations established in the early 1840s by the British following the smuggling of tea seeds from China. Even today, the vast majority of people speak Nepali as a first language and the name Darjeeling continues to be synonymous with tea.

The immigration of Nepali-speaking peoples, mainly Gurkhas, into the mountainous areas of West Bengal was eventually to lead to political problems in the mid-1980s. Resentment had been growing for a number of years among the Gurkhas over what they felt was discrimination against them by the government of West Bengal. Not even their language was one of those recognised by the Indian Constitution and, that being so, government jobs were only open to those who could speak Bengali.

The tensions finally came to a head in widespread riots throughout the hill country which continued for some two years and in which hundreds of people lost their lives and thousands were made homeless. Tourism came to a grinding halt, the 'toy train' put out of action, and the Indian Army was sent in to maintain some semblance of order. The riots were orchestrated by the Gurkha National Liberation Front (GNLF), led by Subash Gheising, which demanded a separate state to be known as Gurkhaland. The Communist Party of India (Marxist) were also responsible for a good deal of the violence since they were afraid of losing the support which they had once enjoyed among the hill peoples.

A compromise was eventually hammered out in late 1988 whereby the Hill Council was to be given a large measure of autonomy from the state government and fresh elections to the Council were to be

held in December of that year. These resulted in the GNLF gaining 26 of the 28 seats in the Hill Council.

Since then, tempers have certainly cooled but sporadic violence still continues between supporters of the GNLF and the CPI (Marxist) but this is unlikely to affect travellers to the area. Whether the fragile peace will hold, on the other hand, remains to be seen but at least a semblance of normality has definitely returned to the area.

Climate

The best time to visit Darjeeling is between April and mid-June and between September and November. During the monsoon months (June to September) clouds obscure the mountains and the rain is often so heavy that whole sections of the road from the plains are washed

1	Ropeway (Chairlift)	27	Dekevas Restaurant
2	Himalayan Mountaineering Institute Zoo	28	New Dish Restaurant
3	Happy Valley Tea Estate	29	Hotel Apsara
4	Tibetan Refugee Centre	30	Hotels Kadambari & Nirvana
5	Raj Bhavan	31	Railway Station & Tourist Reception Centre
6	Deputy Commissioner's Lodge	32	Buses to Gangtok (Sikkim Nationalised Transport)
7	Darjeeling Tourist Lodge & Gymkhana Club	33	Himalayan Restaurant
8	Youth Hostel	34	Shabnan Restaurant
9	Ghoom Monastery	35	Foreigners' Registration Office
10	Monastery	36	Grindley's Bank
11	Tiger Hill	37	Kathmandu Buses
12	New Elgin Hotel	38	GPO
13	Hotel Alice Villa	39	Tibetan Restaurants
14	Buses to Kalimpong & Siliguri	40	State Bank of India
15	Market	41	Timber Lodge & Washington Restaurant
16	Windamere Hotel		
17	Star Dust Restaurant	42	Prestige Hotel
18	Pineridge Hotel	43	Hotel Springburn
19	Gleneary's	44	Tara Hotel
20	Bellevue Hotel, Tourist Office & Indian Airlines	45	Hotel Pagoda
		46	Shamrock Hotel
21	Snow Lion Restaurant	47	Hotels Purnima & Broadway
22	Shangri La Restaurant	48	Hotels Valentino, Continental & Daffodil
23	Central Hotel		
24	Planter's Club	49	Everest Luxury Lodge
25	Keventer's Snack Bar	50	Sinclair's Hotel
26	Taxi Stand	51	Hotel Pradham

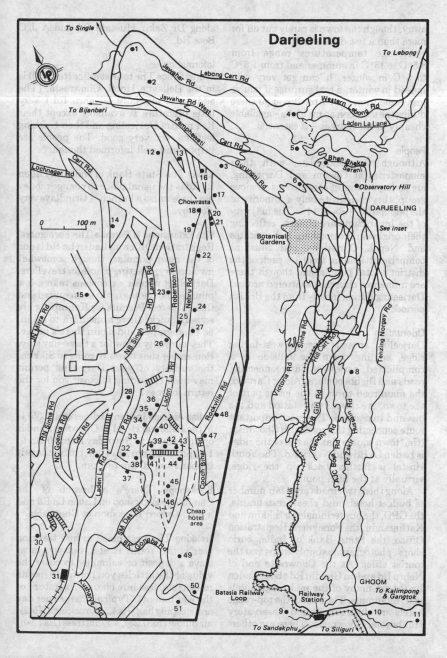

away, though the town is rarely cut off for more than a few days at a time.

Average temperatures range from 8.5°C to 15°C in summer and from 1.5°C to 6°C in winter. It can get very cold indeed in winter, a real surprise if you've just come from Calcutta. If you go there during the monsoon an umbrella – available cheaply in the market – is essential.

People

Although the Buddhists, with their monasteries at Ghoom and Darjeeling, are perhaps the most conspicuous religious group, they constitute only a minority of the population – about 14%. The majority of the inhabitants are Hindus, reflecting their origins in the northern Indian states and Nepal. Christians and Muslims comprise little more than 3% each of the district's total population, though there are numerous churches scattered around Darjeeling dating mostly from the British period.

Orientation

Darjeeling sprawls over a west-facing ridge, spilling down the hillside in a complicated series of interconnecting roads and flights of steps. Along Cart Rd, the main road through the lower part of the town, are the railway station and the bus and taxi stand. The most important route connecting this road with Chowrasta (the 'town square') at the top of the ridge is Laden La Rd and Nehru Rd. The Youth Hostel is further back up the ridge, virtually at the high point.

Along these two roads are a fair number of budget hotels and cheap restaurants, the GPO, the bus terminals for Sikkim and Kathmandu, the Foreigners' Registration Office, the State Bank of India, curio shops, photographic supply shops and the tourist office. At the Chowrasta end of Nehru Rd and on Gandhi Rd above Laden La Rd are many of the mid-range hotels and restaurants. The bulk of the top-range hotels are clustered around Observatory Hill beyond Chowrasta. There are others along Dr Zakir Hussain Rd and A J C Bose Rd.

Information

Tourist Office The tourist office (tel 2050) is in the Bellevue Hotel, Chowrasta. (The address is officially 1 Nehru Rd.) Very little literature is available except their Rs 1 map of Darjeeling and their trekking leaflet – not very good. The people are helpful and well informed though.

Banks The State Bank of India on Laden La Rd is the usual place to change money but there's also a branch of Grindlays very close by.

Visa Extensions & Permits The Foreigners' Registration Office on Laden La Rd is one of the most popular, though somewhat involuntary, meeting places for travellers. Darjeeling permit extensions take a few minutes, no photographs are required and there's no fee. Permits for Kalimpong are equally quick; there's one form to fill in, no photographs and again there's no fee. They normally allow for a three-day stay. Remember that if you're going to Sikkim, the validity of your Darjeeling permit may need extending to cover you for the return journey.

Indian Airlines Indian Airlines (tel 2355) is in the Bellevue Hotel at Chowrasta and is open Monday to Saturday from 10 am to 1.15 pm and from 2 to 4 pm. On Sundays it is open from 10 am to 1 pm.

Bookshops There's a branch of the Cambridge Bookshop on Laden La Rd and a good Oxford Bookshop at Chowrasta.

Trekking The best place to hire trekking gear is the Youth Hostel, but you must leave a deposit or valuables to cover the value of the articles you borrow (deposits returnable, less hire charges, on return of the equipment). Typical charges per day are: sleeping bag (Rs 4.50), rucksack (Rs 2), air pillow (Rs 0.25), air mattress (Rs 1.50), bed roll (Rs 2.50), two-person tent (Rs 6), and aluminium camp cot (Rs 4).

The hostel keeps a very interesting and useful book in which trekkers write comments and suggestions about the routes.

Tiger Hill

The highest spot in the area at 2590 metres, Tiger Hill is near Ghoom, about 11 km from Darjeeling. The hill is famous for its magnificent dawn views over Kanchenjunga and other eastern Himalayan peaks. On a clear day even Mt Everest is visible. Accommodation is available at a *Tourist Lodge*. A pleasant excursion is to walk to the lodge from Darjeeling; it takes about two hours and there are several monasteries along the way. Next morning, after the sunrise view, you can walk to the Ghoom station and catch the toy train back to Darjeeling. If you can't leave your gear elsewhere in Darjeeling the tourist office will look after it for you.

The tourist office also offers bus tours to Tiger Hill to see the sunrise when demand warrants it. The buses leave the Tourist Lodge at 4.30 am and also pick up at Alice Villa and at the taxi rank. The cost is Rs 20 and you should book in advance at the tourist office.

Senchal Lake

Close to Tiger Hill is Senchal Lake, which supplies Darjeeling with its domestic water. It's a particularly scenic area and popular as a picnic spot with Indian holiday-makers. Entrance to the lake costs Rs 0.50.

Kanchenjunga

The best uninterrupted views of this mountain are to be had from Bhan Bhakta Sarani. From Chowrasta, take the road to the right-hand side of the Windamere Hotel and continue about 300 metres.

Ghoom Buddhist Monastery

This is probably the most famous monastery in Darjeeling and is about eight km from town, just below Hill Cart Rd and the railway station near Ghoom. It enshrines an image of the Maitreya Buddha (the coming Buddha). Foreigners are allowed to enter the shrine and take photographs. A small donation is customary and the monks are very friendly. There is another monastery nearby in Ghoom itself.

Aloobari Monastery

Nearer Darjeeling, on Tenzing Norgay Rd, this monastery welcomes visitors and the monks often sell Tibetan and Sikkimese handicrafts and religious objects (usually hand bells). If the monastery is closed you can get the keys from the cottage next door.

Dhirdham Temple

The most conspicuous Hindu temple in Darjeeling, this is just below the railway station and is built along the lines of the famous Pashupatinath Temple in Kathmandu.

Himalayan Mountaineering Institute

Entered through the zoo, on Jawahar Rd West about two km from the town, the institute is the only one of its kind and exists to train mountaineers. It also has a museum containing an interesting collection of historic mountaineering equipment, specimens of Himalayan flora and fauna (though not one of the Abominable Snowman!) and a relief model of the Himalaya.

The institute is open from 9 am to 1 pm and 2 to 4.30 pm and entry costs Rs 0.50.

Zoological Park

Next to the Mountaineering Institute, the park has a collection of high-altitude fauna including the Siberian tiger, Himalayan black bear, deer, panda and a bird collection. Most of the animals are housed in miserable and squalid conditions. The entrance fee is Rs 1 and hours are 8 am to 4 pm.

Botanical Gardens

Below the bus and taxi stand near the market, these gardens contain a representative collection of Himalayan plants, flowers and orchids. The hot-houses are well worth a visit. The gardens are open between 6 am and 5 pm; entrance is free.

Tibetan Refugee Self-Help Centre

The centre was established in October 1959 to help rehabilitate Tibetan refugees who fled from Tibet with the Dalai Lama following the Chinese invasion. Religious importance is attached to this place, as the 13th Dalai Lama (the present is the 14th) stayed here during his visit to India in 1919-22. The centre produces superb carpets, woollens, woodcarvings and leatherwork, and has various Tibetan curios for sale (coins, banknotes, jewellery, etc).

You can wander at leisure through the workshops and watch the work in progress. The weaving and dyeing shops and the woodcarving shop are particularly interesting and the people who work there are very friendly. Their prices, however, are on a par with those in the curio shops of Chowrasta and Nehru Rd. It's an interesting place to visit apart from the workshops, and the views are magnificent.

Curio Shops

The majority of these are on Chowrasta and along Nehru Rd. All things Himalayan are sold here – *thankas*, brass statues, religious objects, jewellery, woodcarvings, woven fabrics, carpets, etc – but if you're looking for bargains you have to shop judiciously and be prepared to spend plenty of time looking. Thankas in particular are nowhere near the quality of 10 years ago. They may look impressive at first sight, but on closer inspection you will find that little care has been taken over the finer detail. The brocade surroundings (said to originate from China) are often of much finer quality.

If you're looking for bronze statues, the real goodies are kept under the counter and cost in multiples of US$100! You have

to indicate that you are not interested in the mass-produced stuff on display before they get the better ones out.

Woodcarvings tend to be excellent value for money. Most of the shops accept international credit cards. There is also a market off Cart Rd next to the bus and taxi stands. Here you can find excellent and relatively cheap patterned woollen sweaters. If you need an umbrella these can be bought here for around Rs 20. Made out of bamboo, they are collectors' items themselves!

Bengal 'Manjusha' Emporium

On the Cart Rd about two km from town on the way to Ghoom and opposite the Ava Art Gallery, this emporium sells Himalayan handicrafts, silk and handloomed products from West Bengal. It's open on all working days from 8 am to 5 pm.

Tea Plantations

Tea is, of course, Darjeeling's most famous export. From its 78 gardens 10.5 million kg are produced annually – 15% of India's total. The industry employs over 46,000 people in the area.

The most convenient garden to visit is the Happy Valley Tea Estate only two km from the centre of town, where tea is still produced by the 'orthodox' method as opposed to the 'Curling, Tearing and Crushing' (CTC) method adopted on the plains. The process is a fascinating one to observe and you should set aside half a day to visit the estate. It's open daily from 8 am to 12 noon and between 1 and 4.30 pm except on Mondays and Sunday afternoons.

After picking, the fresh green leaves are placed 15 to 25 centimetres deep in a 'withering trough' where the moisture content is reduced from 70% to 80% down to 30% to 40% using high-velocity fans. When this is complete the withered leaves are rolled and pressed to break the cell walls and express their juices onto the surface of the leaves. Normally two rollings at different pressures are undertaken, and in between rolls the leaves are sifted to separate

Rajasthan Top: Palace of the Winds, Jaipur (TW)
Left: Shri Chamundaji, Mandore, Jodhpur (TW)
Right: Musicians, Jodhpur Fort (TW)

Rajasthan Top: City Palace, Udaipur (TW)
Left: Wall painting, Udaipur Palace (PC)
Right: Doorman, Rambagh Palace Hotel, Jaipur (TW)

the coarse from the fine. Next the leaves, coated with their juices, are allowed to ferment on racks in a high-humidity room, a process which develops their characteristic aroma and flavour. This fermentation must be controlled carefully since either over or under-fermentation will ruin the tea.

The process is stopped by passing the fermenting leaves through a dry air chamber at 115°C to 120°C on a conveyer belt to further reduce the moisture content to around 2% to 3%. The last process is the sorting of the tea into grades. In their order of value they are: Golden Flowery Orange Pekoe (unbroken leaves), Golden Broken Orange Pekoe, Orange Fannings and Dust (the latter three consisting of broken leaves).

In the last few years modern agricultural practices have been brought to the tea estates to maintain and improve their viability. They were one of the first agricultural enterprises to use clonal plants in their replanting schemes, though very little of this has been done and most of the tea trees are at least 100 years old and nearing the end of their useful or even natural lives. Although Darjeeling produces some of the world's finest tea, the ageing plants and deteriorating soil causes grave concern. Tea is not only a major export item but also provides much employment in the area.

The Passenger Ropeway

At North Point, about three km from town, this was the first passenger ropeway to be constructed in India. It is five km long and connects Darjeeling with Singla Bazaar on the Little Ranjit River at the bottom of the valley. This is a superb excursion, though not one for vertigo sufferers. The fare is Rs 10 one-way and Rs 20 return. There are departures from the top station at 8.30, 9.30 and 10.30 am and 12.30, 1.30 and 2.30 pm. In the opposite direction, there are departures on the hour from 9 am to 3 pm except at 12 noon.

Other Activities

Beware of the pony-wallahs who congregate in Chowrasta. They'll come along with you as a guide and at the end you'll find you're paying for a second pony and for their guiding time! Usual charge is around Rs 10 an hour, but make sure of the price first.

The video craze has hit India everywhere, particularly Darjeeling and some other hill stations. Lots of places have set themselves up as mini-cinemas; a blackboard outside indicates what they're showing. Often it's western films that would have had trouble getting by the censor in the old days.

A British traveller wrote of the joys of a visit to the Darjeeling Gymkhana Club in the last edition:

This majestic ghost of the Raj offers snooker, badminton, rollerskating, table tennis, tennis and squash, and membership is Rs 5 per day or Rs 25 for a week. The building is a grand reminder of how the Brits enjoyed themselves in Darjeeling, with magnificently wood-panelled foyer and stairs and an old ballroom and auditorium on the ground floor redolent of former glories. Streamers hang dusty in the ballroom – from Christmas in the 1980s or 1920s? The place has not been cleaned, it seems, since the British Army officers' wives' social club spring clean in 1935!

We played snooker for an afternoon – good tables, fine old cues and rests. We had a keen snooker-wallah re-spot the balls, hand us the rest, score and encourage us with frequent 'nice shot, sirs'. More out of respect for our citizenship than our snooker prowess. Afterwards you may retire to the members' bar for a tipple after your sporting exertions.

Matt Simmonds, UK

That description is still not too far from the truth except that these days the club is being used partially as a barracks for the Indian Army. If the troubles in Darjeeling continue to subside, however, things may soon return to normal.

Tours

Almost all the bus tours operated by the tourist office were curtailed in 1987 because of the political troubles. The exception is the sunrise trip to Tiger Hill which leaves daily at 4.30 am if demand warrants it. The cost is Rs 20 and you need to book in advance at the tourist office.

Places to Stay

There are a great number of places to stay in Darjeeling. Those that follow are only a limited selection. Prices vary widely with the season; as far as possible those listed are for the high season. In the low season middle-range places costing Rs 250 might drop to Rs 100, bottom-end places costing up to Rs 100 can drop to Rs 25 to Rs 40.

The high seasons are 15 March to 15 July and 15 September to 15 November.

Places to Stay – bottom end

The *Youth Hostel* (tel 2290), above Dr Zakir Hussain Rd right on the top of the ridge, is very popular with trekkers and other budget travellers although it's a 15-minute walk from the centre. From the railway station simply walk straight up the hill. There are two rooms (Rs 25) and dormitories (Rs 6 members, Rs 10 nonmembers). Couples can't get a room together because the manager 'doesn't want to have to ask people if they are married'! The hostel is clean and well maintained, the manager is friendly, meals can be provided, there are cooking facilities and the rooftop view of the mountains is excellent. The hostel also rents trekking gear and keeps an informative book of trekkers' comments and suggestions.

Nabins Lodge is a small guest house just below the Youth Hostel, between Dr Zakir Hussain Rd and A J C Bose Rd. The rooms are a bit spartan and can be cold because the guest house is on the shadowed side of the hill, but it's good value. There's another good hostel alternative just two doors up at 52 Dr Zakir Hussain Rd. If the hostel is full the warden will suggest good alternatives in the vicinity.

The *Hotel Kadambara* is down on the road below the railway station and has concrete box rooms with bathrooms (buckets of hot water available at no extra cost). There's one single at Rs 60 and doubles are Rs 85 and Rs 90. It's a relatively clean place and run by friendly staff but it is getting tatty. The lounge and dining room on the top floor offer excellent views across the valley. Next door the *Hotel Nirvana* is similar in quality and costs Rs 50 a double – no singles. Again, it's run by friendly people.

Going up Laden La Rd from the railway station you'll come to the *Apsara Hotel* which is a typical Indian boarding house with singles/doubles/triples for Rs 75/175/200 with bathroom. The rooms are nothing special but there are good views from the upstairs rooms.

Just beyond the post office there is a whole cluster of cheap hotels either on Laden La Rd or on the alleys and steps running off it. Take the stone steps uphill just beyond the post office and on the right you'll find the *Timber Lodge*. It's popular with people on a very tight budget and the manager is friendly but the rooms are definitely on the decrepit side of rustic. Much better value is the *Hotel Prestige* further up the steps which offers clean, carpeted rooms with bathroom and geyser (hot water) for Rs 60/120 for singles/doubles. Kerosene heaters are available on request (extra charge) and the staff are very pleasant.

Right at the top of the steps and left a few metres along Nehru Rd is the *Hotel Springburn*. It's essentially a concrete box and the furnishings are tatty but otherwise it's OK for a short stay.

Similar in price and quality to the Prestige is the *Shamrock Hotel*, about 100 metres further along the tarmac from the Timber Lodge. The upstairs rooms are more expensive than the downstairs ones, but this Tibetan-run place is very friendly and well kept and there is a fire at night in winter.

Turning right along the gravel track above the post office and in front of the *Shrestha Lodge* and the *Hotel Himalchuly* (both very basic) you'll come across another string of cheapies. They're all pretty basic, but get better the further you walk away from Laden La Rd, and include the *Agarwal, New Indian Hotel* (for derelicts only), *Blue Diamond, Flora* and *Lalit Lodge*.

Going up in price, there's another collection of hotels above the taxi stand on Nehru Rd including the *Hotel Crystal, Holiday Home, Kundus, Shree Anapurna* and the *Capital*. There's not too much to choose between them and they're all similar in price but the views from the front rooms are definitely superior to those from the hotels further down the hill off Laden La Rd.

Further up the hill from this cluster on Rockville Rd is another group which includes the hotels *Purnima, Broadway, La Bella, Ashoka, Rockville, Continental* and *Daffodil*. The Hotel Purnima, for example, charges Rs 130 to Rs 160 a double. The rooms have a bath and hot water and the hotel has its own restaurant. There are no singles.

Further away from this area along Nehru Rd are a number of other cheapies. The fairly modern *Hotel Pradhan* offers singles for Rs 60 to Rs 80, and doubles for Rs 125 to Rs 200. Rooms have a bath with constant hot water (geyser) and the manager is very pleasant. Close by is the *Everest Luxury Hotel* which is anything but luxurious though it does have good views.

Places to Stay – middle

At the bottom end of this category is the *Hotel Tara*, Nehru Rd at the top of the steps leading up from Laden La Rd. It's good value at Rs 250 a double with bath and is run by friendly Tibetan people. There are no singles but the hotel has its own restaurant. Also fairly cheap is the large *Pine Ridge Hotel* at the junction of Nehru Rd and Chowrasta. There are no singles and no discounts for single occupancy but doubles cost Rs 200 with bath and constant hot water.

Excellent value is the *Bellevue Hotel* on Chowrasta which is very well kept and run by a friendly Tibetan lady. There are no singles but a variety of doubles at Rs 200 to Rs 300, all with bath and hot water. Room

49 has the best views and also has a separate sitting room. The hotel has its own restaurant.

Another very well kept hotel with some of the best views in Darjeeling is the *Hotel Valentino* (tel 2228), Rockville Rd, with singles/doubles at Rs 250/350. There are also rooms with four beds for Rs 550. All rooms have a bath, hot water and optional heating. The hotel has its own bar and restaurant (reputedly one of the best in town).

Further down the hill towards the market is the *Central Hotel* (tel 2033), Robertson Rd, which has seen better days and is somewhat run-down but still not bad value at Rs 200/300 for singles/doubles. Rooms have a bath and hot water and the doubles also have a sitting room with a fireplace. Wood for a fire costs Rs 35. The hotel has its own bar and restaurant.

Better value than the Central is the *New Elgin Hotel* (2182), off Robertson Rd, which is a delightful old place though slightly tatty at the edges. The staff are friendly and singles/doubles cost Rs 200/250. The older rooms have fireplaces and fuel for them costs Rs 30. The other rooms have optional heating. There's a popular bar, restaurant and garden/patio.

Another delightful old place to stay and one which has been popular for years is the *Darjeeling Club* above Nehru Rd. Formerly the Tea Planters' Club in the days of the Raj, you can get a room for Rs 265 a double including breakfast or Rs 500 with full board and afternoon tea. There's a billiard room, a musty library, plenty of memorabilia, fires in the bedrooms (buckets of coal cost Rs 15) and lots of pleasant sitting areas. It's all run with considerable old-fashioned style and children are welcome.

The West Bengal Tourist Corporation's *Tourist Lodge* is quite some way from the centre past Loreto College and next to the Gymkhana Club. There are 30 rooms in all which cost Rs 241, Rs 293 and Rs 398 a double (depending on size) and Rs 362 a triple. Single occupancy rates are Rs 200 to Rs 252. All the rooms have a bathroom with hot water and the price includes obligatory breakfast and dinner. Lunch is also available for Rs 35. There's nothing special about this place and the staff are just as indifferent to their work as any other civil servant.

The Tourist Corporation also runs the *Tourist Lodge* at Tiger Hill near Ghoom which is where people go to watch the sunrise over Kanchenjunga. Room rates are similar to those at the Darjeeling lodge. Advance booking is advisable.

Places to Stay – top end

If you have plenty of money to spend then you probably can't beat staying at the *Windamere Hotel* (tel 2841, 2397), on the slopes of Observatory Hill. It's one of the oldest established hotels in Darjeeling and a gem of a leftover from the Raj. This rambling edifice set in beautifully maintained gardens and consisting of a main block with detached cottages and dining room is for all lovers of nostalgia. Owned since the 1920s by Mrs Tenduf-La, a Tibetan lady now in her early 80s, the hotel describes its attitude to hotel management as:

The Windamere remains firmly resistant to the rash modern concept of hotel standardisation... It defies fashion and the cramping dictates of an 'amusement' industry which sees personalised service as an obsolete indulgence. In the face of dreary uniformity, the hotel has simply stood still and elbowed change away with gentle insistence... Very deliberately, the hotel has no TV, video or central heating... It has, however, a log fire in almost every room, a library and a bar...

All this is true and the cosy preprandial gatherings over drinks in the library in front of a roaring fire are one of the major attractions of this hotel. All the same, what can only be described as 'spotless decrepitation' in some of the detached cottages cannot be euphemised away with words such as 'tradition'. There is an urgent need for sensitive restoration particularly in the bathrooms. In summer,

such issues may seem totally irrelevant; in winter, they are not. This, of course, is no reflection on the staff who are paragons of protocol and attendant on your every need.

Rooms cost Rs 490 a single, Rs 745 a double, and cottages Rs 860. The prices include all meals. Fuel for a fire in your room costs Rs 40 extra. Naturally, the staff will make your fire for you on request.

Nothing else in this bracket comes vaguely close to matching the Windamere but if you prefer a modern hotel then there is the *Hotel Sinclair's* (tel 2930), 18/1 Nehru Rd. Singles/doubles cost Rs 560/825 including all meals. All the rooms have bath, hot water and central heating. There's a restaurant and bar and the hotel has its own generator.

Places to Eat

There are numerous cheap restaurants along Laden La Rd all clustered together between the State Bank of India and the post office. Several of them are Tibetan-run while the remainder offer Indian cuisine of various sorts. It's probably unfair to make any particular recommendations since they're all pretty similar and everyone has their own favourite but some of them are definitely in need of a good scrub-down. Take your pick. They include *Shabnam's Restaurant*, the *Golden Dragon, Vineet, Cafe Himalaya, Ulsang, Potala, Lhasa, Penang, Washington* and *Beni's*.

Further up Laden La Rd at the junction with Nehru Rd and Robertson Rd is *Keventer's Snack Bar*, upstairs above the shop. It's a good place for breakfast – they've got ham, bacon, sausages, cheese, and other unusual delicacies from their own farm. Across the road, on Nehru Rd overlooking the small square, is the *Dekevas Restaurant*. It's a neat, clean, shiny little place with great pizzas for up to Rs 25 – ideal for a quick Indian escape – plus they have other food in the same price bracket.

Continue uphill again and you soon come to *Glenary's*, an excellent place with surprisingly reasonable prices and a definite ghost-of-the-Raj air to it. There's a bakery shop underneath it. Across the road is the *Shangri-La Restaurant* which offers Indian and Chinese food. Prices are reasonable and the restaurant has a log fire on winter evenings. Higher up the hill and essentially attached to the Bellevue Hotel is the *Snow Lion Restaurant* with more expensive but very good Chinese and Tibetan food.

On Chowrasta itself the *Star Dust Restaurant* is an open-air restaurant offering south Indian vegetarian snacks. It's a good place to sit and watch the activity on the square but the quality of the food is only very average. The masala dosa I had here (Rs 6) was cold and limp.

For a splurge, the *New Embassy Chinese Restaurant* in the Hotel Valentino is highly recommended and is a popular place to eat. Another splurge would be to eat dinner at the *Windamere Hotel* but, if you're a nonresident, you must book in advance since they usually only cater for their guests.

If you're staying at the youth hostel and don't want to make the trek into town, the *Ratna Restaurant* and the *Little Corner Restaurant* are two good little places nearby.

Getting There & Away

Kurseong is the usual midtrip halting place between Siliguri on the plains and Darjeeling. If you want to overnight there, the *Tourist Lodge* (tel 409) has doubles for Rs 130; or there is the much cheaper *Jeet Hotel*.

Air The nearest airport to Darjeeling is at Bagdogra down on the plains near Siliguri, about 90 km from Darjeeling. From Bagdogra you can get to Darjeeling by road or, if the toy train is running, by rail. There are daily Calcutta/Bagdogra, Bagdogra/Calcutta flights by Indian Airlines. The journey takes 55 minutes. There's also a daily Delhi/Bagdogra/Gawahati/Imphal flight.

There are Indian Airline offices at Siliguri (tel 21201), Kalimpong (tel 241), Darjeeling (tel 2355) and Bagdogra Airport (tel 20366).

If you fly into *and* out of Bagdogra then you are exempted from the permit requirements for Darjeeling. On arrival at Bagdogra your passport will automatically be endorsed for a 15-day visit to Darjeeling. The permit office is right outside the main door of the airport terminal. Flying into and out of Bagdogra does not exempt you from the permit requirements for Sikkim.

Train See the Siliguri section for rail details to or from Calcutta and other centres. If the toy train is operating, you can make reservations at the Darjeeling station for trains out of New Jalpaiguri.

Although a bus or taxi is the fastest means of getting from New Jalpaiguri or Siliguri to Darjeeling, the most interesting way of doing this last stage of the journey is to take the toy train – if it's working – though this will add at least three hours to the journey.

Toy Train The journey to Darjeeling from New Jalpaiguri or Siliguri on the famous miniature railway is a superb experience which shouldn't be missed.

Unfortunately, services on the toy train line were discontinued in 1986 because of the political troubles which plagued the hill country area and subsequent landslides appeared to have sealed its fate. Following the political accommodation, however, between the GNLF and the West Bengal government, major repairs began on the line and it should either be open now or in the near future; check before you go.

If the train is running there should be two or three departures daily (and sometimes more) in either direction though departure times from New Jalpaiguri don't necessarily follow the official timetable (though they may do from Darjeeling). The journey takes seven hours and you stop en route long enough to grab something to eat. If you can't face the whole trip, you can simply make the short excursion between Ghoom and Darjeeling. If you walk up to Tiger Hill, near Ghoom, to watch the Himalayan dawn, you can ride the toy train back.

Until the late 1800s, all supplies for Darjeeling and all exports from the town had to be transported by bullock cart along the Siliguri road. This road, which is still known as the Hill Cart Rd, was so called because its gradient is such that even bullock carts could climb it. Naturally, this form of transportation was slow and expensive. Rice which sold in Siliguri for Rs 98 a ton fetched Rs 240 a ton by the time it reached Darjeeling.

The idea of a railway to Darjeeling was put forward by Franklin Prestage, an agent working for the Eastern Bengal Railway, in 1870. The scheme was accepted and construction begun in 1879. It was completed in 1881, and in 1885 a further km extension was added to take the line into the market area (now in disuse). Later on,

in 1914, it was further extended south towards Kishanganj close to the Nepalese border to cope with the transport of jute and, in 1915, from Siliguri to 15 km beyond Sevok on the way to Kalimpong. The cost of the original section to Darjeeling was Rs 1,700,000 including rolling stock.

The whole line is an ingenious feat of engineering and includes four complete loops and five switchbacks, some of which were added after the initial construction had been completed to ease the line's gradient at certain points. One of the most important additions was the Batasia loop on the final descent into Darjeeling. Altogether, there are 132 unsupervised level crossings!

Bus Most of the buses from Darjeeling depart from the Bazaar bus stand (Cart Rd). Most jeeps and taxis depart from the taxi stand, Robertson Rd/Laden La Rd. There are many different companies operating buses, jeeps and taxis. Buses to Calcutta, Kathmandu and other points further afield generally go through Siliguri.

Watering the toy train, Darjeeling

New Jalpaiguri/Siliguri There are numerous buses, jeeps and taxis in either direction daily between 6 am and 10 pm. The journey takes 3½ to four hours by bus (sometimes less) and costs Rs 16. A taxi costs Rs 55 per person.

Bagdogra West Bengal Tourist Corporation buses connect with the arrival of flights from Calcutta and New Delhi. The fare is Rs 35 and the journey takes 3½ hours including a 15-minute stop at Kurseong for refreshments. In the opposite direction, they depart from the tourist lodge in Darjeeling at 8 am daily and also pick up from Alice Villa Hotel (below the Windamere) and the taxi stand. Buses from Darjeeling must be booked in advance at the tourist office.

Kalimpong Land Rovers, taxis and buses make this 2½-hour trip regularly. Land Rovers cost Rs 25 and taxis Rs 20 and are so much more convenient than the buses that they're worth the extra expense. Land Rovers and buses go from the Bazaar bus stand, taxis from the Robertson Rd/Laden La taxi stand. Your permit for Kalimpong will be checked by the military at Teesta bridge.

Gangtok If you don't want to go by taxi or jeep, there is only one bus line to Gangtok. This is run by Sikkim Nationalised Transport (SNT), which has its Darjeeling office in the first building below the GPO on Laden La Rd (it's unmarked and easy to miss as it's next to a burnt-out decayed building). There is one minibus daily in either direction, and as there are few seats available, early booking is essential. The bus departs at 8 am, takes seven hours and costs Rs 40. If you don't fancy the cramped conditions of the public bus then get a group together and hire a taxi. Your permit will be inspected before you cross the bridge at Rangpo, and at Rangpo itself you will have to visit the police station to fill in the visitors' book. On the way out your permit will be collected at Rangpo.

Other Places Deluxe buses are also available to Calcutta, Patna, Gawahati, Shillong, Silchar and Agartala.

Kathmandu There are several companies which operate daily buses between Darjeeling and Kathmandu but the main ones are Assam Valley Tours & Travels, opposite the post office, and Mahendra Tours (tel 3245) on Laden La Rd above the main block of budget restaurants. Neither one of these companies run direct buses and you have to change at Siliguri.

The usual arrangement is that the agents will sell you a ticket as far as Siliguri (Rs 16) but guarantee you a seat on the connecting bus with the same agency (for which you pay a further Rs 150 on average). You arrive at the border around 3 pm (Kakarbhitta is the name of the town on the Nepalese side), leave again around 4 pm and arrive in Kathmandu around 9 or 10 am the next day.

It's almost as easy to get from Darjeeling to Kathmandu on your own though it involves four changes – bus from Darjeeling to Siliguri (Rs 16), bus from Siliguri to the border (Rs 3), rickshaw across the border to Kakarbhitta (Rs 2), bus from Kakarbhitta to Kathmandu (Nepalese Rs 170). This is cheaper than the package deal, you get a choice of buses from the border, plus you have the option of travelling during the day and over-nighting along the way. There are day buses from Kakarbhitta that go to a number of other towns on the Nepalese *terai* (plains) including Janakpur (NRs 60), and night buses direct to Pokhara (NRs 170).

There is no Nepalese consulate in Darjeeling; the nearest one is in Calcutta, but seven-day visas are available at the border, and these can be extended in Kathmandu. In 1989, the Nepal-India border was affected by a dispute over the terms of a border agreement, and all land crossings except for those at Kakarbhitta, Birganj and Bhairawa were closed to travellers. At the time this book went to press the situation was not resolved so, if possible, check that the crossing at Kakarbhitta is still open and that the Nepalese are still issuing visas.

When the border dispute is resolved other crossings from Bihar and Uttar Pradesh will open again.

Once in Nepal, buses travel west as far as Narayangadh on the Mahendra Highway, skirting the foothills and passing a number of interesting places and sights on the terai; from Narayangadh the road climbs through the Siwalik Hills to Mugling and the Trisuli River valley where you double back towards Kathmandu. If it isn't too hot, consider travelling by day, so you can see the sights and stop in Janakpur and/or the Royal Chitwan National Park.

Avalanches and floods can sometimes delay the bus. The road is in very poor condition in the vicinity of the Kosi Barrage and there's another very bad section on the Prithvi Highway (the Pokhara to Kathmandu road) between Mugling and Kathmandu. Here is one traveller's experience of the Darjeeling to Kathmandu trip during the monsoon:

. . .took us three days to do the trip due to the landslides and bridges being destroyed. Got some incredible shots of us wading through thigh-deep water in swirling, full-flowing rivers to get across and hopefully find another bus to the next disaster. Never again!

TREKS IN THE DARJEELING REGION

The best months to trek in this region are April, May, October and November. There may be occasional showers during April and May but, in a way, this is the best time to go as many shrubs are in flower, particularly the rhododendrons. There may be occasional rains during the first half of October if the monsoon is prolonged. November is generally dry and visibility excellent during the first half of December, though it's usually cold by then. After the middle of December there are occasional snowfalls.

In planning what clothes to take, bear in mind that you will be passing through valley bottoms as low as 300 metres and over mountain ridges as high as 4000 metres, so you'll need clothing for low,

tropical climates and high mountain passes. No matter what time of year you go, it's a good idea to take a light raincoat which can be folded up and put inside your rucksack since the weather can be unpredictable, particularly at high altitudes.

Trek 1
Darjeeling – Rimbik – Raman – Phalut – Sandakphu – Rimbik – Bijanbari – Darjeeling

This is currently one of the most popular treks and is documented by numerous travellers in the Youth Hostel's trekking book. It offers fine mountain views and avoids too much climbing, and some food is available along the route.

Buses run as far as Rimbik from Darjeeling; the trip takes five hours and costs Rs 12. Chetak, Monokamana and the Government of West Bengal all operate buses there. From Rimbik it's a half-hour walk to the very popular *Shiva Pradhan Hotel* which has very cheap beds and meals. Other accommodation is available in Rimbik as well, and if you need supplies there is a small bazaar.

From Rimbik you can walk to Raman in four hours. The trek starts level, then drops steeply for a km to Shirikhola River. After crossing the river the trail is more or less level for nine km to Raman, where there is a *Youth Hostel*.

It's three km from Raman to the Raman River, which is crossed by a bridge. The walk takes you through dense forests of rhododendrons, silver firs, chestnuts, oaks, magnolias and hemlocks. From the river there's a steep ascent along a forest bridle path for the remaining 11 km to Phalut. The day's walk takes six to seven hours. At Phalut there's a *Dak Bungalow* and on a clear day you can see both Kanchenjunga and Everest. Nepal, Sikkim and West Bengal meet at this point.

The third day of the trek starts with a steep zig-zag descent from Phalut. The next 13 km are fairly level before the final steep ascent to Sandakphu. The day's walk again takes six to seven hours. There is another *Dak Bungalow* at Sandakphu and the views are similar to Phalut. Kanchenjunga is only 144 km from here as the crow flies. Day four takes you back to Rimbik, but rather than bus back from there to Darjeeling you can continue to Jhepi and bus back via Bijanbari. The next day's walk begins with a fairly steep descent over about eight km to the bridge across the Lodoma River. After this the path levels out and passes through cultivated land until it reaches Jhepi Bungalow, 17 km from Rimbik. From Jhepi the road climbs some 150 metres over two km to a spur on which Kaijali sits, and then drops down to Bijanbari six km further on. You can either take a jeep from here to Darjeeling 36 km away, or walk there via Pulbazar and Singtam.

The bus from Jhepi to Bijanbari is irregular; you may have to walk. If the only hotel/restaurant in 'town' is full you can stay for free at the government *Haryana Bhawan* – very basic but nobody complains. The key (no one lives there) can be borrowed from the shop on the corner diagonally opposite the hotel/restaurant in the main street. A bus back to Darjeeling from Bijanbari costs Rs 15.

Trek 2

Darjeeling – Manaybhanjang – Tonglu – Sandakphu – Phalut and return (118 km to Sandakphu and 160 km to Phalut return)

This is another good trek with excellent views of Kanchenjunga and Everest. The route passes through superb tropical countryside.

On the first day, either walk or take a jeep or taxi to Manaybhanjang, 26 km from Darjeeling. The first day's walk to Tonglu is a fairly steep climb of 11 km via a succession of zig-zags all the way up to the

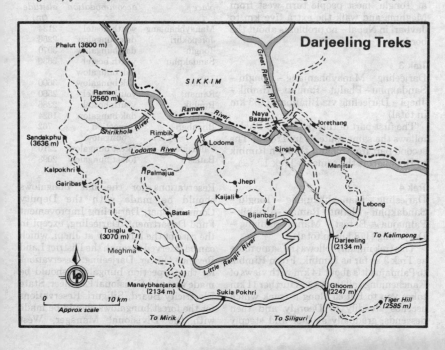

Darjeeling Treks

Phalut (3600 m)
SIKKIM
Raman (2560 m)
Great Rangit River
Ramam River
Naya Bazaar
Jorethang
Sandakphu (3636 m)
Shirikhola River
Rimbik
Lodoma
Singla
Lodoma River
Kalpokhri
Palmajua
Jhepi
Manjitar
Gairibas
Kaijali
Bijanbari
Lebong
Batasi
Tonglu (3070 m)
Darjeeling (2134 m)
To Kalimpong
Meghma
Little Rangit River
Manaybhanjang (2134 m)
Sukia Pokhri
Ghoom (2247 m)
Tiger Hill (2585 m)
0   10 km
Approx scale
To Mirik
To Siliguri

bungalow. Tonglu looks directly on Darjeeling and commands an excellent view of Kanchenjunga.

The next day's walk to Sandakphu covers 22 km and initially passes through bamboo thickets with many ascents and descents until Kalapokhri is reached. About five hours should be allowed for this part of the trek. The last part up to Sandakphu Bungalow involves a steep climb and should take about three hours. The mountain views from here are excellent. You can either continue on to Phalut from Sandakphu or return to Darjeeling. This last stage to Phalut and back is as on Trek 1.

It's possible to return to Manaybhanjang from Phalut in one day if you start out early enough (allow about eight hours of continuous walking), or you can return in two days at a more leisurely pace by breaking the journey at Tonglu.

Due to disrepair of the accommodation at Tonglu, most people turn west from Meghma and walk the extra five km to Javbari in Nepal – no problems about the border.

Trek 3

Darjeeling – Manaybhanjang – Tonglu – Sandakphu – Phalut – Raman – Rimbik – Jhepi – Darjeeling via Bijanbari (153 km in total)

The first part of this trek up to Phalut follows the same route as in Trek 2. The second part from Phalut through Rimbik to Bijanbari is the same as Trek 1.

Trek 4

Darjeeling – Manaybhanjang – Tonglu – Sandakphu – Phalut – Raman – Rimbik – Palmajua – Batasi – Manaybhanjang – Darjeeling (178 km in total)

This trek initially follows the same route as Trek 3 as far as Rimbik. From Rimbik to Palmajua it's about 14 km with views of Kanchenjunga all the way. A further 11 km takes you to Batasi along a track which ascends steadily to Deoraly and then descends, gradually at first and steeply

towards the end, to Batasi. The next day's walk takes you over the final 14 km to Manaybhanjang, where you can either take a jeep or walk to Darjeeling.

Places to Stay

There are enough bungalows and youth hostels along the trekking routes, though advance reservations should be made if possible for the bungalows before you leave Darjeeling. This isn't necessary with the youth hostels.

The bungalows are fairly well furnished and have cooking equipment, sheets and blankets. Firewood can be bought from the chowkidah. The youth hostels provide, as you might expect, somewhat more basic accommodation and usually only have mattresses and blankets, though some do have basic cooking equipment. There are bungalows and youth hostels in the following places:

place	accommodation	altitude (m)
Manaybhanjang	youth hostel	2134
Jorepokhri	dak bungalow	2256
Tonglu	dak bungalow	3070
Sandakphu	youth hostel dak bungalow	3636
Phalut	dak bungalow	3600
Raman	youth hostel	2560
Rimbik	youth hostel	2286
Jhepi	dak bungalow	1624
Bijanbari	inspection bungalow	762
Palmajua	forest bungalow	2210
Batasi	forest bungalow	2098

Reservations for the dak bungalows should be made with the Deputy Commissioner, Darjeeling Improvement Fund Department, Darjeeling, except in the case of the bungalow at Jhepi, which can be reserved through the District Land Revenue Officer, Darjeeling. Reservations for the inspection bungalows should be made with the Divisional Engineer, State Electricity Board, Siliguri. Reservations for the forest bungalows should be made with the Divisional Manager, West

Bengal Forest Development Corporation, Darjeeling.

Rice, dhal, eggs, chicken, onions and potatoes can be bought at most places en route, though they're likely to be more expensive than in Darjeeling. In addition there are small chai shops en route at Sandakphu, Meghma, Garibas, Rimbik, Jhepi, Lodoma and Bijanbari. If you would be happy with this kind of diet then you need carry no food with you. If not, take your own supplies from Darjeeling.

Note Before you go on any of these treks you're advised to browse through the Darjeeling Youth Hostel's book in which trekkers write their comments about the routes.

KALIMPONG

Kalimpong is a bustling and rapidly expanding, though still relatively small, bazaar town set amongst the rolling foothills and deep valleys of the Himalaya at an altitude of 1250 metres. It was once part of the lands belonging to the rajas of Sikkim until the beginning of the 18th century, when it was taken from them by the Bhutanese. In the 19th century it passed into the hands of the British and thus became part of West Bengal.

Kalimpong's attractions include Catholic churches built like Tibetan monasteries, two excellent private libraries for study of Tibetan and Himalayan language and culture, two Buddhist monasteries and the fine views over the surrounding countryside. The most interesting part of a trip to Kalimpong is the journey there from Darjeeling via the Teesta River Bridge. If you have no permit for Sikkim then the town is worth visiting just for the journey, but if you do have a permit then you could by-pass Kalimpong without missing a great deal. The market here is overrated.

Information & Orientation

Though it's a much smaller town than Darjeeling, Kalimpong has a similar kind

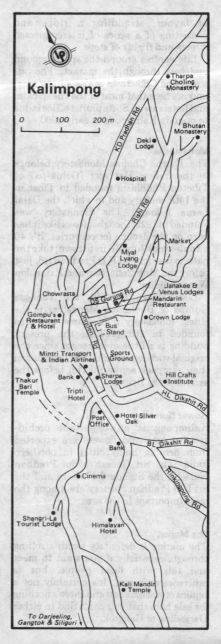

Kalimpong

0   100   200 m

Tharpa Choling Monastery
Bhutan Monastery
Deki Lodge
Hospital
KD Pradhan Rd
Rishi Rd
Market
Myal Lyang Lodge
Chowrasta
DS Gurung Rd
Janakee & Venus Lodges
Mandarin Restaurant
Gompu's Restaurant & Hotel
Ondem Rd
Bus Stand
Crown Lodge
Mintri Transport & Indian Airlines
Sports Ground
Hill Crafts Institute
Thakur Bari Temple
Bank
Sherpa Lodge
HL Dikshit Rd
Tripti Hotel
Post Office
Hotel Silver Oak
Bank
BL Dikshit Rd
Cinema
Rinkingpong Rd
Shangri-La Tourist Lodge
Himalayan Hotel
Kali Mandir Temple
To Darjeeling, Gangtok & Siliguri

of layout, straddling a ridge and consisting of a series of interconnected streets and flights of steps.

Life centres around the sports ground and east through the market. The bus stand and Chowrasta is also a busy area, and it's here that most of the cheap cafes and hotels are. A State tourist office is due to open in Kalimpong in early 1990.

Monasteries

The Tharpa Choling Monastery belongs to the Yellow Hat sect (Geluk-pa) of Tibetan Buddhism founded in Tibet in the 14th century and to which the Dalai Lama belongs. The monastery was founded in 1922, though it looks like it has been on the decline for centuries. It's 40 minutes walk (uphill) from town; take the path to the right off K D Pradhan Rd, just before the Milk Collection and Extension Wing Building.

Lower down the hill, the Thongsa Gompa or Bhutanese Monastery is the oldest monastery in the area and was founded in 1692 though the present building is a little more recent since the original was destroyed by the Gurkhas in their rampage across Sikkim before the arrival of the British.

Flower Nurseries

Kalimpong is an important orchid-growing area and flowers are exported from here to many cities in northern India. The Sri Ganesh Moni Pradhan Nursery, the Standard Nursery and the Sri L B Pradhan Nursery are among the most important in the area.

The Market

The market is definitely worth strolling through, especially if you want to meet and talk with local people, but is otherwise overrated. It's certainly not a replica of Kathmandu and there's nothing for sale here that you can't find in either Darjeeling or Gangtok.

Places to Stay – bottom end

The majority of the really cheap places on the far side of the bus stand look like the ceiling would fall on your head if you raised your voice and they're definitely only for desperadoes. Such places include the *Punjabi Lodge*, right opposite the bus stand, and the *Venus Lodge* close by.

Many travellers stay at *Gompu's Restaurant & Hotel* on Chowrasta which has doubles for Rs 80 with bath (no singles). It's run by friendly Tibetans and the restaurant here is rated highly by local people. If it's full then the *Sherpa Lodge*, Ongden Rd, is a good bet at Rs 30/60 for singles/doubles with bath though the only water available may be in bucket form because of local shortages. It's run by very pleasant people who speak fluent English.

A similar place is the *Myal Lyang Lodge*, Rishi Rd, which has singles/doubles for Rs 35/50 with bath but cold water only. The manager is friendly and the restaurant downstairs offers Indian and Chinese meals for around Rs 10 to Rs 14 per dish.

Away from this area on the road down to the Teesta Bridge is another very popular place – the *Shangri-La Tourist Lodge* (tel 230). It's a clean old wooden place with pleasant staff and it offers dorm beds for Rs 11.55 (seven in total) and double rooms with bath for Rs 50. Breakfast and dinner are available. The hotel isn't signposted so, if walking out of Kalimpong, watch for a cinema on the left-hand side and then take the small dirt path downhill on the right-hand side shortly afterwards.

Up the scale a bit is the *Crown Lodge*, a few metres down a side street off H L Dikshit Rd. It's quiet, clean and good value at Rs 66/110 for singles/doubles with bath and hot water. The staff are pleasant but the hotel has no restaurant.

Places to Stay – top end

If you have the money, there's no better place to stay in Kalimpong than the beautiful old stone-built *Himalayan Hotel* (tel 248) on the right-hand side about 300 metres up the hill past the post office. It is the former home of a British trade agent with Tibet named David MacDonald who wrote *20 Years in Tibet* and *Land of the Lamas*. The hotel is surrounded by superb gardens looking across to the snow-covered peaks of Kanchenjunga. The present manager, Dr R K Sprigg, is an English scholar of the Tibetan language. He was Reader in Tibetan phonetics at the School of Oriental & African Studies at London University and his knowledge of the area is unsurpassed. His daily walks (if you can keep up) take him to many scenic and interesting places. Dr Sprigg and his wife are what make this place so mellow and so fascinating. It's a bargain at Rs 350/450 for a single/double including all meals and bathrooms with bucket hot showers. If you don't want meals the tariffs are reduced. Log fires in the rooms are extra. For a group of eight people or more the charges are Rs 250 per person including all meals. The dining room with its log fire and genuine Tibetan antique memorabilia will be a memory you will cherish for many years and long to revisit.

By contrast, there is the West Bengal Tourist Corporation's *Hotel Silver Oaks* (tel 260), Upper Cart Rd, about 50 metres up hill from the post office. It's not a patch on the Himalayan Hotel but, as modern hotels go, it is very pleasant if somewhat devoid of life and it does have good views. It's pretty expensive at Rs 650/750 for singles/doubles without meals but with a bathroom and constant hot water (geysers).

The *Kalimpong Park Hotel* (tel 304) has singles ranging from Rs 225 to Rs 345 and doubles from Rs 320 to Rs 560.

Places to Eat

Gompu's Restaurant, Chowrasta, is a pleasant restaurant with friendly staff and highly recommended both by local people and travellers alike. They serve Tibetan, Indian and Chinese food and western breakfasts (omelettes, toast and so on). Also very good is the *Mandarin Restaurant* opposite the bus stand which does Chinese food. Another restaurant, similar in quality, is at *Myal Lyang Lodge*.

For a cheap simple meal, the *Usha Restaurant*, a tiny and very friendly chai shop between the Crown Lodge and the bus stand, is worth trying. Those looking for standard Indian food should try one of the restaurants along the main street such as that at the *Tripti Hotel*.

Getting There & Away

Darjeeling There are frequent jeeps (Rs 25) and taxis (Rs 20) in either direction for the three-hour trip. The buses are so much less frequent, slower and more uncomfortable that it's hardly worth the small cost saving. All the transport leaves from the Bazaar bus stand other than the taxis. Kalimpong Motor Transport Syndicate is the main operator.

Siliguri Buses cost Rs 14 for this three-hour trip. There are also Land Rovers and taxis. The road to Siliguri follows the Teesta River after the bridge so it's much cheaper and quicker than going via Darjeeling. The views are magnificent.

Gangtok (Sikkim) Several bus companies operate this route from the bus stand – try Sikkim Nationalised Transport or Jayshree (otherwise spelt Joy Shree). There are several buses daily for the four-hour trip, and the fare is around Rs 20. They're fond of dubbing the buses 'luxury', which is a joke and should be treated as such.

Bagdogra Mintri Transport Ltd operates one bus daily to Siliguri and the Bagdogra airport at 8 am from their office (which is also the Indian Airlines office) on Main Rd. The trip takes about three hours and costs Rs 35.

Phuntsholing If you're one of those rare and lucky people who have managed to get hold of a Bhutanese visa, then transport is available from Kalimpong to Phuntsholing on the Bhutanese border.

Sikkim

Population: 380,000
Area: 7214 square km
Capital: Gangtok
Main language: Nepali

Until 1975, Sikkim, or 'New House', was an independent kingdom, albeit under a treaty which allowed the Indian government to control Sikkim's foreign affairs and defence. However, following a period of political crises and riots in the capital, Gangtok, India annexed the country in 1975 and Sikkim became the 22nd Indian state. The move sparked widespread criticism, but tensions have now cooled. The central government has been spending relatively large sums of money to subsidise Sikkim's road building, electrification, water supply and agricultural and industrial development.

Much of this activity was no doubt motivated by India's fear of Chinese military designs on the Himalayan region. Even today, there's still a lot of military activity along the route from Darjeeling to Gangtok, though much of it has been connected over the last three years with the violence accompanying the Gurkha National Liberation Front's demand for a separate state.

For many years, Sikkim was regarded as one of the last Himalayan 'Shangri Las' because of its remoteness, spectacular mountain terrain, varied flora and fauna and ancient Buddhist monasteries. It was never easy to visit and, even now, you need a special permit from the central government. Don't bother trying to get into Sikkim without a permit – you'll be refused entry at the state border (Rangpo). With further permission from Delhi, foreign visitors are allowed to trek up into the remote Dzongri region of western Sikkim but the eastern part of Sikkim along the Tibetan border remains out of bounds.

History

The country was originally home to the Lepchas, a tribal people thought to have migrated from the hills of Assam around the 13th century. The Lepchas were pacifist forest foragers and small-patch cultivators who worshipped nature spirits. They still constitute some 18% of the total population of Sikkim, though their ability to lead their traditional lifestyle has been severely limited by immigration from Tibet and, more recently, from Nepal.

The Tibetans started to emigrate into Sikkim during the 15th and 16th centuries to escape religious strife between various Lamaist sects. In Tibet itself, the Yellow Hat sect, or Geluk-pa (to which the Dalai Lama belongs), gradually gained the upper hand. In Sikkim, however, the Red Hat sect, or Nyingma-pa, remained in control and was the official state religion until the country became a part of India. In the face of the waves of Tibetan immigrants, the Lepchas originally retreated to the more remote regions. A blood brotherhood was eventually forged between their leader, Thekong Tek, and the Bhutias leader, Khye-Bumsa, and spiritual and temporal authority was imposed on the anarchistic Lepchas. In 1641, the Dalai Lama in Lhasa appointed Penchoo Namgyal as the first king of Sikkim. At that time, the country included the area contained by the present state as well as a part of eastern Nepal, the Chumbi Valley (Tibet), the Ha Valley (Bhutan) and the Terai foothills from the present border down to the plains of India, including Darjeeling and Kalimpong.

Between 1717 and 1734, during the reign of Sikkim's fourth king, a series of wars fought with the Bhutanese resulted in the loss of much territory in the southern foothills, including Kalimpong, then a very important bazaar town on the trade route between Tibet and India. More territory was lost after 1780 following the Gurkha invasion from Nepal, though the invaders were eventually checked by a Chinese army with Bhutanese and Lepcha assistance. Unable to advance into Tibet, the Gurkhas turned south where they came into conflict with the British East India Company. The wars between the two parties ended in the treaty of 1817 which delineated the borders of Nepal. The Gurkhas also ceded to the British all the Sikkimese territory they had taken; a substantial part was returned to the Raja of Sikkim in return for British control of all disputes between Sikkim and its neighbours. The country thus became a buffer state between Nepal, Tibet and Bhutan.

In 1835, the British, seeking a hill station as a rest and recreation centre for their troops and officials, persuaded the raja to cede the Darjeeling area in return for an annual stipend. The Tibetans objected to this transfer of territory. They continued to regard Sikkim as a vassal state, and Darjeeling's rapid growth as a trade centre had begun to make a considerable impact on the fortunes of Sikkim's leading lamas and merchants. Tensions rose and, in 1849, a high-ranking British official and a botanist, who were exploring the Lachen region with the permission of both the Sikkimese raja and the British government, were arrested. Although the two prisoners were unconditionally released a month later following threats of intervention, the British annexed the entire area between the present Sikkimese border and the Indian plains and withdrew the raja's stipend (the stipend was eventually restored to his son).

Further British interference in the affairs of this area led to the declaration of a protectorate over Sikkim in 1861 and the delineation of its borders. The Tibetans, however, continued to regard these actions as illegal and, in 1886, invaded Sikkim to reassert their authority. The attack was repulsed by the British, who sent a punitive military expedition to Lhasa in 1888 in retaliation. The powers of the Sikkimese raja were further reduced and high-handed treatment by British officials prompted him to flee to Lhasa in 1892, though he was eventually persuaded to return.

Keen to develop Sikkim, the British encouraged immigration from Nepal, as they had done in Darjeeling, and a considerable amount of land was brought under rice and cardamom cultivation. This influx of labour continued until the 1960s and, as a result, the Nepalese now make up approximately 75% of the population of Sikkim. The subject of immigration became a topic of heated debate in the late '60s and the raja was constrained to prohibit further immigration. New laws regarding the rights of citizenship were designed to placate those of non-Nepalese origin, but they served to inflame the opposition parties.

There was also a great deal of grass-roots support for a more popular form of government than Sikkim's *chogyal*. The British treaties with Sikkim had passed to India at independence and the Indian government had no wish to be seen propping up the regime of an autocratic raja while doing their best to sweep away the last traces of princely rule in India

Sikkim

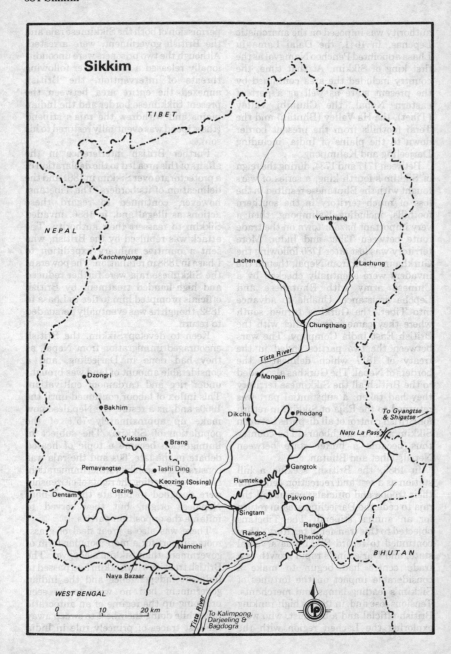

itself. However, the chogyal resisted
demands for a change in the method of
government until the demonstrations
threatened to get out of control and he was
eventually forced to ask India to take over
the country's administration. In a 1975
referendum, 97% of the electorate voted
for union with India. Despite significant
international resentment at the time, the
political situation has cooled down and
Sikkim is now governed by its own
democratic congress with representatives
in the central government in New Delhi.

The current population of Sikkim is
approximately 18% Lepcha and 75%
Nepalese; the other 7% are Bhutias and
Indians from various northern states.
About 60% of the population is Hindu and
28% Buddhist, although the two religions
exist, as in many parts of Nepal, in a
syncretic form. The ancient Buddhist
monasteries, of which there are a great
many, are one of the principal attractions
of a visit to Sikkim.

Permits
See the section on permits to Darjeeling
and Sikkim in the West Bengal chapter.

GANGTOK (population 17,000)
Gangtok, the capital of Sikkim, occupies
the west side of a long ridge flanking the
Ranipool River. The scenery is spectacular
and there are excellent views of the entire
Kanchenjunga range from many points in
the vicinity. Many people expect Sikkim
to be a smaller version of Kathmandu
overflowing with ancient temples, palaces,
monasteries and narrow, colourful bazaars
– it's not! Gangtok only became the
capital in the mid-1800s (previous
capitals were at Yuksam and Rabdantse)
and the town has undergone rapid
modernisation in recent years.

Information & Orientation
To the north is Raj Bhavan, the former
British and later Indian Residency. Above
is the Tourist Lodge and Enchey
Monastery. The palace of the former

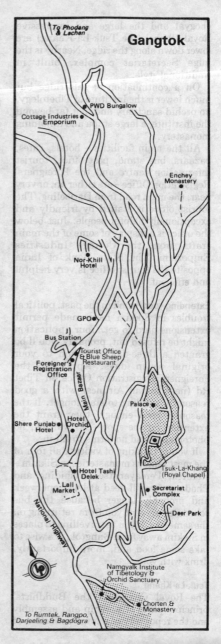

chogyal and the large and impressive Royal Chapel (the Tsuk-La-Khang) are lower down along the ridge. Nearby is the huge Secretariat complex, built in traditional style.

On a continuation of this ridge but much lower is the Institute of Tibetology, an orchid sanctuary and, not far beyond the institute, a large stupa and adjoining monastery.

All the main facilities – hotels, cafes, bazaars, bus stand, post office, tourist information centre and the Foreigners' Registration Office – are either on, or very near, the main road from Darjeeling. The tourist office is staffed by friendly and exceptionally helpful people. Just below the office is a display of some of the main crafts from the Cottage Industries Emporium. The State Bank of India opposite the tourist office is very helpful and efficient.

Extending your Permit In the past, political troubles in Sikkim have made permit extensions hard to get. Your application might be refused but, probably, you'll be granted a three-day extension to your original seven days. Apply at the Foreigners' Registration Office on Tibet Rd (near Indian Airlines) with a good reason for needing to stay longer. If the reason is good enough, they grant the extension on the spot – no waiting, no photographs and no forms to fill in.

If you're thinking of visiting all four of the most famous monasteries in Sikkim – Rumtek, Pemayangtse, Tashiding and Phodang – you'll need at least one week and probably longer because the bus schedules prevent you from returning on the same day. If you're travelling to places in Sikkim away from Gangtok, it's wise to take some food and, more importantly, drink with you.

Tsuk-La-Khang
The Royal Chapel is the Buddhists' principal place of worship and assembly and the repository of a large collection of scriptures. It's a beautiful and impressive building, its interior covered with murals. Lavishly decorated altars hold images of the Buddha, bodhisattvas and Tantric deities and there are also a great many fine woodcarvings. It's not always open to visitors, particularly in the off season, and no photography is allowed inside.

The chapel is the site for such important festivals as the mid-September one to the god of Kanchenjunga, and the New Year celebration when the famous Black Hat dance portrays the triumph of good over evil.

Namgyalk Institute of Tibetology
Established in 1958 and built in traditional style, this unique institute promotes research on the language and traditions of Tibet, as well as on Mahayana Buddhism. It has one of the world's largest collection of books and rare manuscripts on the subject of Mahayana Buddhism, many religious works of art and a collection of astonishingly beautiful and incredibly finely executed silk-embroidered thankas. The director of the institute is a very friendly man who will spend time showing you around if you care to approach him. The institute is open from 10 am to 4 pm, Monday to Saturday, and there is no entrance fee.

Orchid Sanctuary
Surrounding the institute and itself enclosed by a peaceful forest is the Orchid Sanctuary, where you can see many of the 454 species of orchid found in Sikkim. The best times to visit are April-May, July-August and October-November.

Chorten & Monastery
The gold apex of a huge white chorten, about a km beyond the institute, is visible from many points in Gangtok. Next to it is a monastery for young lamas with a shrine containing huge images of Guru Padmasambhava, the Indian teacher of Buddhism in Tibet, and his manifestation, Guru Snang-Sid Zilzon.

Institute of Cottage Industries

High up on the main road above the town, the Cottage Industries Emporium specialises in producing hand-woven carpets, blankets, shawls, Lepcha weaves, patterned decorative paper and 'Choktse' tables, exquisitely carved in relief. It's open from 9 am to 12.30 pm and 1 to 3.30 pm daily, except Sundays and every second Saturday. In addition to the shop, there is a smaller display of craftwork on the ground floor of the tourist office.

Deer Park

This popular viewpoint is on the edge of the ridge next to the Secretariat building. In it, as you might expect, are deer and a replica of the Buddha image at Sarnath in India.

Enchey Monastery

Next to the Tourist Lodge, about three km from the centre of town, the 200-year-old Enchey Monastery is well worth a visit, particularly if you're in Gangtok when religious dances are performed in December.

Lall Market

If you've been to markets in Kathmandu or Darjeeling, this one will come as a disappointment as it has none of their colour and magic, nor their range of products.

Tours

The Department of Tourism offers daily tours of Rumtek Monastery and Gangtok's various points of interest from February to May and from October to December. For reservations, contact the Department of Tourism, Gangtok Bazaar (tel 664).

The morning tour includes visits to Tashi View Point, the Deer Park, Enchey Monastery, the Royal Chapel, the Secretariat, the Cottage Industries Institute, the Institute of Tibetology and the nearby chorten and orchid sanctuary.

Places to Stay – bottom end

The *Shere Punjab* (tel 2823), just below the Hotel Orchid, has rooms at Rs 20/30, Rs 55 for a double with bath. At the *Doma Hotel*, rooms with common bath are similarly priced.

Accommodation at the *Sinouchu Lodge* costs Rs 50/75, Rs 80/120 for deluxe rooms. The hotel is managed by the Government of Sikkim Tourist Department and is about 40 minutes walk, or Rs 25 by taxi, from town. 'The sunrises viewed from your window are right out of the Book of Genesis' enthused one biblically minded traveller.

The *Hotel Orchid* (tel 2381) has rooms with bath for Rs 65, Rs 40 with common bath. There are also larger three and four-bed rooms, and prices are lower in the off season. Avoid the top-floor rooms at the back. The place is clean and has friendly staff, attractive rooms with excellent views of Kanchenjunga, hot water when the electricity is on (there are frequent power cuts in Gangtok) and a restaurant and bar on the top floor. However, solo women may find this place a bit difficult.

The *Green Hotel* (tel 2254) is a little way up the main bazaar from the tourist office, on the same side of the road. It has a restaurant and a wide variety of rooms; the 3rd-floor singles for Rs 100 are good. Again, prices are lower in the off season and the rooms are possibly slightly better than those at the Orchid. The *Karma Hotel* has bathless rooms at Rs 20/45 and doubles with bath for Rs 65.

The *Hotel Kanchen View* (tel 2086) has dorm beds, as well as rooms priced from Rs 35 to Rs 65. Other hotels include the *Deeki Hotel* (tel 2301), described by one unimpressed traveller as 'a nasty pimple on the face of Indian accommodation', the rock-bottom *Leden La Hotel* and the *Holiday Inn* (no relation to the international chain).

If you can get in, the *PWD Bungalow* is high up on the National Highway, beyond the Cottage Industries Emporium. There are only two double rooms available and these cost Rs 16 per person. Book with the

Executive Engineer, CPWD North, Sikkim Highway, Gangtok.

At the top of this range is the Tibetan-run *Hotel Tibet* (tel 2523) on Stadium Rd. Singles/doubles here cost between Rs 60/80 to Rs 145/195, all with bath. There's a bar, restaurant, currency exchange facilities and a laundry service, and the staff are friendly and helpful.

Places to Stay - top end
There are a surprising number of more expensive hotels in Gangtok. The centrally located *Nor-Khill Hotel* (tel 3186/7) has singles/doubles for Rs 450/550 including all meals. There's a bar, library, currency exchange facilities and a restaurant which offers continental, Chinese and Indian food.

Though officially a four-star hotel, the *Hotel Tashi Delek* (tel 2991, 2038) is similarly priced and offers much the same facilities as the Nor-Khill. It has singles/doubles at Rs 300/500 including all meals, Rs 150/200 without meals.

Places to Eat
Most restaurants are attached to the hotels, such as the Hotel Tibet's excellent *Snow Lion Restaurant*. The *Hotel Orchid's* restaurant is also popular with good chicken curry, vegetables, fried dhal and so on. In the Orchid's bar, beer is cheap and a tot of Sikkimese spirit is even cheaper. Although not quite up to the standard of the Orchid, the *Green Hotel's* restaurant also has very good food.

The excellent *Blue Sheep Restaurant*, in the tourist office complex, has good food. The *Tashi Delek* has a restaurant where you can sit outside - pleasant in summer - while the *Kho-Chi Restaurant*, on the corner of Gandhi Marg and National Highway, offers good Chinese food. *Durga Sweets* and *Lazmi Sweets*, diagonally across from the Green Hotel, have excellent snacks such as puris and idli vada.

Other than this, you can obtain basic food at very low prices from a number of simple vegetarian cafes around the bus stand and along the main bazaar. About 500 metres uphill from the bus stand on the National Highway, where a road branches off to the stadium and Nor-Khill Hotel, there is a cafe which serves tea, coffee and snacks.

Try *thungba* from a chang shop in the market - a large bamboo mug full of millet to which you add hot water to get fresh *chang*.

Getting There & Away
Air An Indian Airlines helicopter service operates daily between Bagdogra airport and Gangtok. It departs Gangtok at 11.30 am and Bagdogra at 1.30 pm. The journey takes about half an hour.

Train The nearest railheads are at Siliguri/New Jalpaiguri and Darjeeling.

Bus Sikkim Nationalised Transport (SNT) is the main bus operator to Gangtok but, as their buses are almost always hopelessly overcrowded, it's far preferable to take a taxi or Land Rover if possible.

Siliguri The trip to or from Gangtok takes about five hours; there are some half a dozen buses a day and the fare is Rs 25. Apart from SNT, buses are also operated by North Bengal Services, Apsara and other companies.

Bagdogra SNT have a daily bus connecting with flights from Bagdogra airport. The journey takes five hours.

Darjeeling SNT and North Bengal Services run buses on this route. The journey takes six or seven hours and costs Rs 40. SNT uses what is probably its best minibus for this trip. The service is heavily booked, so plan well in advance. If the bus is full you can always go via Kalimpong, as there are more buses operating between Gangtok and Kalimpong and frequent Land Rovers from Kalimpong to Darjeeling. The road house at Rangpo, on the border between West Bengal and Sikkim, is the only place you can get food

between Sikkim and Darjeeling, apart from snacks at the Teesta Bridge. The service is impossibly slow so perhaps it's better to bring some food with you.
Kalimpong SNT, Jayshree and Sangam operate on this route. The trip takes about four hours and costs about Rs 20.

AROUND GANGTOK
Rumtek Monastery
Rumtek, on the other side of the Ranipool Valley, is visible from Gangtok though it's 24 km away by road. The monastery is the seat of the Gyalwa Karmapa, the head of the Kagyu-pa sect of Tibetan Buddhism. The sect was founded in the 11th century by Lama Marpa, the disciple of the Indian guru Naropa, and later split into several subsects, the most important of which are Druk-pa, Kagyu-pa and Karma-pa. The teachings of the sect are transmitted to the disciples orally.

The main monastery is a recent structure, built by the Gyalwa Karmapa in strict accordance with the traditional designs of his monastery in Tibet. Visitors are welcome and there's no objection to your sitting in on the prayer and chanting sessions. They'll even bring you a cup of salted butter tea when it's served to the monks. Mural work is still being done; if you're interested in the Tibetan style of religious painting, Rumtek is a must.

If you follow the tarmac road for two or three km beyond Rumtek, through a gate off to the left you'll find another interesting, but smaller, monastery which was restored in 1983. Opposite is an old and run-down monastery with leather prayer wheels.

Places to Stay The *Kunga Delak Hotel & Restaurant* is off the square in front of the monastery and has cheap rooms. It's dirty, with no water (although the rooms have bathrooms) and the bus will probably arrive too late in the evening for you to get any food.

The *Hotel Sangay* is 100 metres down

the motor road from the monastery. It's basic but clean and blankets and candles are provided (there's no electricity most of the time). Beautifully quiet and peaceful, the Sangay is run by friendly people. The price of the rooms is negotiable but should be around Rs 15 per bed. Just below the lodge is a small chai shop where eggs and fresh bread are served in the morning, chow-chow in the evening.

Getting There & Away A daily bus leaves from Gangtok in the late afternoon and returns from Rumtek early the next morning, forcing you to spend at least two nights in Rumtek. The journey takes about two hours (half a day return) and Land Rovers or Ambassador taxis are available. Count on paying around Rs 200 return per car.

Pemayangtse & Tashiding Monasteries
Pemayangtse Monastery, at a height of 2085 metres, is the second oldest monastery in Sikkim. It belongs to the Tantric Nyingma-pa sect, which was established by the Indian teacher, Padmasambhava, in the 8th century. All the sect's monasteries are characterised by a prominent image of this teacher, together with two female consorts, and this monastery is the head of all others in Sikkim. The sect followers wear red caps.

Pemayangtse is about six km from the bus terminus at Gezing, while Tashiding is a full-day hike up a ridge from Pemayangtse. The hike starts with a 1½-hour uphill walk to Tashiding village. The monastery itself, hidden by pine trees, is further up the hill, near the summit, a walk of about 15 minutes from the village. Sangacholing Monastery is also in the vicinity.

At present, permits to visit Pemayangtse appear to be very restricted.

Places to Stay Gezing has a choice of at least four basic lodges for around Rs 20 a room – any number of people can share a room. Food of the rice, dhal and eggs variety is available.

If you want something slightly better, try the *PWD Rest House*, about two km up the hill from Gezing towards Pemayangtse. It's excellent value but prior booking is necessary; do this at the CPWD in Gangtok between 9.30 am and 4.30 pm. The chowkidah cooks excellent meals for a further charge.

There is a *Forestry Department Bungalow* at Tashiding but you must bring your own blankets and sheets. To stay here, you need authorisation from either the tourist office in Gangtok or the Forestry Department in Gezing. Good meals are available in the village chai shop and, if you eat there, you'll have the whole village for company!

For luxury accommodation, the *Pemayangtse Tourist Lodge* (tel 73) has rooms for around Rs 400 including all meals. Contact the tourist office in Gangtok for reservations.

Getting There & Away Between Gangtok and Gezing (sometimes spelt Geyshing), one bus per day operates in either direction and leaves in the morning. The journey takes seven to eight hours. Pemayangtse is about six km from Gezing but, if the bus is late, basic accommodation is available in Gezing. A trip to Pemayangtse will take at least three days, so make sure your permit covers you for this period.

As with Rumtek, you can hire a car or jeep for around Rs 800 round trip, depending on the route taken.

Phodang Monastery

This is as far as you are allowed to go in eastern Sikkim without further bureaucratic entanglement. Phodang Monastery at Thumlong, 40 km north of Gangtok, has recently been rebuilt but, at Labrang Gompa just above it, the original construction is still intact. Labrang is accessible on foot along a bitumen road,

Lady from Sikkim

40 minutes walk from Phodang. If you're permitted to go further up the road to Mangan and Singhik, you'll get a clear unobstructed view of Kanchenjunga. The Phodang Monastery is sometimes closed.

Places to Stay The *Yak & Yeti*, along the highway to Mangan, has big clean rooms for around Rs 20 per bed. The food here – rice, dhal, vegetables, momos and so on – is excellent, as is the chang and *raksi*. The people are very friendly and charge you no more than the locals.

Getting There & Away There are several daily buses to Phodang, some of which continue on to Mangan. The trip takes around 2½ hours and the fare is Rs 8. Allow plenty of time if you want to see anything of Phodang and the other monasteries in the area.

A car or jeep costs about Rs 350 for the half-day return trip.

TREKKING IN SIKKIM

You can trek in western Sikkim but you need a further endorsement on your permit. Though the regulations are somewhat elastic, you're officially allowed to trek to Dzongri for up to 10 days so long as: 1) you're accompanied by a travel agent recognised by the Indian Tourist Development Corporation and a liaison officer or guide provided by the government of Sikkim; 2) you travel by air from Calcutta to Bagdogra; and 3) you take either the Nayan Bazaar/Pemayangtse/Yuksam/Dzongri route or the Rangpo/Gangtok/ Yuksam/Dzongri one.

In other words, you have little choice but to go with an organised tour unless you have political clout with the Sikkimese bureaucracy. The travel agents which organise these treks are Yak & Yeti Travels, Snow Lion Travels or Sikkim Himalayan Adventure, all in Gangtok. They also hire trekking gear. The best time to trek is mid-February to late May and October to December.

Travellers' Notebook

Communications

Communication in India has special rules, not altogether unlike those in other places in Asia but totally unlike those that prevail in the west. Use any answer rather than a negative one, for example.

'Will the bus stop here?'

'Yes'. Which could equally mean 'No, but I'd hate to disappoint you by telling you so'. Or 'I've got no idea' or 'I simply can't raise the energy to think about that question'.

'Am I heading in the right direction for the Grand Hotel?'

'Yes'. Which might mean 'Good grief, you've come so far in the wrong direction already I'd hate to be the one to tell you'.

The solution is to always word questions so that a commitment must be made. Not 'Is this the way?' but 'Which is the way?'. But then you can fall for the any answer rather than no answer syndrome – 'Down that way and round the corner, then straight for a km' might mean 'I've got no idea at all'. Never ask directions just once.

More annoying than fouled-up communications are no communications at all. Many Indians (and away from the main tourist centres, taxi or auto-rickshaw drivers are particularly prone to this) feel that communicating with a foreigner is completely impossible. Hop in an auto-rickshaw and ask for the 'Grand Hotel'. Complete incomprehension. Pronounce 'Grand Hotel' 20 different ways but, despite the fact that the Grand Hotel is the town's number-one landmark, it's not getting through. Eventually an English-speaking passer-by is found. 'Where do you want to go?', he asks. 'Grand Hotel' you tell him, 'Grand Hotel', he says to the auto-rickshaw driver and you're saved.

Even more annoying than that is the precognated communication. The driver knows better than you do what you want. The fact that you're saying airport quietly, loudly or even screaming it has no bearing on his conviction that you really want a hotel and if he can get you into the Hotel Super he'll get a commission!

Tony Wheeler

North-East Frontier

state	capital	area (sq km)	population
Assam	Gawahati	78,000	24,000,000
Manipur	Imphal	22,300	1,700,000
Meghalaya	Shillong	22,400	1,500,000
Nagaland	Kohima	17,000	900,000
Tripura	Agartala	10,400	2,400,000
Arunachal Pradesh	Itanagar	84,000	720,000
Mizoram	Aizawi	21,000	590,000

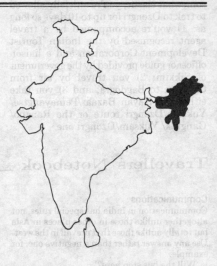

The north-east region is the most varied and at the same time the least-visited part of India. Before independence the whole region was known as Assam Province, but it was finally split into five separate states and two Union Territories – Mizoram and Arunachal Pradesh.

In many ways the north-east is unlike the rest of India. It is the country's chief tribal area, with a great number of tribes speaking many different languages and dialects – in Arunachal Pradesh alone over 50 distinct languages are spoken! These tribal people have many similarities to the hill tribes across the sweep of the country at the eastern end of the Himalaya, which extends from India through Burma (Myanmar) and Thailand into Laos. Also, the north-east has a high percentage of Christians, particularly in the more isolated areas where the population is predominantly hill tribespeople.

For a number of reasons India has always been touchy about the north-east, and a visit to the region is a tricky proposition. For a start the north-east is a sensitive border zone where India meets Bhutan, China, Burma and Bangladesh. Equally important, the region is remote – only the narrow Siliguri corridor connects it to the rest of India, and before independence the usual route to Assam would have been through Bangladesh. Today, going far into the north-east by train involves a long journey by metre-gauge rail. Roads have been improved dramatically but there are still very few of them compared with the rest of India.

The Indian government has been sensitive about visitors and in the past only permitted them to go to Assam and Meghalaya. The other five regions, all bordering China or Burma, were for all practical purposes off limits. Even a visit to Assam and Meghalaya required a special permit, although this was readily available, at least for specific tourist attractions.

Then in the early '80s the north-east was the scene for violence, terrorism and a whole series of riots and strikes, leaving it off limits for a time to outsiders. There were a number of reasons for this unrest, including a feeling of central government neglect (poor transport links and lack of infrastructure development were the main complaints). This feeling strengthened as oil prices rose since Assam has a substantial part of India's small, but important, oil reserves. Very little of this oil wealth found its way back to improve Assam's industrial development, and the whole region remains overwhelmingly agricultural.

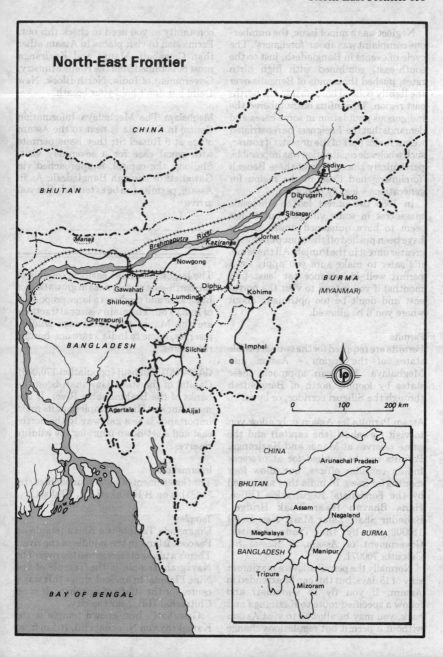

Neglect was a minor issue; the number-one complaint was about 'foreigners'. The cycle of events in Bangladesh, just to the south-east, combined with high birth rates, pushed thousands of Bengalis over the lightly policed borders into the north-east region. This influx outnumbered the indigenous population in some cases and demands that the 'foreigners' be repatriated were a major part of the unrest. Of course, such wholesale repatriation was impossible, particularly since many of these Bengali 'foreigners' had lived in the region for generations – legally or not.

In 1983 the unrest led to wholesale massacres in some villages, but things seem to have quietened down. Events have been pushed off the front page by the greater unrest in the Punjab. All the same, it's safer to make sure you apply for a permit well in advance (at least four months) if you intend to visit the north-east and don't be too optimistic about where you'll be allowed.

Permits

Permits are required for the two accessible states of the region – Assam and Meghalaya. You can approach these states by looping north of Bangladesh through the Siliguri corridor, or by air.

Assam Permits for Assam only allow you to visit Gawahati (the capital) and the game reserves at Manas and Kaziranga. Permits can be applied for at overseas Indian consular offices, but allow four months for issue. In India they are issued by the Foreigners' Registration Office, Hans Bhavan (near Tilak Bridge), Bahadur Shah, Zafar Marg, New Delhi 110002; or by the Trade Adviser, Government of Assam, 8 Russel St, Calcutta 700071.

Normally the permit allows a maximum stay of 15 days, but this can be extended in Assam. If you fly to Gawahati and follow a specified route to Kaziranga and back, you may be allowed to visit Assam without a permit but regulations change constantly so you need to check this out. Permission to visit places in Assam other than Gawahati, Manas and Kaziranga must be obtained from the Home Ministry, Government of India, North Block, New Delhi but don't hold your breath.

Meghalaya The Meghalaya Information Centre in Calcutta is next to the Assam office at 9 Russel St; they issue permits with equal ease for a seven-day visit. Shillong, the capital, is approached via Gawahati or through Bangladesh. As in Assam, permits can be extended after you arrive.

Assam

The largest and most easily accessible of the north-east states, Assam grows 60% of India's tea and produces a large proportion of India's oil. The main visitor attractions are the Manas and Kaziranga wildlife reserves, home to India's rare one-horned rhinoceros.

GAWAHATI (Gauhati) (population 170,000) Capital of the state, Gawahati is on the banks of the Brahmaputra River. It has many ancient Hindu temples but its main importance is as a gateway to the north-east and a set-down point for the wildlife reserves.

Information

The Government of India tourist office (tel 31381) is on B K Kakati Rd, Ulubari.

Temples

Umananda Temple is a Shiva temple on Peacock Island in the middle of the river. There's a pleasant ferry across the river. The Navagrah Temple is the Temple of the Nine Planets. In ancient times this was a centre for the study of astrology. It is on Chitrachal Hill, near the city.

Gawahati's best-known temple is the Kamakshya on Nilachal Hill, 10 km from

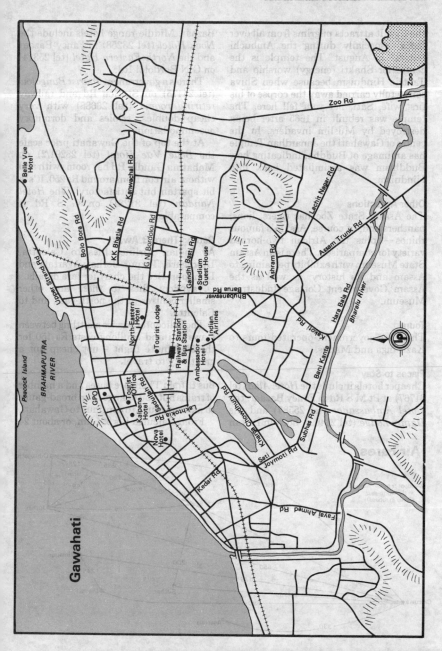

the city. It attracts pilgrims from all over India, especially during the Ambuchi festival in August. The temple is the centre for Shakti (energy) worship and Tantric Hinduism because when Shiva sorrowfully carried away the corpse of his first wife, Sati, her *yoni* fell here. The temple was rebuilt in 1665 after being destroyed by Muslim invaders. In the centre of Gawahati the Janardhan Temple has an image of Buddha, indicating how Buddhism was assimilated back into Hinduism.

Other Attractions
The Assam State Zoo has tigers, lions, panthers and, of course, Assam's famous rhinos – plus the African two-horned variety for comparison. There is an Assam State Museum with exhibits pertaining to Assam and its history, as well as the Assam Government Cottage Industries Museum.

Tours
There are government-operated tours to Kaziranga and Manas.

Places to Stay
Cheaper hotels include the *Hotel Alka* (tel 31767) at Pt M S Rd in Fancy Bazaar, the *Hotel Ambassador* (tel 25587) and the *Happy Lodge* (tel 23409), both in Paltan Bazaar. Middle-range hotels include the *Nova Hotel* (tel 23258) in Fancy Bazaar and the *North-Eastern Hotel* (tel 25314) on G N Bordoloi Rd.

There's a government *Tourist Bungalow* (tel 24475) on Station Rd and railway *retiring rooms* (tel 26688) with very cheap doubles, triples and dormitory accommodation.

At the top of the Gawahati price scale the *Belle Vue Hotel* (tel 28291/2) on Mahatma Gandhi Rd has rooms with and without air-con from around Rs 250. It's 'a bit spartan but satisfactory'. The *Hotel Nandan* (tel 31281) on G S Rd is comparable.

Getting There & Away
Air Indian Airlines flies to Calcutta, Dibrugarh, Tezpur, Jorhat, Agartala and Dimapur. See the chart for fare details.

Vayudoot flies to these and other smaller centres in the north-east, and to Calcutta.

The helicopter service shuttling between Gawahati and Shillong costs Rs 150 for the 35-minute flight – not cheap but a great way to travel.

Bus & Train There are buses and a number of trains but you change from broad-gauge to narrow-gauge to continue to Gawahati.

From Calcutta it's 991 km, or about 24

Air Fares

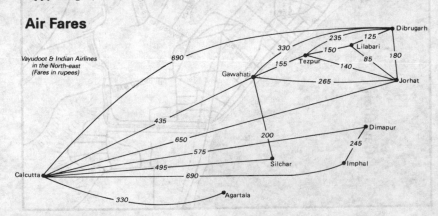

Vayudoot & Indian Airlines
in the North-east
(Fares in rupees)

hours, to Gawahati and costs Rs 91 in 2nd class, and Rs 344 in 1st. It's about 19 hours to Dibrugarh, or 560 km, and costs Rs 59 in 2nd class and Rs 218 in 1st. New Delhi is 2050 km and 36 hours away, even on the fastest train, the NE Express.

The Shillong to Gawahati bus takes 3½ hours and costs Rs 24.

AROUND GAWAHATI
Hajo

On the north bank of the Brahmaputra, 24 km from Gawahati, Hajo is an important pilgrimage centre for Buddhists and Muslims. Some Buddhists believe that Buddha attained nirvana here, and they flock to the Hayagriba Madhab Temple. For Muslims the Pao Mecca Mosque is considered to have one-quarter (*pao*) the sanctity of the great mosque at Mecca.

Sualkashi

Also across the river from Gawahati, 20 km away, this is a famous silk-weaving centre where the Endi, Muga and Pat silks of Assam are made in a small household weaving centre. There is a regular ferry across the river and a bus several times daily.

Other Attractions

Basistha Ashram is 12 km south of Gawahati, and the *rishi* or sage, Basistha, once lived here. It's a popular picnic spot. The beautiful natural lagoon at Chandubi is 64 km from Gawahati.

Darranga, 80 km away on the Bhutan border, is a great winter trading area for the Bhutias mountain folk. Barpeta, with a monastery and the shrine of a Vaishnavaite reformer, is 145 km north-west of Gawahati.

WILDLIFE PARKS

Assam is famous for its rare one-horned Great Indian Rhinoceros – when Marco Polo saw it he thought he had found the legendary unicorn! Kaziranga and Manas are the two well-known parks in Assam.

There are smaller parks at Orang and Sonai.

Kaziranga

North-east of Gawahati, on the banks of the Brahmaputra River, is the Kaziranga Wildlife Reserve famous as the last major home of *Rhinoceros unicornis*. The 430-square-km park is thought to have a rhino population approaching 1000, although in 1904 they were on the verge of extinction. The park became a game sanctuary in 1926, and by 1966 the numbers had risen to about 400.

The park also has wild gaur (buffalo), deer, elephants, tigers, bears and many water bird species including pelicans, which breed here. One of the standard ways of observing the wildlife is from elephant-back, and the rhinos are said to have become accustomed to elephants carrying camera-toting tourists.

Information The park is at its best from February to May. There is a tourist information centre (tel 23) at Kaziranga, but you're supposed to give 10 days' notice for booking accommodation or transport. They have a minibus and a jeep and also organise those elephant rides into the long grass. There's an entry fee for the park and an additional charge for a still camera, plus higher charges for telephoto lenses (!) or movie cameras.

Places to Stay There is a variety of accommodation around the park, including *Forest Inspection Bungalows* at Beguri (no bedding or mosquito nets), Arimarh (no electricity) and Kohora. Or there is a *Soil Conservation Inspection Bungalow*, a very cheap *PWD Inspection Bungalow* at Kaziranga and two *Tourist Bungalows*. At the top of the price scale there are rooms at the *Kaziranga Forest Lodge* from around Rs 250, with and without air-con.

Getting There & Away Calcutta/Jorhat flights land 84 km from the park.

Furketing is the most convenient railway station, 72 km away; from here buses run to Kaziranga. Gawahati is 233 km away on Highway 37. There are state transport buses from Gawahati.

Jorhat

A little beyond Kaziranga, this is the gateway to the north-east of Assam. Sibsagar, 55 km away, has the huge Jay Sagar Tank and many temples in the environs; it was the old capital of the Ahom kingdom. There's a small *Tourist Bungalow* by the tank.

Manas

In the foothills of the Himalaya, north-west of Gawahati, Manas Wildlife Sanctuary is on the Bhutan border. Three rivers run through the sanctuary, which has abundant bird and animal life. The rare pygmy hog and the golden langur (monkey) are amongst the notable animals here, although you may also see rhinos.

Information Manas is best from January to March; there is excellent fishing from November to December. Mothangiri is the main town in the park but the tourist information centre (tel 49) is in Barpeta Rd. Entry and camera charges are the same as Kaziranga. Boats can be hired for excursions or fishing trips on the Manas River.

Places to Stay *Manas Tourist Lodge* has rooms in the upper bungalow and the lower bungalow from around Rs 20 per bed up to Rs 65 or more per room. You can camp if you have a tent. The *Forest Bungalow* doesn't have electricity but it is cheaper, and includes bedding and mosquito nets. There is a *Rest House* at the Barpeta Road Tourist Centre.

Getting There & Away Gawahati, 176 km away, has the nearest airport. Barpeta Road, 40 km from Mothangiri, is the nearest

railway station. Transport from here to Mothangiri must be arranged in advance.

Meghalaya

Created in 1971, this state is the home for Khasia, Jantia and Garo tribespeople. The hill station of Shillong is the state capital while Cherrapunji, 58 km away, is said to be the wettest place on earth with an average annual rainfall of 1150 centimetres, nearly 40 feet! In one year 2300 centimetres (75 feet) of rain fell. It's no wonder Meghalaya means 'abode of clouds'.

Other places of interest around the state include Jakrem with its hot springs, Kayllang Rock at Mairang, Mawjymbuin Cave at Mawsynram and Umiam Lake. Recently Mawsynram had an annual rainfall total that even surpassed the record at Cherrapunji.

SHILLONG (population 200,000)

This pleasant hill station, standing at 1496 metres, is renowned for its climate and breathtaking views; it's even had the label 'Scotland of the East' applied to it! Around town you can pass the time observing the tiny red-light district behind the Delhi Hotel, as there's not a lot to do apart from pass through. The people around Shillong, the Khasias, are matrilineal, passing down property and wealth through the female rather than the male line.

Information

Police Bazaar has a Government of Meghalaya tourist office (tel 6054) and a Government of India tourist office (tel 25632) on G S Rd. The GPO is also on G S Rd.

Things to See

The State Museum covers the flora, fauna, culture and anthropology of the state. The town has a number of parks and gardens and a Botanic Garden and Botanical Museum beside the central Ward Lake. The Crinoline Waterfalls are near Lady Hydari Park, and there are various other waterfalls around Shillong. The town takes its name from the 1960-metre-high Shillong Peak, from which there are fine views. It's 10 km from the centre.

The Anglical graveyard and All Saints' Cathedral may be of interest to fans of the Raj; the gravestones have inscriptions such as 'killed in the great earthquake' or 'murdered by headhunters'.

Tours
There are morning tours of the city area, and day tours to Cherrapunji and the hot springs at Jakrem.

Places to Stay & Eat
There's a good *Tourist Bungalow* near the polo grounds with rooms and dormitory accommodation. There are many other middle-priced hotels around, and cheap accommodation can be found in the Police Bazaar near the tourist office. There's good food at the *Lhasa Restaurant*; there are several other restaurants around town.

Mr Bhuyan's *Snack Bar a la Carte* (tel 24909) has good accommodation for Rs 150 with hot water by the bucket. Mr Bhuyan is very friendly and a good source of information.

The *Hotel Pinewood Ashok* (tel 23116, 23765) is Shillong's premier hotel (and Ashok's worst, said a visitor), with rooms from Rs 250. The disgruntled visitor reported that it was damp and mouse infested.

Getting There & Away
A good road runs the 100 km from Gawahati in Assam to Shillong. Cherrapunji is 58 km south of Shillong, and there are daily buses; if it's not raining the views from here over Bangladesh are superb. Permission is required from the Commissioner of Police to visit the area, but it's given readily.

Coming from Bangladesh, you cross the border (if it's open) at Dawki, from where it's a 1½-km walk to the town, and then a 3½-hour trip to Shillong.

Other States & Territories

The other north-eastern regions are generally hard to get permission to visit even at the best of times. All of them border either with China or Burma (Myanmar). The following information is for interest only.

Transport in the Region
The only railway to these states and territories terminates at Ledo, but the roads have been improved lately. Both Indian Airlines and Vayudoot operate a comprehensive service to the region from Calcutta.

ARUNACHAL PRADESH
The furthest north-east of the regions, this was known as the North-East Frontier Agency under the British. Arunachal Pradesh borders with Bhutan, China and Burma and is a mountainous, remote and predominantly tribal area. The old 'Stillwell Road' used to run from Ledo in the south of Arunachal Pradesh to Myitkyinya in the north-east of Burma. Built in 1944 by General 'Vinegar Joe' Stillwell, it must rate as one of the most expensive roads in the world. The 430 km cost US$137 million way back then, and after opening for just a few months it has hardly been used since. All road routes into Burma are closed.

NAGALAND
South of Arunachal Pradesh and north of Manipur, the remote and hilly state of Nagaland is bordered by Burma. Kohima, the capital of Nagaland, was the furthest

point Japanese troops advanced into India during WW II.

MANIPUR

South of Nagaland and north of Mizoram, Manipur also borders with Burma. The state is inhabited by over two dozen different tribes, many of them Christians. It is famous for its Manipuri dances and handloomed textiles.

Imphal (population 130,000), the capital, is surrounded by wooded hills and lakes and has the golden Shri Govindaji Temple. During WW II a road was built from Imphal to Tamu on the Burma border but, as with the Stillwell Road further north, this route into Burma is also closed.

MIZORAM

This finger-like extension in the extreme south-east of the region pokes between Burma and Bangladesh. The name means hill people's land – Mizo, 'man of the hill', and ram, 'land'. It's a picturesque place where the population is both predominantly tribal and overwhelmingly Christian.

TRIPURA

The tiny state of Tripura is almost totally surrounded by Bangladesh. It's a lush, wooded region with many beautiful waterfalls. Agartala is the capital; near it is the lake palace of Nirmahal. Here, too, the population is largely tribal.

Travellers' Notebook

Indian Airlines

Flying Indian Airlines is a much more restful experience since they've computerised. Well, booking Indian Airlines flights is much more restful, anyway. At their Calcutta office each terminal has a floor fan standing behind it since somebody forgot to design a cooling fan into the computer terminals!

New computers or not, they can still dish up some truly terrible food though. They get it right on some of the longer flights, but on short

hops 'meals' are usually sandwiches which look as dreadful as they taste. The real surprise, however, is that often they're not prepared by Indian Airlines but by the local top-notch hotel which, with commendable honesty but considerable lack of marketing sense, even add their name card to the junk they prepare. Would anybody deign to eat at the Taj Mahal Hotel in Bombay after they'd seen a Taj cheese sandwich on an IA flight?

Tony Wheeler

Rajasthan

Population: 41 million
Area: 342,214 square km
Capital: Jaipur
Main languages: Rajasthani & Hindi

Rajasthan, the 'Land of the Kings', is India at its exotic and colourful best. It is the home of the Rajputs, a group of warrior clans who have controlled this part of India for 1000 years according to a code of chivalry and honour akin to that of the medieval European knights. While temporary alliances and marriages of convenience were the order of the day, pride and independence were always paramount. The Rajputs were therefore never able to present a united front against a common aggressor. Indeed, much of their energy was spent squabbling amongst themselves and the resultant weakness eventually led to their becoming vassal states of the Moghul Empire. Nevertheless, the Rajputs' bravery and sense of honour were unparalleled.

Rajput warriors would fight on against all odds and, when no hope was left, chivalry demanded that *jauhar* be declared. In this grim ritual, the women and children committed suicide by immolating themselves on a huge funeral pyre, while the men donned saffron robes and rode out to meet the enemy and certain death. In some of the larger battles, tens of thousands of Rajput warriors lost their lives in this way. Three times in Chittorgarh's long history, the women consigned themselves to the flames while the men rode out to their martyrdom. The same tragic fate befell many other fortresses around the state. It's hardly surprising that Akbar persuaded Rajputs to lead his army, nor that subsequent Moghul emperors had such difficulty controlling this part of their empire.

With the decline of the Moghul Empire,

the Rajputs gradually clawed back their independence through a series of spectacular victories but, by then, a new force had appeared on the scene in the form of the British. As the Raj inexorably expanded, most Rajput states signed articles of alliance with the British which allowed them to continue as independent states, each with its own maharaja (or similar title), subject to certain political and economic constraints. The British, after all, were not there for humanitarian reasons but to establish an empire and gain a controlling interest in the economy of the subcontinent in the same way as the Moghuls.

These alliances proved to be the beginning of the end for the Rajput rulers. Indulgence and extravagance soon replaced chivalry and honour so that, by the early 1900s, many of the maharajas spent most of their time travelling the world with a vast army of wives, concubines and retainers, playing polo, racing horses, gambling and occupying whole floors of the most expensive hotels in Europe and America. While it suited the British to indulge them in this respect, their profligate waste of Rajputana's resources was socially and educationally disastrous. When India gained its independence, Rajasthan had one of the subcontinent's lowest life expectancy and literacy rates.

At independence, India's ruling Congress Party was forced to make a deal with the nominally independent Rajput states in order to secure their agreement to join the new India. The rulers were allowed to keep their titles, their property holdings were secured and they were paid an annual stipend commensurate with their status. It couldn't last forever, given India's socialist persuasion, and the crunch came in the early 1970s when Indira Gandhi abolished both the titles and the stipends and severely sequestered their property rights.

While some of the rulers have survived this by turning their forts into museums and their palaces into luxury hotels, many have fallen by the wayside, unable to cope with the financial and managerial demands of the late 20th century.

Although the fortunes of its former rulers may be in tatters, the culture of Rajasthan, with its battle-scarred forts, its palaces of amazing luxury and whimsical charm, its riotous colours and even its romantic sense of pride and honour, is still very much alive. It is certainly part of India, yet it's visibly unique. That visibility extends from the huge pastel-coloured turbans and soup-strainer moustaches sported by the men and the bright mirrored skirts and chunky silver jewellery of the women, to the manner in which these people deal with you. In some parts of India, you can never be sure that agreements will be kept. There are always exceptions, of course, but an agreement struck in Rajasthan is generally solid. Tourism has obviously made inroads here, but it will be a long time before it corrupts the traditional sense of honesty or destroys the cultural vitality of these people.

The land itself is somewhat dry and, in parts, inhospitable. Geographically, it's

very varied. The state is diagonally divided into the hilly and rugged south-east region and the barren north-east Thar Desert, which extends across the border into Pakistan. Like all deserts, the Thar offers oases of magic and romance. There are plenty of historic cities, incredible fortresses awash with legends, and rare gems of impressionistic beauty, such as Udaipur, which combine water with earth and sky to create a pastiche of paradise. There are also a number of centres which attract travellers from far and wide, such as peaceful Pushkar with its holy lake, and the exotic desert city of Jaisalmer which resembles a fantasy from *The Thousand & One Nights*.

No-one visits Rajasthan without taking home superb memories, an address book full of friends (who keep in touch with you!) and, often, a bundle of embroidery and jewellery.

Art & Architecture

Rajasthan has a school of miniature painting, the style deriving from the Moghul but with some clear differences – in particular, the palace and hunting scenes are complemented by religious themes, relating especially to the Krishna legends. This art carried through to the elegant palaces built by the Rajputs when they were freed from confrontation with the Moghuls. Many are liberally covered with colourful frescoes.

Most of Rajasthan's early architecture was damaged or destroyed by the first waves of Muslim invaders. Fragments remaining from that period include the Adhai-din-ka-jhonpra Mosque in Ajmer, which is basically a converted Hindu temple of great elegance, and the ruined temples at Osian, near Jodhpur. There are many buildings dating from the 10th to 15th century, including the superb Jain temples at Ranakpur, Mt Abu and Jaisalmer. Most of the great forts date, in their present form, from the Moghul period.

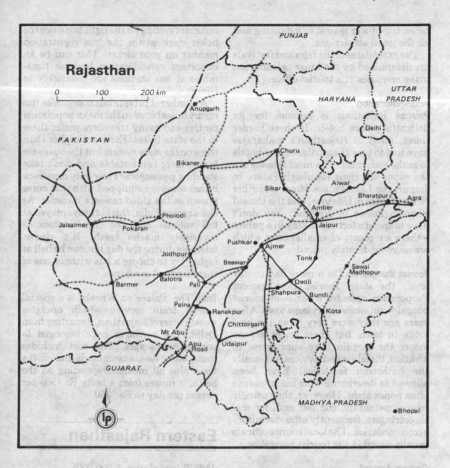

Rajasthan

0   100   200 km

PUNJAB

HARYANA

UTTAR
PRADESH

PAKISTAN

Anupgarh

Delhi

Churu

Bikaner

Alwar

Sikar

Bharatpur

Agra

Amber

Pholodi

Jaipur

Jaisalmer

Pokaran

Pushkar

Ajmer

Tonk

Jodhpur

Beawar

Sawai
Madhopur

Barmer

Balotra

Pali

Deoli

Shahpura

Bundi

Palna

Kota

Ranakpur

Chittorgarh

Mt Abu

Udaipur

Abu
Road

GUJARAT

MADHYA PRADESH

Bhopal

LP

Festivals

Rajasthan has all the usual Hindu and Muslim festivals, some celebrated with special local fervour, as well as a number of festivals of its own. The spring festival of Gangaur (late March to early April) is particularly important, as is Teej (early to late August) which welcomes the monsoon. The state is at its most beautiful when the monsoon rains fill the many lakes and tanks.

Rajasthan also has many fairs, some traditional and others the creation of the state Tourist Development Corporation. Best known of the fairs is the immense and colourful Pushkar camel and cattle fair, held annually in early to mid-November. Similar, but less well known, are the Nagaur festival (late January to early February), about halfway between Bikaner and Jodhpur, and the fair at Bikaner (mid to late November).

The Desert Festival at Jaisalmer (early to mid-February) is a modern creation designed to foster local folk arts and music and to promote tourism. It features camel races, tug-of-war teams, folk dancing and all the usual attractions.

The exact dates of the fairs and festivals are determined by the lunar calendar, so make enquiries at a tourist office.

Accommodation

Palaces Rajasthan is famous for its delightful palace hotels. In these harder times, many of Rajasthan's maharajas have had to turn their palaces into hotels to make ends meet. The most famous are the super-luxurious Rambagh Palace in Jaipur, the Lake Palace Hotel and Shiv Niwas Palace in Udaipur, and the Umaid Bhawan Palace in Jodhpur. You don't have to spend a fortune to stay in a palace – there are plenty of smaller ones which are more moderately priced.

Tourist Bungalows On a more day-to-day level, the state Tourist Development Corporation operates a series of tourist bungalows in almost every large town. A few years ago they were very often the best value in town, but their prices are no longer the bargain they once were. In addition, the fabric and services (especially the bathroom facilities) have been allowed to deteriorate with maintenance often nonexistent. However, they usually have a restaurant and bar and, for real shoestringers, frequently offer dormitory accommodation. The local tourist office is usually found in the tourist bungalow.

Getting Around

Bus Rajasthan has an extensive and reasonably good state bus system. On most sectors, there is a choice of ordinary and express buses. You're advised to stick to expresses since the ordinary buses stop frequently, make a lot of detours off the main route and take a long time to get anywhere.

If you're taking a bus from a major bus stand, it's worth buying a ticket from the ticket office rather than on board the bus. It guarantees (or at least comes closer to guaranteeing) a seat, and you're also certain of getting on the right bus since the ticket clerk writes the bus registration number on your ticket. This can be an important consideration because time-tables at bus stations are invariably in Hindi.

A number of private bus companies run luxury buses between the major population centres and many travellers prefer these to the state buses. Fares are higher than those on the state system but the buses are faster, more comfortable and don't take standing passengers. Their only drawback is that some are equipped with that curse known as the video cassette recorder. As elsewhere in India, this is always played at full volume and the film content is invariably macho trash. It's almost tolerable during the day but can be hell at night. Try to choose a bus without one of these infernal machines.

Train The 'Palace on Wheels' is a special tourist train service which operates weekly tours of Rajasthan, departing from Delhi. The carriages once belonged to various maharajas. The cost includes tours, entry fees, accommodation on the train plus all meals. Depending on the berth, it ranges from a hefty Rs 1500 per person per day to Rs 2550.

Eastern Rajasthan

JAIPUR (population 1,200,000)
The capital city of the state of Rajasthan is popularly known as the 'pink city' because of the pink-coloured sandstone from which the buildings in its old, walled city are constructed. In contrast to the cities on the Ganges plain, Jaipur has broad avenues and a remarkable harmony. The city sits on a dry lake bed in a wild and somewhat arid landscape, surrounded by barren hills surmounted by fortresses and crenellated walls. Jaipur long ago out-stripped the confines of its city wall yet retains a less crowded and more relaxed

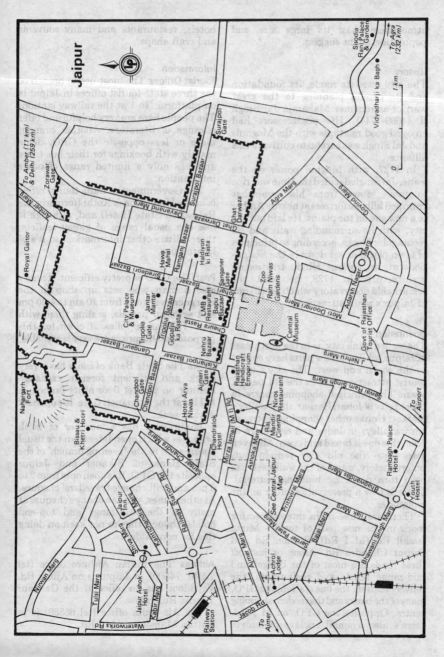

atmosphere than its large size and population might suggest.

History

The city owes its name, its foundation and its careful planning to the great warrior-astronomer Maharaja Jai Singh II (1699-1744). His predecessors had enjoyed good relations with the Moghuls and Jai Singh was careful to cultivate this alliance.

In 1727, with Moghul power on the wane, Jai Singh decided the time was ripe to move down from his somewhat cramped hillside fortress at nearby Amber to a new site on the plains. He laid out the city, with its surrounding walls and six rectangular blocks, according to principles of town planning set down in the *Shilpa-Shastra*, an ancient Hindu treatise on architecture. In 1728, he built the remarkable observatory which is still one of Jaipur's main attractions.

Orientation

The walled 'pink city' is in the north-east of Jaipur, while the new parts have spread to the south and west. The city's main tourist attractions are in the old part of town. The principal shopping centre in the old city is Johari Bazaar, the jeweller's market. Unlike other shopping centres in narrow alleys in India and elsewhere in Asia, this one is broad and open. All seven gates into the old city remain but, unfortunately, much of the wall itself has been torn down for building material. There is now a preservation order on the remainder.

There are three main interconnecting roads in the new part of town – Mirza Ismail Rd (M I Rd), Station Rd and Sansar Chandra Rd. Along or just off these roads are most of the budget and mid-range hotels and restaurants, the railway station, the bus station, the GPO, many of the banks and the modern shopping centre. Opposite the GPO, on M I Rd, there's also a small enclave of budget hotels, restaurants and many souvenir and craft shops.

Information

Tourist Offices The most useful branch of the three state tourist offices in Jaipur is on platform No 1 at the railway station. The people here are very helpful and offer a range of literature. Another branch, more or less opposite the GPO, deals mainly with bookings for their bus tours and has only a limited range of other information.

The Government of India tourist office is in the Hotel Khasa Kothi (formerly the Rajasthan State Hotel) and, although it has the usual range of glossy leaflets, there's little other information, so it's of limited use.

Post The GPO is pretty efficient. There's also a man who sets up shop in the entrance every day from 10 am to 4.30 pm and sews up parcels, sealing them with wax. He has supplies of cloth for this purpose and his prices are very reasonable.

Banks The State Bank of India has a very quick and efficient foreign exchange counter on the 1st floor of its branch in M I Rd at the Sanganeri Gate. It's open six days a week.

Jaipur also has a number of bank branches which open later than the usual hours, such as the 'evening branch' of the State Bank of Bikaner and Jaipur opposite the GPO. It is open only from 2 to 6 pm and will change travellers' cheques. At other times, you can change cheques at many of the mid-range and top-end hotels, though they're not keen on doing this for nonresidents.

Airlines The Indian Airlines office (tel 72940, 74500) in Jaipur is on Ajmer Rd. Vayudoot has an office at the Gangaur Tourist Bungalow.

The Air India office (tel 65559) is in Rattan Mansion on M I Rd.

Bookshops There's an excellent range of English-language hardbacks and paperbacks as well as magazines and guide books at Books Corner, next to Niro's Restaurant. They even stock this book.

The bookshop at the Rambagh Palace Hotel also has a good choice. A smaller but thoughtfully chosen selection can be found at the Arya Niwas Hotel.

Old City

The old city is partially encircled by a crenellated wall with seven gates – the major gates are Chandpol, Sanganeri and Ajmeri. Broad avenues, over 30 metres wide, divide the pink city into neat rectangles.

It's an extremely colourful city and, in the evening light, the pink and orange buildings have a magical glow which is complemented by the brightly clothed Rajasthanis. Camel-drawn carts are a characteristic of Jaipur's passing street scene, along with the ubiquitous Ambassador taxis and the more modern Maruti vans and cars. The major landmark in this part of town is the Iswari Minar Swarga Sul, the 'minaret piercing heaven', near the Tripolia Gate, which was built to overlook the city.

The main bazaars in the old city are Johari Bazaar (for jewellery and saris), Tripolia Bazaar (for brassware, carvings and lacquerware), Bapu Bazaar (for perfumes and textiles) and Chandpol Bazaar (for modern trinkets and bangles).

Hawa Mahal

Built in 1799, the Hawa Mahal, or 'Palace of the Winds', is one of Jaipur's major landmarks, although it is actually little more than a facade. This five-storey building, which looks out over the main street of the old city, is a stunning example of Rajput artistry with its pink, semioctagonal and delicately honeycombed sandstone windows. It was originally built to enable ladies of the royal household to watch the everyday life and processions of the city. You can climb to the top of the Hawa Mahal for an excellent view over the city. The palace was built by Maharaja Sawaj Pratap Singh and is part of the City Palace complex. There's a small archaeological museum on the same site.

Entrance to the Hawa Mahal is from the rear of the building. To get there, go back to the intersection on your left as you face the Hawa Mahal, turn right and then take the first right again through an archway. It's signposted. Hours are 9 am to 4.30 pm and entry costs Rs 0.60.

City Palace

In the heart of the old city, the City Palace occupies a large area divided into a series of courtyards, gardens and buildings. The outer wall was built by Jai Singh but other additions are much more recent, some dating to the start of this century. Today, the palace is a blend of Rajasthani and Moghul architecture. The former maharaja still lives in part of the palace.

The seven-storey Chandra Mahal is the centre of the palace and commands fine views over the gardens and the city. The ground and 1st floor of the Chandra Mahal form the Maharaja Sawai Man Singh II Museum. The apartments are maintained in luxurious order and the museum has an extensive collection of art, carpets, enamelware and old weapons. The paintings include miniatures of the Rajasthani, Moghul and Persian schools. The armoury has a collection of guns and swords dating back to the 15th century, as well as many of the ingenious and tricky weapons for which the warrior Rajputs were famous. The textile section contains dresses and costumes of the former maharajas and maharanis of Jaipur.

Other points of interest in the palace include the Diwan-i-Am, or 'Hall of Public Audiences', with its intricate decorations and manuscripts in Persian and Sanskrit, and the Diwan-i-Khas, or 'Hall of Private Audiences', with a marble-paved gallery. There is also a clock tower and the newer Mubarak Mahal.

Outside the buildings, you can see a large silver vessel in which a former maharaja used to take drinking water with him to England. Being a devout Hindu, he could not drink the English water! The palace and museum are open daily, except on public holidays, between 9.30 am and 4.45 pm. Entry is Rs 6 (Rs 3 for students).

City Palace guards, Jaipur

Observatory

Adjacent to the entrance to the City Palace is the observatory, or Jantar Mantar, begun by Jai Singh in 1728. Jai Singh's passion for astronomy was even more notable than his prowess as a warrior and, before commencing construction, he sent scholars abroad to study foreign observatories. The Jaipur observatory is the largest and the best preserved of the five he built and was restored in 1901. The others are in Delhi (the oldest, dating from 1724), Varanasi and Ujjain. The fifth, the Muttra observatory, has now disappeared.

At first glance, Jantar Mantar appears to be just a curious collection of sculptures but, in fact, each construction has a specific purpose, such as measuring the positions of stars, altitudes and azimuths, or calculating eclipses. The most striking instrument is the sundial with its 30-metre-high gnomon. The shadow this casts moves up to four metres an hour. It's very accurate, but operates on Jaipur local time! Admission to the observatory is Rs 1, free on Mondays; hours are 9 am to 5 pm.

Those interested in the theory behind the construction of these monumental instruments should buy a copy of *A Guide to the Jaipur Astronomical Observatory* by B L Dhama (Rs 15), which can be purchased on site.

Central Museum

The museum is housed in the architecturally impressive Albert Hall in the Ram Niwas Gardens, south of the old city. The upper floor contains portraits of the Jaipur maharajas and many other miniatures and artworks. The ground floor has a collection of costumes and woodwork from different parts of Rajasthan and a description of the people and life in the rural areas of the state. The collection, which started in 1833, is also notable for its brassware, jewellery and pottery. Entry to the museum is Rs 1, free on Mondays. It is open every day except Friday from 10 am to 5 pm.

Other Attractions

The Ram Niwas Gardens also have a zoo with birds, animals and a crocodile breeding farm. Jaipur has a modern art gallery in the 'theatre' near the zoo. To visit it you need to make enquiries as it's normally locked. Phone 62227 to arrange a visit to the Kripal Kumbh, B-18/A Shiv Marg, where Jaipur's famous blue pottery is made. The Rambagh Palace Hotel puts on an hour-long cultural programme of Rajasthani folk dances in the evening. Admission is Rs 30 but the standard of dancing is not high.

Finally, if you go to only one Hindi

movie while you're in India, see it at the Raj Mandir. This opulent, grandiose and extremely well-kept cinema is a Jaipur tourist attraction in its own right and is always full, despite its immense size. They don't build them like this in the west anymore. Tickets cost Rs 4 to Rs 8.

Festivals

Jaipur's elephant festival is held in early to mid-March (depending on the lunar calendar) and is actually part of the Holi festival. For the exact dates, ask at a tourist office.

Tours

Jaipur City Both the RTDC and the ITDC offer half-day and full-day bus tours of Jaipur and Amber. All tours visit the Sahib ki Haveli, Hawa Mahal, Amber Fort, Jantar Mantar, City Palace and Museum and include the inevitable stop at a craft shop. Here, the processes of production are explained and you'll be persuaded to buy something. The half-day tours are a little rushed but otherwise alright. If possible, take a full-day tour. Times are 8 am to 1 pm, 11.30 am to 4.30 pm and 1.30 to 6.30 pm. The full-day tours are from 9 am to 6 pm, including a lunch break at Nahagarh Fort. Half-day tours cost Rs 20 and full-day tours Rs 40.

RTDC tours can be booked and picked up from any of the three tourist bungalows, from the RTDC Transport Unit (tel 60239) opposite the GPO or, by prior arrangement, from the Arya Niwas Hotel. ITDC tours can be booked and picked up from the ITDC tourist office (tel 65451) in the Khasa Kothi Hotel.

Those who want to spend more time at places in the old town than tours allow should walk, use a bicycle or hire auto-rickshaws. Catch public buses to Amber.

Other Tours The RTDC operate a number of other long-distance tours, most of which are of little interest to travellers. One which is worth considering, however, is the Wednesday tour to Shekhawati. It

leaves at 7 am, returns at 10 pm and costs Rs 80 (or Rs 40 one way). The small Rajasthani town of Shekhawati is famous for its beautiful murals. To decide whether such a tour is worth your time, get hold of the booklet *The Guide to Painted Towns of Shekhawti* by Ilay Cooper (Rs 35), which can be found at most Jaipur bookshops.

Another tour which might appeal to those with limited time is the one to Bikaner. This two-day tour involves an overnight stay in Bikaner and costs Rs 60 one way, Rs 115 return.

Places to Stay

Getting to the hotel of your choice in Jaipur can be a problem. Auto-rickshaw drivers besiege every traveller who arrives by rail (less so by bus). If you don't want to go to a hotel of their choice, they'll either refuse to take you at all or they'll demand at least double the normal fare. If you do go to the hotel of their choice, you'll pay through the nose for accommodation because the manager will be paying them a commission of at least 30% of what he charges you for a bed (and the charge won't go down for subsequent nights).

Many hotel owners cooperate with this 'mafia' but others refuse. It's very easy to find out which hotels don't cooperate – the auto-rickshaw drivers will either refuse to take you there or demand extortionate rates for transport. It's invariably cheaper in the long run to pay double the normal fare to be taken to the hotel of your choice. If you want to stay at a mid-range hotel, you'll be charged double fare anyway because you can obviously afford it.

Some hotels which don't offer commission to auto-rickshaw drivers are the Jaipur Inn, Atithi Guest House, Arya Niwas Hotel, Evergreen Hotel and the three tourist bungalows.

Places to Stay – bottom end

One of the most popular of Jaipur's budget hotels is the *Jaipur Inn* (tel 66057) in Bani Park which is clean, well run, helpful and friendly. It has a kitchen for guests to use or you can arrange to have meals prepared. Large dormitories cost Rs 20 per person and double rooms are Rs 50 to Rs 100. The more expensive rooms have a bath and hot water. You can even camp on the lawn if you have your own tent. It's also a good place to tune in to the travellers' grapevine.

Another very popular budget hotel is the *Evergreen Guest House* (tel 63446), off M I Rd opposite the GPO. This largish hotel, complete with restaurant, has rooms arranged around a large garden courtyard and a recently added swimming pool. The hotel offers dorm beds for Rs 12 (lockers available), singles/doubles with common bath for Rs 25/30, downstairs doubles with bath for Rs 45 and upstairs doubles/triples with bath for Rs 70/80. Bucket hot water is available for Rs 3. The downstairs rooms are pretty basic and their common bathrooms somewhat scruffy, but the upstairs rooms are fine. The restaurant has an extensive cheap menu and breakfast is excellent value at Rs 9. Checkout time is 10 am and the hotel can arrange air, rail and bus tickets for a Rs 10 service charge. There are a number of other cheap hotels in the same area but they are distinctly inferior to the Evergreen.

The RTDC operates three tourist bungalows in Jaipur, two of which offer higher-priced budget accommodation including dorm beds. Cheaper of these two is the *Swagatam Tourist Bungalow* (tel 67560), close to the railway station. It has a restaurant and offers ordinary singles/ doubles for Rs 50/70, deluxe rooms for Rs 60/90, air-cooled rooms for Rs 100/125 and air-con rooms for Rs 145/175, all with bath and hot water (except the ordinary rooms which only have cold water). There are also dorm beds for Rs 20.

The more expensive *Teej Tourist Bungalow* (tel 74206) has dorm beds for Rs 20, deluxe singles/doubles for Rs 100/ 125, air-cooled rooms for Rs 130/155 and air-con rooms for Rs 200/250. All the rooms have bath and hot water and there's

a bar and restaurant. It's more or less round the corner from the Swagatam so you don't really need an auto-rickshaw to get there from the railway station.

Another budget accommodation option is the *National Hotel* (tel 65766), a tall, thin, modern building overlooking the fruit and vegetable market outside the Chandpol Gate. It has singles/doubles for Rs 40/60 to Rs 80/150, as well as triples and four-bed rooms. The costlier rooms have hot water. There's a 25% discount on these prices if you don't arrive by auto-rickshaw.

Other travellers have recommended the *Hotel Rose* (tel 77422) at B6 Shopping Centre, Subhash Nagar, Bani Park, but it's a very, very long way out from the centre. It has a cheap basement dormitory as well as a variety of private single and double rooms.

Quite a few auto-rickshaw drivers will try to persuade you to stay at the *Hotel Kalyan* (tel 65355), Hathoi Fort, off the Ajmer Rd. If you agree, you'll find yourself paying high prices for substandard accommodation in a distinctly featureless hotel with tatty fittings and grubby decor. It's poor value – a single will cost you at least Rs 100.

The 60-bed *Youth Hostel* (tel 67576) is a long way from the centre of things and few people stay here. Dorm beds are just Rs 12 for members, Rs 9 with a YHA card. They also have singles/doubles for Rs 25/35 and a thali dinner can be bought for Rs 14. The railway *retiring rooms* at the station are also relatively cheap.

Places to Stay - middle

The two best mid-range hotels, and the most popular, are the *Arya Niwas Hotel* (tel 73456), behind the Amber Cinema on Sansar Chandra Rd, and the *Atithi Guest House* (tel 78679), 1 Park House Scheme, Motilal Atal Rd, between M I Rd and Station Rd. The Arya Niwas, the larger and more popular of the two, is run by the dapper Mr Bansels. He is extremely friendly, very keen on maintaining

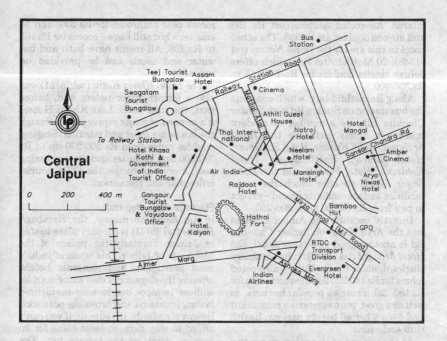

Central Jaipur

Bus Station

Teej Tourist Bungalow

Assam Hotel

Swagatam Tourist Bungalow

Railway Station Road

Cinema

Athiti Guest House

Thai International

Motilal Atal Rd

Natraj Hotel

Hotel Mangal

Sansar Chandra Rd

Amber Cinema

To Railway Station

Hotel Khasa Kothi & Government of India Tourist Office

Neelam Hotel

Arya Niwas Hotel

Air India

Mansingh Hotel

Gangaur Tourist Bungalow & Vayudoot Office

Rajdoot Hotel

Mirza Ismail (M I) Road

Bamboo Hut

GPO

Hotel Kalyan

Hathoi Fort

RTDC Transport Division

Ajmer Marg

Ashoka Marg

Indian Airlines

Evergreen Hotel

0   200   400 m

standards and a mine of information on what's worth seeing around Jaipur. His rooms are spotlessly clean, pleasantly furnished and decorated and he refuses to pay commission to auto-rickshaw drivers (so expect to pay a Rs 10 fare from the railway station). The variety of rooms range in price from Rs 75/90 to Rs 180/250. All rooms have bath and, in the winter months, hot water. There are no service charges or tax added to the room prices. The hotel restaurant serves tasty vegetarian food at very reasonable prices. Also available are money exchange facilities, a parking area, bicycle hire, a pleasant front lawn with tables and chairs and a small bookshop.

Equally good, and with a beautiful home atmosphere, is the smaller Atithi Guest House. Run by the Shukla family, it's superbly maintained, squeaky clean and very friendly and it offers excellent meals. It has not been open very long but you'll be directed here if the Arya Niwas is full. Like the Arya Niwas, it's excellent value at Rs 130/195. All rooms have bath and hot water. The family here are very keen to please and nothing is too much trouble.

The RTDC *Ganguar Tourist Bungalow* (tel 60231) is just off Sansar Chandra Rd. Although it is the most expensive of the tourist bungalows in Jaipur, it's still pretty good value and is better maintained than most others in Rajasthan. Deluxe singles/doubles cost Rs 145/175, air-cooled rooms are Rs 170/200 and air-con rooms are Rs 225/275, all with bath and hot water. There's a pleasant lawn, restaurant and bar.

Close to the Atithi Guest House on Motilal Atal Rd are two other mid-range hotels. Facing you as you come off M I Rd, the *Hotel Neelam* (tel 72215) is pleasant but not used much by travellers. There are no singles but single occupancy rates are offered. Air-cooled doubles cost Rs 195 and air-con doubles are Rs 395. The other hotel in this area is the *Hotel Natraj* (tel 61348), 20 Motilal Atal Rd, which offers deluxe singles/doubles for Rs 135/165 to Rs 350/400.

Along Banasthli Marg, which connects the bus station on Station Rd with Sansar Chandra Rd, are a number of modern mid-range hotels including the *Hotel Archana, Hotel Kumar, Hotel Shalimar, Hotel Gauray, Hotel Goyal, Hotel Kohinoor, Hotel Purohit* and the *Hotel Sagar*. They all offer much the same facilities and are similarly priced – expect to pay from Rs 70/100 to Rs 200/250.

Directly opposite the Amber Cinema and the Arya Niwas on Sansar Chandra Rd is another good mid-range hotel, the *Hotel Mangal* (tel 75216). It has ordinary singles/doubles for Rs 85/110, air-cooled rooms for Rs 180/220 and air-con rooms for Rs 180/220. There's a popular bar here, as well as a good, pure vegetarian restaurant and even a herbal beauty parlour, health club and sauna.

At the top end of this category are two hotels which were formerly minor palaces of the Jaipur aristocracy. Very popular and worth considering if you have the money, the *Hotel Bissau Palace* (tel 74191) is full of old world charm and surrounded by its own well-maintained gardens. One diplomat commented in the visitor's book that this is 'truly a Moghul amongst motels'. Singles/doubles cost Rs 140/180; suites are Rs 250. The hotel has a restaurant, swimming pool (not always filled), tennis court and library and Rajasthani music and folk dances can be arranged on request.

The other is the *Hotel Khetri House* (tel 69183), further up the road from the Bissau. Officially, this is a three-star hotel though, superficially, it's hard to see why. Like the Bissau, Khetri House is full of Rajput nostalgia but it's getting tatty at the edges and has an atmosphere of gloom. Nevertheless, it offers two enormous suites consisting of no less than three

rooms plus bathroom for Rs 330, and 14 smaller – but still huge – rooms for Rs 165 to Rs 198. All rooms have bath and hot water and meals can be provided on request.

The *Hotel Khasa Kothi* (tel 75151) was also a former minor palace and, before that, the state hotel. Like Khetri House, it's in need of major rejuvenation though the lawns are quiet and relaxing. Singles/doubles range from Rs 200/290 up to Rs 390/500 and facilities include swimming pool, money exchange, the ITDC tourist office, bar and restaurant.

Places to Stay – top end

If you have the money, the *Rambagh Palace* (tel 75141) is the only place to stay in Jaipur. Formerly the palace of the Maharaja of Jaipur, this is one of India's most prestigious and romantic hotels, offering the elegance of cool white marble, endless terraces overlooking manicured lawns, fountains and browsing peacocks. By any standards, it's superb. If you can't afford to stay here, at least come for an evening drink on the terrace bar. The cheapest singles/doubles are Rs 900/1000, while the more luxurious suites and rooms go all the way up to Rs 5500/6000 for the royal suite. Meals cost Rs 60 (breakfast), Rs 105 (lunch) and Rs 115 (dinner).

The *Hotel Clarks Amer* (tel 822616), Jawaharlal Nehru Marg, is less expensive but a long way (about 10 km) from the centre of town. Air-conditioned singles/doubles cost Rs 690/740 and the facilities are much the same as those at the Rambagh Palace.

If you can't afford the Rambagh Palace but want to stay in the centre of town, try the *Mansingh Hotel* (tel 787710), off Sansar Chandra Rd, behind the Central Bank of India building. This fairly new five-star hotel has fully air-conditioned singles/doubles for Rs 575/700, suites for Rs 1000 and all the facilities you would expect of a five-star hotel, including a swimming pool.

The four-star *Hotel Jaipur Ashok* (tel

75121), Jai Singh Circle, Rani Park, is one of those hotels which was fine when newly opened but has been on the rapid decline ever since. It is not recommended.

Places to Eat

In Johari Bazaar, near the centre of the old city, *LMB* (Laxmi Mishthan Bhandar) is well known for its excellent vegetarian food, with main courses ranging from Rs 10 to Rs 20. It also has amazingly pristine '50s 'hip' decor – definitely worth seeing. A dessert speciality is LMB kulfi, including dry fruits, saffron and cottage cheese, for Rs 11.50. A complete meal costs Rs 40 to Rs 50 per person. Out front, a snack counter serves good snacks and excellent ice cream and offers a wide range of Indian sweets.

Niro's, on M I Rd, is rated one of Jaipur's best and most expensive restaurants. It's certainly very popular with both locals and tourists and has a bright, busy atmosphere. The food, though good, is not outstanding but everyone seems to eat here at least once. Soups cost Rs 14 to Rs 20, meat dishes Rs 18 to Rs 55 and vegetarian dishes Rs 14 to Rs 26. They offer Indian, Chinese and continental dishes. Next door to Niro's are two good vegetarian restaurants, the *Surya Mahal Restaurant* and the *Natraj Vegetarian Restaurant*.

Further up M I Rd, opposite the GPO, is the *Kwality* which has the range of medium-priced dishes common to this India-wide chain. It's closed on Tuesdays. Close by, near the junction with Ajmer Rd, the relaxed atmosphere of the *Handi Restaurant/Bamboo Hut* makes it a pleasant place to eat good kebabs and tandoori food. Another good choice on M I Rd is the *Minar Restaurant*, between the GPO and Niro's.

Up on Sansar Chandra Rd, opposite the Amber Cinema, the Hotel Mangal's *Rituraj Restaurant* is very reasonably priced. Its very good vegetarian meals are popular with local people as well as with travellers and there's a bar on the same floor. Also good is the *Vaishali Restaurant*

in the Chandragupta Hotel on Station Rd, next to the bus station.

Opposite the Mangal, in the cinema complex, *The Eats* has a self-serve fast-food department and snacks cafe on the ground floor which offers Chinese and south Indian food, pizzas, burgers, soups and ice cream. The deluxe restaurant in the basement serves more substantial meals and is open from 7 pm onwards.

At the other end of the price scale, you can eat in fine style at the *Rambagh Palace* where the food is prepared for the bland tastes of international tourists. You can't stay at the *Circuit House*, in the entranceway to the Hotel Khasa Kothi and the Government of India tourist office, but it is excellent value for breakfast. For less than Rs 10 you get cornflakes, toast, eggs and coffee or tea.

Open-air restaurants in the Ram Niwas gardens serve good masala dosas and other south Indian food.

Things to Buy

Jaipur is well known for precious stones, which seem cheaper here than elsewhere in India, and is even better known for semiprecious stones. For precious stones, find a narrow alley called Haldion ka Rasta off Johari Bazaar (near the Hawa Mahal). Semiprecious stones are sold in another alley, called the Gopalji ka Rasta, on the opposite side of the street. There are many shops here which offer bargain prices, but you do need to know your gems.

Shops around the City Palace and Hawa Mahal are likely to be more expensive, although they do have many interesting items including miniatures and clothes. Marble statues, jewellery and textile prints are other Jaipur specialities. The Rajasthan Government Emporium in M I Rd is reasonably priced; it has a branch in Amber as well as a workshop/sales outlet en route where RTDC tour buses stop. Jaipur's salespeople are hard working and very persuasive, so take care. Many unwary visitors get talked into buying things for resale at inflated prices.

You will find different state emporia, specialising in fabrics, in the courtyard at the back of the Hotel Mansingh. These are well worth visiting if you're looking for cloth.

Getting There & Away
Air Indian Airlines flies Delhi/Jaipur daily, continuing on to Bombay via Jodhpur, Udaipur and Aurangabad (and vice versa). Delhi/Jaipur flights, continuing on to Bombay via Jodhpur and Aurangabad (and vice versa), also operate daily, except Tuesday and Thursday.

Vayudoot connects Jaipur with Jodhpur (Rs 330), Jaisalmer (Rs 615), Kota (Rs 245), Delhi (Rs 265) and Bikaner (Rs 425).

Bus Buses to all Rajasthan's main population centres and to Delhi and Agra are operated by the Rajasthan State Transport Corporation from the bus station, some deluxe (essentially nonstop). A number of private companies cover the same routes and also offer services to Ahmedabad, other cities in Gujarat and Bombay. These companies have their own depots, but the most useful collection is opposite the Hotel Neelam on Motilal Atal Rd, just off M I Rd. The buses are not as frequent as those operated by the state transport corporation and often travel at night. Avoid video buses unless you want a thumping headache the next morning.

State transport deluxe buses to Delhi take five hours. The 306-km trip costs Rs 40, Rs 55 deluxe. Deluxe state transport buses leave for Agra five times daily, taking 4½ hours at a cost of Rs 52. The ordinary buses cost Rs 36.

Deluxe buses run nine times a day to Ajmer and cost Rs 25 for the 2½-hour trip. Five deluxe buses per day take seven hours to reach Jodhpur and cost Rs 69. To Udaipur, there are four deluxe buses daily; they take about 10 hours and cost Rs 89. There are also one or two deluxe buses daily to Kota (Rs 45), and one daily to Jaisalmer (14 hours, Rs 82).

Train The train services from Jaipur are generally slower than buses because they are on metre-gauge rails. The Pink City Express leaves old Delhi railway station at 6 am and reaches Jaipur at 11 am. The Jaipur to Delhi service leaves at 5 pm and arrives at 10.20 pm. Fares for the 308-km trip are Rs 40 in 2nd class, Rs 137 in 1st. All Jaipur trains leave from the old Delhi station.

The Ahmedabad Mail runs overnight, leaving Delhi at 10 pm and arriving in Jaipur at 4.30 am, while the Chetak Express leaves Delhi at 1 pm and arrives in Jaipur at 8.30 pm. These are the most convenient trains, though there are others. The Chetak Express continues through Jaipur to Ajmer and Udaipur.

The daily 'superfast' express between Jaipur and Agra (the Jaipur-Agra Fort Express) takes only five hours. It leaves Jaipur at 6.10 am and Agra at 5 pm.

Getting Around
Airport Transport The airport is 15 km out of town. The airport bus costs Rs 15; a taxi costs about Rs 80.

Local Transport Jaipur has taxis (unmetered), auto-rickshaws and a city bus service which also operates to Amber. A cycle-rickshaw from the station to the Jaipur Inn or Arya Niwas Hotel should cost about Rs 3, Rs 5 from the station to Johari Bazaar, while an auto-rickshaw should cost Rs 4 and Rs 7 on these trips. However, if you're going to a hotel with your baggage and the hotel doesn't pay the drivers commission, you'll be extremely lucky to get a ride for these prices. In such cases, expect to pay two to three times the usual price. If they quote you the normal fare to a hotel whose rates you don't know, it probably means they're guaranteed an especially big commission at your expense.

It is possible to share 'four seaters' or 'six seaters' – larger auto-rickshaw-like devices which travel from the station to the main gates of the city (Sanganer to Rampol) for Rs 1 or Rs 1.50.

Bicycles can be hired from several of the budget hotels, as well as from the Arya Niwas Hotel, at Rs 10 per day.

AROUND JAIPUR

There are several attractions around Jaipur, including some on the road between Jaipur and Amber. Jaipur tours usually stop at some of these sites on the way to or from Amber.

Amber

About 11 km out of Jaipur on the Delhi to Jaipur road, Amber was once the ancient capital of Jaipur state. Construction of the fortress-palace was begun in 1592 by Raja Man Singh, the Rajput commander of Akbar's army. It was later extended and completed by the Jai Singhs before the move to Jaipur on the plains below. The fort is a superb example of Rajput architecture, stunningly situated on a hillside and overlooking a lake which reflects its terraces and ramparts.

You can climb up to the fort from the road in 10 minutes. Riding up on elephant-back is popular, though expensive at Rs 65 per elephant one way (an elephant can carry up to four people). A quick ride around the palace courtyard costs about Rs 5. You can get cold drinks within the palace if the climb is a hot one.

An imposing stairway leads to the Diwan-i-Am, or 'Hall of Public Audiences', with a double row of columns and latticed galleries above. Steps to the right lead to the small Kali Temple. There is also the white marble Sila Devi Temple.

The maharaja's apartments are on the higher terrace – you enter through a gateway decorated with mosaics and sculptures. The Jai Mandir, or 'Hall of Victory', is noted for its inlaid panels and glittering mirror ceiling. Regrettably, much of this was allowed to deteriorate during the '70s and '80s but restoration work has begun. Opposite the Jai Mandir is the Sukh Niwas, or 'Hall of Pleasure',

Amber Palace

with an ivory-inlaid sandalwood door, and a channel running right through the room which once carried cooling water. From the Jai Mandir you can enjoy the fine views from the palace ramparts over the lake below.

Amber palace is open from 9 am to 4.30 pm and entry costs Rs 6 (Rs 3 for students).

Getting There & Away A bus to Amber from the Hawa Mahal in Jaipur costs about Rs 1. The trip takes half an hour and buses depart every few minutes. A taxi costs about Rs 70.

Gaitor

The cenotaphs of the royal family are at Gaitor, 6½ km from Jaipur on the road to Amber. The white marble cenotaph of Maharaja Jai Singh II is the most impressive and is decorated with carved peacocks. Next to it is the cenotaph of his son.

Opposite the cenotaphs is the Jal Mahal water palace in the middle of a lake and reached by a causeway. Or at least it was in the middle of a lake; the water is now all but squeezed out by the infamous weed, water hyacinth. There is another Royal Gaitor just outside the city walls.

Galta

The temple of the Sun God at Galta is 100 metres above the city to the east, a 2½-km climb from the Surya Gate. A deep temple-filled gorge stands behind the temple and there are fine views over the surrounding plain.

Tiger Fort

The Nahargarh Fort overlooks the city from a sheer ridge 6½ km away. The road from Amber through the hills can be travelled by jeep or by rickshaw, but the peak is at the end of 1½ km of zigzag path. The views fully justify the effort and the entry fee. There's a small, almost deserted restaurant on the top. The fort was built in 1734 and extended in 1868.

Jaigarh Fort

The imposing Jaigarh Fort, built in 1726 by Jai Singh, was only opened to the public in mid-1983. It's within walking distance of Amber and offers a great view over the plains from the Diwa Burj watchtower. The fort, with its water reservoirs, residential areas, puppet theatre and the cannon, Jaya Vana, is open from 9 am to 4.30 pm. Entry is Rs 6.

Sisodia Rani Palace & Gardens

Eight km from the city on the Agra road and surrounded by terraced gardens, this palace was built for Maharaja Jai Singh's second wife, the Sisodia princess. The outer walls are decorated with murals depicting hunting scenes and the Krishna legend.

Vidyadhar's Garden

Nestled in a narrow valley, this beautiful garden was built in honour of Jai Singh's chief architect and town planner, Vidyadhar.

Sanganer

The small town of Sanganer is 16 km south of Jaipur and is entered through the ruins of two *tripolias*, or triple gateways. In addition to its ruined palace, Sanganer has a group of Jain temples with fine carvings to which entry is restricted. The town is noted for handmade paper and block printing.

Balaji

The Hindu exorcism temple of Balaji is about 1½ km off the Jaipur to Agra road, about 1½ hours by bus from Bharatpur. The exorcisms are sometimes very violent and those being exorcised don't hesitate to discuss their experiences. Two morning buses leave for Balaji from the bus terminal in Delhi.

BHARATPUR

A must for those with an interest in ornithology, Bharatpur is now best known for its bird sanctuary, the Keoladeo

Ghana National Park but, in the 17th and 18th centuries, was a Jat stronghold. Before the arrival of the Rajputs, the Jats inhabited this area and were able to retain a high degree of autonomy, both because of their prowess in battle and because of their chiefs' marriage alliances with various Rajput princes. They successfully opposed the Moghuls on more than one occasion and their fort at Bharatpur, constructed in the 18th century, withstood a four-month siege by the British in 1805. This siege eventually led to the signing of the first treaty of friendship between the Indian states of north-west India and the East India Company. Only the inner wall of this fort, the palace and the moat which surrounded it remain, but it houses an interesting archaeological museum and is worth a visit.

The town itself, which was once surrounded by an 11-km-long wall (now demolished), is of little interest. Bring insect repellent with you as the shallow lakes of the bird sanctuary are ideal breeding grounds for mosquitoes.

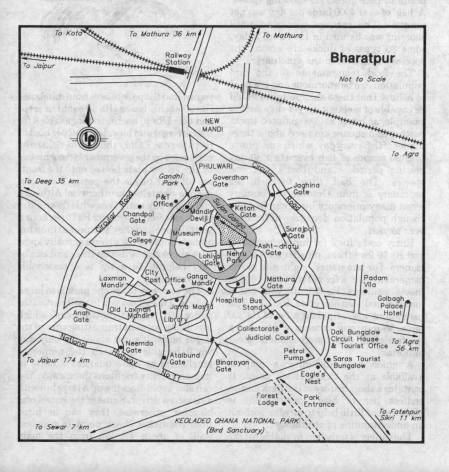

Bird Sanctuary

No less than 328 kinds of birds have been sighted at the Keoladeo sanctuary, 117 of which migrate from as far away as Siberia and China. The sanctuary was formerly a vast semiarid region, filling during the monsoon season only to rapidly dry up afterwards. To prevent this, the Maharaja of Bharatpur diverted water from a nearby irrigation canal and, within a few years, birds began to settle in vast numbers. Naturally, his primary concern was not the environment but, rather, his desire to take guests on shooting sprees. A 'bag' of over 4000 birds per day was not unusual. The carnage continued until shooting was banned in 1964 and, today, some 80 types of ducks are among the species which nest in the sanctuary.

The food requirements of the bird population can be enormous and it's hard to believe that these shallow lakes would be capable of meeting it – yet they do. For example, as many as 3000 painted storks nesting in a square km need about three tonnes of fish every day, which amounts to over 90 tonnes of fish over their 40-day nesting period – and that's just one species. The best time to visit the sanctuary is from October to February when many migratory birds can be seen, though population densities differ from year to year.

Entry costs Rs 2 for Indian nationals and Rs 10 for others, plus Rs 2 for a still camera. For 'amateurs', eight-mm movie cameras attract a fee of Rs 10 and 16-mm movie cameras Rs 25; if you are a 'professional', either costs Rs 100. The regulations also stipulate a fee of Rs 200 for a 35-mm still camera if you are a 'professional'. Do professionals wear uniforms?

A guide book including a map is available at the ticket check point. It contains a short history of the park and an endless list of bird species, but is otherwise of little help to anyone without an understanding of ornithology.

The variety of transport available to take you around the park ranges from minibuses (Rs 30 each), buses (Rs 50 each) or jeeps and cars (Rs 10 each), to tongas (Rs 8 for the carriage) and bicycles (Rs 2 per hour or Rs 10 per day). Only those auto-rickshaws authorised by the government (recognisable by the yellow plate bolted onto the front) are allowed inside the park – beware of anyone who tells you otherwise! Although you don't pay entry fees with these auto-rickshaws, you'll be up for Rs 15 per hour if you take one and they'll expect a tip on top of that. Some of the drivers actually know a lot about the birds you'll see and can be very helpful, so a tip is a reasonable request.

The best way to see the park is to hire a bicycle. This allows you to easily avoid the motorised tourist bottlenecks which inevitably occur at the nesting sites of the larger birds. It's just about the only way you'll be able to watch the numerous kingfishers at close quarters – noise or human activity frightens them away. You can also avoid clocking up a large bill with a rickshaw driver. Some of the hotels rent bicycles; otherwise, they can be hired from the ticket check point (a pleasant walk of about 1½ km from the main entrance gate). If you plan to visit the sanctuary at dawn (one of the best times to see the birds), you'll have to hire your bicycle the day before.

Boats can also be hired from the ticket check point for Rs 5 per person per day (minimum charge of Rs 20). This is a very good way of getting close to the wildlife in this park.

There's a snack bar and drinks kiosk about halfway through the park, next to the so-called Keoladeo Temple (hardly a temple – more a small shrine).

This is one bird sanctuary which even nonornithologists should visit.

Lohagarh Fort

The 'Iron Fort' was built in the early 18th century and took its name from its supposedly impregnable defences. Maharaja Suraj Mal, the fort's constructor and founder of Bharatpur, built two towers within the ramparts, the Jawahar Burj and Fateh Burj, to commemorate his victories over the Moghuls and the British. The fort is open from 10 am to 5 pm daily and admission is free.

Inside the fort are three palaces. The oldest dates from Badan Singh's time and houses the museum. Founded by the Maharaja of Bharatpur in 1944, this museum contains a number of interesting exhibits. It's closed on Fridays.

Places to Stay

If, like most people, you've come to Bharatpur to see the bird sanctuary, bear in mind the fact that the park entrance is about seven km from the railway station. If you stay near the station, transport is going to cost you quite a lot unless you hire a bicycle. Christmas and New Year are very busy times so, if possible, book accommodation in advance.

Most travellers stay at the *Saras Tourist Bungalow* (tel 3700), about 500 metres from the park entrance, as it has some of the cheapest accommodation. It suffers from the lack of maintenance which characterises many RTDC bungalows and the hot water is limited but, otherwise, it's OK. Dorm beds are Rs 20, singles/doubles range from Rs 100/120 to Rs 175/200, or you can camp for Rs 8 per person. The bungalow has a characterless bar and the restaurant is pretty average, though it can occasionally put on an excellent spread.

Directly opposite the Saras Bungalow is the *Eagle's Nest*. Expansion is planned but, at present, it has only four double rooms at Rs 200. Food is available with advance notice.

Somewhat further away from the entrance to the park, on the Agra road, the huge, very mellow *Golbagh Palace Hotel* (tel 3349) is straight out of the hunting days of the maharajas. It is surrounded by its own gardens. There are more tigers' heads lining the panelled walls here than there are tigers in the Ranthambhor sanctuary, all of them supposedly shot in Bharatpur (where they're now extinct). Otherwise, it's a very civilised place to stay and has its own bar and restaurant. Rooms in the annexe cost Rs 100/125, Rs 140/175 in the main building. Only the double rooms have baths. Book in advance, if possible, as they only have 18 rooms.

If you want to stay in the national park

itself, the ITDC *Forest Lodge* (tel 2260, 2322) is about one km beyond the entrance gate. It's a very pleasant place to stay but not cheap at Rs 375/500 from October to March. During the rest of the year it costs Rs 180/260, Rs 310/400 with air-con. Meal charges are Rs 45 for breakfast and Rs 70 for lunch or dinner and there's also a bar.

The only other place near the park is the *Hotel Paradise* (tel 3791), Neemda Gate, on the National Highway. It's not the best, but the rooms are clean, though overpriced at Rs 125/160 for singles/doubles with bath. Good meals are available on request but are similarly overpriced. The main problem here is the deafening TV which roars until midnight in the lounge.

All the other hotels are much closer to the railway station. They also seem to pay the rickshaw drivers commission, so you pay more. These hotels include the *Hotel Alora* (tel 2616), Kumher Gate, Rs 40/75, the *Hotel Avadh* (tel 2462), Kumher Gate, Rs 60/120, *Hotel Tourist Complex*, the *Hotel Nannd* (tel 3119) and the *Hotel Kohinoor* (tel 3733). The Tourist Complex is six km from the park entrance and the Nannd and Kohinoor are about three km from the entrance.

Getting There & Away

Bus Bharatpur is on the Agra to Jaipur road, just two hours by bus from Agra or an hour from Fatehpur Sikri – buses cost about Rs 6. The Agra and Fatehpur Sikri buses pass the front door of the Tourist Bungalow and will stop there if you ask.

Buses from Jaipur take about 4½ hours and the fare is Rs 25. However, as the state transport corporation seems to select their most decrepit buses for this run, the train is preferable.

Train Bharatpur is on the New Delhi to Bombay broad-gauge line as well as the Delhi/Agra/Jaipur/Ahmedabad metre-gauge line, ensuring a good choice of trains. Be certain that the one you choose

is going to stop at Bharatpur – not all trains do. The 188-km journey from Jaipur takes about four hours and costs Rs 93 in 1st class, Rs 28 in 2nd class.

Getting Around

You can use tongas, auto-rickshaws and cycle-rickshaws to get around town, and the state tourist office has a minibus (see the tourist officer in the Tourist Bungalow). You can hire bicycles for Rs 10 a day (plus your passport or Rs 500 bond).

DEEG

Very few travellers ever make it to Deeg, about 36 km from Bharatpur. This is unfortunate because this small town with its massive fortifications, stunningly beautiful palace and busy market is much more interesting than Bharatpur itself.

History

Built by Suraj Mal in the mid-18th century, Deeg was formerly the second capital of Bharatpur state and the site of a famous battle in which the maharaja's forces successfully withstood a combined Moghul and Maratha army of some 80,000 men. Eight years later, the maharaja even had the temerity to attack the Red Fort in Delhi! The booty he carried off included an entire marble building which can still be seen.

Gopal Bhawan

Suraj Mal's palace, Gopal Bhawan, has to be one of India's most beautiful and delicately proportioned buildings. It's also in an excellent state of repair and, as it was used by the maharajas until the early 1970s, most of the rooms still contain their original furnishings.

Built in a combination of Rajput and Moghul architectural styles, the palace fronts onto a tank, the Gopal Sagar, and is flanked by two exquisite pavilions which were designed to resemble pleasure barges. The tank and palace are surrounded by well-maintained gardens which also contain the Keshav Bhawan, or summer pavilion, with its hundreds of fountains, many of which are still functional though only turned on for local festivals.

The palace is open daily from 8 am to 12 noon and 1 to 7 pm; admission is free. Deeg's massive walls (up to 28 metres high) and 12 bastions, some with their cannons still in place, are also worth exploring.

Places to Stay

Deeg is essentially an agricultural town and few visitors ever come here, so the choice of accommodation is very limited. The *Deeg Dak Bungalow* (tel 18) is a possibility, with beds for less than Rs 20.

SARISKA TIGER RESERVE & NATIONAL PARK

Situated 107 km from Jaipur and 200 km from Delhi, the sanctuary is in a wooded valley surrounded by barren mountains. It covers 800 square km (including a core area of 498 square km) and has blue bulls, sambar, spotted deer, wild boar and, above all, tigers. Project Tiger has been in charge of the sanctuary since 1979.

As at Ranthambhor, the park contains ruined temples as well as a fort, pavilions and a palace (now a hotel) built by the maharajas of Alwar, the former owners of this area. The sanctuary can be visited year-round, except during July-August when the animals move to higher ground, but the best time is between November and June.

You'll see most wildlife in the evening or at night, though tiger sightings are becoming more common during the day. The night outings that can be arranged at the Tourist Bungalow or the Hotel Sariska Palace are not particularly cheap and suffer from the usual drawbacks. One traveller succinctly commented: 'You see mainly deer during the two-hour tour, most of them fleeing in panic at the approach, at tremendous speed, of a lurching minibus full of screaming tourists with a man halfway out of the cab waving a spotlight and shouting excitedly'.

A better way to see game is to book a 'hide' overlooking one of the waterholes for Rs 20 (Rs 10 for Indians). Take along food, drink and a sleeping bag (mattresses are provided).

Entry to the park costs Rs 10 for foreigners and Rs 2 for Indians.

Places to Stay

Most travellers stay at the RTDC *Tiger Den Tourist Bungalow* (tel 42). It is very good, but somewhat expensive at Rs 125/150 for deluxe singles/doubles, Rs 150/175 air-cooled and Rs 225/275 with air-con, though they do have a Rs 20 dormitory. The bungalow has a bar and restaurant. There's also a *Forest Rest House* where rooms are cheaper.

Today a two-star hotel, the *Hotel Sariska Palace* (tel 22), at the park entrance, is the former hunting lodge of the maharajas of Alwar. It offers air-cooled singles/doubles for Rs 275/330 and air-con doubles/suites for Rs 500/600. All rooms have heating in winter and bath with constant hot water. There's a bar and restaurant so, even if you don't stay here, it warrants a visit.

Getting There & Away

Sariska is 35 km from Alwar, which is a convenient town from which to approach the sanctuary. There are direct buses to Alwar from Delhi (170 km) and Jaipur (146 km). Though some people attempt to visit Sariska on a day trip from Jaipur, this option is expensive and, largely, a waste of time.

ALWAR

Alwar was once an important Rajput state which emerged in the 18th century under Pratap Singh by pushing back the rulers of Jaipur to the south and the Jats of Bharatpur to the east, and by successfully resisting the Marathas. It was one of the first Rajput states to ally itself with the fledgeling British Empire, though British interference in Alwar's internal affairs meant that the partnership was not always amicable.

Bala Quila Fort

This huge fort, with its five km of ramparts, stands 300 metres above the city. Predating the time of Pratap Singh, it's one of very few forts in Rajasthan which was constructed before the rise of the Moghuls. Unfortunately, because the fort now houses a radio station, it can only be visited with special permission.

Palace Complex

Below the fort sprawls the huge city palace complex, its massive gates and tank lined by a beautifully symmetrical chain of ghats and pavilions. Today, most of the complex is occupied by government offices, but there is a museum (closed on Fridays). Examples of miniature writing, miniature paintings of the Bundi school and ivory, sandalwood and jade *objets d'art*, as well as the usual armoury displays, are among the museum's unusual exhibits.

Places to Stay

If you're in the area, the RTDC *Lake Castle Tourist Bungalow* (tel 22991) at Siliserh is an ideal place to unwind, though it is some 20 km from Alwar. It is a former palace, built by Vinay Singh, Alwar's third ruler, and overlooks a lake. It's also relatively cheap at Rs 100/140 for deluxe singles/doubles, with more expensive rooms for Rs 135/175, and has a bar and restaurant.

In Alwar itself there is a variety of cheaper hotels, including the *Alka Hotel* (tel 2796) and the *Ashoka Hotel* (tel 2027), and the railway has *retiring rooms*.

AJMER (population 340,000)

South of Jaipur is Ajmer, a green oasis on the shore of the Ana Sagar Lake, hemmed in by barren hills. Historically, Ajmer always had great strategic importance and was sacked by Mahmud of Ghanzi on one of his periodic forays from Afghanistan.

Later, it became a favourite residence of the great Moghuls. One of the first contacts between the Moghuls and the British occurred in Ajmer when Sir Thomas Roe met with Jehangir here in 1616.

The city was subsequently taken by the Scindias and, in 1818, it was handed over to the British, becoming one of the few places in Rajasthan controlled directly by the British rather than being part of a princely state. Ajmer is a major centre for Muslim pilgrims during the fast of Ramadan but, although it has some superb examples of early Muslim architecture, a fort overlooking the town and a lively bazaar, Ajmer is just a stepping stone to nearby Pushkar for most travellers.

Information & Orientation

The tourist office (tel 20430) is in the Tourist Bungalow and has a good range of literature. The tourist officer, Mr Hazarilal Sharma, is very keen to help – he's one of those rare tourist officers who takes an active interest in his job. The State Bank of India, next to the Tourist Bungalow, changes only Thomas Cook travellers' cheques. Other types must be negotiated at the very efficient Bank of Baroda, diagonally opposite the GPO on the 1st floor.

The bus stand is close to the Tourist Bungalow on the Jaipur side of town. The railway station and most of the hotels are on the other side of town.

Ana Sagar Lake

This artificial lake was created in the 12th century by damming the River Luni. On its bank is a fine park, the Dault Bagh, containing a series of marble pavilions erected in 1637 by Shah Jahan. It's popular for an evening stroll. The lake tends to dry up if the monsoon is poor, so the city's water supply is taken from Foy Sagar Lake, five km further up the valley. There are good views from the hill beside the Dault Bagh.

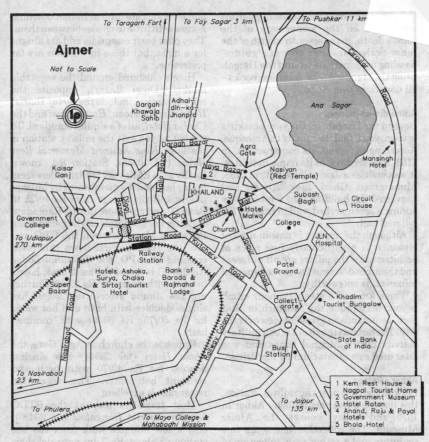

Ajmer

Not to Scale

To Taragarh Fort
To Foy Sagar 3 km
To Pushkar 11 km

Circular Road

Ana Sagar

Mansingh Hotel

Dargah Khawaja Sahib

Adhai-din-ka-Jhonpra

Dargah Bazar

Agra Gate

Nasiyan (Red Temple)

Subash Bagh

Circuit House

Kaisar Ganj

Naya Bazar
2

KHAILAND
5
3 4
Hotel Malwa

College

JLN Hospital

Government College

Madar Gate
GPO
Prithviraj
Church

1
Station Road

Railway Station

Kutchery Road

Jaipur Road

Patel Ground

Khadim Tourist Bungalow

To Udaipur 270 km

Hotels Ashoka, Surya, Chalsa & Sirtaj Tourist Hotel

Bank of Baroda & Rajmahal Lodge

Super Bazar

Collectorate

State Bank of India

To Nasirabad 23 km

Nasirabad Road

Railway Colony

Bus Station

To Phulera

To Mayo College & Mahabodhi Mission

To Jaipur 135 km

1 Kem Rest House & Nagpal Tourist Home
2 Government Museum
3 Hotel Ratan
4 Anand, Raju & Payal Hotels
5 Bhola Hotel

Dargah

At the foot of a barren hill in the old part of town, this is one of India's most important places for Muslim pilgrims. The Dargah is the tomb of a Sufi saint, Khwaja Muin-ud-din Chishti, who came to Ajmer from Persia in 1192. Construction of the shrine was completed by Humayun and the gate was added by the Nizam of Hyderabad. Akbar used to make the pilgrimage to the Dargah from Agra once a year.

As you enter the courtyard, removing your shoes at the gateway, a mosque constructed by Akbar is on the right. The

large iron cauldrons are for offerings which are customarily shared by families involved in the shrine's upkeep. In an inner court, there is another mosque built by Shah Jahan. Constructed of white marble, it has 11 arches and a Persian inscription running the full length of the building.

The saint's tomb is in the centre of the second court. It has a marble dome and the actual tomb inside is surrounded by a silver platform. The horseshoes nailed to the shrine doors are offerings from successful horse dealers! The tomb attracts hundreds of thousands of pilgrims every year on the anniversary of the saint's death, in the seventh month of the lunar calendar. Beware of 'guides' hassling for donations around the Dargah using the standard fake donation books – all donations over Rs 50!

Adhai-din-ka-jhonpra

Beyond the Dargah, on the very outskirts of town, you'll find the ruins of this mosque. According to legend, its construction, in 1153, took 2½ days, as its name indicates. It was built as a Jain college but, in 1198, Muhammad Ghori took Ajmer and converted the building into a mosque by adding a seven-arched wall in front of the pillared hall.

Although the mosque is now in need of repair, it is a particularly fine piece of architecture – the pillars are all different and the arched 'screen', with its damaged minarets, is noteworthy.

Three km and a steep 1½-hour climb beyond the mosque, the Taragarh, or 'Star Fort', commands an excellent view over the city. The fort was the site of much military activity during Moghul times and was later used as a sanatorium by the British.

Akbar's Palace

Back in the city, near the railway station, this imposing fort was built by Akbar in 1570 and today houses the Ajmer Museum. The collection has some fine sculpture and a rather poor collection of Moghul and Rajput armour. The museum is closed on Fridays and charges a small admission fee.

Nasiyan Temple

The 'Red Temple' on Prithviraj Marg is a Jain temple built last century. Its double-storey hall contains a series of large, gilt wooden figures from Jain mythology which depict the Jain concept of the ancient world. It's certainly worth a visit.

Places to Stay – bottom end

With some exceptions, most of Ajmer's budget hotels are typical Indian boarding houses with little to choose between them. They offer basic essentials and are alright for a night, but those in Pushkar are far preferable.

Hotels clustered around the vegetable market (Diggi Bazar), opposite the railway station, include the *Sirtaj Tourist Hotel*, *Hotel Ashoka*, *Hotel Surya* and the *Chalsa Hotel*, all of a similar standard. To the left as you exit the railway station is the huge *King Edward Memorial Rest House* (tel 20936), Station Rd, known locally as 'KEM'. Very few travellers seem to stay here and it's mainly used by Muslim pilgrims. Rooms range from Rs 10/25 to Rs 45/60 and cost more during Ramadan.

Better budget hotels can be found along Prithviraj Marg, between the GPO and the Red Temple. First down this road, opposite the GPO, the *Rajmahal Lodge* (tel 21347) is one of the most basic hotels in town with rooms for Rs 25/40. Further up, the *Anand Hotel* (tel 23099) has singles/doubles with bath and hot water for Rs 50/75, Rs 30/40 with common bath.

Opposite the church at Agra Gate, the *Bhola Hotel* (tel 23844) has singles/doubles for Rs 40/70 with bath and constant hot water. The vegetarian restaurant is excellent.

Most travellers stay at the RTDC *Khadim Tourist Bungalow* (tel 20490), only a few minutes walk from the bus station or about Rs 7 by auto-rickshaw from the railway station. There's a range of rooms available priced from Rs 55/75 to Rs 175/225 with air-con, as well as a Rs 20 dormitory. It's certainly a pleasant setting but hotel maintenance is virtually nonexistent.

Places to Stay – top end

The only top-end hotel in Ajmer is the brand new *Mansingh Hotel* (tel 30855), Circular Rd, overlooking Ana Sagar. In comparison to other hotels of this chain elsewhere, it's excellent value at Rs 299/399 for singles/doubles; suites cost Rs 599/699. It's beautifully decorated and furnished and everything is provided.

Places to Eat
Few restaurants in Ajmer stand out as worthy of special mention. One exception is the vegetarian restaurant at the *Bhola Hotel*. The food is very tasty, the restaurant is well maintained and few items cost more than Rs 10.

For a minor splurge, try either the *Honeydew* or the *Elite* restaurants which flank the KEM (King Edward Memorial) Rest House near the railway station.

For a real treat, have a meal at the *Mansingh Hotel*.

Getting There & Away
Bus There are buses from Jaipur to Ajmer every 15 minutes, some nonstop. The trip costs Rs 21 and takes 2½ hours. From Delhi, 20 buses run daily in either direction at a cost of Rs 61.

State transport buses also go to Jodhpur (210 km, 4½ hours, Rs 34), Udaipur (303 km via Chittorgarh, Rs 45), Chittorgarh (190 km, Rs 29), Kota (200 km via Bundi, Rs 25 to Rs 31), Bharatpur (305 km, Rs 48) and Bikaner (277 km, Rs 42). In addition, buses leave for Agra (385 km, Rs 58) each morning at 7.30, 8 and 10 am and for Jaisalmer (490 km, Rs 73) daily at 8 am. As not all these buses are 'deluxe', limited stop or nonstop, you need to check beforehand.

Also available are private deluxe buses to Ahmedabad (Rs 110), Udaipur (Rs 65), Jodhpur (Rs 50), Mt Abu, Jaisalmer, Bikaner, Delhi and Bombay. If you don't like video buses, make enquiries before buying a ticket.

Train Ajmer is on the Delhi/Jaipur/Marwar/Ahmedabad line and most trains on this line stop at Ajmer. The 135-km journey from Jaipur costs Rs 20 in 2nd class, Rs 72 in 1st. The Pink City Express takes about the same time as the buses to cover the distance.

Getting Around
Ajmer is a relatively small town and easy enough to get around on foot, but there are plenty of auto-rickshaws and cycle-rickshaws.

PUSHKAR
Like Goa or Dharamsala, the mellow, quiet and interesting little town of Pushkar is one of those travellers' centres where people go for a little respite from the hardships of life on the Indian road. It's only 11 km from Ajmer but separated from it by Nag Pahar, the 'Snake Mountain', and right on the edge of the desert.

The town clings to the side of the small but beautiful Pushkar Lake with its many bathing ghats and temples. For Hindus, Pushkar is a very important pilgrimage centre. It's also world famous for the huge camel and cattle fair which takes place here each October or November. At this time, the town is thronged with tribal people from all over Rajasthan, pilgrims from all over India and film-makers and tourists from all over the world. If you're anywhere within striking distance at the time, it's an event not to be missed.

Some guide books would have you believe that Pushkar is a centre for that endangered species, the hippie. While this may have been true in the past, it's hardly the case these days. 'Ordinary' travellers with interests far removed from the esoteric or the exotic far outnumber hippies – whatever they are.

The Camel Fair
The exact date on which the Camel Fair is held depends on the lunar calendar but, in Hindu terminology, it falls on the full moon of Kartik Poornima. Each year, up to 200,000 people flock to Pushkar for the Camel Fair, bringing with them some 50,000 camels and cattle for several days of pilgrimage, horse dealing, camel racing and colourful festivities.

The Rajasthan tourist office has promoted the fair as an international attraction by adding Rajasthan dance programmes and other cultural events and by putting up a huge tent city for the Indian and foreign visitors. It's one of India's biggest and most colourful festivals. In 1990, the festival will be held from 31 October to 2 November and, in 1991, the dates are 18 November to 21 November.

Temples

Pushkar boasts temples, though few are as ancient as you might expect at such an important pilgrimage site since many were destroyed by Aurangzeb and subsequently rebuilt. The most famous is what is said to be the only temple in India dedicated to Brahma. It's marked by a red spire and over the entrance gateway is the *hans*, or goose symbol, of Brahma, who is said to have personally chosen Pushkar as its site. The Rangji Temple is also important.

The one-hour trek up to the hilltop temple overlooking the lake is best made early in the morning; the view is magnificent.

Ghats

Numerous ghats run down to the lake, and pilgrims are constantly bathing in the lake's holy waters. If you wish to join them, do it with respect – remove your shoes, don't smoke and don't take photographs. This is not Varanasi and the pilgrims here can be very touchy about insensitive intrusions by non-Hindus.

Places to Stay

Pushkar is such a small but popular town that it can be difficult to find accommodation, especially if you arrive late in the day. Advance booking is advisable for rooms at the better places. If you can't do this, take whatever is available on arrival and look for something better the following day.

If you arrive in Pushkar at the Marwar bus stand rather than the Ajmer bus stand, you'll have to run the gauntlet of the touts who hang out there. They'll tell you that all the hotels are full, except the one to which they want to take you (where they'll collect a commission). If it's still light, ignore them and make your own enquiries. If it's dark, they may actually be telling the truth.

Most of the available hotels are very basic with a bed, common bathroom facilities and no hot water. Many have just string beds with no mattress or sheets. On the other hand, they're generally clean and freshly whitewashed. You should ask to see a few rooms before deciding as many have a cell-like atmosphere due to the small or nonexistent windows. Mosquitoes come with most rooms, so bring insect repellent.

Perhaps the best of the bunch is the very popular *Pushkar Hotel* whose lawn ends right at the lakeside. It's very clean, pleasant, freshly whitewashed and has a vegetarian restaurant. The hotel offers a variety of rooms, ranging from dorm beds at Rs 8 and double rooms with common bath at Rs 15, right up to suites for Rs 200. Get there early in the day if you want a room.

Next to the Pushkar Hotel, but approached from a different entrance, the RTDC *Sarovar Tourist Bungalow* (tel 40) is set in its own spacious grounds at the far end of the lake and has a vegetarian restaurant. It's much better value than the Tourist Bungalow in Ajmer with dorm beds for Rs 25, ordinary singles/doubles for Rs 60/80 and deluxe rooms from Rs 80/100. Part of this hotel was once a small palace belonging to the Maharaja of Jaipur.

The popular *Everest Guest House* is also excellent value. It's a warren of a place, but it is mellow, quiet and very clean and the family running it is extremely friendly. There are also great views from the roof. Rooms cost Rs 15/20 with common bath and Rs 50 for a double with bath. Constant hot water is available and meals can be arranged.

A similar place is the *Oasis Hotel* (tel 100), near the Ajmer bus stand. It has an internal garden area, comfortable beds and

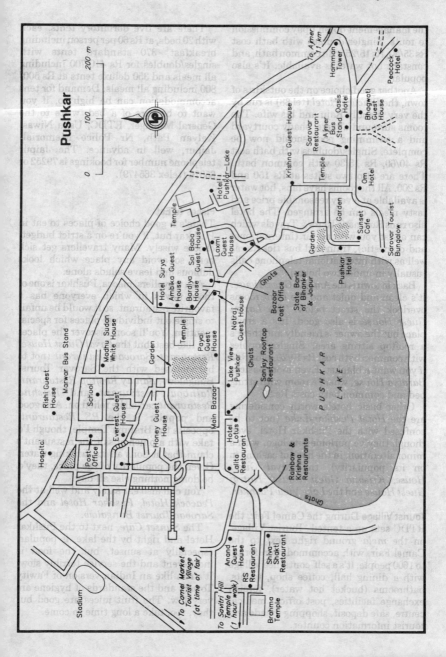

Pushkar

0   100   200 m

To Amer
11 km

Hamman
Tower

Peacock
Hotel

Ajmer
Bus
Stand

Bhagwati
Guest
House

Oasis
Hotel

Krishna Guest House

Sarovar
Restaurant

Om
Hotel

Garden

Sunset
Cafe

Garden

Sarovar Tourist
Bungalow

Pushkar
Hotel

Hotel
Pushkar

Lake

Temple

Sai Baba
Guest House

Laxmi
Guest
House

Bardiya
House

Hotel Surya

Ambika Guest
House

Natraj
Guest House

Bazaar
Post Office

State Bank
of Bikaner
& Jaipur

Ghats

Payal
Guest
House

Madhu Sudan
White House

Temple

Garden

P U S H K A R
L A K E

Ghats

Lake View
Pushkar

Sanjay Rooftop
Restaurant

Ghats

Marwar Bus Stand

Rishi Guest
House

School

Everest Guest
House

Honey Guest
House

Main Bazaar

Hotel
Lotus

Lalita
Restaurant

Rainbow &
Krishna
Restaurants

Ghats

Hospital

Post
Office

Stadium

To Camel Market &
Tourist Village
(at time of fair)

To Savitri Hill
Temple (1 hour walk)

Anand
Guest
House

RS
Restaurant

Shiva-
Shakti
Restaurant

Brahma
Temple

the management doesn't pay commission to touts. Singles/doubles with bath cost Rs 35/50, Rs 15/25 with common bath, and constant hot water is available. It's also popular.

Another good choice on the outskirts of town, the *Peacock Hotel* (tel 88) is run by the very friendly Raju and his wife. The rooms surround a large, shady courtyard and a swimming pool should now be complete. Singles/doubles with bath cost Rs 40/60, Rs 15/30 with common bath. There are also two suites at Rs 150 and Rs 200. All the rooms have fans, hot water is available at a very reasonable price and tasty meals can be arranged. The hotel also runs Rukmani Tours & Travels which can assist you with all air (international and domestic), train and bus tickets, as well as with international telephone calls (usually in under two hours).

Back in town is the *Ambika Guest House*. It's clean and quiet and the front rooms overlook the street below. The *Laxmi Guest House* is also good. It's a small place but the owner is friendly and there's a rooftop sitting area. Singles/doubles with common bath cost Rs 10/20, plus Rs 3 if you want a blanket. Even more basic is *Bardiya House*, where a room with string bed and common bath costs Rs 20.

Other basic hotels worth considering are the *Hotel Pushkar-Lake* (not to be confused with the Pushkar Hotel, even though they've purloined its logo, with a minor alteration, in the hope of cashing in on its popularity), the *Payal Guest House*, *Krishna Guest House*, *Natraj Guest House* and the *Lake View Pushkar*.

Tourist Village During the Camel Fair, the RTDC sets up a tented 'Tourist Village' on the *mela* ground right next to the Camel Fair, with accommodation for up to 1600 people. It's a self-contained village with a dining hall, coffee shop, toilets, bathrooms (bucket hot water), foreign exchange facilities, post office, medical centre, safe deposit, shopping arcade and tourist information counter.

There are five dormitory tents, each with 20 beds, at Rs 60 per person including breakfast, 370 standard tents with singles/doubles for Rs 410/700 including all meals and 350 deluxe tents at Rs 500/800 including all meals. Demand for tent accommodation can be high so, if you want to be sure of a bed, write to the General Manager, RTDC, Usha Niwas, Kalyan Path, Nr Police Memorial, Jaipur, well in advance. The Jaipur telephone number for bookings is 79252 or 65076 (telex 365479).

Places to Eat

There's a good choice of places to eat in Pushkar but, if you're on a strict budget, choose wisely. Many travellers get sick here, so avoid any place which looks dubious and leave salads alone.

As a travellers' mecca, Pushkar is one of those towns in which everyone has a favourite restaurant, so it would be unfair to single out individual places for special mention. You'll soon discover the places you like best, but the *Payal Guest House/Restaurant*, *Sarovar Restaurant* (not to be confused with the Sarovar Tourist Bungalow), *Sanjay Rooftop Restaurant*, *Rainbow Restaurant* and *Krishna Restaurant* can all be relied on. Also good and popular is the *RS Restaurant*, opposite the Brahma Temple, though I'd take with a pinch of salt the restaurant's claim that it boils all its drinking water. Given the popularity of the place, they'd be doing nothing else all day!

You can also eat safely and well at the *Peacock Hotel*, *Pushkar Hotel* and the *Sarovar Tourist Bungalow*.

The *Sunset Cafe*, next to the Pushkar Hotel and right by the lake, is popular, especially at sunset, but the food is indifferent and the service terribly slow. It's run like an Indian version of Fawlty Towers and the standards of hygiene are very low. The fruit juices are good but they, too, take a long time to come.

Things to Buy

Pushkar has a wide selection of handicraft shops all along the main bazaar and is especially good for embroidered fabrics such as wall hangings, bed covers, cushion covers and shoulder bags. A lot of what is stocked here actually comes from the Barmer district south of Jaisalmer and other tribal areas of Rajasthan. There's something to suit all tastes and pockets though you'll have to haggle over prices. The shopkeepers here have been exposed to tourists with plenty of money and not much time, so there's the usual nonsense about 'last price' quotes which aren't negotiable. Take your time and visit a few shops. Once your face is known you can start serious negotiations.

In between these shops are the inevitable clothing shops catering to styles which were in vogue in Goa and Kathmandu at the end of the '60s. You may find occasional timeless items, but most of it is pretty clichéd.

The music shops (selling tapes and records), on the other hand, are well worth a visit if you're interested in picking up some examples of traditional or contemporary classical Indian music. The shops here don't seem to stock the usual banal current film-score rages.

Three places sell English-language books, one along the main bazaar and the other two between the bazaar post office and the Om Hotel. Most books are trade-ins which travellers have brought with them, but there is a good selection.

Getting There & Away

Buses depart Ajmer frequently from both the railway station and the state bus stand near the Tourist Bungalow. Buses from the state bus stand stop at the Marwar bus stand on the main road in Pushkar, but those from the Ajmer railway station stop at the Ajmer bus stand on the opposite side of town. Although both cost Rs 3, it's preferable to arrive in Pushkar at the Ajmer bus stand where there are very few touts. Most travellers seem to make the mistake of arriving at the Marwar stand and have to run the gauntlet. It's a spectacular climb up and over the hills – if you can see out of the window!

It is possible to continue straight on

Pushkar

from Pushkar to Jodhpur without having to backtrack to Ajmer, but the buses go there via Merta and can take eight hours. It's much faster to go to Ajmer and take the 4½-hour express bus.

RANTHAMBHOR NATIONAL PARK

Near the town of Sawai Madhopur, midway between Bharatpur and Kota, Ranthambhor National Park is one of the prime examples of Project Tiger's conservation efforts in Rajasthan. There are 42 tigers in this park and good chances of a sighting on your first safari though, to be sure, you should plan on two safaris and, preferably, three. Other game, especially the larger and smaller herbivores, are more numerous.

The park itself covers some 400 square km and its scenery is very beautiful. A system of lakes and rivers is hemmed in by steep high crags and, on top of one of these, there's an extensive and well-preserved fortress containing temples and the remains of palaces. The lower-lying ground alternates between open bushland and fairly dense forest and is peppered with ruined pavilions, *chhatris* (tombs) and 'hides' – the area was formerly a hunting preserve of the maharajas.

A good network of gravel tracks criss-crosses the park and safaris are undertaken in open-sided jeeps driven by a ranger. If you've ever been on safari in Africa, you might think this is an unduly risky venture but the tigers appear unconcerned by jeep loads of garrulous tourists touting cameras only metres away from where they're lying. No-one has been mauled or eaten – yet!

The best time to visit the park is between September and April since, during the monsoon months, the animals have no need to stay close to the lake system for water and spread out into the more remote areas of the park. Early morning and late afternoon are the best times to view game.

There's a Rs 10 entry fee to the park, plus Rs 10 for a camera. You'll also have to pay the entry fee for your driver/guide

(compulsory) and an additional Rs 10 if you have your own jeep.

The park entrance is about 15 km from the Sawai Madhopu railway station.

Places to Stay

Advance booking is essential during the busy Christmas and New Year periods. There's a tourist information bureau at the Project Tiger office in Sawai Madhopur so, if you have no accommodation booked, it's best to check here first before moving off.

If you're most interested in wildlife and the sounds of the jungle then the best, though not the cheapest, place to stay is the *Jogi Mahal*, right next to the main entrance gate and overlooking one of the lotus-studded lakes. It's the only accommodation within the park itself. This former hunting lodge, which once belonged to the maharajas, is the one featured in all the glossy tourist brochures. It's a beautiful place to stay but, as they have only four rooms which are always in heavy demand, advance booking is essential. Rooms cost Rs 300 per person, including all meals. Meals are not available to nonresidents.

Most travellers stay at the equally pleasant RTDC *Castle Jhoomar Baori* (tel 2495). This hotel is stunningly sited on the hillside to the right of the road between Sawai Madhopur and the main entrance gate, about seven km from the railway station. It was formerly a maharaja's palace, then a jail (what a pleasant place in which to be incarcerated!). The 11 rooms are comfortable, spacious and well furnished and have modern toilet and bathroom facilities with hot water. There's also a beautiful lounge as well as open rooftop areas. The ordinary air-cooled rooms cost Rs 145/175. There's also a Panther Suite for Rs 250 and a Tiger Suite for Rs 350. A considerable discount applies between May and September. The bar and restaurant (with a sensible menu) are open to nonresidents. Transport to or from Sawai Madhopur railway station costs Rs 15 per person, but there's a minimum charge of Rs 60.

Also relatively close to the main entrance gate is the *Tented Camp* about 2½ km from the Jhoomar Baori, alongside the main road, and a branch of *Indian Adventures* at Sherpur village which offers relatively expensive all-inclusive package deals and chalet accommodation. To get to it, take the left-hand fork in the main road just past the Tented Camp, where you'll see a hoarding for the Bank of Baroda.

Closer to Sawai Madhopur, about three km from the railway station on the road to the park entrance, the former Maharaja of Jaipur's hunting lodge, now called the *Sawai Modhpur Lodge,* offers full board for a mere Rs 900. If the price doesn't deter you, book through the City Palace at Jaipur. Almost opposite, the very modern *Amrat Resort* is not a cheap option.

In Sawai Madhopur itself, there are a number of basic hotels including the *Swagat Hotel* which costs Rs 50 a double. Although accommodation in Sawai Madhopur is certainly cheap, transport to the park entrance is expensive.

Getting There & Away

Sawai Madhopur is on the main Delhi to Bombay broad-gauge railway line and, as most trains stop here, there's a wide range from which to choose. It's also the junction of the metre-gauge spur to Jaipur and Bikaner. Only one train per day travels along this spur in either direction. It leaves Jaipur at 6.55 am, arriving in Sawai Madhopur at 10.15 am and, in the opposite direction, leaves Sawai Madhopur at 5.30 pm and arrives in Jaipur at 8.45 pm.

Getting Around

Jeeps can be hired from several places, the main ones being the RTDC Castle Jhoomar Baori, the Tented Camp and the main entrance gate/Jogi Mahal. RTDC-operated jeeps from the main entry gate cost Rs 30 per person (minimum charge

Rs 150) and will take up to six people excluding the driver/guide. Private jeeps are usually available from the same place at negotiable prices. Hired from Castle Jhoomar Baori, jeeps cost Rs 20 per person (minimum charge Rs 100). This may seem somewhat cheaper but it works out to almost the same because you have to add on the cost of getting to the entrance gate from the lodge and it's quite a distance.

Safari times are 7 to 8.30 am, 8.30 to 10 am, 2.30 to 4 pm and 4 to 5.30 pm. Officially, only nine jeeps are allowed into the park at any one time, but this is rarely enforced.

Southern Rajasthan

KOTA (population 347,000)

Following the Rajput conquest of this area of Rajasthan in the 12th century, Bundi was chosen as the capital with Kota as the land grant of the ruler's eldest son. This situation continued until 1624 when Kota became a separate state, remaining so until it was integrated into Rajasthan following independence. Building of the city began in 1264 following the defeat of the Bhil chieftains but Kota didn't reach its present size until well into the 17th century when Rao Madho Singh, a son of the ruler of Bundi, was made ruler of Kota by the Moghul emperor Jehangir. Subsequent rulers have all added to the fortress and palaces which stand here today.

Today, Kota serves as an army headquarters. It's also Rajasthan's industrial centre (mainly chemicals), powered by the hydroelectric plants on the Chambal River – the only permanent river in the state – and the nearby atomic plant. Very few tourists visit Kota, which is surprising because the fortress and part of the palace complex are now open to the public and the Rao Madho Singh Museum has to be one of the best in Rajasthan.

Information & Orientation

Kota is strung out along the east bank of the Chambal River. The railway station is well to the north, the Tourist Bungalow, a number of other hotels and the bus stand are in the middle, and Chambal Gardens, the fort and the Kota Barrage are to the south.

The tourist office is at the Chambal Tourist Bungalow. The staff here are keen and a range of leaflets is available.

Changing money in Kota can be a problem. The only bank which will change travellers' cheques is the State Bank of Bikaner and Jaipur on Aerodrome Circuit, quite a way from the centre of things. The Hotel Brijraj Bhawan will change cheques for guests at the standard rate, but they don't issue an exchange certificate.

City Palace & Fort

Standing beside the Kota Barrage, overlooking the Chambal River, the City Palace and Fort is one of the largest such complexes in Rajasthan. Some of its buildings are now occupied by schools but most of the complex is open to the public. Entry is from the south side through the Naya Darwaza, or 'New Gate'.

Just inside the New Gate is the small Government Museum. It has a collection of stone idols and other such fragments but is otherwise of only mild interest and desperately needs a major revamp. In theory, it's open between 10 am and 4.30 pm daily, except Friday, but the staff rarely arrive before 11 am. Entry costs Rs 1.

The Rao Madho Singh Museum, in contrast, is superb. It's on the right-hand side of the complex's huge central courtyard and is entered through a gateway topped by rampant elephants like those at the Bundi Fort. Inside, you'll find displays of weapons, clothing and some of the best-preserved murals in the state. Indeed, everything about this former palace is colourful. The museum is open daily, except Friday, from 11 am to

5 pm and entry costs Rs 3, plus Rs 5 for a still camera (Rs 10 for a movie camera).

After visiting the museum, it's worth wandering around the rest of the complex just to appreciate how magnificent this place must have been in its heyday. Unfortunately, a lot of it is falling into disrepair and the gardens are no more, but there are some excellent views over the old city, the river and the huge industrial complex with its enormous twin chimneys across the river.

Chambal Gardens

The gardens south of the fort at Amar Niwas are popular for picnics and feature a pond well stocked with garwhal crocodiles. In the past, these reptiles were common all along the river but, by the middle of this century, they had been virtually exterminated through over-hunting. The pond is also home to some flamingoes, which appear remarkably unbothered by their companions.

Jagmandir

Between the City Palace and the Tourist Bungalow is the picturesque artificial tank of Kishore Sagar, constructed in 1346. Right in the middle of the tank, on a small island, is the enchanting little palace of Jagmandir. Built in 1740 by one of the maharanis of Kota, it's best seen early in the morning but is exquisite at any time of day. It doesn't appear to be open to the public, though you might be able to persuade one of the boat owners to take you around it.

Just below the tank, beside the tourist bungalow, is a curious collection of somewhat neglected but impressive royal tombs, or chhatris, in the Chhattar Bilas Gardens.

Places to Stay

Although there are a number of pretty good hotels close to the railway station, few people choose to stay such a long way from the centre of things. If you do want accommodation in this area, try either the

Rajasthan Top: Amber Fort (GC)
Left: Amber Palace (HF)
Right: Amber Fort (GC)

Top: Wall painting, Udaipur, Rajasthan (TW)
Left: Hilltop Jain temples at Palitana, Gujarat (GC)
Right: Padlock salesman, Ahmedabad, Gujarat (TW)

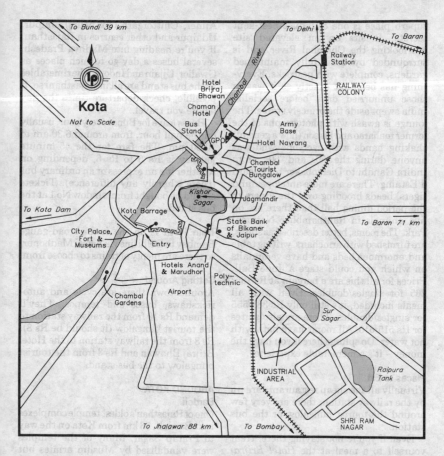

Kota

Not to Scale

To Bundi 39 km
To Delhi
To Baran
Railway Station
RAILWAY COLONY
Chambal River
Hotel Brijraj Bhawan
Chaman Hotel
Bus Stand
GPO
Army Base
Hotel Navrang
Chambal Tourist Bungalow
Kishor Sagar
Jagmandir
To Kota Dam
Kota Barrage
City Palace, Fort & Museums
Entry
State Bank of Bikaner & Jaipur
To Baran 71 km
Hotels Anand & Marudhor
Poly-technic
Airport
Chambal Gardens
Sur Sagar
Raipura Tank
INDUSTRIAL AREA
To Jhalawar 88 km
To Bombay
SHRI RAM NAGAR

Hotel Shri Anand or the *Gaytri Hotel* (tel 23230).

Most travellers to Kota head for the RTDC *Chambal Tourist Bungalow* (tel 26527). While the staff are very friendly and the hotel is surrounded by gardens, it's a poor choice. Once, it was probably a very pleasant place to stay but, these days, it's in an advanced state of decay and infested with mosquitoes. The staff will tell you that everything works and it does – until you want to use it. Dorm beds cost Rs 15 or there are deluxe singles/doubles for Rs 70/90, Rs 175/200 with air-

con. Meals are available, but order in advance if there are not many guests.

The *Hotel Navrang* (tel 23294), close to the GPO on Station Rd, Civil Lines, is better value. They have singles/doubles with bath and hot water for Rs 80/120. It's a modern, pleasant place and the staff speak English. For something cheaper, try the *Chaman Hotel* (tel 23377), closer to the bus station, also on Station Rd.

However, by far the best hotel in Kota is the *Hotel Brijraj Bhawan* (tel 23071), once a palace of the maharaos of Kota and also the former British Residency. This superb place is one of India's best-kept secrets. It sits on an elevated site overlooking the Chambal River and is surrounded by beautifully maintained gardens, complete with peacocks. Everything has been left exactly as it was in those unhurried days before socialist India swept aside the princely states. The lounge is awash with photographs of the former maharao and his son (now a general) shaking hands with everyone who was anyone during the '50s and '60s, from Indira Gandhi to Diefenbaker to Giscard d'Estaing. There are more antelopes' and tigers' heads brooding over the diners in the period dining hall than there are on live animals in Ranthambhor National Park. The rooms, better described as suites, are furnished with armchairs, writing table and enormous beds and have verandahs on which you could stage a June Ball. Prices for all this are a bargain at Rs 135/265 for singles/doubles. Even with all meals included, it's still only Rs 385/555 for singles/doubles. There are also suites for Rs 515/610. All rooms have bath with hot water. Do splurge here if you have the money – it's a memorable experience.

Places to Eat

Virtually all the cheap restaurants are up by the railway station; there are very few around the tourist bungalow or the bus station.

Even if you're not staying there, treat yourself to a meal at the *Hotel Brijraj Bhawan* – you need to make advance arrangements. The quality of the food and the variety of dishes is superb. So, too, is the manner in which it is served. Everyone eats at the same huge table on a crisp, white linen tablecloth with silver-plated cutlery and, afterwards, you can enjoy a long postpradial drink on the outside verandah or in the commodious lounge complete with grand piano. Fairlawn Hotel (Calcutta), eat your heart out!

Getting There & Away

Bus There are bus connections to Bundi,

Ajmer, Chittorgarh (six hours), Jaipur, Udaipur and other centres in Rajasthan. If you're heading into Madhya Pradesh, several buses a day go to such places as Gwalior, Ujjain and Indore. The timetables at the bus stand are all in Rajasthani so, if possible, check departure times the day before you travel.

Buses leave for Bundi every hour, usually on the half hour, from around 6.30 am to 10.30 pm. The fare for the 45-minute journey is Rs 5 to Rs 6, depending on whether it's an express or an ordinary bus (there's hardly any difference). Tickets should be bought from window No 1 at the bus stand.

Train Kota is on the main broad-gauge Bombay to Delhi line via Sawai Madhopur, so there are plenty of trains to choose from.

Getting Around

Around town there are cycle and auto-rickshaws, buses and tempos. They'll demand Rs 10 from the railway station to the tourist bungalow (it should be Rs 8), Rs 8 from the railway station to the Hotel Brijraj Bhawan and Rs 3 from the tourist bungalow to the bus stand.

AROUND KOTA
Bardoli

One of Rajasthan's oldest temple complexes is at Bardoli, 56 km from Kota on the way to Pratap Sagar. Many of the temples were vandalised by Muslim armies but much remains and it warrants a visit. If you are short of time, you can see a lot of the sculptures from these 9th-century temples displayed in the Government Museum in Kota. The Pratap Sagar Dam is the Chambal's second dam.

Jhalara-Patan

At Jhalara-Patan, some 80 km south of Kota on the Jhalawar road, are the ruins of a huge 10th-century Surya, or Sun God, temple containing magnificent sculptures as well as one of the best-preserved idols of Surya in the whole of India.

Jhalawar itself, about seven km from the temple, is also worth a visit and has a good collection of sculptures from nearby temples displayed in the Government Museum.

Gagron Fortress

While you're in this area, you should also take a look at the Gagron Fortress, 10 km from Jhalawar. Though perhaps not as famous as others like Chittorgarh, Jodhpur and Jaisalmer, this huge fort occupies a prominent place in the annals of Rajput chivalry and has been fought over for centuries.

If you like to explore in peace and quiet, this is the fort for you. Very few tourists even suspect its existence. The fort is close to (and visible from) the road between Kota and Ujjain and Indore. Local buses run from Kota to Jhalawar and you can arrange transport to the fort from there.

BUNDI (population 50,000)

Bundi, only 39 km west of Kota, was the capital of a major princely state during the heyday of the Rajputs. Although its importance dwindled with the rise of Kota during Moghul times, it maintained its independence until its incorporation into the state of Rajasthan in 1947. Kota itself was part of Bundi until its separation in 1624 at the instigation of the Moghul emperor Jehangir.

Today, Bundi is a picturesque little town whose medieval atmosphere more or less remains. It's also well off the beaten track, so there are very few tourists here. The town's Rajput legacy is well preserved in the shape of the massive Taragarh Fort which broods over the town in the narrow valley below and the huge palace which stands beneath it. In this palace are found the famous Bundi murals – similar to those in the Rao Madho Singh Museum in Kota. Since there's very little accommodation in Bundi, many travellers prefer to stay in Kota and come here on a day trip. This can be the best way to see the palace and fort since most of the

palace is under lock and key and the guardians only appear willing to open it up for prearranged package tour groups, not individual travellers.

Orientation

The bus station is at the Kota (east) end of town. It's relatively easy to find your way to the palace on foot through the bazaar – once you pass through the city gate, there are only two main roads through town and the palace is visible from many points. Auto-rickshaws are also available and can be hired for Rs 5 from outside the bus station.

Taragarh Fort & Palace

The Star Fort was built in 1354. It is reached by a steep road leading up the hillside to its enormous gateway, topped by rampant elephants. Inside are huge reservoirs carved out of solid rock and the Bhim Burj, the largest of the battlements, on which is mounted a famous cannon. Views over the town and surrounding countryside are excellent.

The palace itself is reached from the north-western end of the bazaar, through a huge wooden gateway and up a steep cobbled ramp. Only two parts of the outer perimeter of the palace, known variously as the Chitra Mahal and Ummed Mahal, are usually open to the public. Some of the famous Bundi murals can be seen on the upper level. Unfortunately, they're deteriorating rapidly and absolutely nothing is being done to preserve them. Nor is anything being done to preserve the actual fabric of the palace itself. There are other murals inside the main part of the palace, but you're very unlikely to be able to persuade the guardians to unlock the place and let you in.

Directly below the Chitra Mahal is the ruined Ratan Daulat, or horse stables, used these days as a public toilet.

Nawal Sagar

Also visible from the fort is the square artificial lake of Nawal Sagar. In the

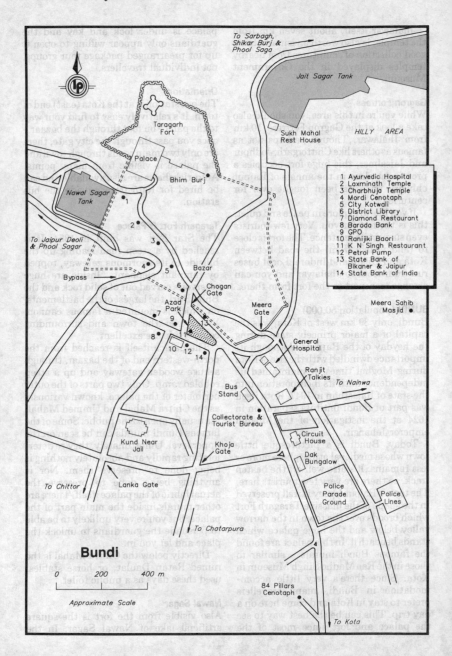

To Sarbagh,
Shikar Burj &
Phool Saga

Jait Sagar Tank

HILLY AREA

Taragarh
Fort

Palace

Bhim Burj

Nawal Sagar
Tank

Sukh Mahal
Rest House

To Jaipur Deoli
& Phool Sagar

1

2

3

4   5

Bazar

Chogan
Gate

6

Azad
Park

9

7

8

11

10 12 14
13

Bypass

Meera
Gate

Meera Sahib
Masjid

1 Ayurvedic Hospital
2 Laxminath Temple
3 Charbhuja Temple
4 Mordi Cenotaph
5 City Kotwali
6 District Library
7 Diamond Restaurant
8 Baroda Bank
9 GPO
10 Ranijiki Baori
11 K N Singh Restaurant
12 Petrol Pump
13 State Bank of
   Bikaner & Jaipur
14 State Bank of India

General
Hospital

Ranjit
Talkies

To Nainwa

Bus
Stand

Collectorate &
Tourist Bureau

Circuit
House

Dak
Bungalow

Kund Near
Jail

Khoja
Gate

To Chittor

Lanka Gate

Police
Parade
Ground

Police
Lines

To Chatarpura

Bundi

0   200   400 m

Approximate Scale

84 Pillars
Cenotaph

To Kota

centre is a temple to Varuna, the Aryan god of water.

Other Attractions

Bundi's other attractions are all out of town and difficult to reach without transport. The modern palace, with its beautiful artificial tank and gardens, is several km out of town on the Ajmer road, alongside Phool Sagar. Shikar Burj is a nearby small hunting lodge and picnic spot along the same road. The cenotaphs of Bundi's rulers are close to here at Khshar Bagh. There's another beautiful palace, the smaller Sukh Mahal, closer to town on the edge of Jait Sagar, which has been converted into a hotel.

Places to Stay

The obvious places to stay, such as the *Circuit House* and the *Dak Bungalow*, both near the bus stand, seem to have a policy of discouraging foreigners and are unlikely to offer you a bed.

The only other option is the *Sukh Mahal Rest House* on the edge of Jait Sagar Tank. To get there, take an autorickshaw or taxi from the bus station. A former palace of the rulers of Bundi, the rest house is not cheap but it's a very pleasant place to stay. Make enquiries about booking at the tourist office (tel 27695) in Kota.

Getting There & Around

It takes about five hours by bus from Ajmer to Bundi. From Kota, it's only 45 minutes to Bundi. Buses also go from Bundi to Chittorgarh and Udaipur.

CHITTORGARH (population 36,000)

The hilltop fortress of Chittorgarh epitomises the whole romantic, doomed ideal of Rajput chivalry. Three times in its long history, Chittor was sacked by a stronger enemy and, on each occasion, the end came in textbook Rajput fashion as jauhar was declared in the face of impossible odds. The men donned the saffron robes of martyrdom and rode out

from the fort to certain death, while the women and children immolated themselves on a huge funeral pyre. Honour was always more important than death.

History

Chittor's first defeat occurred in 1303 when Ala-ud-din Khilji, the Pathan king of Delhi, besieged the fort in order to capture the beautiful Padmini, wife of the Rana's uncle, Bhim Singh. When defeat was inevitable the Rajput noblewomen, including Padmini, committed *sati* and Bhim Singh led the orange-clad noblemen out to their deaths.

In 1535 it was Bahadur Shah, the Sultan of Gujarat, who besieged the fort and, once again, the medieval dictates of chivalry determined the outcome. This time, the carnage was immense. It is said that 13,000 Rajput women and 32,000 Rajput warriors died following the declaration of jauhar.

The final sack of Chittor came just 33 years later, in 1568, when the Moghul emperor Akbar took the town. Once again, the fort was defended heroically but, once again, the odds were overwhelming and the women performed sati, the fort gates were flung open and 8000 orange-robed warriors rode out to their deaths. On this occasion, Maharana Udai Singh fled to Udaipur where he re-established his capital. In 1616, Jehangir returned Chittor to the Rajputs but there was no attempt at resettlement.

Orientation

The fort stands on a 280-hectare site on top of a 180-metre-high hill, which rises abruptly from the surrounding plain. Until 1568, the town of Chittor was also on the hilltop within the fort walls but today's modern town, known as Lower Town, sprawls to the west of the hill. A river separates it from the bus stand, railway line and modern part of the town.

Information

The tourist office (tel 2273) is in the Janta

Avas Grah (the RTDC Tourist Bungalow), near the railway station. It's open from 8 am to 12 noon and 3 to 6 pm.

The Fort

Bhim, one of the Pandava heroes of the *Mahabharata*, is credited with the fort's original construction. All of Chittor's attractions are within the fort. A zigzag ascent of over one km leads through seven gateways to the main gate on the western side, the Ram Pol.

On the climb, you pass two chhatris, memorials marking spots where Jaimal and Kalla, heroes of the 1568 siege, fell during the struggle against Akbar. Another chhatri, further up the hill, marks the spot where Patta fell. The main gate on the eastern side of the fort is the Suraj Pol. Within the fort, a circular road runs around the ruins and there's a deer park at the southern end.

Today, the fort of Chittor is a virtually deserted ruin, but impressive reminders of its grandeur still stand and those with imagination should easily be able to tune in to the romantic heroism which lingers in the air of this incredible monument. The main sites can all be seen in half a day (assuming you're not walking) but, if you like the atmosphere of ancient sites, then it's worth spending longer as this is a very mellow place and there are no hassles whatsoever.

Rana Kumbha Palace Entering the fort and turning right, you come almost immediately to the ruins of this palace. It contains elephant and horse stables and a Shiva temple. One of the jauhars is said to have taken place in a vaulted cellar. Across from the palace is the archaeological office and museum, and the treasury building or Nau Lakha Bhandar.

Fateh Prakash Palace Just beyond the Rana Kumbha Palace, this palace is much more modern (Maharana Fateh Singh died in 1930). It houses an interesting museum and statues and armoury are found in various buildings in the fort. The museum is open daily from 10 am to 5 pm. Entry costs Rs 1.

Tower of Victory Continuing anticlockwise around the fort, you come to the Jaya Stambh, or 'Tower of Victory'. Erected by Rana Kumbha to commemorate his victory over Mahmud Khilji of Malwa in 1440, the tower was constructed between 1458 and 1468. It rises 37 metres in nine storeys and, for Rs 0.50, you can climb the narrow stairs to the top. Watch your head on the lintels!

Hindu sculptures adorn the outside of the tower, but the dome was damaged by lightning and repaired during the last century. Close to the tower is the Mahasati, an area where the ranas were cremated during Chittorgarh's period as the Mewar capital. There are many sati stones here. The Sammidheshwar Temple stands in the same area.

Gaumukh Reservoir Walk down beyond the temple and, at the very edge of the cliff, is this deep tank. A spring feeds the tank from a carved cow's mouth in the cliffside – from which the reservoir got its name. The opening here leads to the cave in which Padmini and her compatriots are said to have committed jauhar.

Padmini's Palace Continuing south, you come to Padmini's Palace, built beside a large pool with a pavilion in its centre. Legends relate that, as Padmini stood in this pavilion, Ala-ud-din was permitted to see her reflection in a mirror in the palace. This glimpse was the spark that convinced him to destroy Chittor in order to possess her.

The bronze gates in this pavilion were carried off by Akbar and can now be seen in the fort at Agra. Continuing round the circular road, you pass the deer park, the Bhimlat Tank, the Suraj Pol Gate and the Neelkanth Mahadev Jain Temple, and reach the Tower of Fame.

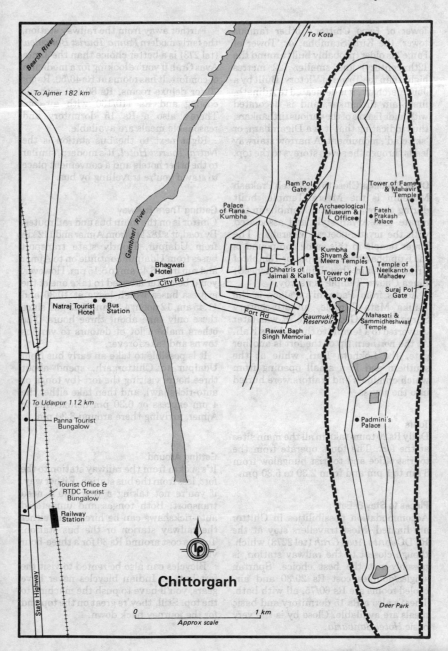

To Kota

Beach River

To Ajmer 182 km

Gambheri River

Ram Pol
Gate

Palace
of Rana
Kumbha

Tower of Fame
& Mahavir
Temple

Archaeological
Museum &
Office

Fateh
Prakash
Palace

Kumbha
Shyam &
Meera Temples

Bhagwati
Hotel

Chhatris of
Jaimal & Kalla

Tower of
Victory

Temple of
Neelkanth
Mahadev

City Rd

Suraj Pol
Gate

Natraj Tourist
Hotel

Bus
Station

Fort Rd

Mahasati &
Sammidheshwar
Temple

Gaumukh
Reservoir

Rawat Bagh
Singh Memorial

To Udaipur 112 km

Panna Tourist
Bungalow

Padmini's
Palace

Tourist Office &
RTDC Tourist
Bungalow

Railway
Station

State Highway

Chittorgarh

0   1 km

Approx scale

Deer Park

Tower of Fame Chittor's other famous tower, the Kirti Stambha, or 'Tower of Fame', is older (probably built around the 12th century) and smaller (22 metres high) than the Tower of Victory. Built by a Jain merchant, it is dedicated to Adinath, first Jain tirthankar, and is decorated with nude figures of the various tirthankars, thus indicating that it is a Digambara, or 'sky clad', monument. A narrow stairway leads through the seven storeys to the top.

Other Buildings Close to the Fateh Prakash Museum is the Meera Temple, built during the reign of Rana Kumbha in the ornate Indo-Aryan style and associated with the mystic-poetess Meerabai. The larger temple in this same compound is the Kumbha Shyam Temple, or Temple of Vriji. The Jain (but Hindu-influenced) Singa Chowri Temple is nearby.

Across from Padmini's Palace is the Kalika Mata Temple, an 8th-century Surya, or Sun God, temple. It was later converted to a temple to the goddess Kali. At the northern tip of the fort is another gate, the Lokhota Bari, while at the southern end is a small opening from which criminals and traitors were hurled into the abyss.

Tours
Daily Rs 20 tours take in all the main sites at the fort. The tours operate from the tourist office and tourist bungalow from 8 am to 1 pm and from 2.30 to 5.30 pm.

Places to Stay & Eat
Accommodation possibilities in Chittor are limited. Most travellers stay at the RTDC *Janta Avas Grah* (tel 2273) which, though closest to the railway station, is possibly not the best choice. Spartan singles/doubles cost Rs 20/30 and air-cooled rooms are Rs 60/75, all with bath. There's also a Rs 15 dormitory and basic meals are available. Close by is the very basic *Hotel Sanvaria*.

Further away from the railway station, the fairly modern *Panna Tourist Bungalow* (tel 273) is a better choice than the Janta Avas Grah if you're looking for a modicum of comfort. It has rooms at Rs 40/50, Rs 55/70 for deluxe rooms, Rs 80/110 with air cooling and Rs 110/130 with air-con. There's also a Rs 15 dormitory and reasonable meals are available.

Right next to the bus station is the *Natraj Tourist Hotel*. It's modern, similar to the other hotels and a convenient place to stay if you're travelling by bus.

Getting There & Away
Chittor is on the main bus and rail routes. By road, it's 182 km from Ajmer and 112 km from Udaipur. Hourly state transport buses from Udaipur continue on to Ajmer and run from 6.45 am to 5.15 pm. However, you'd be better advised to take one of the express buses which leave at 10.30 and 11.45 am, 12 noon, 4.15 and 5.15 pm, since these only take about three hours. The others make a lot of detours to various towns and take forever.

It is possible to take an early bus from Udaipur to Chittorgarh, spend about three hours visiting the fort (by tonga or auto-rickshaw), and then take either the 4 pm express or 6.30 pm deluxe bus to Ajmer, arriving there around 8.30 pm.

Getting Around
It's six km from the railway station to the fort, less from the bus station. Either way, if you're not taking a tour you'll need transport. Both tongas and unmetered auto-rickshaws can be hired from either the railway station or the bus station. Tongas cost around Rs 30 for a three-hour visit.

Bicycles can also be rented to visit the fort but, as Indian bicycles never have gears, you'll have to push the machine to the top. Still, they're great on the top and for the journey back down.

AROUND CHITTORGARH
Menal
On the Bundi to Chittorgarh road, 48 km from Bundi, Menal is a complex of Shiva temples built during the Gupta period.

Bijolia
Bijolia, 16 km from Menal, was once a group of 100 temples. Today, only three are left standing, one of which has a huge figure of Ganesh.

Mandalgarh
A detour between Menal and Bijolia takes you to Mandalgarh. It is the third fort of Mewar built by Rana Kumbha – the others are the great fort of Chittorgarh and the fort at Kumbhalgarh.

Nagri
One of the oldest towns in Rajasthan, Nagri is 14 km north of Chittor. Hindu and Buddhist remains from the Mauryan to the Gupta period have been found here.

UDAIPUR (population 300,000)
Possibly no city in Rajasthan is quite as romantic as Udaipur, even though the state is replete with fantastic hilltop fortresses, exotic fairy-tale palaces and gripping legends of medieval chivalry and heroism. The French Impressionist painters, let alone the Brothers Grimm, would have loved this place and it's not without justification that Udaipur has been called the 'Venice of the East'. Jaisalmer is certainly the 'Beau Geste' of the desert; Udaipur is the Versailles.

Founded in 1567 by Maharana Udai Singh following the final sack of Chittorgarh by the Moghul emperor Akbar, Udaipur rivals any of the world-famous creations of the Moghuls with its Rajput love of the whimsical and its superbly crafted elegance. The Lake Palace is certainly the best late example of this unique cultural explosion, but Udaipur is full of palaces, temples and havelis ranging from the modest to the extravagant. It's also proud of its heritage as a centre for the performing arts, painting and crafts. And, since water is relatively plentiful in this part of the state (in between the periodic droughts), there are plenty of parks and gardens, many of which line the lake shores.

Until recent times, the higher uninhabited parts of the city were covered in forests but, as elsewhere in India, most of these have inevitably been turned into firewood. There is, however, a movement afoot to reverse this process. The city was once surrounded by a wall and, although the gates and much of the wall over the higher crags remain, a great deal of it has disappeared. It's sad that this fate should have befallen such a historic place but the essence remains.

In common with all Indian cities, Udaipur's urban and industrial sprawl goes beyond the city's original boundaries and pollution of various kinds can be discouraging. This will be your first impression of Udaipur if you arrive at the railway or bus station. Ignore it and head for the old city where a different world is waiting for you.

Information & Orientation
The old city, bounded by the remains of a city wall, is on the east side of Lake Pichola. The railway station and bus station are both just outside the city wall to the south-east. The tourist office (tel 3509) and the Tourist Bungalow are also outside the city wall, to the north-east and only a km or so from the bus stand. Tourist office hours are 10 am to 5 pm Monday to Saturday.

There are also tourist information counters at the railway station and airport. The GPO is directly north of the old city, behind the movie theatre at Chetak Circle, but the poste restante is at the post office at the junction of Hospital Rd and the road north from Delhi Gate, close to the Tourist Bungalow. It's efficient and the staff are friendly and helpful.

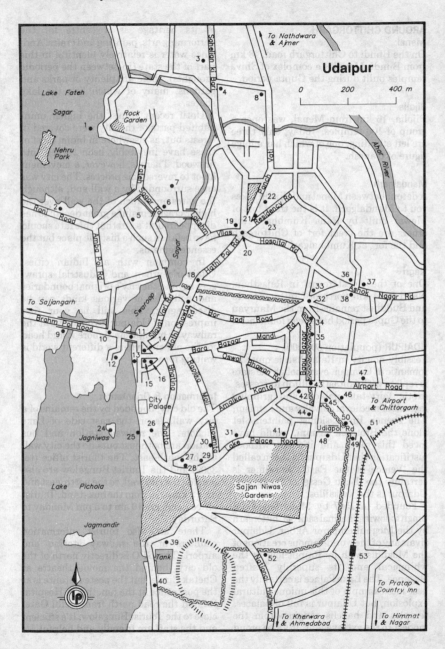

Udaipur

To Nathdwara & Ajmer

0   200   400 m

To Sajjangarh

To Pratap Country Inn

To Airport & Chittorgarh

To Kherwara & Ahmedabad

To Himmat & Nagar

Lake Fateh Sagar

Nehru Park

Rock Garden

Rani Road

Ahar River

Lake Pichola

Jagniwas

Jagmandir

Sajjan Niwas Gardens

City Palace

Tank

Fateh Sagar Rd

Amba Mata Rd

Sagar

Swaroop Sagar Rd

Brahm Pol Road

Sahelion ki Bari

Sajjan Rd

Chetak

Ashok Nagar Rd

Residency Rd

Hospital Rd

Hathi Pol Rd

Bhatiyani Chohatta

Bar Hadi Rd

Mandi Rd

Bara Bazaar

Bhawan Rd

Oswal

Airport Road

Udaipol Rd

Lake Palace Road

Bhatias Mori

Chetak Chouraha

Amalka

Kanta

Chougan

Bapu Bazaar

National Highway 8

1	Lake boat moorings	28	Craft Shops
2	Hotel Lakend	29	Hotel Rangiwas Palace
3	Saheliyon ki Bari	30	Badi Haveli Hotel
4	Chandralok Hotel	31	Hotel Chandra Prakash &
5	Hotel Hill Top		Mahendra Prakash
6	State Hotel	32	Delhi Gate
7	Laxmi Vilas Palace Hotel &	33	Indian Airlines
	Hotel Anand Bhawan	34	Alka Hotel
8	Hotel Fountain	35	Parkview Restaurant
9	Brahm Pol	36	Poste Restante
10	Amba Pol	37	Tourist Office &
11	Chand Pol		Kajri Tourist Bungalow
12	Lake Pichola Hotel	38	Ashok & Prince Hotels
13	Jagat Niwas Hotel	39	Cafe Hill Park
14	Lalghat Guest House	40	Jal Burj Cafe
15	Lake Ghat Guest House &	41	Garden Hotel
	Shri Karni Guest House	42	Patel's Soda Factory
16	Jagdish Temple	43	Suraj Pol Gate
17	Clock tower	44	Hotel Maan
18	Hathi Pol	45	International Tourist &
19	Berry's Restaurant		Sadhana Hotels
20	Chetak Circle	46	Hotel Apsara
21	Kwality	47	Keerti Hotel
22	Bhartiya Lok Kala Museum	48	Hotel Shalimar
	(Folk Museum)	49	Hotel Welcome
23	GPO	50	Hotel Yatri
24	Lake Palace Hotel	51	Long Distance Bus Terminal
25	Lake Palace Boat Jetty	52	Kishan Pol
26	Rang Niwas Palace Hotel	53	Railway Station
27	Roof Garden Cafe		

Lake Pichola

The beautiful Lake Pichola was enlarged by Maharana Udai Singh after he founded the city. He built a masonry dam, known as the Badi Pol, and the lake is now four km in length and three km wide. Nevertheless, it remains fairly shallow and can actually dry up in severe droughts. At these times, you can walk to the island palaces from the shore. Fortunately, this doesn't happen often. The City Palace extends a considerable distance along the east bank of the lake. South of the palace, a pleasant garden runs down to the lake. North of the palace, you can wander along the lake, where there are some interesting bathing and dhobi ghats.

Out in the lake are two islands –

Jagniwas and Jagmandir. One-hour boat rides around the lake can be boarded at the City Palace jetty at any time during daylight hours. They cost Rs 20 per person. The Lake Palace Hotel also operates a barge tour at 5 pm each day, complete with musicians from the Lake Palace Hotel. This tour actually visits the two islands and costs Rs 55 per person.

Islands

Jagniwas, the Lake Palace island, is about 1½ hectares in size. The palace was built by Maharana Jagat Singh II in 1754 and covers the whole island. Today, it has been converted into a luxury hotel with courtyards, fountains, gardens and a swimming pool. It's a delightful place and, even if you can only dream of staying there, it's worth the trip out to have a look around. Launches cross to the island from the City Palace jetty but casual visitors are discouraged unless they plan to eat there. The easiest way to do this is to splurge one evening on the smorgasbord buffet dinner. The cost is Rs 150 per head (collected at the jetty), including a free barge trip in either direction.

The other island palace, Jagmandir, may also eventually become a hotel. It was commenced by Maharana Karan Singh, but takes its name from Maharana Jagat Singh (1628-1652) who made a number of additions to it. It is said that the Moghul emperor Shah Jahan derived some of his ideas for the Taj Mahal from this palace after staying here in 1623-24 while leading a revolt against his father, Jehangir. The view across the lake from the southern end, with the city and its great palace rising up behind the island palaces, is a scene of rare beauty. A couple

of the cheap hotels have absolutely superb views across the lake.

City Palace & Museum

The huge City Palace, towering over the lake, is the largest palace complex in Rajasthan. Actually a conglomeration of buildings added by various maharanas, the palace manages to retain a surprising uniformity of design. Building was started by Maharana Udai Singh, the city's founder. The palace is surmounted by balconies, towers and cupolas and there are fine views over the lake and the city from the upper terraces.

The palace is entered from the northern end through the Bari Pol of 1600 and the triple Tripolia Gate of 1725 with its eight carved marble arches. It was once a custom for maharanas to be weighed under the gate and their weight in gold or silver distributed to the populace.

The main part of the palace is now

View of Udaipur from Hotel Badi Haveli

preserved as a museum with a large and varied, albeit somewhat run-down, collection. The museum includes the Mor Chowk with its beautiful mosaics of peacocks, the favourite Rajasthani bird. The Manak, or 'ruby', Mahal has glass and porcelain figures while Krishna Vilas has a remarkable collection of miniatures. In the Bari Mahal, there is a fine central garden. More paintings can be seen in the Zanana Mahal. The Moti Mahal has beautiful mirror work and the Chini Mahal is covered in ornamented tiles. Other exhibits include the princely Rolls Royces.

Enter the City Palace Museum through the Ganesh Deori which leads to the Rai Angam, or 'Royal Courtyard'. The museum is open from 9.30 am to 4.30 pm and entry is Rs 4, plus Rs 5 for a camera. There's also a government museum within the palace complex. Exhibits include a stuffed kangaroo and Siamese-twin deer.

The other part of the palace is up against the lake shore and, like the Lake Palace, it has been converted into a luxury hotel known as the Shiv Vilas Palace Hotel. The swimming pool here is open to nonresidents but costs Rs 100 per day!

Jagdish Temple

Only 150 metres north of the entrance to the City Palace, this fine Indo-Aryan temple was built by Maharana Jagat Singh in 1651 and enshrines a black stone image of Vishnu as Jagannath, Lord of the Universe. A brass image of the Garuda is in a shrine in front of the temple and the steps up to the temple are flanked by elephants.

Lake Fateh Sagar

North of Lake Pichola, this lake is overlooked by a number of hills and parks. It was originally built in 1678 by Maharana Jai Singh but, after heavy rains destroyed the dam, it was reconstructed by Maharana Fateh Singh. A pleasant lakeside drive winds along the east bank of the lake. In the middle of the lake is Nehru Park, a popular garden island with a boat-shaped cafe, although recent reports suggest that it is now closed. You can get there by boat from the bottom of Moti Magri Hill for Rs 3 return.

Pratap Samak

Atop the Moti Magri, or 'Pearl Hill', overlooking Fateh Sagar Lake, is a statue of the Rajput hero Maharana Pratap, who frequently defied the Moghuls. The path to the top traverses elegant gardens, including a Japanese rock garden. The park is open from 9 am to 6 pm and admission is Rs 2.

Bhartiya Lok Kala Museum

The interesting collection exhibited by this small museum and foundation for the preservation of folk arts includes dresses, dolls, masks, musical instruments, paintings and - the high point of the exhibits - puppets. The museum is open daily from 9 am to to 6 pm and admission costs Rs 2. Regular puppet shows in the theatre at the museum are advertised in many of the hotels. They usually take place between 6 and 7 pm. Watch for the advertisements or call 24296 for details.

Rajasthani Folk Dances & Music

There are regular performances on Tuesday, Thursday and Saturday from 7.30 to 8.30 pm at the Meera Rangshala Theatre (tel 23976), Sector 11, Hiran Magari, Udaipur. They cost Rs 15 per head and are well worth attending. You can expect to see not only a whole range of tribal dances, but also some more spectacular acts which involve balancing numerous pots on top of the head while dancing on broken glass or unsheathed sabres. An auto-rickshaw to the auditorium from the City Palace area costs Rs 10 (shared by up to three people).

Saheliyon ki Bari

The Saheliyon ki Bari, or 'Garden of the Maids of Honour', is in the north of the city. This small ornamental garden, with its fountains, kiosks, marble elephants and delightful lotus pool, is open from 9 am to 6 pm. Entry is Rs 1. It costs Rs 2 to have the fountains turned on and the camera fee is Rs 5.

Ahar Museum
East of Udaipur are the remains of an ancient city. Here, you'll find a small museum and the cenotaphs of the maharanas of Mewar.

Other Attractions
Patel or Sukhadia Circle is north of the city. The huge fountain in the centre is illuminated at night. Sajjan Niwas Gardens have pleasant lawns, a zoo and a children's train ride (if it's operating). Beside it is the Rose Garden, or Gulab Bagh. Don't confuse the Nehru Park opposite Bapu Bazaar with the island park of the same name in Lake Fateh Sagar. The city park has some strange topiary work, a giant cement teapot and

children's slides incorporating an elephant and a camel.

On the distant mountain range, visible from the city, the former maharaja's Monsoon Palace is visible from the city as a gleaming white edifice. Now deserted, the views from the top are incomparable. The round trip takes about three hours.

Tours
A five-hour tour starts at the tourist bungalow at 8 am each day. It costs Rs 20 and takes in all the main city sights. An afternoon tour (2 to 7 pm) goes out to Eklingi, Haldighati and Nathdwara and costs Rs 45.

Places to Stay – bottom end
There are four main clusters of budget hotels in Udaipur, but those around the Jagdish Temple are definitely preferable to the others. Next best are those between the City Palace and the bus station, mainly along Lake Palace Rd. The third

Inside the Lake Palace Hotel, Udaipur

cluster is along the main road between the bus station and the Delhi Gate. This is one of the noisiest, dirtiest and most polluted roads in India and you have to be desperate or totally lacking in imagination to stay here. The last cluster is around the tourist bungalow and, although it's better than staying on the main road, it's somewhat inconvenient.

Although not the most popular, the best of the hotels around the Jagdish Temple is the *Badi Haveli*. This magical little labyrinth has narrow staircases, terraces, a leafy courtyard and two rooftops with superb views over the lake and old city. The eight rooms (one single and seven doubles) are all different and vary in price between Rs 41 and Rs 91, all with bath and fan. Close by, down near the ghat, is the *Lalghat Guest House* (tel 25301). This has been a very popular place for many years and renovations/extensions were recently completed. It has a large courtyard with tables and chairs, rooftop areas with excellent views across the lake and a back terrace which overlooks the ghats. A variety of different rooms are available, ranging from Rs 30/40 up to Rs 125 for a double with bath. All the rooms have fans and mosquito nets.

Across the road from the Lalghat, the *Lake Ghat Guest House* is also popular but lacks some of the atmosphere of the Lalghat or the Badi Haveli. Again, there's a wide range of accommodation with dorm beds at Rs 15, singles/doubles without bath for Rs 25/40 and doubles with bath for Rs 75 to Rs 125. There are also three and four-bed rooms with bath for Rs 100. While some of the cheaper rooms are very dark and cell-like, there's a good rooftop area and the management are friendly. The restaurant offers a limited choice of food.

Just behind the Lake Ghat Guest House is the much smaller *Shri Karni Guest House*. It's very basic and has only five rooms (all doubles or triples) but, if the visitors' book is any indication, people who stay here really like it. It costs Rs 20 to

Rs 30 downstairs and Rs 20 to Rs 60 upstairs, all with common bath and cold water only. Close by, on the waterfront, the *Jeel Hotel* is somewhat more expensive.

On Lake Palace Rd are two very popular places right next to each other – the *Hotel Chandra Prakash* (tel 28109) and the *Hotel Mahendra Prakash* (tel 23015). They're both modern buildings and similar in standard, though the owner of the Mahendra Prakash takes a much greater interest in his guests' welfare and, with the right group on request, will lay on a traditional Rajasthani evening in his own house at the rear of the hotel. Smaller rooms at either hotel cost Rs 50 to Rs 80 and larger air-cooled rooms are Rs 125 to Rs 150. All rooms have bath and hot water and both hotels have garden areas.

Not far away, off Udaipol Rd, the *Hotel Shalimar* (tel 26319) has doubles at Rs 60, air-cooled doubles at Rs 75 and four-bed rooms at Rs 80; there are no singles. All rooms have bath and constant hot water. On the other side of the road from the tourist bungalow and back one block is a group of three hotels. The *Prince Hotel* (tel 25355) offers ordinary rooms for Rs 30/50 and deluxe singles/doubles for Rs 50/70. All rooms have a bath and the deluxe rooms have constant hot water. Bucket hot water is available for the other rooms at Rs 2. The *Alka Hotel* (tel 25130) is similar. It is a very large place with singles/doubles for Rs 25/60 and bigger rooms for Rs 100 to Rs 150. The more expensive rooms are air-cooled and have constant hot water. Reasonably priced vegetarian meals are served. The nearby *Ashok Hotel* is very similar in price and standard.

For those who don't mind the noise and pollution of the main road, there are a number of choices. Best of the group is probably the *Hotel Apsara*, a huge place where the rooms front onto an internal courtyard making them relatively quiet. There are dorm beds for Rs 20 and singles/doubles for Rs 30/50 to Rs 150/275. The more expensive rooms have constant hot water. Close to the bus station, next to Udai Pol, is the *Hotel Yatri*. It has no singles but offers doubles with bath and constant hot water for Rs 75. Better, but more expensive, is the *Hotel Welcome* on the other side of the gate.

Other travellers have recommended the *Keerti Hotel* (tel 3639) on Sarsvati Marg (Airport Rd), a short stroll out from the Suraj Pol Gate. It used to be a popular place, especially for those catching an early bus, but it's a fairly long way from the centre of things. Rooms are cheap and basic, with bath but no hot water. Behind the Keerti on College Rd, the *Ghunghru Guest House* is a reasonable overflow place with cheap rooms and a pleasant garden.

The *Mewar Inn Hotel* (tel 27093) at 42 Residency Rd has been recommended by many travellers. It has rooms from Rs 18/28 and a Rs 7 dorm.

There's also an interesting place at Titadha village, seven to eight km outside Udaipur – the *Pratap Country Inn*. It's operated by the same people who manage the Keerti, so go there first and they'll arrange transport to Titadha. City buses run there every hour for about Rs 1, or you can ride out on a bicycle. Accommodation in tents and rooms costs as little as Rs 20 or as much as Rs 300. There's a swimming pool, restaurant, free horse and camel riding, beautiful surroundings and a very relaxed atmosphere, but it's straight-forward and fairly primitive. If you come out here expecting any luxuries, you'll be disappointed.

Places to Stay – middle

The best of the mid-range places is the *Rang Niwas Palace Hotel* (tel 23891), Lake Palace Rd. This interesting, pleasant and very relaxed hotel is surrounded by its own gardens and, as its name suggests, was formerly a small palace. Downstairs rooms with shared bath (cold water only) start at just Rs 40, Rs 75 with bath (hot water). The much larger upstairs rooms

cost Rs 125, Rs 150 and Rs 200 with bath and hot water. A restaurant in a separate building offers a limited range of Indian and continental dishes, as well as standard breakfast fare. It's a very popular hotel and close to the centre of things.

Like many of the RTDC tourist bungalows in the state, the *Kajri Tourist Bungalow* (tel 23509), at the traffic circle on Ashoka Rd, has seen better days. Still, it isn't too bad if you're prepared to take one of the higher-priced rooms. Deluxe singles/doubles are Rs 100/125, air-cooled rooms Rs 120/150 and air-con rooms Rs 200/250. There's a bar and restaurant and you can arrange boating and bus tours from here. A much better place than the tourist bungalow is the brand new *Jagat Niwas Hotel*, right on the lakeside below the Jagdish Temple close to the Lalghat Hotel.

Between Lakes Pichola and Fateh Sagar are two other mid-range hotels. The *Hotel Hill Top* (tel 28708), 4 Ambavgarh, offers air-con rooms with bath and constant hot water for Rs 325/375. There's a bar and restaurant and folk dances and puppet shows can be arranged on request. As the name suggests, the hotel overlooks Lake Fateh Sagar. Not far away along Rani Rd is the *Hotel Lakend* (tel 23841). Rooms are Rs 175/300, Rs 250/350 with air-con. There's a swimming pool, bar, restaurant and a garden running down to the Fateh Sagar lakeside.

Towards the north of the city, another mid-range hotel worth considering is the *Hotel Fountain* (tel 26646), 2 Sukhadia Circle. It has a restaurant and offers air-cooled singles/doubles for Rs 110/160 and air-con rooms for Rs 210/250. All rooms have bath with constant hot water.

Places to Stay – top end

Without a doubt, the best of the lower-priced top-range hotels is the *Lake Pichola Hotel* (tel 29197), Chand Pol, which looks out across to the dhobi ghats, the Jagdish Temple and the northern end of the City Palace. It's a stunningly beautiful building and extremely well maintained and managed. All rooms have air-con, TV, telephone, carpet and bath with constant hot water. They cost Rs 300/400 for singles/doubles and suites are available for Rs 500/600. There's a money exchange facility, bar and restaurant.

Between Pichola and Fateh Sagar lakes are two upper-notch hotels side by side. The ITDC-operated *Laxmi Vilas Palace Hotel* (tel 24411) is a four-star hotel where rooms cost Rs 425/550, Rs 625/750 with air-con. There's a swimming pool, bar and restaurant. Next door is the *Hotel Anand Bhawan* (tel 23256) which has air-con rooms with bath and constant hot water for Rs 250/310. The restaurant serves vegetarian and non-vegetarian food.

About three km out of town on the Ahmedabad road is the four-star *Shikarbadi Hotel* (tel 25321) where air-con singles/doubles cost Rs 390/550. It's a small but pleasant hotel set in beautiful grounds with swimming pool, lawns and a small lake. It has a deer park and a stud farm – horse and elephant rides are available. The food here is excellent and there's a choice of continental, Indian and tandoori dishes.

At the very top end of the scale are two of India's most luxurious hotels, facing each other across Lake Pichola. The incomparable *Lake Palace Hotel* (tel 23241/5) is on the smaller of the lake's two islands. It's the very image of what a maharaja's palace should be like and most people with sufficient money to spend would not pass up an opportunity to stay here. It offers every conceivable comfort, including a mango-tree-shaded swimming pool. The cheapest rooms are Rs 900/1000 and suites cost Rs 5000. Most of the rooms overlook the lake.

The equally luxurious *Shiv Niwas Palace Hotel* (tel 28239/ 41) forms part of the City Palace complex. The cheapest rooms cost Rs 600, super deluxe suites are Rs 1800 and historic suites cost Rs 2500. There's also a Royal Suite for Rs 4000 and

an Imperial Suite for Rs 5000, but you need prior permission from the manager to stay in these.

If you want accommodation in either of these 'palace' hotels, you have to plan ahead – there's heavy demand for rooms.

Places to Eat

Udaipur is not overendowed with good places to eat. The *Tourist Bungalow* restaurant has the usual menu with variable results. Sometimes the food is surprisingly good, sometimes not, but you'd probably only eat here if you were staying in one of the rooms. Just round the corner from the Rang Niwas Palace Hotel, facing the City Palace, the *Roof Garden Cafe* has the appearance of a Hanging Gardens of Babylon. The food here is slightly expensive but there's a good menu and live folk music several nights per week.

The popular *Natural Attic* is a good cheap place to eat if you're staying in the vicinity of the Jagdish Temple. There's always a crowd of budget travellers eating here.

For a minor splurge, *Berry's Restaurant* on Chetak Circle is popular with middle-class Indians and western tourists and, although relatively expensive, the food is good. A soup, main course and drink will cost you around Rs 40. Opposite is a branch of *Kwality* which offers the usual selection and is somewhat cheaper than Berry's. Another good place for a treat is *The Feast* at Saheliyon ki Bari.

South of the Sajjan Niwas Gardens, on the hill overlooking Lake Pichola, the *Cafe Hill Park* is worth a visit just for the views. They offer cheap south Indian dishes and snacks.

Patel's Soda Factory, near the Suraj Pol Gate, is a clean and friendly spot for a cold drink; the fruit juices (orange Rs 4) are terrific. They have an autographed picture of Roger Moore from the filming of the James Bond 007 epic *Octopussy* in Udaipur in late 1982. There's no sign in

English but the place is not hard to find.

Just about everybody with a bit of spare cash goes to the *Lake Palace Hotel* for a buffet dinner at least once while they're in Udaipur. For Rs 150 you can eat as much as you like and the range of dishes is mind boggling. It need hardly be said that the quality of the food is excellent. Residents have a separate dining room which you're not allowed to use, but you can wander around the place, use the bar and watch the folk music and dancing which takes place between 9 and 10 pm each evening around the inner fountains and swimming pool. To get there, go down to the boat jetty below the Rang Niwas Palace Hotel in the late afternoon or early evening. The Rs 150 is collected there and includes the return boat trip.

Things to Buy

Udaipur has countless small shops and many interesting local crafts, particularly paintings in the Rajput-Moghul style. There's a good cluster of these shops on Lake Palace Rd, next to the Rang Niwas Palace Hotel, and others around the Jagdish Temple.

Getting There & Away

Air Indian Airlines flies Delhi/Jaipur/ Jodhpur/Udaipur/Aurangabad/Bombay, and vice versa, daily. Fares to or from Udaipur include Delhi Rs 560, Jaipur Rs 340, Jodhpur Rs 330, Aurangabad Rs 605 and Bombay Rs 670. The direct flight between Udaipur and Aurangabad can save a great deal of bus or train time. The Indian Airlines office (tel 23952) is at Delhi Gate.

Bus Frequent state transport buses run from Udaipur to other regional centres, as well as to Delhi and Ahmedabad. If you use these buses, make sure you take an express bus since the ordinary stopping buses take forever, make innumerable detours to various towns off the main route and can be very uncomfortable. For long-distance travel, it's best to use private buses. The tourist office has a full list of bus timetables.

Destinations served by express buses include Jaipur (nine hours, nine daily), Ajmer (11 daily), Kota/Bundi (six daily), Jodhpur (eight to 10 hours) via either Ranakpur (six daily) or Nathdwara (two daily) and Chittorgarh (three hours, five daily).

There are quite a few private bus companies which operate to such places as Ahmedabad (Rs 60), Baroda (Rs 80), Bombay (Rs 150), Delhi (Rs 140), Indore (Rs 70), Jaipur (Rs 80), Jodhpur (Rs 50), Kota (Rs 50) and Mt Abu (Rs 55). Most have their offices along the main road from the bus station to Delhi Gate (Khangipir Rd), but there are others opposite the Rang Niwas Palace Hotel. Book in advance.

Train The best train between Delhi and Udaipur, the daily Chetak Express, takes nearly 21 hours. On Wednesday, Friday and Sunday, part of the Delhi to Jaipur Pink City Express continues on to Udaipur as the Garib Nawaz Express. Fares for the 739-km trip are Rs 75 in 2nd class, Rs 275 in 1st. The trains go via Jaipur and Ajmer.

There is also a daily express in either direction between Udaipur and Ahmedabad. The 297-km trip takes about 10 hours and costs Rs 37 in 2nd class, Rs 134 in 1st.

Getting Around

Airport Transport The airport is 25 km from the city and, as there's no airport bus, the cheapest way to get into the city is to walk to the main road (about 500 metres) and take a regular bus from there. A taxi costs around Rs 80.

Local Transport Udaipur has a reasonably good city bus service. Taxis and autorickshaws are unmetered so you need to agree on a fare before setting off. The standard fare for tourists anywhere within the city appears to be Rs 10, and you'll be very lucky to get it for less since there are too many well-heeled tourists around who pay the first price asked.

Udaipur is small enough and vehicle traffic slow enough to make getting around on a bicycle quite enjoyable. You can hire bicycles all over town for around Rs 2 an hour or Rs 10 per day.

AROUND UDAIPUR
Eklingi (22 km)
This interesting little village with a number of ancient temples is only a short bus ride north of Udaipur. The Shiva temple in the village itself was originally built in 734 AD, although its present form dates from the rule of Maharana Raimal between 1473 and 1509. The walled complex includes an elaborately pillared hall under a large pyramidal roof and features a four-faced Shiva image of black marble. The temple is open at rather odd hours – 5 to 7 am, 10 am to 1 pm and 5 to 7 pm.

At Nagada, about a km off the road and a km before Eklingi, are three old temples. The Jain temple of Adbudji is essentially ruined, but its architecture is interesting and it's very old. The nearby Sas Bahu, or 'Mother and Daughter-in-Law', group has very fine and intricate architecture and carvings, including some erotic figures. You can reach these temples most conveniently by hiring a bicycle in Eklingi itself, though this isn't always easy.

Getting There & Away Buses run from Udaipur to Eklingi every hour from 5 am onwards. There's a small guest house in the village if you want to stay overnight.

Haldighati (40 km)
This is where Maharana Pratap valiantly defied the superior Moghul forces of Akbar in 1576. The site is a battlefield and the only thing to see is the chhatri to the warrior's horse, Chetak, a few km away.

Places to Stay The RTDC runs a *Rest House* here. It has two clean rooms which

cost Rs 20/30 and good meals are available on request.

Getting There & Away A state transport bus to Haldighati leaves Udaipur daily at 9 am and private buses depart at 11.45 am and 12.30 pm.

Nathdwara (48 km)
The important 18th-century Vishnu temple of Sri Nathji stands here. It's a popular pilgrimage site, but non-Hindus are not allowed inside. The black stone Vishnu

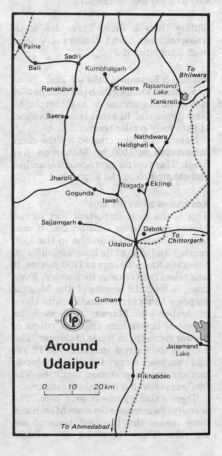

image was brought here from Mathura in 1669 to protect it from Aurangzeb's destructive impulses. According to legend, when an attempt was later made to move the image, the getaway vehicle, a wagon, sank into the ground up to the axles, indicating that the image preferred to stay where it was!

Places to Stay The RTDC *Gokul Tourist Bungalow* (tel 85) offers air-cooled singles/doubles for Rs 120/150. There's also a dormitory with beds for Rs 20, as well as a bar and restaurant.

Getting There & Away There are state transport buses from Udaipur every hour from 5 am onwards.

Kankroli & Rajsamand Lake (65 km)

At Kankroli, Dwarkadhish (an incarnation of Vishnu) is similar to the temple at Nathdwara and, like that temple, is open at extremely erratic hours.

Nearby is a lake created by the dam constructed in 1660 by Maharana Raj Singh. There are many ornamental arches and chhatris along the huge bund.

Kumbhalgarh Fort (84 km)

This is the most important fort in the Mewar region after Chittorgarh. It was built by Maharana Kumbha in the 15th century and, due to its inaccessibility on top of the Aravalli range at 1100 metres, it was taken only once in its history. Even then, it took the armies of the Moghul emperor Akbar in combination with those of Amber and Marwar to breach its defences. It was here that the rulers of Mewar retreated in times of danger. The walls of the fortress stretch some 12 km and enclose many temples, palaces, gardens and water storage facilities. The fort was renovated in the last century.

There's also a game reserve here. The scarcity of waterholes between March and June makes this the best time to see animals. There is a lot of wildlife including antelope, panther and bear, and it's a good area for walking.

Getting There & Around There are state transport buses from Udaipur to Kumbhalgarh at 7.30 and 11 am, 3.30 and 5 pm. Private buses are also available. From where the bus drops you, you'll have to walk or hire a jeep, so it's a good idea to come here as part of a small group and share the cost.

Jaisamand Lake (48 km)

This stunningly sited artificial lake, created by damming the Gomti River, was built by Maharana Jai Singh in the 17th century. There are beautiful marble chhatris around the embankment, each with an elephant in front. The summer palaces of the Udaipur queens are also here and a wildlife sanctuary is nearby.

Places to Stay There's a good *Tourist Bungalow* on the shores of the lake.

Getting There & Away Hourly state transport buses from Udaipur run from 5.30 am onwards.

Ranakpur (98 km)

One of the biggest and most important Jain temples in India, the extremely beautiful Ranakpur complex lies in a remote and peaceful valley of the Aravalli range. The main temple in the complex is the Chaumukha, or 'Four-Faced' Temple, dedicated to Adinath. Built in 1439, this huge, beautifully crafted and well-kept marble temple has 29 halls supported by 1444 pillars, no two alike. Within the complex are two other Jain temples to Neminath and Parasnath and, a little distance away, a Sun Temple. One km from the main complex is the Amba Mata Temple.

The temple is open to non-Jains from noon to 5 pm. Shoes and all leather articles must be left at the entrance.

Places to Stay & Eat The RTDC *Shilpi Tourist Bungalow* has deluxe singles/doubles for Rs 80/100, air-cooled rooms for Rs 100/130, good dormitory beds for Rs 20 and a dining room.

For a donation, you can stay at the dharamsala within the temple complex. If you arrive at a meal time, you can get a good thali in the dining hall, just inside the main entrance to the complex on your left, again for a donation (set at Rs 6). Staying overnight at Ranakpur breaks up the long trip between Udaipur and Jodhpur.

Getting There & Away Ranakpur is 39 km from Palna (or Falna) Junction on the Ajmer to Mt Abu rail and road routes. From Udaipur, there are five state transport express buses per day, and even these take up to five hours. Although it's just possible to travel through from Ranakpur to Jodhpur or Mt Abu on the same day, it's hardly worth it since you'll arrive well after dark. It's better to stay for the night and continue on next day. There's also a daily bus from Mt Abu which terminates at Sadri, only seven km from Ranakpur.

Ghanerao

The attractive town of Ghanerao can make a good base for explorations of the various attractions around Udaipur. The Ghanerao Royal Castle's helpful owners can arrange a trek from Ghanerao to Kumbhalgarh with an overnight stay at their hunting lodge, Bagha ka Bagh, en route.

Places to Stay About a km out of town, the *Ghanerao Royal Castle* is a small castle/palace with six well-kept rooms at Rs 150/200.

MT ABU (population 15,500)

Rajasthan's only hill station sprawls along a 1200-metre-high plateau in the south of the state, close to the Gujarati border. It's a pleasant hot-season retreat from the plains for both Rajasthan and Gujarat, but you won't find many western

travellers here. The predominantly Indian visitors include many honeymooners. Mt Abu's pace is easygoing and relaxed.

Mt Abu has more to attract visitors than its cooler conditions – it has a number of important temples, particularly the superb Dilwara group of Jain temples, five km away. Also, like many other hill stations in India, it has its own artificial lake.

Hand stencil

Information & Orientation

Mt Abu is on a hilly plateau about 22 km long by six km wide, 27 km from the nearest railway station, Abu Road. The main part of the town extends along the road in from Abu Road, down to Nakki Lake. Coming in by bus, you first pass the Tourist Bungalow, up a hill to your right, then a string of hotels, before you arrive at the bus stand. The tourist office (tel 51) is opposite the bus stand and is open from 8 to 11 am and 4 to 8 pm.

Continuing through the town, you pass more hotels and restaurants, the small market to your right and, eventually, arrive at the lake. The GPO is on Raj Bhavan Rd, opposite the art gallery and museum. Several banks and a number of top-end hotels will change money.

Nakki Lake

Virtually in the centre of Mt Abu, the small lake takes its name from the legend that it was scooped out by a god, using only his nails, or *nakk*. It's a short and easy stroll around the lake – look for the strange rock formations. The best known,

Toad Rock, looks just like a toad about to hop into the lake. Others, like Nun Rock, Nandi Rock or Camel Rock, require more imagination. The 14th-century Ragunath Temple stands beside the lake.

You can hire boats and row (or be rowed) out on the lake. Costs are around Rs 20 per half hour.

Viewpoints

Of the various viewpoints around town, Sunset Point is the most popular. Hordes stroll out here every evening to catch the setting sun, the food stalls and all the usual entertainments. Other popular points include Honeymoon Point, which also offers a view of the sunset, the Crags and Robert's Spur.

Museum & Art Gallery

Maintenance of the small museum leaves a lot to be desired. Although it's not very interesting, the museum does have some items from archaeological excavations which date from the 8th to 12th centuries, as well as Jain bronzes, carvings, brasswork and local textiles. 'Art gallery' is hardly an accurate description of the

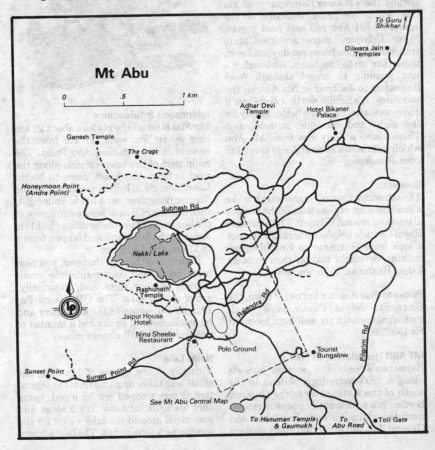

Mt Abu

0   .5   1 km

To Guru Shikhar

Dilwara Jain Temples

Adhar Devi Temple

Hotel Bikaner Palace

Ganesh Temple

The Crags

Honeymoon Point (Andra Point)

Subhash Rd

Nakki Lake

Rajendra Rd

Raghunath Temple

Jaipur House Hotel

Nina Sheeba Restaurant

Polo Ground

Pilgrim Rd

Tourist Bungalow

Sunset Point

Sunset Point Rd

See Mt Abu Central Map

To Hanuman Temple & Gaumukh

To Abu Road

Toll Gate

collection of half a dozen pictures. The museum, on Raj Bhavan Rd, is open from 10 am to 4.30 pm daily, except Fridays, and admission is free. There is also a Rajasthan Emporium back towards the market.

Adhar Devi Temple

Three km out of the town, 200 steep steps lead to this Durga temple built in a natural cleft in the rock. You have to stoop to get through the low entrance to the temple. There are good views over Mt Abu from up here.

Madhuban

This is the Brahma Kumaris World Spiritual University, not far from the lake. Meditation and Raja Yoga courses are held here regularly; they offer free introductory courses. There's also a museum on the site.

Tours

The RTDC and several private companies offer daily tours of all the main sites. They're clustered around the bus stand and tourist office and cost the same – Rs 20 plus all entry and camera fees. Tour times are 8.30 or 9 am to 1.30 pm and 1.30 to 6 pm (later in summer). The afternoon tours finish at Sunset Point. They tend to be heavily booked in the high season, so plan ahead.

Places to Stay

There are literally scores of hotels to choose from, with new ones being opened all the time. Most are along or just off the main road through to Nakki Lake.

The high season lasts from mid-March to mid-November. As most hotel owners raise prices to whatever the market will bear at those times, it can be an expensive place to stay.

In the low season (with the exception of Christmas and New Year), discounts of up to 50% are available and mid-range accommodation can be an absolute bargain. The hotels usually have a 9 am

checkout time as most of the buses leave Mt Abu early in the morning.

Places to Stay – bottom end

The very popular *Hotel Lake View* (tel 240) overlooks picturesque Nakki Lake but, although the views are certainly good, it's really only an average hotel and the manager is somewhat pompous. In winter, rooms on the front side are Rs 80 a double and, on the back side, Rs 40 to Rs 60. The minimum summer rate is Rs 100 but charges can be as high as Rs 150 (back side) and Rs 250 (front side). All rooms have bath and hot water is available between 6 and 11 am.

Also very popular is the *Tourist Guest House* (tel 160), just off the main road below the Tourist Bungalow. It's a quiet and pleasant place and the owner is very friendly. In winter, prices are Rs 30/40 for singles/doubles but, in summer, they can go as high as Rs 200 to Rs 300 a double. All rooms have bath, constant hot water and mosquito nets. Food is available in the rooms between 6.30 and 11 pm at reasonable prices.

Close by is the *Hotel Vishram*, on the main road. It is somewhat more primitive but clean and reasonably good value at Rs 30 for a double with bath. There are no singles. Bucket hot water is available for Rs 1.50. Further up the main road towards the lake is the *Hotel Veena* which is similar. It offers singles/doubles in the low season for Rs 30/40 and doubles in the high season for Rs 60 to Rs 100. Bucket hot water is available.

If you take the right-hand fork going up the hill opposite the taxi stand and polo ground, you'll find several other budget hotels. The *Hotel Natraj* (tel 432) has reasonable singles/doubles/triples with bath and constant hot water (geysers) for Rs 52/75/100 in the low season. Prices go up to Rs 200 a double in the high season. On the opposite side of the road, the *Rajendra Hotel* (tel 74) has singles/doubles with bath for Rs 20/25 in the low season and Rs 75/100 in the high season.

Bucket hot water costs Rs 2. They prefer nonsmokers and good Gujarati vegetarian food is available. Several other budget hotels are close by.

On the far side of the polo ground, the *Purjan Niwas Youth Hostel* (tel 185) offers dormitory beds for Rs 20 but there are a lot of beds in each dormitory. Food is available here.

The *Hotel Nakki Vihar* (tel 361), above but not overlooking the lake, is also cheap and offers rooms for Rs 20 to Rs 40 in the low season, Rs 40 to Rs 60 in the high season, all with bath. Bucket hot water is available for Rs 2. However, it's very basic, often noisy and has been painted a sickening puce colour.

At the top end of this category, the RTDC *Shikar Tourist Bungalow* (tel 29, 69), back from the main road and up a steepish path, is the biggest place in Mt Abu with about 100 rooms. Although fairly popular, it's certainly not the best value in town. During the low season (July-August and January-March) it offers ordinary singles/doubles for Rs 40/50 and deluxe rooms for Rs 60/75, Rs 90/150 with air-con. In the high season, these prices rise to Rs 80/100, Rs 110/150 and Rs 155/200. All rooms have bath and hot water part of the time. There's also a Rs 20 dorm, a somewhat indifferent bar and a restaurant.

Other budget hotels include the *Hotel Panghat*, *Hotel Ambika* and *Gujarat Hotel*.

Places to Stay – middle

The new *Hotel Sheratone* (tel 273), alongside the main road, is a friendly place. All the rooms are air-cooled and have TV and channel music. In the low season, a single costs Rs 60 and doubles are Rs 60 to Rs 100, all with bath and hot water from 6 to 11 am. In the high season, these prices are at least double. Close by, a little further up the main road, is the *Hotel Madhuban*. Doubles with bath cost Rs 125 and hot water is available from 6 to 11 am. There are no singles. Back from the main road, opposite the bus stand, the largish *Hotel Vrindavan* (tel 47) is very pleasant indeed and excellent value. The cheapest rooms (all doubles) are Rs 150, deluxe rooms are Rs 200 and suites cost Rs 260, all with bath and hot water. The restaurant serves Gujarati thalis and snacks.

The *Hotel Samrat* and *Hotel Navijan* (tel 73, 53), on the top side of the polo ground, are basically the same hotel although they appear to be separate. It's a large place with off-season singles/doubles for Rs 80/100, all with bath and hot water. High season prices are Rs 100/300. The hotel also has a restaurant. The *Hotel Maharaja International* (tel 61) directly opposite is of a similar standard and price.

At the bottom end of the polo ground is the *Hotel Abu International*. Doubles here cost Rs 275 to Rs 300 in the high season, with discounts of 30% to 60% in the low season. The hotel restaurant offers Punjabi and Gujarati meals.

Those looking for the fading splendour of the Rajputs or the Raj should seriously consider staying at either the *Mount Hotel* (tel 55) or the *Hotel Connaught House* (tel 260). The Connaught is a little further up the road from the Natraj and Rajendra Hotels and belongs to the former Maharaja of Jodhpur. This beautiful old place is set in extensive gardens and its somewhat gloomy and claustrophobic interior features numerous period photographs of members of the Indian aristocracy and polo-playing British officers. It offers off-peak doubles for Rs 200 (Rs 300 high season) and triples for Rs 300 (Rs 400 high season), all with bath and hot water. Meals are available but should be ordered in advance.

The Mount Hotel once belonged to a British army officer and has changed little since those days, except for the installation of hot water in the bathrooms. It's now run by a man who was previously manager of the Air India office in Singapore. He's extremely friendly and very keen on

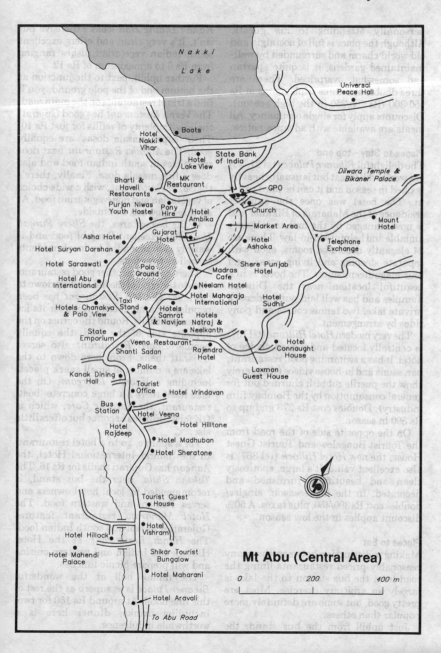

Mt Abu (Central Area)

0   200   400 m

personally attending to his guests. Although the place is full of nostalgia and old world charm and surrounded by well-maintained gardens, it is quite spartan and somewhat overpriced. There are three double and three triple rooms at Rs 150/300 (Rs 200/350 in the high season). Discounts apply for single occupancy. All meals are available with advance notice.

Places to Stay - top end

The delightful *Bikaner Palace* (tel 21, 33) is a worthwhile treat but is usually heavily booked in season and it can be hard to get in. The hotel was once the summer residence of the Maharaja of Bikaner and is now managed by the maharaja's very amiable and helpful son-in-law. There are 24 elegantly decorated rooms, each with separate sleeping and living areas, and four magnificent suites. The hotel is in a beautiful location near the Dilwara Temples and has well laid-out gardens, a private lake, two tennis courts and pony rides by arrangement.

The very modern *Hotel Hilltone* (tel 137) is centrally located and a good choice of hotel. It has a swimming pool, restaurant, bar, sauna and in-house videos (they rarely show the puerile rubbish churned out for general consumption by the Bombay film industry). Doubles cost Rs 273 and up to Rs 390 in season.

On the opposite side of the road from the Tourist Bungalow and Tourist Guest House, the new *Hotel Hillock* (tel 367) is also excellent value. It's large, spotlessly clean and beautifully furnished and decorated. In the high season, singles/doubles cost Rs 390/450, plus taxes. A 50% discount applies in the low season.

Places to Eat

Making a distinction between the many reasonably priced restaurants lining the road from the bus station to the lake is largely an arbitrary exercise. Most are pretty good, but some are definitely more popular than others.

Just uphill from the bus stand, the *Kanak Dining Hall* looks expensive but isn't. It's very clean and offers excellent south Indian vegetarian dishes ranging from Rs 6 to a maximum of Rs 12.

Further uphill, next to the junction at the bottom end of the polo ground, you'll find a trio of restaurants on the main road. The *Veena Restaurant* has good Gujarati thalis with plenty of refills for just Rs 10. Their 'super masala dosas' are equally good. The *Ambika Restaurant* next door specialises in south Indian food and also does a fine masala dosa. Finally, there's the *Sagar Restaurant*, with a wide choice of vegetarian and non-vegetarian food. At all three, you can sit outside.

In the bazaar area, the *Shere Punjab Hotel* has excellent Punjabi food and is warmly recommended by local residents as well as travellers.

There are several other good restaurants close to the crest of the hill leading down to the lake. The *MK Restaurant* has been popular for a number of years for its ice cream and thalis. Round the corner on the opposite side of the road, the equally popular *Bharti Restaurant* also serves Gujarati thalis. From here down to the lake are a number of small snack places, including a *Havmor Icecream*. On the lake itself there's a large concrete 'boat' restaurant, the *Sarovar Cafe*, which is OK for a cup of tea or coffee but offers little else.

For a splurge, go to a hotel restaurant. In the Samrat International Hotel, the *Aangan* has Gujarati thalis for Rs 15. The *Taksha Shila*, near the bus stand, is recommended by local hotel owners and serves Punjabi and western food. The *Hotel Maharaja* restaurant features Gujarati, Punjabi and south Indian food. The *Handi Restaurant* at the Hotel Hilltone has Indian and western cuisine and will prepare picnic lunches.

The dining hall at the wonderful *Bikaner Palace* is as superb as the rest of this fine hotel. At around Rs 150 for two, including drinks, dinner here is a worthwhile indulgence.

Things to Buy

The Rajasthan Emporium is on Raj Bhavan Rd and there are quite a few shops on the road down to the lakefront. Jewellery shops have a good selection. As in most of India, jewellery is usually sold by weight.

Getting There & Away

Bus From 6 am onwards, regular buses make the 27-km climb from Abu Road up to Mt Abu. The trip takes about an hour and costs Rs 5. Shared jeeps (which take up to 10 people, sometimes more) cost Rs 10 per person. A taxi, which you can share with up to five people, costs Rs 100. As you enter Mt Abu, there's a toll gate where passengers are charged Rs 3. Some state transport buses go all the way to Mt Abu, while others terminate at Abu Road, so make sure you get the one you want.

The bus schedule from Mt Abu is extensive and, to many destinations, you will find a direct bus faster and more convenient than going down to Abu Road and waiting for a train.

Private buses are more expensive but definitely preferable to state transport buses and there's plenty of choice. Most have their offices along the main road but, according to local people, they're not all necessarily reliable. This can be critical if you have to make a connecting flight from, say, Ahmedabad. Shobha Travels and Baba Travels are reliable and both companies have buses to Ahmedabad (two daily, six hours, Rs 65) and Udaipur (two daily, five hours, Rs 55).

Train Abu Road, the railhead for Mt Abu, is on the metre-gauge line between Delhi and Ahmedabad via Jaipur and Ajmer. There's a variety of trains, the best being the daily 'superfast' Delhi to Ahmedabad Ashram Express. Fares for the 187-km journey from Ahmedabad are Rs 28 in 2nd class, Rs 93 in 1st. The 440-km journey from Jaipur costs Rs 52 in 2nd class, Rs 185 in 1st.

Direct trains also run from Abu Road to Ajmer, Jodhpur and Agra. For Bhuj and the rest of the Kathiawar Peninsula in Gujarat, change trains at Palanpur.

Getting Around

Buses from the bus stand go to the various sites in Mt Abu, but it takes a little planning to get out and back without too much hanging around. Some buses go just to Dilwara, while others will take you out to Achalgarh, so you'll need to decide which place to visit first, depending on the schedule. The trip to Achalgarh takes about 40 minutes and the fare is Rs 2; to Dilwara, it's Rs 1.

There are plenty of taxis with posted fares to anywhere you care to mention, but Mt Abu's unique form of transport is the large 'baby pram' in which you can sit and be wheeled around! They all seem to be operated by Abu Enterprises, but are mainly used by parents to transport their children.

AROUND MT ABU

Dilwara Temples (5 km)

These Jain temples are Mt Abu's main attraction and amongst the finest examples of Jain architecture in India. The complex includes two temples in which the art of carving marble has reached unsurpassed heights.

The older of the temples is the Vimal Vasahi, built in 1031 and dedicated to the first tirthankar, Adinath. The central shrine has an image of Adinath, while around the courtyard are 52 identical cells, each with a Buddha-like cross-legged image. Forty-eight elegantly carved pillars form the entrance to the courtyard. In front of the temple stands the 'House of Elephants' with figures of elephants marching in procession to the temple entrance.

The later Tejpal Temple is dedicated to Neminath, the 22nd tirthankar, and was built in 1230 by the brothers Tejpal and Vastupal. Like Vimal, they were ministers in the government of the ruler of Gujarat. Although the Tejpal Temple is important as an extremely old and complete example of a Jain temple, its most notable feature is the fantastic intricacy and delicacy of the marble carving. The carving is so fine that, in places, the marble becomes almost transparent. In particular, the lotus flower which hangs from the centre of the dome is an incredible piece of work. It's difficult to believe that this huge lace-like filigree actually started as a solid block of marble. The temple employs several full-time stone carvers to maintain and restore the work. There are three other temples in the enclosure, but they all pale beside the Tejpal and Vimal Vasahi.

The complex is open from 12 noon to 6 pm and there is a Rs 10 camera charge (or, supposedly, Rs 20 if you have a zoom or wide-angle lens). As at other Jain temples, all articles of leather have to be left at the entrance – shoes, belts and even camera cases. You must also observe a number of other regulations which include 'no smoking, no chewing, no drinking, no umbrellas, no transistor or tape recorders and no videos', and there's a dire warning for women: 'Entry of ladies

in monthly course is strictly prohibited. Any lady in monthly course if enters any of the temples she may suffer'.

You can stroll out to Dilwara from the town in less than an hour, or take a taxi for about Rs 10.

Achalgarh (11 km)

The Shiva temple of Achaleshwar Mahandeva has a number of interesting features, including a toe of Shiva, a brass Nandi and, where the Shiva lingam would normally be, a deep hole said to extend all the way to the underworld.

Outside, by the car park, is a tank beside which stand three stone buffaloes and the figure of a king shooting them with a bow and arrows. A legend states that the tank was once filled with ghee, but demons in the form of buffaloes came down and drank each night – until the king shot them. A path leads up the hillside to a group of colourful Jain temples with fine views out over the plains. There's a camera fee of Rs 20.

Guru Shikhar (15 km)

At the end of the plateau is Guru Shikhar, the highest point in Rajasthan at 1721 metres. A road goes almost all the way to the summit. At the top is the Atri Rishi Temple, complete with priest and good views all around.

Below the temple is a soft drinks and snacks restaurant.

Gaumukh Temple (8 km)

Down on the Abu Road side of Mt Abu, a small stream flows from the mouth of a marble cow, giving the shrine its name. There is also a marble figure of the bull Nandi, Shiva's vehicle. The tank here, Agni Kund, is said to be the site of the sacrificial fire, made by the sage Vasishta, from which four of the great Rajput clans were born. An image of Vasishta is flanked by figures of Rama and Krishna.

Dilwara Temples

Tejpal
House of Elephants
Entrance
Vimal Vasahi
Parasnath
Dharamsala
To Mt Abu

ABU ROAD

This station down on the plains is the rail junction for Mt Abu.

Places to Stay

In the main market area, the *Bhagwati Guest House* is only five minutes from the train and bus stations. It has singles for Rs 20 and doubles with bath for Rs 35, as well as dorm beds for Rs 12. It's OK for one night and there are other simple places around. The station has railway *retiring rooms*.

Getting There & Away

Although there are state transport buses from Abu Road to other cities such as Jodhpur, Ajmer, Jaipur, Udaipur and Ahmedabad, there's little point in catching them here as they're all available from Mt Abu itself. Buses operated by private companies also run from Mt Abu.

Western Rajasthan

JODHPUR (population 600,000)

The largest city in Rajasthan after Jaipur, Jodhpur stands at the edge of the Thar Desert. The city is totally dominated by the massive fort, topping a sheer rocky hill which rises right in the middle of the town. Jodhpur was founded in 1459 by Rao Jodha, a chief of the Rajput clan known as the Rathores. His descendants ruled not only Jodhpur, but also other Rajput princely states. The Rathore kingdom was once known as Marwar, the 'Land of Death'.

The old city of Jodhpur is surrounded by a 10-km-long wall, built about a century after the city was founded. From the fort, you can clearly see where the old city ends and the new begins. It's fascinating to wander around the jumble of winding streets in the old city. Eight gates lead out from the walled city. It's one of India's more interesting cities and, yes, it was from here that those baggy-

tight horse-riding trousers, jodhpurs, took their name. Today, you're more likely to see them worn in Saurashtra in Gujarat than here.

Orientation

The tourist office, railway stations and bus stand are all outside the old city. High Court Rd runs from the Raika Bagh railway station, directly across from the bus stand, past the Umaid Gardens, the Tourist Bungalow and tourist office, and round beside the city wall towards the main station and the GPO. Most trains from the east stop at the Raika Bagh station before the main station – quite handy if you want to stay at the Ghoomar Tourist Bungalow.

The GPO is not far from the main station – to get to it, take the road which goes under the tracks. It's on the right-hand side shortly after you emerge from the tunnel.

Information

The tourist office (tel 21900) is at the Tourist Bungalow and is open Monday to Saturday from 8 am to 12 noon and 3 to 6 pm. Nonresidents can use the subterranean swimming pool at the Umaid Bhawan Palace Hotel (tel 22316) for a fee.

Meherangarh Fort

Still run by the former Maharaja of Jodhpur, the 'Majestic Fort' is just that. Sprawled across the 125-metre-high hill, this is the most impressive and formidable fort in fort-studded Rajasthan. A winding road leads up to the entrance from the city below. The first gate is still scarred by cannon balls, indicating that this was a fort which earned its keep. The gates include the Jayapol, built by Maharaja Man Singh in 1806 following his victory over the armies of Jaipur and Bikaner, and the Fatehpol, or 'Victory Gate', erected by Maharaja Ajit Singh to commemorate his defeat of the Moghuls. The final gate is the Lahapol, or 'Iron Gate', beside which there are 15 handprints,

Jodhpur market & clock tower

the sati marks of Maharaja Man Singh's widows who threw themselves upon his funeral pyre in 1843. They still attract devotional attention and are usually covered in red powder.

Inside the fort, there is a whole series of courtyards and palaces. The palace apartments have evocative names like the Moti Mahal, or 'Pearl Palace', the Sukh Mahal, or 'Pleasure Palace' and the Phool Mahal, or 'Flower Palace'. They house a fantastic collection of the trappings of Indian royalty, including an amazing collection of elephant howdahs, used when the maharajas rode their elephants in glittering procession through their capitals, miniature paintings of a variety of schools, superb folk music instruments and the inevitable Rajput armoury, palanquins, furniture and costumes. In one room, there's even an exhibit of baby-rocking cradles. Finally, there's an enormous, luxurious and stunningly

beautiful tent, originally made for the Moghul emperors but carried off as booty by the Rajputs following one of their many battles. The palace apartments are beautifully decorated and painted and have delicately carved latticework windows of red sandstone. It's one of the best palace museums in Rajasthan.

At the southern end of the fort, old cannons look out from the ramparts over the sheer drop to the old town beneath. There's no guard rail and you can clearly hear voices and city sounds carried up by the air currents from the houses far below. The views from these ramparts are nothing less than magical. From here, you can also see the many houses painted blue to distinguish them as those of Brahmins. The Chamunda Temple, dedicated to Durga, stands at this end of the fort.

The fort is open from 9 am to 5 pm and admission is Rs 10 (Rs 4 for Indians). There's an additional charge of Rs 10 to use a camera, Rs 15 for a flash and Rs 25 for a movie camera. The fee includes a semiguided tour by liveried attendant, but they generally expect a small tip at the end. A group of musicians usually stands near the entrance and strike up a merry Rajasthani number to herald your arrival – it helps set the mood for a visit to this superb fort and they, too, appreciate a tip.

Jaswant Thanda

This white marble memorial to Maharaja Jaswant Singh II is part of the way down from the fort, just off the fort road. The cenotaph, built in 1899, was followed by the royal crematorium and three later cenotaphs which stand nearby. Inside are portraits of the various Jodhpur rulers.

Clock Tower & Markets

The clock tower is a popular landmark in the old city. The colourful Sardar Market is close to the tower, and narrow alleys lead from here to bazaars selling textiles, silver and handicrafts.

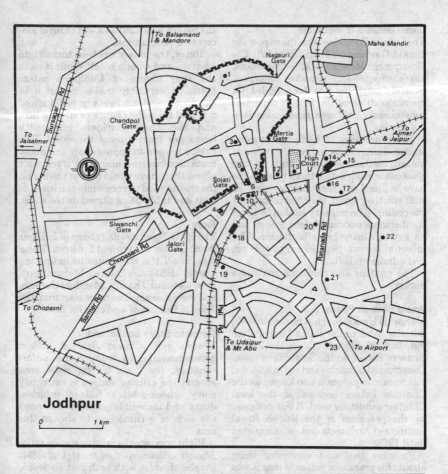

Jodhpur

0   1 km

1	Jaswant Thada
2	Fort Meherangarh
3	Market & Clock Tower
4	Ardash Niwas Hotel &
	Kalinga Restaurant
5	Hotel Soner
6	Chanderlok Hotel
7	Hotel Priya
8	Jodhpur Coffee House
9	Agra Sweet House
10	Hotel Arun
11	Galaxy Hotel
12	Zoo & Government Museum
13	Tourist Office, Indian Airlines &
	Ghoomer Tourist Bungalow
14	Bus Terminus
15	Raika Bagh Railway Station
16	Raika Bagh Palace
17	Antique Shops
18	Main Railway Station
19	GPO
20	Ajit Bhawan Palace Hotel
21	Vama Restaurant
22	Umaid Bhawan Palace
23	Hotel Ratanada International

Umaid Gardens & Museums

The Tourist Bungalow is on the edge of the Umaid Gardens on High Court Rd. The Government Museum, within the gardens, has a unique and amusing collection. Scarcely anything has been added (or maintained) since the British departed; consequently, it's a frozen-in-time Raj-era display.

There are lots of badly moth-eaten stuffed animals, including a number of almost featherless desert birds in two glass cases, each with a thorn bush. Some have toppled off their perches and lie stiffly on the ground, their feet pointing at the ceiling! The military section includes cumbersome wooden biplane models and an extraordinary brass battleship. The museum is open from 10 am to 4.30 pm and admission is Rs 1.

The gardens also contain a zoo and a library.

Umaid Bhawan Palace

Maharaja Umaid Singh, who died in 1947, initially lived in the Raika Bagh Palace but, in 1928, began building the Umaid Bhawan Palace on the outskirts of town. Constructed of marble and red sandstone, this immense palace is also known as the Chhittar Palace because of the local Chhittar sandstone used. It was designed by the president of the British Royal Institute of Architects and not completed until 1943.

Probably the most surprising thing about this grandiose palace is that it was built so close to independence. It seems to have escaped the attention of the maharaja and his British advisers that the upheavals of independence were just around the corner, and that maharajas, princely states and the grand extravagances common to this class would soon be a thing of the past, or that works of a socially beneficial nature might have been more appropriate. Such considerations, however, seem rarely to have impinged on the consciences of rulers anywhere in the world. It's been suggested by some that

the palace was built as a sort of royal job-creation programme!

Today, the palace has been turned into a hotel – and what a hotel! While it lacks the zany charm of Udaipur's palace hotels, it certainly makes up for it in spacious grandeur. Few who could afford it would miss the chance of staying here and the hotel corridors echo with languages from around the world. The palace is open to nonresidents and many come here for an evening meal. If you can't afford that, have a cold beer at the bar on the colonnaded terrace while you listen to sitar and tabla being played on the steps.

Tours

The RTDC operates daily tours of Jodhpur from 8.30 am to 1 pm and 2 to 6 pm. These take in all the main sites including the Umaid Bhawan Palace, Meherangarh Fort, Jaswant Thanda, Mandore Gardens and the museum. The tours start from the Tourist Bungalow and cost Rs 20.

Places to Stay – bottom end

There's not a great deal of budget accommodation in Jodhpur and, unfortunately, the main budget hotel area around the railway station is extremely noisy, chock-a-block full of vehicles, dusty and incredibly polluted. You need the hide of a rhinoceros to stay in this area.

Right opposite the railway station is the *Shanti Bhawan Lodge* (tel 21689). Singles/doubles with bath cost Rs 35/55, rooms with common bath are Rs 25/40 and rooms with bath and air cooler cost Rs 65/75. Next door, the *Charli Bikaner Lodge* (tel 23985) is similarly priced but scruffier.

There are better hotels near the Sojati Gate and the road which goes over the railway lines. Here, you'll find the *Chanderlok Hotel*, where singles/doubles with common bath cost Rs 40/60; doubles with bath are Rs 85. The staff appear somewhat disinterested and don't do a lot, so don't expect too much. On the other

Rajasthan Top: Udaipur at dusk (GC)
Bottom: Temple carving, Rajasthan (GC)

Orissa Top: Dhauli Peace Pagoda, near Bhubaneswar (TW)
Left: Sculptures on the Temple of the Sun, Konarak (TW)
Right: Strange three-part fishing boat, Puri (TW)

side of the road, the well-maintained *Galaxy Hotel* (tel 20796) is a much better choice and similar in price.

Most people stay at the *Ghoomar Tourist Bungalow* (tel 21900), High Court Rd. It has ordinary singles/doubles for Rs 60/80, deluxe rooms for Rs 100/120, air-cooled rooms for Rs 120/150 and air-con rooms for Rs 175/225. Dorm beds cost Rs 20. There's a bar and restaurant here, as well as the tourist office and the Indian Airlines office. It's a reasonably good place to stay and there's generally live folk music and dancing each evening between 6.30 and 7.30 pm, except Sundays, in the upstairs lounge (open to nonresidents). There's no charge for this, but the performers are paid so little that a tip is appreciated. Those in a hurry can safely leave bags here during the day (even if you're not staying) while seeing Jodhpur's sights. Many people do this and then take the night train to Jaisalmer.

Places to Stay – top end

At the bottom end of this bracket is the delightful *Ajit Bhawan Palace Hotel* (tel 20409) on Airport Rd, a very popular place to stay and great for a small splurge. The rooms actually consist of a series of 20 stone cottages arranged around a well-tended and very relaxing garden with fish-stocked pools. All the cottages are differently furnished in their own whimsical style but they're all equipped with very clean, modern bathrooms. It's a whole world away from the noise and pollution around the railway station. The cottages cost Rs 385 a double or Rs 275 for single occupancy plus Rs 70 for an extra bed. The meals here are excellent. Rajasthani folk music and dancing is put on every evening between 6 and 8 pm and a skeleton band continues on until late.

Jodhpur's finest hotel is the *Umaid Bhawan Palace* (tel 22316), the residence of the former Maharaja of Jodhpur. As the sales blurb says, 'To create luxury we did not change history'. They are not wrong! This has to be one of the world's most

incredible hotels but, in comparison to what you would pay for something vaguely similar anywhere else in the world, it's an absolute bargain. It has everything from an indoor swimming pool to golf, badminton, tennis and croquet, a billiard room, endless manicured lawns, bars, a vast dining hall which would seat the entire United Nations Assembly, countless tigers' heads hanging from the walls and every conceivable service. Armies of cleaners keep every square inch squeaky clean and there are fine views across to the fort. The rooms are, of course, palatial and cost Rs 775/875. There are also suites for Rs 1500, Rs 2000 and Rs 2500.

The only other hotel in this category is the *Hotel Ratanada International* (tel 25911), a new place on Residency Rd, some distance out towards the airport. It's somewhat more expensive than the Ajit Bhawan. Nonresidents can use the swimming pool here for Rs 35 (men), Rs 30 (women).

Places to Eat

The *Kalinga Restaurant* in the Adarsh Niwas Hotel, near the railway station, has excellent non-vegetarian food. Many travellers come here for an evening meal before taking the overnight train to Jaisalmer. It's a surprisingly bright place and a very complete meal, including drinks and dessert, costs about Rs 50 per person.

Opposite the Kalinga, behind the trees, the *Renuka Restaurant* is a small snacks/drinks place. The *Fruit & Juice Centre* outside sells excellent fresh fruit juice. While you're in Jodhpur, try makhania lassi, a delicious thick cream variety of that most refreshing of drinks. The lassi bar in the gateway to the central market, near Sojati Gate, is so popular that they claim to sell over 1000 glasses a day at Rs 3 each. Other popular dessert specialties in Jodhpur include *mawa ladoo* and the baklava-like *mawa kachori*. *Dhood fini* is a cereal dish consisting of fine threads of wheat in a bowl with milk and sugar.

There are essentially only two places to go for a splurge and you should make sure that you go to one or the other whilst you're in Jodhpur, if only for the experience and the live music and dance which each present. The cheaper of the two is the *Ajit Bhawan Palace Hotel* where a fixed-price smorgasbord dinner in the main courtyard costs Rs 60, plus tax. The food is excellent and comes complete with a bonfire, Rajasthani folk music and dances. Nonresidents should book in advance, though this isn't always necessary.

More expensive of the two is the *Umaid Bhawan Palace*. A meal here is better described as a memorable banquet because it's served in what has to be the largest of the palace's halls and is accompanied by a live sitar, sarod and tabla recital by nationally renowned musicians. The food is superb and the range of dishes endless. Do make it here at least once. Advance booking is not necessary as a rule, but it's a good idea to check beforehand in the high season. If you can't afford the dinner, have a lunch or dinner on the terrace overlooking the lawns (Rs 50 plus tax, fixed menu) or simply come here and sip a cold beer (expensive at Rs 44 including tax). Musicians also play here in the evening.

Things to Buy

The usual Rajasthani handicrafts are available here, but Jodhpur specialises in antiques. The greatest concentration of antique shops is along the road connecting the Ajit Bhawan with the Umaid Bhawan and the well-known Abani Handicrafts is next to the Tourist Bungalow. However, the existence of these shops is well known to western antique dealers who come here with suitcases full of money and wallets stuffed with plastic cards. As a result, you'll be hard pressed to find any bargains, though this is no reflection on the generally excellent quality of the goods available.

Getting There & Away

Air Indian Airlines flies daily to Delhi, Jaipur, Udaipur, Aurangabad and Bombay. The Indian Airlines office (tel 20909) is in the Tourist Bungalow and is open daily from 10 am to 1.15 pm and 2 to 5 pm.

Vayudoot operates daily flights to Delhi (Rs 535), Jaipur and Jaisalmer (Rs 330) and, sometimes, to Bikaner.

Bus Both state transport buses (from the State Roadways bus stand at Raika Bagh) and private luxury buses connect Jodhpur with other cities and places of interest in Rajasthan. Road distances from Jodhpur include Barmer 220 km, Bikaner 240 km, Jaipur 340 km, Jaisalmer 290 km, Mt Abu 264 km, Ranakpur 175 km and Udaipur 275 km.

The best bus to Jaisalmer is the daily super deluxe which departs from the Ghoomar Tourist Bungalow at 6 am and arrives in Jaisalmer five hours later. The fare is Rs 55. The cheaper buses from the State Roadways bus stand take up to 10 hours. Buses to Udaipur take eight to 10 hours and are much faster than the train. The fare is Rs 40 to Rs 55, depending on the bus. The six-hour trip across the desert to Bikaner costs Rs 35. Buses to Ajmer go hourly, take 4½ hours and cost Rs 30. The fastest state transport buses to Mt Abu leave from the bus stand at 6.30 am and 6 pm, take six hours and cost Rs 39. Private luxury buses are also available.

Train There are 'superfast' expresses between Delhi and Jodhpur (14 hours) and Ahmedabad and Jodhpur (nine hours). Other expresses take a couple of hours longer. Fares for the 626-km trip from Delhi are Rs 67 in 2nd class, Rs 242 in 1st.

Not many people make the trip from Delhi straight through. Most take the train from Jaipur. Jaipur to Jodhpur takes seven hours and the 318-km trip costs Rs 41 in 2nd class, Rs 141 in 1st.

There are both overnight and day trains to Jaisalmer, both taking around nine hours. The 295-km journey costs Rs 37 in 2nd class, Rs 134 in 1st. See the Jaisalmer section for more details.

There is a tourist booking office on platform No 1 at the main railway station.

Getting Around

Airport Transport The airport is only five km from the centre and it costs about Rs 10 in an auto-rickshaw but they often demand Rs 20. A taxi costs around Rs 30.

Bus There are regular city buses to places around Jodhpur like Mandore, Balsamand and Mahamandir.

Taxi & Auto-Rickshaw Jodhpur has unmetered taxis and allegedly metered auto-rickshaws, as well as tongas. Auto-rickshaw drivers are rapacious, particularly if they pick you up from outside the Ajit Bhawan Palace Hotel or the Umaid Bhawan Palace. Quite rightly, they assume that if you can afford to stay or eat at either place, you're not short of money. You'd have difficulty getting through the narrow lanes of the old city in anything wider than an auto-rickshaw.

Bicycle Jodhpur is a good place to explore by bicycle. They can be rented from several places, including one right next to the Charli Bikaner Lodge opposite the main railway station. Expect to pay Rs 5 per day.

AROUND JODHPUR

Maha Mandir (2 km)

The 'Great Temple' is a small walled town north-east of the city. It is built around a 100-pillared Shiva temple but is not of great interest.

Balsamand Lake & Palace (7 km)

Originally constructed in 1159, this lake and garden are to the north of the city. A palace, built in 1936, stands by the lakeside. This is a popular excursion spot and the gardens are open from 8 am to 6 pm. Entry is Rs 1.

West of Jodhpur, the larger Pratap Sagar Lake and Kailana Lake (where there is also a garden) provide the city's water supply.

Mandore (9 km)

Further north, Mandore was the capital of Marwar prior to the foundation of Jodhpur. Today, its extensive gardens with high rock terraces make it a popular local attraction. The gardens also contain the cenotaphs of Jodhpur rulers, including Maharaja Jaswant Singh and, largest and finest of all, the soaring temple-shaped memorial to Maharaja Ajit Singh.

The 'Hall of Heroes' contains 15 figures carved out of a rock wall. The brightly painted figures represent Hindu deities or local heroes on horseback. The Shrine of 33 Crore (330 million) Gods is painted with figures of gods, spirits and divinities. Regular buses run to Mandore from Jodhpur.

Osian (65 km)

The ancient Thar Desert town of Osian was a great trading centre between the 8th and 12th centuries when it was dominated by the Jains. Today, it's a desert oasis with numerous peacocks. The wealth of Osian's medieval inhabitants allowed them to build lavish and beautifully sculpted temples, most of which have withstood the ravages of time. The largest of the 16 Jain and Brahmanical temples is that dedicated to Mahavira, the last of the Jain tirthankars. The sculptural detail on the Osian temples rivals that of the Hoysala temples of Karnataka and the Sun Temple of Konarak in Orissa so, if you have the time, make the effort to visit this place.

Getting There & Away About six buses a day make the two-hour trip from Jodhpur. The fare is Rs 9.

Nagaur (135 km)

Nagaur has a historic fort and palace and also sports a smaller version of Pushkar's cattle and camel fair. The week-long fair takes place in late January or early February and attracts thousands of rural people from far and wide. As at Pushkar, the fair includes camel races and various cultural entertainment programmes.

Sardar Samand Lake (55 km)

The route to this wildlife centre passes through a number of colourful villages. There is a summer palace of the maharaja here and accommodation can be arranged.

Dhawa, or Doli, is another wildlife sanctuary with many antelope, 45 km from Jodhpur on the road to Barmer.

JAISALMER (population 25,000)

Nothing else in India is remotely similar to Jaisalmer. Jodhpur certainly has one of the country's most spectacular fortress-palace complexes and both Chittorgarh and Khumbhalgarh far surpass Jaisalmer in fame and sheer size. Yet this desert fortress is straight out of the *Tales of the Arabian Nights* and you could easily be forgiven for imagining that you'd somehow been transported back to medieval Afghanistan. This magic, incomparably romantic and totally unspoiled city has been dubbed the 'Golden City' because of the colour imparted to its stone ramparts by the setting sun. Jaisalmer is all of this and much more besides. No-one who makes the effort to get to this remote outpost leaves disappointed.

Centuries ago, Jaisalmer's strategic position on the camel train routes between India and central Asia brought it great wealth. The merchants and townspeople built magnificent houses and mansions, all exquisitely carved from wood and from the golden-yellow sandstone. These havelis, as they are known, can be found elsewhere in Rajasthan but nowhere are they quite as exotic as in Jaisalmer. Even the humblest shops and houses display something of the Rajput love of the decorative arts in its most whimsical form. It's likely to remain that way, too, for a long time to come since the city fathers are keen to ensure that all new buildings blend in with the old.

The rise of shipping trade and the port of Bombay saw the decline of Jaisalmer. At independence, partition and the cutting of the trade routes through to Pakistan seemingly sealed the town's fate, and water shortages could have pronounced the death sentence. But the 1965 and 1971 Indo-Pakistan wars revealed Jaisalmer's strategic importance, and the Rajasthan Canal, to the north, is beginning to restore life to the desert. Paved roads and a railway now link it to the rest of Rajasthan, and even electricity has finally reached this remote part of India.

Today, tourism will soon rival military bases as the pillar of the city's economy. The military bases hardly impinge at all on the life of the old city and only the occasional sound of war planes landing or taking off in the distance ever disturbs the tranquility of this desert gem.

It's not always been so peaceful, of course, since fortresses have rarely been constructed for aesthetic reasons and medieval desert chieftains were not known for their pacific temperaments. Chivalric rivalry and ferocity between the various Rajput clans were the order of the day and the Bhatti Rajputs of Jaisalmer were regarded as a formidable force throughout the region. While Jaisalmer largely escaped direct conquest by the Muslim rulers of Delhi, it did experience its share of sieges and sackings with the inevitable jauhar being declared in the face of inevitable defeat. There is, perhaps, no Rajasthani city in which you can more easily conjure up the spirit of those times. It's a city where every stone has a story to tell.

Information & Orientation

Finding your way around Jaisalmer is not really necessary – it's a place to simply

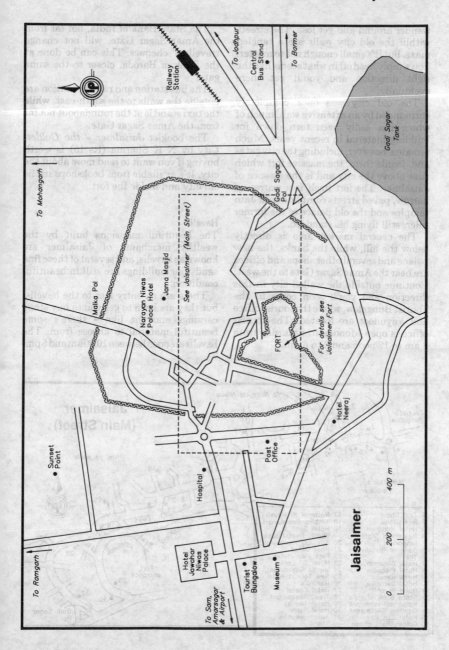

Jaisalmer

To Ramgarh

To Mohangarh

Railway Station

To Jodhpur

Central Bus Stand

To Barmer

Gadi Sagar Tank

Malka Pol

Narayan Niwas Palace Hotel

Jama Masjid

Gadi Sagar Pol

See Jaisalmer (Main Street)

FORT

For details see Jaisalmer Fort

Hotel Neeraj

Sunset Point

Hospital

Post Office

Hotel Jawahar Niwas Palace

Tourist Bungalow

Museum

To Sam, Amarsagar & Airport

0   200   400 m

wander around and get lost. The streets within the old city walls are a tangled maze, but it's small enough not to matter. You simply head off in what seems like the right direction and you'll get there eventually.

The old city was once completely surrounded by an extensive wall, much of which has sadly been torn down for building material in recent years. Much remains, however, including the city gates and, inside them, the massive fort which rises above the city and is the essence of Jaisalmer. The fort itself is a warren of narrow, paved streets complete with Jain temples and the old palace of the former ruler, still flying his standard.

The central market area is directly below the hill, while the banks, the new palace and several other shops and offices are near the Amar Sagar Gate to the west. Continue outside the walled city in this direction and you'll soon come to the Tourist Bungalow, where the tourist office and Vayudoot are located. The tourist office is open Monday to Saturday from 8 am to 12 noon and 3 to 6 pm.

The State Bank of India, not far from the Amar Sagar Gate, will not change travellers' cheques. This can be done at the Bank of Baroda, closer to the same gate.

The bus station and railway station are outside the walls to the south-east, while the taxi stand is at the roundabout not far from the Amar Sagar Gate.

The booklet *Jaisalmer – the Golden City* by N K Sharma (Rs 15) is worth buying if you want to read more about the city. It's available from bookshops in the old city and inside the fort.

Havelis

The beautiful mansions built by the wealthy merchants of Jaisalmer are known as havelis, and several of these fine sandstone buildings are still in beautiful condition.

There are no entry fees to the havelis, but they are keen to get you to buy stone carvings and the like – there's some beautiful material to choose from. The havelis are open between 10.30 am and 5 pm.

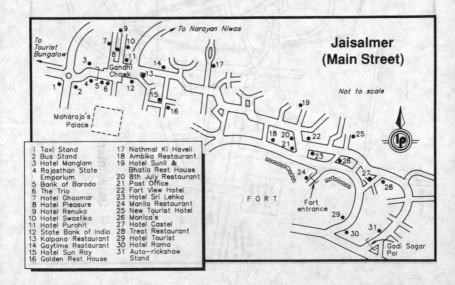

1 Taxi Stand	17 Nathmal Ki Haveli
2 Bus Stand	18 Ambika Restaurant
3 Hotel Manglam	19 Hotel Sunil &
4 Rajasthan State	Bhatia Rest House
Emporium	20 8th July Restaurant
5 Bank of Baroda	21 Post Office
6 The Trio	22 Fort View Hotel
7 Hotel Ghoomar	23 Hotel Sri Lehka
8 Hotel Pleasure	24 Manila Restaurant
9 Hotel Renuka	25 New Tourist Hotel
10 Hotel Swastika	26 Monica's
11 Hotel Purohit	27 Hotel Castel
12 State Bank of India	28 Treat Restaurant
13 Kalpana Restaurant	29 Hotel Tourist
14 Gaytime Restaurant	30 Hotel Rama
15 Hotel Sun Ray	31 Auto-rickshaw
16 Golden Rest House	Stand

Patwon ki Haveli This most elaborate and magnificent of all the Jaisalmer havelis stands in a narrow lane. One of its apartments is painted with beautiful murals. You can go inside the mansion and there is a fine view from the roof.

Salim Singh ki Haveli This haveli was built about 300 years ago and is still partially lived in. Salim Singh was the prime minister when Jaisalmer was the capital of a princely state, and his mansion has a beautifully arched roof with superb carved brackets in the form of peacocks. The mansion is just below the hill and, it is said, once had two additional wooden storeys in an attempt to make it as high as the maharaja's palace. The maharaja had the upper storeys torn down!

Nathmal ki Haveli This late 19th-century haveli was also a prime minister's house. The left and right wings of the building were carved by brothers and are very similar, but not identical. Yellow sandstone elephants guard the building, and even the front door is a work of art.

Gadi Sagar Tank
This tank, south of the city walls, was once the water supply of the city and there are many small temples and shrines around it. A wide variety of water birds flock here in winter.

The beautiful gateway which arches across the road down to the tank is said to have been built by a famous prostitute. When she offered to pay to have this gateway constructed, the maharaja refused permission on the grounds that he would have to pass under it on going down to the tank, and he felt that would be unseemly. While he was away, she built the gate anyway, adding a Krishna temple on top so the king could not tear it down.

Fort
Built in 1156 by Rawal Jaisal, the fort crowns the 80-metre-high Trikuta hill. About a quarter of the old city's

population resides within the fort walls, which have 99 bastions around their circumference. It's fascinating to wander around this place. Nothing has changed here for centuries and if ever an effort were made to pack as many houses, temples and palaces into the smallest possible area, this would be the result. It's honeycombed with narrow, winding lanes, all of them paved in stone and with a remarkably efficient drainage system which keeps them free of excrement and effluent. It's also quiet – vehicles are not allowed up here and even building materials have to be carried up by camel cart. The fort walls provide superb views over the old city and surrounding desert. Strolling around the outer fort ramparts at sunset is a popular activity, but be warned that the entire outer rampart is used as a public toilet, so watch your step!

The fort is entered through a forbidding series of massive gates leading to a large courtyard. The former maharawal's seven-storey palace fronts onto this. The square was formerly used to review troops, hear petitions and present extravagant entertainment for important visitors. Part of the palace is open to the public, but opening times can be erratic.

Jain Temples Within the fort walls are a group of beautifully carved Jain temples built between the 12th and 15th centuries. They are dedicated to Rikhabdevji and Sambhavanthji.

The Gyan Bhandar, a library containing some extremely old manuscripts, is also in the temple complex. The temples are only open in the morning until 12 noon and the library only opens between 10 and 11 am. There are also Shiva and Ganesh temples within the fort.

Festivals
The annual Desert Festival is supposed to have camel races and dances, folk music, desert ballads and puppeteers, but it seems to have quickly become a purely

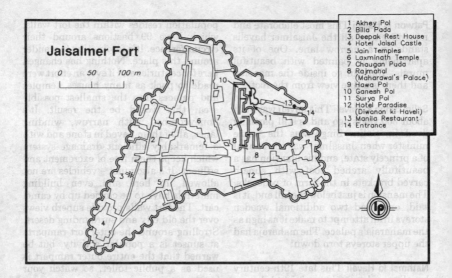

Jaisalmer Fort

0   50   100 m

1 Akhey Pol
2 Billa Pada
3 Deepak Rest House
4 Hotel Jaisal Castle
5 Jain Temples
6 Laxminath Temple
7 Chaugan Pada
8 Rajmahal
   (Maharawal's Palace)
9 Hawa Pol
10 Ganesh Pol
11 Surya Pol
12 Hotel Paradise
   (Diwanon ki Haveli)
13 Manila Restaurant
14 Entrance

commercial tourist trap. The state Tourist Development Corporation sets up a special 'Tourist Village' at this time, similar to the one in Pushkar. The festival takes place between late January and mid-February, depending on the lunar calendar. Make enquiries at a tourist office for the exact dates.

Places to Stay – bottom end
There's quite a travelling community in Jaisalmer these days, and many cheap hotels have sprung up to meet the demand. Almost all of them offer very similar standards though some are distinctly better than others in terms of amenities and position. If you arrive by train, you'll be besieged by a gaggle of earnest, eager to please, honest johns who will spare nothing in their efforts to convince you that the hotel to which they want to take you cares not a jot about money and everything about the welfare of its guests. One of Jaisalmer's most disarming features is that at least 90% of them are sincere.

Staying at one of the hotels within the fort itself is the most imaginative choice,

but don't take this to imply that there aren't equally good hotels outside the fort walls. Jaisalmer is also one of those places where travellers fervently defend their choice of hotel over all others, so this selection will undoubtedly create controversy.

There's a good choice of budget hotels in the streets around the Amar Sagar Gate. The popular *Hotel Swastika* (tel 2483), Chainpura St, is very well kept and has friendly staff and great views from the roof. The hotel sends a taxi to meet incoming trains. Dorm beds are Rs 10, singles/doubles cost Rs 20/40 and rooms with bath are Rs 50/60. Bucket hot water is available. The owners are Brahmins, so non-vegetarian food and alcohol are prohibited.

The *Hotel Renuka*, a little further up the same street, is equally good and very pleasant. It's run by an exceptionally friendly family and, like the Swastika, has great rooftop views. It offers singles/doubles at Rs 20/40, doubles with bath for Rs 60 and deluxe doubles with bath for Rs 70. Another good alternative is the *Hotel Pleasure* (tel 2323) on the next street over. Run by Didi and his wife, it's very small but exceptionally clean and has mattresses on the roof (with sheets and blankets) for Rs 10 and singles/doubles with common bath for Rs 25/40. Bucket hot water, a somewhat ancient washing machine and a refrigerator are available, as is vegetarian food on request. Off to the right, a little further away from the gate, the *Golden Rest House* and the *Hotel Sun Ray* are also reasonable choices.

Across the other side of the old town is another group of budget hotels, close to the entrance to the fort. By far the most popular is the *Fort View Hotel* and two of the reasons for this are the fine views from the roof and its live-wire owner. Can this man talk? He's irrepressible! Fortunately, he's a mine of information and knows what he's talking about. There are dorm beds for Rs 10, doubles with bath on the lower floors for Rs 33 to Rs 55 and doubles on the top floor for Rs 66 and Rs 88. Bucket hot water is available but, if they have to use electricity, there's a small charge. This is one of the few budget hotels which actually has a restaurant – it overlooks the small square below. You can change travellers' cheques and arrange air, rail and bus tickets here.

The *Hotel Sunil, Bhatia Rest House, Hotel Sri Lekha* and the *New Tourist Hotel* are nearby.

Further away from this area, to the south and south-east of the fort and quite a walk from the bazaar, you'll find several other places, some of which are popular. The *Hotel Rama* has a good atmosphere, a garden area with restaurant and a range of doubles for Rs 30 to Rs 150. The higher-priced rooms have bath and hot water. Opposite, the *Hotel Tourist* is of a similar standard.

The cheapest budget hotel within the fort itself is the *Deepak Rest House*. It's actually part of the fort wall and offers stunning views from its rooftops. The hotel is run by a very mellow young guy and has a total of 14 rooms, six with bath and eight with common bath. Room No 9 is the best

one since it has its own balcony (the top of one of the bastions). Next best is room No 8. Both of these rooms cost Rs 60 a double. Other doubles are upwards of Rs 40. There are also singles for Rs 20 and Rs 30 and a dorm for Rs 7, or you can sleep on the roof for Rs 5. The cheaper rooms are somewhat cell-like and have no views. Hot water is available round the clock at no extra charge. To find this place, keep your eyes skinned for a tiny sign on the main alley and then go under an archway.

Also in the fort, and of a much better standard, is the relatively new *Hotel Paradise*. You'll see it on the far side of the main square from the palace as you come through the last gate into the fort. It's a kind of haveli, with 18 rooms arranged around a leafy courtyard and excellent views from the roof. Doubles downstairs cost Rs 35 and those upstairs cost Rs 40 to Rs 50, all with common bath, while upstairs doubles with bath are Rs 60 to Rs 120. Hot water is available and the more expensive rooms have their own balcony.

Places to Stay – middle

The only place worth considering in this price bracket is the *Hotel Jaisal Castle* (tel 2362). Basically a haveli which has been tastefully restored with the addition of unobtrusive modern bathroom facilities, its biggest attraction is its position high up on the ramparts looking out over the desert. The views from the rooftop of this hotel are the best in Jaisalmer. It's also a bargain at Rs 200/230 for singles/doubles, and meals are available. You can always get an ice-cold beer and local musicians are engaged to play on the rooftop most evenings. This is one of the most memorable hotels you're ever likely to visit, but try to book in advance as they only have 11 rooms. It's not signposted, but entry is through a large wooden doorway in front of a small courtyard at the far side of the fort.

The RTDC *Moomal Tourist Bungalow* (tel 92, 192) is reasonable value. Between August and March, singles/doubles range from Rs 60/75 to Rs 175/225 and, at other times, there are significant reductions.

The only other hotel in this category is the *Hotel Neeraj* (tel 2442), which offers singles/doubles with bath and hot water for Rs 240/300 in the high season, Rs 60/125 in the low season. The hotel is often used by overland tour groups, but it's characterless and the high-season prices are definitely way over the top. It's also in a lousy position and a long walk from anywhere else.

Places to Stay – top end

There are only two top-end hotels in Jaisalmer. The better of the two is the *Narayan Niwas Palace* (tel 2408), on the hill at the back of the old town. Beautifully designed to simulate the atmosphere of a Rajput ruler's desert camp, it's festooned with local crafts and *objets d'art*. If the Jaisal Castle is full and you have the money, stay here. Rooms cost Rs 300/390 for singles/doubles. Meals

are available and local musicians play in the courtyard while dinner is served.

Next door, the much smaller *Sri Narayan Vilas* (tel 108) is very similar in standard and has a captivating desert atmosphere. It has only eight rooms, all with bath and constant hot water. The hotel's restaurant is also similar to that at the Narayan Niwas but is often full.

Places to Eat

Like all travellers' centres, Jaisalmer sports a clutch of budget restaurants/juice bars which seem to attract their own cliques of long-time stayers. Everyone has a favourite but *Gaytime, Kalpana Restaurant* and the *8th July Restaurant* have been popular for years. *Monica's* is currently recommended for lassi and other cold drinks.

The Trio, a new restaurant next to the Bank of Baroda near the Amar Sagar Gate, is the current favourite for a minor splurge. It's run by the same people who

Nathmal ki Haveli

operate the Sri Narayan Vilas hotel and has a mellow atmosphere. The food is very good and local musicians play here every evening. It's open for breakfast, lunch and dinner and dishes cost up to Rs 40, although Rs 20 to Rs 30 is the usual price range.

For a major treat, try a meal at the *Hotel Jaisal Castle* or the *Narayan Niwas Palace*, but ring beforehand and make a booking.

Things to Buy

Jaisalmer is famous for embroidery, Rajasthani mirror work, rugs, blankets, old stonework and antiques. Tie dye and other fabrics are made at Kadi Bundar, north of the city.

Getting There & Away

Air Vayudoot flies Delhi/Jaipur/Jodhpur/ Jaisalmer and vice versa three times a week. On the Jodhpur to Jaisalmer route, flights often go via Bikaner. Fares from Jaisalmer are Rs 330 (Jodhpur or Bikaner), Rs 615 (Jaipur) and Rs 785 (Delhi). You can pay in rupees for these flights and no bank receipt is necessary.

Bus There's a choice of two state transport buses and two private deluxe buses per day to and from Jodhpur. They take around eight hours. The fare on state transport buses is Rs 40; private buses are more expensive.

Similarly, between Bikaner and Jaisalmer, two state transport buses and two private deluxe buses per day run in each direction. The journey takes eight to nine hours and costs Rs 50 by private bus, less by state transport bus.

A daily state transport bus links Jaipur and Jaisalmer, and vice versa, via Jodhpur. The trip in either direction takes about 13 hours and costs Rs 85. Every day, there are five state transport buses each way between Jaisalmer and Barmer. They take around four hours and cost Rs 24.

Train There's a day and a night train in either direction between Jodhpur and Jaisalmer, the 295-km trip takes around

10 hours. Fares vary slightly, but are about Rs 140 in 1st class, Rs 37 in 2nd. The reservations office in Jaisalmer is only open from 10 am to 1 pm, 2 to 4 pm and in the chaotic period just before departure.

The train journey from Jodhpur, at least by day, can be made rather gruelling by the dust and coal smuts which swirl in and turn your hair to wire. Still, fleeting glimpses of gazelles, or the still rarer bustard, compensate. At night, it can get very cold out in the desert.

If you're going through from Jaisalmer to Jaipur, the train connection at Jodhpur is missed so often that it might be worth not buying a through ticket in case you have to change to a bus at Jodhpur.

Getting Around

Airport Transport The airport is the same as that used by the military, but the civil 'terminal' is just a corrugated shack. A minibus runs from the Tourist Bungalow to the airport and costs Rs 15.

Taxi & Jeep Unmetered taxis and jeeps are available. From the railway station, expect to pay Rs 12 to Rs 15 to the Tourist Bungalow and less to the old town.

Quite a few of the hotels provide their own transport from the station which is free if you're going to stay there. Those hotels which own jeeps generally also hire them out for visits to the surrounding area. Prices vary but are usually around Rs 2 per km shared between up to six people. A visit to the sand dunes at Sam, for instance, is about Rs 30 per person. Mahendra Travels, near the State Bank of India, offer trips to Sunset Point at 3.30 pm each day for Rs 30 per person. The Tourist Bungalow's jeep can be hired at similar rates.

The best way to get quickly around Jaisalmer itself is to hire a bicycle.

AROUND JAISALMER

There are some fascinating places in the area around Jaisalmer, although it soon fades out into a barren sand-duned desert which stretches across the lonely border into Pakistan.

Camel Safaris

The most interesting means of exploring the desert around Jaisalmer is on a camel safari and virtually everyone who comes here goes on one of them. Indeed, you can hardly avoid doing so, especially if you stay at a budget hotel, since the managers will hassle you until you agree to book with them. Naturally, they all offer *the best* safari and spare no invective in pouring scorn on their rivals' safaris.

The truth is more mundane. None of the hotels have their own camels – these are all independently owned by the drovers – so the hoteliers and the travel agents are just middlemen, though the hotels often organise the food and drink supplies. In addition, there's a lot of cut-throat competition to offer the cheapest safaris and this has resulted in many complaints when promises have been made and not kept.

Everyone has a different tale to tell, so you need to consider a few things before jumping at what appears to be a bargain. Hotel owners typically pay the camel drovers Rs 35 to Rs 40 per camel per day to hire them so, if you're offered a safari at Rs 50 per day, this leaves only Rs 15 a day for food and the agent's profit. It's obvious that you can't possibly expect three reasonable meals a day on these margins, but this is frequently what is promised. As a result, a lot of travellers feel they've been ripped-off when the food doesn't eventuate. It's a moot point which of the parties ought to shoulder the responsibility for this – is it the hotel owners who make impossible promises or the travellers who have unrealistic expectations?

If you pay Rs 50 to Rs 60 per day, you cannot expect anything more than the most basic food (say, rice/chappati and dhal) and, sometimes, not even a cup of coffee. For Rs 80 per day, you should get at least this much and perhaps a little more. Anyone expecting three decent meals a day, enough drinking water and tea or coffee should think in terms of at least Rs 100 to Rs 120 per day. If you're thinking of going in some style and eating well-cooked western or Indian food, having a beer in the evenings and sleeping in semicomfort, you're looking at up to Rs 350 per day. However much you decide to spend, make sure you know exactly what is being provided and make sure it's there before you leave Jaisalmer. You should also make sure you know where they're going to take you. Attempting to get a refund on your return for services not provided is a waste of time.

Most safaris last three to four days and, if you want to get to the most interesting places, this is a bare minimum. Bring something very comfortable to sit on – many travellers neglect to do this and come back with very sore legs and/or backsides! A wide-brimmed hat (or Rajput-style turban), sun cream and a personal water bottle are also essential. October to February is the best time for a safari.

The usual circuit takes in such places as Amar Sagar, Lodruva, Mool Sagar, Bada Bagh and Sam, as well as various abandoned villages along the way. Normally, the tourist sits in front with feet in stirrups and a camel driver perched behind, on top of a large fodder bag. The reins are fastened to the camel's nose peg, so the animals are easily steered. At resting points, the camels are completely unsaddled and hobbled. They limp away to browse on nearby shrubs while the camelmen brew sweet chai or prepare food. The whole crew rests in the shade of thorn trees by a tank or well.

It's a great way to see the desert, which is surprisingly well populated and sprinkled with ruins. You constantly come across tiny fields of millet, girls picking berries or boys herding flocks of sheep or goats. The latter are always fitted with tinkling neckbells and, in the desert silence, it's music to the ears. Camping out at night in the Sam sand dunes,

huddling around a tiny fire beneath the stars and listening to the camel drivers' yarns can be quite romantic. You may even hear tales of their other source of income apart from tourists – smuggling trips over the border into Pakistan!

The camel drivers will expect a tip or gift at the end of the trip. Don't neglect to do this.

Due to the troubles in Punjab and alleged arms smuggling across the border from Pakistan, all of Rajasthan west of National Highway No 15 is now a Restricted Area. Special permission is required from the Collector's office in Jaisalmer if you want to go there, and this is only issued in exceptional circumstances. The only places exempted are Amar Sagar, Bada Bagh, Lodruva, Kuldhara, Akal, Sam and Ramkunda.

Amar Sagar

North-west of Jaisalmer, this once pleasant formal garden has now fallen into ruins. The lake here dries up several months into the dry season.

A beautifully carved Jain temple is being painstakingly restored by crafts-people brought in from Agra. Commenced in the late '70s, this monumental task is expected to take many years.

Lodruva (15 km)

Further out, beyond Amar Sagar, are the deserted ruins of the town which was the ancient capital before the move to Jaisalmer. The Jain temples, rebuilt in the late '70s, are the only reminders of the city's former magnificence. The temples have ornate carved arches at the entrance and a Kalputra, the 'divine-tree', within. In the temple is a hole from which a snake is said to emerge every evening to drink an offering of milk. Only the 'lucky' can see it.

At the same time that they rebuilt the temples, Jain benefactors had the road out from Jaisalmer sealed, but it deteriorates into a desert track immediately beyond Lodruva.

Mool Sagar (9 km)

Directly west of Jaisalmer, this is another pleasant small garden and tank. Continuing in this direction you reach the Sam sand dunes, about 40 km from the town. This is the nearest real Sahara-like desert to Jaisalmer.

Khuri (40 km)

Khuri is a village south-west of Jaisalmer, out in the desert, in the touchy area near the Pakistan border. It's a delightfully peaceful place with houses of mud and straw decorated like the patterns on Persian carpets.

Bada Bagh & Cenotaphs

North of Jaisalmer, Bada Bagh is a fertile oasis with a huge old dam. Much of the city's fruit and vegetables are grown here and carried into the town each day by colourfully dressed women.

Above the gardens are royal cenotaphs with beautifully carved ceilings and equestrian statues of former rulers. In the early evening, this is a popular place to watch the setting sun turn Jaisalmer a beautiful golden brown.

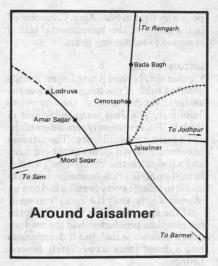

Around Jaisalmer

Map labels: To Ramgarh, Bada Bagh, Lodruva, Cenotaphs, Amar Sagar, To Jodhpur, Mool Sagar, Jaisalmer, To Sam, To Barmer

Other Places

Three km off the road to Barmer, at a point 14 km from Jaisalmer, the 180-million-year-old fossils of trees can be seen.

A desert national park has been established in the Thar Desert near Sam village, but a separate permit is required to enter it.

POKARAN

The junction where the Jaisalmer to Bikaner and Jaisalmer to Jodhpur roads split is the site of another magnificent Rajasthan fortress. The yellow sandstone fort rises from the yellow desert sands and shelters a tangle of narrow streets lined by balconied houses decorated with parrots, elephants and Rajasthan's inevitable peacocks. The usually quiet town springs to life during its annual cattle fair. It must also have sprung to life in May 1974 when a nuclear explosion took place nearby!

BARMER

Barmer is a centre for woodcarving, carpets, embroidery, block printing and other handicrafts and its products are famous throughout Rajasthan. Otherwise, this desert town, 153 km from Jaisalmer and 220 km from Jodhpur, isn't very exciting. There's no fortress here and the most interesting part is probably the journey there through small villages, their mud-walled houses decorated with the characteristic geometrical designs of each different village. Whilst walking around Barmer, I was stopped by an army captain driving a jeep. He asked me, 'Why have you come to Barmer? There's nothing here!' By the end of the day, I found myself in substantial agreement with him.

There's also hardly anywhere to stay here. The only obvious hotel I came across was the *Agra Rest House* on Station Rd, though there must be others.

Buses run between Barmer and Jaisalmer. Barmer is also connected to Jodhpur by metre-gauge railway. Although the line continues on to the Pakistani border, there are no through trains to that country and, in any case, foreigners are not allowed to cross the border at this point.

BIKANER (population 345,000)

This desert town in the north of the state was founded in 1488 by Rao Bikaji, a descendant of the founder of Jodhpur, Jodhaji. Like many others in Rajasthan,

Rajasthani embroidery

the old city is surrounded by a high battlemented wall and, like Jaisalmer, its smaller sister to the south, it was once an important staging post on the great caravan trade routes.

The city is chiefly interesting for its superb large fort, but it is also known for the fine camels bred here. There is a government camel breeding farm near the city. The Gang Canal, built between 1925 and 1927, irrigates a large area of previously arid land around Bikaner.

Information & Orientation

The old city is encircled by a seven-km-long city wall with five entrance gates, constructed in the 18th century. The fort and palace, built of the same reddish-pink sandstone as Bikaner's, are outside the city walls.

The tourist office is in Junagarh Fort and is open from 10 am to 5 pm, closed on Sundays. The GPO is at the collectorate, while the city post office is inside Kote Gate.

Junagarh Fort

Constructed between 1588 and 1593 by Raja Rai Singh, a general in the army of the Moghul emperor Akbar, the fort has a 986-metre-long wall with 37 bastions and two entrances. The Suraj Pol, or 'Sun Gate', is the main entrance to the fort. The palaces within the fort are at the southern side and make a picturesque ensemble of courtyards, balconies, kiosks, towers and windows. A major feature of this fort and its palaces is the superb quality of the stone carving – it rivals the best anywhere in the world.

Among the places of interest are the Chandra Mahal, or 'Moon Palace', with paintings, mirrors and carved marble panels. The Phool Mahal, or 'Flower Palace', is also decorated with glass and mirrors. The Karn Mahal was built to commemorate a notable victory over the Moghul Aurangzeb.

Other palaces include the Rang Mahal, Bijai Mahal and Anup Mahal. The contents include the usual Rajput weapon

collection, not to mention the decaying pieces of a couple of old WW I biplanes. The Durga Niwas is a beautifully painted courtyard while the Ganga Niwas, another large courtyard, has a finely carved red sandstone front. Har Mandir is the royal temple, dedicated to Lord Shiva.

The fort is open from 10 am to 4.30 pm and is closed on Fridays. Admission is Rs 5, plus Rs 10 for a still camera or Rs 20 for a movie camera. The fee includes a Hindi-speaking guide (not compulsory). If you prefer, you can wander around on your own. Guardians stationed at various points will direct you.

Lalgarh Palace

Outside Bikaner, about three km from the city centre, the 'Red Fort' was built by Maharaja Ganga Singh (1881-1942) in memory of his father Maharaja Lal Singh. The Bikaner royal family still lives in part of the palace, which is made of red sandstone and has beautiful latticework. The rest of the palace has been turned into a luxury hotel, and a museum known as the Shri Sadul Museum. The museum houses a collection of old photographs and the usual exhibition of Indian wildlife, shot and stuffed. It is open from 10 am to 5 pm, closed Wednesdays.

Ganga Golden Jubilee Museum

This small museum near the Tourist Bungalow contains pre-Harappan, Gupta and Kushan pieces and a wide collection of weapons, terracottas, pottery and paintings, particularly miniatures of the Bikaner school. It is open from 10 am to 5 pm, closed on Fridays.

Places to Stay – bottom end

The pleasantly quiet *Dhola Maru Tourist Bungalow* (tel 5002) is on Pooran Singh Circle. The deluxe singles/doubles for Rs 65/80, air-cooled rooms for Rs 90/120 and air-con rooms for Rs 125/175 are reasonably good value, but the fabric has been allowed to deteriorate and cleaning

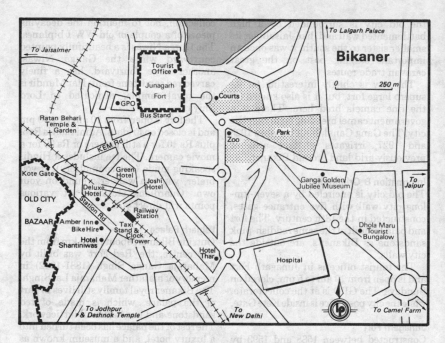

standards leave much to be desired. There's a bar and restaurant, but the food is very average and somewhat expensive because of the tax loading. It's quite a long way from the town centre and the fort so you'll have to take an auto-rickshaw. The fare should be Rs 5 but they often ask for more.

There is a string of low-priced hotels near the station on Station Rd. They include the *Deluxe Hotel* (tel 192) and the *Green Hotel* (tel 296), which are similar in standard and have singles/doubles with bath for Rs 25/40. Bucket hot water is available for Rs 2. The rooms are basic with mattress, single sheet and blanket and no mosquito nets. Also cheap is the nearby *Grand Hotel*. It is essentially a doss house for single men (there are no doubles) and costs Rs 25. All rooms have bath and bucket hot water is available.

Slightly more expensive is the *Hotel Shantiniwas* (tel 5025) down the street, opposite the railway station on the right-hand side. It has singles without bath for Rs 20 and singles/doubles with bath and hot water for Rs 28/55. It was redecorated recently and the floors and bathrooms are kept clean, but the bed covers are often grubby so you may have to insist on clean sheets.

Other nearby budget hotels are the *Delight Hotel, Roopan Hotel* (tel 373) and, near the railway crossing on Station Rd, the *Sankhla Rest House* (tel 3949).

Places to Stay – middle

The *Joshi Hotel* is also near the railway station. It offers singles/doubles for Rs 150/200 and air-cooled deluxe rooms for Rs 200/250. All rooms have bath and hot water. Try not to get a room too close to the lounge area which is always packed with a boisterous crowd watching videos at full volume.

Another fairly new mid-range hotel is

the *Hotel Thar*, on the left-hand side of Hospital Rd on the way to the Tourist Bungalow. Rooms with bath and constant hot water cost Rs 160/200 and 40 dorm beds are also available. There's a discount of 20% between April and August. The hotel has a restaurant and Rajasthani music and folk dances are put on during the high season.

Places to Stay - top end
Bikaner's sole top-end hotel is the *Lalgarh Palace Hotel* (tel 3263), which is part of the maharaja's modern palace of the same name. It offers air-cooled rooms with bath and constant hot water for Rs 285/375, less a 20% discount during May, June and July. There's a swimming pool, restaurant and billiard room and Rajasthani music and folk dances can be arranged if you're willing to pay for the troupe.

Places to Eat
Bikaner has very few outstanding places to eat. The *Chhotu Motu Joshi Restaurant* is just down from the Green Hotel towards the station and has good, cheap vegetarian food, icy-cold lassi and lots of Indian sweets. The *Green Hotel* and the *Deluxe Hotel* both have similar small, clean restaurants serving snacks and drinks.

Across the road from these hotels, you can get cheap vegetarian food at a number of open-air places like *Krishan, Laxmi* and *Ganesh*, but they're all pretty grubby. The more expensive *Amber Restaurant* is on Station Rd.

Getting There & Away
Air Vayudoot operates three flights a week on the Delhi/Jaipur/Bikaner route. Jaipur/Bikaner takes just over an hour. Vayudoot also flies from Jaisalmer to Jodhpur three times a week, but this flight sometimes goes via Bikaner. If that's the connection you want to make, ask at a Vayudoot office. The airport is 15 km from the city centre.

Bus On the edge of the Thar Desert, Bikaner is connected by road with the rest of Rajasthan. There is a sealed national highway to Jaipur (320 km) and to Jaisalmer (330 km).

Although there are state transport buses between Jaisalmer and Bikaner, most travellers opt for one of the private luxury buses. The offices of these companies are clustered together opposite the GPO. The Rathore Travels (tel 6427) bus leaves Bikaner daily at 9.30 pm and arrives in Jaisalmer around 5.30 am, including a half-hour stop en route. The fare is Rs 50. Jodhpur is 240 km away and costs Rs 38 by express bus. The Dhola Maru Tourist Bungalow offers a daily luxury bus to Jaipur which leaves at 10 pm and costs Rs 60.

Train Day and night trains take about 12 hours to make the 463-km trip from Delhi to Bikaner. Fares are Rs 53 in 2nd class, Rs 194 in 1st. There are also trains to Jodhpur and Jaipur.

An alternative way of travelling from Jaisalmer to Bikaner is to take the Jodhpur-bound night train as far as Phalodi, arriving there at 1.30 am, then catch the connecting bus at 2 am. This gets to Bikaner around 6 am.

Getting Around
Auto-rickshaws are unmetered. Bikaner also has tongas and there are lots of bicycle-hire places along Station Rd, across from the railway station.

AROUND BIKANER
Bhand Sagar Temple (5 km)
The 16th-century Jain temple to the 23rd tirthankar, Parasvanath, is the most important of the complex. Others include the Chintamani Temple of 1505 and the Adinath Temple. There is a fine view of the city wall and surrounding countryside from the park behind the temple.

Devi Kund (8 km)
This is the site of the royal chhatris (cenotaphs) of many of the Bika dynasty

rulers. The white marble chhatri of Maharaja Surat Singh is among the most imposing.

Camel Breeding Farm (10 km)

This government-managed camel breeding station is probably unique in Asia. There are hundreds of camels here and it's a great sight at sunset as the camels come back from grazing. The British army had a camel corps drawn from Bikaner during WW I. Rides are available.

You'll have no difficulty finding transport to the camel farm – half the auto-rickshaw and taxi drivers in Bikaner appear to be on the lookout for tourists to take out there.

Gajner Wildlife Sanctuary (32 km)

A number of animals can be seen in this reserve on the Jaisalmer road. Imperial sand grouse migrate here in winter.

The old royal summer palace stands on the bank of the lake and is sometimes used as a hotel.

Karni Mata Temple (33 km)

At Deshnok on the Jodhpur road, this temple is dedicated to the mystic Karni Mata. The huge silver gates to the temple and the marble carvings were donated by Maharaja Ganga Singh and a golden umbrella tops the temple.

The main interest here, however, is the rats. Like cows in the rest of India, the rats here are regarded as holy and are fed by the priests, who care for them in the belief that they will be reincarnated as mystics or holy men. Strolling around this temple with rats playing leapfrog over your bare feet can be a little unnerving. There's a Rs 5 camera fee at the temple.

Getting There & Away You can reach the temple on the hourly bus from Bikaner for about Rs 5, or hire a taxi or jeep from in front of the railway station for about Rs 90 round trip.

Gujarat

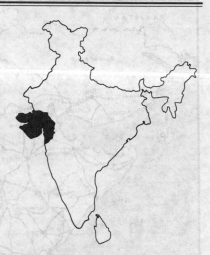

Population: 42 million
Area: 195,984 square km
Capital: Gandhinagar
Main language: Gujarati

The west coast state of Gujarat is not one of India's busiest tourist destinations. Although it is quite easy to slot Gujarat in between Bombay and the cities of Rajasthan, few people pause to explore this interesting state. Yet Gujarat has a long and varied history and a great number of interesting places to visit. If you want to go right beyond history into the realms of legend, then the Temple of Somnath was actually there to witness the creation of the universe! Along the south coast are the sites where many of the great events in Lord Krishna's life took place.

On firmer historic footing, Lothal was the site of a Harappan or Indus Valley Civilisation city over 4000 years ago. The main sites of this very ancient culture are now in Pakistan, but it is thought that Lothal may have survived the great cities of the Sind by as much as 500 years. Gujarat also featured in the exploits of the great Buddhist emperor Ashoka, and one of his rock edicts can be seen near Junagadh.

Later, Gujarat suffered Muslim incursions from Mahmud of Ghazni and subsequent Moghul rulers and was a battlefield between the Moghuls and the Marathas. It was also an early point of contact with the west and the first British commercial outpost was established at Surat. Daman and Diu survived as Portuguese enclaves within the borders of Gujarat until 1961. More recently, Gujarat had close ties with the life of the father of modern India, Mahatma Gandhi. It was in Gujarat that the Mahatma was born and spent his early years and it was to Ahmedabad, the great city of Gujarat, that he returned to wage his long struggle with the British for independence.

Gujarat has always been a centre for the Jains, and some of its most interesting sights are Jain temple centres like those at Palitana and Girnar. The Jains are an influential and energetic group and, as a result, Gujarat is one of India's wealthier states with a number of important industries, particularly textiles. Apart from its Jain temples, Gujarat's major attractions include the last Asian lions, in the Gir Forest, and the fascinating Indo-Saracenic architecture of Ahmedabad.

Geographically, Gujarat can be divided into three areas. The eastern (mainland) region includes the major cities of Ahmedabad, Surat and Baroda. The Gulf of Cambay divides the mainland strip from the flat, often barren, plain of the Kathiawar Peninsula, also known as Saurashtra. This was never incorporated into British India, but survived in the form of more than 200 princely states right up to independence. In 1956, they were all amalgamated into the state of Bombay but, in 1960, this was in turn split, on linguistic grounds, into Maharashtra and Gujarat. The Gulf of Kutch divides

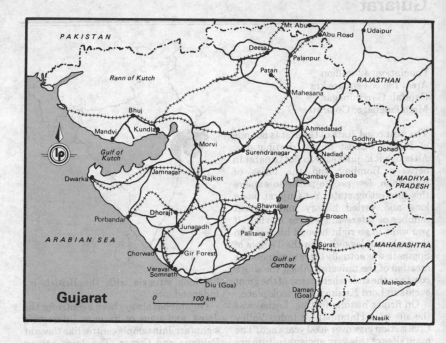

Gujarat

0   100 km

Saurashtra from Kutch, which is virtually an island, cut off from the rest of Gujarat to the east and Pakistan to the north by the low-lying 'Ranns' of Kutch.

Gujarat has provided a surprisingly large proportion of India's emigrants, particularly to the UK and USA. More than half of the 100,000 Indians in the New York area are Gujaratis; there, the popular Gujarati surname 'Patel' has come to be commonly identified as Indian.

Gujarati Food

The strict vegetarianism of the Jains has contributed to Gujarat's distinctive regional cuisine. Throughout the state, you'll find the Gujarati variation of the thali – it's the traditional all-you-can-eat vegetarian meal with an even greater variety of dishes than usual. For those without a sweet tooth, however, it can be overpoweringly sweet.

Popular dishes include *kadhi*, a savoury curry of yoghurt and fried puffs, flavoured with spices and finely chopped vegetables. *Undhyoo* is a winter speciality of potatoes, sweet potatoes, broad beans and aubergines roasted in an earthenware pot which is buried upside down (undhyoo) under a fire. In Surat, the local variation of this dish is more spicy and curry hot. *Sev ganthia*, a crunchy fried chickpea-flour snack, is available from *farsan* stalls.

In winter, try Surat's *paunk*, a curious combination of roasted cereals, or *jowar*, garlic chutney and sugar. Then there's *khaman dhokla*, a salty steamed chickpea-flour cake, and *doodhpak*, a thick, sweetened, milk-based dessert with nuts. *Srikhand* is a dessert made from yoghurt and spiced with saffron, cardamom, nuts and candied fruit. *Gharis* are rich sweets made of milk, clarified butter and dried fruits – another Surat specialty. In summer, *am rasis* is a popular mango drink.

The Gujaratis make superb ice cream which is available throughout western India. The brand name is Vadelal and it comes in about 20 flavours, some of which are seasonal – 'custard apple', for example, can only be bought in January and February. Many of the varieties have chunks of real fruit in them and, of course, no chemical additives.

Things to Buy

With its busy modern textile works, it's not surprising that Gujarat offers a number of interesting buys in this line. Extremely fine, and often extremely expensive, Patola silk saris are still made by a handful of master craftspeople in Patan. From Surat comes the *zari*, or gold-thread embroidery work. Surat is also a centre for silk saris. On a more mundane level, but still beautiful, are the block prints of Ahmedabad. At Madhupura Rani-no-Hajiro on Mirzapur Rd, near the Ahmedabad GPO, you will also find cloth, hand painted in the traditional black, red, maroon and ochre.

Jamnagar is famous for its tie-dye work, which you'll see in Saurashtra as well as in the bazaar shops of Jamnagar. Brightly coloured peasant embroideries and beadwork are also found in Saurashtra, along with woollen shawls, blankets and rugs, while brass-covered wooden chests are manufactured in Bhavnagar and embroidered stuffed toys are made in Kutch. In Ahmedabad, antique shops sell wooden carvings, such as window frames, shutters and doorways from old houses, and most Gujarati handicrafts are on display at Gujari or Handloom House, both on Ashram Rd.

Festivals & Fairs

Gujarat has a busy calendar of events. Some of the main ones include:

January
   Mankar Sankranti This end-of-winter

festival is celebrated with kite-flying contests.
January-February
   Muharram Tazias, large replicas of the tombs of two Muslim martyrs, are paraded in the evening, particularly in Surat, Junagadh and Ahmedabad.
September-October
   Navarati Nine nights of music and dancing celebrate this festival of the mother goddess Amba. The Dandiya Ras, which Lord Krishna danced with his milkmaids or gopis, is featured. Champaner celebrates this festival with particular fervour.
October
   Dussehra The 10th day of Navarati culminates in the celebration of Rama's victory over the evil Ravana in the *Ramayana*.
October-November
   Sharad Purnima Song and dance celebrate the end of the monsoon on the night of the full moon in the month of Sharad.

Gujarat has many fairs in its temple towns and small villages. They offer a chance to see religious festivals and celebrations and, in the villages, also function as a shop window for local handicrafts. The village of Ambaji, 177 km north of Ahmedabad, celebrates four major festivals each year. The Bhavnath Fair, held at the foot of Mt Girnar in the month of Magha (January-February), is a fine opportunity to hear local folk music and see folk dances.

The tribal Adivasi people have a major festival at Dangs near Surat – it's known as the Dangs Durbar. Lord Krishna's birthday, or Janmashtamia, falls in August and his temple at Dwarka is the place to be. Along the coast at Porbandar, the Madhavrai Fair is held in the month of Chaitra (March-April) to celebrate Lord Krishna's elopement with Rukmini. In the same month, a major festival takes place at the foot of Pavagadh Hill by Champaner, near Baroda, honouring the goddess Mahakali. Somnath has a large fair at the full moon of Kartika Purnima in November-December. Lord Shiva, the three-eyed one, or Trinetreshwar, has an important festival in his honour in Bhadrapada (August-September) in Ternetar village – you'll see colourful local tribal costumes here.

Eastern Gujarat

AHMEDABAD (population 3,000,000)
Ahmedabad, Gujarat's principal city, is one of the major industrial cities in India. It has been called the 'Manchester of the East' due to its many textile industries. Today, it is destined to be the earth station for India's satellite TV project. Ahmedabad is also very noisy and incredibly polluted; only on Sunday mornings is there any respite.

Visitors in the hot season should bear in mind the derisive title given to Ahmedabad by the Moghul emperor Jehangir: Gardabad, 'the city of dust'. Nevertheless, this comparatively little-visited city has a number of attractions for travellers. Gandhi's ashram at Sabarmati is open to tourists and features a small museum. In the city, there are some of the finest examples of Islamic architecture in India, as well as a number of other interesting buildings, both religious and secular. Ahmedabad is one of the best places to study the blend of Hindu and Islamic architectural styles known as the Indo-Saracenic.

The new capital of Gujarat, Gandhinagar, is 23 km from Ahmedabad.

History
Over the centuries, Ahmedabad has had a number of periods of grandeur, each followed by decline. It was originally founded in 1411 by Ahmed Shah and, in the 17th century, was thought to be one of the finest cities in India. In 1615, the noted English ambassador Sir Thomas Roe judged it to be 'a goodly city, as large as London' but, in the 18th century, it went through a period of decline. Its industrial strength once again raised the city up,

and, from 1915, it became famous as the site of Gandhi's ashram and the place where he launched his famous march against the Salt Law.

In recent years, Ahmedabad has seen outbursts of communal violence, mainly between Muslims and Hindus. Some fear that the city will eventually be divided into areas, strictly segregated on religious grounds but, at the moment, there is little evidence of this.

Orientation
The city lies on both sides of the Sabarmati River. On the eastern bank, two main roads run away from the river to the railway station, about three km away. They are Tilak Rd (Relief Rd) and Gandhi Rd. The airport is off to the north-east of the city, while the Gandhi Ashram is on the west bank of the Sabarmati River, to the north of the city. Virtually all the city walls are now demolished, but some of the gates remain.

Information
Tourist Office The state tourist office is just off Sri R C Rd, across the river from the town centre. Hours are 10.30 am to 1.30 pm and 2 to 5.30 pm. They're late starters, even by Indian standards. The office has excellent maps of Ahmedabad (Rs 4) and Gujarat state (Rs 1) and a free list of their own chain of hotels/resort centres with current prices. They can also arrange various tours of the state in their own buses, as well as car hire. Many rickshaw drivers don't know where this place is and don't understand where you want to go. This is hardly surprising as it's not at all obvious. Have them stop and ask if you feel you're heading in the wrong direction.

Post The poste restante at the GPO routinely pigeonholes letters according to the first name on the address, so you need to check all combinations.

Airlines Indian Airlines is on Tilak Rd, close to the Nehru Bridge, on the right-

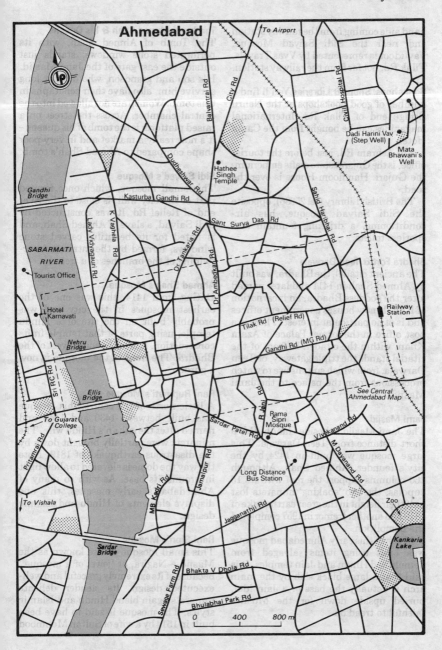

Ahmedabad

To Airport

City Rd

Balvantrai Rd

Chhotanagar Rd

Gandhi Hospital Rd

Dadi Harini Vav
(Step Well)

Mata
Bhawani's
Well

Hathee
Singh
Temple

Gandhi
Bridge

Dudheshwar Rd

Kasturba Gandhi Rd

K Vaghela Rd

Sabid Haribhai Rd

Sant Surya Das Rd

Lady Vidyagaun Rd

SABARMATI
RIVER

Tourist Office

Dr Tankaria Rd

Dr Ambedkad Rd

Hotel
Karnavati

Railway
Station

Nehru
Bridge

Tilak Rd (Relief Rd)

Gandhi Rd (MG Rd)

Sri RC Rd

Ellis
Bridge

See Central
Ahmedabad Map

R Jani Rd

Rama
Sipri
Mosque

To Gujarat
College

Pritamrai Rd

Sardar Patel Rd

Vivekanand Rd

M Dayanand Rd

Jamalpur Rd

Long Distance
Bus Station

Zoo

To Vishala

MB Kadri Rd

Jagganathji Rd

Kankaria
Lake

Sardar
Bridge

Bhakta V Dhola Rd

Sewage Farm Rd

Bhulabhai Park Rd

0   400   800 m

hand side coming from the railway station and near the Sidi Saiyad Mosque. Vayudoot is represented by Vyas Travels, Tilak Rd, not far from the railway station.

Bookshops, Shops & Libraries You'll find a number of good bookshops at the Nehru Bridge end of Tilak Rd. International magazines can be bought from the Cama Hotel.

On Ashram Rd, just before the tourist office, is the Gujarat state crafts emporium, the Gujari. Handloom House is over the road.

The British Library (tel 25686), opposite the Sidi Saiyad Mosque, has air-conditioning, a drinking fountain and spotless toilets.

Bhadra Fort & Teen Darwaja
The ancient citadel, the Bhadra, was built by Ahmed Shah in 1411 and later named after the goddess Bhadra, an incarnation of Kali. It now houses government offices and is of no particular interest. There is a post office in the former Palace of Azam Khan, within the citadel. In front of the citadel stands the triple gateway, or Teen Darwaja, from which sultans use to watch processions from the palace to the Jami Masjid.

Jami Masjid
The Jami Masjid is beside Gandhi Rd, a short distance from Teen Darwaja. This large mosque was built in 1424 by the city's founder, Ahmed Shah. Although 260 columns support the roof with its 15 cupolas, the two 'shaking' minarets lost half their height in the great earthquake of 1819 and another tremor in 1957 completed the demolition.

Much of this early Ahmedabad mosque was built using items salvaged from demolished Hindu and Jain temples. It is said that a large black slab by the main arch is actually the base of a Jain idol, buried upside down for the Muslim faithful to tread on.

Tombs of Ahmed Shah & his Queens
The Tomb of Ahmed Shah, with its perforated stone windows, stands just outside the east gate of the Jami Masjid. His son and grandson, who did not long survive him, also have their cenotaphs in this tomb. Women are not allowed into the central chamber. Across the street on a raised platform is the tomb of his queens – it's now really a market and in very poor shape compared to Ahmed Shah's tomb.

Sidi Saiyad's Mosque
This small mosque, which once formed part of the city wall, is close to the river end of Relief Rd. It was constructed by Sidi Saiyad, a slave of Ahmed Shah, and is noted for its beautiful carved stone windows, formed by the intricate inter-twining of the branches of a tree.

Ahmed Shah's Mosque
Dating from 1414, this was one of the earliest mosques in the city and was probably built on the site of a Hindu temple, using parts of that temple in its construction. It is in the south-west of the Bhadra. The front of the mosque is now a garden.

Rani Rupmati's Mosque
A little north of the centre, this mosque was built between 1430 and 1440 and named after the sultan's Hindu wife. The minarets were partially brought down by the disastrous earthquake of 1819. Note the way the dome is elevated to allow light in around its base. As with so many of Ahmedabad's early mosques, this one displays elements of Hindu and Islamic design.

Rani Sipri's Mosque
This small mosque is also known as the Masjid-e-Nagira, or 'jewel of a mosque', because of its extremely graceful and well-executed design. Its slender delicate minarets again blend Hindu and Islamic styles. The mosque is said to have been built in 1514 by a wife of Sultan Mehmood

Begada after he executed their son for some minor misdemeanour. It's to the south-east of the town centre.

Sidi Bashir's Mosque & Shaking Minarets

Just south of the railway station, outside the Sarangpur Gate, the Sidi Bashir Mosque is famed for its shaking minarets, or Jhulta Minar. When one minaret is shaken, the other rocks in sympathy. This is said to be a protection against earthquake damage. Whether or not this is true, you won't be allowed to confirm it. In any case, the mosque is usually closed and the opening hours posted outside appear to bear no relation to reality.

The Raj Babi Mosque, south-east of the railway station in the suburb of Gomtipur, also had shaking minarets, one of which was partially dismantled by an inquisitive Englishman in an unsuccessful attempt to find out how it worked. It's worth a visit but, once again, you're specifically prohibited from shaking the remaining minaret (even if that were possible). Expect to be hassled for a contribution when visiting this mosque.

A little to the north of the railway station, other minarets are all that remain of a mosque which was destroyed in a battle between the Moghuls and Marathas in 1753.

Hathee Singh Temple

Just outside the Delhi Gate, to the north of the old city, this Jain temple is built in typical style and, as with so many Jain temples, is made of white marble. Built in 1848, it is dedicated to Dharamanath, the 15th Jain tirthankar.

Dada Harini Vav (Step Well)

Step wells, or baolis, are strange constructions, unique to northern India, and this is one of the best. The curious well, built in 1499, has a series of steps leading down to lower and lower platforms, eventually terminating in a small octagonal well. The depths of the well are cool, even on the hottest day, and it must once have

Shaking Minarets, Ahemedabad

been quite beautiful. Today, it is completely neglected and often bone dry, but it's a fascinatingly eerie place with galleries above the well and a small portico at ground level.

The best time to visit and/or photograph the well is between 10 and 11 am; at other times, the sun is in the wrong place and doesn't penetrate to the various levels. There's no entry or camera fee. Behind the well is the equally neglected Mosque and Rauza 'Tomb' of Dada Harini. The mosque has a tree motif like the one on the windows of Sidi Saiyad's Mosque.

There is a second step well, that of Mat Bhawani, a couple of hundred metres north of Dada Harini's. Ask children to show you the way. Thought to be several hundred years older, it is much less ornate and is now used as a crude Hindu temple.

Kankaria Lake

South-east of the city, this artificial lake,

complete with an island summer palace, was constructed in 1451 and has 34 sides, each 60 metres long. Once frequented by Emperor Jehangir and Empress Nur Jahan, it is now a local picnic spot. The huge zoo and children's park by the lake are outstanding and the Ghattamendal pavilion in the centre houses an aquarium.

Other Mosques & Temples

It's very easy to get bored with mosques in Ahmedabad. If your enthusiasm for them is limited, don't go further than Sidi Saiyad's and the Jami Masjid. If you have real endurance, you could continue to Dastur Khan's Mosque near the Rani Sipri Mosque, or to Haibat Khan's Mosque, Saiyad Alam's Mosque, Shuja'at Khan's Mosque, Shaikh Hasan Muhammed Chisti's Mosque and Muhafiz Khan's Mosque.

Then, for a complete change, you could plunge into the narrow streets of the old part of town and seek out the brightly painted Swami Narayan Temple. Enclosed in a large courtyard, it dates from 1850. To the south of this Hindu temple are the nine tombs known as the Nau Gaz Pir, or 'Nine Yard Saints'.

Around the Town

Ahmedabad can be an interesting place around which to wander. The bazaar streets are narrow, crowded and colourful, and lots of the houses have ornately carved wooden facades. In many streets, there are Jain bird-feeding places known as *parabdis*. Children catch and release pigeons for the fun of it. The older parts of the city are divided into totally separate areas known as *pols*. It's easy to get lost.

The Victoria Gardens beside M G Rd are pleasant and about the only place where you'll get some relief from the weekday noise and pollution.

The western side of Ahmedabad across the river is a late 20th-century creation full of modern buildings such as the Ahmedabad Mill Owner's Association building and the museum, both designed by Le Corbusier, who also had a hand in the new capital of Gandhinagar.

Unlike so many other large cities, Ahmedabad has little evidence of the British period. The chief landmarks of the era are the tall smokestacks that ring this industrial city. On the sandy bed of the Sabarmati River, traditional block-printed fabrics are still stretched out to dry, despite the 70-plus large textile mills. The river dries to a mere trickle in the hot season.

Other places of interest in and around town include the ruined tomb of Darya Khan, north-west of the Hathee Singh Temple. Built in 1453, the tomb has a particularly large dome. Nearby is the Chhota Shahi Bagh; the Shahi Bagh is across the railway line. Ladies of the harem used to live in the chhota 'small' garden. In Saraspur, east of the railway line, the Temple of Chintaman is a Jain temple originally constructed in 1638 and converted into a mosque by Aurangzeb.

Museums

Ahmedabad has a number of museums. The Calico Museum of Textiles (tel 5100) exhibits antique and modern textiles including rare tapestries, wall hangings and costumes. Also on display are old weaving machines. The museum is in Sarabhai House, a former haveli, in the Shahi Bagh gardens. It is open from 10 am to 12.30 pm and 2.30 to 5 pm, closed on Wednesdays, and admission is free. The interesting little museum shop sells cards, books and reproductions of some of the pieces.

The N C Mehta Museum of Miniatures (tel 78369) at Sanskar Kendra, Paldi, has excellent examples of the various schools of Indian miniature painting. It is open from 9 to 11 am and 4 to 7 pm daily, except Mondays. The building was designed by Le Corbusier.

The Shreyas Folk Museum displays the folk arts and crafts of Gujarat. There's also the National Institute of Design, the Tribal Research & Training Institute

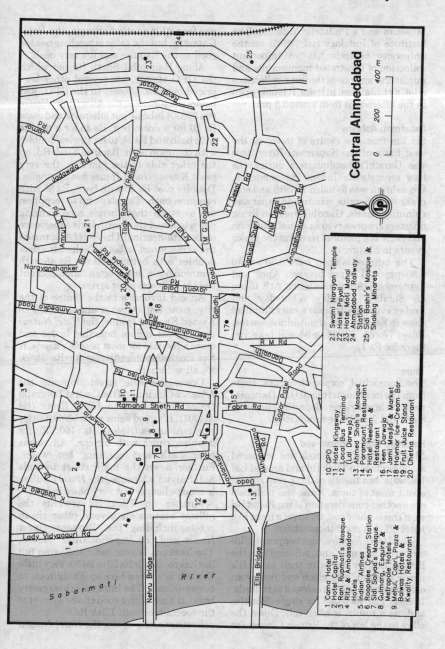

Central Ahmedabad

0   200   400 m

1 Cama Hotel
2 Hotel Capital
3 Rani Rupmati's Mosque
4 Ritz & Ambassador
   Hotels
5 Indian Airlines
6 Roopalee Cream Station
7 Sidi Saiyad's Mosque
8 Gulmarg, Esquire &
   Metropole Hotels
9 Mehul, Capri, Plaza &
   Balwas Hotels &
   Kwality Restaurant

10 CPO
11 Hotel Kingsway
12 Local Bus Terminal
    (Lal Darwaja)
13 Ahmed Shah's Mosque
14 Paramount Restaurant
15 Hotel Neelam &
    Restaurant
16 Teen Darwaja
17 Jami Masjid & Market
18 Havmor Ice-Cream Bar
19 Fruit Juice Stand
20 Chetna Restaurant

21 Swami Narayan Temple
22 Hotel Payall
23 Hotel Moti Mahal
24 Ahmedabad Railway
    Station
25 Sidi Bashir's Mosque &
    Shaking Minarets

Museum and a Philatelic Museum. The Institute of Indology (tel 78295) on the university campus has an important collection of illustrated manuscripts and miniatures and one of the finest collections relating to Jainism in India. It is only open in the afternoons from around 3 pm.

Sabarmati Ashram

Six km from the centre of town, on the west bank of the Sabarmati River, this was Gandhi's headquarters during the long struggle for Indian independence. His ashram was founded in 1918 and still makes handicrafts, handmade paper and spinning wheels. Gandhi's spartan living quarters are preserved as a small museum and there is a pictorial record of the major events in his life.

The ashram is open from 8.30 am to 6.30 pm (till 7 pm between April and September). Admission is free. At 8.15 pm on Sunday, Tuesday, Thursday and Friday evenings, there is a son et lumière show in English for a small admission fee. Buses No 81, 82, 83 or 84 will take you there for Rs 1.

Tours

The municipal corporation runs tours from the local bus terminal (Lal Darwaja) near Nehru Bridge, departing daily at 8 am and 2 pm. The fare is Rs 20.

Places to Stay - bottom end

Most of the cheap hotels are scattered along or close to Tilak Rd and around Lal Darwaja, but there's nothing very special about most of them. Noise and pollution are another consideration along Relief Rd so, if this bothers you, try to get a room in a hotel off this main thoroughfare.

The *Hotel Esquire*, right opposite Sidi Saiyad's Mosque and adjacent to the British Library, is better than most. It's newly painted, very clean and run by an oldish woman who cares about standards. It costs just Rs 34/68 for singles/doubles and, as a result, is often full. Down the alley to the left of the British Library (as

you face it) is another cheapie, the *Hotel Gulmarg*, but the value is nowhere near as good as the Esquire and it's very basic.

Along Ramanlal Sheth Rd, on which the GPO stands, are several other low-priced options. Closest to the GPO, just before the junction, the *Alka Guest House* (tel 20830) is basic but adequate and costs Rs 20 for a dorm bed, Rs 45 for a double with bath and Rs 34/40 for singles/doubles with common bath. Back on Tilak Rd, on the other side of the junction, the very basic *Kamal Guest House* has no singles. Doubles cost Rs 45 with bath, Rs 35 with common bath. The steps up to reception are so steep that there's rope hanging down to assist those with little experience of mountaineering! The *Hotel Ashiana* on the same street is better value. It offers doubles with bath for Rs 50, Rs 45 with common bath, and is often full. Checkout time is 24 hours after arrival.

An old favourite in the centre of the city, near Lal Darwaja and adjacent to Ahmed Shah's Mosque, the *Hotel Natraj* is a typical Indian boarding house and quite adequate for most people's needs. It has singles/doubles/triples for Rs 34/69/95, all with bath.

Down the side street opposite the Advance Cinema and the Central Telegraph Office is the modern *Hotel Relax* (tel 354301). It's good value at Rs 50/69/120 for singles/doubles/triples, Rs 150/175 for doubles/triples with air-con. All rooms have bath and constant hot water. Further down the main street towards Sidi Saiyad's Mosque, the *Hotel Cadilac* is much cheaper but very basic indeed.

Further up Tilak Rd towards the railway station are several other cheap hotels including the *Yamuna Guest House* and the *Imperial Guest House*. The Yamuna is very basic and often full but has rooms for Rs 20 to Rs 50. Very little English is spoken here so it's difficult to communicate. The Imperial is also pretty basic. It's not such a good choice as most of the rooms face onto Tilak Rd.

Further along again, the *Hotel Naigra*

(tel 384977) looks expensive but is surprisingly cheap. Singles/doubles/triples with bath are Rs 44/82/100 and singles with common bath cost Rs 34. It's often full but, as most of the rooms face onto a side alley rather than onto Tilak Rd, it's worth checking out.

Places to Stay – middle

The *Moti Mahal Guest House* (tel 339091), Kapasia Bazar, is visible from the railway station off to the right. It is very clean and good value at Rs 141/182 for singles/doubles, Rs 232/256 with air-con. All rooms have bath and constant hot water and the hotel has a restaurant (vegetarian and non-vegetarian).

Further down Tilak Rd, the *Amber Hotel* (tel 335012) is cheaper than the Moti Mahal with singles/doubles for Rs 103/134. All rooms have a bath with hot water and the staff are friendly. Almost at the end of Tilak Rd, down a side alley opposite Electric House and round the corner from the Hotel Capri, is the *Hotel Metropole* (tel 354988). Quite a few travellers stay here and it's pretty good value at Rs 103/134 for singles/doubles, Rs 167/194 with air-con, all with bath and hot water. This hotel's only disadvantage is that most of the rooms face the lounge area where a noisy TV is turned on much of the time.

Very close to the Metropole, the *Hotel Balwas* (tel 351135), 6751 Tilak Rd, has singles/doubles for Rs 154/182, Rs 232/256 with air-con. Deluxe air-con rooms are also available for Rs 193 a single and Rs 230 a double. All rooms have bath and constant hot water, there's a same-day laundry service and the hotel has a terrace restaurant.

Similar to the Balwas in quality and price is the *Hotel Kingsway* (tel 26221/5), Ramanlal Sheth Rd, close to the junction with Tilak Rd. Singles/doubles cost Rs 219/256, Rs 297/330 with air-con, and all rooms have bath, constant hot water and a colour TV.

Outside this area, just off Dr Tankaria Rd (which runs north from Sidi Saiyad's Mosque), is the *Bombay Hotel* (tel 351746), KB Commercial Centre, near the Dinbai Tower and the Gujarat Samachar Building. The hotel is on the 3rd floor and not very obvious from street level, but it has 30 rooms priced from Rs 46/89 to Rs 97/134. All rooms have bath and telephone and checkout is based on the 24-hour principle. It's fairly grubby so, if you can't find it, you're not missing much.

On the borderline between middle and top-end are two hotels on the river bank, very close to Nehru Bridge. By far the more interesting of the two is the *Ritz Hotel* (tel 353637/9). This place is a real find – a haven of peace in an urban jungle. Set in a quiet, leafy garden overlooking the river, it has the feel of a rural hunting lodge with its mellow old buildings and beautiful verandahs, and the staff are very friendly indeed. Singles/doubles cost Rs 128/230, Rs 348/399 with air-con, and all rooms have bath with constant hot water, colour TV and telephone. There's a garden terrace, liquor shop (a rarity in Gujarat, with permits issued on the spot), laundry service, ample car-parking facilities, currency exchange and restaurant. This place is highly recommended but it's often full during the week. You also need to watch the 9 am checkout time and the restaurant taxes which can total 22%!

Just round the corner from the Ritz, the *Hotel Ambassador* (tel 353244), Khanpur Rd, is also popular. Rooms cost Rs 180/230, Rs 245/295 with air-con, and there are also deluxe singles/doubles for Rs 278/328. It's modern and very clean and all rooms have bath with constant hot water. In addition, the staff are pleasant and helpful.

If you don't mind staying some distance out of town, the modern *Gandhi Ashram* is close to the river. It has just nine rooms, each with bath and balcony, so it's wise to book ahead. Phone 867652 or contact the tourist office (tel 449683).

Places to Stay – top end

Close to the river end of Tilak Rd is the
Hotel Capri (tel 24643/6), one of the
cheapest of the top-end hotels. Rooms
cost Rs 245/295, Rs 375/425 with air-con,
all with bath and constant hot water.
Checkout time is 12 noon.

The other two main top-end hotels are
alongside the river on Khanpur Rd. The
Cama Hotel (tel 25281/5) offers singles/
doubles for Rs 580/640, plus more expensive
suites. It has all the facilities you would
expect of a multistar hotel including a
swimming pool, liquor shop, currency
exchange, bookshop and restaurants.
Singles/doubles at the nearby *Rivera
Hotel* (tel 24201) cost Rs 407/555 and
deluxe rooms are available for Rs 472/620.
The Rivera has similar facilities to the
Cama.

Across the river on Ashram Rd is
the centrally air-conditioned *Hotel
Karnavati* (tel 402161) where singles/
doubles cost Rs 550/650 and deluxe rooms
are Rs 715/750. On the same road, the
four-star *Hotel Nataraj* (tel 448747) has
rooms at Rs 390/450.

Places to Eat

Ahmedabad is a good place to sample a
Gujarati thali; see the Gujarat food
section. One of the best thali specialists in
Ahmedabad is the *Chetna Restaurant* on
Tilak Rd, where the all-you-can-eat thali
costs Rs 15. It can be a little hard to locate
since the sign is not in Roman script, but it
almost adjoins the Krishna Cinema
(although their sign is also in an Indian
script) and is directly across the road from
the Oriental Building. It's so popular that
you may have to queue to get in, and a
special waiter is provided to ply the
waiting customers with water. 'We ate all
we could', reported one gourmand, 'and
had to lie down in a park to recover'.

The *Hotel Payall* at Khadia Char Rasta
is even more anonymous and charges Rs 15
for their standard Gujarati thali and Rs 5
for dessert. There's a waiting area before
you reach the main restaurant. Another

traveller recommended 'the little hole-in-
the-wall *Vepari Hotel*' between Teen
Darwaja and Manek Chowk, back from
the street along a narrow lane and up
flights of stairs. It's so crowded that you
always have to wait 15 minutes for a table.
'The thalis are great and it's also a good
place for a real taste of old Ahmedabad
and its bustle and energy'.

Plenty of other restaurants in the
central area serve Indian and western
food, but check the menu prices and
service charges before ordering because
you can often end up paying the same for a
meal here as you would at one of the
restaurants in the top-end hotels. Near
Teen Darwaja, the *Neelam Hotel* and the
Paramount are good for western food,
although a meal at the somewhat
pretentious Neelam can set you back Rs 60.
Likewise, at the *Kwality* on Tilak Rd near
the Capri Hotel, a meal of ordinary fish &
chips, alu gobi, nan, lemon soda and ice
cream can cost Rs 60.

If you have this sort of money to spend
on a meal, you might as well eat at either
the *Cama Hotel* or the *Rivera Hotel*.
Although the restaurants at both these
hotels look very expensive, they're
surprisingly cheap with most dishes
averaging around Rs 20 and very
reasonably priced soups, breads and
desserts. The standard of cooking is also
far higher than that at the apparently less
expensive places and you never have to
wait for a table.

On the other side of the river, the air-
conditioned *Sankalp Restaurant* (tel
446231), off Ashram Rd near Dinesh Hall,
is definitely worth at least one visit. This
has to be one of the best south Indian
vegetarian restaurants in India and the
prices are very reasonable indeed. You
won't find a crisper, fresher masala dosa
anywhere and the restaurant boasts the
longest dosas in India – four feet long! Get
a group together and ask the extremely
pleasant manager to cook you one of these
culinary wonders. The restaurant is very
close to the tourist office.

Also on this side of the river, the *Collegian Restaurant* is popular with students from the Gujarat College opposite. The food is mainly Punjabi with lots of variety and is reasonably priced.

For ice cream fans, there are any number of *Havmor* parlours – two along Tilak Rd alone – which also offer snacks and cold flavoured milk. There are a number of clean milk bars where you can get bottles of milk in curious flavours. On the corner of Tilak Rd and Dr Ambedkar Rd, across from the second Havmor, a large open-air fruit juice stand serves superb fruit juices. The *Roopalee Cream Station*, near Indian Airlines and the Roopalee Cinema, is good for drinks, ice cream and snacks, if they finally get round to serving you. I waited a full 25 minutes for an orange juice one afternoon while I watched others who arrived after me being served. By the time I got the drink, they'd already left!

Very close to the Teen Darwaja Gate is the tiny *Gandhi Cold Drinks Bar* with more good ice cream (Rs 2 to Rs 4) and cold drinks.

For an interesting night out in Ahmedabad, try *Vishala*, a rural complex on the southern edge of town which evokes the atmosphere of a Gujarat village. Here, you'll dine in Indian fashion, seated on the floor, while watching puppet shows and local dancing. It's peaceful, friendly and very well done. The cost is Rs 28 for lunch (11 am to 1 pm) and Rs 35 for dinner (7 to 11 pm).

Getting There & Away
Air Indian Airlines flies from Bombay to Ahmedabad (and vice versa) daily, except Monday, Friday and Saturday when there are two flights per day. Another useful connection is the six times a week Delhi/Jaipur/Jodhpur/Ahmedabad/Bombay (and vice versa) flight. There's also a Madras/Bangalore/Ahmedabad flight three times a week and a Bombay/Ahmedabad/Lucknow/Patna/Calcutta flight, also three times a week.

Fares are Rs 740 to Delhi and Rs 1460 to Calcutta, making these about the most expensive internal flights in the country.

Bus Plenty of buses operate around Gujarat and to neighbouring states, but the Gujarat State Transport Corporation buses are almost all standard-issue meat wagons, battered and crowded. If you're travelling long-distance, private buses are preferable. There are a number of agencies running luxury buses to most of the main centres of population. Their only drawback is the ear-splitting macho garbage which blasts from the TV/VCR at the front of the bus.

One such agency in Ahmedabad is Punjab Travels (P) Ltd, with offices at Delhi Gate, Shahpur Rd (tel 23111), Embassy Market (tel 449777), off Ashram Rd, and Shefali Shop Centre (tel 77111), near Paldi Char Rasta. It operates luxury buses to many places within Gujarat, as well as to various cities in Rajasthan, Madhya Pradesh, Maharashtra and Bombay. To Bhavnagar, for instance, the fare is Rs 40 and the journey takes about 4½ hours.

If you're heading north into Rajasthan, a direct bus to Mt Abu (seven hours) is probably faster than a train to Abu Road and a bus from there. A bus takes about six hours to Udaipur and 11 hours to Bombay.

Train Ahmedabad is not on the main broad-gauge line between Delhi and Bombay, although there is a broad-gauge line running south to Bombay and a metre-gauge line running north to Delhi via the major towns of Rajasthan. The trip from Delhi to Ahmedabad is 938 km and takes around 24 hours, except on the four-times-weekly Ashram Express (17 hours) or the twice-weekly Sarvodaya Express (18½ hours). The latter train takes the broad-gauge line from Delhi via Kota and Ratlam to Baroda, then turns north to Ahmedabad. Fares between Delhi and Ahmedabad are Rs 85 in 2nd class, Rs 317 in 1st.

There are plenty of daily trains between Ahmedabad and Bombay. The 492-km trip takes 10 to 15 hours, with the fastest mail trains making the journey in around nine hours. Fares are Rs 54 in 2nd class, Rs 197 in 1st. The Delhi trains on the northward metre-gauge line will get you to Abu Road in about five hours (186 km), to Ajmer in 12 hours (491 km) and to Jaipur in 15 hours (626 km).

Getting Around

Airport Transport Indian Airlines operates a bus between Lal Darwaja and the airport. It connects with all flights and the fare is Rs 10. An auto-rickshaw costs at least Rs 25 and usually more since they refuse to use the meter, while a taxi is upwards of Rs 50.

Local Transport Ahmedabad has the usual local buses and taxis and hordes of completely reckless auto-rickshaw drivers. It is well on the way to displacing Lagos as the world's craziest city as far as traffic is concerned and the auto-rickshaw drivers are hellbent on making each journey a Rambo-like adventure. Venturing out in an auto-rickshaw is a nerve-shattering experience not to be undertaken lightly. I had climbed into one outside the railway station when my Manson-like driver was attacked by a lathi-wielding policeman who managed to dent the cab and very nearly caved in my head. I never found out why. And that was relaxing in comparison to the stunts the driver tried to pull on the way down Tilak Rd. I'd swear he was intent on killing someone. You'll also find that very few of them are willing to use the meters so negotiate fares before you set off and, if you're using them for sightseeing, strike a cast-iron deal before you even sit down. 'Waiting time' is an excuse to double the fare.

The local bus terminal is known universally as Lal Darwaja. The routes, destinations and fares are all posted in Gujarati.

AROUND AHMEDABAD

Sarkhej

The suburb of Sarkhej is only eight km from the centre of Ahmedabad. It is noted for its elegant group of buildings, including the Mausoleum of Azam and Mu'assam, built in 1457 by the brothers who were responsible for Sarkhej's architecture. The architecture here is interesting because the style is almost purely Hindu, with little evidence of the Saracenic influence felt so strongly in Ahmedabad.

As you enter Sarkhej, you pass the Mausoleum of Mahmud Begara and, beside the tank and connected to his tomb, that of his queen, Rajabai (1460). Also by the tank is the tomb of Ahmad Khattu Gaj Buksh, a renowned Muslim saint and spiritual adviser to Ahmed Shah. The saint is said to have died in 1445 at the age of 111. Next to this is the fine mosque – 'the perfection of elegant simplicity'. Like the other buildings, it is notable for the complete absence of arches, a feature of Muslim architecture. The palace, with pavilions and a harem, is also around the tank. The Dutch established a factory in Sarkhej in 1620 to process the indigo grown here.

Batwa

South-east of Ahmedabad, the suburb of Batwa has tombs of a noted Muslim saint (himself the son of another saint) and the saint's son. Batwa also has an important mosque.

Adalaj Vav

Nineteen km north of Ahmedabad, this is one of the finest of the Gujarati step wells, or baolis. It was built by Queen Rudabai in 1499 and provided a cool and secluded retreat during the hot summer months. Buses run here regularly for a fare of about Rs 4.

Cambay

The old seaport of Ahmedabad is to the south-west, at the northern end of the

Gulf of Cambay. At the height of Muslim power in Gujarat, the entire region was known as Cambay and, when the first ambassadors arrived from England in 1583, they bore letters from Queen Elizabeth addressed to Akbar, the 'King of Cambay'. Dutch and Portuguese factories were established in the port before the British arrived, but the rise of Surat eclipsed Cambay and, when its port silted up, the city's decline was inevitable.

Nal Sarovar

Between November and February, this 116-square-km lake is home to vast flocks of indigenous and migratory birds. Ducks, geese, pelicans and flamingoes are best seen early in the morning and in the evening. A *Holiday Home* offers accommodation near the lake which has to be booked through the tourist office in Ahmedabad.

Lothal

About 80 km south of Ahmedabad, towards Bhavnagar, this site is of great interest to archaeologists. The city which stood here 4500 years ago was clearly related to the Indus Valley cities of Moenjodaro and Harappa, both in Pakistan. It has the same neatly laid-out street pattern, the same carefully assembled brickwork and the same scientific drainage system.

The name Lothal actually means 'mound of the dead' in Gujarati, as does Moenjodaro in Sindhi. At its peak, this was probably one of the most important ports on the subcontinent and trade may have been conducted with the civilisations of Mesopotamia, Egypt and Persia.

Places to Stay The Tourist Corporation of Gujarat runs the *Toran Holiday Home*, which has 10 dorm beds for Rs 15 each and two double rooms for Rs 50. Checkout time is 9 am.

Getting There & Away Lothal is a day trip from Ahmedabad. You can reach it by rail, disembarking at Bhurkhi on the Ahmedabad to Bhavnagar railway line,

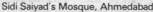

Sidi Saiyad's Mosque, Ahmedabad

from where you can walk or take a bus. Alternatively, there are direct buses from Ahmedabad.

Modhera

The ruined Sun Temple of Modhera was built by King Bhimdev I (1026-27) and bears some resemblance to the later, and far better known, Sun Temple of Konarak in the state of Orissa. Like that temple, it was designed so that the dawn sun shone on the image of Surya, the Sun God, at the time of the equinoxes. The main hall and shrine are reached through a pillared porch and the temple exterior is intricately and delicately carved. As at Somnath, this fine temple was ruined by Mahmud of Ghazni. The temple is open from 8 am to 6 pm daily.

Places to Stay There is a *PWD Rest House* but foreigners find it difficult to get a bed here for the night.

Getting There & Away Modhera is 106 km north-west of Ahmedabad. There are direct buses to Modhera, or you can take the train to Mahesana and then catch a bus for the 40 km trip to Modhera.

Unjha

A little north of Mahesana and a base for those visiting the Modhera Temple, the town of Unjha is interesting for the marriage customs of the Kadwakanbis who live in this region. Marriages occur only once every 11 years and, on that day, every unmarried girl over 40 days old must be wed. If no husband can be found, a proxy wedding takes place and the bride immediately becomes a 'widow'. She later remarries when a suitable husband shows up.

Further north again is Sidhpur where you'll find the very fragmented ruins of an ancient temple. This region was an important centre for growing opium poppies.

Patan

About 120 km north-west of Ahmedabad,

this was an ancient Hindu capital before being sacked by Mahmud of Ghazni in 1024. Now a pale shadow of its former self, it still has over 100 Jain temples and is famous for the manufacture of beautifully designed Patola silk saris. There's also another step well here.

Places to Stay The only hotel is the *Hotel Neerav*, about 500 metres from the bus station, next to Kohinoor Talkies. Double rooms cost Rs 60.

Getting There & Away Patan is 25 km north-west of the Mahesana railway station, which also serves as a departure point for Modhera.

GANDHINAGAR (population 30,000)

Although Ahmedabad initially became the capital of Gujarat state when the old state of Bombay was split into Maharashtra and Gujarat in 1960, a new capital was planned 32 km north-east on the west bank of the Sabarmati. Named Gandhinagar after Mahatma Gandhi, who was born in Gujarat, it is India's second planned city after Chandigarh and, like that city, is laid out in numbered sectors. Construction of the city commenced in 1965 and the secretariat was moved there in 1970.

Places to Stay

Gandhinagar has an excellent *Youth Hostel* in sector 16 and, in sector 11, there is the *Panthik Ashram* government rest house. You'll find other rest houses and guest houses at Pethapur and opposite Sachivalaya. The tourist information centre (tel 2211) is also at Sachivalaya but is more or less moribund.

Getting There & Away

Buses from Ahmedabad cost about Rs 2.

BARODA (Vadodara) (population 600,000)

Baroda was the capital of the princely Gaekwad state prior to independence. Today, it is a pleasant, medium-sized city with some interesting museums and art galleries and a fine park. It's a good place for a short pause.

Information & Orientation

The railway station, bus stand and a cluster of cheaper hotels are all on one side of the city. The tourist office is in a small, upstairs room across from the station to the left. A road runs straight out from the station, across the river by the Sayaji Bagh and into the main part of town.

Sayaji Bagh & Baroda Museum

This extensive park is a popular spot for an evening stroll and also has a small zoo. A minirailway encircles the park. Within the park is the Baroda Museum & Art Gallery, open from 9.30 am to 4.45 pm daily, except Saturday when it opens at 10 am. The museum has various exhibits, while the gallery has Moghul miniatures and a collection of European masters.

Also within the park grounds is the relatively new planetarium where there is an English-language performance each evening,

Maharaja Fateh Singh Museum

A little south of the centre, this royal art collection includes European works by Raphael, Titian and Murillo and examples of Greco-Roman, Chinese and Japanese art, as well as Indian exhibits. The museum is in the palace grounds and is open from 9 am to 12 noon and 3 to 6 pm between July and March, 4 to 7 pm from April to June. It is closed on Mondays.

Other Attractions

The flamboyant Laxmi Vilas Palace has a large collection of armour and sculptures but is not normally open to the public. The Naulakhi Well, a fine baoli, is 50 metres north of the palace. These interesting

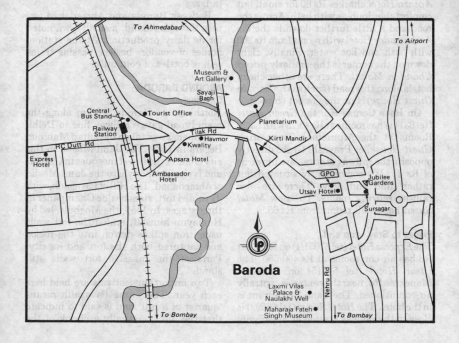

multilevel wells are unique to western India. There are others in Ahmedabad as well as just outside the city.

The Railway Staff College now occupies the Pratap Vilas Palace; there are a number of other palaces in the city. The Gaekwad rulers' family vault, the Kirti Mandir, is decorated with murals created by Indian artist Nandial Bose. The town centre is built around a lake swarming with fish – vendors sell food to throw to them.

Tours

Check with the tourist office about the daily tours of Baroda.

Places to Stay – bottom end

There are a lot of cheaper hotels within walking distance of the railway station. If you head straight out from the station and take the second road on the right, you'll find the *Laxmi Lodge* where rooms start at Rs 65. The pleasant and well-kept *Apsara Hotel* charges Rs 80 for small but comfortable doubles with bath. Across the road and a little further down is the big *Ambassador Hotel* with rooms from Rs 200 with bath and hot water. Finally, right down on the corner is the similarly priced *Chandan Mahal*. There are other cheap hotels along this road (such as the *Baroda Guest House*), but they're not so good.

On Race Course Rd, the *Green Hotel* (tel 63111) has rooms at Rs 40/75 with bath. Rooms at the *Municipal Corporation Guest House*, or Pravashi Gruh, directly opposite the railway station, are upwards of Rs 40. It's conveniently situated but rather drab and grey. There are also railway *retiring rooms*. The new *Motel Suren* has small rooms from Rs 65.

Places to Stay – top end

The *Express Hotel* (tel 67051/4) on R C Dutt Rd has air-con rooms at Rs 450/550. The *Utsav Hotel* (tel 51415) on Professor Manekrao Rd, near the centre, is centrally air-conditioned. The Tana Restaurant is in the hotel. The *Hotel Surya* (tel 66592) is close to the railway station at Sayajigunj

and has rooms at Rs 200/290, Rs 350/400 with air-con.

Places to Eat

The *Ambassador Hotel* is popular for its excellent thalis. Along the main road from the station towards the gardens and the river, there's a reasonable *Kwality*, with good lunch-time snacks on its verandah, and a *Havmor*. The railway station also has a good restaurant.

Getting There & Away

Air There are flights to Baroda from Bombay and Delhi.

Train Baroda is 112 km south of Ahmedabad and 419 km north of Bombay. As it's on the main Bombay to Ahmedabad railway line, plenty of trains pass through, or you can go by bus. Rail fares to Bombay are Rs 51 in 2nd class, Rs 178 in 1st. Fares to Ahmedabad are Rs 16 in 2nd class, Rs 64 in 1st.

Between Baroda and Ahmedabad you pass through Anand, a small town noted for its dairy production. At the station, hordes of vendors besiege passing trains selling bottles of cold milk.

AROUND BARODA
Champaner

North-east of Baroda, 47 km along the main broad-gauge railway line to Delhi, Champaner was taken by Sultan Mahmud Begara in 1484. The Jami Masjid in this city is one of the finest mosques in Gujarat and is similar in style to the Jami Masjid of Ahmedabad. The Hill of Pavagadh, with its ruined fort, rises beside Champaner in three stages. In 1553, the Moghuls, led by Humayun himself, scaled the fort walls using iron spikes driven into the rocks, and captured both the fort and its city. Parts of the massive fort walls still stand.

Two important festivals are held here each year. The name Pavagadh means 'quarter of a hill' and is said to indicate that the hill is actually a chunk of the

Places to Stay The state tourist organisation runs the *Hotel Champaner*. It has 15 dorm beds for Rs 20 per person and 32 double rooms for Rs 100.

Dabhoi Fort

The 13th-century fort of Dabhoi is 29 km south-east of Baroda. A fine example of Hindu military architecture, it is notable for the design of its four gateways – particularly the Hira, or 'Diamond Gate'.

Dakor

Equidistant from Baroda and Ahmedabad, the Temple of Ranchodrai in Dakor is sacred to Lord Krishna and is a major centre for the Sharad Purnima festival in October or November.

BROACH (Bharuch) (population 120,000)

This very old town was mentioned in historical records nearly 2000 years ago. In the 17th century, English and Dutch factories were established here. The fort overlooks the wide Narbada (or Narmada) River from its hilltop location and, at its base, is the Jami Masjid, constructed from a Jain temple. On the riverbank, outside the city to the east, is the Temple of Bhrigu Rishi, from which the city took its name, Bhrigukachba, later shortened to Bharuch.

The town of Suklatirth near Broach has a State Tourism Corporation of Gujarat *Toran Holiday Home* (tel 38) with double rooms for Rs 30. The nearby island of Kabirwad, in the river, features a gigantic banyan tree which covers a hectare.

SURAT (population 600,000)

Surat stands on the banks of the River Tapti and was once one of western India's major ports and trading towns. Two hundred years ago, it had a bigger population than it does today and was far more important than Bombay. Parsis first settled in Surat in the 12th century; they had earlier been centred 100 km south in Sanjan, where they had fled from Persia five centuries before. In 1573, the city fell to Akbar after a prolonged siege. It then became an important Moghul trading port and also the point of departure for Mecca-bound Muslim pilgrims.

Surat soon became a wealthy city and, in 1612, the British established a trading factory there, followed by the Dutch in 1616 and the French in 1664. Portuguese power on the west coast had been severely curtailed by a crushing naval defeat at the hands of the British settlement in India. In 1664, Moghul power and prestige suffered a severe blow when the Maratha leader Shivaji sacked the town. In a classic display of the British stiff upper lip, Sir George Oxenden sent a message to Shivaji from the strongly defended English factory, saying that he should 'save the labour of his servants running to and fro on messages and come himself with all his army'. Perhaps Shivaji took him seriously because the English factory was not attacked.

Although the English factory later

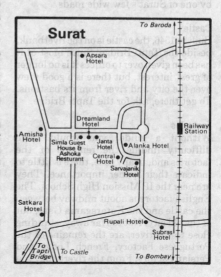

transferred its 'presidency' to Bombay, Surat continued to prosper. A dock was built in 1720, followed by two British shipyards. By 1759, when the British took virtually full control over the city's ruler, Moghul power was long past its prime and, by 1800, the city was in British hands. Surat is no longer of any importance as a port, but it is a major industrial centre, especially for the manufacture of textiles and chemicals.

Despite its industrial importance, the city is of little interest to travellers, except those with a fascination for urban decay, noise and pollution. If Ahmedabad is bad in this respect, Surat is horrific. It might just be tolerable if the city had even one redeeming feature, but it doesn't.

Orientation
An eight-km-long wall once encircled Surat on one side, while the Tapti River forms the other. The walls were made of mud but, after the sack of the city by Shivaji, they were reconstructed in brick. The railway station, with many cheaper hotels in its immediate vicinity, is connected to the old fort beside the river by one of Surat's few wide roads.

Castle
Built in 1546, the castle is on the riverbank, beside the Tapti Bridge. Since most of it has been given over to offices it is no longer of great interest, but there is a good view over the city and river from its bastions. To get there, ask for the Tapti Bridge.

Factories
Without a guide, you would have difficulty finding the remains of the factories and, in any case, there is little to indicate their former importance. They are near the IP Mission High School. The English factory is about midway between the castle and the Kataragama Gate, out of the old city. Not too far away, standing close to the river, are the remains of the Portuguese Factory, French Lodge and Persian Factory. From the riverbank, you

can see the Tapti Bridge to your left and, across the river to your right, you'll see the mosque-studded suburb of Rander. There's a small temple by the river which is dedicated to Hanuman.

Cemeteries
The now very run-down, overrun and neglected English Cemetery is just beyond the Kataragama Gate, to the right of the main road. Many of the tombstones mark the graves of children under five years of age. As you enter the cemetery, the huge mausoleum to the right is that of Sir George Oxenden, who died in 1669. The structure is actually a tomb within a tomb, since his brother was buried here 10 years earlier and a larger mausoleum was constructed over that tomb. Another large tomb next to it is said to be that of Gerald Aungier, the next president of the English factory. Like any scrap of waste ground in India, the English Cemetery has become a public toilet and the imposing mausoleums are in a sorry state.

Back track towards the city and, about 500 metres after the Kataragama Gate and some 100 metres off the road to the left (to the right if you are coming from the centre), you'll find the Dutch Cemetery. The massive Mausoleum of Baron Adriaan van Reede, who died in 1691, was once decorated with frescoes and woodcarvings. Note the inscription on the wall; 'Souratta' rates capital letters while lesser 'bombai' is in lower case. Adjoining the Dutch Cemetery is the Armenian Cemetery.

Other Attractions
Surat has a number of mosques and Jain, Hindu and Parsi temples. Cotton, silk and the manufacture of bangles are important industries here. Nearby Rander, five km across the Hope Bridge, was built on the site of a very ancient Hindu city which had been taken by the Muslims in 1225. Swally (Suvali) was the old port for Surat, 19 km to the west. It was off Swally, in 1615, that Portuguese colonial aspirations in India were ended by the British navy.

Places to Stay – bottom end

There are lots of hotels near the railway station but none stand out. They're all within walking distance. In the rock-bottom bracket, the *Rupali Hotel* has dorm beds for Rs 15, doubles with bath for Rs 65 and singles with common bath for Rs 33. Facilities are basic. Very similar to this are the adjacent *Adarsh Guest House, Pavas* and *Subras*.

On the left, down the road facing the station, the *Janta Hotel* has doubles with bath for Rs 45 and singles/doubles with common bath for Rs 20/40. You'll get a good idea of the hotel's standards as you climb the greasy, filthy stairs to the 2nd-floor reception area. The staff are not particularly helpful. On the same street, the *Simla Guest House* is better value but otherwise unremarkable. It has doubles with bath for Rs 110 and singles/doubles with common bath for Rs 34/68. Another cheapie close to the station is the large *Central Hotel* where ordinary singles/doubles cost Rs 61/110 and deluxe singles/doubles are Rs 79/152.

Places to Stay – middle

Good value at the lower end of this category is the new *Sarvajanik Hotel*, close to the railway station. It's pleasant, though the staff are indifferent, and offers singles for Rs 73 to Rs 85 and doubles for Rs 122, all with bath and hot water. The returnable deposit of Rs 100 pays for a lock and key.

In the same block as the Rupali, the *Hotel Amar*, a new building with very friendly staff, is also good. Singles/doubles/triples cost Rs 70/122/150 and deluxe air-con doubles are also available for Rs 200. All rooms have bath and hot water.

Surat's best hotel is on top of the textile market, about two km from the railway station. The *Tex Palazzo Hotel* (tel 43002), Ring Rd, has singles/doubles for Rs 150/275, Rs 230/350 with air-con. It has all the usual services and a restaurant.

Places to Eat

The *Tex Palazzo Hotel* boasts India's first revolving restaurant and, as with so many revolving restaurants around the world, the food takes a distant second place to the view. At least it's not outrageously expensive, but the splendours of Surat unfold below you through windows nearly as dirty as those on the average Indian bus! Back at ground level, the same hotel serves a good Gujarati thali.

Close to the railway station and next to the Central Hotel, the *Gaurav Restaurant* offers excellent and very cheap south Indian dishes (masala dosa costs Rs 3.50). It's clean, popular and highly recommended. For a more substantial meal, try the *Hotel Ashoka* (actually a restaurant, not a hotel), next to the Simla Guest House. It's run by Sikhs and the food is good without being really special.

AROUND SURAT

There are a number of beaches near Surat. Only 16 km away, Dumas is a popular health resort. Hajira is 28 km from the city and Ubhrat is 42 km out, while Tithal is 108 km away and only five km from Valsad on the Bombay to Baroda rail line.

Twenty-nine km south of Surat, Navsari has been a headquarters for the Parsi community since the earliest days of their settlement in India. Udvada, only 10 km north of Vapi, the station for Daman, has the oldest Parsi sacred fire in India. It is said that the fire was brought from Persia to Diu, on the opposite coast of the Gulf of Cambay, in 700 AD. Sanjan, in the extreme south of the state, is the small port where they first landed. A pillar marks the spot.

DAMAN

Right in the south of Gujarat, the 56-square-km enclave of Daman was, along with Diu, taken from the Portuguese at the same time as Goa. For a time, Daman and Diu were governed from Goa but both are now Union Territories governed from New Delhi. Daman's main role now seems to be as a place to buy alcohol, since the surrounding state of Gujarat is completely 'dry'. The streets of Daman are lined with bars selling beer, 'Finest Scotch Whisky – Made in India' and various other spirits such as feni (distilled from fermented cashew nuts or coconuts).

The Portuguese seized Daman in 1531 and were officially ceded the region by Bahadur, Shah of Gujarat, in 1559. There is still a lingering Portuguese flavour to the town, with its fine old forts and a number of churches, but it is definitely not a smaller version of Goa. The town is divided by the Damao Ganga River. The northern part of the town is known as Nani Daman, or 'little' Daman, and contains the hotels, restaurants, bars and so on. In the southern part, known as Moti Daman, or 'big' Daman, government buildings and churches are enclosed within an imposing wall.

Like Goa, Daman is beside the sea but its beaches bear no relation to the glowing, golden stretches of sand further south. Daman's beaches are grey, drab, dirty and dismal and function as local latrines.

Churches

The Se Cathedral in the Moti Daman fort dates from the 17th century and is totally Iberian. It's less impressive than the Church of Our Lady of the Rosary, where ancient Portuguese tombstones are set into the cool, damp floor. The altar is a masterpiece of intricately carved, gold-painted wood. Light filters through the dusty windows, illuminating wooden panels painted with scenes of Christ and the apostles.

Other Attractions

You can walk around the ramparts of the Nani Daman fort. They're a good place from which to watch the fish market and the activity on the small fishing fleet which anchors alongside, but there's otherwise nothing of much interest.

Near the river on the Nani Daman side is an interesting Jain temple. If you enquire in the temple office, a white-robed caretaker will show you around. The walls inside are completely covered with glassed-over 18th-century murals depicting the life of Mahavira, who lived around 500 BC.

Places to Stay

Most of the hotels are on Seaface Rd. The *Hotel Brighton* is popular and is therefore often full. It offers doubles (no singles) with common bath for Rs 30 downstairs and Rs 40 upstairs. Although there's no hot water, it's a pleasant place to stay. The *Hotel Sovereign*, almost opposite, is fairly basic. Ground-floor singles/doubles/triples with common bath cost Rs 25/30/40 and upper-floor singles/doubles/triples with bath are Rs 30/50/60.

Just off Seaface Rd, the *Hotel Marina* is one of the few surviving Portuguese-style houses. The reception area indicates that it must once have been a very fine house but, although it still has a lot of character, it's unfortunately been allowed to decay and can only be described as very basic. The rooms are large and airy but the bed sheets are far from clean and full of holes. Singles/doubles with common bath cost Rs 30/40. The staff are friendly and there's a bar and restaurant downstairs.

Although more expensive, the very popular *Hotel Gurukripa* (tel 446/7) is good value at Rs 75/100 for singles/doubles, Rs 175/200 with air-con. The rooms are clean and pleasant, the staff are friendly and a restaurant on the ground floor serves very tasty food, though it's not cheap. It's undoubtedly the best restaurant in town. Checkout time is 12 noon.

Next to the taxi stand are two other mid-range hotels, the *Hotel Diamond* and the *Hotel Paradise*. Both are modern, clean and well kept with friendly staff. Prices are roughly the same at Rs 75/100 for singles/doubles and Rs 200 for air-con doubles.

Houses can be rented on the Moti Daman side of town.

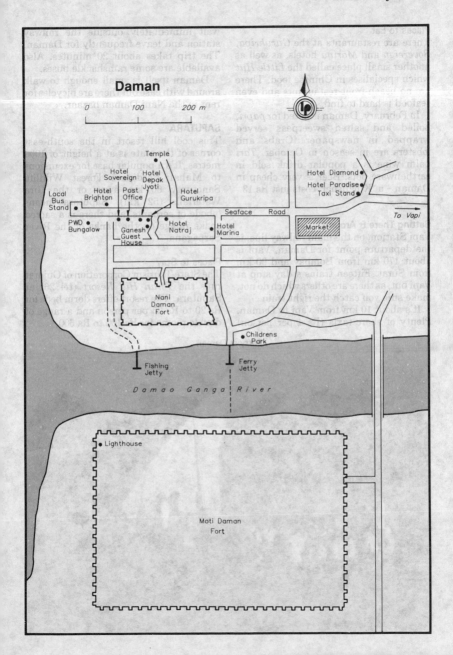

Daman

0   100   200 m

Temple

Hotel Sovereign

Hotel Depak Jyoti

Hotel Gurukripa

Hotel Brighton

Local Bus Stand

Post Office

Hotel Diamond

Hotel Paradise

Taxi Stand

PWD Bungalow

Ganesh Guest House

Hotel Natraj

Hotel Marina

Seaface   Road

Market

To Vapi

Nani Daman Fort

Childrens Park

Fishing Jetty

Ferry Jetty

Damao Ganga River

Lighthouse

Moti Daman Fort

Places to Eat

There are restaurants at the *Gurukripa, Sovereign* and *Marina* hotels, as well as another small place called the *Little Hut* which specialises in Chinese food. There are no beach-front restaurants and even seafood is hard to find.

In February, Daman is noted for *papri*, boiled and salted sweetpeas served wrapped in newspaper. Crabs and lobsters are in season in October. *Tari* palm wine is a popular drink sold in earthenware pots. Beer is very cheap in Daman – a 'Kingfisher' costs just Rs 13.

Getting There & Around

Vapi Station, on the main railway line, is the departure point for Daman. Vapi is about 170 km from Bombay and 90 km from Surat. Fifteen trains a day stop at Vapi but, as there are others which do not, make sure you catch the right train.

It's about 10 km from Vapi to Daman. Plenty of share-taxis (Rs 4 per person) wait immediately outside the railway station and leave frequently for Daman. The trip takes about 20 minutes. Also available are some ramshackle buses.

Daman itself is small enough to walk around with ease but there are bicycles for rent in the Nani Daman bazaar.

SAPUTARA

This cool hill resort in the south-east corner of the state is at a height of 1000 metres. It's a popular base for excursions to Mahal Bardipara Forest Wildlife Sanctuary 60 km away or the Gira Waterfalls (52 km). Saputara means 'abode of serpents' and there is a sacred snake image on the banks of the River Sarpagana.

Places to Stay

The State Tourism Corporation of Gujarat runs the *Toran Hill Resort* (tel 26) at Saputara. The resort offers dorm beds for Rs 20 to Rs 25 per person and a range of double rooms for Rs 100 to Rs 600.

Ferry at Daman

Saurashtra

The often bleak plains of Saurashtra on the Kathiawar Peninsula are inhabited by colourful, friendly but reserved people. Those in the country are distinctively dressed – the men wear white turbans, cross-laced smocks (short-waisted and long-sleeved) and jodhpurs (baggy seat and drainpipe legs) and often sport golden ear-studs. The women are nearly as colourful as the women of Rajasthan and wear embroidered halter-neck tops.

Although somewhat off the main tourist routes, Saurashtra is a pleasant area to travel around with very interesting – sometimes spectacular – temple sites and cities to explore, not to mention some beautiful beaches and the Sasan Gir Lion Sanctuary. The network of metre-gauge railway lines is extensive but the trains are very slow and most people choose buses, preferably of the limited-stop deluxe variety.

The peninsula took its name from the Kathi tribespeople who used to roam the area at night stealing whatever was not locked into the many village forts, or *kots*. Around Kathiawar, you may notice long lines of memorial stones known as *palias* – men are usually depicted riding on large horses while women ride on wheels, showing that they were in carriages.

BHAVNAGAR (population 300,000)
Founded as a port in 1723, Bhavnagar is still an important trading post for the cotton goods manufactured in Gujarat. The Bhavnagar lock gate keeps ships afloat in the city's port at low tide. On the surface, Bhavnagar isn't the most interesting place to visit and few travellers get here. It does, however, have a beautiful old bazaar area with overhanging wooden balconies, thousands of little shops, lots of local colour and not a tourist in sight.

Orientation
Bhavnagar is a very sprawling city with distinctly separate old and new sections. The bus station is in the new part of town and the railway station is at the far end of the old town around 2½ km away. To complicate matters, private bus companies usually have their own depots which are sometimes a long way from the bus station.

There are no cheap hotels around the bus station so, if you're on a budget, take an auto-rickshaw into the old town. Even there, the choice is very limited.

The Bazaar
The bazaar is well worth a day's exploration if you enjoy taking in the sights, sounds and smells of an extremely busy and colourful old town untouched by tourism.

Takhteshwar Temple
This temple sits on the highest hillock in Bhavnagar. The views over the city and out into the Gulf of Cambay are excellent but the temple itself is of minor interest.

Places to Stay – bottom end
The only cheap hotels in Bhavnagar are in the old bazaar area and there's very little choice. Perhaps the best value is the *Shital Hotel* (tel 28360), Amba Chowk, Mali Tekra, right in the middle of the bazaar area. It's clean and newly painted and the manager speaks English. Singles/doubles with bath cost Rs 30/45, Rs 25/35 with common bath. Dorm beds are also available for Rs 15 per person. Not far from here is the *Vrindavan Hotel*. It's well signposted but the entrance can still be quite difficult to find. This huge, rambling old place has a somewhat Dickensian atmosphere, though the exterior has been freshly painted. Inside, it's pretty basic. Singles/doubles with bath are Rs 30/50 and rooms with common bath cost Rs 25/40. Going up in price, the extremely pleasant *Hotel Mini* (tel 23113), Station Rd, is about two minutes walk from the railway station. It's very clean and quiet with a mellow atmosphere

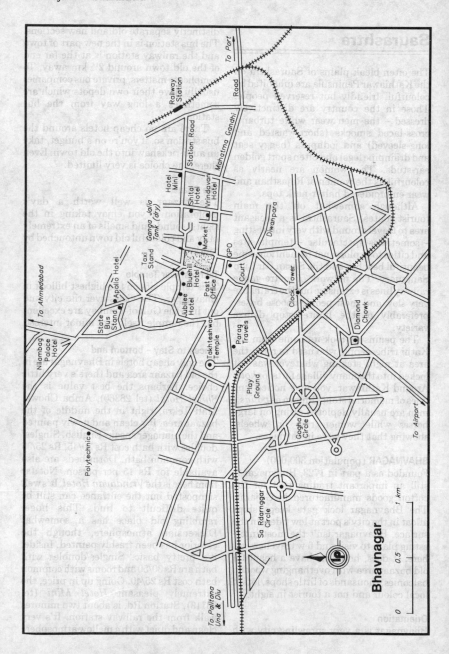

Bhavnagar

and is run by a very gentle old man who speaks fluent English. Singles/doubles with bath cost Rs 45/75, Rs 110/135 with air-con.

Places to Stay – middle

Directly opposite the bus station, the *Apollo Hotel* (tel 25249) is where most travellers seem to stay, though it's somewhat overpriced. The cheapest rooms cost Rs 115/146 and there are more expensive air-con rooms for Rs 202/246 and Rs 219/269.

Down the road a little from the Apollo and across the other side of the park/gardens are two adjacent newly built mid-range hotels, next to the taxi stand. The *Bluehill Hotel* (tel 26591/4) is extremely pleasant and immaculately maintained. Most of the rooms have a balcony and all have wall-to-wall carpeting, colour TV and bathroom with constant hot water. Singles/doubles cost Rs 125/150, Rs 180/250 with air-con, and there are two vegetarian restaurants. The *Jubilee Hotel* (tel 26624) offers similar facilities but is slightly cheaper at Rs 115/140 for singles/doubles and Rs 167/218 for air-con rooms. The hotel has two restaurants, one vegetarian, the other non-vegetarian.

Places to Stay – top end

If you can possibly afford it, the most interesting place to stay is the *Nilambag Palace* (tel 29323/4), above the bus station on the road in from Ahmedabad. As its name suggests, the Nilambag is a former maharaja's palace packed with memorabilia from a bygone age and surrounded by well-tended gardens. Rooms are surprisingly cheap with singles/doubles at just Rs 180/295, more expensive rooms at Rs 310/425 and 'executive' rooms at Rs 498/620. Breakfast (Rs 55), lunch (Rs 90) and dinner (Rs 100) are available and, at these prices, you can expect a meal fit for a king and served accordingly. The staff here are very friendly indeed.

Places to Eat

Apart from the usual hole-in-the-wall cafes in the bazaar area, Bhavnagar has very few cheap restaurants. Just about the only readily accessible place is the *Nataraj Restaurant* which has good food and a two-page menu of ice-cream goodies! Look for the Vadelal Ice Cream sign on the far side of the now-dry tank (Ganga Jalia).

Also convenient are the restaurants at the *Apollo, Bluehill* and *Jubilee* hotels. Prices at all three are pretty reasonable and the food is good – a thali at the Bluehill, for instance, costs Rs 20 with no charge for refills.

Getting There & Away

Air Indian Airlines flies Bombay/Bhavnagar/Rajkot and vice versa daily. Vayudoot flies between Surat and Bhavnagar and vice versa several times per week.

Bus State transport buses connect Bhavnagar with Ahmedabad and other centres in the region but they're pretty ramshackle affairs and most travellers prefer the private buses. The timetable at the state bus stand in Bhavnagar is entirely in Gujarati.

The main private bus company is Punjab Travels (tel 26333), Parag Travel Agency, Waghawadi Rd, just below the Takhteshwar Temple. It operates buses to Ahmedabad at 6.30 am and 4 pm each day. These cost Rs 40 and take 4½ hours.

If you're heading from Bhavnagar to Diu or Sasan Gir Lion Sanctuary, take a state transport bus to Una and change there. Ordinary buses leave for Una daily at 5.30, 6.30 and 8.30 am and a 'semiluxury' bus departs at 5 pm. You can use the same buses to get to Palitana, with services to this town much more frequent than those to Una.

A private taxi from Bhavnagar to Diu and return costs Rs 500 (Rs 1.50 per km) so you'd have to get a group together to make it worthwhile.

Train Bhavnagar is 244 km by road from Ahmedabad and about 270 km by rail. The rail trip takes about seven hours and costs Rs 34 in 2nd class, Rs 123 in 1st.

PALITANA

Situated 56 km from Bhavnagar, the town of Palitana is little more than a gateway to Shatrunjaya, the 'place of victory'. The 600-metre ascent from the town to the hilltop is a walk of some two km. Over a period of 900 years, 863 temples have been built here. The hilltop is dedicated entirely to the gods; at dusk, even the priests depart from the temples, leaving them deserted.

Almost all the temples are Jain and this hill, one of Jainism's holiest pilgrimage places, is another illustration of their belief that merit is derived from constructing temples. The hilltops are bounded by sturdy walls and the temples are grouped into nine enclosures or *tunks* – each with a central major temple and many minor ones clustered around. Some of the earliest temples here were built in the 11th century but, in the 14th and 15th centuries, the Muslims destroyed them, so the current temples date from the 16th century onwards.

The hilltop affords a very fine view in all directions; on a clear day you can see the Gulf of Cambay beyond Bhavnagar. The most notable of the temples is dedicated to Shri Adishwara, the first Jain tirthankar. Note the frieze of dragons around the temple. Adjacent to this temple is the Muslim shrine of Angar Pir. Women who want to have children make offerings of miniature cradles at this shrine.

Built in 1618 by a wealthy Jain merchant, the Chaumukh, or 'four-faced' shrine, has images of Adinath facing out in the four cardinal directions. Other important temples are those to Kumar Pal, Sampriti Raj and Vimal Shah. There are so many marble temples on the hill

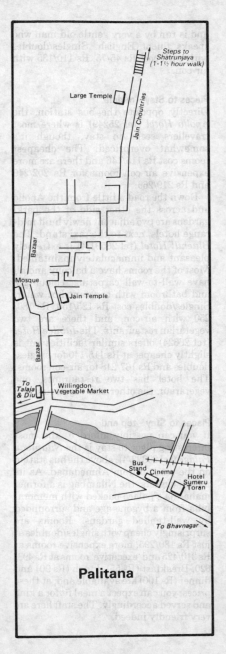

Palitana

summit that, from a distance, it looks like a giant, glistening white wedding cake. The temples are open from 7 am to 7 pm; temple jewels are shown between 9 am and 3 pm. Image washing is at 9.45 am, puja at 10.45 am.

You'll need a photography permit to take a camera up the hill – enquire at your hotel. You will be asked for the permit at the main entrance. (There are two entrances – the main one is reached by taking the left-hand fork as you near the top and the other by the right-hand fork.)

A horse cart to the base of the hill costs Rs 3 per person or Rs 5 if you're alone. The walk is time consuming but not strenuous. You can be carried up the hill in a *dooli* swing chair for Rs 30 (Rs 40 round trip), as do quite a few affluent and obese pilgrims.

Valabhipur

North of Palitana, this ancient city was once the capital of this part of India. Extensive ruins have been located and archaeological finds are exhibited in a museum, but there's little to see apart from scattered stones.

Places to Stay

Palitana has scores of choultries (pilgrims' rest houses) but, unless you're a Jain, you're unlikely to be allowed to stay at any of them. The *Hotel Sumeru Toran* (tel 227) on Station Rd is a Gujarat Tourism enterprise which offers excellent accommodation at reasonable prices. Double rooms with bath and balcony are Rs 100 a double, Rs 200 with air-con, and there are a total of 32 dorm beds at Rs 20 per person. Meals are available at the hotel.

The *Hotel Shravak* (tel 328), opposite the bus station, has rooms at Rs 40/70 and more expensive rooms with air-con. Beds in the rather crowded dormitories cost Rs 15, but there are no lockers so the Sumeru Toran dorms are better.

Places to Eat

The *Sumeru Toran* and *Shravak* have excellent restaurants with full Gujarati thalis for Rs 12 (Sumeru) or Rs 10 (Shravak) as well as Punjabi food. Down the alley towards the cinema, beside the Shravak, a wildly busy 24-hour snack place offers puris, sabzi, curd, roasted peppers and *ganthia*, varieties of fried dough.

Getting There & Away

Air There are flights to Bhavnagar, the nearest airport, from Bombay (Indian Airlines) and Surat (Vayudoot).

Bus If you're coming from the north, plenty of state transport buses make the 30 to 45-minute (or more) trip from Bhavnagar. The fare is Rs 5 (pay on the bus) but, as they tend to be very crowded, it's advisable to buy a Rs 1 seat reservation ticket beforehand.

Train Express trains make the trip from Ahmedabad in nine to 11 hours with a change at Sihor shortly before Palitana. Express buses take 4½ hours, an hour less than the ordinary ones, and the fare is Rs 20. Trains between Bhavnagar and Palitana take about two hours.

To/from Diu The route between Palitana and Diu, taken by most travellers, is Palitana/Talaja/Mahuva/Una/Diu. If you're going in that direction, it's advisable to travel early in the day (before 10 am). As soon as the temperature rises, local people behave as though a pack of lepers was advancing down the main street intent on mischief. Even Kerala buses are like a vicarage tea party by comparison.

The first part of the journey isn't too trying, even if you set off late. If you're interested in Jain temples, Talaja also has hilltop monuments though they're nowhere near as extensive as those at Palitana. However, most of the buses which pass through Talaja originate elsewhere (usually in Bhavnagar, Mahuva or Una) and are always full to bursting when they arrive. Despite the obvious impossibility of getting on, a good percentage of those who have been waiting manage this feat – including Geoff, who then spent 2½ hours hanging from a roof rail, a pack on his back and a shoulder bag in one hand, being jostled like crazy every time the bus stopped (which was frequently) because nobody could get past him.

Frequent buses make the one-hour trip along the rough road from Palitana to Talaja. Take the 7 am bus if you're heading for Diu. The Talaja to Mahuva (pronounced 'Mauwa') route is serviced by fairly regular buses through the morning and early afternoon, but very few run in the late afternoon. The trip takes one to 1½ hours. Some buses from Palitana continue to Una so you won't have to change.

Between Mahuva and Una, there are plenty of buses all day until 5 pm. They take about 3½ hours. Bus fares from Palitana to Una total less than Rs 20. Few buses connect Una and Ghoghla, the tiny sliver of mainland Diu, so most people take an auto-rickshaw, motorcycle-rickshaw or shared taxi. The locals pay Rs 2.50 for this trip, but you'll be asked for Rs 10 to Rs 15, even Rs 25 to Rs 50 in some cases.

Tell them firmly where to go! The journey takes about 20 minutes and your passport (and, very occasionally, your pack) may be checked as you cross from Gujarat to Diu. Rickshaws and other transport to Ghoghla doesn't leave from outside the bus stand in Una but from another street about three minutes walk away. Rickshaw drivers will, naturally, offer to take you there for Rs 2 to Rs 3.

Transport between Ghoghla and Diu is by ferry, though a very expensive and totally unnecessary bridge is being constructed between the mainland and the island. You'll be dropped off at the entrance to Ghoghla and must then walk about a km down the main street to the ferries. They cross when full throughout the day and evening. The crossing takes three or four minutes and costs Rs 0.50.

DIU (population 36,000)

One of India's undiscovered gems, this was the first landing point for the Parsis when they fled from Persia, although they stayed only three years. Like Daman and Goa, Diu was a Portuguese colony until taken over by India in 1961. Along with Daman, it is still governed from New

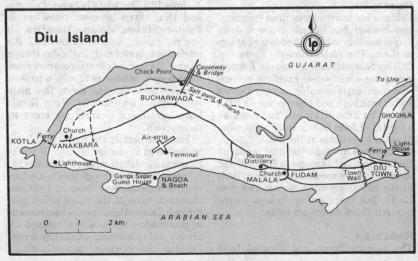

Delhi as a Union Territory rather than as part of Gujarat. The former colony includes the island of Diu itself, about 11 km long by three km wide, separated from the coast by a narrow channel. There are also two tiny mainland enclaves. One of these, on which the village of Ghoghla stands, is the entry point to Diu if you arrive through the town of Una. Diu's crowning glory is the huge fort, a sight which justifies all the trials and tribulations of getting here on public transport.

The northern side of the island, facing Gujarat, is tidal marsh and salt pans while the southern coast alternates between limestone cliffs, rocky coves and sandy beaches, the best of which are at Nagoa. The somewhat windswept and arid island is riddled with quarries from which the Portuguese removed vast quantities of limestone to construct their huge fort, city walls, monuments and buildings. The rocky or sandy interior reaches a maximum height of just 29 metres, so agriculture is limited although there are extensive stands of coconut and other palms. Branching palms (Hyphaene species) are very much a feature of the island and were originally introduced from Africa by the Portuguese.

The Indian government appears to have an official policy of playing down the Portuguese era. Seven Rajput soldiers (six of them Singhs) and a few civilians were killed in Operation Vijay, which ended Portuguese rule. After the Indian Air Force unnecessarily bombed the airstrip and terminal, near Nagoa, it remained derelict until the late 1980s. The old church in Diu Fort was also bombed and is now a roofless ruin. It's said that the Portuguese blew up Government House to stop it falling into 'enemy' hands.

History

These days, it's hard to understand why the Portuguese should have been interested in capturing and fortifying such an apparently unimportant and isolated outpost but, in the 14th to 16th centuries,

Diu was an important trading post and naval base from which the Ottoman Turks controlled the shipping routes in the northern part of the Arabian Sea.

After an unsuccessful attempt to capture the island in 1531, during which the Sultan of Gujarat was assisted by the Turkish navy, the Portuguese finally secured control in 1534 by taking advantage of a quarrel between the sultan and the Moghul emperor Humayan. Humayan had sent an army into the sultan's territory in search of Mirza Zamal, who had made an attempt on the emperor's life. Not wanting to fight on two fronts, the sultan concluded a treaty with the Portuguese which allowed them to stay in Diu in return for providing 500 infantry men to serve with the sultan. The treaty was soon cast to the wind and, although both Bahadurshah, the Sultan of Gujarat, and his nephew, Sultan Mahmad III, attempted to contest the issue, the peace treaty which was eventually signed in 1539 ceded the island of Diu and the mainland enclave of Ghoghla to the Portuguese. Soon after the signing of this treaty, the Portuguese began constructing their fortress.

Information

The tourist office is open Monday to Friday from 9.30 am to 1.15 pm and 2 to 5.45 pm. It has all the bus, train and air travel information and is a nice place to sit and read the *Times of India*.

The State Bank of Saurashtra is the most efficient place to change travellers' cheques. The main post office opens remarkably early for India and there's another post office at Ghoghla, a walk of about 10 minutes from the jetty on your left. Manesh Medical Store is the only pharmacy in town and there's a doctor in the same building.

Diu Town

The island's main industry would have to be fishing, followed by booze and salt. A distillery at Malala produces rum from sugar cane grown on the mainland. The town boasts quite a few bars where visitors from the 'dry' mainland can enjoy a beer (or stronger IMFL – 'Indian Made Foreign Liquor').

The town is sandwiched between the massive fort to the east and a huge city wall to the west. The main gateway in the wall has some nice carvings of lions, angels and a priest, while just inside the gate is a miniature chapel with an icon, dating to 1702. Diu Town has two churches, St Paul's and St Francis of Assisi, and a third which has been converted into a hospital. It's said that there are now only 15 Christian families left on the whole island.

Unlike Daman, the buildings in Diu show a significant Portuguese influence. The town is a maze of narrow, winding streets and, although many of the wooden balconies have been allowed to decay, you could easily imagine yourself to be in one of the former Portuguese Moroccan enclaves such as Essaouira or El Jadida. Many of the houses are well ornamented and brightly painted. Further away from this tightly packed residential quarter, the streets turn into meandering and often leafy lanes reminiscent of rural Iberia.

All the buses operate from the main 'town square' on the northern shore. The post office and banks (three of them) are nearby, along with Goa Travels, customs, a few bars and the tourist office. A gateway with a bell leads off the square down to the ferry quay. At the back of this square, there's also a tiny but interesting bazaar where most of life's necessities can be found. In a small park on the esplanade, between the square and the police station, the Marwar Memorial, topped by a griffin, commemorates the liberation of the island from the Portuguese. It also sports a tiny crocodile 'farm'.

Constructed in 1547, the massive Portuguese fort with its double moat (one tidal) must once have been virtually impregnable, but sea erosion and neglect are leading to its slow, inevitable collapse. Piles of cannon balls litter the place and the ramparts have a superb array of cannons, many old and in good condition. Dating from 1624, one was built by Don Diego de Silva Conde de Porta Legre in the reign of Don Philippe, Rex d'Espana – all legible. There's also a museum of sorts within the fort but it's rarely open. Since the fort also serves as the island's jail, it closes at 5 pm each day. Entry is free. Signs prohibit photography but I've never seen anyone observing this rule and no-one will hassle you once you move away from the main gate.

Places to Stay

Diu Town The *PWD Rest House* towards the fort is clean, quiet, well run and incredible value at Rs 15 a double, but it's usually full. Meals, other than breakfast, have to be ordered in advance. Lunch is a thali; good fish and prawn dishes are available on request.

Most budget travellers stay at the *Nilesh Guest House*. It has a range of available rooms which vary in price from Rs 20 to Rs 50, depending on size and position. The more expensive rooms have baths. This place is OK but the atmosphere is entirely dependent on the clientele. There's a bar and restaurant on the ground floor.

Another cheapie which has become popular in the last few years is the *Hotel Mozambique*, an old Portuguese-style house facing the vegetable market. The potential of this place is enormous but, alas, unrealised and likely to remain so without more imagination on the part of the management. Doubles cost Rs 30 and Rs 40 (there are no singles) and there's a top floor 'suite' for Rs 50. All rooms have bath but no hot water and there's a bar and a basic restaurant on the ground floor.

Somewhat out of the main area, the clean and tidy *Hare Krishna Guest House* has doubles for Rs 20 and Rs 25. The manager is very friendly and helpful and

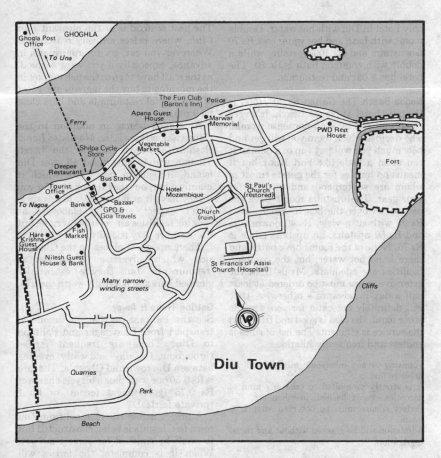

GHOGHLA

Ghogla Post Office

To Una

Ferry

The Fun Club (Baron's Inn)

Police

Apana Guest House

Marwar Memorial

PWD Rest House

Shilpa Cycle Store

Vegetable Market

Deepee Restaurant

Bus Stand

Tourist Office

Hotel Mozambique

St Paul's Church (restored)

Fort

To Nagoa

Bank

Bazaar
GPO & Goa Travels

Church (ruin)

Hare Krishna Guest House

Fish Market

St Francis of Assisi Church (Hospital)

Nilesh Guest House & Bank

Many narrow winding streets

Cliffs

Diu Town

Quarries

Park

Beach

speaks fluent English. The hotel restaurant is only open to residents and meals must be ordered in advance.

Higher in price is the *Baron's Inn* which was recently renamed *The Fun Club* – a most inappropriate name which gives a totally false impression of the place. On the Old Fort Rd, halfway between the ferry quay and the PWD Rest House, this fine old Portuguese villa is right by the sea, overlooking the channel between Diu Town and Ghoghla. Nothing has changed here for years and, with luck, things will stay the same since the friendly management

are keen to retain the inn's ambience. Spacious rooms with fan and bath (cold water only) cost Rs 90 a double, Rs 60 for single occupancy, plus Rs 20 for an extra bed if there are three of you. The food here is excellent – fish, prawns, chips and salad as well as the usual breakfast items – and prices are very reasonable. The restaurant is open to nonresidents for meals and drinks. It's very unlikely to be full so, if you're told it is, hang on and see what happens.

Very close by on the same road, the more modern *Apana Guest House* is the only hotel in Diu with hot water. Double rooms with bath and hot water cost Rs 70 downstairs and Rs 100 upstairs, while a double with common bath is Rs 50. The hotel has a bar and restaurant.

Nagoa Beach The *Ganga Sagar Hotel* is the only hotel at Nagoa Beach. It's very clean and run by a no-nonsense woman who decides which room you will get and how much you will pay (up to a point). It can seem a little like Fort Knox but it means no hassles for the guests (most of whom are westerners) and security for your gear. The upstairs rooms have the best views over the beach. Singles cost Rs 30 without a view, Rs 40 downstairs and Rs 50 upstairs; an upstairs triple is Rs 75. None of the rooms have baths and there is no hot water, but the common facilities are adequate. Meals from the extensive menu must be ordered at least half a day in advance – otherwise, they will definitely not cater for you. On the other hand, the food is good and fresh and the service is efficient. The list of rules is endless and frequently hilarious:

Vomiting or any inheigenic misdeed will be liable to fine.
It is strictly prohibited to take any kind of narcotics – ganja, hashish, heroihen, etc.
Perfect silence must be observed after 2100 hours.
Admission will be granted without any racial eggrigation.

It's also possible to rent palm-roofed cottages in the village for Rs 50 to Rs 100 per month but all you get is a roof. You'll have to buy beds and cooking facilities for yourself so this is only a viable option if you plan to stay for a while.

Places to Eat
Although there are plenty of bars in Diu Town, there are very few restaurants which are not attached to hotels. The bars may offer rice and dhal, or something similar, but that's about the limit. This means that you'll have to eat at one of the hotels.

The best seafood is at the pleasant *Fun Club*, where prices are very reasonable. Wherever you eat, try to order meals in advance, especially if you want seafood, as the staff have to go to the fish market in the morning to buy the ingredients. Most of Diu's hotel restaurants and bars close by 9 pm.

At Nagoa beach, in addition to the Ganga Sagar there is the *Mombasa Bar & Restaurant*, next door to the hotel. Though widely advertised all over Diu island, it's just a tiny place which is mainly a bar, but they'll cook food for you if they have it or if you order in advance. Don't expect anything elaborate as cooking facilities are relatively crude, but the staff are very friendly.

There are a few places on the Ghoghla side which advertise themselves as 'restaurants' but they're essentially glorified bars and not really worth the trip.

Getting There & Away
See the Palitana section for details of transport from Bhavnagar and Palitana to Diu. There are frequent ferries throughout the day and early evening between Diu town and Ghoghla. The fare is Rs 0.50 one way, plus a bicycle charge of Rs 0.75 (government ferries) or Rs 1 (private ferries).

A bridge across the channel from Diu town to Ghoghla is being constructed but it won't be finished for some time yet. When it is complete, the ferries will become obsolete and direct buses will run between Una and Diu. For the present, however, to get to Una you need to take the ferry to Ghoghla, walk about 800 metres down the main street to the old gate and catch an auto-rickshaw, bus or other form of transport from there. The buses cost Rs 2.50 and run about six times daily.

Air Rehabilitation of the airport on Diu should now be complete. Vayudoot plans to fly between Bombay and Diu but, should this not happen, the nearest airport is at Keshod, about 150 km away.

There are flights to Keshod from Bhavnagar and Bombay.

Bus Daily state transport buses run from the main square in Diu to places like Veraval (Rs 10), Junagadh (Rs 15), Rajkot (Rs 20), Palitana, Bhavnagar and Ahmedabad. They're very crowded and a major hassle to negotiate with a rucksack, so be there early and get a seat as you cannot reserve one in advance.

Goa Travels, with an office on the main square, operates a daily 'luxury' bus between Diu and Bombay via Bhavnagar, Anand and Vapi (for Daman) which leaves around 8.30 am. The trip takes more than 20 hours and costs Rs 130. It's a popular bus so you need to book in advance, though it's rarely full on weekdays. The Bombay agent is Hirup Travel Service (tel 358186, 359856), Prabhakar Sadan, ground floor, Khetwadi Back Rd, 12th Line, Bombay 400004. In Daman, the agent is Satish General Stores, Nani Daman.

Train Only about eight km from Diu, Delwada is the nearest railhead. A shared auto-rickshaw from here to Ghoghla costs about Rs 2. Trains run from Delwada to Sasan Gir or Junagadh.

Taxi You can hire a taxi to various other main centres within Gujarat from the office on the left-hand side of the Casa Luxo bar, on Diu's main square. Quite a few travellers take advantage of this option, though you need a group to make it viable as you also have to pay for the driver's return journey. A taxi from Diu to Sasan Gir, for instance, costs Rs 400 shared between up to five people.

Getting Around
There are no rickshaws or tongas on the island but the two local bus services, Diu/Nagoa/Vanakbara and Diu/Bucharwada/Vanakbara, operate daily buses on a fairly frequent basis. Fares are Rs 0.75 to Nagoa and Rs 1 to Vanakbara.

Cycling around Diu is the best way to get to know this island and most travellers prefer the greater freedom of movement allowed by a bicycle. The best place to hire them is the Shilpa Cycle Store on the main square. The 'store' is actually one of the wooden huts on the left-hand side of the gate leading to the ferry quay. They cost Rs 7 per day and the friendly man who rents them doesn't usually ask for a deposit – you simply record your name and hotel in a book. You can also rent bicycles from the Krishna Cycle Store near the fish market and the State Bank of Saurashtra.

AROUND DIU
Other Villages
There are a number of interesting villages on Diu island.

Fudam Close to Diu, the village of Fudam has a huge abandoned church, Our Lady of Remedies. A large old carved wooden altar with Madonna and child remains inside but the vestry has become a manger, full of straw!

Vanakbara At the extreme west of the island, Vanakbara has a church (Our Lady of Mercy), fort, lighthouse, small bazaar, post office and fishing fleet. A ferry crosses from here to Kotla village on the mainland and you can get a bus from Kotla to Kodinar.

Nagoa Nagoa, Diu's premier beach, is reminiscent of Goa in the 1960s. This beautiful palm-fringed beach is still largely deserted, safe for swimming and the place to shed all your worldly cares. You'll find an interesting mix of people here from defiant ex-hippies to Hemingway clones in search of the world's last island paradise.

Samudra Beach
Just over the state border beyond Ghoghla stands one of Gujarat State Tourism's prestige developments, the *Samudra*

Beach Resort (tel Una 116). Crores of rupees have been spent on this ambitious but quite sensitively designed answer to the lures of Diu. It could be a beautiful place to stay and there's no criticising the ethnic furnishings, the decor or the maintenance. Unfortunately, however, it's an organisational disaster and staffed by people who simply don't seem to care. Furthermore, when Russian tourists are staying there, they won't even let you in! And, despite the fact that the Diu border is within spitting distance, you cannot even have a beer with your meal, let alone anything stronger. This is puritanism with a vengeance. Where do they think the Russians go for an aperitif? To Diu, of course! Even if you're thinking of going for a splurge, you can't just turn up and order a meal because they won't have the food. They're not worried about it either. The ultimate piece of nonsense is that the glossy literature advertising this place (known otherwise as Ahmedpur-Mandvi) sites the hotel way out beyond the Gulf of Kutch! There is a Mandvi out there, but no Samudra Beach Resort!

If none of this bothers you, you can stay at the beach resort for Rs 310/360; there's also a 'loft' for Rs 590. Meals are extra – they'll no doubt cater for you if you're a guest.

JUNAGADH (population 120,000)

Few travellers make the trip out to Junagadh, but it's an interesting town situated right at the base of the temple-studded Girnar Hill. Junagadh is also the departure point for visits to the Gir Forest, last home of the Asian lion.

The city takes its name from the fort which enclosed the old city. Dating from 250 BC, the Ashokan edicts near the town testify to the great antiquity of this site. At the time of partition, the Nawab of Junagadh opted to take his tiny state into Pakistan. However, the inhabitants were predominantly Hindu and the Nawab soon found himself in exile, perhaps explaining the sorry state of his former palace and fort. This city is full of derelict and very exotic old buildings which makes it a fascinating place to explore, but very few tourists come this way.

Information

Visiting the tourist office in the Hotel Girnar is a waste of time. The best source of current information is the Hotel Relief, the city's unofficial information centre and the only one worth checking out. Just inside the entrance to the fort you'll see a man selling literature. It's worth paying Rs 3 for the booklet *Girnar Guide* by Mohanlal Desai. It supposedly describes the holy mountain of the same name but is somewhere between a barrel of laughs and a barrel of bullshit. If any publication deserves a Nobel Prize for pure, unadulterated nonsense (let alone typos), this is it. It's money well spent!

Uparkot

This very old fort, from which the city derives its name, stands on the eastern side of Junagadh and has been rebuilt and extended many times in its history. In places, the walls are 20 metres high and an ornate triple gateway forms the entrance to the fort. It's said that the fort was once besieged, unsuccessfully, for a full 12 years and, in all, it was besieged 16 times. It is also said that the fort was abandoned from the 7th to 10th centuries and, when rediscovered, it was completely overrun by jungle. The plateau-like area formed by the top of the old fort is covered in lantana scrub. Paths lead from one point of interest to the next and entry to the fort is free.

The Jami Masjid, the mosque inside the fort, was built from a demolished Hindu temple. Other points of interest include the Tomb of Nuri Shah and two fine wells known as the Adi Chadi and the Naughan. The Adi Chadi is named after two of the slave girls who fetched water from it. The Naughan is reached by a magnificent circular staircase. Cut into the hillside close to the mosque are some

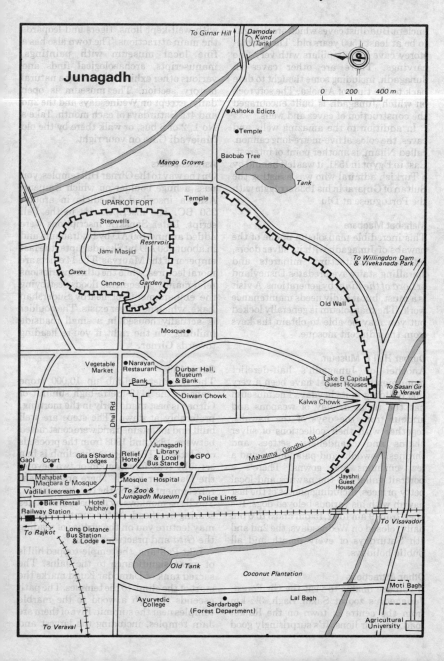

Junagadh

To Girnar Hill

Damodar Kund (Tank)

0   200   400 m

Ashoka Edicts

Temple

Baobab Tree

Mango Groves

Tank

Temple

UPARKOT FORT

Stepwells

Reservoir

Jami Masjid

Caves

Cannon

Garden

To Willingdon Dam & Vivekananda Park

Old Wall

Mosque

Vegetable Market

Narayan Restaurant

Bank

Durbar Hall, Museum & Bank

Diwan Chowk

Lake & Capital Guest Houses

To Sasan Gir & Veraval

Kalwa Chowk

Dhal Rd

Gaol

Court

Gita & Sharda Lodges

Relief Hotel

Junagadh Library & Local Bus Stand

GPO

Mahatma Gandhi Rd

Jayshri Guest House

Mahabat Maqbara & Mosque

Vadilal Icecream

Mosque Hospital

To Zoo & Junagadh Museum

Bike Rental
Railway Station

Hotel Vaibhav

Police Lines

To Rajkot

Long Distance Bus Station & Lodge

To Visavador

Old Tank

Coconut Plantation

Moti Bagh

To Veraval

Ayurvedic College

Sardarbagh (Forest Department)

Lal Bagh

Agricultural University

ancient Buddhist caves which are thought
to be at least 1500 years old. The double-
storey cave has six pillars with very fine
carvings. There are other caves in
Junagadh, including some thought to date
back to the time of Ashoka. The soft rock
on which Junagadh is built encouraged
the construction of caves and wells.

In addition to the amazing wells and
caves, the colossal five-metre-long cannon,
called Nilam, is another point of interest.
Cast in Egypt in 1531, it was left behind by
a Turkish admiral who was assisting the
Sultan of Gujarat in his 1538 struggle with
the Portuguese at Diu.

Mahabat Maqbara
This incredible mausoleum of one of the
nawabs of Junagadh with its silver doors,
intricate architecture, minarets and
spiralling stairways predates Disneyland
or *Lord of the Rings* by generations. A visit
is a must, but it badly needs maintenance
work. The mausoleum is generally locked
but you may be able to obtain the keys
from the adjacent mosque.

Durbar Hall & Museum
Another of Junagadh's half-derelict
monuments, this must have been a very
fine building in its heyday. The museum
has the usual display of weapons and
armour from the days of the nawabs,
together with their collections of silver
chains and chandeliers, settees and
thrones, howdahs and palanquins, and a
few cushions and gowns. There's a
portrait gallery of the nawabs and local
petty princes, including photos of the last
nawab with his various beloved dogs. It's
open from 9 am to 12.15 pm and 3 to 6 pm
daily, closed on Wednesdays, the 2nd and
4th Saturdays of every month and all
public holidays.

Other Attractions
If you are unable to visit the Gir Forest,
Junagadh's zoo at Sakar Bagh, 3½ km
from the centre of town on the Rajkot
road, has Gir lions. It's surprisingly good

with well-kept lions, tigers and leopards
the main attractions. The town also has a
fine local museum with paintings,
manuscripts, archaeological finds and
various other exhibits including a natural
history section. The museum is open
daily, except on Wednesdays and the 2nd
and 4th Saturdays of each month. Take a
No 1, 2 or 6 bus, or walk there by the old
Majevadi Gate on your right.

Ashoka Edicts
On the way to the Girnar Hill temples, you
pass a huge boulder on which Emperor
Ashoka inscribed 14 edicts in around
250 BC. His inscription is in the Pali
script. Later Sanskrit inscriptions were
added around 150 AD by Rudradama and
in about 450 AD by Skandagupta, the last
emperor of the Mauryas. The 14 edicts are
moral lectures, while the other inscriptions
refer mainly to recurring floods destroying
the embankments of nearby Sudershan
Lake, which no longer exists. The boulder
is actually housed in a small roadside
building, on the right if you're heading
towards Girnar.

Girnar Hill
The 600-metre climb up 10,000 stone
steps to the 1118-metre-high summit of
Girnar is best made early in the morning,
preferably at dawn. The steps are well
built and maintained and were constructed
between 1889 and 1908 from the proceeds
of a lottery. The start of the climb is in a
scrubby teak forest, a km or two beyond
the Damodar Kund. There are frequent
refreshment stalls on the two-hour ascent.
You'll see monkeys by the path and eagles
soaring overhead. At the summit, sadhus
may lecture you on the virtues of reading
the *Gita* and practising yoga.

Like Palitana, the temple-topped hill is
of great significance to the Jains. The
sacred tank of Damodar Kund marks the
start of the climb to the temples. The path
ascends through a wood to the marble
temples near the summit. Five of them are
Jain temples, including the largest and

oldest – the 12th-century temple of Neminath, the 22nd Jain tirthankar. There is a large black image of Neminath in the central shrine and many smaller images around the temple.

The nearby triple temple of Mallinath, the 9th tirthankar, was erected in 1177 by two brothers. During festivals, this temple is a favourite gathering place for sadhus and a great fair is held here during the Kartika Purnima festival in November or December. On top of the peak is the temple of Amba Mata, where newlyweds are supposed to worship at the shrine of the goddess in order to ensure a happy marriage.

A local No 3 or 4 bus from the stand opposite the GPO will take you to Girnar Taleti at the base of the hill. Buses run about once an hour, cost Rs 0.50 and go by the Ashoka edicts.

Places to Stay

Junagadh has neat, clean railway *retiring rooms* for Rs 15/25 and dorm beds for Rs 10. Just outside the railway station are two very basic hotels, the *Gita Lodge* and the *Sharada Lodge*, but you'd have to be penniless to consider staying there.

The hotels around Kalwa Chowk, one of the two main squares in Junagadh, are better, but an inconvenient distance from the centre of town. In this area, you'll find the *Lake Guest House* and the *Capital Guest House* offering accommodation of much the same standard. Singles/doubles/triples cost Rs 15/25/36, all with common bath, and bucket hot water is available for Rs 2. As you might expect at that price, they're very basic.

Somewhat closer to the centre on Mahatma Gandhi Rd is another fairly basic hotel, the *Jayshri Guest House*, which is worth trying if the others are full.

By far the best hotel is the *Relief Hotel* (tel 20280), Chittakhana Chowk, within easy walking distance of both the bus stand and the railway station. The manager here is a real live wire and very

keen to make sure you're comfortable and have everything you need. He is also full of accurate information about the area. None of the other hotels are a patch on this place. The Relief is immaculately clean and well maintained and the cheap restaurant on the ground floor is excellent. It offers a variety of rooms ranging in price from Rs 30 for a single with bath (Rs 25 with common bath) to between Rs 40 and Rs 100 for a double with bath. All the bathrooms have hot water and the most expensive double also has air-con. Bicycles can be hired from the hotel.

Halfway between the Relief and the bus station is the *Hotel Vaibhav* (tel 21070/1) which costs Rs 54 for an ordinary double, Rs 83.60 for a deluxe double and Rs 153 for an air-con suite. There are no singles. All rooms have bath and bucket hot water is available at no extra charge. The hotel also has an air-conditioned restaurant.

Junagadh's top-end hotel is the state-operated *Hotel Girnar* (tel 21201), Majwadi Darwaja. It has dorm beds for Rs 20 to Rs 25, doubles for Rs 100 and air-con doubles for Rs 150.

Places to Eat

Cheap all-you-can-eat thalis can be found at the *Sharada Lodge* opposite the railway station. Nearby, a *Vadelal* ice-cream parlour offers flavours which include 'pinepal' and 'stro bary'.

Only slightly more expensive is the food at the *Relief Hotel*, which is probably where you'll eat if you're staying there.

For something of an eye-opener, try the restaurant at the *Hotel Vaibhav*. It has an amazingly flashy air-conditioned mirrored dining hall where you can get the 'ultimate' all-you-can-eat thali for Rs 16, plus Rs 5 for dessert.

Junagadh is famous for its fruit, especially *kesar* mangoes and *chiku* (sapodilla) which are popular in milkshakes in November-December.

Getting There & Away

Air Keshod, 40 km from Junagadh, and

Rajkot, 102 km from Junagadh, are the nearest airports. Indian Airlines flies Bombay/Bhavnagar/Rajkot/Bombay daily; Vayudoot flies Surat/Bhavnagar/Keshod. There is no Indian Airlines office in Junagadh, but the manager at the Relief Hotel will put you in touch with a travel agency which can make bookings or reconfirmations.

Bus The timetable at the state bus stand is entirely in Gujarati. Buses leave for Rajkot every hour (the 8.30 am bus is nonstop) for a fare of Rs 12, Sasan Gir at 8.45 and 10 am, 12.30 and 1.30 pm for Rs 7, Una (for Diu) at 5, 6 and 7 am, Bhuj at 5.45 and 7.15 am, Palitana at 5.30 am, Veraval every hour and Ahmedabad daily at 9.45 pm.

Train The Somnath Mail (No 23-24) and Girnar Express (No 45-46) run between Ahmedabad and Veraval via Junagadh. (The Somnath Mail is a multipart train, so make sure you get into the right part.) The No 37-38 Veraval-Rajkot Mail runs between Rajkot and Veraval via Junagadh, while the 380-km trip from Ahmedabad to Junagadh takes about 11 hours and costs Rs 46 in 2nd class, Rs 163 in 1st. A daily passenger train to Sasan Gir and on to Delwada, near Diu, leaves Junagadh daily at 6 am.

Getting Around
You can rent bicycles for Rs 7 per day from either the Relief Hotel or the small yellow shack near the railway station. Most other places in town seem reluctant to rent bikes to foreigners!

VERAVAL
Only a few km from Somnath, Veraval was the major seaport for Mecca pilgrims before the rise of Surat. It still has some importance as one of India's major fishing ports; over 1000 boats are based here. As you might imagine, the place stinks of fish depending on the prevailing wind. Dhows are still being built and some run across to

Bombay – you could probably get a ride by asking around.

There's not a lot to see in Veraval, despite its size. Pigs abound in the streets. Between Veraval and Somnath, a large ship lies (spectacularly) wrecked on the shore.

Places to Stay
Accommodation in Veraval can be hard to find; places are often full and prices get jacked up. Veraval has the *Toran Tourist Bungalow* (tel 20488), College Rd, and a *Circuit House* near the lighthouse which has fine views of the sunset over the sea. The Tourist Bungalow is quiet and has doubles for Rs 75, a dorm with six beds for Rs 120 and a dorm with four beds for the same price. Meals have to be ordered in advance.

The *Hotel Satkar* (tel 120) near the bus stand is clean and well maintained. It has all sorts of rooms, from dorm beds at Rs 20 or regular rooms from Rs 35 to rooms with air-con from Rs 180. Their prices may rise during an accommodation squeeze. There are railway *retiring rooms* at the station, the *Chandrani Guest House* is nearby and the *Sri Niwas Guest House* and the *Hotel Supreme* are a little further away.

In Somnath, about halfway between the bus stand and the temple and some 100 metres north of the road, the *Sri Somnath Temple Trust* has a vast guest house. The 100 double rooms are a bit dingy but they're not that old and, at Rs 18, they're good value. The signs for the guest house are in Hindi and Gujarati only, but you can ask for directions.

Places to Eat
Veraval has few eating places. The *Hotel Satkar*, near the bus station, does good Gujarati thalis with plenty of refills for Rs 22. The *Hotel La'Bela* is actually a restaurant which offers (hot) thalis. The *New Apsara*, not far from the station, serves vegetarian thalis and dosas downstairs and non-vegetarian food (including local fish) upstairs, but it's

fairly basic. Street stalls all over town sell green drinking coconuts.

Getting There & Away

Air Keshod, the nearest airport, is serviced by Vayudoot but there's no Vayudoot office in Veraval. Somnath Travels (tel 162) in Satta Bazaar will obtain tickets for a fee. There is a good road to Keshod – the bus takes only an hour and costs Rs 6.

Bus Daily buses run from the bus station to Diu via Kodinar; the fare is Rs 9. Buses also go along the coast road to Porbandar via Chorwad and Mangrol. Bhavnagar is nine hours away and the trip costs Rs 27.

Train It's 459 km from Ahmedabad to Veraval. Fares for the 13-hour trip are Rs 53 in 2nd class, Rs 189 in 1st. There's also a passenger (slow) train which goes to Delwada, near Una (for Diu).

Getting Around

An auto-rickshaw to Somnath, six km away, costs about Rs 12. There are municipal and local buses to Somnath for Rs 1.50.

AROUND VERAVAL
Chorwad

The summer palace of the Junagadh nawabs, situated at the popular beach resort of Chorwad, 70 km from Junagadh and 20 km from Veraval, was converted by the Gujarat State Tourism Department into the beautiful *Palace Beach Resort* (tel 96/7). The hotel is surrounded by well-tended gardens and overlooks the sea. It has a total of 24 rooms in the main palace building and 16 detached cottages. Doubles in the cottages and the palace annexe cost Rs 150, Rs 350 with air-con, while rooms without air-con in the former palace itself cost Rs 250. Meals have to be ordered in advance.

Somnath

The Temple of Somnath, at Somnath

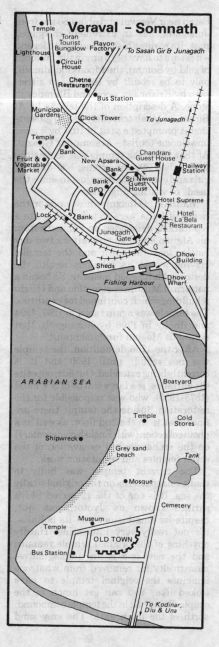

Patan near Veraval and about 80 km from Junagadh, has an extremely chequered past. Its earliest history fades into legend – it is said to have been originally built out of gold by Somraj, the Moon God himself, only to be rebuilt by Rawana in silver, then by Krishna in wood and Bhimdev in stone. A description of the temple by Al Biruni, an Arab traveller, was so glowing that it prompted a visit in 1024 by a most unwelcome tourist – Mahmud of Ghazni. At that time, the temple was so wealthy that it had 300 musicians, 500 dancing girls and even 300 barbers just to shave the heads of visiting pilgrims.

Mahmud of Ghazni, whose raids on the riches of India were to gain him quite a reputation, descended on Somnath from his Afghan kingdom and, after a two-day battle, took the town and the temple. Having looted its fabulous wealth, he destroyed it for good measure. So began a pattern of Muslim destruction and Hindu rebuilding which continued for centuries. The temple was again razed in 1297, 1394 and finally in 1706 by Aurangzeb, that notorious Moghul fundamentalist.

After the 1706 demolition, the temple was not rebuilt until 1950 and it is currently being extended. Outside, opposite the entrance, is a large statue of S V Patel (1875-1950), who was responsible for the restoration. Inside the temple there are fine views from the 2nd floor, as well as a photo collection (with English commentary) on the archaeological excavation of the seven temples and restoration work.

The current temple was built to traditional patterns on the original site by the sea. It is one of the 12 sacred Shiva shrines known as Jyotorlingas but, despite its long history and its holiness, it's not really very interesting. Hardly anything of the original temple remains and the new one is an unimaginative monstrosity far removed from what one imagines the original temple to have looked like. You can get lunch in the simple dining hall in the temple compound, north of the main gate. The grey sand beach right outside the temple is OK for a swim, although there's no shade.

Down the lane from the temple is a museum, open from 9 am to 12 noon and 3 to 6 pm, closed Wednesdays and holidays. Admission is Rs 0.20, plus Rs 0.20 for each photograph you take. They're not very serious about keeping count. Remains of the old temple can be seen here as a jumble of old carved stones littering a courtyard. There are pottery shards, a seashell collection and a (strange) glass case of water bottles containing samples from the Danube, Nile, St Lawrence, Tigris, River Plate and even the Australian Murray, as well as seawater from Hobart and New Zealand.

Other Somnath Sites

The town of Somnath Patan is entered from Veraval by the Junagadh Gate. This very ancient triple gate was the one through which Mahmud finally broke to take the town. Close to the second gate is an old mosque dating from Mahmud's time. The Jami Masjid, reached through the town's picturesque bazaar, was constructed using parts of a Hindu temple and has interesting bo tree carvings at all four corners. It is now a museum with a collection from many of these temples.

About a km before the Junagadh Gate, coming from Veraval, the finely carved Mai Puri was once a Temple of the Sun. This Hindu temple was converted into a mosque during Mahmud's time and is surrounded by thousands of tombs and palias. Two old tombs are close by and, on the shore, the Bhidiyo Pagoda probably dates from the 14th century.

To the east of the town is the Bhalka Tirth where Lord Krishna was mistaken for a deer and wounded by an arrow while sleeping in a deerskin. The legendary spot is at the confluence of three rivers. You get to it through the small Sangam (confluence gate), which is simply known as the Nana, or 'small gate'. North of this sacred spot is the Suraj Mandir, or 'Temple of the Sun', which Mahmud also had a go at knocking down. This very old temple, a frieze of lions with elephant trunks around its walls, probably dates from the same time as the original Somnath Temple. Back inside the small gate is a temple which Ahalya Bai of Indore built as a replacement for the Somnath Temple.

SASAN GIR LION SANCTUARY

The last home of the Asian lion is 54 km from Junagadh via Keshod. Fewer than 200 lions survive. The sanctuary covers 1400 square km of dry scrubland and is best visited between October and June. Apart from the lions there are also bears, hyenas, foxes and a number of species of deer and antelope. The deer include the largest Indian antelope (the nilgai), the graceful chinkara gazelle, the chousingha and the barking deer. You may also see parrots, peacocks and monkeys.

The lions themselves are elusive and it may be several days before you catch sight of one or, better still, a pair. On the other hand, it's true to say that some of the rangers (who also act as jeep drivers) are better at finding the lions than others, so it's definitely worth asking around to

ascertain who has worked in the forest longest. To be sure of seeing lions, set aside at least three days, though you may be lucky and, like Geoff, come across a mating pair on your very first safari. Whatever else you do, take a jeep and not a minibus. While the latter stick to the main tracks, the jeeps can take the small trails where you're much more likely to come across lions.

Before you can go on safari, you must get a permit. These are issued on the spot at the Sinh Sagar Forestry Lodge office and cost Rs 15 per person plus Rs 7.50 for a camera and Rs 7.50 for a driver/guide (shared between however many people are in the jeep). Jeeps are available from the same office every day between 7 and 10 am and 4 and 6.30 pm. They cost Rs 2.25 per km and take up to six passengers. If possible, book in advance, though they're rarely full.

Places to Stay & Eat There are two very pleasant places to stay at Sasan Gir village. Directly opposite the railway tracks, the *Sinh Sagar Forestry Lodge* has good singles/doubles with mosquito nets and baths for Rs 60/80. It's popular because of the price, so try to make advance reservations. There's a restaurant here which serves thalis but it sometimes runs out of food, in which case you'll have to eat at the other lodge.

The State Tourism Corporation of Gujarat's *Lion Safari Lodge* (tel 21/8) is down by the river, about 200 metres from the Sinh Sagar, surrounded by well-maintained gardens. It has 20 dorm beds (four beds per dorm) for Rs 30, doubles for Rs 150 and rooms with air-con for Rs 115/350. The double rooms are excellent value, very tastefully furnished and decorated and have balconies and bathrooms with hot water, towels, soap and toilet paper. The restaurant on the ground floor serves good thalis (Rs 20) and other dishes and, despite the notice at the dining hall entrance, you don't have to order meals in advance. This is one of the few state tourist lodges where the staff appear to take a pride in their work.

You can also get snacks at the shacks opposite the Sinh Sagar Lodge, but the food is very basic and hygiene is lacking.

Getting There & Away State transport buses make the two-hour trip between Junagadh and Veraval via Sasan Gir four times a day. They leave Junagadh at 8.45 and 10 am and 12.30 and 1.30 pm and cost Rs 7. The buses can be very crowded so it's much better to take a shared taxi – if there's one available, which is not very often. You simply have to wait around at the food shacks opposite the Sinh Sagar and see what comes through. If you find one, it will cost Rs 20 per person and take about one hour to get to Junagadh. Some travellers even take a tempo all the way to Junagadh – it's cheaper, but expect at least 18 people to pile onto the back end.

The daily slow train direct from Junagadh to Sasan Gir takes 2½ hours and costs just Rs 6. The train continues on to Delwada near Diu. The railway station is only 10 minutes walk from the Forest Lodge.

JAMNAGAR (population 420,000)

Prior to independence, the princely state of Jamnagar was ruled by the Jadeja Rajputs. The city was built around a lake and linked by bridge to an island in the middle, though there's little evidence of this today and the city now sprawls in all directions. Few tourists make the special effort to visit Jamnagar as there's precious little to see or do here. This bustling city has a long history of pearl fishing and a local variety of tie dyeing.

Orientation

The state bus stand (known locally as 'ST') and the new railway station are several km apart and both are a long way from the centre of the city, so you'll need to take an auto-rickshaw.

Street maps of Jamnagar are unobtainable. The police headquarters has one on the wall (as does the fire station) but you're not allowed to copy it for 'security reasons'. When I requested permission to copy it the response was, 'Why do you want a map? You don't need one. Jamnagar is a small city. Take an auto – you'll get anywhere within an hour.' So I tried this. I asked an auto-rickshaw driver to take me to the railway station. He did – the derelict old one. That's why we've included a basic plan of the city.

The Indian Airlines office is open from 10 am to 4.30 pm (closed for lunch from 1 to 1.45 pm). The office is efficient but does not provide a minibus to the airport which is a long way out. Auto-rickshaw drivers demand Rs 20 – it's a rip-off but they refuse to use the meters.

Places to Stay

It can be hard to find accommodation in Jamnagar at certain times of year, especially during the 'marriage season' (around the end of January) when even expensive hotels can be full.

Places to Stay – bottom

At the bottom end of the market, Jamnagar offers some of the worst hotels in the whole of India and you'd be well advised to give these disgusting dosshouses a miss. They're mostly clustered around the former railway station and include the *Everest Lodge, Jai Hind Lodge, Palace Guest House, Dreamland Guest House, and the Grand Hotel*, as well as the *Evergreen Lodge* further out.

A good place for those on a budget is the centrally located *Ashiana Hotel* (tel 77421/2), New Super Market, a vast, rambling place on the top floor of the supermarket complex. The huge sign above the supermarket is easily seen from the road below. There's a range of singles/ doubles here for Rs 30/55, Rs 105/125 with air-con.

If the Ashiana is full, the *Janki Guest House/Gokul Hotel*, on the 3rd floor of a building nearby, is of a similar standard. It offers singles/doubles without air-con at Rs 45/75 and air-con doubles at Rs 150, all

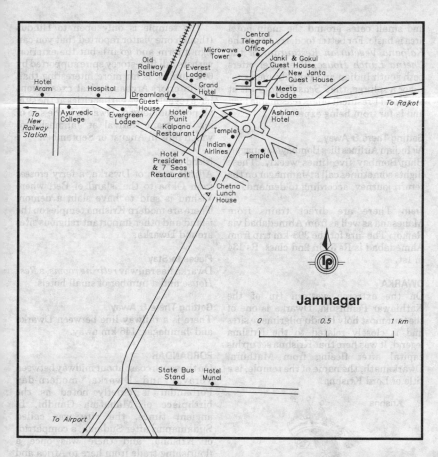

Jamnagar

0   0.5   1 km

with bath. Bucket hot water is available at no extra charge. If you want to stay near the state bus stand, there's really only the very basic *Hotel Munal* on the 3rd floor of the shopping arcade to the right of the bus stand as you face it. It's not easily seen so you may need to ask.

Places to Stay – middle

Right in the centre of town is the modern *Hotel President* (tel 70516), Teen Batti. Singles/doubles cost Rs 140/180, Rs 180/230 with air-con, all with bath and constant hot water. The hotel has a

restaurant (the *7 Seas Restaurant*), currency exchange facilities and also accepts credit cards.

Further out along the road to the new railway station, the *Hotel Aram* (tel 78521/5), Nand Niwas, Nehru Marg, is a very pleasant, older type of building set in its own gardens and with its own restaurant. Singles/doubles cost Rs 90/130, Rs 170/220 with air-con. It's a popular place and often full.

Places to Eat

The cuisine at the numerous food stalls

and small cafes around the main hotel area is basic. For better food, try either the *Kalpana Vegetarian Restaurant* or the *Chetna Lunch House*. The latter offers both south Indian and Punjabi meals.

For a splurge, the *7 Seas Restaurant* at the Hotel President offers reasonable food and is far from being expensive.

Getting There & Away
Air Indian Airlines flies Bombay/Jamnagar/ Bhuj/Bombay five times weekly. These flights sometimes call at Jamnagar on the return journey, according to demand.

Train There are direct trains from Mahesana as well as from Ahmedabad via Rajkot. The fare for the 308-km trip from Ahmedabad is Rs 37 in 2nd class, Rs 134 in 1st.

DWARKA
On the extreme western tip of the Kathiawar Peninsula, Dwarka is one of the four most holy Hindu pilgrimage sites and is closely related to the Krishna legend. It was here that Krishna set up his capital after fleeing from Mathura. Dwarkanath, the name of the temple, is a title of Lord Krishna.

Krishna

The temple is only open to Hindus (though one visitor reported that you can sign a form and go in), but the exterior, with its tall five-storey spire supported by 60 columns, is far more interesting than the interior. Archaeological excavations have revealed five earlier cities at the site, all now submerged. Dwarka is the site of an important festival at Janmashtami which falls in August or September.

Island of Bet
A little north of Dwarka, a ferry crosses from Okha to the island of Bet, where Vishnu is said to have slain a demon. There are modern Krishna temples on the island and other important religious sites around Dwarka.

Places to Stay
Dwarka has railway *retiring rooms*, a *Rest House* and a number of small hotels.

Getting There & Away
There is a railway line between Dwarka and Jamnagar, 145 km away.

PORBANDAR
On the south coast about midway between Veraval and Dwarka, modern-day Porbandar is chiefly noted as the birthplace of Mahatma Gandhi. In ancient times, the city was called Sudamapuri after Sudama, a compatriot of Krishna, and there was once a flourishing trade from here to Africa and the Persian Gulf. The Africa connection is apparent in the number of Indianised blacks, called Siddis, who form a virtually separate caste of Harijans.

Porbandar has several large cement and chemical factories and a textile mill. A massive breakwater was recently constructed to shelter a deep-water wharf and fishing harbour. Dhows are still being built here and fish drying is an important activity, lending a certain aroma to the town!

Swimming near the Tourist Bungalow is not recommended. The beach, called

Maharashtra Top: Entrance to the Bhaja Caves (GC)
Left & Right: Maharashtran tribal women at Ellora Caves (GC)

ANY ONE CREATING NUISANCE BY
EASING HIMSELF ON THE BEACH OR IN
ANY MANNER WILL BE PROSECUTTED.

दर्या देगेक कोणेय कसल्याय रीतीन घाण
केल्यार ताजेर कायदेशीर करणी करतले.

समुद्र किनाऱ्यावर कोणत्याही इसमाने
घाण केल्यास त्यांच्यावर कायदेशीर
कारवाई करण्यात येईल.

Goa Top: Panaji (HF)
    Left: Sunset at Colva Beach (TW)
    Right: Ferry from Bombay docked at Panaji (TW)

Chowpatty, is used as a local toilet and there is a factory drain outlet by the Hazur Palace. Swimming is said to be OK a few km down the coast towards Veraval.

Kirti Mandir

The Kirti Mandir, Gandhi's birthplace, houses one of India's many collections of Gandhian memorabilia. A swastika on the floor in a small room marks the actual spot! There is also an exhibit of photographs, some with English captions, and a small bookshop.

Planetarium

Across the muddy creek, which is spanned by the Jynbeeli (once Jubilee) Bridge, are the Nehru Planetarium and the Bharat Mandir. Flocks of flamingoes are an unexpected sight along the creek. Men and women enter the planetarium from the verandah by separate doors whose panels celebrate Indian nonalignment, showing Shastri with Kosygin on one side and Nehru with JFK on the other! The planetarium has afternoon sessions in Gujarati. The projection equipment is a

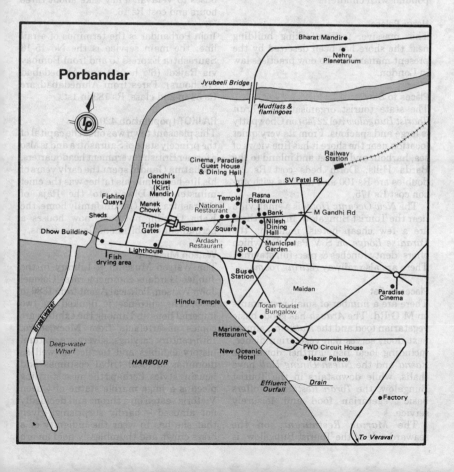

little antiquated and stars chase one another across the domed roof to the sound of whirring machinery.

Bharat Mandir

The large Bharat Mandir hall is in a charming irrigated garden opposite the planetarium. On the floor inside is a huge relief map of India and the building's pillars are brilliantly painted with bas-reliefs of over 100 religious figures and legendary persons from Hindu epics. The verandah's six distorting mirrors are popular with children.

Hazur Palace

This massive, forlorn-looking building near the shore has been deserted by the present maharana who now practises law in London.

Places to Stay

The state tourist organisation's *Toran Tourist Bungalow* (tel 22745) on Chowpatty is large and spacious. From its very quiet location near the shore it has fine views of sea, harbour and sunset and inland to the Barda Hills. Dorm beds cost Rs 20, doubles are Rs 100 and doubles with air-con cost Rs 175.

The *New Oceanic Hotel* is a small villa near the Tourist Bungalow. In town there are a few cheap hotels, including the *Paradise Lodge* on S V Patel Rd which offers 'denty lunches & piecefull staying'. There are also railway *retiring rooms*.

Places to Eat

There are a number of small restaurants on M G Rd. The *Ardash* has good, basic vegetarian food and the *National*, almost next door, serves non-vegetarian dishes, including local fish. Further down, the *Rasna* and the *Nilesh Dining Hall* have thalis, while downstairs in the Tourist Bungalow, the *Toran Restaurant* offers basic vegetarian food and leisurely service.

The *Marine Restaurant*, on the seaward side of the Tourist Bungalow, is

an 'ephemeral' snack bar. On Sunday evenings, a vast crowd of well-dressed middle-class citizens flock here to parade themselves on the Esplanade, and stalls on wheels feed them cane juice, peanuts and so on. You can sit in the Marine 'Rest' and enjoy excellent samosas or ice cream.

Getting There & Away

Air Vayudoot services the airport at Porbandar.

Bus There are a couple of early-morning buses to Veraval. They take about three hours and cost Rs 16.

Train Porbandar is the terminus of a rail line; the main service is the No 15-16 Saurashtra Express to and from Bombay via Rajkot (6½ hours) and Ahmedabad (10 hours). Fares from Ahmedabad are Rs 53 in 2nd class, Rs 189 in 1st.

RAJKOT (population 420,000)

This pleasant town was once the capital of the princely state of Saurashtra and is also a former British government headquarters. Mahatma Gandhi spent the early years of his life here while his father was the chief minister, or Diwan, to the Raja of Saurashtra. The Gandhi family home, the Kaba Gandhi no Delo, now houses a permanent exhibition of Gandhi items.

Watson Museum

The Watson Museum & Library in the Jubilee Gardens commemorates Colonel John Watson, Political Agent from 1886 to 1889. The entrance is flanked by two imperial lions and among the exhibits are copies of artefacts from Moenjodaro, 13th-century carvings, silverware, natural history exhibits and textiles as well as dioramas of local tribal costumes and housing styles. Perhaps the most startling piece is a huge marble statue of Queen Victoria seated on a throne and decidedly not amused – hardly surprising, given that she has to wear the indignity of a brass crown and thumblessly hold an orb and sceptre. This section also has two plaster Venuses and many splendid portraits of colonial bigwigs. It's well worth the Rs 0.20 entry fee.

Places to Stay – bottom end

On Lakhajiraj Rd, the road leading into the heart of the bazaar area, are a number of hotels. At the upper end of this group, the *Hotel Intimate* offers 'laxurious living'; singles/doubles with bath cost Rs 40/60. More or less opposite is the *Himalaya Guest House*, a huge place where singles/doubles with bath are Rs 28/

55. It's basic, but clean and quite adequate, and bucket hot water is available at no extra charge. The entrance to this place is right inside the shopping complex over which it stands. A similar hotel is the *Anand Guest House*, behind the Hotel Intimate.

You'll find two other cheapies at the back of the bus station, the *Jyoti Guest House* (no English spoken) and the *Jayshree Guest House* which offers singles/doubles/triples with bath for Rs 25/38/50.

Very close to the bus station on the main

To Jamnagar

Railway Station

Rajkot

0   100   200m

Jubilee Gardens

M Gandhi Rd

Bazaar

Playing Fields

Lakhajiraj Rd

Rajendra Prasad Rd.

To Junagadh & Veraval

1	Flats
2	Stadium
3	Water Tower
4	Ambedkar Statue
5	Court
6	Bank
7	Women's Hospital
8	Fruit Market
9	GPO
10	Temple
11	Galaxy Hotel
12	Havmor Restaurant
13	Bank
14	Cemetary
15	Telegraph Office
16	Gandhi School & Statue
17	Library
18	Watson Museum
19	Information Centre
20	Bhabha Guest House & Dining Hall
21	Taj Restaurant
22	Indian Airlines
23	Sindh Punjab Restaurant
24	Ashok Guest House & Municipal Office
25	Bus Station
26	Ashok Hotel
27	Library
28	Hotel Intimate
29	Himalaya Guest House
30	Rainbow Restaurant
31	Anand Guest House
32	Vishram Restaurant
33	Jyoti Guest House
34	Jayshree Guest House
35	Ruby & Jeel Hotels
36	Hotel Tulsi & Kanchan Restaurant

road are the two branches of the *Ashok Hotel*. Both are basic boarding houses and offer a variety of rooms at Rs 25/35 for singles/doubles with bath, Rs 23 for singles with common bath and Rs 85 for deluxe doubles.

Places to Stay - middle

By far the best top-end hotel in Rajkot is the *Galaxy Hotel* (tel 31781/7) on Jawahar Rd. It has a good atmosphere, the staff are pleasant and helpful and the beautiful spacious rooms are kept spotlessly clean. The front rooms overlook the Maidan. Rooms cost Rs 90/140 for singles/doubles, Rs 200/260 with air-con. All rooms have bath with constant hot water. Most international credit cards are accepted and travellers' cheques can be cashed, but there's no restaurant.

The *Hotel Tulsi* (tel 33991/3), Kanak St, is a fairly new high-rise building and similar in price. Rooms cost Rs 100/150 for singles/doubles, Rs 175/225 with air-con and colour TV. There are foreign exchange facilities, credit cards are accepted and the hotel has its own restaurant, the Kanchan.

Other mid-range hotels include the *Hotel Jayson* (tel 26170) on S V P Rd (Canal Rd) and the *Hotel Mohit International* (tel 33338) on Sir Harilal Gosaliya Marg.

Places to Eat

For cheap vegetarian food and thalis, try the popular *Vaibhav Restaurant* attached to the Ashok Hotel. The thalis served in the *Bhabha Dining Hall* at the Bhabha Guest House on Panchnath Rd, not far from the Galaxy Hotel, is excellent though somewhat more expensive.

There's good, cheap south Indian food at the *Rainbow Restaurant* opposite the Hotel Intimate. A masala dosa, coffee and soft drink comes to just Rs 7.50.

The better class *Havmor*, near the Galaxy Hotel, serves Indian, Chinese and western food. Also nearby, but in the other direction, is the vegetarian *Taj Restaurant*.

The *Sindh Punjab* in the Municipal Office offers cheap vegetarian and non-vegetarian food.

For a splurge, try the *Kanchan* restaurant at the Hotel Tulsi.

Getting There & Away

Air Indian Airlines flies Bombay/Bhavnagar/Rajkot/Bombay daily. A mini-bus between the Indian Airlines office in town and the airport connects with the flights.

Bus Each day, there are a number of 'luxury' buses from the state bus stand between Rajkot and Veraval and between Rajkot and Jamnagar in each direction. Pay your fare on the bus. For either service, it's also advisable to buy a seat reservation ticket in advance for Rs 1. The trip from Rajkot to Veraval via Junagadh takes about five hours and costs Rs 20. Rajkot to Jamnagar is a two-hour journey and costs Rs 18. It's advisable to avoid the ordinary buses – they're very crowded and you'll have to fight your way onto them.

There are also a number of private buses which operate to such places as Ahmedabad. Eagle Travels, Moti Tati Shop (a 10-minute walk from the bus station), has daily luxury buses to Ahmedabad (Rs 80) and Bombay (Rs 160).

Train The overnight (broad gauge) Saurashtra Express connects Rajkot with Ahmedabad 246 km away. Fares are Rs 32 in 2nd class and Rs 109 in 1st. There are other fast trains to and from Jamnagar and Hapa (broad gauge), Porbandar and Veraval (metre gauge).

AROUND RAJKOT
Wankaner

Like so many Indian palaces, the Royal Palace of Wankaner, about 50 km from Rajkot, is now a hotel and holiday resort. The regal palace has a swimming pool, museum and game reserve, not to mention the maharana's collection of vintage cars. Reservations must be made in advance if you wish to stay; it's mainly used for groups. From here, you can make excursions to the Little Rann of Kutch or to the palace and monuments of Halvad.

Surendrangar (Wadhwan)

This town on the route from Ahmedabad to Rajkot features the very old temple of Ranik Devi, who became involved in a dispute between local rulers Sidh Raja (who planned to marry her) and Rao Khengar (who carried her off and did marry her). When Sidh Raja defeated Rao Khengar, she chose sati over dishonour and Sidh Raja built the temple as her memorial.

Kutch (Kachchh)

The western-most part of Gujarat is virtually an island; indeed, during the monsoon period from May, it really is an island. The Gulf of Kutch divides Kutch from the Kathiawar Peninsula while, to the north, Kutch is separated from the Sind region of Pakistan by the Great Rann of Kutch.

The salt in the soil makes this low-lying marsh area almost completely barren. Only on scattered 'islands' which rise above the salt level is there vegetation. During the dry season, the Rann is a vast expanse of hard, dried mud. Then, with the start of the monsoon in May, it is flooded first by sea water, then again by the fresh water from rivers as they fill. Kutch is also separated from the rest of Gujarat to the east by the Little Rann of Kutch.

During the winter, the Gulf of Kutch is a breeding ground for flamingoes and pelicans. The Indian wild ass lives in the Little Rann of Kutch and part of the area has been declared a sanctuary for this rare animal. Because of their isolation, the people of Kutch have preserved their local customs and traditions to a much greater

degree than elsewhere in the state and you're in for a very colourful experience. Very few tourists ever visit this part of India.

BHUJ (population 60,000)

Bhuj, the major town of Kutch, is an old walled city – until very recently the city gates were still locked each night from dusk to dawn. It's one of those places which leaps right out of the pages of Rudyard Kipling. Bhuj is the Jaisalmer of Gujarat except that, in this case, the walls not only enclose the palace but almost the entire bazaar area and a lake too! The bazaar is lively and extremely colourful.

You can lose yourself for hours in the maze-like streets and alleyways of this town. There are walls within walls, crenellated gateways, old palaces with intricately carved wooden pavilions, Hindu temples decorated with the gaudy, gay abandon of which only tribal people seem capable, equally colourful tribes-people and camels pulling huge cartfuls of produce into the various markets. All this exists right next to one of the largest Indian Air Force bases in the country, with aircraft taking off, on average, every 20 minutes. In short, there's never a dull moment.

Bhuj resembles much of India before the tourist invasion. You can expect stares from just about everyone because they don't see many westerners. On the other hand, because people remain largely unaffected by what goes on outside the area, you're much more likely to come across that disarming hospitality which was once the hallmark of rural India. Where else would someone offer you a lift on their bicycle?

Information

The State Bank of India on Station Rd, near the Indian Airlines office, changes money with amazing speed.

Indian Airlines itself has a minibus which connects with all incoming and outgoing flights; it costs Rs 5.

Palace & Museum

The Kachchh Museum was originally known as the Fergusson Museum after its founder, Sir James Fergusson, a Governor of Bombay under the British Raj. Built in 1877, it's the oldest museum in Gujarat and has an excellent collection. The well-maintained and labelled (in English and Gujarati) exhibits include a picture gallery, an anthropological section, archaeological finds, textiles, weapons, musical instruments, a shipping section and, of course, stuffed animals. The museum is open every day, except Wednesdays and the 2nd and 4th Saturday of each month, from 9 to 11.30 am and 3 to 5.30 pm. Entry costs Rs 0.20. This is one of the best museums in India.

Rao Pragmalji's Palace is an ornate Italianate marble and sandstone building which was constructed in the latter part of the 19th century. Parts of it are now used for government offices but the vast Darbar Hall and the clock tower are open to the public. High up on the walls of this hall are portraits of past maharaos while down below is the usual mausoleum of big game driven to the verge of extinction by egotism and pompous stupidity. It's said that the beautiful inlaid wood and ivory door of the palace was coveted for some time by the British Museum. The correspondence relating to the British attempt to 'borrow' this priceless object many years ago is solemnly set out next to the door. Perhaps it's a pity that they never did borrow it because it's in an advanced state of disrepair. The clock tower adjacent to the Darbar Hall is well worth climbing for the superb views over the town and surrounding countryside.

The old palace, built in traditional Kutchi style, is across the courtyard from the new palace. It's a pity that the palace is not open to the public but it's been sadly neglected and is in urgent need of major renovation.

Entry to the palace and clock tower costs Rs 2; remove your shoes at the door. There's a sign saying, 'Photography prohibited' as you enter and, although it's usually enforced in the Darbar Hall itself, there's no-one at the top of the tower to stop you clicking away to your heart's content. Opening times for the palace are the same as those for the Kachchh Museum.

Other Attractions

A huge old wall stretches around the hills overlooking the city – the view is best from near the railway station. Unfortunately, you cannot explore as this is all a restricted military area. The dilapidated Maharao Palace to the north of the lake is noted for its quaint pillars. Stone statues flank the entrance but, inside, many statues are now headless and deteriorating.

The colourful and richly decorated Swaminarayan Temple is near the bazaar. Descriptions and photographs of this temple have featured in many travel magazines around the world. Non-Hindus are allowed inside but, if you want to take photographs, it's probably best to enlist (for a small fee) one of the people who hang around outside the temple offering their services as guides.

Around Bhuj

The city is connected by road with the old port of Mandvi to the south-west and by road and rail to the new port of Kandala. It is intended that Kandala should substitute for Karachi as a port for this area. There is a boat service from Kandala to Navlakhi, which is on the Kathiawar Peninsula and connected to Morvi and Wankaner by rail.

The new town of Gandhidham, near Kandala, was established to take refugees from the Sind following partition. About 150 km north-east of Bhuj, the remains of Indus Valley civilisation fortifications have been discovered.

Places to Stay – bottom end

Many travellers seem to stay at the *Sagar Guest House*, over the road from the bus stand. It's fairly cheap at Rs 10 for dorm beds and Rs 30/40/50 for singles/doubles/

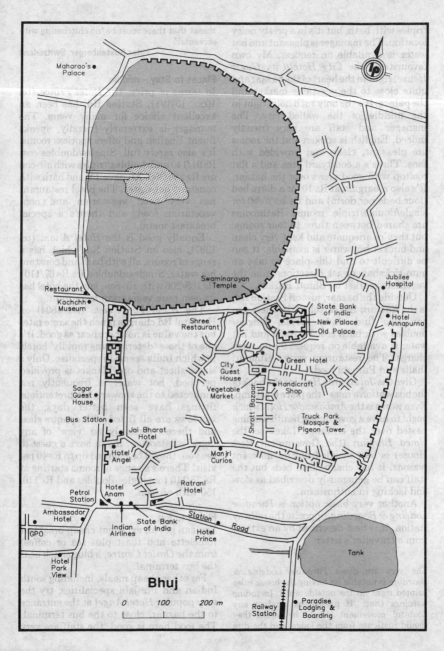

Maharao's Palace

Jubilee Hospital

Restaurant

Kachchh Museum

Swaminarayan Temple

State Bank of India

New Palace
Old Palace

Hotel Annapurna

Shree Restaurant

Green Hotel

Sagar Guest House

City Guest House

Handicraft Shops

Bus Station

Vegetable Market

Shrott Bazaar

Truck Park Mosque & Pigeon Tower

Jai Bharat Hotel

Hotel Angel

Manjri Curios

Hotel Anam

Ratrani Hotel

Petrol Station

Ambassador Hotel

GPO

Indian Airlines

State Bank of India

Station Road

Hotel Prince

Hotel Park View

Tank

Bhuj

0   100   200 m

Paradise Lodging & Boarding

Railway Station

triples with bath, but it's in a pretty noisy location. The manager is pleasant and hot water is available on request. My own favourite is the *City Hotel/City Guest House*, right in the heart of the bazaar and quite close to the vegetable market and the palace. It's the only such hotel right in the middle of the walled city. The manager and staff are very friendly indeed, English is spoken and the rooms are pleasant, clean and provided with fans. There's a courtyard area and a flat rooftop with good views over the bazaar. It's also a bargain at Rs 10 for a dorm bed (four beds per dorm) and Rs 20/25/50 for single/double/triple rooms. Bathrooms are shared between three to four rooms, but they're adequate and kept very clean and bucket hot water is available. It can be difficult to find this place so take an auto-rickshaw or ask directions from the vegetable market on Shrott Bazaar.

Outside the bazaar, just off Station Rd, is the *Ratrani Hotel* (tel 1607) where you can also find cheap rooms. Singles/doubles with bath cost Rs 20/30 and hot water is available on request for no extra charge. The restaurant serves Gujarati thalis and Punjabi food.

Give the *Jai Bharat Hotel* at the back of the bus station a miss – the place is a dump. Even worse is the *Ambassador Hotel* which ought to have a government health warning pasted over the entrance. Likewise, the *Umed Bhavan* (the Government Rest House) is best avoided but for different reasons. It has cheap dorm beds but the staff can be generously described as slow and lacking in enthusiasm.

Another very basic option is *Paradise Lodging & Boarding*, opposite the railway station. It is best described by an extract from a traveller's letter:

The very run-down *Paradise Lodging & Boarding* is notable for having the house rules painted right on the outside walls. Including warnings that: 'If passengers conduct any doubtful movement should be found they should rusticate from the lodge' and the dire threat that there must be 'no chitcheting with servents!'

Peter Russenberger, Switzerland

Places to Stay – middle

In terms of price, the *Hotel Prince* (tel 1095, 1370/1), Station Rd, has been an excellent choice for many years. The manager is extremely friendly, speaks fluent English and offers spotless rooms. It's also rarely full. Singles/doubles cost Rs 91/140 and doubles/triples with air-con are Rs 256/395. All have TV and bath with constant hot water. The hotel restaurant has very good vegetarian and non-vegetarian food, and there's a special breakfast menu.

Equally good is the *Hotel Anam* (tel 1397), also on Station Rd, which has a range of rooms, all with bath and constant hot water. Singles/doubles are Rs 67/110 , Rs 165/206 with air-con, and the hotel has its own pure vegetarian restaurant.

The *Hotel Park View* (tel 1804) on Hospital Rd charges much the same rates but the value is nowhere near as good. It's one of those 'deteriorating rapidly' hotels in which India seems to specialise. Only a single sheet and one blanket is provided per bed, hot water is frequently not connected to the showers, the pretentious fittings have seen better days, the windows are all fitted with opaque glass and there's certainly no 'view' of any 'park' whatsoever. If you have a guest to see you, they'll be charged up to Rs 40 per visit! There's a range of rooms starting at Rs 75/110 for singles/doubles and Rs 110/150 with air-con.

Places to Eat

You can get an excellent cheap breakfast (omelette and toast plus tea or coffee) from the *Omlet Centre*, a blue shack near the bus terminal.

For other cheap meals, including south Indian and Punjabi specialities, try the very popular *Hotel Angel* at the entrance to the bazaar, close to the bus terminal. The food here is good, the staff are very friendly and the restaurant is on three floors – choose your level!

Perhaps the best vegetarian thalis in town can be found at the air-conditioned restaurant on the ground floor of the *Hotel Anam*. They cost Rs 16 without dessert, Rs 20 with dessert. The restaurant is open for lunch from 10.30 am to 3 pm and for dinner from 7 to 10 pm, except on Sundays when it opens only for lunch. For a splurge, have a meal at the *Hotel Prince*. It has both vegetarian and non-vegetarian dishes but doesn't serve thalis.

The nearest restaurant to the City Hotel is the *Green Hotel*, down a small alley opposite the vegetable market. It offers cheap meals and snacks, with a range of available dishes.

If you're wandering around the bazaar or visiting the palace, the *Shree Restaurant*, opposite the top end of the Swaminarayan Temple, is a good place to have a cold drink or a snack and watch the world go by. The staff are very friendly.

Things to Buy
Ramnik K Shah, Gopiani St, Shroff Bazaar, is a very friendly person who speaks English and is involved in the import/export trade. His crafts shop is on the map. For the renowned Kutchi embroideries, you must go out to the villages and deal directly with the local people.

Getting There & Away
Air Indian Airlines flies Bombay/Jamnagar/Bhuj/Bombay daily, except Monday and Thursday. These flights sometimes call at Jamnagar on the return journey too.

Flights to or from Bhuj are often delayed because of military activity at the airport, so it's a good idea to call at the Indian Airlines office around noon to see whether the flight to Bombay has been delayed.

Bus Buses run to other centres in Gujarat including Ahmedabad, Rajkot and Kandala Port. You can also take taxis between Bhuj and Rajkot. These depart from near the state bus stand and cost about Rs 30 per seat. N K Travels at the north end of the bus station have an overnight deluxe bus to Ahmedabad for Rs 75. It's a long two-day bus trip north from Bhuj through Barmer to Jaisalmer in Rajasthan.

Train There is a daily rail connection with Ahmedabad, 310 km away, but some trains take a much longer route via Palanpur. Fares are Rs 37 in 2nd class, Rs 134 in 1st. There are also trains between Bhuj and Kandala Port.

A fast way of getting to Bhuj from Bombay is to take the daily superfast express from Bombay to Gandhidham via Ahmedabad, broad-gauge all the way. Plenty of buses are available for the two-hour trip from Gandhidham to Bhuj.

Getting Around
Airport Transport You're advised to take the Rs 5 minibus which runs from the Indian Airlines office to the airport to connect with flights – the taxi and auto-rickshaw drivers are rapacious. They'll demand Rs 30 but accept Rs 20 after much haggling. Even so, it's a rip-off since the airport is only four km out of town (though they'll tell you it's nine km).

Local Transport When you're not just wandering around the bazaars there are plenty of auto-rickshaws.

Madhya Pradesh

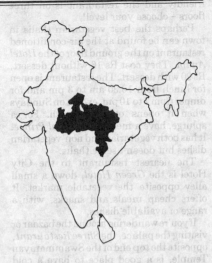

Population: 62 million
Area: 442,841 square km
Capital: Bhopal
Main language: Hindi

The large state of Madhya Pradesh is the geographical heartland of India. Most of the state is a high plateau and in summer it can be very dry and hot. Virtually all phases of Indian history have left their mark on Madhya Pradesh, historically known as Malwa. There are still many pre-Aryan Gond and Bhil tribal people in the state, but Madhya Pradesh is overwhelmingly Indo-Aryan with the majority of the people speaking Hindi and following Hinduism.

Two of Madhya Pradesh's attractions are remote and isolated: Khajuraho, in the north of the state, is a long way from anywhere and most easily visited when travelling between Agra and Varanasi; Jabalpur, with its marble rocks, is in the centre of the state.

Most of the state's other attractions are on or near the main Delhi to Bombay rail line. From Agra, just outside the state to the north, you can head south through Gwalior (with its magnificent fort), Sanchi, Bhopal, Ujjain, Indore and Mandu. From there you can head west to Gujarat or south to the Ajanta and Ellora caves in Maharashtra.

History

The state's history goes back to the time of Ashoka, the great Buddhist emperor whose Mauryan Empire was powerful in Malwa. At Sanchi you can see the Buddhist centre founded by Ashoka, the most important reminder of him in India today. The Mauryans were followed by the Sungas and then by the Guptas, before the Huns swept across the state. Around 1000 years ago the Parmaras ruled in south-west Madhya Pradesh – they're chiefly remembered for Raja Bhoj, who gave his name to the city of Bhopal and also ruled over Indore and Mandu.

From 950-1050 AD the Chandellas constructed the fantastic series of temples at Khajuraho in the north of the state. Today Khajuraho is one of India's main attractions. Between the 12th and 16th centuries the region saw continuing struggles between Hindu and Muslim rulers or invaders. Often the fortified city of Mandu in the south-west was the scene for these battles, but finally the Moghuls overcame Hindu resistance and controlled the region, only to fall to the Marathas who, in turn, fell to the British.

Northern Madhya Pradesh

GWALIOR (population 650,000)

In the extreme north-west of Madhya Pradesh and a few hours from Agra by train or road, Gwalior is famous for its old and very large fort. Within the fort walls

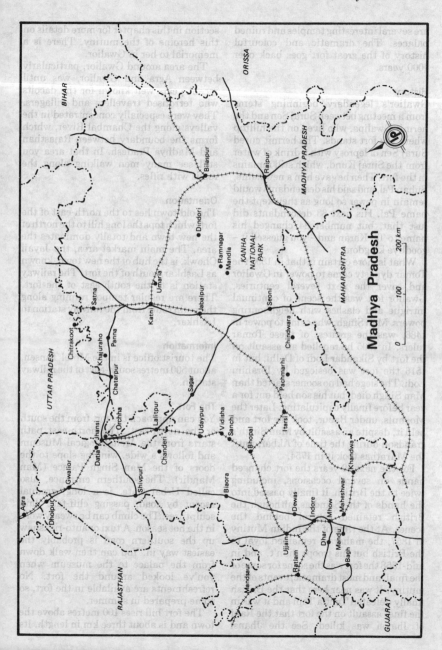

are several interesting temples and ruined palaces. The dramatic and colourful history of the great fort goes back over 1000 years.

History

Gwalior's legendary beginning stems from a meeting between Suraj Sen and the hermit Gwalipa, who lived on the hilltop where the fort stands. The hermit cured Suraj Sen of leprosy with a drink of water from the Suraj Kund, which still remains in the fort. Then he gave him a new name, Suhan Pal, and said his descendants would remain in power so long as they kept the name Pal. His next 83 descendants did just that, but number 84 changed his name to Tej Karan and – you guessed it – goodbye kingdom.

What is more certain is that in 1398 the Tomar dynasty came to power in Gwalior and, over the next several centuries, Gwalior fort was the scene of continual intrigue and clashes with neighbouring powers. Man Singh, who came to power in 1486, was the greatest of these Tomar rulers. In 1505 he repelled an assault on the fort by Sikandar Lodi of Delhi, but in 1516 the fort was besieged by Ibrahim Lodi. The siege had no sooner started than Man Singh died, but his son held out for a year before finally capitulating. Later the Moghuls, under Babur, took the fort and held it, despite an assault by Man Singh's grandson during the time of Akbar, until the Marathas took it in 1754.

For the next 50 years the fort changed hands on several occasions, including twice to the British. It finally passed into the hands of the Scindias, although the British retained control behind the scenes. At the time of the Indian Mutiny in 1857, the maharaja remained loyal to the British but his troops didn't, and in mid-1858 the fort was the scene for some of the final, and most dramatic, events of the mutiny. It was near here that the British finally defeated Tantia Topi and it was in the final assault on the fort that the Rani of Jhansi was killed. See the Jhansi section in this chapter for more details on this heroine of the mutiny. There is a memorial to her in Gwalior.

The area around Gwalior, particularly between Agra and Gwalior, was until recent years well known for the dacoits who terrorised travellers and villagers. They were especially concentrated in the valleys along the Chambal River, which forms the boundary between Rajasthan and Madhya Pradesh. In that area you still see many men walking along the roads with rifles.

Orientation

The old town lies to the north-east of the fort, which tops the long hill to the north of the new town and totally dominates the area. The main market area, the Jayaji Chowk, is the hub of the new town, known as Lashkar, south of the fort. The railway station is to the south-east of the fort. There are regular tempos running along the main route from the railway station to Lashkar.

Information

The tourist office is in the Motel Tansen, about 500 metres south-east of the railway station.

The Fort

You can approach the fort from the south or the north-east. The north-east path starts from the Archaeological Museum and follows a wide, winding slope to the doors of the Man Singh Palace (Man Mandir). The southern entrance, also called Urbai Gate, is a long, gradual ascent by road, passing cliff-face Jain sculptures. The climb can be sweaty work in the hot season. A taxi or auto-rickshaw up the southern road is probably the easiest way in. You can then walk down from the palace to the museum when you've looked around the fort. No refreshments are available in the fort, so come prepared in summer.

The fort hill rises 100 metres above the town and is about three km in length. Its width varies from nearly a km to less than 200 metres. The fort walls, which continue around almost the entire hilltop, are 10 metres high and imposingly solid. Beneath the walls, the hill face is a sheer drop away to the plains. On a clear day the view from the fort walls is superb; old Gwalior itself clings to the northern and north-eastern end of the fort hill. The view extends far out over the surrounding plains.

There are several things to see in and around the fort, although most of the enclosed area is simply open space and fields.

Gwalior Fort

Archaeological Museum The museum is within the Gujri Mahal Palace, at the start of the north-east ascent to the fort. The palace was built in the 15th century by Man Singh for his favourite queen, Mrignayani. The building is now rather deteriorated but the museum has a collection of Hindu and Jain sculptures and copies of the Bagh Caves' frescoes.

The museum is open from 10 am to 5 pm daily but is closed on Mondays.

North-East Entrance There is a whole series of gates as you ascend the path to the Man Singh Palace (Man Mandir). At one time the path had steps, but they have now been smoothed into one long ascent, though they're still more suitable for feet than wheels. The first of the six gates is the Alamgiri Gate, dating from 1660. It was named after Aurangzeb, who took the title of Governor of Alamgiri in this region.

The second gate dates from the same period as the Gujri Mahal and is known as the Badalgarh, after Badal Singh, Man Singh's uncle, or as the Hindola Gate after a swing, or *hindol*, which used to stand here. The third gate, the Bansur, or 'archer's gate', has disappeared.

The interesting fourth gate was built in the 1400s and named after the elephant-headed god, Ganesh. There is a small pigeon house or Kabutar Khana here and a small four-pillared Hindu temple to the hermit Gwalipa, after whom the fort and town were named. Next you pass a Vishnu shrine dating from 876 AD known as Chatarbhujmandir, shrine of the four-armed. A tomb nearby is that of a nobleman killed in an assault on this gate in 1518. From here a series of steps lead to rock-cut Jain sculptures at the north-east of the fort. They are not of the same size, quality and importance as the sculptures on the southern side. There are other Hindu sculptures along this same face.

The Hathiya Paur, or 'elephant gate', forms the entrance to the palace. Within the palace was the final gate, the Hawa Gate, but this has also been removed.

Man Singh Palace The palace, or Man Mandir, is a delightfully whimsical building, also known as the Chit Mandir or 'painted palace' because of the tiled and painted decorations of ducks, elephants and peacocks. Painted blue, with hints of green and gold, it still looks very good today.

The palace was built by Man Singh between 1486 and 1516 and repaired in 1881. It has four storeys, two of them underground and all of them now deserted. The subterranean ones are cool, even in the summer heat, and were used as prison cells during the Moghul period. The emperor Aurangzeb had his brother Murad imprisoned and executed here. The east face of the palace, with its six towers topped by domed cupolas, stands over the fort entrance path.

The museum in the palace is open from 8 am to 5 pm, Tuesday to Sunday.

Other Palaces There are other palaces clustered within the fort walls at the northern end. None are as interesting or as well preserved as the Man Singh Palace. The Karan Palace, or Kirti Mandir, is a long, narrow two-storey palace on the western side of the fort. At the northern end are the Jehangir and Shah Jahan palaces with a very large and deep tank, the Jauhar Kund, named after the jauhar, or ritual Rajput suicide, that took place here in 1232.

Sasbahu Temples The 'mother-in-law' and 'daughter-in-law' temples stand close to the eastern wall about midway along that side of the fort. The two temples are similar in style and date from the 9th to 11th centuries. The larger temple has an ornately carved base and figures of Vishnu over the entrances, and four huge pillars carry the heavy roof.

Teli-Ka-Mandir On the opposite side of the fort, beyond the Suraj Kund tank, this temple probably dates from the 9th century and has a peculiar plan and design. The roof is Dravidian while the decorations (the whole temple is covered with sculptures) are Indo-Aryan. A Garuda tops the 10-metre-high doorway. This is the highest structure in the fort.

Southern Entrance The long ascent on the southern side climbs up through a ravine to the fort gate. Along the rock faces flanking this road are many Jain sculptures, some impressively big. Originally cut into the cliff faces in the mid-1400s, they were defaced by the forces of Babur in 1527 but were later repaired.

The images are in five main groups and are numbered. In the Arwahi group, image 20 is a 17-metre-high standing sculpture of Adinath, while 22 is a 10-metre-high seated figure of Nemnath, the 22nd Jain tirthankar. The south-eastern group is the most important and covers nearly a km of the cliff face with more than 20 images.

Jai Vilas Palace & Museum

Located in the 'new town', which actually dates from 1809, this was the palace of the Scindia family. Although the current maharaja still lives in the palace, a large part of it is used as a museum. It's full of the bizarre items Hollywood maharajas are supposed to collect, such as Belgian cut-glass furniture, including a rocking chair, or what looks like half the tiger population of India, all shot, stuffed and moth-eaten. Then there's a little room full of erotica, including a life-sized marble statue of Leda having her way with a swan. But the *pièce de résistance* is a model railway that carried brandy and cigars around the dining table after dinner.

It's a long way from the palace entrance around the part still in use to the museum section. If you go there by auto-rickshaw, get dropped off at the museum, not at the palace entrance. The museum is open daily, except Mondays, from 10 am to 5 pm; admission is Rs 5.

The palace is in Lashkar, meaning 'camp', after the camp that Daulat Rao Scindia set up here in 1809 when he took control of Gwalior.

Old Town

The old town of Gwalior lies to the north and north-east of the fort hill. The 1661 Jami Masjid mosque is a fine old building, constructed of sandstone quarried from the fort hill. Mohammed Gaus, a Muslim saint who played a key role in Babur's acquisition of the fort, has his fine, large tomb on the eastern side of the town. It has hexagonal towers at its four corners, and a dome which was once covered with glazed blue tiles. It's a very good example of early Moghul architecture.

Close to the large tomb is the smaller Tomb of Tansen, a singer much admired by Akbar. Chewing the leaves of the tamarind tree near his grave is supposed to do wonders for your voice, although a few years ago some enthusiasts got somewhat carried away and ate the whole tree – roots and all! It is a place of pilgrimage for musicians during December-January. To find it, follow the Fort Rd from the north-eastern gate for about 15 minutes and turn right onto a small road.

Places to Stay – bottom end

There's nothing much near the railway station. As you go out the main gate, turn left and a minute or so away is the extremely basic *Hotel Ashok* with accommodation at Rs 20 per person. Straight across the road is the rather better but more expensive *Hotel India* (tel 24983), with singles/doubles at Rs 60/80. The *Hotel Safari* in the same area charges Rs 75/90 for singles/doubles.

The station has *retiring rooms*, but a female traveller suggested that the 2nd-class ladies' waiting room is almost as comfortable and free – so long as you can tolerate the mosquitoes and the constant comings and goings.

About half a km from the station, accessible on foot or by auto-rickshaw (Rs 4), is the state government's *Motel Tansen* (tel 21568) at 6 Gandhi Rd. It's comfortable and has well-kept rooms with bath for Rs 90/130 or Rs 200/250 with air-con. Camping in the garden is possible and the food is good and reasonably priced; it's a popular place with foreign visitors. The *Hotel President* and *Hotel*

Meghadoot are both cheaper with rooms for less than Rs 100.

None of Gwalior's accommodation is concentrated in one area – there's nothing much around the bus station in Lashkar either. On M L B Rd in Lashkar, the *Regal Hotel* has singles/doubles for Rs 80/110 or Rs 150/180 with air-con, but we've had some complaints about concealed peepholes in the bathrooms!

The friendly *Hotel Hemsons* at Phalke Bazaar, one of the few places in Lashkar, has very basic rooms from Rs 20.

At the top of this bracket, the *Hotel Vivek Continental* (tel 23624) is centrally located in Topi Bazaar and has rooms for Rs 90/120 or Rs 110/170 with air-con.

Places to Stay – top end

Gwalior's top hotel is the *Welcomgroup Usha Kiran Hotel* (tel 22049, 23453) at Jayendraganj, Lashkar. It's right behind the Jai Vilas Palace, and the 25 rooms are all either air-conditioned or air-cooled; singles/doubles are Rs 550/750.

Places to Eat

There's the usual selection of places to eat, including a *Kwality Restaurant* and a *Wengier's Restaurant*, both between the station and Lashkar. The Kwality has air-conditioning of arctic intensity. In the city centre at Jayaji Chowk, the *Hotel Saraswati Mahal* has good thalis for Rs 12.

Getting There & Away

Air There is a daily flight from Delhi through Gwalior to Bhopal (Rs 375), Indore (Rs 525) and Bombay (Rs 955) and vice versa. To Delhi the fare is Rs 330.

Bus There are regular bus services from Gwalior to Delhi, Agra, Ujjain, Indore, Bhopal, Jabalpur and Khajuraho, as well as to nearby centres like Shivpuri.

Train Gwalior, on the main Delhi to Bombay rail line, is 317 km from Delhi, 118 km from Agra and 1225 km from

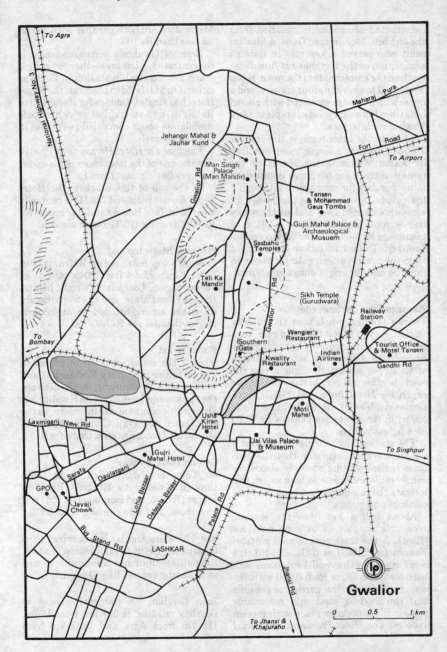

To Agra

National Highway No. 3

Maharaj Pura

Fort Road

To Airport

Jehangir Mahal & Jauhar Kund

Man Singh Palace (Man Mandir)

Gwalior Rd

Tansen & Mohammad Gaus Tombs

Gujri Mahal Palace & Archaeological Musuem

Sasbahu Temples

To Bombay

Teli Ka Mandir

Gwalior Rd

Sikh Temple (Gurudwara)

Railway Station

Wengier's Restaurant

Southern Gate

Kwality Restaurant

Indian Airlines

Tourist Office & Motel Tansen

Gandhi Rd

Moti Mahal

Usha Kiran Hotel

Laxmiganj New Rd

Jai Vilas Palace & Museum

To Singhpur

Gujri Mahal Hotel

Sarafa

Daulatganj

GPO

Lohia Bazaar

Daliwala Bazaar

Palace Rd

Jayaji Chowk

Bus Stand Rd

LASHKAR

Jhansi Rd

Gwalior

0   0.5   1 km

To Jhansi & Khajuraho

Bombay. From Delhi the express or mail trains take about six hours to Gwalior, and the fare is Rs 41 in 2nd class, Rs 141 in 1st.

It's only two hours between Agra and Gwalior and the fares are Rs 23 in 2nd class, Rs 83 in 1st. The Taj Express from Delhi to Agra continues on to Gwalior three times a week. The fastest train from Delhi is the superfast Shatabdi Express which takes only 3½ hours and costs Rs 140, including meals.

Getting Around
There are taxis, rickshaws, auto-rickshaws and tempos in Gwalior. Auto-rickshaw drivers will not use their meters, so arrange the fare before you depart. Tempos run regular services around the city; from the railway station to Bada, the main square in Lashkar, the fare is about Rs 2.

AROUND GWALIOR
Shivpuri
The old summer capital of Shivpuri is 114 km south-west of Gwalior and 94 km west of Jhansi. The road runs through a national park where you sometimes come across animals. Near Shivpuri is a pleasant lake surrounded by gardens. The road from Gwalior passes through Narwar with its large old fort.

Places to Stay The *Chinkara Motel* (tel 297) in Shivpuri has rooms at Rs 65/100. On the main road right in the middle of town, the *Harish Lodge* has well-kept rooms for just Rs 35 and a good restaurant.

Towards Agra
Between Gwalior and Agra, actually on a part of Rajasthan that separates Madhya Pradesh and Uttar Pradesh, is Dholpur. It was near here that Aurangzeb's sons fought a pitched battle to determine who would succeed him as emperor of the rapidly declining Moghul Empire. The Shergarh fort in Dholpur is very old and now in ruins. Near Bari is the Khanpur

Mahal, a pavilioned palace built for Shah Jahan but never occupied.

Towards Jhansi
To the east of the railway line, 61 km south of Gwalior towards Jhansi, a large group of white Jain temples is visible scattered along a hill. They're one of those strange, dream-like apparitions that so often seem simply to materialise in India. Sonagir is the nearest railway station.

Only 26 km north of Jhansi is Datia, with the deserted seven-storey palace of Raj Bir Singh Deo. The town is surrounded by a stone wall and the palace is to the west of the town.

CHANDERI
At the time of Mandu's greatest power, this was an important place, as indicated by the many ruined palaces, serais, mosques and tombs – all in a Pathan style similar to Mandu. The Koshak Mahal is a ruined Muslim palace which is still being maintained. Today the town is chiefly known for its gold brocades and saris. Chanderi is 33 km west of Lalitpur, which is 90 km south of Jhansi on the main railway line. Accommodation in the town includes a *Circuit House* and the *Rest House* near the bus stand.

JHANSI (population 270,000)
Jhansi, situated 101 km south of Gwalior, is actually in Uttar Pradesh, a part of that state extends into Madhya Pradesh, but for convenience we'll include it here. Although Jhansi has played a colourful role in Indian history, most visitors to the town today go there simply because it's a convenient transit point for Khajuraho. This is the closest the Delhi to Bombay rail line runs to Khajuraho, and there are good connections with Delhi and Agra; it's only three hours by bus from Jhansi to Khajuraho.

Orchha, only 18 km south of Jhansi, has a well-preserved 18th-century fort which is worth visiting if you're passing through.

Bir Singh Deo ruled from Orchha between 1605 and 1627 and built the Jhansi fort. A favourite of the Moghul prince Salim, he feuded with Akbar and in 1602 narrowly escaped the emperor's displeasure; his kingdom was all but ruined by Akbar's forces. Then in 1605 Prince Salim became Emperor Jehangir, and for the next 22 years Bir Singh was a powerful figure. In 1627, Shah Jahan became emperor and Bir Singh once again found himself out of favour; his attempt to revolt was put down by 13-year-old Aurangzeb.

In the 18th century Jhansi became an important centre, eclipsing Orchha, but in 1803 the British East India Company got a foot in the door and gradually assumed control over the state. The last of a string of none-too-competent rajas died without a son in 1853 and the British, who had recently passed a neat little law allowing them to take over any princely state under their patronage when the ruler died without a male heir, pensioned the rani off and took full control.

The Rani of Jhansi, who wanted to rule in her own right, was unhappy about this enforced retirement, so when the Indian Mutiny burst into flame four years later, she was in the forefront of the rebellion at Jhansi. The British contingent in Jhansi were all massacred, but the following year the rebel forces were still quarrelling amongst themselves and the British retook Jhansi. The rani fled to Gwalior and, in a valiant last stand, she rode out against the British, disguised as a man, and was killed. She has since become a heroine of the Indian independence movement, a sort of central Indian Joan of Arc.

The Jhansi fort was once used by the Indian Army but can now be visited. There are excellent views from its ramparts. The British ceded the fort to the Maharaja of Scindia in 1858, but later exchanged it for Gwalior in 1866. It was built in 1613 by Maharaja Bir Singh Deo of Orchha. Watch out for the monkeys, they often snatch things.

Information & Orientation

The old city is behind the fort, which is two km from the railway station. The town is quite spread out so you'll need to use auto-rickshaws to get around.

The Uttar Pradesh and Madhya Pradesh state governments have tourist booths at the railway station, although neither of them is particularly good.

Places to Stay & Eat

There are dorm beds in the railway *retiring rooms* and a handful of cheap places close to the station. The *Ashok Hotel* charges Rs 45/75 for singles/doubles and has more expensive air-con rooms.

The *Hotel Beerangana*, run by Uttar Pradesh Tourism, has rooms from Rs 50/75 up to Rs 175/225 with air-con. At the top of the scale the *Jhansi Hotel* is the best in town and has a fairly good restaurant and bar; rooms range from Rs 150 to Rs 300.

Most of the good restaurants are in the Cantonment area, near the Jhansi Hotel. The *Nav Bharat Restaurant* and the *Holiday* both serve good food. *Sharma's* has excellent sweets.

Getting There & Away

Bus Buses to Khajuraho leave from the railway station. They start early in the morning taking about three hours at a cost of Rs 25. To Orchha they leave from the bus stand, three km away.

Train Jhansi is on the main Delhi/Agra/Bhopal/Bombay railway line. The 414-km trip from Delhi takes only 5½ hours on the AP Express and costs Rs 51 in 2nd class, Rs 178 in 1st. To Bombay, it's 1128 km which takes about 21 hours and costs Rs 98 in 2nd class, Rs 380 in 1st. Agra is 215 km and four hours away.

There are also direct trains from Jhansi to Bangalore, Lucknow, Madras, Pune and Varanasi.

ORCHHA

This well-preserved city on an island in the Betwa River is worth a visit. It was

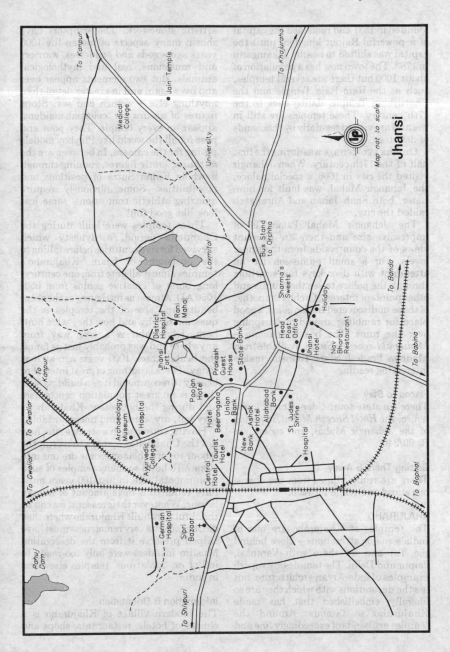

founded in 1531 and remained the capital of a powerful Rajput kingdom until the capital was shifted to nearby Tikamgadh in 1783. The town now has a population of about 1000 but there are several temples, such as the Ram Raja Temple and the Chaturbhuj Temple, dating back to the 17th century. These temples are still in use and are visited regularly by thousands of devotees.

Orchha's golden age was during the first half of the 17th century. When Jehangir visited the city in 1606, a special palace, the Jehangir Mahal, was built for him. Later, both Shah Jahan and Aurangzeb raided the city.

The Jehangir Mahal Palace is of impressive size and there are pleasant views of the countryside from the upper levels. For a small admission fee an attendant with door keys takes visitors through the palace to see the murals and other points of interest. Orchha is another of those undiscovered Indian gems, a good place for rambling around and tripping over the ruins. The booklet *Orchha – Medieval Legacy in Stone*, available from Madhya Pradesh State Tourism, makes interesting reading.

Places to Stay

There's a state tourist department guest house, the *Hotel Sheesh Mahal*, in a wing of the Jehangir Mahal, and rooms are Rs 90/240.

Getting There & Away

There are regular buses from the Jhansi bus stand to Orchha for Rs 5.

KHAJURAHO

The temples of Khajuraho are one of India's major attractions – close behind the Taj and up there with Varanasi, Jaipur and Delhi. The temples are superb examples of Indo-Aryan architecture, but it's the decorations with which they are so liberally embellished that has made Khajuraho so famous. Around the temples are bands of exceedingly fine and artistic stonework. The sculptors have shown many aspects of Indian life 1000 years ago – gods and goddesses, warriors and musicians, real and mythological animals. But two elements appear over and over again and in greater detail than anything else – women and sex. Stone figures of *apsaras* or 'celestial maidens' appear on every temple. They pout and pose for all the world like Playboy models posing for the camera. In between are the *mithuna*, erotic figures, running through a whole Kama Sutra of positions and possibilities. Some obviously require amazing athletic contortions, some just look like good fun!

These temples were built during the Chandella period, a dynasty which survived for five centuries before falling to the onslaught of Islam. Khajuraho's temples almost all date from one century-long burst of creative genius from 950-1050 AD. Almost as intriguing as the sheer beauty and size of the temples is the question of why and how they were built here. Khajuraho is a long way from anywhere and was probably just as far off the beaten track 1000 years ago as it is today. There is nothing of great interest or beauty to recommend it as a building site, there is no great population centre here and during the hot season Khajuraho is very hot, dry, dusty and uncomfortable.

Having chosen such a strange site, how did the Chandellas manage to recruit the labour to turn their awesome dreams into stone? To build so many temples of such monumental size in just 100 years must have required a huge amount of human labour. Whatever their reasons, we can be thankful they built Khajuraho where they did, because its very remoteness must have helped preserve it from the desecration Muslim invaders were only too ready to inflict on 'idolatrous' temples elsewhere in India.

Information & Orientation

The modern village of Khajuraho is a cluster of hotels, restaurants, shops and stalls around the bus station. A little north from there are three government-run hotels. By the bus stand are the museum, tourist office (tel 47) and post office. The temples are in three groups. By the modern part of Khajuraho is the western group, most of its temples in a well-kept enclosure; it includes the largest and most important temples.

A km or so east of the bus stand is the old village of Khajuraho; around it are the temples of the eastern group. Finally, the two southern groups of temples are further south. Small images of the gods can be bought from the shops in Khajuraho – plus lots of postcards.

Terminology

The Khajuraho temples follow a fairly consistent design pattern unique to Khajuraho. Understanding the architectural conventions and some of the terms will help you enjoy the temples more. Basically all the temples follow a five-part or three-part layout.

You enter the temples through an entrance porch, known as the *ardha-mandapa*, behind this is the hall or

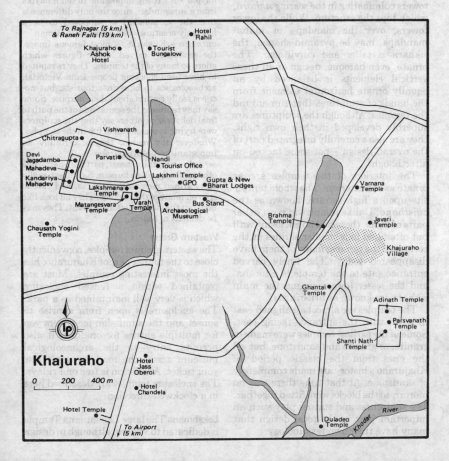

To Rajnagar (5 km) & Raneh Falls (19 km)

Hotel Rahil

Khajuraho Ashok Hotel

Tourist Bungalow

Chitragupta

Devi Jagadamba

Mahadeva

Kandariya Mahadev

Vishvanath

Parvati

Nandi

Tourist Office

Lakshmi Temple

GPO

Gupta & New Bharat Lodges

Lakshmana Temple

Matangesvara Temple

Varah Temple

Bus Stand

Archaeological Museum

Brahma Temple

Varnana Temple

Javari Temple

Khajuraho Village

Chausath Yogini Temple

Ghantai Temple

Adinath Temple

Parsvanath Temple

Shanti Nath Temple

Khajuraho

0   200   400 m

Hotel Jass Oberoi

Hotel Chandela

Hotel Temple

To Airport (5 km)

Duladeo Temple

Khodar River

mandapa. This leads into the main hall, or *mahamandapa*, supported with pillars and with a corridor around it. A vestibule or *antarala* then leads into the *garbhagriha*, the inner sanctum, where the image of the god to which the temple is dedicated is displayed. An enclosed corridor, the *pradakshina*, runs around this sanctum. The simpler three-part temples delete part 2 (the mandapa) and part 5 (the pradakshina), but otherwise follow the same plan as the five-part temples.

Externally the temples consist of successive waves of higher and higher towers culminating in the soaring *sikhara*, which tops the sanctum. While the lower towers, over the mandapa or maha-mandapa, may be pyramid-shaped, the sikhara is taller and curvilinear. The ornate, even baroque, design of all these vertical elements is balanced by an equally ornate horizontal element from the bands of sculptures that run around the temples. Although the sculptures are superbly developed in their own right, they are also a carefully integrated part of the overall design – not some tacked-on afterthought.

The interiors of the temples are as ornate as the exteriors. The whole temple sits upon a high terrace, known as the *adisthana*. Unlike temples in most other parts of India, these had no enclosing wall but often had four smaller shrines at the corners of the terrace; many of them have disappeared today. The finely carved entrance gate to the temple is a *torana*, and the lesser towers around the main sikhara are known as *urusringas*.

The temples are almost all aligned east to west, with the entrance facing east. Some of the earliest temples were made of granite, or granite and sandstone, but all the ones from the classic period of Khajuraho's history are made completely of sandstone. At that time there was no mortar, so the blocks were fitted together. The sculptures and statues play such an important part in the total design that many have their own terminology:

apsara – heavenly nymph, beautiful dancing woman.

salabhanjika – woman figure with tree, which together act as supporting brackets in the inner chambers of the temple. Apsaras also perform this bracket function.

surasundari – when a surasundari is dancing she is an apsara. Otherwise she attends the gods and goddesses by carrying flowers, water, ornaments, mirrors or other offerings. She also engages in everyday activities like washing her hair, applying make-up, taking a thorn out of her foot, fondling herself, playing with pets and babies, writing letters, playing musical instruments or posing seductively.

nayika – it's really impossible to tell a nayika from a surasundari, since the only difference is that the surasundari is supposed to be a heavenly creature while a nayika is human.

mithuna – Khajuraho's most famous image, the sensuously carved, erotic figures which adorn so many of the temples. They're reputed to have been shocking people from Victorian archaeologists to blue-rinse tourists, but no-one is really certain about their purpose. Some say they represent the sexual side of the path to final deliverance, others say that the sculptors were trying to include all of life in the temples. Whatever the reason, they're certainly an important part of Khajuraho.

sardula – a mythical beast, part lion, part some other animal or even human. Sardulas usually carry armed men on their backs, and can be seen on many of the temples. They all look like lions but the faces are often different. They may be demons or *asuras*.

Western Group

The western group of temples, conveniently close to the tourist part of Khajuraho, has the most interesting temples. Most are contained within a fenced enclosure which is very well maintained as a park. The enclosure is open from sunrise to sunset and the admission fee covers you for multiple entries for one day. It also permits entry to the archaeological museum across the road, so don't lose your ticket. Admission is free on Fridays. The enclosure temples are described here in a clockwise direction.

Lakshmana The large Lakshmana Temple is dedicated to Vishnu, although in design it is similar to the Kandariya Mahadev and Vishvanath temples. It is one of the earliest of the western enclosure temples, dating from around 930-950 AD, and also one of the best preserved with a full five-part floor plan and four subsidiary shrines. Around the temple are two bands of sculpture instead of the usual three; the lower one has fine figures of apsaras and some erotic scenes.

On the subsidiary shrine at the south-west corner you can make out an architect working with his students – it is thought this may be the temple's designer including himself in the grand plan. Around the base of the temple is a continuous frieze with scenes of battles, hunting and processions. The first metre or two of the frieze consists of a highly energetic orgy, including one gentleman proving that a horse can be a person's best friend, while a stunned group of women look aside in shock.

Lakshmi & Varah Facing the large Lakshmana Temple are these two small shrines. The Varah Temple, dedicated to

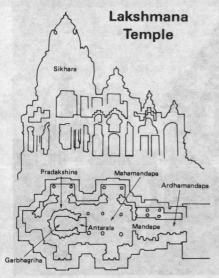

Lakshmana Temple

Vishnu's boar incarnation or Varah Avatar, actually faces the Matangesvara Temple which is outside the enclosure. Inside this small, open shrine is a huge, solid and intricately carved figure of the boar.

Kandariya Mahadev The first of the temples on the common platform at the back of the western enclosure is the one temple to see in Khajuraho above all others. The Kandariya Mahadev is not only the largest of the temples, it is also artistically and architecturally the most perfect. Built between 1025 and 1050, it represents Chandella art at its finest. Although the four subsidiary shrines which once stood around the main temple have long disappeared, the central shrine is in superb condition and shows the typical five-part design of Khajuraho temples.

The main spire is 31 metres high, and the temple is lavishly carved. The English archaeologist Cunningham counted 226 statues inside the temple and a further 646 outside – 872 in total with most of them nearly a metre in height. The statues are carved around the temple in three bands and include gods, goddesses, beautiful women, musicians and, of course, some of the famed erotic groups. The mithuna on the Kandariya Mahadev include some of the most energetic eroticism to be seen at Khajuraho. In the sexual Olympics there would definitely be some gold-medal winners here.

Mahadeva This small and mainly ruined temple stands on the same base as the Kandariya Mahadev and the Devi Jagadamba. Although small and insignificant compared to its mighty neighbours, it houses one of Khajuraho's best sculptures – a fine figure of a person (man or woman, observers have been unable to decide), caressing a lion.

Devi Jagadamba The third temple on the common platform is slightly older than the Kandariya Mahadev and of a simpler, three-part design. It was probably originally dedicated to Vishnu, but later changed to Parvati and then Kali. Some students believe it may still be a Parvati temple and that the Kali image (or Jagadamba) is actually an image of Parvati, painted black. The sculptures around the temple are again in three bands. Many of the two lower band images are of Vishnu with sardulas in the inner recesses. But on the third and uppermost band the mithuna again come out to play, and some feel that this is Khajuraho's most erotic temple.

Chitragupta The fourth temple at the back of the western enclosure does not share the common platform with the other three. Similar in design to the Devi Jagadamba, this temple is probably slightly newer and is unique at Khajuraho in being dedicated to Surya, the Sun God.

Attempts have obviously been made to restore the temple but it is not in as good condition as other temples. Nevertheless it has some very fine sculptures that include processions, dancing girls, elephant fights and hunting scenes. In the inner sanctum, Surya can be seen driving his chariot and seven horses, while on the central niche in the south facade you can see an 11-headed statue of Vishnu. The central head is that of Vishnu himself; the 10 others are of his incarnations.

Parvati Continuing around the enclosure, you come to the Parvati Temple on your right. The name is probably incorrect since this small and not so interesting temple was originally dedicated to Vishnu and now has an image of Ganga riding on the back of a crocodile.

Vishvanath Temple & Nandi Believed to have been built in 1002, this temple has the complete five-part design of the larger Kandariya Mahadev Temple, but two of its four subsidiary shrines still stand. That it is a Shiva shrine is made very clear

Khajuraho

by the large image of his vehicle, the bull Nandi, which faces the temple from the other end of the common platform. Steps lead up to this high terrace, flanked by lions on the northern side and elephants on the southern side. The sculptures around the temple include the usual Khajuraho scenes, but the sculptures of women are particularly notable here. They write letters, fondle a baby, play music and, perhaps more so than at any other temple, languish in provocative poses.

Matangesvara Temple Standing next to the Lakshmana Temple, this temple is not within the fenced enclosure because it is still in everyday use, unlike all the other old Khajuraho temples. It is one of the older temples at Khajuraho, dating from around 900-925 AD. The temple has a simpler floor plan than the other, more highly developed temples and does not have the same profusion of carvings. Inside the shrine is a highly polished 2½-metre-high lingam.

Chausath Yogini Standing beyond the tank, some distance from the other western group temples, this ruined temple is probably the oldest at Khajuraho, dating from 900 AD or earlier. It is also the only temple constructed entirely of granite and the only one not aligned east to west. Chausath means 64 – the temple once had 64 cells for figures of the 64 yoginis who attended the goddess Kali. A 65th cell sheltered Kali herself. A further half km west is the Lalguan Mahadev Temple, a small, ruined shrine dedicated to Shiva and constructed of granite and sandstone.

Archaeological Museum
Close to the western enclosure and across the road from the post office, the museum has a fine collection of statues and sculptures rescued from around Khajuraho. It's small and definitely worth a visit. Opening hours are from 9 am to 5 pm daily except Fridays, and admission is included in the western enclosure entrance fee.

Temple sculpture, Khajuraho

Opposite the museum, in the Archaeological Survey of India's compound beside the Matangesvara Temple, there are many more rescued sculptures – but the area is off limits.

Eastern Group
The eastern group of temples can be subdivided into two groups. The first is made up of the interesting Jain temples in the walled enclosure. The other four temples are scattered through the small village of Khajuraho. The easiest way to see these temples is to take a rickshaw out to the Jain enclosure and then walk back to your hotel through Khajuraho village. Alternatively, you can visit all the temples en route to the southern group.

Parsvanath The largest of the Jain temples in the walled enclosure is also one of the finest temples at Khajuraho. Although it does not approach the western enclosure temples in size, and does not attempt to compete in the sexual activity stakes, it is notable for the exceptional skill and precision of its construction, and for the beauty of its sculptures. Some of the best known figures at Khajuraho can be seen here, including the classic figure of a woman removing a thorn from her foot and another of a woman applying eye make-up. Although it was originally dedicated to Adinath, an image of Parsvanath was substituted about a century ago and the temple takes its name from this newer image.

Adinath Adjacent to the Parsvanath Temple, the smaller Adinath has been partially restored over the centuries. It has fine carvings on its three bands of sculptures and, like the Parsvanath, is very similar to the Hindu temples of Khajuraho. Only the image in the inner sanctum indicates that it is Jain rather than Hindu.

Shanti Nath This temple is a relatively modern one built about a century ago, but it contains many components from older temples around Khajuraho and a fine collection of Jain sculpture. The Jain compound also contains a small museum.

Ghantai Walking from the eastern Jain temple group towards Khajuraho village, you come to this small, ruined Jain temple. Only its pillared shell remains, but it is interesting for the delicate columns with their bell and chain decoration and for the figure of a Jain goddess astride a Garuda which marks the entrance.

Javari Walk through the village, a typical small Indian settlement, to this temple. Dating from around 1075-1100 AD, it is dedicated to Vishnu and is a particularly fine example of Khajuraho architecture on a small scale. The exterior has more of Khajuraho's delightful women.

Vamana About 200 metres north of the Javari Temple, this temple is dedicated to Vamana, the dwarf incarnation of Vishnu. Slightly older than the Javari Temple, the Vamana Temple stands out in a field all by itself. It's notable for the relatively simple design of its shikara. The bands of sculpture around the temples are, as usual, very fine with numerous 'celestial maidens' adopting interesting poses.

Brahma Turning back towards the modern village, you pass this granite and sandstone temple, one of the oldest at Khajuraho. It was actually dedicated to Vishnu and the definition of it as a Brahma temple is incorrect. Taking the road directly from the modern village to the Jain enclosure, you pass a temple dedicated to Hanuman with a large image of the monkey god.

Southern Group
There are only two temples in the southern group, one of which is several km south of the river.

Temple sculpture, Khajuraho

Duladeo A dirt track runs to this isolated temple, about a km south of the Jain enclosure. This is the latest temple at Khajuraho, and experts say that at this time the skill of Khajuraho's temple builders had passed its peak and the sculptures are more 'wooden' and 'stereotyped' than on earlier temples. Nevertheless, it's a fine and graceful temple with figures of women in a variety of pin-up poses and a number of mithuna couples.

Chaturbhuja South of the river, about three km from the village and a healthy hike down a dirt road, this ruined temple has a fine three-metre-high image of Vishnu.

Tours

There are walking tours around the western group of temples. Sometimes the Archaeological Survey of India in Khajuraho provides cheap tours by competent guides. Licensed private guides are also available for hire.

Places to Stay – bottom end

The state government *Hotel Rahil* (tel 62), fairly close to the Khajuraho Ashok Hotel, has singles/doubles with hot showers for Rs 80/100; there are also 72 dormitory beds at Rs 20 each. This place is pretty basic so don't expect too much. Similar in standard and also run by the state government is the *Tourist Village* which has singles or doubles for Rs 60. Meals are available at both places.

There's a cluster of cheap hotels near the bus station, many quite reasonable. Try the *New Bharat Lodge* (tel 82), popular with travellers, or the *Jain Lodge* (tel 52); doubles in both these places cost around Rs 65. The *Shita Lodge* is clean and good value at Rs 35 a double. Others include the *Gupta Lodge* and the *Laxmi Lodge*.

The *Hotel Sunset View* (tel 77) has doubles with bath for Rs 60 and is very clean and modern. Rooms face into a courtyard in this pleasant hotel, and

there's also a Rs 15 dorm. Don't buy jewellery from its crafts shop! It's on the main road from the airport, just before the town. The *Hotel Surya*, with rooms at Rs 40 has been recommended, as has the *Yadar Lodge* on Jain Temple Rd.

More expensive is the state government *Tourist Bungalow* (tel 64) which has singles/doubles for Rs 100/150. All meals are available here.

Places to Stay – top end

The state tourist department's *Hotel Payal* (tel 76) has spacious singles/doubles for Rs 100/150 or Rs 250/300 with air-con. It's clean, well kept and everything seems to work, although the service is slow. There's a bar, and average meals are available in the hotel's restaurant.

The *Hotel Chandela* (tel 54) is south of the modern village, towards the airport. It's the number one hotel at Khajuraho and its 102 air-con rooms cost Rs 700/900 a single/double. Nonguests can use the hotel's swimming pool for Rs 30.

The *Khajuraho Ashok Hotel* (tel 24, 42), a short walk north of the modern village, is cheaper at Rs 220/260; more with air-con. Both hotels have restaurants, but at the Khajuraho Ashok 'the staff hang around like vultures waiting for tips'; this is yet another Ashok hotel getting a decisive thumbs-down from visitors. The *Hotel Jass Oberoi* (tel 85), on Bypass Rd, has rooms at Rs 600/850 plus a swimming pool, central air-con and other mod cons.

Places to Eat

Opposite the entrance to the western enclosure, *Raja's Cafe* is run by a Swiss woman. The large shady tree in the restaurant's courtyard is a popular gathering spot, although recent reports suggest that standards may be slipping. They also operate a free book-swap system. The *New Bharat Restaurant* does good thalis (Rs 10) and other food plus really good tea – if you're heartily sick of the usual overmilky, oversweet tea in

India. The *Gupta Restaurant* has reasonable food.

Getting There & Away

Getting to Khajuraho can be a major pain. It is really on the way from nowhere to nowhere, and is not near any railway station. Although many travellers slot it between Varanasi and Agra, it involves a lot of travelling to cover not particularly great distances. If you can afford to fly, then do; you'll save a lot of time.

Air Indian Airlines have a daily Delhi/ Agra/Khajuraho/Varanasi flight that returns by the same route to Delhi. It's probably the most popular tourist flight in India and can often be booked solid for days by tour groups. Delhi to Khajuraho costs Rs 510.

Bus & Train From the west there are bus services from Agra (391 km, 12 hours), Gwalior (280 km) and Jhansi (175 km). Jhansi is the nearest approach to Khajuraho on the main Delhi to Bombay rail line, and there are half a dozen buses a day on the Jhansi to Khajuraho route. This is the most popular route to Khajuraho by public bus, and it's a five or six-hour trip.

There is no direct route to Varanasi from Khajuraho. Satna, 120 km from Khajuraho, is the nearest railhead for visitors from Varanasi, Calcutta or Bombay. It's on the Bombay to Allahabad line. From Varanasi it takes six to nine hours to Satna on the faster express services. The 322-km trip costs Rs 41 in 2nd class, Rs 145 in 1st. The only daytime expresses from Varanasi leave from Mughal Sarai station. The daily Bombay Mail leaves at 8 am, arriving in Satna around 2.15 pm. Once there, it's about two km to the local bus station and about four hours direct to Khajuraho. Buses depart Satna for Khajuraho at 6.45 am and 3.30 pm.

Another alternative from Khajuraho to Varanasi is to take the hourly bus to Mahoba (four hours) and a train from there, but it's a rather slow passenger train. Harpalpur is 99 km from Khajuraho, closer than Satna. Buses make the four-hour trip twice daily.

There are two direct night buses from Khajuraho to Bhopal (11 hours), which are good for getting to Sanchi. There are also buses from Khajuraho to Jabalpur (10 hours) and Indore (16 hours).

Getting Around

There is an airport bus or taxis into town. The western temples can all be viewed on foot; take a rickshaw to the eastern or southern group. You can go out to the Jain enclosure and walk back from there, or make a round trip to Duladeo. All the rickshaw-wallahs have 'fixed rates' to any temple or group of temples you care to name, but it's for show. The rates are really for a round trip for two people. Bicycles can be hired in Khajuraho for Rs 7 a day.

SATNA

You may find it convenient or necessary to stay overnight here on your way to or from Khajuraho.

Places to Stay

The *Park Hotel* (tel 2646) has clean rooms from Rs 40 and is 1½ km from the railway station. Directly opposite the bus stand is the *India Hotel*, which is not so clean but rather cheaper – maybe OK for one night.

The *Hotel Natraj* is also marginally cheaper. The state tourist department's *Tourist Motel* (tel 2941) has rooms at Rs 100/150; more with air-con. The *Tourist Bungalow* has rooms at Rs 60, or you can sleep in the railway *retiring rooms* for Rs 22.

Getting There & Away

There are buses to Khajuraho at 6.45 am and 3.30 pm, and these take about four hours. There are direct trains from Satna to Calcutta, Varanasi, Bombay and Madras.

Central Madhya Pradesh

SANCHI

Beside the main railway line, 46 km north of Bhopal, a hill rises from the plain. It's topped by some of the oldest and most interesting Buddhist structures in India. Although this site had no direct connection with the life of Buddha, it was the great Emperor Ashoka who built the first stupas here in the 3rd century BC, and a great number of stupas and other religious structures were added over the succeeding centuries.

As Buddhism was gradually absorbed back into Hinduism in its land of origin, the site decayed and was eventually completely forgotten. In 1818 a British officer rediscovered the site, but in the following years amateur archaeologists and greedy treasure hunters did immense damage to Sanchi before a proper restoration was first commenced in 1881. Finally, between 1912 and 1919, the structures were carefully repaired and restored to their present condition by Sir John Marshall.

Despite the damage which was wrought after its rediscovery, Sanchi is a very special place and is not to be missed if you're anywhere within striking distance. The sculptures here are full of vitality and a freshness of perception only possible at the beginning of a cultural era. The site itself is one of the most mellow in India.

Information & Orientation

Sanchi is little more than a small village at the foot of the hill. The site is open daily from dawn to dusk and there's a nominal entry fee except on Sundays when it's free. The quickest access is via the stone track off to the left of the tarmac road.

There's a small museum at the foot of the hill which costs Rs 0.50 entry and is open daily except on Fridays. At this museum you can buy copies of the guidebook *Sanchi*, published by the Archaeological Survey of India.

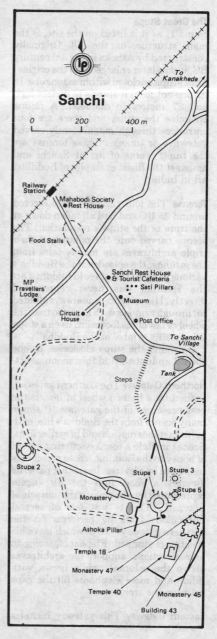

The Great Stupa

Stupa 1, as it is listed on the site, is the main structure on the hill. Originally constructed by Ashoka in the 3rd century BC, it was later enlarged and the original brick stupa enclosed within a stone one. In its present form it stands 16 metres high and 37 metres in diameter. A railing encircles the stupa and there are four entrances through magnificently carved gateways or toranas. These toranas are the finest works of art at Sanchi and amongst the finest examples of Buddhist art in India.

Toranas The four gateways were erected around 35 BC and had all fallen down at the time of the stupa's restoration. The scenes carved onto the pillars and their triple architraves are mainly tales from the *jatakas*, the episodes of the Buddha's various lives. At this stage in Buddhist art the Buddha was never represented directly. His presence was always alluded to through symbols such as the bo tree, the wheel of law or his footprint. Even a stupa is in itself a symbol of the Buddha.

Go round the stupa clockwise, as one should around all Buddhist monuments.

Northern Gateway The northern gateway, topped by a broken wheel of law, is the best preserved of the gateways. It shows many scenes from the Buddha's life, both in his last incarnation and in earlier lives. Scenes include a monkey offering a bowl of honey to the Buddha, whose presence is indicated by a bo tree. In another panel he ascends a road into the air (again represented by a bo tree) in the 'miracle of Sravasti'. This is just one of several miraculous feats he performs on the northern gateway – all of which leave his spectators stunned. Elephants, facing in four directions, support the architraves above the columns, while horses with riders and more elephants fill the gaps between the architraves.

Eastern Gateway This gateway includes scenes of the Buddha's entry to nirvana on a pillar. Across the front of the middle architrave is the 'great departure', where the Buddha (symbolised by a riderless horse) renounces the sensual life and sets out to find enlightenment. Maya's dream of an elephant standing on the moon, which she had when she conceived the Buddha, is also shown on one of the columns. The figure of a yakshi maiden, hanging out from one of the architraves, is one of the best known images of Sanchi.

Southern Gateway The oldest of the gateways, this includes scenes of the Buddha's birth and also events from Ashoka's life as a Buddhist. As on the western gateway, the tale of the Chhaddanta Jataka features on this gateway.

Western Gateway The western gateway, with the architraves supported by dwarves, has some of the most interesting scenes. The rear face of one of the pillars shows the Buddha undergoing the temptation of Mara, while demons flee and angels cheer his resistance. Mara also tempts on the back of the lowest architrave. The top front architrave shows the Buddha in seven different incarnations, but since he could not, at the time, be represented directly, he appears three times as a stupa and four times as a tree. His six incarnations prior to the seventh, Gautama Buddha, are known as the Manushi Buddhas.

The colourful events of the Chhaddanta Jataka are related on the front face of the bottom architrave. In this tale the Buddha, in a lower incarnation, took the form of a six-tusked elephant, but one of his two wives became jealous; she managed to reincarnate as a queen and then arranged to have the six-tusked elephant hunted and killed. The sight of his tusks, sawn off by the hunter, was sufficient for the queen to die of remorse! Pot-bellied dwarves support the architraves on this gateway.

Pillars Scattered around the site are pillars or the remains of pillars. The most important is pillar 10, which was erected by Ashoka and stands close to the southern entrance to the great stupa. Only the base of this beautifully proportioned and executed shaft now stands, but the fine capital can be seen in the museum. The three back-to-back lions, which once topped the column, are an excellent example of the Greco-Buddhist art of that era at its finest. They now form the state emblem of India and can be seen on every bank note.

Pillars 25 and 35, both dating from the 5th century AD, are not as fine as the earlier Ashoka pillar. Pillar 35, also broken, stands close to the northern gateway of the great stupa; again, the capital figure is in the museum.

Buddhist gateway

Other Stupas

There are many other stupas on the hill, some of them tiny votive ones less than a metre high. They date from the 3rd century AD. Eight were built by Ashoka but only three remain, including the great stupa. Stupa 2, one of the most interesting of the lesser stupas, is halfway down the hill to the west. If you come up from the town by the main route you can walk back down via stupa 2. There are no gateways to this stupa, but the 'medallions' which decorate the surrounding wall are of great interest. Their design is almost childlike, but full of energy and imagination. Flowers, animals and people – some mythological – are found all around the stupa.

Stupa 3 stands north-east of the main stupa and is similar in design, though smaller in size, to the great stupa. It has only one gateway and is thought to have been constructed soon after the completion of the great stupa. Stupa 3 once contained relics of two important disciples of the Buddha. They were removed and taken to London in 1853 but returned to Sanchi in 1953. Stupa 2, down the hill, also contained relics of important Buddhist teachers, but it is thought this lower spot was chosen for their enshrinement because the top of the hill was reserved for shrines to the Buddha and his direct disciples. Almost totally destroyed, stupa 4 stands right behind stupa 3. Between stupa 1 (the great stupa) and stupa 3 is stupa 5, unusual in that it once had an image of the Buddha, now displayed in the museum.

Temples

Immediately south of stupa 1 is temple 18, a *chaitya* hall which in style is remarkably similar to classical Greek-columned buildings. It dates from around the 7th century AD but traces of earlier wooden buildings have been discovered beneath it. Beside this temple is the small temple 17, also Greek-like in style. The large temple 40, slightly south-east of these two temples, in part dates back to the Ashokan period.

Temple 6 stands between 40 and 18. It is

known as the Gupta Temple and dates back to the 4th century AD. The flat-roofed structure is made of stone slabs, and also shows a Greek influence, probably stemming from the work of Bactrian artisans. This temple is interesting in that it displays the Indian temple style with a porch leading to the central shrine, which was later developed in classical Hindu temples at Khajuraho and Orissa.

Monasteries

The earliest monasteries on the site were made of wood and have long since disappeared. The usual plan is of a central courtyard surrounded by monastic cells. Monasteries 45 and 47 stand on the higher, eastern edge of the hilltop. They date from the later period of building at Sanchi, a time of transition from Buddhism to Hinduism, and show strong Hindu elements in their design. There is a good view of the village of Sanchi and Bhilsa (Vidisha) from this side of the hill. Monastery 51 is partway down the hill on the western side toward stupa 2.

Other Buildings

The modern vihara (monastery) on the hill was constructed to house the returned relics from stupa 3. The design is a poor shadow of the former artistry of Sanchi. Close to monastery 51 is the 'great bowl' in which food and offerings were placed for distribution to the monks. It was carved out of a huge boulder. The *Sanchi* guidebook describes all these buildings, and many others, in much greater detail.

Places to Stay

It's possible to take in all that Sanchi has to offer in just two or three hours – less if you're pushed for time – so few people stay overnight. If you'd like to do so, however, there's a choice of accommodation.

Best value for money in Sanchi is probably (and surprisingly) the railway *retiring rooms*. There are just two of them but they're big, spacious and spotlessly clean. Just outside the station is the *Sri*

Lanka Mahabodhi Society Rest House which is rather more spartan and has rooms and dorm beds. In theory you should make reservations in advance, but in practice you can just drop in. Ask around for the caretaker if it looks closed.

Continuing on across the main road and towards the site you come to the Madhya Pradesh Tourism's *Tourist Cafeteria* (tel 43) which offers singles/doubles for Rs 90/130. As the name suggests, meals are available here and the restaurant is also open to nonresidents. At the back of this place is the Gothic-looking and decidedly derelict *Sanchi Rest House*. It's still possible to find a cheap room here but don't expect too much in the way of facilities. If there's no-one around, ask at the house across the courtyard.

On the main road to Bhopal about 250 metres from the crossroads is the *Travellers' Lodge* (tel 23). This is also run by Madhya Pradesh Tourism and offers singles/doubles for Rs 90/130 or Rs 200/250 with air-con. There's a bar and restaurant at the lodge.

Places to Eat

For food you've got a choice of the *Tourist Cafeteria, Travellers' Lodge* or the cluster of food stalls at the crossroads. The stalls don't look too sanitary but they're no worse than any others in India and there's plenty of choice.

Getting There & Away

Bus Local buses connect Bhopal with Sanchi (and other towns and villages in the area) about every hour from dawn to dusk, but there are two possible routes. The longer route goes via Raisen (an interesting town with an extensive hilltop fortress), takes three hours for the 68-km trip and costs Rs 10. The shorter route follows the railway line to Delhi, takes up to two hours and costs Rs 7. In Bhopal, tickets for the buses are sold at counter No 7 (all the numbers are in Hindi).

Karnataka Top: Devaraja Market, Mysore (HF)
Bottom: Sravanabelagola (HF)

Karnataka Top: Hampi (HF)
Bottom: Sadhus at Hampi (HF)

Train Sanchi is on the main Delhi to Bombay railway line only 46 km north of Bhopal, although certain mail and express trains do not stop at Sanchi. First-class passengers who have travelled a minimum distance to Sanchi can request the train be halted for them. Obviously it is necessary to arrange this in advance.

AROUND SANCHI

In the immediate vicinity of Sanchi there are more Buddhist sites, although none are of the scale or as well preserved as Sanchi's sites. Sonari, 10 km south-west of Sanchi, has eight stupas, two of them important. At Satdhara, west of Sanchi on the bank of the Beas River, there are two stupas, one 30 metres in diameter. Another eight km south-east is Andher, where there are three small but well-preserved stupas. These stupas were all discovered in 1851, after the discovery of Sanchi.

Other places of interest around Sanchi include:

Vidisha (Bhilsa or Besnagar)
Vidisha was an important town in

Ashoka's time; his wife came from here. Today the city is known as Besnagar, and Bhilsa railway station has an important collection of antiques discovered in the area. The Khamb Baba pillar is one of the more interesting attractions. It was erected by Heliodorus, a Greek ambassador to the city from Taxila (now in Pakistan). The pillar celebrates his conversion to Hinduism and is dedicated to Vishnu. Also in town is the Bija Mandal, a mosque built from the remains of Hindu temples.

Udayagiri (Udaigiri)
The Gupta caves here date from 320-606 AD; two are Jain, the other 18 Hindu. In cave 5 there is a superb image of Vishnu in his boar incarnation. Cave 7 was cut out for King Chandragupta II's personal use. The caves are seven km west of Vidisha. From Bhopal take a Sanchi bus or train to Vidisha, and from there take a tonga to the caves.

Raisen
On the road to Bhopal, 23 km south of Sanchi, the huge and colourful hilltop fort has temples, cannons, three palaces, 40 wells and a large tank. This Malwa fort was built around 1200 AD and although initially the centre of an independent kingdom, it later came under Mandu control.

Gyaraspur
There are tanks, temples and a fort dating from the 9th and 10th centuries AD at this town, 51 km north-east of Sanchi. The town's name is derived from the big fair which used to be held here in the 11th month, Gyaras.

Udayapur
Reached through Basoda and Gyaraspur, Udayapur is 90 km north of Sanchi. The large Neelkantheswara Temple is thought to have been built in 1059 AD. It's profusely and very finely carved with four prominent decorated bands around the sikhara. The temple is aligned so that the

first rays of the morning sun shine on the Shiva lingam in the sanctum. It's a particularly fine example of Indo-Aryan architecture and is reached via the railway station at Bareth, seven km away.

BHOPAL (population 800,000)

The capital of Madhya Pradesh, Bhopal was built on the site of the 11th-century city of Bhojapal founded by the legendary Raja Bhoj who is credited with having constructed the lakes around which the city is built. The present city was laid out by the Afghan chief Dost Mohammed Khan who was in charge of Bhopal during Aurangzeb's reign, but took advantage of the confusion following his death in 1707 to carve out his own small kingdom.

Today, Bhopal presents a multifaceted profile. On the one hand there is the old city with its crowded marketplaces, huge old mosques visible from far afield, and the palaces of the former begums who ruled over the city from 1819-1926. To the north sprawl the huge industrial suburbs and the slums which these developments inevitably attract in India. The new city with its broad avenues, sleek high-rise offices and leafy residential areas lies to the west. In the centre of Bhopal are two lakes which, while providing recreational facilities, are also the source of its plagues of mosquitoes.

The city, of course, is famous as the site of one of the world's worst industrial tragedies. On 2 December 1984, a tank at the Union Carbide plant containing methyl isocyanate (a base for the manufacture of pesticides) ruptured and released a deadly cloud of highly poisonous gas. By the time it had dispersed, over 1000 people had died and tens of thousands had their health destroyed for the rest of their lives. The tragedy still haunts the city but what is perhaps worse is that responsibility for it has yet to be determined. Until then, those who were affected but survived will have to wait with diminishing hope for any adequate compensation to come their

way. Meanwhile, the only people who seem to be benefiting from the interminable legal wrangling are the lawyers for the two sides.

An excellent account of the whole affair can be found in the book *Bhopal. The Lessons of a Tragedy* by Sanjoy Hazarika (Penguin 1987).

Orientation

Both the railway station and bus station are within easy walking distance of the main hotel area along Hamidia Rd. For hotels along Berasia Rd, it's best to take an auto-rickshaw. When arriving by train, you need to leave the station by platform No 4 or 5 exit to reach Hamidia Rd. The railway booking offices are on platform No 1.

The new part of the city is a long way from either of the transport terminals so you'll have to take an auto-rickshaw or taxi. Auto-rickshaw drivers almost always use their meters except at night when you'll have to negotiate the fare.

Information

There is a tourist information office at the railway station. The staff are helpful but have no street maps of Bhopal. The main tourist office (tel 67173) is in the Gangotri Complex, 4th floor, T T Nagar, in the new town.

Indian Airlines is also in the Gangotri Complex as is the Vayudoot agent, Lucky Travel Agency (tel 66125), on the ground floor. The main office for Vayudoot is at the Mayur Hotel (tel 77094/5/6/7), Berasia Rd.

The GPO is near Hamidia Hospital.

Taj-ul-Masjid

Commenced by Shah Jahan Begum, but never really completed, the Taj-ul-Masjid is one of the largest mosques in India, if not the largest. It's a huge pink mosque with two massive white-domed minarets and three white domes over the main building.

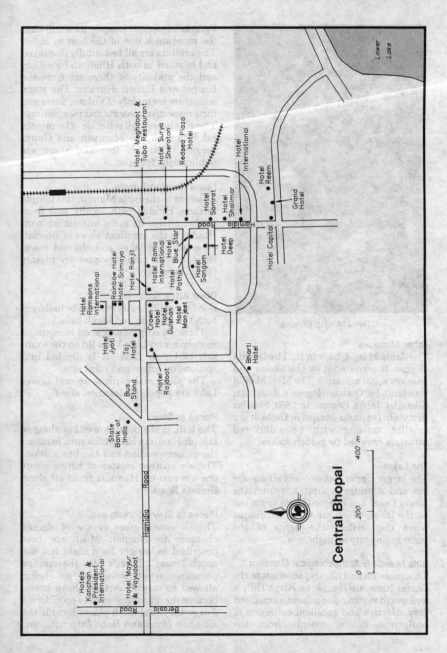

Tal-ul Masjid, Bhopal

Other Mosques

The Jama Masjid, built in 1837 by Qudsia Begum, is surrounded by the bazaar and has very squat minarets. The Moti Masjid was built by Qudsia Begum's daughter, Sikander Jahan Begum, in 1860. Similar in style to the Jama Masjid in Delhi, it is a smaller mosque with two dark-red minarets crowned by golden spikes.

The Lakes

The larger Upper Lake covers six square km and a bridge separates it from the Lower Lake. You can rent boats to get out on the lakes, which are very picturesque when they reflect the lights of the surrounding city at night.

Birla Mandir & Archaeological Museum

This museum and library, adjacent to the Laxmi Narayan Temple on Arera Hill, is well worth visiting. It contains a small but very selective and excellent collection of sculptures dating mainly from the Paramana period. Despite its small size, the museum is one of the best in India. The exhibits are all beautifully displayed and labelled in both Hindi and English, and the majority of them are from the Bhopal and Raisen districts. The stone sculptures are mainly of Vishnu, Shiva and their respective consorts and incarnations. There's also a small selection of terracotta exhibits from the Mauryan and Gupta periods. Entry is free and there are publications for sale.

Laxmi Narayan Temple

Adjacent to the Birla Mandir, this temple attracts Hindus both locally and from further afield. Its main interest for non-Hindus is the excellent views of Bhopal, especially the lakes and the old town. Bhopal's two main mosques are plainly visible from here.

Other Attractions

Good views of the city can also be had from both the Shamla and Idgah hills.

There's a surprisingly good museum of modern art on Lake View Rd on the south side of Upper Lake. It is divided into sections on urban and rural arts.

The parks and gardens around Lower Lake are popular relaxation areas.

Places to Stay

The bulk of the hotels are either along or just off Hamidia Rd, which runs between the railway station and the bus station. There's another cluster of hotels about one km east up Hamidia Road off along Berasia Road.

Places to Stay - bottom end

There's not a great choice of decent cheapies in Bhopal. Most are best described as 'alright for a night but not much longer'. There's also the strange phenomenon of foreigners not being allowed to stay in certain cheap hotels because the management have no 'C' forms – or so they say! Such places include the *Rainbow Hotel* and *Hotel International*.

The cheapest places to stay would have to be the *Grand, Capital* or *Reem* close to the flyover, but this is an extremely noisy junction and can't seriously be recommended. Better is the *Crown Hotel*, Hamidia Rd, which has singles/doubles for Rs 40/60 and 'delux' doubles for Rs 70/90, all with bath and hot water. Similar is the *Hotel Gulshan*, also on Hamidia Rd, which has singles with common bath for Rs 30 and singles/doubles/triples with private bath for Rs 40/70/85.

The *Hotel Meghdoot* (tel 76961), Hamidia Rd, has singles/doubles for Rs 50/70 and 'delux' doubles for Rs 115 to Rs 150, all with bath. The hotel has its own restaurant.

Two places to recommend in this bracket are the *Hotel Manjeet* (tel 76794), Hamidia Rd, and the *Bharti Hotel*. The Manjeet has singles for Rs 50 to Rs 65 and doubles for Rs 65 to Rs 110, all with bath and hot water. The Bharti offers good, clean rooms with bed linen, bath and hot water for Rs 50/70. Another cheapie worth trying is the *Hotel Rama International*, Hamidia Rd, an older type building with singles/doubles for Rs 55/80, 'delux' air-con rooms for Rs 100/125, and 'super delux' air-con for Rs 150/200. At the top end of this bracket, the *Hotel Deep* (tel 72900) has singles/doubles at Rs 50/80 and 'delux' doubles for Rs 125, all with bath and hot water plus there's a restaurant. A similar place is the *Hotel Shalimar* (tel 72563), Hamidia Rd, with singles/doubles/triples for Rs 55/80/100 and 'delux' doubles for Rs 105.

Definitely excellent value is the *Hotel Jyoti* (tel 76838), 53 Hamidia Rd, which is very clean, well-maintained and costs Rs 65/95 for singles/doubles; TVs and air-coolers cost extra. The hotel is managed by Gujaratis so there's no bar and all the food is pure vegetarian.

The *Hotel Ranjit* (tel 75211) at 3 Hamidia Rd, is good value with singles/doubles for Rs 60/80 and 'delux' rooms for Rs 80/90, all with bath, hot water, TV and telephone. The hotel has a restaurant and bar.

There are railway *retiring rooms* and a *Youth Hostel* (tel 63671) but the latter is a long way from anywhere in North T T Nagar, between the lakes. In addition, it has only dormitory beds which you can find at the railway station in any case.

Places to Stay – middle

Unlike the bottom-end section, there's a good choice of mid-range hotels available.

The *Hotel Pathik* (tel 77252), Hamidia Rd, has singles from Rs 75 to Rs 100 and doubles from Rs 100 to Rs 125; 'delux' rooms go for Rs 150/140, and air-con 'delux' for Rs 200/250. The *Hotel Rajdoot* (tel 72692), Hamidia Rd, has singles/doubles for Rs 90/140 with bath and hot water. Similar but with a very friendly manager is the *Hotel Sangam* (tel 77161), over Bridge Rd, with doubles at Rs 80, 'delux' doubles at Rs 100 and 'super delux' doubles at Rs 140. Another good choice is the *Hotel Srimaya* (tel 75454), Hamidia Rd, with air-cooled singles/doubles for Rs 100/150 and air-con rooms for Rs 175/225, all with baths and hot water. There's no restaurant and checkout time is 24 hours after arrival.

An old favourite in this bracket is the *Hotel Ramsons International* (tel 72299), Hamidia Rd, which offers singles/doubles for Rs 130/190 or Rs 210/270 with air-con, all with bath and hot water, colour TV, English and Hindi videos and a verandah. Checkout is 12 noon, and there's an air-con bar and restaurant with average meal prices of Rs 22 (breakfast), Rs 45 to Rs 50 (lunch and dinner).

Round the corner from Ramsons is the brand-new *Taj Hotel* (tel 73161), 52 Hamidia Rd, with singles/doubles at Rs 125/175 and air-con 'delux' rooms for Rs 250/300. Checkout is 12 noon.

The *Hotel Surya Sheraton* (tel 76925), Hamidia Rd, is reasonably good value and has prices almost identical to the Taj. Away from this area is the *Hotel Mayur* (tel 76418), Berasia Rd, which is another very modern hotel. It offers a range of singles/doubles from Rs 130/170 up to

Rs 280/320. The higher priced rooms are air-conditioned, and checkout time is 24 hours after arrival. Also on Berasia Rd are two other mid-range hotels, the *Hotel Kanchan* and the *Hotel President International*.

Places to Eat

The cheapest places to eat are the street stalls surrounding the bus station, and the railway refreshment room where you can get a tasty thali for just Rs 7.

Many of the hotels along or just off Hamidia Rd have good restaurants/bars where you can eat for between Rs 25 and Rs 40. Excellent Gujarati vegetarian dishes are available at the *Hotel Jyoti*. All these restaurants are open to nonresidents.

The *Bagicha Restaurant & Bar* next door to the Crown Hotel on Hamidia Rd is a popular place for grilled food, though they also have the usual range of Indian curries. You have the choice here of eating alfresco in the garden, or inside. The only drawback with the garden in the evenings are the clouds of mosquitoes which seem to descend on the place, so bring insect repellent. Prices range from moderate to high. The *Tuba Restaurant* is also a popular place.

For specialist Chinese food, try the *Dragon Chinese Restaurant* next door to the Bagicha.

Getting There & Away

Air Indian Airlines connects Bhopal with Bombay, Indore, Gwalior and Delhi daily except Tuesday. There are Vayudoot flights from Bhopal to: Delhi (Rs 600), Gwalior (Rs 375), Indore and Jaipur. If you book a Vayudoot ticket from an agency make sure it's a confirmed ticket and not just a provisional booking or you may find that you haven't got a seat.

Bus There are numerous daily buses from Ujjain, Indore and Jabalpur to Bhopal but it's much easier and more comfortable to travel by train.

There is supposedly a direct bus between Bhopal and Khajuraho which takes about 12 hours and travels overnight, but it's really only for masochists. The trip to Khajuraho from Allahabad in Uttar Pradesh or via the Jabalpur to Allahabad rail link is much less traumatic.

Train Bhopal is on one of the two main Delhi to Bombay railway lines. It's 705 km from Delhi, which takes 11 to 13 hours and costs Rs 73 in 2nd class, Rs 264 in 1st. From Bombay it's 837 km and takes 13 to 16 hours with fares of Rs 82 in 2nd class, Rs 303 in 1st. Sanchi is only 46 km north of Bhopal, but note the warning in the Sanchi section on nonstop trains.

AROUND BHOPAL

Bhojpur

The legendary Raja Bhoj (1010-53) not only built the lakes at Bhopal but also built another one, estimated at 400 square km, in Bhojpur, 28 km south-east of the state capital. History records that the lake was held back by massive earthen dams faced on both sides with huge blocks of sandstone set without mortar. Unfortunately, the lake no longer exists having been destroyed by Hoshang Shah, the ruler of Mandu, in a fit of destructive passion in the early 15th century. It's said that the lake took three years to empty and that the climate of the area was radically affected by the loss of this enormous body of water.

What does survive here is the huge, but uncompleted, Bhojeshwar Temple which originally overlooked the lake. Dedicated to Shiva, it has some very unusual design features and sports a lingam 2.3 metres high by 5.3 metres in circumference. The earthen rampart used to raise stones for the construction of the dome still remains. Nearby is another incomplete monolithic temple, this time a Jain shrine containing a colossal statue of Mahavira over six metres in height. Though a long way from rivalling the 17-metre-high statue of

Gomateshvara at Sravanabelagola in Karnataka, this has to be one of the largest Jain statues in India.

Bhimbetka

Like the Australian Aboriginal rock paintings in the outback, the cave paintings of the Bushmen in the Kalahari Desert in Africa or the Neolithic Lascaux caves of France, the Bhimbetka caves are a must. Only recently, some 700 rock shelters were discovered amongst dense forest and craggy cliffs 40 km south of Bhopal. These caves contain hundreds of paintings depicting the life and times of the people who once lived here. They date from the Upper Paleolithic right through to medieval times. There's everything from figures of bison, bears, tigers and rhinoceros to hunting scenes, initiation ceremonies, childbirth, communal dancing and drinking scenes, religious rites and burials.

Because of the natural pigments which the painters used, the colours have been remarkably well preserved and it's obvious in certain caves that the same surface has been used by different people at different times.

Buses connect Bhopal with Bhimbetka.

Other Places

Of the lesser important sites, Neori, only six km from Bhopal, has an 11th-century Shiva temple and is a popular picnic spot. Islampur, 11 km from Bhopal on the Berasia Rd, was built by Dost Mohammed Khan and has a hilltop palace and garden. At Ashapuri, six km north of Bhopal, there are ruined temples and Jain palaces with statues scattered on the ground. Chiklod, 45 km out, has a palace in a peaceful sylvan setting.

PACHMARHI

At an altitude of 1100 metres near Itarsi on the Bombay to Jabalpur and Allahabad railway line, Pachmarhi is Madhya Pradesh's hill station. There are fine views out over the surrounding red sandstone hills and some interesting walks.

Places to Stay

The state tourist organisation has a variety of accommodation at Pachmarhi. The cheapest are the *Holiday Homes* (tel 99) near the bus stand which cost Rs 30 for a single or double and Rs 10 for extra beds. There's a bar and restaurant. Next are the *Panchvati Cottages* (tel 96) near Tehsil, and one-bedroom cottages cost Rs 60/90 for singles/doubles and two-bedroom cottages cost Rs 100 for singles or doubles; the complex includes a restaurant.

Somewhat more expensive is *Amaltas* (tel 98) near Tehsil with singles/doubles at Rs 90/130, and the *Satpura Retreat* (tel 97), on Mahadeo Rd, with deluxe singles/doubles at Rs 120/150. Both places have a restaurant and the Amaltas also has a bar.

Western Madhya Pradesh

UJJAIN (population 340,000)

Only 80 km from Indore, on the right bank of the River Shipra, Ujjain is one of India's holiest cities for Hindus. It gets its sanctity from an ancient Hindu mythological tale about the churning of the oceans by the gods and demons in search of the nectar of immortality. The first thing to come to the surface were 14 gems that were followed by Lakshmi, the goddess of wealth. When the coveted vessel of nectar was finally found there followed a mad scramble across the skies with the demons pursuing the gods in an attempt to take the nectar from them. In the process four drops were spilt and they fell at Hardwar, Nasik, Ujjain and Prayag (Allahabad). As a result, Ujjain is one of the sites of the triennial Kumbh Mela. It comes to Ujjain next in 1992 and if it shapes up into anything like the one which took place at Allahabad in 1989 then it will be spectacular. On the main day of the festival at Allahabad, no less than 16 million people came to bathe in the river!

Despite its relative obscurity today, Ujjain ranks equal as a great religious centre with such places as Varanasi, Bodh Gaya and Kanchipuram. It has provided a home for Shaivism, Vaishnavism and its various subsects as well as Jainism and Buddhism. Even Tantricism once flourished in this city. On the other hand, non-Hindus may very well find Ujjain a relatively boring city. There's not much of interest going on here most of the year and by no stretch of the imagination is this Varanasi.

Sadhu

History

Ujjain has a long and distinguished history whose origins are lost in the mists of time. It was an important city in the kingdom ruled by Ashoka's father, when it was known as Avanti. Later it was so attractive to Chandragupta II (380-414 AD), one of the Gupta kings, that for a long period he ruled from here rather than his actual capital, Pataliputra. It was at his court that Kalidasa, one of Hinduism's most

revered poets, worked and, in one of his most famous poems, the *Meghdoot*, there is a lyrical description of the city and its people.

With the passing of the Guptas and the rise of the Paramaras, Ujjain became the centre of much turmoil in the struggle for control of the Malwa region of which it was, for a time, the capital. The last of the Paramaras, Siladitya, was captured alive by the Muslim sultans of Mandu, and Ujjain thus passed into the hands of Moghul vassals.

Muslim rule was sometimes violent, sometimes benign. An invasion by Altumish in 1234 resulted in the wholesale desecration of many temples but that was halted during the reign of Baz Bahadur of Mandu. Bahadur himself was overthrown by the Moghul emperor, Akbar, who ordered a city wall be constructed around the city. Little of this remains today. Later on, during the reign of Aurangzeb, a great deal of reconstruction of the temples was undertaken using grants provided by the emperor.

Following the demise of the Moghuls, Maharaja Jai Singh (of Jaipur fame) became the governor of Malwa and during his rule the observatory and several new temples were constructed at Ujjain. With his passing, Ujjain experienced another period of turmoil at the hands of the Marathas until finally taken by the Scindias in 1750. When the Scindia capital was moved to Gwalior in 1810, Ujjain's commercial importance declined rapidly.

Orientation

The railway line divides the city roughly in half with the old section, along with the bazaar and most of the temples and ghats, off to the north-west of the city, and the new section, including the cantonment area and Vikram university, off to the south-east. The majority of hotels are in front of the railway station.

Temples

Mahakaleshwar Temple One of the most

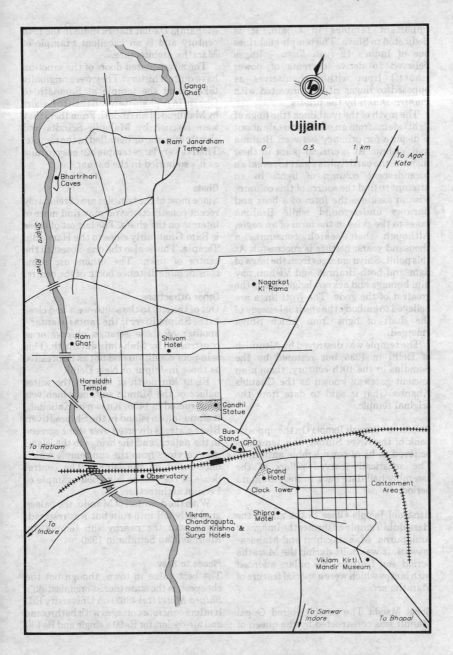

Ujjain

0   0.5   1 km

To Agar
Kota

Ganga
Ghat

Ram Janardham
Temple

Bhartrihari
Caves

Shipra
River

Nagarkot
Ki Rama

Ram
Ghat

Shivom
Hotel

Harsiddhi
Temple

Gandhi
Statue

To Ratlam

Bus
Stand

GPO

Grand
Hotel

Cantonment
Area

Observatory

Clock Tower

Vikram,
Chandragupta,
Rama Krishna &
Surya Hotels

Shipra
Motel

To
Indore

Vikiam Kirti
Mandir Museum

To Sanwar
Indore

To Bhopal

important temples in Ujjain, it is dedicated to Shiva. The temple enshrines one of India's 12 *jyoti linga* – lingas believed to derive currents of power (*shakti*) from within themselves as opposed to lingas ritually invested with *mantra-shakti* by the priests.

The myth of the jyoti linga (the linga of light) stems from an old Hindu tale about a dispute for primacy between Brahma and Vishnu. At a critical point in their dispute, the earth splits apart to reveal an incandescent column of light. In an attempt to find the source of this column, Vishnu assumes the form of a boar and burrows underground while Brahma takes to the skies in the form of an eagle. Although their search consumes a thousand years, neither is successful. At this point, Shiva emerges from the linga of light and both Brahma and Vishnu pay him homage and acknowledge him as the greatest of the gods. The jyoti linga are believed to embody the spiritual energy of the shaft of light from which Shiva emerged.

The temple was destroyed by Altumish of Delhi in 1235 but restored by the Scindias in the 19th century, though an ancient gateway known as the Chaubis Khanba Ghaj is said to date from the original temple.

Chintaman Ganesh Temple On the opposite bank of the River Shipra, this temple is believed to be of considerable antiquity. The artistically carved pillars of the assembly hall date back to the Paramara period.

Harsiddhi Temple Close to the ghats, the Harsiddhi Temple enshrines the images of Annapurna, Mahalakshmi and Mahasaraswati. It was built during the Maratha period and features two pillars adorned with lamps which were a special feature of Maratha art.

Gopal Mandir The marble-spired Gopal Mandir was constructed by the queen of

Maharaja Daulat Rao Scindia in the 19th century and is an excellent example of Maratha architecture.

The silver-plated doors of the sanctum have quite a history. They were originally taken from the temple at Somnath to Ghazni in Afghanistan and then to Lahore by Mahmud Shah Abdati. From there they were rescued by Mahadji Scindia and shortly afterwards installed in the temple. This is a very large temple but easy to miss as it's so buried in the bazaar.

Ghats

Since most of the temples are of relatively recent construction you may find more of interest on the ghats. The largest of these is Ram Ghat fairly close to the Harsiddhi Temple. This is also the one closest to the centre of town. The others are some considerable distance north of the centre.

Other Attractions

Out of the city to the south-west and close to the Shipra River is the Jantar Mantar – another of those strange observatories constructed by Maharaja Jai Singh. This is in poor condition and not as impressive as those in Jaipur or New Delhi.

Eight km north of town is the water palace of the Mandu sultans which was constructed in 1458. Known as Kaliadah, it stands on an island in the Shipra River. River water is diverted over stone screens in the palace, and the bridge to the island uses carvings from the sun temple which once stood on the island. The central dome of the palace is a good example of Persian architecture.

With the downfall of Mandu, the palace gradually fell into ruin but was restored, along with the nearby sun temple, by Madhav Rao Scindia in 1920.

Places to Stay

The best value in town, though not the cheapest, is the state tourist organisation's *Shipra Motel* (tel 4862) on University Rd. It offers concrete cottages with bathrooms and air-coolers for Rs 90 a single and Rs 130 a double, and there's a restaurant. It's on a quiet road and the setting is very pleasant.

Just over the railway bridge and not far from the Shipra Motel is the *Grand Hotel*. This hotel certainly looks grand from the outside with its well-maintained ornamental gardens but inside it's a dreadful replica of a series of interrogation cells. Singles are Rs 25 and doubles range from Rs 54 to Rs 100, all with bathrooms, but there's hot water only in the doubles.

Most of the other hotels face the railway station and there's a reasonable choice. The cheapest is the huge *Vikram Hotel* but it's a pretty decrepit place and perhaps best avoided. Better is the *Hotel Rama Krishna* (tel 5912) which has singles for Rs 35 right up to Rs 100, and doubles for Rs 45 to Rs 125, all with bathrooms. The hotel also boasts an 'Entrocommunication facility' – whatever that is! – and a restaurant. Close by is the *Hotel Chandragupta*, which has singles/doubles for Rs 45/60 and deluxe rooms for Rs 75/115, all with bathrooms. Bucket hot water is available at no extra charge and there's a restaurant and bar.

More expensive is the *Hotel Surya* at Rs 120 a double with bath (Rs 100 for single occupancy). The rooms are pretty good and fairly quiet.

Places to Eat

There are few restaurants to choose from outside of the hotels; the best available face the railway station.

Getting There & Away

Bus There are frequent daily buses between Ujjain and Indore which cost Rs 8 and are generally faster than the train. There are also much less frequent buses which connect Ujjain with Kota in Rajasthan. You need to make enquiries about these as the schedules are entirely in Hindi and are rarely followed.

Train Ujjain is connected to one of the main broad-gauge lines from Delhi to Bombay by a track from Nagda; using this line involves a change of train at Nagda. It is also connected to the other broad-gauge line from Delhi to Bombay by a track from Bhopal via Indore. The 184-km trip from Bhopal costs Rs 27 in 2nd class and Rs 92 in 1st, and takes 3½ hours.

There is also a broad-gauge line connecting Ujjain with Indore, Bhopal, Jabalpur and Bilaspur. A daily express connects all these cities and the 80-km trip from Indore to Ujjain costs Rs 13 in 2nd class and Rs 50 in 1st, and takes about 2½ hours.

Getting Around

Many of Ujjain's sights are a long way from the centre of town so you'll probably find yourself using quite a few auto-rickshaws. The drivers here are rapacious so make sure you fix the price before setting off.

INDORE (population 1,000,000)

Indore is not of great interest, but it makes a good departure point for visiting Mandu. It's an affluent-looking town and a major textile-producing centre, with plenty of new houses and flats. The Khan and Sarasvati rivers run through the town. From 1733, Indore was ruled by the Holkar dynasty who were firm supporters of the British, even during the mutiny.

Information & Orientation

The older part of town is on the western side of the railway line, the newer part on the east. The railway line forms a rough north to south dividing line, while Mahatma Gandhi Rd bisects the town in an east to west direction. The railway and bus stations are close together but separated by a complicated flyover system.

If arriving by train, leave the station by platform No 1 for the east side of town and by platform No 4 for the west side. A footbridge connects the two.

The tourist office (tel 38888) is at the Tourist Bungalow at the back of the R N

Tagore Natya Griha Hall, R N Tagore Rd. They have a fair selection of leaflets and a good map of Madhya Pradesh but no street maps. This is the best place to make enquiries about tours to Mandu.

Travellers' cheques can be changed quickly at the State Bank of India (Main Branch) near the GPO. Other branches don't offer this facility.

Rupayana, by the Central Hotel, is a reasonably good bookshop.

Palaces

In the old part of town the multistorey gateway of the Rajwada or 'old palace' looks out onto the palm-lined main square in the crowded streets of the Kajuri Bazaar. Much of the palace is in ruins but the bulk of what remains has been given over to government offices and a hospital. There is, however, an open stone gallery overlooking the courtyard which can be reached by the flight of stairs to your left as you face the gateway from inside the courtyard. There are no entry fees.

The Manik Bagh, to the south of the city, and the Lal Bagh, to the south-west, also have palaces.

The Kajuri Bazaar streets are a good place to take a stroll. They're always very busy and there are many examples of old houses with picturesque overhanging verandahs. Unfortunately, these are disappearing fast as concrete rapidly replaces wood.

Kanch Mandir

On Jawahar Rd, not far from the Rajwada, is the Kanch Mandir or Seth Hukanchand Temple. This Jain temple is very plain externally, but inside is completely mirrored with pictures of sinners being tortured in the afterlife.

Museum

The museum, near the GPO, has one of the best collections of medieval and premedieval Hindu sculpture in Madhya Pradesh. Most are from Hinglajgarh in the Mandasaur district of western

Madhya Pradesh and range from early Gupta to Paramana times. Some pieces are stunning in their delicacy but one wonders why they were brought here. Many appear to have been carelessly hacked away from whatever they used to be attached to and a lot of damage has been done in the process. Not only that, but the pieces are poorly displayed, there are hardly any labels, and much of the collection appears to have been dumped at random pending cataloguing, except that this latter task has never been done. It's a great pity to see such treasures treated so apathetically.

Entry to the museum is free and it's closed on Mondays.

Chhatris

The chhatris, or memorial tombs, of the region's former rulers are now neglected and forgotten. They stand in the Chhatri Bagh on the banks of the River Khan. The cenotaph of Malhar Rao Holkar I, founder of the Holkar dynasty, is the most impressive.

Places to Stay – bottom end

The railway station and the Sarwate bus station are only a few minutes walk apart, and it's in this area that you'll find the budget hotels. Most have signs in Hindi but the buildings are obviously boarding houses so they're easy to recognise. Around the bus station you'll be approached by commission touts with a pocketful of hotel cards. These people are useful if everywhere seems to be full but probably best avoided otherwise. The area is lively, dirty, polluted and noisy. None of the budget hotels could be described as a bargain and most are overpriced.

The Hotel Ashoka (tel 37391) (sign in English), opposite the bus station, has been a popular place for many years. The management are friendly and singles/ doubles cost Rs 55/75 with bathroom and hot water. Very similar in standard and price is the Janata Hotel (tel 37695) (sign in Hindi) next door.

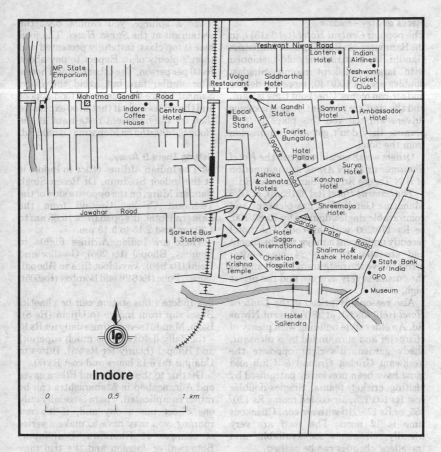

Indore

0   0.5   1 km

The *Hotel Sailendra* (sign in Hindi), opposite the entrance to the Christian Hospital, is a rip-off at Rs 75/100 for singles/doubles and western visitors are distinctly unwelcome. Touts will bring you here since they give commission.

Women should check out the *YWCA* opposite the GPO as they may have room. You'll need to take an auto-rickshaw to get there since it's quite a way from the transport terminals.

There are also railway *retiring rooms* at the station.

Up the scale a bit is the *Tourist Bungalow* (tel 38888), on R N Tagore Rd, at the back of the Tagore Natya Griha Hall. It's small but clean and comfortable and singles/doubles cost Rs 70/90, or Rs 150/200 with air-con. All air-con rooms have baths with hot water and bucket hot water is available in the others (no extra charge). Checkout time is 9 am.

Also good value is the *Siddhartha Hotel* (tel 39099), at 564 Mahatma Gandhi Rd, with singles/doubles from Rs 70/90 up to Rs 145/165. The staff are pleasant, there's a bar and restaurant and checkout is 24 hours after arrival.

Places to Stay - middle

The popular *Central Hotel* (tel 32131), in the Rampurawala Building at 27 Mahatma Gandhi Rd, is attractively old-fashioned with large, well-kept rooms. Singles/doubles are Rs 100/140, more for deluxe and air-con rooms. Checkout time is 9 am, and the staff are pleasant. Auto-rickshaw drivers will tell you this place is 'full' because they don't get any commission from the hotel.

Others worth considering are the *Hotel Shalimar* or *Hotel Ashok* at the junction of R N Tagore Rd and Sardar Patel Rd.

The *Samrat Hotel* (tel 32185/8), at 18/5 Mahatma Gandhi Rd, has pleasant and comfortable singles/doubles for Rs 80/100, or Rs 175/200 with air-con. The hotel recently underwent a major refurbishment and checkout time is 24 hours after arrival. Give the restaurant here a miss as the cuisine is very average and the prices high.

Also reasonably priced is the *Lantern Hotel* (tel 135327), at 28 Yeshwant Niwas Rd. An older style building with plenty of character and surrounded by a pleasant, shady garden, it's right opposite the Yeshwant Cricket Ground & Club and must have been previously patronised by visiting cricket teams. Singles/doubles cost Rs 100/125, air-cooled rooms Rs 120/155, or Rs 175/210 with air-con. Checkout time is 12 noon. The staff are very friendly, all meals are available, and travellers' cheques can be cashed.

Places to Eat

There are several good places offering standard Indian fare close to the bus stand. The restaurant at the *Janata Hotel* is also good value.

The *Volga Restaurant*, near the Mahatma Gandhi statue on the road of the same name, has good vegetarian food and aggressive air-conditioning. Another good place for snacks and coffee is the *Indore Coffee House*, a little further up Mahatma Gandhi Rd from the Central Hotel.

For a splurge, you cannot beat the restaurant at the *Surya Hotel*. The food here is top class, tastefully presented and there's plenty of it. Expect to pay about Rs 50 per person. The other top-end hotels offer similar fare but avoid the *Hotel Samrat* where the quality of food is poor and the prices high. If that's too expensive then try the basement restaurant at the *Hotel Siddhartha* on Mahatma Gandhi Rd.

Getting There & Away

Air The Indian Airlines office in Indore is at the Indoor Stadium, Dr Rosen Singh Bandari Marg, on the opposite side of the Yeshwant Cricket Ground from the Lantern Hotel. It's open from 10.05 am to 1.30 pm and 2.15 to 5.15 pm.

There are Indian Airlines flights to Bombay, Bhopal (Rs 205), Gwalior and Delhi (Rs 940). Vayudoot flies to Bhopal, Jaipur, Pune (Rs 645) and Bombay (Rs 505).

Bus Indore's bus station can be chaotic. Buses run from Indore to Ujjain (Rs 8), Bagh, Mandu (several times daily for Rs 15 – the daily deluxe bus is much superior) and Bhopal (hourly for Rs 25). Buses to Udaipur take 12 hours and cost Rs 60.

Getting to the Ajanta and Ellora caves and Aurangabad in Maharashtra can be rather complicated. There is usually only one direct bus a day and, if it's not running, you may have to make a series of changes at Khandwa, Burhanpur, Bhusawal or Jalgaon and the trip may take up to 14 exhausting hours. It's much better to take a train to Jalgaon, but even this involves changes.

Train Indore is on neither of the main broad-gauge lines between Delhi and Bombay but is connected to them by tracks from Nagda via Ujjain in the west and Bhopal in the east. There is one direct train per day in either direction between New Delhi and Indore. The 264-km trip from Bhopal costs Rs 34 in 2nd class, Rs 123 in 1st, and takes five hours.

The other broad-gauge line runs from

Indore to Bilaspur via Ujjain, Bhopal and Jabalpur. A daily express connects all these cities. The 80-km trip from Ujjain takes about 2½ hours and costs Rs 13 in 2nd class, Rs 50 in 1st.

There is also a metre-gauge line through Indore. Services run on this line from Ajmer and Chittorgarh, north of Indore in Rajasthan, south-east to Khandwa, Nizamabad and Secunderabad.

Getting Around

Indore's railway station and the Sarwate bus stand are close together, but separated by a complicated flyover system. Not surprisingly, a large number of gaps have appeared in the fences by the railway lines and most people just march straight across the lines between the two terminals.

There are plenty of taxis, auto-rickshaws and tempos in Indore. The auto-rickshaws are cheap and drivers automatically use their meters – if not, walk away and find another. The only trouble is that few auto-rickshaw-wallahs speak English, so while they understand hotel names, 'bus station' and 'railway station', they understand precious little else. If you don't want to be taken on a very frustrating wild goose chase (at your expense), make sure they understand where you want to go before you set off.

AROUND INDORE
Omkareshwar

This island at the confluence of the Narmada and Kaveri rivers has drawn Hindu pilgrims for centuries on account of its jyoti linga, one of the 12 throughout India, at the Shiva temple of Shri Omkar Mandhata. (For an explanation of the myth of the jyoti linga refer to the section on Ujjain.)

The temple is constructed from local soft stone which has enabled its artisans to achieve a rare degree of detailed work particularly in the friezes on the upper parts of the structure.

There are other temples on this island including the Siddhnath, a good example of early medieval Brahminic architecture, and a cluster of other Hindu and Jain temples. Though damaged by Muslim invaders in the time of Mahmud of Ghanzi (11th century), these temples and those on the nearby riverbanks remain essentially intact. The island temples present a very picturesque sight and are well worth visiting.

Places to Stay There are many dharamsalas offering basic accommodation at Omkareshwar, and also the *Holkar Guest House* at Omkareshwar Mandir, but they're mainly for Hindu pilgrims.

Getting There & Away Omkareshwar Road, on the Ratlam/Indore/Khandwa line, is the nearest railway station. Omkareshwar itself is 12 km from here by road.

There are regular local buses to Omkareshwar from Indore (88 km), Ujjain and Khandwa.

Maheshwar

Maheshwar was once an important cultural and political centre at the dawn of Hindu civilisation and was mentioned in the *Ramayana* and *Mahabharata* under its former name of Mahishmati. It languished in obscurity for many centuries after that until revived by the Holkar queen, Rani Ahilyabai, of Indore in the late 18th century. It's from these times that most of the temples and the fort complex of this riverside town date.

The principal sights are the fort which is now a museum displaying heirlooms and relics of the Holkar dynasty (open to the public), the three ghats lining the banks of the Namada River, and the many-tiered temples distinguished by their overhanging balconies and intricately worked doorways.

Places to Stay There is a *Government Rest House*, the *Ahilya Trust Guest House* and a number of basic dharamsalas.

Getting There & Away Maheshwar is best

reached by road as the nearest railhead is 39 km away. Local buses run here on a regular basis from Barwaha and Dhar both of which, in turn, can be reached by local bus from Indore.

Maheshwar is often included on bus tours from Indore to Mandu when these are operating.

Dhar

Founded by Raja Bhoj, the legendary founder of Bhopal and Mandu, this was the capital of Malwa until Mandu rose to power. There are good views from the ramparts of Dhar's well-preserved fort. Dhar also has the large stone Bhojashala Mosque with ancient Sanskrit inscriptions, and the adjoining tomb of the Muslim saint Kamal Maula.

Dhar is best visited en route to or from Mandu.

MANDU

The extensive and now mainly deserted hilltop fort of Mandu is one of the most interesting sights in central India. There is accommodation in Mandu, or you can make a day trip from Indore if your time is short.

Mandu is on an isolated outcrop separated from the tableland to the north by a deep and wide valley, over which a natural causeway runs to the main city gate. To the south of Mandu the land drops steeply away to the plain far below and the view is superb. Deep ravines cut into the sides of the 20-square-km plateau occupied by the fort.

Entry to Mandu costs Rs 1. There are soft drink and fruit stalls at most of the major sites.

History

Mandu, known as the 'city of joy', has had a chequered and varied history. Founded as a fortress and retreat in the 10th century by Raja Bhoj (see Bhopal), it was conquered by the Muslim rulers of Delhi in 1304. When the Moghuls invaded and

took Delhi in 1401, the Afghan Dilawar Khan, Governor of Malwa, set up his own little kingdom and Mandu embarked on its golden age. Even after it was added to the Moghul Empire by Akbar, it retained a considerable degree of independence, until the declining Moghuls lost control of it to the Marathas. The capital of Malwa was then shifted back to Dhar, and Mandu became a ghost town. For a ghost town it's remarkably grandiose and impressive, and worth a day's inspection at the very least. Mandu has one of the best collections of Afghan architecture to be seen in India.

Although Dilawar Khan first established Mandu as an independent kingdom, it was his son, Hoshang Shah, who shifted the capital from Dhar to Mandu and raised it to its greatest splendour. Warlike as he was, Hoshang's rule from 1405 was marked by the construction of the Delhi Gate, the Jami Masjid, his own fine tomb and the extensive and complex fortifications.

Hoshang's son ruled for only a year before being poisoned by Mahmud Shah, who became king himself and ruled for 33 years. During his reign Mandu was in frequent and often bitter dispute with neighbouring powers. There are few architectural remains of his reign because his most imposing structures, such as his own tomb, were poorly designed and built, and soon collapsed. Nevertheless his constant war-making raised Mandu to great importance and prosperity.

In 1469, Mahmud Shah's son, Ghiyas-ud-din, ascended the throne and spent the next 31 years devoting himself to women and song – not wine, for he was reputed to be teetotal. His son, Nasir-ud-din, became so fed up with waiting for over-indulgence to finish off his father that he poisoned him in 1500, when he was 80 years old. The son lived only another 10 years before dying, some say of guilt. In turn his son, Mahmud, had an unhappy reign during which his underlings, like Gada Shah and Darya Khan, often had more influence than he did. Finally, in 1526,

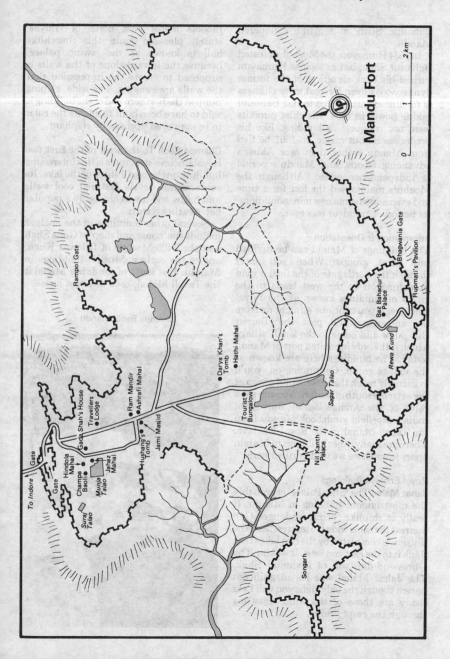

Mandu Fort

2 km
0   1

Bhagwania Gate
Rupmati's Pavilion

Rampol Gate

Darya Khan's Tomb

Hathi Mahal

Baz Bahadur's Palace

Rewa Kund

Ram Mandir
Ashrafi Mahal

Travellers Lodge
Gada Shah's House

Tourist Bungalow

Sagar Talao

Jami Masjid

Hushang's Tomb

Hindola Mahal
Champa Baoli
Jahaz Mahal
Munja Talao

Gate

To Indore Gate

Suraj Talao

Nil Kanth Palace

Songarh

Bahadur Shah of Gujarat conquered Mandu.

In 1534 Humayun, the Moghul, defeated Bahadur Shah, but as soon as Humayun turned his back an officer of the former dynasty took over. Several more changes of fortune eventually led to Baz Bahadur taking power in 1554. His chief pursuits were not conquest or building, like his predecessors, but music. In 1561 he fled from Mandu rather than face Akbar's advancing troops, and Mandu's period of independence ended. Although the Moghuls maintained the fort for a time and even added some new minor buildings, its period of grandeur was over.

Information & Orientation

The buildings of Mandu can be divided into three groups. When you enter through the north gate of the fort, a road branching off to the west leads to the group of buildings known as the Royal Enclave. If you continue straight on from the entrance you'll pass the Tourist Bungalow and come to the small village which is the only inhabited part of Mandu today. The buildings here are known as the village group. Continuing on, you'll eventually reach the Rewa Kund group at the extreme south of the fort. You can get a copy of the Archaeological Survey of India's excellent guidebook *Mandu* from the Taveli Mahal in the Royal Enclave. There are many other buildings in Mandu apart from those we've described here.

Royal Enclave Buildings

Jahaz Mahal The 'Ship Palace' is probably the most famous building in Mandu. It really is shiplike, being far longer (110 metres) than it is wide (15 metres), and the illusion is completed by the two lakes that flank it to the east and west. It was built by Ghiyas-ud-din, son of Mahmud Shah. The Jahaz Mahal was his magnificent harem though the only sighs you will hear today are those of the wind whistling through the empty ruins.

Hindola Mahal Just north of Ghiyas' stately pleasure dome, this churchlike hall is known as the 'swing palace' because the inward slope of the walls is supposed to create the impression that the walls are swaying. The wide, sloping ramp at the northern end of the building is said to have been built to enable the ruler to be conveyed upstairs by elephant.

Champa Baoli To the west of the first two Royal Enclave structures is this interesting building on the north shore of the lake. Its subterranean levels featured cool wells and baths and it was obviously a popular hot-weather retreat.

Several other buildings in the enclave include the 'house and shop' of Gada Shah and the 1405 Mosque of Dilawar Khan, one of the earliest Muslim buildings in Mandu. Just south of the Jahaz Mahal is the Taveli Mahal, used as a rest house.

Champa Baoli, Mandu

Village Group Buildings

Jami Masjid This huge mosque built in 1454 dominates the village of Mandu. It is claimed to be the finest and largest example of Afghan architecture in India. Construction was commenced by Hoshang Shah, who patterned it on the great mosque in Damascus, Syria. The mosque features an 80-metre-square courtyard.

Hoshang's Tomb Immediately behind the mosque is the imposing marble tomb of Hoshang, who died in 1435. The tomb is entered through a domed porch and the interior is lit by stone *jali* screens – typical of the Hindu influence on the tomb's fine design. It has a double arch and a squat, central dome surrounded by four smaller domes. It is said that Shah Jahan sent his architects to Mandu to study this tomb before they embarked upon the design of the Taj Mahal.

To one side of the tomb enclosure is a long, low colonnade with its width divided into three by rows of pillars. Behind is a long, narrow hall with a typically Muslim barrel-vaulted ceiling. This was intended as a shelter for pilgrims visiting Hoshang's tomb.

Ashrafi Mahal The ruin of this building stands directly across the road from the Jami Masjid. Originally built as a *madrasa* (religious college), it was later extended by its builder, Mahmud Shah, to become his tomb. The design was simply too ambitious for its builders' abilities and it later collapsed. The seven-storey circular tower of victory, which Mahmud Shah erected, has also fallen. A great stairway still leads up to the entrance to the empty shell of the building.

Rewa Kund Buildings

Palace of Baz Bahadur About three km south from the village group, past the large Sagar Talao tank, is the Rewa Kund group. Baz Bahadur was the last independent ruler of Mandu. His palace, constructed around 1509, is beside the Rewa Kund and there was a water lift at the northern end of the tank to supply water to the palace. The palace is a curious mix of Rajasthani and Moghul styles, and was actually built well before Baz Bahadur came to power.

Rupmati's Pavilion At the very edge of the fort, perched on the hillside overlooking the plains below, is the pavilion of Rupmati. The Malwa legends relate that she was a beautiful Hindu singer, and that Baz Bahadur persuaded her to leave her home on the plains by building her this pavilion. From its terraces and domed pavilions Rupmati could gaze down on the Narmada River, winding across the plains far below.

It's a romantic building, the perfect setting for a fairytale romance – but one with an unhappy ending. Akbar, it is said, was prompted to conquer Mandu partly due to Rupmati's beauty. And when Akbar marched on the fort Baz Bahadur fled, leaving Rupmati to poison herself.

Darya Khan's Tomb & Hathi Mahal To the east of the road, between the Rewa Kund and the village, are these two buildings. The Hathi Mahal or 'elephant palace' is so named because the pillars supporting the dome are of massive proportions – like elephant legs. Nearby is the tomb of Darya Khan, which was once decorated with intricate patterns of mosaic tiles.

Nil Kanth Palace This palace, at the end of one of the ravines which cuts into the fort, is actually below the level of the hilltop and is reached by a flight of steps down the hillside. At one time it was a Shiva shrine, as the name – 'the god with the blue throat' – suggests. Under the Moghuls it became a pleasant water palace with a cascade running down the middle. Though once one of Emperor Jehangir's favourite retreats, it has once again become a Shiva temple and a playground for monkeys.

Tours

There are no longer any regular day tours from Indore to Mandu operated by the tourist office so you need to ask around (at the tourist office or hotel reception desks) if that's what you're looking for. You'll be directed to a private bus company which runs day tours on Saturdays and Sundays.

Places to Stay & Eat

It may still be possible to find cheap accommodation at the *Archaeological Rest House* by the Jahaz Mahal in the Royal Enclave but don't count on this. It's often reserved for Archaeological Survey of India workers.

Other accommodation is expensive and, because it's used a lot by well-heeled package-tour groups from Europe, advance booking is more or less essential if you want to be sure of a bed. Do this at the tourist office in Indore.

The best place is the *Travellers' Lodge* (tel 21) which has eight double rooms at Rs 150 with bathroom, hot water and breakfast (toast, eggs, tea or coffee). Other meals are available on request. Despite the fact that there are only eight rooms, the lodge can accommodate up to 24 people with extra beds at Rs 30 each. The manager is friendly and the lodge is well organised plus there are good views over the ghats.

The *Tourist Bungalow* (tel 35) consists of a series of cottages overlooking the large tank. The cottages have two beds at Rs 130 (Rs 90 for single occupancy) but are without hot water. The deluxe cottages have four beds in two rooms at Rs 150 per room (Rs 120 for single occupancy) plus hot water. All meals are available and there's a bar. The dining room/bar is very tatty and in need of a major face-lift but the rooms aren't so bad.

For those not eating at the lodges, there are several small eating places in the village.

Getting There & Away

There are buses from Bhopal, Mhow,

Ujjain, Dhar and Indore to Mandu. From Indore buses depart three times daily at 8.30 am, 12 noon and 3.15 pm. The fare is Rs 13 for the four-hour trip.

The alternative to the erratic tours is to get a group together and hire a car. The best place to do this is at the tourist office in Indore. Four types of car are available but the cheapest are private Ambassadors at Rs 1.75 per km plus waiting time. This works out at around Rs 425 return for the day. More expensive are cars operated by Madhya Pradesh Tourism. Advance booking is usually necessary.

Getting Around

Be prepared for lots of walking if you haven't come on a tour. On the other hand, this is a fine area for walking and it's pleasantly unpopulated.

There is one tempo for hire in Mandu village but, of course, it only leaves when more or less full.

OTHER PLACES

Bagh Caves

The Bagh Caves are seven km from the village of Bagh and three km off the main road. Bagh is about 50 km west of Mandu, on the road between Indore and Baroda in Gujarat. The Buddhist caves date from 400-700 AD and all are in very bad shape. Cave-ins, smoke and water damage have reduced them to such poor condition that restoration work is barely worthwhile. Compared to the caves of Ajanta or Ellora, the Bagh Caves are hardly worth the considerable effort of getting to them.

In the Archaeological Museum in Gwalior you can see reproductions of the wall paintings from Cave 4, known as Rang Mahal or the 'Painted Hall', when they were in much better condition than today.

There is a *PWD Dak Bungalow* at the caves.

Ratlam & Mandsaur

The railway line passes through Ratlam,

capital of a former princely state whose ruler died in one of those tragically heroic Rajput battles against the might of the Moghuls.

At Mandsaur, north of Ratlam, a number of interesting archaeological finds were made in a field three km from the town. Some others are displayed in the museum at Indore. Two 14-metre-high sandstone pillars are on the site, and an inscription commemorates the victory of a Malwa king over the Huns in 528 AD. In the fort are some fine pieces from the Gupta period.

Eastern Madhya Pradesh

JABALPUR (population 900,000)
Almost due south of Khajuraho and east of Bhopal, the large city of Jabalpur, the second largest in the state, is principally famous today for the gorge on the Narmada River known as the Marble Rocks. It's also the departure point for a visit to the Kanha National Park further south.

The city was constructed in the 1860s after the British overran the Maratha territories following the latter's defeat in 1818. The original settlement in this area was ancient Tripuri and the rulers of this city, the Hayahaya, are mentioned in the *Mahabharata*. It passed successively into Mauryan and then Gupta control until, in 875 AD, it was taken by the Kalchuri rulers. In the 13th century it was overrun by the Gonds and by the early 16th century it had become the powerful state of Gondwana.

Though besieged by Moghul armies from time to time, Gondwana survived until 1789 when it was conquered by the Marathas. Their rule was unpopular, due largely to the activities of the 'thuggies' (from which the word 'thug' is derived). These people engaged in ritual murders,

strangling their victims with a silken cord in order to please the goddess Kali. It took the best part of 50 years for the British to fully wipe out the practitioners of this cult, and the officer who was given the job of doing this, Colonel Sleeman, gave his name to the town of Sleemanabad between Jabalpur and Satna.

These days, Jabalpur is a major administrative and educational centre and the army headquarters for the states of Orissa and Madhya Pradesh. It also has an unusual number of Christian schools, colleges and churches scattered throughout the cantonment area and, judging from the names on the houses, a large community of Goans.

Information
The tourist office (tel 2211) is at the railway station. It's open Monday to Saturday from 10 am to 5 pm, except for the second Saturday of the month, and is closed on Sundays and public holidays. They have the usual range of leaflets available but can't book accommodation for you at Kanha National Park, though they can tell you the state of the booking so you know if there's room available at Kisli.

Money can be changed at the main branch of the State Bank of India and at Jackson's Hotel.

The best bookshop is A H Wheeler on platform No 1 at the railway station. English-language newspapers *Newsweek, National Geographic*, etc, can be bought at the Janta Newsagency opposite Shyam Talkies, Malviya Chowk. It's a tiny place next to Jain Book/Stationers.

Bazaar
The old bazaar area of Jabalpur is huge and full of typically Indian smells, sights, sounds and goods for sale. Put aside a whole morning or afternoon to stroll through it. You'll be lucky to see another tourist though you may well see quite a few east African students.

The Rani Durgavati Museum, south of the bazaar, is also worth a visit.

Madan Mahal

This ancient Gond fortress is on the route to the Marble Rocks, perched on top of a huge boulder. The Gonds, who worshipped snakes, lived in this region even before the Aryans arrived, and maintained their independence right up until Moghul times.

Places to Stay & Eat

There are two main hotel areas, one relatively close to the railway station and the other in the streets around the bus station. You'll need an auto-rickshaw to get between the two as they're about two km apart.

Places to Stay - bottom end

There are hardly any cheap hotels around the railway station. The only exception is the *Simla Lodge* (tel 21260) and even this is not that close to the station. It's a fairly tatty place but has singles/doubles with bath for Rs 25/40 and checkout is 24 hours after arrival.

The other cheap places to stay are down by the bus station. Best value is the modern *Swayam Hotel* at Rs 30/40 for singles/doubles with bath and bucket hot water. Also cheap is the *New Central Lodge*, a very basic, typical Indian boarding house with singles/doubles at Rs 17/30 with common bath. Next door is the *Meenakshi Lodge* of similar standard. Going up in price, the *Hotel Anand* is a good choice at Rs 40/50 for singles/doubles with bath and hot water supplied on request, Rs 100 for doubles with TV. The staff are very friendly and the hotel has a restaurant – the *Roopali*.

Similar is the modern *Hotel Rahul* which looks pricey but is reasonable at Rs 65/80 for singles/doubles with bath and hot water. The hotel has its own restaurant, the *Goofa Restaurant*. Another good choice is the new but relatively cheap *Lodge Shivalaya* at Rs 40/59 for singles/

doubles with bathroom and bucket hot water available between 6 and 11 am.

Jackson's Hotel (tel 25366) in Civil Lines must have been the best hotel in town at one time, and it still has fading touches of the Raj with its extensive gardens and badminton court. It's very popular with travellers who don't mind spending a little extra to enjoy its mellow atmosphere. There's a whole range of rooms from Rs 50/80 for singles/doubles up to Rs 350 for air-con rooms, all with bath and hot water, and some have balconies overlooking the gardens. The staff are very friendly and helpful. The hotel has a bar and restaurant and the varied food is excellent. They have a licence for changing travellers' cheques and excess baggage can be left here safely while you visit Kanha National Park. In the hotel compound there's a post office, bookshop and a travel agent.

Back down towards the bus station is the *Hotel Ambassador* (tel 21771), Russel Crossing, another fairly old building with singles/doubles for Rs 40/60 and deluxe singles for Rs 60; there are also air-con doubles for Rs 270. All rooms have a shower and toilet with bucket hot water available; air-con rooms have running hot water. Similar is the *Hotel Samrat*, Russel Crossing, with singles/doubles at Rs 45/60, air-cooled rooms at Rs 58/90 and air-con rooms at Rs 200/240. All rooms have a shower, toilet and TV.

Places to Stay - middle

The cheapest of the mid-range hotels is the state tourist corporation *Hotel Kalchuri* (tel 27411, 27491), a very modern, well-maintained building with singles/doubles at Rs 120/150 or Rs 250/300 with air-con, including breakfast. All rooms have a bath and hot water. There's a bar and restaurant and the manager is very pleasant.

The other hotel in this bracket is the *Sidharth Hotel* (tel 27580, 29247), Russel Crossing, a modern, high-rise building with air-cooled singles/doubles at

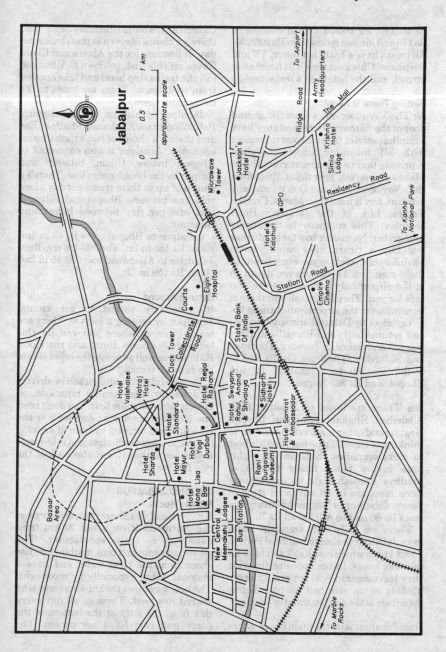

Jabalpur

approximate scale

0   0.5   1 km

To Airport

Ridge Road

Army
Headquarters

The Mall

Krishna
Hotel

Jackson's
Hotel

Simla
Lodge

Microwave
Tower

Residency   Road

GPO

Hotel
Kalchuri

To Kanha
National Park

Station   Road

Empire
Cinema

Courts

Elgin
Hospital

State Bank
of India

Collectorate   Road

Clock Tower

Hotel
Vaishalee

Natraj
Hotel

Hotel
Regal & Rahans

Hotel
Standard

Hotel Swoyam,
Rahul, Anand
& Shivalaya

Sidharth
Hotel

Hotel
Sharda

Hotel
Mayur

Hotel
Yogi
Durbar

Hotel Samrat
& Ambassador

Rani
Durgavati
Museum

Bazaar
Area

Hotel
Mona Lisa
& Bar

New Central &
Meenakshi Lodges

Bus
Station

To Marble
Rocks

Rs 95/140, air-cooled deluxe doubles at Rs 175 and air-con rooms from Rs 200/250. All rooms have a bath, hot water, TV and telephone. Checkout time is 24 hours after arrival, and the hotel has a restaurant.

Getting There & Away
Air The Vayudoot office is on the ground floor of the Sidharth Hotel and they have a minibus service to the airport to connect with all incoming/outgoing flights. A private taxi to the airport costs Rs 80. Make sure you buy your ticket direct from the Vayudoot office. Don't, on any account, buy it from their agents, Chadha Travels Ltd, at the Jackson's Hotel complex. This company is thoroughly untogether. No matter how far in advance you buy a ticket, they won't inform Vayudoot of the fact so you won't be on the flight manifest. This means you'll turn up at the airport only to discover there's no seat for you. They'll also tell you there is no minibus to the airport – an outright lie.

Vayudoot fly Delhi/Allahabad/Jabalpur and return daily, and Bhopal/Jabalpur/Nagpur and return on Tuesday, Thursday and Saturday. The fares are Rs 910 to Delhi, Rs 380 to Allahabad, Rs 315 Bhopal, and Rs 325 Nagpur.

Bus There are buses to Jabalpur from Allahabad, Khajuraho, Varanasi, Bhopal, Nagpur and other main centres. If you're thinking of travelling by bus then it's best to make enquiries about private night-time luxury buses rather than take Madhya Pradesh state transport buses since most are in an advanced state of decay. Jabalpur to Nagpur by luxury bus costs Rs 60 and to Allahabad Rs 70.

There are daily state transport buses from Jabalpur to Kanha National Park at 7 and 11 am which cost Rs 22 and take six to seven hours. In the opposite direction they leave around 8.30 am and 12 noon. Tickets go on sale half an hour before departure at the city bus stand in Jabalpur.

Train Jabalpur is on the main broad-gauge Calcutta/Allahabad/Bombay line and there's a choice of seven express trains per day. If heading for the Ajanta and Ellora Caves on this line, go down to Bhusaval (all the trains stop here) and take another train to Jalgaon. There are buses to the caves from there.

Jabalpur is also on the broad-gauge Patna/Varanasi/Allahabad/Madras line and there's a choice of two express trains each day. Jabalpur is also connected to Bhopal, Indore, Ujjain, Bilaspur and Raipur by the broad-gauge line. There's a choice of up to three trains per day along this line between Bhopal and Bilaspur and one per day between Indore and Bilaspur.

Jabalpur to Bhopal costs Rs 43 in 2nd class, Rs 153 in 1st. The 369-km trip from Jabalpur to Allahabad costs Rs 45 in 2nd class, Rs 159 in 1st.

Getting Around
It's probably easiest to get around Jabalpur by renting a bicycle. There are several places where you can do this between Jackson's Hotel and the Hotel Kalchuri as well as across the other side of the railway tracks.

Be careful with auto-rickshaw drivers in Jabalpur, they can be rapacious, so always agree on a fare first. You don't need one if you're staying at Jackson's or the Kalchuri and arriving by train. If arriving by bus, most of the budget and mid-range hotels are within 10 minutes walk of the city bus stand.

AROUND JABALPUR
Marble Rocks
Known locally as Bhegaghat, this gorge on the Narmada River about 20 km from Jabalpur is truly spectacular. The gleaming white and pink marble cliffs rise sheer from the clear water and have a magical effect, especially by moonlight. The best way to see the km-long gorge is by shared row boat. These go all day every day from the jetty at the bottom of the gorge and cost Rs 3 per person. The

boaties give you a running commentary (in Hindi) and point out peculiar formations which they've naturally given fanciful names to such as the Hathi-ka-paon 'elephant's foot' and the 'monkey's leap'. The cliffs at the foot of the gorge are floodlit at night.

At the head of the gorge is the spectacular Dhuandhar or 'smoke cascade'. All around the falls are hundreds of stalls selling marble carvings, much of it fairly clichéd but there are some beautiful pieces if you shop around. Foreign tourists naturally get quoted inflated prices so you'll need to do some solid bargaining if you want to buy anything.

Above the lower end of the gorge, a flight of over 100 stone steps leads to the Chausath Yogini or Madanpur Temple. The circular temple has damaged images of the 64 yoginis, or attendants of the goddess Kali.

Places to Stay & Eat Marble Rocks is a very mellow place to stay and the best accommodation is at the state tourist corporation *Motel Marble Rocks* (tel 38), which overlooks the foot of the gorge and has a restaurant. The motel has only four rooms for Rs 90/130 a single/double with bath, so it's best to book in advance. There are plenty of cheap cafes in the village and at the falls but there is nowhere to stay at the falls themselves.

Getting There & Away Local buses and tempos run to the Marble Rocks from the city bus stand in Jabalpur for a few rupees. A taxi hired from Jabalpur costs about Rs 130 return including waiting time. An alternative way to get there is to hire a bicycle. The road is flat most of the way and there are plenty of stalls to stop at along the way.

KANHA NATIONAL PARK

Kanha, south-east of Jabalpur, is one of India's largest national parks covering 1945 square km including a core zone of 945 square km. It's a beautiful area of forest and lightly wooded grassland with many rivers and streams, and it supports an excellent variety of wildlife. It is also a part of Project Tiger, one of India's most important and successful conservation efforts, along with 16 other national parks across the subcontinent.

Wildlife was first given limited protection here as early as 1933 but it wasn't until 1955 that the area was declared a national park. Additions to the park were made in 1962 and 1970. Kanha is a good example of what can be achieved under a determined policy of wildlife management; between 1973 and 1981 the tiger population increased from 43 to 83, leopards from 30 to 54, chital from 9000 to 17,000, sambar from 1058 to 1712 and barasingha from 118 to 451. Only the gaur decreased in numbers during those years but this was due to an outbreak of rinderpest in 1976 and their numbers are again on the increase.

The park is very well organised and a

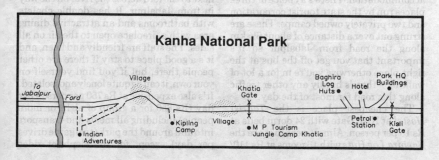

Kanha National Park

To Jabalpur — Ford — Village — Khatia Gate — Baghira Log Huts — Hotel — Park HQ Buildings — Petrol Station — Kisli Gate — Village — M P Tourism Jungle Camp Khatia — Kipling Camp — Indian Adventures

popular place to visit. You're almost guaranteed one or even more sightings of tiger, gaur and many herbivores on every safari, especially if you go on elephant-back. Indeed, the tigers in this park appear to be so accustomed to bunches of camera-toting visitors on elephant-back that the mahout will often take the elephant right up to a tiger. It can be quite disconcerting to be staring into the eyes of a wild tiger literally only a few feet away but, so far, no-one has come off the worse for wear. It's certainly a very exciting experience.

There's no 'best time of the year' to visit Kanha but the park is closed from 1 July to 31 October due to the monsoons. The hottest months are May and June when the temperature can reach 42°C in the afternoons. December and January are the coldest months and, although it's warm enough to do without a sweater during the day, as soon as the sun sets the temperature quickly plunges to zero and below. Since the best times to go on safari are early morning and late afternoon, you're going to need plenty of warm clothes.

There are no facilities for changing travellers' cheques at Kanha. The nearest places to do this are at Mandla and Jabalpur (State Bank of India).

Entry to the park costs Rs 10 per person per day.

Places to Stay & Eat

Kisli is the main entrance and centre of accommodation. There's a choice of three places run by the state tourist corporation and two privately owned camps. These are strung out over a distance of about 6½ km along the road from Jabalpur so it's important that you get off the bus at the right place otherwise you're in for a lot of walking – there's hardly any other traffic along this road for most of the day.

The cheapest place is the *Tourist Hostel* at Kisli Gate with 24 dorm beds at Rs 15 per person. Almost next to it are the *Baghira Log Huts* with 16 rooms at Rs 110/

150 a single/double, and extra beds for Rs 30 each. Meals are available and this is where you must also eat if staying at the hostel. Back down the road some four km is the Khatia Gate where the *Jungle Camp Khatia* has 18 rooms at Rs 30 for singles or doubles, plus extra beds for Rs 15 each. Meals are available here.

All these places are run by the state tourist organisation and it's advisable to book in advance, though not essential if you're happy with a dorm bed. Bookings more than 10 days in advance have to be made at one of these MP State Tourism offices:

Bhopal
   4th Floor, Gangotri, T T Nagar (tel 65154)
Bombay
   74 World Trade Centre, Cuffe Parade, Colaba (tel 217603)
Calcutta
   Room 7, 6th Floor, Chitrakoot Building, 230A A J C Bose Rd (tel 448543)
New Delhi
   2nd Floor, Kanishka Shopping Plaza, 19 Ashok Rd (tel 3327264).

Bookings between four and 10 days in advance have to be made through the tourist office (tel 22111) at the railway station in Jabalpur. If you can't book more than four days in advance then this same tourist office can tell you what accommodation will be available to you.

Of the privately run accommodation, the furthest from Kisli is *Indian Adventures*, next to the ford across the river on the way in from Jabalpur. It has double chalets with bathrooms and an attractive dining area with a fireplace open to the air on all sides. The staff are friendly and keen, and it's a good place to stay if there are other people there, but if you find yourself on your own, it can be quite lonely and isolated. It's also expensive at Rs 750 per person per day (Rs 650 for a group of eight or more people) including all meals and transport into and around the park (two game drives per day) except for the elephant rides which are extra. Their Maruti jeep is quiet and comfortable and they don't skimp on time. Food, on the other hand, is only of average quality and the 'packed breakfasts' very poor. Bookings should be made through Indian Adventures (tel 6422925), 257 S V Road, Bandra, Bombay 400050, at least 10 days in advance (15 days for groups of eight or more people). Bookings less than 10 days in advance can be made through Chadha Travels (tel 22178), Jackson's Hotel, Civil Lines, Jabalpur.

The other private camp is *Kipling Camp* about one km closer to Kisli than Indian Adventures. It's run by an Englishman, Bob Wright, who can be contacted through the Tollygunge Club (tel 46 1922) 120 D P Sasmal Rd, Calcutta. It's not cheap at Rs 600 per day, but prices include all meals and transport, guides, etc. It's open from 1 November to 30 April and does not take people who just roll up, so bookings must be made in advance.

There are no small Indian boarding houses where you can stay at Kisli but there are two small cafes at the Khatia Gate.

Finally, there's the state tourist organisation *Kanha Safari Lodge* at Mukki on the other side of the park from Kisli. Singles/doubles cost Rs 110/150 or Rs 170/200 with air-con, plus Rs 30 in either for extra beds. There's a bar and restaurant. Mukki isn't easy to get to without your own transport but the lodge is open all year, unlike accommodation at Kisli which is closed during the monsoons. Bookings should be made in the same way as for the accommodation at Kisli.

Getting There & Away

There are direct state transport buses from the city bus station in Jabalpur to Kisli Gate twice daily at 7 am (six hours) and 11 am (seven hours) which cost Rs 22. Tickets go on sale about 15 minutes before departure. In the opposite direction, the buses depart Kisli at around 8.30 am and 12 noon but the early bus can be late starting in winter. These are ramshackle old buses and crowded as far as Mandla though there are generally spare seats after that. Don't bring too much baggage as there's hardly anywhere to put it. On the Kisli to Jabalpur run you may have to change buses at Mandla.

Make sure you get off at the right place if you are staying at Indian Adventures, Kipling Camp or Khatia Gate.

Getting Around

Jeep Jeeps are for hire at both Khatia and Kisli Gates and cost Rs 4 per km shared by up to six people, plus Rs 3 per hour for a compulsory guide. Park entry fees are extra. Excursion times are sunrise to 12 noon and 3 pm to sunset from 1 November to 15 February; sunrise to 12 noon and 4 pm to sunset from 16 February to 30 April, and sunrise to 11 am and 5 pm to sunset from 1 May to 30 June. An average distance covered on a morning excursion would be 60 km; less in the afternoon. As in other Indian national parks, drivers tend to drive too fast and not wait around long enough for game to appear. If you think they're being impatient, tell them to slow down.

Elephant The other transport available is elephant safaris. This is an excellent way to see the park as elephants go where the jeeps cannot – into the long grass, along river courses, etc – so you're far more likely to see tigers. Elephants cost Rs 20 per hour shared between up to four people and the ride usually lasts two to three hours. Safaris leave at 3 pm between 1 November and 15 February, 4 pm between 16 February and 15 April, and 5 pm between 16 April and 30 June. Book your elephant at the Kisli Gate in the morning. The elephants are stabled several km inside the park at the Forest Department's camp so you'll also need to hire a jeep to get there.

There's also the so-called 'Tiger Show' which usually occurs in the mornings around 11 am. What happens here is that certain tigers seem to favour certain spots in the park and the trackers know where these are. The jeep which you've hired goes back to Kisli Gate and the park officials give you a 'quota'. The jeep then takes you to the spot where the tigers are and there you transfer to an elephant for the final 100 metres or so. The 'show' costs Rs 5 per person plus Rs 10 per elephant shared between up to four people.

BANDHAVGARH NATIONAL PARK
This national park is north-east of Jabalpur in the Vindhyan mountain range. Like Kanha it has a wide variety of wildlife but it's not part of Project Tiger. This doesn't mean that you won't see tigers but the population here is relatively small – around 25 at present. The famous white tiger of Rewa was also discovered in this area.

Bandhavgarh covers an area of 104 square km and is named after an ancient fortress built on top of cliffs which are 800 metres high. Being fairly small, the park has a fragile ecology but it supports such animals as nilgai, wild boar, jackal, gaur, sambar and porcupine as well as many species of birds. The ramparts of the fort provide a home for vulture, blue rock thrush and crag martin.

Places to Stay
The *White Tiger Forest Lodge*, run by the state tourist organisation, is the only place to stay. Singles/doubles cost Rs 90/130 and extra beds Rs 30. The manager is friendly and the food good though don't

expect anything too elaborate. Advance booking is advisable (addresses and telephone numbers in Kanha section).

Getting There & Around
Umaria, on the Katni to Bilaspur rail line, is the nearest railhead. Local buses are available from there.

Jeeps and elephants can be hired for the same rates as at Kanha.

OTHER PLACES
Mandla & Ramnagar
Mandla is about 100 km south of Jabalpur on the road to Kanha. Here there is a fort on a loop of the Narmada River built so that the river protects it on three sides while a ditch protects it on the fourth. Built in the late 1600s, the fort is now subsiding into the jungle although some of the towers still stand.

About 15 km away is Ramnagar where there is a ruined three-storey palace overlooking the Narmada. This palace, and the fort at Mandla, were both built by Gond kings, retreating south before the advance of Moghul power. Also near Mandla is a stretch of the Narmada where many temples dot the riverbank.

Bilaspur & Raipur
These are larger towns in the east of the state on the Bombay to Calcutta railway line. Ratanpur, 25 km north of Bilaspur, was the capital of the old kingdom of Chattisgarh, the 'kingdom of 36 forts'.

Orissa

Population: 31 million
Area: 155,842 square km
Capital: Bhubaneswar
Main language: Oriya

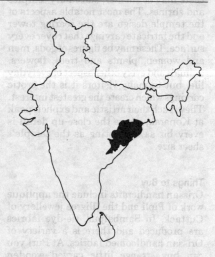

The state of Orissa lies along the eastern seaboard of India, south of Bengal. Its main attractions are the temple towns of Puri and Bhubaneswar and the great Sun Temple at Konarak. These three sites make a convenient and compact triangle, and Bhubaneswar is on the main Calcutta to Madras railway route. It is predominantly rural, with fertile green coastal plains rising to the hills of the Eastern Ghats.

Orissa is tapping the hydroelectric potential of its many rivers, and fledgling industries are being started. The state is mineral-rich and a big exporter of iron ore with a large factory at Rourkela. However, the state is still largely a region of green fields and small villages.

History

Orissa's hazy past focuses with the reign of Kalinga. In 260 BC he was defeated by Ashoka, the great Indian emperor, but the bloody battle left such a bitter taste with Ashoka that he converted to Buddhism and spread that gentle religion far and wide. Buddhism soon declined in Orissa, however, and Jainism held sway until Buddhism reasserted itself in the 2nd century AD. By the 7th century AD Hinduism had, in turn, supplanted Buddhism and Orissa's golden age was in full swing.

Under the Kesari and Ganga kings the Orissan culture flourished and countless temples from that classical period still stand today. The Orissans managed to defy the Muslim rulers in Delhi until the region finally fell to the Moghuls during the 16th century. Many of Bhubaneswar's temples were destroyed at that time.

Temple Architecture

Orissan temples – whether it is the mighty Lingaraj in Bhubaneswar, the Jagannath in Puri, the Sun Temple at Konarak, or the many smaller temples – all follow a similar pattern. Basically there are two structures – the *jagamohan* or entrance porch, and the *duel* where the image of the temple deity is kept and above which the temple tower rises. The design is complicated in larger temples by the addition of other entrance halls in front of the jagamohan. These are the *bhoga-mandapa* or 'hall of offering' and the *nata-mandir* or 'dancing hall'.

The whole structure may be enclosed by an outer wall and within the enclosure

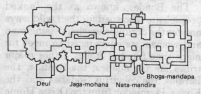

Deul   Jaga-mohana   Nata-mandira   Bhoga-mandapa

Lingaraja Temple

there may be smaller, subsidiary temples and shrines. The most notable aspects of the temple design are the soaring tower and the intricate carvings that cover every surface. These may be figures of gods, men and women, plants and trees, flowers, animals and every other aspect of everyday life, but to many visitors it is the erotic carvings which create the greatest interest. They reach their artistic and explicit peak at Konarak, where the close-up detail is every bit as interesting as the temple's sheer size.

Things to Buy

Orissan handicrafts include the appliqué work of Pipli and the filigree jewellery of Cuttack. In Sambalpur, tie-dye fabrics are produced and there is a variety of Orissan handloomed fabrics. At Puri you can buy strange little carved wooden replicas of Lord Jagannath and his brother and sister. At Balasore lacquered children's toys are manufactured.

Tribal People

Orissa has no less than 62 distinct tribal groups of aboriginal people who were there prior to the Aryan invasion of India. They constitute about 25% of the state's population and live mainly in the hilly area of central Orissa. Amongst the better known tribes are the Kondhs, who still practise colourful ceremonies, although animal sacrifices have been substituted for the human ones which the British took so much trouble to stop – particularly around Russelkonda (Bhanjanagar).

The Bondas, known as the 'naked people', are renowned for their wild ways and for the dormitories where young men and women are encouraged to meet for night-time fun and frolics. Other major tribes are the Juangs, the Santals, the Parajas, the colourful Godabas and the Koyas. Permission from the Orissa Home Ministry is needed to visit tribal villages except those along the main highways.

BHUBANESWAR (population 219,000)

The capital of Orissa is known as the temple town because of its many temples in the extravagant Orissan style. At one time the Bindusagar tank had over 7000 temples around it. Today there are about 500, but most of these are decayed fragments. Perhaps a dozen are of real interest, including the great Lingaraj Temple, one of the most important temples in India. The temples are in a variety of Orissan styles and date from the 8th to the 13th century AD.

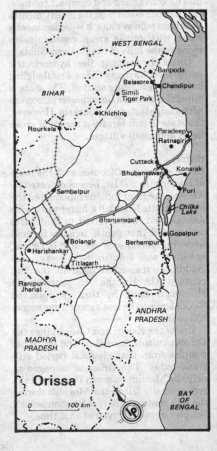

Orissa

Information & Orientation

Bhubaneswar is a sprawling town divided into old and new parts – the railway line forms the approximate dividing line. The bus stop and the Indian Airlines office are both in the new town, as are most of the hotels. The Tourist Bungalow and the ITDC Ashok Hotel are across the tracks.

The tourist office is down the lane beside the Panthanivas Tourist Bungalow. There's also a Government of India tourist office nearby. Most of the temples are within reasonable walking distance of the Tourist Bungalow.

Lingaraj Temple

The great temple of Bhubaneswar is off limits to all non-Hindus. Close to the wall, on the northern side, is a viewing platform, originally erected for Lord Curzon during the days of the Raj. It's the best view you'll get of the temple and you really need binoculars to see anything. You'll be asked for a donation at the viewing platform.

The temple is dedicated to Tribhuvaneswar or 'Lord of the Three Worlds', also known as Bhubaneswar. In its present form it dates from 1090-1104 AD, although parts of it are over 1400 years old. The granite block which represents Tribhuvaneswar is said to be bathed daily with water, milk and bhang (hashish). The temple compound is about 150 metres square and is dominated by the 40-metre-high temple tower.

The ornately carved tower is intricately sculptured. From the viewing platform you can easily see the lions crushing elephants, said to be a representation of the re-emergence of Hinduism over Buddhism. More than 50 smaller temples and shrines crowd the enclosure. In the north-east corner a smaller temple to Parvati is of particular interest.

There is also an annual chariot festival in the temple in April.

Bindu Sagar

The 'Ocean Drop' tank just north of the great temple is said to contain water from every holy stream, pool and tank in India. Consequently, when it comes to washing away sin this is the tank that washes whitest. There are a number of temples and shrines scattered around the tank, several with towers in imitation of the ones at the Lingaraj Temple. In the centre of the tank is a water pavilion where, once a year, the Lingaraj Temple's deity is brought to be ritually bathed.

Siddharanya

Close to the main Bhubaneswar to Puri road, on the same side as the Lingaraj Temple, the 'Grove of the Perfect Beings' is a cluster of about 20 smaller temples, including some of the most important in Bhubaneswar. Right by the road the small, 11-metre-high Mukteswar Temple is finely detailed with some excellent carving, but unfortunately much of it is defaced. The dwarves are particularly nice. The Mukteswar features an arched torana showing clear Buddhist influence.

Also by the road, across the path from the Mukteswar, the Kedareswar is one of the older temples at Bhubaneswar and has a small tank. Close to the Mukteswar is Siddheswar Temple, an interesting old temple with a fine standing Ganesh figure. If you follow the path from these temples towards the Lingaraj you soon come to the Parsurameswar on your right. It's the best preserved of the early (7th century AD) temples and has interesting bas-reliefs of elephant and horse processions. All its fine carvings are vigorous and alive.

If you work up a thirst while temple hunting, the shop beside the cinema near the junction has cold, cheap soft drinks.

Raj Rani

Across the road and about 100 metres to the right, the Raj Rani stands alone in a green field. It's one of the latest of the Bhubaneswar temples and is particularly finely sited. Statues of nymphs, embracing couples, elephants and lions fill the niches and decorate the pillars. As it's no longer

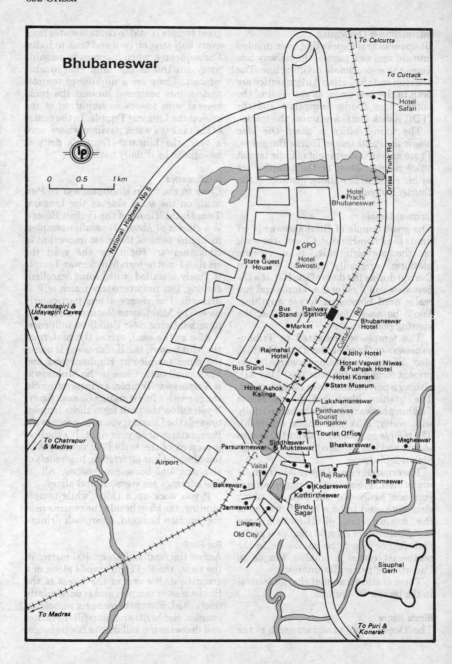

Bhubaneswar

To Calcutta

To Cuttack

0   0.5   1 km

National Highway No 5

Orissa Trunk Rd

Hotel Safari

Hotel Prachi Bhubaneswar

GPO

State Guest House

Hotel Swosti

Khandagiri & Udayagiri Caves

Bus Stand

Railway Station

Market

Cuttack Rd

Bhubaneswar Hotel

Rajmahal Hotel

Jolly Hotel

Bus Stand

Hotel Vagwat Niwas & Pushpak Hotel

Hotel Konark

Hotel Ashok Kalinga

State Museum

Lakshamaneswar

To Chatrapur & Madras

Panthanivas Tourist Bungalow

Tourist Office

Parsurameswar

Siddheswar & Mukteswar

Bhaskareswar

Megheswar

Airport

Vaital

Raj Rani

Brahmeswar

Bakeswar

Kedareswar

Jameswar

Kottirtheswar

Lingaraj Old City

Bindu Sagar

Sisuphal Garh

To Madras

To Puri & Konarak

used for worship you are free to wander at will.

Brahmeswar

About a km east of the main road, the Brahmeswar Temple stands in a courtyard flanked by four smaller structures. It's notable for its very finely detailed sculptures with erotic and sometimes amusing elements – such as the young lady with the surprised look on her face, no doubt due to her lover's hand in her pants! The temple dates from the 9th century.

Close by are two other temples which are not of such great interest. The Bhaskareswar has an unusual stepped design in order to accommodate an unusually large, three-metre lingam it once contained. The Megheswar is in a courtyard and its shrine entrance is topped by a figure. Beside it is a tank.

Other Temples

Close to the Bindu Sagar Tank, the Vaital has a double-storey 'wagon roof', an influence from Buddhist cave architecture. Further north the Lakshamaneswar is a very plain temple. Dating from the 7th century, it is one of the earliest specimens of Orissan architecture and acts as a gateway to the city.

Museum

The museum is opposite the Hotel Ashok Kalinga and has an interesting collection relating to Orissan history, culture and architecture and to the various Orissan tribes. The Tribal Research Bureau is also here. The museum is open from 10 am to 1 pm and from 2 to 4 pm daily, except Mondays. Entry is Rs 0.25.

Dhauli Edicts

South of Bhubaneswar and to the right of the Puri road, King Ashoka carved his famous edicts into a five metres by three metres rock. The great Buddhist emperor related the horrors he experienced in the Kalinga wars, which he won, and his

Raj Rani Temple, Bhubaneswar

subsequent conversion to Buddhism. These 13 inscriptions are still remarkably clear after more than 2000 years. The rock is at the base of the small rocky hill. The adjacent larger hill is topped by a shiny new Peace Pagoda built by the Japanese in the 1970s. You can get to the place where you turn off the main road on any Puri or Konarak bus for Rs 1.

Other Attractions

The partly excavated ruins at Sisupal Garh are thought to be the remains of an Ashokan city. At Nandankanan, 30 km from Bhubaneswar, there is a garden divided into a wildlife sanctuary, botanical garden and lake. The wildlife sanctuary has tigers, crocodiles and even a lion safari. You can rent boats on the lake too.

Tours

During the season various tours operate from the Tourist Bungalow, including a tour of temples and caves of Bhubaneswar for Rs 30 or a Puri to Konarak tour for Rs 40. The latter tour runs from 9 am to 6.30 pm. The Bhubaneswar tour spends too long at a zoo/nature reserve and not long enough at the caves and temples.

Places to Stay - bottom end
Most of Bhubaneswar's cheaper hotels are close to the museum, behind the railway station. Some are of similar standard to the Tourist Bungalow but much cheaper. A particularly good-value hotel is the *Bhubaneswar Hotel* (tel 51977) directly behind the railway station, with singles/doubles at Rs 45/65 or Rs 100/125 with air-con. Also excellent value, the *Pushpak Hotel* (tel 50545) has rooms with bath for Rs 50 and a good restaurant serving south Indian food. Another reasonable place is the *Hotel Vagwat Niwas* (tel 54481), very close to the Pushpak, which has singles at Rs 25 or rooms with fan and bath for Rs 60. The *Hotel Gajapati* (tel 50843) at 77 Budha Nagar has rooms at Rs 50/60 or Rs 150 with air-con. The *Hotel Anarkali* (tel 54031) is another station-area hotel with rooms at Rs 75/90. If you're looking for something cheaper, try the *Jolly Hotel*, Cuttack Rd, opposite the Pushpak.

The centrally located *Rajmahal Hotel* (tel 52448) has its own bar and restaurant and is excellent value at Rs 30/40 for singles/doubles with bath. Round behind it the *Hotel Venus* has doubles at Rs 50 but it's nothing special. There are a lot of other small cheap lodges along the main road between the Rajmahal and the expensive Hotel Konark.

The Government of Orissa has an *Inspection Bungalow* on Old Station Bazaar, Satyanagar. The railway station has *retiring rooms* (tel 52233), as does the bus station. Out at the Udayagiri and Khandagiri hills there's a very run-down building claiming to be the Khandagiri *Youth Hostel*.

Places to Stay - middle
The government-run tourist bungalows throughout Orissa are all similarly priced and offer very similar standards. They're well kept, all rooms have bathrooms, and there's a reasonably priced restaurant. In Bhubaneswar the still popular *Panthanivas Tourist Bungalow* (tel 54515) is conveniently near the many temples. Rooms with bath are Rs 100, or Rs 150 with air-con. There are also a couple of four-bed rooms which can be used as dormitories at a very pricey Rs 30 per bed.

The *Hotel Prachi Bhubaneswar* (tel 52689) at 6 Janpath has rooms at Rs 150/200, and Rs 325/425 with air-con.

Places to Stay - top end
Not far from the Tourist Bungalow is the *Hotel Ashok Kalinga* (tel 53318), opposite the museum. It's modern, centrally air-conditioned, and has a good restaurant and bar. Singles/doubles cost Rs 395/595 in the new block. There are some cheaper rooms without air-con for Rs 275/375. Continue across the railway line towards the centre of town where the *Hotel Konark* (tel 53330, 54330/1) has rooms with bath for Rs 425/525. The hotel is centrally air-conditioned and there's a restaurant, bar, swimming pool and bookshop.

By far the best value among the top-end places is the *Hotel Swosti* (tel 54178). Singles/doubles cost Rs 295/375. The *Hotel Oberoi* (tel 56618) is on the outskirts of town. It is a beautiful building and charges Rs 630/750 for air-con singles/doubles.

Places to Eat
The *Tourist Bungalow* has a reasonably priced, if monotonous, dining hall. Amongst the eating places in town you could try the *South Indian Hotel*, behind the Rajmahal Hotel and under the Venus Lodge, for a thali. The restaurant at the *Hotel Swosti* has excellent food.

The *Pinky Restaurant* has been recommended as friendly and cheap. The *Hotel Ashok Kalinga* is an excellent place for an escape to air-con comfort and good food – say Rs 60 to Rs 70 per person for a complete meal. They have a pleasant bar with free peanuts or other snacks.

Getting There & Away
Air Bhubaneswar is connected by Indian Airlines flights to Delhi (Rs 1200), Raipur, Varanasi (Rs 650), Calcutta (Rs 430), Nagpur and Hyderabad (Rs 895).

Bus There are frequent private buses from Bhubaneswar to Puri. The trip takes 1½ to two hours and costs Rs 6. It takes the same time, and Rs 6.40, to Konarak. See Konarak for Puri to Konarak information. If it is not possible to get a direct bus to Konarak, all Puri buses go through Pipli, where the Konarak road branches off.

Train Bhubaneswar is 437 km from Calcutta and 1226 km from Madras. Since it is on the main Calcutta to Madras railway line there are plenty of trains to Bhubaneswar as well as the trains terminating at Puri. The crack Coromandel Express departs Calcutta at 4 pm and arrives in Bhubaneswar just over seven hours later. Other trains are rather slower; the Madras Mail leaves at 8 pm and takes eight hours. Fares are Rs 52 in 2nd class, Rs 185 in 1st.

From Madras the Coromandel Express takes about 20 hours, the Howrah Mail about 24 hours and other trains 30 or more hours. Fares from Madras are Rs 104 in 2nd class, Rs 406 in 1st. Trains terminating in Puri take 1½ to two hours longer from Calcutta or Madras.

There are one or two trains a day from Delhi to Bhubaneswar and Puri and they take 34 to 42 hours. Delhi to Bhubaneswar is 2074 km and the fares are Rs 144 in 2nd class, Rs 590 in 1st.

Getting Around
Airport Transport The airport is very close to the town. A taxi costs Rs 25 but you could also get a rickshaw for Rs 10.

Local Transport From the Tourist Bungalow a rickshaw to town or the Lingaraj Temple

is about Rs 3. If you plan on staying at one of the hotels along Cuttack Rd, at the back of the station, it isn't worth getting a rickshaw – simply cross the railway tracks at the southern end of the station and walk through.

AROUND BHUBANESWAR
There are two interesting sites close to Bhubaneswar, both dating from the Buddhist period.

Udayagiri & Khandagiri Caves
About five km out of Bhubaneswar, the two hills flanking the road on each side are riddled with caves. On the right of the road, Udayagiri, or 'Sunrise Hill', has the more interesting caves scattered at various levels up the hill. All are numbered. At the base of the hill, round to the right, is the two-storey Rani ka Naur or 'Queen's Palace Cave' (1). Both levels

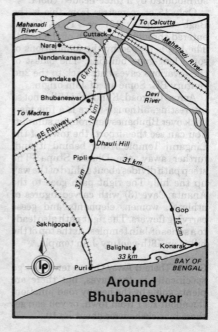

Around Bhubaneswar

have eight entrances and the cave is extensively carved.

Return to the road via the Chota Hathi Gumpha (3), with its carvings of elephants coming out from behind a tree. The Jaya Vijaya Cave (5) is again double-storeyed and a bo tree is carved in the central compartment. Back at the entrance, ascend the hill to cave 9, the Swargapuri, and 14, the Hathi Gumpha or 'Elephant Cave'. The latter is plain but an inscription relates in 117 lines the exploits of its builder, King Kharaveli of Kalinga, who ruled from 168 to 153 BC.

Circle round the hill to the right, to the single-storey Ganesh Gumpha (10), which is almost directly above the Rani ka Naur. The carvings here tell the same tale as in the lower-level cave but are better drawn. Retrace your steps to cave 14, then on to the Pavana Gumpha or 'Cave of Purification' and the small Sarpa Gumpha or 'Serpent Cave', where the tiny door is surmounted by a three-headed cobra.

Only 15 or so metres from this is the Bagh Gumpha (12) or 'Tiger Cave', entered through the mouth of the beast. The hill is topped by the foundations of some long-gone building. The oldest of these various caves date back to the 2nd century BC. Some are of Jain origin.

Across the road, Kandagiri Hill is not so interesting, although there is a fine view back over Bhubaneswar from its summit. You can see the airport, the tower of the Lingaraj Temple rising behind it and, further away, the Dhauli Stupa. The steep path divides about a third of the way up the hill. The right path goes to the Ananta Cave (3) with carved figures of athletes, women, elephants and geese carrying flowers. The right path also leads to a series of Jain temples. At the top of the hill is an 18th-century Jain temple.

Getting There & Away Only a few buses go specifically to the caves, but there are plenty going by the nearby road junction. It's about Rs 1 from town, or you can get there by rickshaw for about Rs 10.

PURI (population 100,000)

On the coast, 55 km from Bhubaneswar, Puri is one of the four holiest cities in India. The city revolves around the great Jagannath Temple and its famous Rath Yatra or 'Car Festival'. It is thought that Puri was the hiding place for the Buddha tooth of Kandy before it was spirited away to Sri Lanka. There are similarities between the Rath Yatra and the annual Kandy procession.

Many Indian companies and government departments have vacation homes here but the town is most visited by Bengali holidaymakers.

According to one traveller, it is definitely worth getting up before sunrise and watching the fishing boats heading out to sea. For a few rupees the fishers will take you with them – 'it was the highlight of my trip witnessing the dawn over the sea and fishing boats'.

Information & Orientation

There is only one wide road in Puri, the Baradand or Grand Rd which runs from Jagannath Temple to the Gundicha Mandir. Buses stop along this road. Most of the hotels are along the seafront but there are two distinct beach areas – Indians to the west, travellers to the east.

The tourist office is on Station Rd and there's a counter (open longer hours) at the railway station.

Jagannath Temple

The temple of Jagannath, Lord of the Universe, is not open to non-Hindus, but its considerable popularity amongst Hindus is partly due to the lack of caste distinctions – all are welcome before Lord Jagannath. Well, almost all – Indira Gandhi was barred from entering as she had married a non-Hindu. Nonbelievers can look down into the temple from the roof of the Raghunandan Library, opposite the main entrance to the temple. You'll be asked for a donation.

The temple enclosure is nearly square,

Balabhadra, Subhadra & Lord Jagannath

measuring almost 200 metres on each side. The walls of the enclosure are six metres high. Inside, a second wall encloses the actual temple. The conical tower of the temple is 58 metres high and is topped by the flag and wheel of Vishnu. It is visible from far out of Puri. The temple was built in its present form in 1198.

In front of the main entrance is a beautiful pillar, topped by an image of the Garuda, which originally stood in front of the temple at Konarak. The main entrance is known as the Lion Gate from the two stone lions guarding the entrance, and it is also the gate used in the chariot procession. The southern, eastern and northern gates are guarded by statues of men on horseback, tigers and elephants respectively.

In the central jagamohan, pilgrims can see the images of Lord Jagannath, his brother Balbhadra and sister Subhadra. Non-Hindus are not, of course, able to see them but the many shop stalls along the road outside the temple sell small wooden replicas. The curious images are carved from tree trunks, in a childlike caricature of a human face. The brothers have arms but the smaller Subhadra does not. All three are garlanded and dressed for ceremonies and the various seasons.

The temple employs 6000 men to perform the temple functions and the complicated rituals involved in caring for the gods. It has been estimated that in all, 20,000 people are dependent on Jagannath, and the god's immediate attendants are divided into 36 orders and 97 classes!

Rath Yatra (Car Festival)

One of India's greatest annual events takes place in Puri each June or July when the fantastic festival of the cars sets forth from the Jagannath Temple. It commemorates the journey of Krishna from Gokul to Mathura. The images of Jagannath, his brother and his sister are brought out from the temple and dragged in huge 'cars', known as raths, down the wide Baradand to the Gundicha Mandir or 'Garden House' over a km away.

The main car of Jagannath stands 14 metres high, over 10 metres square and rides on 16 wheels, each over two metres in diameter. It is from these colossal cars that our word 'juggernaut' is derived and, in centuries past, devotees were known to have thrown themselves beneath the wheels of the juggernaut in order to die in the god's sight. To haul the cars takes over 4000 professional car-pullers, all employees of the temple. Hundreds of thousands of pilgrims (and tourists) flock from all over India to witness this stupendous scene. The huge and unwieldy cars take an enormous effort to pull, are virtually impossible to turn and once moving are nearly unstoppable.

Once they reach the other end of the road the gods take a week-long summer break, then they are reloaded onto the cars and trucked back to the Jagannath Temple, in a virtual repeat of the previous week's procession. Following the festival the cars are broken up and used for firewood in the communal kitchens inside the temple, or for funeral-pyre fuel. New cars are constructed each year. At intervals of eight, 11 or 19 years (or combinations of those numbers depending on various astrological occurrences) the gods themselves are also disposed of and new images made. In the past 150 years there have been new images in 1863, 1893, 1931, 1950, 1969 and 1977. The old ones are buried at a site near the northern gate.

Gundicha Mandir

The Garden House, in which the images of

the gods reside for seven days each year, is off limits to non-Hindus. The walls enclose a garden in which the temple is built. Puri has a number of other temples, but these too are off limits to non-Hindus.

The Beach

Puri has a fine stretch of white sand from which Indian pilgrims bathe in their customary, fully attired manner. Orissan fishers, wearing conical straw hats, guide bathers out through the surf. You can hire your own lifeguard for Rs 4 a morning or afternoon, but their main function is to guard people's clothes. They're unlikely to be much help should trouble arise, as an elderly English traveller reported: 'I called out to my husband: There's going to be a rescue! – when to our amazement the lifeguards turned back having done only 10 yards and the swimmer (or nonswimmer?) disappeared for good. Too late for anyone else to go by then. The victim was a young man of 19'. This, it turned out, was not

the only recent drowning and the 'lifeguards' have no equipment or real ability.

Further east you come to the travellers' beach, in front of the cluster of popular budget hotels like the Z Hotel and the Shankar International. Beyond this is the local fishing village. The fishers' crude boats are quite unusual – they're made of solid tree trunks and are enormously heavy. Buoyancy comes purely from the bulk of the wood. They're made in two or three pieces, split longitudinally and bound together. When not in use they're untied and the pieces laid out on the beach, presumably to dry. There is an enormous number of them, and since each one uses so much wood entire forests must have fallen to construct this fishing fleet. The other thing on the beach in enormous quantity is shit.

Tours

Tours operate out of Puri daily, except

Puri beach

Monday, to Konarak, Pipli, Dhauli, Bhubaneswar and the Udayagiri and Khandagiri hills. They depart at 6.30 am, return at 6.30 pm and cost Rs 45. Three days a week there is a Rs 60 tour to Chilka Lake.

Places to Stay - bottom end

Almost all the accommodation in Puri is along the seafront. Most of the budget hotels popular with travellers are at the east end of the beach towards the fishing village, along or off Chakra Tirath Rd. In the centre are most of the mid-range and top-end hotels, while at the west end is a mixture of mid-range and budget hotels – the latter catering mainly to Indian pilgrims.

Near the Tourist Bungalow the pleasant *Sea Side Inn* (tel 2531) has doubles with bath for Rs 66. The big and modern *Youth Hostel* (tel 424) has separate dormitory accommodation for men and women at Rs 8 per bed, Rs 5 if you're a YHA member. Some of the dorms have only two or three beds but others are larger. The hostel has its own restaurant, which does good thalis. Checkout time is 12 noon and there's a 10 pm curfew.

A number of popular budget hotels are clustered together a little further east. The very popular *Z* (Zed you Americans!) *Hotel* is an old, rambling, well-maintained building with large, airy rooms, many of them facing the sea. It was actually the palace of a very minor maharaja of a very minor state in what is now West Bengal. The management is friendly and easygoing, there's a terrific ocean view, it is quiet and pleasant and serves good seafood. Singles are Rs 30, doubles Rs 50 to Rs 80 depending on whether they have shared or private bathroom. You can also get a dorm bed for Rs 15; the beds are in an open area on the top floor.

The *Sea Foam Hotel* is fairly small with a friendly, intimate atmosphere and clean communal showers and toilets. Rooms are Rs 40/60 a single/double and they are extremely basic. The food is indifferent,

so although most people eat breakfast here they take lunch and dinner out at one of the nearby restaurants.

Towards the beach from the Sea Foam is the popular *Shankar International*. There are a number of new rooms facing the sea which cost Rs 60 to Rs 100 a double. The *Milli Hotel* is close to the Shankar and is run by the friendly Mr Milli.

Other possibilities include the *Hotel Casuarina*, between the Shankar and the Sea Foam, or the *Travellers' Inn* beside the Z Hotel. The *Bay View Hotel* is a quiet and very pleasant place with rooms from Rs 25 to Rs 60 and a nice verandah area for sitting out on. Across the road is the *Holiday Home*.

Among the several very cheap lodges further down the beach road in the fishing village, the family-run *Balaji Hotel* charges Rs 30 for a double, Rs 40 with bath. It is clean and one of the cheapest in the area. At the railway station, *retiring rooms* cost Rs 23 per person and there's a Rs 12 dormitory.

At the pilgrims' beach, about a km west, there are numerous hotels along Marine Parade. Most of them only offer all-inclusive rates and are patronised almost 100% by Indian pilgrims. The *Sea View Hotel* (tel 117) advertises on its cards a 'Full View of Refreshing Sea – Rubberised Coir Mattress Beds – Attached Baths & Homely Living' (all true!). Full board is Rs 60 per person per day depending on the room.

Alternatively the big *Puri Hotel* (tel 2114) has rooms from Rs 60 to Rs 65 for singles, Rs 70 to Rs 130 for doubles. There are also air-con rooms from Rs 90 to Rs 180. This is the most popular hotel among middle-class Indians. Rates inclusive of meals are available.

The *Hotel Panthabhawan* is run by Orissa Tourism and is on the western end of the beach, south of the temple. It charges Rs 40 for its double rooms.

Places to Stay - middle & top end

First of the hotels at the east end of the

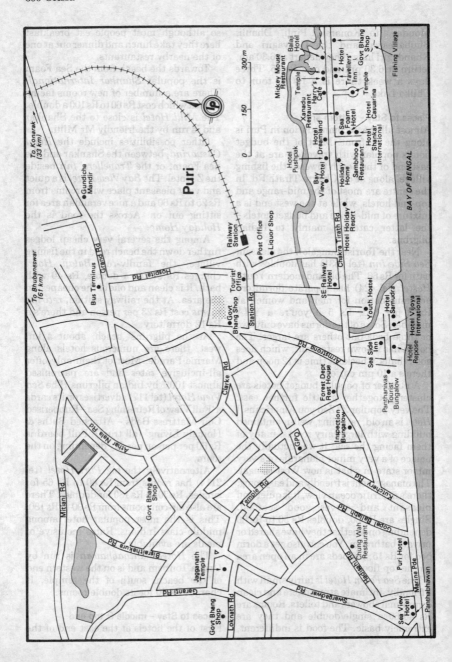

Puri

To Konarak
(33 km)

To Bhubaneswar
(61 km)

Gundicha
Mandir

Bus Terminus

Grand Rd

Hospital Rd

Railway
Station

Post Office

Liquor Shop

Govt
Bhang Shop

Tourist
Office

Station Rd

SE Railway
Hotel

Chakra Tirath Rd

Youth Hostel

Hotel
Samudra

Hotel Vijoya
International

Hotel
Repose

Sea Side
Inn

Armstrong Rd

Clarke Rd

Forest Dept
Rest House

Panthanivas
Tourist
Bungalow

Inspection
Bungalow

GPO

Kutchery Rd

Temple Rd

Gobal Ballabh Rd

Chung Wah
Restaurant

Puri Hotel

Marine Pde

Swargadwar Rd

Panthabhawan

Jagganath
Temple

Garant Rd

Loknath Rd

Sea View
Hotel

Govt Bhang
Shop

Biratkhura Rd

Mitiani Rd

Govt Bhang
Shop

Atnal Nala Rd

Mickey Mouse
Restaurant

Xanadu
Restaurant

Harry's
Café

Balaji
Hotel

Z Hotel

Travellers'
Inn

Govt Bhang
Shop

Hotel
Temple

Hotel
Casuarina

Sea
Foam
Hotel

Hotel
Shankar
International

Sambhoo
Restaurant

Holiday
Home

Hotel
Dreamland

Hotel
Pushpak

Bay
View Hotel

Hotel Holiday
Resort

Fishing Village

BAY OF BENGAL

300 m

150

0

beach is the *Panthanivas Tourist Bungalow* (tel 562), where doubles with bath and fan cost Rs 110. Some rooms in the new building have excellent views of the sea. It's well kept, well located and, as usual, has a dining hall.

There are several new hotels along the beach from the Tourist Bungalow. The *Hotel Repose* charges Rs 100 for doubles and is good value. The *Hotel Vijoya International* (tel 2701/2) has rooms at Rs 250 with air-con. The adjacent *Hotel Samudra* (tel 2705) is right on the beach; each room has a balcony and looks out on the sea. Rooms are Rs 110/150 or Rs 210/250 with air-con.

A little back from the beach on the main road is the delightfully 'olde worlde' *South-Eastern Railway Hotel* (tel 62). Singles/doubles, including all meals, cost Rs 270/430, or Rs 360/525 with air-con. It has a pleasant lounge, bar, dining hall and an immaculate stretch of lawn. Non-residents can eat here; lunch or dinner costs Rs 55 and the food is good.

Further along the road the new *Hotel Holiday Resort* (tel 2440) has beautiful views of the sea and a pleasant lawn. It charges Rs 180 to Rs 300 for double rooms. The ITDC *Hotel Neelachal Ashok* charges Rs 375/450 for air-con rooms. The *Hotel Prachi Puri* (tel 26850) has rooms ranging from Rs 100 to Rs 300.

The new *Hotel Toshali Sands* is on the beach between Puri and Konarak. It has 27 cottages and a swimming pool. Rooms cost between Rs 300 and Rs 500.

Places to Eat

Although Puri is nowhere near as developed as the other popular travellers' beaches, you can still get excellent seafood in pleasant and congenial surroundings at the *Xanadu* or the *Sambhoo Restaurant*. Both offer lobsters, prawns, fish, chips and a range of salads as well as a variety of sweets. Most dishes cost Rs 3 (fish curry) to Rs 7 (prawn curry), although naturally you pay more for a lobster (Rs 30) or a whole fish. The tuna steaks at the Xanadu

have been described as 'divine'. Next door is *Brady's*, a new place with a decent sound system.

Across the road from the Z Hotel is the very popular *Mickey Mouse Restaurant* which has loud music. Great name for Puri! The Shankar's *Om Restaurant* does good seafood and great chips.

The *Puri Hotel* has a good vegetarian thali for Rs 18. There are a number of other small cafes down at this end of the beach. In the old town there are countless vegetarian places like the *Jagannath South Indian Restaurant* on Grand Rd. Down the road beside the Puri Hotel there's even a Chinese restaurant, the *Chung Wah*.

One traveller reported that the *Sandy Village Restaurant* on the beach serves fresh lobster.

Things to Buy

Puri is one of those delightfully eccentric Indian towns where the use of ganja and bhang is not only legal, the government very thoughtfully provides for smokers' requisites in the form of shops selling high-quality weed at very reasonable prices. Should you be unfortunate enough to be suffering from Delhi Belly, they do a nice medicinal line in opium. There are several of these shops, one of them close to the railway station and another just beyond the Z Hotel.

You'll come across quite a few craft and salespeople offering fabric, bead and bamboo work. Some of it is well worth a second look. Prices are negotiable, as always with this sort of thing. There are also plenty of people trying to sell snake and animal skins in such numbers that one dreads to think what is happening to the wildlife in the Orissan forests.

Getting There & Away

Bus Puri doesn't really have a bus station – just a stretch of street where buses depart and arrive. It can be chaotic. There are state transport buses to Calcutta daily at 6.15 am and 4.45 pm. A number of private buses also go to Calcutta, most of them departing around 6.30 pm. See Konarak for Puri to Konarak transportation details.

Train The Puri railway booking office is open daily from 9 am to 1 pm and 1.30 to 4.30 pm. There's a city booking office on Grand Rd just opposite the town police station. It has its own berth quota (2nd class only), and it might be worthwhile booking ahead in the pilgrim season when trains to Madras and Calcutta are often booked out five to 10 days ahead.

All trains into and out of Puri pass through Bhubaneswar, the Orissa state capital. If you want to travel between these two places the buses are faster and more convenient than the trains. By train it's about two hours and costs Rs 12 in 2nd class. Buses, which run every half-hour throughout the day, take about 1½ hours and cost Rs 6.

If you're going to Madras, take a train to Bhubaneswar and then one of the Calcutta to Madras expresses from there. There are one or two trains to Delhi every day from Puri.

Getting Around
A rickshaw from the Puri bus stand to the hotels along the beach is around Rs 4.

KONARAK
Konarak is on the coast, 64 km from Bhubaneswar and only about 33 km north of Puri. The site consists of little more than the mighty temple and a handful of shops, stalls and places to stay. The Temple of the Sun was constructed some time during the 13th century but remarkably little is known about its early history. Thought to have been built by an Orissan king to celebrate a military victory, it has been in ruins for centuries and until the early 1900s it was simply an interesting ruin of impressive size.

Then in 1904 debris and sand were cleared from around the temple base and the sheer magnitude of its architect's imagination was revealed. The entire temple was conceived as a chariot for the Sun God, Surya. Around the base of the temple are 24 gigantic carved-stone wheels. Seven mighty horses haul at the temple and the immense structure is covered with carvings, sculptures, figures and bas-reliefs. It is not known if the construction of the temple was ever completed. If the tower was completed it would have soared to 70 metres and archaeologists wonder if the sandy foundations could have supported such a structure. Part of the tower was still standing in 1837 but by 1869 had collapsed. Today the temple's interior has been filled in to support the ruins.

The main entrance, from the Tourist Bungalow side, is guarded by two stone lions crushing elephants. Steps rise to the main entrance, flanked by straining horses. The jagamohan still stands, but the duel behind it has collapsed. The three images of Surya still stand, and they are designed to catch the sun at dawn,

Sun Temple, Konarak

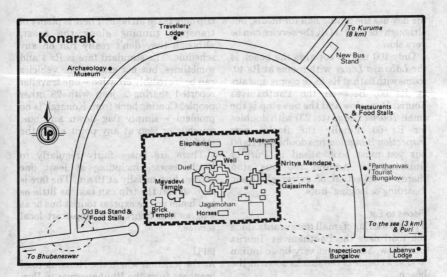

noon and sunset. Between the main steps up to the jagamohan and the entrance enclosure is an intricately carved dancing hall. To the north is a group of elephants and to the south a group of horses rearing and trampling men.

Around the base of the temple and up the walls and roof is a continuous procession of carvings. Many are in the erotic style for which Konarak, like Khajuraho, is famous. These erotic images of entwined couples, or solitary exhibitionists, can be minute images on the spoke of a temple wheel or life-size figures higher up the walls.

Outside the temple enclosure is a museum (open from 10 am to 5 pm, closed Fridays) containing many sculptures and carvings found during the temple excavation. For more information, the *Sun Temple - Konarak* by Mitra is on sale at the Archaeological Survey of India for Rs 6, but not at the temple.

The sea is three km from the temple; you can walk there or hire a cycle-rickshaw. The temple was once known as the Black Temple by sailors, in contrast to the whitewashed temples of Puri. It was said to contain a great mass of iron which would draw unwary ships to the shore.

Places to Stay

As there is a direct, sealed road along the coast between Puri and Konarak, there's no real need to stay here. If you take an early morning bus from Puri and a late bus back (or on to Bhubaneswar) in the afternoon then you're going to have all the time in the world to have a look at the temple. Of course there are always people who disagree with anything; we've had letters recommending staying in Konarak and visiting Puri from there! The sunsets, the superb beach and, of course, the temple, could encourage long stays. Sunbathing or swimming at this very pleasant beach is likely to draw a crowd.

The *Panthanivas Tourist Bungalow* (tel 21) is very close to the temple's main entrance. Rooms are more reasonably priced than the Puri and Bhubaneswar tourist bungalows. Here doubles with a bathroom and fan are Rs 50, dorm beds Rs 15. It's well kept, pleasantly located and has a dining hall and the tourist office. Many people coming from Puri for the day use the dining hall for meals, but although the food is OK the service can be very slow.

Only 100 metres towards the beach is the *Labanya Lodge* with rooms at Rs 40, rooms with bath at Rs 45, or rooms upstairs at Rs 60. Between the Panthanivas Tourist Bungalow and the bus stop is the small *Tourist Lodge* (tel 23) with doubles for Rs 60. Finally the flashy new *Inspection Bungalow* has doubles at Rs 50 but you must book ahead in Puri or Bhubaneswar. Around the bus stop there's a collection of extremely basic 'boarding & lodging' huts.

Places to Eat

There is a string of small restaurants along the road near the Panthanivas Tourist Bungalow. You can get very basic Indian food at a couple of the shacks down at the beach.

Getting There & Away

There is a direct route along the 33 km of coast between Puri and Konarak and the

Sun Temple, Konarak

trip only takes an hour. There is plenty of transport running along the coast, although they don't really run on any schedule. The standard fare is Rs 4 and sometimes, but not always, the vehicles can be incredibly crowded – one traveller reported sharing a jeep with 28 other people! Coming back from Konarak is no problem – simply flag down any bus, minibus or jeep at any point along the road.

There are buses fairly regularly to Bhubaneswar, including at least one express bus, usually at 10 am. The fare is Rs 6.40 and the trip can take as little as two hours on the express tourist bus or as long as four hours on a stop-start local service.

PIPLI

At the junction where the Konarak road branches from the Bhubaneswar to Puri road, this small village is notable for its appliqué craft. The colourful materials are used to make temple umbrellas and wall hangings.

CHILKA LAKE

South of Puri, Chilka Lake is dotted with islands and is noted for the many migratory birds which flock here in winter (December to January). The shallow lake is about 70 km long and averages 15 km wide, and is supposedly one of the largest brackish-water lakes in the country. It is separated from the sea only by a narrow sand bar. The railway line and the main road run along the inland edge of the lake. Rambha at the lake is 130 km from Bhubaneswar. There is another Ashokan rock edict at Jangada.

Enquire at the Rambha Tourist Bungalow for information on hiring power boats and yachts.

Places to Stay

There are *Tourist Bungalows* at Rambha, at the southern end of the lake, and at Barkul, six km north of the railway station of Balugaon and 32 km north of Rambha.

The *Barkul Tourist Bungalow* has 18 rooms and charges Rs 70 for doubles.

GOPALPUR-ON-SEA

This popular but decaying little beach resort is 18 km from Berhampur, where there is a railway station. There are regular buses between Berhampur and Gopalpur. From here you can make excursions to the hot springs at Taptapani, 45 km away.

Places to Stay

At the bottom end of the scale there is a 16-bed *Youth Hostel* (Rs 8) and a selection of local hotels. The *Hotel Sea Breeze* has doubles for Rs 50 to Rs 60, while the *Hotel Holiday Home* is marginally more expensive and the *Wroxham House Tourist Lodge* is cheaper.

The *Motel Mermaid* on Beach Rd is flashy, clean, modern and right on the beach. Rooms are Rs 180/275, although with bargaining you can get a fine room for around Rs 50. The food is good too and the beers are very cold.

At the top end there is the 21-room *Oberoi Palm Beach Hotel* with rooms from Rs 700/940 including meals.

CUTTACK (population 270,000)

Only 35 km north of Bhubaneswar, this riverine city was the capital of Orissa until the new city was constructed at Bhubaneswar. Only a gateway and the moat remain of the 14th-century Barabati Fort. The stone revetment on the Kathjuri

Detail of filligree jewellery from Cuttack

River, which protects the city from seasonal floods, dates from the 11th century. Today the town is a chaotic and largely uninteresting place.

Places to Stay

The *Panthanivas Tourist Bungalow* (tel 23867) has doubles for Rs 50 and dorm beds for Rs 15. The *Hotel Orienta* (tel 24249) in Buxi Bazaar has rooms at Rs 90/120 or with air-con for Rs 140/160, while the *Hotel Anand* (tel 21936) on Canal Bank Rd is a little cheaper. There are a number of other small hotels, but if you wish to visit Cuttack it is probably easier to day-trip from Bhubaneswar.

BALASORE & CHANDIPUR

Balasore is the first major town on the railway line from Calcutta in north Orissa. It was once an important trading centre with Dutch, Danish, English and French factories. In 1634 it was the first British East India Company factory in Bengal. Remina, eight km away, has the Gopinath Temple, an important pilgrimage centre.

Chandipur, 16 km away on the coast, is a beach resort where the beach extends six km at low tide! There are buses twice a day from Balasore.

Places to Stay

There are a few small hotels in Balasore such as the *Hotel Sagarika* or the *Hotel Moonlight*. The Municipal Tourist Bungalow, known as *Deepak Lodging*, is very pleasant and reasonably priced. Walk from the station to the main road, turn left and it's on the right-hand side, two blocks from the corner and across the street from the cinema. In Chandipur there is a *Tourist Bungalow*.

SIMILIPAL NATIONAL PARK

The Similipal National Park is in the north-east of the state, 250 km from Calcutta and 320 km from Bhubaneswar. It is well known for its varied wildlife including tigers, leopards and elephants.

Places to Stay

There are several *Forest Houses* in the park itself, or you can stay at the village of Baripada 20 km away. Hotels here include the *Hotel Durga* (tel 330) and the *Hotel Mayura* (tel 343), both of which charge about Rs 40 for a double.

OTHER PLACES

In the north of Orissa, about 200 km inland from the coast, Khiching was once an ancient capital and has a number of interesting temples, temple ruins and a small museum. Further inland is the important industrial city of Rourkela with a major steel plant.

North-east of Cuttack, about 100 km from Bhubaneswar, there are Buddhist relics and ruins at the three hilltop complexes of Ratnagiri, Lalitgiri and Udayagiri. The Ratnagiri site has the most interesting ruins. At Lalitgiri artisans make replicas of stone sculptures.

In the extreme west of the state, the twin villages of Ranipur-Jharial are 30 km from Titlagarh and are noted for the extensive collection of temples on a rock outcrop. They include a circular 64-yogini temple, similar to the one at Khajuraho. Harishankar, near Bolangir in the west, has a number of temples and a waterfall.

In the south-west of the state is Gupteswar Cave; this is the region of the Bonda tribespeople. A little north-west of Cuttack is the Shiva temple of Kapilas.

Travellers' Notebook

Watch Out

You've got to be on your toes in India. Officially they drive on the left but in practice it's more usually optional, so don't just look for traffic the way it *should* be coming. There will often be a bicycle, rickshaw or even truck sneaking down in the opposite direction. They'll create a third line of traffic right over on the opposite side of the road or take short cuts along the wrong lane of divided roads.

Watch out for your head too. Many Indian buildings seem to have been constructed without recourse to preliminary drawings or plans. Half-way up the flight of steps the builders have suddenly realised it's not going to get to the next level in time so a corner is hurriedly inserted. But oops, that hasn't been allowed for down below (or up above) and we now have (as Californians would say) 'radically impaired vertical clearance'. For tall and unwary westerners this means frequent cracks on the skull at turns in the stairs.

Tony Wheeler

Bombay

Population: 10 million
Main languages: Hindi & Marathi

Bombay is the capital of Maharashtra

Bombay is the economic powerhouse of India. It's the fastest moving, most affluent, most industrialised city in India. It also has India's busiest international airport and the country's busiest port, handling nearly 50% of the country's total foreign trade. It's the stronghold of free enterprise in India; a major manufacturing centre for everything from cars and bicycles to pharmaceuticals and petrochemicals. It's the centre for India's important textile industry as well as the financial centre and an important base for overseas companies. Nariman Point is rapidly becoming a mini-Manhattan with India's tallest buildings. Yet once upon a time Bombay was nothing more than a group of low-lying, swampy and malarial mud flats passed on to the British by its Portuguese occupiers as a wedding dowry!

When the Portuguese arrived on the scene Bombay consisted of seven islands occupied by simple fisherfolk known as Kolis. In 1534 the seven islands, from Colava in the south to Mahim in the north, were ceded to Portugal by the Sultan of Gujarat in the Treaty of Bassein. The Portuguese did little with them and the major island of the group, Mumbadevi, was part of the wedding dowry when Catherine of Braganza married England's Charles II in 1661. In 1665 the British government took possession of all seven islands and in 1668 leased them to the East India Company for an annual £10 in gold.

Soon after the British takeover Bombay started to develop as an important trading port. One of the first signs of this was the arrival of the Parsis, who settled in Bombay in 1670 and built their first Tower

of Silence in 1675. In 1687 the presidency of the East India Company was transferred from Surat to Bombay and by 1708 it had become the trading headquarters for the whole west coast of India.

Although Bombay grew steadily for the next century, it was around the middle of the 1800s that its most dynamic development took place. The first railway was laid out of Bombay in 1854, and one of the effects of the Mutiny of 1857 was to further improve the city's image as a 'safe' place, far from the insurrections of the north. Then the American Civil War provided Bombay's young cotton and textile industries with an enormous boost as supplies of cotton from the US dried up. In 1862 a major land-reclamation project joined the original seven islands into a single land mass and a year later the governor, Sir Bartle Frere, dismantled the old fort walls, sparking a major building boom.

During this century Bombay has further extended its position as the major commercial, industrial, financial and trading centre of India. Its role as an economic magnet, the Indian city with streets paved with gold, has also contributed to enormous slum problems and over-crowding. The problem is exacerbated by the fact that there is no room for further expansion. It really has become a city bloated by uncontrolled transmigration. Travelling from the airport to the centre (particularly if you take the back road) you pass through one of the worst slums in Asia – one hell of an introduction to urban India at its very worst.

Nevertheless Bombay is an active, alive city, full of interest in its own right and yet an ideal gateway to the states around it.

Orientation

Bombay is an island connected by bridges to the mainland. Low, swampy areas indicate where it was once divided into several islands. The principal part of the city is concentrated at the southern end of the island; the northern end is comparatively lightly populated. Sahar International Airport is in the suburb of

Bombay Docks

Santa Cruz, 26 km north of the city centre.

There are three main railway stations in the city centre. Churchgate and Victoria Terminus are central, but Bombay Central is some distance out.

Orientation in Bombay is relatively simple. The southern promontory is Colaba Causeway and the northern end of this peninsula is known as Colaba. Most of the cheap hotels and restaurants, together with a number of Bombay's top-notch establishments, are here. Bombay's two main landmarks, the Gateway of India and the Taj Mahal Hotel, are also at Colaba.

Directly north of Colaba is the area known as Bombay Fort, since the old fort was once here. Most of the impressive buildings from Bombay's golden period during the last 40 years of the last century are here, together with the GPO, offices, banks, tourist office and the two main railway stations.

To the west of the fort is Back Bay, around which sweeps Marine Drive. The southern end of this drive is marked by Nariman Point. This is the modern business centre of Bombay, with more international-class hotels, skyscrapers, airline offices (including Indian Airlines and Air India) and banks. The other end of the drive is Malabar Hill, a classy residential area.

Bombay (now officially Mumbai) has had lots of official name changes which everyone completely ignores. Colaba Causeway is not known as Shahid Bhagat Singh Rd, Wodehouse Rd is not known as N Parekh Marg. Wellingdon Circle is not known as Dr S P Mukherjee Chowk; in fact it's usually known as Regal after the cinema there. Veer Nariman Rd is sometimes called that; the rest of the time it's still Churchgate St. Victoria Terminus is always VT.

Information
Tourist Offices The Government of India tourist office (tel 293144) is at 123 Maharishi Karve Rd, Churchgate, directly

across from Churchgate station. It's open from 8.30 am to 6 pm Monday to Friday, and 8.30 am to 1.30 pm every second Saturday and public holidays; it's closed on Sundays. This main office has a comprehensive leaflet and brochure collection and is one of the most helpful and efficient offices in the country. They also have a counter at the international (Sahar) airport (tel 6325331, ext 253) and in the domestic terminal (tel 6149200, ext 278) and these are supposedly open around the clock.

There is a Maharashtra Tourism Development Corporation office (tel 2026713) at CDO Hutments, Madame Cama Rd. They offer city and suburban tours of Bombay and operate long-distance buses to Mahabaleshwar, Aurangabad and Panaji. This is where you book the ferry to Goa, assuming that it's operating.

Post & Telephone The GPO is an imposing building in Nagar Chowk near Victoria Terminus. The efficient poste restante service is open from 8 am to 6 pm Monday to Friday. The parcel post office is around the back of the main building, on the 1st floor. It's open from 10 am to 4.30 pm on weekdays and if you're lucky you'll be out of there within an hour. On the footpath outside the GPO is a guy who will wrap your parcel in cotton and seal it in the required way, and supply you with the necessary forms, all for a few rupees.

The Central Telegraph Office is open 24 hours a day and is right by Flora Fountain on Veer Nariman Rd. International calls can be dialled direct to most countries with minimal delays.

Banks The American Express office (tel 2048278) is at 276 Dadabhoy Naoroji Rd. The banking facilities at the airport are relatively fast and efficient. In the Air India Building at Nariman Point you can change money after hours.

Bookshops & Publications The Nalanda bookshop in the Taj Hotel is excellent.

Other good bookshops are Strand, just off Sir P M Rd (parallel to Churchgate behind Horniman Circle and Flora Fountain), and Bookpoint, in the Ballard Estate.

City of Gold, the Biography of Bombay is a good book to read about the city. An indication of Bombay's relative affluence and fast-moving nature is that the city even has its own fortnightly 'what's on' magazine, *Bombay*.

Travel Agencies Travel Corner Ltd, Marine Drive, near the Ambassador Hotel, is a reliable agency for discounted tickets. Transway International (tel 269941) at Pantaky House, 3rd floor, 8 Maruti Cross Lane, Fort, has also been recommended as quick, efficient and reasonably priced. Space Travels (tel 2864458) give good service and are at Nanabhoy Mansion, Sir P M Rd.

If you are shipping a vehicle you'll need a customs agent to clear it. Perfect Cargo Movers (tel 275621) at 28 Mombay Smachar Marg have been recommended as efficient and helpful.

Curiously enough, despite the great number of airlines flying through Bombay it is not as good a centre for cheap tickets as New Delhi.

If you need passport photos there's an automatic machine (typically, it provides a job for an attendant) at Central station. It's a real experience: 'You get a brief training course and your photos held in front of a fan by the attendant as part of the service. Difficult for us self-conscious Brits as the whole performance attracts a crowd who peer at the ghastly images!'

Airlines If you're staying in the Colaba area of Bombay and want to make bookings/reservations with Indian Airlines, you don't have to go all the way to Nariman Point as there's an Indian Airlines desk in the Taj Mahal Hotel.

Many airline offices are in the big Air India building on Nariman Point. The airport buses depart from here, and there

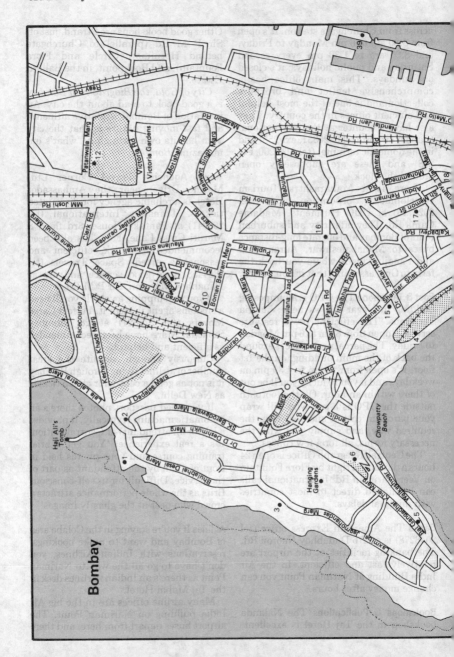

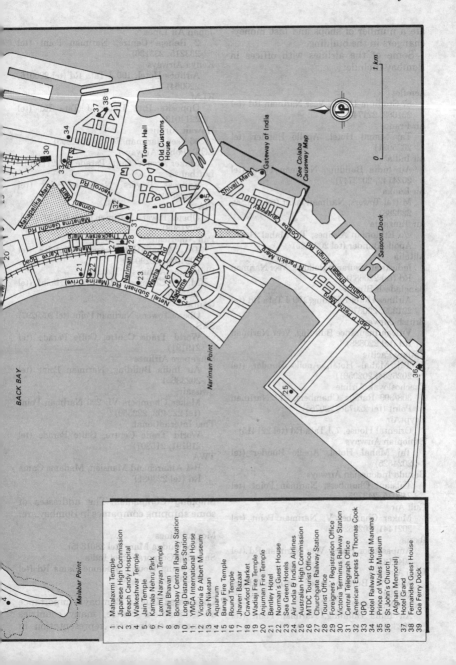

1 km

0

Malabar Point

BACK BAY

Nariman Point

Town Hall

Old Customs House

Gateway of India

See Colaba Causeway Map

Sassoon Dock

1   Mahalaxmi Temple
2   Japanese High Commission
3   Breach Candy Hospital
4   Walkeshwar Temple
5   Jain Temple
6   Kamala Nehru Park
7   Laxmi Narayan Temple
8   Mani Bhavan
9   Bombay Central Railway Station
10 Long Distance Bus Station
11 YMCA International House
12 Victoria & Albert Museum
13 Siva Niketan
14 Aquarium
15 Banaji Fire Temple
16 Round Temple
17 Jhaveri Bazaar
18 Crawford Market
19 Wadiaji Fire Temple
20 Anjuman Fire Temple
21 Bentley Hotel
22 Norman's Guest House
23 Sea Green Hotels
24 Air India & Indian Airlines
25 Australian High Commission
26 MTDC Tourist Office
27 Churchgate Railway Station
28 Tourist Office
29 Foreigners Registration Office
30 Victoria Terminus Railway Station
31 Central Telegraph Office
32 American Express & Thomas Cook
33 GPO
34 Hotel Railway & Hotel Manama
35 Prince of Wales Museum
36 St John's Church
    (Afghan Memorial)
37 Hotel Grand
38 Fernandes Guest House
39 Goa Ferry Dock

are a number of shops and fast money-changers in the building.

Some of the airlines with offices in Bombay include:

Aeroflot
87 Stadium House, Veer Nariman Rd (tel 221682, 221743)

Air France
Taj Mahal Hotel, Apollo Bunder (tel 2025021)

Air India
Air India Building, Nariman Point (tel 2024142, 2023747)

Air Lanka
Mittal Towers, Nariman Point (tel 223299, 223288)

Air Tanzania
c/o Ethiopian Airlines, Taj Mahal Hotel, Apollo Bunder (tel 2024525)

Alitalia
Industrial Assurance Building, Veer Nariman Rd (tel 220683)

Bangladesh Biman
Airlines Hotel Building, 199 J Tata Rd (tel 221339, 220676)

British Airways
Vulcan Insurance Building, Veer Nariman Rd (tel 220888)

Cathay Pacific
Taj Mahal Hotel, Apollo Bunder (tel 2025234, 2029561)

Czechoslovak Airlines
308/309 Raheja Chambers, 213 Nariman Point (tel 220736, 220765)

EgyptAir
Oriental House, 7 J Tata Rd (tel 221415)

Ethiopian Airways
Taj Mahal Hotel, Apollo Bunder (tel 2024525)

Garuda Indonesian Airways
Tulsiani Chambers, Nariman Point (tel 243075, 243725)

Gulf Air
Maker Chamber V, Nariman Point (tel 2021441, 2021626)

Iberia
Ambassador Hotel, Veer Nariman Rd (tel 2041131)

Iraqi Airways
May Fair Building, Veer Nariman Rd (tel 221399)

Indian Airlines
Air India Building, Nariman Point (tel 2023031)

Japan Air Lines
2 Raheja Centre, Nariman Point (tel 233215, 233136)

Kenya Airways
Airlines Hotel, 199 J Tata Rd (tel 220015, 220064)

KLM
Opposite Ritz Hotel, J Tata Rd (tel 2214013)

Kuwait Airlines
86 Veer Nariman Rd (tel 2041395)

LOT (Polish Airways)
Maker Arcade, Cuffe Parade (tel 211440)

Lufthansa
Express Towers, Nariman Point (tel 2023430)

PIA
Oberoi Towers, Nariman Point (tel 2021373, 2021598)

Pan American
Taj Mahal Hotel, Apollo Bunder (tel 2024024, 2029048)

Philippine Airlines
Maker Chambers II, Nariman Point (tel 224580)

Qantas
Oberoi Towers, Nariman Point (tel 2029297)

SAS
World Trade Centre, Cuffe Parade (tel 219191)

Singapore Airlines
Air India Building, Nariman Point (tel 2023365)

Swissair
Maker Chambers VI, 220 Nariman Point (tel 222402, 222559)

Thai International
World Trade Centre, Cuffe Parade (tel 219191, 215207)

TWA
B-1 Amarchand Mansion, Madame Cama Rd (tel 223081)

Shipping Companies The addresses of some shipping companies in Bombay are:

Moghul Lines
GN Vaidya Marg (tel 2861835)

Shipping Corporation of India
Shipping House, Madame Cama Rd (tel 2026666)

Consulates Due to Bombay's importance as a business centre, many countries maintain diplomatic representation in

Bombay as well as in the capital, New Delhi. They include:

Australia
   Maker Towers, E Block, Cuffe Parade (tel 211071)
Denmark
   L & T House, N Morarjee Marg, Ballard Estate (tel 268181)
France
   Tata Prasas N Gamadia Rd, off Peddar Rd (tel 4949808, 4948277)
Germany (West)
   Hoechst House, Nariman Point (tel 232422)
Japan
   1 B Dahanukar Marg (tel 4923847)
Netherlands
   16 M Karve Rd (tel 296840)
Sri Lanka
   Sri Lanka House, Homi Mody St (tel 2045861)
Sweden
   Indian Mercantile Chambers, R Kamani Marg (tel 262583)
Switzerland
   Manek Mahal, Veer Nariman Rd (tel 293550)
Thailand
   Krishnabad Building, Bhulabhai Desai Rd (tel 8226417)
UK
   Hong Kong & Shanghai Bank Building, Mahatma Gandhi Rd (tel 274874)
USA
   Lincoln House, Bhulabhai Desai Rd (tel 8223611)

The honorary Irish consul can be found in the Royal Bombay Yacht Club by India Gate!

Cultural Centres The British Council Library (tel 223560) is at Mittal Tower A Wing, Nariman Point. Although it is ostensibly for members only, it is possible to get in to read the British newspapers.

The French Alliance Française (tel 291867) is at Sophy Hall, New Marine Lines.

Movies
Quickly, what are the biggest film-producing city and country in the world? Hollywood and the USA? Wrong twice – Bombay and India! The Indians turn out 500 to 600 full-length feature films a year and, of these, nearly half are made in Bombay. Calcutta makes some arty, intellectual films; Madras some family comedies or musicals; but for extravaganzas, action dramas, the 'starcast' A features, it's Bombay all the way.

A visit to a film studio is a real education, as we found when we turned up at Famous Film Studios. For a start the film production company and the studios are totally separate. Bombay has about 12 studios and far more film-makers. When they want to make a film they simply hire the studio by the day. Nor are Indian films made one at a time as in the west. A big star could be involved in a number of films simultaneously – shooting a day on one, a week on another, a morning on a third. This involves phenomenal scheduling problems and also means that Indian films generally take a long time to make.

A glance at Indian film posters or film magazines gives you the impression that Indian movie actors are a band of escapees from weight-watchers. Well, there's no glamour in being thin in India. Every beggar in the street is skinny; it's the well-padded look which appeals. It's amusing to see how this works on western films shown in India – familiar European and American film stars become remarkably rotund when they're repainted for the Indian posters.

Our image of these chubby, smug actors was quickly shattered when we were asked into the dressing room to meet the star of the film we went to see. He was friendly, very open about the problems involved in making films in India – and not a kg overweight! Life for a lot of Indians is not all that much fun and illiteracy is still widespread. Bombay film-makers are not trying to produce something for a sophisticated and intellectual audience. It's pure, straight-forward, down-to-earth entertainment. Escapism and nothing more.

Indian films are always a bit of everything – drama, action, suspense, music, dancing, romance – all mixed together into one extravagant blend. They've even got a name for them – 'masala films', since masala is the all-purpose word for spices, something you add to make it tasty.

Within their commercial constraints Indian movie-makers often do a surprisingly good job, particularly the camerapeople and technicians, who manage to produce reasonable standard films from hopelessly outdated equipment. Apart from the restrictions on importing new equipment, a large slice of the proceeds goes to the Indian government. Film admission prices may be only Rs 3, 4 or 5, but the government gulps down about 75% of that figure. To make an Indian movie and earn money out of it, you really have to know what you're about.

Tony Wheeler

Gateway of India

In the days when most visitors came to India by ship and when Bombay was India's principal port, this was indeed the 'gateway' to India. Today it's merely Bombay's principal landmark. The gateway was conceived following the visit of King George V in 1911 and officially opened in 1924. Architecturally it is a conventional Arch of Triumph, with elements in its design derived from the Muslim styles of 16th-century Gujarat. It is built of yellow basalt and stands on the Apollo Bunder, a popular Bombay

meeting place in the evenings. The Taj Mahal Inter-Continental Hotel overlooks the Apollo Bunder and launches run from here across to Elephanta Island. Close to the gateway are statues of Swami Vivekananda and of the Maratha leader, Shivaji, astride his horse.

Colaba Causeway

The streets behind the Taj Mahal Hotel are the travellers' centre of Bombay. Here you will find most of the cheap hotels and restaurants. Colaba Causeway, now renamed Shahid Bhagat Singh Rd, extends to the end of the Colaba promontory, the southern end of Bombay Island. Sassoon Dock is always interesting to visit around dawn, when the fishing boats come in and unload their catch in a colourful scene of intense activity. There's an old lighthouse at the end of the promontory, although the actual lighthouse used today is further south on a rocky island.

The Gateway of India

St John's Church

This church, also known as the Afghan Church, was built in 1847 and is dedicated to the soldiers who fell in the Sind campaign of 1838 and the First Afghan War of 1843.

Prince of Wales Museum

Beside the Wellingdon Circle, close to the Colaba hotel enclave, the Prince of Wales Museum was built to commemorate King George V's first visit to India in 1905 while he was still Prince of Wales. The first part of this interesting museum was opened in 1923. It was designed in the Indo-Saracenic style and has sections for art and paintings, archaeology and natural history. Among the more interesting items is a very fine collection of miniature paintings, images and bas-reliefs from the Elephanta Caves, and Buddha images. Put aside at least half a day to explore this fascinating place.

The museum (tel 244484) is open from 10 or 10.30 am to 6 or 6.30 pm, depending on the time of year. It is closed on Mondays and entry is Rs 2 (children Rs 1), except on Tuesdays when it is free.

Jehangir Art Gallery

Within the compound of the museum stands Bombay's principal art gallery. There are often special exhibitions of modern Indian art here. The gallery also has public phones, public toilets and a good snack bar. It opens at 10.30 am.

University & High Court

Along K B Patel Marg, overlooking Cross Maidan, there are several imposing public buildings erected during Bombay's period of great growth under the British. The university is in Gothic 14th to 15th-century style and is dominated by the 80-metre Rajabai Tower. This impressive clock tower rises above the university library.

Statues of Justice and Mercy top the huge High Court building beyond the university. It was built in Early English style and completed in 1878.

Flora Fountain

This is the business centre of Bombay, around which many of the major banks and business offices are centred. Now officially renamed Hutatma Chowk, it was erected in 1869 in honour of Sir Bartle Frere, who was governor of Bombay from 1862 to 1867, during which time Bombay experienced its most dramatic growth due to the world-wide cotton shortage caused by the American Civil War.

Close to the fountain is the Cathedral of St Thomas, begun by Gerald Aungier in 1672 and finally formally opened in 1718. There are several interesting memorials inside the cathedral, which has had a series of additions and alterations over the years.

Horniman Circle

Several interesting old Bombay buildings stand close to Horniman Circle. If you're walking from the GPO back to Colaba some time, it's worth pausing to have a glance at some of these buildings. The old Mint was completed in 1829 and has an Ionic facade. It was built on land reclaimed in 1823 and adjoins the Town Hall. Behind the Town Hall stand the remains of the old Bombay Castle.

Opened in 1833, the Town Hall still houses the library of the Royal Asiatic Society. Ascend the imposing steps at the front of the Town Hall and have a short wander inside. You'll see statues of a number of the government officials and wealthy benefactors of Bombay's golden period, including Sir Bartle Frere and Sir Jamsetjee Jeejeebhoy. Continuing on, you pass the old Customs House built in 1720. The old Bombay dockyards are behind this building.

Marine Drive

Now officially renamed Netaji Subhash Rd, Marine Drive is built on land reclaimed in 1920. It runs along the shoreline of Back Bay, starting at Nariman Point and sweeping around by Chowpatty Beach and up to Malabar Hill. The road is backed with high residential buildings and this is one of Bombay's most popular promenades.

Taraporewala Aquarium
Constructed in 1951, the aquarium on Marine Drive has both freshwater and saltwater fish. It's open Tuesday to Saturday from 11 am to 8 pm, Sunday from 10 am to 8 pm, and admission is Rs 1. It is closed on Mondays.

Also along Marine Drive, before the aquarium, is a series of cricket pitches where in summer there always seems to be games underway.

Chowpatty Beach
Bombay's famous beach attracts few bathers and even fewer sunbathers – neither activity has much of a following in India, and in any case the water is none too healthy. Chowpatty has plenty of other activities though. It's one of those typical Indian slices of life where anything and everything can happen, and does. Sand-castle sculptors make elaborate figures in the sand, contortionists go through equally elaborate contortions and family groups stroll around. In between there are kiosks selling Bombay's popular snack, bhelpuri, and kulfi ice cream.

Chowpatty Beach is also the scene for the annual Ganesh Chaturthi festival, during which large images of the elephant-headed god are immersed in the sea.

Mani Bhavan
At 19 Laburnum Rd, near August Kranti Maidan, is the building where Mahatma Gandhi stayed during his visits to Bombay between 1917 and 1934. Today it has a pictorial exhibit of incidents in Gandhi's life and contains a library of books by or about the Mahatma. It is open from 9.30 am to 6 pm; entry is Rs 2.

Malabar Hill
At the end of Back Bay, Marine Drive climbs up to Malabar Hill. This is an expensive residential area, for not only is it a little cooler than the sea-level parts of the city, but there are fine views over Back Bay and Chowpatty Beach to the town. At the end of the promontory is Raj Bhavan, the old British government headquarters.

Close by is the temple of Walkeshwar, the 'sand lord', an important Hindu pilgrimage site. According to the *Ramayana*, Rama rested here on his way from Ayodya to Lanka to rescue Sita. He constructed a lingam of sand at the site. The original temple was built about 1000 years ago but was reconstructed in 1715.

Jain Temple
This marble temple was built in 1904 and is dedicated to the first Jain tirthankar, Adinath. It's typical of modern Jain temples in its gaudy, mirrored style. The walls are decorated with pictures of incidents in the lives of the tirthankars.

Hanging Gardens
On top of Malabar Hill, these gardens were laid out in 1881 and are correctly known as the Pherozeshah Mehta Gardens. They take their name from the fact that they are built on top of a series of reservoirs that supply water to Bombay. The formally laid out gardens have a notable collection of hedges shaped like animals and there are good views over the city.

Kamala Nehru Park
Directly across the road from the Hanging Gardens, this park offers more superb views over Bombay. It was laid out in 1952 and was named after Nehru's wife. An unusual feature is a large nursery-rhyme 'old woman's shoe' which children love to play in.

Towers of Silence
Beside the Hanging Gardens, but carefully shielded from viewers, are the Parsi

Towers of Silence. The Parsis hold fire, earth and water as sacred and thus will not cremate or bury their dead. Instead the bodies are laid out within the towers to be picked clean by vultures (if there are any vultures in Bombay; maybe it's crows).

Elaborate precautions are taken to keep ghoulish sightseers from observing the towers, despite which a *Time-Life* book on Bombay provided a bird's-eye view of one of the towers. Parsi power in Bombay is sufficiently strong that the book was black-ink censored. Tour guides, always fond of a tall story for tourists, like to tell you that the reason the Hanging Garden reservoirs were covered over was that the vultures had an unpleasant habit of dropping the odd bit in the water supply.

Mahalaxmi Temple

Descending from Malabar Hill and continuing around the coastline, you come to the Mahalaxmi Temple, the oldest in Bombay and, appropriately for this city of business and money, dedicated to the goddess of wealth. The images of the goddess and her two sisters were said to have been found in the sea.

Near here is the Mahalaxmi Racecourse, said to be the finest in India, where horse races are held each Sunday from December to May. The road along the seashore by the racecourse was once known as the Hornby Vellard, and was constructed in the 18th century to reclaim the swampland on which the course is now constructed.

Haji Ali's Tomb

This tomb and mosque are devoted to a Muslim saint who drowned here. The buildings are reached by a long causeway which can only be crossed at low tide. Here a scene of typical Indian ingenuity and resourcefulness takes place. Hundreds of beggars line the length of the causeway waiting for the regular stream of pilgrims. At the start of the causeway is a small group of moneychangers who, for a few

paise commission, will change a Rs 1 coin into 100 one-paise coins. Thus a pilgrim can do their soul the maximum amount of good for the minimum expenditure.

No doubt at the ebb tide the mendicants can change their one-paise coins into something a little more manageable, thus giving the moneychangers their small change for the next low tide and no doubt providing them with another commission rake-off.

Victoria Gardens

These gardens, which contain Bombay's zoo and the Victoria & Albert Museum, have been renamed the Veermata Jijabai Bhonsle Udyan. The museum has some interesting exhibits relating to old Bombay. Just outside the museum building is the large stone elephant removed from Elephanta Island in 1864, and after which the island was named.

The museum (tel 8727131) is open from 10.30 am to 5 pm, the zoo from sunrise to sunset. Both are closed on Wednesday and charge Rs 0.50 admission.

Other Attractions

The Nehru Planetarium is on Dr Annie Besant Rd at Worli near the Haji Ali Tomb. There are shows in English at 3 and 6 pm daily except on Mondays when it is closed. Admission is Rs 5.

Falkland St is the centre for Bombay's notorious red-light district known as 'the cages'. The ladies stand behind metal-barred doors, hence the name. A No 130 bus from the museum passes through this fascinating area.

Tours

There are numerous tours of Bombay but they tend to be more expensive than in most Indian cities and, as usual, are impossibly rushed. Daily city tours are operated by the ITDC, the Travel Corporation of India and the Maharashtra Tourist Development Council. Morning tours generally last from 9 am to 1 or 2 pm and cost Rs 35 with the ITDC or Rs 40 with the MTDC. Afternoon tours last from 1.45 or 2 pm to 6 or 7 pm and cost Rs 35 or Rs 40.

The MTDC also have an all-day suburban tour which operates from 10 am to 7 pm and costs Rs 70. This goes to the Kanheri Caves, Juhu Beach and other fascinating places such as the airport.

Launch services and tours to Elephanta leave regularly from Apollo Bunder (Taj Mahal Hotel) and can be booked at the kiosk there. The round trip takes four hours. The ITDC and the MTDC have some tours further afield, such as four-day tours to Aurangabad and the Ajanta and Ellora caves (MTDC, Rs 820). Check at the tourist office for details.

Places to Stay

Bombay is India's most expensive city for accommodation, so if your funds are limited you should plan on spending as little time as possible here. Not only that,

but it's a magnet for Middle East and Gulf Arabs who come here for holidays, shopping expeditions and business. They invariably bring with them their entire entourage. Not all of these visitors are super-rich oil sheikhs who can afford to stay in the Taj Mahal Inter-Continental, so the pressure for accommodation – even at the bottom end of the market – is intense.

There is no guarantee that you will be able to find a room in the price range you expected to pay and, at least for the first night, you may well have to settle for something considerably more expensive. As though that were not enough, the standard of accommodation at the bottom end of the market is often poor.

The only way to give yourself a fighting chance, not only for a room, but for something halfway decent, is to arrive in Bombay as soon as possible after dawn. Luckily, most international flights into

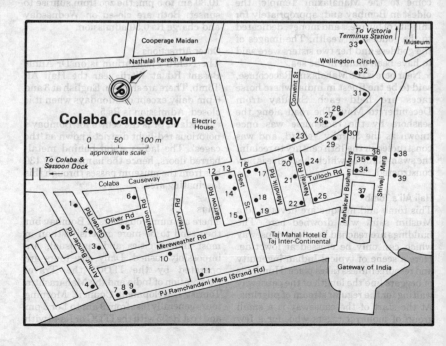

Bombay arrive in the early morning. The same is true of the ferry from Panaji, Goa (when it's operating).

It's also a distinct advantage to be part of a small group (impromptu or otherwise), since if the first place you try is full, then one or two of you can look after the baggage while the rest fan out in search of somewhere else. If you should be unlucky enough not to find anything in the price range that you can afford on the first day, try making a booking for the following day.

1	Hotel Ascot
2	Godwin Hotel
3	Garden Hotel
4	Hotel Mukund
5	Bentley's Hotel
6	Cowie's Guest House
7	Shelley's Guest House
8	Strand Hotel
9	Sea Palace Hotel
10	Whalley's Guest House
11	Hotel Prosser
12	Kamat Hotel (restaurant)
13	Ananda Punjabi
14	Dipti's Pure Drinks
15	Salvation Army Red Shield Hostel
16	Cafe Apsara
17	Food Inn
18	Rex & Stiffles Hotel
19	Hotel Diplomat
20	Leopold Restaurant
21	Laxmi Vilas
22	Carlton Hotel
23	Olympic Coffee House
24	Apollo Restaurant
25	Alps
26	Delhi Durbar
27	Canteena
28	Hotel Majestic (restaurant)
29	Crystal Hotel
30	Cafe Mondegar
31	Sahakari Bhandar Canteen
32	Woodside Pizza
33	YWCA International Guest House
34	Apollo Hotel & Restaurant
35	Suba Guest House
36	Naval & Military Restaurant
37	Royal Bombay Yacht Club
38	Cottage Industries Emporium
39	Mandarin & Hong Kong Restaurants

The tourist office or the desk at the airport can sometimes be helpful in finding an empty room, but in Bombay even budget accommodation is expensive.

Places to Stay – bottom end

Colaba The majority of the budget hotels are in the Colaba area directly behind that useful landmark, the Taj Mahal Inter-Continental. Best known are the *Rex* (tel 2020363) and *Stiffles* (tel 2021518) at 8 Best Rd; it's here that many travellers start their search for a room. The Rex is on floors 3 and 4, the Stiffles on 1 and 2. A great deal has been said and written over the years about the standard of accommodation at these two places – some of it good, most of it bad.

Given the standards of Bombay, these places aren't bad although every square cm of space has been converted into rooms, so some are cramped and windowless while others have weird and wonderful ways of entering them. Also, you must get there early in the morning if you want any chance of finding a room. The management is pleasant and gear left in your room is secure. At the Rex (marginally the better of the two) doubles cost from Rs 85 without a window or bath, up to Rs 155 with both. Stiffles charges Rs 75/105 for singles/doubles without bath, Rs 116/135 with bath, and air-con doubles go for Rs 196.

Across the road on the corner of the street is another old favourite, the *Salvation Army Red Shield Hostel* (tel 241824), at 30 Mereweather Rd. Full board costs Rs 60 in the dormitory, Rs 40 just for bed & breakfast. There are also a few double rooms for Rs 200 with breakfast although these are only let out to married couples (and you have to prove it!). Safe-deposit lockers can be hired for a returnable deposit of Rs 50 plus Rs 1 per day. Checkout time is 9 am and you need to be there early in the morning in order to be well up the line when 9 am rolls round. Some say that there's usually more room for women than men.

Another cheapie in the Colaba area is the *Carlton Hotel* (tel 2020642) at 12 Mereweather Rd. It's an interesting old place with singles/doubles at Rs 59/100 without windows. Doubles with a window cost Rs 119 and are relatively good value. Opinions of this place vary widely: 'The grottiest place I saw in *all* of India', wrote one traveller. 'Excellent, a good deal', wrote another!

Another reasonable place is *Hotel Prosser's* (tel 241715), on the corner of Henry Rd and P J Ramchandani Marg, which has small hardboard partitioned rooms with shared bath for a steep Rs 100/160 for a single/double.

There's a whole collection of small hotels on various floors along the noisy and somewhat sleazy Arthur Bunder Rd. The *Seashore Hotel* and the *Hotel Mukund* (tel 2873240) at Kamal Mansion are both fairly clean, friendly and have decent-sized rooms, although you'll be lucky to get a window. For double rooms they charge from Rs 110 to Rs 150 depending on the size.

Others along Arthur Bunder Rd include the *Janata Guest House, Imperial Guest House, India Guest House, Gateway Guest House, Gulf Hotel* and *Hotel Al-Hijaz*. Many of them look like they ought to be cheap, but don't let appearances fool you and remember that prices and standards vary enormously.

If you're really stuck there are a couple of ultra-basic places on Colaba Causeway which may have room. These places have no signs but there are always touts hanging around who will willingly lead the way. Expect to pay about Rs 60 for an airless single room of such minute proportions that there's a fair chance you'll trip over the bed as you walk in the door. Clean sheets? – you'd be lucky. One such place is the *Moghal Guest House*, not far from the Leopold Restaurant.

Elsewhere Away from the Colaba area, one of the most popular places – deservedly so – is the 3rd-floor *Lawrence Hotel* (tel

243618), on Ashok Kumar Lane (signposted as Rope Walk Lane) off K Dubash Marg at the back of the Prince of Wales Museum. It's often full since it only has nine rooms, but is excellent value at Rs 100 for doubles with common bath. Some of the rooms have balconies.

There are several cheapies on P D'Mello Rd just to the east of the GPO/Victoria Terminus but they are certainly nothing special. The *Railway Hotel* (tel 266705), 249 P D'Mello Rd, has basic singles from Rs 50 up to Rs 124 for a double with bath. It's definitely for those who don't care too much about windows and hardboard partitioning. At 239 the *Rupam Hotel* (tel 266225) is more expensive, with singles/doubles from Rs 72/80 up to Rs 187 for an air-con double with bath. The management are friendly and it's clean despite being somewhat run-down.

Also on P D'Mello Rd, the *Hotel Manora* (tel 267450) at 243 has singles/doubles for Rs 80/130, or Rs 115/150 with bath.

The *City Lodge* (tel 265515) is directly across from VT station and the GPO and is above a tailor shop. The management are friendly and the rooms are extremely shabby but it would do at a pinch. It is not all that cheap at Rs 100 for doubles with common bath.

Between here and Colaba at Ballard Pier, the very pleasant and quiet *Fernandez Guest House* (tel 260554) in the Balmer Lawrie Building, 5 J N Heredia Marg, is very similar to the Lawrence Hotel. The cost is Rs 50 per person and this includes breakfast. It's not that easy to find and, like the Lawrence, is invariably full – there are just seven rooms.

The Ys Like other Indian cities, Bombay has its share of YMCAs and YWCAs. Although very good value for money, they're invariably full. The most popular is the *YWCA International Centre* (tel 2020445), in Colaba at 18 Madame Cama Rd. It takes women, and men if they are part of a couple or family, and offers bed &

breakfast for Rs 71/139 plus Rs 10 membership charges (valid for one month). It's sometimes booked out up to three months in advance.

The *YMCA International Guest House* (tel 891191) is at 18 YMCA Rd near Central railway station. This is rather a long way from downtown Bombay and the popular Colaba area. The rooms are pleasant and well kept but are expensive at Rs 137/253, or Rs 165/320 with bathroom. These prices include all meals. There's also a Rs 40 per person transient membership charge, valid for 90 days.

Other Places For men only there is excellent dormitory accommodation for Rs 15 or rooms for three people at Rs 20 per person at *Siva Niketan* (tel 372395) on J Jijibhoy Rd. This is in the northern part of the city, near Byculla railway station on the suburban line from VT.

There are no purpose-built youth hostels as such in Bombay, but during university/college vacations you may be able to find cheap accommodation at *Bhavan's College* (tel 572192), Versova Rd, Bhavan's Camp, Andheri; *University Hostel* (tel 472425), L A Kidwai Rd; or *Podar College of Commerce Hostel* (tel 472414), 193 Sion Koliwada Estate.

Finally, both Bombay Central and Victoria Terminus have *retiring rooms*. At Central they cost Rs 65 for a double, or Rs 130 with air-con.

Places to Stay – middle
Many of the middle-bracket hotels – along with the Taj Inter-Continental and most of the cheapies – are in the Colaba area. The other main group is clustered along Marine Drive (Netaji Subhash Rd) between Madame Cama Rd and Veer Nariman Rd, and along Veer Nariman Rd itself. The ones in the Colaba area tend to be less expensive than those along Marine Drive.

Colaba *Hotel Cowie's* (tel 240232), 15 Walton Rd, offers large singles/doubles for Rs 125/200 with bath, or Rs 240/300 with air-con and bath. All rooms have colour TV and phone. *Whalley's Guest House* (tel 221802), 41 Mereweather Rd, is a plain place charging Rs 125/225 for rooms with bath including breakfast, although windows are rare.

On Colaba Causeway near the Leopold Restaurant, the *Hotel Crystal* (tel 2020673) has reasonable singles/doubles for Rs 125/175, or Rs 250 for an air-con double. Rooms have windows but these are a mixed blessing as the street noise can be horrendous at times.

Bentley's Hotel (tel 241733) at 17 Oliver Rd has singles/doubles for Rs 95/145. Prices include breakfast and bath. Rooms in this good-value place are large and have colour TV. Just off Shivaji Marg (the road running back from the Gateway of India) the *Suba Guest House* (tel 2021845) has rooms at Rs 125, and Rs 225 with bath. There are no windows but the rooms are clean.

Still in the Colaba area are a number of hotels along the waterfront. The *Sea Palace Hotel* (tel 241828), 26 P J Ramchandani Marg (Strand Rd), is a large building with reasonable singles/ doubles with bath for Rs 315/465. The hotel has a restaurant. Next door is the *Strand Hotel* (tel 241624) which has singles/doubles for Rs 275/375. Bathrooms are shared between two rooms. It's very worn and not special value. At the end of the same block is *Shelly's Hotel* (tel 240229), 30 P J Ramchandani Marg, which offers air-con rooms with bath and window for Rs 200/255.

There are three popular places on Garden Rd but these are more expensive. The *Ascot Hotel* (tel 240020), 38 Garden Rd, has air-con singles/doubles with bath for Rs 417/492 including breakfast. A few doors down, the *Godwin Hotel* (tel 241226), 41 Garden Rd, offers accommodation of a similar standard for Rs 415/525. The *Garden Hotel* (tel 241476) at 42 Garden Rd has air-con singles/doubles with bath for Rs 487/525 as well as two very ritzy deluxe rooms. This hotel also has its own bar and restaurant.

The *Hotel Diplomat* (tel 2021661), at 24 Mereweather Rd on the corner of Best Rd, has its own bar and restaurant. Singles/doubles are Rs 421/534, an extra bed costs Rs 84. Like many other Bombay hotels, it's poor value and the rooms are not very clean.

VT Station Area At 221-225 P D'Mello Rd near Victoria Terminus the *Hotel Manama* (tel 263860) has only double rooms, and these cost Rs 160, or Rs 225 with air-con. It's good value but is often full. Also on P D'Mello Rd, the *Embassy Hotel* (tel 866255) is opposite the Dockyard Rd suburban railway station and has air-con doubles for Rs 230.

Marine Drive Moving to the Marine Drive (Netaji Subhash Rd) area, you can try the *Sea Green Hotel* (tel 222294) at No 145, where rooms are Rs 192/275, or with air-con Rs 264/345. Next door is the *Sea Green South Hotel* (tel 221662), where prices are similar. These charges include breakfast. Both these hotels are popular and often full.

On the corner of Marine Drive and D Rd, the clean and simple *Norman's Guest House* (tel 294234) has a few singles at Rs 153, doubles at Rs 212 or Rs 300 with bath. The *Bentley Hotel* (tel 291244) on the other corner has rooms with common bath at Rs 120/154, although some of them are very small.

Nearby is the *Chateau Windsor Guest House* (tel 2043376), 86 Veer Nariman Rd, which has a wide selection of rooms with and without air-con and bath, and varying widely in size. Some of the windowless little boxes are poor value but rooms range from Rs 192 for a single with common bath to Rs 405 for a double with bath, up to over Rs 600 for very large air-con rooms. The lift has a sign announcing that 'servants may only use the lift if accompanied by children'.

Places to Stay – top end

Hotels in this category usually have a 10% service charge and 7% state 'luxury' tax tagged on top of the room charge – as do some of the middle-range places.

Bombay has the hotel reputed to be the best in India. It certainly has an air of glamour. Most of Bombay's cheap hotels cluster right behind it, and the hotel has a comfortable air-conditioned lounge and one of the best bookshops in the city, so you'll find a fair number of backpackers around it too! The *Taj Mahal Hotel* is an elegant turn-of-the-century building on Apollo Bunder near the Gateway of India. More recently the *Taj Inter-Continental* was added to it, so it is now known as the *Taj Mahal Hotel & Taj Inter-Continental* (tel 2023366). There are 650 rooms with singles/doubles from Rs 1450/1600. The affluence in the Taj is amazing; this is one place in India where you see BMWs and Mercedes parked outside and where people look rich!

On Nariman Point, and in an equally high price range, the *Hotel Oberoi-Towers* (tel 234343) has singles/doubles at Rs 1095/1195 plus a variety of restaurants, bars, coffee bars and a swimming pool. Right next door is the amazing new *Hotel Oberoi* (tel 2024440). It's worth wandering in just to have a look at the lobby. A room here will set you back a mere Rs 1650/1800, or if you're feeling flush, the Kohinoor Suite is yours for Rs 9000 – compare that to what most Indians earn in a month, or a year.

The rather out-of-the-way *Hotel President* (tel 4951090) is at 90 Cuffe Parade, about halfway down Colaba Causeway. Rooms are Rs 750/880 for singles/doubles.

Centrally located on Veer Nariman Rd in Churchgate, the *Ambassador Hotel* (tel 2041131) is topped by a revolving restaurant and has rooms at Rs 750/850. Close by on J Tata Rd, the *Hotel Ritz* (tel 220141) has rooms for Rs 500/625.

Ballard Estate is to the east side of Bombay, between Colaba and the GPO. In this central but relatively quiet area you'll find the *Grand Hotel* (tel 268211) at 17 Sprott Rd with rooms at Rs 555/632, although we've had a couple of complaints about it recently.

Places to Stay – Airport & Juhu

There are a number of hotels out by the airport and a lot of them along Juhu Beach. They're mainly at the more expensive end of the market and, unless you have some compelling reason to be near the airport, there's little incentive to stay there. It's also hard to think of a good reason to stay at Juhu Beach.

Airport Right outside the domestic terminal (Santa Cruz) is the *Centaur Hotel* (tel 6126660), a large circular hotel with conference facilities, all the usual amenities of a five-star hotel including a swimming pool, and rooms from Rs 700/800.

There are several other hotels very close by, either beside the Centaur or just across the road. They're all air-conditioned and offer good but expensive facilities. The *Hotel Airport Plaza* (tel 6123390) is at 70-C Nehru Rd, Vile Parle 'Veelay Parlay' and has rooms for Rs 521/626. It also has a swimming pool. The *Hotel Airport International* (tel 6122883) has rooms at Rs 380/520. The *Hotel Airport Palace* is a good deal cheaper at Rs 150.

Also close to the domestic terminal, the *Hotel Aircraft International* (tel 6123667) is at 179 Dayaldas Rd, Vile Parle, and has rooms at Rs 305/347. The comfortable and well-kept *Hotel Jal* (tel 6123820) on Nehru Rd costs Rs 300/450. The *Sabena Restaurant* next door has good food and a varied selection of beers. Also on Nehru Rd, the *Hotel Transit* (tel 6129325) costs Rs 390/525.

If you're departing within 24 hours, the *retiring rooms* at the domestic airport are Rs 75 per person. Ask at the airport manager's office.

By the international terminal, the five-star *Leela Penta* (tel 6363636) has rooms for Rs 1050/1150.

Juhu Beach Hotels at Juhu are generally at the expensive end of the price range. Don't even consider swimming at Juhu – one look at the untreated sewage which slithers sluggishly out to sea from the vast slum encampments from Dadar to Juhu will convince you.

Cheaper hotels (in Juhu) include the *Kings Hotel* (tel 579141), 5 Juhu Tara Rd, which provides air-con rooms for Rs 250/310, and the *Sea Side Hotel* (tel 621972) on the beach road.

Other places to try at the cheaper end of the market are the *Sea View Hotel* and the *Purnima Guest House* (tel 541215).

Right at the top is the *Holiday Inn* (tel 571425), Balraj Sahani Marg, which has air-con singles/doubles for Rs 825/925, a swimming pool and other facilities. The *Palm Grove Hotel* (tel 6149343) is another five-star hotel with rooms at Rs 600/700. The *Sun-n-Sand Hotel* (tel 571481) has a variety of rooms from Rs 500 to Rs 700.

The *Citizen Hotel* (tel 6123159) at 960 Juhu Beach Rd is not bad value at Rs 400/500. The *Welcomgroup Searock* (tel 6425421) at Bandstand, Bandra, has 401 rooms. Singles/doubles cost Rs 750/900.

Places to Eat

The accommodation shortage certainly doesn't spill over into restaurants. Bombay probably has the best selection of restaurants of any major Indian city. As in other cities, a meal in a better-class restaurant can be one of India's bargains. A foray into the more expensive places is a worthwhile investment, even for backpackers.

Less Expensive There are plenty of places to eat around Colaba. *Dipti's Pure Drinks*, near the Rex and Stiffles, is popular for its wonderful fruit juices (Rs 6 to Rs 8), fruit salads and lassis (Rs 6 to Rs 10). The relatively high prices don't put people off this tiny establishment. On Navroji Furounji Rd, *Laxmi Vilas* has excellent vegetarian thalis for Rs 7 and lassi for Rs 4.50. On Wodehouse Rd (alias the extension of Colaba Causeway alias Shahid Bhagat Singh Rd) the *Ananda Punjabi* is more expensive but tasty, say Rs 40 for two. A couple of doors down, the *Kamat Hotel* has excellent vegetarian food and it's air-conditioned upstairs.

The *Apsara Restaurant* is a popular place with good Indian and Chinese food; about Rs 40 for two. Nearby, the *Food Inn* is also popular and very clean and shiny looking although their tea is 'in the face of some stiff competition, the worst in Bombay'.

The *Leopold Restaurant* is a very popular place, not only for breakfast, lunch and dinner, but for hanging around and enjoying a cold beer. And not only for travellers; indeed some good Muslim Gulf Arabs seem to spend all day and night here making the most of the cold beer (Rs 19) – even at breakfast! The Leopold has a very pleasant atmosphere, although the service is only average. The food, however, is pretty good, the place is fairly hygienic and the prices reasonable, and you'll never be short of someone to chat with.

The *Cafe Mondegar*, a pleasant coffee bar in the next block towards Wellingdon Circle, is very similar. Across the road, the *Hotel Majestic* is a big vegetarian plate-meal specialist; Rs 7 for a standard thali, Rs 11 with pulao and sweet. Directly across from the Leopold, the *Olympic Coffee House* is a traditional old coffee bar with wonderful decor.

Right by Wellingdon Circle, the *Sahakari Bandar Canteen* is tacked on to an old building but the food is good and very cheap.

The *Cafe Samovar* in the Jehangir Art Gallery is a good place for a cold drink or a quick snack. At the top of Garden Rd, next to the garage, the *Edward VIII Restaurant* is a well-kept little place with good fruit juices.

Colaba is renowned for fine prawns and seafood. You can get fish & chips in a few places, including right beside the Marine

Drive aquarium! Bhelpuri is a Bombay speciality – a tasty snack of crisp noodles, spiced vegetables and other mysterious ingredients for Rs 1 or less. It's available from stalls all over town, but particularly on Chowpatty Beach. There are several restaurants along the beach road.

There's a couple of places if you want a meal, a snack or just a drink while you read the mail you've just picked up from the GPO. *Kohinoor* is virtually opposite the GPO. At 204 D Naoroji Rd, from the GPO and Victoria Terminus back towards Colaba, the small *Swidha* restaurant in the National Insurance Building has excellent vegetarian food although it's crowded at lunch time.

Bombay also has its own string of fast-food places called *Open House*. The closest one to the centre is on Veer Nariman Rd near the footbridge. They have good burgers for Rs 10 to Rs 15, and pizza for Rs 15 to Rs 20.

If you're in the Nariman Point area, the very popular air-con *Woodlands Restaurant* is close to the Air India Building in Mittal Chambers. The Rs 20 thali is good value; even better is the Rs 35 version which consists of soup, rice, puris, vegetable curries, raitha, chutney, pickles, curd, papadam, a sweet and pan! At lunch times you may have to wait for a table, but they also do takeaway.

More Expensive The Taj Mahal Hotel has a whole range of restaurants and snack bars, including the *Harbour Bar* where a beer for just Rs 35 almost seems a bargain. The *Apollo Bar* on the rooftop caters for western tastes and has fine views, although a beer here is a cool Rs 80. The *Shamiana Bar* has light meals – a buffet breakfast is Rs 60 and not all that good. The *Tanjore* is probably the best place for a splash-out meal – traditional Indian food (most dishes Rs 50 to Rs 80) accompanied by sitar music and classical Indian dancing in the evenings. They have thalis for no less than Rs 85. Formal dress is required in all the Taj's restaurants, and these days they even have the temerity to evict 'shabby' travellers from the deliciously cool lobby. There's a wonderful pastry shop in the new Oberoi Hotel at Nariman Point.

Along K Dubash Marg, just across from the Jehangir Art Gallery and Prince of Wales Museum, the newly renovated *Copper Chimney* has a typical non-veg menu.

In Colaba the *Delhi Darbar* doesn't serve alcohol but it does have an extensive menu. This is a good place to try the Parsi dish *dhaansak* – vegetable dhaansak is Rs 23.50. They have very good milkshakes and ice cream (try the pista kulfi).

Bombay has a particularly good selection of Chinese restaurants. Some say the *Nanking*, on Shivaji Marg in Colaba, has the best Chinese food in India. Directly across the road, the *Mandarin* is marginally more expensive. The adjacent *Hong Kong* does excellent Szechuan food – 'the best Chinese food we've ever found anywhere', reported a Canadian traveller. The *Kabab Corner* in the Hotel Nataraj on Marine Drive has excellent food and a sitar player in the evenings.

At Nariman Point, past the Air India Building, is the *Rangoli Restaurant* in the performing arts complex. The excellent buffet lunch is fantastic value at Rs 75. Near Churchgate station, the *Samrat* vegetarian restaurant has been recommended for its good food. Here you can try the local apéritif known as jal jeera – 'very popular but it smells like rotten eggs and is very salty' according to one unimpressed drinker.

One of the best splurges in the country and an absolute must in Bombay is the buffet lunch at the *Taj Mahal Hotel*. For Rs 125 you can gorge yourself on a mind-boggling array of both Indian and western dishes. This spread is laid on in the ballroom and there's even live piano accompaniment.

Daba Lunches

Mr Bombay Business-Wallah sets off from home, boards his train or bus and heads into the city every morning – just like his office-worker counterpart in Australia, England or America. Just like many of his overseas office-wallah brothers, he'd like to take his lunch with him and eat in the office. But an Indian lunch isn't as simple as a couple of sandwiches and an apple. A cut lunch could never satisfy an Indian – there has to be curry and rice and parathas and spices and a lot of things that take a lot of time to prepare and would hardly slip into a brown paper bag in the briefcase.

Naturally there's a supremely complex, yet smoothly working, Indian solution to this problem – it's called the daba lunch system. After he's left for work, his wife – or the cook or bearer – sets to and fixes his lunch. When it's prepared it's packed into a metal container about 15 cm in diameter and 30 cm high. On the lid there's a mysterious colour-coded notation. The container is then carried down to a street corner pick-up point where it meets up with lots of other lunch containers and heads towards their city office destination. From the pick-up point they're conveyed to the nearest train station where they're transported to the appropriate city station.

In the city they're broken down to their separate destinations, and between 11 and 12 in the morning thousands upon thousands of individually coded lunches pour out of Victoria Terminus, Churchgate, Bombay Central and other stations. On the heads of porters, carried in carts, slung from long poles, tied on bicycle handlebars, those lunch containers then scatter out across the city. Most of the daba-wallahs involved in this long chain of events are illiterate, but by some miracle of Indian efficiency, when Mr Business-Wallah opens his office door at lunchtime there will be his lunch by the door. Every day, without fail, they never lose a lunch.

Things to Buy

Bombay has a number of intriguing markets and some feel it's much better for shopping than Delhi. Chor Bazaar is Bombay's thieves' market. It's off Grant Rd (Maulana Shaukatali Rd) and here you'll find a phenomenal collection of 'antiques', jewellery, wooden items, leather and general bric-a-brac. Mutton

St has a particularly interesting collection of shops for miscellaneous 'junk'. Shops are generally open from 10 am but are closed on Fridays. The shopkeepers here really know the value of their stuff but it's still possible to pick up some interesting items.

Crawford Market, officially renamed Mahatma Phule Market, is the centre for flowers, fruit, vegetables, meat and fish in Bombay. This is the place to look for Bombay's two famous fish – the pomfret and the 'Bombay duck'. The market building was constructed in 1867 and is one of the most colourful and photogenic places in Bombay. Nearby is Javeri Bazaar, the jewellery centre off Mumbadevi Rd. There is some fantastic stuff here, especially silver belts and old statues and charms. Nearby is the brass bazaar on Kalbadevi Rd.

There are all sorts of places selling handicrafts, artefacts, antiques and art around the Colaba area. Shops in the Taj Hotel specialise in high quality – and high prices. Check the Jehangir Gallery by the Prince of Wales Museum too. The street stalls along S B Singh Rd in Colaba are good places to buy things, especially 'export reject' clothes which are incredibly cheap – good men's shirts for Rs 25. Also good is the Khadi Village Industries Emporium (tel 2043288) at 286 D Naoroji Rd, and the Central Cottage Industries Emporium (tel 2022491) at Apollo Bunder.

If Bombay is your last (or only) stop, you can also pick up souvenirs from all over the country from the various state government emporiums. In the World Trade Centre in Cuffe Parade are those operated by Madhya Pradesh, Himachal Pradesh, Maharashtra and Jammu & Kashmir. Others run by Uttar Pradesh and Bihar are on Sir P M Rd.

Getting There & Away
Air There is an extensive network of flights operating to and from Bombay's Sahar and Santa Cruz airports. The domestic terminal (Santa Cruz) is some distance away from the international terminal. Bombay is the main international gateway to India, with far more flights than New Delhi, Calcutta or Madras. It also has the busiest network of domestic flights.

Between Delhi and Bombay there are frequent daily flights, including a number of direct Airbus connections. There are a couple of daily flights to and from Calcutta and Madras, and connections with numerous other cities in India:

Ahmedabad	Rs 450
Aurangabad	Rs 330
Bangalore	Rs 835
Calicut	Rs 915
Calcutta	Rs 1460
Cochin	Rs 1010
Coimbatore	Rs 885
Dabolim (Goa)	Rs 435
Delhi	Rs 1075
Hyderabad	Rs 690
Madras	Rs 1015
Mangalore	Rs 715
Pune	Rs 180
Trivandrum	Rs 1165
Udaipur	Rs 670

Bus Long-distance buses depart from the State Transport Terminal opposite Bombay Central station. It's fairly chaotic and there is almost nothing in English.

The state bus companies of Maharashtra, Gujarat, Karnataka and Madhya Pradesh all have offices here and bookings can be made (tel 374272) between 8 am and 11 pm. There is computerised advance booking available for journeys by deluxe buses.

Some travel times and approximate costs include:

Aurangabad	11 hours	Rs 51 (Rs 77*)
Bangalore	25 hours	Rs 161 (Rs 203*)
Indore	16 hours	Rs 78 (Rs 85*)
Hyderabad	16 hours	Rs 92 (Rs 145*)
Mangalore	25 hours	Rs 157 (Rs 199*)
Panaji (Goa)	17 hours	Rs 73 (Rs 132*)

*deluxe buses

The MTDC operates daily deluxe buses to

Mahabaleshwar (6½ hours, Rs 70) and to Goa (18 hours, Rs 139). These are better than a lot of other deluxe buses as they are not the dreaded video coaches and the drivers don't seem to have the suicide wish that is common among Indian bus drivers. Bookings should be made in advance at the CDO Hutments, Madame Cama Rd.

Train Two railway systems operate out of Bombay. Central Railways handles services to the east and south, plus a few trains to the north. The booking office (tel 2043535) at Victoria Terminus is a marvel of modern technology. Reservations are computerised and the booking hall is air-conditioned and extremely fancy. There are over 70 ticket windows and you can queue up at any one after you fill in a form (available downstairs). Windows 1 and 2 are specifically for dealing with foreigners and this is where you buy Indrail passes. Despite all this, however, if you want to get a tourist-quota ticket, it still has to be arranged through the Foreign Tourist Guide in the kiosk on the main railway station concourse. The booking office is open daily from 9 am to 1 pm and 1.30 to 5 pm.

The other system operating out of Bombay is Western Railways, which has services to the north from Churchgate and Central stations. Bookings in 1st class can be made at the Western Railways booking office (tel 291952) next to the Government of India tourist office opposite Churchgate, between 8 am and 8 pm Monday to Saturday, and 9 am to 4 pm Sunday. Tourist-quota tickets are issued from here, but only between 9.30 am and 3 pm and must be paid for in foreign currency. The exchange rate is the same as the bank so you don't lose out. Refunds and change are given only in rupees. With the exception of the tourist quota, 2nd class has to be booked from Bombay Central (tel 375986) between 9 am and 4 pm.

There are a number of Central Railways trains that do not depart from either Central or Churchgate but from Dadar station, further north of Central. These trains can still be booked at Central station and include the Dadar to Madras Express, the fastest train to Madras.

From Bombay it is 1588 km and 17 hours to Delhi, and the fare is Rs 121 in 2nd class, Rs 484 in 1st. The Rajdhani Express is the fastest train; it's a special one-class train which costs Rs 350 in the air-con chair car, Rs 645 in an air-con sleeper. Fares include tea, dinner, coffee and breakfast on board.

Bombay to Calcutta is a lengthy 1968-km trip taking 32 hours and costing Rs 141 in 2nd class, Rs 575 in 1st. Bombay to Madras is 1279 km and takes from 27 hours at a cost of Rs 106 in 2nd class, Rs 418 in 1st.

Boat See Goa for more details on the Bombay to Goa ferry. The service was operated by the Shipping Corporation of India, although in 1988 the service was suspended as all boats were either under repair or had been called into service ferrying troops and supplies to Sri Lanka. Hopefully this is only a temporary situation.

When it is operating, departures are every day except Tuesday, but the service is suspended during the monsoon between June and September.

Getting Around

Airport Transport The airport bus service operates between the Air India Building at Nariman Point and Santa Cruz (domestic) and Sahar (international) airports. The journey from Nariman Point to Santa Cruz takes about one hour and costs Rs 20. To Sahar it takes about 1½ hours and costs Rs 27. From Nariman Point departures are every 30 minutes from around 3 am to 11 pm. In peak hour the trip through Bombay's horribly congested streets can take well over two hours so don't cut things too fine.

Tickets for the buses are bought either on the buses themselves, at the Air India Building or at the terminals. Buses between the terminals depart every 15 minutes and cost Rs 10.

For those die-hards determined to get there on the cheap regardless of inconvenience, it is possible to get from Sahar Airport to central Bombay for less than Rs 15. First take the airport bus from the international to the domestic terminal, then an ordinary bus to Vile Parle (No 321), followed by a suburban train to Churchgate. If you're carrying more than a toothbrush, avoid doing anything as defiant as this in rush hours.

A taxi to the domestic airport on the meter costs about Rs 85 from Colaba, Rs 80 from Churchgate, Rs 60 from Dadar, Rs 35 from Juhu. It's a bit further to the international airport. During rush hours you won't find anyone who's prepared to use the meter, so expect to pay more. From the airport there is a police-operated taxi booth where you pay a set fare and are then assigned to a taxi. You give the driver your slip and there's no further fuss. You do, however, pay a bit more than the meter fare (plus adjustment card) - the official fare from the domestic airport to Colaba is Rs 114.

An auto-rickshaw from Sahar to Juhu costs about Rs 15.

Bus Bombay has one of the best public transport systems of any major Indian city. There are lots of well-kept double-decker buses with fares beginning from Rs 0.50. They tend to be crowded, especially during rush hours, and Bombay's pickpockets are notoriously adept. Take care.

The buses are operated by BEST (Bombay Electric Supply & Transport) and have separate route maps for their extensive city and suburban services. From the Victoria Terminus railway station take a No 1, 6 Ltd, 7 Ltd, 103 or 124 to 'Electric House', a useful landmark in Colaba. From Bombay Central take a No 43, 70 or a 124. Ltd means 'limited stops'.

Train Bombay has an extensive system of electric trains, and it's virtually the only place in India where it's worth taking trains for intra-city travel. But *avoid* rush hours when they are so crowded that you have to make your way towards the door at least three stops before you want to get out to have any chance of getting off, *and* you need to know which side the platform will be on - forget it. First class is also packed solid even though it is comparatively expensive.

The main suburban route of interest to travellers is Churchgate to Bombay Central and Dadar, with many other stops in between. There's a train every two to five minutes in either direction between 4.30 am and 10.30 pm. The fare between Churchgate and Central is Rs 1.50 in 2nd class and Rs 13 in 1st. A taxi over the same distance would cost you about Rs 20 on the meter. If you arrive at Bombay Central on the main railway system, your ticket covers you for the journey from there to the more convenient Churchgate station.

Taxi Bombay has a large fleet of metered taxis but you'll often have to try a few before you find one willing to go where you want, especially during peak periods. As usual, the meters are out of date so you pay according to a fare conversion card which all drivers carry, regardless of how reluctant they are to pull them out when they'd prefer to tell you the first figure that comes into their head. At last count the metered flagfall was Rs 1 but the adjustment was meter times 4½!

You probably won't have any difficulties about drivers resetting the meters from dawn until late evening, but between midnight and dawn they're reluctant to take you anywhere on the meter so you'll have to negotiate a price.

AROUND BOMBAY
Elephanta Island

The island of Elephanta is about 10 km north-east from Apollo Bunder and is

Bombay's major tourist attraction due to the four rock-cut temples on the island. They are thought to have been cut out between 450 and 750 AD, and at that time the island was known as Gharapuri, the 'fortress city'. When the Portuguese arrived they renamed it Elephanta after the large stone elephant near the landing place. This figure collapsed in 1814 and the remaining pieces were removed to the Victoria Gardens in Bombay in 1864 and reassembled in 1912.

Unfortunately the Portuguese took their traditional disdain for other religions to its usual lengths at Elephanta, and did considerable damage to the sculptures. Although some people feel that Elephanta is not as impressive as the rock-cut temples of Ellora, the size, beauty and power of the sculptures are without equal.

The caves are reached by a stairway up the hillside from the landing place. Palanquins are available for anybody in need of being carried up. There is one main cave with a number of large sculptured panels, all relating to Shiva, and a separate lingam shrine.

The most interesting of the panels includes one of Trimurti, or the three-headed Shiva, where he also takes the role of Brahma, the creator, and Vishnu, the preserver. In other panels Shiva appears as Ardhanari, where he unites both sexes in one body – one side of the sculpture is male, one side female.

There are figures of Shiva and his wife Parvati and of their marriage. In another panel Shiva dances the Tandava, the dance that shakes the world. Parvati and their son, Ganesh, look on a little astonished. One of the best panels is that of Ravana shaking Kailasa. The demon king of Lanka decided to carry Shiva and his companions off by the simple expedient of removing their Himalayan home, the mountain Kailasa. Parvati became panic-stricken at his energetic attempts to jerk the mountain free, but Shiva calmly pushed the mountain back

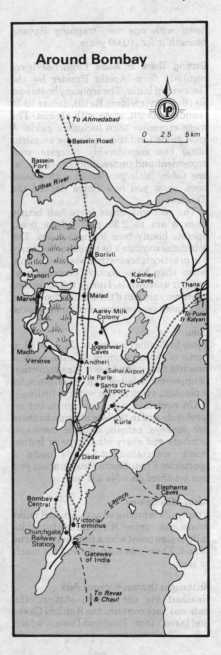

Around Bombay

0   2.5   5 km

To Ahmedabad

Bassein Road

Bassein Fort

Ulhas River

Borivli

Manori

Kanheri Caves

Thana

Marve

Malad

Aarey Milk Colony

To Pune & Kalyan

Madh

Versova

Jogeshwari Caves

Andheri

Juhu

Vile Parle

Sahar Airport

Santa Cruz Airport

Kurla

Dadar

Elephanta Caves

Bombay Central

Launch

Victoria Terminus

Churchgate Railway Station

Gateway of India

To Revas & Chaul

down with one toe, trapping Ravana beneath it for 10,000 years.

Getting There & Away Launches leave regularly from Apollo Bunder by the Gateway of India. The economy boats cost Rs 16 return (children Rs 10), deluxe Rs 30 (children Rs 20), more with air-con. The more expensive trips include a guide. A good guide (and there are some excellent ones) can considerably increase your enjoyment and understanding – even, as one tubby little gentleman with glasses does, show you how Shiva danced the Tandava.

The economy boats leave half-hourly from 8 am to 2.30 pm; deluxe boats operate hourly from 9 am to 2 pm. The schedules shouldn't be taken too seriously – in practice it seems that boats leave only when they have enough passengers to make it worthwhile. During the monsoon, boats may not run if the water is too rough. Elephanta gets very crowded on weekends.

Juhu
Close to Bombay's airports, Juhu is 18 km north of the city centre. It's the nearest beach to the city and has quite a collection of upper-notch hotels, but it's no place for a pleasant swim as the water is filthy.

On weekdays it is fairly quiet, but on weekends and in the late afternoons there are donkeys, camels, dancing monkeys, acrobats and every other type of Indian beach entertainment – it's quite a spectacle. From Santa Cruz station you can get there on a No 231 bus.

Aarey Milk Colony
Fresh milk is produced at this model milk-production centre. It's notable also for its hilltop viewpoint with a fine view over the island. There's an entry fee and not much to see.

Krishnagiri Upavan National Park
Reached via the Borivli station, the national park contains the Kanheri Caves and lakes Vihar, Tulsi and Powari, which act as reservoirs for much of Bombay's water supply.

At the entrance to the park there's a huge outdoor movie lot, including a fort frontage partly constructed from old oil drums. Also near the park entrance is, believe it or not, a Lion Safari Park. It's open from 9 am to 5 pm daily except Mondays (Tuesdays if Monday is a public holiday) and trips are made through the park in a 'safari vehicle'.

Kanheri Caves Within the national park, about 42 km from Bombay, 109 caves line the side of a rocky ravine. The caves are Buddhist and date from around the 2nd to 9th century AD. Although there are so many of them, most are little more than holes in the rock and only a handful are of real interest. The most important is cave 3, the 'Great Chaitya Cave', which has a long colonnade of pillars around the *dagoba* at the back of the cave. Further up the ravine are some good views out to the sea.

Kanheri can be visited on the regular suburban tours, or you can take a train to Borivli station and then a taxi for the 10 km or so to the caves. On Sundays and holidays there is a bus service from the station to the caves.

Other Beaches
Bombay's best known beach, Juhu, is too close to the city and not sanitary enough for a pleasant swim, but there are more remote beaches on the island. Manori beach is about 40 km out of the city. You can get to it via the station at Malad, 32 km out. There's an interesting fishing village and an old Portuguese church nearby.

A nice place to stay near the village of Manori is the *Manoribel Hotel* (tel 241707), which has double rooms with bath from Rs 100. Or there's the friendly *Hotel Dominica* with rooms at Rs 100 to Rs 150. To get there, take the suburban electric train to Malad, then a bus (No 272) to Marve ferry, cross on the ferry and walk to the Manoribel. The walk to the

Snake charmer at Juhu Beach

at Montpezir near Borivli. The Jogeshvari Caves are near the Andheri station.

Bassein

Just across the river which separates the mainland from Bombay island is Bassein, a Portuguese fortified city from 1534 to 1739. The Portuguese took Bassein at the same time as Daman, further north in Gujarat. They built a fort containing a city of such pomp and splendour that it came to be known as the 'Court of the North'. Only the Hidalgos or aristocracy were permitted to live within the fort walls, and by the end of the 17th century there were 300 Portuguese and 400 Indian-Christian families here, with a cathedral, five convents and 13 churches.

Then in 1739 the Marathas besieged the city and the Portuguese surrendered after three months of appalling losses. Today the city walls are still standing and you'll see the ruins of some of the churches and the Cathedral of St Joseph.

Bassein is 11 km from the Bassein Road (Vasai Road in Marathi) railway station. About an hour by bus from the station are the Vajreshwari hot springs.

Chaul

South of Bombay, this was another Portuguese settlement, although not as important as Bassein. They took it in 1522 and lost it to the Marathas at the same time as Bassein. There are a few remains and old ruined churches within the Portuguese fortifications. Looking across to the Portuguese fort from the other side of the river is the hilltop Muslim Korlai Fort.

Ferries run to Revas from the New Ferry Wharf, a 1½-hour trip. From there you've got a 30-km bus trip to Chaul. It's possible to continue on from here by road to Mahabaleshwar, or to join the Bombay to Pune road.

beach is a km and a bit from where the ferry stops at Manori.

Aksa Beach, also reached by bus No 272 or by an auto-rickshaw from Malad, is OK. It's probably the best beach within easy reach of Bombay. Other beaches around Bombay include Madh, 45 km out and also reached via Malad. Versova is 29 km from the city, reached via Andheri station, but is very dirty too. Getting to Uran involves a 74-km trip, the last 10 km by sea. Launches leave from the New Ferry Wharf.

Montpezir & Jogeshvari Caves

There are a few Hindu caves, one of which was converted into a Portuguese church,

Maharashtra

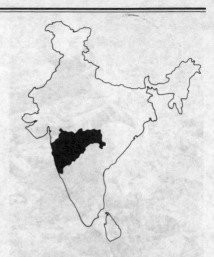

Population: 75 million
Area: 307,762 square km
Capital: Bombay
Main language: Marathi

The state of Maharashtra is one of the largest in India, both in terms of population and in area. Its booming capital, Bombay, makes it not only one of the most important states economically, but also a major gateway for overseas visitors. From Bombay you can head off into India in a number of directions, but most travellers will either be going south to Goa through Pune (Poona), with its famous ashram, or north-east to the amazing cave temples of Ajanta and Ellora. Most of the state stands on the high Deccan Plateau. Historically this was the main centre for the Maratha Empire, which defied the Moghuls for so long, and which under the fearless rule of Shivaji carved out a large part of central India as its domain.

Cave Architecture

The rock-cut caves in Maharashtra have several distinct design elements. The Buddhist caves, which are generally the older ones, are either chaityas (temples) or viharas (monasteries). Chaityas are usually deep and narrow with a stupa at the end of the cave. There may be a row of columns down both sides of the cave and around the stupa.

The viharas are usually not as deep and narrow as the chaitya caves. They were normally intended as living and sleeping quarters for the monks and often have rows of cells along both sides. In the back there is a small shrine room, usually containing an image of the Buddha. At Ajanta, the cliff face into which the caves are cut is very steep and there is often a small verandah or entrance porch in front of the main cave. At Ellora the rock face is

more sloping and the verandah or porch element generally becomes a separate courtyard.

The cave temples reach their peak of complexity and design in the Hindu caves at Ellora, and particularly in the magnificent Kailasa Temple. Here they are hardly caves any longer, for the whole enclosure is open to the sky. In design they are much like other temples of that era – except that instead of being built up from the bottom they were cut down from the top. They are an imitation of the conventional architecture of that period.

Though the caves are notable for their sculptures and paintings, the famous Ajanta 'frescoes' are not, technically speaking, frescoes at all. A fresco is a painting done on a wet surface which absorbs the colour. The Ajanta paintings are, more correctly, tempera, since they were painted on a dry surface. The rough-hewn rock walls were coated with a centimetre-thick layer of clay and cow-dung mixed with rice husks. A final coat of lime was then applied to produce the finished surface on which the artist painted. This surface was then polished to produce a high gloss.

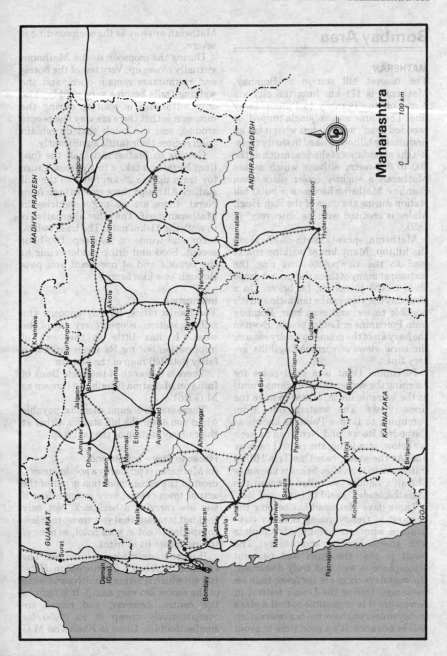

Maharashtra

0 _____ 100 km

Bombay Area

MATHERAN

The nearest hill station to Bombay, Matheran is 171 km from the city via Neral on the Bombay to Pune railway line. The name means 'jungle topped' or 'wooded head', which is just what it is – an undulating hilltop cloaked in shady trees. It's the abundance of shade as much as the 700 to 800-metre altitude which makes Matheran a slightly cooler place than Bombay. Matheran became a popular hill station during the days of the Raj; Hugh Malet is credited with its 'discovery' in 1850.

Matheran sprawls north-south along the hilltop. Many km of walking tracks lead to the viewpoints that ring the station; at many of them the ground drops sheer to the plains far, far below. On a clear day the view can be fantastic and it's possible to see, and even hear, Bombay from Porcupine or Louisa points. Even in the hazy air of the premonsoon dry season, the eerie views of surrounding hills are very fine.

Porcupine Point is a good place for catching the sunset, but Panorama Point, at the extreme north, is said to have the finest views. The western side, from Porcupine to Louisa Point, is known as Cathedral Rocks, and Neral can be seen far below, straddling the central railway line. At the south, near One Tree Hill, a trail down to the valley below is known as Shivaji's Ladder, so called because the Maratha leader is said to have used it.

These days Matheran has become the hangout of trendy young Bombay daytrippers who come equipped complete with ghetto blasters and whisky. The result is that the quiet and peaceful atmosphere is well and truly disturbed. On weekdays there are far fewer than on weekends. During the Diwali festival in November it is impossible to find a place to stay unless you have made a reservation well in advance. It's a good time to avoid Matheran anyway as the overcrowding is severe.

During the monsoon season Matheran virtually closes up. Very few of the hotels and restaurants remain open, and the walking trails become very muddy. The only advantage of visiting during the monsoon is that there are very few people around, and the hotels that do remain open reduce their tariffs significantly.

Getting to Matheran is half the fun; from Neral you take a tiny narrow-gauge toy train up the 26-km route to the hill station. Although there are also taxis from Neral, there are no motor vehicles in Matheran itself. The other alternative is to walk the 11-km path. The train twists, turns and winds on its steep, two-hour ascent. Food and drink vendors cling to the outside and at one point you pass through 'one kiss tunnel'.

Information

The tourist office, directly opposite the railway station, is open every day of the week. It has little in the way of information but for Rs 1 you can buy a fairly detailed map of the plateau.

There is a branch of the State Bank of India on Mahatma Gandhi Rd (known as M G Rd).

There is a Rs 5 'capitation tax' payable when you enter the hill station, either at the railway station or the taxi stop.

Places to Stay – bottom end

As Matheran is primarily a holiday resort, most of the accommodation is out of the actual town centre; very inconvenient if you are carrying a backpack. Not only that but it means that you are more or less compelled to eat at your hotel, as none of the paths are lit at night.

Budget accommodation is limited. The cheapest is *Khan's Cosmopolitan Hotel* (tel 40) which is rather primitive and some of the rooms are very damp. It is right in the centre, however, and rooms are comparatively cheap at Rs 30/50 for singles/doubles. Close to Khan's on M G

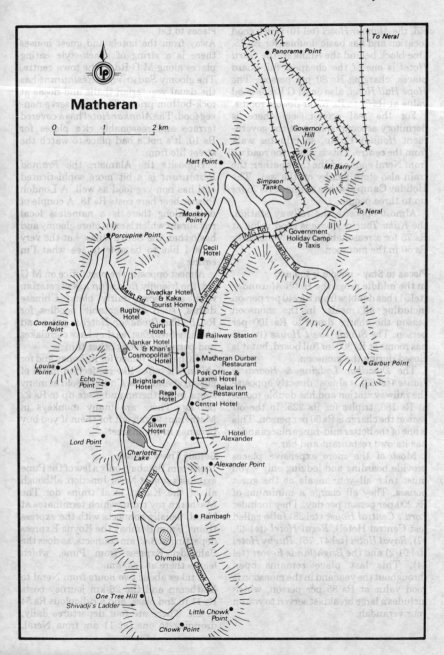

Matheran

0   1   2 km

To Neral

Panorama Point

Governor Hill

Mt Barry

Hart Point

Simpson Tank

Monkey Point

Porcupine Point

Cecil Hotel

Mallet Rd

Divadkar Hotel & Kaka Tourist Home

Rugby Hotel

Coronation Point

Guru Hotel

Alankar Hotel & Khan's Cosmopolitan Hotel

Railway Station

Louisa Point

Echo Point

Brightland Hotel

Regal Hotel

Matheran Durbar Restaurant

Post Office & Laxmi Hotel

Relax Inn Restaurant

Central Hotel

Lord Point

Silvan Hotel

Hotel Alexander

Charlotte Lake

Alexander Point

Rambagh

Olympia

One Tree Hill

Shivaji's Ladder

Little Chowk Point

Chowk Point

To Neral

Government Holiday Camp & Taxis

Garbut Point

MG Rd

Mahatma Gandhi Rd

Garbut Rd

Panorama Rd

Shivaji Rd

Little Chowk Rd

Rd, the *Alankar Hotel* (tel 10) is in a good location and has basic doubles for Rs 75. One block behind the Alankar, the *Guru Hotel* is one of the cheapest full-board places, charging Rs 80 per person. The *Hope Hall Hotel*, also on M G Rd, is good value at Rs 60 to Rs 75 for double rooms.

For the real economisers there is dormitory accommodation at the government *Holiday Camp*, 45 minutes walk from the centre. This is where the road up from Neral ends and the taxis gather; the train also stops nearby on the way. The Holiday Camp also has rooms at Rs 75 for up to three people.

Almost opposite the railway station, the *Kaka Tourist Home* is good value at Rs 75 for a reasonable double with bath; Rs 50 in the monsoon.

Places to Stay – middle & top end

In the middle range the *Hotel Alexander* (tel 51) has doubles from Rs 240 per person including all meals. In the monsoon season the charge drops to Rs 100 per person. The *Silvan Guest House* (tel 74) has rooms at Rs 300 for full board, but it is closed during the monsoon.

The *Divadkar Lodging & Boarding House* (tel 23) is almost directly opposite the railway station and has double rooms at Rs 180, triples for Rs 225. In the off season the charge is Rs 60 per person. This is one of the better mid-range places and it has its own restaurant and bar.

Most of the more expensive places provide boarding and lodging only – you must take all your meals at the guest houses. They all charge a minimum of Rs 200 per person per day. They include: *Lord's Central House* (tel 28) (also called just Central Hotel), *Regal Hotel* (tel 43, 87), *Royal Hotel* (tel 47, 75), *Rugby Hotel* (tel 91/2) and the *Brightlands Resort* (tel 44). This last place remains open throughout the year and in the monsoon is good value at Rs 85 per person, which includes a large breakfast served to you on your verandah.

Places to Eat

Away from the hotels and guest houses there is a string of snack-style eating places along M G Rd in the town centre. The gloomy *Sadya Vijay Restaurant* has the usual vegetarian thalis and dosas at rock-bottom prices. They also serve non-veg food. The *Alankar Hotel* has a covered terrace and reasonable rice plates for Rs 10. It's not a bad place to watch the street life from.

Opposite the Alankar, the *Pramod Restaurant* is a bit more sophisticated and has non-veg food as well. A London Pilsner beer here costs Rs 18. A couple of doors along there is a nameless local restaurant which is even more gloomy and basic than the Sadya Vijay – at the very least I like to be able to see what I'm eating.

Almost opposite the post office on M G Rd, the friendly *Relax Inn* has vegetarian food, and some fairly bland Chinese dishes, such as vegetable noodles for Rs 15. The *Divadkar Hotel* is not a bad place for breakfast, as they have cornflakes and porridge, among other things.

Matheran is famed for its honey and for *chikki* – a toffee-like confection made of gur-sugar and nuts. Chikki is sold at many shops in Matheran and costs up to Rs 22 per kg. There are many monkeys in Matheran; watch out for them if you buy bananas in the market!

Getting There & Away

Train From Bombay, only a few of the Pune expresses stop at Neral Junction, although all of the Karjat local trains do. The Matheran toy train, which terminates at Neral, usually connects with the express trains. From Bombay the Koyna Express departing at 8.45 am connects, as does the Sahyadri Express from Pune, which leaves there at 7.25 am.

It takes about two hours from Neral to Matheran and the 26-km journey costs Rs 11 in 2nd class, and a ridiculous Rs 54 in 1st. There are four departures daily, dropping to one (at 11 am from Neral,

2.30 pm from Matheran) during the monsoon, and even this is suspended if there has been really heavy rain.

When arriving at Neral to catch the toy train, ignore the touts who try and con you into taking a taxi by telling you that the train is full and takes three hours, etc.

Taxi Share taxis cost Rs 22 per person and they leave when full, although your idea of full might not tally with the driver's – there were nine paying passengers in the one I caught! The trip takes half an hour.

Getting Around
In Matheran itself the only transport is by rickshaw – one man pulls, two push (or hold it back on the descents). If your gear is too heavy to carry very far, and you're staying a long way from the station, you may want to use one to get your bags to the hotel. Ponies can also be hired for riding on the many trails that wind around Matheran.

The taxis stop 45 minutes walk from the centre. A pony costs Rs 20, a rickshaw Rs 30. If you want to walk into the centre, take the track for about 100 metres and then turn left along the railway track as the ascent is much more gradual.

The railway station is right in the centre of town.

KARLA & BHAJA CAVES
Situated 126 km south-east of Bombay on the main rail line to Pune, Lonavla (sometimes spelt Lonavala) is the place from which to visit the Karla and Bhaja caves. There is nothing of interest in the town itself. It is possible to visit the caves in a day-trip from either Bombay or Pune if you don't mind rushing and hiring an auto-rickshaw from Lonavla for the day.

The Karla Cave is about 11 km from Lonavla, about 1½ km off the main road. The Bhaja Caves are about three km off the other side of the main road. If you plan on walking to the latter, take a local train from Lonavla to Malavli first.

Information
The tourist office outside Lonavla station is fairly useless although they do sell a Rs 6 booklet which has a good detailed map of the area if you want to do some exploring.

Karla Cave
It's a steep half-km climb up the hillside to Karla Cave. The cave temple is Hinayana Buddhist and was completed around 80 BC. One of the best preserved of its type in India, it dates from the time when this style of temple was at its height in terms of design purity.

A beautifully carved 'sun window' filters the light in towards the small stupa at the inner end of the deep, narrow cave. Unfortunately an ugly little modern temple has been erected just outside the cave entrance. Inside, the pillars are topped by two kneeling elephants and two seated figures with their arms over each other on the elephants. Generally the figures are male and female, but sometimes

Sculpture at Karla Cave

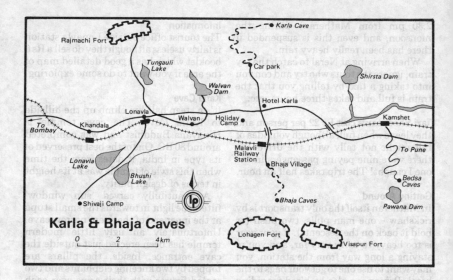

Karla & Bhaja Caves

they are two women. The roof of the cave is ribbed with teak beams said to be original; there may once have been such beams at Ajanta and Ellora, but they are now gone. On the sides of the vestibule are carved elephant heads which once had real ivory tusks.

Other carvings can also be seen along the sides. A pillar topped by four back-to-back lions, an image usually associated with Ashoka, stands outside the cave. It may be older than the cave itself.

There are some small monastery, or vihara, caves at Karla, further round the hillside. Some of these have been converted into Hindu shrines.

If possible, avoid going to the Karla Cave at weekends or on public holidays, when it is invaded by the transistor radio and picnic mobs from Bombay. The noise and mess which they create isn't going to do anything for your appreciation of this beautiful site. Bhaja is too far from the main road for this to happen on the same scale, but it does get its fair share too.

Bhaja Caves

It's a fairly rough route from the main road to the 18 Bhaja Caves. They're in a lusher, greener setting than the Karla Cave's dry hillside, and are thought to date from around 200 BC. Cave 12, a chaitya cave similar in style to the Karla Cave, is the most important. About 50 metres past this is a strange group of 14 stupas, five inside and nine outside the cave. The last cave on the south side has some fine sculptures.

A few minutes walk past the last cave is a beautiful waterfall which during the monsoon has enough water for a good swim. From the waterfall you can see the old forts on the hilltops.

Other Caves & Forts

Further along the line, six km south-east of Kamshet station, are the Bedsa Caves. They are thought to be newer than the better executed Karla Cave. At one time the roof of the main cave was probably painted.

There are a number of old forts in the vicinity, including the hilltop Lohagen Fort, six km from Malavli, which was taken twice by Shivaji, and lost again on each occasion. Above the Bhaja Caves is Visapur Fort.

Khandala, before Lonavla, is picturesquely situated overlooking a ravine. In the wet season there is a fine waterfall near the head of the ravine.

Places to Stay

Lonavla Like Khandala and Mahabaleshwar, Lonavla is regarded as a kind of hill station by people from Bombay, so there's quite a range of accommodation here. It's a compact town and there are several places close to the bus and railway stations. The *Hotel Purohit* (tel 2695) is one of these. It is tolerably grubby and double rooms cost Rs 60. It's about the best for the money.

The *Adarsh Hotel* (tel 2353) is also good value at Rs 60/75, or Rs 120/150 with aircon, although the staff are more than just a little unhelpful.

The *Hotel Girikunj* (tel 2529) has rooms with bathroom from Rs 80 as well as a vegetarian restaurant. The *Janata Hotel* (tel 2689) opposite has similar prices. Both places are quite OK for a night.

On the main road the *Hotel Annapurna* is noisy, and overpriced at Rs 75/100 for singles/doubles with bath. Avoid the *Hotel Mahalaxmi* opposite the Adarsh Hotel. It is totally uninhabitable and a complete rip-off at Rs 60.

The *Hotel Swiss Cottage* (tel 2561) is one of the better places and costs Rs 150 for a double, Rs 200 with air-con. It's about a 10-minute walk from the bus station. The *Hotel Chandralok* has been completely rebuilt and is now one of the more expensive places in Lonavla.

Karla It is possible to visit the caves from the government-run *Holiday Camp* (tel 30) just off the Bombay to Pune road near the caves. The problem is that it's a long walk from anywhere and you have to take your meals at the camp. There are rooms ranging from Rs 75 for a triple up to Rs 200 for four in a 'super deluxe suite'. From July to September there's a discount of 10% on weekends and 25% on weekdays.

The *Hotel Karla* is in a good location, at the Karla Caves junction, but the rooms are filthy and it's not in any way a pleasant place to stay.

Places to Eat

Lonavla The *Plaza Restaurant* on the main highway has good vegetarian food – they even have toasted butter sandwiches! Cold Golden Eagle beer costs Rs 18.

Sagar Snacks is a good place for masala dosas and other vegetarian snacks. They have what must be one of the few espresso coffee machines in the country – pity they don't use it.

The *Central Restaurant* in the old part of town on the west side of the railway tracks is one of the few places serving non-veg food. Good for a breakfast omelette.

Getting There & Away

Lonavla is on the main Bombay to Pune road and railway line so there are plenty of trains and buses from both cities.

Bombay to Lonavla takes about three hours, and fares for the 128-km trip are

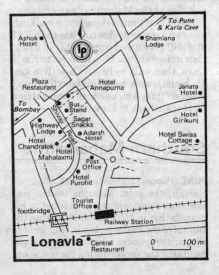

Lonavla

Rs 20/68 in 2nd/1st class. From Pune long-distance express trains as well as passenger shuttles run the 64 km to Lonavla. The expresses take about one to 1½ hours, the passenger trains about two hours. The fare is Rs 12 in 2nd class, Rs 42 in 1st.

Getting Around

In theory there are local buses about a dozen times a day between Lonavla and Karla and to the Rajmachi Fort. Unfortunately the timetable seems to be imaginary; the buses arrive full and leave even fuller, everybody fights like crazy to get on and you never know which buses are going where because there are no signs. You can save a lot of time and frustration by hiring an auto-rickshaw but this works out quite expensive, especially if you are alone. The prices are fairly standard: Lonavla to Karla Rs 30, Rs 50 for the return trip including waiting time, and Rs 100 for Lonavla/Karla/Bhaja/Lonavla including waiting time at both sites. Even if you do hire an auto, there is still quite a walk to both sites from the car parks. In the monsoon the road to Bhaja is closed to vehicles at the Malavli railway crossing.

If you don't mind doing some walking, you can keep costs down to less than Rs 3 and still get around comfortably in a day. Catch the 9 am bus from Lonavla to Karla Cave, then walk to Bhaja Cave (five km, 1½ hours), walk back to Malavli railway station (three km, one hour) and catch a local train back to Lonavla.

Southern Maharashtra

PUNE (Poona) (population 2,000,000)
Shivaji, the great Maratha leader, was raised in Pune, which was granted to his grandfather in 1599. Later it became the capital of the Peshwas, but in 1817 went to the British, under whom it became the capital of the region during the monsoon.

It has a rather more pleasant climate at that time than muggy Bombay.

With the express commuter train, the Deccan Queen, connecting Pune to Bombay in just over three hours, many people who can't afford the sky-high prices of accommodation in Bombay actually commute daily between the two cities. As a result some of the big-city influence has rubbed off on Pune, so fashion shops and fast-food outlets are springing up all the time.

Although Pune has a number of points of interest and can be conveniently visited if you're heading from Bombay to Aurangabad (for Ajanta and Ellora) or to Goa, its major attraction for western visitors is the Shree Rajneesh Ashram (now known as Rajneeshdham). The ashram is so well known that it is even included on the city bus tour, where, in a superb reversal of roles, Indians flock to view westerners.

1	Panchaleshwar Temple
2	Shivajinagar Railway Station
3	Shanwarwarda Palace
4	City Post Office
5	Raja Kellar Museum
6	Parvati Temple
7	Hotel Saras
8	Hotel Avanti
9	City Bus No 4
10	Swargate State & Municipal Bus Terminal
11	Pune Railway Station
12	Wilson Gardens
13	Tourist Office
14	Woodlands Hotel
15	National Hotel
16	GPO
17	Indian Airlines
18	Hotel Salimar
19	Ritz Hotel
20	Food Stalls & Juice Bars
21	Venky's
22	Coffee House
23	Rajneesh Ashram
24	Bund Gardens
25	Marina Hotel
26	Rajneeshdham
27	Gandhi National Memorial

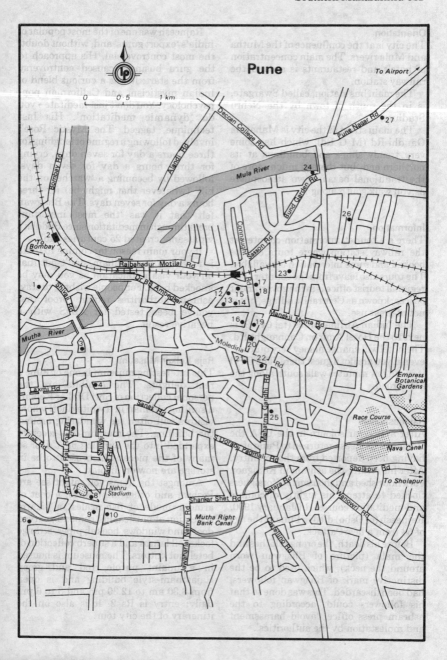

Pune

To Airport

To Bombay

Deccan College Rd

Mula River

Pune Nagar Rd

Bombay Rd

Arandi Rd

Bund Garden Rd

Connaught Wasson Rd

Raibahadur Motilal Rd

Dr Br Ambedkar Rd

Shivaji Rd

Mutha River

Manekji Mehta Rd

Moledina

Rd

Empress
Botanical
Gardens

Laxmi Rd

Saras Rd

Shivaji Rd

Mahatma Gandhi Rd

Race Course

Nava Canal

Tilak Rd

Bhagte Fail Foa Rd

Bajrao Rd

S Dorabji Padmal Rd

Satara Rd

Sholapur Rd

To Sholapur

Nehru Stadium

Shankar Shet Rd

Wanowri Rd

Jawaharlal Nehru Rd

Mutha Right
Bank Canal

Castellino Rd

0   0.5   1 km

Orientation

The city is at the confluence of the Mutha and Mula rivers. The main concentration of hotels and restaurants is around the railway station.

The main bus station, called Swargate, is in the south of town by the Nehru Stadium.

The main street of the city is Mahatma Gandhi Rd (M G Rd), which has some very trendy shops and buildings at its northern end, but there is much more of the traditional bazaar-town atmosphere as you walk south along it.

Information

There's a tourist information counter at the railway station where tours can be booked and some information is available. The tours also leave from the counter. The regional tourist office is in the government offices, known as Central Buildings, but is not of great use.

The Indian Airlines office (tel 64189) is next to the Hotel Amir on Connaught Rd. The hotel will change money very quickly, even if you are not a guest there. The GPO is just a few minutes walk south along the same road.

Rajneeshdham

After a 4½-year sojourn in the USA the Bhagwan Rajneesh returned to Pune after having been deported from that country. After his return, the ashram in Koragaon Park flourished and thousands of foreigners flocked to attend his nightly discourses and meditation courses. In January 1990, Rajneesh (or Osho) died in Pune at the age of 58 from a heart attack.

Before his death, the orange clothes and the mala (picture of Bhagwan worn around the neck), which used to be the distinctive mark of Bhagwan followers, had been discarded. This was done so that his followers could, according to the ashram press office, 'avoid harassment and molestation by the authorities'.

Rajneesh was one of the most popular of India's 'export gurus' and, without doubt, the most controversial. His approach to the guru business caused controversy from the start; it was a curious blend of Indian mysticism and Californian pop-psychology. You don't just meditate – you do 'dynamic meditation'. His last technique, tagged 'The Mystic Rose', involved following a regime of laughing for three hours a day for seven days, crying for three hours a day for seven days, followed by becoming a 'watcher on the hill' (whatever that might be) for three hours a day for seven days. The Bhagwan felt that it was 'the most important breakthrough in meditation since Buddha's vipassana, created 25 centuries ago'.

If your main reason for coming to India is to visit Rajneeshdham, don't put that on your visa application as you may be knocked back. For people wishing to stay, ashram authorities require proof that you've been tested for AIDS with a negative result.

Raja Kelkar Museum

This interesting museum is one of Pune's real delights. The exhibits are the personal collection of Shri Dinkar Kelkar, a smiling old man in a white dhoti whom visitors will often see wandering around the building. The museum has recently expanded into the building next door so many of the pieces which used to be in storage are now on display.

Amongst the items you might see are Peshwa and other miniatures, a coat of armour made of fish scales, a bizarre collection of musical instruments, carved doors and windows, hookah pipes, strange locks, oil lamps and a superb collection of betel-nut cutters. The museum is housed in a quaint purple, red and green Rajasthani-style building and is open from 8.30 am to 12.30 pm and 3 to 6 pm daily; entry is Rs 2. It is also on the itinerary of the city tour.

Shanwarwada Palace

In a section of the town where narrow and winding streets form a maze, stands the imposing, fortress-like Shanwarwada Palace. Built in 1736, the massive walls enclosed the palace of the Peshwa rulers – until it was burnt down in 1828. Today there is a pleasant two-hectare garden inside and little signs proclaiming which rooms used to stand where. The palace is entered through sturdy doors studded with spikes in order to dissuade enemy elephants from leaning too heavily against the entrance! In a nearby street the Peshwa rulers used to execute offenders by having elephants trample them.

Tribal Museum

Just south of the railway line is this excellent museum. It is open daily from 10 am to 5 pm.

Temples & Gardens

The Empress Botanical Gardens have fine tropical trees and a small zoo nearby. The moated Saras Buag Ganesh Temple is in Peshwa Park. The Bund Gardens, on the banks of the river, are a popular place for an evening stroll. The bridge here crosses the river to Yeravda and the Gandhi National Memorial (formerly the Aga Khan's Palace). The Parvati Temple is on the outskirts of the town on a hilltop. There's a good view from the top, where the last Peshwa ruler is said to have watched his troops being defeated by the British at Kirkee.

The rock-cut Panchaleshwar Temple, a small 8th-century temple similar in style to the much grander rock temples of Ellora, is fairly central. The story goes that it was excavated in one night. There's a fine equestrian statue of Shivaji close by.

The 150-metre-long Wellesley Bridge crosses the Mutha River to Sangam, the promontory of land where the Mutha and Mula join. It dates from 1875.

Gandhi National Memorial

Across the river in Yeravda is this fine memorial set in 6½ hectares of gardens. In the past it was the Aga Khan's palace but he donated it to India in 1969.

At one time Mahatma Gandhi and other leaders of the movement for Indian independence were interned here, and today it is maintained as another memorial to Gandhi. Kasturba Gandhi, the Mahatma's wife, died here while interned and her memorial tomb stands in the palace grounds.

Some of the scenes from the movie *Gandhi* were shot in this building. It is open from 9 am to 4.45 pm daily; entry is Rs 2. The easiest way to see it is on the city tour which stops here for half an hour or so.

Tours & Courses

There are morning and afternoon tours daily from the railway station in Pune – they last four hours, cost Rs 20 and cover all the main sights but it is the usual breathless rush. They are convenient, however, as the town's sights are spread out.

Kasturba & Mohandas Gandhi

As well as the Rajneesh ashram, Pune has numerous courses in yoga and ayurvedic medicine.

Places to Stay - bottom end

There is the usual collection of grubby, drab and/or dismal places close to the railway station. Wilson Gardens is a small street behind the National Hotel and is a good place to start looking. The *Central Lodge* (tel 61414) at 13 Wilson Gardens is a filthy pit but if price is your main concern, you won't beat this place at Rs 35 for a double. If you value your health more than your rupees, the *Green Hotel* across the road is a good deal more hygienic and costs Rs 40/70 for singles/doubles. Also in Wilson Gardens, the *Shree Mathura Lodge* (tel 66246) at No 20 has reasonable doubles at Rs 50.

Still in Wilson Gardens, the *Alankar Hotel* is none too friendly but is not bad value at Rs 58/75. There are quite a few other places in the immediate vicinity if you draw a blank at those mentioned so far - but some are of extremely poor quality, quite uninhabitable.

At the top of this range, the friendly *National Hotel* (tel 68054) is in a rambling old mansion directly opposite the railway station. It has recently undergone renovation so the rooms, although spartan, are clean and have a western-style bathroom complete with hot water. Double rooms cost Rs 90; no singles.

Also in this range is the *Ritz Hotel* (tel 62995) near the GPO. The rooms are big, tatty and clean, and the ones at the back don't suffer from the traffic noise. There are no single rooms; doubles are Rs 90. At 18 Wilson Gardens the *Hotel Jinna-Mansion* (tel 667158) is run by a friendly woman. There's hot water in the mornings only, and room charges are Rs 75/100.

If you want to be near Swargate bus station for an early morning departure, the *Hotel Avanti* (tel 445975) is excellent value at Rs 80 for a clean, airy double room with hot water. It's quite a way from the centre, however.

There are good *retiring rooms* at the railway station with rooms from Rs 25. Just along from the Rajneesh ashram, the *Hotel Sundaban* is quite cheap but is usually full of Rajneesh followers.

Places to Stay - middle

If you follow the road in front of the station to the left you'll soon come to Connaught Rd. The *Hotel Gulmohr* (tel 61773) is to the right at No 15. Single rooms cost Rs 88, doubles Rs 145. They also have air-con doubles at Rs 320. Along the lane next to the National Hotel, the huge *Woodlands Hotel* (tel 61111) is in a quiet spot and has a pleasant courtyard. All rooms have telephone and hot water, and cost Rs 150/200 for singles/doubles, Rs 200/225 with air-con.

In the thick of things at 77 M G Rd is the *Marina Hotel* (tel 669141). Single/double rooms at this somewhat noisy hotel go for Rs 100/135.

Places to Stay - top end

The *Hotel Amir* (tel 61841) is very close to the railway station at 15 Connaught Rd. This is one of the best places in Pune, with rooms at Rs 200/260 and Rs 310/350 with air-con. It has the usual mod cons, a vegetarian restaurant and a good (and fairly reasonably priced) snack bar if you're in need of something non-Indian.

Places to Eat

On Station Rd, near the corner of Connaught Rd, *Neelam Restaurant* is pleasant and the *Hotel Madhura* (only a very small sign in English but it's in the big Hotel Metro building) has excellent thalis, good lassi and super-cool drinks. A couple of doors further along there's the *Savera Restaurant*, which is a bit more expensive but is a good place. They also have an air-con dining hall here. Be warned that the 'omelettes' served in these vegetarian places have not had an egg so much as waved near them.

There is a stack of meals places along the road which runs from the railway station towards the tourist office; the *Shri Krishna Palace* is a typical place.

In the evening, stalls are set up along a side street not far from the GPO (see map). They sell excellent fresh juices and some have a variety of hot snacks. The owners are fairly anxious to get you to sit down at their stall and competition is fierce. Juices such as pineapple, orange, apple and pomegranate cost between Rs 4 and Rs 6.

On Moledina Rd near the top end of M G Rd, the *Coffee House* is Pune's trendy hangout and is definitely the place to be seen. *Venky's* is an expensive fast-food place nearby which has good burgers and milkshakes.

The *Hotel Amir* has a more expensive restaurant if you feel like something other than curry.

Getting There & Away

Air There are daily Pune/Bombay flights (Rs 180), and Pune/Delhi flights (Rs 1215). Four times a week there are flights to Bangalore (Rs 790), and twice weekly to Hyderabad (Rs 535) and Ahmedabad (Rs 565).

Bus There are daily regular and air-con buses between Bombay and Pune. The MTDC operates deluxe buses to Mahabaleshwar (Rs 75) and Panaji (Rs 109.50). Reservations can be made at the tourist information counter at the railway station.

To Aurangabad for the Ajanta and Ellora caves there are regular buses from the Shivaji Nagar bus stand. Pune to Aurangabad takes about six hours.

Private deluxe buses run to Bangalore (Rs 180) and Mangalore (Rs 150) from opposite the Nehru Stadium near the Swargate bus station.

Pune has three bus stations: the railway bus stand for points south including Goa, Belgaum, Kolhapur, Mahabaleshwar and Panchgani; the Shivaji Nagar bus stand for points north and north-east – Ahmednagar, Aurangabad, Belgaum,

Lonavla and Nasik; and the Swargate bus stand for Sinhagad.

Train Pune is 192 km from Bombay. Trains take four or five hours and cost Rs 28 in 2nd class, Rs 94 in 1st. The fastest train between the two cities is the Deccan Queen which leaves Pune at 7.15 am and arrives at 10.40 am. In the other direction it leaves Bombay at 5.15 pm. It's necessary to reserve a seat as it is usually solidly booked with commuters, although the booth on the platform at Pune can usually allocate you a seat at the last minute.

If you're heading for Matheran, the only train which stops at Neral is the Sahyadri Express departing at 7.25 am. This connects with the toy train.

Taxi Long-distance share-taxis also connect Pune and Bombay. They leave from the taxi stand in front of the railway station.

Getting Around

Bus The local buses are relatively uncrowded. The main bus which you are likely to use is the No 4, which runs from the railway bus stand to Swargate via the Shivaji Nagar bus station. The Marathi number '4' looks like an Arabic '8' with a gap at the top.

Auto-Rickshaw There are lots of auto-rickshaws. From the railway station to the Swargate bus stand or the Saras Hotel costs about Rs 8, to the Shivaji Nagar bus stand is about Rs 6. As usual, the meters are out of date so you pay by the card.

Bicycle If you are feeling brave, bicycles can be rented all over the place. There's one place just near the entrance to the National Hotel.

AROUND PUNE

Sinhagad

Sinhagad, the 'lion fort', is 25 km south-west of Pune and was the scene of another of Shivaji's daring exploits. It makes an excellent day trip from Pune, which will give you a good chance to get some fresh air into your lungs and clear your head.

The fortress stands near the tele-communications mast at 1270 metres, on top of a steep hill. Although the fort itself is largely ruined, there are a number of old bungalows up here, including one where Gandhi met with Tilak in 1915. Obviously the fort itself dates back much further. In 1670 Shivaji's general, Tanaji Malusre, led a force of men who scaled the steep hillside in the dark and defeated the unprepared forces of Bijapur.

Legends about this dramatic attack relate that the Maratha forces used trained lizards to carry ropes up the hillside! There are monuments at the spot where Tanaji died, and also at the place where he lost his left hand before his death.

The climb up from the end of the road takes a sweaty 1½ to two hours but the views from the top are superb. Although there is a tea stall and cool drinks available at the top, it's a good idea to bring some water and food with you from Pune. There are also lassi-wallahs at various intervals on the trail up but give them a miss unless you feel the need for some exotic germs in your stomach.

Getting There & Away The Pune city bus No 50 takes you to Sinhagad village at the end of the road. The buses run frequently from 5.25 am to 8 pm from the stop opposite the Nehru Stadium and the trip takes about 45 minutes.

MAHABALESHWAR

This popular hill station was the summer capital of the Bombay presidency during the days of the Raj. At an altitude of 1372 metres, Mahabaleshwar has pleasant walks and good lookouts (the sea, 30 km away, is visible on a clear day), and the area has interesting historical connections with Shivaji. The station was founded in 1828 by Sir John Malcolm.

As with most hill stations, Mahaba-leshwar closes right up tight for the monsoon season. During the period from mid-June to mid-September the local buildings are clad with *kulum* grass to stop them being damaged by the torrential rain. In this three-month period Mahabaleshwar receives an unbelievable six *metres* (around 235 inches) of rain!

The local tourist information brochure has this to say:

The weather of Mahabaleshwar is healthy and contains the ideal 20% of oxygen which is often augmented in foggy weather of late summer and early monsoon. When the Mahabaleshwar plateau is covered in mist, it helps to make you more healthy. The water contains a meagre percentage of iron which helps increasing haemoglobin in your blood provided you digest your food by any exercise such as walking, boating, etc. You will be surprised to note that at Mahabaleshwar all old leaves do not become yellow some become red.

Elphinstone Point, Babington Point, Bombay Point, Kate's Point and a number of other lookouts around the wooded plateau offer fine views over the plains below. Arthur's Seat, 12 km from Mahabaleshwar, looks out over a sheer drop of 600 metres to the coastal strip between the ghats and the sea, known as the Konkan. There are pleasant waterfalls such as Chinaman's Waterfall (2½ km), Dhobi Waterfall (three km) and Lingmala Waterfalls (six km).

Most of the walking trails are well signposted, although the moss growing over the signs can make them difficult to read these days. The riding paths have quaint old names such as Lamington Ride, Malcolm Path, Lady Wilingdon Gallop and Duchess Ride.

Venna Lake, within Mahabaleshwar, has boating and fishing facilities. In the village of Old Mahabaleshwar there are three old temples, although they are badly ruined. The Krishnabai, or Panchganga 'five streams', Temple is said to contain five streams, including the Krishna River.

Places to Stay

There are plenty of hotels at Mahabaleshwar but most are closed during the monsoon. The cheaper lodges are all in the town centre in the bazaar area, but even these are not cheap by local standards. If you arrive by bus there are plenty of touts at the station who will find you a room.

The *Hotel Saraswati* on Mari Peth has doubles with hot water for Rs 110 in season. The off-season price of Rs 30/40 for singles/doubles is good value. The *Poonam Hotel* (tel 291) is very central but charges Rs 220 for a double. Other cheaper lodges near the centre include the *Vyankatesh* (tel 397), *Samartha* (tel 416), and the *Ajantha* (tel 272), all on Mosque St.

The *Ripon Hotel* (tel 257) is a 20-minute walk from the bus stand. It is run by a very friendly elderly gentleman and there are fine views over the lake. Rooms cost Rs 50 per person including breakfast (closed during monsoon).

There is a state government-operated *Holiday Camp* (tel 318) about two km from the centre, which has a variety of rooms ranging from Rs 60 for a double in the 'renovated type C Block' up to Rs 295 for a four-bed cottage. Reservations can be made through the Maharashtra Tourism Development Corporation (tel 2024482) at Express Towers, Nariman Point, Bombay.

More expensive hotels include the *Dreamland Hotel* (tel 228), *Regal Hotel* (tel 317), *Dina Hotel* (tel 246) and *Fredrick Hotel* (tel 240). These places generally quote all-inclusive prices in the Rs 120 to Rs 250 per person range.

Places to Eat

The *Shere-e-Punjab* is right in the bazaar and does good non-veg food. During the monsoon this is about the only place open. At the far end of the same road, *Imperial Stores* does takeaway toasted sandwiches, burgers and other small snacks.

Getting There & Away

Pune is the normal departure point for Mahabaleshwar although Satara Road is the closest convenient railway station. Mahabaleshwar is 120 km from Pune via Panchgani, which is 19 km before it.

There are daily buses to Kolhapur (seven hours, Rs 25), Satara (one hour, Rs 8), Pune (three hours, Rs 15) and Panchgani (Rs 2.50). There is also an MTDC state transport deluxe bus to Bombay daily (Rs 72, seven hours).

Getting Around

Mahabaleshwar has a wonderful collection of old Dodge limousines as its taxis. It's possible to hire one to take you around the main viewpoints for Rs 100. To Panchgani it costs Rs 50 for the whole vehicle.

AROUND MAHABALESHWAR
Panchgani

'Five Hills' is just 19 km from Mahabaleshwar and, at 1334 metres, just 38 metres lower. It's also a popular hill station but is overshadowed by better-known Mahabaleshwar. On the way up to Panchgani you pass through Wai, a site featured in the *Mahabharata*.

Places to Stay & Eat As in Mahabaleshwar, there are various hotels. The most expensive is the *Aman Hotel* (tel 211). Cheaper places include the *Prospect Hotel* (tel 263), *Hotel Western* (tel 288) and the *Malas Guest House* (tel 321).

The *Hotel Five Hills* is run by the MTDC and has rooms for Rs 125/150. The attached *Silver Oaks Restaurant* is reasonably priced and has excellent food.

Pratapgarh Fort

Built in 1656, this fort is about 24 km from Mahabaleshwar. It's connected with one of the more notable feats in Shivaji's dramatic life. Outnumbered by the forces of Bijapur, Shivaji arranged to meet with the opposing General Afzal Khan. Neither was supposed to carry any weapon or wear armour; but neither, it turned out, could be trusted.

When they met, Afzal Khan pulled out

a dagger and stabbed Shivaji, but the Maratha leader had worn a shirt of mail under his white robe and concealed in his left hand was a *waghnakh*, a deadly set of 'tiger's claws'. This nasty weapon consisted of a series of rings to which long, sharpened metal claws were attached. Shivaji drove these claws into Khan and disembowelled him. Today a tomb marks where their encounter took place, and a tower was erected over the Khan's head. There is a statue of Shivaji in the ruined fort. There is another Shivaji fort at Raigarh, 80 km from Mahabaleshwar.

SATARA

On the main road from Pune to Belgaum and then Goa, but 15 km off the railway line from Satara Road, this town houses a number of relics of the Maratha leader Shivaji. A building near the new palace contains his sword, the coat he wore when he met Afzal Khan and the *waghnakh* with which he killed him. The Shivaji Maharaj Museum is opposite the bus station.

The Fort of Wasota stands in the south of the town – it has had a colourful and bloody history, including being captured from the Marathas in 1699 by the forces of Aurangzeb, only to be recaptured in 1705 by means of a Brahmin who befriended the fort's defenders, then let in a band of Marathas.

KOLHAPUR

With a population of nearly 300,000, this was once the capital of an important Maratha state. One of Kolhapur's maharajas died in Florence, Italy, and was cremated on the banks of the Arno where his chhatri (cenotaph) now stands. The last maharaja, Major General His Highness Shahaji Chhatrapati II, died in 1983.

There's little of interest in the town itself, although the palace is worth a visit if you're passing through.

Maharaja's Palace

The old maharaja's palace has been turned into the Shahaji Chhatrapati Museum and it contains a weird and wonderful array of the maharaja's old possessions including his clothes, old hunt photos and the memorial silver spade used by the maharaja to 'turn the first sod of the Kolhapur State Railway' in 1888. There's even his Prince Shiraji Pig-Sticking Trophy. The gun and sword collection is comprehensive, and the ashtrays and coffee tables made from tigers' and elephants' feet, not to mention the lamp stands from ostrich legs, are unbelievably gross.

Only a few rooms are open to the public and there are officious men employed to make sure you don't wander off. The palace is a few km to the north of town. Rent a bicycle, or take an auto-rickshaw (Rs 3), but make sure you ask for the 'new palace' or you'll end up at the Shalini Palace Ashok Hotel by the lake.

Places to Stay

The main hotel and restaurant area is around the square opposite the bus station, five minutes walk from the centre of town and the railway station. The cheapest place is the *Hotel Anand Malhar* (tel 25091) which charges Rs 30 for a single without bath, Rs 50 for a double with bath. There's also a good restaurant. The *Hotel Sahyadri* (tel 24581) is of a similar standard but gets a bit noisy.

The *Hotel Maharaja* (tel 29025) is a bit better at Rs 50/70, while the *Hotel Girish* has good clean rooms for Rs 73/84. All the rooms in this friendly place have TV, phone and piped music (mercifully there's a switch to kill it).

At the top of the scale, the *Shalini Palace Ashok* (tel 20401) is in a grand old palace by the lake, five km from the bus or railway station. Simple rooms cost Rs 165/220, or with air-con Rs 275/330.

There are *retiring rooms* at the railway station, and these cost Rs 25/35.

Places to Eat

The restaurants are also concentrated around the square. The *Subraya Restaurant* has north Indian veg and non-veg dishes, and good thalis for Rs 9.

In the evening dozens of snack stalls are set up in the street to the right of the bus station (as you leave it). They whip up great omelettes and other goodies – a very economical and interesting place to eat.

Getting There & Away

Bus The bus station is not too chaotic but, as usual, there is nothing written in English. For buses originating in Kolhapur it is possible to book 24 hours in advance between 8 am and 12 noon and 2 and 4.30 pm.

There are daily departures for Satara, Bijapur, Mahabaleshwar, Pune, Ratnagiri and Belgaum.

Train The railway station is close to the centre of town. The broad-gauge line connects Kolhapur with Miraj, from where there are daily trains to Pune, Bombay, Madras and Margao (Goa).

The daily Koyna Express goes all the way to Bombay, taking 13 hours.

OTHER PLACES IN THE SOUTH

Ratnagiri

Ratnagiri, on the coast 135 km west of Kolhapur, was the place where Thibaw, the last Burmese king, was interned by the British from 1886 until his death in 1916.

Panhala & Pawangarh

These are interesting hill stations. At Panhala there is a fort with a long and convoluted history; it was originally the stronghold of Raja Bhoj II in 1192. The Pawala Caves are nearby, plus a couple of Buddhist cave temples.

Sholapur

If you have an hour or two to kill in Sholapur (changing buses or trains on your way to or from Bijapur), check out the superbly decorated municipal offices. The *Hotel Rajdhani* near the railway station is a reasonable place to stay.

Northern Maharashtra

AHMEDNAGAR (population 155,000)

On the road between Pune (82 km away) and Aurangabad, Ahmednagar has had a colourful history. It was here that the Emperor Aurangzeb died in 1707, aged 97. The town's imposing fort was erected in 1550, and at one time Nehru was imprisoned here by the British.

Places to Stay

There are various hotels, including the *Ashoka Tourist Hotel* (tel 3607) and the *Hotel Sablok*. The Ashoka is at King's Gate, about a km from the centre, and has rooms with and without air-con.

NASIK (population 240,000)

This interesting little town with its picturesque bathing ghats makes a good stopover on the way from Bombay to Aurangabad. The town is actually about eight km north-west of the station, which is 187 km from Bombay.

Nasik stands on the Godavari River, one of the holiest rivers of the Deccan. Like Ujjain, this is the one of the sites for the triennial Kumbh Mela which comes here every 12 years. The riverbanks are lined with steps above which stand temples and shrines. Although there are no particularly notable temples in Nasik, the Sundar Narayan Temple, to the west of the city, is worth seeing.

Other points of interest in Nasik include the Sita Gupha Cave from which Sita, the deity of agriculture and wife of Rama, was supposed to have been carried off to the island of Lanka by the evil king Ravana, according to the *Ramayana*. Near the cave, in its grove of large banyan trees, is the fine house of the Panchavati family. Also nearby is the Temple of Kala Rama, or 'black Rama', in a 96-arched enclosure. The Kapaleswar Temple upstream is said to be the oldest in the town.

Kumbh Mela

Aeons ago the gods and demons, who were constantly at odds, fought a great battle for a *kumbh* or pitcher, drinking the contents of which would ensure immortality. They had combined forces to raise the pitcher from the bottom of the ocean, but once it was safely in their hands Vishnu grabbed it and ran. After a struggle lasting 12 days the gods eventually defeated the demons and drank the nectar – it's a favourite scene in illustrations of Hindu mythology. During the fight for the pitcher's possession four drops of nectar spilt on the earth, at Allahabad, Hardwar, Nasik and Ujjain. The mela is held every three years, rotating among the four cities. Thus each has its own mela every 12 years (for a god's day is a human's year).

Places to Stay

At the *Hotel Siddhartha* (tel 73228) on the Nasik to Pune road, singles/doubles are Rs 75/90, more with air-con.

On Trimbak Rd, two km from the centre, the *Green View Hotel* (tel 72231/4) is more expensive at Rs 90/125, more with air-con. The *Hotel Samrat* (tel 77211) near the central bus station is similarly priced. There are many other places to stay in Nasik, including a *Tourist Bungalow*.

At Dhule, on the highway between Nasik and Indore, the *Hotel Dina* on Sakri Rd has rooms at Rs 75/100.

AROUND NASIK
Pandu Lena

About eight km south-west of Nasik, close to the Bombay road, are these 21 Hinayana Buddhist caves. They date from around the 1st century BC to the 2nd AD. The most interesting caves are 3, 10 and 18. Cave 3 is a large vihara with some interesting sculptures. Cave 10 is also a vihara and almost identical in design to

cave 3, although it is much older and finer in its details. It is thought to be nearly as old as the Karla Cave. Cave 18 is a chaitya cave thought to date from the same time as the Karla Cave. It too is well-sculpted and its elaborate facade is particularly noteworthy. Cave 20 is another large vihara. The other caves are not of great interest.

Trimbak

This is the source of the Godavari River, 33 km from Nasik. From this source high on a steep hill, the river dribbles into a bathing tank whose waters are reputed to wash away sins. From this tiny start the Godavari eventually flows down to the Bay of Bengal, clear across India.

AURANGABAD (population 210,000)

It's easy to think of Aurangabad simply as a place to stay when visiting the cave temples of Ajanta and Ellora. In fact Aurangabad has a number of attractions and could easily stand on its own were it not so overshadowed by the famous caves. The city is named after Aurangzeb, but earlier in its history it was known as Khadke.

Information & Orientation

The railway station, tourist office and a variety of cheaper hotels and restaurants are clustered in the south of the town. There's a fairly open gap from here to the more crowded and older part of the town to the north, where you'll also find the bus station. In comparison to other Deccan towns Aurangabad is remarkably un-crowded and quiet except for the occasional political rally.

The more expensive hotels are between the old town and the railway station or on the road out to the airport. There is a not particularly useful state tourist office (tel 4713) in the MTDC Holiday Resort, Station Rd (East), while on Station Rd (West) is a more useful Government of India tourist office (tel 4817). Even so, it's the usual 'sit around, do nothing and rely on what out-of-date publications they

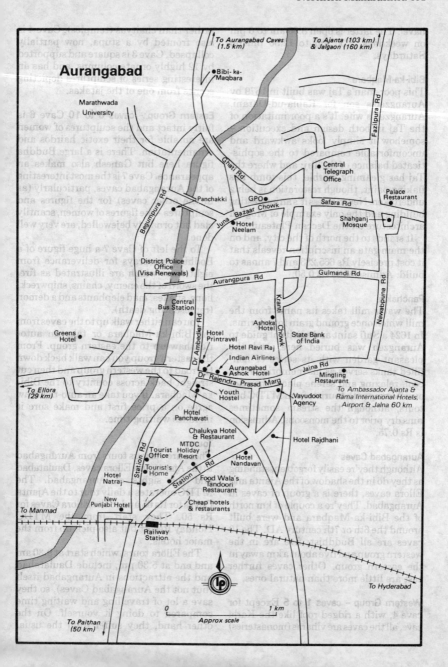

Aurangabad

To Aurangabad Caves (1.5 km)

To Ajanta (103 km) & Jalgaon (160 km)

Bibi- ka-Maqbara

Marathwada University

Fazilpura Rd

Ghati Rd

Central Telegraph Office

Palace Restaurant

Panchakki

GPO

Safara Rd

Shahganj Mosque

Begumpura Rd

Juna Bazaar Chowk

Hotel Neelam

Gulmandi Rd

District Police Office (Visa Renewals)

Aurangpura Rd

Nawabpuna Rd

Central Bus Station

Dr Ambedkar Rd

Hotel Printravel

Ashoka Hotel

State Bank of India

Kranti Chowk

Greens Hotel

Hotel Ravi Raj

Indian Airlines

Aurangabad Ashok Hotel

Dr Rajendra Prasad Marg

Jaina Rd

Mingling Restaurant

Youth Hostel

Vayudoot Agency

To Ambassador Ajanta & Rama International Hotels, Airport & Jalna 60 km

To Ellora (29 km)

Hotel Panchavati

Chalukya Hotel & Restaurant

Hotel Rajdhani

Tourist Office

MTDC Holiday Resort

Station Rd

Tourist's Home

Hotel Nandavan

Hotel Natraj

Station Rd

Food Wala's Tandoori Restaurant

New Punjabi Hotel

Cheap hotels & restaurants

To Manmad

Railway Station

To Hyderabad

To Paithan (50 km)

1 km

Approx scale

have'. The latter is open 8.30 am to 6 pm on weekdays, 8.30 am to 12.30 pm on Saturdays.

Bibi-ka-Maqbara

This poor-man's Taj was built in 1679 by Aurangzeb's son for Rabia-ud-Darani, Aurangzeb's wife. It's a poor imitation of the Taj in both design and execution – somehow it simply looks awkward and uncomfortable compared to the sophisticated balance of the Taj; and where the Taj has gleaming marble, this tomb has flaking paint, though restoration is being undertaken. Nevertheless it's an interesting building and the only example of Moghul architecture on the Deccan Plateau.

It stands to the north of the city, and on the main gate an inscription reveals that it cost precisely Rs 665,283 and 7 annas to build. Admission is Rs 0.50.

Panchakki

The water mill takes its name from the mill which once ground grain for pilgrims. In 1624 a Sufi saint and spiritual guide to Aurangzeb was buried here, and the pleasant garden with its series of fish-filled tanks serves as his memorial. It's a cool, relaxing and serene place when not overflowing with tourists from MTDC bus tours, although the stream sometimes runs dry prior to the monsoons. Admission is Rs 0.75.

Aurangabad Caves

Although they're easily forgotten, standing as they do in the shadow of the Ajanta and Ellora caves, there is a group of caves in Aurangabad. They're a couple of km north of the Bibi-ka-Maqbara and were built around the 6th or 7th century AD. The 10 caves are all Buddhist; five are in the western group and five about a km away in the eastern group. Other caves further east are little more than natural ones.

Western Group – caves 1 to 5 Except for cave 4, with a ridged roof like the Karla cave, all the caves are viharas (monasteries) rather than chaityas (temples). Cave 4 is also fronted by a stupa, now partially collapsed. Cave 3 is square and supported by 12 highly ornate columns, and has an interesting series of sculptures depicting scenes from one of the jatakas.

Eastern Group – caves 6 to 10 Cave 6 is fairly intact and the sculptures of women are notable for their exotic hairdos and ornamentation. There is a large Buddha figure here but Ganesh also makes an appearance. Cave 7 is the most interesting of the Aurangabad caves, particularly (as in the other caves) for the figures and sculptures – the figures of women, scantily clad but ornately bejewelled, are very well done.

To the left of Cave 7 a huge figure of a Bodhisattva prays for deliverance from eight fears which are illustrated as fire, the sword of the enemy, chains, shipwreck, lions, snakes, mad elephants and a demon (representing death).

You can either walk up to the caves from the Bibi-ka-Maqbara or take an auto-rickshaw up to the eastern group. From the eastern group you can walk back down the road to the western group and then cut straight back across country to the Bibi-ka-Maqbara. If you take an auto-rickshaw agree on a price first and make sure it includes waiting time.

Tours

There are various tours from Aurangabad to the Ajanta and Ellora caves, Daulatabad and the sights of Aurangabad. The MTDC operates a daily tour to the Ajanta Caves for Rs 65 and to the Ellora Caves for Rs 50. They start from the MTDC Holiday Resort but also pick up from the major hotels.

The Ellora tours, which start at 9.30 am and end at 5.30 pm, include Daulatabad and the attractions in Aurangabad itself (but not the Aurangabad Caves), so they save a lot of travelling and waiting time compared to doing it yourself. On the other hand, they suffer from the usual

Aurangabad Caves - Western group

attempt to pack in too many places (some of which aren't worth seeing) thus leaving you with not enough time at the Daulatabad Fort and Ellora. Likewise, because the Ajanta Caves are quite a long way from Aurangabad, these tours don't really give you enough time to fully explore them, so many travellers prefer to take local transport and stay overnight.

The state transport buses also run daily tours to the same places but only in season. They start from the railway station and are considerably cheaper than the MTDC tours. The Ellora tour, for instance, costs Rs 31.

Places to Stay - bottom end

Most of Aurangabad's cheaper hotels are close to the railway station and there are infinite variations on the Punjab, Punjabi, New Punjabi, Shere-Punjab name theme. The notable exception outside this area is the excellent *Youth Hostel* midway

between the railway station and the main part of town. There are 40 dorm beds at Rs 10 each (Rs 6 for YHA members) and the place is spotlessly clean. It has hot and cold water, and breakfast and evening meals are available. There's also one family room for three people. Check-in times are 7 to 11 am and 4 to 8 pm; check-out time is 9 am. The people who run this place are very friendly but it's sometimes closed when there are water shortages.

A hundred metres or so from the station is the MTDC *Holiday Resort*, where you'll also find the state government tourist office. Doubles with bathroom cost Rs 80 to Rs 125, and there are similar rooms with three beds (Rs 75) and four beds (Rs 100) but without bathroom. Aircon rooms with bathroom cost Rs 225. Mosquito nets are provided. The Holiday Resort staff are a long way short of helpful – check-out time is 8 am and they positively will not look after baggage for you, even if you are going on one of their tours.

Between the Holiday Resort and the station there is a string of very cheap and basic places such as the *Ashoka Lodging*, *Ambika Lodge*, *New Punjabi Hotel* and the *Ashoka Tourist Hotel*. They're all of a similar standard and there's not much to choose between them. Expect to pay around Rs 40 for a room.

Better value are the two hotels on the west arm of Station Rd. The first is the *Hotel Natraj* which is a typical Indian boarding house with singles/doubles at Rs 40/50 with bathroom. The hotel has a vegetarian restaurant. The other is the *Tourist's Home* which is basic but very clean and pleasant. Singles/doubles with common bath cost Rs 30 and doubles with bath cost Rs 50. Bucket hot water is available for Rs 1.

Over towards the old part of town, between the bus station and post office, is the *Hotel Neelam* (tel 4561/2) which is a newer looking building with rooms at Rs 50 to Rs 60 with bath.

At the top of this range is the *Hotel*

Printravel (tel 4707, 6407) which has singles/doubles for Rs 55/100 all with attached bath and hot water. Check-out time is 12 noon. Similar is the *Hotel Panchavati*, next to the Youth Hostel, which has singles/doubles at Rs 50/70 with attached bath and hot water in the mornings. It's basic but the building is relatively new and the staff are friendly. Check-out time is 24 hours after arrival, and the hotel has a restaurant and bar.

Places to Stay - middle

The *Hotel Ravi Raj* (tel 3637, 3627), Dr Rajendra Prasad Marg close to the junction with Station Rd, is a convenient place to stay, but it's definitely seen better days. Singles/doubles cost Rs 160/220 and Rs 250/310 with air-con. There are also air-con suites for Rs 375 and Rs 575. All the rooms have bathrooms. The hotel has two restaurants, one indoor and the other outdoor, and there's a bar. Checkout time is 12 noon.

Better value though less convenient is the *Hotel Rajdhani* (tel 6103), on Station Rd, which is a new building and very clean. Rooms cost Rs 175/225, and Rs 225/275 with air-con. All rooms have a bath and hot water.

Similar but older is the *Hotel Nandanvan* (tel 3311), also on Station Rd, about one km from the railway station. Rooms cost Rs 80/115 for singles/doubles, and Rs 190 for air-con doubles. All rooms have a bath with hot water. The hotel has a restaurant and bar, travellers' cheques can be cashed and there's a same-day laundry service. Checkout time is 12 noon.

At the top end of this range is the *Hotel Amarpreet* (tel 4615, 4306), Nehru Marg, which is centrally air-conditioned, tastefully decorated and very well maintained. Singles/doubles cost Rs 200/250 and Rs 250/325 with air-con. All rooms have a bath and constant hot water. There's a laundry service, two restaurants, coffee/snack bar, and a bar. MTDC tour buses call here.

Places to Stay - top end

There are two 'international-standard' hotels almost next to each other a couple of km out of town towards the airport. The *Ambassador Ajanta* (tel 82211/5), Chikalthana, is a beautiful hotel with air-conditioning, swimming pool, sports facilities, currency exchange, a restaurant offering Continental, Indian and Chinese dishes, and a bar. Singles/doubles cost Rs 600/750, plus they have suites for Rs 800 to Rs 2000. The *Rama International* (tel 8455/9) is of a similar standard and price.

The *Aurangabad Ashok* (tel 4520/9), Dr Rajendra Prasad Marg, is beside the Indian Airlines office and costs Rs 395/595 for singles/doubles. All the rooms are centrally air-conditioned with a bath and constant hot water, plus there are all the usual facilities including a swimming pool, restaurant, bar and currency exchange. It's a very pleasant hotel.

Places to Eat

There's a string of rock-bottom restaurants along Station Rd (East) near the railway station and this is where most budget travellers come to eat. None of these places stand out as deserving particular mention but the food is usually good and cheap. The *Prem Popular Punjab* must set a record for the number of switches on the panel above the cashier.

More expensive but excellent vegetarian food can be found at *Food Wala's Bhoj Restaurant* in front of the Printravel Hotel at the junction of Dr Rajendra Prasad Rd and Station Rd. This is a very popular place to eat and the food is very tasty. You can eat as much as you like if you order a thali (Rs 18). They also have south Indian specialities including masala dosa (Rs 5) – excellent! This restaurant has a branch on Station Rd (East) beyond the MTDC Holiday Resort called *Food Wala's Tandoori Restaurant & Bar* which offers what its name implies. Meals here are definitely more expensive, as you might expect, but the restaurant is good for a splurge.

Another very good place to splurge at is the *Chalukya Hotel & Restaurant/Bar* a little further up the road from the tandoori restaurant.

Some travellers have recommended the *Mingling Restaurant* opposite the Hotel Amarpreet as having good, reasonably priced Chinese food though it's quite a way from the centre of town. Others have recommended the *Palace Restaurant* in the centre of the old town at Shahganj opposite the Shahganj Mosque. It's a typical Muslim restaurant with so-so biryanis and other dishes.

For a major splurge, go for lunch or dinner to one of the three top-end hotels. The *Ambassador Ajanta* is particularly recommended but it is expensive.

Getting There & Away

The cave groups at Ajanta and Ellora are off the railway lines and are usually approached from either Aurangabad (Ellora 30 km, Ajanta 106 km) or from Jalgaon (Ajanta 59 km). Jalgaon is on the main broad-gauge line from Bombay to Allahabad, but Aurangabad is off the main line and getting there requires a change to metre-gauge line at Manmad. On the other hand Aurangabad is the access point from Pune (by road) or Hyderabad (by rail). Aurangabad also has an airport served by Indian Airlines and Vayudoot.

Air The Indian Airlines office is on Dr Rajendra Prasad Marg next to the Aurangabad Ashok. The Vayudoot agent is Welworth Travels, Kranti Chowk, right on the roundabout.

Indian Airlines flies Bombay/Aurangabad/Udaipur/Jodhpur/Jaipur/Delhi and vice-versa daily. It's a popular tourist route and the flights can be booked up several days in advance.

Vayudoot also fly Aurangabad/Bombay (Rs 330) but their flights, too, are usually booked up several days in advance.

Vayudoot also connects Aurangabad and Pune (Rs 350).

Bus There are bus connections between Aurangabad and Pune, Nasik, Indore and Bombay. Several luxury buses are available to Bombay. TPH Tours & Travels at the Hotel Rajdhani, Station Rd, go daily to Bombay at 9 pm. The journey takes 10 hours and costs Rs 120. Likewise, the Government of India tourist office has two daily buses which take 10½ hours. The ordinary bus costs Rs 95 and the luxury bus Rs 120. You can also book these buses at Food Wala's Bhoj Restaurant.

Train Jalgaon is 420 km from Bombay; the trip takes about eight hours by rail and costs Rs 51 in 2nd class, Rs 178 in 1st. From Jalgaon there are frequent buses to Ajanta and Aurangabad (the bus station in Jalgaon is a long way from the railway station so you'll need to take an auto-rickshaw or tonga). By rail direct to Aurangabad you change trains at Manmad, 261 km from Bombay, for the 113-km trip to Aurangabad. Travelling time is about eight hours, plus the time changing trains. The cost is Rs 34 in 2nd class, Rs 123 in 1st. From Hyderabad (Secunderabad), which is on the same metre-gauge line as Manmad, the distance is 517 km. The journey takes 12 hours and costs Rs 57 in 2nd class, Rs 208 in 1st.

Getting Around

Airport Transport An auto-rickshaw to or from the airport costs Rs 20. Almost all the Aurangabad auto-rickshaw wallahs use their meters so you shouldn't have any problems about being charged the correct price.

To Ellora & Ajanta Caves Aurangabad is a good base for visiting either the Ellora or Ajanta caves. Unless you're planning on doing a day-tour from Aurangabad to Ajanta, you'll probably find it more convenient to actually stay at Ajanta. Bus fares from Aurangabad are Rs 5 to Ellora (every half hour), Rs 13.30 to Ajanta (about every hour, takes three hours), Rs 20.30 to Jalgaon (hourly, takes 4½ hours). From Ajanta to Jalgaon costs Rs 7 (takes 1½ hours).

Most of the Ajanta accommodation is actually at Fardapur, about five km from the caves – Rs 0.75 by the reasonably frequent buses. Not all the Aurangabad to Jalgaon buses go up to the end of the turn-off where the Ajanta Caves are situated, so if it's the caves you specifically want and not Fardapur, make sure you get on the right bus. On the other hand, it's not that far to walk from the turn-off on the main road.

AURANGABAD TO ELLORA
Daulatabad
Between Aurangabad and the Ellora Caves is the magnificent hilltop fortress of Daulatabad. The fort is surrounded by five km of sturdy walls, while the central bastion tops a 200-metre-high hill. In the 14th century the somewhat unbalanced Mohammed Tughlaq, Sultan of Delhi, conceived the crazy plan of not only building himself a new capital here, but marching the entire population of Delhi 1100 km south to populate it. His unhappy subjects proceeded to drop dead like flies on this forced march, and 17 years later he turned round and marched them all back to Delhi. The fort remained.

It's worth making the climb to the top for the superb views over the surrounding country. Along the way you'll pass through a complicated and ingenious series of defences, including multiple doorways to prevent elephant charges, and spike-studded doors just in case. A magnificent tower of victory, the Chand Minar, built in 1435, soars 60 metres high. The Qutab Minar in Delhi, five metres higher, is the only loftier victory tower in India. On the other side of the entrance path is a mosque built from the remains of a Jain temple.

Higher up is the blue-tiled Chini Mahal Palace where the last king of Golconda was imprisoned for 13 years until his death. Finally you climb the central fort to a huge six-metre cannon, cast from five different metals and engraved with Aurangzeb's name. The final ascent to the top goes through a pitch-black, spiralling tunnel down which the fort's defenders could hurl burning coals at any invaders. Of course, your guide may tell you, the fort was once successfully conquered despite these elaborate precautions – by the simple expedient of bribing the guard at the gate.

If you take one of the MTDC bus tours to Daulatabad and Ellora you won't have time to climb to the summit.

The hill on which the fort stands was originally known as Devagiri, the 'hill of the gods', but Mohammed Tughlaq renamed it Daulatabad, the 'city of fortune'.

Rauza
Also known as Khuldabad, the 'heavenly abode', this walled town is only three km from Ellora. It is the Karbala or holy shrine of Deccan Muslims. A number of historical figures are buried here, including Aurangzeb, the last great Moghul emperor. Aurangzeb built the crenellated wall around the town, which was once an important centre although today it is little more than a sleepy village.

The emperor's final resting place is a simple affair of bare earth in a courtyard of the Alamgir Dargah at the centre of the town. Aurangzeb's pious austerity extended even to his own tomb, for he stipulated that his mausoleum should be paid for with money he earned himself by copying out the Koran. Within the building there is also supposed to be a robe worn by the Prophet Mohammed; it is only shown to the faithful once each year. Another shrine across the road from the Alamgir Dargah is said to contain hairs of the Prophet's beard and lumps of silver from a tree of solid silver, which miraculously grew at this site after a saint's death.

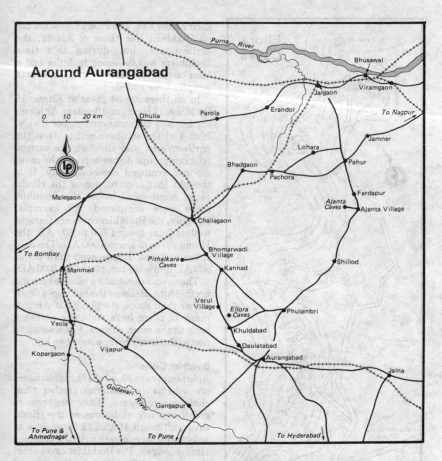

Around Aurangabad

0   10   20 km

Purna River

Bhusawal
Viramgaon

Jalgaon

To Nagpur

Dhulia   Parola   Erandol

Jamner

Lohara
Pahur

Bhadgaon   Pachora

Fardapur

Malegaon   Ajanta
Caves   Ajanta Village

Chalisgaon

Bhomarwadi
Village

To Bombay

Shillod

Pithalkara
Caves

Manmad   Kannad

Verul
Village

Ellora
Caves   Phulambri

Yeola

Khuldabad

Daulatabad

Kopargaon   Vijapur   Aurangabad

Jalna

Godavari River

Gangapur

To Pune &
Ahmednagar   To Pune   To Hyderabad

Guidebooks

At many sites in India you can buy excellent, locally produced guidebooks very cheaply which will help give you a deeper appreciation of what you are seeing. The caves of Ajanta and Ellora are no exception, and both *Aurangabad, Daulatabad, Ellora & Ajanta* by Professor Dr S Siddiqui and *Ajanta, Ellora & Aurangabad Caves – an Appreciation* by T V Pathy are worthwhile investments. The former has good black and white pictures, which help in the identification of the actual sculpture or painting being described. The latter guide has more examples of the delightful way Indians have with English. The author describes a

statue as being a 'semi-nude dryad with a slender waist, pouting lips and abundant mammalian equipment. . .' What a fine way of saying she had big breasts.

ELLORA CAVES

The caves of Ellora are about 30 km from Aurangabad. Whereas the Ajanta Caves are noted for their paintings, here it's the sculpture that is remarkable. Chronologically the Ellora Caves start where the Ajanta Caves finish – it's thought that the builders of Ajanta moved to Ellora when they suddenly ceased construction at

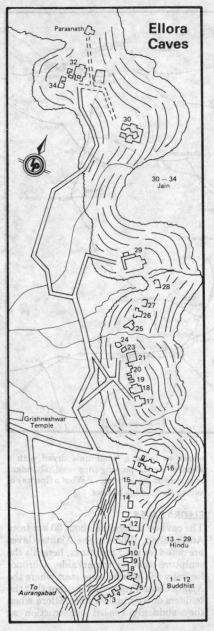

Ellora Caves

their earlier site. The Ellora Caves are not all Buddhist like those of Ajanta; the earliest are, but during this time Buddhism was declining in India and a later series of Hindu and Jain cave temples were added.

In all there are 34 caves at Ellora: 12 Buddhist, 17 Hindu and five Jain. Although the temples are numbered consecutively, from 1 at the southern end to 34 at the northern end, and although the various religious groups do not overlap, the caves are not arranged chronologically. It is thought that construction of the Hindu caves commenced before the Buddhist caves were completed, for example. Roughly, the Buddhist caves are thought to date from around 600 to 800 AD, the Hindu caves to around 900 AD. The Jain caves were not commenced until about 800 AD and were completed by 1000 AD.

The caves are cut into a hillside running north-south. Because the hill slopes down rather than drops steeply, as at Ajanta, many of them have elaborate entrance halls to the main shrines. From south to north, the caves cover about two km.

Buddhist Caves

Apart from cave 10, all the Buddhist caves are viharas (monasteries) rather than chaityas (temples). They are not as architecturally ambitious as the Hindu caves, although 11 and 12 show signs of attempting to compete with the complex Hindu designs. The Buddhist caves chart the period of Buddhism's division and decline in India.

Caves 1 to 4 These are all vihara caves. Cave 2, with its ornate pillars and figures of the Buddha, is quite interesting. Caves 3 and 4 are earlier, simpler and less well preserved.

Cave 5 This is the biggest vihara cave. The rows of stone benches indicate that it may have been an assembly or dining hall.

Caves 6 to 8 In cave 6 there is a large seated

Buddha in the shrine room, but this ornate vihara also has a standing figure thought to be either the Hindu goddess of learning, Saraswati, or her Buddhist equivalent, Mahamayuri. Caves 7 and 8 are not so interesting.

Cave 10 The Viswakarma or 'carpenter's cave' is the only chaitya cave in the Buddhist group. It takes its name from the ribs carved into the roof, in imitation of wooden beams. The temple is entered by steps to a courtyard, followed by further steps to the main temple. A finely carved horseshoe window lets light in and a huge seated-Buddha figure fronts the nine-metre-high stupa.

Cave 11 The Do Thal 'two-storey' Cave is also entered by a courtyard. Curiously, it actually has three storeys but the third was not discovered until 1876. Construction of the middle floor was never completed.

Cave 12 The Teen Thal 'three-storey' Cave also has three storeys and is entered through a courtyard. It contains a very large seated Buddha and a number of other figures. The walls are carved with relief pictures, as in the Hindu caves.

Hindu Caves

The Hindu caves are the most dramatic and impressive of the Ellora cave temples. In size, design and energy they are in a totally different league from the Buddhist or Jain caves. If calm contemplation describes the Buddhist caves, then dynamic energy is the description for the Hindu caves. The sheer size of the Kailasa Temple (cave 16) is overwhelming. It covers twice the area of the Parthenon in Athens and is 1½ times as high. Remember that this whole gigantic structure was cut out of solid rock! It has been estimated that carving out the Kailasa entailed removing 200,000 tons of rock! It is, without doubt, one of the wonders of the world!

All these temples were cut from the top

down, so that it was never necessary to use any scaffolding – their builders started with the roof and moved down to the floor. It's worth contemplating the skill and planning that must have gone into such a process – there was no way of adding a panel or a pillar if things didn't work out as expected.

Cave 14 The first Hindu cave, cave 13, is not impressive, but cave 14, the Rava Kakhai, sets the scene for the others. Like them it is dedicated to Shiva, who appears in many of the carvings. You can see Shiva dancing the tandava, a victory dance over the demon Mahisa, or playing chess with his wife Parvati, or defeating the buffalo demon. Parvati also appears in the form of Durga. Vishnu makes several appearances too, including one as Varaha, his boar incarnation. The seven 'mother goddesses' can also be seen, and Ravana makes yet another attempt to shake Kailasa.

Cave 15 The Das Avatara Cave is one of the finest at Ellora. The two-storey temple is reached by a long flight of steps. Inside there is a modern image of Shiva's vehicle, the bull Nandi. Many of the familiar scenes involving Shiva can be found again here, but you can also see Vishnu resting on a five-hooded serpent or rescuing an elephant from a crocodile. Vishnu also appears as the man-lion, Narsimha, while Shiva emerges from his symbolic lingam and in another panel he marries Parvati.

Cave 16 The mighty Kailasa Temple is the central attraction at Ellora. Here Indian rock-cut temple architecture reaches its peak. Kailasa is, of course, Shiva's Himalayan home, and the Kailasa Temple is a representation of that mountain. The temple consists of a huge courtyard, 81 metres long by 47 metres wide and 33 metres high at the back. In the centre, the main temple rises up and is connected to the outer enclosure by a bridge. Around the enclosure are galleries, while towards the front are two large stone elephants with two massive stone 'flagstaffs' flanking the Nandi pavilion, which faces the main shrine.

As in the previous two caves, there is a variety of dramatic and finely carved panels, the most impressive being the image of Ravana shaking Kailasa. In the *Ramayana* the demon king Ravana flaunted his strength by lifting up Shiva's mountain home. Unimpressed, Lord Shiva simply put his foot down on the top and pressed the mountain and the upstart Ravana back into place. Vishnu also appears along one gallery as Narsimha once again; in this legend he defeats a demon, who could not be killed by man or beast, by the simple expedient of becoming a man-lion, neither man nor beast.

Other Caves The other Hindu caves pall beside the majesty of the Kailasa, but several of them are worth at least some study. Cave 21, known as the Ramesvara, has a number of interesting interpretations of scenes also depicted in the earlier temples. Shiva once again marries Parvati and plays dice with her, and the goddesses Ganga and Yamuna once again appear. The figure of Ganga, standing on her crocodile or *makara*, is particularly notable.

The very large cave 29, the Dumar Lena, is similar in design to the Elephanta Cave at Bombay. It is thought to be a transitional model between the simpler hollowed-out caves and the fully developed temples exemplified by the Kailasa.

Jain Caves
The Jain caves mark the final phase of Ellora. They do not have the drama and high-voltage energy of the best Hindu temples nor are they as ambitious in size, but they balance this with their exceptionally detailed work. There are only five Jain temples, several hundred metres north of the last Hindu temple.

Cave 30 The Chota Kailasa or 'little

Kailasa' is a poor imitation of the great Kailasa Temple and was never completed. It stands by itself some distance from the other Jain temples, which are clustered closely together.

Cave 32 The Indra Sabha or 'Assembly Hall of Indra' is the finest of the Jain temples. The ground-floor plan is similar to that of the Kailasa, but the upstairs area, reached by a stairway, is as ornate and richly decorated as downstairs is plain. There are images of the Jain tirthankars Parasnath and Gomatesvara, the latter surrounded by vegetation and wildlife. Inside the shrine is a seated figure of Mahavira, the 24th and last tirthankar, and founder of the Jain religion. Traces of paintings can still be seen on the roof of the temple.

Other Caves Cave 31 is really an extension of 32. Cave 33, the Jagannath Sabha, is similar in plan to 32 and has some particularly well-preserved sculptures. The final temple, the small cave 34, also has interesting sculptures. On the hilltop over the Jain temples a five-metre-high image of Parasnath looks down on Ellora. An enclosure was built around it a couple of hundred years ago.

Grishneshwar
Close to the Ellora Caves in the village of Verul, this 18th-century Shiva temple has one of the 12 jyotorlingas in India, so it's an important place of pilgrimage for Hindus.

Places to Stay
Although most people stay in Aurangabad, some accommodation is available at the caves. The relatively expensive *Hotel Kailasa* very close to the caves has rooms from Rs 60, all with bath. A restaurant attached to the hotel is cheaper than the other government restaurant here, which is intended for tour groups.

AJANTA CAVES
The caves of Ajanta predate those of

Ellora, so if you want to see the caves in chronological order you should visit these first. Although the Ellora Caves are easily visited using Aurangabad as a base, it's much easier to stay near the Ajanta Caves rather than make a day trip to them. Unlike the Ellora Caves, which are Buddhist, Hindu and Jain, the Ajanta Caves are all Buddhist; and whereas at Ellora the caves are masterpieces of sculpture, at Ajanta it's the magnificent paintings for which the caves are famous.

After their abandonment with the move to Ellora and the decline of Buddhism, the Ajanta Caves were gradually forgotten and their rediscovery was dramatic. In 1819 a British hunting party stumbled upon them, and their remote beauty was soon unveiled. Their isolation had contributed to the fine state of preservation in which some of the paintings remain to this day. The caves are cut into the steep face of a deep rock gorge. There are 29 caves in a curve of the gorge, and there is a good viewpoint across the ravine. They date from around 200 BC to 650 AD and do not follow the chronological order that the

Ellora Caves generally do; the oldest are mainly in the middle and the newer ones are to each end.

The cave paintings initially suffered some deterioration after their rediscovery, and some heavy-handed restoration also caused damage. Between 1920 and 1922 two Italian art experts conducted a meticulous restoration process and the paintings have been carefully preserved since that time. Many of the caves are dark, and without a light the paintings are hard to see – it's worth paying for a lighting ticket which will ensure that the cave guards turn the lights on for you. Or you could try tagging along with a tour party, although normally the doors are shut after each party enters a cave.

Five of the caves are chaityas or temples while the other 24 are viharas or monasteries. Caves 8, 9, 10, 12 and 13 are the older Hinayana caves, while the others are Mahayana. In the simpler, more austere Hinayana school the Buddha was never represented directly – his presence was always alluded to by a symbol such as the footprint or wheel of law. The Ajanta paintings are not, strictly

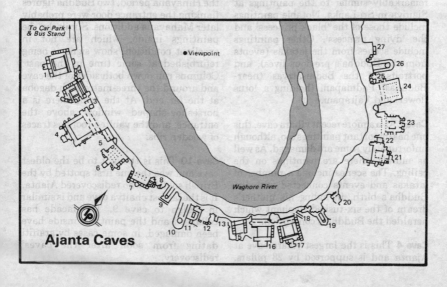

To Car Park & Bus Stand

Viewpoint

Waghore River

Ajanta Caves

speaking, frescoes but tempera paintings – a difference purely of technique. Although the Ajanta paintings are particularly notable, there are also many interesting sculptures here.

The caves are open daily from 9 am to 5.30 pm. Entry costs Rs 0.50 plus Rs 5 for a lighting fee (optional but more or less essential).

Avoid, if at all possible, coming here at weekends or on public holidays. On those days, Ajanta seems to attract half the population of India and it's bedlam. The Calcutta rush hour has nothing on this place at those times – hardly the contemplative atmosphere which its monks and builders had in mind!

Cave 1 This vihara cave is one of the most recent and also most fully developed of the Ajanta Caves. A verandah at the front leads to a large square hall with elaborate carvings and paintings and a huge Buddha statue. Cave 1 is notable for both its sculpture and its paintings.

Amongst the interesting sculptures is one of four deer sharing a common head. There are many paintings of women, some remarkably similar to the paintings at Sigiriya in Sri Lanka. Notable paintings include those of the 'black princess' and the 'dying princess'. Other paintings include scenes from the jatakas (events from the Buddha's previous lives), and portraits of the Bodhisattvas (near-Buddhas) Padmapani (holding a lotus flower) and Vajrapani.

Cave 2 Also a more recent vihara cave, this one has important paintings too, although unfortunately some are damaged. As well as murals, there are paintings on the ceiling. The scenes include a number of jatakas and events connected with the Buddha's birth, including his mother's dream of the six-tusked elephant which heralded the Buddha's conception.

Cave 4 This is the largest vihara cave at Ajanta and is supported by 28 pillars.

Although it was never completed, the cave has some fine sculptures, including scenes of people fleeing from the 'eight great dangers' to the protection of the Buddha's disciple Avalokitesvara. One of the great dangers is an angry-looking elephant in pursuit of a man and woman. Caves 3, 5 and 8 were never completed.

Cave 6 This is the only two-storey cave at Ajanta, but parts of the lower storey have collapsed. Inside is a seated figure of the Buddha with an intricately carved door to the shrine. Upstairs the hall is surrounded by cells with fine paintings on the doorways.

Caves 7 & 8 Cave 7 is of unusual design in that the verandah does not lead into a hall with cells down the sides and a shrine room at the rear. Here there are porches before the verandah, which leads directly to the four cells and the elaborately sculpted shrine. Cave 8 is used solely for the generating equipment which lights the caves.

Cave 9 This is a chaitya cave and one of the earliest at Ajanta. Although it dates from the Hinayana period, two Buddha figures flanking the entrance door were probably later Mahayana additions. Similarly, the paintings inside, which are not in excellent condition, show signs of being refurbished at some time in the past. Columns run down both sides of the cave and around the three-metre-high dagoba at the far end. At the front there is a horseshoe-shaped window above the entrance, and the vaulted roof has traces of wooden ribs.

Cave 10 This is thought to be the oldest cave and was the one first spotted by the British soldiers who rediscovered Ajanta. It is the largest chaitya cave and is similar in design to cave 9. The facade has collapsed and the paintings inside have been damaged, in some cases by graffiti dating from soon after the caves' rediscovery.

Caves 11 to 14 Caves 11, 12 and 13 are not of great interest – they are all relatively early, either Hinayana or early Mahayana. Cave 14 is an incompleted vihara, standing above cave 13, which is an early Mahayana vihara.

Cave 16 Some of Ajanta's finest paintings can be seen in this, one of the later vihara caves. It is thought that cave 16 may have been the original entrance to the entire complex, and there is a very fine view of the river from the front of the cave. Best known of the paintings here is the 'dying princess'. Sundari, wife of Buddha's half-brother Nanda, is said to have expired at the hard news that her husband was renouncing the material life (and her) in order to become a monk. This is one of the finest paintings at Ajanta. Nanda features in several other paintings, including one of his conversion by Buddha.

Cave 17 This is the cave with the finest paintings at Ajanta. Not only are they in the best condition, they are also the most numerous and varied. They include beautiful women flying overhead on the roof while carved dwarfs support the pillars. A popular scene shows a woman, surrounded by attendants, applying make-up. In one there is a royal procession, while in another a couple engage in a little private lovemaking. In yet another panel the Buddha returns from his enlightenment to his own home to beg from his wife and astonished son.

A detailed panel tells the story of Prince Simhala's expedition to Sri Lanka. With his 500 companions he is shipwrecked on an island where ogresses appear as beautiful women, only to seize and devour their victims. Simhala escapes on a flying horse and returns to conquer the island.

Cave 19 The facade of this chaitya cave is remarkably detailed and includes an impressive horseshoe-shaped window as its dominant feature. Two very fine standing Buddha figures flank the entrance. Inside this excellent specimen of a chaitya cave is a tall dagoba with a figure of the Buddha on the front.

There are also some fine sculptures and paintings, but one of the most important is outside the cave to the west, where there is an image of the Naga king with seven cobra hoods arrayed around his head. His wife, hooded by a single cobra, is seated beside him.

Caves 20 to 25 These caves are either incomplete or not of great interest, although cave 24 would have been the largest vihara at Ajanta, if finished. You can see how the caves were constructed from this example – long galleries were cut into the rock, and then the rock between them was broken through.

Cave 26 The fourth chaitya cave's facade has fallen and almost every trace of its paintings has disappeared. Nevertheless there are some very fine sculptures remaining. On the left wall is a huge figure of the 'reclining Buddha', lying back as he prepares to enter nirvana. Other scenes include a lengthy depiction of the Buddha's temptation by Mara. In one scene Mara attacks the Buddha with demons, and then his beautiful daughters tempt him with more sensual delights. However, the Buddha's resistance is too strong, and the final scene shows a glum and dejected-looking Mara having failed to deflect the Buddha from the straight and narrow.

Caves 27 to 29 Cave 27 is virtually a vihara connected to the cave 26 chaitya. There's a great pond in a box canyon 200 metres upstream from the cave. Caves 28 and 29 are higher up the cliff face and relatively hard to get to.

Places to Stay & Eat
There is an MTDC *Travellers' Lodge* right by the entrance to the caves but it's in an appalling state of repair. When we researched this edition, the toilet in the

restaurant part had a broken cistern hanging off the wall, there was shit all over the floor and walls, and the place stank to high heaven. Rooms cost Rs 30/50 for singles/doubles with common bath. If the common bath is anything like the one attached to the restaurant then you're in for a shock. Checkout time is 8 am. The restaurant itself, however, is half-decent and the food reasonably good. Prices are moderate.

Most people stay at Fardapur, five km from the caves, where there is the excellent MTDC *Holiday Resort* run by the state government. Rooms along the pleasant verandah cost Rs 77 for a single or double with bath (cold water only). Each room has two beds, clean sheets, mosquito nets and a fan. You have to pay in advance plus a Rs 50 returnable deposit. The hotel is run by a no-nonsense manager, so gear left in the rooms is secure.

The only other place in Fardapur is the *Pavan Tourist House* – at least, there's a sign to that effect nailed onto a tree outside the Holiday Resort, but I never found the place.

There are a number of shacks along the main road where you can buy cheap tea and snacks but nothing that you could vaguely call a meal. The only restaurant is the *Vihara Restaurant* attached to the Holiday Resort. It only functions in the evening, only offers thalis (Rs 12) and the food is very average. If possible, order in advance or they may not buy sufficient food to cater for you.

Getting There & Away

It's Rs 13.30 from Aurangabad to Ajanta by local bus and it takes about three hours. From Jalgaon it's Rs 7 to Fardapur by local bus and this trip takes about 1½ hours. The caves are a couple of km off the main road from Aurangabad to Jalgaon, and Fardapur is a little further down the main road towards Jalgaon. There are regular buses between Fardapur and the Ajanta Caves which cost Rs 0.75 but not

all buses travelling along the main road call at the caves. Make sure you get on the right one otherwise you'll have to walk the last two km.

There's a 'cloak room' at the Ajanta Caves where you can leave gear, so that it is possible to arrive on a morning bus from Jalgaon, look around the caves, and continue to Aurangabad in the evening, or vice versa.

LONAR METEORITE CRATER

At the small village of Lonar, three hours by bus north-east of Jalna or 4½ hours south-east of Ajanta, is this huge impressive meteorite crater. It's about two km in diameter and several hundred metres deep, with a shallow lake at the bottom. A plaque on the rim near the town states that this is 'the only natural hypervelocity impact crater in basaltic rock in the world'.

There are several Hindu temples on the crater floor, and langur monkeys inhabit the bushes by the lake. The crater is only about five minutes walk from the bus station – ask for Lonar Tank.

It's possible to visit Lonar in a day en route between Fardapur and Aurangabad, but this would be rushing things.

Places to Stay

There is a basic hotel by the bus station in Lonar, and others in Buldhana three hours to the north.

Getting There & Away

From Lonar there are buses to Buldhana from where it's easy to catch a bus for the bumpy 1½-hour journey to Fardapur. Heading south from Lonar there are direct buses to Jalna, from where there are trains and buses to Aurangabad, a total of about five hours.

NAGPUR (population 1,600,000)

Situated on the River Nag, from which the town takes its name, Nagpur is the orange-growing capital of India. It was once the capital of the central province, but was later incorporated into Maharashtra. Long ago it was a centre for the aboriginal Gond tribes who remained in power until the early 18th century. Many Gonds still live in this region. Later it went through a series of changes before eventually falling to the British.

Places to Stay

There are all sorts of hotels in Nagpur. Among the centrally located cheaper places is the *Hotel Shyam* (tel 24073) on Pandit Malviya Rd, with rooms at around Rs 80. The *Hotel Blue Diamond* (tel 47461/9) at 113 Dosar Square Central Ave has a variety of rooms from Rs 40 to Rs 150.

Other more expensive places include the *Hotel Upvan* (tel 34704/5), 65 Mount Rd, which has air-cooled rooms for Rs 150/200 and air-con for Rs 200/250.

OTHER PLACES IN THE NORTH
Ramtek

About 40 km north-east of Nagpur, Ramtek has a number of picturesque 600-year-old temples surmounting the 'Hill of Rama'. In summer this is one of the hottest places in India. The old British cantonment of Kemtee is nearby, and a memorial to the Sanskrit dramatist Kalidasa is just along the road from the Tourist Bungalow, which has a spectacular view of the town.

Wardha & Sevagram

About 80 km south-west of Nagpur, near Wardha station, is Sevagram, the 'Village of Service', where Gandhi established his ashram in 1933. For the 15 years from then until India achieved independence, this was in some ways the alternative capital of India.

The Centre of Science for Villages (Magan Sangrahalaya) is a museum

intended to explain and develop Gandhi's ideals of village-level economics. The huts of his ashram are still preserved in Sevagram and there is a photo exhibit of events in the Mahatma's life at Mahadev Bhawan, beside the Sevagram hospital.

Only three km from Sevagram is the ashram of Vinoba Bhave, Gandhi's follower who walked throughout India persuading rich landlords to hand over tracts of land for redistribution to the landless and poor.

Jalgaon

The railway station and the bus station in Jalgaon are a long way from each other and you'll need to take a tonga or auto-rickshaw between the two.

Places to Stay For those en route to the caves, the *Morako* and the friendly *Tourist Hotel* are lower middle-range places. The *Tourist Hotel*, one km from the railway station, has rooms at around Rs 80 and a popular non-vegetarian restaurant. The *PWD Rest House*, just behind the Tourist Hotel, has been recommended, has rooms for Rs 55 and is much better. The railway *retiring rooms* at Jalgaon are good value.

Amraoti & Akola

These two towns are between Jalgaon and Nagpur. Amraoti has the biggest cotton market in India and the old Amba temple near the walled city. The town has a famous sports college with old-fashioned wrestling pits.

Places to Stay You can try the *Maharaja Guest House* at Amraoti or the *Hotel Dreamland* at Akola – the latter is another of those places on the downhill path to Indian hotel oblivion.

Goa

Population: 1.2 million
Area: 3702 square km
Main languages: Konkani, Marathi, & Gujarati. English is widely spoken and many of the older generation also speak Portuguese.

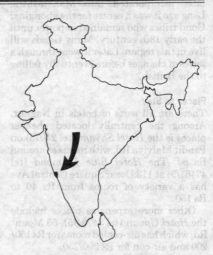

The former Portuguese enclave of Goa, one of India's gems, has enjoyed a prominent place in the travellers' lexicon for many years. The main reason for this is its magnificent palm-fringed beaches and 'travellers' scene'. Yet it offers much more than just the hedonism of sun, sand and sea. Goa has a character quite distinct from the rest of India. Despite nearly three decades of 'liberation' from Portuguese colonial rule, Roman Catholicism remains the predominant religion, skirts far outnumber saris, and the people display an easygoing tropical indulgence, humour and civility which you'll find hard to beat even in Kerala.

Gleaming whitewashed churches with Portuguese-style facades pepper the hillsides, rice paddies and dense coconut palm groves, while crumbling forts guard rocky capes and estuary entrances. Markets are lively colourful affairs; and siesta is widely observed during the hot afternoon hours. Carnival explodes onto the streets for five riotous days and nights prior to Lent. Not only that, but there seems to be a total lack of the excessive shyness which Hindu women display towards men, and there are very good reasons for that. One of them relates to the Goan laws of property which ensure that a married woman is entitled to 50% of the couple's estate - a far cry from what applies in the rest of India.

With a bit of luck you'll come across that peculiar colonial anachronism, the *escrivão*, an older Hindu civil servant wearing a three-piece suit with tie, socks and shoes, a solar hat and a dhoti!

Until recently, the other two former Portuguese coastal enclaves of Daman and Diu were also governed from Goa. These have now been detached and are ruled from New Delhi as Union Territories. They are both dealt with in the Gujarat chapter of this book.

If you're interested in a sympathetic yet satirical cartoon essay on Goa from a Goan point of view, then get hold of the booklet *Goa with Love* by Mario Miranda (Goa Tours, Goa, 1982) - it's superb!

History

Goa's history stretches back to the 3rd century BC when it formed part of the Mauryan Empire. It was later ruled by the Satavahanas of Kolhapur at the beginning of the Christian era and eventually passed to the Chalukyans of Badami, who controlled it from 580 to 750 AD. Over the next few centuries it was ruled successively by the Shilharas, the Kadambas and the Chalukyans of Kalyani.

Goa fell to the Muslims for the first time in 1312, but the invaders were forced to evacuate it in 1370 by Harihara I of the Vijayanagar Empire, whose capital was at Hampi in Karnataka state. The Vijayanagar rulers held on to Goa for nearly 100 years, and its harbours became important landing places for ships carrying Arabian horses on their way to Hampi to strengthen the Vijayanagar cavalry.

In 1469, Goa was conquered by the Bahmani Sultans of Gulbarga, and when this dynasty broke up, the area passed to the Adil Shahis of Bijapur, who made Goa Velhaa their second capital. The present Secretariat building in Panaji is the former palace of Adil Shah, and it was later taken over by the Portuguese viceroys as their official residence.

The Portuguese, having been unable to secure a base on the Malabar coast further south, arrived in Goa in 1510 under the command of Alfonso de Albuquerque. This was due to opposition from the Zamorin of Calicut and stiff competition from the Turks who, at that time, controlled the trade routes across the Indian Ocean.

Blessed as it was by natural harbours and wide rivers, Goa was the ideal base for the seafaring Portuguese, who were intent on their quest for control of the spice route from the east and the desire to spread Christianity. For a while their control was limited to a small area around Old Goa, but by the middle of the 16th century it had expanded to include the provinces of Bardez and Salcete.

The eventual ousting of the Turks and the fortunes to be made from control of the spice trade led to Goa's 'golden age'. The colony became the viceregal seat of the Portuguese Empire of the east which included various East Africa port cities, East Timor and Macau. Decline set in, however, due to competition from the British, French and Dutch in the 17th century combined with Portugal's inability to adequately service its far-flung empire.

Goa reached its present size in the 18th century as a result of further annexations, first in 1763 when the provinces of Ponda, Sanguem, Quepem and Canacona were added, and later in 1788 when Pednem, Bicholim and Satari were added.

The Marathas nearly vanquished the Portuguese in the late 18th century and there was a brief occupation by the British during the time of the Napoleonic Wars in Europe. It was not until 1961, however, when India ejected the Portuguese in a near bloodless operation, that the Portuguese finally disappeared from the subcontinent. The other enclaves of Daman and Diu were also taken over at the same time. Though dubbed the 'liberation' by Nehru at the time, it would appear that many Goans, given the choice, might have preferred independence; the matter is still a bone of contention in the Indian Supreme Court. A recent ruling made 'invasion' the legally accepted term.

Nudism & Local Sensibilities

Goa is a part of the Indian subcontinent overlaid with much Hindu culture. You should never make the mistake of thinking that because Goa is so welcoming, friendly and liberal, that you're at liberty to exploit it or flagrantly disregard local sensibilities.

Too many people did that in the late '60s and '70s by nude (or seminude) bathing, and Goa became famous for it. Of course, there are still plenty of opportunities to lie around in your birthday suit and plenty of people do, but don't do it where families bathe. Probably no-one will bother you (that's Goa), but remember that it's merely tolerated.

This guidebook has come in for varying degrees of criticism for suggesting that nudism, whether partial or complete, was acceptable on Goan beaches. One newspaper article bitterly attacked the 'disgusting unabashedness' with which we suggested that, if you were tired of wearing clothes, to take them off since everyone else did. It went on to condemn the 'pernicious attempt to cash in on nudism by making it one of the artificially created resources for tourism promotion'.

The truth of the matter is that signs

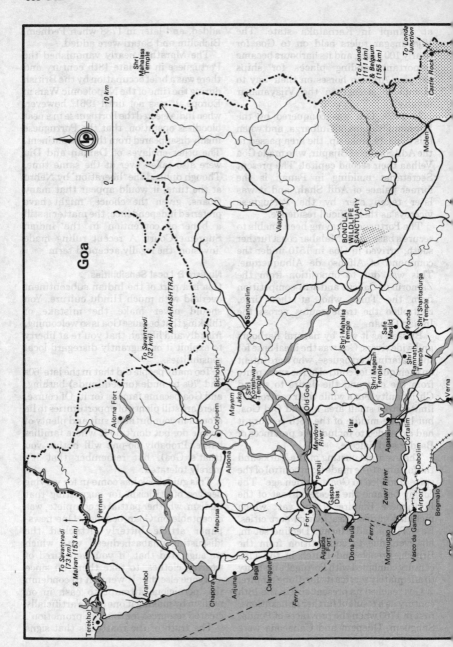

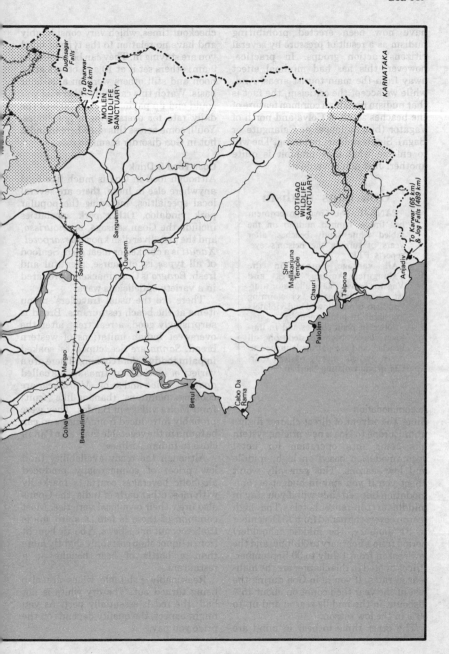

have now been erected prohibiting nudism as a result of pressure by several citizens' action groups. In practice, however, this has had minimal effect away from the main tourist areas. And, while we accept the criticism, the fact is that nudism remains a common feature of the beaches south of Colva and north of Vagator (but no longer at Calangute or Baga). Signboards are one thing. The will to enforce what they prohibit is quite another. Just don't overdo it!

Goa bans nudism

PANAJI: The Goan government has finally banned nudism on the fabled white sandy beaches, after years of turning the nelson's eye, reports PTI.

All vantage points on the Calungute, Anjuna, Baga and Vagator beaches have all major tourist draw billboards proclaiming "nudism is not allowed and violaters are liable to punishment."

Police in plain clothes and in uniform have been posted on all beaches and sea patrols launched to desist nudists, mostly western tourists, from violating the ban.

Accommodation

Since the advent of direct charter flights from Europe to Goa a new pricing system has come into operation for hotel accommodation based on high, middle and low seasons. This generally won't affect you if you stay in budget accommodation but certainly will if you stay in middle or top-range hotels. The high season covers the period from 15 December to 31 January, the middle (shoulder) period from 1 February to 30 June, and the low season from 1 July to 30 September. Prices quoted in this chapter are the high-season rates. If you're in Goa during the rest of the year then count on about 15% discount in the middle season and up to 50% in the low season.

The other thing to bear in mind are checkout times, which vary considerably and have no relation to the type of hotel you are staying in. They can be as early as 9 am; others set it at 10 am, others at 12 noon and still others work on a 24-hour basis. Watch this carefully otherwise you could end up paying an extra 50% of the daily rate for overstaying a few hours. You'll come across this elsewhere in India but in Goa disorder seems to rule.

Goan Food & Drink

Although food in Goa is much like food anywhere else in India, there are several local specialties, including the popular pork vindaloo. Other pork specialties include the Goan sausage, or *chourisso*, and the pig's liver dish known as *sarpotel*. *Xacutí* is a chicken or meat dish. Seafood of all types is, of course, plentiful and fresh. *Bangra* is Goan mackerel, prepared in a variety of delicious ways.

There are the usual travellers' menu items at the beach restaurants. Bread is surprisingly good, a real treat after the oversweet Indian imitations of western bread. *Sanna* are rice 'cupcakes' soaked in palm toddy before cooking. There are a variety of special Christmas sweets called *dodol*, *bebinca* and so on. *Moira kela* are cooking plantains (banana-like fruit) from Moira village in Bardez. They were probably introduced from Africa and can be found in the vegetable market in Panaji close to Indian Airlines.

Although the ready availability (and low price) of commercially produced alcoholic beverages contrasts markedly with most other parts of India, the Goans also brew their own local varieties. Most common of these is feni, a spirit made from coconut or cashews. A bottle bought from a liquor shop costs only slightly more than a bottle of beer bought at a restaurant.

Reasonably palatable wines are also being turned out. The dry white is not bad; the red is essentially port. As you might expect, the quality depends on the price you pay.

Festivals

The Christian festivals in Goa take place on the following dates:

6 January
Feast of Three Kings at Reis Magos, Cansaulim and Chandor

2 February
Feast of Our Lady of Candelaria at Pomburpa

February/March
Carnival

Monday after 5th Sunday in Lent
Procession of the Franciscan Order at Old Goa

1st Sunday after Easter
Feast of Jesus of Nazareth at Siridao

16 days after Easter
Feast of Our Lady of Miracles at Mapusa

24 August
Festival of Novidades

1st fortnight of October
Fama de Menino Jesus at Colva

3rd Wednesday of November
Feast of Our Lady of the Rosary

3 December
Feast of St Francis Xavier at Old Goa

8 December
Feast of Our Lady of Immaculate Conception at Panaji and Margao

25 December
Christmas

Hindu festivals are harder to date because of the different calendar but they include:

January
Festival of Shantadurga Prasann at the small village of Fatorpa, south of Margao in Quepem province. There is a night time procession of chariots bearing the goddess and as many as 100,000 people flock to the festival.
The Shri Bodgeshwar *zatra*, or temple festival, takes place just south of Mapusa.

February
The three day zatra of Shri Mangesh takes place in the lavish temple of that name in the Ponda district.

In the old Fontainhas district of Panaji the Maruti zatra draws huge and colourful crowds. Maruti is another name for Hanuman.

March

In Goa the festival of Holi is called Shigmo. There's a parade in Panaji and numerous temple festivals around Goa.

In the Procession of Umbrellas at Cuncolim, south of Margao, a solid silver image of Shantadurga is carried in procession over the hills to the original temple site wrecked by the Portuguese in 1580. The route taken is the same one by which the image was spirited away to safety outside the Portuguese borders. It's a colourful and dramatic event.

PANAJI (Panjim)

Panaji is one of India's smallest and most pleasant state capitals. Built on the south bank of the wide Mandovi River, it became the capital of Goa in 1843, though the Portuguese viceroys had shifted their residence from the outskirts of Old Goa to the former palace of Adil Shah at Panaji as early as 1759.

The old town has preserved its Portuguese heritage remarkably well; there are narrow winding streets, old houses with overhanging balconies and red-tiled roofs, whitewashed churches and numerous small bars and cafes. Portuguese signs are still visible over many shops, cafes and administrative buildings.

People are friendly and the atmosphere is easygoing. The main attraction is Old Goa, nine km east of Panaji and the former capital founded by Alfonso de Albuquerque in 1510, but Panaji is well worth a visit for its own sake.

Panaji's 'sights' are few, but among those worth visiting are the old Church of the Immaculate Conception (on the hillside at one end of the Municipal Gardens) and the Mahalaxmi Temple. If you're staying in Panaji rather than on the beaches of Goa then the nearest beach is at Miramar three km along the road to Dona Paula.

Information

Tourist Office The tourist office (tel 3396, 3903) is in the Tourist Home (a kind of youth hostel with dorm-type accommodation) in a complex between the bus stand and Ourem River – turn left when you get to the bridge which leads into town (it's signposted). The staff here are very keen and their information is reliable. Excellent maps of Goa and Panaji are available for Rs 6.50.

There is also a Government of India tourist office (tel 3412) in the Communidade Building, Church Square.

Post & Telephone The poste restante at the GPO is efficient. They give you the whole pile to sort through yourself and will willingly check other pigeon holes if expected letters are not arriving. It's open from 9.30 am to 1 pm and 2 to 5.30 pm Monday to Saturday.

International telephone calls are handled at the Central Telegraph Office, Dr Atmaram Borkar Rd, and not at the GPO. It is also possible to dial direct international calls from private phones. We dialled Australia direct one evening from a private phone and had a connection within seconds, and the charge was considerably less than what it would have been from a hotel or restaurant.

Visa Extensions Visas can no longer be renewed in Goa except in cases of emergency such as illness and then only for a few days. The nearest places to get an extension are Bombay and Bangalore.

Tax Clearance If you've stayed in India so long that you need a tax clearance certificate before you depart, then the Taxation Department is in the Shanta Building at the end of Emidio Gracia Rd.

Airlines & Travel Agents Indian Airlines (tel 3822) is at Dempo Building, D Bandodkar Marg, on the riverfront, and it's computerised. Air India is at the Fidalgo Hotel on 18th June Rd.

Georgeson & Georgeson (tel 2150) opposite the GPO (1st floor) is a travel agent which seems to be reasonably reliable and efficient. MGM Travel is similar and has a branch office at Calangute Beach. If you have to reconfirm international flights, check if Air India will do it first. Some travel agents charge heavily for this service.

Vayadoot have no office in Panaji and just a solitary desk at Dabolim Airport, but tickets are sold by many travel agents in Panaji. There's one on the ground floor of the Hotel Mandovi.

Books & Newspapers The hotels Mandovi and Fidalgo both have good bookshops. *Inside Goa* by Manohar Mulgaokar with illustrations by Mario Miranda is excellent, though somewhat expensive. The *Herald Tribune, Time, Newsweek* and other international magazines are also available.

Two local English language newspapers are published in Panaji. The 'establishment' paper is the *Navhind Times* and the 'independent' paper is the *Herald*.

Ganja The dreaded weed is readily available in Goa (it's usually from Kerala). Travellers who've come from Kashmir or the Kulu Valley may offer you resin but the quality varies. Test before buying. It is, of course, illegal.

Goans are also justifiably concerned about the spread of heroin addiction among local youths and the police have begun to crack down heavily. If you're a smoker, discretion and care is the name of the game.

Tours
Tours of Goa are offered both by the tourist office (book there or at the Panaji interstate bus terminal, tel 6515), and by private agencies. Apart from tours to the temples and churches of Goa and the excursion to Bondla Wildlife Sanctuary, the tours aren't very good because they pack too much into a short day so you end up seeing very little. The beach tours are only for voyeurs hoping to catch a glimpse of nude or seminude western bodies.

The North Goa tour visits Panaji, Datta Mandir, Mayem Lake, Mapusa, Vagator, Anjuna, Calangute and Fort Aguada. The South Goa tours take in Miramar, Dona Paula, Pilar Seminary, Mormugao, Vasco da Gama, Colva, Margao, Shantadurga Temple, Mangesh Temple and Old Goa. The tours cost Rs 40 and depart daily at 9 and 9.30 am respectively. They return to Panaji at 6 pm. The beach tour is Rs 20 and lasts from 3 to 7 pm. The Bondla Wildlife Sanctuary tour costs Rs 35 and departs daily at 9.30 am, returning at 5 pm.

There are also two daily river cruises along the Mandovi River at 6 (Sunset Cruise) and 7.15 pm (Sundown Cruise) which last an hour and cost Rs 30. They're good value and include a cultural programme of Goan folk songs and dances. Drinks and snacks are available. Make sure you get the government-operated boat, the *Santa Maria*, which leaves from the former Bombay steamer jetty by the customs office. The other boats, in front of the Tourist Hostel, are privately owned and departures are more random.

Places to Stay
Whenever there is a religious festival in Goa – especially the festival of St Francis Xavier (several days on either side of 3 December) – it can be difficult to find accommodation in Panaji, especially at the small, inexpensive lodges. There is no accommodation at Old Goa.

Places to Stay - bottom end
A couple of years ago, most of the budget hotels in Panaji were at the dim and dusty end of basic. Some still are but there's now a much better choice of perfectly adequate accommodation in this price bracket.

Popular at the lower end of the scale is the *Republica Hotel* (tel 4630), Jose Falca Rd, at the back of the Secretariat block. It's an old place with fine views over the Mandovi River. Singles/doubles without

1	Children's Park	18	O Pastelaria
2	Hotel Campal	19	Hotel Nova Goa
3	Museum	20	Hotel Rajdhani
4	Hotel Palacio de Goa	21	Central Telegraph Office
5	Hotel Samrat	22	Municipality
6	Indian Airlines	23	Hotel Neptune
7	Municipal Market	24	Police Headquarters, Immigration Office
8	El Dorado Theatre		& Registration of Foreigners
9	Hotel Delmon	25	Collectorate
10	Hotel Summit	26	Central Library
11	Hotel Fidalgo, Passport Office & Air India	27	Ferry Ramp
12	Ashok Samrat Theatre	28	Azad Maidan
13	Junta House & National Parks Office	29	Hotel Mandovi
14	Hotel Keni's	30	State Bank of India
15	Hotel Mayfair	31	Godinho Restaurant
16	Mahalaxmi Temple	32	Cine National
17	Goenchin Restaurant	33	New Punjab Restaurant

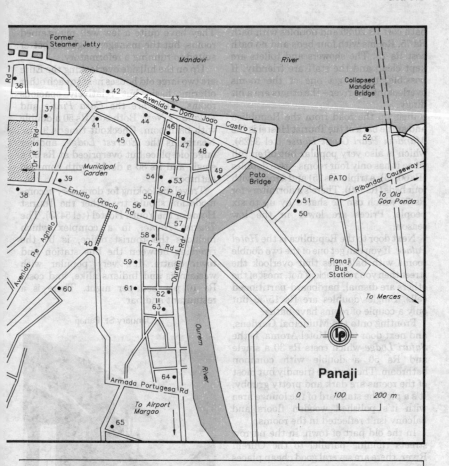

34	Safari Lodge	50	Tourist Office & Tourist Home
35	Hotel Aroma	51	Lord's Hotel
36	Directorate of Customs & Central Excise	52	Fishing Jetty
37	Karnataka Tourist Office	53	Baretons Hotel
38	Kamat Hotel	54	Elite Boarding & Lodging
39	Church of the Immaculate Conception	55	Orav's Guest House
40	School	56	Orlando's Nest & Casa Pinho
41	Republica & Palace Hotels	57	Income Tax Office
42	Secretariat	58	Everest Lodge
43	River Cruises Jetty	59	Park Lane Lodge
44	Tourist Hostel	60	Alliance Francaise
45	Mandovi Pearl Guest House	61	Church
46	Hotel Venite	62	Tourist Home
47	Udipi Boarding & Lodging	63	Panjim Inn
48	GPO	64	Historical Archives
49	Hotels Flamingo & Sona	65	Sangam Deluxe Lodge

bath cost Rs 20/35 and doubles with bath Rs 75. Rooms with four beds and no bath cost Rs 73. The showers and toilets are kept clean and the staff are friendly. If possible, try to get one of the rooms overlooking the river – the others are a bit dingy.

Just up the road from the Republica and at the back of the Tourist Hostel is the *Mandovi Pearl Guest House* (tel 3928), which is also very popular but often full since it has only four rooms – two doubles (Rs 60/75), a triple (Rs 75) and a room with four beds (Rs 100). There's a dormitory for Rs 75 which can be shared by up to six people. Prices are lower in the low season.

Next door to the Republica is the *Hotel Palace*. If you can get one of the two double rooms with balconies that overlook the street then you're in luck, if not, most of the others are dismal, hardboard-partitioned cells. Singles/doubles are Rs 15/30 but only a couple of rooms have baths.

Fronting onto the Municipal Gardens, and next door to the Hotel Aroma, is the *Safari Lodge* which costs Rs 30 a single and Rs 50 a double with common bathroom. The staff are friendly but most of the rooms are dark and pretty grubby. It's a pity the standard of the lounge area with it's polished wooden floors and balcony isn't reflected in the rooms.

In the old part of town, in the narrow streets running parallel to the Ourem River, there are several good cheap places to stay. One of my own favourites because of its superb atmosphere and very friendly staff is the *Hotel Venite*, 31 January Rd. They only have four basic but clean rooms (one of them with two small balconies overlooking the street) and the common toilet/bathroom facilities are scrubbed out daily. The rooms have fans and cost Rs 30/40 for singles/doubles. Get there early if you want a room. Close by are the *Udipi Boarding & Lodging* and the *Elite Boarding & Lodging*. The latter costs Rs 30 to Rs 40 a double with common bath and Rs 50 a double with private bath.

They have quite a few well maintained rooms, but the manager might be better suited to running a reformatory.

Up on the hillside overlooking the Elite are two large old houses next to each other offering basic but relatively spacious rooms. They are the *Casa Pinho* and *Orlando's Nest*. Both cost Rs 50 a double with bathroom. Checkout time is 9 am. Nearby is the *Everest Lodge*, another large old place but overpriced at Rs 50 a single and Rs 80 a double with common bathroom.

Travellers looking for dormitory accommodation should try either the Tourist Home or the Youth Hostel (tel 5433). The *Tourist Home*, in a complex which includes the tourist office, is by the riverside between the bus station and town centre. It's very popular with westerners and Indians alike, and costs Rs 10 per bed per night. There is a restaurant and bar.

January St, Panaji

The *Youth Hostel* is out at Miramar Beach and has a superb location right next to the beach. It has dorm beds for Rs 8 (Rs 10 for nonmembers) and a solitary double room with bath for Rs 50. Officially the hostel is closed between 1 and 4 pm, but they're not strict about it. Its only drawback is the distance from the centre of town, but regular buses will get you there within five minutes.

Also at Miramar beach, the *Hotel Solmar* (tel 4555/6), Avenida Gaspar Dias, and the rustic *Belvila Lodge*, on the main road opposite the turn-off for the Youth Hostel, have reasonably priced rooms.

Back in town but going up in price, there is the multistorey *Tourist Hostel* (tel 3903, 3396) fronting onto the Mandovi River. This place is a bargain at Rs 70 a single, Rs 80 a double and Rs 120 a triple, all with bath and hot water. It's only drawback is that it can be booked out for weeks in advance. There's a terrace restaurant (small portions), bar, bookshop and handicraft shop on the ground floor. Similar is the other *Tourist Home*, Ourem Rd, which quite a few travellers stay at.

In the streets parallel to the Ourem River, in the old part of town, are a number of other places. Prominent among them is the family-run *Park Lane Lodge* at Rs 60 a single, Rs 75 a double, Rs 85 a triple and Rs 95 for a four-bed room. It comes complete with a crazy dog and friendly owner. Checkout is 12 noon. Nearby and similar are the *Maureen Inn* and *Punam Lodge*.

Also good in this upper budget bracket is *Orav's Guest House*, 31 January Rd, which is a relatively new place and very clean. It costs Rs 80 a double with bath. There are no single rooms.

In the new part of town is the *Hotel Neptune* (tel 5727), Malaca Rd, which offers rooms for Rs 60/90 a single/double and Rs 150 with air-con. All the rooms have baths and hot water, and there's a 'posh restaurant with bar attached'. It's often full.

Places to Stay – middle

One of the best places to stay at the lower end of this bracket is the *Panjim Inn* – a beautiful old mansion with a large 1st-floor verandah and leafy garden. It's a popular place and the staff are friendly. Rooms cost Rs 110 a single and Rs 140 a double with bathroom.

Equally popular, and fronting onto the Municipal Gardens, is the modern *Hotel Aroma* (tel 3519), Cunha Rivara Rd, which has rooms for Rs 126 a single and Rs 164 a double with bathroom. There are clean sheets, fans and a laundry service but the hot water is often a figment of the imagination. The tandoori restaurant on the 1st floor is one of the best in Panaji.

Similarly priced but less attractive is the *Hotel Sona* (tel 4426), Ourem Rd, which costs Rs 118 a double and Rs 168 a triple. All rooms have a bath but with hot water in the mornings only.

More expensive, but a pleasant place to stay, is the *Mayfair Hotel* (tel 5952), Dr Dada Vaidya Rd, which has rooms for Rs 135, or Rs 170 with air-con. All rooms have their own bathroom with hot and cold water plus there's a bar and restaurant with Goan, continental, vegetarian and non-vegetarian cuisine. The manager is a very friendly guy. Similar is the *Hotel Summit* (tel 5309), Menezes Braganza Rd, which costs Rs 170/195/270 for singles/doubles/triples and Rs 295 for air-con doubles. All rooms have their own bathroom with hot and cold water 24 hours a day.

Other hotels in this bracket include the *Hotel Samrat* (tel 3318), Dr Dada Vaidya Rd, and *Keni's Hotel* (tel 4581), 18th June Rd. The Samrat charges Rs 145/200/250 for singles/doubles/triples. All rooms have a bath with hot water plus there's a restaurant, bar and rooftop garden. They can also change travellers' cheques and accept most credit cards. Keni's Hotel is also popular with travellers in need of a touch of luxury. They offer singles/doubles for Rs 113/184 and air-con doubles for Rs 261 with bath, hot water and colour

TV. The hotel includes a bar, restaurant and shopping arcade. Keni's Hotel is actually classified as a three-star hotel so don't be too surprised if you're quoted high prices when the rooms without air-con are full.

Also good in this bracket is the *Hotel Rajdhani* (tel 5362), Dr Atmaram Borkar Rd, which charges Rs 180/200/250 for singles/doubles/triples; Rs 220/250/300 with air-con. 'Ideal', as the hotel describes itself, 'for honeymooners, pleasure seekers and visiting businessmen'.

Places to Stay - top end

For many years, two top of the range hotels dominated the Panaji scene. They were the *Hotel Fidalgo* (tel 3321), 18 June Rd, and the *Hotel Mandovi* (tel 6270), Dayamond Bandokar Marg. They're both still there and have all the usual facilities. The Fidalgo costs Rs 395/550 for singles/doubles. The Mandovi costs Rs 275/495 for singles/doubles. Both hotels offer more expensive suites.

Many other multistar hotels now offer the same standard of accommodation but are more imaginatively designed, some of them with swimming pools, and some of them considerably cheaper than the two just mentioned.

Foremost among them is the *Hotel Nova Goa* (tel 6231/9), Dr Atmaram Borkar Rd, and the *Hotel Palácio de Goa* (tel 4289), Dr Gama Pinto Rd. The Nova Goa offers rooms for Rs 200 to Rs 320 a single and Rs 250 to Rs 370 a double. There are more expensive suites (Rs 370 to Rs 400) and a shaded swimming pool. The Palácio de Goa is a sensitively designed five-storey hotel with each room having a Portuguese-style balcony overlooking the street. Rooms cost just Rs 165 for a double and Rs 225 for an air-con double – an incontestable bargain at today's prices. The only trouble with the Palácio is that it caters mainly for Gujarati families so it's pure vegetarian food and no alcohol. But so what? Goa is replete with seafood restaurants and bars.

Places to Stay - around Panaji

Most of the hotels outside of Panaji – south of Calangute and north of Colva but excluding Vasco da Gama and Mormugao – are beach resorts that cater largely for affluent tourists and those seeking water sports. One of them was chosen during Indira Gandhi's time as the venue for a Commonwealth Heads of Government conference.

Seventeen km west of Panaji, on the opposite side of the Mandovi River, is the *Fort Aguada Beach Resort* (tel 7501), Sinquerim. It has 120 rooms and costs Rs 1150 for singles or doubles in the high season and Rs 800/900 during the rest of the year; there's a further discount during the low season.

Seven km south of Panaji and facing Mormugao Bay is the *Cidade de Goa* (tel 3301), Vainguinim Beach, Dona Paula, which has 101 rooms and costs Rs 800/900 for singles/doubles in the high season and Rs 700/800 during the rest of the year. There are further discounts during the low season. Even further south, on the far side of the Mormugao peninsula but only three km from the airport, is the *Oberoi Bogmalo Beach* (tel 2191) which has 119 rooms. They cost Rs 1100 a single or double in the high season and there are discounts for the low season. All these five-star hotels offer the usual luxuries plus a whole range of water and land-based sports facilities.

A new hotel has recently been opened a little upriver from the Cidade de Goa but still facing Mormugao Bay. It is the *Green Valley Beach Resort* (tel 6499), Bambolim Village, eight km south-east of Panaji. It offers air-con doubles at Rs 500 (high season) and Rs 300 (low season), water sports and an open-air thatched restaurant surrounding an enormous banyan tree. The resort is owned by two Goan brothers, Vero and Savio Nunes. They aim to give the five-star resorts a run for their money, offering much the same facilities, but at bargain basement prices.

Places to Eat

Panaji is full of restaurants, many of them attached to hotels, which cater for every taste and every pocket. One of the best – if not *the* best – is at the *Hotel Venite*, 31 January Rd. This beautiful old place on the 1st floor has polished wooden floors, flower-decked balconies overlooking the street and bags of atmosphere. Run by Luis de Souza and an enthusiastic band of well-trained and meticulous young chefs and waiters, this restaurant attracts a colourful crowd of local people and travellers every day of the week. The Goan and seafood cuisine is superb, the servings are generous and all the food is bought fresh from the market each day. Prices are surprisingly moderate for such quality – generally Rs 16 to Rs 20 per plate and you'll be hard-pressed to find a friendlier place. It's also a great spot for a cold beer or two during siesta. The Venite is open for breakfast, lunch and dinner.

Other restaurants have tried to copy the style of the Venite but without success. One of them is the *Udipi Boarding & Lodging*, one street east of the Venite. The Udipi also has a 1st floor restaurant with balcony overlooking the street. Although cheap, it isn't anywhere near as popular, but is worth checking out. Another is the *Godinho* around the back of the Hotel Aroma. When it first opened a few years ago, its good range of Goan, seafood and Indian non-vegetarian dishes was about as close as you could get to anything with a Portuguese flavour in Panaji. Unfortunately, that atmosphere has largely been destroyed with the partitioning of the restaurant into areas with and without air-con. The food, however, is still pretty good, moderately priced and it's a popular place to eat, but servings are small. Lunchtime is probably the best time for a meal as most of the evening clientele come here to talk over bottles of beer rather than to eat.

The *New Punjab Restaurant* in the Municipal Gardens offers excellent Punjabi food and is a cheap and popular place to eat, though tandoori specialities are more expensive. It's closed on Saturdays. Diagonally opposite is the good vegetarian *Kamat Hotel*, while off the gardens at the opposite end is the *Jesmal Cafe* which has excellent milkshakes (particularly mango). Also in the Municipal Gardens is the tandoori restaurant on the 1st floor of the *Hotel Aroma*. There's an extensive menu and the food is good but you should expect to pay more for a meal here than you would in those places already mentioned.

Upstairs at the Tourist Hostel is the *Chit Chat Restaurant* with its pleasant open-air verandah overlooking the Mandovi River. It's a good place for breakfast, the food is reasonable and it's used by many travellers, but the lunch and dinner servings (especially of seafood) are minuscule so it's not particularly good value.

Other good restaurants include the *Shere Punjab Restaurant* on 18 June Rd, and the *Shalimar* and *Taj Mahal* restaurants next to each other on Mahatma Gandhi Rd. The former is non-vegetarian and the latter vegetarian.

Going up in price, the best place for a Chinese meal is the *Goenchin*, just off Dr Dada Vaidya Rd. The food here is excellent but it's definitely a splurge. It's open from 12.30 to 3 pm and 7.30 to 11 pm daily. Another excellent place to splurge is the *Chilliya Restaurant* next to the Hotel Summit on Menezes Braganza Rd. This restaurant specialises in Mughlai vegetarian and non-vegetarian dishes and is open for lunch and dinner. The rooftop restaurant at the *Mandovi Hotel* is also worth trying both for the food and the views but it's expensive. For much less expensive food and similar views, try the restaurant on the banks of the Mandovi River right opposite the Mandovi Hotel adjacent to the ferry landing.

Most of the small inexpensive restaurants in Panaji tend to close by 10 or 11 pm, but if you feel like partying on or even going for a meal at that time of night then there are a few places in Miramar along the main road to Dona Paula (Dayamond Bandokar Marg) which stay open until late. It's best to take a taxi and see what's happening because they only stay open if there are sufficient clients to warrant it. One good place is *Dany's* at Miramar Children's Park.

For fruit juices, probably the best place in town is the *Juicy Corner* right opposite the Secretariat (Adil Shah's old palace) in the centre of town. It's a very popular place especially with travellers. Cake freaks should head for *A Pastelaria* next to the Goenchin Chinese restaurant. There's another cake shop of the same name which is part of the Mandovi Hotel complex.

Finally, some Goans rate the food at *O'Coquiero* in Porvorim as the best in Goa. It's several km north of Panaji at the junction where the Mapusa and Calangute roads split. It might be worth the effort to get there if you don't mind taking a taxi (about Rs 15 each way) or a much cheaper bus heading for Mapusa. Charles Sobhraj, the international serial-murderer, certainly thought it was worth the effort since this is the place where he was recaptured in 1986 after escaping from prison in New Delhi. Prices are not excessive but it's definitely a splurge.

Getting There & Away

Air Indian Airlines have two to three flights a day between Bombay and Goa. The fare is Rs 435. There are also daily flights to and from Bangalore, Delhi and Cochin. Vayadoot flies daily to and from Pune (Rs 460) and Hyderabad (Rs 560).

Bus Many private companies offer 'luxury/deluxe', 'super deluxe' and 'super deluxe video' buses to Bombay, Bangalore, Pune and Mangalore from Panaji and Margao daily. The buses generally depart at night but if you have any designs on sleeping then avoid the video buses. Most of the companies have offices in Panaji, Mapusa and Margao but they're scattered

around the respective towns. The trip to Bombay is supposed to take 14 hours but can take 18. The cheapest fare is Rs 110, with others ranging from Rs 120 to Rs 170 depending on the type of bus.

Buses go to Londa (where you can get a direct railway carriage to Mysore every day), Hubli (a railway junction on the main Bombay to Bangalore line, where you can also get trains to Gadag for both Bijapur & Badami and Hospet & Hampi) and Belgaum. A bus to Hubli takes seven hours and costs Rs 23 on Karnataka State Transport and Rs 25 on Kadamba. From Hubli to Hospet is another 4½ hours.

There are daily buses to Mysore for Rs 76, Rs 88 or Rs 92, which take 16 hours. Mangalore is an 11-hour trip for Rs 66 ('luxury'), Rs 57 on Karnataka State Transport and Rs 79 on Kadamba. Other buses include Pune for Rs 113 (Kadamba, but cheaper on other buses), Bangalore for Rs 103 (KRTC) and Rs 111 (Kadamba).

Train The railhead in Goa is at Vasco da Gama (it actually continues on to Mormugao but very few of the main trains start from there). See the Getting Around section for details of getting to Vasco from Panaji. The other main station in Goa is at Margao. Seats and sleepers on the trains can be booked at Vasco da Gama, Margao or the South Central Out-Agency booking office at counter No 5 in the Panaji bus station *except* for Indrail Pass holders who must book at Vasco da Gama and nowhere else (there's a special tourist quota allocated to them at this station). The Out-Agency booking office is open from 10 am to 1 pm and 2 to 5.30 pm daily except Sundays.

Apart from the main trains from Vasco da Gama and Margao, some local trains run between Kolamb (another Goan town further up the line) and Mormugao but they're of little interest to travellers.

Trains to Bangalore take about 24 hours. There are some through carriages from Margao, so you do not have to change trains at Londa. Fares for the 689-km trip are Rs 70 in 2nd class, Rs 260 in 1st. It takes 21 to 25 hours to Bombay and involves a change of train at Miraj. Fare for the 788-km trip is Rs 79 in 2nd class, Rs 286 in 1st.

Getting to New Delhi from Goa involves several changes of train, usually at Miraj and Bombay. Total journey time is about 48 hours and the fare for the 2400-km trip is Rs 161 in 2nd class, Rs 664 in 1st.

If you are heading for inland Karnataka – Hampi, Bijapur or Badami – there are two through carriages on the No 205 Miraj Passenger (departing Vasco da Gama at 9 pm), which get detached at Londa and hook up with the No 238 Miraj Link Express to Hubli, arriving there at 6.30 am. Hubli is a major railway junction from where there are express trains to Bombay and Bangalore, and passenger steam trains to Hospet (for the Vijayanagar ruins at Hampi), Badami and Bijapur.

Ferry The bad news is that the ferry service between Bombay and Goa has been suspended until further notice. The ship that used to do the trip was sold to the Indian Navy at the time of the Sri Lankan emergency in 1986. The good news is that the service may be resumed. Following discussions between the governments of the USSR and the states of Maharashtra, Goa and Kerala, a ferry is supposed to connect Bombay with Panaji and Cochin from 1990. The journey time between Panaji and Bombay is expected to be 10 hours. Make enquiries locally.

Getting Around

Airport Transport Kadamba operate buses from the Indian Airlines office in Panaji to Dabolim Airport near Vasco da Gama in time for flights. They generally leave two hours before flights depart but the posted timetable is a mass of alterations so turn up early. The fare is Rs 15.

A taxi costs about Rs 150 to Rs 160 (fixed fare) and takes about 40 minutes. You can share this with up to five people.

Bus Over the last few years the Kadamba Bus Company has almost completely taken over the internal Goan bus network. They're cheap and they run to just about everywhere. Services are frequent and destinations at the bus stations are in English so there are no worries about finding the bus you want. Pay your fare on the bus.

The only trouble is that the conductors have the same mentality as sardine-can manufacturers so, if you want a seat, get on at a bus station otherwise you'll have to join the crush. The good news, on the other hand, is that Goans have a very mellow attitude to being packed into a tin can. There's no crazy panic and no-one will try to claw you out of the way in their manic attempt to board a bus. Seated passengers may even offer to take your bags if you're standing. The buses are, however, fairly slow since they make many stops.

The bridge across the Mandovi River from Panaji to Betim collapsed in 1986 with the loss of several lives. The tragedy aside, the main joke going around Goa at the time was that it stood for only half as long as it took to construct. A new bridge is under construction but, at the rate it is going, will take years to complete. In the meantime, all buses north of Panaji leave from the north side of the Mandovi River and you must take a ferry to get to them. Buses south of Panaji are not affected.

Some of the more popular routes from Panaji include:

Vasco da Gama & Mormugao There are two ways of getting there. You can either go via the ferry from Dona Paula to Mormugao, or road via Agassaim and Cortalim. Unless you know there will be a ferry waiting for you on arrival at Dona Paula, the route via Agassaim and Cortalim is the quicker of the two. Either way it costs about Rs 3 to Rs 4 and will take you about one hour – the exact cost depends on the sort of bus.

Margao You can get to Margao either via Agassaim & Cortalim or via Ponda. The former is the more direct route and takes about 1½ hours. It's Rs 3.40 to Rs 4.50 depending on what type of bus you take. Via Ponda it takes about an hour longer and costs a little more.

Old Goa Take one of the frequent buses going straight to Old Goa or any bus going to Ponda. The journey costs Rs 1 and takes 20 to 30 minutes.

Calangute There is a frequent service throughout the day and evening. The journey takes about 35 to 45 minutes and costs Rs 1.30.

Mapusa Buses cost Rs 1.20 and take about 25 minutes. There are also three buses daily direct to Chapora Village via Mapusa. Mapusa is pronounced 'Mapsa', and this is what the conductors shout.

Taxis & Auto-Rickshaws The official posted rates for taxis are Rs 3.85 for the first km plus Rs 3.30 for each subsequent km. Equivalent rates for auto-rickshaws are Rs 2.20 and Rs 2 respectively. Both taxis and auto-rickshaws are entitled to charge up to 60% of the actual fare to cover a return trip but rarely do in practice except after dark. Many taxi drivers will actually quote *below* meter rates for long trips (Rs 10 to Rs 20), so it's worth asking around. Taxis can, of course, be shared by up to five people.

Typical fares from Panaji include Calangute, Rs 35 to Rs 40; Colva, Rs 130 to Rs 150; and Dabolim Airport, Rs 150 (negotiable) plus Rs 3 for the Zuari River bridge toll.

Local Ferries One of the joys of travelling around Goa are the ferries across the many rivers in this small state. Almost without exception they are combined passenger/car ferries. The main ferries are:

Panaji to Betim These are the ferries that connect with buses, motorbikes and taxis going north of Panaji. There are nonstop passenger/car ferries around the clock across the Mandovi River. These ferries are free for passengers and bicycles but you have to pay a small charge for motorbikes and cars (buy the ticket for this before boarding the ferry). For Aguada, Calangute and Baga the ferry landing is opposite the Mandovi Hotel. For Mapusa and points further north the ferry landing is opposite the Tourist Hostel.

Dona Paula to Mormugao This ferry runs between September and May only. There are regular crossings but they are infrequent and, at certain times of the day, you could find yourself waiting about two hours. The crossing takes 30 to 45 minutes and costs Rs 1.20. Buses wait on either side for the arrival of boats. This is a passenger ferry only, but it's the best way of getting from Panaji to Vasco da Gama.

Old Goa to Piedade Ferries every 30 minutes.

Other Ferries These include: Aldona to Corjuem; Colvale to Macasana; Pomburpa to Chorao; Ribander to Chorao and Siolim to Chopdem. There are also launches from the central jetty in Panaji to Aldona (once daily), Britona (twice daily), Naroa (twice daily) and Verem.

Bicycle There are plenty of places to hire bicycles in all the major towns and beaches in Goa. Standard charges are Rs 1.50 per hour or Rs 8 for a full day (8 am to 6 pm) plus Rs 2 if you keep it overnight. Occasionally you'll be asked for more. If you object, go to a different place.

Motorbike Hiring a motorbike in Goa is easy, and many long-term travellers do just that. The machines available are old Enfields (which often need loving care on the spark plugs) and Rajdoots (Indian manufacture which one of the authors of this book asserts, from experience, are the worst in the world). Obviously what you pay for – with certain exceptions – is what you get, but Rs 400 per week would be about right for an Enfield. On a daily basis you're looking at around Rs 100 per day for a fairly new Rajdoot. You'll need your passport and a sizeable deposit before they'll let you go.

While it might be more expensive than the buses – and with all due respect to the conservationist lobby – the freedom it gives you cannot be measured. If you don't agree then rent a bicycle – but getting down to Palolen or up to Terekhol is something else on a bicycle!

OLD GOA
History
Even before the arrival of the Portuguese, Old Goa was a thriving and prosperous city and the second capital of the Adil Shahi dynasty of Bijapur. At that time it was a fortress surrounded by walls, towers and a moat, and contained many temples and mosques as well as the large palace of Adil Shah. Today none of these structures remain except for a fragment of the gateway to the palace. What there is dates from the Portuguese period.

Under the Portuguese the city grew rapidly in size and splendour, eventually coming to rival Lisbon itself, despite an epidemic in 1543 which wiped out a large percentage of the population. Many huge churches, monasteries and convents were erected by the various religious orders which came to Goa under royal mandates. The Franciscans were the first to arrive.

Old Goa's splendour was short-lived, however, because by the end of the 16th century Portuguese supremacy on the seas had been replaced by that of the British, Dutch and French. The city's decline was accelerated by the activities of the Inquisition and a devastating epidemic which struck the population in 1635. Indeed, if it had not been for the treaty between the British and the Portuguese, it is probable that Goa would either have passed to the Dutch or been absorbed into British India.

The city muddled on into the early 19th century as the administrative capital of Portugal's eastern empire which consisted of Goa, Daman and Diu in India, a string of port cities along the East African coast, Timor in Indonesia, and Macau in China.

Today it's a small village surrounded by huge churches and convents built during its heyday. Some of them remain in active use while others have become museums maintained by the Archaeological Survey of India – a maintenance very necessary because if the lime plaster which protects the laterite structure was not renewed frequently, the monsoons would soon reduce the buildings to ruin. The city attracts visitors from many parts of the world.

Information
The Archaeological Survey of India publishes *Old Goa* by S Rajagopalan (New Delhi 1975), an excellent booklet about the monuments. It's available from the Archaeological Museum in Old Goa.

Se Cathedral
The largest of the churches in Old Goa, Se Cathedral was begun in 1562 during the reign of King Dom Sebastião (1557-78) and substantially completed by 1619, though the altars were not finished until 1652. The cathedral was built for the Dominicans and paid for by the Royal Treasury out of the proceeds of the sale of Crown property.

Architecturally, the building is Portuguese-Gothic in style with a Tuscan exterior and Corinthian interior. There were originally two towers, one on either side of the facade, but one collapsed in 1776. The remaining tower houses a famous bell, one of the largest in Goa, often called the 'Golden Bell' because of its rich sound. The main altar is dedicated to St Catherine of Alexandria, and old paintings on either side of it depict scenes from her life and martyrdom.

Convent & Church of St Francis of Assisi
This is one of the most interesting buildings in Old Goa. It contains gilded and carved woodwork, old murals depicting

scenes from the life of St Francis, and a floor substantially made of carved gravestones – complete with family coats of arms dating back to the early 1500s. The church was built by eight Franciscan friars who arrived here in 1517 and constructed a small chapel consisting of three altars and a choir. This was later pulled down and the present building was constructed on the same spot in 1661.

The convent at the back of this church is now the Archaeological Museum. It houses many portraits of the Portuguese viceroys, most of them inexpertly touched up; fragments of sculpture from Hindu temple sites in Goa, which show Chalukyan and Hoysala influences; stone Vetal images from the animist cult which flourished in this part of India centuries ago; and a model of a Portuguese caravel minus the rigging (surely someone could get it together to do the rigging!).

Professed House & Basilica of Bom Jesus

The Basilica of Bom Jesus is famous throughout the Roman Catholic world. It contains the tomb and mortal remains of St Francis Xavier who, in 1541, was given the task of spreading Christianity among the subjects of the Portuguese colonies in the east. A former pupil of St Ignatius Loyola, the founder of the Jesuit Order, St Francis Xavier made missionary voyages in the east that became legendary and, considering the state of communications at the time, were nothing short of miraculous.

Arriving in Goa in 1542, St Francis Xavier spent the next few years spreading the Christian faith along the Malabar and Coromandel coasts, until news reached him that Christianity had begun to make inroads in the Molucca Islands (now Maluku in Indonesia). Wishing to make sure that the converts properly comprehended their new faith, he set out on a voyage to those islands, returning to Goa in 1548. He stayed in Goa only a short time however, and soon embarked on a voyage

to Japan where he sought permission from the King of Yamaguchi to teach Christianity. Though permission was granted, Francis made little headway due to the opposition of the Bonzes (Buddhist priests). Disappointed, he boarded a ship bound for Goa but got off at Sancian Island just off the coast of China. There he fell ill and died in December 1552 at the age of 46.

His body was buried on Sancian but subsequently taken to Melaka (Malacca) and placed in the Church of Our Lady of the Mount. Four months later in 1554, Francis' successor had the grave opened in order to pay his respects and, finding that the body was still fresh and lifelike, had it sent to Goa. First kept in St Paul's College, it was then transferred to the Professed House in 1613. After canonisation the body was removed to the Basilica of Bom Jesus. The body is exposed to public view once every 10 years (1994 is the next occasion) on the anniversary of St Francis' death.

Unfortunately, however, it's no longer whole, having been through some weird and wonderful mutilations at the hands of relic seekers, both lay and ecclesiastical. While in Melaka, the body was kept in too small a grave, which resulted in the neck being broken. One of the toes was bitten off in 1554 by a Portuguese woman who wanted a relic of the saint. In 1615 part of the right hand was cut off and sent to Rome where it is venerated in the Church of Gesu, and in 1619 the remaining part of the hand was removed and sent to the Jesuits in Japan. Portions of the intestines have been removed from time to time and distributed to various places!

As well as the 10-year cycle of expositions, a festival is held in Old Goa every year on the anniversary of the saint's death (3 December). The normally sleepy little village becomes a madhouse of pot and pan stalls, food and beer tents, trinket sellers, balloons, firecrackers, buses from all over Goa and even further afield, and thousands of pilgrims, many of whom doss down in the cloisters of the

Basilica. When Mass is said there isn't a square cm of space left in the church.

Apart from the richly gilded altars, the interior of the church is remarkable for its simplicity, and this is the only church which is not plastered on the outside. Construction began in 1594 and the church was completed in 1605. The centre of interest inside the church is, of course, the Tomb of St Francis, the construction of which was underwritten by the Duke of Tuscany and executed by the Florentine sculptor Giovanni Batista Foggini. It took 10 years to build and was completed in 1698. The remains of the body are housed in a silver casket which at one time was covered in jewels. On the walls surrounding it are murals depicting scenes from the saint's journeys, including one of his death on Sancian Island.

The Professed House, next door to the basilica, is a two-storey laterite building covered with lime plaster which was completed in 1585 despite much opposition to the Jesuits. Part of the building burned down in 1663 but was rebuilt in 1783. There's a modern art gallery attached to the basilica.

Church of St Cajetan
Modelled on the original design of St Peter's in Rome, this church was built by Italian friars of the Order of Theatines, who were sent by Pope Urban III to preach Christianity in the kingdom of Golconda (near Hyderabad). The friars were not permitted to work in Golconda and so settled down at Goa in 1640. The construction of the church began in 1655. Historically, it's of much less interest than the other churches.

Church of St Augustine Ruins
All that is left of this church is the enormous 46-metre-high tower which served as a belfry and formed part of the facade of the church. What little is left of the other parts of the church is choked with creepers and weeds, and access is difficult. The church was constructed in 1602 by Augustinian friars who arrived at Goa in 1587.

It was abandoned in 1835 due to the repressive policies of the Portuguese government, which resulted in the eviction of many religious orders from Goa. The church fell into neglect and the vault collapsed in 1842. Many years later, in 1931, the facade and half the tower fell down, followed by more parts in 1938.

Church & Convent of St Monica
This huge, three-storey laterite building was commenced in 1606 and completed in 1627, only to burn down nine years later. Reconstruction started the following year, and it's from this time that the buildings date. Once known as the Royal Monastery due to the royal patronage which it enjoyed, the building is now used by the Mater Dei Institute as a nunnery which was inaugurated in 1964. Visitors are allowed inside if they are reasonably dressed. There are fading murals on the western inside walls.

Other Buildings
Other monuments of minor interest in Old Goa are the Viceroy's Arch, Gate of Adil Shah's Palace, Royal Chapel of St Anthony, Church of St John of God, Chapel of St Catherine, the ruins of the Church of the Carmelites, and the Church of Our Lady of the Mount.

Getting There & Away
If you're a lover of old buildings and exotic ruins you'll need the best part of a day to wander around Old Goa. Otherwise, a morning or an afternoon would be sufficient.

There are frequent buses to Old Goa from the bus stand at Panaji; you can also use all buses from Panaji to Ponda as they also pass through Old Goa. The trip takes 20 to 30 minutes and costs Rs 1. Whenever there is a festival at Old Goa (such as the Festival of St Francis Xavier on 3 December) boats ply between Panaji and Old Goa. This 45-minute trip is a very pleasant way of getting there. The boats used to depart from the former Bombay steamer jetty but as this is now defunct you'll need to make enquiries.

MARGAO (Madgaon)

The capital of Salcete Province, Margao is the main population centre of southern Goa and a pleasant provincial town which still displays many reminders of its Portuguese past. In itself it's not of great interest to travellers, though the old Margao church is worth a visit and the covered market is the best of its kind in the whole of Goa. Its importance, however, is as a service and transport centre for people staying at Colva Beach. If you're planning on staying at Colva you must first head for Margao, which is connected to the rest of Goa and to the neighbouring states by bus, train and taxi.

The covered market is a fascinating place to wander through, even if you don't want to buy anything. If you'll be staying at Colva for some time and renting a house, the other, smaller market behind the Secretariat building is excellent for pots, pans and other kitchen equipment.

If you're coming to Margao from outside Goa, the last bus to Colva Beach leaves at 8 pm. After that you will either have to hire a motorcycle or taxi to get to Colva or stay overnight in Margao.

Information & Orientation

The tourist office is in the Secretariat building on the bottom side of the Municipal Gardens. The staff are friendly and helpful though, as elsewhere in India, they're limited in what they can offer due to lack of funds.

The main bus station (Kadamba bus station) is about 1½ km from the centre of town on the road to Panaji. Auto-rickshaws, motorcycles and taxis are available for transfer between the two.

The main taxi stand is behind the Secretariat building.

Rau Raje Deshprabhu, in the Old Market, is an Indian Airlines agent. The

poste restante is not in the GPO on the top side of the Municipal Gardens, but in a separate office about 300 metres away.

Places to Stay - bottom end

A very pleasant place in this bracket is the *Woodlands Hotel* (tel 21121), Miguel Loyola Furtado Rd, which has friendly staff and its own bar and restaurant. Singles/doubles are Rs 40/55 with bath, and air-con rooms are Rs 90 a double.

Most of the other cheapies are strung out along Station Rd between the central Municipal Park and the railway station. I'd nominate the friendly *Rukrish Hotel*, opposite the Bank of India, as the best of the bunch. Here you can get a good, clean single with a small balcony overlooking the street for Rs 30, or doubles with bath for Rs 40 to Rs 50.

Other hotels of similar standard along Station Rd include the *Milan Kamat Hotel* (tel 22715) and the *Sanrit Hotel* (tel 21226) in front of the railway station. *Centaur Boarding & Lodging*, around the corner from the Sanrit, is in the same category. Across the other side of the railway tracks, close to the turn-off for Benaulim, is the *Hotel Annapurna* (tel 22760).

Near the market in the middle of town the government-run *Tourist Hostel* (tel 21966) has singles/doubles for Rs 50/60 (or Rs 45/50 in the low season). It's of a similar standard to the Tourist Hostel in Panaji. Another place worth checking out is the *Twiga Lodge* (tel 20049), 413 Abade Faria Rd, which has singles/doubles for under Rs 50. It's off the main road so there's no traffic noise.

At the top of this bracket, the *Mabai Hotel* (tel 21653/8), conveniently located on the top side of the Municipal Gardens, has singles/doubles for Rs 50/82, Rs 82/126 with air-con. The rooms are large, airy and pleasantly decorated and there's a restaurant, bar and roof garden.

Similar is the *Hotel La Flor* (tel 21591), Erasmo Carvalho St, which has singles/doubles for Rs 55/75 and air-con

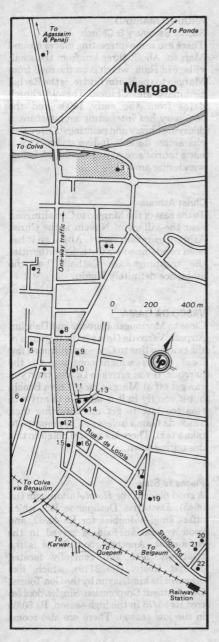

1	Kadamba Bus Station
2	Twiga Lodge
3	Margao Church
4	Hotel Metropole
5	Poste Restante
6	Goa Woodlands
7	Bank
8	GPO
9	Mabai Hotel
10	Marliz
11	Kandeel Restaurant
12	Tourist Office & Bar & Kamat Hotel
13	Buses to Colva
14	La Marina
15	Market
16	Rukrish Hotel
17	Paradise Bar & Restaurant
18	Centaur Lodging
19	Milan Kamat Hotel
20	Vishranti Lodge
21	Sangram Boarding
22	Hotel Sanrit

singles/doubles from Rs 100/120 up to Rs 150/170.

Places to Stay – middle

The *Hotel Metropole* (tel 21169), Avenida Concessão, a short walk from the centre of town, offers singles/doubles for Rs 125/150 and air-con singles/doubles for Rs 200/250. There are two restaurants, a roof garden, bar, disco and bookshop.

Places to Eat

The partially air-conditioned *Kandeel* is beside the Municipal Gardens and the friendly staff serve superb Goan-style food. Try the Goan fish, masala chicken and rice which come complete with chappati, papadam, salad and pickles. They also have ice-cold beers.

Close by is *La Marina Cafe* which is a very reasonable restaurant although they don't have everything their extensive menu promises. There is a bakery next door. Directly opposite the tourist office, the charming *Longuinhos* does ultra-hot curries ('recommended only for fire eaters') and good sweets and cakes.

For snacks and breakfasts, the *Marliz*

on the top side of the Municipal Gardens is an extremely popular cafe and has been so for many years. It's always crowded – and for very good reasons as its snacks are excellent. They include sandwiches, vegetarian and non-vegetarian pasties, cakes and coffee.

Getting There & Away
Colva Beach Buses run to Colva via Benaulim approximately every hour. The first bus from Margao leaves at about 7.30 am and the last at 8 pm. The fare is Rs 1.20 and the journey takes 20 to 25 minutes.

Alternatively, you can take a motorcycle for Rs 8 (no objection to rucksacks) or a taxi. The fares of the latter are government regulated so it should cost Rs 25 during the day but more at night because they're entitled to charge 50% of the cost of the return journey. You can share this with up to five people.

Panaji Buses depart approximately every half-hour from dawn to 8 pm, take about 1½ hours and cost Rs 3.40. It's a picturesque journey, if you get a seat, as there are many old, whitewashed churches and monasteries to be seen en route.

Other Buses You can find buses to most towns in Goa from the Kadamba bus stand in Margao. Timetables are approximate (the buses leave when full) but they're fairly frequent to the major centres of population in central and southern Goa. To the smaller towns, such as Betul south of Colva, they're much less frequent so it's best to make enquiries at the bus station in advance. Get there early if you want a seat.

Train Trains are dealt with in the Panaji section but bookings for all classes can be made at Margao station *except* for Indrail Pass holders who must go to Vasco da Gama to make bookings.

AROUND MARGAO
Rachol Seminary & Church
There are some interesting places around Margao. About three km from the small village of Raia, which is on the road from Margao to the Borim bridge, is the Rachol Seminary and Church. The old church dates from the early 1600s and the seminary has interesting architecture, a decaying library and paintings of Christian characters done in Indian styles. This is not a tourist site so you should ask before wandering around.

Christ Ashram
To the east of the Margao to Cortalim road near the village of Nuvem is the Christ Ashram exorcism centre. Although it has been condemned by Catholic authorities the trappings are Catholic but the ambience definitely Hindu.

VASCO DA GAMA
Close to Mormugao Harbour and Dabolim Airport, Vasco da Gama is the terminus of the railway line to Goa – apart from a few local trains which continue to the harbour. If you arrive in Goa by train you can get off at Margao, near Colva Beach, but if you fly in it is possible to arrive in Goa too late to get much further than Vasco da Gama unless you're prepared to take a taxi. There are several hotels in this unexciting town.

Places to Stay
A good place is the *Hotel Annapurna* (tel 3645), Dattatria Deshpande Rd, which offers singles/doubles for Rs 40/60, and good vegetarian food is served in the restaurant. Another good choice is the relatively new and centrally located *Tourist Hostel* (tel 3119), which, like others of its kind, is run by the Goa Tourist Development Corporation. Singles/doubles cost Rs 55/75 in the high season, Rs 50/65 in the low season. There are also rooms

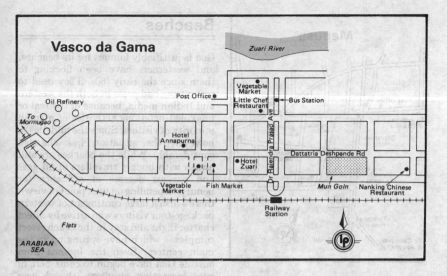

Vasco da Gama

with four beds for Rs 90 (high season) and Rs 70 (low season).

Other cheap hotels include the *Hotel Manish* (tel 2419), F L Gomes Rd, the *Sultan Lodge* (tel 2507) and the *Hotel Zuari*. The *Hotel La Paz Gardens* (tel 2121/6), Swatantra Path, has air-con singles/doubles for Rs 175/300.

Places to Eat

The *Nanking Chinese Restaurant*, three blocks east of the railway station, is a friendly place with good food. You can also get excellent, though somewhat expensive, food at the *Hotel Zuari*. Travellers in search of something resembling western fast food should try the *Little Chef*.

MAPUSA

Mapusa (pronounced locally as 'Mapsa') is the main centre of population in the northern provinces of Goa and the main town for supplies if you are staying either at Anjuna or Chapora. If you're staying at Calangute or Baga, you have a choice of Panaji or Mapusa as a service centre. In itself, there's nothing to see in Mapusa,

though the Friday market is worth a visit. You may, however, need to stay here overnight if you're catching a bus to Bombay the following day – there's no need to go to Panaji for long-distance buses unless you particularly want to.

Places to Stay

There's no need to actually stay in Mapusa – accommodation at the nearby beaches of Anjuna, Vagator and Chapora is far preferable. If you have to stay here, the *Hotel Bardez* (tel 2607) is a good choice. It has rooms for Rs 50/70 with bath.

Also reasonable value is the *Tourist Hostel* (tel 2794), on the roundabout at the entrance to Mapusa, which has singles/doubles for Rs 55/70 and rooms with four beds for Rs 80 in the high season. In the low season the tariff is Rs 50/60 and Rs 60 respectively.

At the top end of the scale is the *Satyahara Hotel* (tel 2849), near the Maruti Temple. Rooms cost Rs 50/80 for singles/doubles and Rs 140/225 with air-con.

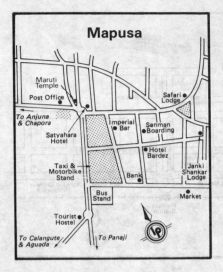

Mapusa

Maruti Temple
Post Office
To Anjuna & Chapora
Satyahara Hotel
Safari Lodge
Imperial Bar
Sanman Boarding
Hotel Bardez
Taxi & Motorbike Stand
Bank
Janki Shankar Lodge
Bus Stand
Market
Tourist Hostel
To Calangute & Aguada
To Panaji

Places to Eat

The *Tourist Hostel* has a large dining hall. The *Imperial Bar & Restaurant* serves good non-vegetarian food and cold beers. It's clean, easygoing and popular with local people.

Getting There & Away

As at Panaji, schedules are only approximate (buses leave when full), but bus services are frequent. Buses to Anjuna and Chapora can be very crowded – mostly with westerners staying on the beaches. Mapusa to Panaji takes about 25 minutes and costs Rs 1. There are also buses to Calangute and to other population centres in northern Goa.

Instead of buses you can take either a taxi or a motorcycle. A motorbike to Anjuna or Calangute costs Rs 12 and takes about 15 minutes. Taxi fares are government controlled so you should only be paying about Rs 25 to Rs 30 (shared by up to five people).

Beaches

Goa is justifiably famous for its beaches, and westerners have been flocking to them since the early '60s. They used to suffer from bad press in both the western and Indian media, because of the real or imagined nefarious activities of a small minority of visitors. Since the mid-1980s, however, the situation has changed considerably. While the beaches are still awash with budget travellers of all ages and various degrees of affluence (or penury, depending on your point of view), there's also a large contingent of western package-tour visitors who arrive by direct charter flight and stay in the beach resort complexes which have sprung up in the main centres. Even the Indians from outside Goa have begun to come here in ever increasing numbers, though you won't find them swimming or sunbathing!

The only problem is deciding which beach to head for. Much depends on how long you intend to stay. Renting a room at a hotel is an expensive way of staying long-term and most budget travellers prefer to either rent a simple room at one of the beach cafes or to rent a private house on a monthly basis (shared, if desired, with a group of friends). Such rooms and houses can be found at all the main centres but there's heavy demand for the latter in the winter (high) season, so it might take you several days to track one down. In the meantime, stay at a cafe or hotel and do a lot of asking around.

Colva & Benaulim, Calangute & Baga, Vagator & Chapora and Anjuna are the main beaches where travellers congregate. Instant accommodation is easiest at Colva & Benaulim and Calangute & Baga. At the others you may have to do quite a bit of legwork before you find somewhere to stay as there are no real hotels as such (if you disregard the relatively expensive Vagator Beach Resort).

All these beaches are well touristed, so if what you have in mind is that near-deserted beach, then you'll have to look further afield. Arambol (or Harmal as it's spelt on some maps), near the northern tip of Goa, is one such place. Betul, south of Colva, and Palolen, even further south, are two others. The 'real' freaks have gone even further south over the border into Karnataka to a place called Gokarn, off the main Panaji to Mangalore road, though a few still hang in at Arambol.

The Aguada and Bogmalo beaches are essentially for affluent tourists staying at the beach resorts there.

Just a word of warning. When using the beaches, it pays to be a little security conscious. Things do get stolen on the beaches so don't leave valuables unattended. Better still, don't bring them to the beach at all unless you're going to take turns looking after them.

COLVA & BENAULIM

Colva stretches sun-drenched, palm-fringed and virtually deserted for km after

km. Fifteen years ago precious little disturbed its soft white sands and warm crystal-clear turquoise waters, except the local fishers who pulled their catch in by hand each morning, and a few of the more intrepid hippies who had forsaken the obligatory drugs, sex and rock & roll of Calangute for the soothing tranquillity of this corner of paradise. Since there were only two cottages for rent and one restaurant (Vincy's), most people stayed either on the beach itself or in palm-leaf shelters, which they took over from departing travellers or constructed themselves.

Those days are gone forever. Even in days of yore the property speculators and developers had begun to sniff around in search of a fast rupee. Today, you can see the results of their efforts – air-conditioned resort complexes, close-packed ranks of tourist cottages, discos, trinket stalls and cold-drink stalls. You'll be lucky if you see an angler around the main area and,

Colva Beach

anyway, most have acquired motorised trawlers which stand anchored in a line offshore. Likewise, you won't come across anyone sleeping out on the beach these days or throwing up a palm-leaf shelter. The changing times and the determination of the average male Indian day-tripper to catch a glimpse of a scantily clad western female body put paid to all that.

It's only fair to point out that this development is concentrated in a relatively small area at the end of the road from Margao, and that it's simplicity itself to get away from it. Walk two km either side of there, and you'll get close to what it used to be like before the cement mixers began chugging away. It could be said we have only ourselves to blame for making the beach so popular in the first place, but Colva still has a long way to go before it gets as developed as Calangute, or a lot of other beaches I could think of around the world. It's still the best of the Goan beaches, and if you like a really quiet life you can always head further south to Benaulim, Betul or Palolen.

Information

The nearest post office is in Colva village. Letters can be sent poste restante there rather than to Margao if you like. At present there is no bank in the village, but the Silver Sands Hotel may be prepared to change travellers' cheques. The nearest banks are in Benaulim village (Bank of Baroda) and Margao.

Places to Stay

The best deal – if you're going to stay here for a while – is to rent a house with a number of other people. If you're not already part of a large enough group, ask around in the cafes at Colva and Benaulim, or take a walk along the road which runs parallel to the beach from Colva village in both directions, and ask every time you see a likely looking place. It shouldn't take more than a few days. Obviously you get what you pay for, but around Rs 400 per month would be

reasonable. Between November and March competition is stiff, so get there before then if possible. There are very few places to rent on a long-term basis on the beach itself; most houses are a good 15 to 20 minutes walk from the beach.

The price of hotel accommodation varies according to the season. The peak season stretches from 16 November to 15 February, the shoulder from 16 February to 15 June and 16 September to 15 November, and the low season from 16 June to 15 September. Unless otherwise stated, peak season rates are quoted in what follows. In the shoulder period you can expect up to 20% less; in the low season it is 50% to 60% less.

Colva For short-term accommodation there is a wide choice. At the cheaper end of the market are various places strung out along the beach, north of the main area. They're usually just a few simple rooms attached to a restaurant but prices have risen considerably over the last few years so don't expect too many bargains. In the high season you're looking at about Rs 60 a double. The rooms at the *Lucky Star Restaurant*, for example, are Rs 60 a double with bath and fan. There are similarly priced rooms at the *Summer Queen Cottage* next to the Sunset Restaurant.

Also popular in this bracket is the *Vailankanni Cottages* at Rs 60 for a double downstairs with common bath and Rs 80 a double upstairs with private bath. All the rooms have fans and mosquito nets and it's run by a very friendly family. The place has its own good and reasonably priced restaurant. Further away from the beach is the *Tourist Nest* which offers ordinary doubles for Rs 50 and Rs 65 and 'luxury' doubles with bath for Rs 85. Slightly more expensive, but very close to the beach, is *Jymi's Cottages* which charges Rs 70 a double downstairs and Rs 90 a double upstairs. All the rooms have baths.

More expensive but excellent value for

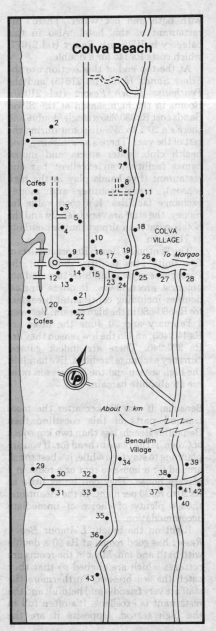

Colva Beach

1	Lucky Star Restaurant
2	Longuinhos Beach Resort
3	Colmar Hotel
4	Tourist Complex
5	Cycle Hire
6	Andorinho Restaurant
7	Umita Corner Restaurant
8	Tourist Nest
9	Bus Stop
10	Skylark Cottages
11	Bicycle Hire
12	Vincy Hotel
13	Mar E Sol Hotel
14	Silver Sands Hotel
15	Lactancia Restaurant
16	Colva Beach Resort
17	Johnny Cool
18	Nosso Bar & Restaurant
19	Man Mar Inn
20	Penthouse Beach Resort
21	Jymi's Cottages
22	Sukhsagar Hotel
23	Williams Resort
24	Vailankanni Cottages
25	General Store
26	Church
27	Post Office
28	Paloma Restaurant
29	Pedro's Bar & Johnney's
30	L'Amour Beach Resort
31	O Palmar Cottages
32	Green Garden Tourist Cottages
33	Liteo Cottages
34	Kencro Tourist Cottages
35	Savio Rest House
36	Bar Dominic
37	Cacy-Rose Restaurant
38	Maria Hall
39	Fridola's Restaurant
40	Caravan Tourist Home
41	Church
42	Brito's Tourist Home
43	Palm Grove Cottages

money is the government-owned *Tourist Complex* (or Tourist Cottages) (tel 22287) which consists of a double-storied terrace of rooms facing the sea (each with their own balcony), a separate block of cottages, a restaurant, bar, reception area and garden. The rooms cost Rs 80/120 a double complete with clean sheets, fan and bathroom. There's also a dormitory for Rs 20 per bed. In the low season prices drop to Rs 60/80 a double and Rs 10 for a dormitory bed. The place is very well maintained and the staff are friendly.

Similar, but without the favourable aspect, is the *Sukhsagar Hotel* (tel (08342) 20224) which offers doubles for Rs 130 and Rs 230 with air-con. In the low season prices drop to Rs 55/60 for singles/doubles, Rs 110/120 with air-con. All rooms have baths with hot and cold running water. The hotel has a bar but no restaurant.

At a similar price are the *Skylark Cottages* at Rs 126 a double with bathroom. It's a new place and the rooms are very clean. In the low season prices drop by around 30%, and there are also new air-con rooms. The *Vincy Hotel* (tel 22276), once the only bar/restaurant in the area, has been through many changes as Colva changed from an obscure fishing village to a major resort area. The original Indo-Portuguese structure has sadly long since disappeared and Vincy's has joined the 20th century with a vengeance. It now offers double rooms with bath and hot and cold running water for Rs 150. More rooms have recently been built. There's a vast restaurant on the ground floor, and although it has no atmosphere, the food is good.

There are six other places here but they're definitely in the top-end bracket. Cheapest is the *Colmar Hotel* (the former White Sands Hotel) (tel 21253) which has double rooms with common bathroom for Rs 100, doubles with bathroom for Rs 200 and chalets for Rs 350. The hotel has its own restaurant and bar, money exchange facilities and is used by overland tour groups.

A similar place is the *Longuinhos Beach Resort* (tel 22918), a pleasant, self-contained hotel with its own bar and restaurant adjacent to the beach. Rooms with bath and hot water cost Rs 200 a double. Further away from the beach is the *Colva Beach Resort* with doubles for Rs 175 and air-con doubles for Rs 300, both

with bath and hot water. There's no restaurant at this hotel. Also in this category is *William's Resort* (tel 21077) which costs Rs 145 for a double.

At the top end of this section are the *Silver Sands Hotel* (tel 21645) and the *Penthouse Beach Resort* (tel 21030). Rooms in the high season at the Silver Sands cost Rs 330/395 a single/double and there's a 20% to 35% discount during the rest of the year. There's a swimming pool, health club, water sports and indoor games facilities, an excellent bar and restaurant (live bands play in the high season), travel counter and money exchange facilities. It's good value for money, the staff are very friendly and the hotel operates an airport shuttle bus daily at 11.30 am.

The Penthouse Beach Resort consists of five units plus facilities built in the Portuguese style of architecture and set amongst green lawns. It offers singles/doubles including continental breakfast for Rs 560/580 in the high season. Between 1 February and 30 June the rates are Rs 440/460, and in the low season they are Rs 220/240. There are indoor games, currency exchange facilities, live bands in the high season and the low-season rates are an absolute bargain.

Benaulim If you hanker after the more tranquil parts of this coastline then Benaulim Beach, less than two km south of Colva, is the place to head for. If you are planning to stay for a while, it's best to ask around for a house to rent or a room in a private house. They can be as little as Rs 20 to Rs 30 per night. In the meantime, there's plenty of choice of immediate accommodation.

Right on the beach, *L'Amour Beach Resort* has good rooms at Rs 80 a double with bath and fan. Most of the rooms are cottages which are aligned so that they catch the sea breezes. Furthermore the staff are very friendly and helpful, and the restaurant is excellent. It's often full in the high season. Opposite it are the

O Palmar Beach Cottages which cost the same and have a fan and bathroom. If there's nobody around, enquire at Pedro's Bar & Restaurant by the beach.

Most of the other places are scattered around the village of Benaulim about one km back from the beach, and accommodation here is generally cheaper than that available at the beach itself. The first places you'll come to walking back from the beach are the *Tansy Tourist Cottages* and the *Liteo Cottages*. The latter is a modern two-storey building with verandahs; you should make enquiries at the house opposite. A little further on is the *Green Garden Tourist Cottage*.

Turn left at the first crossroads and you'll find the *Kencro Tourist Cottages*; or turn right and you'll find the *Savio Rest House* and the *Palm Grove Cottages*. The latter is a delightful place set in very colourful gardens. A more tranquil setting is hard to imagine. It's quite a walk, however, from the turn-off past the Bar Dominic and over a small bridge (about one km in total).

Benaulim village is at the second crossroads and, off to the right, you'll find the *Caravan Tourist Home*, a small place with a few rooms to let. The best place to stay in Benaulim itself, however, is *Brito's Tourist Home* which has doubles for Rs 50 including bathroom and cooking facilities with gas provided. If it's full they have two rooms at their own house close by for Rs 40 a double. Many people stay here for months and come back year after year. It's owned by Edmund Brito who is a very mellow, friendly and interesting man who will regale you with tales of what Goa used to be like in the old days. Attached to the building is a small general store which is also where you will find Edmund.

Bogmalo North of Colva and close to the airport is Bogmalo where the *Oberoi Bogmalo Beach* (tel 2191/2) has 118 rooms with singles/doubles for Rs 800/925 at the height of the season. Substantial discounts are available in the low season. There's a swimming pool, water sports and all the other five-star facilities.

Places to Eat

If you're at the beach you naturally want to eat outside, and there's plenty of alfresco restaurants. It doesn't matter how good the food is if it's spoilt by having to eat it inside glass and concrete and away from the sights and sounds that attracted you to Goa in the first place.

Colva The most popular places to eat (and drink) around Colva itself are the string of open-air wooden restaurants which line the beach on either side of where the road ends. They're all individually owned and, because of the competition, the standard of food is pretty high. Seafood is, of course, *de rigeur* and the restaurants are well tuned in to what travellers like for breakfast. Virtually all of them have a sound system but the variety and quality of the tapes which they play varies enormously – best to bring your own if possible. Cold beer and spirits are available at all of them.

It would be unfair to single out individual restaurants for special mention since every traveller has a favourite and that often depends on the particular crowd which eats there. This naturally changes constantly. There is one thing you do need to watch at these restaurants, however. If you're eating fish, you'll be asked whether you want a large or small piece. The menu prices are for 'small' pieces and if you ask for a large piece the price of a meal can double despite the fact that there's precious little difference in size. The other restaurants in Colva that are back from the beach don't operate this pernicious system so, although their prices are generally higher, you can often eat a substantial meal there for less than what it would cost at the beach huts. Perhaps the system only operates during the high season when there are plenty of well-heeled tourists around who don't baulk at the 'hidden extras'.

Apart from the beach huts, there are plenty of established restaurants to choose from. One of the cheapest is the *Lucky Star Restaurant*. It's been a popular place for years and has a reasonable sound system. You can eat here for between Rs 15 and Rs 20. Other cheapies close to the beach are the *Sunset Restaurant* and the *Lactancia Restaurant* but their days of glory as travellers' meccas have long since passed.

Further back from the beach along the back road are a number of popular places. They include the *Man Mar Inn*, the *Nosso Lar Bar & Restaurant*, *Umita Corner Restaurant & Bar* and the *Andorinho Restaurant*. The Nosso Lar is an interesting old place with some Portuguese flavour but if you want to eat here in the evening then call in earlier in the day and let them know what you'd like. Other travellers have recommended the improbably named *Johnny Cool*. The sort of night you have at any one of them depends largely on the crowd which turns up but the food is generally good.

The *Vincy Hotel* was Colva's original restaurant, but although it now occupies about three times its former space and still attracts a fair share of customers, it sports the atmosphere of a fast-food outlet. Prices, however, are still reasonable and, despite the lack of atmosphere, the food is very good and the portions generous. The garlic prawns here are excellent. The *Peacock Bar & Restaurant* at the Hotel Mar E Sol is similar.

Going up somewhat in price, the *Dolphin* at the Hotel Colmar is still good but the restaurant is enclosed so there are no sea breezes to enliven the cuisine. The same is true of the restaurant at the *Tourist Complex* though they do have a good variety of Indian curries as opposed to seafood on the menu.

For a splurge, there's a choice of three places – *Longuinhos Beach Resort*, *Silver Sands Hotel* and *Penthouse Beach Resort*. The cuisine and service at these places is what you would expect from multistar hotels but they all offer Goan, Indian and continental dishes as well as seafood. Both the Silver Sands and the Penthouse have live bands during the high season and dinner is often an 'all you can eat' smorgasbord for a set price. They're all good value and not beyond a budget traveller's pocket but, if alfresco is your preference, then head for the Penthouse. The other restaurants are enclosed.

Benaulim Down at Benaulim, the *L'Amour Beach Resort* restaurant offers a wide variety of seafood plus chips. Some recent reports, however, suggest that the food and service is not as good as it used to be, though the prices are reasonable. *Pedro's Bar & Restaurant* on the beach at Benaulim is a mellow place and has been popular for years. The only problem about this place is finding someone to order from, and the service tends to be erratic. Very similar are the two beach huts below Pedro's which include the popular *Johnney's*.

There are a number of places back from the beach at Benaulim village. One of the most popular at present is the *Cacy-Rose Bar & Restaurant*, very close to the cross-roads opposite Maria Hall. It's also a good place to ask around for accommodation in the village. Also very popular, especially for evening meals, is *Fridola's Restaurant*, a little way down the road to Colva.

If you're staying at either the Savio Rest House or Palm Grove Cottages then the *Bar Dominic* should be able to fix you up with a meal if you order in advance.

Getting There & Around

Buses run from Colva to Margao every hour and take 25 minutes. The fare is Rs 1. The first bus from Colva departs around 7.30 am and the last one back leaves about 8 pm.

A taxi from Colva to Margao costs Rs 25 shared between up to five or six people (or more if the driver is willing). Colva to Dabolim Airport costs Rs 120 and to Panaji costs Rs 150. The fare to Panaji is negotiable and it's relatively easy to get it down to Rs 130.

If you like the wind through your hair, the easiest way to get between Margao and Colva is to take a motorcycle. The standard fare is about Rs 10. Backpacks are no problem.

There are plenty of places to rent bicycles from in both Colva and Benaulim. The most convenient places in Colva are at the back of the Tourist Complex just past the Skylark Cottages and close to the Tourist Nest on the back road. The usual charge is Rs 1.50 an hour or Rs 8 for a full day plus a further Rs 2 if you keep it overnight. Some places charge more so you'll have to negotiate. At low tide you can ride down the beach to the picturesque fishing port of Betul at the southern end. It's possible to get a boat across the estuary and then cycle back via Margao.

If the weekly flee market at Anjuna Beach is operating, you will see large signs advertising buses in many of the beach restaurants and at some of the hotels in Colva and Benaulim. If you're not planning on staying at any of the northern beaches then it's worth making the day trip – but it will take you the best part of a day. The cost is minimal. Doing this trip by public buses involves umpteen changes and a lot of messing about. It's also possible to hire one of the wooden ex-fishing boats to take you there but for this you're going to have to get a group together as they're relatively expensive.

CALANGUTE & BAGA

Until recently, Calangute was the beach all self-respecting hippies headed for, especially around Christmas when all psychedelic hell broke loose and the beach was littered with more budding rock stars than most people have hot dinners. If you enjoyed taking part in those mass pujas with their endless half-baked discussions about 'when the revolution comes' and 'the vibes, man', then this was just the ticket. You could frolic around with not a stitch on, be ever so cool and liberated,

and completely disregard the feelings of the local inhabitants. You could get totally out of your head every minute of the night and day on every conceivable variety of ganja from Timor to Tenochtitlan, exhibit the most bizarre behaviour, babble an endless stream of drivel and bore everybody shitless. Naturally, John Lennon or The Who were always about to turn up and give a free concert. Ah, Woodstock! Where did you go!

Calangute's heyday as the Mecca of all expatriate hippies has passed and the place has settled down to the more bourgeois pursuits of selling handicrafts, jewellery and woven fabrics to the tourists. It no longer provides the Indian press with a permanent shock-horror story about the decadent, drug-crazed (not to mention naked) fiends who were supposed to be rotting the moral fibre of Indian youth. Calangute isn't one of the best Goan beaches – there are hardly any swaying palms to grace the shoreline, much of the sand is contaminated with red soil and the beach drops pretty rapidly into the sea – but there's plenty going on and people who find Colva too quiet may find Calangute just the place.

Only two km north of Calangute is Baga, where the beach is much better and where there's a good choice of restaurants and accommodation. Indeed, Baga has become more popular with travellers than Calangute over the last few years and it's easy to see why. There's nowhere near the same degree of commercialisation as there is at Calangute, the atmosphere is much mellower and the landscape more interesting. Development is definitely creeping closer and closer but there's still a sort of *cordon sanitaire* between the two.

Information & Orientation

The tourist office and the post office are next to each other where the road forks to Baga and Calangute Beach. Across the road is an excellent second-hand bookshop offering books in most languages you could care to name. You can buy, sell or exchange here. Halfway between these places and Calangute village, and next to the Hotel Orfil, is a branch of the State Bank of India where you can change travellers' cheques and cash.

Close to the tourist office are two travel agents – MGM and Space Travels – which offer discount tickets to other parts of the world at rates similar to those you can get in Bombay. There are numerous stalls all the way from the crossroads to the beach selling genuine and reproduction Tibetan and Rajasthani crafts. Most of them are well made and some of them stunningly beautiful, but they aren't cheap. Interesting jewellery, bangles and other ethnic trinkets (usually Tibetan, Kashmiri and Indian tribal in origin) are available.

Places to Stay

Just like Colva Beach, the price you pay for accommodation here depends on the season. The high season stretches from 15 December to 31 January, the shoulder from 1 February to 30 June and 1 October to 14 December, and the low season is from 1 July to 30 September. Finding budget accommodation – or even higher priced accommodation – in the high season is not always easy so you may initially have to stay in whatever is available and put a lot of effort into asking around. Baga is the place to head for if you don't want to pay through the nose for the first few days.

Over the last few years there's been a tremendous spate of building activity around Calangute and the place is now awash with hotels, most of them in the mid to upper-range bracket.

Calangute Despite the building boom it's still possible to find privately owned rooms or part houses here for as little as Rs 15 per night – but there aren't many of them. Don't expect anything other than a bed without linen, a couple of chairs and access to a well for this price. A good place

to ask about these is Pete's Bar & Restaurant.

There's a fair choice of budget accommodation south of the road which leads to the beach. The *Souza Lobo Restaurant* (tel 79) has quite a few attractively constructed bamboo matting doubles for Rs 50 with common bathroom. They're clean and a table fan is provided but, unfortunately, the rooms don't have windows and the verandah is taken up by the restaurant.

Better perhaps, are the various houses owned by the Fernandes family. The first you'll come to on the back road heading south is the *Fernandes Beach Resort*. Despite the name, it's just a cottage with a few rooms to rent for around Rs 60 a double. Enquire here or at Pete's Bar & Restaurant a few metres down the road. On the opposite side of the road and into the coconut palm groves is *Angela P Fernandes Guest House* which is a large place offering doubles for Rs 50 with common bath and Rs 95 with private bath. It's good value, a popular place to stay and the staff are very friendly. All the rooms have fans.

Similar in price and standard is the *Calangute Guest Paradise*, just before Fernandes Beach Resort, and the *Alfa Guest House* close to the end of this road.

Off to the left down a side track is the very pleasant *Coco Banana* where the rooms surround a quiet courtyard. Rooms here cost Rs 75 a single and Rs 130 to Rs 150 a double, all with bathrooms. The place is very clean, the beds comfortable, fans are provided and the staff are friendly and helpful. Similar is the *Hotel A'Canôa* which has doubles for Rs 100 with bathroom.

Other places in the budget hotel bracket in this area but closer to the sea include the *International Guest House* and *Francisco's Sun Shine Guest House*. The nearby *Calangute Beach Guest House* is a modern place and looks more expensive than it is. The rooms are spacious and

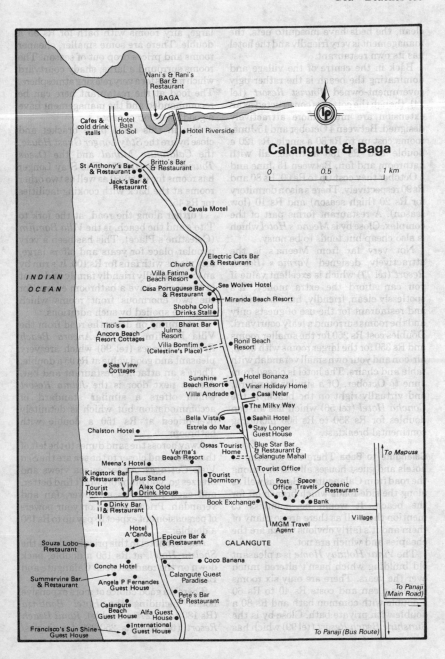

Calangute & Baga

0   0.5   1 km

INDIAN OCEAN

BAGA

Nani's & Rani's Bar & Restaurant

Hotel Baia do Sol

Cafes & cold drink stalls

Hotel Riverside

St Anthony's Bar & Restaurant

Britto's Bar & Restaurant

Jack's Bar & Restaurant

Cavala Motel

Electric Cats Bar & Restaurant

Church

Villa Fatima Beach Resort

Sea Wolves Hotel

Casa Portuguese Bar & Restaurant

Miranda Beach Resort

Shobha Cold Drinks Stall

Tito's

Bharat Bar

Ancora Beach Resort Cottages

Julma Resort

Vilia Bomfim (Celestine's Place)

Ronil Beach Resort

Sea View Cottages

Sunshine Beach Resort

Hotel Bonanza

Vinar Holiday Home

Villa Andrade

Casa Nelar

The Milky Way

Bella Vista

Saahil Hotel

Estrela do Mar

Stay Longer Guest House

Chalston Hotel

Oseas Tourist Home

Blue Star Bar & Restaurant & Calangute Mahal

To Mapusa

Varma's Beach Resort

Meena's Hotel

Tourist Office

Kingstork Bar & Restaurant

Bus Stand

Alex Cold Drink House

Tourist Dormitory

Post Office

Space Travels

Oceanic Restaurant

Tourist Hotel

Dinky Bar & Restaurant

Book Exchange

Bank

Village

Hotel A'Canôa

Epicure Bar & Restaurant

MGM Travel Agent

CALANGUTE

Souza Lobo Restaurant

Concha Hotel

Coco Banana

Summervine Bar & Restaurant

Angela P Fernandes Guest House

Calangute Guest Paradise

Pete's Bar & Restaurant

To Panaji (Main Road)

Calangute Beach Guest House

Alfa Guest House

Francisco's Sun Shine Guest House

International Guest House

To Panaji (Bus Route)

clean, the beds have mosquito nets, the management is very friendly and the hotel has its own restaurant.

Back in the centre of the village and dominating the beach is the rather ugly government-owned *Tourist Resort* (tel 24), though the cottages constructed as an extension are much more attractively designed. Between 4 October and 15 June, rooms cost up to Rs 80 a single, Rs 120 a double and Rs 130 a triple, all with bathroom and fan. Between 15 June and 3 October they cost up to Rs 60, Rs 80 and Rs 90 respectively. There's also a dormitory for Rs 20 (high season) and Rs 10 (low season). A restaurant forms part of the complex. Close by is *Meena's Hotel* which is also cheap but tends to be noisy.

Not very far from Meena's is the attractively designed *Varma's Beach Resort* (tel 77) which is excellent value if you can afford the extra money. It's spotlessly clean, friendly, has its own bar and restaurant for the use of guests only and the rooms surround a leafy courtyard. Doubles cost Rs 250 for the smaller rooms and Rs 350 for the larger rooms with bath, air-con and your own small verandah with table and chairs. The hotel is closed from June to October. Of a similar standard, and virtually right on the beach, is the *Concha Hotel* (tel 56) which has air-con doubles for Rs 350 to Rs 500 including continental breakfast.

Calangute to Baga There are a string of hotels and guest houses all the way along the road from Calangute to Baga as well as along the side roads which branch off for the beach. It would be pointless to mention them all as there are so many of them and it's fairly obvious which are the cheapies and which are not.

The *Vinar Holiday Home* is a pleasant old building which hasn't altered much over the years. There are only six rooms but it's clean and costs Rs 40 to Rs 60 a double with common bath and Rs 80 a double with private bath. Close by is the *Sunshine Beach Resort* (tel 99) which has

large, airy rooms with bath for Rs 95 a double. There are some smaller, cheaper rooms and prices drop out of season. The rooms surround a large, shady courtyard which makes for a very relaxing atmosphere. The food at the restaurant here can be recommended and the management have a good selection of tapes.

Also in this same price bracket and close by are the *Stay Longer Guest House*, the *Calangute Mahal* and the *Oseas Tourist Home* (tel 65). The Stay Longer has rooms for Rs 50/60 as well as two other rooms at the back with cooking facilities for Rs 45.

Further along the road, at the fork to Tito's and the beach, is the *Villa Bomfim* (Celestine's Place). This has been a very popular place for years and offers large, airy rooms with fans for Rs 100. It's run by an exceptionally friendly family and most of the rooms have a bathroom except for the two enormous front rooms which would be spoiled by such additions.

Continuing on down the road from the Villa Bomfim are the *Ancora Beach Resort Cottages* (tel 96) which are very pleasant and good value at Rs 95 a double. There's an attached restaurant and bar. Almost next door is the *Julma Resort* which offers a similar standard of accommodation but which is definitely over-priced at Rs 150 a double with bathroom.

Away across the sand dunes to the left of the Julma and closer to the sea are the *Sea View Cottages*. As far as sea views and breezes go, you probably won't find better, and each room has a shower, fan and verandah. Prices depend on your powers of persuasion but expect to pay up to Rs 150 a double.

Another hotel in this price bracket is the *Shelsta Hotel*, at Rs 150 a double, back down on the road between Calangute and Baga.

There's a good choice of more expensive hotels including the *Hotel Bonanza* (Rs 180 to Rs 275 a double), *Ronil Beach Resort* (tel 68) (Rs 250/300 for singles/

doubles, Rs 300/350 with air-con), *Miranda Beach Resort* and *Sea Wolves Hotel*.

The place I'd nominate as best in this bracket, however, is the *Estrela do Mar* (tel 14) which has to be the Raffles Hotel of Calangute. No anonymous concrete similarity here! All the rooms are different and have their own character. Flowering vines cover the walls and the surrounding gardens are lush and colourful. The open-air bar and restaurant is an ideal place to relax and enjoy excellent food plus the beach is a short trip over the sand dunes. Doubles cost Rs 350 in the high season and Rs 287 in the shoulder season. Larger discounts are available in the low season. Advance booking is recommended in the high season.

Baga On the way into Baga, right next to the Casa Portuguese Bar & Restaurant, you'll come across the *Villa Fatima Beach Resort* set back from the road amid the coconut palm groves. It's a somewhat grandiose name for what is essentially a three-storey building attached to a private house, but it's a very popular place to stay, especially long-term. The family who runs it is really pleasant. Double rooms cost Rs 80 (top floor), Rs 70 (middle floor) and Rs 60 (bottom floor). There are also two other rooms with cooking facilities for Rs 100. It's often full in the high season.

Further in towards Baga is the *Cavala Motel* (tel 90) which offers doubles with their own verandah and bathroom for Rs 120 to Rs 160. There's no restaurant at this hotel.

In Baga itself, you come across a cluster of bar & restaurants alongside the main road – Jack's, Britto's and St Anthony's, with the Two Sisters' Bar & Restaurant a little further off to the right. These are the places to ask around for a room or for a house to rent. It will literally take you minutes to find something. Prices vary from around Rs 15 for just a cubicle and a bed, to Rs 35 for a room with common shower or Rs 75 for a room with shower.

There are also a number of houses and cottages for rent across the river but they're often occupied for weeks and months at a time by long-term visitors, so you'll have to play it by ear. You cross over to the northern side of the river by a most extraordinary bridge which has to be seen to be believed. Somebody was apparently given an unlimited amount of concrete and told to construct the ugliest and most extravagant bridge they could imagine. The upshot was a covered footbridge that could support an army of tanks and survive a direct nuclear hit.

As for hotel accommodation, there's little choice. The cheapest is the *Hotel Riverside* at Rs 180 a double with bathroom and fan. The rooms are very pleasant and clean, and the staff are friendly, plus the hotel has its own bar and restaurant.

More expensive is the two-star *Hotel Baia do Sol* (tel 84/5), a modern hotel set in an attractive flower garden. Singles/doubles here cost from Rs 100/125 to Rs 250/280. Air-con in any of these rooms cost Rs 50 extra per night. The hotel has its own restaurant and bar.

Places to Eat

There are any number of small restaurants all the way from Calangute village to the beach, especially around the bus stand, and a whole collection of them on the beach at Baga. As at Colva, seafood features prominently on the menus of most restaurants though some do also offer meat dishes. Genuine vegetarian food is often hard to find – what you usually get if you order it is a double helping of whatever vegetables would be served with fish or meat. Indian curries are also hard to find, the *Tourist Resort* being one of the few places where they're available.

Right on the beach at Calangute, one of the best places to eat is the *Souza Lobo Restaurant* which has an excellent setting and is a perfect place to watch the sunset or relax in the early afternoon (though it closes between 3 and 6 pm for the benefit of the guests). The food is very good and cheap and it's a popular place to eat. At least as good if not better is the *Dinky Bar & Restaurant* where prices are about the same. The seafood and meat dishes here are extremely tasty.

Another popular place to eat or sit around with a few cold beers is *Pete's Bar & Restaurant* near Angela P Fernandes Guest House. Other travellers have recommended the *Alex Cold Drink House* opposite the Tourist Resort, the *Kingstork Bar & Restaurant* (part of the Tourist Resort), and the *Oceanic Restaurant* up the road past the tourist office and close to the bank.

Along the road to Baga, the *Blue Star Bar & Restaurant* attracts a varied clientele as does the restaurant at the *Sunshine Beach Resort*.

One of the most popular restaurants in this area, however, is *Tito's*, almost at the end of the road which branches off at the Villa Bomfim and heads towards the beach. Formerly known as Richdavy Restaurant, this place has been a travellers' haunt for years on account of its excellent food and pleasant setting overlooking the sea. Prices are generally higher than the restaurants in Calangute and Baga but the taste and the portions match the price. Expect to pay between Rs 20 and Rs 40 for a meal depending on whether you have fish or prawns.

Further up along the main road to Baga is the *Casa Portuguese Bar & Restaurant*. This is a good place for a minor splurge with its old-world charm and pleasant setting among the coconut palms, though not everyone rates the cuisine too highly.

At Baga itself, take your pick of the open-air restaurants – *Jack's Bar & Restaurant*, *Britto's Bar & Restaurant*, *St Anthony's Bar & Restaurant* or the *Two Sisters' Bar & Restaurant*. They're all popular and offer the same sort of fare at a similar price – western breakfast staples, seafood, fruit juices, beer and other drinks.

For a very mellow afternoon or night out, try *Nani's & Rani's Bar & Restaurant* on the other side of the river from the Hotel Baia do Sol (cross the river via the bridge next to the Hotel Riverside). This place doesn't attract a large or consistent clientele so it might be best to order specific meals in advance.

The restaurant at the *Hotel Riverside* has also been recommended by many travellers.

Getting There & Away

There are frequent buses to Panaji and Mapusa from Calangute throughout the day. The fare is Rs 1.30 from Calangute to Panaji and the trip takes 35 to 45 minutes.

Taxis are also available and worth the extra cost if there is a small group of you and you want to save time. Panaji to Calangute or Baga costs Rs 30 to Rs 35 for the car and takes about 15 minutes.

Getting Around

Most of the buses between Panaji and Calangute terminate at Calangute. Very few continue on to Baga so, if you're reliant on buses, make sure you know the schedules.

Bicycles can be hired at many places in Calangute and Baga at the usual rates – Rs 1.50 per hour or Rs 8 for a full day plus Rs 2 for the night, though many places ask for Rs 10 per day. Get there early in the morning if you want the best bicycles – maintenance is only undertaken under duress.

Motorbikes – old Enfields and Rajdoots – are also available for hire at the usual rates (see under Panaji). Hiring by the week or the month is much more economical than by the day. You need basic maintenance skills to keep these machines running – spark plugs oil-up constantly.

AGUADA

South of Calangute, near the mouth of the Mandovi River, Aguada is Goa's jet-set beach. Its main attraction is the 16th century Portuguese Aguada Fort in which the main hotel is built.

Places to Stay

There are several hotels here, all very much at the top end. The five-star *Fort Aguada Beach Resort* (tel 7501/9) is built within the ramparts of the old fort and has air-con rooms or individual cottages at Rs 700 to Rs 995, and Rs 800 to Rs 995 for singles and doubles. The resort has a swimming pool, tennis courts, shops, boats and canoes to rent, and bicycles. They also have a number of villas known as the *Aguada Hermitage* costing Rs 1750/3250 for singles/doubles.

ANJUNA

This is the beach that everyone went to when Calangute had been filmed, recorded, reported and talked about into the sand. There's a weird and wonderful collection of overlanders, monks, defiant ex-hippies, gentle lunatics, artists, artisans, seers, searchers and peripatetic expatriates who normally wouldn't be seen out of the organic confines of their health-food emporia in San Francisco or London.

There's no point in trying to define what Anjuna is or what it's like – it's many different things to many different people. The only way to find out is to stay here for a while and make some friends. Full moon is a particularly good time to be here. Unlike Calangute, the place has retained its charm and there's no hotel development going on here. Nude bathing, on the other hand, is very much on the decline as are the once freely available drugs. Local outrage and official concern about the excesses of a certain minority has led to periodic clampdowns and an exodus to more remote beaches like Arambol to the north and Gokarn over the border in Karnataka to the south.

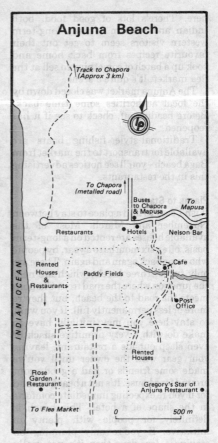

Information

There is a post office to which you can have mail sent but there's no bank.

Flea Market

The Wednesday flea market at Anjuna is a major attraction for people from all the Goan beaches. It's a wonderful blend of Tibetan traders, colourful Gujarati tribal women, blissed-out '60s-style hippies plus just about anybody else you might meet in India. Whatever you need, from a used paperback to read to a new *tanga* (G-string monokini) for the beach, you'll find it here. There's lots of good food, both Indian and western – many long-term western visitors seem to get out their favourite recipes from back home and cook up a batch of something to sell at the flea market. It's quite a scene.

The Anjuna market was closed down by the local authorities some time back. Before heading off, check to see if it has reopened.

Traditional-style fishing boats are available for transport to the market from Baga beach – you'll see notices advertising this in the restaurants.

Places to Stay

It isn't easy to find a place to stay between November and March. Most of the available houses are rented on a long-term basis, often six months to a year, by people who come back again and again. There are only two or three hotels, which are near the junction where the road from Chapora meets the road to the beach, but they're more or less permanently full. If you want to stay here you may initially have to make do with a very primitive shack or even sleep outside a restaurant, leaving your gear with the owner until you've made some friends or had a good scout around for a house. It's not a beach to head for if you're expecting immediate comforts in the shape of a hotel. This beach is definitely for people with plenty of initiative. If you're only planning on staying a few days then it's not really worth coming here except for the market.

Places to Eat

There are any number of restaurants and cafes strung out along the road to the beach and all along the beachfront. Which one you choose as your favourite will depend largely on what sort of person you are and who you meet. The *Rose Garden Restaurant* has excellent seafood and cold beer and is one of the more popular places.

Back from the beach and difficult to find, so ask directions, is *Gregory's Star of*

Anjuna which has a particularly good reputation – people come here from Calangute to eat. It's only open in the evenings and the food is strictly western.

Getting There & Away

There are buses every one to two hours to Anjuna and Chapora from Mapusa. They can be very crowded at certain times of the day. It's usually a lot easier and certainly quicker to take a motorcycle (Rs 12, about 15 minutes) or to get a group together and hire a taxi (Rs 30).

CHAPORA

This is one of the most beautiful, interesting and unspoilt areas of Goa and a good deal more attractive than Anjuna either for a short or a long stay. Much of the inhabited area nestles under a canopy of dense coconut palms and the village is dominated by a rocky hill on top of which sits an old Portuguese fort. The fort is fairly well preserved and worth a visit, and

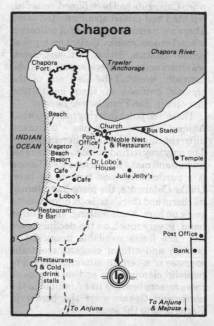

the views from its ramparts are excellent. Secluded sandy coves are found all the way around the northern side of this rocky outcrop, though the main beaches face west towards the Indian Ocean.

Many westerners stay here on a long-term basis but it's not a ghetto. The local people remain friendly and since the houses available for rent are widely scattered and there are many beaches and coves to choose from, only rarely will you see large groups of travellers together in one place.

Quite a lot of traditional boat building goes on along the shores of the Chapora River.

Places to Stay

There are few places where you can find cheap instant accommodation in Chapora. This is one of the things which makes it such a pleasant place to stay, particularly as most people who do come here stay for a long time. Initially, you'll have to take whatever is available and ask around, or stay at Mapusa, Calangute or Baga and 'commute' until you've found something.

At the top end of the market is the *Vagator Beach Resort* (tel Siolim 41), on the beach of the same name. The resort, in palm-shaded grounds, comprises a main block containing the restaurant, bar and reception area, and two types of cottages. It's a friendly place and, as beach resorts go in Goa, deserves top billing. The cottages cost Rs 180 to Rs 390 a double depending on the facilities which they offer.

At the bottom end of the market you can find a room either at *Dr Lobo's* house – a very friendly family but the facilities are somewhat basic – or at the *Noble Nest & Restaurant*, opposite the church at the bottom of the track which leads to Dr Lobo's, where doubles are Rs 40.

Most people who stay in Chapora come on a long-term basis and find a house or room to rent. If you're particular about where you want to stay, this can take some time. It helps if you get here before most of the others – try September and October when there are only a few people about. On the other hand, it isn't particularly difficult to find somewhere to live – just make it your top priority and keep asking around in the stores and cafes.

Wherever you decide to live, make sure you have a torch (flashlight) handy. There are no street lights, and finding your way along the paths through coconut palms late at night when there's no full moon is a devil of a job! Houses for rent cost between Rs 150 to Rs 400 a month depending on their size and location.

Places to Eat

There are numerous restaurants along the main street of Chapora village, opposite the church, at the back of the Vagator Beach Resort and along the beach south of the road which leads to Vagator. Most are pleasant and serve good seafood, but *Lobo's* (not to be confused with Dr Lobo's house in the village) is exceptionally good and they have cold beers. It's a superb little restaurant, but turn up early as seating is limited. It's closed on Sundays. *Julie Jolly's* is also very popular.

Getting There & Away

There are fairly frequent buses to Chapora from Mapusa throughout the day for Rs 1.20 as well as the occasional direct buses from Panaji which follow the coast and do not go via Mapusa. The bus stand is near the road junction in Chapora village. It's often easier and much quicker to rent a motorbike from Mapusa or to get a group together and hire a taxi.

ARAMBOL (Harmal)

A few years ago, when the screws were tightened at Anjuna in an attempt to control what local people regarded as the more outrageous activities (nudism and drug use) of a certain section of the travelling community, the die-hards cast around for a more 'sympathetic' beach. Arambol, north of Chapora, was one of those which they chose.

Initially, only those willing to put up with very primitive conditions and a total lack of facilities came here. That has changed due to the laws of supply and demand, even if some of those who come here look askance at the developments. Nevertheless, development has so far been minimal.

Buses from Mapusa take you as far as Arambol where there is a chai shop and a few other tiny shops. From here a road branches off to the village by the sea where kids will offer you a room for around Rs 10 a day. All you get is bare walls and no beds, apart from the rooms in an old hotel/house which is always full in any case. You can rent mattresses, cookers and all the rest from two shops at the village – obviously one comes here for at least a week. In the village there are 10 or so chai shops that serve 'westernised-Indian' food.

The seashore is beautiful and the village quiet and friendly with just a few hundred locals, mostly fishers, and a couple of hundred western residents in the November to February high season. Over a rocky hill, 10 minutes walk from the village beach, there's another beach where the last of the hippies hang out. Here it's possible to live in huts made of palm leaves on the slopes of a jungle valley alongside a river that makes an inland lake, just 20 metres from the sea. It's what Colva was in the late '60s. Naturally, you'll have to take with you whatever you'd normally expect to find.

Getting There & Away

There are occasional buses from Mapusa to Arambol which take three hours. Alternatively, get a group together and hire a taxi but remember that if you do this you'll have to pay the fare both ways since the driver is unlikely to be able to pick up passengers for the return journey. Another way to get there is to take the ferry across the river from Siolim, north-east of Chapora, to Chopdem and hitch from there.

OTHER BEACHES

If you'd like to get right out of the way of all the tourist development in Goa then it's worth considering a trip to either Terekhol in the extreme north-west corner of Goa or Palolen way down south near Chauri.

At Terekhol there's a large old Portuguese fort which has been converted into a government-owned hotel, the *Terekhol Fort Tourist Rest House* (tel Reddy 48), which offers a range of accommodation. Ordinary singles/doubles cost Rs 45/60 and 'special' singles/doubles Rs 75/100 between 4 October and 15 June. Between 16 June and 3 October they cost Rs 30/40 and Rs 60/75 respectively. There's also a dormitory which costs Rs 15 in the high season and Rs 10 in the low season.

There are very occasional buses between Mapusa or Pernem to Querim on the opposite (south) side of the river from Terekhol. Between Querim and Terekhol there is a flat-bottomed ferry.

At Palolen there's only basic accommodation available as yet. To get there, take a bus from Margao to Chauri.

OTHER ATTRACTIONS IN GOA
Bondla Wildlife Sanctuary

Up in the lush foothills of the Western Ghats, Bondla is a good place to see sambar and wild boar, among other things. It's the smallest of the Goan wildlife sanctuaries but the easiest one to gain access to at present.

Bookings for accommodation and transport should be made either with the Chief Wildlife Warden (tel 4747, 5926) 3rd floor, Junta House, Panaji, or with the Deputy Conservator of Forests, Wildlife Division, 4th floor, Junta House, Panaji.

Places to Stay & Eat Overnight accommodation is available inside the park at the *Tourist Cottages* which cost Rs 15 per person for a cottage or Rs 3 for a dormitory bed. Meals are available for those who book in advance.

Getting There & Around To get to the park, take a public bus to Ponda followed by a minibus or taxi to the park entrance.

There is usually a minibus to take you around the park once you're there but the times vary and it may be better if you can arrange to hire a motorbike from the nearby town of Usgao.

Molen & Cotigao Wildlife Sanctuaries

Both these wildlife sanctuaries are larger than the Bondla sanctuary but neither is easy to get to and you would need your own transport.

Places to Stay & Eat Accommodation is available at Molen in the *Tourist Complex* (tel 38). Room rates are Rs 25/40 for singles/doubles between 4 October and 15 June and Rs 20/25 between 15 June and 4 October. There's also a dormitory for Rs 15 in the high season and Rs 10 in the low season. Meals are available for those who book in advance.

There's no accommodation available at the Cotigao sanctuary.

Temples

When the Portuguese arrived in Goa they destroyed every Hindu temple and Muslim mosque they could lay hands on, so temples in Goa are generally back from the coast and comparatively new although some date back about 400 years. The temples have been rebuilt from the original temples destroyed by the Portuguese, and their lamp towers are a distinctive Goan feature. Despite their earnest attempts to spread Roman Catholicism, only 38% of Goans today are Christian.

Five of the most important Hindu temples are close to Ponda on the inland route between Panaji and Margao. The Shiva temple of Shri Mangesh is at Priol-Ponda Taluka, about 22 km from Panaji. The tiny temple with its white tower, a local landmark, is on top of a small hill. Less than two km further down the road is Shri Mahalsa, a Vishnu temple.

About five km from Ponda are Shri Ramnath and Shri Nagesh, and nearby is the Shri Shantadurga Temple. Dedicated to Shantadurga, the goddess of peace, the latter temple sports a very unusual, almost pagoda-like structure with a roof made out of long slabs of stone. Further south are the temples of Shri Chandreshwar, west of Quepem; the Shantadurga, east of Betul; and the Shri Mallikarjuna, east of Chauri.

Mosques

The only mosque remaining in Goa is the Safa Shahouri Masjid at Ponda, built by Ali Adilshah in 1560. When first built it matched in size and quality the mosques at Bijapur but was allowed to decay during the Portuguese period. Little remained of its former grandeur by the time the Portuguese left but the Archaeological Survey of India has now undertaken its restoration using local artisans. If what has already been completed is anything to go by, it will look superb when finished.

Forts

There are quite a few old Portuguese forts dotted around Goa, mostly on the coast, and most are in a reasonable state of preservation and worth visiting if you have the time. The one at Chapora is particularly recommended. Two of them – Aguada and Terekhol – have been converted into hotels.

Karnataka

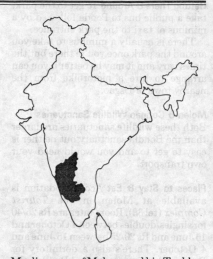

Population: 44 million
Area: 191,773 square km
Capital: Bangalore
Main language: Kannada

The state of Karnataka, formerly known as Mysore, is one of the more easygoing Indian states. It's a state of strong contrasts, with the modern, industrialised city of Bangalore at one extreme and expanses of rural farming areas at the other. Karnataka also has some of the most interesting historic architecture in India, and a varied and tumultuous history.

History

It was to Sravanabelagola, Karnataka, in the 3rd century BC that Chandragupta Maurya, India's first great emperor, retreated after he had renounced worldly ways and embraced Jainism. Later, the mighty 17-metre-high statue of Gomateshvara, which celebrated its 1000th anniversary in 1981, was erected at Sravanabelagola. Fifteen hundred years ago at Badami, in the north of the state, the Chalukyans built some of the earliest Hindu temples in India. All later south Indian temple architecture stems from the Chalukyan designs at Badami, the Pallavas at Kanchipuram and Mahabalipuram in Tamil Nadu.

Other important Indian dynasties, such as the Cholas and the Gangas, have also played their part in Karnataka's history, but it was the Hoysalas, who ruled between the 11th and 14th centuries, who left the most vivid evidence of their presence. The beautiful Hoysala temples at Somnathpur, Belur and Halebid are gems of Indian architecture with intricate and detailed sculptures rivalling anything to be found at Khajuraho (Madhya Pradesh) or Konarak (Orissa).

In 1327, Hindu Halebid fell to the Muslim army of Mohammed bin Tughlaq, and in the succeeding centuries Karnataka was held by first the followers of one religion, then the other. Founded in 1336, the Hindu kingdom of Vijayanagar, with its capital at Hampi, is one of the least visited and most surprising of India's ruined kingdoms. Vijayanagar reached its peak in the early 1550s, but in 1565 it fell to the Deccan sultans and Bijapur became the most important city of the region. Today, Bijapur is just a small city surrounded by an imposing wall and packed with a fascinating collection of mosques and other reminders of its glorious past.

Finally, Hyder Ali took control of the area in 1761 and the seat of power moved back south to Srirangapatnam near Mysore. His son, Tipu Sultan, with help from the French, further extended his father's kingdom and put the British in their place on more than one occasion, before being defeated and killed in 1799.

The British installed a Hindu ruler when they brought the region under their control, and a series of enlightened and progressive rulers held power right through to independence. The maharaja

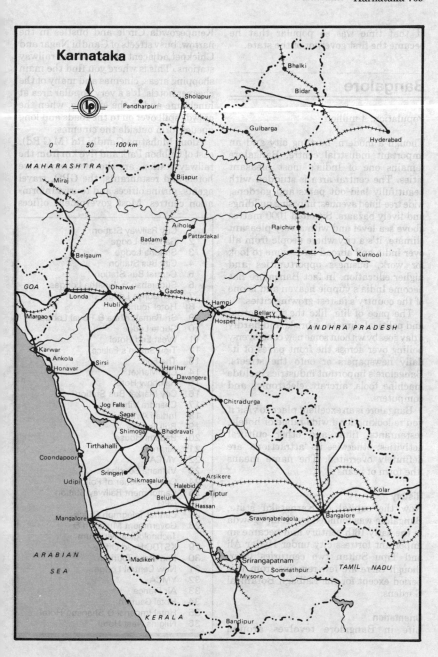

Karnataka

0   50   100 km

MAHARASHTRA

Miraj

Pandharpur

Sholapur

Bhalki

Bidar

Gulbarga

Hyderabad

Bijapur

Aihole

Badami   Pattadakal

Belgaum

Raichur

Kurnool

GOA

Dharwar   Gadag

Londa

Hubli   Hampi

Margao   Hospet   Bellary

Karwar   ANDHRA PRADESH

Ankola   Sirsi

Honavar

Harihar

Davangere

Jog Falls   Chitradurga

Sagar

Shimoga   Bhadravati

Coondapoor   Tirthahalli

Sringeri   Arsikere

Udipi   Chikmagalur   Halebid

Belur   Tiptur   Kolar

Hassan

Mangalore   Sravanabelagola   Bangalore

ARABIAN

SEA

Madikeri   Srirangapatnam

Somnathpur   TAMIL NADU

Mysore

Bandipur

KERALA

at that time was so popular that he became the first governor of the state.

Bangalore

Population: 4 million

Though a modern, bustling city and an important industrial centre, Bangalore remains one of India's most pleasant cities. The central area is studded with beautifully laid out parks and gardens, wide tree-lined avenues, imposing buildings and lively bazaars. Situated 1000 metres above sea level and with a very pleasant climate, it's a city where people from all over India and abroad have come to look for work, business opportunities and higher education. In fact Bangalore has become India's yuppie heaven and is one of the country's fastest growing cities.

The pace of life, like the intellectual and political climate, is brisk, and hardly a day goes by without some new controversy boiling over across the front pages of its daily newspapers or onto the streets. Bangalore's important industries include machine tools, aircraft, electronics and computers.

Bangalore is an excellent place to visit if you're looking for a wide range of hotels, restaurants, films and other cultural activities; otherwise its 'attractions' are definitely overrated. The name means 'the town of beans'.

History

Now the capital of Karnataka state, Bangalore was founded by Kempegowda in the early 16th century and became an important fortress city under Hyder Ali and Tipu Sultan two centuries later, though there are few remains from this period except for the Lalbagh Botanical Gardens.

Orientation

Life in Bangalore revolves around Kempegowda Circle and bustles in the narrow, busy streets of Gandhi Nagar and Chickpet adjacent to the bus and railway stations. This is where you find the main shopping areas, cinemas and many of the cheaper hotels. It's a very popular area at lunchtime and in the evening, when the crowds spill over on to the roads and long queues form outside the cinemas.

Along Mahatma Gandhi Rd (M G Rd), east of Cubbon Park and five km from the railway station, are the more expensive hotels and restaurants, the GPO, travel agents, airline offices and tourist information centres. Most government offices

1	City Railway Station
2	Ganesha Lodge
3	Soudha Lodge
4	City Bus Station
5	Central Bus Station
6	Sudarshan & Janatha Lodges
7	Samadhya Lodge
8	Hotel Tourist
9	Sri Ramakrishna & Royal Lodges
10	Gupta Lodge
11	West End Hotel
12	Tipu Sultan's Palace
13	The Fort
14	City Market
15	Rainbow Hotel
16	City Market Bus Station
17	Chandra Vihar
18	Indian Airlines
19	Bull Temple
20	Badami House
21	Air India
22	YMCA
23	Vidhana Soudha
24	Commissioner of Police
25	Cantonment Railway Station
26	GPO
27	Central Telegraph Office
28	Government Museum & Technological Museum
29	KSTDC Head Office
30	Karnataka Tourism
31	New Central Lodge
32	YMCA
33	Air France
34	Hotel Gautam
35	Hotel Imperial & Shansug Hotel
36	Nilgiris Nest Hotel

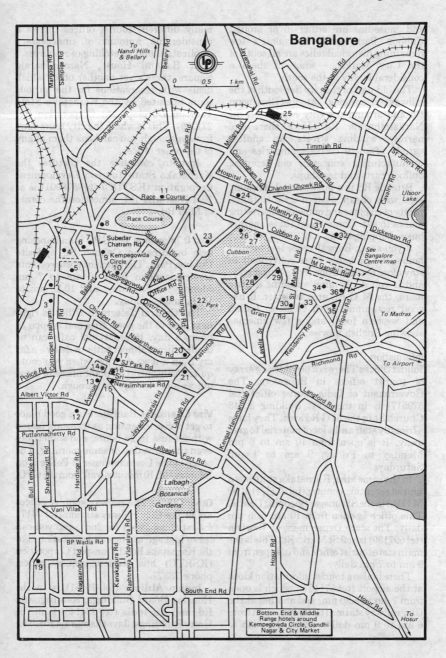

Bangalore

To Nandi Hills & Bellary

Bellary Rd

Jayamahal Rd

Borebank Rd

0   0.5   1 km

Margosa Rd

Sampige Rd

Seshadripuram Rd

Old Butts Rd

Sankey's Rd

Palace Rd

Miller's Rd

Cunningham Rd

Queen's Rd

Broadway Rd

St John's Rd

Timmiah Rd

Cavalry Rd

Dickenson Rd

Ulsoor Lake

Hospital Rd

Chandni Chowk Rd

11 Race Course Rd

24

Infantry Rd

Cubbon St

31   32

See Bangalore Centre map

8 Race Course

7
6

Subedar Chatram Rd

23

26
27

Cubbon

IM Gandhi Rd

4

9 Kempegowda Circle

10

Kempegowda Rd

Seshadri Rd

Palace Rd

28   29

MG Marks St

34   36

Post

1

5

Balepet

2

Office Rd

District Office Rd

18

Nrupathunga Rd

22 Park

Kasturba Rd

35

Brigade Rd

To Madras

30   33

Grant Rd

Lavelle St

Presidency Rd

To Airport

3

Cottonpet Bhashyam Rd

Chickpet Rd

Nagarthrpet Rd

20

Richmond Rd

Langford Rd

To Airport

Police Rd

14   16

SJ Park Rd

17

Sri Narasimharaja Rd

21

Lalbagh Rd

Kengal Hanumanthiah Rd

Albert Victor Rd

13

Avenue Rd

15

Jayachamaraja Rd

Lalbagh Fort Rd

12

Puttannachetty Rd

Shankarmutt Rd

Hardinge Rd

Lalbagh Botanical Gardens

Bull Temple Rd

Vani Vilas Rd

BP Wadia Rd

Nagasandra Rd

Kanakapura Rd

Rashtreeya Vidyalaya Rd

19

South End Rd

Hosur Rd

To Hosur

Bottom End & Middle Range hotels around Kempegowda Circle, Gandhi Nagar & City Market

and museums are either in or around Cubbon Park, while Bangalore's few remaining historical relics are all south of the City Market – some of them a considerable way to the south.

The old part of the city lies south of the railway station along Cottonpet Bhashyam Rd and around the City Market on Sri Narasimharaja Rd. Here there are narrow, winding streets, an endless variety of small cottage industries and manufacturing concerns, old temples, bullock carts and tea shops.

Brigade Rd is a busy central shopping area with cheap western-style clothing, plenty of cinemas and numerous interesting places to eat. Commercial Rd is another busy shopping area.

If you are in Bangalore for less than 24 hours, it's probably more convenient to stay close to the station. For a longer stay, and if you don't mind spending a little more, the M G Rd area is better. It has good restaurants with Chinese, Indian and western food, and a few cinemas showing English movies.

Information

Tourist Offices There is a bewildering array of tourist offices in Bangalore. The Government of India tourist office (tel 579517) is in the KFC Building at 48 Church St in the M G Rd area. They have a friendly staff and a lot of material to give away. It is open from 10 am to 6 pm Monday to Friday, 9 am to 1 pm Saturdays.

In the same area, Karnataka state has a tourist reception counter (tel 572377) at 52 M G Rd in the Shrunagar Shopping Centre. This office is open from 10 am to 6 pm daily. The state Department of Tourism (tel 597139) is at 9 St Marks Rd. This is the main state tourist office and it's open from 9 am to 7 pm daily.

There is also a tourist information kiosk at the airport (tel 571467), which is open from 7 am to 8.30 pm, and another at the City railway station (tel 70068), open from 6 am to 9 pm daily. Obviously, with so

many different tourist offices there's a considerable amount of unnecessary duplication and stretching of resources.

At Badami House, Narasimharaja Square, there's yet another office which deals with reservations for the various tours operated by the Karnataka State Tourism Development Corporation (tel 221299). This is where the city tours start from, although you can book them at any of the other offices.

Just to complete the picture, the Karnataka State Tourism Development Corporation (KSTDC) (tel 578901) is at 10/4 Kasturba Rd, almost on the corner of M G Rd.

Post & Telephone The GPO is an imposing new building on Cubbon St, opposite Cubbon Park. The efficient poste restante service is open from 10 am to 7 pm Monday to Saturday, and 10.30 am to 1.30 pm on Sunday.

The Central Telegraph Office is right next door to the post office and is open 24 hours a day. International calls can be dialled direct almost without delay – a far cry from a few years ago when you could quite easily spend all night in one of these offices and still not get through.

Visa Extensions Bangalore is a good place to get a visa extension as these are issued without fuss in 24 hours, and sometimes even the same day or same morning. The office of the Commissioner of Police is on Infantry Rd, 10 minutes walk from the GPO.

Other Offices The railway enquiry offices are at the City railway station (tel 74172 for 1st class, 29511 for 2nd), and you can leave luggage at the railway station. For the Karnataka Road Transport Corporation (KSRTC) bus station enquiry office, phone 73377.

Indian Airlines (tel 76851) is in the Housing Board Buildings, Kempegowda Rd, and Air India (tel 224143) is in the Unity Buildings, Jayachamaraja Rd. The

Vayudoot agent is Paramount Travels, Embassy Centre, Race Course Rd.

Thomas Cook (tel 571066) is at 55 M G Rd, and this is an excellent place to change money if you have Cook's cheques. You'll be out of the place in under five minutes.

Bookshops There are various book stalls on Brigade Rd, Residency Rd and Avenue Rd (west of Cubbon Park) but the best bookshops are all on M G Rd. Gangaram's Book Bureau is the best, and almost next door is a branch of Higginbotham's.

The Bangalore Tract & Book Society on the corner of St Marks and M G Rd is not bad, despite its unpromising name, mainly because it's an agent of Oxford University Press.

The British Library on St Mark's Rd has lots of current British newspapers and magazines, and they don't seem to mind if you rest awhile and catch up on the news. It's open from 10.30 am to 6.30 pm Tuesday to Saturday.

Vidhana Soudha

This is one of Bangalore's, and indeed one of India's, most spectacular buildings. Built of granite in the neo-Dravidian style of architecture and located at the northern end of Cubbon Park, it houses both the Secretariat and the State Legislature. The cabinet room is famous for its massive door made of pure sandalwood, and the building is floodlit on Sunday evenings and on public holidays.

If you want to pay a visit it is open from 3 to 5.30 pm on weekdays. The entrance is on the ground floor behind the grand steps. You are allowed only into the entrance lobby where you can admire the impressive dome and the gaudy colour scheme.

Cubbon Park & the Museums

One of the main 'lungs' of the city, this beautiful shady park, full of flowering trees, covers an area of 120 hectares and was laid out in 1864. In it are the red

Vidhana Soudha

Gothic buildings which house the Public Library, the High Court, the Government Museum and the Technological & Industrial Museum. Also in the gardens is a huge children's park where, in a reversal of the usual roles, adults are not allowed in unless accompanied by children.

The Government Museum, one of the oldest in India, was established in 1886 and houses collections on geology, art, numismatics and relics from Moenjodaro (one of the cradles of Indian civilisation, dating back 5000 years). There are also some good pieces from Halebid and Vijayanagar. Admission costs Rs 0.50 and the museum is open daily, except Wednesdays and public holidays, from 9 am to 5 pm.

The Technological & Industrial Museum, also on Kasturba Rd and adjacent to the Government Museum, is open daily, except Mondays and public holidays, between 10 am and 5 pm; admission costs

Rs 1. Its theme is the application of science and technology to industry and human welfare. It is full of happy children pressing the buttons of exhibits that reflect India's technological progress. However, it is nothing special and you can skip it if you are short of time.

Lalbagh Botanical Gardens

This is a beautiful and popular park in the southern suburbs of Bangalore. It covers an area of 96 hectares and was laid out in the 18th century by Hyder Ali and his son Tipu Sultan. It contains many centuries-old trees (most of them labelled), lakes, lotus ponds, flower beds, a deer park and one of the largest collections of rare tropical and subtropical plants in India. Refreshments are available at several places within the park.

The gardens are open daily from 8 am to 8 pm.

The Fort

Located on Krishnarajendra Rd close to the City Market, this was originally a mud-brick structure built in 1537 by Kempegowda. It was later rebuilt in stone in the 18th century by Hyder Ali and Tipu Sultan, but much of it was destroyed during the wars with the British and you would be missing little if you left it out of your itinerary. It is supposed to be open daily from 8 am to 6 pm, but this isn't always the case.

Tipu Sultan's Palace

This palace on Albert Victor Rd, near the junction with Krishnarajendra Rd, was begun by Tipu Sultan's father, Hyder Ali, and completed by Tipu in 1791. It resembles the Daria Daulat Bagh at Srirangapatnam near Mysore, but has been sadly neglected and is falling into disrepair. You may find the temple next to it of far greater interest. The palace is open daily from 8 am to 6 pm; admission is free.

Bull Temple

Situated on Bugle Hill at the end of Bull Temple Rd, this is one of Bangalore's oldest temples. Built by Kempegowda in the Dravidian style, it contains a huge monolith of Nandi similar to the one on Chamundi Hill, Mysore. Non-Hindus are allowed to enter and the priests are friendly. You will be offered jasmine flowers and are expected to leave a small donation.

Other Attractions

The remains of the four watchtowers built by Kempegowda are worth a visit if you're in the vicinity of the Bull Temple. They are about 400 metres to the west of the temple. Ulsoor Lake, to the north-east of Cubbon Park, has boating facilities and a swimming pool which is far from clean. The Karnataka Folk Art Museum at Kumara Park West has displays of folk art, costumes, toys and an extensive recorded music collection.

Tours

The Karnataka State Tourism Development Corporation (KSTDC) offers the following tours, all starting at Badami House:

Bangalore City The tours operate twice daily from 7.30 am to 1 pm and 2 to 7.30 pm. The places visited are Tipu's Palace, Bull Temple, Lalbagh Botanical Gardens, Ulsoor Lake, Government Soap Factory, Vidhana Soudha, Government Museum, Technology Museum and Art Gallery. The tours cost Rs 35 but about half of the time is spent at government-owned emporiums that sell silks and handicrafts. Tourist attractions such as the park, the Bull Temple and Tipu Sultan's Palace are not that interesting and you can easily visit the museums on your own. Unless you are in Bangalore just for a day and would like to rush things there is little point in taking this tour.

Srirangapatnam, Mysore & Brindavan Gardens Daily tours begin at 7.15 am and return at 10.45 pm. The tour includes

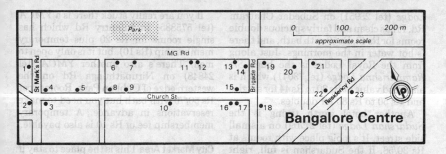

1 Bangalore Tract & Book Society
2 British Library
3 Koshy's Restaurant
4 KC Das
5 Ginza
6 Chit Chat Restaurant
7 Lakeview Milk Bar
8 Berrys Hotel
9 Govt of India Tourist Office
10 Blue Heaven Chinese Restaurant
11 Higginbotham's Book Store
12 Gangaram's Book Bureau
13 Thomas Cook
14 Rice Bowl Restaurant
15 Hotel RR
16 Mac's Fast Food
17 Oasis & The Pub
18 Waikikee Restaurant
19 Cauvery Arts & Crafts Emporium
20 Brindavan Hotel
21 Karnataka Govt Sari Emporium
22 Bus from Station
23 Hotel New Victoria

visits to Ranganathaswamy Temple, the Fort, Gumbaz and Daria Daulat Bagh at Srirangapatnam, St Philomena's Cathedral, Chamundi Hill, the Palace, Art Gallery and Cauvery Arts & Crafts Emporium at Mysore. The tour costs Rs 100 by deluxe bus. Mysore is such a pleasant city that it is better to visit it on your own unless your time is very limited.

Hampi & Tungabhadra Dam This is a two-day tour which departs on Fridays at 10 pm and returns to Bangalore at 10 pm on Sunday. It includes visits to Mantralaya

(the village associated with the Hindu saint, Raghavendra Swami), Tungabhadra Dam and Hampi. Overnight accommodation is at the *Hotel Mayura Vijayanagar* at Tungabhadra dam. The cost of the tour is Rs 260, including accommodation.

Mysore & Ooty This is a three-day tour to Srirangapatnam, Mysore, Ooty and the Bandipur Game Sanctuary. It costs Rs 425 including accommodation for two nights and departs Bangalore every Monday and Friday during the season.

Tirupathi A two-day tour to Tirupathi costs Rs 210, but it's much more convenient to visit Tirupathi en route to Madras if you're heading that way.

All these tours can be booked at any of the KSTDC tourist offices.

Places to Stay – bottom end
Bus Station Area There are a couple of cheap and extremely noisy hotels along Cottonpet Bhashyam Rd, south of the bus station. An old favourite is the *Sudha Lodge* (tel 60542) at No 6, although these days it's definitely on the skids. Rooms cost Rs 25/34/45 for singles/doubles/triples. Close by, and equally basic, is the *Sri Ganesha Lodge* (tel 609144) with rooms for Rs 22/30, Rs 2 more with bath.

On the east side of the bus station are a dozen or more hotels and lodges to suit most budgets. One of the best is the *Royal*

Lodge (tel 28951) on Subedar Chatram Rd. It has clean and fairly spacious double rooms for Rs 40, Rs 50 with bath, and there is hot water in the mornings. Just along from the Royal Lodge is the huge *Sri Ramakrishna Lodge* (tel 73041) which is also good value at Rs 30 to Rs 44 for singles and Rs 50 to Rs 80 for doubles.

Another hotel worth trying is the *Sudarshan Lodge* (tel 27709) on a small side street. It's a big place with rooms at Rs 30/58. If the Sudarshan is full, right next door is the *Janatha Lodge* (tel 27237) with rooms for Rs 30/45. The *Hotel Tourist* (tel 72381), around the corner on Race Course Rd, is good value at Rs 25/40 and there's hot water in the morning.

Up the scale a bit, the brand-new *Hotel Adora* (tel 76225) at 47 Subedar Chatram Rd has good rooms for Rs 48/80, and there's hot water in the morning. The *Samadhya Lodge* (tel 74064) at 70 Subedar Chatram Rd has similar prices.

The railway *retiring rooms* can be a good fall-back, although they are often full by the afternoon. There are no singles, and doubles cost Rs 50; there's one with air-con for Rs 75. Dorm beds cost Rs 15.

M G Rd Area Budget accommodation is limited in this area but there are a couple of good places. The *Hotel Imperial* (tel 577421) is at 95 Residency Rd, one block south of M G Rd. Clean and airy rooms cost Rs 42 a single, Rs 73 a double.

Conveniently situated on M G Rd, the *Brindavan Hotel* (tel 573271) at No 108 has a variety of rooms ranging from Rs 42/84. You get hot water in the mornings and a newspaper under your door. The hotel is set back off the street so it doesn't suffer from the traffic noise – recommended. There's also a good 'meals' dining hall here.

North of M G Rd, on the other side of the park, is the *New Central Lodge* (tel 571395) at 56 Infantry Rd. There are no single rooms and doubles cost Rs 80 with private bath or Rs 60 with common bath.

If you are really stuck there is a *YMCA* (tel 575885) in Infantry Rd which has single rooms for Rs 20 plus temporary membership (Rs 10), but it is only open to men. There's also another *YMCA* (tel 24848) on Nirupathunga Rd on the western edge of Cubbon Park. Rooms cost Rs 50/70 with bath but you need to make reservations in advance. A temporary membership fee of Rs 10 is also payable.

City Market Area This is the place to stay if you want to be in the real thick of things. It's the area of Bangalore with the noise, bustle and local atmosphere. To get there on foot from either the railway station or bus station, go south down Cottonpet Bhashyam Rd as far as the Kangeri Police Station (on the right-hand side), and then turn left. This is Police Rd, though there are no signs to tell you this. Continue down Police Rd for several hundred metres and you will find yourself outside City Market. It is 25 minutes walk from the railway station.

The *Rainbow Hotel* (tel 602235) is on Sri Narasimharaja Rd right opposite the City Market bus stand. It's very good value at Rs 30/45, and their air-con rooms at Rs 85 a double are the cheapest you'll find in Bangalore.

Close by on Avenue Rd, the *Delhi Bhavan Lodge* (tel 75045) is cheap and gloomy at Rs 30/53, while the *Chandra Vihar* (tel 224146) opposite is marginally better and charges Rs 42/74.

Places to Stay – middle
Most of the hotels in this price range are in the more expensive M G Rd area near the city centre, flashy restaurants, shopping centre and cinemas.

The *Hotel New Victoria* (tel 570336) at 47 Residency Rd is set in a beautiful garden, and there's a touch of class and old-world charm about it. Rooms here cost Rs 86/176 and there's a restaurant. Close by at 171 Brigade Rd, the *Nilgiris Nest Hotel* (tel 577501) has big rooms for Rs 99/145, or Rs 154/210 with air-con.

The *Berrys Hotel* (tel 573331) is just off M G Rd at 46 Church St and charges Rs 107/145 for singles/doubles, Rs 188/250 with air-con. Another mid-range place with a good location is the *Hotel Gautam* (tel 577461) at 17 Museum Rd. All rooms cost Rs 80/130 and have a bath and phone.

Places to Stay – top end

Bangalore also has its share of top-end hotels. The three-star *Hotel Westend* (tel 29281) on Race Course Rd has a pleasant garden and a pool, and singles/doubles cost Rs 475/595. The *Hotel Taj Residency* (tel 568888) is on the eastern end of M G Rd. All rooms have air-con and cost from Rs 400/460.

The *ITDC Hotel Ashok* (tel 79411) at Kumara Krupa, close to the city centre, has all the mod cons from tennis courts, shops and a swimming pool to full air-conditioning. Singles/doubles cost from Rs 600/720.

The *Hotel Bangalore International* is at 2A-B Crescent Rd, High Grounds, and is rather smaller than the large Hotel Ashok. Singles/doubles cost from Rs 160/240 or Rs 220/330 with air-con. Another cheaper top-end hotel is the *Hotel Cauvery Continental* (tel 29350) at 11/37 Cunningham Rd. Rooms are Rs 220/300 with air-con and there are vegetarian and non-vegetarian restaurants as well as monkeys in the garden.

Places to Eat

Bangalore has some excellent places to eat, with not only Indian but also western and Chinese food available. Most of the better restaurants are in the M G Rd area. The popular though expensive *Rice Bowl*, owned by the Dalai Lama's sister, is one of the best places. It is gloomy in the tradition of all 'good' Indian restaurants, but has very good Chinese and Tibetan food and is packed in the evening. The wonton soups are excellent and they have a good tape collection and cold beer. Another good place for Chinese food is the *Blue Heaven* in Church St, although you won't get out of there cheaply.

Also on Church St, the very popular *Mac's Fast Food*, which strongly imitates western fast-food chain restaurants, is just the place if you're hanging out for some good old-fashioned junk food. It has everything from fish & chips (Rs 17), pizza and burgers (Rs 8 to Rs 12) to steak, egg & chips and roast chicken. It can be difficult to get a seat in here at times. Next door to Mac's is *The Pub*, which is also popular. It's the closest thing you'll find to an English pub in India and there is beer on tap.

On M G Rd, the *Indian Coffee House* is a good cheap place for a non-veg breakfast or a coffee. As with the other cafes in this chain, the waiters are all done up in shabby white suits replete with cummerbunds and hats. Just a few doors further along, the *Chit-Chat* is a very flash new place complete with fountain and coloured lights. The food is only average and includes pizzas and sausages. In the same area, the *Lakeview Milk Bar* has excellent shakes and sundaes.

For an Indian meal in the M G Rd area, the *Shanbag Cafe* (not to be confused with the New Shanbag a couple of doors along) on Residency Rd does an excellent thali in its air-con dining hall. The meal starts with a sweet, followed by a soup, then you move on to puris, three vegetable curries, sambar, pepper water, papadam, chutney, pickles and curd, followed by a sizeable vegetable biryani and finally a fruit salad. Excellent value at Rs 16. Also good value is the Rs 5 'mini meal' in the dining hall of the Brindavan Hotel.

The *Waikikee* on Brigade Rd does good north Indian non-veg dishes. The steaks and pizzas at *Casa Piccolo*, 131 Residency Rd, have received good raves from a number of travellers.

K C Das, on the corner of Church St and St Mark's Rd, is a well-known snack-and-sweet shop whose headquarters is in Calcutta. Try their famous rasgullas. On Brigade Rd, opposite the Kwality

Restaurant, is the *Nilgiris* supermarket where you can get such goodies as whole-wheat bread, cheese and Danish pastries.

The many restaurants in the bus station area offer mainly Indian food. The *Kamat Hotel* on Subedar Chatram Rd has good vegetarian meals and snacks, while next door the *Sagar Hotel* has vegetarian meals for Rs 10, non-veg for Rs 14. Most of these restaurants (eating rooms is perhaps a more accurate description) are typical cheap veg and non-veg Indian eateries, although the standards of hygiene leave something to be desired – there was a dead cockroach lurking under my omelette in one of these places.

Things to Buy

Like its sister establishment at Mysore, the Cauvery Arts & Crafts Emporium (tel 571418) at 23 M G Rd stocks a huge range of superb handcrafted tables, carvings (many of them in sandalwood), jewellery, ceramics, carpets and incense (*agarbathi*). If anything, there is a better selection here than in the store in Mysore. Few things are cheap, but this emporium stocks some of the best craftwork in India, and they're good at packing and posting.

For silk saris the Government Emporium, next to the Symphony Theatre on M G Rd, sells good quality noncreasable 'crepe' saris for around Rs 600.

Getting There & Away

Air Indian Airlines have flights at least daily connecting Bangalore with Bombay (Rs 835), Delhi (Rs 1825), Hyderabad (Rs 535) and Madras (Rs 315). There are also regular connections to Ahmedabad (Rs 1230), Calcutta (Rs 1475), Goa (Rs 485), Madurai (Rs 365), Mangalore (Rs 340) and Pune (Rs 790).

Vayudoot have flights from Bangalore to Bellary (Rs 370), Hyderabad (Rs 535), Mysore (Rs 175) and Tirupathi (Rs 250).

Bus Bangalore's huge and well-organised

Central bus station is directly in front of the City railway station.

There are four buses daily to Bombay. Regular state buses cost Rs 204 and take 24 hours or more. Luxury video buses departing from outside the bus station cost Rs 250. To Hospet there are regular daily buses plus a luxury KSTDC bus. The 340-km journey takes nine hours and costs Rs 65.

The Madras run takes about nine hours and there are 10 buses daily; ordinary buses cost Rs 37 and deluxe buses Rs 45. There are four buses daily to Mangalore, and the 357-km journey takes eight hours and costs Rs 53.

There are very frequent and remarkably civilised buses to Mysore, and the trip takes 3½ hours and costs Rs 25. KSTDC deluxe buses to Mysore leave every 15 minutes or so when full.

Other important routes include Bijapur (four buses daily, 14 hours), Calicut (two buses daily), Ernakulam (three buses daily), Hassan (12 buses daily, 185 km), Ooty (two buses daily), Vellore (two buses daily), Puttapathy, Jog Falls, Goa (two buses daily) and Kodaikanal (one bus daily, 12 hours).

All the regular buses are operated by the Karnataka State Road Transport Corporation (KSRTC). Andhra Pradesh State Road Transport Corporation (APSRTC) and Thiruvalluvar Transport Corporation (the Tamil Nadu state bus company) also run buses from Bangalore, and their offices are at stand 13 of the Central bus station. There are six daily APSRTC services to Hyderabad costing Rs 91. Thiruvalluvar also run buses to Madras 18 times daily, and the fare is Rs 48 (super deluxe). The buses go via Chittore or Vellore; the latter route is cheaper. Thiruvalluvar also have 10 buses to Madurai for Rs 46, and three daily to Coimbatore for Rs 40.

In addition to the various state buses, numerous private companies offer buses between Bangalore and the other major cities in central and southern India. You'll find them all over the bus station area. Their prices are higher than the state service but their buses are better and there's more leg room – important on long journeys. The thing you need to watch out for is the dreaded video coach. Find a nonvideo bus if you want to retain your sanity, let alone your hearing.

Train Train reservations in Bangalore are computerised so it's not too painful. However, there is no tourist quota on any trains and bookings are heavy on most routes. It is usually possible for travellers to get into the emergency quota. The booking office is outside Bangalore City station and is open from 7 am to 1 pm and 1.30 to 7 pm Monday to Saturday, only in the morning on Sunday.

Bangalore is connected by direct daily express trains with all the main cities in southern and central India. But, as elsewhere in India where there is more than one express per day, you should be careful to choose the right train if speed is your priority, as journey times vary considerably from one express to the next.

The Trivandrum Express leaves daily at 5.45 pm and costs Rs 82 in 2nd class, Rs 305 in 1st. The 855-km trip takes about 18 hours. To Cochin there is one through train daily at 5.45 pm, arriving in Cochin at 8 am the next day. The fare is Rs 67 in 2nd class, Rs 245 in 1st.

Various expresses operate between Bangalore and Bombay, and some require a change of train at Miraj. The trip varies from 1129 to 1211 km depending on the route and takes 24 to 27 hours. Fares are about Rs 100 in 2nd class, Rs 400 in 1st.

There are several express services between Bangalore and Madras. The 358-km journey takes six to seven hours and the fare is Rs 44 in 2nd class, Rs 156 in 1st. Various trains operate between Bangalore and Hyderabad, and the daily Bangalore to Hyderabad Express leaves at 5.15 pm. The 789-km trip takes about

16 hours and costs Rs 79 in 2nd class, Rs 286 in 1st.

There are half a dozen daily trains to Mysore, the fastest being the Tippu Express which takes about three hours. Fares for the 139-km journey are Rs 20 in 2nd class, Rs 73 in 1st.

The daily Karnataka Express to New Delhi departs from Bangalore at 10.30 pm and arrives in New Delhi 42 hours later. Fares for the 2444-km journey are Rs 163 in 2nd class, Rs 687 in 1st.

Getting Around

Airport Transport If you take a taxi or auto-rickshaw from the airport be careful you don't get stuck with the parking fee, which a sign clearly states is the driver's responsibility. Since the airport is outside the city limits you'll probably have to agree on an over-the-meter fee.

Bus Bangalore has a comprehensive local bus network. The main bus station, near the railway station, is also the centre for local buses.

To get from the railway station to the M G Rd area, catch a No 131, 315 or 333 to the fire station on Residency Rd. For Kadugodi (Sai Baba Ashram), take a No 331 bus.

Auto-Rickshaw As is often the case, the auto-rickshaw drivers may be unwilling to take you to certain hotels as they will be missing out on a commission. The meters are current so you don't have to pay extra. Expect to pay about Rs 6 from the railway station to M G Rd.

AROUND BANGALORE
Nandi Hills
This hill station, 68 km from Bangalore, was a popular summer retreat even in Tipu Sultan's days. Tipu's Drop, a 600-metre-high cliff face, provides a good view over the surrounding country. There are two ancient temples here.

Places to Stay Department of Horticulture

rest houses cost Rs 25 for a double or Rs 30 for a cottage. Reservations can be made through the Department either in Nandi Hills (tel 21) or Bangalore (tel 602231).

The KSTDC operates the *Hotel Mayura Pine-Top* (tel 1) in Nandi Hills. Rooms cost Rs 65/85, and reservations need to be made in advance in Bangalore (tel 578901).

Kolar Gold Fields

These mines, 100 km east of Bangalore, are the major gold producers for India and are said to have the deepest shafts in the world, reaching over 2400 metres below the surface. Visits can be arranged.

Mysore

Population: 580,000

Sandalwood City! Everywhere you go in this beautiful city you'll find yourself surrounded by the lingering aromas of sandalwood, jasmine, rose, musk, frangipani and many others. Whenever you smell them again, you'll be reminded of this place. It's one of the major centres of incense manufacture in India, and scores of small, family-owned agarbathi (incense) factories are scattered all over town, their products exported all over the world.

Every one of the incense sticks is handmade, usually by women and children, and a good worker can turn out at least 10,000 a day! They are made with thin slivers of bamboo, dyed red or green at one end, onto which is rolled a sandalwood putty base. The sticks are then dipped into small piles of powdered perfume and laid out to harden in the shade. You can see them being made if you enquire at any of the small firms you come across.

Mysore is also a crafts centre, and there are numerous shops selling a large range of sandalwood, rosewood and teak carvings, and furniture. Probably the most stunning display can be seen at the Cauvery Arts & Crafts Emporium in the centre of town. Their rosewood tables and elephants, intricately inlaid with ivory and other woods, are perhaps the best you will see anywhere. It's not unusual to visit the post office and see travellers sending a package back home!

There are plenty of other reasons why you would not want to miss Mysore. Until independence the city was the seat of the maharajas of Mysore, a princely state covering about a third of present-day Karnataka, and their walled Indo-Saracenic palace in the centre of the city is a major attraction drawing visitors from all over the world. Just south of the city is Chamundi Hill, which is topped by an important Shiva temple.

Outside the city to the north lie the extensive ruins of the former capital of Mysore, the fortress city of Srirangapatnam, built by Hyder Ali and Tipu Sultan on an island in the middle of the Cauvery River. Tipu Sultan fought the last of his battles with the British here in the closing years of the 18th century. Probably the biggest attraction outside the city is the beautiful temple of Somnathpur.

Mysore, at an altitude of 770 metres, is a travellers' Mecca and it's easy to see why. Apart from offering many attractions, it's a friendly, easygoing city with plenty of shady trees, well-maintained public buildings, clean streets and a good climate, yet it's small enough not to overwhelm.

Don't miss Mysore's eccentric evening newspaper the *Star of Mysore*.

Orientation

The railway and bus station (two km apart) are both conveniently close to the city centre and only 10 minutes walk from all the main hotels and restaurants. The main shopping street is Sayaji Rao Rd, which runs from New Statue Square on the north side of the Maharaja's Palace, across Irwin Rd to the north of the city.

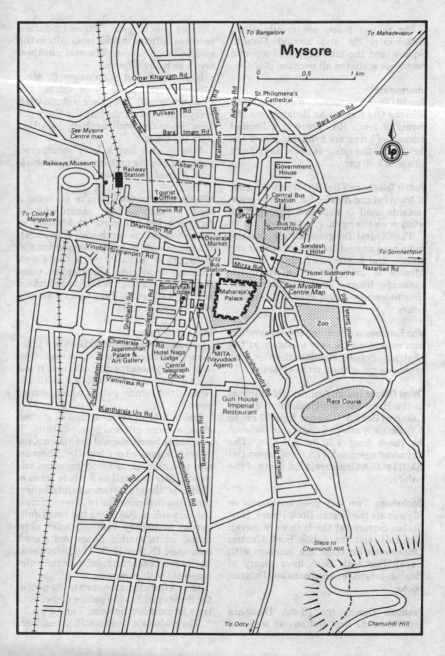

Mysore

0   0.5   1 km

To Bangalore

To Mahadevapur

Omar Khayyam Rd

St Philomena's
Cathedral

Pulikesi   Rd

Bara   Imam Rd

Bara Imam Rd

See Mysore
Centre map

Akbar Rd

Government
House

Railways Museum

Railway
Station

Tourist
Office

Central Bus
Station

To Coore &
Mangalore

Irwin Rd

GPO

Bus to
Somnathpur

Dhanvantri Rd

Devaraja
Market

Sandesh
Hotel

To Somnathpur

Vinoba (Sivarampet) Rd

City
Bus
Station

Mirza Rd

Hotel Siddhartha

Nazarbad Rd

See Mysore
Centre Map

Sudarshan
Lodge

Maharaja's
Palace

Zoo

Chamaraja
Jaganmohan
Palace &
Art Gallery

Rd
Hotel Naga
Lodge
Central
Telegraph
Office

MITA
(Vayudoot
Agent)

Vanivilasa Rd

Gun House
Imperial
Restaurant

Race Course

Kantharaja Urs Rd

Medhvachray Rd

Steps to
Chamundi Hill

To Ooty

Chamundi Hill

The budget hotels are mostly along Dhanvantri Rd and around Gandhi Square, and the mid-range and top-end hotels are scattered all over the place.

Information

Tourist Office The tourist office (tel 22096) is in the Old Exhibition Building, on the corner of Irwin Rd. There is a limited amount of literature available if you ask for it, and the office is open daily from 10 am to 5.30 pm.

Post & Telephone The GPO is on the corner of Irwin Rd and Ashoka Rd, and the poste restante mail is delivered through the window on the right.

The Central Telegraph Office is on the main road around the eastern side of the palace, and is open 24 hours a day. As Mysore is not yet on an electronic exchange, international calls take some time to connect – allow at least a couple of hours.

Visa Extensions According to one traveller, visa extensions are easy to obtain at the District Police Headquarters – 'no problems, no queues, no baksheesh'.

Other Offices Indian Airlines (tel 21486) is in the Hotel Mayura Hoysala on Jhansi Lakshmi Bai Rd. It's open from 10 am to 5.15 pm daily except Sunday, but is closed for lunch from 1.30 to 2.15 pm. The Vayudoot agent is MITA travel agent (tel 20031) at 66A Chamaraja Rd, south of the palace.

Bookshops Two very good bookshops in Mysore are the Geetha Book House, New Statue Square (at the bottom of Sayaji Rao Rd), and the Ashok Book Centre, Dhanvantri Rd (near the junction with Sayaji Rao Rd). Both have plenty of English-language paperbacks and Penguin books.

Festivals During the 10-day Dussehra festival in the first and second weeks of October each year, accommodation becomes difficult to find, especially in the middle-range places. The real cheapies aren't as badly affected.

If you can find somewhere to stay, Mysore is the place to be during the Dussehra festival. The palace is illuminated every night and on the last day there is a huge procession with elephants, starting from the palace.

Mysore also has a busy racecourse, patronised by the maharaja. The season is from August to October.

Wildlife Sanctuaries If you're planning a visit to the wildlife sanctuaries of Bandipur (80 km north of Mysore) or Nagarhole (93 km south-west of Mysore), it's advisable to book accommodation and transport in advance with the Forest Officer, Woodyard, Ashokpuram (near the Siddhartha High School in a southern suburb of the city). Take a rickshaw or a No 61 city bus there.

Maharaja's Palace

The beautiful profile of this walled Indo-Saracenic palace, the seat of the maharajas of Mysore, graces the city's skyline. It was built in 1907 at a cost of Rs 4.2 million to replace the former palace which burned down.

Inside it is an extravaganza of stained glass, mirrors, gilt and gaudy colours. 'It could have been designed by Citizen Kane on acid', suggested one traveller. There are also beautiful carved wooden doors and mosaic floors as well as a whole series of mediocre, though historically interesting, paintings depicting life in Mysore during the Edwardian Raj. Note the beautifully carved mahogany ceilings, solid silver doors, white marble floors and superb columned Durbar Hall. The palace even has its own Hindu temple inside the walls, complete with gopuram.

Only a few rooms are open to the public. On Sunday nights the palace is spectacularly illuminated between 7 and 8 pm.

The maharaja's son is still in residence

Maharaja's Palace, Mysore

at the back of the palace, and here the Residential Museum (Rs 2) is a must. During the 10-day festival of Dussehra, held in the first and second weeks of October each year, the maharaja's son leads one of India's most colourful processions. Richly caparisoned elephants, liveried retainers, cavalry, and the gaudy and flower-bedecked images of deities make their way through the streets to the sound of jazz and brass bands, and through the inevitable clouds of incense.

Depending on how many tourist coaches there are outside in the parking lot, the palace can sometimes rival the departure lounge of a major international airport. Check this out before you go in! Entry is from the south gate only and the palace is open daily from 10.30 am to 5.30 pm. Tickets cost Rs 2 and you must leave your shoes and camera at the deposit (there's a charge for this).

Chamundi Hill

You can spend a very pleasant half-day walking up (or, more sensibly, down) the 1000-odd steps to the top of this hill, where the temple to Sri Chamundeswari stands 1062 metres above sea level. There's some shade on the way and the views over the city and surrounding countryside are superb.

Three-quarters of the way up the hill you will come across the famous Nandi (Shiva's bull) carved out of solid rock which, at five metres high, is one of the largest in India. It's always garlanded in flowers and constantly visited by bevies of pilgrims offering *prasad* to the priest in attendance there.

The temple is a huge structure with a seven-storey 40-metre-high gopuram which is visible from far away. The goddess Chamundi was the family deity of the maharaja, and the statue at the top of the temple is that of the demon

Mahishasura who was one of Chamundi's victims. Visiting hours for the temple (non-Hindus are allowed inside) are from 8 am to 12 noon and 5 to 8 pm. The priests are quite enthusiastic to show you around.

There are buses approximately every half-hour from the City bus station in Mysore to the terminus on Chamundi Hill which is about 300 metres from the temple. Demand for buses can be very heavy on Sundays (I've seen 500 people waiting for a bus!). It's quite a good walk down and this bypasses the problem of ridiculously overcrowded buses. Buses up the hill are not so crowded. Refreshments, snacks and south Indian plate meals are available at cafes around the temple.

Though local guidebooks and tourist literature will tell you that the summit is 13 km from the city, this refers to the winding and switchbacked road only. Going via the steps it's only about four km.

Devaraja Fruit & Vegetable Market
This market stretches along Sayaji Rao Rd from Dhanvantri Rd to New Statue Square and is one of the most colourful in India. It provides excellent subject material for photographers.

Jaganmohan Palace
Another place worth a visit is the Jayachamarajendra Art Gallery in Jaganmohan Palace. Not only does it display paintings, particularly by Ravi Varma, but it has handicrafts, historical objects of interest and rare musical instruments. The palace itself was built in 1861 and served as a royal auditorium. Visiting hours are from 8 am to 5 pm daily and entry is Rs 1.50. Photography is prohibited.

St Philomena's Cathedral
This cathedral is interesting if you want to see what the Christians got up to in Mysore earlier this century. It's one of the largest churches in India and it is built in neo-Gothic style.

India Milk Bar, Mysore

Railway Museum
Across the line from the railway station is a small but interesting railway museum with a maharani's saloon carriage, complete with royal toilet, dating from around 1888. It's open from 10 am to 1 pm and 3 to 5 pm daily except Monday; entry is Rs 0.40.

Tours
There are several government tours available from Mysore, including one of Mysore, Somnathpur, Srirangapatnam, Brindavan Gardens and, in season, the Ranganathittu Bird Sanctuary. The daily tour starts at 7.15 am, finishes at 8.30 pm and costs Rs 30. Frankly, this tour attempts to do too much in one day, but if you're in a hurry. . .

The tour to Belur, Halebid and Sravanabelagola visits two Hoysala temples and the Jain pilgrimage centre where the immense statue of Lord

Gomateshvara stands. The tours operate on Wednesdays, Fridays and Sundays, starting at 7.30 am and finishing at 9 pm. The cost is Rs 60 but the buses sometimes break down and guides are not always provided, although they are supposed to be. A number of travellers have written to complain bitterly about this tour; a few have written to commend it!

From April to June there is also a daily tour to Ootacamund, the hill station in the Nilgiris. It starts at 7 am, finishes at 9 pm and costs Rs 60.

All these tours are operated by the KSTDC and can be booked at the office in the Mayura Hoysala Hotel, 2 Jhansi Lakshmi Bai Rd. The tours also start and end there.

Places to Stay – bottom end

Mysore has plenty of budget hotels. The main areas are Gandhi Square, Dhanvantri Rd and in the streets around the Jaganmohan Palace.

Around Gandhi Square, the *Hotel Durbar* (tel 20029) is popular and charges Rs 25/40 for rooms with common bath, Rs 30/50 with private bath. The rooftop restaurant here is also good. In the same area the *Hotel Srikanth* (tel 26111) is a bit more expensive at Rs 35/65 but does offer hot water in the mornings.

The *Hotel Mona* has good rooms for Rs 30/50 with bath. Close by, the *Hotel Maurya* on Hanumantha Rd near Gandhi Square is good value at Rs 50 for a double with bath. On Sayaji Rao Rd opposite the Devaraja market the *Hotel Anugraha* (tel 30768) is a big place with clean rooms for Rs 42/63. Avoid the front rooms, however, as the road is very noisy.

East of the clock tower and north of the palace, *Green's Boarding & Lodging* (tel 22415) is very cheap, basic and good value at Rs 20/30 for huge singles/doubles.

Up the price scale a bit, but still in the Gandhi Square area, the *Hotel Dasaprakash* (tel 24444) is one of a chain of hotels through south India and is ideal for budget travellers. It is a huge place and

has a variety of somewhat shabby rooms ranging from Rs 50/80 up to Rs 75/125 for 'deluxe' rooms, although the only difference between the rooms seems to be that you get a few more switches to play with. All rooms have hot water in the morning and you get a paper under your door. The rooms also have telephones and the switchboard operator will book international calls for guests.

One of the better new hotels in Mysore is the *Hotel Siddhartha* (tel 26869) at 73/1 Government Guest House Rd. It's clean and good value for Rs 52/95 or Rs 84/150 with air-con. The *Parklane Hotel* (tel 30400) is in the same area at 2720 Curzon Park Rd. It's a good place and small rooms cost Rs 52/84 with bathroom and mosquito nets, although the latter are not really necessary most of the year.

In the Dhanvantri Rd area, the cheapest on offer is the *New Gayathri Bhavan* (tel 21224) which has singles/doubles with common bath for Rs 20/42, slightly more with private bath. A similar place is the *New Vishnu Bhavan* (tel 25466), also on Dhanvantri Rd. There are no singles and doubles cost Rs 53.

The *Agrawal Lodge* (tel 22730), just off Dhanvantri Rd, is a clean and friendly place with single/double/triple rooms for Rs 37/63/75. The relatively new *Hotel Aashriya* (tel 27088) has good double rooms but tiny, claustrophobic singles for Rs 32/73. Still in the Dhanvantri Rd area, the big *Hotel Chalukya* (tel 27374) has a range of rooms at Rs 35/74, and Rs 56 for a double bed in a single room.

The lodges around the Jaganmohan Palace tend to be a bit cheaper than elsewhere. A good place is the *Sudarshan Lodge* (tel 26713) with somewhat gloomy rooms for Rs 20/40 with common bath. Of a similar standard is the *Palace Lodge* (tel 20416) right opposite the palace. It is hardly palatial but is clean and adequate. Rooms cost Rs 50 a double with bath. The *Hotel Palace View* (tel 21416) is in the same street and has some reasonable singles/doubles for Rs 30/50 with bath.

Old Santhepet Rd connects the Jaganmohan Palace area with the market area. It is a street full of warehouses and is always full with rucks, carts and drays loading and unloading. Despite this, it is not too noisy and there are a couple of cheap lodges. The *Hotel Naga Lodge* (tel 26704) at No 155 Old Santhepet Rd is a friendly place and the large rooms cost Rs 30/45. The *Lakshmi Lodge* (tel 27178) on Sivarampet is not bad value at Rs 34/63. For the really impecunious, the *Sri Ram Lodge* close by has gloomy but otherwise OK rooms for Rs 20/35 with common bath.

At the railway station there are good *retiring rooms* for Rs 50 and dorm beds for Rs 15. There is a *Youth Hostel* (tel 36753) five km from the centre of town to the north-west. It costs only Rs 5, or Rs 8 for nonmembers, but its inconvenient location is a definite detraction. If you are keen, take a bus No 27, 41, 51, 53 or 63 from the City bus station.

The *Hotel Mayura Hoysala* (tel 25349), 2 Jhansi Lakshmi Bai Rd, opposite the Hotel Metropole, is operated by the KSTDC and offers spacious, pleasantly decorated singles/doubles with bath for Rs 74/98. The tours operated by KSTDC start from this hotel.

Close to the Central bus station is the *Ritz Hotel* (tel 22668) which has doubles for Rs 78. It's an older building with very pleasant staff who display a remarkably sardonic sense of humour about the hotel's facilities. There's a sign up in the bar saying: 'There's no place like home – after the bar closes', which is 11 pm. Also close to the bus station is the *Hotel Mannars* (tel 35060) where you'll get a room for Rs 78/100.

Of similar standard is the *Sandesh Hotel* (tel 23210), 3 Nazarbad Rd, which has an air-con bar and restaurant, money-changing facilities, laundry service and a car-rental counter. Rooms cost Rs 88/99/135 for singles/doubles/triples. All rooms have bathrooms and hot water. It's used mainly by Indian middle-class holiday-makers and businesspeople.

Places to Stay – middle

The *Hotel Metropole* (20681) at 5 Jhansi Lakshmi Bai Rd is tucked away in its own spacious and well-kept grounds. The service is erratic but the place has a pleasant ambience, and rooms are Rs 190/250 or Rs 285/405 with air-con. There is a restaurant serving Indian, Chinese and

1	Railway Station
2	Commercial Superintendents Office (Tourist Quota)
3	Tourist Office
4	Hotel Hoysala & Indian Airlines
5	Hotel Kings Court
6	Hotel Metropole
7	Grandpas Kitchen Restaurant
8	Shanghai Chinese Restaurant
9	Sri Ram Lodge
10	Lakshmi Lodge
11	New Gayathri Bhavan
12	Kwality Restaurant
13	New Vishnu Bhavan
14	Hotel Indra Bhavan
15	Hotel Aashriya
16	Agrawal Lodge
17	Hotel Chalukya
18	Devaraja Market
19	Punjabi Restaurant
20	Cauvery Arts & Crafts Emporium
21	State Bank of Mysore
22	Hotel Anugraha
23	Paras Restaurant & Indra Sweets
24	Geetha Book House
25	Palace
26	Hotel Maurya
27	Hotel Mona
28	Hotel Srikanth
29	Shilpashri Restaurant & Bar
30	Hotel Dasaprakash
31	Hotel Durbar
32	Gandhi Square
33	Hotel RRR
34	GPO
35	Central Bus Station
36	Hotel Mannars
37	Bus to Somnathpur
38	Ritz Hotel
39	Mysore Hotel Complex
40	Clocktower
41	Parklane Hotel & Green's Boarding and Lodging

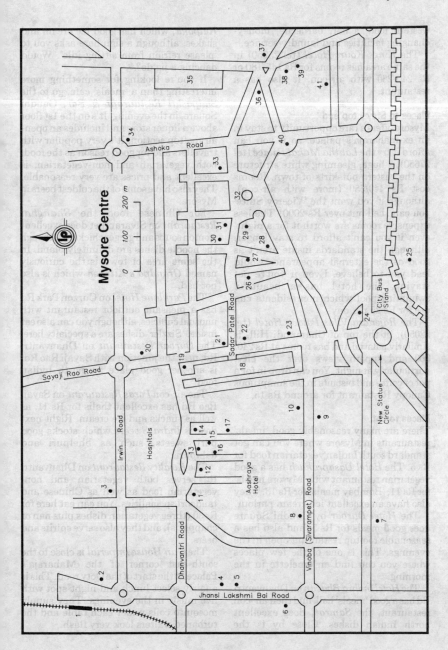

western food, a bar, barbecue, money-changing facilities and laundry service.

The *Kings Kourt Hotel* (tel 25250) in the same area has rooms for Rs 145/180 or Rs 240/280 with air-con. It also has a restaurant.

Places to Stay – top end

Mysore offers a rare opportunity to stay in an ex-maharaja's palace, so if you can afford it try the *Lalitha Mahal Palace* (tel 27650), a huge, gleaming white structure on the eastern outskirts of town. Rooms cost Rs 440/550 (more with air-con), although if you want the 'Viceroy Suite' you can shell out over Rs 2000! The less expensive rooms are worth it for a night, even if you can't afford to stay longer, although the standards inside aren't as good as the external appearance would lead you to believe. Even if you're not staying, the hotel has a beautiful swimming pool which nonresidents can use for Rs 25 per day.

The *Rajendra Vilas Palace Hotel* (tel 22050), at the top of Chamundi Hill, is similarly palatial and has rooms at Rs 240/360 and superb views over the city, particularly at night. You can drop in for a pot of coffee and biscuits in the sumptuous Canopy Restaurant for around Rs 15.

Places to Eat

There are many reasonably good 'meals' restaurants in Mysore where you can get standard south Indian vegetarian food for Rs 5. The *Hotel Dasaprakash* has a good vegetarian restaurant with 'Mysore meals' for Rs 11, 'Bombay meals' for Rs 13. They also have an excellent ice-cream parlour.

The *Hotel Durbar* by Gandhi Square does good meals for Rs 5, and also has a reasonable rooftop restaurant open in the evenings. This is one of the few places where you can find an omelette in the morning.

The *Hotel Indhra Bhavan* on Dhanvantri Rd has a good 'meals' hall, and their air-con restaurant, the *Samrat*, does excellent north Indian dishes. Close by is the *Kalpaka*, which has good ice cream and shakes, although a sign here asks you to 'please refrain from sitting idle'. Would dancing a jig do?

If you're looking for something more interesting than a 'meals' cafe, go to the *Shilpashri Restaurant & Bar*, Gandhi Square, in the evening. It's on the 1st floor above a liquor store and includes an open-air rooftop section. It's very popular with travellers and for good reason as the food, both vegetarian and non-vegetarian, is excellent and prices are very reasonable. They also have some of the coldest beers in Mysore.

For Chinese food the *Shanghai Restaurant* on Sivarampet does excellent wonton soups and ginger chicken, although the noodle dishes are definitely bland. In the same area of town is the curiously named *Grandpa's Kitchen* which is also not bad.

The *Parklane Hotel* on Curzon Park Rd has a pleasant outdoor restaurant with unusual cubicles, although you can also eat inside. 'Sizzler' dishes are a specialty here. The *Durbar Restaurant* on Dhanvantri Rd, near the junction with Sayaji Rao Rd, is another good place for north Indian food.

The air-con *Paras Restaurant* on Sayaji Rao Rd has excellent thalis for Rs 11, as well as snacks and ice cream. Right next door is *Indra Sweets* which stocks good puri sweets, such as bhelpuri and dahipuri.

The *Kwality Restaurant* on Dhanvantri Rd serves both vegetarian and non-vegetarian food as well as Chinese and tandoori specialities. You can eat here for Rs 30 (three vegetarian dishes plus nan or chappatis), and they also serve spirits and beers.

The *Gun House Imperial* is close to the south-east corner of the Maharaja's Palace at the start of the Ooty road. This is a fairly select lunch and night spot with live music in the evenings. They supply mosquito coils under each table and the turbaned waiters look very flash.

Finally, some places at the top and bottom of the price scale. The deluxe *Lalitha Mahal Palace Hotel* has an excellent evening buffet and the decor is impressive; 'like eating inside a giant Wedgewood pot' was how one overawed diner described it. Or at the other end of the scale you can look for the street stalls selling steamed chickpeas, puris stuffed with potatoes, dhal and raw carrots, all for a rupee. Their colourful, glass-sided carts, marked 'Welcome', are found by the clock tower in the evening.

Things to Buy

Mysore is famous for carved sandalwood and ivory articles, inlay works, silk saris and incense. The best place to see the whole range is at the Cauvery Arts & Crafts Emporium on Sayaji Rao Rd. It's open daily, except Thursdays, from 10 am to 2 pm and 3.30 to 7.30 pm (Sundays from 10 am to 2 pm). They accept credit cards, foreign currency or travellers' cheques and will arrange packing (they do a very good job) and export. There are always a number of street hawkers outside the Cauvery Emporium. They sometimes have interesting and cheap bangles, rings and old coins. Few of the larger things are cheap by Indian standards (the smallest of the inlaid tables costs about US$100), but the place is worth a visit even if you're not going to buy anything.

There are many other crafts shops along Dhanvantri Rd with similar prices. Some of them specialise in ivory chess sets, but a 10-cm set can cost you up to US$1500, and anyway, the ivory looks much better left on the elephant. The best bargains are the carved sandalwood images of Indian deities. They retain their scent for years and come in a huge array of sizes and configurations.

Getting There & Away

Air There are no Indian Airline flights to Mysore, but Vayudoot operate services to Bangalore (Rs 175), Bellary (Rs 545) and Hyderabad (Rs 700).

Bus The Central bus station is not far from the centre of Mysore, just north of the Ritz Hotel, and it handles all the long-distance buses. You can make reservations three days in advance. The City bus stand, near the Palace by New Statue Circle, is for city and Srirangapatnam buses.

There are a few direct buses daily to Somnathpur from the corner diagonally opposite the Ritz Hotel. It's more likely that you'll have to catch a bus to T Narisipur first (from the same place, Rs 3.50), then change for Somnathpur (Rs 1). These buses leave often and the total journey time is around 1½ hours. You can also get to Somnathpur by taking a bus from Mysore to Bannur and then another one from there. There are also buses direct from Bannur to Srirangapatnam.

There are plenty of buses from the City bus stand to Srirangapatnam. The No 125 goes only as far as Srirangapatnam; others pass through on their way to somewhere else. There's no problem getting back to Mysore along the same route. As an alternative to the bus, it's also possible to get there by taking a Bangalore train from Mysore station. It's also possible to catch a bus from Srirangapatnam on to Somnathpur.

Buses to Arsikere depart a dozen times daily from the Central bus stand. You can use Arsikere as a base from which to visit Belur, Halebid and Sravanabelagola, though Hassan is the more usual base. There are a couple of dozen buses daily from Mysore to Hassan for Rs 20, and the journey takes 2½ hours.

Nonstop deluxe buses to Bangalore depart every 20 to 30 minutes from early morning to late evening; the ordinary service with stops runs approximately every hour.

The daily bus to Bellary is the one to take if you want to visit the Vijayanagar ruins at Hampi direct from Mysore. There are three buses daily to Bandipur.

There are two or three buses daily from Mysore to Coimbatore, Cannanore, Nagarhole and Udupi. Half a dozen buses a day go to Calicut, and several of them continue to Ernakulam. This is an interesting trip through the Bandipur Sanctuary (watch for elephants) and over the Nilgiri Mountains. The Cochin to Mysore service also goes via Calicut; it takes about 13 hours.

There are half a dozen buses to Chikmagalur daily via Belur. A dozen buses daily go to Mangalore and the trip takes six hours. There are half a dozen buses daily to Ootacamund which you can take to get to the wildlife sanctuaries of Bandipur and Mudumalai. The trip takes five hours and costs Rs 20. A similar number of buses go to Sravanabelagola. Finally, there's a daily overnight service to Panaji in Goa, although the train to Jog Falls might be more interesting and easier on the nerves.

Train The booking office at Mysore station is very good and rarely has more than two or three people in it. If you're trying to book sleeper tickets on trains from Mysore and you're told that the quota is full for the day you're hoping to leave, buy a ticket anyway and go to the Commercial Superintendent's Office, the entrance is just near the railway station entrance. Find the office marked, 'Concession Orders Issued Here' (it's on your right as you enter) and ask for the Tourist Quota. Have your ticket handy – you can't do this without a ticket for the journey – fill in a form, wait for five minutes, and you'll get that sleeper. The quota here has precedence over the official waiting list compiled at the station ticket office.

If you're heading for Bombay from Mysore but don't want to go through Bangalore, there's a service to Miraj where you can take an express to Bombay; the whole trip takes about 40 hours. The 2700-km trip to Delhi costs Rs 175 in 2nd class, Rs 732 in 1st. It's 2170 km to Calcutta and the fare is Rs 149 in 2nd class, Rs 612 in 1st.

There are half a dozen express trains daily on the 140-km trip to Bangalore.

The trip usually takes around 3½ hours and costs Rs 20 in 2nd class, Rs 73 in 1st. There are also slower passenger trains to Bangalore, and these go through Maddur from where you can get to Srirangapatnam.

There are three passenger trains daily to Arsikere via Hassan. If you plan on visiting the Hoysala temples of Belur and Halebid and the Jain centre of Sravanabelagola, and if you're going to use Hassan as a base, then these are the trains to take. To Hassan the 130-km journey takes 4½ hours and costs only Rs 11 as these are not express trains.

One of the daily passenger trains to Arsikere connects with the daily train from Bangalore and goes right through to Vasco da Gama (Goa). It's painfully slow as it runs as a passenger train most of the way and takes a full 50 hours from Mysore. The 700-km journey costs Rs 70 in 2nd class, Rs 260 in 1st. If you're heading for Goa an alternative to that train and the bus is to take the overnight through-service to Jog Falls. One carriage goes all the way through to Talguppa (a few km from Jog) via Arsikere and Birur. The train departs Mysore at 6.05 pm, arriving in Talguppa at 9.10 am. The 372-km journey costs Rs 46 in 2nd class, Rs 173 in 1st.

Getting Around

Bus Bus No 150 goes to Brindavan Gardens. For Chamundi Hill, take No 101 from the City bus stand. They run approximately every 40 minutes and cost Rs 2.50.

Auto-Rickshaw There are plenty of auto-rickshaws if you prefer this form of transport. The drivers use the meters only with a good deal of persuasion.

AROUND MYSORE
Srirangapatnam

Sixteen km from Mysore on the Bangalore road stand the ruins of Hyder Ali and Tipu Sultan's capital from which they ruled much of southern India during the 18th century. In 1799, the British, allied with

The Gumbaz, Srirangapatnam

disgruntled local leaders and with the help of a traitor, finally defeated them. Tipu's defeat marked the real beginning of British territorial expansion in southern India.

There isn't much left of Srirangapatnam as the British did a good job of demolishing the place, but the extensive ramparts and battlements and some of the gates still stand. The dungeon where Tipu held a number of British officers has also been preserved. Inside the fortress walls there's also a mosque and the Sri Ranganathaswamy Temple, a popular place of pilgrimage with Hindus. Non-Hindus can go all the way inside except to the inner sanctum, where there is a black stone image of sleeping Vishnu. The population of the town inside the fort is about 20,000.

Across the other side of the main road from Srirangapatnam stands the Daria Daulat Bagh (Tipu's summer palace) and the Gumbaz (Tipu's mausoleum). These are perhaps the most interesting parts of a visit to Srirangapatnam. The Daria Daulat Bagh was later used as a residence by Colonel Arthur Wellesley in 1777. It stands in well-maintained ornamental gardens and is now a museum which houses some of Tipu's belongings as well as many ink drawings of him and his family. It also has 'artists' impressions' of the last battle, drawn by employees of the British East India Company. All around the internal walls of the ground floor are paintings depicting Tipu's campaigns, with the help of French mercenary assistance, against the British. The Daria Daulat Bagh is open daily until 5 pm.

Places to Stay Srirangapatnam can comfortably be visited in a day trip from Mysore, but it is also possible to stay here. The KSTDC operates the beautifully located *Hotel Mayura River View* (tel 114), a few km from the bus stand and railway station. Cottages cost Rs 84 for a double and there is a restaurant.

Just up the main road from the bus stand in Srirangapatnam are a couple of basic lodges which would do for an overnight stay.

Getting There & Around There are scores of buses every day to and from the Central bus station in Mysore, and the fare is Rs 2.50. It's also possible to take any of the Mysore to Bangalore trains.

Walking around the sights is not really an option as the points of interest are well spread out. The best plan is to hire a bicycle in Srirangapatnam. There are a couple of hire shops in the main street, about 500 metres from the bus stand or railway station. All the roads are well signposted so it's not difficult to find your way around.

If cycling is not your bag, there are tongas and auto-rickshaws for hire.

Somnathpur
The Sri Channakeshara, built around

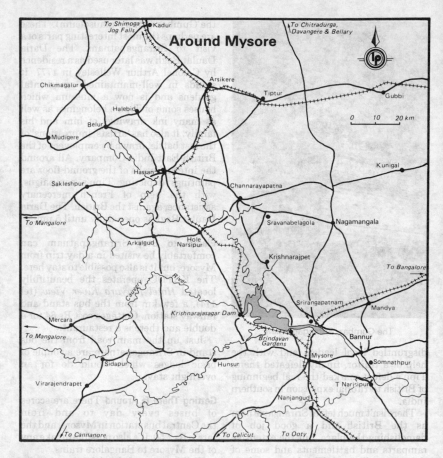

Around Mysore

1260 AD during the heyday of the Hoysala kings, is at Somnathpur, 45 km east of Mysore. It's an extremely beautiful and interesting building, although it doesn't quite match up to the other Hoysala temples at Belur and Halebid north of Mysore. Unlike these other two, however, it is complete.

The walls of the star-shaped temple are literally covered with superb sculptures in stone depicting various scenes from the *Ramayana*, *Mahabharata*, *Bhagavadgita* and the life and times of the Hoysala kings. No two friezes are alike.

The temple is open daily from 9 am to 5 pm.

Information A useful booklet, *The Hoysalas* by P K Mishra, is on sale at the temple for Rs 6.

Places to Stay Just outside the temple compound is a KSTDC *Tourist Home & Restaurant*. The pleasantly decorated rooms with bathrooms and carpeted floors are great value from Rs 40, yet they're rarely full. The restaurant serves decent food.

Getting There & Away See the Mysore section for details on how to get to Somnathpur by public transport.

Bandipur Wildlife Sanctuary

Eighty km south of Mysore on the Mysore to Ootacamund road, this wildlife sanctuary covers 874 square km and is part of a larger national park which also includes the neighbouring wildlife sanctuaries of Mudumalai in Tamil Nadu and Wynad in Kerala. In the days of the Mysore maharajas this was their game reserve.

The sanctuary is one of the 15 selected across the country for Project Tiger, a scheme launched in 1973 by the World Wildlife Fund to save the tiger and its habitat. The sanctuary is noted for its herds of bison, spotted deer, elephant, sambar and leopard. There are supposed to be two dozen tigers but they are rarely seen.

The Forestry Department has jeeps and trucks available for hire and, as in Mudumalai, you can go on elephant-back safari. Boats are available for use on the river. Motorised transport and accommodation in the sanctuary must be booked in advance if you want to be sure of them.

Food and accommodation at the park are very good. The best time to go is May and June, and again from September to November, although one traveller wrote of seeing elephant, bison, jungle fowl, peacocks, monkeys, mongoose, sambar and deer in February! If there is a drought, the park may not be worth visiting, as the animals migrate to the adjoining park at Mudumalai in Tamil Nadu for water. Entry is only possible from 6 to 9 am and 4.30 to 6.30 pm. For reservations contact any of the following:

Assistant Director, Bandipur National Park, Bandipur (tel 21)
Chief Wildlife Warden, Aranya Bhavan, 18th Cross, Malleswaram, Bangalore (tel 341993)
Forest Officer, Forest Dept, Woodyard, Ashokpuram, Mysore

Places to Stay There are huge deluxe *bungalows* at the park with bathrooms, mosquito nets, hot water and a big lounge for Rs 25 per night plus a one-time charge of Rs 15. The caretaker (or somebody) will fix excellent meals, and you can see chital (spotted deer) right from your windows. Films are shown at the centre each night.

Getting There & Around You can make a day trip to Bandipur by catching the 5.30 am bus from Mysore to Ooty. You'll arrive at the Bandipur office two or three hours later and can take a jeep trip (Rs 5 per person per km) or hire an elephant and guide (Rs 30 for four people). Doing both, you'll still be in time to catch the last bus back to Mysore around 5.30 pm. Jeeps are better than trucks, which tend to be crowded and noisy.

Ranganathittoo Bird Sanctuary

The sanctuary is on one of three islands in the Cauvery River, three km from Srirangapatnam. If you're interested in birds this is a good place to visit at any time

of year, though it's best between May and November. Access is by a motorable road, open all year. Boats are available for use on the river but there is no accommodation.

Brindavan Gardens

These ornamental gardens are laid out below the Krishnarajasagar Dam across the Cauvery River, 19 km from Mysore. They're popular for picnics and pleasant enough, but probably not worth a special visit although they are colourfully lit for two hours each night – 'cosmic kitsch' is how somebody described the lighting – and there's a musical fountain!

Entry costs Rs 2 plus Rs 20 (!) if you have a camera. One of the tours operated by the KSTDC will bring you here, or there are buses (No 150) from the Mysore City bus stand every half-hour. The lights are on from 7 to 9 pm, and the fountain from 7.30 to 7.40 pm.

Places to Stay There are two places to stay at the gardens. The *Hotel Krishnarajasagar* (tel Belagola 22) is an expensive western-style hotel with all the mod cons, and rooms cost Rs 150/220, or Rs 190/255 with air-con.

The KSTDC *Hotel Mayura Ca*~*ory* (tel Belagola 52) is similar to the one at Somnathpur, and doubles with bathroom cost from Rs 40.

Bylakuppe

At Bylakuppe, 80 km to the west of Mysore, is a Tibetan refugee settlement called Rabgayling – which means 'Good Progress Place' although nobody calls it that! There are 15 villages scattered over low, rolling hills in a grid pattern – lovely to see against the green cornfields. There are two monasteries, one of them a Tantric college, both involved in the village life.

The two carpet factories are glad to produce Tibetan carpets to your own design. Thankas are painted at the Tantric college. There's no commercial accommodation in the area although two small cafes serve momos, noodles and curd.

Southern Karnataka

BELUR & HALEBID

The temples at Belur and Halebid, along with that at Somnathpur east of Mysore, are the cream of what remains of one of the most artistically exuberant periods of Hindu cultural development. The sculptural decoration on these superb temples even rivals the temples of Khajuraho (Madhya Pradesh) and Konarak (Orissa) or the best of European Gothic art.

The wealth of sculptural detail on the Hoysaleswara Temple at Halebid makes it easily the most outstanding example of Hoysala art. Every cm of the outside walls and much of the interior are covered with an endless variety of Hindu deities, sages, stylised animals and birds, and friezes depicting the life and times of the Hoysala rulers. No two are alike. Scenes from war, hunting, agriculture, music and dancing, and some very sensual sculptures explicitly portraying the après-temple activities of the dancing girls are represented here, together with two huge Nandis (Shiva's bull) and a monolithic Jain statue of Lord Gomateshvara.

The Hoysala temples are squat and low, more human in scale than the soaring temples found elsewhere in India. What they lack in size they make up in the sheer intricacy of their sculptures. The Hoysaleswara Temple at Halebid was constructed about 10 years after the temple at Belur, but despite 80 years' labour was never completed. There is also a smaller temple, the Kedareswara, at Halebid.

At Belur, the Channekeshava Temple is the only one at the three Hoysala sites still used as a functioning temple. Non-Hindus are allowed inside. It is very similar to the others in design but here much of the decoration has gone into the internal supporting pillars and lintels, and the larger but still very delicately carved images of deities and guardian beasts. As at Halebid, the external walls are covered in friezes. The other, lesser, Hoysala temples at Belur are the Channigaraya and the Viranarayana.

The Hoysalas, who ruled this part of the Deccan between the 11th and 13th centuries, had their origins in the hill tribes of the Western Ghats and were for a long time feudatories of the Chalukyas. They did not become fully independent until about 1190 AD, though they first rose to prominence under their leader Tinayaditya (1047-78 AD), who took advantage of the waning power of the Gangas and Rashtrakutas. Under Bittiga (1110-52 AD), better known by his later name of Vishnuvardhana, they began to take off on a course of their own and it was during his reign that the temples of Belur and Halebid were built.

Vishnuvardhana's conversion to Vishnu worship was one of the main factors which led to a decline of Jainism, but it was not the only one. Corruption among the priesthood and the public defeat of the Jain texts by Ramanuja also undermined its influence, but it was by no means extinguished and at least one of Vishnu-vardhana's wives and a daughter continued to practise that faith. Later Hoysala rulers also continued to patronise the religion. This normally easy coexistence between Shaivites, Vaishnavites and Jains explains why you will find images of all these various sects' gods, their consorts and associated companions in Hoysala temples.

The early temples of this dynasty closely followed the style of those of their Chalukyan overlords, but by Bittiga's time they had developed a distinctive style of their own. Typically, the temple is a relatively small star-shaped structure set on a platform to give it some height, with most of the attention devoted to sculptural embellishment.

It's quickly apparent from a study of these sculptures that the arts of music and dancing reached a high point in grace and perfection during the Hoysala period. As with Kathakali dancing in Kerala, the arts were used to express religious fervour, the joy of a victory in battle, or simply to give domestic pleasure. It's obvious that these were times of a relatively high degree of sexual freedom and prominent female participation in public affairs. Most Indian books which describe these temples and the ones at Khajuraho bend over backwards to play down the sensuality of these sculptures. Perhaps this embarrassment reflects the repressed attitudes of the average urban Indian today regarding all matters physical. Of course a century ago our Victorian ancestors were also slightly shocked by some Indian temples!

The Hoysala temples at Halebid and Belur are open every day. A spotlight is available inside to enable you to see the sculptural work (it's quite dark otherwise), but if it's not already turned on you'll be charged Rs 2 for the privilege. Entry to Halebid is free although, as at Belur, there is a Rs 0.20 charge for the shoe-minder. The Halebid temple is maintained by the Archaeological Survey of India, and there is a small museum adjacent to the temple but it's of little interest.

Places to Stay

Halebid Though Halebid was once the capital city of the Hoysala rulers, it is now little more than a rural village. KSTDC *Tourist Cottages* adjoin the Halebid temple, and rooms with bath cost from Rs 50. It's a very pleasant place with catering facilities. There is nowhere else to stay. An old sign in the village centre indicates that the temple is one mile (1.6 km) away; someone can't measure since it's less than one-third of that distance.

Belur Belur is just a small town. The KSTDC *Hotel Mayura Velapuri* (tel 9) is only 200 metres from the temple and five minutes walk from the bus stand. Rooms cost Rs 47/75 and meals can be supplied with advance notice.

There's also the basic *Shri Praghavendra*

Tourist Home just to the right of the temple entrance. Rooms have nothing more than a couple of mattresses on the floor and cost Rs 25 with bath.

The *New Gayatri Hotel* (tel 55) and the *Hotel Vishnu Prasad* (tel 63) are both on the main road through the town and charge around Rs 30 for a double. They also have restaurants and are a two-minute walk from the bus stand.

Though it's possible to stay in either Halebid or Belur – and this is a good idea if you want to spend a day at each temple – most people use Hassan as a base. Arsikere is another possibility. Accommodation and transport facilities at both of these places are covered later in this chapter.

SRAVANABELAGOLA (population 3500)

This is one of the oldest and most important Jain pilgrimage centres in India, and the site of the huge 17-metre-high statue of Lord Bahubali (Gomateshvara), said to be the world's tallest monolithic statue. It

The statue of Lord Bahubali

overlooks the small town of Sravanabelagola from the top of the rocky hill known as Indragiri and is visible from quite a distance. Its simplicity is in complete contrast to the complexity of the sculptural work at the temples of Belur and Halebid. The word 'Sravanabelagola' means 'the monk on the top of the hill'.

History

Sravanabelagola has a long historical pedigree going back to the 3rd century BC when Chandragupta Maurya came here with his guru, Bhagwan Bhadrabahu Swami, after renouncing his kingdom. In the course of time Bhadrabahu's disciples spread his teachings all over the region and thus firmly established Jainism in the south. The religion found powerful patrons in the Gangas who ruled the southern part of what is now Karnataka between the 4th and 10th centuries, and it was during this time that Jainism reached the zenith of its influence.

Information

The tourist office is right by the entrance to the hill and is open from 10 am to 1 pm and 3 to 5.30 pm daily. It's staffed by a friendly and helpful man – a stark contrast to many tourist offices in India where monosyllabic grunts and general indolence are the order of the day.

Gomateshvara Statue

The statue of Lord Bahubali was created during the reign of the Ganga king, Rachamalla. It was commissioned by a military commander in the service of Rachamalla and built by the sculptor Aristanemi in 981 AD.

Entry to the site is Rs 2, and you have to leave your shoes at the entrance. This creates a real problem in the summer as you then have to scamper up the 614 rock-cut steps which become scolding hot. Coir mats are laid down but these don't cover the entire distance. Get there before the heat of the day to avoid this small bit of purgatory.

The statue is the subject of the spectacular Mahamastakabhisheka ceremony, which takes place once every 12 to 14 years when the small town of Sravanabelagola becomes a mecca for thousands of pilgrims and tourists from all over India and abroad. The climax of the Mahamastakabhisheka involves the anointing of Lord Bahubali's head with thousands of pots of coconut milk, yoghurt, ghee, bananas, jaggery, dates, almonds, poppy seeds, milk, gold coins, saffron and sandalwood from the top of a scaffolding erected for the purpose. There must be a lot of work for cleaners after this event! The last one was in 1981. The rest of the time, Sravanabelagola reverts to a quiet little country town which is a very pleasant place to stay for a few days. The people are friendly, the pace is unhurried and the place is full of cosy little chai shops.

Other Temples

In addition to the statue of Lord Bahubali there are several very interesting Jain *bastis* (temples) and *mathas* (monasteries) both in the town and on Chandragiri Hill, the smaller of the two hills between which Sravanabelagola nestles. Two of these, the Bhandari Basti and the Akkana Basti, are in the Hoysala style, and a third, the Chandragupta Basti, is believed to have been built by Emperor Ashoka the Great. The well-preserved paintings in one of the temples are like a 600-year-old comic strip of Jain stories.

Places to Stay & Eat

The only accommodation is the *Shriyans Prasad Guest House* pilgrims' quarters next to the bus station, at the foot of the hill. Double rooms cost Rs 40.

There is a very basic refreshment canteen in the bus station, and there are a couple of vegetarian restaurants in the street leading up to the entrance to the hill.

Getting There & Away

There are direct buses from Sravanabelagola to Arsikere, Hassan, Mysore and Bangalore. See the Hassan transport section for full details of buses in this area.

If your time is short and you have to see Belur, Halebid and Sravanabelagola in one day, your only choice is the very rushed KSTDC tours from Mysore.

HASSAN

Hassan is probably the most convenient base from which to explore Belur, Halebid and Sravanabelagola. It has little of interest; it's simply a place for accommodation and transport.

Information

The tourist office is a total waste of time. The guy who staffs it speaks very poor English and seems to spend a good deal of time examining the backs of his eyelids while resting his head on the desk.

Places to Stay - bottom end

There are quite a few hotels in Hassan. Only a few minutes walk from the bus station is *Vaishnavi Lodging* (tel 7413). This new lodge is excellent value at Rs 35/52, and all rooms have a bath, mosquito netting on the windows and are big, clean and airy.

About 10 minutes walk from the bus station in the centre of the town is the *Hotel Lakshmi Prasanna* (tel 8391). Rooms in this basic hotel are a good size and cost Rs 30/50. Right next door is the *Hotel Sanman* (tel 8024) which is one of the cheapest around at Rs 22/42. It's also quite OK for an overnight stay. In the same area, the *IJV Lodge* (tel 8574) is dirt cheap at Rs 18/28; unfortunately it is not only cheap but also dirty.

The *Sathyaprakash Lodge* (tel 8521) almost next door to the bus station is also good at Rs 25/34 for rooms with bath. The *Hotel Dwaraka* next door is to be avoided at all costs. It has the dubious distinction of not only being uninhabitable (not altogether uncommon) but also of being the filthiest pit I saw in 10,000 km of travel in south India.

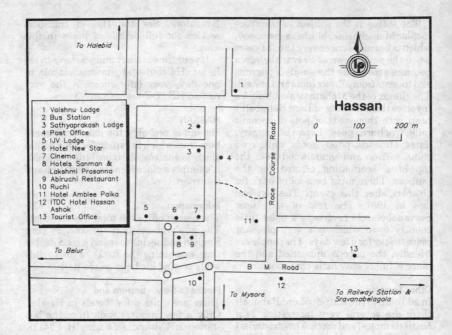

1 Vaishnu Lodge
2 Bus Station
3 Sathyaprakash Lodge
4 Post Office
5 IJV Lodge
6 Hotel New Star
7 Cinema
8 Hotels Sanman &
  Lakshmi Prasanna
9 Abiruchi Restaurant
10 Ruchi
11 Hotel Amblee Paika
12 ITDC Hotel Hassan
   Ashok
13 Tourist Office

Hassan

To Halebid

Race Course Road

0   100   200 m

To Belur

B M Road

To Mysore

To Railway Station &
Sravanabelagola

There's just one *retiring room* at the railway station, and it costs Rs 7.50/15.

Places to Stay - middle & top end

The relatively new *Hotel Amblee Palika* (tel 7145) is very clean and well maintained. The rooms are large and comfortable and have mosquito netting on the windows. Rooms are Rs 75 for singles and doubles, or there are deluxe rooms for Rs 120, more if you want carpets and a few more light switches to play with.

The *Hotel Hassan Ashok* (tel 8731) is the best hotel in town and one of the chain of ITDC hotels you will find all over India. Rooms with bath cost Rs 200/300 or Rs 400/550 with air-con and there is a restaurant.

Places to Eat

The *Hotel Sanman* has a very popular vegetarian restaurant which serves a good thali for Rs 5. They also have excellent dosas and idli. The restaurant at the *Hotel Lakshmi Prasanna* is much the same.

An old favourite for years has been the restaurant under the Sathyaprakash Lodge. It has undergone a few name changes over the years; in its present incarnation it's known as the *Shanthala Restaurant*. The thalis are still good although the waiters have the annoying habit of hovering for a tip.

For something a bit better, the Hotel Amblee Palika has the *Malanika Restaurant* and a bar. For non-vegetarian food, a good choice is the *Hotel New Star*. It is open quite late and does good mutton and beef curries. For north Indian and Chinese dishes, the *Abiruchi Restaurant* is not bad although it's a little expensive by local standards – a good meal costs about Rs 20.

On the city circle *Ruchi* does good fruit drinks and excellent ice creams and desserts.

Getting There & Away

Bus If you're planning on visiting Belur and Halebid in one day, then there's no need to return to Hassan after you've seen one of the places, as there are buses in either direction between Belur and Halebid. In addition to these bus services, there are at least 20 buses daily to Mysore (Rs 15.50) and the same number to Bangalore (Rs 34 super deluxe, Rs 23.50 ordinary).

Belur There are about 20 buses daily from Hassan to Belur; the first leaves at 6.15 am. The journey takes 1½ hours and costs Rs 5. Ignore the claim on the timetable about some of the buses being 'express', it's a figment of the imagination.

From Belur there are infrequent buses to Halebid, ask at the bus stand in Belur. Once the bus arrives don't hang about – there is always a mad rush. This bus takes about half an hour and costs Rs 1.50. There are also small and crowded private minibuses operating on this route.

Halebid There are 10 buses daily from Hassan to Halebid. The journey takes one hour and costs Rs 3.75. The first bus departs at 8 am, and the last bus back to Hassan leaves Halebid at 6.15 pm. It's more convenient to visit Halebid first, as there are many more buses from Belur to Hassan and they run until much later at night.

Sravanabelagola There are three buses daily to Sravanabelagola and the 1½-hour journey costs Rs 5. The first bus is at 9 am. It's better to get an early start from Hassan and catch a bus first to Chanrayapatna at 6.30 am (one hour, Rs 5), then take another to Sravanabelagola from there at 7.45 am (30 minutes, Rs 1.75). Late in the afternoon bus paranoia sets in and the usual chaos results.

There are also direct buses from Sravanabelagola to Mysore, Arsikere and Bangalore.

Arsikere Buses to Arsikere depart many times daily, though the exact times are hard to ascertain as the bus schedule is entirely in Kannada. The journey takes about 1½ hours along a good road and costs Rs 7.

Goa It's 8½ hours to Hubli and another 5½ hours to Panaji at a total cost of about Rs 85. An interesting alternative, if you have a few days to spare, is to spend a few days winding through the hills and forests of the Western Ghats to Goa. This does involve quite a bit of bus travel but the buses on this route are fairly new and uncrowded. The first stage is to Sringeri (four hours), from where there are buses to Sagar (five hours, Rs 15) and on to Jog Falls (one hour, Rs 3), and from there buses go to Karwar (six hours, Rs 22) to connect with buses to Panaji (four hours, Rs 10). This trip takes you through a variety of untouristed territory. There is accommodation in Sringeri (at the temple), Jog Falls and Karwar.

Train The station at Hassan is about two km from the centre of town, so either hire an auto-rickshaw (about Rs 3) or walk.

There are three passenger trains to and from Mysore daily. The 119-km journey takes 4½ hours and costs Rs 11. These trains from Mysore also continue on to Arsikere, taking 1½ hours, although there are a couple of express trains along this 47-km sector. The fare is Rs 8 express, or Rs 4 passenger.

There are also passenger trains to Mangalore which take eight hours to cover the 189 km; the daily express is marginally quicker at 6½ hours. The cost in 2nd class is Rs 16 passenger and Rs 28 express. This line is closed during the monsoon season from June to September.

ARSIKERE

Like Hassan, this is a convenient base from which to explore the temples of Belur and Halebid and the Jain centre of Sravanabelagola, but unlike Hassan it has a Hoysala temple of its own. Unfortunately, much of the temple has been defaced and vandalised, and many contemporary structures have been added so it's no longer very representative.

It's about a 15-minute walk down the road next to the Co-operative Bank on the main road just up from the bus station.

Arsikere is also a railway junction with express trains to Bangalore, Bombay, Jog Falls and Goa.

Places to Stay

Just outside the railway station is the clean, quiet and friendly *Geetha Lodge*. Rooms cost Rs 15/25 with bath.

The *Hotel Mayura* (tel 358) is in the centre of town near the bus station. The staff are helpful and they have rooms for Rs 22/35. The *Janata Hotel* (tel 471) opposite the bus station has rooms where you stand a sporting chance of surviving for a night without being eaten alive, and it's cheap at Rs 15/25.

There are two *retiring rooms* at the railway station, and these cost Rs 15/30.

Places to Eat

The *Janata Hotel* has an excellent 'meals' dining hall on the ground floor – Rs 4 for all you can eat. In the non-veg department, the *Elite Hotel* is just up from the bus stand on the main road.

Getting There & Away

Bus The bus schedule here is entirely in Kannada, which is bad news if you've just mastered the rudiments of Tamil or Hindi (or Malayalam or Telugu or. . .), but there are plenty of buses – just ask.

Train There is no sleeping-accommodation quota on the Bangalore-Miraj Mail at Arsikere. Arsikere to Bangalore is 156 km and the fare is Rs 24 in 2nd class, Rs 80 in 1st. They do, however, have a quota on the express to Bombay.

There is a direct train from Arsikere to Goa departing daily at 12.30 am. The journey takes 19 hours and costs Rs 70 in 2nd class, Rs 260 in 1st.

If you're heading for Mysore there are three passenger trains daily. If you're trying to get from Arsikere to Hospet (for the Vijayanagar ruins at Hampi), take the passenger train to Harihar and then a bus from there. The bus station at Harihar is just opposite the railway station.

Coast & Western Ghats

MADIKERI (Mercara) (population 25,000)
The small town of Madikeri, the capital of Coorg region, is 124 km west of Mysore. Until 1956, when it was included in Karnataka, Coorg (or Kodagu) was a ministate in its own right. It is a mountainous area in the south-west of the state where the Western Ghats start to tumble down towards the sea. It is green, scenic, fertile and an important coffee-growing area. The view from Raja's Seat, the local scenic lookout, is wonderful.

There is a fort here which has played an important part in Karnataka's tumultuous history, and there's also the Omareswara Temple. The temple is one km from the centre of town back towards Mysore. There is a small museum housed in an old church within the walls of the fort, while the old palace itself is now used as the local municipal headquarters.

The town is well spread out along a series of ridges but the bus station and the bulk of the hotels and restaurants are in a compact area. There is very little to do in this quiet and unhurried hill station other than walk around and take in the cool air.

Information

There is a tourist office in the PWD Bungalow on the main road into town. Their hand-out is full of the usual non-English mumbo-jumbo and speaks of the coffee plantations and 'orange grooves'.

Places to Stay

The quiet *Anchorage Guest House*, visible from the State bus stand, is on a large bare block of land. Double rooms cost Rs 35 with bath. Also very close to the bus station is the *Hotel Sri Venayaka Lodge* with dull but adequate rooms for

Rs 25/50. There are a few other rock-bottom places in the main street but they're not very good.

The *Hotel Cauvery* (tel 6292) is five minutes walk from the bus station and next to the cinema. Rooms in this clean and friendly place cost Rs 30/60 with bath, and there is hot water in the mornings.

The KSTDC *Hotel Mayura Valley View* (tel 6387) is on the edge of the ghats, half a km up behind the Town Hall. It's about Rs 4 by auto-rickshaw or 20 minutes on foot, and the views from the hotel are excellent. Rooms cost Rs 68/84 during October to May, but are a good deal cheaper for the rest of the year.

Places to Eat
The *Chitra Lodge* in the main street does a good standard 'meal' for Rs 4.50. Also on the main street is the *Popular Restaurant*, which in no way lives up to its name.

For something a bit more sophisticated, the *Hotel Capitol*, next to the Hotel Cauvery, is mainly a bar but also serves good food. The menu is limited and the service slow but there's not much choice in Madikeri. The vegetable fried rice is worth the wait.

Getting There & Away
The State bus stand is right in the centre of town and, as Madikeri is on the main Mysore to Mangalore road, there are plenty of buses running to both places. To Mysore buses take three hours and cost Rs 15; to Mangalore it's 3½ hours and Rs 18. There are 10 buses daily to Bangalore (six hours), and at least one a day to Hassan, Arsikere, Belur and Chikmagalur.

NAGARHOLE NATIONAL PARK
This 573-square-km wildlife sanctuary is in the south-east of Coorg. The name derives from two Kannada words: 'nagar' meaning snake, and 'hole' meaning streams.

The best time to visit the park is from October to May. In theory, the Forest Department has jeeps available for wildlife viewing from 6 to 9 am and 4 to 6.30 pm for a cost of Rs 10 per person for two hours. In practice things probably work a lot differently.

The park entry fee is Rs 2 and there is a Rs 1 camera fee.

Places to Stay
There are three *government lodges* operating, with tariffs ranging from Rs 25 to Rs 50 for a double.

The privately run *Kabini River Lodges* are just a fraction more expensive at Rs 80 per person for full board.

The government lodges can be booked in advance from any of the following:

Range Forest Officer, Nagarhole National Park, Kutta (tel Kutta 21)
Chief Wildlife Warden, Aranya Bhavan, 18th Cross, Malleswaram, Bangalore (tel 341993)
Forests Officer, Forest Dept, Woodyard, Ashokpuram, Mysore

MANGALORE (population 400,000)
The west coast railway line through Kerala crosses the border into Karnataka and terminates at this port. At one time Mangalore was a port of great importance and the major seaport and shipbuilding centre of Hyder Ali's kingdom. Even today it is a major centre for the export of coffee and cashew nuts, but its attractions are very limited – in fact it has none. If Mangalore is on your way it can make a convenient overnight stop, but otherwise don't lose any sleep if you have to pass it by.

The only remnant from the past is the Sultan's Battery on the headland to the old port. It really doesn't rate as one of the not-to-be-missed wonders of India. To get to it take a No 16 bus from the centre of the city, or it costs about Rs 10 by auto-rickshaw for the round trip.

Orientation
Mangalore is a hilly place so the streets twist and wind all over the place. For this reason navigation can be difficult. Fortunately all the hotels and restaurants

are in or around the hectic city centre, as is the railway station. The bus station is a few km to the north and you'll need to catch an auto-rickshaw (about Rs 5).

Information

There is a tourist office at the Hotel Indraprastha, in the centre of town, but the guy staffing it seems to be permanently out to lunch. In the same hotel is an office of KSRTC, the state bus company. The GPO is about 15 minutes walk downhill (south) from the centre, just past Chetty Circle.

The Indian Airlines and Air India offices (tel 21300) are in the Poonja Arcade of the fancy new Poonja International Hotel on K S Rao Rd in the centre of town. Unlike many Indian Airlines offices, this one is very quiet and, as it's all computerised, can be a good place to make reservations. The office is open from 9 am to 1 pm and 1.45 to 4 pm daily.

Places to Stay – bottom end

Mangalore's hotels are concentrated along K S Rao Rd in the centre of the city. The huge Hotel Vishnu Bhavan (tel 24622) is extremely basic but passably clean and habitable. As is so often the case, the rooms at the front of the building are extremely noisy, those at the back are much better. Rooms cost Rs 33 a double with bath.

Also on K S Rao Rd is the Hotel Vasanth Mahal (tel 22311) with single/ double rooms for Rs 34/52. The Hotel Roopa (tel 21271) is on the other side of Light House Hill Rd and rooms cost Rs 32/ 42, or Rs 158 for an air-con double.

If you want to stay near the bus station, the Panchami Boarding & Lodging, right opposite, is good for an overnight stop. Rooms are adequate and cheap at Rs 30/40. Another cheap one-night option are the railway retiring rooms which cost Rs 25/ 50, or Rs 15 for a dormitory bed.

Places to Stay – middle & top end

For something a bit better try the Hotel

Navaratna (tel 27941) on K S Rao Rd. Rooms at this friendly hotel cost Rs 52/94 for singles/doubles, and Rs 126/158 with air-con. Another place on K S Rao Rd is the Hotel Maurya (tel 32316) where you pay Rs 89/115, more with air-con.

On Light House Hill Rd just up from the centre of the city is the KSTDC Hotel Indraprastha (tel 31641). All rooms have phone and hot water, and those at the front have balconies with views out over the city and the ocean. The tariff is Rs 63/80 for singles/doubles and you get a paper under your door in the morning. At the top of the scale is the brand new multistorey Hotel Poonja International on K S Rao Rd.

Eleven km south of the city is the Summer Sands Beach Resort at Ullal Beach. It makes a quiet escape from the city. To get there take a No 44A, 44C or 44D bus.

Places to Eat

The Safa Dine is a small non-veg restaurant in the lower level next to the Roopa Hotel. They serve excellent biryani and Ceylon paroda.

The Roopa Hotel itself has a couple of restaurants – the Shin Min Chinese Restaurant is acceptable, and there's also the Vyshaki Non-Veg Corner, the Kamadhenu Veg Restaurant and the Big Daddy Ice Cream Parlour.

In the arcade just below the Hotel Indraprastha the Panchali Restaurant is a popular 'meals' place.

The Hotel Maurya has a lunchtime buffet on weekdays but at Rs 20 it's not fantastic value. The main attraction seems to be the cowboy movies on the video (at full volume of course), and the air-con.

Getting There & Away

Air The airport is 20 km from the town centre. Indian Airlines have at least daily flights to Bombay (Rs 715) and four flights a week to Bangalore (Rs 340).

Vayudoot have flights to Cochin for Rs 465.

Bus The main bus station is fairly quiet and well organised. Daily departures include Hassan (four hours, Rs 22), Hospet (Rs 60), Karwar (Rs 38), Goa (Rs 54), Madras (Rs 90), Bombay (Rs 158), Mysore (Rs 34) and Bangalore (Rs 47).

Train The twice-weekly Bangalore to Mangalore fast passenger train takes about 16 hours for the 447-km trip. Fares are Rs 42 in 2nd class, Rs 168 in 1st. Trivandrum to Mangalore takes about 17 hours for the 921-km trip via Calicut, Ernakulam and Quilon. Fares are Rs 86 in 2nd class, Rs 324 in 1st.

Madras to Mangalore is a 900-km trip taking around 18 hours with fares of Rs 85 in 2nd class, Rs 317 in 1st. Direct trains between Delhi and Mangalore take 2½ days for the 3033-km trip, and fares are Rs 191 in 2nd class, Rs 811 in 1st.

On the Mangalore to Hassan run there are two trains daily which take 6½ hours to cover the 189 km up through the Western Ghats. The fare is Rs 28 in 2nd class, Rs 93 in 1st. Trains on this line are suspended during the monsoon season if the rain has been particularly heavy.

Getting Around
Mangalore's local buses are privately owned, and there's a confusing array of them. The only one you're likely to need is the No 16 out to Sultan's Battery.

As always, there are plenty of auto-rickshaws.

AROUND MANGALORE
If you liked Sravanabelagola (near Mysore) and would like to visit other famous Jain pilgrimage centres, there are several fairly close to Mangalore:

Dharmastala
A little south of the Mangalore to Belur road, about halfway between the two, there are a number of Jain bastis at Dharmastala, including the famous Manjunatha Temple. There is also a 14-metre-high statue of Lord Bahubali which was erected in 1973.

Venur
Midway between Mangalore and Dharmastala, 41 km from the latter, Venur has eight bastis and the ruins of a Mahadeva temple. An 11-metre-high statue of Lord Bahubali stands on the south bank of the Gurupur River, where it was installed in 1604.

Mudabidri
At this site, 22 km from Venur, there are 18 bastis, the oldest of which is the Chandranatha Temple with its 1000 richly carved pillars.

Karkal
A further 31 km north of Mudabidri are several important temples and a 13-metre-high statue of Lord Bahubali, which was completed in 1432.

SRINGERI
In the lush coffee-growing hills of Chikmagalur, near Harihar, Sringeri is the southern seat of the orthodox Hindu hierarchy. The other three centres founded by Shankaracharya are Joshimath in the Himalaya (north), Puri (east) and Dwarka (west). The very interesting Vidyashankar Temple has zodiac pillars and a huge paved courtyard. A beautifully clean second temple is dedicated to Sharada, the goddess of learning. The Tunga River flows past the old monastery in this charmingly unspoilt town.

Places to Stay & Eat As this is a major pilgrimage centre, there is a range of pilgrim accommodation available in different buildings around the town. A charge of Rs 15 per person is made for spartan single or double rooms with bath. You must report to the small office at the temple entrance to be allocated a room.

There's a vegetarian meals restaurant in the bus station, which is in the centre of town.

Getting There & Away There are plenty of buses from Sringeri to virtually all points in Karnataka, including Mysore, Hassan, Chikmagalur, Sagar and Bangalore.

JOG FALLS

Near the coast, 348 km north-west of Mysore and not far from the terminus of the Birur Junction railway line, Jog Falls are the highest in India. The Shiravati River drops 253 metres in four separate falls known as the Rani, the Rocket, the Raja and the Roarer.

During the dry season the falls are less impressive and in the wet they may be totally obscured by mist and fog. The best time to see them is just after the monsoon. The most exciting view is from the top of the Raja, where you can see it fall over the Roarer! Even in the dry season the ever-changing fans of rainbows over the falls are superb.

To get to the falls from the hotels, take the road towards Sirsi, cross the bridge, turn left and take the second path on your left. Don't fall off the cliff!

The view of the falls from in front of the Inspection Bungalow is also excellent, and there are steps leading down the side of the cliff.

By the Hotel Woodlands there's a swimming pool with diving platforms although the water is usually green and home to dozens of frogs.

Places to Stay & Eat

The basic *Hotel Woodlands* (tel Jog 22) has cavernous rooms for Rs 35/50. The Karnataka Government *Tourist Home* charges Rs 20 for a single and Rs 35 for a huge double, 'and resident rat, bed bugs, mosquitoes and a few cockroaches thrown in for good measure', wrote a keen entomologist. You may have to hunt around for the manager, especially in the off season.

The *PWD Inspection Bungalow* commands the best position but is almost always full.

The food options are even more limited.

The *Hotel Woodlands* has a spartan restaurant where you can have omelettes or omelettes, or there are a couple of decrepit stalls selling chai and bananas.

Getting There & Away

Bus There is a daily bus from Karwar (seven hours, Rs 22) which leaves in the early afternoon and returns from Jog Falls on the following morning.

There are plenty of local buses to Sagar, 30 km south-east of Jog Falls, from where you can head south through the forests and coffee plantations of the Western Ghats to Tirthahalli, Sringeri, Chikmagalur and Hassan. It's a pleasant two-day journey to Hassan, stopping overnight at the temple in Sringeri.

Train Talguppa railway station is a few km east of Jog Falls, and it's the end of the line. There are a couple of passenger trains daily to Birur, one of which goes on to Arsikere and Bangalore. One carriage of this train gets unhooked at Arsikere and is attached to one of the Mysore trains, so it can be a useful way of getting from Jog Falls to Hassan or Mysore. It's an unreserved carriage but it is usually not too full.

UP THE COAST

Ankola

There's a little-used beach at this small village. Near the main road are the ruined walls of King Sarpamalika's Fort, and a temple (Shri Venkatraman) which dates back to the same period, about the 15th century. In an unmarked mud-brick garage near the temple are two giant wooden chariots, large enough to be pulled by elephants and carved all over with scenes from the *Ramayana*. Near Ankola is the village of Gokarna, an important pilgrimage place due to the Mahabaleshwara Temple.

Places to Stay & Eat

Jai Hind Lodge is a 'dingy, wretched pit' but at Rs 15 for a single it's cheap; the toilets smell. *Azab's Cold Drinks* is nice. There are no restaurants to speak of, just meals places.

Karwar

Karwar, only a short distance south of Goa and 56 km north of Gokarna, has excellent beaches. However, the whole nature of the town is likely to change in the near future as it has been chosen as the site of a major new naval base.

You can make trips up the Kali River from Karwar, or take a walk to see the spectacular bridge over the Kalinadi River north of town – it's about a 45-minute walk, or a Rs 4 ride by rickshaw.

Places to Stay & Eat

There's a range of budget places in Karwar. Close to the bus station is the *Hotel Ashok* (tel 6418), or the *Tourist Home* (tel 6380). Other hotels include the *Savan* (tel 6481) and the *Govardhan* (tel 6456). The *Anand Bhavan Lodge* (tel 6356) is good value at Rs 25 for doubles with bath.

One km back along the coast road to Panaji is the very pleasant *Inspection Bungalow*.

Probably the best place in town to eat is the vegetarian restaurant in the bus station itself. The *Hotel Ashok* has non-veg food.

Getting There & Away

The Karwar bus station, close to the centre of town, is total madness at times as hordes of people battle for limited seats.

There are Kadamba buses almost hourly for the 4½-hour journey to Panaji; Rs 10.

There are at least daily departures for Hubli, Bijapur, Belgaum, Mangalore, Bellary, Belur, Sringeri, Chikmagalur and Jog Falls (Kargal).

Central Karnataka

HAMPI (population 800)

The Vijayanagar city ruins at Hampi are one of the most interesting and least visited historical sites in south India. It is set in a strange and beautiful landscape – hill country strewn with enormous, rounded boulders – with the Tungabhadra River running along the northern edge of it. It has a magic quality and the ruins are superb, though scattered over a large area.

It is possible to see all the main sites in one day on foot if you start early. Signposting on the site is somewhat inadequate and a lot of the land between the ruins is planted out with sugar cane and other crops. All the same, even where the trail is indistinct, there are plenty of local villagers so you can't really get lost.

History

Hampi (Vijayanagar) was once the capital of one of the largest Hindu empires in Indian history. Founded by the Telugu princes Harihara and Bukka in 1336, it reached the height of its power under Krishnadevaraya (1509-29), when it controlled the whole of the peninsula south of the Krishna and Tungabhadra rivers, except for a string of commercial principalities along the Malabar coast.

Comparable to Delhi in the 14th century, the city, which covered an area of 33 square km, was surrounded by seven concentric lines of fortification and was reputed to have had a population of about half a million. It maintained a mercenary army of over one million according to the Persian ambassador, Abdul Razak, which included Muslim mounted archers to defend itself from the Muslim states to the north.

Hampi's wealth was based on control of the spice trade to the south and the cotton industry of the south-east. Its busy bazaars, described by European travellers

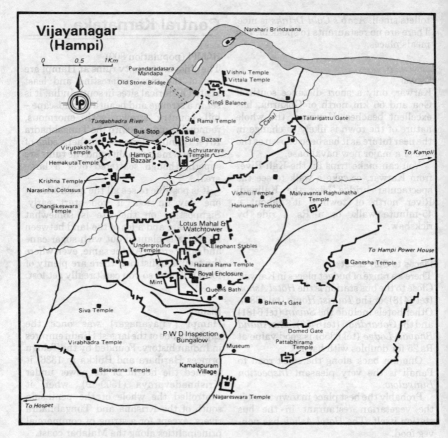

Vijayanagar (Hampi)

0   0.5   1Km

Narahari Brindavana

Purandaradasara Mandapa

Old Stone Bridge

Vishnu Temple
Vittala Temple

King's Balance

Tungabhadra River

Rama Temple

Bus Stop

Talarigattu Gate

Sule Bazaar

Virupaksha Temple

Hampi Bazaar

Achyutaraya Temple

To Kampli

Hemakuta Temple

Krishna Temple
Narasinha Colossus

Vishnu Temple

Malyavanta Raghunatha Temple

Chandikeswara Temple

Hanuman Temple

Lotus Mahal & Watchtower

To Hampi Power House

Underground Temple

Elephant Stables

Ganesha Temple

Hazara Rama Temple

Royal Enclosure

Siva Temple

Mint

Queens Bath

Bhima's Gate

P W D Inspection Bungalow

Domed Gate

Virabhadra Temple

Museum

Pattabhirama Temple

Basavanna Temple

Kamalapuram Village

To Hospet

Nagareswara Temple

such as Nunez and Paes, were centres of international commerce. The religion was a hybrid of current Hinduism with the gods Vishnu and Shiva being lavishly worshipped in the orthodox manner though, as in the Hoysala Kingdom, Jainism was also prominent. Brahmins were privileged, sati (the burning of widows on the funeral pyres of their husbands) was widely practised and temple prostitution was common. Brahmin inscriptions discovered on the site date the first Hampi settlement back to the 1st century AD and suggest that there was a Buddhist centre nearby.

The empire came to a sudden end in 1565 after the disastrous battle of Talikota when the city was ransacked by the confederacy of Deccan sultans (Bidar, Bijapur, Golconda, Ahmednagar and Berar), thus opening up southern India for conquest by the Muslims.

Information

There are good Archaeological Survey of India maps of the area available in Hampi Bazaar. A publication entitled *Hampi* by D Devakunjari and published by the Archaeological Survey is on sale at the museum in Kamalapuram for Rs 4. It gives a history of the Vijayanagar Empire and a description and layout of the ruins. For a good overview of the site there is a large scale model in the courtyard of the museum at Kamalapuram. There's also a completely useless tourist office in Hampi Bazaar.

Things to See

The best plan for a visit to the ruins is to start and finish in Hampi Bazaar. From here it's possible to walk to all the main sites and down to the museum at Kamalapuram, from where there are buses back to Hospet, or you can walk back to Hampi along the road in 40 minutes. It's at least one full day's outing, and it's a good idea to bring some food and water along, although there are restaurants in both Hampi and Kamalapuram. Of course if you can afford to stick around for a few days (highly recommended) you can take your time.

The old Hampi Bazaar is now a bustling village, and the locals have inhabited the old bazaar buildings which line the main street. The town is becoming a minor travellers' centre and is a very atmospheric place to stay and get a feel for the ruins, but those who want anything in the way of conveniences will find Hospet the better bet.

The village is dominated by the Virupaksha Temple with its 52-metre-high gopuram. The temple dates back to the middle of the 15th century and is popular with Indian tourists. A sign in the temple courtyard reads: 'Please keep off the Plantains from the sight of the Monkies', which translates to something like, 'Watch out or the monkeys will pinch your bananas'.

From the far end of the bazaar a track leads left to the highlight of the ruins, the Vittala Temple. This temple is a World Heritage Monument (one of only three in south India, the others being at Thanjavur and Mahabalipuram in Tamil Nadu) and is in a very good state of preservation. Although it was never finished or consecrated, the incredible sculptural

work is of the highest standard and is the pinnacle of Vijayanagar art. The outer pillars are known as the musical pillars as they reverberate when tapped, although this practice is being actively discouraged as the pillars are somewhat the worse for wear. The stone cart, which replaces the usual wooden temple cars, has some fine detail – even the wheels used to turn!

Not far away from the temple is the deserted Sule Bazaar, which gives you some idea of what Hampi Bazaar might look like if it wasn't taken over by villagers. At the southern end of this area is the Achyutaraya Temple which also has some fine carvings.

South of Sule Bazaar, in the middle of the site, are two of Hampi's other major attractions: the Lotus Mahal and the Elephant Stables. The former is a delicately designed pavilion in a walled compound known as the Zanana enclosure. The building gets its name from the lotus bud carved in the centre of the domed and

Stone cart, Vittala Temple

vaulted ceiling. The Elephant Stables consist of a grand building with eleven domed chambers for housing the state elephants.

Other buildings worth visiting are the Royal Enclosure with its various temples, and the Queen's Bath, both at the southern end of the ruins.

Excavation at Hampi was started in 1976 by the Archaeological Survey of India in collaboration with the Karnataka state government, and is still continuing.

The museum at Kamalapuram has some

very fine sculptures and coins and is worth a visit. It is open from 10 am to 5 pm.

Places to Stay

If you'd prefer to stay near the ruins rather than in Hospet, then there are some rooms available to rent from the villagers. Most have only grass mats and primitive facilities, and the average charge is Rs 5 per person. The owner of the *Sri Sangameshwara Hotel*, next to the tourist office in Hampi Bazaar, has one good, clean room with electricity and

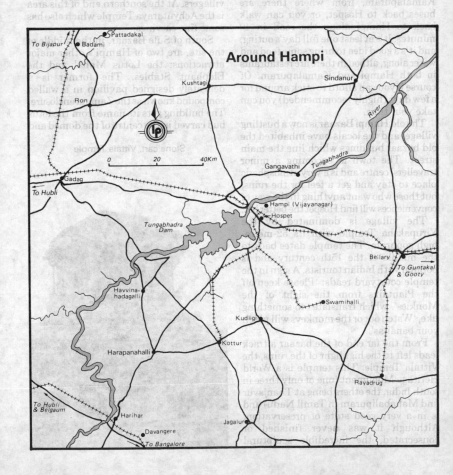

toilet. There are plenty of others – just ask around.

There's also a couple of lodges in Hampi. The *Heeralal Guest House* is one but I'd have reservations about even keeping a mangy dog there, although you can sleep on the roof.

In the Virupaksha Temple there are some extremely basic rooms for Rs 4 to Rs 6 per person.

At the southern end of the ruins is the *PWD Inspection Bungalow*. It is actually an old temple which was converted to a residence by an early British governor. It's rarely occupied and there are only a couple of rooms, which cost Rs 20. Meals are available if ordered in advance from the chowkidah. There are also a couple of basic eateries close by in Kamalapuram village.

Places to Eat

You can get a typical 'meal' at any one of a number of vegetarian places along Hampi Bazaar. One block behind the bazaar is the outdoor *Ramsingh Trishul Tea Shop* which has good travellers' food such as muesli, porridge, flavoured lassis and meals. It's owned by the Sri Aurobindo Ashram in Pondicherry, and the guy running it can also find rooms for you.

Set amongst the ruins is the KSTDC *Hotel Mayura Lotus Mahal Restaurant* between the Hazarama Temple and the palace site. The menu is very limited although they do have ice-cold beers.

Getting Around

Hampi is 13 km from Hospet, the town which most people use as a base. There are two main points of entry to the ruins, Hampi Bazaar and Kamalapuram, and buses run frequently to these two places from Hospet.

As an alternative to the buses you could hire a bicycle in Hospet, although at the site itself it could become something of a liability as the track to the Vittala Temple and many others are only negotiable on foot.

If you're walking around the site, expect to cover at least seven km just to see the main sites. It is possible to see most of the ruins in a day, though two or more days would allow a more leisurely pace.

HOSPET (population 114,000)

Most people who come to see the Vijayanagar ruins at Hampi use Hospet as a base. It's a fairly typical Karnataka country town with dusty roads, plenty of bullock carts, bicycles, dilapidated buses, and an unobtrusive industrial area near Tungabhadra Dam.

For much of the year Hospet is not a particularly interesting place in itself, but because it has a large Muslim population it comes alive during the festival of Moharam. If you're here at this time don't miss the firewalkers, who walk barefoot across the red-hot embers of a fire that's been going all day and night. Virtually the whole town turns out to watch or take part and the excitement gets to fever pitch around midnight. The preliminaries, which go on all day, appear to be a bewildering hybrid of Muslim and Hindu ritual, quite unlike any other Muslim festival I've ever seen.

Information

The tourist office has absolutely no information and there's no reason to visit it unless you want to take the KSTDC tour which leaves from here daily at 9 am. It costs Rs 25 and, in keeping with the Indian preoccupation with dams, includes a visit to the Tungabhadra Dam and spends little time at the ruins. Still, if you're in a hurry. . .

Places to Stay

Hospet is an anomaly amongst Indian towns in that there is an oversupply of cheap, clean and respectable hotels. One of the best, and an old favourite among travellers, is the friendly *Malligi Tourist Home* (tel 8101), by the canal. Rooms with bath cost Rs 22/35. There's a very helpful self-styled tourist office here and the guy

even rents out Asterix and Tintin books for Rs 2 per day! You can also book the KSTDC tour from here.

On Station Rd opposite the bus station, the new *Hotel Vishwa* has large, clean rooms which are very good value at Rs 24/45. Also on Station Rd, but further from the centre of town, is the *Hotel Priyardarshini* (tel 8838). It too has large rooms for Rs 25/45, and Rs 100 for an air-con double. The *Hotel Sandarshan* (tel 8128) is virtually next door and houses the telegraph office. Rooms cost Rs 22/42 with bath.

For something a bit cheaper, there's the *Hotel Mayura* (tel 8418) with rooms at Rs 13/23, but it's poor value compared with what else is on offer.

There are railway *retiring rooms* at the station but this is none too convenient as it is more than one km from the centre of town. A double room is Rs 20, single Rs 15.

Places to Eat
The *Shanthi Restaurant* in the Vishwa Hotel does excellent vegetarian meals at lunchtime for Rs 5.50, and snacks the rest of the day. A similar place is the *Amruth Garden* at the Malligi Tourist Home.

For something a bit better, try the outdoor *Eagle Garden Restaurant* opposite the Malligi. The food is good and the service prompt, although it's a bit more expensive, count on about Rs 50 for two. Cold beers are Rs 18. They also have an amazing menu with no fewer than 53 ways to have your chicken served – everything from Chicken Skylob and Chicken Hens to Chicken Dry and Chicken Bullet! There's even a Chinese soup called Chicken Sings Poor (Singapore, I think!) and good biryanis, even chicken ones. Or how about Egg Cycloned Parrots! This place is about the only non-veg restaurant in Hospet.

As the Eagle Garden doesn't open for breakfast until 9 am, if you want an omelette, try the humble *Janatha Hotel* between the Mayura Hotel and the canal. The building it's in looks like it's ready to collapse at any moment.

Getting There & Away
Bus Ten express buses run daily between 7 am to 11.45 pm on the 358-km trip from Hospet to Bangalore. There's also a luxury overnight KSTDC bus from the tourist office at 10 pm which costs Rs 65; regular buses take hours longer.

Heading for Goa there are three buses daily for the 3½-hour trip to Hubli. Hyderabad is 445 km away and there's one express bus daily. The daily bus from Hospet to Badami, 170 km away, takes six hours to do the trip. There's also one direct bus to Bijapur, the 190-km trip takes eight hours.

Buses depart almost hourly to Bellary. Other services include Davanegere, Shimoga, Mangalore, Hassan and Karwar.

Train The Hospet railway station has a healthy quota allotment for the express trains between Hubli and Bangalore and they are rarely booked up more than one day in advance. If you are heading to Hospet from Goa either by train or bus it is necessary to change at Hubli. Hospet to Hubli takes about four hours; see the Hubli section for onward travel.

If you're heading to or from Badami there is a daily passenger train in each direction; the 152-km trip takes nearly six hours and costs Rs 14.

Getting Around

The Hospet railway station is a 20-minute walk or Rs 2 by cycle rickshaw from the centre of town.

Buses run frequently to Hampi from stand No 10 at the bus station and the trip takes about half an hour and costs Rs 2. The first bus is at 6.30 am, and they depart almost hourly from then on. The last one back from Hampi in the evening departs at 8 pm. The terminus is at Hampi Bazaar, but you can also get off at Kamalapuram and walk into the ruins from there, or rent a bicycle in Hospet. A taxi costs around Rs 100 for a round trip to Hampi but a share-taxi is only about Rs 4 per person.

Buses depart frequently from Hospet to Tungabhadra Dam. The 15-minute trip costs Rs 0.80. If you find yourself waiting a long time for a bus back to Hospet from the dam, walk down to the junction at the bottom of the road, as there are more frequent buses to Hospet from there.

AROUND HOSPET

Tungabhadra Dam

If you have half a day to kill in Hospet, it might be worth a trip out here, although there's little of interest, despite what the tourist literature might tell you.

Places to Stay Naturally, the KSTDC has built a hotel below the dam where tourists are encouraged to stay but it's very inconvenient for anything other than the dam. It's called the *Hotel Mayura Vijayanagar* (tel 8270) and the rooms, all with bathroom, cost Rs 50/70.

The *Vaikunt Guest House* (tel 8254)

overlooks the dam on the hilltop. For reservations contact the Executive Officer (tel 8241), HLC Division, Tungabhadra Dam.

HUBLI

Hubli is important to the traveller principally as a major railway junction on the routes from Bombay to Bangalore, Goa and north Karnataka. Other than this it's an industrial city and there's precious little to see. It's only included because you may have to spend the night here on your way to somewhere else.

All the main services (hotels, restaurants, etc) are conveniently close to the railway station. The bus station is at the far end of Lamington Rd, 15 minutes walk from the railway station.

Places to Stay

The highly recommended *Hotel Ajanta* (tel 62216) is a short distance off the main street and visible from the railway station. It's a huge place and you'll always be able to find accommodation here. Rooms with fan and bath cost Rs 32 to Rs 45. On the ground floor there is a 'meals' cafe.

The *Modern Lodge* (tel 62654) is on the main street before you get to the Hotel Ajanta. This is a typical cheap hotel with basic facilities. Rooms cost Rs 25 to Rs 35 and although they have a fan and bath you must provide your own sheets. There is a 'meals' cafe on the ground floor.

The *Ashok Hotel* (tel 62271) is on Lamington Rd, which is parallel to the railway line, 500 metres from the station. Rooms are good value at Rs 33/68.

For something better, try the *Hotel Kailash* (tel 66601), also on Lamington Rd. It's five minutes walk from the bus station and has clean doubles with hot water for Rs 50/80.

If you're just waiting for the evening train to Goa, a bed in the railway *retiring rooms* dorm is a good investment at Rs 12 as it gives you somewhere to rest and have a shower. Double rooms are Rs 20 per person, or Rs 35 for two.

Places to Eat

Kamat's Wasant Bhavan Hotel, opposite the railway station, offers fairly good plate meals at lunchtime for Rs 5. There's also an air-con dining hall upstairs, and during the rest of the day coffee and tiffin are available.

For non-veg food, the *New Delhi Dharbar Restaurant*, 100 metres along from the Modern Lodge, is not bad but the menu is somewhat limited. Better is the *Hotel Vaishali* a couple of doors down from the Modern Lodge. They have excellent biryanis for Rs 11 to Rs 14.

Getting There & Away

Bus Hubli has a large and busy bus station. Buses to Panaji (Goa) take 11 hours and leave three times a day. These Goa government Kadamba buses are semi-lux and should be booked in advance from 6.30 am to 12 noon and 2 to 3.30 pm.

Other bus destinations from Hubli include Bangalore (four daily), Mysore (two daily), Mangalore (daily), Bijapur (four daily), Bombay (two daily) and Pune (two daily).

Opposite the bus station are plenty of private companies operating super-deluxe, whizz-bang video coaches. These buses run to Bombay and Bangalore, but don't expect any sleep with the confounded video blaring away all day and night.

Train Hubli is a major rail junction on the Bombay to Bangalore route and for trains to Bijapur and Hospet. If you're heading for Goa (either Vasco da Gama or Margao) the No 237 Gadag to Miraj Link Express has a 2nd-class three-tier sleeping coach and another combined 1st and 2nd-class two-tier sleeping coach attached to the train, and these go all the way to Vasco da Gama, thus avoiding the need to change at Londa. At Londa these coaches are detached from the 237 and added to the 206 Miraj to Vasco da Gama Gomantak Express at about 3.30 am.

There's a quota for the three-tier sleeper, the two-tier sleeper and for 1st class at Hubli station. The full quota is rarely taken up even on the day of departure, but you may have to opt for 1st class, and booking closes at 5 pm. After that time you have to apply for reservations at the ticket collector's office, but don't count on getting one at that time. The fare for the 302-km trip is Rs 34 in 2nd class, Rs 137 in 1st.

The railway reservation office is open from 8.30 am to 12 noon and 2.30 to 5 pm.

Northern Karnataka

BELGAUM (population 300,000)
In the north-west corner of the state and on the Bombay/Pune/Goa bus and rail route, Belgaum was a regional capital in the 12th and 13th centuries. Today there's an old town area, a more modern cantonment, and 'Sunset Point' on the old racetrack road which offers fine views.

Fort

The old oval-shaped stone fort is near the bus terminus, but it's of no real interest unless you like malarial moats, although Gandhi was locked up here once. Outside the fort gate to the left is the local cattle market, which is colourful and aromatic.

Mosques, Temples & Other Buildings

The Masjid-Sata Mosque dates from 1519. There are also two interesting Jain temples, one with an extremely intricate roof, while the other has some fine carvings of musicians. Belgaum's watch-tower gives a nice panorama of the countryside.

Gokak Falls

A little north of Belgaum, eight km off the railway line from Gokak Road, are Gokak Falls where the Ghataprabha River takes a 52-metre drop.

Places to Stay & Eat

The *Hotel Sheetal* (tel 25483) in Khade

Andhra Pradesh Top: 'Vote Bicycle' - election campaign in Hyderabad (TW)
Left: Charminar triumphal arch, Hyderabad (TW)
Right: Golconda Fort, near Hyderabad (TW)

Kerala Top: Backwaters between Alleppey and Quilon (HF)
Bottom: Chinese fishing nets, Cochin (HF)

Bazaar is clean, bright, efficient and very comfortable. Ordinary rooms are Rs 30/45, deluxe ones Rs 35/60. The *Hotel Tapuam* – turn right when you are outside of the bus station and walk for 20 minutes – has singles with shower for Rs 20 and is reportedly good value.

The railway *retiring rooms* cost Rs 20/30.

The bus station canteen has excellent and inexpensive snack foods. Belgaum also has lots of sweet shops.

CHALUKYAN CAVES & TEMPLES

Set in beautiful countryside amongst red sandstone hills, rock-hewn 'tanks' (artificial lakes) and peaceful farmlands, the three small rural villages of Badami, Aihole and Pattadakal were once the capital cities of the Chalukyan Empire which ruled much of the central Deccan between the 4th and 8th centuries AD. Here you can see some of the earliest and finest examples of Dravidian temples and rock-cut caves. The forms and sculptural work at these sites provided inspiration for the later Hindu empires which rose and fell in the southern part of the peninsula before the arrival of the Muslims.

Though principally promoters of the Vedic culture, the Chalukyans were tolerant of all sects, and elements of Shaivism, Vaishnavism, Jainism and even Buddhism can be found in many of their temples, especially in the rock-cut caves at Badami.

Badami (population 16,000)

Badami, the later capital from about 540 until 757 AD when the Chalukyans were overthrown by the Rashtrakutas, is magnificently nestled in a canyon and is famous for its rock-cut temples. Cut into the cliff-face of the red sandstone hill and overlooking the picturesque tank of Agastyatirtha (itself constructed in the 5th century), these caves display the full range of religious sects which have grown up on Indian soil.

There are five caves altogether, four of

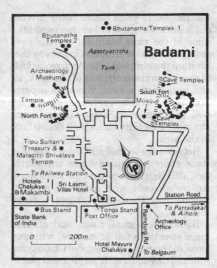

them artificial and one natural, all connected by flights of steps. Of the rock-cut temples, two are dedicated to Vishnu, one to Shiva and the fourth is a Jain temple. The natural cave is a Buddhist temple. There are excellent views over the town and surrounding plains from the caves.

The caves are only one of the many things to be seen at Badami. All over the sides and tops of the hills, which enclose the tank on three sides, are temples, fortifications, carvings and inscriptions dating not just from the Chalukyan period but from other times when the site was occupied as a fortress. After it fell to the Rashtrakutas, Badami was occupied successively by the Chalukyans of Kalyan (a separate branch of the Western Chalukyans), the Kalachuryas, the Yadavas of Devagiri, the Vijayanagar Empire, the Adil Shahi kings of Bijapur and the Marathas.

All these various rulers have left their mark at Badami, and there's even a Pallava inscription dating back to 642 AD when their king, Narasimhavarman, briefly overwhelmed the Chalukyans and occupied

Badami for 13 years before being driven out again. Of these other monuments, some of the most beautiful are the two groups of lakeside temples (known as the Bhutanatha temples). The Archaeological Museum, on the north side of the tank, is also well worth a visit. It houses superb examples of sculpture collected locally, as well as the remarkable Lajja-Gauri images of a fertility cult which flourished in the area.

Between the second and third cave is a stone staircase leading up to the south fort, although it seems that the steps were cut by someone with a grudge against anyone less than about three metres tall.

Badami is a small town, and off the main street it's full of narrow, winding lanes, old houses, the occasional Chalukyan ruin and tiny squares. It's a pleasant place and people are friendly, but the street kids can be incredibly persistent in hassling you for pens and money. They'll follow you down the streets in packs chanting 'Ta ta, Ta ta!', or 'One pen, one pen!'. Of course you get this elsewhere in India, in most places in fact, but it's the persistence with which they do it here that's surprising. Somehow they've even got their English so confused that they say something like 'Campindipenlo', or just 'Penlo' for short.

Information & Orientation

Badami, Pattadakal and Aihole are fairly close to each other and can be visited from a single base, either Badami or Aihole, though Badami is the more popular and has the better facilities. There are no accommodation facilities at Pattadakal.

Local buses connect Badami, Pattadakal and Aihole, and you can easily see the three sites in a day using these buses.

At the first cave temple in Badami you can occasionally buy a copy of *The Cave Temples of Badami* by A M Annigeri for Rs 4. It's worth buying if you'd like more detail about the cave temples or the other monuments at Badami, though it's

Cave sculpture, Badami

written in typically verbose Indian English and peppered with nonsense like, 'This shows dwarfs dancing in different poses... Some of them have interesting hair-styles... They are also engaged in different activities... Visitors forget themselves at the sight of these delightful dwarfs' and 'These dwarfs are very amusing and create laughter... These arrest the attention of the visitors'.

Places to Stay

Badami There are a few lodges along the main street of Badami. The *Hotel Chalukya* has small basic rooms for Rs 20/30 with bath. Next door the *Hotel Mukambi* is better but overpriced at Rs 50 for a double.

The *Shri Laxmi Vilas Hotel* has double rooms with bath and balcony for Rs 30, although some of them are filthy.

The KSTDC *Hotel Mayura Chalukya* (tel 41), about a half km from the centre of town, is undoubtedly the best place to stay. Rooms with bathroom cost Rs 52/68 and have mosquito nets and hot water. It's an excellent place to stay, but don't leave your door open for too long as the resident monkeys are fond of pinching things.

Places to Eat

The best place to eat in Badami is the *Hotel Sanman*, next to the Sri Mahakuteshwar Lodge. It has vegetarian and non-vegetarian meals, cold beers, other alcoholic drinks and loud music from current Indian films which the proprietor is loathe to turn down.

There are plenty of small cafes, especially around the tonga stand on the main road, but most of them serve only tiffin. The *Shri Laxmi Vilas Hotel* has a good vegetarian restaurant serving meals for Rs 5, as well as idlis and dosas. The *Hotel Brindavan* opposite the tonga stand serves excellent dosas.

The food at the *Hotel Mayura Chalukya* is quite good but, as is so often the case in these government-run places, you have to wait an age for even the simplest order to arrive.

Getting There & Away

Bus To Bijapur there is one bus daily and the four-hour journey costs Rs 17. There are daily buses to Bagalkot, Hospet, Hubli, Bangalore, Kolhapur and Gadag.

Train All the trains from Badami station are passenger trains; there are no express trains. If you're heading for Bijapur you can take the train either to Bijapur or Sholapur. Similarly, if heading for Gadag you can take the train either for Gadag, Hubli or Hospet. The journey from Badami to Bijapur takes four hours and costs Rs 11.

For Hospet and the Vijayanagar ruins at Hampi, there is one passenger train daily via Gadag. The trip takes six hours and costs Rs 14.

Getting Around

Badami railway station is five km from the village itself and a tonga from outside the station costs Rs 2 to Rs 3. The locals pay less than a rupee but you need brown skin, black hair, brown eyes and fluency in Kannada to get it for that! Local buses and minibuses also run approximately hourly between the station and village.

The best way to explore the area is by local buses as they are fairly frequent and run pretty much to schedule. Take the 8.15 am bus from Badami to Aihole. It takes a tedious two hours and seems to go halfway around outback Karnataka. From Aihole there is a bus at 1 pm back to Pattadakal, from where there are frequent buses and minibuses back to Badami. As there's nowhere much to eat in Aihole, it's a good idea to bring some food along.

Aihole (population 3000)

At Aihole, the regional capital between the 4th and 6th centuries, you can see Hindu temple architecture in its embryonic stage from the earliest Ladkhan Temple to the later and more complex structures like the Kunligudi and Durgigudi temples. The Durgigudi is particularly interesting, probably unique in India, being circular in shape and surmounted by a primitive gopuram, those structures which typify the temples throughout Tamil Nadu.

There are over 70 structures in and around this village which are monuments to the vigorous experimentation in temple architecture undertaken by the Chalukyans. Most are in a good state of preservation.

Places to stay

Accommodation is available at the KSTDC *Tourist Bungalow* (tel Aminagad 41), and rooms with bathroom cost Rs 20 to Rs 35. It's not as good as the Hotel Mayura Chalukya at Badami, the food is OK although you can grow old waiting for a meal to arrive.

Pattadakal

Pattadakal reached the height of its glory during the 7th and 8th centuries, when most of the temples here were built. It was not only the second capital of the Badami Chalukyans, but the place where all coronations took place. The most important monument here, the Lokeshwari or Virupaksha Temple, is a huge structure with sculptures that narrate episodes from the Hindu epics, the *Ramayana* and *Mahabharata*, as well as throw light on the social life of the early Chalukyans. The other main temple, Mallikarjuna, has sculptures which tell a different story – this time from the *Bhagavadgita*, the story of Lord Krishna. The old Jain temple with its two stone elephants, about a km from the centre, is also worth visiting.

BIJAPUR (population 150,000)

Bijapur is the Agra of the south, full of ruined and still-intact gems of 15th to 17th-century Muslim architecture – mosques, mausoleums, palaces and fortifications. Like Agra, it has its world-famous mausoleum, the Golgumbaz. This enormous structure with its vast hemispherical dome, said to be the world's second largest, dominates the landscape for miles around.

The austere grace of the monuments in this city is in complete contrast to the sculptural extravaganza of the Chalukyan and Hoysala temples further south. The Ibrahim Roza mausoleum, in particular, is one of the most beautiful and finely proportioned Islamic monuments anywhere.

Bijapur was the capital of the Adil Shahi kings (1489-1686), one of the five splinter states formed when the Bahmani Muslim kingdom broke up in 1482. The others, formed at roughly the same time, were Bidar, Golconda, Ahmednagar and Gulbarga. Like Bijapur, all these places have their own collection of monuments dating from this period, though the ones at Bijapur are definitely more numerous and generally in a better state of preservation.

Bijapur is well worth a visit. It's a pleasant garden town, still strongly

Muslim in character and small enough not to be overwhelming, although in some ways it is more like the cities of the north than those of the south. You will need at least a day to see the monuments in a fairly leisurely manner since they are spread out across the city.

Orientation

The two main tourist attractions, the Golgumbaz and the Ibrahim Roza, are at opposite ends of the town. Almost all the major hotels and restaurants are in the main street, M G Rd, along with statues of Gandhi, Ambedkar and a local hero. The bus stand is a five-minute walk from M G Rd, near the citadel ruins, while the railway station is two km east of the centre.

Information

The tourist office is in the Hotel Mayura Adil Shaha. They have sketch maps of the city and verbose leaflets which don't tell you a great deal and take up lots of paper.

It seems that the local authority is running a road safety campaign, as on each electricity pole as you go through the town are signboards with messages such as 'Better to Safe then Sorry' (sic), and, 'Jay walking – a short cut to the Mortuary'. The last sign reads 'Avoid Reading boards while driving'!

There's a very colourful market area just off M G Rd near the centre of town.

Golgumbaz

The largest and most famous monument, though not the most beautiful, is the Golgumbaz. Built in 1659, it is a simple building with four walls that enclose a majestic hall 1704 square metres in area, and are buttressed by octagonal seven-storied towers at each of the corners. This basic structure is capped by an enormous dome said to be the world's second largest (St Peter's in the Vatican City, Rome, has the largest). St Peter's dome diameter is

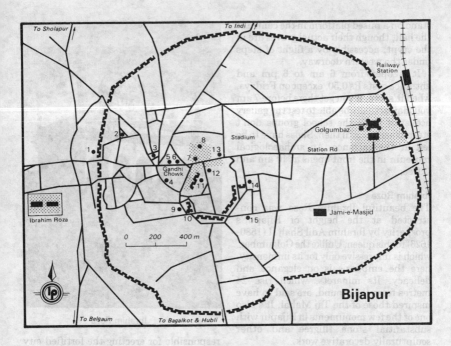

Bijapur

1	Malik-i-Maidan Cannon
2	Upil Buruj
3	Market
4	State Bank of India
5	Hotel Tourist
6	Post Office
7	Midland & Mysore Lodges
8	Bara Kaman (Ali II Roza)
9	Bus Station
10	Hotel Lalita Mahal
11	Citadel (Gagan Mahal, Sat Manzil Anand Mahal & Mecca Masjid)
12	Tourist Office
13	Hotel Mayura Adil Shaha Annexe
14	Asar Mahal
15	Mehtar Mahal

42 metres, St Paul's in London is 33 metres, the Golgumbaz is 38 metres.

Around the base of the dome at the top of the hall is a three-metre-wide gallery known as the 'whispering gallery', since the acoustics here are such that any sound made is repeated 10 times over (some guidebooks claim it's repeated 12 times over). Fortunately, you won't have the chance to get embroiled in that controversy as the 'whispering gallery' is permanently full of kids running amok and screaming at the top of their voices. 'Bedlam gallery' would be a more appropriate name. Access to the gallery is via a narrow staircase up one of the towers.

The views over Bijapur from the base of the dome are superb. You can see virtually every other monument and almost the whole of the city walls from here. The views are best in the early morning. The monument is set in well manicured gardens which are stunningly green during and just after the monsoon season.

The Golgumbaz is the mausoleum of Mohammed Adil Shah (1626-56), his two wives, his mistress (Rambha), one of his daughters and a grandson. Their caskets stand on a raised platform in the centre of the hall, though their actual graves are in the crypt, accessible by a flight of steps under the western doorway.

It is open from 6 am to 6 pm and entrance costs Rs 0.50, except on Fridays, when it's free. If you get there before 7 am you may actually be able to test the gallery acoustics too – the school groups don't start to arrive until then. Shoes have to be left at the entrance. An archaeological museum in the front opens at 10 am and is free.

Ibrahim Roza

The beautiful Ibrahim Roza was constructed at the height of Bijapur's prosperity by Ibrahim Adil Shah II (1580-1626) for his queen. Unlike the Golgumbaz, which is impressive only for its immensity, here the emphasis is on elegance and delicacy. Its minarets, which rise 24 metres from the ground, are said to have inspired those of the Taj Mahal. It's also one of the few monuments in Bijapur with substantial stone filigree and other sculpturally decorative work.

Buried here are Ibrahim Adil Shah, his queen Taj Sultana, his daughter, two sons, and his mother Haji Badi Sahiba. There is no entrance charge, but shoes should be left on the steps up to the platform on which the mausoleum stands.

Jami-e-Masjid

This is another finely proportioned building with graceful arches, a fine dome and a large inner courtyard containing fountains and a reservoir. It's quite a large monument covering an area of 10,800 square metres and has room for 2250 worshippers. Spaces for them are marked out in black on the polished floor of the mosque.

There's very little ornamentation here, the whole concept being one of simplicity. The flat roof is accessible by several flights of stairs. This mosque was constructed by Ali Adil Shah I (1557-80), who was also

Ibrahim Roza

responsible for erecting the fortified city walls and Gagan Mahal, and for installing a public water system.

Asar Mahal

To the east of the citadel, the Asar Mahal was built by Mohammed Adil Shah in about 1646 to serve as a Hall of Justice. The rooms on the upper storey are profusely decorated with fresco paintings, many of them using foliage and flower motifs, some portraying male and female figures in various poses. The latter have all been defaced. The building was also used to house two hairs from the Prophet's beard. The front of the building is graced with a square tank still fed by conduits from Begum Tank.

Women are not allowed inside the main structure.

The Citadel

Surrounded by its own fortified walls and wide moat in the city centre, the citadel once contained the palaces, pleasure gardens and Durbar Hall of the Adil Shahi kings. Unfortunately, most of them are now in ruins although some superb fragments remain.

Of the important fragments, the Gagan Mahal probably gives the best impression of the scale on which things were built here. This monument was built by Ali Adil Shah I around 1561 to serve the dual purpose of a royal residence and a Durbar Hall. Essentially it's an enormous hall completely open to the north, so that an audience outside the hall had a full and unobstructed view of the proceedings on the raised platform inside. The hall was flanked by small chambers used to house the families of the royal household.

Nearby, the Sat Manzil, Mohammed Adil Shah's seven-story palace, is now substantially in ruins and the remaining parts of it are used for public offices, but just across the road stands one of the most delicate pieces of architecture in Bijapur. This is the Jala Manzil or Jala Mandir, a water pavilion no doubt intended as a cool and pleasant place to relax in the days when it was surrounded by secluded courts and gardens within the palace precincts. Opposite the citadel on the other side of Station Rd are the graceful arches of Bara Kaman, the ruined mausoleum of Ali Roza.

Malik-e-Maidan

This huge cannon must be one of the largest medieval guns ever made. It measures over four metres long and almost 1½ metres in diameter, and is estimated to weigh 55 tons! It was cast in 1549 by Mohammed-bin-Hasan Rumi, a Turkish officer in the service of the King of Ahmednagar, from an alloy of copper, iron and tin. It was brought to Bijapur as a trophy of war and set up here with the help of 10 elephants, 400 oxen and hundreds of men. Its outer surface is polished dark green and adorned with inscriptions in Persian and Arabic, one of them attributed to the Moghul emperor Aurangzeb says

that he subdued this gun. The name of the cannon, Malik-e-Maidan, means 'Monarch of the Plains'.

Upli Buruj

This watchtower, 24 metres high and on high ground near the western walls of the city, was built by Hyder Khan, a general in the service of Ali Adil Shah I and Ibrahim II, in about 1584. The tower can be climbed by a flight of steps which winds around the outside of the building. The top commands a good view of the city and is well furnished with guns, powder chambers and water cisterns. The guns are much longer than the Malik-e-Maidan (nine metres and 8½ metres respectively), but of much narrower bore, only 29 cm.

Other Monuments

There are a number of other monuments worth visiting in Bijapur, the most important being the Anand Mahal and the Mecca Masjid, both in the citadel, and the Mehtar Mahal. The much-photographed Mehtar Mahal is typical of the architecture of Bijapur and has been richly decorated with sculptural work. It serves as an ornamental gateway leading to a small mosque.

Places to Stay

The KSTDC *Hotel Mayura Adil Shaha* (tel 934), just off Station Rd near the entrance to the citadel, is quiet. The rooms cost Rs 42/56 and have bathrooms, mosquito nets (there are hordes of mozzies) and are set around a pleasant courtyard.

If your budget doesn't stretch that far, then there are some dives on Station Rd. The *Mysore Lodge* is barely habitable, but cheap at Rs 18/30. Next door is the *Midland Lodge* (tel 299) which is not much of an improvement.

A better cheapie is the big *Hotel Lalita Mahal* (tel 21641) near the bus station. The front rooms cop the bus station noise but the others are quite acceptable at Rs 25/42.

The *retiring rooms* at the railway station cost Rs 10 per person in the dorm, or Rs 15/25 for a room.

The *Hotel Mayura Adil Shaha Annexe* is expensive for what it offers, which is really nothing more than the other Adil Shaha. Rooms here cost Rs 64/94.

Places to Eat

For just a snack, the *Prabhu Cafeteria* on the ground floor next to the Hotel Tourist is a popular place serving excellent dosas, bhelpuri, lassis and other snacks. On the 1st floor of the same building, the *Swapna Lodge Restaurant* has good veg and non-veg food as well as cold beers (Rs 18). The lodge itself is not a good place to stay.

The *Hotel Mayura Adil Shaha* has a restaurant in the middle of the courtyard, and it's a reasonable place to eat, although it's not somewhere you'd go to pick up a quick bite. Thalis cost Rs 9 and cold Kingfisher beer is Rs 20.

Getting There & Away

Bus Buses run from Bijapur to Badami (two daily, one goes via Kerur), Bangalore (630 km, six daily in the evening only), Belgaum (12 buses daily), Bidar, Hubli (11 daily), Hyderabad (two daily), Hospet (daily), Pune (daily), Kolhapur (five daily) and Sholapur (12 daily, the trip takes three hours).

Train Bijapur station has a healthy quota of sleeping berths allotted to it on all the main trains which pass through Sholapur and Gadag. These are rarely taken up more than one day in advance. The trip from Bijapur to Gadag is a slow but entertaining ride as it's the permanent pitch of at least three lots of buskers. Bijapur to Badami takes 3½ hours and costs Rs 11.

Bijapur to Hubli takes about seven hours for the 258-km trip and costs Rs 33 in 2nd class, and Rs 118 in 1st on the daily express train. In addition there are two slower (and cheaper) passenger trains each day.

There's a daily passenger train to Hospet which takes nine hours and costs Rs 22 for the 285-km journey.

Getting Around

Bus There's a surprisingly uncrowded local bus system which has only one route: from the railway station, along Station Rd to the gate at the western end of town. Buses run approximately every 15 minutes and the standard fare is Rs 0.50.

Cycle-Rickshaw & Tonga Bijapur has plenty of cycle-rickshaws, but they must have been designed by an ergonomist who had his legs amputated at the knee! Expect to pay Rs 3 from the bus station to the Hotel Adil Shaha, although it is easy walking distance.

The tonga drivers are eager for business and hassle you at every opportunity. It's about Rs 5 for a round trip out to Ibrahim Roza and Malik-e-Maidan, although you'll need to bargain fiercely. A ride from the centre of town to the railway station should only cost Rs 3, but Rs 5 is the going rate for foreigners.

THE NORTH-EAST

Bidar

This little-visited town in the extreme north-east corner of the state was the capital of the Bahmani Kingdom from 1428, and later the capital of the Barid Shahi dynasty. It's a pleasant town with a splendid old 15th-century fort containing the Ranjeenmahal, Chini Mahal and Turkish Mahal palaces. The impressive Khwaja Mahmud Gawan Madrasa and the tombs of the Bahmani and Barid kings are also worth seeing.

Places to Stay & Eat The KSTDC *Hotel Mayura Barid Shahi* on Yadgir Rd near the bus station has rooms from Rs 45, or you can try the *Sri Venkateshwara Lodge* on the main street. The adjoining *Kalpana Hotel* has good food.

Gulbarga (population 190,000)

This town was the Bahmani capital from 1347 until its transfer to Bidar in 1428. Later the kingdom broke up into a number of smaller kingdoms – Bijapur, Bidar, Berar, Ahmednagar and Golconda. The last of these, Golconda, finally fell to Aurangzeb in 1687. Gulbarga's old fort is in a much deteriorated state, but has a number of interesting buildings inside.

The Jami Masjid, inside the fort, is reputed to have been built by a Moorish architect during the late 14th or early 15th century who imitated the great mosque in Cordoba, Spain. The mosque is unique in India, with a huge dome covering the whole area, four smaller ones at the corners, and 75 smaller still all the way around. The fort itself has 15 towers. Gulbarga also has a number of imposing tombs of Bahmani kings, a shrine to an important Muslim saint and the Temple of Sharana Basaveshwara.

Places to Stay There are a number of hotels in the town including the KSTDC *Hotel Mayura Bahamani*.

Andhra Pradesh

Population: 64 million
Area: 276,754 square km
Capital: Hyderabad
Main language: Telugu

Andhra Pradesh was created by combining the old princely state of Hyderabad with the Telugu-speaking portions of the former state of Madras. Most of this large state stands on the high Deccan Plateau, sloping down to the low-lying coastal region to the east where the mighty Godavari and Krishna rivers meet the Bay of Bengal in wide deltas.

Andhra Pradesh was once a major Buddhist centre and part of Ashoka's large empire until it broke apart. Traces of that early Buddhist influence still remain in several places. Later, in the 7th century, the Chalukyas held power but they, in turn, fell to the Chola Kingdom of the south around the 10th century.

In the 14th century, Muslim power finally reached this far south and, for centuries, the region was an arena for Hindu-Muslim power struggles. Finally, in 1713, it was taken over by a general of the Moghul emperor Aurangzeb. His successors, the nizams of Hyderabad, ruled the state right through to independence.

The final Nizam of Hyderabad was reputed to be one of the richest men in the world, but Andhra Pradesh itself is one of the poorest and least developed states in India. New dams and irrigation projects are improving the barren, scrubby land of the plateau, but much of the state remains economically backward.

There is not a great deal to attract the traveller to Andhra Pradesh apart from the capital, Hyderabad, and the amazing temple complex of Tirumala. Visitors with a keen interest in architecture or archaeology may wish to visit some of the excavations or old temple sites.

HYDERABAD & SECUNDERABAD
(population 3 million)
Like Bijapur to the west in neighbouring Karnataka state, Hyderabad is an important centre of Islamic culture and central India's counterpart to the Moghul splendours of the northern cities of Delhi, Agra and Fatehpur Sikri. Consisting of the twin cities of Hyderabad and Secunderabad, it is the capital of Andhra Pradesh and famous as the former seat of the fabulously wealthy nizams of Hyderabad.

Here, lively crowded bazaars surround huge and impressive Islamic monuments dating from the 16th and 17th centuries. The city, India's sixth largest, was founded in 1590 by Muhammad Quli, the fourth of the Qutab Shahi kings. They ruled this part of the Deccan from 1512 until 1687, when the last of their line was defeated by the Moghul emperor Aurangzeb following failure to pay the annual tribute to their nominal suzerain in Delhi.

Before the founding of Hyderabad, the Qutab Shahi kings ruled from the fortress city of Golconda, 11 km to the west. The extensive ruins of this fort, together with

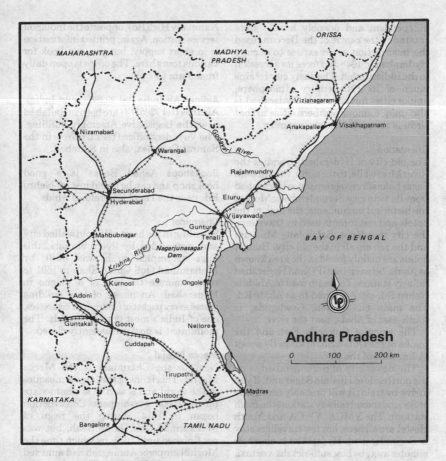

Andhra Pradesh

ORISSA

MAHARASHTRA

MADHYA
PRADESH

Vizianagaram

Anakapalle • Visakhapatnam

• Nizamabad

Warangal

Godavari River

Rajahmundry

Secunderabad

Hyderabad

Eluru

Vijayawada

• Mahbubnagar

Guntur
Tenali

Krishna River

*Nagarjunasagar
Dam*

BAY OF BENGAL

Kurnool

Ongole

• Adoni

Guntakal • Gooty

Nellore

Cuddapah

0   100   200 km

Tirupathi

KARNATAKA

Chittoor

Madras

Bangalore

TAMIL NADU

the nearby tombs of the Qutab Shahi
kings, are the principal attractions of a
visit to Hyderabad.

After Aurangzeb's death in 1707,
Moghul control over this part of India
rapidly waned and the viceroys who had
been installed to look after the interests of
the Moghul Empire broke away to
establish their own independent state,
taking first the title of Subedar and, later,
that of Nizam. These new rulers, allied to
the French, became embroiled in the
French-British rivalry for control of India
during the latter half of the 18th century.

However, the defeat of the French and
subsequent Maratha raids seriously
weakened their kingdom and they were
forced to conclude a treaty with the
British, relinquishing most of their
power.

When Indian independence was declared
in 1947, the Nizam toyed with the idea of
declaring an independent state and went
so far as to allow an Islamic extremist
group to seize control. However, this led to
his downfall when the Indian government,
mindful of Hyderabad's Hindu majority
of around 85% and unwilling to see an

independent and possibly hostile state created in the centre of the Deccan, used the insurrection as an excuse to occupy Hyderabad in 1948 and force its accession to the Indian union. The dusty city retains much of its 19th-century atmosphere, unlike cities further south. Hyderabad is also unique among southern cities in that Urdu is the major language spoken.

Orientation

The old city of Hyderabad straddles the River Musi while, to the north, the Hussain Sagar Lake effectively separates Hyderabad from its twin city Secunderabad. Most of the historical monuments, the bulk of the hotels and restaurants used by travellers, the city bus depot, Salar Jang Museum and the zoo are all in the old city. Budget hotels are mainly found in the area known as Abids, between the GPO and Hyderabad railway station. The main road to Abids is Nehru Rd, often referred to as Abids Rd. The main bus station, Gowliguda, is south-east of Abids, near the river.

The ruins of Golconda Fort and the tombs of the Qutab Shahi kings lie about 11 km west of the city.

The newer city of Secunderabad is on the north side of Hussain Sagar and, if you arrive by train, it will probably terminate at Secunderabad railway station (the main station). The YMCA, YWCA and Youth Hostel are all here, but few travellers stay in Secunderabad. Hyderabad is about 20 minutes away by bus, auto-rickshaw or taxi.

Information

Tourist Offices There are tourist information kiosks at both Secunderabad and Hyderabad railway stations but neither is very good. The Government of India tourist office (tel 66877) is in the Sendozi Building at 26 Himayatnagar Rd. The only information they hand out is a fairly inaccurate map of the city.

The Andhra Pradesh Travel & Tourist Development Corporation (APTTDC) (tel 556493) is in the Gagan Vihar Complex on M J Rd (the continuation of

Nampally High Rd), opposite the Indianoil service station. Again, printed information is in short supply, but you can book for various tours here. The office is open daily from 9 am to 7 pm.

Airlines Air India (tel 222883) and Indian Airlines (tel 72051/3) are both in Saifabad near the Legislative Assembly building. The Vayudoot office (tel 232625) is in the Samrat Complex, also in Saifabad.

Bookshops Ashad Books is a good bookshop and can be found just off Nehru Rd, near the Hotel Emerald in Abids.

Charminar

Standing in the heart of the old walled city and surrounded by lively bazaars, this huge triumphal arch was built by Muhammad Quli Qutab Shah in 1591 to commemorate the end of a plague in Hyderabad. An image of this building graces every packet of Charminar cigarettes, one of India's most popular brands. The monument is now permanently closed.

Mecca Masjid

Next to the Charminar is the Mecca Masjid. This is one of the largest mosques in the world and is said to accommodate up to 10,000 worshippers. Construction began in 1614, during the reign of Muhammad Quli Qutab Shah, but was not finished until 1687, by which time the Moghul emperor Aurangzeb had annexed the Golconda Kingdom. The colonnades and door arches are made from single slabs of granite. According to historical records, these massive stone blocks were quarried 11 km away and dragged to the site by a team of 1400 bullocks! The minarets were originally intended to be much higher, but the enormous cost of erecting the main part of the building apparently forced the ruler to settle for something less grand.

Unfortunately, this beautiful and impressive building has been disfigured by huge chicken wire awnings, erected in

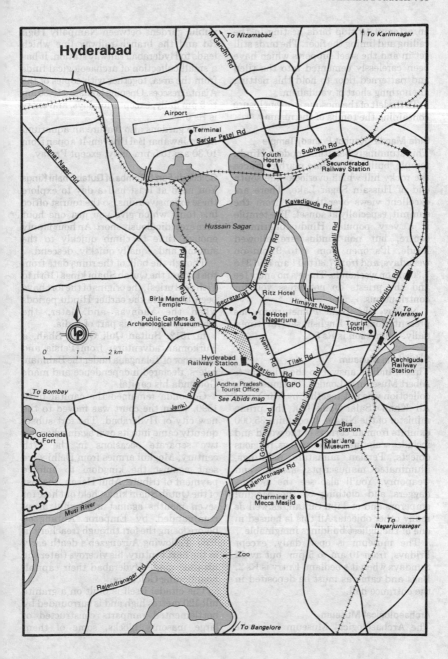

Hyderabad

To Nizamabad
To Karimnagar

M Gandhi Rd

Airport

Terminal
Sardar Patel Rd

Youth Hostel

Subhash Rd

Secunderabad Railway Station

Sanat Nagar Rd

Kavadiguda Rd

Hussain Sagar

Tankbund Rd

Chickadpalli Rd

University Rd

Raj Bhavan Rd

Birla Mandir Temple

Secretariat Rd

Ritz Hotel

Himayat Nagar

To Warangal

Public Gardens & Archaeological Museum

Hotel Nagarjuna

Nehru Rd

Tourist Hotel

Hyderabad Railway Station

Station Rd

Tilak Rd

Kachiguda Railway Station

To Bombay

Prasad Rd

Janki

Andhra Pradesh Tourist Office

See Abids map

GPO

Gosharmahal Rd

Maharganj Jhansi Rd

Golconda Fort

Bus Station

Salar Jang Museum

Musi River

Rajendranagar Rd

Charminar & Mecca Masjid

To Nagarjunasagar

Zoo

Rajendranagar Rd

To Bangalore

0   1   2 km

an attempt to stop birds nesting in the ceiling and liming the floor. The birds still get in and the steel supports which have been carelessly cemented into the tiled and patterned floor to hold this netting are nothing short of vandalism.

To the left of the mosque is an enclosure containing the tombs of the nizams.

Birla Mandir (Naubat Prahad) Temple

This stunningly beautiful modern Hindu temple, built out of white marble, graces the rocky hill which overlooks the south end of Hussain Sagar Lake. There are excellent views over the city from the summit, especially at sunset. The temple is a very popular Hindu pilgrimage centre, but non-Hindus are allowed inside. It's open from 4 to 9 pm on weekdays, and from 7.30 to 11 am and 3 to 7.30 pm on weekends. There's no entry fee and the priests do not press you for contributions.

Nearby, the Birla Planetarium has presentations in English several times daily. Admission is Rs 5.

Salar Jang Museum

This is India's answer to the Victoria & Albert Museum in London. The museum's collection was put together by Mir Yusaf Ali Khan (Salar Jang III), the prime minister of the Nizam. It contains 35,000 exhibits from all corners of the world and includes sculptures, woodcarvings, religious objects, Persian miniature paintings, illuminated manuscripts, armour and weaponry. You'll also see the swords, daggers and clothing of the Moghul emperors and of Tipu Sultan, as well as many other objects. All this is housed in one of the ugliest buildings imaginable.

The museum is open daily, except Fridays, from 10 am to 5 pm, but avoid Sundays when it's bedlam. Entry is Rs 2. Bags and cameras must be deposited in the entrance hall.

Archaeological Museum

The Archaeological Museum is in the public gardens between Nampally High Rd and the branch railway line which leads to Hyderabad railway station. It has a small collection of archaeological finds from the area, together with copies of the Ajanta frescoes. Opening hours are 10.30 am to 5 pm daily, except Mondays, and entry is Rs 0.25.

The gardens also feature an aquarium in the Jawahar Bal Bhavan. It's open from 10.30 am to 5 pm daily, except Friday.

Golconda Fort & Tombs of Qutab Shahi Kings

You need at least half a day to explore these extensive ruins, so the tourist office bus tours which give you just one hour here are ridiculously short. An hour is only enough time to climb quickly to the summit and, equally quickly, descend.

Though the bulk of the ruins date from the time of the Qutab Shahi kings (16th to 17th centuries), the origins of the fort have been traced to the earlier Hindu periods when the Yadavas and, later, the Kakatiyas ruled this part of India.

In 1512, Sultan Quli Qutab Shah, a Turkoman adventurer from Persia and Governor of Telangana under the Bahmani rulers, declared independence and made Golconda his capital.

Golconda remained the capital until 1590, when the court was moved to the new city of Hyderabad. The fort subsequently came into its own again when, on two separate occasions in the 17th century, Moghul armies from Delhi were sent against the kingdom to enforce payment of tribute. Abul Hasan, the last of the Qutab Shahi kings, held out here for seven months against a Moghul army commanded by Emperor Aurangzeb before losing the fort through treachery in 1687. Following Aurangzeb's death early in the next century, his viceroys (later the nizams) made Hyderabad their capital, abandoning Golconda.

The citadel itself is built on a granite hill 120 metres high and is surrounded by battlemented ramparts constructed of large masonry blocks, some of them

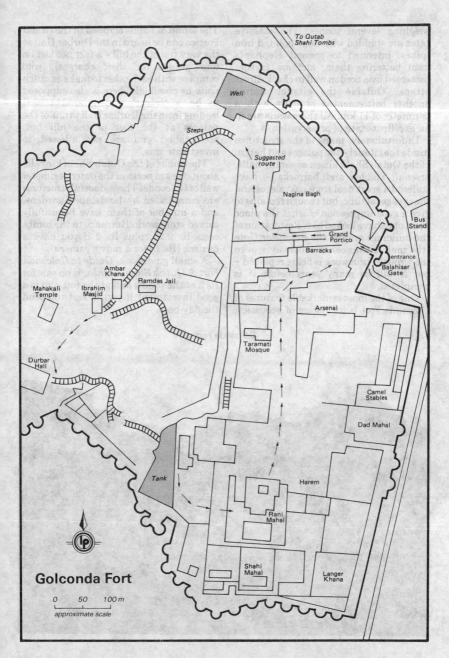

To Qutab
Shahi Tombs

Well

Steps

Suggested
route

Nagina Bagh

Grand
Portico

Bus
Stand

Barracks

entrance

Balahisar
Gate

Ambar
Khana

Ramdas Jail

Arsenal

Mahakali
Temple

Ibrahim
Masjid

Durbar
Hall

Taramati
Mosque

Camel
Stables

Dad Mahal

Tank

Harem

Rani
Mahal

Shahi
Mahal

Langer
Khana

Golconda Fort

0   50   100 m

approximate scale

weighing several tonnes. The massive gates are studded with large pointed iron spikes, intended to prevent elephants from battering them, and are further protected by a cordon wall to check direct attack. Outside the citadel stands another battlemented rampart with a perimeter of 11 km. All these walls are in an excellent state of preservation.

Unfortunately, many of the structures inside the citadel – the palaces and harem of the Qutab Shahi kings, assembly halls, arsenal, stables and barracks – have suffered a great deal from past sieges and the ravages of time, but enough remains to give a good impression of what the place must once have looked like. Restoration of the buildings around the Balahisar Gate (the main entrance) is underway – even the wrought iron work is being replaced – but it will be many years before it is completed.

One of the most remarkable features of Golconda Fort is its system of acoustics.

The sound of hands clapped in the Grand Portico can be heard in the Durbar Hall at the very top of the hill – a fact not lost on tour guides (or their charges), who compete with each other to make as much noise as possible! There is also supposed to be a 'secret' underground tunnel leading from the Durbar Hall to one of the palaces at the foot of the hill but, predictably, you are not allowed to investigate this.

The tombs of the Qutab Shahi kings lie about one km north of the outer perimeter wall of Golconda. These graceful structures are surrounded by landscaped gardens, and a number of them have beautifully carved stonework. Entrance to the tombs costs Rs 0.25, plus Rs 2 if you have a camera (Rs 10 for a movie camera).

A small guidebook, *Guide to Golconda Fort & Qutab Shahi Tombs*, is on sale for Rs 2 at the tombs and at the fort and is a good investment if you intend to spend the day here.

Golconda Fort

City buses No 119 and No 142 take you from Nampally High Rd, outside the public gardens, to the main fort entrance at Balahisar Gate. The 11-km trip takes an hour and costs about Rs 2. An auto-rickshaw costs at least Rs 10 each way.

Nehru Zoological Park

One of the largest zoos in India, the Nehru Zoological Park is spread out over 1.2 square km of landscaped gardens with animals living in large, open enclosures. They don't look any less bored than animals in zoos anywhere else in the world, but at least an effort has been made here, which is more than can be said for most Indian zoos.

The park is open from 9 am to 6 pm daily, except Mondays.

Tours

The APTTDC offers daily tours of the city. The tours start at 8 am, run to 6 or 6.30 pm and cost Rs 40. In addition, you usually have to pay your own entrance fees. Tours visit Osmania University, Venkateswara Temple, Birla Mandir, Qutab Shahi Tombs, Golconda Fort, Gandipet, Salar Jang Museum, Charminar, Mecca Masjid and the zoo.

Unfortunately, the time allowed for each sight is ludicrously short. Five and 10-minute stops are the order of the day, and a lot of time is wasted on an inconsequential visit to Gandipet Lake. Even Golconda Fort only gets an hour and the tombs of the Qutab Shahi kings are allocated just over an hour.

Places to Stay - bottom end

The best of the cheap places are all in the Abids area between Abids Circle and Hyderabad railway station. The *Royal Lodge* is on Nampally High Rd, near the junction with Station Rd. There are plenty of rooms in this huge place; singles/doubles cost Rs 40/70. In the same enclave, around a courtyard, are several other 'Royal' hotels – the *Royal Home, Royal Hotel, Neo Royal Hotel and Gee*

Osmania University

Royal Lodge. Good grief! The Royal Hotel offers singles from Rs 25 and doubles with shower for Rs 50. Rooms at the Neo Royal cost Rs 40/75 and, across the road, the extremely basic *Asian Lodge* has singles from Rs 20.

The *Hotel Imperial* (tel 235436) is right on the corner of Station Rd and Nampally High Rd. It has singles/doubles for Rs 40/58, all with bath, but the rooms on the roof are unbearably hot in summer. The hotel restaurant serves vegetarian and non-vegetarian food.

Another budget hotel in the Abids area is the *Everest Lodge* on Tilak Rd, near the junction with Nehru Rd. Rooms cost Rs 25/45 so it tends to fill up early.

Away from Abids, the *Tourist Hotel* (tel 665691) is close to the Kachiguda railway station, which makes it convenient if you're heading for Guntakal, Bangalore or Madras by rail, but otherwise it's out of the way. Singles/doubles cost Rs 40/55.

Even further from the central Abids area, the *Youth Hostel*, behind the Boat Club at the north-eastern end of Hussain Sagar in Secunderabad, offers the cheapest dormitory-type accommodation in town. There are 51 beds at only Rs 5 per night if you have a YHA card, Rs 8 if you don't, but it's so far out of the way that it's hard to think of another good reason to stay here.

Only Secunderabad railway station (tel 70144/5) has *retiring rooms* and these cost Rs 50 a double. Surprisingly, there is no dormitory accommodation.

Up the scale a bit, the big *Sri Brindavan Hotel* (tel 237970) on Station Rd near Abids Circle has large, airy rooms with fan and bath for Rs 66/88. Avoid the noisy rooms over the main road at the front; most of the rooms are built around a quiet courtyard well off the road. The staff are friendly (but watch out for extra charges) and, in the morning, hot water is available and there's even a daily newspaper pushed under your door.

On the corner of Nehru Rd and King Kothi Rd, the sprawling *Hotel Taj Mahal* (tel 237988) has singles/doubles at Rs 70/110 and doubles with air-con for Rs 253. Closer to the station but still on Station Rd, the *Hotel Kakatiya* (tel 40186) has clean and well-kept rooms at Rs 88/125.

The *Hotel Suhail* (tel 41286) is clean, quiet and good value at Rs 71/93 for singles/doubles, Rs 143/176 with air-con. It's well hidden behind the GPO; the easiest way to find it is to walk through the carpark of the Ramakrishna Cinema and turn left. The hotel is up a little further, on the left.

Places to Stay – middle
The *Hotel Annapurna* (tel 557931), also on Station Rd, has singles/doubles for Rs 115/154, Rs 176/220 with air-con, and a good restaurant.

Still in Abids, the *Hotel Jaya International* (tel 223444) is just off to the left on Bank St as you face the GPO. This very

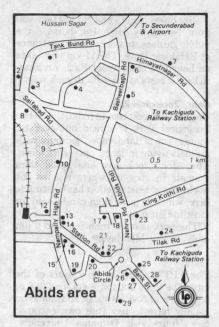

Abids area

pleasant modern hotel has singles/doubles at Rs 90/120, Rs 143/198 with air-con. All rooms have bathrooms and the hotel has its own restaurant. The *Emerald Hotel* (tel 237835), just off Nehru Rd on Chirag Ali Lane, has rooms for Rs 147/176, Rs 275/330 with air-con.

Places to Stay – top end
The small, old and well-kept *Ritz Hotel* (tel 233571) is pleasantly situated on Hill Fort Rd, Basheer Bagh, and has all the usual mod cons, from air-conditioning to swimming pool and tennis courts. Singles/doubles cost Rs 420/540.

The *Hotel Nagarjuna* (tel 237201) is on Basheerbagh Rd, the extension of Nehru Rd from Abids. The hotel is centrally air-conditioned and rooms are Rs 220/300, Rs 330/430 with air-con.

Places to Eat
Good, cheap vegetarian meals can be

1	Birla Mandir Temple
2	Hotel Kamut
3	Indian Airlines
4	Ritz Hotel
5	Nagarjuma Hotel
6	Nirala's Open House
7	Government of India Office
8	AP Legislative Assembly Building
9	Public Gardens & Archeology Museum
10	Nampally Bus Stop (for Golconda)
11	Hyderabad Railway Station
12	Deluxe Bus Companies
13	Royal Lodges
14	Imperial Hotel
15	New Punjab Hotel
16	Kakatiya Hotel
17	Hotel Emerald
18	Ashad Books
19	AP Tourist Office
20	Annapurna Hotel
21	Sri Brindavan Hotel
22	State Bank of India
23	Hotel Taj Mahal
24	Everest Lodge
25	Liberty Restaurant
26	GPO
27	Grand Hotel
28	Hotel Jaya International
29	Ramakrishna Cinema

found at any *Kamat Hotel*, where the standard fare costs Rs 5. There's one in Abids on Station Rd, near the junction with Nampally High Rd, and another near the Indian Airlines office. Almost opposite the Kamat on Station Rd, the small *New Punjab Hotel* serves excellent north Indian non-vegetarian food.

The *Priya Hotel* is at the other end of Station Rd, opposite the Sri Brindavan Hotel. It's air-conditioned and has good vegetarian and non-vegetarian lunchtime meals for Rs 11. Food at the *Hotel Swagat* almost next door is also good. Meals cost Rs 9.

Nirala's Open House is a modern fast-food place on Himayatnagar Rd, near the corner of Basheerbagh Rd. It offers typical western food such as chips, pizza, sandwiches, milkshakes and ice creams.

The *Grand Hotel*, just around from the post office on Bank St, is hardly grand but has good cheap non-vegetarian food such as biryanis (Rs 10 to Rs 13) and mutton cutlets (Rs 4). Opposite the Grand, the *Liberty Restaurant* is another of the new western-style places and serves Chinese and Indian dishes.

The *Annapurna Hotel* on Station Rd has an air-conditioned vegetarian restaurant where you can get good food, including thalis for Rs 10, 'Bombay' thalis for Rs 17 and 'Annapurna Special' thalis for Rs 30. The ice cream is good too. Near the Royal Hotel, at the station end of Station Rd, the *Gop Milk Shop* sells lassi and curd.

Things to Buy
Hyderabad is famous for glass bangles and these can be bought in Lud Bazaar, the street running to the right of the Charminar (when coming from Abids). Prices range from as little as Rs 8 for a box of a dozen or so up to Rs 30 for one.

Getting There & Away
Air There are Indian Airlines flights at least daily from Hyderabad to Bangalore (Rs 535), Bombay (Rs 690), Calcutta (Rs 1245), Delhi (Rs 1165) and Madras (Rs 545). Connections to other places, including Bhubaneswar (Rs 895) and Pune (Rs 535), are less frequent.

Vayudoot operates services from Hyderabad to Tirupathi (Rs 450), Warangal (Rs 175), Goa (Rs 560) and Bangalore (Rs 535).

Bus Buses leave from the main bus station, Gowliguda, for all parts of the state. Unfortunately, the timetable is completely in Telugu.

Private deluxe buses connect Hyderabad with Bangalore (Rs 120), Bombay (Rs 150), Madras (Rs 120) and Tirupathi (Rs 100). There are also direct buses through to Aurangabad; the trip takes 16 hours. You can book these buses from the offices opposite the Royal Lodge, at the entrance to Hyderabad railway station.

Train The main railway station is at Secunderabad. Hyderabad railway station is only a branch line, although some trains do start from here. If you're staying in Abids and heading south to Guntakal, Bangalore or Madras, you can board the train at Kachiguda station instead of going all the way to Secunderabad. As elsewhere, the fastest night express trains are booked up days in advance, so reserve your seat or sleeper as early as possible.

The reservation system at Hyderabad station (and, in fact, throughout Andhra Pradesh) is extremely sensible and should be implemented throughout the country. You fill in your reservation form and take it to the enquiries window, where you are given a window number and a token number. You then go to the relevant window and wait for your token number to be called. This means that, although you still have to wait, at least you can sit down and read a book rather than having to do battle in the 'queue' while half a dozen locals squeeze in before you. At Secunderabad, the reservation office is inconveniently located 15 minutes walk (Rs 3 by auto-rickshaw) from the station. Ask for directions.

The 1675-km trip from New Delhi to Secunderabad on the Andhra Pradesh Express takes 26 hours and costs Rs 125 in 2nd class, Rs 500 in 1st. The Hazrat Nizamuddin Express takes the same time and goes to and from Hyderabad station.

The quickest route from Calcutta is to take the daily Coromandel Express from Howrah station and change at Vijayawada. If you're coming from Nagpur, change at Kazipet, just west of Warangal.

From Hyderabad, the 862-km trip to Madras takes 13½ hours on the daily Charminar Express; the fare is Rs 83 in 2nd class, Rs 310 in 1st. The 790-km trip from Hyderabad to Bangalore takes 17 hours and costs Rs 79 in 2nd class, Rs 286 in 1st.

The line from Secunderabad to Aurangabad is metre gauge – the 517-km trip takes 12 hours at a cost of Rs 57 in 2nd class, Rs 208 in 1st. The express continues through Aurangabad to Manmad, on the Bombay to Delhi line, via Bhopal and Agra. The Secunderabad to Ajmer line is also metre gauge. This 1138-km route passes through Khandwa, Mhow, Indore, Ratlam and Chittorgarh, a 39-hour journey which costs Rs 107 in 2nd class, Rs 422 in 1st.

The daily Venkatadri Express connects Secunderabad with Tirupathi 741 km away. The trip takes 18 hours and costs Rs 75 in 2nd class, Rs 275 in 1st.

Getting Around

Airport Transport There is no airport bus, but an auto-rickshaw to or from Abids costs about Rs 15 by the meter. Don't trust the auto-rickshaw wallahs at the airport – make sure the meter is switched on and starts at zero.

Bus Getting on any city bus in Hyderabad, other than at the terminus, is (as one traveller put it) 'like staging a banzai charge on Guadalcanal'. He wasn't exaggerating! Buses you might find useful include: No 2 – Secunderabad railway station to Charminar; No 7 – Secunderabad railway station to Afzalganj and return (this is the one to catch if you're heading for Abids, as it goes down Tankbund Rd and Nehru Rd via the GPO); No 8 – connects Secunderabad and Hyderabad railway stations; No 119 and 142 – Nampally High Rd to Golconda Fort.

Auto-Rickshaw Unlike those in many other Indian cities, the drivers here need no prompting to use the meter. Sample fares are: the YHA to Abids, Rs 6; Abids to the Charminar, Rs 4; Secunderabad to the GPO, Rs 7.

NAGARJUNAKONDA & NAGARJUNASAGAR

Nagarjunakonda, 150 km south-east of Hyderabad on the Krishna River, was one of the largest and most important Buddhist centres in southern India from the 2nd century BC until the 3rd century AD. Known in those days as Vijayapur, Nagarjunakonda takes its present name from Nagarjuna, one of the most revered Buddhist monks, who governed the *sangha* for nearly 60 years around the turn of the 2nd century AD. The Madhyamika school he founded attracted students from as far afield as Sri Lanka and China.

The site was discovered in 1926. Subsequent excavations, particularly in the '50s and '60s, have unearthed the remains of stupas, viharas, chaityas and mandapas, as well as some outstanding examples of white marble carvings and sculptures depicting the life of the Buddha. These finds were taken to an island following the decision to flood this entire area to build the Nagarjunasagar Dam. The dam is touted as one of the largest masonry constructions in the world and India claims that it will create the world's third largest artificial lake.

Places to Stay

The choice of accommodation maintained by the APTTDC (tel Hyderabad 556523) includes the *Vijay Vihar Complex*, which has double air-con rooms for Rs 75 and cottages for Rs 100. For reservations, contact the Assistant Manager (tel 69).

Also operated by the APTTDC is the *Project House* with doubles for Rs 40. Make reservations through the Assistant Manager (tel 3633).

Getting There & Away

The easiest way to visit Nagarjunakonda and Nagarjunasagar is to take the deluxe tourist bus from Hyderabad organised by the APTTDC. It departs daily (if demand warrants it) at 6 am, returns at 9 pm and costs Rs 58. The tour includes visits to the Nagarjunakonda Museum, Pylon (an engraved granite monolith from the Buddhist period), Nagarjunasagar Dam and the working model of the dam.

If you'd prefer to make your own way there, regular buses link Hyderabad, Vijayawada and Guntur with Nagarjunasagar. The nearest railway station is at Macherla – a branch line running west from Guntur – and regular buses leave there for Nagarjunasagar.

Getting Around

Boat If you're not taking one of the local tours or those organised from Hyderabad, launches to Nagarjunakonda Museum depart at 9.30 am and 1.30 pm at a cost of Rs 10 per person.

WARANGAL (population 190,000)

This was once the capital of the Kakatiya Kingdom, which spanned the greater part of present-day Andhra Pradesh from the latter half of the 12th century until it was conquered by the Tughlaqs of Delhi early in the 14th century. The Hindu Kakatiyas were great builders and patrons of the arts, and it was during their reign that the Chalukyan style of temple architecture and decoration reached the pinnacle of its development.

If you have an interest in the various branches of Hindu temple development and have either visited or intend to visit the early Chalukyan sites at Badami, Aihole and Pattadakal in neighbouring Karnataka state, then an outing to Warangal is worthwhile. Facilities are adequate for an overnight stopover, or it can be visited in a long day-trip from Hyderabad.

There's a colourful wool market a couple of hundred metres past the bus stand.

The Fort

Warangal's main attraction is the enormous abandoned mud-brick fort, which has a terrific atmosphere and many interesting features. Carved stones from wrecked Chalukyan temples are set indiscriminately in the massive stone walls which form a distinct fortification almost a km inside the outer mud walls.

Chalukyan Temples

The most notable remaining Chalukyan

temples are the 1000-Pillared Temple on the slopes of Hanamkonda Hill (one shrine of which is still in use), Bhadrakali Temple on a hillock between Warangal and Hanamkonda, and Shambu Lingeswara or Swayambhu Temple (originally a Shiva temple). Built in 1162, the 1000-Pillared Temple is, however, inferior to those found further south. It is in a sad state of disrepair, and looters have removed many of the best pieces and chiselled away the faces of statues.

Tours

The APTTDC has weekend day-tours to Warangal for Rs 100. The tours leave Hyderabad at 7 am on Saturdays and Sundays, returning at 9.30 pm the same day.

Places to Stay & Eat

Accommodation facilities are modest. Most of the hotels are on Station Rd, which runs parallel to the railway line; turn left as you leave the station. The *Vijya Lodge* (tel 5851) is excellent value at Rs 35/40, and has an attached restaurant serving both vegetarian and non-vegetarian food.

The *Hotel Shanthi Krishna* (tel 5305) is behind the post office, which is also on Station Rd. Rooms in this modern hotel cost Rs 30/45.

Up behind the bus station and near the huge market, the basic *Vikas Lodge* (tel 5943) has rooms with bath for Rs 22/35, Rs 3 more with a telephone.

There are also a couple of *retiring rooms* at the railway station, and these cost Rs 30 for a double.

Getting There & Away

Air Vayudoot has three flights a week between Hyderabad and Warangal. The fare is Rs 175.

Bus Regular buses run between Warangal and Hyderabad, Nizamabad and other major centres. Local buses connect Warangal with Kazipet and Hanamkonda.

Train Many expresses stop at Warangal. The 152-km journey to Hyderabad or Secunderabad takes about 3½ hours. Warangal to Vijayawada takes about the same time and costs Rs 30 in 2nd class, Rs 90 in 1st.

Getting Around

The bus station is directly opposite the entrance to the railway station. As usual, the timetable is printed completely in Telugu.

Bus No 28 will take you the five km to the fort at Mantukonda.

TIRUPATHI & TIRUMALA

The 'holy hill' of Tirumala, 20 km from its service town of Tirupathi in the extreme south of Andhra Pradesh, is one of the most important pilgrimage centres in all India because of the Temple of Lord Venkatesa. This is the god whose picture graces the reception areas of most lodges and restaurants in southern India. He's the one with his eyes covered (since his gaze would scorch the world) and garlanded in so many flowers that only his feet are visible.

Among the powers attributed to Lord Venkatesa by his devotees is the granting of any wish made in front of the idol at Tirumala. On the basis of such a legend, pilgrims flock here from all over India. There are never less than 5000 here at any one time and, in a day, the total is often as high as 100,000, although the average is a mere 30,000. The temple staff alone number nearly 6000!

Such popularity makes the temple one of the richest in India, with an annual income of a staggering five billion rupees, but a lot of this money is ploughed back into schemes to help the poor and into providing shelter for pilgrims on their way to Tirumala.

It's considered auspicious to have your head shaved when visiting the temple, so if you see people with shaved heads in south India, you can be pretty sure they've recently been to Tirupathi – this applies to

Pilgrims at Tirumala

men, women and children. The practice is known as *tonsuring*.

In order to cope with the army of pilgrims, everything at Tirupathi and Tirumala is organised to keep the visitors fed, sheltered and moving. Most are housed in special pilgrim accommodation (known as choultries) in both Tirupathi and Tirumala. However, the private hotels and lodges are in Tirupathi, so a whole fleet of buses constantly ferries pilgrims between Tirupathi and Tirumala from before dawn until well after dark.

The temple is one of the few in India which will allow non-Hindus into the sanctum sanctorum. After paying Rs 25 for 'special darshan', you're allowed into the temple. Special darshan means you can enter ahead of all those who have paid nothing for ordinary darshan and who have to queue up – often for 12 hours and more – in the claustrophobic wire cages which ring the outer wall of the temple. To find the start of the queue, follow the signs

to Sarvadarshan, around to the left of the temple entrance. 'Special darshan' is supposed to get you to the front of the queue in two hours, but on weekends when the place is much busier it can take as long as five hours, and you still have to go through the cages. A signboard at the entrance tells you how long you can expect it to take.

As you face the entrance to the temple, there is a small museum at the top of the steps to the left. Among other things, it has a good collection of musical instruments, including a tabla-type drum called a Ubangam!

It's an engrossing place where you can easily spend a whole day just wandering around and, despite the huge numbers of pilgrims here, the place sees very few foreign visitors.

Information
The Indian Airlines office (tel 2369) is in the Hotel Vishnupriya complex, opposite the main bus station in Tirupathi.

Tours
The APTTDC runs weekend tours to Tirumala from Hyderabad. The tours include accommodation and 'special darshan' and cost Rs 275. It is possible to take the bus only, and this costs Rs 100 one way. The tour leaves Hyderabad at 4 pm on Friday, returning at 6 am on Monday.

There are also daily tours to Tirumala from Madras run by the Tamil Nadu Tourist Development Corporation, but this is guided-tour madness at its very worst. The tour takes about 15 hours, at least 12 of which are spent on the bus to and from Madras. In addition, the schedule allows for a two-hour wait for 'special darshan' (included in the tour price), but if the wait is much longer (as it is on weekends), it's not uncommon for the bus to return to Madras at midnight and even as late as 3 am!

However, if your endurance is unbounded and you still want to do it, the buses leave the tourist office in Mount Rd at 6 am and return at 9 pm (with luck). The price is Rs 100 on the ordinary bus, Rs 200 for air-con, and this includes breakfast, lunch and 'special darshan'. As the tour is a popular one, you need to book in advance.

Places to Stay
Tirupathi Tirupathi is the village at the bottom of the hill and the transport hub. It has plenty of hotels and lodges, so there's no problem finding somewhere to stay. The *Bhimas Hotel* has singles/doubles with bath for Rs 35/75. The reception desk is at the Bhimas Hotel Annexe across the street.

Directly opposite the railway station, the noisy *Gopi Krishna Deluxe Lodge* (tel 3149) has small rooms for Rs 50 with bath. The colour schemes in these rooms are really something.

Almost next door to the Bhimas Hotel is the *Bhima's Deluxe Hotel* (tel 2501) at 42 G-Car St. It's much more expensive, with singles from Rs 82, but has good rooms. A whole group of better class hotels can be found around the main bus station, 500 metres from the centre of town, and there are *retiring rooms* at the railway station for Rs 40 a double.

Tirumala Tirumala has only one hotel offering private rooms – most pilgrims stay in the vast dormitories which ring the temple. This pilgrim accommodation is open to anyone. If you want to stay there, check in at the accommodation reception in Tirumala and you'll be allocated a bed or a room. It's best to avoid weekends when the place becomes outrageously crowded.

The Tamil Nadu Tourist Development Corporation has tourist cottages for rent at Tirumala. These can be booked at the office in Madras, or ask at cottage No 304 near the bus station in Tirumala.

Places to Eat
Tirupathi The *Lakshmi Narayana Bhavan* is a good vegetarian restaurant opposite

Tirumala Temple

the main bus station. The *Hotel Bhimas* also has a good vegetarian restaurant, including an air-conditioned dining hall. On the same street, you can get non-vegetarian north Indian tucker at the *Restaurant Peacock*.

Tirumala Huge dining halls serve more than 3000 free meals daily to keep the pilgrims happy. Other than that, there are a few no-frills 'meals' places.

Getting There & Away
Air Indian Airlines has daily flights from Tirupathi to Madras (Rs 140), Vijayawada and Hyderabad.

Vayudoot operates flights between Tirupathi and Bangalore (Rs 250), and between Tirupathi and Madras (Rs 140).

Bus It is possible to see Tirumala on a long day trip from Madras if you make a very early start, but staying overnight makes it far less rushed.

Thiruvalluvar have express buses (route No 802) from the Thiruvalluvar bus station in Madras at 8.15 am, 3.30 and 8.30 pm. There are also many other ordinary buses, although these are not particularly recommended as they take circuitous routes. The express buses take four hours, cost Rs 18 and can be booked in advance in Madras. The expresses to Madras from Tirupathi leave at 9.30 am, 1.15 and 8.30 pm.

There are plenty of buses to Madras, but again, only a few are expresses. The normal buses (route Nos 200 and 201) cost Rs 17.50.

Train As a popular pilgrimage centre, Tirupathi is well served by express trains. The 147-km trip to Madras takes 3½ hours and costs Rs 22 in 2nd class, Rs 77 in 1st; there are three trains daily.

The daily Rayala Seema Express connects Hyderabad and Tirupathi. The trip takes 16 hours and costs Rs 73 in 2nd class, Rs 268 in 1st.

There are three expresses to Vijayawada daily and one of these, the Tirupathi Express, goes on to Puri. The trip to Vijayawada is 389 km, takes eight hours and costs Rs 47 in 2nd class, Rs 189 in 1st. The 1207-km trip to Puri takes 18 hours and costs Rs 103 in 2nd class, Rs 400 in 1st.

Getting Around

Tirumala Link buses operate from both the main bus stand, and the Tirumala bus stand in the centre of Tirupathi. The 20-km trip takes 45 minutes and costs Rs 4.50 one way, or Rs 8.50 return. To get on a bus in either Tirupathi or Tirumala, you have to go through a system of crowd-control wire cages which are definitely not for the claustrophobic. At busy times (weekends and festivals), it can take up to two hours to file through the cages and get onto a bus. If you're staying in Tirupathi, it's worth buying a return ticket which saves you some queuing time in the cages at the

top of the hill. There are no cages at the main bus station.

Finding the queue for the buses in Tirupathi can also be a task. The entrance to the choultry (through which you have to walk to reach the cages and ticket office) is opposite the bottom of the foot-bridge over the railway line – just follow the crowd. There's always a steady stream of people filing in.

The road to Tirumala winds precariously upwards and the bus drivers have perfected the art of maniacal driving. The road they drive down is the old one and is very narrow and winding. It has 57 hairpin bends, which means 57 adrenalin rushes for you as the buses hurtle down – total lunacy.

Taxi If you're in a hurry, or don't like the cages, there are share taxis running up and down the hill all the time. Seats cost around Rs 20, depending on demand.

SOUTH OF HYDERABAD
Puttaparthi

Prasanthi Nilayam, the ashram of Sri Sathya Sai Baba, is in Puttaparthi. Sai Baba's followers are predominantly Indian but he also has many western followers. When he celebrated his 60th birthday in late 1985, 400,000 people came to his ashram. Known as the Abode of Highest Peace, it is spacious and beautiful with good food and accommodation – at least when the numbers aren't over-whelming. It does get very dry here in the hot season.

Getting There & Away Puttaparthi is in Andhra Pradesh, but it is most easily reached from Bangalore, 150 km away. Take a train or bus to Dharmavaram or Anantapur, the nearest railway station.

EAST COAST

Although the main Calcutta to Madras railway line runs along the east coast of Andhra Pradesh, few travellers stop south of Orissa. During the monsoon, the extensive deltas of the Godavari and Krishna rivers may flood, forcing trains between Calcutta and Madras to detour further inland through Raipur, Nagpur and Hyderabad.

Waltair & Visakhapatnam
(population 720,000)

These two towns have really merged into one and the local people do not recognise any distinction between them. The northern residential area can be thought of as Waltair and the booming southern business and industrial area towards the docks as Visakhapatnam (abbreviated as Vizag). The railway station, roughly in the centre, is called Visakhapatnam Junction.

Waltair, a popular seaside resort, boasts rocks and pools as well as several km of sand. There are two beaches: Mission Beach, about three km from the centre, and Lawson Beach, a distance of about six km. Simhachalam Hill, about 10 km north of Waltair, has an 11th-century Vishnu temple in fine Orissan style.

There is a tourist office in the railway station but, according to one disgruntled visitor, it's 'moderately to severely useless'.

Places to Stay Vizag has plenty of hotels right up to five-star quality. The excellent bus station has *retiring rooms*. Cheap hotels include the *Hotel Poorna* (tel 62344) on Main Rd, where rooms with attached bath start at Rs 25/45. On the same road, the *Hotel Prasanth* (tel 65282) has rooms for Rs 35/50 and a dormitory. The *Hotel Apsara* (tel 64861) on Waltair Main Rd is more expensive, with rooms from Rs 100.

The *Ocean View Inn* (tel 64828) is near the better (northern) end of the beach and is very comfortable, peaceful and friendly, with singles/doubles for Rs 75/100. Rooms with air-con cost Rs 150/175. All rooms have TV and in-house videos. The

centrally located *Hotel Daspalli* has rooms for Rs 120/150, more with air-con.

Getting There & Away Vizag is linked by broad-gauge railway line to Raipur, and by Indian Airlines directly to Calcutta, Hyderabad and Madras. There's a new and well-organised bus station in Vizag which is quite different from the usual bus station confusion. Good services run to and from Puri and Vijayawada.

Vijayawada (population 650,000)

On the banks of the mighty Krishna River, only 149 km south of Rajahmundry and the Godavari River, Vijayawada is the junction for the railway line to Warangal and Hyderabad. It's a fairly hectic town and there's little reason to stop here, except perhaps to have a look at the river, or to break a long journey along the east coast.

Two thousand years ago, this was an important Buddhist area and there are interesting excavations upstream at Amaravathi (now much damaged) and Nagarjunakonda. See the Nagarjunakonda section for more information. To reach Amaravathi you have to continue south to Guntur, then turn back north, a distance of about 65 km.

Only a few km from Vijayawada, but across the river, are the ancient Hindu cave temples of Undavalil. Masulipatam, 80 km from Vijayawada on the coast, once had English, Dutch and French factories and was the subject of violent Anglo-French rivalry.

Places to Stay & Eat The main hotel area is quite a walk from either the bus or railway station. If you have any luggage, you'll need a cycle-rickshaw – Rs 4 from the railway station, Rs 3 from the buses. Best value is the *Hotel Swapna Lodge* (tel 72172) on Durgaiah St. It's both friendly and clean and rooms cost Rs 40/60, more with air-con.

The *Ashoka Hotel* is dingy, but cheap at Rs 30/50. Its other saving grace is its location, only a few minutes' walk from the bus station.

The town's best is the *Hotel Mamata*, visible from the bus station, where rooms cost Rs 110/165.

There are good *retiring rooms* at the railway station, but this is convenient only for the train traveller. Double rooms cost Rs 50, and a bed in the eight-bed dorm is Rs 15. At the station, there's a good vegetarian and non-vegetarian restaurant which opens at 6 am.

Getting There & Away Vayudoot has flights to Madras (Rs 425) and Vizag (Rs 375).

The bus station in Vijayawada is totally chaotic. From here, buses travel to all parts of Andhra Pradesh, and also to Madras.

Vijayawada is on the main Madras to Calcutta and Madras to Delhi lines and all the expresses stop here. The quickest train from Vijayawada to Madras is the Calcutta to Madras Coromandel Express, which does the 432-km journey nonstop in a shade under six hours. The fare is Rs 52 in 2nd class, Rs 185 in 1st. In the opposite direction, the same train takes just 27 hours for the 1236-km journey to Calcutta. The fare is Rs 104 in 2nd class, Rs 403 in 1st. There are slower expresses, such as the Tirupathi Express, which you can catch to Puri.

The 351-km trip to Hyderabad takes seven hours and costs Rs 44 in 2nd class, Rs 156 in 1st. The Tamil Nadu Express takes 50 hours to cover the 1761 km to New Delhi. The fare is Rs 129 in 2nd class, Rs 523 in 1st.

There are also direct trains to Bangalore, Kanyakumari, Trivandrum and Varanasi.

Kerala

Population: 30 million
Area: 38,864 square km
Capital: Trivandrum
Main language: Malayalam

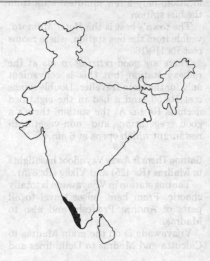

Kerala, the land of green magic, is a narrow, fertile strip on the south-west coast of India, bordered by the Western Ghats. These high mountains have sheltered Kerala from invaders from the rest of India but, at the same time, Kerala has a very long history of contact with the outside world. In Cochin, there is still a small community descended from Jewish settlers who fled Palestine 2000 years ago. Christianity has also been in Kerala for as long as it has been in Europe! When the Portuguese arrived here 500 years ago, they were more than a little surprised to find Christianity already established along the Malabar coast, and more than a little annoyed that these Christians had never heard of the Pope.

Long before Vasco da Gama led the Portuguese to India, the coast had been known to the Phoenicians, who came in search of spices, sandalwood and ivory. Kerala was not only a spice centre in its own right, but a trans-shipment point from the Moluccas. The Arabs and Chinese also made their mark on Kerala, and local fishermen use Chinese fishing nets to this day.

The present-day state of Kerala was created in 1956 from Travancore, Cochin and Malabar. Malabar was formerly part of Madras State, while both Travancore and Cochin were princely states ruled by maharajas. Unlike some maharajas in other parts of India who exploited and terrorised their people, the maharajas of Travancore and Cochin paid considerable attention to the provision of basic services and education for their subjects.

The people of Kerala speak Malayalam, a language derived from Tamil hundreds

of years ago. In 1957, Kerala became the first place in the world to freely elect a communist government. Although the communists currently hold power, they have not always been in government since that initial election success. The princely state of Travancore had already implemented a far-sighted land ownership policy over a century ago. Today, land distribution in Kerala is more equitable than almost anywhere else in India, and this has resulted in unusually intensive cultivation and far more equality of income distribution than is found elsewhere in India. This policy of equity also applies to health and education. Infant mortality in Kerala is relatively low, and the literacy rate is 70%, twice the all-India average and the highest in the country, yet still growing faster than in the rest of India. These results have been achieved without spending a higher proportion of state income on health or education than other states. It's also the only Indian state in which females outnumber males.

Kerala offers visitors one of the best beaches in India at Kovalam, an intriguing blend of cultures and some unusual ways of travelling around. Perhaps more than anywhere else in India, getting around can be half the fun, particularly on the backwater trips along the coastal lagoons. Best of all, Kerala has an easygoing, relaxed atmosphere unlike the bustle you find elsewhere in India.

Religions

The population of Kerala is roughly 60% Hindu, 20% Muslim and 20% Christian. Christianity was established here earlier than almost anywhere else in the world. In 52 AD, St Thomas the Apostle, or 'Doubting Thomas', is said to have landed on the Malabar coast near Cranganore, where a church with carved Hindu-style columns supposedly dates from the 4th century AD. Further south, there is the 9th-century Syrian church of Vallia Palli. Kerala's Syrian Christians were here by 190 AD – a visitor at that time reported seeing a Hebrew copy of the gospel of St Matthew. Kerala's main Christian area is in the central part of the state, around Cochin and Kottayam. Hindus are mainly concentrated in southern Kerala, around Trivandrum.

The diminishing Jewish population of Kerala also made a very early appearance on the subcontinent. The 'black Jews' are said to have fled here in 587 BC when Nebuchadnezzar occupied Jerusalem. Their descendants have now intermarried with the Hindu population, but there is still a small number of the later 'white Jews' in Cochin. Kerala's Muslims are mainly in the northern part of the state, near Calicut.

NORTH OF CALICUT
Mahé (Pondy)

Mahé, 60 km north of Calicut, was a small French dependency handed over to India at the same time as Pondicherry. Today, its main function is to supply passing truck drivers with cheap Pondicherry beer. Mahé is still part of the Union Territory of Pondicherry.

The English factory established here by

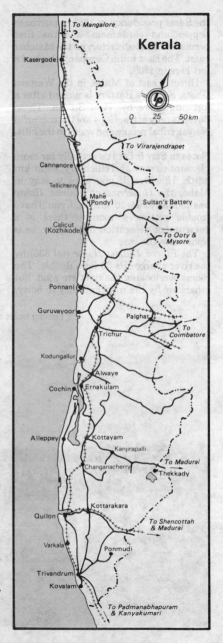

the Surat presidency in 1683 to purchase pepper and cardamom was the first permanent English factory on the Malabar coast. The East India Company also had a fort here in 1708.

Directly east of Mahé, in the Western Ghats, Sultan's Battery is named after a fort built here by Tipu Sultan. These days, its only attractions are the colourful Naiyak tribal people and walks in the hills.

Places to Stay & Eat It's actually far more pleasant to stay at Tellicherry, eight km north. However, if you want to stay in Mahé, the *Government Tourist Home* has doubles for Rs 20, although you'll have trouble getting a room if there is a government delegation in the area, as is sometimes the case.

The *Rivera Tourist Home* (tel 536) by the river charges Rs 30 for a double. The rooms overlooking the river are good, but others are by the road and they're noisy.

The hotel's *Rainbow Restaurant* has passable food.

Getting There & Away Mahé is too small to warrant a bus station. Instead, buses stop on the northern side of the bridge, outside the Rivera Tourist Home.

There are regular buses to Mangalore and Calicut.

Tellicherry

Tellicherry is a typical Keralan fishing village (and smells like it) right off the tourist circuit. Perhaps its biggest claim to fame is as the home town of many Indian circus performers. It's certainly not worth a special detour but, if you are making your way along the coast, it's a pleasant, unhurried place to stop for a night. Tourists are definitely a rare breed here.

The town's fishing fleet returns in the late afternoon, and the beach becomes an

Fishing boats at Tellicherry

animated impromptu fish market as people haggle over the catch.

Places to Stay & Eat The friendly *Paris Lodge* (tel 600) is five minutes walk from the bus stand and 10 minutes from the railway station (Rs 2 by auto-rickshaw). The rooms are clean, bright and airy and cost Rs 35 for a double with bath, Rs 110 with air-con. The *Taj Lodging House* (tel 22291) is quite OK; rooms with bath are Rs 22/29.

The *Hotel New West End* in the busy main shopping square has good non-vegetarian food – their fish curry is excellent. Also in the square, the *Lazza Ice Cream* shop has a variety of food, including delicious kulfi.

Getting There & Away Frequent trains and buses head up the coast to Mangalore and south to Calicut and Cochin.

CALICUT (Kozhikode) (population 650,000) Vasco da Gama landed at Calicut in 1498, becoming the first European to reach India via the sea route around the southern cape of Africa. His arrival heralded the period of Portuguese supremacy in India. The history of Calicut after 1498 was certainly dramatic. The Portuguese attempted to conquer the town, a centre of Malabar power under the Zamorins or 'Lords of the Sea', but their attacks in 1509 and 1510 were both repulsed, although the town was virtually destroyed in the latter assault. Tipu Sultan laid the whole region to waste in 1789, and British rule was established in 1792.

Despite its colourful past, there is nothing to see in Calicut. It does have a beach but, as is often the case in India, this is covered with human excrement and other refuse.

Information
There's a tourist information counter at the railway station, but what is there to ask?

The Indian Airlines office (tel 65482) is in the Eroth Centre on Bank Rd, close to the junction with Mavoor Rd (also known as Indira Gandhi Rd). These are Calicut's two main streets. The State Bank of India is also on Bank Rd in this area.

Places to Stay – bottom end
The *Metro Tourist Home* (tel 65216) is one of several hotels within a few minutes walk from the bus station on Mavoor Rd. Rooms here are good value at Rs 25/45, Rs 75/90 with air-con.

The *NCK Tourist Home* (tel 65331) is a large new place on Mavoor Rd, five minutes walk to the left as you exit the bus station. It's clean, with spacious rooms and a good vegetarian restaurant downstairs. Rooms cost Rs 37/62 with bath, Rs 88/121 with air-con. Also here is the *Hotel Sajina* (tel 64983), with rooms at Rs 33/55.

Closer to the railway station, the *Coronation Lodge* (tel 76051) on M P Rd has rooms for Rs 25/40, although it does fill up early. To get there from the railway station, turn left as you exit, then right at the T-junction. Ask for directions from there – it's only a couple of minutes walk. Finally, there are single/double *retiring rooms* at the railway station for Rs 35/50, and a six-bed dormitory at Rs 15 per person.

The *Hotel Foura* (tel 63601) is on Mavoor Rd, not far from the bus station. There are only three singles but lots of doubles, and rooms cost Rs 35/58. It's good value and the rooms on the upper three floors get the benefit of a sea breeze.

Moving up-market a bit, the *Hotel Hyson* (tel 65221), close to the Metro Tourist Home, is better again, and has double rooms for Rs 55, Rs 130 with air-con. There are no single rooms in this hotel.

Places to Eat
The *Ruchi Restaurant* in the Hotel Foura does a terrific vegetarian thali for Rs 6 which includes a sweet, three vegetable curries, curd and papadams. Next door to

the Foura, the *Hotel Sarovar* serves very mediocre non-vegetarian food.

The *Hotel Sea Shell* is a small restaurant in the bazaar area, tucked away at the top of a stairway near the Cosmopolitan Lodge. It serves good non-vegetarian food, including an excellent fish korma.

On Bank Rd, opposite the 'tank', the pleasant open-air *Park Restaurant* is open in the evenings when this area is lively with buskers and other footpath entertainers.

Getting There & Away

Air Indian Airlines has four flights a week to and from Bombay (Rs 925).

Bus The main bus station is on Mavoor Rd, a few minutes walk from Bank Rd. For a change, the timetable is in English, which greatly simplifies matters. There are regular departures to Bangalore, Mangalore, Mysore, Ooty, Madurai, Coimbatore, Pondicherry, Trivandrum, Alleppey, Cochin and Kottayam.

The bus to Ooty or Mysore climbs up and over the Western Ghats. Sit on the left for the best views of this spectacular scenery. The trip to Mysore takes 5½ hours.

Train The railway station is not far from the town centre and within walking distance of the bazaar area. It costs about Rs 3 by auto-rickshaw from the bus station and the hotels in the Bank Rd area.

Regular trains go north to Mangalore. It's a 222-km journey which takes three hours and costs Rs 31 in 2nd class, Rs 107 in 1st.

Heading south-east, there are trains via Palghat to Coimbatore, Bangalore, Madras and Delhi. Following the coast due south, it's five hours and 200 km south to Ernakulam at a cost of Rs 28 in 2nd class, and Rs 95 in 1st. The 414-km trip to Trivandrum takes 10 hours and costs Rs 51 in 2nd class, Rs 178 in 1st.

Getting Around

There's no shortage of auto-rickshaws in Calicut, but it is difficult to get the drivers to use the meters. It should only cost about Rs 3 from the railway station to the bus station or hotels on Bank Rd.

TRICHUR

Trichur, 74 km north of Ernakulam, has the old Temple of Guruvayur (Hindus only), a museum and a zoo with a notable collection of snakes. The annual Pooram festival, held in April-May, is one of the biggest in the south, with fireworks and colourful processions, including brightly decorated elephants.

Places to Stay & Eat

The *Hotel Elite International* (tel 21033) on Chemboottil Lane has rooms with bathroom for Rs 50/80, Rs 130/185 with air-con. The *Casino Hotel* (tel 24699) on T B Rd is slightly more expensive. The railway *retiring rooms* cost Rs 20/40.

The *Hotel Bharat* has 'state-of-the-art south Indian food', one traveller reported.

COCHIN & ERNAKULAM

Cochin population 800,000
Ernakulam population 160,000

With its wealth of historical associations and its beautiful setting on a cluster of islands and narrow peninsulas, the interesting city of Cochin reflects the eclecticism of Kerala perfectly. Here, you can see the oldest church in India, winding streets crammed with 500-year-old Portuguese houses, cantilevered Chinese fishing nets, a Jewish community whose roots go back to 1000 AD, a 16th-century synagogue, a palace built by the Portuguese and given to the Raja of Cochin (later renovated by the Dutch, it contains some of India's most beautiful murals) and a performance of the world-famous Kathakali dance-drama.

The older parts of Fort Cochin and Mattancherry are an unlikely blend of medieval Portugal, Holland and an

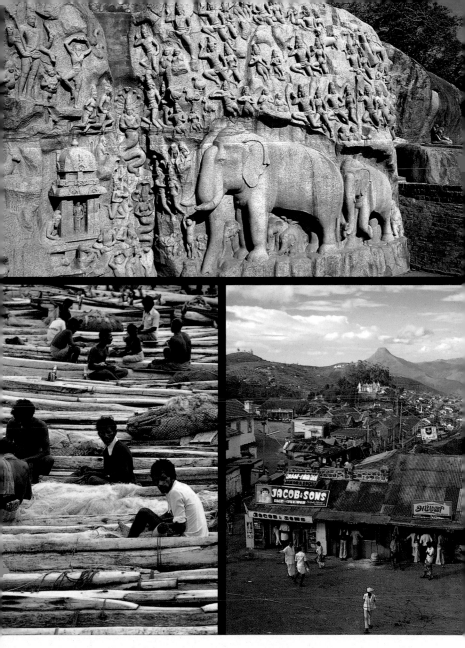

Tamil Nadu Top: Arjuna's Penance, Mahabalipuram (TW)
　　　Left: Fishing boats on the beach, Kanyakumari (HF)
　　　Right: Kodaikanal (HF)

Tamil Nadu Top: Krishna's Butterball, Mahabalipuram (TW)
Left: Temple priest, Trichy (HF)
Right: Vishnu's boar avatar, Mahabalipuram (TW)

English country village grafted onto the tropical Malabar coast – a strange contrast to the bright lights and big hotels of mainland Ernakulam.

Fort Cochin is also one of India's largest ports and a major naval base. On any day of the year, the misty silhouettes of huge merchant ships can be seen anchored off the point of Fort Cochin, waiting for a berth in the docks of Ernakulam or Willingdon Island. This artificial island, created with material dredged up when the harbour was deepened, also provides a site for the airport.

Orientation

Cochin consists of mainland Ernakulam, the islands of Willingdon, Bolgatty and Gundu in the harbour, Fort Cochin and Mattancherry on the southern peninsula, and Vypeen Island north of Fort Cochin, all linked by ferry. In addition, there are bridges and a road connecting Ernakulam with Willingdon Island and the Fort Cochin/Mattancherry peninsula. The railway station, bus station, Tourist Reception Centre and most hotels and restaurants are in Ernakulam.

Almost all the historical sites are in Fort

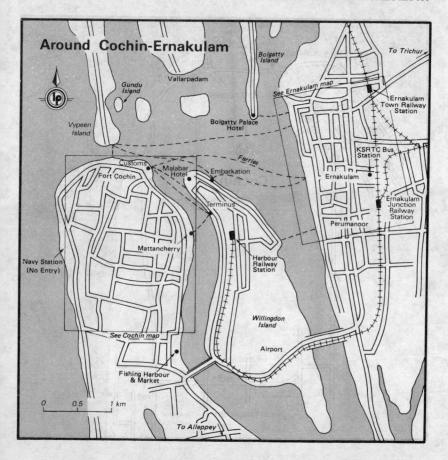

Cochin or Mattancherry, but the area's accommodation and restaurant facilities are limited to a few budget-type hotels. The airport is on Willingdon Island. At the tip of the island, opposite Fort Cochin, is the main tourist office and Cochin's top hotel, the Malabar.

Information

Tourist Offices The Tourist Reception Centre (tel 353234) on Shanmughan Rd in Ernakulam has friendly, helpful staff but not much literature. They'll organise

accommodation for you at the Bolgatty Palace Hotel and arrange your conducted boat cruise around the harbour. The office is open from 8 am to 6 pm.

The Government of Kerala tourist information centre is in the Old Collectorate building on Park Rd. It has a useful booklet entitled *Kerala – Travel Facts*, compiled by the Department of Tourism.

The Government of India tourist office (tel 6045) is next to the Malabar Hotel on Willingdon Island. The people here are friendly and helpful and offer a range of leaflets and maps.

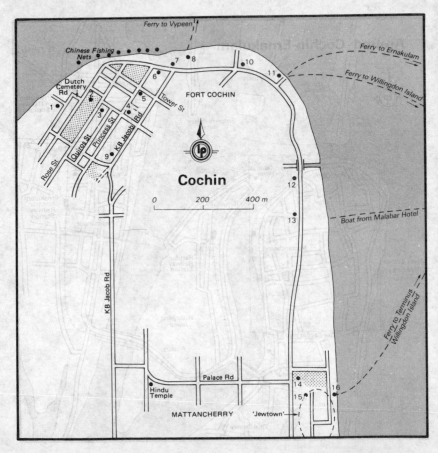

Post & Telephone The GPO (including the poste restante) is at Fort Cochin. The Ernakulam Telegraph Office is on the 2nd floor of the Jos Annex Building on M G Rd, next to the Anantha Bhavan Lodge. It's open 24 hours a day and international calls are connected fairly quickly.

Visa Extensions Apply for visa extensions at the office of the Commissioner of Police, at the northern end of Shanmughan Rd. An extension takes 10 days, which is totally ridiculous, *and* you have to leave your passport at the office during that time.

Airlines The Indian Airlines office (tel 352465) is in Durbar Hall Rd, next to the Bharat Tourist Home. Air India (tel 365485) is on M G Rd, a couple of blocks south of the Chinese Garden Restaurant.

Bookshops Bhavi Books on Convent Rd is an excellent bookshop.

Fort Cochin

St Francis Church This is India's oldest European-built church. Vasco da Gama, the first European to reach India by sailing around Africa, died in Cochin in 1524 and was buried here for 14 years before his remains were transferred to

1	PWD Bungalow
2	St Francis Church
3	GPO
4	Elite Hotel
5	Uncle Sam's Chinese Restaurant
6	Sabala Restaurant
7	Fort Cochin Bus Stand
8	Ferry to Vypeen
9	Santa Cruz Cathedral
10	Hotel Sea Gull
11	Ferry to Ernakulam
12	State Bank of India
13	Port View Hotel
14	Mattancherry Palace (Dutch Palace)
15	Jewish Synagogue
16	Ferry to Willingdon

Lisbon in Portugal. His tombstone still stands.

The church was built in 1503 by Portuguese Franciscan friars who accompanied the expedition led by Pedro Alvarez Cabral. The original structure was wood, but the church was rebuilt in stone around the mid-16th century – the earliest Portuguese inscription found in the church is dated 1562. In 1663, the Protestant Dutch captured Cochin and the church, which they later restored in 1779. After the occupation of Cochin by the British in 1795, it became an Anglican church and, at present, it is used by the Church of South India.

Also in Fort Cochin is the much later Santa Cruz Cathedral, which is worth a visit.

Chinese Fishing Nets Strung out along the tip of Fort Cochin opposite Vypeen Island, these cantilevered fishing nets were introduced by traders from the court of Kublai Khan. You can also see them along the backwaters between Cochin and Kottayam, and between Alleppey and Quilon. They're mainly used at high tide.

Mattancherry

Mattancherry Palace The palace was built by the Portuguese in 1557 and presented to the Cochin raja, Veera Kerala Varma (1537-61), as a gesture of goodwill (and, probably, as a means of securing trading privileges). It was substantially renovated by the Dutch after 1663, hence its other name, the 'Dutch' Palace. The double-storeyed quadrangular building surrounds a courtyard containing a Hindu temple. The central hall on the 1st floor was the Coronation Hall of the rajas of Cochin; on display are their dresses, turbans and palanquins.

The most important feature of this palace, however, is the astonishing murals in the bedchambers and other rooms, which depict scenes from the *Ramayana* and Puranic legends connected with Shiva, Vishnu, Krishna, Kumara and Durga. These murals are undoubtedly some of the most beautiful and extensive to be seen anywhere in India. You can pick up numerous Indian tourist pamphlets containing breathless descriptions of the murals at Ajanta but never see a mention of these, although they are one of the wonders of India. The Shiva temple in Ettumanur (a few km north of Kottayam) has similar murals.

The palace is open Sunday to Thursday from 10 am to 5 pm, closed Fridays. Entrance is free. Flash photography is prohibited, effectively precluding photography altogether, which is a great pity as there are no books or postcards for sale. The murals can be photographed quite well by holding your camera on the railing, wrote one visitor. There are three black-and-white photographs of the murals in the Archaeological Survey of India's booklet, *Monuments of Kerala* by H Sarkar (1978, Rs 3.25). Other books in which they're illustrated are *Cochin Murals* by V R Chitra & T N Srinivasan (Cochin, 1940), and *South Indian Paintings* by C Sivaramamurti (New Delhi, 1968).

The Jewish Synagogue Constructed in 1568, this is the oldest synagogue in the Commonwealth. An earlier one, built at Kochangadi in 1344, has since disappeared, although a stone slab from this earlier building, inscribed in Hebrew, can be found on the inner surface of the wall which surrounds the current synagogue.

The present building was destroyed by shelling during a Portuguese raid in 1662 and was rebuilt two years later when the Dutch took over Cochin. It's an interesting little place with hand-painted, willow-pattern floor tiles (no two alike) brought from Canton, China, in the mid-18th century by Ezekial Rahabi who had trading interests in that city. He was also responsible for the erection of the clock tower which tops the building.

The synagogue is open daily from 10 am to 12 noon and from 3 to 5 pm, except Saturdays and Jewish holidays. Entrance is Rs 0.50. The synagogue guardian is very friendly and keen to tell you about the history of the place and the Jewish community here, and to talk about what's happening in the rest of the world. He speaks fluent English.

This unexpected and isolated Jewish community dates back to the time of St Thomas the Apostle's voyage to India in AD 52. The first Jewish settlement was at Cranganore, north of Cochin. Like the Syrian Orthodox Christians, the Jews became involved in the trade and commerce of the Malabar coast – preserved in the synagogue are a number of copper plates inscribed, in an ancient script, with the grant of the village of Anjuvannam (near Cranganore) and its revenue to a Jewish merchant, Joseph Rabban, by King Bhaskara Ravi Varman I (962-1020). You may view these plates with the permission of the synagogue guardian.

The concessions given by Ravi Varman I included permission to use a palanquin and parasol – in those days the prerogative of rulers – and so, in effect, sanctioned the creation of a tiny Jewish kingdom. On Rabban's death, his sons fought each other for control of the 'kingdom' and this rivalry led to its break-up and the move to Mattancherry.

A lot of research has been done into this community. One particularly interesting study by an American professor of ethnomusicology found that the music of the Cochin Jews contained strong Babylonian influences and that their version of the Ten Commandments was almost identical to a Kurdish version housed in the Berlin Museum Archives. Naturally, there's also been much local influence and many of the hymns are similar to ragas.

The area around the synagogue is known as Jewtown and is one of the centres of the Cochin spice trade. Scores of small firms huddle together in old, dilapidated buildings and the air is filled with the pungent aromas of ginger, cardamom, cumin, tumeric and cloves.

Many Jewish names are visible on business premises and houses, but the community has diminished rapidly since Indian independence and now numbers less than 30. As there has been no rabbi within living memory, all the elders are qualified to perform religious ceremonies and marriages. There are many interesting curio shops on the street leading up to the synagogue.

Ernakulam

Kathakali Dancing The origins of India's most spectacular dance-drama go back some 500 years to a time when open-air performances were held in a temple courtyard or on the village green. There are over 100 different arrangements, all of them based on stories from the *Ramayana* and *Mahabharata*, those two epics of Indian mythology, and they were designed to continue well into the early hours of the morning. Since most visitors don't have the inclination to stay up all night, the centres which put on the dance in Ernakulam offer shortened versions lasting about 1½ hours.

Kathakali isn't simply another form of dancing – it incorporates elements of yoga and ayurvedic (traditional Indian) medicine. All the props are fashioned from natural materials – powdered minerals and the sap of certain trees for the bright facial make-up; the beaten bark of certain trees, dyed with fruits and spices, for wigs; coconut oil for mixing up the colours; burnt coconut oil for the black paint around the eyes; and eggplant flowers tucked under the eyelids to turn the whites of the eyes deep red. Usually, you're welcome to watch the make-up process before the dance – quite a show in its own right. The dancers are accompanied by two drummers and another musician, who plays finger cymbals. A government-run school, near Palghat in northern Kerala, teaches Kathakali dancing.

Both of the companies which put on performances start the evening with an explanation of the symbolism of the facial expressions, hand movements and ritualistic gestures involved in the dance-drama. This is followed by an actual dance-drama lasting about one hour. 'Bring mosquito coils', suggested one visitor. The centres offering Kathakali are:

The Cochin Cultural Centre (tel 37866), Durbar Hall Grounds, Durbar Hall Rd. Entry to the daily performances is Rs 25, plus a Rs 10 camera 'donation'. Advance booking is not required. The dance is held in the 'cultural centre' – a slapdash shed of bricks and fibrocement sheeting in front of the museum on Durbar Hall Rd.

Devan Gurukalum, in Kalathiparambil Lane near the Piazza Lodge. This centre is at Mr Devan's home and he gives an amusing preshow chat on dance history and a somewhat simplistic explanation of Hinduism. This is by far the better of the two shows and lasts from 7 to 8.30 pm; get there at 6 pm to see the make-up routine. Entry costs Rs 25.

Cochin Museum

The museum is housed in what was previously Durbar Hall on Durbar Hall Rd – an enormous building constructed in traditional Keralan style. Although it contains collections of 19th-century oil paintings, old coins, sculptures and Moghul paintings as well as exhibits from the Cochin royal family, it's hardly anything special. The museum is open daily, except Mondays and public holidays, from 9.30 am to 12 noon and 3 to 5.30 pm. Entry is free.

Gundu Island

The smallest island in Cochin harbour, Gundu Island is close to Vypeen Island. The only building on the island is a coir factory, where attractive doormats are made out of coconut fibre. You come across these mats all over Cochin. The only way to get there is on the Kerala Tourist Development Corporation boat tour.

Tours

The Kerala Tourist Development Corporation's daily conducted boat cruises around Cochin harbour visit Willingdon

Island, Mattancherry Palace, the Jewish Synagogue, Fort Cochin (including St Francis Church) and Bolgatty Island. The first tour is from 9 am to 1 pm, the second from 2 to 6 pm. This very worthwhile tour costs Rs 15.

For reservations, contact either the Tourist Reception Centre (tel 353234), Shanmughan Rd, Ernakulam, or the manager, Bolgatty Palace Hotel (tel 355003) Bolgatty Island. The tour starts and finishes at the Sealord boat jetty in front of the Sealord Hotel, Shanmughan Rd, Ernakulam. You can also board the boat at the tourist office jetty at Willingdon Island, 20 minutes after the start of each tour.

Places to Stay

The top-range hotels are in Ernakulam and on Willingdon Island. You'll find mid-range hotels at Ernakulam and Bolgatty Island and, if you want a budget hotel, try Ernakulam or Fort Cochin, although the choice is better in Ernakulam.

Places to Stay – bottom end

If the sleepy, laid-back atmosphere of the old part of the city appeals, head for Fort Cochin. There are only a few places, all very basic. Ernakulam is certainly more hectic than Fort Cochin but is still fairly easygoing.

Fort Cochin The friendly *Elite Hotel* (tel 25733), very close to St Francis Church, has double rooms with bath for Rs 44, or with common bathroom and toilet for Rs 25. The popular non-vegetarian cafe on the ground floor is excellent value. Nearby, the *Princess Lodge* is none too clean and the rooms are damp.

For the really impecunious, the *Port View Lodge* (tel 352140) is about halfway between Fort Cochin and Mattancherry, 10 minutes walk from the Embarkation ferry stop. It's one of the very few places in that area that can be classified as a budget hotel, although there are a few incredibly decrepit dosshouses along this road. The

1	High Court Jetty & Ferry to Bolgatty
2	Commissioner of Police
3	Vypeen Island Ferry Jetty
4	Sealord Jetty
5	Sealord Hotel & Sealord Restaurant
6	Post Office
7	Athul Jyoti Restaurant
8	State Bank of India
9	Hakoba Hotel
10	KTDC Tourist Reception Centre
11	Chick-Chow Restaurant
12	Hotel Blue Diamond
13	Modern Guest House
14	Hotel Abad Plaza & Regency Restaurant
15	Stadium
16	State Bus Stand
17	Ninan's Tourist Lodge
18	Hotel Luciya
19	Bhavi Books
20	Basoto Lodge
21	Deepak Lodge
22	Jetty for Ferries to Willingdon Island & Fort Cochin
23	Indian Coffee House
24	Biju's Tourist Home
25	GPO
26	Mini Stadium
27	Grand Hotel
28	Pandal Restaurant
29	Woodlands Hotel & Jaya Cafe
30	Geetha Lodge
31	Shiva Temple
32	Kerala Tourist Information Centre
33	Bharat Tourist Home
34	Indian Airlines
35	Museum & Cultural Centre
36	Anantha Bhavan Lodge
37	Indian Coffee House
38	Bimbi's & Khyba Restaurant
39	Hotel Sangeetha
40	Shaziya Hotel
41	Ernakulam Tourist Bungalow
42	Hotel KK International
43	Premier Tourist Home
44	Central Lodge
45	Piazza Lodge
46	Bus to Fort Cochin
47	Devan Gurukalum
48	Art Kerala
49	Chinese Garden Restaurant

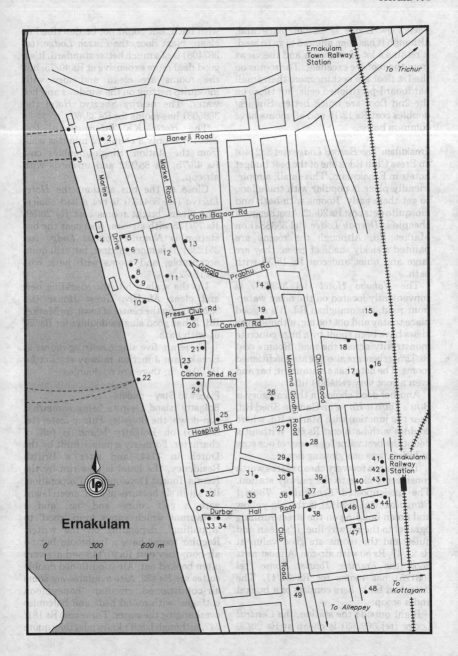

Ernakulam
Town Railway
Station

To Trichur

Banerji Road

Market Road

Cloth Bazaar Rd

Marine Drive

Gopala Prabhu Rd

Press Club Rd

Convent Rd

Canon Shed Rd

Hospital Rd

Mahatma Gandhi Road

Chittoor Road

Ernakulam
Railway
Station

Durbar Hall Road

Club Road

Ernakulam

0   300   600 m

To Kottayam

To Alleppey

Port View Lodge is an old place and, although it has been allowed to go to seed, it retains a lot of character and the views from the roof are excellent. The rooms on the 1st floor are nothing more than small hardboard-partitioned cells, but those on the 2nd floor are much better. Singles/doubles cost Rs 12/15 and all rooms have common baths.

Ernakulam The *Basoto Lodge* (tel 352140) on Press Club Rd is one of the best budget hotels in Ernakulam. This small, simple, friendly place is popular with travellers, so get there early. Rooms with bath and mosquito nets cost Rs 20/32. Another good cheapie is *Deepak Lodge* (tel 353882) on Market Rd. Although the rooms are painted a sickly shade of green, they are large and quiet and cost Rs 15/30 with bath.

The *Hakoba Hotel* (tel 353933) is conveniently located on the noisy waterfront road, Shanmughan Rd. It's a good place to stay and not too big, although the views have been spoilt by a huge concrete monstrosity across the road. Rooms cost Rs 32/54; there are also five air-conditioned rooms. The hotel has a restaurant, bar and even a (not very reliable) lift.

Another good choice in this category is *Biju's Tourist Home* on Cannon Shed Rd, near the junction with Market Rd, where doubles with bath cost Rs 66. 'Without a doubt the best value for money of our stay in India', was one glowing report.

There are a few very cheap places worth considering close to the railway station. The unsignposted *Ernakulam Tourist Bungalow* (tel 352412) is the big yellow and green building on the street running parallel to the railway line. It's clean and quiet and the rooms are good value at Rs 22/47, Rs 80 with air-con. Almost next door, the *Premier Tourist Home* (tel 368125) has rooms for Rs 31/47. The 'attached bath' here consists of a bucket and a scoop.

Right outside the station, the *Central Lodge* (tel 369263) is cheap at Rs 20/30 with bath, but could not be described as clean. Next door, the *Piazza Lodge* (tel 367408) is of a much better standard. It's a good deal more expensive at Rs 40/75, but the rooms are clean and airy with mosquito netting on the windows and hot water. The nearby *Shaziya Hotel* (tel 369508) has rooms for Rs 33/60.

The *Hotel KK International* (tel 366010) is only a couple of minutes walk from the station. Singles/doubles cost Rs 43/75, Rs 88/132 and upwards with air-con.

Close to the bus station, the *Hotel Luciya* (tel 354433) is not a bad choice. The clean, bright rooms cost Rs 29/59, Rs 77/125 with air-con. Also near the bus station is *Ninan's Tourist Lodge* (tel 351235). It is more modest, but still quite acceptable, and rooms with bath cost Rs 16/32.

Up the scale a bit, the sparkling new and clean *Modern Guest House* (tel 352130) is in the centre of town, on Market Rd. It has good singles/doubles for Rs 35/64 with bath.

There are five single *retiring rooms* at Ernakulam Junction railway station for Rs 30 each; there are no doubles.

Places to Stay – middle

Bolgatty Island Despite being somewhat run-down, the *Bolgatty Palace Hotel* (tel 355003) on Bolgatty Island is full of character. Formerly a palace built by the Dutch in 1744, and later a British Residency, the hotel is now run by the Kerala Tourist Development Corporation. It's set in six hectares of lush, green lawns with a golf course and bar, and a restaurant which varies from 'good' to 'appalling', depending on the writer! Regular rooms have a bathroom but no air-con; they cost Rs 97/145 and are very often booked out. Air-conditioned double suites are Rs 432. Also available are some air-conditioned circular 'honeymoon cottages' with round beds and balconies overhanging the water. These cost Rs 181/242, although I don't know why they quote a single tariff for a 'honeymoon cottage'! 'Staying in the honeymoon cottages is like having a honeymoon in a zoo – it could lead to divorce!' wrote one disgruntled guest.

A regular ferry (Rs 0.20) leaves the High Court Jetty every 20 minutes between 6 am and 10 pm but, if you want to get across at any other time, rowboats are available (price negotiable).

Fort Cochin Overlooking the harbour, the *Hotel Sea Gull* (tel 28128) is about halfway between the two ferry stops. The hotel has been created by converting a number of old houses and warehouses. Doubles (there are no singles) cost Rs 50, Rs 100 with air-con. They also have some windowless boxes which cost the same. The hotel has a bar and a restaurant from which you can watch the ships come and go.

The shabby *PWD Rest House* is rarely full. Its very spacious rooms cost Rs 30/50.

Ernakulam The *Bharat Tourist Home* (tel 353501) on Durbar Hall Rd is a good hotel and charges Rs 88/110, Rs 200 for doubles with air-con. Another very pleasant mid-range hotel is the *Hotel Blue Diamond* (tel 353221) on Market Rd, where singles/doubles cost Rs 60/121, Rs 88/154 with air-con. It has a roof garden, restaurant and air-conditioned bar, the rooms are pleasant and it's very good value. Furthermore, the staff are friendly.

The *Woodlands Hotel* (tel 351372) on M G Rd is good value. Rooms with bathroom are Rs 95/145, Rs 156/200 with air-con, and the hotel has an air-conditioned vegetarian restaurant. The *Hotel Sangeetha* (tel 368736) is on Chittoor Rd, not far from the railway station. Rooms here are very clean and spacious and cost Rs 55/100, Rs 120/145 with air-con. The *Hotel Ganaam* (tel 367123), behind the Sangeetha, has rooms for Rs 90/170, 140/205 with air-con.

Places to Stay – top end
Willingdon Island Cochin's best hotel, the *Malabar Hotel* (tel 6811), is superbly located at the tip of Willingdon Island, overlooking the harbour. It has recently been renovated and expanded, and the fabulous rooms, at Rs 660/770, have all the extras you'd expect in this price range. The Government of India tourist office is next door.

The *Casino Hotel* (tel 6821) has 35 rooms, starting at Rs 375/450. 'The mosquitoes were voracious, but slow fliers', reported one particularly observant visitor.

Ernakulam On Shanmughan Rd, the *Sealord Hotel* (tel 352682) has air-conditioned singles/doubles from Rs 200/265. The *Hotel Abad Plaza* (tel 361636) on M G Rd offers singles/doubles for Rs 300/350 and deluxe rooms for Rs 385/440, all with TV and video. This conveniently located hotel is centrally air-conditioned and has a seafood restaurant, as well as what they describe as a 'fast-food joint'.

Places to Eat
Ernakulam As is usual in Keralan towns, an *Indian Coffee House* offers good snacks and breakfasts. There are two in Ernakulam, one not far from the railway station and the other on the corner of Canon Shed Rd and Park Ave. They are popular with local people and always busy. The waiters are very quaint in their cummerbunds and shabby white uniforms.

Opposite the Indian Coffee House near M G Rd, the popular *Bimbi's* is a modern, self-serve, fast-food restaurant offering both Indian and western dishes. It has a huge sweet store in the front, and the more expensive air-conditioned *Khyber Restaurant* upstairs. Towards the railway station, on the same street, the *Shaziya Hotel* does good vegetarian meals for Rs 6 and various non-vegetarian Indian dishes, including an excellent fish curry for Rs 3, although the size of the piece of fish makes sardines look enormous. They also have Chinese dishes.

Another good 'meals' place is the *Jaya*

Cafe, in the Woodlands Hotel on M G Rd. A vegetarian thali costs Rs 9 and their lassis are excellent. There's an air-conditioned dining hall too. The *Chick-Chow Restaurant* on Broadway has good chicken dishes and also serves western breakfasts.

For a western escape, the *Pandal Restaurant* opposite the Grand Hotel on M G Rd gets the thumbs up from many travellers. It serves good pizza, hamburgers and banana splits, as well as absolutely superb north Indian food, although the portions are stingy. Also relatively expensive, the *Chinese Garden Restaurant* is just off M G Rd, south of Durbar Hall Rd. The service here is very attentive and the food is good. Expect to pay around Rs 30 to Rs 50 per person at either of these places.

At the *Sealord Restaurant* on Shanmughan St, fish stuffed with grapes and baked cheese is delicious. This is a good place for a splurge and even has good live western music in the evenings!

On the 2nd floor of the Abad Plaza Hotel, the classy but reasonably priced *Regency Restaurant* offers good Indian, Chinese and western food.

Fort Cochin The eating options in Fort Cochin are severely limited. The very popular *Elite Hotel*, near St Francis Church, is recommended for its good non-vegetarian meals at Rs 3, particularly the fish curry.

Uncle Sam's Chinese Restaurant is nearby; it's only open in the evenings. The government-run *Sabala Restaurant*, across the road from the fishing nets, does some good food, although the service is slow.

In the Mattancherry Palace area, *Cool of Cools* serves great fresh fruit juices for just a few rupees.

Willingdon Island The plush *Rice Boats* restaurant in the Malabar Hotel has a lunchtime buffet from 12 noon to 3 pm.

You can pig out for Rs 73, but think twice before ordering a beer – it costs Rs 44!

Getting There & Away
Air Indian Airlines has three or four flights daily between Bombay and Cochin for Rs 1010. There are also regular flights to Bangalore (Rs 395), Goa (Rs 635), Delhi (Rs 1930), Madras (Rs 655) and Trivandrum (Rs 225).

Vayudoot has flights to Mangalore (Rs 465), Madras (Rs 655), Coimbatore (Rs 195) and Madurai (Rs 290).

Bus The bus stand is right by the railway tracks in Ernakulam, between the railway stations. Because Ernakulam is almost in the middle of Kerala, the routes of many buses starting in places north and south of here pass through Ernakulam. It's often possible to get a seat on these buses, but you can't make advance reservations. You simply have to join the scrum when it turns up. All the buses listed in this section originate in Ernakulam.

You can make reservations up to five days in advance on many of the buses which start in Ernakulam. The timetable is in English as well as Malayalam and the station staff are usually quite helpful. The monthly booklet *Time Table* (Travel & Tourist Guide), published by Jaico, is helpful. It costs Rs 2.50 and is available at the bus station and at hotels and bookshops around town. It gives a complete rundown of the schedules, journey times and fares for all KSRTC bus routes, together with details of buses for which it's possible to make advance reservations. It also contains train and air schedules, and a list of the better hotels.

Going South More than a dozen buses a day go to Alleppey (62 km), including a couple of limited-stop buses. You can also get to Alleppey on any of the express buses heading south to Quilon and Trivandrum. The fare is Rs 8 and the journey takes 1½ hours.

There are numerous Fast Passenger

services to Quilon, 150 km away, the first at 9.40 am. The fare for the four-hour journey is Rs 21. You can reach Quilon at other times of the day by taking a Trivandrum bus via Alleppey.

There are two routes to Trivandrum (221 km), one via Alleppey and the other via Kottayam. About 15 buses take the Alleppey route daily, another four the Kottayam route. The fare is Rs 29 by Fast Passenger (6½ hours) and Rs 34 by Express (about five hours).

A bus leaves at 10 am each morning on the 302-km journey to Kanyakumari. It takes nine hours and costs Rs 46.

Going East Four buses a day make the 324-km trip to Madurai in Tamil Nadu (Rs 44, 9¼ hours). To Madras, there's one bus daily at 3.30 pm (Rs 86, 16 hours).

There are about 10 buses a day to Kottayam (76 km). The fare is Rs 10 and the journey takes 2¼ hours. To Thekkady (Kumily) (192 km), there are three buses daily, the most convenient leaving at 6.30 am. The fare for the seven-hour journey is Rs 27.50.

Going North Interstate express buses originate in Ernakulam; they make the 565-km trip to Bangalore in 15 hours at a cost of Rs 82.

There are also three buses daily to Calicut (Kozhikode). The 219-km trip takes 6½ hours and the fare is Rs 32. The 360-km trip to Palghat takes 4½ hours and costs Rs 23. There are four or five buses daily.

Train Ernakulam has two stations; Ernakulam Junction is more central than Ernakulam Town. Very few trains go as far as the Cochin Harbour station on Willingdon Island. The booking office at Ernakulam Junction station has no tourist quota and is usually busy. It is open from 7 am to 1 pm and 1.30 to 7.30 pm. A quaint sign inside says: 'Only self, relatives, servants or peons of travelling party will be allowed to form the queue.'

The weekly Himasagar Express connects Delhi and Ernakulam. The 2833-km trip

takes 56 hours and costs Rs 183 in 2nd class, Rs 767 in 1st.

The 221-km trip to Trivandrum takes four hours on the Vanchinad Express. The train leaves at 6 am and costs Rs 31 in 2nd class, Rs 107 in 1st. In the opposite direction, it leaves Trivandrum at 5.20 pm. This is a very fast train, stopping only in Kottayam and Quilon.

Ernakulam to Bangalore is a 629-km trip taking 14 hours. The fare is Rs 67 in 2nd class, Rs 242 in 1st on the Cochin-Ahmedabad Express. Bombay is 1841 km and 35 hours away on the three-times-weekly Netravati Express. The trip costs Rs 134 in 2nd class, Rs 542 in 1st. The daily Cochin Express to Madras takes 14 hours to cover the 708 km at Rs 73 in 2nd class, Rs 264 in 1st.

If you're heading to or from Ooty, there are quite a few expresses which stop at Coimbatore. The 198-km trip takes about six hours and costs Rs 28 in 2nd class, Rs 95 in 1st.

The Malabar Express makes a daily run along the Kerala coast from Mangalore to Trivandrum, through Calicut, Trichur, Ernakulam, Kottayam and Quilon. Other trains follow part of this coastal route.

Getting Around

Bus & Auto-Rickshaw There are no convenient bus services between Fort Cochin and the Mattancherry Palace/Jewish Synagogue, but it's a pleasant half-hour walk through the busy warehouse area along the port-side road. Auto-rickshaws are also available.

In Ernakulam, auto-rickshaws are the most convenient mode of transport. The trip from the bus station to the tourist reception centre on Shanmughan Rd should cost about Rs 3 but, unfortunately, the drivers have a strong aversion to using the meters.

The buses are fairly good and cheap – minimum fare is Rs 0.50 for a long journey, such as Hotel Hakoba to the airport. An auto-rickshaw on this route costs Rs 12.

If you have to get to Fort Cochin after the ferries stop running, catch a bus in Ernakulam on M G Rd, just south of Durbar Hall Rd. The fare is Rs 1.40. Auto-rickshaws will try to charge an outrageous Rs 50, but the buses run until at least 9.30 pm.

Taxi Taxis charge round-trip fares between the islands, even though you only go in one direction.

A taxi from Ernakulam to the airport costs Rs 25.

Ferry This is the main form of transport between the various parts of Cochin. The ferry stops are all named, which helps to identify them on the timetable at Ernakulam. The stop on the northern side of Willingdon Island is called Embarkation, the one around the corner opposite Mattancherry is Terminus; this is not the tourist office and Malabar Hotel stop. The main stop at Fort Cochin is known as Customs; the other one (for Vypeen Island) is unnamed.

Ernakulam to Mattancherry via Fort Cochin (Customs) & Willingdon Island (Terminus). This, the most useful ferry, runs 30 times daily from 6.30 am to 9.40 pm. The fare to both Fort Cochin and Mattancherry is Rs 0.80.

Ernakulam to Vypeen Island via Willingdon Island (Embarkation). Ferries run every 15 to 30 minutes between 5.30 am and 10.30 pm. The fare to Vypeen is Rs 0.80. There are also ferries to Vypeen from near the Police Station on Shanmughan Rd.

Fort Cochin (Customs) to Malabar Hotel & Tourist Office Ferries leave approximately once every half-hour, or you can take a motorised boat for Rs 3 per person.

Fort Cochin to Vypeen Island Ferries cross this narrow gap virtually nonstop from 6 am until 10 pm. There is also a vehicular ferry every half-hour or so.

KOTTAYAM

Kottayam was a centre for the Syrian Christians of Kerala and there are several of their churches, including Cheria Palli and Vallia Palli, about five km north-west of the railway station. Today, Kottayam is also a centre for Indian rubber production. Its main street is busy and colourful.

As there are direct buses from here to Periyar Wildlife Sanctuary, as well as ferries to Alleppey, you may well find yourself passing through. There is a regular ferry service (more than 10 boats a day) through the lagoons from Alleppey to Kottayam – a fascinating alternative to the Quilon backwater trip. Many people think that this trip is actually more interesting because the scenery is more varied.

Places to Stay

The *Hotel Ambassador* (tel 3293) is on K K Rd, 15 minutes walk from the bus station. It's good value for money at Rs 32/53 for singles/doubles with bath, Rs 75 with air-con. The hotel is set back off the road, so the driveway is easy to miss.

Almost opposite the bus station on T B Rd, the basic *Anurag Lodge* is OK for an overnight stay. Rooms cost Rs 25/40. *Kaycees Lodge* (tel 3440), on YMCA Rd near the central square, has good rooms with bath and telephone for Rs 30/50.

The railway station *retiring rooms* cost Rs 25/40, but there's no dormitory.

For something better, try the *Anjali Hotel* (tel 3661) on K K Rd, also near the square. It has air-conditioned rooms only, and these cost Rs 132/190 with bath.

Places to Eat

An *Indian Coffee House* a couple of doors along from the Anurag Lodge serves the usual snacks and breakfast. It's open from 8 am to 9 pm. A bit further along the street, the *Hotel Black Stone* has good vegetarian food.

The *Hotel Vysak* on K K Rd, just up from the Hotel Anjali, serves non-vegetarian meals. The railway station has vegetarian and non-vegetarian 'refreshment rooms', although the menus are a bit limited.

Getting There & Away

Bus The busy bus station is in the centre of town and, as at Cochin, the timetable is in English. Most of the buses are coming through from somewhere else, so you may have to sharpen your elbows to get a seat.

There are plenty of buses to Trivandrum and Cochin, and six daily to Thekkady (and Periyar, four hours), three of which continue on to Madurai (seven hours).

Train Kottayam is well served by express trains running between Trivandrum and Cochin.

Boat Ten boats daily make the 2½-hour trip to Alleppey, the first at 6.30 am and the last at 8.30 pm. This interesting trip is good if you don't have the time or the inclination for the longer one between Quilon and Alleppey.

Getting Around

The railway station, bus station and ferry jetty are well apart, so you need to catch an auto-rickshaw from one to another. An auto-rickshaw from the railway station to the ferry (ask for 'jetty') is Rs 6; it's Rs 3 from the bus station to the ferry.

The bus station is very central but, from either the ferry or train, you'll need to take an auto-rickshaw into the centre. A map on a signboard at the entrance to the GPO gives you a good idea of the town layout.

AROUND KOTTAYAM
Kumarakom

Sixteen km west of Kottayam is a KTDC *Tourist Complex* on Vembanad Lake. The hotel is actually a British plantation family's old house. There's plenty of birdlife and rubber is still processed.

PERIYAR WILDLIFE SANCTUARY

This 800-square-km sanctuary in the Thekkady district, on the Tamil Nadu border, is one of the most important in India. Once, you could reasonably expect to see elephants, bison, antelope, sambar, wild boar, monkeys and, if you were very lucky, those elusive tigers. These days, wildlife sightings are usually limited to a few elephants and bison, especially if you only take the sightseeing boat around the lake. One guide said he hasn't seen a tiger since 1976. Unless you are travelling between the Kerala coast and Madurai, it's hardly worth the long haul up from the coast just for this.

The park is centred around a large artificial lake, and there's a choice of private or KTDC accommodation. Unfortunately, if this is as far as you get, you won't see much in the way of wildlife, as there's too much human activity and traffic noise around the lodges. Indeed, at weekends, they're inundated by day trippers and tourist coaches, and the only things you will hear are transistor radios and the ape-like noises of fellow human beings.

Elephants are the animals you're most likely to see although, as with any wildlife sanctuary, it's quite possible to see nothing at all. They're worth seeking at the right time of year.

If you don't have four or five days to spare, you'll have to take one of the launch trips down the lake. These are OK as far as they go, but you'll be lucky to see much in the way of game. 'As soon as a shy animal sticks its head up,' reported one visitor, 'all aboard shout and scream until it goes again'.

It's advisable to bring warm clothes and waterproof clothing to Periyar. Kumily is the nearest place to buy supplies if you're going to stay in one of the forest rest houses/observation towers, although these are booked out weeks in advance.

The best time for a visit is between September and May.

Information & Orientation

Periyar means the whole park; Thekkady is used to refer to the area where Aranya Nivas and Periyar House are located. Kumily is a separate village with accommodation, restaurant facilities and

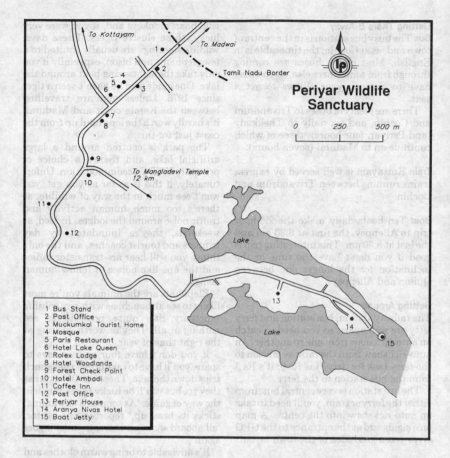

Periyar Wildlife Sanctuary

0   250   500 m

To Kottayam

To Madwai

Tamil Nadu Border

To Mangaladevi Temple
12 km

Lake

Lake

1 Bus Stand
2 Post Office
3 Muckumkal Tourist Home
4 Mosque
5 Paris Restaurant
6 Hotel Lake Queen
7 Rolex Lodge
8 Hotel Woodlands
9 Forest Check Point
10 Hotel Ambadi
11 Coffee Inn
12 Post Office
13 Periyar House
14 Aranya Nivas Hotel
15 Boat Jetty

a bus station. These three place names tend to be used synonymously and confusingly.

The buses stop at the station in Kumily and continue down to the lake, to the Aranya Nivas Hotel.

The tourist office at the Hotel Ambadi, between Kumily and the lake, is not a government office and is just an attempt by the hotel to attract custom. The staff member's local knowledge is strictly limited – he tried to convince me that the Mangaladevi Temple was 60 km away.

Mangaladevi Temple

A visit to this temple, 28 km from Kumily, is an interesting excursion. Although the temple is just a few ruins, the views are magnificent. You can hire a bicycle and ride there, but it's uphill all the way (coast back). Alternatively, rent a jeep (about Rs 150) for the trip – three to four hours with a lunch stop.

Places to Stay

Thekkady The Kerala Tourist Development Corporation runs three hotels in the park and, if you're visiting on a weekend, advance reservations are necessary.

Periyar House (tel Kumily 26) is the cheapest of the three and is very popular so, unless you get there early or make advance reservations, it will almost certainly be full, although you can be lucky. Singles/doubles cost Rs 41/94. The restaurant serves good vegetarian and non-vegetarian food and, considering you have no choice, the prices are reasonable.

Aranya Nivas (tel Kumily 23) is considerably more expensive – it offers ordinary, deluxe and VIP rooms with prices ranging from Rs 180/270 to Rs 400/600. There's a restaurant, bar, postal and banking facilities and a handicrafts showroom. The Aranya Nivas is at the end of the road leading into the park from Kumily. Periyar House is about half a km back along the road.

The most expensive of the three hotels, the *Lake Palace* (tel Kumily 24), is on the lake shore, a long way into the park. If you can afford it (doubles with full board are Rs 765), this is a delightful place to stay and you can actually see animals from your room. There is a restaurant, bar, postal and banking facilities and a handicrafts showroom. To stay at the Lake Palace, you must be at the Aranya Nivas launch jetty by 4 pm at the latest. The ferry trip is included in the tariff.

There are observation towers and forest rest houses in the park itself. Ask at the boat jetty about their availability.

If possible, try to book government accommodation at Periyar in advance. You can do this at any Kerala tourist office.

Kumily If the government places are full, or you want something cheaper, stay in Kumily. The four km to the lake make a pleasant shady walk, or you can hire a bicycle or catch a share jeep.

There's a fair selection of cheap accommodation in Kumily. One of the better choices is the *Muckumkal Tourist Home* (tel 70) on the main street (it's virtually a one-street town), a couple of

minutes walk from the bus station. The hotel has its own generator, which is a mixed blessing if you're in one of the back rooms as it makes an incredible racket when switched on. The rooms cost Rs 27/42 with bath.

The *Rolex Lodge* (tel 81), on the road to the park, has basic rooms with bath for Rs 30/40. Close by, the *Hotel Woodlands* (tel 77) is a bit gloomy but, at Rs 15/25 with bath, it's the cheapest around.

The *Hotel Lake Queen* (tel 84) is the largest building in town. Although it's popular with Indian holidaymakers, you can usually find space here. Rooms cost Rs 25/50. Closer to the park, 500 metres from Kumily, the *Hotel Ambadi* (tel 11) is at the forest checkpost. The cottages here are not all that old, but little time appears to be spent on maintenance. They cost Rs 80, or there are two four-bed rooms for Rs 60.

Places to Eat

If you're staying in Thekkady, the government lodges have reasonable food. Halfway between Thekkady and Kumily, the outdoor *Coffee Inn* has a good selection of music and good travellers' food. In the evenings, they serve fabulous home-made brown bread with honey. It's open from 7 am to 10 pm and, in the tradition of popular Indian travellers' restaurants, the food takes a while to arrive. Take a torch if you eat here at night – it can be a dark walk back to Kumily or Thekkady.

The restaurant at the *Hotel Ambadi* is quite good and you can expect to pay about Rs 50 for a full meal for two.

The tiny *Paris Restaurant* in the main street has only two tables, but the food is good and it's popular with travellers. Try the real Italian pasta here. For a vegetarian meal, the dining hall in the *Muckumkal Lodge* is OK.

Getting There & Away

Bus The bus station in Kumily is just a bit of spare land at the northern edge of town, near the barrier on the state border. It's chaotic when more than three buses are there at once.

All buses originating in Kumily start and finish at Aranya Nivas by the lake, but also stop at the bus station.

There are direct connections with Kottayam (six daily, four hours), Ernakulam (three daily, six hours), Trivandrum (three daily, eight hours) and Kovalam (one daily, nine hours) in Kerala, as well as buses to Kodaikanal (one daily, six hours) and Madurai (four daily, four hours) in Tamil Nadu.

Getting Around
Jeeps down to the lake cost Rs 20 for the vehicle. If you pay on a Rs 2 per person basis, you have to wait for the jeep to fill up. It's also possible to walk or, better still, rent a bicycle in the main street of Kumily. There's not much traffic on this road.

The launches operating on the lake supposedly run to schedule but, if that's the case, the schedule must be infinitely flexible. Basically, it's a matter of paying your Rs 7 and waiting for the boat to fill up, which can take over an hour. When you finally get under way, the tour lasts for two hours. The level of the lake has been steadily dropping in the last few years and, if the trend continues much longer, the launches may stop running altogether.

The Aranya Nivas Hotel rents boats for Rs 150 per hour. This is a better option than the organised tours if you can get a few people together to share the cost.

OTHER SANCTUARIES
Thattekkad Bird Sanctuary is 20 km from Kothamangalam, on the Ernakulam to Munnar road.

The Parambikulam Wildlife Sanctuary, 48 km south of Palghat, stretches around the Parambikulam, Thunacadavu and Peruvaripallam dams – there are lots of crocodiles in the dam reservoirs. There are *forest rest houses* at Thunacadavu, the

sanctuary headquarters, and at Thellikal and Elathode. For more details and reservations, contact the Divisional Forest Officer (tel Pollachi 33), Teak Plantation Division, Thunacadavu, via Pollachi.

ALLEPPEY (population 210,000)
Like Quilon, this is a pleasant, easygoing market town surrounded by coconut-palm plantations and built on the canals which service the coir industry of the backwaters. While there's precious little to see in Alleppey for most of the year, there is one event which you should not miss if you're anywhere in the vicinity on the second Saturday of August. This is the snakeboat race for the Nehru Cup. On this day, scores of long, low-slung dugouts with high decorated sterns and up to 100 rowers compete for the cup, watched from the banks by thousands of spectators. The only reasons to pass through here on any other day of the year are, of course, to make the backwater trip to Quilon or, if you're coming from Quilon, to stay here overnight before heading further north. For full details of the unforgettable backwaters trip, refer to the section on Quilon.

Alleppey is infamous for its drinking water – dysentery is a speciality. Even if you normally drink the tap water in other places, it's advisable to give it a miss here.

Orientation
The bus station and boat jetty are conveniently close to each other on the canal, and there are plenty of hotels within walking distance.

Places to Stay – bottom end
There are a few hotels worth trying just north of the canal. The cheap and habitable *Sheeba Lodge* has doubles for Rs 30. The *Karthika Tourist Home* (tel 2554) in the same area is good value; its large rooms with bath cost Rs 15/30.

Right opposite the boat jetty, the *Sree*

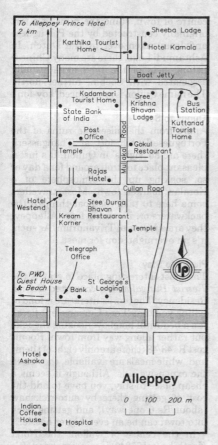

To Alleppey Prince Hotel 2 km

Sheeba Lodge

Karthika Tourist Home

Hotel Kamala

Boat Jetty

Kadambari Tourist Home

Sree Krishna Bhavan Lodge

Bus Station

State Bank of India

Kuttanad Tourist Home

Post Office

Temple

Gokul Restaurant

Rajas Hotel

Mullakal Road

Cullan Road

Hotel Westend

Sree Durga Bhavan Restaurant

Kream Korner

Temple

Telegraph Office

To PWD Guest House & Beach

St George's Lodging

Bank

Hotel Ashoka

Alleppey

0   100   200 m

Indian Coffee House

Hospital

The friendly new *Hotel Komala* (tel 3631), north of the canal, is not the cheapest in town at Rs 35/55, but it is clean and offers good value for money.

Close to the beach and a Rs 4 rickshaw ride from the centre of town, the *PWD Guest House* is a good place to stay. Rooms cost Rs 30/45 and meals are available for Rs 6 if ordered in advance.

Places to Stay – middle

The *Kuttanad Tourist Home*, between the bus station and boat jetty, is a brand-new place where double rooms cost around Rs 100 with bath.

Places to Stay – top end

Two km north of town is the *Alleppey Prince Hotel* (tel 3752). All the rooms have air-con, bath and telephone. The hotel boasts the town's only swimming pool although, at the time of writing, it was nothing more than a slimy green frog pond. Rooms cost Rs 275/330, but this is negotiable if business is slow.

Places to Eat

The pleasant *Indian Coffee House* is 15 minutes walk south of the southern canal, opposite the hospital. As usual, the waiters display a touch of the Raj in their white uniforms, cummerbunds and frilly turbans. They serve cheap non-vegetarian food and excellent real coffee – of course – and prices are very reasonable.

The *Arun Restaurant* in the Komala Hotel, on the other side of the canal bridge, is the best eatery in town. For cheap non-vegetarian food, the small *Kream Korner* restaurant on Cullan Rd does good chicken dishes. On the same road, the non-vegetarian *Rajas Hotel* is also cheap.

On the main street, the *Gokul Restaurant* serves good vegetarian meals and dosas.

Getting There & Away

Bus There are eight to 10 buses to Quilon each day and at least 30 to Trivandrum. About 40 buses daily go to Ernakulam;

Krishna Bhavan Lodge (tel 3453) has small, basic rooms around a courtyard. It's OK (just) for a night's stay and costs Rs 15/25.

On the main street, right in the centre of town, the *Kadambari Tourist Home* (tel 4210) is new, clean and well worth the Rs 20/35 charged for a room with bath.

St George's Lodging (tel 3373) is on the southern of the two canals, 15 minutes walk from the boat jetty and bus station. It's cheap at Rs 20/39 with bath, but the maintenance is minimal and the place looks decidedly shabby these days.

the 1½ to two-hour trip costs Rs 10. If you are heading for Fort Cochin rather than Ernakulam, you can get off this bus just before the bridge which connects Cochin and Willingdon Island. Take a local bus or auto-rickshaw from there into either Mattancherry or Fort Cochin. This saves you a lot of messing about with ferries when you get to Ernakulam.

There are also daily buses to Cannanore, Calicut (Kozhikode) and Palghat.

Boat See the Quilon section for details of the backwater trip.

Boats to Kottayam take 2½ hours to cross Lake Vembanad and cost Rs 3. There are about 10 boats daily and they give a short taste of the backwaters.

Another good trip is to Changanacherry, on the road and railway line 18 km south of Kottayam, 78 km north of Quilon. There are about 10 boats daily which take three hours and cost Rs 3.50. They are especially good if you are heading south, as there is only a night service to Quilon and no indication that the daytime boat will be reinstated.

QUILON (population 170,000)
Nestled amongst coconut palms and cashew tree plantations on the edge of Ashtamudi Lake, Quilon is a typical small Keralan market town, with old wooden houses whose red-tiled roofs overhang winding streets. If you're coming up from the south, it's also the gateway to the backwaters of Kerala. The trip by boat to Alleppey through these backwaters is a unique and fascinating experience.

Quilon dates back many centuries and, in fact, the Malayalam era is calculated from the founding of this town in the 9th century. Quilon's history is interwoven with the rivalry between the Portuguese, Dutch and English for control of commodities grown in this part of the subcontinent, and of the trade routes across the Indian Ocean.

At Thangasseri, only three km from the centre of town, stand the ruins of a fort originally constructed by the Portuguese and later taken over by the Dutch. In Ashtamudi Lake, there are many Chinese fishing nets of the type more usually associated with Cochin, further north. The name Quilon is pronounced 'koy-lon'.

Things to See
Apart from the miserable ruins of the Portuguese/Dutch fort at Thangasseri, there are no 'sights' in Quilon. It's just a pleasant place to stroll around for a day or so, soaking up the atmosphere of a Keralan market town. Most travellers come here to take the boat through the backwaters or, if coming from Alleppey, they are en route to Trivandrum. As such, it's an overnight stop for most.

Places to Stay
The most interesting place to stay is the *Tourist Bungalow* – a converted British Residency. The tourist literature is fond of telling you that 'Lord Curzon slept here'. It's a beautiful hotel overlooking the lake but rather a long way from town. Rooms cost Rs 43/48 (there are only eight of them) and, while meals are available, they're on the expensive side. Although it seems a cheap place to stay, you have to add the cost of getting there by auto-rickshaw (about Rs 6 one way), and getting back into town can be an even bigger hassle.

In the centre of Quilon, the *Hotel Karthika* (tel 76240) is recommended. It's a large place built around a central courtyard. Whoever did the interior decorating should be shot, or made to stay in one of the rooms – some are painted in the most horrendous and depressing colour schemes, although others are quite OK. There is mosquito netting on the windows (a big plus) and all rooms have a bath. The tariff is Rs 33/51.

The *Iswarya Lodge* (tel 78101) in Main St charges Rs 32/50 for good-sized rooms, Rs 72/111 with air-con. The cheap *Mahalakshmi Lodge* is directly opposite the bus station. Rooms cost Rs 12/20 with

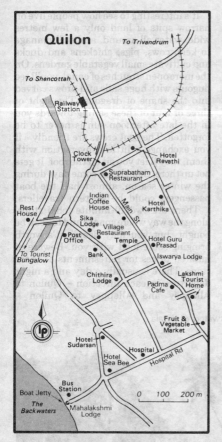

Quilon

To Trivandrum

To Shencottah

Railway Station

Clock Tower

Hotel Revathi

Suprabatham Restaurant

Indian Coffee House

Hotel Karthika

Rest House

Sika Lodge

Village Restaurant

Post Office

Temple

Hotel Guru Prasad

Bank

Iswarya Lodge

To Tourist Bungalow

Chithira Lodge

Padma Cafe

Lakshmi Tourist Home

Fruit & Vegetable Market

Hotel Sudarsan

Hospital

Hotel Sea Bee

Hospital Rd

Bus Station

Boat Jetty

The Backwaters

Mahalakshmi Lodge

0   100   200 m

Main St

located near the bus station and boat jetty. Singles/doubles with bath cost Rs 43/66, Rs 82/110 with air-con. Similar in standard is the *Hotel Sudarsan* (tel 3755), between the post office and the boat jetty. It's looking a bit tatty these days but is still a good place. Rooms with bath and hot water cost Rs 44/66, Rs 115/180 with air-con. The hotel has two restaurants and a bar.

The *retiring rooms* at the station cost Rs 20/30; a dorm bed is Rs 10.

Places to Eat

The restaurant on the ground floor of the *Iswarya Lodge* has good vegetarian food. The *Hotel Guru Prasad*, Main St, is another vegetarian place which serves excellent food. It does delicious banana shakes for Rs 2. The *Indian Coffee House* on Main St is, as usual, good value. Opposite, the *Azad Hotel* does good vegetarian meals.

The *Village Restaurant*, next to the Sika Lodge, is only open in the evenings. It serves excellent chicken dishes. If you are staying at the Karthika, the *Suprabatham Restaurant* near the clock tower is a convenient place to eat. It's a typical south Indian 'meals' restaurant.

Quilon is a cashew-growing centre and, at Rs 10 per 100 grams roasted and salted, the nuts are cheaper than you'll find anywhere else – a good buy.

Getting There & Away

Bus Many of the buses leaving the Quilon bus station are en route from somewhere else. There are a couple of dozen buses to Trivandrum daily and the two-hour trip costs Rs 11.

Half a dozen buses a day go to Alleppey or Shencottah, and there are about 15 to Ernakulam. Plenty of other buses go further up the coast and to intermediate towns.

The daily service to Kumily (Periyar Wildlife Sanctuary) takes eight hours. If you catch this bus, you may have to change at Kottayam.

common bath and, basically, you get what you pay for. Another ultra-basic place is the *Padma Cafe* in Main St. It has singles for only Rs 12. Also for the impecunious is the *Sika Lodge* (tel 7096), about 100 metres down the road from the bridge across the river. It's reasonable value at Rs 20/35 with bath and fan, although the rooms are fairly small and, according to one guest, 'the fans suck you to the ceiling'. There is a fairly good vegetarian restaurant on the ground floor.

The *Hotel Sea Bee* (tel 3631) is relatively new and very conveniently

Train Quilon is 156 km south of Cochin. The three or four-hour train trip costs Rs 24 in 2nd class, Rs 80 in 1st. The Trivandrum Mail from Madras goes through Quilon, as does the Bombay to Kanyakumari Express and the Mangalore to Trivandrum coastal service.

There are also trains between Quilon and Madras Egmore via Madurai (760 km, eight hours, Rs 77 in 2nd class, Rs 280 in 1st). The trip across the Western Ghats is a pure delight. Passenger trains between Quilon and Trivandrum are very slow, but there are plenty of expresses.

Backwater Boat Trip This trip to Alleppey is one of the highlights of a visit to Kerala. It takes you across shallow, palm-fringed lakes studded with cantilevered Chinese fishing nets, and along narrow shady canals where coir (coconut fibre), copra (dried coconut meat) and cashews are loaded onto dugouts. Along the way, you call at many small settlements.

It's interesting to see how people live on narrow spits of land only a few metres wide, water all around, and still manage to keep cows, pigs, chickens and ducks and cultivate small vegetable gardens. On the more open stretches of canal, you'll see dugouts with huge sails and prows carved into the shape of dragons. The sight of three or four of these sailing towards you in the late afternoon sun is never to be forgotten. The boat crews are friendly – if you exchange a little conversation with them, they'll let you sit on the roof. It gets hot up there, though. On some days during the winter season, almost half the boat passengers could be western travellers.

There are two 10-minute 'chai stops' along the way where snacks and tea can be bought, but you may decide it's worth bringing some food with you. Beware of inflated prices for refreshments at these stops. There is usually a day and a night departure in each direction – Quilon to Alleppey and Alleppey to Quilon –

Along the backwaters of Kerala

although the morning departure from Alleppey seems to have gone the way of the Ark. Some travellers have reported that, with a full moon, the night trip can be interesting, but you really should do it by day. The trip takes approximately 8½ hours and costs only Rs 6.70 per person. The morning departure from Quilon is at 10.30 am, so it's possible to come from Trivandrum, or even Kovalam, if you start out early enough.

Most people find the trip from Quilon to Alleppey too long for comfort. After a few hours, it can become hot, crowded and monotonous. It is possible, however, to make shorter trips. The best option is to take a bus or train from Quilon to Changanacherry (78 km); from there, 10 boats daily make the three-hour trip to Alleppey. Another alternative is to go all the way to Kottayam by train or bus and take a boat from there to Alleppey.

Getting Around
The transport facilities are at opposite ends of the town, three km apart. This means that, if you arrive by rail and want to get to the bus station or the boat jetty, you'll need to take an auto-rickshaw (Rs 4).

VARKALA
Only 19 km south of Quilon and 55 km north of Trivandrum, the seaside resort of Varkala boasts a mineral-water spring on the beach and the Janardhana Temple. One of the earliest British East India Company trading posts was established at nearby Anjengo in 1684.

Places to Stay
There is no accommodation in Varkala itself, although there are a couple of basic places out at the beach, two km away. The problem is that the only eating places are back in town!

TRIVANDRUM (population 625,000)
As you stroll around this friendly, relaxed city built over seven forested hills, it's hard to imagine that it is a state capital.

The 'City of the Sacred Snake' is unlike other Indian state capitals and has managed to retain the magic ambience so characteristic of Kerala in general – red-tiled roofs, narrow winding lanes, intimate corner cafes, dilapidated municipal buses and necessary business accomplished in a friendly manner with a relatively high degree of efficiency.

At least, this is how it is when political tensions between the various factions haven't reached the stage where they erupt into violence on the streets. Political slogans, emblems and flags, especially those of the communist parties, dominate the urban landscape of Kerala. Luckily, even when there is violence, it rarely affects the visitor and is generally an indication that you'll be drawn into some very lively discussions in the cafes and restaurants.

On the other hand, there isn't a great deal to see in Trivandrum itself, and non-Hindus aren't allowed into the famous Sri Padmanabhaswamy Temple. The main reason people come to Trivandrum is to stay at magnificent Kovalam Beach, 16 km south. You might also find yourself here for a day or so if you plan to fly to Sri Lanka (political climate permitting) or the Maldive Islands.

Orientation
Trivandrum covers a large area, but most of the services and places of interest are on or very close to Mahatma Gandhi Rd – the main road running through the centre of the city from the zoological gardens to Sri Padmanabhaswamy Temple. The long-distance bus terminal, railway station and tourist office are all within a few metres of each other, as are many of the budget hotels. The municipal bus stand is 10 minutes walk from the railway station, opposite Sri Padmanabhaswamy Temple.

The museum, zoo and airline offices are all in the north of the city and you'll need an auto-rickshaw to reach them.

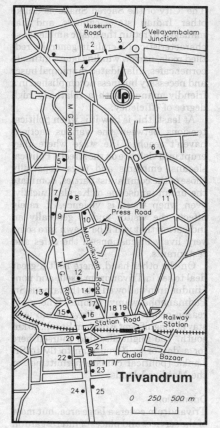

1 Mascot Hotel & Indian Airlines
2 Museum
3 Air India
4 Tourist Office
5 Indian Coffee House
6 Air Lanka
7 Hotel Pankaj
8 Secretariat
9 Central Telegraph Office
10 British Library & YMCA
11 Commissioner of Police
12 Bhaskara Bhavan Tourist Paradise
13 GPO
14 Pravin Tourist Home
15 Omkar Cafe & Safari Restaurant
16 Chicken Corner
17 Hotel Highland &
    Manacaud Tourist Paradise
18 Tourist Office & Chaithram Hotel
19 Central Bus Station
20 Nalanda Tourist Home
21 Indian Coffee House
22 Padmanabhaswamy Temple
23 Fort Bus Station
24 Hotel Luciya Continental
25 Kovalam Buses & Taxis

The poste restante counter is open from 8 am to 6 pm.

The Central Telegraph Office is on M G Rd, midway between Station Rd and the museum and 20 minutes walk from either. It is open 24 hours a day.

Visa Extensions Apply for visa extensions at the Office of the Commissioner of Police (tel 60555) on Residency Rd, Rs 4 by auto-rickshaw from the railway station. Extensions take between four days and a week to issue but you don't have to leave your passport there. It speeds things up if you give the name of a Trivandrum hotel as your address rather than somewhere in Kovalam. Surprisingly, this office is open on Saturdays as well as weekdays, from 10 am to 5 pm.

Airlines The Air India office (tel 64837) is on Museum Rd, by Vellayambalam Circle. Indian Airlines (tel 66940) is on the same road, next to the Mascot Hotel. The

Information

Tourist Office There is a tourist office (tel 75031) in the Chaithram Hotel, near the railway station and central bus station, and another near the museums. At the Chaithram Hotel office, you can book tours of Trivandrum and tours to Kanyakumari, Periyar Wildlife Sanctuary and Kodaikanal.

Post & Telephone The GPO is tucked away down a small side street off M G Rd, about 10 minutes walk from the Station Rd area.

Air Lanka office (tel 68767) is in the Geethanjali Building at 15/1289/1 Ganapathy Kovil Rd, east of the Secretariat building. The agent for Maldives Airways is the S&J Sales Corporation (tel 66105), in the Glass House Building north of the bus station.

Bookshops & Libraries The British Library (tel 68716), in the YMCA grounds near the Secretariat building, is supposedly only open to members, but they seem to welcome visitors. It has three-day-old British newspapers and a variety of magazines.

There's a branch of Higginbothams bookshop on M G Rd, just up from Station Rd.

Museum, Gallery & Zoo
These are all in the same area, in the park at the north end of the city. They are open daily, except Monday and Wednesday mornings, between 10 am and 4.45 pm.

Housed in an attractive building, the Napier Museum has a good collection of bronzes, historical and contemporary ornaments, temple carts, ivory carvings and life-size figures of Kathakali dancers in full regalia. Entrance is Rs 1. The Science & Industry Museum is not that interesting unless you are a high-school science student.

On display at the Sri Chitra Art Gallery are paintings of the Rajput, Mughal and Tanjore schools, together with works from China, Tibet, Japan and Bali. There are also many modern Indian paintings, especially those of Ravi Varma. Entrance is Rs 2.

Although the Zoological Gardens are among the best laid-out zoos in Asia, set amongst woodland, lakes and well-maintained lawns, some of the animal enclosures are still miserable. The zoo's botanical garden includes examples of almost every tropical tree.

Sri Padmanabhaswamy Temple
This temple, thought to be to the 'presiding deity' of Trivandrum, is

dedicated to Vishnu. It was constructed in the Dravidian style by a maharaja of Travancore in 1733. Only Hindus are allowed inside, and even they have to wear a special dhoti which can be rented for Rs 1. There is a pool in which the faithful bathe.

Tours
City Tour The Trivandrum city tour leaves daily at 8 am, returning at 7 pm, and costs Rs 40 per person. It includes visits to Sri Padmanabhaswamy Temple (for Hindus only), the museum, art gallery, Kovalam Beach and the zoo. This tour is not worth taking unless your time is severely limited.

Kanyakumari The daily Kanyakumari (Cape Comorin) tour departs at 7.30 am, returns at 9 pm and costs Rs 60. It includes visits to Padmanabhapuram Palace and Cape Comorin.

Periyar Wildlife Sanctuary The tour to this sanctuary, in the mountains of Kerala near the Tamil Nadu border, departs every Saturday at 6.30 am and returns the following evening at 9 pm. It costs Rs 100, excluding board and lodging. This must be one of the silliest tours in India, since there's no way you're going to have the time to see any wildlife at all – even if it were that easy!

Places to Stay – bottom end
There are many cheap lodging places in the Station Rd area (near the railway station and bus stand), but they're often full, many are very basic and this road is busy and noisy.

Manjalikulam Rd, a small road heading north off Station Rd, is a good hunting ground for both bottom-end and mid-range hotels. It's quiet and convenient. The friendly *Pravin Tourist Home* (tel 75343) has large rooms for Rs 28/44. Close by, the hopefully named *Bhaskara Bhavan Tourist Paradise* (tel 79662) is a bit gloomy but otherwise OK, and the rooms are good value at Rs 20/37. Also on Manjalikulam Rd is the *Sundar Tourist*

Home (tel 76632). It is extremely basic and has rooms for Rs 14/28.

Up the scale a bit, the clean and well-kept *Sivada Tourist Home* (tel 75320), in the same street, has rooms around a pleasant courtyard for Rs 35/60. In the same category and location is the new *Manacaud Tourist Paradise* (tel 75360), close to Station Rd. The rooms are clean, large and good value at Rs 27/47 with bath.

South of the railway line is the *Nalanda Tourist Home* (tel 71864) on busy M G Rd. Rooms towards the back are not too noisy, and it's cheap at Rs 26/42.

The *retiring rooms* at the railway station cost Rs 35/50, and there's an eight-bed dorm for Rs 15 per bed.

Places to Stay – middle

The brand new *Chaithram Hotel* is run by the Kerala Tourism Development Corporation. It's on Station Rd, just a one-minute walk from the bus and train stations. Rooms cost Rs 75/90, Rs 125/175 with air-con. Later in the day, it's often full.

Back on Manjalikulam Rd, just up from Station Rd, the *Hotel Highland* (tel 78440) is the tallest building in the area and visible from some distance. The hotel has a lift, good-sized rooms and friendly staff. The rooms cost Rs 48/80 with bath and a big window – good value.

Places to Stay – top end

Most people seeking five-star comfort head for the *Kovalam Ashok Beach Resort* at Kovalam Beach (20 minutes from Trivandrum by taxi). In Trivandrum itself, the KTDC-run *Mascot Hotel* (tel 68990) is one of the best value hotels in its price category in southern India. It's near the museums in the northern part of the city and has rooms at Rs 100/140, Rs 175/235 with air-con.

The *Hotel Pankaj* (tel 76257) is a fine hotel, conveniently situated opposite the Government Secretariat. It has two restaurants, one on the roof overlooking

the city, with a choice of Mughlai, Tandoori, Chinese and western cuisine. Singles/doubles are Rs 120/150, Rs 200/250 with air-con.

The *Hotel Luciya Continental* (tel 73443) is a good top-end hotel at East Fort. Singles/doubles are Rs 125/225 or Rs 175/300 with air-con which, in this category, is very good value. The hotel also has two good restaurants.

Places to Eat

The *Athul Jyoti* on M G Rd, near the Secretariat, serves good vegetarian food, and a thali with a variety of vegetables, dhals and curd for only Rs 5.50. Despite the name, the *Sri Ram Sweet Stall* is actually a very good vegetarian restaurant. It's at the entrance to the Pankaj Hotel on M G Rd.

Also on M G Rd, but down near Station Rd, the small *Omkar Cafe* does an unusual thali with a tangy curd sauce for Rs 5.50. A couple of doors down, the *Safari Restaurant* is none too popular but a good place if you're just after a beer.

Almost opposite the Safari is the *Chicken Corner Restaurant*, specialising in chicken dishes at around Rs 11 to Rs 14. The *City Queen Restaurant* in the Highlands Hotel does good Chinese dishes and also serves Indian and western food.

The *Indian Coffee House* is the usual good value. There are two in Trivandrum, both on M G Rd. One is just north of the Secretariat, the other south of the railway line near East Fort.

On Station Rd, you'll find a few vegetarian restaurants serving the usual common or garden thali for a few rupees. There's not much difference between them.

Getting There & Away

Air Trivandrum is a popular place from which to fly to Colombo (Sri Lanka) and Male (Maldives). The fare to Colombo is Rs 561; Air Lanka has flights five days a week although, with the ethnic problems in Sri Lanka, tourists aren't going there much these days.

Indian Airlines flies to Male three times a week. The fare is Rs 673, but foreigners have to pay the rupee equivalent of US$63 which works out to be considerably more.

Domestically, there are flights to and from Bombay (Rs 1165), Cochin (Rs 225), Dabolim (Goa, Rs 800), Delhi (Rs 2050) and Madras (Rs 630).

Bus The bus station, opposite the railway station, is total chaos. Although there is a timetable in English, it's largely a fiction and, as there are no bays, you have to join the scramble every time a bus arrives just in case it happens to be the one you want. The law of the jungle applies each time a battered old bus comes to a screeching halt in a cloud of dust. There are frequent buses to all the main cities in Kerala and to Kanyakumari. Also available are long-distance buses to Madras and Bangalore, but it's better to take a train if you're going that far.

There are 10 buses daily for Kanya-kumari; the 2½-hour trip costs Rs 12. Buses between Trivandrum and Nagercoil are more frequent and, from Nagercoil, it's easy to get buses to the Cape.

Departures start at 7.30 am for Ernakulam/Cochin, passing through Quilon. The trip to Quilon, where you can start the backwater trip, takes two hours. Three daily buses make the eight-hour trip to Thekkady (for Periyar Wildlife Sanctuary).

Train Although the buses are much faster than the trains, Kerala State Road Transport buses, like most others in southern India, make no concessions to comfort and the drivers are pretty reckless. If you like to keep your adrenalin levels down, the trains are a pleasant alternative.

The reservation office is relatively efficient and there are plenty of tourist quota tickets on most trains. Even so, it's

a good idea to book your ticket at least a few days in advance. The office is open Monday to Saturday from 7 am to 1 pm and 1.30 to 7.30 pm; on Sunday, it's open from 9 am to 5 pm.

The trains passing through Trivandrum go right down the coast via Ernakulam and Quilon. The daily Kerala to Mangala Express departs from New Delhi and arrives in Trivandrum 52 hours later. The 3054-km trip costs Rs 195 in 2nd class, Rs 822 in 1st.

To and from Madras, there's the daily Trivandrum Mail. The 925-km trip costs Rs 86 in 2nd class, Rs 324 in 1st, and takes 16 hours.

The daily Malabar Express on the Mangalore to Trivandrum coastal route takes 16 hours to travel the full distance of 634 km. The fare is Rs 67 in 2nd class, Rs 234 in 1st. It's 65 km from Trivandrum to Quilon (Rs 12 in 2nd class, Rs 42 in 1st), and 201 km between Trivandrum and Ernakulam (Rs 30 in 2nd, Rs 99 in 1st). Trivandrum to Calicut is 414 km (Rs 51 in 2nd, Rs 178 in 1st).

Trivandrum to Bangalore takes 18 hours; fares for the 855-km trip are Rs 82 in 2nd class, Rs 305 in 1st. The 2062-km trip from Bombay takes a lengthy 45 hours and costs Rs 144 in 2nd class, Rs 590 in 1st. This train continues on to Kanyakumari (87 km, Rs 13 in 2nd class, Rs 53 in 1st).

It's a nine-hour journey to Coimbatore (for Mettupalayam and Ooty) on the Ahmedabad Express (427 km, Rs 51 in 2nd class, Rs 183 in 1st).

Getting Around

Airport Transport The disorganised little airport is six km from the city centre. A No 14 local bus will take you there for less than Rs 1. A taxi costs Rs 30; an auto-rickshaw is Rs 15.

Local Transport There are very crowded local state government buses, as well as auto-rickshaws and taxis. For transport around the city itself, auto-rickshaws are probably your best bet. The drivers are reluctant to use the meters, but Rs 3 takes you most places.

Bus No 111 for Kovalam Beach departs 25 times daily from stand 19 of the Fort Bus Depot. This platform is actually on M G Rd, 100 metres south of the bus station, directly opposite the Hotel Luciya. The first bus leaves on the half-hour journey at 6.20 am and the last at 9 pm. Although the bus starts out ridiculously overcrowded, it rapidly empties. A share taxi from the bus stop in Trivandrum to Kovalam Beach should not cost more than Rs 5 per person; they leave when full, which usually means when they can't squash another body in – eight passengers is fairly standard. An auto-rickshaw costs Rs 20.

AROUND TRIVANDRUM
Padmanabhapuram Palace
Although actually in Tamil Nadu, this fine palace is easily visited from Trivandrum. See the Kanyakumari (Tamil Nadu) section for more details. To get there, you can either catch a local bus from Trivandrum (or Kovalam Beach) or take one of the Kanyakumari tours organised by the Kerala Tourist Development Corporation. The palace is closed on Mondays.

KOVALAM
Kovalam, just south of Trivandrum, is one of India's best beaches – perhaps *the* best – and the favourite watering hole of travellers in southern India. It consists of a few small, palm-fringed bays separated by rocky headlands. There is good surf on most days although, unless you are a strong swimmer, you should approach the water cautiously until you're familiar with the rip – one or two people drown here every year. Lifeguards patrol the main two bays during daylight hours, and flags indicate where it's safe to swim.

There are plenty of cheap places to stay and a choice of simple restaurants, many right on the water's edge. Most offer excellent seafood.

If anything, the atmosphere at Kovalam is even more mellow than on the beaches of Goa, and many people who turn up here intending to stay for a few days find themselves staying considerably longer. It takes a little time and effort to get to Kovalam, and most people have given India a chance to seep into their pores by the time they arrive here. This is one of the reasons for the interesting collection of people on the beach.

Back from the beach and on either side of the two main coves, life goes on as it always has. The local people continue to cultivate their rice, coconuts, bananas, pawpaws and vegetables, and the fishers still row their dugouts out to sea and pull in their nets by hand. The influx of westerners hasn't radically affected the lifestyles of the people who live at the back of the two main coves. It has meant that extra income can be earned selling fruit and other produce to the sun-and-waves worshippers, and anyone who can is offering rooms for rent or doing something to make this possible.

Information & Orientation
The nearest post office is in Kovalam village. The branch of the Central Bank of India at the Kovalam Ashok Beach Resort changes travellers' cheques without fuss or form-filling. It is only open from 10.30 am to 2 pm Monday to Friday, and 10.30 am to 12 pm on Saturday.

You can buy general-store commodities from the stalls at the bus stop.

Kovalam is spread out and finding a place can involve a bit of a walk – especially difficult if you're carrying all your gear. It's about 15 minutes on foot from the bus stop to the second cove and most of the hotels and restaurants.

The paths through the coconut palms and around the back of the paddy field are hard to negotiate at night without a full moon, unless you're familiar with them.

The stalls just below the bus stop have an excellent stock of second-hand books for sale or hire – choose from literally

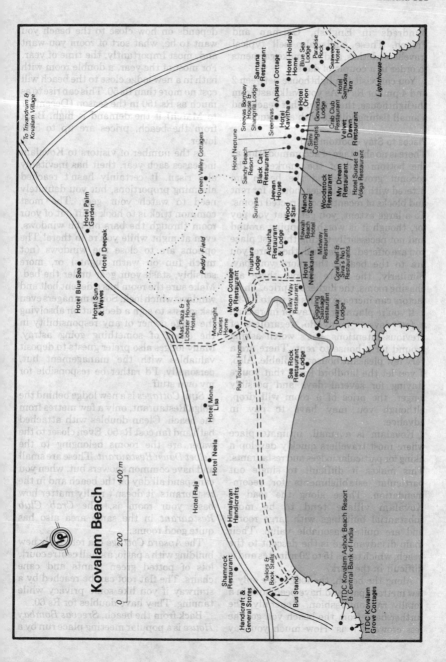

hundreds in English, German and French. These stalls also sell typical travellers' clothes, and will make garments to order in a couple of days.

You can visit the lighthouse between 2 and 4 pm for Rs 1. As you walk east from the lighthouse, there is another beach and a small fishing village with a mosque.

Places to Stay - bottom end

There is no shortage of accommodation at the bottom end of the market - the coconut groves behind the beach are littered with small lodges, houses for rent and blocks of recently constructed rooms. To a large extent, you get what you pay for, though it is worth shopping around and not necessarily taking the first place you are offered. In general, the nearer you are to the beach, the more you pay. Similarly, the more people there are chasing rooms, the higher the price. These factors can increase tariffs by up to Rs 30.

If you're planning to stay for more than a few days - many do, regardless of previous intentions - it's worth asking around for a house to rent. There are a very few pleasant houses available. Also, if you let the landlord know that you're staying for several days and possibly longer, the price of a room will drop, although you may have to pay in advance.

Kovalam is a small, intimate place where most travellers quickly develop a liking for particular lodges and restaurants. This makes it difficult to single out particular establishments for recommendation. Those along the road to Kovalam village tend to be more substantial buildings with large rooms and are quite reasonable value. Their main disadvantage is the descent to the beach, which takes 15 to 20 minutes and is difficult in the dark.

Along the beach, the lodges are only a few metres apart and have been built in a totally random fashion. Generally, the further back from the beach you go, the less crowded it is. How much you pay depends on how close to the beach you want to be, what sort of room you want and, most importantly, the time of year. For most of the year, a double room with bath in a new lodge close to the beach will cost no more than Rs 50. This can rise to as much as Rs 150 in the season (December to March) if the demand is high. Back from the beach, prices are up to 50% lower.

As the number of visitors to Kovalam increases each year, theft has inevitably also risen. It certainly hasn't reached alarming proportions, but you definitely need to watch your gear. The most common trick is to hook stuff out of your room through the bars on the windows, even at night while you're in there! The options are to close the windows (not much fun on warm nights) or, more sensibly, stash your gear under the bed. Make sure the room has a decent bolt and windows which lock. Some managers even ask guests to sign a declaration absolving the lodge owner of any responsibility in the event of something going astray. Many lodges also prefer guests to deposit valuables with the management but, personally, I'd rather be responsible for my own stuff.

Simi Cottages is a new lodge behind the Volga Restaurant, only a few metres from the beach. Clean doubles with attached bath and fan cost Rs 50. Even closer to the water are the rooms belonging to the *Velvet Dawn Restaurant*. These are small and have common showers but, when you can spend all day on the beach and in the restaurants, it doesn't really matter how basic your room is. The *Crab Club Restaurant* in the same area also has quite good rooms.

The *Apsara Cottage* is a relatively new building with a patio, a small centre court, lots of potted green plants and cane chairs. The flat roof can be reached by a stairway if you like some privacy while tanning. They have doubles for Rs 60.

Back from the beach, *Sreevas Bombay House* is a popular meeting place run by a retired army sergeant who speaks good English. The nearby *Shangrila Lodge* is similar.

Right on the beach, you have the choice of half a dozen places. The *Hawah Beach Hotel* has free video movies every evening (nonguests welcome) or, if there's a Test match being played somewhere in India, you can watch the live telecast.

If you want to be right away from things, the *Green Valley Cottages* on the far side of the paddy field are cheap, clean and well run. There are at least a dozen other bottom-end lodges, and new ones pop up all the time.

Places to Stay – middle

If you prefer accommodation close to the road and away from the beach, the *Hotel Raja* is good value at Rs 80 a double, especially compared to some similar places closer to the beach. The new *Hotel Palm Garden* has large single rooms for Rs 50. The *Hotel Blue Sea* has a variety of rooms (Rs 100 for a double) and a nice garden. If you want to enjoy both the beach and a garden during your stay in Kovalam, this traditional-style mansion is the place to be. Of a similar standard and a bit closer to the beach are the *Mas Plaza Hotel* and the *Lobster House Hotel*. The latter has good double rooms for Rs 75.

Right on the beach, the *Sea Rock Lodge* is a good choice. The front rooms have balconies overlooking the water and, at Rs 110 for a double, they're good value.

The best hotel in this price range is the *Hotel Rockholm*. Although not at the beach, it commands a beautiful view from its superb location at the top of the cliff on the next bay, above the Seaweed Hotel. It has a small library, TV and a good restaurant. Singles/doubles cost Rs 210/ 240 but are worth it if you can afford them.

Just below the lighthouse, at the far end of the beach, a cluster of mid-range accommodation is fairly accessible by auto-rickshaw from the lighthouse road. The pleasant *Seaweed Hotel* is one of the cheaper places at Rs 75/100 for singles/ doubles. The *Paradise Rock Lodge* has a new, two-storey addition in front of the cheaper original rooms. The rooms are huge and have balconies overlooking the beach.

The KTDC *Hotel Samudhra Tara* is another in this group. Rooms have balconies and cost Rs 150 for a double. Others here include the *Blue Sea Lodge* and the *Hotel Holiday Home*.

Places to Stay – top end

The most luxurious place to stay is the ITDC *Kovalam Ashok Beach Resort* (tel Trivandrum 68010), on the headland just above the bus stop. Studio rooms, double rooms and cottages are expensive at Rs 900 a single and Rs 1050 a double. The hotel has every facility you would expect, including air-con, swimming pool, bar, crafts shop and boats for hire. It's a beautiful place and a lot of effort has obviously been put into its design and construction. Despite the high prices, quality of service and facilities can be lacking.

Places to Eat

Restaurants line the beachfront, but others just as good are scattered among the coconut palms. Almost all of them cater to an international palate with western-style breakfasts (porridge, muesli, eggs, toast, jam, pancakes), seafood (fish, prawns with French fries, lobster) and a variety of fruit salads and custard-based sweets. Everyone has their favourite, but there isn't much difference between them in quality or price – they all tend to be pretty good.

However, the restaurants vary widely in size of helpings, how long you have to wait before a meal arrives, distractions in the meantime (music or no music) and lighting facilities. Some places have definitely bitten off much more than they can chew and will attempt to cater for up to two dozen customers on a single-burner stove. This isn't just a commendable case of overenthusiasm – it's clearly impossible, which is why you'll still be waiting for the first course three hours after you ordered it. Things are obviously worst during the high season; the rest of the time, it's not too bad.

The *Volga* on the beach has generous servings of good food. Their special muesli is particularly tasty. Others on the beach include the *Black Cat*, *My Dream* and *Woodstock*, all of which seem to rate raves when they manage to get the food out and protests when they take hours. The *Crab Club* has excellent barbecued fish and real crème caramel.

The *Coral Reef* and the *Giggling Sausage* are also popular, although the former only seems to have one cassette (Kate Bush), which gets more than a little monotonous on the third consecutive hearing! The Coral Reef's saving grace, however, is its home-made brown bread.

The *Santana*, behind the Apsara Cottages, is the first on the block to get a compact disc player. It's a real pleasure to listen to after some of the 'Mickey Mouse' cassette players you hear around the place. The food is not bad either.

In addition to the restaurants, a number of local women do the rounds of the sun worshippers on the beach, selling fruit. The ring of, 'Hello, baba. Mango? Papaya? Banana? Coconut? Pineapple?' will soon become a familiar part of your day. Naturally, they'll sell you fruit at any price you're willing to pay so, on your first few encounters, establish what you think is fair for certain fruits. After that, they'll remember your face and you don't have to repeat the performance. They rarely have any change, but they're reliable about bringing it to you later. There are also guys on the beach selling batik longhis and beach mats. Plenty of others offer cheap Kerala grass, which seems to be the main attraction of this place for some people.

Toddy (coconut beer) and feni (spirits made by distilling the fermented mash of either coconuts or cashew nuts – the two varieties taste quite different) are available from shops in Kovalam village, or from the stall at the southern end of the beach.

Beers are sold at both the Kovalam Ashok Beach Resort and the Hotel Raja, but at a price likely to singe the hair on the back of your hand as you reach for your wallet. You can sometimes buy them 'under the counter' for Rs 30 at the beach restaurants. The best bet is a wine store in Trivandrum, although you then have the problem of chilling them.

Getting There & Away

Bus The local No 111 bus to Trivandrum runs 25 times daily, but the schedules are not too believable. The first bus leaves at 6.15 am, the last at 10 pm, from the depot outside the Kovalam Ashok Beach Resort. It costs Rs 1.60.

There are also direct services to Ernakulam and Kanyakumari (Cape Comorin), which are a good way of avoiding the crush at Trivandrum. Cape Comorin is two hours away and there are four departures daily. One bus leaves each morning for Thekkady in the Periyar Wildlife Sanctuary. Direct buses go to Quilon if you want to do the backwater trip.

Taxi & Auto-Rickshaw To travel to or from Trivandrum in a hurry, use share taxis. They leave when full, which usually means waiting for seven or eight passengers, and cost Rs 5 per seat. An auto-rickshaw costs Rs 20 one way.

LAKSHADWEEP

The 36 scattered Lakshadweep islands are 200 to 300 km off the Kerala coast and form a northern extension of the Maldives chain. Ten of the islands are inhabited. They are, in descending order of size, Minicoy, Androth, Kavarathi, Kadmat, Agathy, Ameni, Kalpeni, Kiltan, Chetlat and Bitra. The islands' population is about 42,000, 93% Muslim, and the economy centres around the production of copra from coconuts.

Permits

Tourists need permission to visit Lakshadweep, and this is usually only granted if you are part of a package tour group. Nevertheless, it might be worth applying for a permit anyway. They are issued by the Administrator (tel 69131), Union Territory of Lakshadweep, Indira Gandhi Rd, Willingdon Island, Cochin. Four passport photos are needed.

Generally, foreign tourists are only given permission to visit uninhabited Bangaram Island.

Places to Stay

On Bangaram, there are eight 'family huts' for Rs 80 per day. There are 10 of these huts on Kadmat, and three on Kavarathi.

The all-inclusive price of the seven-day tour is Rs 1290 deck class, Rs 1440 in a two-berth air-conditioned cabin.

Getting There & Away

The Shipping Corporation of India ship, the MV *Bharatseema*, visits the islands three to five times a month. The trip from Cochin takes about 18 hours.

Travellers' Notebook

Ganja

Yes, there's an awful lot of that well-known weed in India. Shiva, the most worshipped of gods, is supposed to devote a fair amount of time to smoking dope in his remote Himalayan home so it would be pretty difficult to ignore it. In fact there are government hashish shops in places like Varanasi, Puri and Jaipur, but effectively it's illegal unless you happen to be a Hindu sadhu or someone similar who clearly needs it!

If you want to find it you'll have little problem anywhere in India. Goa with its large resident travellers' population, Kashmir and the Kulu Valley, where it grows in profusion, and Varanasi, with its religious connections, are all good places. Discretion is the key word wherever you are. Don't smoke in public and don't leave it lying around hotel rooms.

The places to avoid it include the airports and a number of railway stations. Often dope searches are simply ways of extracting a little baksheesh, but it's still wise not to get involved. Along the popular Delhi-Bombay railway route, at Allahabad, in Manali in the Kulu Valley, from Patna up to the Nepalese border, are all places where dope searches have been known to take place. In Delhi there are occasional dope raids on the cheaper hotels, particularly around Paharganj, and in Agra in the cheap hotels just south of the Taj.

Beware of the concentrated powers of bhang-lassi or other mixtures of bhang with foodstuffs. A German traveller wrote to us describing the two-hour search she and some friends made for their hotel in darkest Jaisalmer after partaking of bhang-pakora!

Tony Wheeler

Madras

Population: 5.2 million
Main language: Tamil

Madras is the capital of Tamil Nadu

Madras, India's fourth largest city, is the capital of Tamil Nadu state. It suffers far less from congestion and overcrowding than other big cities in India, but it's still fairly hectic, and the traffic fumes are bad.

Madrassis are zealous guardians of Tamil culture which they regard as inherently superior to the hybridised cultures further north. They also appear to know the meaning of relaxation and efficiency with regard to public services – a remarkable combination, to be found only in isolated pockets elsewhere in India! Here it's possible to use public buses without undue discomfort and the urban commuter trains without a second thought. There are, it is true, slums and beggars but they are far less obtrusive and smaller in number.

The city also has the advantage of a long clean beach front on the Bay of Bengal, which ensures a good supply of refreshing sea air and provides a popular place to relax in the evening.

Though the city has long been important for textile manufacture, a great deal of industrial expansion, including car-assembly plants, railway coach and truck works, engineering plants, cigarette factories, film studios and educational institutes, has taken place in recent years.

As a tourist attraction, Madras is something of a nonevent compared to the real marvels elsewhere in the state. The main reason travellers come here is to transact business or to make a long-distance travel connection.

The city suffers from acute water shortages in the summer months, especially

if the last monsoon season has been a poor one.

History

Madras was the site of the East India Company's first settlement – founded in 1639 on land given by the Raja of Chandragiri, the last representative of the Vijayanagar rulers of Hampi. A small fort was built on the settlement in 1644, and a town which subsequently became known as George Town, in the area of Fort St George, arose north of it. The settlement became independent of Banten, Java in 1683 and was granted its first municipal charter in 1688 by James II. It thus has the oldest municipal corporation in India, a fact which Tamil Nadu state governors are only too keen to point out at every available opportunity.

During the 18th and early 19th centuries, when the British and French competed for supremacy in India, the city's fortunes waxed and waned; it was briefly occupied by the French on one occasion. It was also the base from which Clive of India set out on his military expeditions during the Wars of the Carnatic. During the 19th century it was the seat of the Madras presidency, one of the four divisions of British Imperial India.

Orientation

The city may be conveniently divided into two parts. The older section, known as George Town, is west of the dock area and north of Poonamallee High Rd. In these narrow, busy streets are the offices of shipping and forwarding agents, some cheaper hotels and restaurants, large office buildings, bazaars, the GPO and Thomas Cook. The area's main focal point is Parry's Corner – the intersection of Prakasam Rd (more commonly known as Popham's Broadway) and NSC Bose Rd. Many of the city buses terminate here; the Tamil Nadu State bus stand and the Thiruvalluvar bus stand (the two long-distance bus terminals) are close by on the Esplanade.

The other main part of the city is south of Poonamallee High Rd. Through it runs Madras' main road, Anna Salai, which is still generally known as Mount Rd. Along it are most of the airline offices, theatres, banks, bookshops, crafts centres, consulates, tourist offices and the bulk of the top-range hotels and restaurants.

Egmore and Central, Madras' two main railway stations, are close to Poonamallee High Rd. If you're arriving from anywhere other than Tamil Nadu or Kerala you'll come into Central station. Egmore is the arrival point for most Tamil Nadu and Kerala trains. Egmore also has the largest concentration of bottom and middle-range hotels, although these days it's difficult to get a cheap room after midday.

Information

Tourist Offices The Government of India tourist office (tel 869685) at 154 Mount Rd is open daily, except Sundays, from 9 am to 6 pm; holidays and every Saturday from 9 am to 1 pm. This office is a good one; the staff are knowledgeable, friendly and helpful. A bus (No 11 or 18) from

Parry's Corner or Central station takes you there.

Information counters at the domestic (tel 431686) and international airport terminals are supposedly open daily, but the staff at both counters seem to be out to lunch – permanently.

The India Tourism Development Corporation (ITDC) (tel 474216) is at 29 Victoria Crescent on the corner of Commander-in-Chief (C-in-C) Rd. It's open from 6 am to 8 pm Monday to Saturday, and 6 am to 2 pm Sundays. This is not a tourist office as such, but all the ITDC tours can be booked, and in fact start, here.

The Tamil Nadu Government tourist office (tel 840752) is at 143 Mount Rd. It is open daily from 10 am to 5 pm Monday to Friday. You can book all Tamil Nadu Tourism Development Corporation (TTDC) tours from here. The Tamil Nadu government also maintains offices at Central railway station (tel 563351) and the Thiruvalluvar bus station.

The Automobile Association (tel 586121) is at 187 Mount Rd. Apart from route information, the organisation offers accommodation for members of any foreign automobile association, and car-parking facilities on the premises.

Hallo Madras is a monthly tourist guide to the city with hotels, restaurants, tourist attractions, bus routes – both local and further afield – and lots of addresses. It's available from newsstands and bookshops.

Post & Telephone The GPO is on North Beach Rd, but if you are staying around Egmore or the Mount Rd area (as most people seem to do these days), it is more convenient to use the poste restante service at the Anna Rd post office. The full address is Anna Rd post office, Mount Rd, Madras 600002. It is open for poste restante collection from 8 am to 6 pm.

Both the GPO and the Anna Rd post office have telegraph offices which are open 24 hours a day. Reverse charge

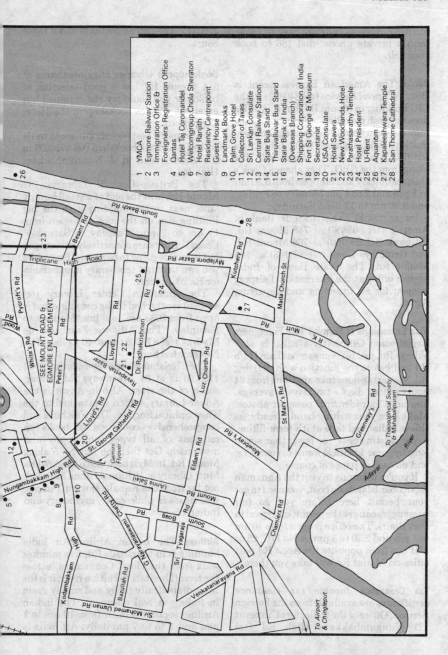

1 YMCA
2 Egmore Railway Station
3 Immigration Office &
  Foreigners' Registration Office
4 Qantas
5 Hotel Taj Coromandel
6 Welcomgroup Chola Sheraton
7 Hotel Ranjith
8 Residency Centrepoint
  Guest House
9 Landmark Books
10 Palm Grove Hotel
11 Sri Lankan Consulate
12 Collector of Taxes
13 Central Railway Station
14 State Bus Stand
15 Thiruvalluvar Bus Stand
16 State Bank of India
   (Overseas Branch)
17 Shipping Corporation of India
18 Fort St George & Museum
19 Secretariat
20 USA Consulate
21 Hotel Savera
22 New Woodlands Hotel
23 Parathasarathy Temple
24 Hotel President
25 U-Rent
26 Aquarium
27 Kapaleeshwara Temple
28 San Thome Cathedral

(collect) overseas calls are easy to make from a private phone; dial 186 to book your call.

Banks The American Express agent is Binny's Travel Service (tel 840803) in the LIC Building in Mount Rd, but this office does not cash travellers' cheques and they may not even be able to replace them very quickly. The Thomas Cook office (tel 524976) is at 20 North Beach Rd, just along from the GPO. They change Cook's cheques quickly and are open from 9.30 am to 1 pm and 2 to 4 pm Monday to Friday, and 9.30 am to 12 noon Saturday.

International banks include Bank of America (tel 863856) at 748 Mount Rd, Citibank (tel 860750) at 768 Mount Rd, and Grindlays Bank (tel 861168) at 164 Mount Rd. The State Bank of India branch office at the international airport is open for all incoming and departing flights.

Visa Extensions & Permits The Foreigners Registration Office (tel 478210) is at 9 Village Rd, just off Nungambakkam High Rd and before the junction with Sterling Rd. Visa extensions take anything from 24 hours to four days – two days is average. You need four *identical* passport photos. Make sure your writing hand is ready, as this is Indian red tape at it's form-filling, paper-wasting best – no fewer than seven lengthy, near-identical forms to complete, and no carbon paper of course.

If you're planning to visit the Andaman & Nicobar Islands by boat, you need to get your permit here before you go (air passengers can get the permit on arrival in Port Blair). The office is open from 10 am to 1 pm and 2.30 to 5 pm. A No 17C, 25 or 25B bus from opposite the Anna Rd post office on Mount Rd will take you there.

Tax Clearance Income tax clearance certificates are available from the Foreign Section, Office of the Collector of Taxes at 121 Nungambakkam High Rd (tel 472011). The procedure takes about three hours.

Bookshops & Libraries Higginbothams at 814 Mount Rd has a good selection of books; or you could try the cramped but excellent Giggles bookshop in the Hotel Connemara.

Perhaps the best bookshop in south India is the Landmark bookshop (tel 479637) in the Apex Plaza at 3 Nungambakkam High Rd.

The British Council Library, 737 Mount Rd, is at the end of a small bumpy lane, next to the building with the big Phillips sign on the roof. It's open from 11 am to 7 pm, Tuesday to Saturday. Casual visitors are not actively encouraged but if you are going to be around for a while you can take out temporary membership for Rs 20 a month.

The American Center Library (tel 477825) is attached to the consulate and is open from 9.30 am to 6 pm, Monday to Saturday. The Alliance Française de Madras (tel 479803) is at 40 College Rd, Nungambakkam.

The Krishnamurty Foundation (tel 416803) is at 64 Greenways Rd, Adyar, south of the river. Also in Adyar is the Adyar Library, which is attached to the Theosophical Society. There's a huge and comprehensive collection of books on religions of all types, philosophy and mysticism. Get there on bus No 5 along Mount Rd. In Mylapore, the Ramakrishna Mutt Library at 16 Ramakrishna Mutt Rd, not far from the Kapaleeshwara Temple, specialises in philosophy, mythology and Indian classics.

Airlines The Indian Airlines/Air India building is in Marshalls Rd, five minutes walk from the Hotel Connemara, across the river (I hesitate to call it a river; it is the most diabolically filthy and smelly drain in India – a real disgrace). The Indian Airlines section is open from 10 am to 1 pm, and 1.45 to 7 pm daily; Air India is open from 9.30 am to 1 pm, and 1.45 to 5.30 pm daily.

Air India
19 Marshalls Rd, Egmore (tel 474477)
Air Lanka
142 Nungambakkam High Rd (tel 471195, 475332)
British Airways
26 C-in-C Rd (tel 477388, 474272)
Indian Airlines
19 Marshalls Rd, Egmore (tel 478333)
Maldives Airways
Crossworld Tours, Rosy Towers, 7 Nungambakkam High Rd (tel 471497)
Malaysian Airlines
189 Mount Rd (tel 868970, 868985)
Singapore Airlines
167 Mount Rd (tel 862871/2)
Vayudoot
Travel Express, Wellington Estate, C-in-C Rd (tel 4342783)

Shipping Agents Shipping Agents in Madras include:

Binny & Co Ltd
65 Armenian St (tel 586894)
KPV Shaik Mohammed Rowther & Co Ltd
202 Linghi Chetty St (tel 510346)
Shipping Corporation of India
Old Bonded Warehouse, opposite the Customs House, North Beach Rd (tel 514537)

Consulates Consulates in Madras include:

Japan
6 Spur Tank Rd, Chetput (tel 865594)
Malaysia
287 TTK Rd (tel 453580)
Singapore
Apex Plaza, 3 Nungambakkam High Rd (tel 473795)
Sri Lanka
9-D Nawab Habibullah Ave, Anderson Rd (tel 472270)
UK
24 Anderson Rd (tel 473136)
USA
Gemini Circle, 220 Mount Rd (tel 473040)
West Germany
22 C-in-C Rd (tel 471747)

Fort St George & St Mary's Church

Built in 1653 by the British East India Company, but much altered from its original design, the fort presently houses the Secretariat and the Legislative Assembly. The 46-metre-high flagstaff out the front is actually a mast salvaged from a shipwreck in the 17th century.

The Fort Museum, open from 10 am to 5 pm but closed on Fridays, has a fascinating collection of memorabilia from the days of the East India Company and the British Raj. Entrance to the museum is free. Upstairs is the Banqueting Hall, built in 1802, around the walls of which hang many paintings of Fort St George's governors and other high officials of the British regime. Just south of the museum is the Pay Accounts Office. It was formerly Clive's house, and one room, known as Clive's Corner, is open to the public.

St Mary's Church, built in 1678-80, was the first English church and the oldest surviving British construction in India. There are reminders in the church of Robert Clive, who was married here in 1753, and of Elihu Yale, the early governor of Madras who went on to found the famous university bearing his name in the USA.

North of the fort is the old 1844 lighthouse, superseded in 1971 by the ugly modern one on the marina, and the High Court, built in 1892.

High Court Building

This red Indo-Saracenic monster at Parry's Corner is the main landmark in George Town. It's said to be the largest judicial building in the world after the Courts of London.

You can wander around, and sit in on one of the courtroom sessions. Court No 13 has the finest furniture and decor.

Government Museum & Art Gallery

The Government Museum & Art Gallery is on Pantheon Rd, near Egmore station. The most interesting parts of the museum are the archaeological section and the bronze gallery.

The archaeological section has an excellent collection of pieces from all the major south Indian periods including Chola, Vijayanagar, Hoysala and Chalukya. There's also a good zoology section.

The bronze gallery has some fine examples of Chola bronze art. The museum and gallery are open daily, except on public holidays, between 8.30 am and 4.30 pm. Entrance is Rs 0.50, and the ticket includes entry to the bronze gallery, which the city tours omit.

The building originally belonged to a group of eminent British citizens, known as the Pantheon Committee, who were charged with improving the social life of the British in Madras.

Kapaleeshwara Temple
Off Kutchery Rd, in the southern part of the city, this ancient Shiva temple has a typical Dravidian gopuram. It's worth a

Kapaleeshwara Temple

visit if your time is limited and you won't be visiting the more famous temple cities of Tamil Nadu. As with other functioning temples in this state, non-Hindus are only allowed into the outer courtyard.

San Thome Cathedral
Near Kapaleeshwara Temple at the southern end of South Beach Rd, close to the seafront, this Roman Catholic church is said to house the remains of St Thomas the Apostle (Doubting Thomas). It was originally built in 1504 but was rebuilt in 1893.

Parathasarathy Temple
On Triplicane High Rd, this temple is dedicated to Lord Krishna. Built in the 8th century during the reign of the Pallavas, it was subsequently renovated by the Vijayanagar kings in the 16th century.

Marina & Aquarium
The sandy stretch of beach known as the Marina extends for 13 km, as far south as the San Thome Cathedral. The tour guides on the city tour insist that this is the longest beach in the world!

The aquarium, on the seafront near the junction of Pycroft's Rd and South Beach Rd, is open daily between 2 and 8 pm, except on Sundays and holidays when it is open from 8 am. Entrance costs Rs 0.50 but it's a miserable place, worth missing just to discourage its continued existence.

Near the aquarium is the 'ice house'. This relic of the Raj era was used 150 years ago to store enormous blocks of ice cut from lakes in the northern USA and sent to India by sailboat. If you wanted a cold drink, that was how you got it in the days before refrigeration.

Guindy Deer & Snake Parks
Close to Raj Bhavan at Guindy, on the southern outskirts of Madras, this is the only place in the world where it is still possible to see large numbers of the fast-dwindling species of Indian antelope

(black buck). It also has small numbers of spotted deer, civet cats, jackals, mongoose and various species of monkeys.

The reptile house is open daily between 9 am and 5.30 pm and entrance costs Rs 0.50. Probably the best way to get to Guindy is to take the urban commuter train from either Beach railway station, opposite the GPO, or from Egmore station. There are also regular buses from the centre of Madras (No 21E from Parry's Corner, or Nos 5 and 5A from Mount Rd opposite the Anna Rd post office).

Other Attractions

From the end of November until the second week of January Madras is host to a dance and music festival. The tourist office has details.

Tours

Both the India Tourism Development Corporation (ITDC) and Tamil Nadu Tourism Development Corporation (TTDC) have tours of Madras, the nearby temple cities and further afield:

City Sightseeing Tour This includes visits to Fort St George, Madras Museum & Art Gallery, Valluvar Kottam, Gandhi Mandapam, Snake Park, Kapaleeshwara Temple and Marina Beach. The daily tours are fairly good value, although rushed as usual. The morning tour is from 8.30 am to 1.30 pm, and the afternoon one from 2 to 6 pm; the cost is Rs 30. The TTDC tour commentary is a nightmare of tautologies and non-English gibberish but the guides are helpful. A disclaimer on the back of the ticket carries the dire warning that 'there will be no refund for any unforeseen calamities which may occur during the tour'!

Kanchipuram, Tirukkalikundram & Mahabalipuram This tour includes visits to three of the four ancient temples at Kanchipuram, the famous hilltop temple of Tirukkalikundram and the 7th-century Pallavan antiquities at Mahabalipuram. A stop is made at the Crocodile Farm on the way back to Madras. There's a breakfast halt in Kanchipuram and a lunch halt in Mahabalipuram. The daily tours start at 6.20 am and finish at 7 pm, and cost Rs 60 or Rs 90 (air-con bus). It's good value if you're strapped for time, but otherwise a breathless dash around too many places.

Tirupathi This all-day return tour to the famous temple of Sri Balaji at Tirumala in southern Andhra Pradesh is good value if you don't have the time or inclination to do it yourself. It is, however, a hell of a long day, with at least 12 hours spent on the bus. The price includes 'special darshan' at Tirumala, and the tour allows two hours for this. That's usually fine on weekdays but on weekends and holidays it can take five hours or more, which means the bus doesn't get back to Madras until midnight or later. The daily tours officially last from 6 am to 9 pm. The fare is Rs 150 (deluxe bus) and Rs 200 (air-con), and includes breakfast, lunch and the Rs 25 'special darshan' fee at Tirumala.

All these tours, operated by TTDC, can be booked at their office, 143 Mount Rd (tel 849803), at the Thiruvalluvar bus stand in Esplanade Rd (tel 561982) between 6 am and 9 pm, or at Central railway station (tel 563351).

The ITDC tours can be booked at the Mount Rd (tel 869685) or C-in-C Rd office (tel 478884).

Places to Stay

There are three main areas for hotels in Madras. The top-range hotels are mainly along Mount Rd (Anna Salai) and the roads off this principal highway. Around Egmore station and along the section of Poonamallee High Rd between Egmore and Central station are mid-range places interspersed with a few budget places. The cheapest hotels are in George Town between Mint Rd, NSC Bose Rd (Parry's Corner/Popham's Broadway) and North Beach Rd.

Egmore station is the most popular area

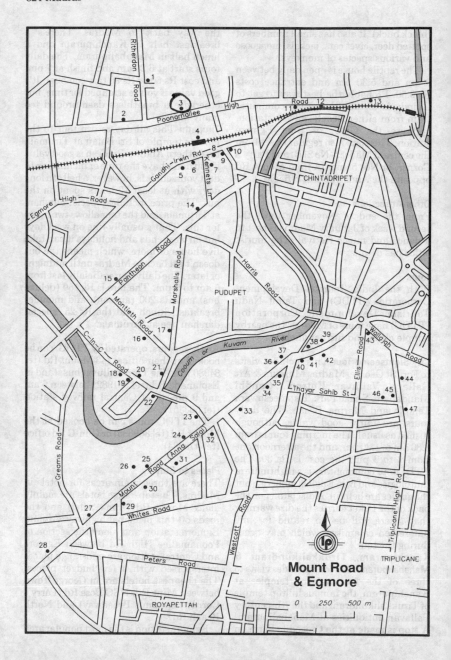

Mount Road & Egmore

0   250   500 m

RYOAPETTAH

TRIPLICANE

CHINTADRIPET

PUDUPET

1	Salvation Army Red Shield Guest House	25	Bank of America
2	Hotel Peacock	26	British Council Library
3	YWCA Guest House	27	Yamuna Restaurant & Madras International Hotel
4	Egmore Railway Station		
5	Tourist Home & Hotel Ramprasad	28	Richy Rich Restaurant
6	Hotel Impala Continental	29	Malaysian Airlines
7	Hotel New Victoria	30	Automobile Association of South India
8	Hotel Imperial		
9	People's Lodge	31	Singapore Airlines, Lufthansa & Grindlays Bank
10	Vaigai & Chandra International Hotels	32	Government of India Tourist Office
11	Everest Boarding & Lodging	33	Tamil Nadu Tourist Office
12	Devi Lodge	34	Binny's Travel Service (American Express)
13	TTDC Youth Hostel		
14	Dayal De Lodge	35	Southern Railways Booking Office
15	Government Museum & Art Gallery	36	Higginbothams
16	Hotel Ambassador Pallava	37	Poompuhar Handicrafts Emporium
17	Hotel Guru	38	Tarapore Tower
18	Hotel Kanchi	39	Anna Road Post Office
19	Indian Tourist Development Corporation (ITDC) Office	40	Hotel Sangam & Buharis Restaurant
20	Vayudoot & Pan Am	41	Chungking Restaurant
21	Air India & Indian Airlines	42	Yadgaar Restaurant
22	British Airways	43	Coronation Durbar Restaurant
23	Hotel Connemara	44	Wheat Hotel
24	Fiesta Restaurant & Spencer's Department Store	45	Maharaja Restaurant
		46	Broadlands
		47	Ganga Restaurant

for travellers these days, but places like Broadlands in the Mount Rd area and the Malaysia Lodge in George Town continue to be well patronised.

Places to Stay - bottom end
Mount Rd Area The very popular *Broadlands* (tel 845573, 848131) is at 16 Vallabha Agraharam St, off Triplicane High Rd, opposite the Star Cinema. It's a beautiful, whitewashed old place with rooms around three interconnected leafy courtyards. The rooms, though simple, have a table and chair, two wicker easy chairs, a coffee table, and beds, of course. There's also a good notice board and you can hire bicycles, but the best thing about Broadlands is the tranquil atmosphere and how well it's run. Straightforward though it is, this is one hotel which is really clean and well kept. You can make international phone calls from here. My

only criticism of this place is their discriminatory anti-Indian policy.

The bulk of the rooms cost Rs 40/78, although there are a few with bathroom at Rs 45/95; dorm facilities (Rs 20) are only available in emergencies. The rooms on the ground floor, especially those near the entrance, can be noisy.

To get there take an auto-rickshaw - most of them know where it is - or bus No 30, 31 or 32 from Esplanade Rd outside the Thiruvalluvar bus stand in the centre of town. From Egmore station take bus No 29D, 22 or 27B - even some of the bus conductors know where Broadlands is! It's about 20 minutes walk from the tourist office - see the map.

Conveniently close to Central station is the *TTDC Youth Hostel* on Poonamallee High Rd. It's only a couple of minutes walk from the station, and although the road is incredibly busy, this place doesn't suffer too badly from the noise. Dorm beds are Rs 20, and there are a couple of doubles for Rs 40, all with shared facilities. It's not a bad place if you're just in Madras overnight.

Places further down Poonamallee High Rd from Central station are assaulted by horrendous noise and pollution from the road in front, the railway line and the 'river' behind. For major emergencies only, you could try *Everest Boarding & Lodging* (tel 30772/3), which has rooms from Rs 45/66.

George Town Another place popular with budget travellers for years is the *Malaysia Lodge* (tel 27053), 104 Armenian St, off Popham's Broadway, at the back of the GPO in George Town. Like the Rex and Stiffles in Bombay, much has been written and said about the Malaysia Lodge over the years – some of it good, most of it bad. It's undeniably cheap and equally basic. Rooms are Rs 18/30 or Rs 20/35 with bath.

The *Hotel Surat* (tel 589236) at 138 Popham's Broadway is above the Madras Cafe. Rooms with bath and phone cost Rs 45/75; if you can get one away from the street, it's not bad value.

Egmore The hotels around Egmore station cover a broad range. This is the real accommodation and travel hub of Madras, and competition for rooms can be fierce. Quite a few places seem to be permanently full, and getting a room in the afternoon can be an exercise in persistence. Cheapest of the lot is the *People's Lodge* (tel 566938) on Whannels Rd. Rooms here cost Rs 30/50, but don't expect too much.

The *Hotel Impala Continental* (tel 561778) on Gandhi Irwin Rd, directly opposite the station, has new rooms around a huge courtyard for Rs 60 a

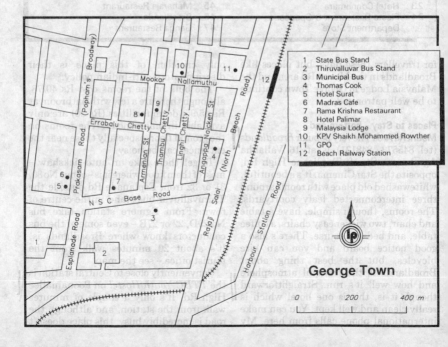

1	State Bus Stand
2	Thiruvalluvar Bus Stand
3	Municipal Bus
4	Thomas Cook
5	Hotel Surat
6	Madras Cafe
7	Rama Krishna Restaurant
8	Hotel Palimar
9	Malaysia Lodge
10	KPV Shaikh Mohammed Rowther
11	GPO
12	Beach Railway Station

George Town

0   200   400 m

double. The *Hotel Ramprasad* (tel 567875) at 22 Gandhi Irwin Rd is better at Rs 77/82 for rooms with hot water and phone. Right next door, the friendly *Tourist Home* (tel 567079) at 21 Gandhi Irwin Rd is more expensive but good value, and the rooms are big. Try to avoid the top floor in summer as these rooms get very hot. The tariff is Rs 88/115 with bath.

A good place to try early in the day is the *Dayal De Lodge* (tel 568359) at 486 Pantheon Rd, not far from Kennets Lane. Rooms in this friendly and relatively spacious lodge cost Rs 47/77.

Also on Gandhi Irwin Rd is the *Chandra International* (tel 568863) at No 6, with rooms for Rs 66/115. Close by at 3 Gandhi Irwin Rd is the *Hotel Vaigai* (tel 567373) which has doubles only, and these cost Rs 110.

Just north of Egmore station at 1086 Poonamallee High Rd is the *YWCA Guest House*. It takes both men and women and has its own restaurant. Singles or doubles cost Rs 45 per person, rooms for four are Rs 40 per person. In addition there's a Rs 10 transient membership fee per head. It is not bad value but always seems to be fully booked. You can also camp in the grounds for a small fee if you have your own vehicle.

In the same area, the *Salvation Army Red Shield Guest House* (tel 33148) is at 15 Ritherdon Rd, 20 minutes walk from Egmore. It's a clean and quiet place, but the Rs 10 dormitory beds are for men only. There are three double rooms with bath for Rs 50. A bit further along at 74 Ritherdon Rd is the *YMCA* (tel 32831), which takes both men and women. Double rooms cost Rs 45 with bath, or there are a few singles with shared facilities for Rs 15.

There are also *retiring rooms* at Central railway station (tel 32218) for Rs 70 a double, Rs 150 with air-con. At Egmore station (tel 848533) they're Rs 50/70 a single/double, Rs 75/150 with air-con.

Places to Stay – middle

One of the biggest in the Egmore area is the *Hotel Imperial* (tel 566176) on Gandhi Irwin Rd. They have a variety of rooms, all with bath and hot water. The cheapest rooms can be fairly small, so try and get one in the block at the rear; those on the side face onto another hotel only one metre away. Rooms cost Rs 82/165, or Rs 160/220 with air-con.

At 1089 Poonamallee High Rd, just north of Egmore station, the *Hotel Peacock* (tel 39081) is good value at Rs 135/190, or Rs 190/265 with air-con. The rooms at the front get the traffic noise. Also on Poonamallee High Rd, the modern *Hotel Blue Diamond* (tel 665981) at No 934 has rooms at Rs 135/175, or Rs 185/240 with air-con.

Some other mid-range places are excellent value. The *Hotel Kanchi* (tel 471100) is at 28 Commander-in-Chief (C-in-C) Rd, just down from the Hotel Connemara. This modern hotel is good value at Rs 128/176, or Rs 160/240 with air-con, and it's got a rooftop restaurant. Close by at 69 Marshalls Rd, Egmore, the *Hotel Guru* (tel 862002) is excellent value and has rooms with bath and hot water for Rs 82/110, or Rs 140/170 with air-con. It's reasonably clean, the staff are helpful and it's conveniently located.

The relatively large *Hotel President* (tel 842211) on Dr Radhakrishnan Rd in Mylapore has air-con rooms at Rs 360/420. It also has a swimming pool and other mod cons. The *New Woodlands Hotel* (tel 473111), 72-75 Dr Radhakrishnan Rd, has air-con singles for Rs 115, doubles for Rs 180.

The *Hotel Ranjith* (tel 470521) at 9 Nungambakkam High Rd is a clean place with rooms for Rs 144/192, or Rs 216/275 with air-con. The food here is also good.

The *Residency Centrepoint Guest House* (tel 456288) is at 167 Kodambakkam High Rd, opposite the Palm Grove Hotel. This is a small, friendly, family-run guest house with modern facilities. There are only three rooms so ring first. Rooms cost Rs 250/300 with air-con and hot water.

Places to Stay – top end

Probably Madras' best known hotel is the old-fashioned but elegant *Hotel Connemara* (tel 810051) on C-in-C Rd, near the tourist office on Mount Rd. The air-con rooms are becoming somewhat run-down and cost Rs 770/880. There is a swimming pool, bar, bookshop and restaurants.

The *Hotel Taj Coromandel* (tel 474849), 17 Nungambakkam High Rd, is probably Madras' most luxurious hotel, with singles at Rs 780, doubles at Rs 960. It's a long way from the centre but like the Connemara does excellent buffet lunches. Another in the same price and quality bracket is the *Welcomgroup Chola Sheraton* (tel 473347), 10 Cathedral Rd, with singles/doubles at Rs 970/1110.

More centrally located at 693 Mount Rd, the *Madras International Hotel* (tel 861811) has rooms for Rs 420/500. The *Hotel Savera* (tel 474700), 69 Dr Radhakrishnan Rd, Mylapore, has rooms for Rs 540/840.

In Egmore, the *Hotel New Victoria* (tel 567738) at 3 Kennets Lane is not bad value at Rs 355/432 with air-con, and the location is very convenient.

Places to Eat

There are numerous vegetarian restaurants in Madras; this is thali territory! On the other hand it is not the place for a beer. You no longer need a 'liquor permit' to buy one, but in return you pay much higher prices – count on at least Rs 30 for a bottle in a restaurant or bar, Rs 17 to Rs 24 in a liquor store. Remember that in south India 'meals' means lunch time; ask for 'tiffin' at other times.

Mount Rd Area There are several good eateries along Mount Rd and close to the Broadlands Hotel. Just around the corner from Broadlands on Triplicane High Rd, the *Maharaja Restaurant* has good toasted sandwiches and lassis, and does snacks right up until midnight. It's become something of a travellers' hangout as it's the best place in the vicinity of Broadlands. Close by, the *Ganga Restaurant* in the Annapurna Hotel has good vegetarian snacks.

The *Coronation Durbar Restaurant* is on Wallajah Rd near the junction with Mount Rd and has a good rooftop terrace which is pleasant in the evenings. The food is good, but even by Indian standards they are a little heavy-handed with the chilli.

On Mount Rd, the *Mathura Restaurant* on the 2nd floor of the Tarapore Tower is an up-market vegetarian restaurant. Thalis here cost Rs 20 and are good value. Their business lunch from 11 am to 3 pm on weekdays for Rs 12 is also good value. Across the road the *Buharis Restaurant* has excellent chicken dishes, and there's an air-con dining hall and an open-air terrace upstairs.

For Chinese food the *Chungking* restaurant almost opposite the Anna Rd post office can't be beaten. It's a very popular place and the food is excellent. Count on around Rs 30 per person.

Another good place to have a meal along Mount Rd – or preferably a cold drink and a snack as the meal prices are quite high – is the *Fiesta Restaurant* in Spencer's Building. This Madras landmark has almost been demolished and is being replaced by a modern shopping complex, but the restaurant and Spencer's department store have survived. Also on Mount Rd is the *Hotel Inland*, close to the Anna Rd post office. It has a rooftop section as well as an air-con room, and an excellent four-course meal costs around Rs 50. The *Manasa* restaurant next to Higginbothams on Mount Rd has also been recommended, as has the *Open House*, also on Mount Rd.

Only a few doors down from the tourist office on Mount Rd, *Aavin* is a stand-up milk bar where you can get lassis, ice cream and excellent cold milk, plain or flavoured.

The *Hotel Connemara* has a wonderful pastry shop, but for a real treat head for the Connemara's Rs 75 buffet. This is a long-running favourite, the food is fantastic and the pianist knows a few good numbers. This place alone makes it worthwhile coming to Madras. Also in the Connemara is the *Raintree* restaurant. It's only open in the evening and is definitely up-market, but the outdoor setting is superb, the service very attentive (you even get a mosquito coil under your table) and there's live classical dancing and music. It's not difficult to spend Rs 120 on a meal for two here. According to one waiter the drinking water is 'very much boiled'.

Further south along Mount Rd, the air-con *Yamuna Restaurant* does an excellent lassi, and the masala dosas and dahi vada are also worth trying.

George Town In the old part of the town there are many vegetarian restaurants. Few stand out, although the *Madras Cafe* on Popham's Broadway does excellent and cheap thalis.

The *Hotel Palimar* on Armenian St is a good air-con vegetarian restaurant – convenient if you're staying at the Malaysia Lodge.

Egmore There are several places to eat along Gandhi Irwin Rd, in front of Egmore station, including the *Rajabhavan* at the entrance to the Hotel Imperial with thalis for Rs 6.50. Nearby is the *Vasanta Bhavan*, next to the Tourist Home, with tasty thalis and fine lassi. This place also has non-vegetarian food.

The *Hotel Impala*, on the corner of Gandhi Irwin Rd and Kennets Lane, does excellent masala dosa for Rs 4. Close by is the *Impala Sweets* and *Impala Snack Bar*.

The *Sherriff Restaurant*, in the Regal Lodge in Kennets Lane, is a cheap non-vegetarian restaurant run by a friendly old Muslim who spends most of the day chanting verses from the Koran.

Things to Buy
The stalls which clutter the footpaths in both Mount Rd and around Parry's Corner are excellent places to pick up cheap 'export reject' clothes. You need to choose carefully, but good shirts for Rs 25 are not hard to find.

For more conventional souvenirs, there's a whole range of craft shops along Mount Rd near the tourist office. Prices aren't cheap but they can be good places to pick up last-minute things.

Getting There & Away
Air Madras is an international arrival point for India as well as an important domestic airport. The brand-new international terminal is well organised and not too heavily used, making Madras a good entry or exit point. There's rarely more than one plane on the ground here at any given time.

There are flights from Singapore (Singapore Airlines, Air India and Indian Airlines), Penang and Kuala Lumpur (Malaysian Airlines), Colombo (Air Lanka and Indian Airlines) and London (British Airways).

The domestic terminal in Madras is also very new and well organised. It's right next door to the international terminal, so walking between the two is quite easy.

Indian Airlines connects Madras with the following towns and cities in India: Bombay (three flights daily, Rs 1015), Delhi (daily, Rs 1405), Calcutta (daily, Rs 1280), Bangalore (five daily, Rs 315), Hyderabad (twice daily, Rs 545), Coimbatore (daily, Rs 510), Tirupathi (twice weekly, Rs 140), Trivandrum (daily, Rs 630), Trichy (11 times weekly, Rs 330), Madurai (11 times weekly, Rs 425), Cochin (daily, Rs 655) and Port Blair (three times weekly, Rs 1255).

Indian Airlines also operate on the international routes to Colombo and Singapore.

Vayudoot has flights from Madras to Coimbatore (Rs 510), Thanjavur (Rs 330), Tirupathi (Rs 140), Madurai (Rs 435), Cochin (Rs 655) and Vijayawada (Rs 425).

Bus The Tamil Nadu state bus company is

called Thiruvalluvar, and the bus station is on the Esplanade in George Town, around the back of the High Court building. This is also known as the Express bus stand, and all interstate buses leave from here.

The reservation office (tel 561835) upstairs is computerised and there is advance booking on most routes. The office is open from 7 am to 9 pm daily. There's a Rs 2 reservation fee, and you have to pay Rs 0.10 for the form! It's worth picking up a copy of the *Bus Route Guide & Map*, Rs 5, which is sporadically available from the enquiry office downstairs. It has a comprehensive list of all Thiruvalluvar bus routes, journey times and fares, and there's also an excellent map of Tamil Nadu.

The Tamil Nadu state bus stand is on the other side of Popham's Broadway. This station is fairly chaotic and there is nothing in English. However, this does not present any real difficulties since an army of young boys attach themselves to every foreigner who enters the terminal and for Rs 0.10 to Rs 0.20 (though, naturally, they try for more) find your bus.

The main reason to use this station is for the buses to Mahabalipuram. There are a number of services, the quickest being No 188. The journey takes two hours and

costs Rs 6.70. The other Mahabalipuram services are Nos 19C, 119A and 188K. There are at least 30 buses daily on this route between about 4.30 am and 9 pm. For other destinations, refer to the table at the bottom of the page.

Train On the 2nd floor of the new building at Madras Central there is an Indrail office which can be immensely useful for foreign visitors. Like the equally wonderful railway tourist offices in New Delhi and Bombay, it handles all manner of tourist railway problems, not just Indrail enquiries and bookings, and is where you go for tourist-quota bookings. It's open from 10 am.

For normal reservations (nontourist quota), there are separate booking offices for 1st and 2nd class on metre-gauge trains, and for all broad-gauge trains. First-class metre-gauge reservations are handled inside the main station building, 2nd-class metre-gauge reservations are upstairs in the small annexe tacked on to the left-hand side of the building. All broad-gauge reservations are now computerised and are handled in the well-organised office on the 2nd floor of the new building, to the left of the main building, and over the incredibly smelly drain (which passes for a river). This reservation office is open from 7.30 am to 1 pm and 1.30 to 7.30 pm

Bus Routes from Madras

	route No	frequency	duration	km	fare
Bangalore	831, 828	17 daily	8 hours	358	Rs 48
Chidambaram	300, 301	6 daily	6 hours	233	Rs 22
Ernakulam	891	1 daily	16 hours	697	Rs 88.60
Hyderabad	898	1 daily	15 hours	647	Rs 92
Madurai	137	16 daily	10 hours	447	Rs 51.50
Mysore	863	1 daily	11 hours	497	Rs 57.50
Ooty	465	1 daily	15 hours	565	Rs 55
Pondicherry	803	20 daily	4 hours	163	Rs 15.50
Rameswaram	166	1 daily	13 hours	550	Rs 52.50
Thanjavur	323	12 daily	8 hours	321	Rs 30.50
Tirupathi	802	3 daily	4 hours	152	Rs 18
Trichy	123	22 daily	8 hours	319	Rs 30.50
Trivandrum	894	4 daily	17 hours	752	Rs 87.50

Monday to Saturday, 7.30 am to 1 pm on Sunday. Although there are more than 25 windows, you still have to queue for up to 30 minutes to get served.

At Egmore, the booking office is open the same hours as at Central, and the phone number for general enquiries is 566565.

The rail journey to Delhi is 2194 km; it takes 40 hours on the Tamil Nadu Express and costs Rs 150 in 2nd class, Rs 620 in 1st. Calcutta is 1669 km away, and the Coromandel Express does it in the relatively quick time of 27 hours at a cost of Rs 125 in 2nd class, Rs 500 in 1st. The Ganga Kaveri Express connects Madras and Varanasi. The 2147-km journey takes 38½ hours at a cost of Rs 148 in 2nd class, Rs 609 in 1st.

The fastest train on the 1279-km trip to Bombay is the Dadar to Madras Express, which takes 24 hours at a cost of Rs 106 in 2nd class, Rs 418 in 1st. The Bombay, Calcutta and Delhi trains all depart from Madras Central station.

The daily Cochin Express runs from Central to Ernakulam (Cochin) – a 708-km trip taking 14 hours and costing Rs 73 in 2nd class, Rs 264 in 1st. To Trivandrum, the Trivandrum Mail is the quickest over the 925 km. It takes 16½ hours at Rs 86 in 2nd class, Rs 326 in 1st.

The overnight Nilgiri Express runs daily from Central, taking 10 hours to make the 530-km trip to Mettuppalayam, from where you continue by the rack train up to Ooty. Fares are Rs 58 in 2nd class, Rs 213 in 1st.

Bangalore, 356 km away, is connected by frequent trains from Central. The fast Brindavan Express takes just six hours and costs Rs 44 in 2nd class, Rs 156 in 1st. You must make a reservation to travel on this commuter train from Madras; there are no unreserved compartments and bookings are heavy, although it is possible to just jump on and occupy a bit of space.

Also from Central the daily Charminar Express whisks you to Hyderabad, a 794-km

journey, in 15 hours for Rs 80 in 2nd class, Rs 291 in 1st. The daily Saptagiri Express covers the 147 km to Tirupathi in 3½ hours at a cost of Rs 22 in 2nd class, Rs 77 in 1st.

From Egmore there are a number of daily trains to Trichy, the fastest being the one-class Vaigai Express which covers the 401 km in five hours for Rs 49 in 2nd class. This train continues on to Madurai – 556 km, 7½ hours, Rs 59 in 2nd class. There is only 2nd-class seating on this train, but the carriages are fairly modern and comfortable – quite adequate for a journey of this length.

The fast overnight Sethu Express to Rameswaram takes only 14½ hours for the 656-km trip. Fares are Rs 68 in 2nd class, Rs 250 in 1st. There are also trains from Egmore to Chidambaram (244 km, six hours) and Thanjavur (351 km, nine hours).

Boat The Shipping Corporation of India (SCI) operates a service to the Andaman Islands (see that section for details).

There is still no service to Malaysia although there are mutterings from time to time that it will be restarted. Check with the SCI, or with their agent K P V Shaik Mohammed Rowther & Co (tel 511535), 202 Linghi Chetty St.

Getting Around

Airport Transport The domestic and international terminals are adjacent to each other, 16 km south of the centre. The easiest way out there is by suburban train from Egmore to Tirusulam, which is right across the road from the terminals. The trains run from 4 am until late at night, and the journey takes about 45 minutes.

Public buses go right by the airport entrance from Mount Rd, but trying to board a bus with a rucksack can be fun and games, especially in peak hour. The buses to use are Nos 18, 18J, 52, 52A, 52B, 52C, 52D and 55A. All buses start and finish at Parry's Corner, but if you want to get on or off at Mount Rd, only the 18 and 18J go along here.

From Egmore station there's a deluxe minibus which operates 30 times a day between 4 am and 1.40 am. It calls in at the Indian Airlines office on the way. The departure point is right outside the Hotel Imperial, and there's a small cabin on the footpath which has the timetable on it. The trip takes 45 minutes and costs Rs 20.

An auto-rickshaw to or from Mount Rd costs Rs 40 and no amount of persuasion will get them to use the meter. At night you can expect to pay more. A taxi costs Rs 80.

Bus The bus system in Madras is less overburdened than in the other large cities and can be used fairly easily, although peak hour is best avoided. The seats on the left-hand side and the rear seat are reserved for women.

Some useful routes include:

Nos 23A & 27C – Egmore (opposite Peoples Lodge) to Mount Rd.
Nos 31, 32 & 32A – Triplicane High Rd (Broadlands) to Central station and Parry's Corner. The No 31 continues on to North Beach Rd for the GPO and the Shipping Corporation of India.
Nos 22 & 27B – Egmore to Wallajah Rd (for Broadlands).

Nos 17C, 25 & 25B – Mount Rd (opposite Anna Rd post office) to Nungambakkam High Rd for Foreigners Registration Office and Income Tax Office.
Nos 9, 10, 17D – Parry's Corner to Central and Egmore stations.
Nos 11, 11A, 11B, 11D, 17A, 18 & 18J – Parry's Corner to Mount Rd.

Taxi Taxis take up to five people and cost Rs 5 for the first 1.6 km and Rs 2 for each subsequent km. Most drivers will use the meters without being reminded of their existence.

Auto-Rickshaw Auto-rickshaws cost Rs 3 for the first 1.6 km, and Rs 1.50 for each subsequent km. A little persuasion may be required before they use the meter.

Moped If you are feeling like a bit of a daredevil (and have an international motorcycle licence) you can hire mopeds or scooters. The cost is Rs 70 per day for a Kinetic Honda scooter, or Rs 40 for a TVS moped. Insurance is an additional Rs 5 and Rs 3 respectively, but the price does include use of a helmet (of sorts). The company which rents them is U-Rent (tel 841345) at 119 Dr Radhakrishnan Rd in Mylapore, not far from the President Hotel.

Tamil Nadu

Population: 58 million
Area: 130,069 square km
Capital: Madras
Main language: Tamil

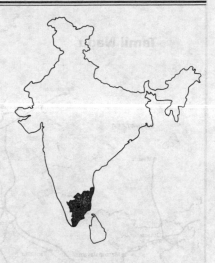

The southern state of Tamil Nadu is the most 'Indian' part of India. The Aryans never brought their meat-eating influence to the extreme south, so this is the true home of Indian vegetarianism. The early Muslim invaders and, later, the Moghuls made only fleeting incursions into the region. As a result, Hindu architecture here is at its most vigorous while Muslim architecture is virtually nonexistent. Even the British influence was a minor one, despite the fact that Madras was their earliest real foothold on the subcontinent.

There were a number of early Dravidian kingdoms in the south. The Pallavas, with their capital at Kanchipuram, were the earliest and were superseded by the Cholas, centred at Thanjavur (Tanjore). Further south, the Pandyas ruled from Madurai, while in the neighbouring region of Karnataka, the Chalukyans were the main power.

Tamil Nadu is the home of Dravidian art and culture, characterised best by the amazingly ornate temples with their soaring towers known as *gopurams*. A trip through Tamil Nadu is very much a temple hop between such places as Kanchipuram, Chidambaram, Kumbakonam, Tiruchirappalli, Thanjavur, Madurai, Kanyakumari and Rameswaram. There are also earlier temples in Tamil Nadu, most notably the ancient shrines of Mahabalipuram. In addition, the state has an important group of wildlife reserves, some fine beaches and a number of pleasant hill stations, including the well-known Ooty.

The people of Tamil Nadu, the Tamils, are familiar faces far from their home state, many having emigrated to Singapore, Malaysia and Sri Lanka. Despite their reputation as hard workers, Tamil Nadu is an easygoing, relaxed state.

Tamil Nadu offers the traveller excellent value, particularly in accommodation. Prices are generally lower than they are further north and standards are often higher. There are many modern, low-priced hotels and the food is also good – you may get heartily sick of thalis while you're here, but they are consistently good value.

Architecture

The Dravidian temples of the south, found principally in Tamil Nadu, are unlike the classically designed temples found further north. The central shrine of a Dravidian temple is topped by a pyramidal tower of several storeys known as the *vimana*. One or more entrance porches, the mandapams, lead to this shrine. Around the central shrine, there is a series of courts, enclosures and even tanks. Many of the larger temples have '1000-pillared halls' although, in fact, there are rarely actually 1000 pillars. At

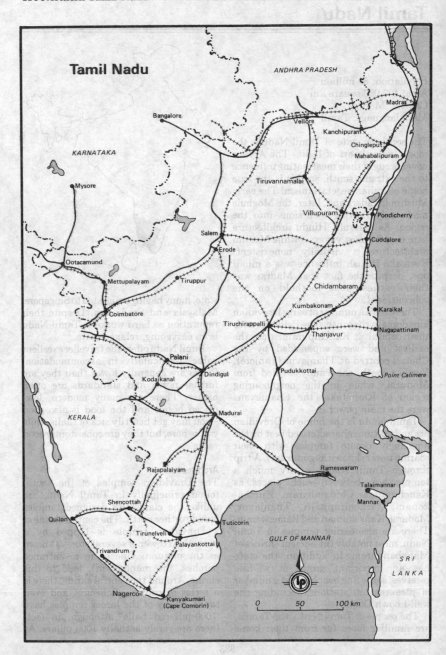

Madurai, there are 997 pillars, the Sri Ranganathaswamy Temple in Trichy has 940, while at Tiruvarur there are only 807.

The whole complex, which often covers an enormous area, is surrounded by a high wall with entrances through towering gopurams. These rectangular, pyramidal towers are the most notable feature of Dravidian design. They are often over 50 metres high, but their interest lies not only in their size – most are completely covered with sculptures of gods, demons, mortals and animals. The towers positively teem with life, as crowded and busy as any Indian city street. Furthermore, many are painted in such technicolour that the whole effect is that of a Hindu Disneyland. This is no recent development – like classical Greek statues, they were all painted at one time.

Northern Tamil Nadu

VELLORE (population 180,000)
Vellore, 145 km from Madras, is a semirural bazaar town full of bullock carts and street markets. It is noteworthy only for the 16th-century Vijayanagar fort and its Jalakanteshwara Temple, and even they are not worth a special detour. Both the moated fort and the temple inside it are in an excellent state of preservation.

Surprisingly, Vellore also has one of the best hospitals in India, and the people who come here from all over India for medical care give the town a cosmopolitan feel. However, there is no tourist office and the bus station, with signs only in Tamil, is absolutely chaotic.

The Fort
The fort is constructed of granite blocks and surrounded by a moat which is supplied by a subterranean drain fed from a tank. It was built in the 16th century by Sinna Bommi Nayak, a vassal chieftain under the Vijayanagar kings, Sada

Sivaraja and Sriranga Maharaja. Later, it became the fortress of Mortaza Ali, the brother-in-law of Chanda Sahib who claimed the Arcot throne, and was taken by the Adil Shahi Sultans of Bijapur. In 1676, it passed briefly into the hands of the Marathas until they, in turn, were displaced by Daud Khan of Delhi in 1708. The British occupied the fort in 1760, following the fall of Srirangapatnam and the death of Tipu Sultan. It now houses various public departments and private offices, and is open daily.

Jalakanteshwara Temple
Jalakanteshwara Temple was built about the same time as the fort (around 1566) and, although it doesn't compare with the ruins at Hampi, it is still a gem of late Vijayanagar architecture. During the invasions by the Adil Shahis of Bijapur, the Marathas and the Carnatic nawabs, the temple was occupied as a garrison and desecrated. Following this, it ceased to be used.

Christian Medical College Hospital
This hospital is a surprising find in such a small town. There are over 1000 beds in the main buildings alone and patients come from as far away as Malaysia, Sri Lanka and the Middle East. Founded by an American missionary in 1900, the hospital has nearly 300 staff members and over 1000 students and trainees. It is supported by 74 churches and organisations worldwide.

Church
The modern church is built in an old British cemetery, which contains the tomb of a captain who died in 1799 'of excessive fatigue incurred during the glorious campaign which ended in the defeat of Tipoo Sultaun'. There is also a memorial to the victims of the little-known 'Vellore Mutiny' of 1806. The mutiny was instigated by the second son of Tipu Sultan, who was incarcerated in

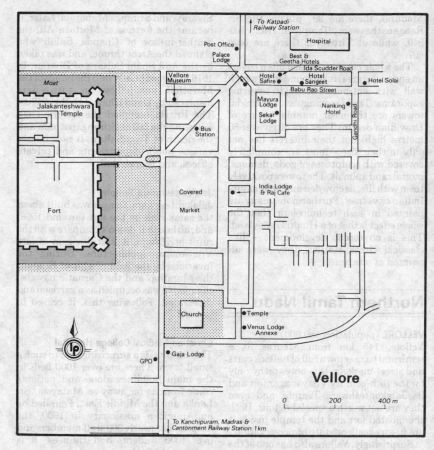

Vellore

0   200   400 m

To Katpadi Railway Station

Post Office
Palace Lodge

Hospital

Best & Geetha Hotels
Ida Scudder Road

Hotel Safire
Hotel Sangeet

Hotel Solai

Babu Rao Street

Vellore Museum

Mayura Lodge
Sekar Lodge

Nanking Hotel

Gandhi Road

Bus Station

Moat

Jalakanteshwara Temple

Covered Market

India Lodge & Raj Cafe

Fort

Church

Temple
Venus Lodge Annexe

Gaja Lodge

GPO

To Kanchipuram, Madras & Cantonment Railway Station 1km

the fort at that time, and was put down by a task force sent from Arcot.

Places to Stay - bottom end

Vellore's cheap hotels are concentrated along Babu Rao St and, to a lesser extent, Ida Scudder St, near the bus station and hospital. One of the best is the *Mayura Lodge* (tel 25488) at 85 Babu Rao St. The rooms are clean and airy, and good value at Rs 25/40/48 for singles/doubles/triples. On the same street, the *Hotel Solai* (tel 22996) is more expensive at Rs 30/44, and the rooms have no windows.

Places to Stay - middle

One km north of Vellore on the Katpadi road is the *Hotel River View* (tel 25768). It is definitely misnamed as it's at least 500 metres from the river with views of nothing more exotic than a smelly drain. However, it's modern and clean. Rooms cost Rs 99 for a double with bath, Rs 198 with air-con, and there are three restaurants.

Places to Eat

In the India Lodge opposite the bazaar, the *Raj Cafe* has good vegetarian meals and excellent dahi vada.

Ida Scudder Rd is dotted with 'meals' restaurants. The *Hotel Geetha* is a good one with excellent masala dosa, while the *Hotel Best* next door serves non-vegetarian food and is a good place for an egg breakfast. For pseudo-Chinese food there's the *Nanking Hotel*, opposite Mani's Mansion on Gandhi Rd.

The *Venus Bakery*, opposite the CMC Hospital on Ida Scudder Rd, has excellent freshly baked biscuits and bread.

Getting There & Away
Bus As elsewhere in Tamil Nadu, the area is serviced by the regional state bus company, (in this case PATC), and the statewide Thiruvalluvar Transport Corporation. The dusty, pot-holed bus station is one of the worst in the country. It is completely disorganised, nothing is in English and an open sewer runs through the middle of it.

Thiruvalluvar buses run to Trichy (Nos 104, 139 & 280, Rs 27.50), Tiruvannamalai (No 104) and Madurai (No 139, Rs 39). All these buses originate in Vellore and can be booked in advance. Others, which pass through en route (and may be full), go to Madras, Bangalore, Tirupathi, Thanjavur and Ooty.

PATC operates 26 buses a day to Kanchipuram, starting at 5 am. The trip takes 2½ hours. There are also PATC buses to Madras (11 daily, Rs 13.30) and Bangalore (11 daily, Rs 21.50).

Train Vellore has two stations on the metre-gauge line between Katpadi and Villipuram, the larger cantonment one being about one km south of the Gaja Lodge. There are daily express and passenger trains to Tirupathi, Tiruvannamalai and Villipuram.

Vellore's nearest broad-gauge railway station is at Katpadi, on the main Bangalore to Madras line. Buses wait outside the station for trains to arrive. The fare into Vellore is Rs 0.80 and the journey takes anything from 10 to 30 minutes.

The trip from Katpadi to Bangalore takes four hours and costs Rs 32 in 2nd class, Rs 109 in 1st. It's 130 km from Katpadi to Madras, and the two-hour journey costs Rs 20 in 2nd class, Rs 68 in 1st.

AROUND VELLORE
Vellamalai
The temple of Vellamalai is only 25 km from Vellore, a one-hour trip on bus No 20M or 20A. The main temple is dedicated to Shiva's son Kartikaya, Murga in Tamil. There's a temple at the bottom of the hill but the main temple, carved from a massive stone, is at the top. Shoes must be removed at the base of the hill. There's a good view of the bleak countryside around Vellamalai – the ground is stony and strewn with boulders. The cloth knots you will see tied to trees are requests that wishes be granted.

THE NORTH-WEST
Hogenekkal
This beautiful, quiet waterfall is 25 km from Dharampuri and 80 km from Bangalore towards Salem. Here, the Cauvery River enters the plains and the river dashing against the rocks is a great sight, particularly impressive in July-August. A huge weekly fair is held in the nearby village of Pennagaram.

Places to Stay The *Hotel Tamil Nadu* (tel 47) has double rooms for Rs 60, or Rs 125 with air-con. Dormitory beds in the attached *Youth Hostel* cost Rs 20.

Yercaud
Yercaud is 33 km uphill from Salem. A quiet and low-priced hill town with many coffee plantations, this is a good place for trekking and boating.

Places to Stay The *Hotel Tamil Nadu* (tel 273) has rooms for Rs 60, and Rs 100 with air-con. Dormitory beds cost Rs 20, or Rs 35 in an air-con dorm.

KANCHIPURAM (population 150,000)

Sometimes known as Siva Vishnu Kanchi, Kanchipuram is one of the seven sacred cities of India and was, successively, capital of the kingdoms of the Pallavas, Cholas and rajas of Vijayanagar. During Pallava times, it was briefly occupied by the Chalukyans of Badami, and by the Rashtrakutas when the battle fortunes of the Pallava kings reached a low ebb.

Kanchipuram is a spectacular temple city and its many gopurams can be seen from a long way away. Many of the temples are the work of the later Cholas and of the Vijayanagar kings. They're spread out all across the city and you need a whole day to see them. The best way to do this is to hire a bicycle or a rickshaw driver for the day (the latter should cost around Rs 20). There are no taxis or autorickshaws.

Have plenty of small change handy when visiting the temples to meet various demands for baksheesh from 'temple watchmen', 'shoe watchers', 'guides' and assorted priests. As it's a famous temple city visited by plenty of pilgrims and tourists, the army of hangers-on is legion.

Kanchi is also famous for its hand-woven silk fabrics. This industry originated in Pallava times, when the weavers were employed to produce clothing and fabrics for the kings.

Kailasanatha Temple

Dedicated to Shiva, Kailasanatha is one of the earliest temples. It was built by the Pallava king, Rayasimha, in the late 7th century, though its front was added later by King Mahendra Varman III. It is the only temple at Kanchi which isn't cluttered with the more recent additions of the Cholas and Vijayanagar kings, and so reflects the freshness and simplicity of early

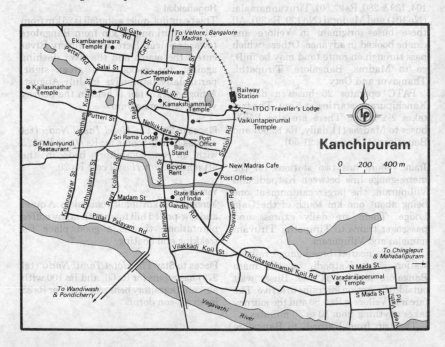

Kanchipuram

0   200   400 m

Dravidian architecture, of which other examples can be seen at Mahabalipuram.

Fragments of the 8th-century murals which once graced the alcoves are a visible reminder of how magnificent the temple must have looked when it was first built.

Vaikuntaperumal Temple

Parameshwara and Nandi Varman II built this temple between 674 and 800 AD, shortly after the Kailasanatha Temple. It is dedicated to Vishnu. The cloisters inside the outer wall consist of lion pillars and are representative of the first phase in the architectural evolution of the grand 1000-pillared halls of later temples.

Ekambareshwara Temple

The Ekambareshwara Temple is dedicated to Shiva and is one of the largest temples in Kanchipuram, covering nine hectares. Its 59-metre-high gopuram and massive outer stone wall were constructed in 1509 by Krishna Devaraja of the Vijayanagar Empire, though construction was originally started by the Pallavas and the temple was later extended by the Cholas. Inside are five separate enclosures and a 1000-pillared hall.

The temple's name is said to be a modified form of Eka Amra Nathar – the Lord of the Mango Tree – and in one of the enclosures is a very old mango tree, with four branches representing the four Vedas. The fruit of each of the four branches is said to have a different taste, and a plaque nearby claims that the tree is 3500 years old. The tree is revered as a manifestation of the god and is the only 'shrine' that non-Hindus are allowed to walk around. You can also partake of the sacred ash (modest contributions gratefully accepted) but, as this is still a functioning Hindu temple, non-Hindus cannot enter the sanctum sanctorum.

A 'camera fee' of Rs 3 goes towards the upkeep of the temple. The visit could cost you more, however, as this is undoubtedly one of the worst temples for hustlers.

Kamakshiamman Temple

Dedicated to the goddess Parvati, this imposing temple is the site of the annual car festival, held on the 9th lunar day in February-March. When not in use, the ornately carved wooden car is kept partially covered in corrugated iron halfway up Gandhi Rd. The temple has a golden gopuram in the centre.

Varadarajaperumal Temple

Like the Ekambareshwara Temple, this is an enormous monument with massive outer walls and a 1000-pillared hall. One of its most notable sculptural features is a huge chain carved from a single piece of stone. The temple is dedicated to Vishnu and was built by the Vijayanagar kings. Entrance costs Rs 0.50 and there is a 'camera fee' of Rs 2.

Other Temples

In addition to the more famous Kanchipuram temples described in this chapter there are many more, both in the city and outside it. Walk in any direction and you will come across others. The small Kailasanatha Temple, for example, is run by the Archaeology Department and is very interesting. It's closed between 12.30 and 4 pm.

Places to Stay

There are a couple of basic lodges in the centre of town, just a few minutes walk from the bus station. The *Sri Rama Lodge* (tel 3195) is at 20 Nellukkara St, the main street. Although the hotel's business card boasts of 'gracious living', the rooms are basic and cost Rs 30/45. There are air-con doubles for Rs 120.

Opposite the Sri Rama, the *Sri Krishna Lodge* (tel 2831) is at 68-A Nellukkara St. It's much the same in quality and price.

The *Hotel Tamil Nadu* (tel 2561) is on Kamatchi Sannathi St, near the railway station. It's the best place in town but is also more expensive, with rooms at Rs 75/100.

Places to Eat

There are many small vegetarian places in the vicinity of the bus stand where you can buy a typical plate meal for around Rs 4. If you're tired of thalis – and there's not much else – you could try the non-vegetarian *Sri Muniyundi Restaurant* on Kossa St near Nellukkara St. If you have plenty of time to wait, the food at the *Hotel Tamil Nadu* is not too bad either.

Getting There & Away

Bus As elsewhere, the timetable here is in Tamil, but there is no problem finding a bus in the direction you want to go. There are a few direct buses to Mahabalipuram (No 212A), but it is usually quicker to take one of the more frequent buses to Chingleput (Rs 3.70), and then another from there to Mahabalipuram.

There are direct Thiruvalluvar buses to Trichy (No 122, Rs 30), Kanyakumari (No 195, Rs 63), Pondicherry (No 804), Madras (No 828) and Bangalore (No 828).

There are also plenty of PATC buses to Madras, Vellore and Tiruvannamalai.

Train Trains run from Kanchipuram to Madras Beach station, and to Arakkonam on the Madras to Bangalore line.

MAHABALIPURAM (Mamallapuram)

World famous for its shore temples, Mahabalipuram was the second capital and sea port of the Pallava kings of Kanchipuram, the first Tamil dynasty of any real consequence to emerge after the fall of the Gupta Empire.

Though the dynasty's origins are lost in the mists of legend, it was at the height of its political power and artistic creativity between the 5th and 8th centuries AD, during which time the Pallava kings established themselves as the arbiters and patrons of early Tamil culture. Most of the temples and rock carvings here were completed during the reigns of Narasimha Varman I (630-668 AD) and Narasimha Varman II (700-728 AD). They are notable for the delightful freshness and simplicity of their folk-art origins, in contrast to the more grandiose monuments built by later larger empires such as the Cholas. The shore temples in particular strike a very romantic theme and are some of the most photographed monuments in India.

The wealth of the Pallava Kingdom was based on the encouragement of agriculture, as opposed to pastoralism, and the increased taxation revenue and surplus produce which could be raised through this settled lifestyle. The early Pallava kings were followers of the Jain religion, but the conversion of Mahendra Varman I (600-630 AD) to Shaivism by the saint Appar was to have disastrous effects on the future of Jainism in Tamil Nadu, and explains why most temples at Mahabalipuram (and Kanchipuram) are dedicated to either Shiva or Vishnu.

The sculpture here is particularly interesting because it shows scenes of day-to-day life – women milking buffaloes, pompous city dignitaries, young girls primping and posing at street corners or swinging their hips in artful come-ons. In contrast, other carvings throughout the state depict gods and goddesses, with images of ordinary folk conspicuous by their absence. Stone carving is still very much a living craft in Mahabalipuram, as a visit to the School of Sculpture shows. The school is diagonally opposite the bus stop and is open from 9 am to 1 pm and 2 to 6 pm, closed Tuesdays.

Today, Mahabalipuram is a very pleasant and easygoing little village of essentially two streets. Positioned at the foot of the low-lying, boulder-strewn hill where most of the temples and rock carvings are to be found, it's very much a travellers' haunt. People rent houses and stay here for some time, and restaurants catering to western tastes – usually seafood – have been set up. After the noise, bustle, fumes and crowding of Madras and other large cities, visiting Mahabalipuram is like coming to another planet. It's a relaxing place with a

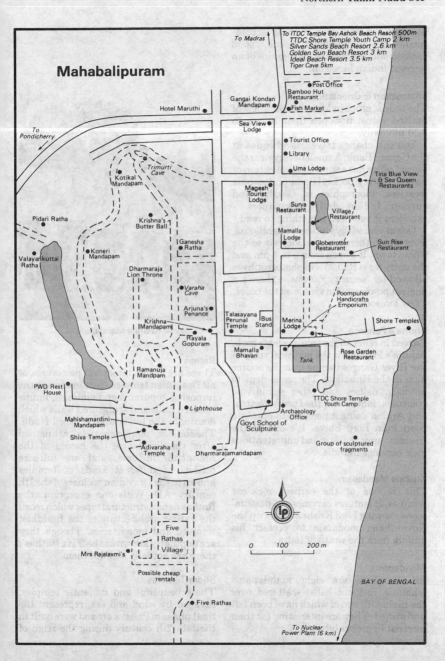

Mahabalipuram

To Madras

To ITDC Temple Bay Ashok Beach Resort 500m
TTDC Shore Temple Youth Camp 2 km
Silver Sands Beach Resort 2.6 km
Golden Sun Beach Resort 3 km
Ideal Beach Resort 3.5 km
Tiger Cave 5km

Post Office
Bamboo Hut Restaurant
Fish Market

Gangai Kondan Mandapam

Hotel Maruthi

Sea View Lodge

To Pondicherry

Tourist Office

Library

Uma Lodge

Tina Blue View & Sea Queen Restaurants

Trimurti Cave

Kotikal Mandapam

Magesh Tourist Lodge

Surya Restaurant

Village Restaurant

Pidari Ratha

Krishna's Butter Ball

Mamalla Lodge

Globetrotter Restaurant

Sun Rise Restaurant

Koneri Mandapam

Ganesha Ratha

Valayankuttai Ratha

Dharmaraja Lion Throne

Varaha Cave

Poompuher Handicrafts Emporium

Arjuna's Penance

Talasayana Perunal Temple

Bus Stand

Merina Lodge

Shore Temples

Krishna Mandapam

Rayala Gopuram

Mamalla Bhavan

Tank

Rose Garden Restaurant

Ramanuja Mandpam

PWD Rest House

Lighthouse

TTDC Shore Temple Youth Camp

Mahishamardini Mandapam

Shiva Temple

Govt School of Sculpture

Archaeology Office

Adivaraha Temple

Dharmarajamandapam

Group of sculptured fragments

0   100   200 m

Five Rathas Village

Mrs Rajalaxmi's

Possible cheap rentals

Five Rathas

BAY OF BENGAL

To Nuclear Power Plant (6 km)

wonderful combination of cheap accommodation, an excellent beach, good seafood *and* the fascinating remains of an ancient Indian kingdom.

Information & Orientation
The tourist office in Mahabalipuram is of limited value; it's open from 10 am to 5.30 pm daily.

You can change travellers' cheques at the Canara Bank. A small library near the tourist office has a surprising collection of novels, history books, Hindu philosophic treatises, biographies of Gandhi and current Indian daily newspapers – excellent if you need something to read.

Orient yourself by visiting the lighthouse, from which there are good views over the whole town. It's open from 2 to 4 pm and the entry fee is Rs 0.25. No photography is allowed for 'security reasons' – there's a nuclear power station visible on the coast, a few km south.

Arjuna's Penance
Carved in relief on the face of a huge rock, Arjuna's Penance is the mythical story of the River Ganges issuing from its source high in the Himalaya. The panel depicts animals, deities and other semidivine creatures, fables from the *Panchatantra*, and Arjuna doing a penance to obtain a boon from Lord Shiva. It's one of the freshest, most realistic and unpretentious rock carvings in India.

Krishna Mandapam
This is one of the earliest rock-cut temples. It features carvings of a pastoral scene showing Lord Krishna lifting up the Govardhana mountain to protect his kinfolk from the wrath of Indra.

Mandapams
In all, there are eight mandapams (shallow, rock-cut halls) scattered over the main hill, two of which have been left unfinished. They are interesting for their internal figure sculptures.

Krishna Mandapam

Rathas
These are the architectural prototypes of all Dravidian temples, demonstrating the imposing gopurams and vimanas, multi-pillared halls and sculptured walls which dominate the landscape of Tamil Nadu. The Rathas, 'temple chariots', are named after the Pandavas, the heroes of the *Mahabharata* epic, and are full-size models of different kinds of temples known to the Dravidian builders of the 7th century AD. With one exception, the Rathas depict structural types which recall the earlier architecture of the Buddhist temples and monasteries. Though they are popularly known as the 'Five Rathas', there are actually eight of them.

Shore Temples
These beautiful and romantic temples, ravaged by wind and sea, represent the final phase of Pallava art and were built in the late 7th century during the reign of

Rajasimha. The two spires of the temples, containing a shrine for Vishnu and one for Shiva, were modelled after the Dharmaraja Ratha, but with considerable modification. Such is the significance of the shore temples that they were recently given World Heritage listing.

The temples are approached through paved forecourts, with weathered perimeter walls supporting long lines of bulls, and entrances guarded by mythical deities. Although most of the detail of the carvings has disappeared over the centuries, a remarkable amount remains, especially inside the shrines themselves.

Tiger Cave

This shady and peaceful group of rathas is five km north of Mahabalipuram and signposted off to the right of the road. The carvings here are similar to those of the other rathas in town, but Tiger Cave is unspoilt by the touts, souvenir junk stalls

and bus loads of rubbernecks. To get there, take any Madras bus or rent a bike.

Beach

The village itself is only a couple of hundred metres from the beach. The beach is very wide and, as there is no shade, it gets uncomfortably hot surprisingly early in the day.

North of the shore temples, the local fishers pull in their boats. The local toilet is also here, and a walk along the beach is an exercise in sidestepping the turds. You need to go south of the shore temples, or 500 metres or so north to the resorts to find a clean piece of beach.

Places to Stay – bottom end

If you don't mind roughing it a bit, it's possible to stay with families in Five Rathas village, a 15-minute walk from the bus stand. Rooms are generally nothing more than thatched cells, with electricity

Shore Temple, Mahabalipuram

and fan if you're lucky, and basic washing facilities. Touts who hang around the bus station will find you accommodation in the village but, of course, you'll pay more if you use them. The usual cost is Rs 80 to Rs 100 per week, or Rs 120 if a tout takes you. *Mrs Rajalaxmi's* is the best in the village. The rooms have fan and electricity, and her back yard shrine is extremely well kept. Meals are available on request. She also does intricate rangolis (the white chalk designs put on the doorsteps of many houses) each morning and is happy to explain their meaning.

The TTDC *Shore Temple Youth Camp* is convenient. A bed in one of the two rather characterless dorms, and a locker to put your gear in will cost you Rs 20. There are no mosquito nets which can make life unpleasant at certain times of year. There are also some mid-range cottages here.

A popular budget hotel right by the bus station, the *Mamalla Bhavan* (tel 250) has clean rooms with bath for Rs 25/40. If the Mamalla Bhavan is full, the next best place is the *Mamalla Lodge*, run by the same people. Double rooms with common showers and toilets cost Rs 25. The place is reasonably clean, but service can be a trifle haphazard.

Also good value is the new *Uma Lodge*, just off the main street. The rooms are large and clean, costing Rs 50 for a double with bath. Further along the same side street, the *Tina Blue View Restaurant*, run by the friendly Xavier, has a few small rooms – overpriced at Rs 70 considering what else is around.

There are a number of other small lodges in Mahabalipuram, including the *Merina Lodge*, the *Magesh Tourist Lodge* and the *Sea View Lodge*. All have rooms in the Rs 20 to Rs 50 bracket, but prices are generally negotiable depending on demand. It would be generous, but dishonest, to describe these places as 'very basic'. In fact, most are filthy, depressing hovels, their walls splattered with the desiccated spittle of generations of previous occupants.

The beds have the appearance of tussocks of paspalum grass and the sheets (where they exist) bear the indelible stains of numberless nuptials and various unthinkable practices. How much does a new sheet and a can of whitewash cost?

Places to Stay – middle & top end

The new *Surya Restaurant* by the small lake has just a couple of cottages with good views from the upper level rooms. These have balconies and cost Rs 150 with fan and bath. The downstairs rooms have neither the balcony nor the view, and are overpriced at Rs 100.

The TTDC *Shore Temple Youth Camp* has cottages from Rs 99 to Rs 132.

Scattered over several km along the Madras road, north of Mahabalipuram, is a string of beach resorts, ranging from the very expensive to the surprisingly reasonable. They all offer fairly similar facilities – swimming pool, bar, restaurant catering to both western and Indian tastes, games, sometimes a discotheque – but vary a lot in terms of the quality and siting of the rooms. Some are obviously pitched at those who are primarily interested in sun-n-sand activities, while others cater more to the businessperson in search of a congenial place to relax or conclude a deal.

Going north, 500 metres from Mahabalipuram, the first of the resorts is the *Temple Bay Ashok Beach Resort* (tel 251). This is the most expensive of them all although, in fact, it doesn't offer much more than the other places. Rooms or cottages cost Rs 470/715. All are air-conditioned and there's a restaurant, bar (fiercely expensive!), swimming pool (Rs 20 per day for nonguests), tennis court and lounge with daily newspapers.

Next to the Temple Bay Ashok Beach Resort, two km from town, is the TTDC *Shore Temple Beach Resort* (tel 235, 268), a Tamil Nadu government enterprise. The rooms are in groups of cottages facing the sea, many of them split-level with a bathroom and lounge downstairs and bedroom upstairs. Singles are Rs 135, doubles Rs 200, and air-conditioned Rs 300. Like the other resorts, it has a swimming pool, restaurant and bar. On paper it sounds like good value, but the place is not maintained as carefully as it might be and, although the food is reasonable, you may well be too old to enjoy it by the time it arrives.

A further 600 metres up the coast is the *Silver Sands Beach Resort* (tel 228, 283). This is the largest of the resorts and has a variety of rooms. It's also very popular with Russian package tourists. Prices vary according to the season, but range from Rs 216 for a single with fan and swing (yes, swing) up to Rs 445 for a deluxe air-con single with 'sitout, balcony, refrigerator and swing'. Doubles are Rs 276 and Rs 590 respectively. Beachfront cottages are more expensive again, ranging from Rs 570 up to Rs 870 with air-con, TV and video. Further back from the beach, the cottages are much cheaper and are actually listed as a separate resort – the *Silver Sands Budget Tourist Complex*. The rooms here cost from Rs 50 to Rs 95 for a single with bath, and Rs 77 to Rs 120 for a double. This is the only one of the resorts without a swimming pool.

Next up the coast, three km from Mahabalipuram, the *Golden Sun Beach Resort* (tel 245, 246) has 50 rooms and a swimming pool. This is another Russian hangout. Rooms cost Rs 170/210, or Rs 210/260 with air-con. The rate for dinner, bed and breakfast is Rs 255/380, or Rs 295/430 with air-con.

The last of the resorts is the *Ideal Beach Resort* (tel 240, 243), 3½ km from town. With only 15 rooms, this is the smallest of the resorts, and the owner wants to keep it that way to preserve the intimate atmosphere. Accommodation costs Rs 120/165, or Rs 220/275 with air-con. There is a restaurant and swimming pool, but no bar.

Places to Eat

When travellers congregate on a beach, you can be pretty sure that, sooner or later, there will be good seafood restaurants. Mahabalipuram is no exception, with several places offering excellent, attractively presented seafood. They're popular, pleasantly relaxed (generally with a good selection of contemporary western music) and they all try hard to please. These restaurants include the *Rose Garden* on Shore Temple Rd, and the *Sun Rise* 100 metres behind it. Neither have fans and they can be incredibly stuffy at the end of a hot day.

The *Globetrotter* is on the lane by the lake and is open until 1.30 am. A bit further along, the *Village Restaurant* is one of the oldest and has fans and excellent food. The *Surya* restaurant is on the same lane in a delightful setting. The food is similar to what you get everywhere.

The *Tina Blue View Restaurant* in the north of town by the beach is a good place in the heat of the day, as the shady upstairs balcony catches any breeze that might be around and there's a good view of the shore temples. The service is slow and the food a shade more expensive than elsewhere. Beers here cost Rs 20. Next door is the *Sea Queen Restaurant*. It's a good place for seafood, and the banana bun cake is also recommended.

Choosing one of these places over another is really just a matter of personal preference – they're all worth trying.

For south Indian vegetarian food, the place to go is *Mamalla Bhavan*, opposite the bus stand. You can eat well and cheaply here. Around the back of the main restaurant, the special thali section serves different thalis every day for Rs 8 – definitely above average, but lunchtime only. The dining hall at the front does regular (but still tasty) thalis and other familiar south Indian snacks.

Things to Buy

Mahabalipuram has revived the ancient crafts of the Pallava stone masons and sculptors, and the town awakes every day to the sound of chisels chipping away at pieces of granite. Some excellent work is turned out. The yards have contracts to supply images of deities and restoration pieces to many temples throughout India and Sri Lanka, and some of the smaller works are available for sale in the crafts shops which line the road from the bus stand to the Five Rathas.

Also for sale in these shops are soapstone images of Hindu gods, woodcarvings, jewellery and bangles made from seashells and other similar products. This is one of the best places to buy soapstone work.

Getting There & Away

Buses No 19C, 119A, 188 and 188K go to Madras. The No 188 bus goes by the most direct route. There are at least 30 buses daily between 4.35 am and 8.50 pm and the 2½-hour trip costs Rs 6.70.

Direct buses leave for Pondicherry five times a day. The journey takes 2½ hours and costs Rs 10. Get there early if you want a seat. There are four direct buses to Kanchipuram. Alternatively, take a bus to Chingleput and then another from there to Kanchipuram.

Getting Around

Bicycles are available for hire in the village if you want to visit Tirukkalikundram, the Crocodile Farm or Tiger Cave. There's a cycle shop about halfway between the Mamalla Lodge and the Mamalla Bhavan. Bicycles cost Rs 8 per day and there's no fuss, no deposit – just provide your name and passport number.

OTHER PLACES AROUND MADRAS

Chingleput

Chingleput is on the road between Madras and Trichy. It is noteworthy for the ruins of an ancient Vijayanagar fort which had a chequered history during the British period.

Covelong

On the coast, Covelong is a fishing settlement with a fine beach. The

expensive TTDC *Fisherman's Cove Resort* (tel 268) has singles from Rs 550 to Rs 600 and doubles from Rs 600 to Rs 700, as well as some cheaper lodges. Food at the Fisherman's Cove is very good and surprisingly reasonable in price.

Tirukkalikundram (Tirukazhukundram)

Fourteen km from Mahabalipuram, this pilgrimage centre with its hilltop temple is famous as the place where two eagles come each day, just before noon, to be fed by a priest. Legend has it that they come

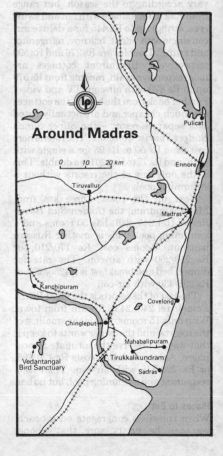

Around Madras

from Varanasi (Benares). Five hundred very steep steps lead to the top of the hill where the soft drink sellers at the top do a brisk trade when it's hot! Some less-fit visitors get themselves carried up in baskets. What most guidebooks ignore about this place, however, is the amazing temple complex with its enormous gopurams at the base of the hill. It's very impressive, yet seems to have few visitors. You can get here from Mahabalipuram by bus or by bicycle.

Crocodile Farm

This farm breeds crocodiles to augment the crocodile populations of India's wildlife sanctuaries. There are now only a few hundred of these reptiles left. Visitors are welcome and you can see crocodiles of all sizes, from the newly hatched to adults. The farm is about 15 km from Mahabalipuram on the road to Madras, and is signposted. Probably the best way to get there is by bicycle, although you can take any Madras bus from Mahabalipuram.

Vedanthangal

Vedanthangal is one of India's major bird sanctuaries. Immediately after the rainy season, great numbers of aquatic birds flock here, 85 km from Madras. The best time to see them is between 3 and 6 pm.

Places to Stay The *Vedanthangal Rest House* is run by the Forests Department. Rooms cost Rs 15/25 and meals are available. Accommodation should be booked in advance with the Wildlife Warden (tel 413947), 49 Fourth Main Rd, Adyar, Madras.

Tiruvannamalai

Further south towards Pondicherry, a 66-km detour inland from Tindivanam will bring you to the temple town of Tiruvannamalai. There are over 100 temples here, but the Shiva-Parvati Temple of Arunachaleswar is said to be the largest in India. The main gopuram is 66 metres and 13 storeys high, and there is

a 1000-pillared hall. The splendid old fortress of Gingee can be visited between here and Pondicherry.

Places to Stay You can stay at the *Park Hotel*, or at the *Modern Cafe* which is clean and has doubles for Rs 25.

Gingee

Gingee (pronounced 'shingee') is about 150 km south-east of Madras, on the road to Tiruvannamalai. There is an interesting complex of forts here, constructed mainly around 1200 AD during the Vijayanagar Empire. The fort is built on three separate hills, joined by three km of fortified walls. The buildings – a granary, audience hall, Shiva temple and a mosque in memory of a favourite general – are fairly ordinary, but the boulder-covered mountain landscape is impressive.

Gingee is pleasantly free of postcard sellers and the like; in fact it's deserted. You can easily spend a whole day here exploring. There's an uneven staircase of stone slabs up Krishnagiri Hill, but the route to Rajagiri Fort is much more difficult to follow. A rickshaw from the town to the hills and back, waiting for you while you explore, costs about Rs 15.

PONDICHERRY (population 300,000)

Formerly a French colony settled early in the 18th century, Pondicherry became part of the Indian Union in the early '50s when the French voluntarily relinquished control. Together with the other former French enclaves of Karaikal (also in Tamil Nadu), Mahé (Kerala) and Yanam (Andhra Pradesh), it now forms the Union Territory of Pondicherry.

The tourist literature gives you the impression that Pondicherry is an enduring pocket of French culture on the Indian subcontinent, but it's nothing of the sort. The only remaining visible French influences are the red *kepis* and belts worn by the local police, the huge French Consulate-General which, together with the predictable Hotel de Ville, dominates the waterfront, and a few streets around the central square which exude a Mediterranean ambience. Otherwise, Pondicherry is as Indian as anywhere else in India, although it is relatively well-lit, paved and laid out. It certainly doesn't compare with Goa's Portuguese or Darjeeling's English flavour. English is spoken everywhere and the signs are in English or Tamil, not French.

The main reason people visit Pondicherry is to see the Sri Aurobindo Ashram and its offshoot, Auroville, 10 km outside town. The ashram, founded by Sri Aurobindo in 1926, is one of the most popular in India with westerners, and is also one of the most affluent. Its spiritual tenets represent a synthesis of yoga and modern science. After Aurobindo's death, spiritual authority passed to one of his devotees, a French woman known as 'The Mother', who herself died in 1973, aged 97. Although the ashram underwrites and promotes a lot of cultural and educational activities in Pondicherry, it's very unpopular with local people because it owns virtually everything worth owning in the union territory but refuses to allow local participation in the running of the society.

Orientation

Pondicherry is laid out on a grid plan surrounded by a semicircular boulevard, so it's easy to find your way around. A north-south canal divides the town into an eastern and a larger western part. In colonial days, the canal separated Pondicherry's European and Indian sections. The French residential area was near the present-day harbour. The main street is now known as Rue Nehru and, at the southern end of the beach road (near the Park Guest House), there is a statue of Duplexis.

The Aurobindo Ashram, its offices, educational institutes and guest houses are clustered around the streets between the waterfront and the canal. The French Consulate-General is also in this area.

The streets in this part of town are very attractive and strongly reflect their French origins.

Most of the hotels are on the west side of the canal, except the Ashram accommodation which is by far the best (although not the cheapest) in town. The railway station is at the southern edge of town, while the bus station is one km west along the main drag, Lal Bahabhur St.

1	GK Lodge
2	Victoria Lodge
3	Market
4	Aristo Hotel
5	India Coffee House
6	Aristo Guest House
7	Amala Lodge
8	Ellora Hotel
9	Hotel Priya (non-veg)
10	Auroville Shop
11	Hotel Priya (veg)
12	Kanchi Hotel
13	Higginbothams Hotel
14	Vak Bookshop
15	Bliss Restaurant
16	Sri Aurobindo Ashram
17	Cottage Guest House
18	International Guest House
19	GPO
20	Snow Lion Restaurant
21	French Consulate-General
22	Kailash French Bookshop
23	Romain Roland Library
24	Seaside Guest House
25	French Library
26	Museum
27	Old Lighthouse
28	Gandhi Memorial
29	Tourist Office
30	Paris Restaurant & Shanthi Guest House
31	Bank
32	Le Transit Restaurant
33	Foreigners' Registration Office
34	Government Tourist Office
35	Water Tower
36	Ajantha Restaurant
37	Blue Dragon Chinese Restaurant
38	Alliance Française
39	Park Guest House
40	Fiesta Restaurant

Pondicherry

To Auroville & Madras

To Youth Hostel & Hotel L'Abri

Thiyaga Raja St

P Covil St

MA Covil St

ID Covil St

KA Covil St

Sri Aurobindo St

Supraya Chettiar St

C Covil St

AH Madam St

Rue Nehru

Rangapillai St

Nidarajapayer St

North Boulevard

B Derichemont St

L Thollendal St

Dupuy St

St Louis St

To Auroville & Madras

Barathi St

SS Pillai St

Anna Salai

St Theresa St

Sinna Pappara St

Lapporth St

Monthorsier St

C Mudhaliar St

Mahatma Gandhi Rd

Mission St

Canteen St

Capr Xavier St

Gingy St

Govt Square

Vict Simonel St

François Martin St

Compagnie St

St Martin St

To Bus Stations, Villupuram & Cuddalore

Lal Bahabhur St

Elai Amman Covil St

Labour Donnai St

Suffren St

Romain Roland St

Dumas St

Goubert Ave

Botanical Gardens

Canal

South Boulevard

0   200   400 m

Railway Station

To TV Station

To New Lighthouse

Main Wharf

1 2 3 4 6 5 7 8 9 10 11 12 13 14 15 16 17 18 19 20 21 22 23 24 25 26 27 28 29 30 31 32 33 34 35 36 37 38 39 40

Information
The tourist office is on Goubert Ave, the road along the waterfront, but it is of absolutely no use.

The GPO is right by the canal in the centre of town, and the telegraph office (open 24 hours) is in the same building.

The Auroville Shop has information and maps of the ashram. The main Auroville Information & Reception Centre is at Bharat Nivas in Auroville, together with their handicrafts shop. The shop is closed on Saturdays and Sundays. There's very little printed information about Auroville here – they mostly seem to sell books on and by Sri Aurobindo and The Mother.

There are quite a few handicraft shops around called Auro-this or Auro-that. They sell excellent handmade goods from Auroville, including leatherwork, pottery and children's clothes.

The Vak Bookshop on Rue Nehru is one of the best in the country for books on religion and philosophy. As the name suggests, the Kailash French Bookshop on Lal Bahabhur St stocks all kinds of French books. There's a branch of Higginbothams on Gingy St, across the canal from the International Guest House.

Sri Aurobindo Ashram
The main ashram building is on Rue de la Marine and is surrounded by other buildings given over to the various educational and cultural activities of the Aurobindo Society. The ashram is open every day and you can be shown around on request. The room in which Aurobindo and The Mother used to meditate (Aurobindo's Samadhi) is open for viewing daily between 11.30 and 11.45 am, by appointment only. Personally, I found its air of self-conscious other-worldliness somewhat contrived.

Opposite the main building is the educational centre where you can sometimes catch a film, slide-show, play or lecture. These very popular events are open to all and audiences are usually half-western and half-Indian. There's usually no entry charge, but a donation is sometimes collected.

Daily 8.30 am ashram tours cost Rs 6, but they are a joke, consisting of being shuffled around by taxi to all the ashram shops and getting the hard sell at each.

Auroville
The brainchild of The Mother and designed by French architect Roger Anger, Auroville was conceived as 'an experiment in international living where men and women could live in peace and progressive harmony with each other above all creeds, politics and nationalities'. Its opening ceremony on 28 February 1968 was attended by the President of India and representatives of 121 countries, who poured the soil of their lands into an urn to symbolise universal oneness. For a time, idealism ran high and the project attracted many foreigners, particularly from France, Germany, the UK, Holland and Mexico. Construction of living quarters, schools, an enormous meditation hall (the Matri Mandir) and dams, and reafforestation, orchard and other agricultural projects were started. The amount of energy and effort invested in Auroville in those early days is obvious even now, and the idealism with which the place began still surfaces in conversations with Aurovillians.

Unfortunately, the death in 1973 of The Mother, undisputed spiritual and administrative head of the Sri Aurobindo Society and Auroville, resulted in a power struggle for control of Auroville. In support of its case for control, the Society quoted The Mother as having said that 'the township with all its property will belong to the Sri Aurobindo Society', but the Aurovillians countered this with her statement that 'Auroville belongs to nobody in particular, (it) belongs to humanity as a whole'.

The struggle soon became acrimonious, with both sides making bitter accusations. On the one hand, the Aurovillians

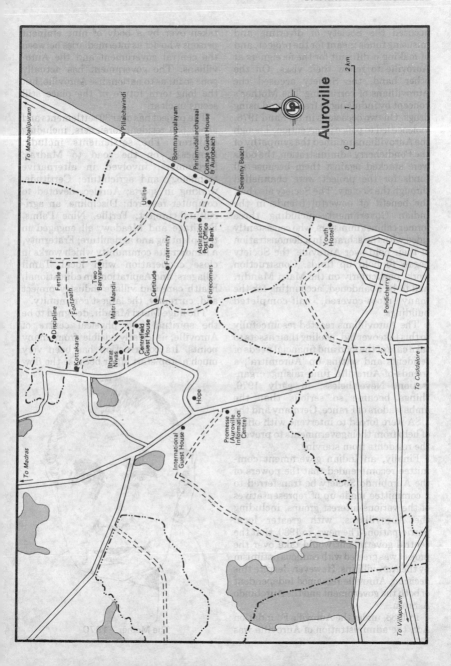

accused the Society of diverting and misusing funds meant for the project, and of making it difficult for the foreigners at Auroville to renew their visas. On the other hand, the Society accused the Aurovillians of corrupting The Mother's concept by indulging in free sex and using drugs. On two occasions in 1977 and 1978, violence led to police intervention. Though the Aurovillians retained the sympathy of the Pondicherry administration, the odds were stacked against them because all funds for the project were channelled through the Society. The Society also had the benefit of powerful friends in the Indian Government, including three former cabinet ministers, who consistently sided with the ashram. In a demonstration of their hold over Auroville, the Society began to hold up funds. Construction work, particularly on the Matri Mandir, had to be abandoned, accounting for the many moss-covered, half-completed buildings.

The Aurovillians reacted resourcefully to this takeover bid, pooling their assets to take care of the food and financial needs of residents and setting up 'Auromitra', a friends-of-Auroville fund-raising organisation. Nevertheless, in early 1976, things became so serious that the ambassadors of France, Germany and the USA were forced to intervene with offers of help from their governments to prevent the residents from starving.

Finally, an Indian government committee recommended that the powers of the Aurobindo Society be transferred to a committee made up of representatives of the various interest groups, including the Aurovillians, with greater local participation. The news, in 1980, that the central government would take over the project was greeted with cautious optimism by the Aurovillians. However, despite this decision, Auroville remained independent of both the government and the Aurobindo Ashram.

In 1988, under the Auroville Foundation Act, the administration of Auroville was taken over by a body of nine eminent persons who act as intermediaries between the central government and the Aurovillians. The government has actually gone so far as to nationalise Auroville, but the long-term future of the place still seems unclear.

The project has over 30 settlements and about 650 resident foreigners, including children. The settlements include: Promesse, on the road to Madras; Forecomers, involved in alternative technology and agriculture; Certitude, working in sports; Aurelec, devoted to computer research; Discipline, an agricultural project; Fertile, Nine Palms, Ermitage and Meadow, all engaged in tree planting and agriculture; Fraternity, a handicrafts community which works in close cooperation with local Tamil villagers; and Aspiration, an educational, health care and village industry project and, currently, the largest community.

The huge Matri Mandir, designed to be the spiritual and physical centre of Auroville, is clearly visible from many points. Its construction has been very much a stop-start affair because the flow

The Mother – 1970

of funds has been less than steady. The frame of the main structure is nearing completion although, at the rate things are going, it will still be a long time before all the finishing touches are added. These include metal discs all over the outside, and a central crystal ball 1½ metres in diameter.

The best way to enter Auroville is from the coast road, at the village of Chinna Mudaliarchavadi. Head towards Aspiration along a small dusty track across an open field. Don't worry about missing this turning because all the local people will point it out for you. It's also possible to enter from the main Madras to Pondicherry road at Promesse. A visit to Auroville makes a good day trip by bicycle from Pondicherry. Everything is so spread out that it's not really practical on foot.

French Institute (Alliance Française)

The French Institute on Dumas St was established in 1955, primarily as a research centre for Indian culture. Its vegetation maps are universally acclaimed. Today, the scope of its activities is far broader and includes French classes and a French restaurant.

Pondicherry Museum

The museum has an eclectic variety of exhibits ranging from French furniture to a history of bead making. It is at 1 Romain Roland St, south of the main square, and is open between 9 am and 5 pm from Tuesday to Sunday.

Places to Stay – bottom end

The cheapest accommodation in Pondicherry is found at the typical Indian hotels west of the canal. The *Hotel Aristo* (tel 24524) at 36 Rue Nehru is not bad, and is certainly cheap at Rs 20/25, but the rooms often seem to be inexplicably 'unavailable'. The *Aristo Guest House* (tel 26728), run by the same people, is around the corner at 50-A Mission St. It has cool clean rooms for Rs 40/60, or Rs 100/125 with air-con.

At the western end of Rue Nehru, the

Victoria Lodge (tel 26367) at No 79 is shabby, but clean enough, and rooms cost Rs 35/50. According to their visiting card, 'air-con suits' are available – sounds like a great idea. Not far away, the *GK Lodge* (tel 23555) is on the very noisy Anna Salai. The rooms don't get too much noise, but from this end of Rue Nehru, it's quite a walk to anywhere. Rooms cost Rs 40/67 with bath.

The friendly *Hotel Kanchi* (tel 25540) is a much better bet. It's on Mission St in a good location, five minutes walk from the GPO. Rooms cost Rs 40/68, and the two huge doubles with balcony at the front are excellent value at Rs 75. *Fenns Lodge*, also on Mission St, has been recommended. Big doubles cost Rs 40.

A few minutes walk south of the main square, in the 'French' part of town, the *Shanthi Guest House* (tel 26473) has large clean rooms for Rs 30/65.

The *International Guest House* (tel 26699) on Gingy St is owned by the Aurobindo Ashram. It is almost always full through long-term group bookings but, if there is room, singles cost Rs 25 and doubles are Rs 30 and Rs 55, or Rs 120 with air-con. There is a 10% discount for ashram members. If you like the ashram atmosphere, you'll probably like this place too. It's near the ashram, two blocks from the sea and a block from the GPO. Rooms are spotlessly clean and contain a photo of The Mother. The only question I had about it is what sort of person pinned the following sign to the notice board: 'Cleanliness is the first indispensable step towards the supramental manifestation. We cannot shelter hippies in our guest house'? I probably wouldn't have noticed it had it not been written in a gold-tinted pseudoartistic scrawl!

Another place belonging to the ashram is the *Cottage Guest House*, just across the canal from the International. It's also almost always full but, if you can get a room, it will cost just Rs 20/30.

The *Park Guest House* (tel 24412) at the southern end of Goubert Ave is probably the best value in town. It is also owned by the Sri Aurobindo Ashram and so has a similar atmosphere. There's a variety of rooms, ranging from a reasonable Rs 45/60 at the back to Rs 75/100 at the front. The cheaper rooms fill up quickly, so get there early. Alcohol and tobacco are prohibited.

Yet another ashram hotel is the *Seaside Guest House* (tel 26494) at 10 Goubert Ave. It's actually an old house, so the rooms are quite spacious but there are few of them. It has doubles only at Rs 75 – quite good value.

Although a little inconveniently located, the *Government Tourist Home* (tel 26376) represents excellent value. It's south of the railway line, a solid 20 minutes walk from any of the restaurants or points of interest. This is not a problem if you rent a bicycle for the duration of your stay. Rooms with bath cost Rs 20/30; an air-con double is a very reasonable Rs 80.

With only two small passenger trains a day to disturb the peace, the *retiring rooms* at the station must be among the quietest in the country. There are two single rooms and one double and these cost Rs 15/30.

There's a *Youth Hostel* on the beach, way out on the northern edge of town, but the inconvenience of the location outweighs any fiscal advantage of staying here. It's only Rs 5 per night, but there's nowhere to eat and no way of cooking anything. The easiest way to get there is by bicycle. Head north along M G Rd, and you'll eventually find black-and-yellow signs directing you to the hostel.

There are a few guest houses out at Auroville, the main one being the *Centrefield Guest House* not far from the Matri Mandir. If you want to stay for a day or two at Auroville, go straight there and they'll find you a place.

Serenity Beach, six km north of Pondicherry and not far from Auroville, is a very basic travellers' hangout. The few lodges are extremely rough-and-ready and really for the die-hards who want to stay maximum time for minimum cost. The *Sunshine Rest House* is little more than a cow shed, with rooms (and I use the word loosely) costing Rs 5. *Chez Mohan* is definitely a notch up the scale and costs Rs 10 with electricity. The best place here is the *Serenité Cottage*, which costs Rs 10 per person. Serenity Beach has one small restaurant, by the beach.

Places to Stay – middle

The brand new *Hotel Mass* (tel 27221) is close to the bus station on Marai Malai Adigal Salai, the continuation of Lal Bahabhur St. Its normal air-con rooms cost Rs 165/220, or there's the deluxe room for Rs 400.

Places to Eat

Pondicherry has some really excellent places to eat Indian, Chinese and even French food.

The popular rooftop restaurant at the *Hotel Aristo* is the best Indian restaurant in town. It has a 207-item menu with everything made to order, so expect to have to wait at least 20 minutes for your food. A lot of effort is put into preparation and presentation.

For Indian snacks or breakfast, the *Indian Coffee House* on Rue Nehru is good value. In the same street, the *Priya Restaurant* has good non-vegetarian Indian food. At the *Bliss Restaurant*, along the canal and Rangàpillai St, straightforward thalis costs Rs 7. This restaurant is closed on Sundays.

Le Transit is a very pleasantly decorated European-style restaurant on Romain Roland St. The menu is limited but the food is excellent – especially the salads. Count on spending at least Rs 50 for two people. Down near the Park Guest House and the Alliance Française, the *Blue Dragon Chinese Restaurant* serves good Chinese food. The *Alliance Française* also has a restaurant which is open in the evenings. The food here is excellent, but expect to pay about Rs 80 for a three-course meal, including the Rs 5 transient membership charge.

Right next door to the Park Guest House, the *Fiesta Restaurant* serves red wine and good food, such as garlic fish (Rs 20) and spaghetti (Rs 12). This is a convenient place for frustrated drinkers and smokers staying at the Park Guest House to indulge themselves.

The *Snow Lion Restaurant*, near the ashram on St Louis St, emphasises Chinese and Tibetan food.

The Sri Aurobindo Ashram *dining hall* is on the northern edge of the main square. If you are staying in one of the ashram guest houses, you can buy meal tickets for Rs 10 per day. The food is unexciting but there's plenty of it.

Getting There & Away

Bus The Thiruvalluvar bus station is on Marai Malai Adigal Salai, the extension of Lal Bahabhur St, 500 metres west of the traffic circle at the junction with Anna Salai. It's quiet and well organised, in stark contrast to the State bus stand 500 metres further west.

The timetable at the Thiruvalluvar stand is in English, and there are buses to Madras at least once an hour (No 803, Rs 15.50), Chidambaram (seven daily, Nos 300 & 324), Tiruvannamalai (Nos 812 & 822), Bangalore (two daily, No 822, Rs 32, 7½ hours), Madurai (daily, No 847, Rs 32, eight hours) and Ooty (daily, No 860, Rs 44.50, 12 hours). Many buses can be booked in advance on the computerised booking system.

From the chaotic State bus stand, there are regular buses to Villupuram, Tiruvannamalai, Mahabalipuram and Chidambaram.

Train Pondicherry does not have the busiest railway station you're likely to come across – most people go by bus. The two daily passenger trains run to Villupuram on the main Madras to Madurai line. From Villupuram, many expresses go in either direction. The

38-km trip between Pondicherry and Villupuram takes two hours and costs Rs 7 in 2nd class, Rs 38 in 1st.

Getting Around

Pondicherry's only public transport is a baffling system of three-wheelers which are a bit like overgrown auto-rickshaws and seem to go all over the place. As there are no signs indicating their destination, they're not much use. It's interesting to watch them on Gingy St – they are often so full that the driver is more out of the vehicle than in and the steering wheel is in front of a passenger. Perhaps it's just as well that it's too complicated to use them.

There are plenty of cycle and auto-rickshaws, but many people hire a bicycle during their stay. This is also a good idea if you plan to visit Auroville. At many of the bike hire shops on M G Rd, you will be asked for Rs 300 or your passport as a deposit. The only way around this is to keep trying until you find a more reasonable place – a deposit of Rs 100 is more appropriate. The usual rental is Rs 8 per day.

Central Tamil Nadu

THANJAVUR (Tanjore) (population 168,000)
Thanjavur was the ancient capital of the Chola kings whose origins, like those of the Pallavas, Pandyas and Cheras with whom they shared the tip of the Indian peninsula, go back to the beginning of the Christian era. Power struggles between these groups were a constant feature of their early history, with one or other gaining the ascendancy at various times. The Cholas' turn for empire building came between 850 and 1270 AD and, at the height of their power, they controlled most of the Indian peninsula south of a line drawn between Bombay and Puri, including parts of Sri Lanka and, for a

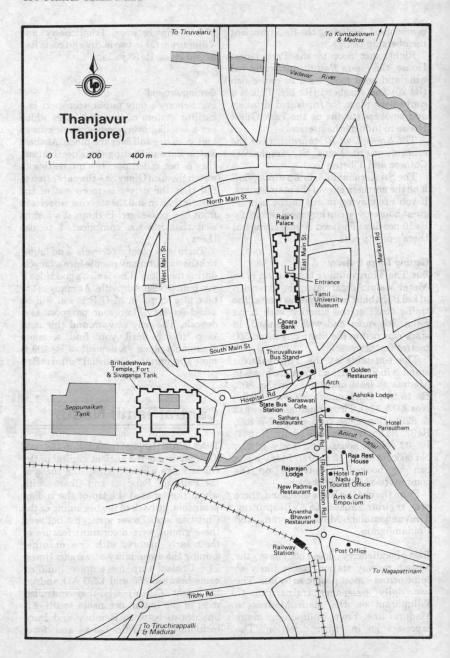

Thanjavur (Tanjore)

To Tiruvaiaru

To Kumbakonam & Madras

Vadavar River

0   200   400 m

North Main St

Raja's Palace

East Main St

Market Rd

West Main St

Entrance

Tamil University Museum

Canara Bank

South Main St

Thiruvalluvar Bus Stand

Brihadeshwara Temple, Fort & Sivaganga Tank

Golden Restaurant

Hospital Rd

Arch

Ashoka Lodge

Seppunaikan Tank

Saraswati Cafe

State Bus Station

Sathars Restaurant

Gandhiji Rd

Anicut Canal

Hotel Parisutham

Railway Station Rd

Raja Rest House

Rajarajan Lodge

Hotel Tamil Nadu & Tourist Office

New Padma Restaurant

Arts & Crafts Emporium

Anantha Bhavan Restaurant

Railway Station

Post Office

To Nagapattinam

Trichy Rd

To Tiruchirappalli & Madurai

while, the Srivijaya Kingdom of the Malay Peninsula and Sumatra.

Probably the greatest Chola emperors were Raja Raja (985-1014 AD), who was responsible for building the Brihadeshwara Temple (Thanjavur's main attraction), and his son Rajendra I (1012-1044 AD), whose navies competed with the Arabs for control of the Indian Ocean trade routes and who was responsible for bringing Srivijaya under Chola control.

Thanjavur wasn't the only place to receive Chola patronage. Within easy reach of Thanjavur are numerous enormous Chola temples. The main ones are at Kumbakonam (40 km away), Thiruvaiyaru (13 km), Thirukandiyur (10 km) and Gangakondacholapuram (71 km). The Cholas also had a hand in building the enormous temple complex at Srirangam near Tiruchirappalli – probably India's largest.

Orientation

The enormous gopurams of the Brihadeshwara Temple dominate Thanjavur. The temple itself, between the Grand Anicut Canal and the old town, is surrounded by fortified walls and a moat. With its winding streets and alleys and the extensive ruins of the palace of the Nayaks of Madurai, the old town was once surrounded by a fortified wall and moat, though most of this has now disappeared.

Between the railway station and the bus stand at the edge of the old city runs Gandhiji Rd, along which are most of the hotels, a number of restaurants, the Poompuhar Arts & Crafts Emporium and the GPO.

Information

The tourist office is in front of the Hotel Tamil Nadu on Gandhiji Rd. It is open from Sunday to Tuesday between 8 am and 8 pm, and from Wednesday to Saturday from 8 to 11 am and 4 to 8 pm. The office has a hand-out map of the area and very little else.

The Canara Bank on South Main St is the only bank in Thanjavur to take Amex cheques, and they do it with a smile!

Brihadeshwara Temple & Fort

Built by Raja Raja (985-1014 AD), the Brihadeshwara Temple is the crowning glory of Chola temple architecture. This superb and fascinating monument is one of only a handful in India with World Heritage listing and is worth a couple of visits. On top of the apex of the 63-metre-high temple, a dome encloses an enormous Shiva lingam (Hindus only). Constructed from a single piece of granite weighing an estimated 81 tonnes, the dome was hauled into place along a six-km earthwork ramp in a manner similar to that used for the Egyptian pyramids. It has since been worshipped continuously for more than 1000 years.

The gateway to the inner courtyard is guarded by one of the largest Nandis (Shiva's bull) in India, also fashioned from a single piece of rock. The carved stonework of the temple, gopurams and adjoining structures is rich in detail and reflects not only Shaivite influences, but also Vaishnavite and Buddhist themes. Recently discovered frescoes adorning the walls and ceilings of the inner courtyard surround have been dated to Chola times and were executed using techniques seen in European fresco work.

Inside the inner courtyard off to the left, the well-arranged Archaeological Museum has some interesting exhibits and photographs showing how the temple looked before much of the restoration work was done, as well as charts and maps detailing the history of the Chola Empire. The museum is open daily from 9 am to 12 noon and 4 to 8 pm, and sells an interesting little booklet titled *Chola Temples* for Rs 2. Also on sale at the entrance is a small booklet called *Thanjavur & Big Temple*. It costs Rs 2.50.

The temple is open every day from 6 am to 12 noon and 4 to 8.30 pm. There is no admittance charge but, as this is still a

Brihadeshwara Temple

functioning Hindu temple, non-Hindus cannot enter the sanctum sanctorum.

Palace, Art Gallery & Saraswati Mahal Library

The huge corridors, spacious halls, observation towers and shady courtyards of this vast labyrinthine building in the centre of the old town were constructed partly by the Nayaks of Madurai around 1550, and partly by the Marathas. Some sections are now in ruins, but a substantial amount remains intact and houses various government offices.

The poorly marked entrance is a wide break in the eastern wall, which leads to a large tree on a traffic circle, and a police station. The palace entrance is off to the left, through the arched tunnel.

The Art Gallery has a superb collection of bronze statues from the 9th to 12th centuries, and the view from the tower on the far side of the courtyard is worth the climb. The gallery is open from 9 am to 1 pm and 2 to 5 pm. Entry costs Rs 1.

The Saraswati Mahal library is next door to the gallery. Established around 1700 AD, the library contains a collection of over 30,000 palm-leaf and paper manuscripts in Indian and European languages, and has a set of prints of prisoners under Chinese torture on its walls! It is open from 10 am to 1 pm and 2 to 5 pm daily, except Wednesday. Don't miss the highly decorated Dharbar Hall off to the left of the library – follow the signs to Mahratta Palace Museum.

The Tamil University Museum contains a good coin collection, and a badly neglected collection of stringed instruments. No-one seems to mind if you pick something up and have a pluck – in fact, the custodian practically thrusts instruments at you.

Places to Stay – bottom end

Many of the hotels are either along

Gandhiji Rd between the bus and railway stations, or at the back of the railway station itself along Trichy Rd – otherwise known as Vallam Rd.

Best value in town is the quiet *Raja Rest House* at the back of the Hotel Tamil Nadu on Gandhiji Rd. The large rooms are arranged around three sides of a huge courtyard, and cost Rs 25/45 with bath. It's about 10 minutes walk from either the bus or railway station.

Closer to the centre, the *Rajarajan Lodge* (tel 21730) is cheaper but noisier, with rooms for Rs 20/40. The *Ashoka Lodge* (tel 20021) is at 93 Abrahem Pandither Rd, just north of the river. It's a big place which has been freshly painted. The rooms on the top floor have the least offensive colour scheme. It's friendly and good value at Rs 30/45, and there are cheaper rooms with common bath.

The *Tamil Nadu Lodge* (tel 22332) on Trichy Rd, south of the railway station, has good clean rooms (if you like bright green) which are not bad value at Rs 25/35. Avoid the *Yagappa Lodge* (tel 22421) across the road – it is grubby and charges the same prices.

The *retiring rooms* at the railway station are good value at Rs 15/30.

Places to Stay – middle

For value in this bracket, you can't beat the *Hotel Tamil Nadu* (tel 21421) on Gandhiji Rd, run by the Tamil Nadu Tourism Development Corporation. It's spacious, spotless and very pleasantly decorated, and the rooms have curtains, fan, desk, wardrobe, comfortable beds, blankets and bathroom with hot water in the mornings. The rooms surround a quiet leafy courtyard, and the staff are helpful. All this costs just Rs 55/77, or Rs 130 for a double with air-con. There is an attached restaurant, and a 'permit room' with cold beer for Rs 20. The hotel is an easy 10-minute walk from either the bus or railway station. The problem with this place is that, with the current scheduling of the TTDC south India tours, it is

booked out by the tour bus passengers every Thursday and Friday night.

Thanjavur's top-notch accommodation is the new *Hotel Parisutham* (tel 21466) on the river at 55 Grand Anicut Canal Rd. It's very flash and charges Rs 104/195 for singles/doubles with bath and phone, Rs 215/275 with air-con.

Places to Eat

There are plenty of simple vegetarian restaurants around the bus stand and along the beginning of Gandhiji Rd, with plate meals for Rs 4. The *Saraswati Cafe* on the corner of Hospital and Gandhiji roads is good for snacks. The *New Padma Restaurant*, almost opposite the Hotel Tamil Nadu, has quite passable meals.

The *Golden Restaurant* on Hospital Rd does good vegetarian meals in its air-conditioned upstairs dining hall. They cost Rs 8 and include a pan at the end. The rooftop is pleasant in the evenings. *Sathars* is a good non-vegetarian restaurant which is open until midnight.

The Hotel Parisutham has the best restaurants in town – the non-vegetarian *Les Repas* serves Indian and Chinese dishes, and the *Geetha* offers vegetarian food. At the *Last Drop* permit room in the basement, beers (Rs 20) come with complimentary nibbles.

The *Hotel Tamil Nadu* restaurant is good for breakfast, but not much else.

Getting There & Away

Air Regular Vayudoot flights go to Madurai (Rs 155) and Madras (Rs 330).

Bus The Thiruvalluvar bus station is fairly well organised but, unusually, there is no timetable in English. The computerised reservation office is open from 7 am to 9 pm. Buses, which can be booked in advance, depart for Madras 12 times daily (No 323, 8¼ hours, Rs 30.50), Pondicherry (No 331, twice daily) and Tirupathi (No 851, daily, Rs 40). There are also quite a few buses passing through on their way to Madurai.

The State bus stand is, as usual, chaotic, with no timetable in any language. Buses to Trichy leave from bays No 9 and 10; the 1½-hour journey costs Rs 7. Kumbakonam buses leave from bays No 7 and 8 on a trip that takes about an hour. There are departures for both destinations every 15 minutes or so.

Train It's nine hours and 351 km between Thanjavur and Egmore station in Madras on the Cholan Express. The fare is Rs 44 in 2nd class, Rs 156 in 1st. The 50-km trip to Trichy takes two hours and costs Rs 8 in 2nd class, Rs 38 in 1st, less (and longer) on a passenger train. The trip to Kumbakonam takes one hour, and it's 2½ hours to Chidambaram. The 192-km trip to Villupuram takes five hours at a cost of Rs 28 in 2nd class, Rs 94 in 1st.

AROUND THANJAVUR

Many of the smaller towns in the Thanjavur area are famous for their huge and impressive Chola temples. The distances of each from Thanjavur are in brackets.

Get a copy of *Chola Temples* by C Sivaramamurti, published by the Archaeological Survey of India. Costing just Rs 2, it describes the three temples in Thanjavur, Dharasuram and Ganga-kondacholapuram. You can buy it at the Brihadeshwara Temple museum in Thanjavur or the Fort St George Museum in Madras.

Thirukandiyur (10 km)

The Thirukandiyur temples are dedicated to Brahma Sirakandeshwara and Harsaba Vimochana Perumal and are noted for their fine sculptural work.

Thiruvaiyaru (13 km)

The famous temple at Thiruvaiyaru is dedicated to Shiva and is known as Panchanatheshwara. Accommodation is completely booked out every January, when an eight-day music festival is held in honour of the saint, Thiagaraja.

Tiruvarur (55 km)

The Shiva temple at Tiruvarur, between Thanjavur and Nagapattinam, was gradually extended over the years. Its 1000-pillared hall actually has just 807 pillars.

Kumbakonam (40 km)

There are five temples in this typical south Indian town. The most important are Sarangapani, Kumbeshwara and Nageshwara, the largest of which is second in size only to the Meenakshi Temple at Madurai. The temples are noted for their colourful semierotic sculpture.

All the temples in Kumbakonam are closed between 12 noon and 4.30 pm.

Thousands of devotees flock to a festival held at the Mahamaham Tank once every 12 years, when the waters of the Ganges are said to flow into the tank. The next such festival will take place in 1992. According to legend, a kumbh (pitcher) came to rest here after a big flood (hence the town name). Shiva broke the pot with his arrow, and its spilled contents

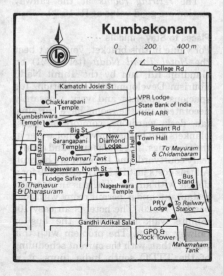

gathered at what is now the sacred Mahamaham Tank.

Kumbakonam also makes an excellent base from which to visit the very interesting nearby towns of Dharasuram and Gangakondacholapuram.

Places to Stay & Eat The *New Diamond Lodge* (tel 20870) at 93 Nageswaran North St has rooms for Rs 20/30, but they can be noisy. The *VPR Lodge* (tel 21949) on Big St is good and clean. Rooms cost Rs 25/40 but the place has so many security bars that it feels more like a prison than a hotel.

The *PRV Lodge* (tel 21820) is at 32 Head Post Office Rd, near the Mahamaham Tank. Its somewhat gloomy singles are Rs 15, and good 'deluxe' doubles with bath cost Rs 35.

The best place in town is the *Hotel ARR* (tel 21234) at 21 Big St. Although it's not very well organised, the rooms are clean and quiet, and cost Rs 55/82 with bath. Air-conditioned rooms cost Rs 115/145.

The railway *retiring rooms* cost Rs 10/20 and are convenient overnight, although the station is not right in the town centre.

Kumbakonam is hardly a gourmet's delight, but the *PRV Lodge* has a good vegetarian 'meals' restaurant and the vegetarian restaurant in the *Hotel ARR* does excellent vegetable biryani. Although the non-vegetarian restaurant is not up to the same standard, it is about the only place in town where carnivores can indulge themselves.

Getting There & Away The bus station is just north of Mahamaham Tank. Once again, there's nothing in English, but there are frequent departures to Thanjavur.

Thiruvalluvar buses use the same station and four buses a day make the 7½-hour journey to Madras (No 305, Rs 27.50). Others pass through here on their way to Madurai, Coimbatore, Bangalore, Tiruvannamalai, Pondicherry and Chidambaram.

The railway station is 500 metres east of the Mahamaham Tank (Rs 4 by cycle-rickshaw from Big St). Trains depart for Madras, Chidambaram, Thanjavur and Trichy.

Dharasuram

The small town of Dharasuram is four km west of Kumbakonam. Set behind the village, the Dharasuram or Airatesvara Temple is a superb example of 12th-century Chola architecture. It was built by Raja Raja II (1146-1163) and is in a fine state of preservation.

The temple is fronted by columns with unique miniature sculptures. In the 14th century, the row of large statues around the temple was replaced with brick and concrete statues similar to those found at the Thanjavur temple. Many were taken to the art gallery in the Raja's Palace at Thanjavur, but have since been returned to Dharasuram. The remarkable sculptures depict Shiva as Kankala-murti (the mendicant) and show a number of sages' wives standing by, dazzled by his beauty. The Archaeological Survey of India has done quite a bit of restoration here in recent years.

Although the temple is used very little at present, there is a helpful and knowledgeable priest who speaks good English. The temple priest mentioned in the previous edition of this book is still there and can quote verbatim what we wrote about him. He is available from 8 am to 8 pm daily and, for a small consideration, will give you an excellent guided tour of the temple.

The best way to visit Dharasuram is to hire a bicycle in Kumbakonam.

Gangakondacholapuram (71 km)

The gopurams of this enormous temple dominate the surrounding landscape. It was built by the Chola emperor Rajendra I (1012-1044) in the style of Brihadeshwara Temple at Thanjavur (built by his father), and is dedicated to Shiva. Many beautiful sculptures adorn the walls of the temple and its enclosures. You'll also see a huge tank into which were emptied vessels of water from the River Ganges, brought to the Chola court by vassal kings. Like the temple at Dharasuram, this one is visited by few tourists and is no longer used for Hindu worship.

Gangakondacholapuram is 35 km north of Kumbakonam and is easily visited from there as a day trip.

Chidambaram

South of Pondicherry, towards Thanjavur, is another of Tamil Nadu's Dravidian architectural highlights – the temple complex of Chidambaram with the great temple of Nataraja, the dancing Shiva. Chidambaram was a Chola capital from 907 to 1310 and the Nataraja Temple was erected during the reign of Vira Chola Raja (927-997). The complex is said to be the oldest in southern India. It covers 13 hectares and has four gopurams, the north and south ones towering 49 metres high. Two of the gopurams are carved with the 108 classical postures of Nataraja, Shiva in his role as the cosmic dancer.

Other notable features of the temple are the 1000-pillared hall, the Nritta Sabha court carved out like a gigantic chariot, and the image of Nataraja himself in the central sanctum. There are other lesser temples in the complex, including ones dedicated to Parvati, Subrahmanya and Ganesh, and a newer Vishnu temple.

The Nataraja Temple courtyard with its many shrines is open from 4 am to 12 noon and 4.30 to 9 pm. The puja ceremony, held at 6 pm every Friday evening, is certainly spectacular with fire rituals and clashing of bells and drums. Although non-Hindus are not allowed right into the inner sanctum, there are usually priests around who will take you in – for a fee, of course.

There is a tourist office at the Hotel Tamil Nadu.

Places to Stay The *Star Lodge* (tel 2743) on South Car St, five minutes walk from the

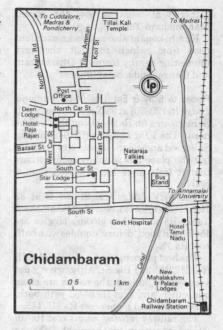

bus station, is the best of the cheap accommodation. Rooms cost Rs 25/35 and are very clean and habitable.

On West Car St, the *Hotel Raja Rajan* (tel 2690) is more expensive at Rs 35/48 with bath. The friendly *Deen Lodge* (tel 2602) close by has reasonable rooms for Rs 20/40.

The new *Hotel Saradha Ram* (tel 2966), near the bus stand, has reasonable singles/doubles for Rs 45/70 and a decent restaurant.

The *Hotel Tamil Nadu* (tel 2323) is the best the town has to offer. Clean rooms here cost Rs 40/75, or Rs 125 for an air-con double. Dormitory beds are occasionally available for Rs 20.

There are a couple more basic lodges by the entrance to the railway station and, at the station itself, there are two *retiring rooms* which cost Rs 10/20.

Places to Eat Meals at the *Hotel Tamil*

Nadu are Rs 10. 'The low point in our culinary experiences' was one evaluation. The *Babu Restaurant*, on the ground floor of the Star Lodge, offers good vegetarian meals.

The *Milky Mist* cafe is opposite the Hotel Tamil Nadu and has excellent snacks and sweets.

Getting There & Away The railway station is 20 minutes walk south of the temple, or Rs 3 by cycle-rickshaw. There are express and passenger trains to Madras, Kumbakonam, Thanjavur, Trichy and Rameswaram.

The bus station is more central and is used by both Thiruvalluvar and local buses. Thiruvalluvar buses leave for Pondicherry and Madras almost every hour (Nos 300 & 326), and others go to Nagapattinam (No 326) and Madurai (No 521). The trip to Pondicherry takes 1½ hours and costs Rs 6.50.

Pichavaram

The sea resort of Pichavaram, with its backwaters and unique mangrove forest, is 15 km east of Chidambaram. A Marine Research Institute is at nearby Porto Novo, a former Portuguese and Dutch port.

Places to Stay The TTDC *Youth Hostel* (tel 32) charges Rs 20 for a dormitory bed.

Tranquebar

Tranquebar, south of Poompuhar, was a Danish trading post in the 18th century and has a church built by the Lutherans. Later, it came under British rule. Danesborg Fort still looks out to sea, impressive and decaying, and there are some fine old colonial houses. Lots of children will pester you to buy Danish coins.

Karaikal

The enclave of Karaikal was part of Pondicherry and is full of French buildings, French gendarmes' capes and so on. It has a well-maintained old Catholic church, although the population

Around Chidambaram

is predominantly Muslim. Hire a bicycle and explore.

Other Places
Nagore (45 km) is an important Muslim pilgrimage centre. Velankanni (90 km) is the site of the famous Roman Catholic Church of Our Lady of Good Health. People of all religions flock to the church, many donating gold or silver models of cured bodily parts! A major festival is held here on 8 September. There's a *PWD Rest House* at Ettukudi, six km away, or write to the vicar of St Mary's Church, Velankanni, about accommodation. The *St Joseph's Pilgrims Quarters* at Velankanni charges Rs 25 for a double with bath, and the *Matha* restaurant next door is good.

Only a small village now stands at the mouth of the Cauvery River. Here, Poompuhar was once a major seaport through which the Chola Empire conducted trade with Rome and with other centres to the east. Poompuhar has a fine beach, a good *Rest House* and some very cheap south Indian vegetarian restaurants.

TIRUCHIRAPPALLI (population 730,000)
This city is usually known by its shortened names of Trichy or Tiruchy. Its most famous landmark is the Rock Fort Temple, a spectacular monument perched on a massive outcrop of rock which rises abruptly from the plain to tower over the old city. There are a few other such outcrops on the way to Thanjavur, one of which has a temple built on it, but none are as large or as tall as the one at Trichy. The Rock Fort Temple is reached by a steep flight of steps cut into the rock, and the views from the summit are magnificent.

The other landmark at Trichy is much less well known, which is surprising because it's probably the largest and one of the most interesting temple complexes in India. This is the Sri Ranganathaswamy Temple (Srirangam), built on an island in the middle of the River Cauvery and covering a staggering 2.5 square km!

There is also another huge temple complex nearby – the Sri Jambukeshwara Temple. Both are visible from the summit of the Rock Fort Temple, shrouded in coconut palms, and it's worth spending a day exploring them.

Trichy itself has a long history going back to the centuries before the Christian era when it was a Chola citadel. In the 1st millennium AD, it changed hands between the Pallavas and Pandyas many times before being taken by the Cholas in the 10th century AD. When the Chola Empire finally decayed, Trichy passed into the hands of the Vijayanagar kings of Hampi and remained with them until their defeat, in 1565 AD, by the forces of the Deccan sultans. The town and its fort, as it stands today, was built by the Nayaks of Madurai and was one of the main centres around which the wars of the Carnatic were fought in the 18th century during the British-French struggle for supremacy in India.

Monuments aside, the city's good range of hotels and facilities makes it a pleasant place to stay. Though spread out, Trichy has an excellent local bus system which doesn't demand the strength of an ox and the skin of an elephant to use.

Orientation
Trichy is scattered over a considerable area. Although you will need transport to get from one part to another, most of the hotels and restaurants, the bus stand, railway station, tourist office, airline offices and GPO are within two or three minutes walk of each other in what is known as the junction (or cantonment) area.

The Rock Fort Temple is 1½ km north of this area, near the banks of the River Cauvery. A further 1½ km north, on an island in the Cauvery, are Trichy's two main temples.

Information
The tourist office is at the front of the Hotel Tamil Nadu, within sight of the bus

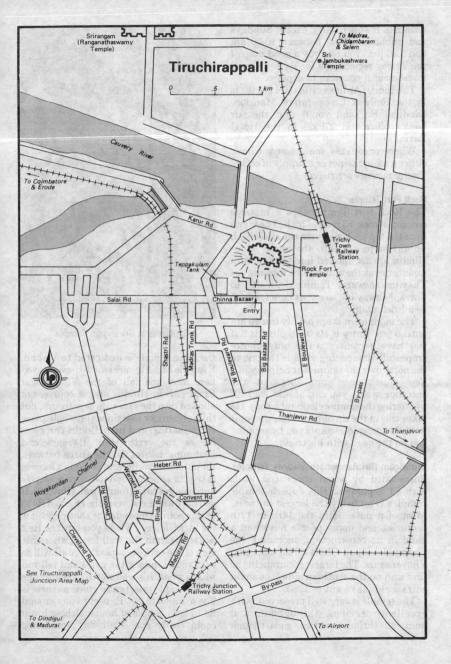

Srirangam
(Ranganathaswamy Temple)

Tiruchirappalli

0   .5   1 km

To Madras,
Chidambaram
& Salem

Sri
Jambukeshwara
Temple

Cauvery River

To Coimbatore
& Erode

Karur Rd

Trichy
Town
Railway
Station

Teppakulam
Tank

Rock Fort
Temple

Salai Rd

Chinna Bazaar

Entry

Shastri Rd

Madras Trunk Rd

W Boulevard Rd

Big Bazaar Rd

E Boulevard Rd

By-pass

Thanjavur Rd

To Thanjavur

Woyakondan Channel

Heber Rd

Werners Rd

Lawsons Rd

Birds Rd

Convent Rd

Cleveland Rd

Madurai Rd

See Tiruchirappalli
Junction Area Map

Trichy Junction
Railway Station

By-pass

To Dindigul
& Madurai

To Airport

terminal. It's open daily, except Sundays and public holidays, between 10.30 am and 5.30 pm. You can buy a good map of the Trichy region here for Rs 3 – a good investment if you plan to explore.

The Indian Airlines office (tel 23116) is in the Railway Co-operative Mansion, Dindigul Rd, and you'll find the Air Lanka office (tel 27952) in the Hotel Laxmi.

Wherever you stay, make sure you have either a mosquito net or a supply of coils – Trichy mozzies are fierce!

Rock Fort Temple

The Rock Fort Temple tops a massive outcrop of rock, 83 metres high. The views from the top are well worth the stiff climb up 437 steps cut into the stone. Non-Hindus are not allowed into the sanctum sanctorum at the summit, or into the Sri Thayumanaswamy Temple dedicated to Shiva, halfway up, so a visit here tends to be a brief affair.

The monument is open daily from 6 am until 8 pm. Entry is Rs 0.50, plus Rs 5 if you have a camera. (The only photographically interesting vista is the one to the north over the temples at Srirangam.) You must leave your shoes at the entrance, where you can amuse yourself by offering the temple elephant a coin. He takes this in the tip of his trunk, passes it to his keeper and rewards you by tapping you on the head with his trunk.

Srirangam (Sri Ranganathaswamy Temple)

Surrounded by seven concentric walls with 21 gopurams, this superb temple complex is probably the largest in India. Most of it dates from the 14th to 17th centuries, and many people have had a hand in its construction, including the Cheras, Pandyas, Cholas, Hoysalas and Vijayanagars. The largest gopuram in the first wall on the southern side (the main entrance) is as recent as 1980.

The temple is very well preserved, with excellent carvings throughout and numerous shrines to various gods, though

Sculpture at Srirangam Temple

the main temple is dedicated to Vishnu. Even the Muslims are said to have prayed here after the fall of the Vijayanagar Empire. Non-Hindus are, of course, not allowed into the sanctum sanctorum, but this is no major loss since the whole place is fascinating, and non-Hindus can go as far as the sixth wall. Bazaars and Brahmins' houses fill the space between the outer four walls, and you don't have to take your shoes off or deposit your bicycle until you get to the fourth wall (Rs 0.20). If you have a camera, you'll be charged Rs 10 at this point. Opposite the shoe deposit is the 'Art Gallery', where you buy the Rs 2 ticket to climb the wall for a panoramic view of the entire complex. A guide will go with you to unlock the gates and tell you what's what. It's well worth engaging one of the temple priests as a guide as there is just so much to see. Expect to pay around Rs 10 for a couple of hours, although you could easily spend all day wandering around this complex. The inner temple is open daily from 6.15 am to 1 pm and from 3.15 to 8.45 pm.

An annual car festival is held here between 15 December and 25 December each year, drawing pilgrims from all over India. Make sure you see it if you're in the area at the time.

Guidebooks

There is a book sold in certain shops in the temple complex called *Sri Ranga Kshetra Mahatmyam* by R Narasimhan Praveen, at Rs 1.50. The author probably intended to produce a guidebook and collection of legends about the temple, but it's full of the most incomprehensible nonsense you're ever likely to encounter. For this reason alone, it's worth buying. Some gems from it include:

Pavithrotsava is conducted to the Lord for nine days from the Sukla-Paksha 'bright fortnight' Ekadasi day. To the negligence committed during all these days in the years in the Pujas, remedy is being sought for otherwise Aparadakshanpana is being sought for.

Thondar-Adi – He is called as Vipra Narayana – He was born in a sacred place called Thirumadangudi. His Janma Nakashatra is Jyeshta in Margazhi month. He was living in Srirangam and engaged himself in presenting Thiru Thuzhai or Thulasi to Sri Tanganatha and garlands of beautiful and scented flowers were daily offered by him to the Lord. He has sung the famous Thirumalai, which is especially in devotion to Lord Sri Ranganatha and no others. His another prabandha named Thiruppalli Yezhuchi is the most important part of the Thirumozhi group to wake up the Lord everyday. It is also spoken as Thirumalai Ariyar – Perumalai Ariyar – ie Those who do not know Lord Sri Ranganatha. Sri Vanamal of Lord Vishnu took the avatar of this Tondar Adi Podi Alwar.

Sri Jambukeshwara Temple

On the opposite side of the main Madras to Salem road to Sri Ranganathaswamy Temple, the Sri Jambukeshwara Temple is dedicated to Shiva and has five concentric walls and seven gopurams. Its deity is a Shiva lingam, submerged in water that comes from a spring in the sanctum sanctorum. Non-Hindus are not allowed in this part of the temple. The complex was built around the same time as Sri Ranganathaswamy Temple and is equally interesting. It's open daily between 6 am and 1 pm and between 4 and 9.30 pm, and there's another Rs 5 camera fee.

St John's Church

Trichy also has some interesting Raj-era monuments. Built in 1812, St John's Church has louvered side doors which can be opened to turn the church into an airy pavilion. It's interesting for its setting and architecture and also for the surrounding cemetery. Rouse the watchman to let you in.

Places to Stay – bottom end

The cheapest habitable place is the *Modern Hindu Hotel* (tel 28858) on Dindigul Rd. It's shabby but clean enough, and rooms cost Rs 30/45. The *Selvam Lodge* (tel 23114) on Junction Rd is also fairly clean and quiet, although the rooms are small and it fills up later in the day. Rooms with bath are Rs 27/47.

The *Vijay Lodge* (tel 24511) is at 13-B Royal Rd, right opposite the State bus stand. It's good value at Rs 30/48 for rooms with bath, as is the *Guru Hotel* (tel 33881) next door at No 13-A. Rooms in this pleasant hotel cost Rs 35/55 with bath. Also in this group is the new *Hotel Rajasugam* (tel 34036) at 13-B/1 Royal Rd, where rooms cost Rs 30/46 with bath.

The *Hotel Tamil Nadu* (tel 253383) is on McDonald Rd, just a couple of minutes walk from the State bus stand. All rooms have bathrooms and cost Rs 45/70, or Rs 99/135 with air-con. It is nowhere near as palatial as the Thanjavur Tourist Bungalow, but the rooms have towels and toilet paper. The tourist office is in this hotel and there's a good restaurant and bar.

The *Hotel Aanand* (tel 26545), 1 Racquet Court Lane, is probably the most attractive of the cheaper places, although it's a bit grubby. Rooms cost Rs 45/70 and air-con doubles are available for Rs 95. There are no air-con singles. All rooms have bathrooms and there is a good restaurant.

The *Arun Hotel* (tel 31231) at 24 State Bank Rd, near the Thiruvalluvar bus stand and the railway station, has recently had a face-lift. The rooms are very clean and pleasant, and are good value at Rs 55/77. Air-con rooms cost Rs 99/132.

The *Hotel Ajanta* (tel 24501), Junction Rd, is huge. It has its own vegetarian restaurant, and rooms cost Rs 35/66.

At the top of this bracket is the *Hotel Aristo* (tel 26565), 2 Dindigul Rd, at the traffic circle. It is set in a pleasant garden and has large quiet rooms. Singles/doubles with bath cost Rs 60/85, or Rs 105/145 with air-con, although the air-conditioned rooms smell damp and musty from a dearth of fresh air.

The *Hotel Ashby* (tel 23652) at 17A Junction Rd merits its description as Trichy's only faded touch of the Raj. If you like the Fairlawn in Calcutta, try the Hotel Ashby. From the road, the place appears about to fall down, but the rooms are not too run-down. They cost Rs 55/66 with bath, or Rs 99/126 with air-con. The hotel has a restaurant and bar.

At the railway station, the *retiring rooms* cost Rs 25/50, and there are dorm beds for Rs 10.

Places to Stay – middle & top end

The fancy *Ramyas Hotel* (tel 31470) is a large new place, right in the centre. Despite appearances, it is remarkably reasonable in price with rooms at Rs 85/105, or with air-con for Rs 154/195.

On the corner of McDonald and Dindigul Rds, the *Rajali Hotel* (tel 31302) has rooms for Rs 154/213, or Rs 230/330 with air-con. It's recommended.

The *Sangam Hotel* (tel 25202) on

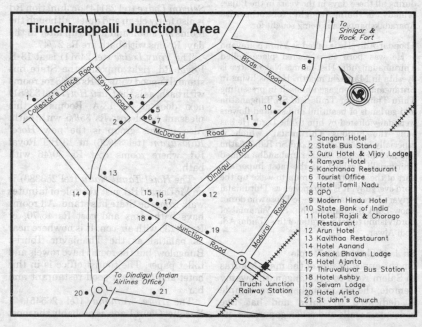

Tiruchirappalli Junction Area

To Srinigar & Rock Fort

1 Sangam Hotel
2 State Bus Stand
3 Guru Hotel & Vijay Lodge
4 Ramyas Hotel
5 Kanchanaa Restaurant
6 Tourist Office
7 Hotel Tamil Nadu
8 GPO
9 Modern Hindu Hotel
10 State Bank of India
11 Hotel Rajali & Chorogo Restaurant
12 Arun Hotel
13 Kavithaa Restaurant
14 Hotel Aanand
15 Ashok Bhavan Lodge
16 Hotel Ajanta
17 Thiruvalluvar Bus Station
18 Hotel Ashby
19 Selvam Lodge
20 Hotel Aristo
21 St John's Church

To Dindigul (Indian Airlines Office)

Tiruchi Junction Railway Station

Collector's Office Rd is the best hotel in town, although it is neither well appointed nor well maintained. Rooms are Rs 370/480, all with air-con. The hotel has one of the few bars in Trichy, but beers are a mite expensive, as is the restaurant. Other hotels with bars are the Hotel Tamil Nadu, the Rajali Hotel and the Ashby.

Places to Eat

There are plenty of cafes serving vegetarian meals around the bus stand and along Junction Rd. One of the best and most popular is the *Vasantha Bhavan Restaurant* on the corner opposite the tourist office. Its 'meals' dining hall has one of the best thalis in south India for Rs 6. There's also a very cheap air-conditioned restaurant at the rear.

The Guru Hotel has the *New Kurunchi Restaurant* and, in the group of shops between it and the corner, the tiny *Maharaja Restaurant* offers good cheap non-vegetarian food from a limited menu.

The *Kanchanaa Hotel* on Williams Rd, just along from the tourist office, is another non-vegetarian restaurant and an agreeable place to sit outside and eat in the evenings.

The vegetarian *Kavithaa Restaurant* in the Kalpana Lodge does excellent highly elaborate thalis for Rs 10, and has an air-conditioned room. The *Ashby* also has good thalis, as well as drinks and excellent service. In the Hotel Aanand, the *Arun Restaurant* serves good food, although one visitor stated that 'the tomato soup was incendiary'.

The *Selvam Lodge* has a rooftop restaurant which is an excellent place for south Indian food in the evenings. There is also a south Indian vegetarian restaurant on the ground floor and a dimly lit, prison-like, air-conditioned restaurant on the 1st floor.

In the Rajali Hotel, the *Chorogo* Chinese restaurant has excellent food, although it's not cheap. Beers cost Rs 27.

Getting There & Away

Air There are daily Indian Airlines flights to Madras (Rs 330), and less frequent connections with Madurai (Rs 155).

Indian Airlines has four flights weekly to Colombo, while Air Lanka has two.

Bus Trichy has a State bus stand, and a Thiruvalluvar bus stand only two minutes walk away. As usual, the State bus stand timetables are only in Tamil. Express buses are distinguished from ordinary buses by the word 'Fast' (in English) on the direction indicator at the front. Services to most places are frequent and tickets are sold by the conductor as soon as the bus arrives. Just buy your ticket and hop on.

Buses to Thanjavur leave every 15 minutes or so, and the one-hour journey costs Rs 5. There are also frequent buses to Madurai, which is a four-hour trip and costs Rs 15.

The Thiruvalluvar buses originating in Trichy can be computer-booked in advance. These buses include: Madras (No 123, 30 daily, eight hours, Rs 30.50), Kanyakumari (No 127, two daily, nine hours, Rs 36) and Tirupathi (No 850, two daily, 9½ hours, Rs 40). In addition, there are many buses passing through and you can usually get a seat on these. Destinations include Bangalore, Pondicherry, Madurai, Kanchipuram, Vellore and Rameswaram.

Train Trichy is on the main Madras to Madurai railway line and some trains run directly from Madras. It's 337 km, takes five to eight hours, and costs Rs 42 in 2nd class, Rs 148 in 1st. Other trains go via Chidambaram and Thanjavur, 64 km further. The Madras to Madurai and Madras to Rameswaram trains also go through Trichy. It's about seven hours from Trichy to Rameswaram, and the 265-km trip costs Rs 34 in 2nd class, Rs 134 in 1st.

It's 155 km from Trichy to Madurai at a cost of Rs 24 in 2nd class, Rs 79 in 1st. The fastest train is the Vaigai Express, which covers the distance in 2½ hours. Slower trains take up to four hours.

Getting Around

Bus Trichy's excellent local bus service is uncrowded and comparatively easy to use. Take a No 7, 63, 63A, 122 or 128 bus to the airport, allowing about half an hour to get there.

The No 1 bus from the State bus stand goes to the Rock Fort Temple, the main entrance to Srirangam and close to the Sri Jambukeshwara Temple. The service is frequent and relatively uncrowded. It takes a full day to do the circuit.

Bicycle The town lends itself well to cycling as it's dead flat. There are a couple of places on Junction Rd, near the Selvam Lodge, where you can hire bicycles for Rs 0.70 per hour.

Heading back from the Rock Fort, the incredibly busy Big Bazaar Rd is one-way traffic (heading north), so you have to get off your bicycle and walk.

OOTACAMUND (Ooty) (population 90,000)

Known in Tamil as Udagamandalam, this hill station near the tri-junction of Tamil Nadu, Kerala and Karnataka is 2268 metres above sea level in the Nilgiri mountains. It was founded by the British in the early part of the 19th century to serve as the summer headquarters of the government of Madras. Before that time, the area was inhabited by the Todas. These tribal people still live there, but today, only 3000 remain. The Todas were polygamists and worshipped buffaloes, and you can see their animist shrines in various places.

Though nestled among some of the most spectacular mountains in southern India, Ooty lacks the fascinating cultures which make the Himalaya so interesting. Indeed, it's more a faded relic of the British Raj and suffers from a bad case of overenthusiasm on the part of the Indian tourist organisation. There's precious little to see and not a great deal to do,

unless you're fond of long walks and boating on the lake. The whole place has a run-down feeling about it, which is not unusual in India. The best part of a visit to Ootacamund is the journey there on the narrow-gauge train which winds upwards through the luxuriant rainforest and tea plantations.

The weather in Ooty can take you by surprise. You will need warm clothing in winter and during the monsoon, as the overnight temperature occasionally drops to 0°C.

The town's general appearance is an unlikely combination of southern England and Australia, with single-storey stone cottages surrounded by twee, fenced flower gardens scattered along leafy, winding lanes with tall eucalypt stands covering the otherwise barren hilltops. Since their introduction back in the 19th century, the eucalypts have spawned a small oil-extraction industry in the area, and bottles of eucalyptus oil are sold in many of the town's shops.

The other main reminders of the British period are the stone churches and the huge boys' school with its landscaped gardens at the bottom end of the lake. There's also the terraced and very English Botanical Gardens, in which Government House stands on the lower slopes of Doddabetta (2623 metres), the highest peak in Tamil Nadu. From the top of Doddabetta you can see Coonoor, Wellington, Coimbatore, Mettupalayam and, on a clear day, as far as Mysore.

Although it quickly became the principal hill station in southern India during the Raj, Ooty was not the first in this area. As early as 1819, the British began to build houses at nearby Kotagiri. This much smaller town survives as a minor hill station, and has a climate midway between that of Ooty and Coonoor.

Orientation

Ooty is spread over a large area amongst rolling hills and valleys. The railway station, bus stand, bazaar, tourist office,

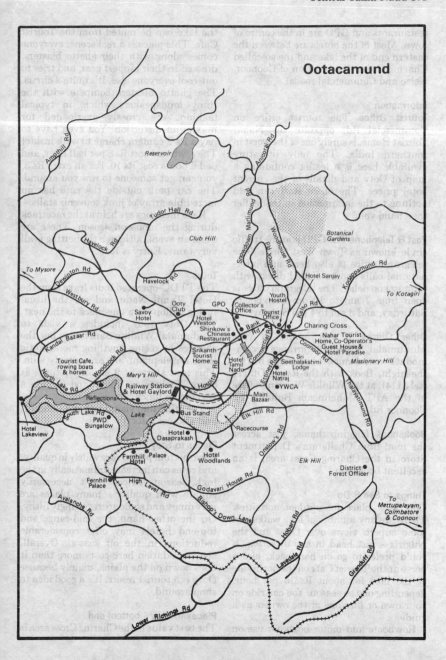

Ootacamund

restaurants and GPO are in the centre of town. Most of the hotels are between the eastern end of the lake and the so-called Charing Cross (the junction of Coonoor, Kelso and Commercial roads).

Information

Tourist Office The tourist office on Commercial Rd, opposite the Nahar Tourist Home, is surely one of the worst in southern India. The only literature available here is a leaflet containing a map of Ooty and details of the current hotel prices. The office staff can add nothing to the information in the leaflet they hand you.

Post & Telephone The GPO is at the traffic circle known as Town West Circle. The telegraph office is also here, and international calls can be dialled direct with (almost) no delay. The telegraph office is open from 7 am to 10 pm Monday to Saturday, and 8 am to 4 pm Sunday.

Other Offices If you intend to visit Mudumalai, it's wise to arrange accommodation in advance to be sure of a bed for the night. Book with the Range Officer (tel 3114), at the Wildlife Warden's office in the APT Mahalingam Building on Coonoor Rd.

Bookshops Higginbothams, just across the road from Chellaram's Department Store in the Charing Cross area, is an excellent bookshop.

Things to See & Do

Ooty is a place for outdoor activities. There are any number of long walks and some superb views over Ooty and the Nilgiris – just head in any direction. If you'd prefer to go on horseback, hire a horse at the Tourist Cafe on the north side of the lake for about Rs 15 per hour, depending on the season. You can ride on your own or hire one of the owners as a guide.

Rowboats and motor boats for use on the lake can be rented from the Tourist Cafe. This place is a real scene; everyone comes along with their ghetto blasters, dressed in their hippest gear, and tries to out-cool everyone else. It's quite a circus. The ghetto blasters compete with the tinny loudspeakers which, in typical fashion, are grossly overloaded for maximum distortion. You even have to pay a Rs 2 camera charge to walk inside! The rowboats cost Rs 8 per half hour, and pedal boats cost Rs 10. For an extra Rs 3, you can get someone to row you around. The car park outside the cafe has an incredible array of junk souvenir stalls.

Race meetings are held at the racetrack during the monsoon season. These are quite an event, although the betting is all very tame. Entry is Rs 5.

Tours

The TTDC-operated tours leave from the Hotel Tamil Nadu and are the usual raring gallop from one place to the next. The Ooty tour includes a visit to Mudumalai Wildlife Sanctuary, but the chances of seeing anything more exotic than an elephant are exceedingly slim. This tour starts at 9 am and returns at 8 pm. Tickets are Rs 60 and include a vegetarian lunch.

The other tour visits Ooty and Coonoor, and also costs Rs 60.

Places to Stay

Rock-bottom places vary widely in quality, and rates can increase dramatically in the high season. Prices don't necessarily equate with quality – many places are very dingy and some are revoltingly filthy. On the other hand, the mid-range and top-end hotels may offer considerable reductions in the off season. Overall, accommodation here costs more than it does down on the plains, mainly because Ooty is a tourist resort. It's a good idea to shop around.

Places to Stay – bottom end

The best value in the Charing Cross area is

the *Hotel Sanjay* (tel 3160). All rooms have a small balcony, and hot water is available between 6 and 10 am. Rooms cost Rs 40/60, or Rs 80/125 in the season. In the same area, the *Co-Operator's Guest House* (tel 2638) has double rooms with a bathroom and small anteroom for Rs 48, and Rs 125 in the season.

There are a number of basic places on Main Bazaar, but the standard varies. The adequate *Hotel Apsara* (tel 3179) has rooms for Rs 40 but, due to an incredibly bad design, only the bathrooms have windows. Rooms in the *Maneck Tourist Home* (tel 3138) are wallpapered in particularly horrific styles, but are cheap at Rs 35/50. Doubles on the ground floor cost Rs 40. The *Vishu Lodge* (tel 2971) has more expensive small rooms for Rs 40/60. Just out of the main bazaar area at the *Sri Seethalakshmi Lodge* (tel 2896), the reasonable rooms are the cheapest you'll find anywhere. They cost Rs 35 for a double with bath.

On the same side of town, the *Hotel Natraj* (tel 3810) on Ettines Rd is a step up the scale, with rooms at Rs 49/70 rising to Rs 150 in the season. The *YWCA*, further along the same road, is in a slightly inconvenient location but not bad value. Rooms cost Rs 60, or Rs 100 in the season. There is a lounge with an open fire, and meals are also available. It's a popular place.

Around the lake on North Lake Rd, 15 minutes walk from the bus or railway station, *Reflections* (tel 3834) has good views of the lake. It charges Rs 48 for doubles, Rs 90 and Rs 125 in season. It has only six rooms, but there is hot water and a homely atmosphere, and the friendly Anglo-Indian manager, Mrs Dique, is a good source of information on the region's history.

For those who really can't afford anything better, the *Pradhiya Lodge* opposite the entrance to the railway station has rooms for Rs 15/25. You get what you pay for here – very little. The railway station has four *retiring rooms*

which cost Rs 30/60, rising to Rs 60/120 in the season.

Up near the Hotel Tamil Nadu, the *Youth Hostel* has beds in large crowded dorms for Rs 20.

Places to Stay - middle

The *Nahar Tourist Home* (tel 2173) is right at Charing Cross. It's a large place with rooms for Rs 120/180, although the off-season rates are less than Rs 100. Not far away is the pleasant *Hotel Tamil Nadu* (tel 2543), on a hill above the tourist office. Rooms cost Rs 140/180 in the season between 1 April and 15 June, dropping to Rs 80/100 in the off season.

Out along Club Rd towards the Ooty Club, the *Hotel Weston* (tel 3500) has small double rooms for Rs 120, half that amount out of season. There are no single rooms.

The *Hotel Dasaprakash* (tel 2434), on the southern side of the racecourse, is not a bad place to stay, although the maintenance is not what it might be. Double rooms cost Rs 220 and deluxe rooms are Rs 400.

At the very western tip of the lake, the *Hotel Lakeview* (tel 2026) is more isolated. The name is not very apt as most of the 'cottages' have a view of nothing more than the back of the 'cottage' in front. The charges are Rs 220, dropping to Rs 110 out of season.

Places to Stay - top end

The *Fernhill Palace* (tel 2055) has rooms from Rs 150 to Rs 300 off season, and from Rs 300 to Rs 600 in season. There are also cottages. This is the best and most expensive hotel in Ooty and is now mainly patronised by the Bombay film set. The former summer palace of the Maharaja of Mysore, it's in a quiet forest setting 1½ km from the railway station. The rooms are magnificent, but slowly decaying, and they can be very cold. The dining room is actually the old ballroom and even if you're not staying, it's worth coming in for a pot of tea (Rs 7), or a Golden Eagle beer in a silver tankard served in the Hunt Room Bar. There's a range of old hunting photographs and other memorabilia around the place.

The *Savoy Hotel* is also luxurious, and rooms cost Rs 450/500 in the off season, Rs 800/950 during the summer.

Places to Eat

In the Charing Cross area, the *Chandan* restaurant in the Nahar Tourist Home serves an excellent 'Madras thali' for Rs 8. The *Blue Hills* next door is popular with non-vegetarians. Next door again, the *Hotel Paradise* is also popular.

There are plenty of basic vegetarian meals places further along Main Bazaar. The friendly *Hotel Shabaha* offers both vegetarian and non-vegetarian dishes. The food is not bad, although the meal I chose was virtually ruined by heavy-handed use of ginger. In the same area, the *Hotel Kaveri* serves excellent biryanis.

Up on Town West Circle, *Shinkow's Chinese Restaurant* has some really good food. It's run by a Chinese family so the Chinese dishes are fairly authentic. The chips are excellent, as is the cassata ice cream. Expect to pay about Rs 20 per person here.

Directly opposite the bus station is a whole gaggle of chai stalls selling snacks and chai.

Getting There & Away

Bus The orderly bus station is fairly central at the western end of the racecourse. From there, it's only about 10 minutes walk to the centre of the bazaar and about 20 to Charing Cross.

Local buses leave hourly on the Rs 4, 1¼-hour trip to Kotagiri. There are a dozen buses daily to Coonoor and the one-hour trip costs Rs 2.

Cheran, the regional bus company, operates buses to Mysore, Bangalore and Coimbatore. There are literally dozens of buses to Coimbatore daily, the last leaving at 8 pm. The trip costs Rs 9.70.

Three KSRTC buses go to Bangalore each day. The eight-hour trip costs Rs 42.30.

The journey to Mysore takes five hours at a cost of Rs 20. This is the bus to take if you're heading for the Mudumalai Wildlife Sanctuary under your own steam. Get off at Theppakadu – the reception centre is here. The trip from Ooty takes about 2½ hours and costs Rs 10. An alternate route to Mudumalai involves taking one of the small buses which go via the narrow and twisting Sighur Ghat road. Most of these buses travel only as far as Masinagudi, but there are plenty of buses from there to Theppakadu.

Seven buses a day go to Calicut in Kerala. Sit on the right-hand side for the spectacular 6½-hour trip down through the western ghats.

Train Like Darjeeling and Matheran, Ooty has a miniature railway connecting it with the lowlands. The trains, with their quaint yellow and blue carriages, are not quite as small as the Darjeeling toy train, but they're still pretty tiny. The unique feature of this line is the toothed central rail onto which the locomotives lock on the steeper slopes. Also unusual is the little locomotive, which is at the back pushing rather than pulling from the front. Each of the four or five carriages has its own brakeman, who sits on a little platform on the front of the carriage. It's quite a circus when the train is about to pull out of a station and each brakeman in turn waves his green flag.

This is an excellent way of getting to Ooty and affords some spectacular views of the precipitous eastern slopes of the rainforest-covered Nilgiris. Views are best from the left on the way up and from the right on the way down.

The miniature railway starts at Mettupalayam, north of Coimbatore, and goes via Coonoor to Ooty. The departures and arrivals at Mettupalayam connect with the Nilgiri Express, which runs between Mettupalayam and Madras. If you're heading for Ooty, the Nilgiri Express departs Madras at 9.05 pm and arrives at Mettupalayam at 7.15 am. You can catch this train from Coimbatore at 6.20 am.

The miniature train leaves Mettupalayam for Ooty at 7.45 am and arrives in Ooty at 12 noon. On the downhill journey, there's a 2.55 pm departure from Ooty to connect with the Nilgiri Express when it departs Mettupalayam at 7.15 pm. The 46-km journey takes about 4½ hours up to Ooty and about 3½ hours going down. During the season, there is an extra departure in each direction daily, and there are also trains which run only between Ooty and Coonoor.

Getting Around

An auto-rickshaw from the railway or bus station to Charing Cross costs about Rs 6. There are also plenty of taxis which, of course, charge more. As is often the case, hiring a bicycle is one of the best ways of exploring.

AROUND OOTY

Kotagiri is a much smaller and quieter hill station, about 28 km from Ooty. From here, you can visit Catherine Falls (eight km away), Elk Falls (eight km) and Kodanad View Point (16 km), where there is a fine panoramic view over the plains and the eastern slope of the Nilgiris.

Places to Stay

There are a few basic lodges in Kotagiri, such as the *Hotel Ram Vihar* where rooms start at Rs 35. The *Queenshill Christian Guest House* has beautifully furnished rooms for Rs 25 and serves excellent western breakfasts.

In Coonoor, the *Hampton Manor Hotel* (tel 244, 961/4) has rooms from Rs 100 to Rs 250. Alternatively, there's the *Ritz Hotel* (tel 6242) on Orange Grove Rd where rooms cost Rs 75/150.

In Mettupalayam, there's a very pleasant two-bed *retiring room* spanning the width of the platform. The *Bhavath*

Bhavanam Hotel has rooms for Rs 15/25 with bath.

COIMBATORE (population 1.1 million)

Coimbatore is a large, busy city at the foot of the Nilgiri mountains, full of 'shirting & suiting' shops. Its main interest for travellers is as a way station en route to Ootacamund and the other Nilgiri hill stations.

Orientation

The bus and railway stations are about two km apart, so you'll need an auto-rickshaw (Rs 5) to get from one to the other. A number of mid-range and budget hotels are clustered around both the bus and the railway stations.

Information

There's a tourist office at the railway station, but it's hard to think of a reason to visit it.

The Indian Airlines (tel 22208) and the Air India offices (tel 23933) are in Indian House on Trichy Rd.

Places to Stay – bottom end

Bus Station Area The *Hotel Sree Shakti* (tel 34225) at 11/148 Sastri Rd is a large, modern hotel with friendly staff. Rooms are pleasantly decorated, reasonably clean, have a fan and bathroom and cost Rs 35/55/80 for singles/doubles/triples. For an extra Rs 10, the rooms have in-house video.

Also on Sastri Rd, the *Sri Ganapathy Lodge* (tel 27365) is behind the bus stand. It's much the same as the Sree Shakti and rooms cost Rs 30/49. The *Zakin Hotel*, Sastri Rd, is a few doors up from the Shakti and is also close to the bus station. Rooms cost Rs 25/34, more with bathroom.

One block further north, Nehru Rd is also lined with hotels. The new *Hotel Blue Star* (tel 37117) offers excellent value at Rs 49/88 with bath. Double rooms with air-con cost Rs 120.

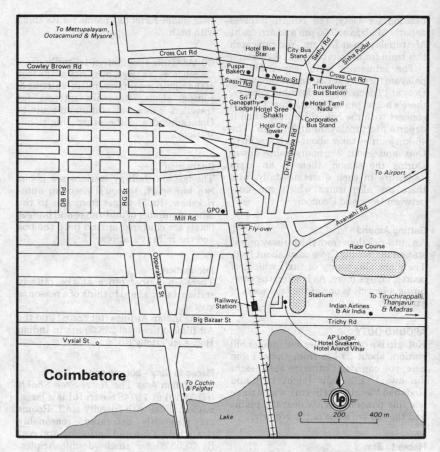

To Mettupalayam,
Ootacamund & Mysore

Cross Cut Rd

Cowley Brown Rd

Hotel Blue
Star

City Bus
Stand

Sathy Rd

Sitha Pudur

Cross Cut Rd

Puspa
Bakery

Sastri Rd

Nehru St

Tiruvalluvar
Bus Station

Sri
Ganapathy
Lodge

Hotel Sree
Shakti

Hotel Tamil
Nadu

Hotel City
Tower

Corporation
Bus Stand

Dr Nanjappa Rd

To Airport

DB Rd

RG Rd

GPO

Mill Rd

Avanashi Rd

Fly-over

Race Course

Opparakkara St

Railway
Station

Stadium

Indian Airlines
& Air India

To Tiruchirappalli,
Thanjavur
& Madras

Big Bazaar St

Trichy Rd

Vysial St

AP Lodge,
Hotel Sivakami,
Hotel Anand Vihar

Coimbatore

To Cochin
& Palghat

Lake

0   200   400 m

Railway Station Area Opposite the railway station, the small Davey & Co Lane is a solid enclave of hotels. They are all fairly quiet as it's one block back from the main road. The new *Hotel Sivakami* (tel 26669) is one of the best in the area. It's well maintained and rooms are good value at Rs 25/40 with bath.

The *Hotel Anand Vihar* (tel 26584) is friendly and helpful and has rooms with bath for Rs 30/50. Up the range a bit, the *AP Lodge* (tel 24773) has large, well-furnished rooms with bath for Rs 61/82.

The noisy railway *retiring rooms* are brand new and significantly more expensive than usual at Rs 50/100, or Rs 250 for an air-con double. The dormitory, in the older building on platform 1, has beds for Rs 20.

Places to Stay – middle
The *Hotel Tamil Nadu* (tel 36311) on Dr Nanjappa Rd is very close to the bus station. Like some other hotels in this government-run chain, it is not maintained as well as it might be and staff seem to have a *laissez-faire* attitude. Rooms cost Rs 77/110, or Rs 115/145 with air-con.

The new *Hotel City Tower* (tel 37681) is

just off Dr Nanjappa Rd, a five-minute walk from the bus station. Rooms in this clean and modern hotel cost Rs 90/130 with bath, Rs 140/180 with air-con. Rooms with TV are Rs 30 more.

Places to Eat
In the railway station area, the small *Hotel Sunrise* restaurant serves reasonable non-vegetarian food and vegetarian meals on a banana leaf for Rs 3.50. The *Royal Hindu Restaurant* on the main road, just north of the station, is a huge place offering good vegetarian meals.

The separate vegetarian and non-vegetarian restaurants at the railway station itself have the usual unimaginative but good-value fare.

The *Hotel Top Form* on Nehru Rd serves interesting non-vegetarian food. Most hotels in this area have their own restaurants, so there are plenty to choose from.

Getting There & Away
Air There are Indian Airlines flights between Coimbatore and Bangalore (Rs 265), Bombay (Rs 885) and Madras (Rs 510).

Vayudoot operates flights to Cochin (Rs 195), Madurai (Rs 255) and Madras (Rs 510).

Bus The large and well-organised Corporation bus station only has timetables in Tamil, except those for buses to Ooty and some interstate buses. The Thiruvalluvar bus stand is on Cross Cut Rd, five minutes walk from the Corporation bus station.

Frequent buses leave for Ooty from both stations. During the season, it can get fairly hectic and you may have to wait for an hour or so before boarding. The Ooty buses leave from the Corporation bus station, platform No 4 stand 12, every 20 minutes or so from 4 am to 7 pm. From the Thiruvalluvar stand, there are 20 buses daily between 4 am and midnight. The trip takes five hours and costs Rs 9.

Other Thiruvalluvar buses include Madras (No 460, five daily, 11½ hours, Rs 57), Madurai (Nos 600 & 626, 19 daily, 5½ hours, Rs 21.50) and Trichy (No 700, 15 daily, 5¼ hours, Rs 20).

Train Coimbatore is a major rail junction and has services to most major centres. Catch the Nilgiri Express at 6.20 am if you're heading for Ooty; it connects with the miniature railway at Mettupalayam. The train trip to Ooty takes 4½ hours.

There are numerous daily trains between Madras Central and Coimbatore, the fastest being the Kovai Express which takes 7½ hours. Other trains take up to nine hours to cover the 494 km. It costs Rs 55 in 2nd class, Rs 201 in 1st.

The daily Rameswaram Express goes through Madurai and takes 5½ hours for the 229-km trip at a cost of Rs 31 in 2nd class, Rs 107 in 1st. The full journey to Rameswaram is 393 km, takes 12 hours and costs Rs 47 in 2nd class, Rs 171 in 1st.

Bangalore is 424 km away. The nine-hour trip costs Rs 51 in 2nd class, Rs 183 in 1st. The daily Kanyakumari Express (from Bombay) takes 13½ hours to travel the 510 km to Kanyakumari and costs Rs 57 in 2nd class, Rs 204 in 1st.

To the Kerala coast, the daily West Coast Express from Madras Central goes to Calicut (185 km, 4½ hours) and on to Bangalore (504 km, nine hours).

Getting Around
Bus Useful buses around Coimbatore include No 20 from the railway station to the airport, and No 12 from the railway station to the bus stations.

Auto-Rickshaw The auto-rickshaw drivers here need a bit of convincing that the meter should be used. It's about Rs 5 from the railway station to the bus stations.

Southern Tamil Nadu

MADURAI (population one million)

Madurai is a bustling city of a million people, packed with pilgrims, beggars, businesspeople, bullock carts and legions of underemployed rickshaw-wallahs. It is one of southern India's oldest cities, and has been a centre of learning and pilgrimage for centuries. Madurai's main attraction is the famous Shree Meenakshi Temple in the heart of the old town, a riotously baroque example of Dravidian architecture with gopurams covered from top to bottom in a breathless profusion of multicoloured images of gods, goddesses, animals and mythical figures. Nothing quite like it exists outside Disneyland! The temple seethes with activity from dawn till dusk, its many shrines attracting pilgrims from every part of India and tourists from all over the world. It's been estimated that there are 10,000 visitors here on any one day!

Madurai resembles a huge, continuous bazaar crammed with shops, street markets, temples, pilgrims' choultries, hotels, restaurants and small industries. Although one of the liveliest cities in the south, it's small enough not to be overwhelming and very popular with travellers. You'll love it!

History

Madurai's history can be divided into roughly four periods, beginning over 2000 years ago when it was the capital of the Pandyan kings. Then, in the 4th century BC, the city was known to the Greeks via Megasthenes, their ambassador to the court of Chandragupta Maurya. In the 10th century AD, Madurai was taken by the Chola emperors. It remained in their hands until the Pandyas briefly regained their independence in the 12th century, only to lose it again in the 14th to Muslim invaders under Malik Kafur, a general in the service of the Deihi Sultanate. Here, Malik Kafur established his own dynasty which, in turn, was overthrown by the Hindu Vijayanagar kings of Hampi. After the fall of Vijayanagar in 1565, the Nayaks ruled Madurai until 1781 AD. During the reign of Tirumalai Nayak (1623-55), the bulk of the Meenakshi Temple was built, and Madurai became the cultural centre of the Tamil people, playing an important role in the development of the Tamil language.

Madurai then passed into the hands of the British East India Company, which took over the revenues of the area after the wars of the Carnatic in 1781. In 1840, the company razed the fort, which had previously surrounded the city, and filled in the moat. Four broad streets – the Veli streets – were constructed on top of this fill and define the limits of the old city to this day.

1	Indian Airlines & State Bank of India
2	Railway Station
3	Bus Stands
4	Hotel International, Central Lodge, TM Lodge & Prem Nivas Hotel
5	New College House
6	Taj Restaurant
7	Santhanam Lodge
8	Mahal Restaurant
9	Amutham Restaurant
10	Ruby Lodge & Subham Restaurant
11	Hotel Tamil Nadu
12	Tourist Office
13	Hotel Aarathus
14	GPO
15	Railway Station
16	State Bus Stand (Periyar Bus Stand)
17	Tiruvalluvar Bus Stand
18	Hotel Devi
19	Meenakshi Temple
20	Tirumalai Nayak Palace
21	Central Telegraph Office
22	YWCA
23	Hotel Madurai Ashok
24	Pandyan Hotel
25	Hotel Tamil Nadu
26	Gandhi Museum
27	Anna Bus Stand
28	Mariamman Theppakulam Tank

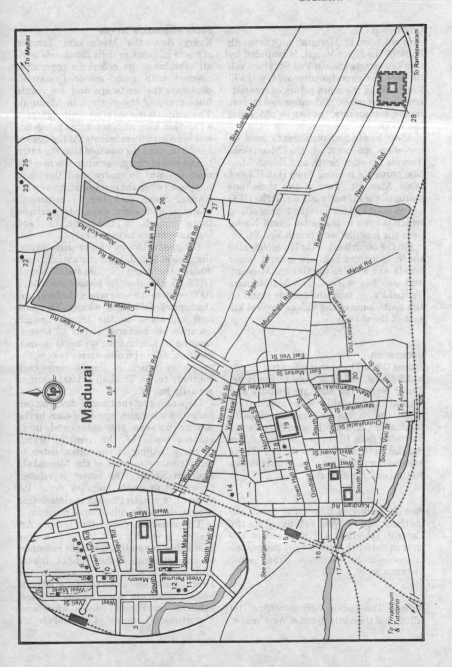

Orientation

The old town of Madurai, on the south bank of the River Vaigai, is bounded by the Veli streets (South Veli St, East Veli St, etc). In this rectangular area, you will find most of the main points of interest, transport services, mid-range and budget hotels, restaurants, the tourist office and the GPO.

Most hotels and restaurants used by travellers are west of the Meenakshi Temple between North and South Masi Sts, particularly along Town Hall Rd and West Masi St. Two of the three bus stations, the railway station and the GPO are on West Veli St. So is the tourist office, which is close to the Hotel Tamil Nadu, near the junction with South Veli St.

On the north bank of the River Vaigai in the cantonment area are several larger hotels, the YWCA, the Gandhi Museum and one bus station. The Mariamman Teppakkulam tank and temple stand on the south bank of the Vaigai, several km east of the old city.

Information

Tourist Office The tourist office (tel 22957) at 180 West Veli St is close to the Hotel Tamil Nadu. The staff are friendly and helpful, and provide some information about the city as well as free maps of Madurai. The office is open Monday to Saturday from 10 am to 5.30 pm, and on Sunday between 10 am and 1 pm. There are also branch offices at Madurai railway station and the airport.

Post & Telephone The GPO is at the northern end of West Veli St, while the Central Telegraph Office is across the river in the north of town – you can see the telecommunications mast from some distance away.

Airlines The Indian Airlines office (tel 26795) is at the northern end of West Veli St.

Shree Meenakshi Temple

Every day, the Meenakshi Temple attracts pilgrims in their thousands from all over India. Its enormous gopurams, covered with gaily coloured statues, dominate the landscape and are visible from many of the rooftops in Madurai. The temple is named after the daughter of a Pandyan king who, according to legend, was born with three breasts. At the time of her birth, the king was told that the extra breast would disappear when she met the man she was to marry, and this duly happened when she met Lord Shiva on Mt Kailas. Shiva told her to return to Madurai and, eight days later, arrived there himself in the form of Lord Sundareshwara to marry her.

Designed in 1560 by Vishwanatha Nayak, the present temple was substantially built during the reign of Tirumalai Nayak (1623-55 AD), but its history goes back 2000 years to the time when Madurai was the capital of the Pandya kings. There are four entrances to the temple, which occupies six hectares. It has 12 towers, ranging in height from 45 to 50 metres, and four outer-rim nine-storey towers, the tallest of which is the 50-metre-high southern tower. The hall of 1000 columns actually has 985.

Depending on the time of day, you can bargain for bangles, spices or saris in the bazaar between the outer and inner eastern walls of the temple, watch pilgrims bathing in the tanks, listen to temple music in front of the Meenakshi Amman Shrine (the music is relayed through the whole complex on a PA system), or wander through the interesting though decidedly dilapidated museum.

The museum, called the Temple Art Gallery, is worth a visit. It contains some beautiful stone and brass images, examples of ancient south Indian scripts, friezes and various attempts to explain the Hindu pantheon and the many legends associated with it, as well as one of the best exhibits on Hindu deities anywhere. Unfortunately, many of the labels are

Shree Meenakshi Temple

missing. Entrance to the Art Gallery costs Rs 1, plus (officially) Rs 5 for a camera if you intend to use it.

On most evenings between 6 and 7.30 pm and 9 and 10 pm, temple music is played outside the Meenakshi Amman Shrine – mantras, fiddle, squeeze box, tabla and bells. Among those who play are some excellent musicians.

The temple is usually open between 5 am and 12.30 pm and again between 4 and 10 pm. Photography inside is only allowed between 12.30 and 4 pm on payment of Rs 10. This is actually a good time to go in even if you don't want to take photographs, because it gives you a chance to wander around without the crowds, though it will cost you Rs 10. Leave your shoes at any of the four entrances, where 'Footwear Safe Custody' stalls will look after them for Rs 0.25.

Many of the priests inside are very friendly and will take the trouble to show you around and explain what's happening.

Licensed guides charge Rs 10 for an hour.

At 9.30 each evening, there's a closing ceremony in which an image of Shiva is carried in procession to Parvati's bedroom. (It's taken back at about 6 o'clock the next morning.) The ceremony starts inside the temple, at the Sri Sudareswara Shrine near the east gopuram.

Tirumalai Nayak Palace

About a km from the Meenakshi Temple (Rs 2 by rickshaw), this Indo-Saracenic palace was built in 1636 by the ruler whose name it bears. Much of it has fallen into ruin, and the pleasure gardens and surrounding defensive wall have disappeared. Today, only the entrance gate, main hall and dance hall remain. The palace was partially restored by Lord Napier, the governor of Madras, in 1866-72, and further restoration work is currently in progress.

The palace is open daily from 9 am to 1 pm and 2 to 5 pm. Entry costs Rs 0.40 and there's no photography charge. The entrance is on the far (eastern) side. You can get there on a No 11, 11A or 17 bus from the Central bus stand, or take the 20-minute walk from the Meenakshi temple through an interesting bazaar area. There is a son et lumière in English, daily at 6.30 pm, telling the history of the city with sound and coloured lights on the temple carvings. The sophistication of both the soundtrack and the lighting is surprising. It's excellent entertainment. Tickets cost Rs 1, 2 and 3 and you should bring mosquito repellent.

Gandhi Museum

Housed in the old palace of the Rani Mangammal, this oddly moving museum provides some little-known facts about the Mahatma, although the only real piece of Gandhi memorabilia is the blood-stained dhoti from the assassination, displayed behind a bulletproof screen. Unfortunately, all the captions are in Tamil or Hindi.

The museum also has an excellent walk-through History of India display with some fine old photographs. The local government museum is in the same grounds, but you needn't waste your time.

To get there, take a No 1 or 2 bus from the State bus stand to the Central Telegraph Office (look for the telecommunications mast). From there, it's a walk of about 500 metres along a shady street.

Mariamman Teppakkulam Tank

This tank, several km east of the old city, covers an area almost equal to that of the Meenakshi Temple. It is the site of the Teppam Festival (Float Festival) in January and February, which attracts thousands of pilgrims from all over India. At other times of year, the empty tank is put to good use by the local kids for cricket games, but it's not really worth a visit then. The Mariamman Teppakkulam Tank was built by Tirumalai Nayak in 1646 and is connected to the River Vaigai by underground channels.

The No 4 bus from the State bus stand terminates at the tank.

Festivals

Madurai's principal festivals are:

Teppam (Float) Festival This very popular festival attracts pilgrims from all over India. Images of Shree Meenakshi and Lord Sundareshwara (Shiva) are mounted on floats and taken to the Mariammam Teppakkulam Tank where, for several days, they are pulled back and forth across the water to the island temple in the tank's centre, before being taken back to Madurai. The annual festival occurs in January or early February.

Chithirai Festival Held in late April-early May, the Chithirai Festival celebrates the marriage of Shree Meenakshi to Lord Sundareshwara.

Avanimoola Festival In late August-early

September, temple cars are drawn round the streets of Madurai.

Places to Stay - bottom end

Finding a room in Madurai can sometimes be difficult. In a pilgrim city of Madurai's size and importance, lots of cheap hotels and lodges offer basic accommodation. Many are just flophouses which bear the scars of previous occupants' bad habits – OK for a night, but not for much longer. On the other hand, there are a few which are clean and very good value. These are mostly found along Town Hall Rd and Dindigul Rd.

The *New College House* (tel 24311) at 2 Town Hall Rd is a huge place where you'll almost certainly get accommodation at any hour of the day or night. The rooms are clean enough and cost Rs 24/48 with bath. Some rooms on the upper floors have distant views of the Meenakshi Temple. Regulation No 4 at this hotel prohibits 'any guests having contagious diseases, unsound mind, suspicious character individuals'.

If you want temple views, you can't beat the friendly *Hotel Devi* (tel 36388) at 20 West Avani St. It's about 15 minutes walk from the bus or train station, but only a minute or two from the temple. The view of the temple from the roof is the best you'll get in the whole city. Try to rouse yourself out of bed for the sunrise. The rooms are good too, and those on the upper two floors have more light. They cost Rs 49 for a double with bath and are reasonably clean.

There are a number of hotels on West Perumal Maistry St. Near Town Hall Rd, the *Ruby Lodge* (tel 32059) at 92 West Perumal Maistry St has small rooms with bath for Rs 20/30. Avoid the noisy and grubby *Hotel Subham* opposite. Further north on the same street, the *Hotel Gangai* (tel 36211) at No 41 is opposite the Prem Nivas Hotel. Its large rooms are good value at Rs 30/49, although a couple of the rooms are much smaller. Still on West Perumal Maistry St, the *KP Lodge* has extremely basic rooms for Rs 15/25 – you get what you pay for.

The *Hotel Grand Central* (tel 36311) is at 47 West Perumal Maistry St and the *Hotel International* (tel 26337) is right next door. Both charge around Rs 35/70 for singles/doubles and are usually full later in the day. The *TM Lodge* (tel 37481) at No 50 is slightly more expensive at Rs 40/77.

At 14 Town Hall Rd, the *Hotel Sri Santhanam* (tel 26585) has quite reasonable rooms for Rs 20/37. Close by at 9 West Marret St, just south of Town Hall Rd, the *Hotel KPS* (tel 24201) is also not bad value at Rs 30/49 with bath. Some of the rooms have temple views.

At the railway station, the *retiring rooms* are noisy and cost Rs 25/40; dorm beds are Rs 10.

Places to Stay – middle

The *Hotel Prem Nivas* (tel 37531) is at 102 West Perumal Maistry St. It's fairly new and very well maintained. Rooms without air-con cost Rs 48/82, doubles with air-con are Rs 132, and each room has a bath with hot and cold running water. It's less than five minutes walk from the railway station, and only about 10 from the bus stands. Right next door, the new *Hotel Supreme* has excellent rooms for Rs 109/140.

On West Veli St, the TTDC *Hotel Tamil Nadu* (tel 37470) is a bit shabby these days and overpriced at Rs 66/99 for singles/doubles, or Rs 115/195 with air-con. The TTDC has another hotel in Madurai. It's also called *Hotel Tamil Nadu* (tel 42461), which can make life a bit confusing. This second one is way across town on Alagarkoil Rd. It's a Rs 10 rickshaw ride and is so inconvenient that it's not worth serious consideration. Rooms cost Rs 99/125, or Rs 180/200 with air-con.

The relatively new and very popular *Hotel Aarathy* (tel 31571), 9 Perumalkoil West Mada St, is similar in standard to the Prem Nivas and just a few minutes walk from the bus station. All rooms have

bathrooms with hot water and cost Rs 49/80, or Rs 90/130 with air-con. It is comfortable and has a nice open-air restaurant.

Places to Stay – top end

Madurai's two best hotels, along with the second Hotel Tamil Nadu, are well out of the town centre across the Vaigai River, along Alagarkoil Rd. An auto-rickshaw should cost no more than Rs 10, although the price will double when they hear where you want to go! City buses No 2, 16 or 20 (among others) will get you there for less than Rs 1.

The *Hotel Madurai Ashok* (tel 42531) and the *Pandyan Hotel* (tel 42470) are both centrally air-conditioned. Rooms have all mod cons, and there are bars and restaurants offering a variety of cuisine (Indian, Chinese and western). The 43-room Ashok costs from Rs 395/595 for singles/doubles and claims to be Madurai's best hotel. The 60-room Pandyan Hotel has rooms for Rs 390/500.

Places to Eat

There are many typical south Indian vegetarian restaurants around the Meenakshi Temple and along Town Hall Rd, Dindigul Rd and West Masi St. The dining hall in *New College House* is very popular and the thalis are good value.

The non-vegetarian *Taj Restaurant* on Town Hall Rd is not bad for breakfast. Just a few doors further along, the air-conditioned *Mahal Restaurant* is very popular with travellers. It is a bit more expensive, but worth it to get out of the heat for a while. The non-vegetarian food is very good and the lassis are excellent.

The non-vegetarian *Subham Restaurant*, next to the Ruby Lodge on West Perumal Maistry St, is also good and much cheaper. It's an outdoor place which is only open in the evenings. The *Indo-Ceylon Restaurant* at 6 Town Hall Rd serves good non-vegetarian meals.

Also on Town Hall Rd is the *Amutham Restaurant*, near the corner of West Masi

St. Again, the food is non-vegetarian. The stuffed parottas (their spelling) are excellent – try chicken & egg.

Getting There & Away

Air Indian Airlines has daily flights to Madras (Rs 425), and less frequent flights to Bangalore (Rs 365). There are also flights from Trichy to Madurai, but not vice-versa.

Vayudoot flies from Madurai to Madras (Rs 435), Cochin (Rs 290), Coimbatore (Rs 255) and Thanjavur (Rs 155).

Bus There are three bus stands in Madurai. Two are next to each other and the third is across the river, north of the centre. The State bus stand (also called Periyar bus stand) is for local city and short-distance buses. The Thiruvalluvar bus stand is for long-distance buses, such as those going to Madras or Kanyakumari. Across the river is the Anna bus stand. Buses leave here for Thanjavur, Trichy and Rameswaram. If your bus terminates at the Anna bus stand, bus No 3 will take you to the State bus stand, or catch an auto-rickshaw for Rs 5.

Plenty of other Thiruvalluvar buses pass through, serving these and other destinations. As these can't be reserved in advance you take potluck, but it's not usually a problem to get a seat. Thiruvalluvar does not run buses to Kodaikanal.

The main bus you are likely to catch from the State bus stand is the bus to Kodaikanal, operated by RMTC and PRC, the regional bus companies. There are seven departures daily and the four-hour trip costs Rs 18. During heavy monsoon rain, the road sometimes gets washed away and the buses have to go via Palani, adding an hour or two to the journey.

Seats on the Thiruvalluvar buses can be reserved in advance; for destinations served from Madurai refer to the table below.

Train The railway station is right on West Veli St, only a few minutes walk from the main hotel area.

The journey from Madras to Madurai takes eight hours via Trichy, longer via Chidambaram and Thanjavur. Fares are Rs 55 in 2nd class, Rs 201 in 1st. The new all-2nd-class Vagai Express is particularly fast and comparatively luxurious.

It takes six hours to cover the 164 km to Rameswaram on the Coimbatore-Rameswaram Passenger. The fare is Rs 14.

If you're heading for Kerala, the best train to take is the morning Madras-Quilon Mail, as the line crosses the Western Ghats through some spectacular mountain terrain, and there are some superb gopurams to be seen at Srivilliputur (between Sivaksi and Rajapalaiyam) and Sankarankovil. This trip takes eight

Thiruvalluvar Bus Timetable					
	route No	frequency	km	hours	fare
Ernakulam	826	2 daily	324	10	Rs 44
Kanyakumari	101	3 daily	253	6	Rs 24
Madras	137	16 daily	447	10	Rs 51.50
Pondicherry	847	1 daily	329	8	Rs 32
Thanjavur	500, 521	8 daily			
Trivandrum	820	8 daily	305	7	Rs 31
Vellore	139	1 daily	413	9	Rs 39

hours and the 268-km journey costs Rs 34 in 2nd class, Rs 123 in 1st. The train gets into Quilon in plenty of time for you to make it to Trivandrum or Kovalam Beach later in the afternoon.

Getting Around
Airport Transport The airport is six km from the city centre and you need to take an auto-rickshaw or taxi.

Bus Some useful local buses include No 3 to the Anna bus stand, Nos 1 and 2 to the Hotel Tamil Nadu and the Gandhi Museum, No 4 to Mariammam Teppakkulam Tank, No 5 to the Tiruparankundram rock-cut temple (eight km outside Madurai) and No 44 to the Alagarkoil Vaishnavite shrine (21 km from Madurai). All these buses depart from the State bus stand.

KODAIKANAL (population 24,000)
Of the three main hill stations of the south – Ootacamund, Kodaikanal and Yercaud – Kodaikanal is undoubtedly the most beautiful and, unlike Ooty, the temperature here rarely drops to the point where you need to wear heavy clothing, even in winter. Kodaikanal is on the southern crest of the Palani Hills, about 120 km north-west of Madurai, surrounded by thickly wooded slopes, waterfalls and precipitous rocky outcrops. Some of the views to the south are quite spectacular, and within easy walking distance of the centre of town – unlike Ooty, where you have to walk several km to find them.

Kodaikanal is not just for those who want to get away from the heat of the plains during the summer months, but also for those seeking a relaxing place to put their feet up for a while and do some occasional hiking. Like Ooty, Kodaikanal has its own landscaped, artificial lake with boating facilities.

Having said that, once you've rowed around the lake, admired the views and put in a few days hiking, there isn't a great deal more to do, especially if you're travelling alone. Apart from one or two restaurants down Hospital Rd, there's really nowhere for people to gather in the evenings, so it's back to your hotel and early to bed, unless you're lucky enough to break into the small 'expatriate' resident community here.

Orientation
For a hill station, Kodai is remarkably compact. The main street is Bazaar Rd (Anna Salai), and the real bottom-end hotels, the restaurants and the bus station are in this area.

The better hotels are some distance from the bazaar, but usually not more than about 15 minutes walk.

Information
There is a tourist office at the bus stand. As usual, they have no information, but do dish out a poor map. The office is open from 10 am to 5 pm Monday to Friday, but don't waste your time. If you want literature about Kodai, try the CLS bookshop more or less opposite.

April to June or August to October are the best times to visit Kodaikanal. April to June is the main season, and prices tend to be higher during these months. The peak of the wet season is November-December. At an altitude of 2133 metres, temperatures here are mild, ranging between 11°C and 20°C in summer and 8°C and 17°C in winter.

There's a railway booking office in the side street off Bazaar Rd where you can book seats on most of the express trains which stop at Kodaikanal Road. It's open from 9.30 am to 12.30 pm and 2.30 to 4.30 pm, Monday to Saturday.

Kodai Walks
The main activity in Kodai is walking around enjoying the sights and views. The rolling lawns of the numerous stone and wood cottages from the British period are edged with flowering shrubs and trees.

The views from Coaker's Walk, where an observatory with telescope is available, and from Pillar Rocks, a seven-km hike,

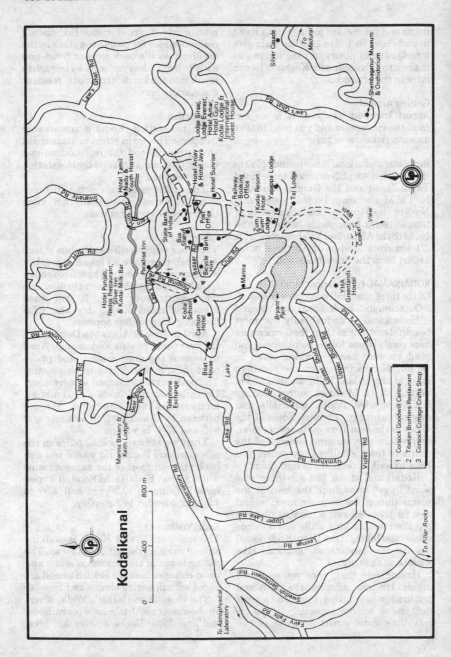

Kodaikanal

0   400   800 m

To Madurai

Silver Casade

Shembaganur Museum & Orchidorium

Law's Ghat Rd

Law's Ghat Rd

Lodge Siraaj,
Lodge Everest,
Hotel Amar,
Hotel Guru,
Kodai Lodge &
International
Guest House

Hotel Anjay
& Hotel Jaya

Hotel Sunrise

Railway
Booking
Office

Yaggapa Lodge

Taj Lodge

Sivanady Rd

Hills Rd

Hotel Tamil
Nadu &
Youth Hostel

State Bank
of India

Post
Office

Bus
Stand

Bazaar Rd

Canara
Bank

Bicycle
Hire

Zum
Lodge

Zum
Kodai Resort
Hotel

Coaker's Walk

View

Paradise Inn

Hotel Punjab,
Nedos Restaurant,
Silver Inn
& Kodai Milk Bar

Fern Hills Rd

Law's Ghat Rd

Hospital Rd

Kodai
School

Carlton
Hotel

Manna

Club Rd

Bryant
Park

St Mary's Rd

YHA
Greenlands
Hostel

Coonoor Rd

Boat
House

Lake

Lower Shola Rd

Upper Shola Rd

Telephone
Exchange

Bear Shola
Rd

Lloyd's Rd

Manna Bakery &
Keith Lodge

Observatory Rd

Lake Rd

Tapp's Rd

Gymkhana
Rd

Gymkhana Rd

Violet Rd

Upper Lake Rd

Levinge
Rd

Swedish Settlement Rd

Fairy Falls Rd

To Astrophysical
Laboratory

To Pillar Rocks

1 Corsock Goodwill Centre
2 Tibetan Brothers Restaurant
3 Corsock Cottage Crafts Shop

are two of the most spectacular in India. Bryant Park is also worth a visit, especially if you have an interest in botany. The park was laid out, landscaped and stocked over many years by the British colonial administrator after whom it is named.

Flora & Fauna Museum

Also worth a visit is the Flora & Fauna Museum at the Sacred Heart College at nearby Shembaganur. It's a six-km hike and all uphill on the way back. The museum is open from 10 to 11.30 am and 3.30 to 5 pm, and is closed on Sundays. There are numerous waterfalls in the area – you'll pass the main one, Silver Cascade, on the road up to Kodai.

Astrophysical Observatory

The Astrophysical Laboratory is built on the highest point in the area, three km uphill from the lake. It houses a small museum which is only open from 10 am to 12 noon on Fridays. The buildings with the instruments are off limits. It's a hard 45-minute uphill walk pushing a bicycle, but it only takes about five minutes to coast back down. Make sure you get a bike with brakes!

Boating & Riding

The lake at Kodai has been wonderfully landscaped, and rowboats are available for Rs 12 per half hour plus a returnable deposit. You can also hire pedal boats for Rs 10. Down by the boathouse, you'll be accosted by people who want to rent you horses. They are not cheap, and you'll be quoted as much as they think you're silly enough to pay. The prevailing rate seems to be Rs 20 per hour and you can ride accompanied or unaccompanied. The saddles are pretty awful, especially if you're used to your own.

Tours

There are tours from the Hotel Tamil

Boating on Kodai Lake

Nadu from 8.30 am to 12.30 pm and from 2.50 to 6.30 pm. This is tourist territory and the hefty price of Rs 45 per person is definitely a tourist rip-off. The tours go to Coakers Walk, the Golf Course, Bryant Park, Silver Cascades waterfall and the lake. Save your money.

Places to Stay – bottom end

The cheap hotels at the bottom (eastern) end of the bazaar are pretty basic places with minimal facilities. Just make sure that they give you blankets, as it gets pretty chilly here. You can usually get a bucket of hot water in the mornings. Prices are fairly negotiable, depending on supply and demand. Pick of the bunch is the *International Tourist Lodge* (tel 542), right at the bottom. The rooms cost Rs 30/40 with attached cubicle and bucket (they call it a bath). There's hot water by the bucket in the mornings.

The *Hotel Amar* and the *Hotel Guru*, a little higher up from the bazaar, are also reasonable value at Rs 30 for a double with attached bucket. The other bazaar hotels verge on the totally uninhabitable.

Away from the bazaar area, the *Zum Zum Lodge* was once popular but is no longer good value at Rs 30/50, as the rooms are damp and gloomy.

Out at the end of Coakers Walk, the *Greenlands Youth Hostel* is very pleasant. Beds in the cosy dorms cost Rs 12.50, and the two double rooms, both with bath, cost Rs 30 and Rs 50. There's also a *Youth Hostel* at the Hotel Tamil Nadu, which is quite a walk from the bus station. Beds cost Rs 20 in the off season, and a hefty Rs 30 in season.

At the start of Coakers Walk, the *Taj Lodge* is in an old house and is very pleasant and quiet with a homely atmosphere. Double rooms cost Rs 75.

On the other side of the lake from the centre, the *Keith Lodge* has just a couple of doubles which are clean and good value at Rs 55, and one deluxe double for Rs 100. The only problem is walking there from the bus stand carrying your pack.

There are a couple of good places at the top of this bracket. The friendly *Hotel Sunrise* (tel 358) is only a few minutes walk from the post office and has double rooms with bath for Rs 80. As with most hotels in Kodai, it has no single rooms. The view from out the front is excellent, and the rooms have individual hot water heaters which they'll switch on for you any time. Just to add a bit of variety to your day, the bathrooms have both Indian and western toilets.

A bit further away, about 20 minutes walk from the bus station, the *Yagappa Lodge* (tel 235) also has good rooms with hot water for Rs 60/80.

Places to Stay – middle

The *Kodai Resort Hotel* (tel 605) is near the start of Coakers Walk. It's fairly new and characterless, and caters mainly to the tour groups, but the cottages are well designed and cost Rs 150 for a double, rising to Rs 250 in the season.

Much closer to the centre, at the end of Hospital Rd, the *Paradise Inn* (tel 674) is another newish place. Rooms cost Rs 125/150. Also near the centre, the new *Hotel Astoria* has similar prices. The *Hotel Tamil Nadu* (tel 481) on Fern Hill Rd has a restaurant and bar. Like the other Hotel Tamil Nadus, this is a state government project. The cheapest doubles cost Rs 110 in the low season, rising to Rs 160 in April, May and June. There are also family rooms with five beds. However, the hotel is 15 minutes walk from the bus stand, or Rs 15 by taxi.

Places to Stay – top end

Kodaikanal's most prestigious hotel is the *Carlton Hotel* (tel 252), Boathouse Rd, which overlooks the lake and has its own restaurant and bar. Singles/doubles are Rs 672/825 in the off season, rising to a steep Rs 912/1045 in the season. These prices include all meals.

Places to Eat

Hospital Rd is a good place to start

looking. For Chinese, Tibetan and some western dishes in this street, try the dilapidated but cosy *Tibetan Brothers Restaurant*, a popular meeting place for travellers and students from the Kodai International School. The noodle soups here are fantastic – a meal in themselves – and the momos are also worth a try. It's certainly the best place in town. Also on Hospital Rd, you'll find the *Silver Inn Restaurant*, which serves reasonable meals, and the *Kodai Milk Bar*.

Another place offering something a bit different is *Manna Bakery* on Bear Shola Rd, near the telephone exchange, run by the very friendly Israel. It's really only a stall, and the location changes from time to time as the authorities make it increasingly difficult to rent a small piece of land. Israel is presently in his fourth location in the last six years, so you may have to look for him! He sells such delicacies as home-made brown bread, vegetable pie, pizza and wonderful apple crumble and custard. He's open for late breakfast and lunch but, if you want to eat here in the evening, you need to place an order by 3 pm.

For Indian meals, there are a few places in the bazaar. The *Pakia Deepam* restaurant at the bus stand is by far the most popular and charges Rs 8.50 for a vegetarian meal.

For a splurge, the *Carlton Hotel* has a Rs 72 evening buffet from 7.30 to 10.30 pm. The variety and quantity of food available is nothing compared to the famous hotel buffets in the bigger cities, but you can still make a fair pig of yourself without too much trouble. As soon as you start ordering drinks, the cost escalates rapidly.

Things to Buy

The Cottage Crafts shop in the main street has some excellent bits and pieces for sale. It is run by Corsock, the Co-ordinating Council for Social Concerns in Kodai. This organisation, staffed by volunteers, sells crafts on behalf of development groups, using the commission charged to help the needy.

Corsock also runs the Goodwill Centre on Hospital Rd. It sells clothing and rents books, with the proceeds again going to needy causes.

Getting There & Away

Bus At least eight buses a day make the four-hour trip to Madurai. Buses to Palani, Dindigul and Kodai Road leave throughout the day. There are no direct buses to Trichy, so catch a bus to Dindigul and then a train or bus from there.

There is a daily bus to Thekkady (Periyar Wildlife Sanctuary) in Kerala, and a KSRTC overnight super-deluxe bus for the 12-hour trip to Bangalore, although booking a ticket on this latter service can be difficult. Hang around the bus station at around 9 am when the bus arrives from Bangalore, and get a ticket from the conductor.

Train The nearest railway stations are Palani to the north, and Kodaikanal Road to the east.

Getting Around

You can hire bicycles at the main intersection at the top of the bazaar. The rate is Rs 2 per hour, which is double and even triple the normal rate. The hills can present quite a problem but, as you'd be walking up them anyway, it's not that much extra hassle to push a bike and at least you can coast down!

AROUND KODAI
Palani

There are fine views of the plains and scattered rock outcrops on the bus ride from Kodaikanal to Palani. The hill temple is dedicated to Lord Maruga, and an electric winch takes pilgrims to the top.

RAMESWARAM (population 13,000)

Rameswaram is the Varanasi of the south and a major pilgrimage centre for both Saivaites and Vaishnavites. Ramana-

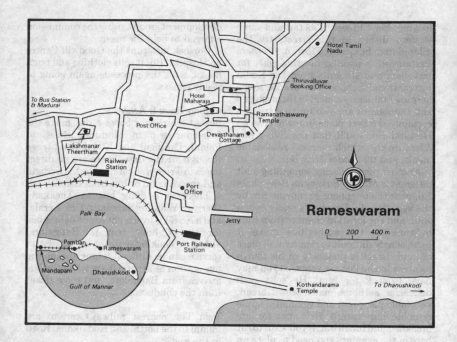

thaswamy Temple is one of the most important southern temples.

This is also the port from which the ferry to Talaimannar (Sri Lanka) used to depart before its suspension due to the turmoil in that country, so the town now has very few foreign visitors.

Information & Orientation

Rameswaram is an island in the Gulf of Mannar, connected to the mainland at Mandapam by rail, and by India's latest engineering wonder, the Indira Gandhi Bridge. The bridge took 14 years to build and was finally opened by Rajiv Gandhi late in 1988.

The town itself is small and dusty, with most of the hotels and restaurants, the ferry jetty, railway station and post office clustered around the Ramanathaswamy Temple. It's not unreasonable to wonder why, with 14 years spent constructing the bridge, some time could not have been

devoted to building a bus station to handle the sudden influx of buses, but no, things don't happen like that in India. The 'bus station' is an expanse of open ground two km west of the town centre. It's totally inadequate, with no facilities of any kind, and finding the right bus can be a problem. The Thiruvalluvar booking office is on North Car St, next to the Hotel Chola.

It can be difficult to get accommodation here if there's a festival on, especially if you arrive late in the day.

At the tourist office in the railway station, you'll find a hand-out map and nothing else. There is a bank on North Car St.

Ramanathaswamy Temple

The town's most famous monument is the Ramanathaswamy Temple, a fine example of late-Dravidian architecture. Its most renowned feature is its magnificent corridors lined with massive sculptured pillars, noted for their elaborate design, style and rich carving. Legend has it that Rama (of the Indian epic the *Ramayana*) sanctified this place by worshipping Lord Shiva here after the battle of Sri Lanka. Construction of the temple began in the 12th century AD and additions were made to the building over the succeeding centuries by various rulers so that today, its gopuram is 53.6 metres high. Only Hindus may enter the inner sanctum. The temple is open from 4 am to 1 pm and 3 to 9 pm. Like Kanyakumari, excessively loud and distorted temple music is blasted out from the temple from about 4.30 am onwards – just in case you had any ideas about sleeping in. It's torture for anyone who is not totally deaf yet, amazingly, the locals go about their business as if nothing is going on.

Kothandaraswamy Temple

This is another famous temple, about three km from the extreme tip of the island.

It was the only structure to survive the 1964 cyclone which washed the rest of the village away. Legend states that Vibishana, brother of Sita's kidnapper Ravana, surrendered to Rama at this spot.

Other Attractions

There is a lovely bathing pool at Dhanushkodi on the very tip of the peninsula, deserted except for friendly fishers. The buses stop at Kothandaraswamy, about three km away, so you have to walk the rest of the way or flag down one of the Public Carrier vans delivering goods to the villagers.

Places to Stay

The best accommodation is the *Hotel Maharaja* (tel 271) on Middle St, the street heading west from the west gopuram of the temple. The hotel is conveniently situated and has pleasant rooms for Rs 30/45 with bath. Its only

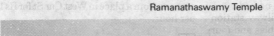
Ramanathaswamy Temple

drawback is that it's right in the line of fire of the temple loudspeakers.

The *Alankar Tourist Home* on West Car St is cheaper, with good rooms for Rs 20/30 with bath. Also on West Car St, the *Lodge Santhya* (tel 329) is a bit more up-market at Rs 40 for a double, Rs 99 with air-con. The *Santhana Lodge* on South Car St has rooms for Rs 20/30 with bath. They're basic but quite acceptable. Cheapest of the lot is the *Nadar Mahajana Sangam Lodge* (tel 240) at 19 New St, five minutes walk south of the temple. It's not bad value at Rs 17/27.

The *Hotel Tamil Nadu* (tel 277) is the best hotel in town but, unless you can make an advance reservation (through the tourist office in Madras), it's virtually impossible to get a room here. The hotel is right on the beach, a few hundred metres from the temple. If you strike it lucky, rooms cost Rs 40/60, or Rs 125 for an air-con double, with signs in each warning of 'thieving crows'. Beds at the *Youth Hostel* attached to the hotel are Rs 20, but here too, it's usually no booking, no bed.

Retiring rooms at the railway station (there's one single, five doubles and four triples) are Rs 20/30/40. There are also 16 dorm beds at Rs 10 each.

Places to Eat

A number of vegetarian restaurants along West Car St serve typical south Indian thalis, all of a pretty dismal standard.

Getting There & Away

Bus The bus station is two km west of town. Thiruvalluvar buses run to Kanyakumari, Trichy, Madurai and Madras, and the local buses run to Madurai (16 daily, four hours), Pondicherry (two daily), Trichy (six daily, six hours) and Thanjavur (daily).

Train There are two expresses (and one passenger train) to Madras daily. The 666-km trip takes 15 hours on the Sethu Express and costs Rs 69 in 2nd class, Rs 253 in 1st.

The daily 784 Rameswaram-Madurai Passenger to Madurai takes 6½ hours to cover the 164 km and costs Rs 14 in 2nd class. The buses are quicker but personally, I'd rather take a slow train than a fast bus any day. I have every intention of living a long life, and I see no need to put it in the hands of an Indian bus driver any more often than is absolutely necessary.

Getting Around

Bus Town buses run backwards and forwards between the temple and the bus station from early morning until late at night.

Auto-Rickshaw, Cycle-Rickshaw & Tonga These ply the streets at all hours. The official fare from the bus stand to the temple is Rs 5, but you'll be doing well to get there for less than Rs 7.

Bicycle Bicycle is a good way of getting around Rameswaram, and out to Dhanushkodi at the tip of the peninsula. You can rent one from a place in West Car St for Rs 1 per hour.

TIRUCHENDUR

South of Rameswaram and Tuticorin is this impressive temple. You may be able to enter the inner sanctums here and watch the enthusiastic proceedings. Just be careful if they offer you a gulp of the holy water. Pouring it over your hands and rubbing them together joyously is an acceptable substitute for drinking it!

Places to Stay

The *Hotel Tamil Nadu* (tel 268) has singles/doubles with bath for Rs 40/60.

KANYAKUMARI (Cape Comorin)

Kanyakumari is the 'Land's End' of India. Here, the Bay of Bengal meets the Indian Ocean and, at full moon, it's possible to enjoy the unique experience of seeing the sun set and the moon rise over the ocean simultaneously. Kanyakumari is also a popular pilgrimage destination of great spiritual significance to Hindus. It is dedicated to the goddess Kanyakumari, 'youthful virgin', who is an incarnation of Devi, Shiva's wife.

Otherwise, Kanyakumari is highly overrated, with its trinket stalls, a lousy beach and one of those places with megaphones at the end of each street which rip your eardrums apart between 4 am and 10 pm. Do Indians collectively suffer from some congenital disability which makes them incapable of perceiving the excruciating levels of noise pollution, or is it a perverse form of merit-garnering

penance? Most interesting are the pilgrims who come here from all over the country, representing a good cross section of India. You can safely give this place a miss if your time is limited but, if you want to stand on the very tip of the subcontinent, it's the place to do it. It also makes an easy day trip from Kovalam if you're feeling energetic.

Information & Orientation

The town is fairly spread out and both transport centres are out of the way. The railway station is almost a km to the

Kanyakumari

0   100   200 m

To Nagercoil & Trivandrum

Railway Station

Sankar's Guest House

Our Lady of Ransom Church

Sri Bhagavathi Lodge

Hotel Sangam & Township Rest House

Manickhan Tourist Home

Post Office

Gopi Nivas Lodge

DKV Lodge

Raja Tourist Home

Chicken Corner Restaurant

Bus Station

Kumari Bhavan Lodge

Vinayakar Kovil

Lighthouse

Youth Hostel

Snack Stalls

Ferry Jetty

Kerala House

Jothi Lodge

Hotel Tamil Nadu

Bank

Tri-Sea Lodge

Tourist Office

Palace Hotel

Gandhi Mandapam

Ranjakumai Temple

Kumari Ghat

Vivekananda Memorial

Main Rd

north, while the bus station is 500 metres west of the town centre.

There is a tourist office near the Gandhi Mandapam – but what could you possibly want to know?

Kanyakumari Temple

Picturesquely located overlooking the shore, the Kumari Ghat attracts pilgrims from all over India to worship and to bathe. According to legend, Devi did penance here to secure Shiva's hand in marriage. When she was unsuccessful, she vowed to remain a virgin (Kanya). The temple is open daily from 4.30 to 11.45 am and from 5.30 to 8.45 pm, but non-Hindus are not allowed into the inner sanctum. Men must remove their shirts, and everyone their shoes, on entering this temple.

Lighthouse

There are excellent views of the countryside from the lighthouse. It is open from 3 to 7 pm and entry costs Rs 0.25. Unfortunately, photography is prohibited.

Vivekananda Memorial

The Vivekananda Memorial is on two rocky islands projecting from the sea about 500 metres offshore. The Indian philosopher Swami Vivekananda came here in 1892 and sat on the rock, meditating, before setting out as one of India's most important religious crusaders. The mandapam which stands here in his memory was built in 1970 and employs architectural styles from all over India. The ferry service to the island every half hour costs Rs 3 per person, plus an entry fee of Rs 2 to the Rock Temple. The islands are open to visitors from 7 to 11 am and 2 to 5 pm.

Suchindram Temple

Dedicated to Indra, the Suchindram Temple is about 13 km from Kanyakumari (Rs 10 by auto-rickshaw) and can be

Vivekananda Memorial

visited by non-Hindus. It's worth joining the Friday sunset ceremonies. You have to hire a special dhoti and a guide will 'rush you around but will paste your forehead, chest and arms with white ash paste'.

Places to Stay - bottom end

Hotels can be heavily booked, which tends to push the prices up. At the bottom end of the market, there are a bunch of cheap hotels clustered just north of the Vinayakar Kovil Temple. Two of these are the *Raja Tourist Home* and *Gopi Nivas Lodge*, with rooms at Rs 25/40. Both are basic but adequate.

The very comfortable *DKV Lodge* is in the same area. Rooms 7 and 9 have excellent views of the town and Vivekananda Memorial, as well as a sea breeze. Double rooms cost Rs 60 with bath; there are no singles.

The *Township Rest House* on Main Rd also has only doubles, and these cost Rs 40. On the town's central street, the *Jothi Lodge* is grubby and gloomy. Rooms are Rs 25/40 with bath.

You can get a bed for Rs 20 in the *Youth Hostel* at the Hotel Tamil Nadu. Accommodation in the tidy dorm at the bus station *lodge* also costs Rs 20. You get a locker under the bed to stow your gear and there is hot water.

The railway *retiring rooms* cost Rs 20/30; a bed in the six-bed dorm is Rs 10.

Places to Stay - middle

The *Hotel Sangam* (tel 351) on Main Rd is next door to the Township Rest House. Rooms - doubles only - cost Rs 100 with bath and hot water. The hotels along the waterfront west of the temple are very pleasant but, unfortunately, you're unlikely to get in without a booking. The *Hotel Tamil Nadu* (tel 257) has doubles for Rs 100, or Rs 125 with air-con. *Kerala House* is run by the Kerala Tourism Development Corporation, but it seems to be monopolised by Kerala government officials.

The relatively new *Manickhan Tourist Home* has doubles for Rs 100. Some of the rooms have a good view of the town and Vivekananda Memorial.

The *lodge* at the bus station has large double rooms for Rs 82 with bath and hot water.

Places to Eat

The popular *Palace Hotel* in the main part of town serves good vegetarian meals on a banana leaf for Rs 5.

Non-vegetarian food is harder to find. The *Chicken Corner* has fish and mutton as well as chicken, and the *Manickhan Tourist Home* also has a non-vegetarian restaurant.

Snack stalls selling chicken, paratha and other dishes are set up on the main intersection in town in the evenings. This is the way to go if you're on a tight budget.

Getting There & Away

Bus The new bus station is an edifice which seems quite out of proportion to the size of the town. Everything here is well organised, with timetables in English, restaurants, waiting rooms and even a lodge upstairs. The reservation office is open from 7 am to 9 pm. The station is a dusty 15-minute walk from the centre.

There are Thiruvalluvar buses to Madurai (No 101, six hours), Madras (No 282, 16 hours), Trivandrum (No 800, 2½ hours) and Rameswaram (No 520, 8½ hours).

Local buses go to Nagercoil, Trivandrum and Kovalam, among other places.

Train Grandiose transport centres are definitely the rage in Kanyakumari. The railway station is almost as over-the-top as the bus station and wouldn't look out of place in Delhi or Bombay.

The one daily passenger train to Trivandrum does the 87 km in a dazzling three hours for a Rs 9 fare.

The Kanyakumari Express travels to Bombay daily in a shade under 48 hours, departing Kanyakumari at 5.15 am. The 2149-km trip costs Rs 148 in 2nd class,

Rs 609 in 1st. This train will also take you to Trivandrum (2¼ hours) and Ernakulam (eight hours).

For the real long-haulers, the weekly Him Sagar Express runs all the way to Jammu Tawi, a distance of 3676 km, taking 10 hours under four days. It's the longest single train ride in India, and leaves from Kanyakumari on Sundays at 11.30 pm, or from Jammu Tawi on Wednesdays at 7.40 pm. This train also goes to Madras (952 km, 12 hours) and Delhi (3141 km, 72 hours) on the way.

AROUND KANYAKUMARI
Padmanabhapuram

Padmanabhapuram, near Nagercoil, was once the seat of the rulers of Travancore, a princely state during the days of the Raj which included a large part of present-day Kerala and the western littoral of Tamil Nadu. There's an old fort and a pagoda-shaped palace with fine 17th and 18th-century murals on the topmost floor which are even finer than those at Matancherry in Cochin, according to one visitor. They are 'less restored, in better condition and staggeringly beautiful'.

The palace is close to the Kerala border, 55 km south of Trivandrum, and is convenient to visit between Kanyakumari and Trivandrum. It's closed on Mondays.

Wildlife Sanctuaries

There are six wildlife sanctuaries in Tamil Nadu, three close to the east coast and the others in the richly forested mountains on the borders of Kerala and Karnataka. The Guindy Deer Park, within the metropolitan boundaries of Madras, is the smallest.

All sanctuaries except Guindy have accommodation and transport facilities. Although it's possible to turn up at any of them without making prior arrangements, it's advisable to book in advance. Rooms in sanctuary lodges and rest houses cannot be allocated to unannounced

guests until very late in the afternoon, when there's no further possibility of anyone arriving with a booking.

Motorised transport can be arranged to the more remote parts of the sanctuaries, where you're far more likely to see animals, which don't often venture too close to main roads or areas of human settlement. Some of the sanctuaries offer elephant rides through the forest which usually don't need to be booked in advance. Although these are great fun, you're unlikely to see many of the animals which live in these sanctuaries from the back of an elephant.

At present, most of the sanctuaries are geared to groups who arrive with their own transport and who have prebooked at least a few days ahead. If you're alone and haven't booked, you could find that a lot of your time is taken up waiting for the arrival of a group to which you can attach yourself. Your choice of accommodation is

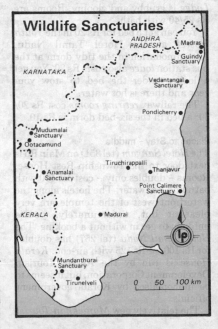

Wildlife Sanctuaries

also limited by a lack of transport, unless you can get a lift. It's time the Indian tourist organisation gave some thought to catering for visitors without their own transport and those who can't make bookings weeks in advance because of the way they travel. Nevertheless, visiting at least one of the sanctuaries can be a very rewarding experience.

MUDUMALAI WILDLIFE SANCTUARY
In the luxuriantly forested foothills of the Nilgiris, Mudumalai is part of a much larger sanctuary which includes Bandipur and Wynad in neighbouring Karnataka and Kerala. The main attractions here are the herds of chital (spotted deer), gaur (Indian bison), elephant, tiger, panther, wild boar, sloth, and the otters and crocodiles which live in the River Moyar. It's possible to see all these animals if you have made arrangements with the Forest Department for a vehicle to take you to the more remote parts of the sanctuary.

The main service area in this sanctuary, Theppakadu, is on the main road between Ootacamund and Mysore. The Wildlife Sanctuary Reception Centre, Sylvan Lodge, Youth Hostel and elephant camp are here. Even around Theppakadu, you can sometimes see spotted deer, elephant and wild boar.

It's advisable to book sanctuary accommodation and transport in advance, either with the Forest Officer in Ooty on Coonoor Rd, or at a Tamil Nadu tourist office. There are entry fees for visitors, vehicles and cameras. Jeeps and minibuses can be hired in the park, and elephant rides are available. The elephants go crashing through the bush over a four to five-km circuit and are great fun, but you'll be lucky to see anything other than spotted deer, wild boar, gaur and monkeys. The elephant rides must be booked in advance in Ooty.

The best time to visit the sanctuary is between February and May, though you can visit at any time of the year, except during the dry season when it may be closed. Heavy rain is common in October and November.

Places to Stay & Eat
Theppakadu The most convenient place to stay is the TTDC *Youth Hostel* (tel Masinagudi 49), where dorm beds cost Rs 20 and basic meals are available. There's no need to book in advance.

The various rest houses cost Rs 40 for a double. The *Sylvan Lodge* is the best and looks out over the river.

The *Abhayaranyam Rest House* has rooms from Rs 25. There's also a dormitory at the *Range Office* a short way from the Rest House.

At the *Reception Centre*, there is an eight-bed dormitory (four per room) with toilet and shower but no catering facilities. If you're staying here, you can eat at the *Sylvan Lodge* or *Youth Hostel* as there are no other restaurants – Theppakadu is not really a village, just the park headquarters on the main road.

Masinagudi Masinagudi is a small village eight km east of Theppakadu. The privately run *Mountania Lodge* (tel 37) has cabins with bath for Rs 140/150. Meals are available here, or you can try the couple of basic 'meals' places in the village.

Bamboo Banks (tel 22) is more expensive again and is inaccessible without your own transport. The *Chital Walk (Jungle Trails) Lodge* (tel Masinagudi 56), eight km east of Masinagudi, is a good place if you have a keen interest in wildlife. It offers double rooms at Rs 125 and dorm beds for Rs 25. Good meals are available. The Sighur Ghat buses to or from Ooty can drop you off on the road near the Valaitotam turn-off if you ask and, from there, it's a few hundred metres off the road.

Right opposite the police station in Masinagudi is a *Travellers Bungalow* with a couple of double rooms for Rs 40.

Getting There & Away The buses from Ooty

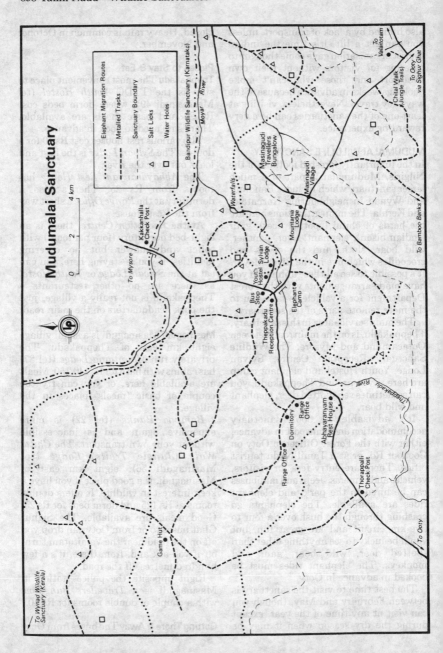

Mudumalai Sanctuary

To Valaitotam

To Ooty
via Sighur Ghat

Chital Walk
(Jungle Trails)

Bandipur Wildlife Sanctuary (Karnataka)

Moyal River

To Bamboo Banks

Masinagudi
Travellers
Bungalow

Masinagudi
Village

Mountania
Lodge

Waterfalls

Kakkanhalla
Check Post

To Mysore

Sylvan
Lodge

Youth
Hostel

Bus
Stop

Thepakadu
Reception Centre

Elephant
Camp

Thepakadu River

Range
Office

Dormitory

Abhayaranyam
Rest House

Range Office

To Ooty

Thorappalli
Check Post

Game Hut

To Wynad Wildlife
Sanctuary (Kerala)

To Ootacamund

N

0   2   4 km

Elephant Migration Routes

Metalled Tracks

Sanctuary Boundary

Salt Licks

Water Holes

to Mysore, Bangalore and Hassan stop at Theppakadu, and it's not too difficult to wave them down.

The more interesting route to or from Ooty involves taking a bus to Masinagudi, then one of the small government buses which make the trip up (or down) the tortuous Sighur Ghat road. It's actually shorter than the main road, but the bends are so tight and the gradient so steep that large buses can't use it. In fact, there's a sign on the road leaving Masinagudi warning that 'you will have to strain your vehicle to reach Ooty'!

You can also visit the sanctuary on tours from Ooty, but you're unlikely to see anything other than elephants.

VEDANTANGAL WATER BIRDS SANCTUARY

This is one of the most spectacular breeding grounds in India. Water fowl gather here for about six months of the year from October-November to March, depending on the monsoons, and their numbers peak in December and January. At the height of the breeding season, you can see up to 30,000 birds at once. The best times to visit are early morning and late afternoon.

Cormorants, egrets, herons, storks, ibises, spoonbills, grebes and pelicans come here to breed and nest, and many other species of migratory birds also visit the sanctuary.

The best way to get there is by bus from Madras to Chingleput, but you will have to hire transport to take you to the *Forest Rest House* – it's the only place to stay, with rooms from Rs 25.

CALIMERE WILDLIFE SANCTUARY

Point Calimere, on the east coast just south of the Pondicherry territory of Karaikal in Thanjavur district, is noted for its congregation of black buck, spotted deer and wild pig, and the vast flocks of migratory water fowl, especially flamingos. Every winter, the tidal mud flats and marshes are covered with masses of birds – teals, shovellers, curlews, gulls, terns, plovers, sandpipers, shanks, herons and up to 3000 flamingos at one time. In the spring, a different set of birds – koels, mynas and barbets – are drawn here by the profusion of wild berries.

Visit between November and January. There is very little activity from April to June, and the main rainy season is between October and December. You can get to Point Calimere either by rail on the Mayavaram to Thiruthuraipoondi section, or by regular bus from either Thanjavur or Mayavaram. A *Forest Rest House* has rooms from Rs 25, but facilities are very basic and no meals are available.

MUNDANTHURAI TIGER SANCTUARY

Mundanthurai is in the mountains near the border with Kerala. The closest railway station is at Amabasamudram, and regular buses run from there to the sanctuary. From Tirunelveli, buses go to Popanasam and, from there, you can catch another bus to the Forest Rest House.

As the name implies, this is principally a tiger sanctuary and the best time to visit is between January and September, though you can come at any time of year.

The main rainy season is between October and December. Tiger sightings are apparently extremely infrequent and, in addition, the *Forest Rest House* is poorly maintained, food is not available and the staff are unhelpful.

ANAMALAI WILDLIFE SANCTUARY

This is the third of the wildlife sanctuaries in the mountains along the border between Tamil Nadu and Kerala. Anamalai is south of Coimbatore and can be reached by regular bus from Coimbatore, or by rail to Pollachi and then bus to the sanctuary. The Reception Centre is at Parambikulam Dam. Anamalai's major attractions are

elephant, gaur, tiger, panther, spotted deer, wild boar, bear, porcupine and civet cat. The Nilgiri tahr, commonly known as ibex, can also be seen here. Transport within the sanctuary can be arranged through the Forest Department.

Accommodation is available at three places: the *Forest Rest House* at Topslip with six rooms, *Varagaliar Rest House* deep in the forest with basic accommodation (but you must take your own provisions as there are no catering facilities), and *Mount Stuart Rest House* with two rooms and meals available. The sanctuary can be visited at any time of the year, and very early morning or late evening is best.

Travellers' Notebook

Coping with Chillies

The majority of Europeans do not know how hot a proper tropically grown chilli is. No-one warned me about chillies before I left for India and as a consequence my trip was ruined. I was travelling in southern India and chillies are in every meal. I had the 'runs' severely, and my intestines became so inflamed that the food just went straight through me. I got so thin (because my inflamed intestines could not absorb the digested food) that I felt I had to leave India and find a place where I could eat without ingesting chilli. I went to Singapore and lived on bread and jam for two weeks until I shitted out the whole lining of my guts. However, I did stay in the east and after two years I could eat the hottest green chilli raw and with relish.

I suggest that the the prospective India-bound traveller try adding chilli powder to tomato soup and see how they get on.

Remember that a south Indian samba contains about five tablespoons of chilli powder in the same volume as an ordinary tin of tomato soup! Travellers should make their insides chilli conscious by regularly eating food with gradually increasing amounts of chilli powder in it.

Steve Ridgeway, England

Damaged Money

Never accept any money with the slightest tear in it. Indians will gladly pass it on to you but will *never* let you pass it onto them. If you get a bad note go right back to the shop and ask for a perfect one. Look the bills over carefully, a slight hole is alright – they often pin their money together– but not a large one.

Ruth Hopf, USA

Andaman & Nicobar Islands

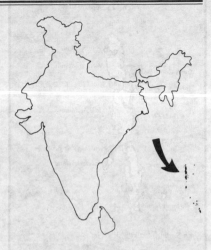

Population: 188,000
Area: 8293 square km on 319 islands
Capital: Port Blair
Main languages: various tribal

This string of over 300 richly forested tropical islands lies in the middle of the Bay of Bengal, two-thirds of the way between India and Burma (Myanma), and stretches almost to the tip of Sumatra. Ethnically, the islands are not part of India and, until fairly recently, they were inhabited by six distinct tribes with different physiognomies and speaking different languages.

These tribes, which constitute about 20% of the present population, fall into two main groups. The first is Negroid in origin and includes the Onges, Sentinelese, Andamanese and Jarawas, all resident in the Andaman Islands. The second group is of Mongoloid descent and includes the Shompens and Nicabarese.

The Onges, concentrated mainly on Little Andaman, are small, dark-complexioned hunters and gatherers who wear no clothes other than tasselled genital decorations and are fond of colourful make-up. They number only about 100; at the turn of the century, there were at least 600 Onges.

The 150 remaining Sentinelese live on North Sentinel Island and still fiercely resist any attempts to integrate them. The Jarawas are the largest grouping and inhabit the west coasts of Middle and South Andaman islands. The Andamanese tribe, once 4000 strong, now lives on tiny Strait Island and numbers only about 20.

The Nicabarese, whose home is on Car Nicobar, are a fair-complexioned people who have begun to adapt to contemporary Indian society. They are the largest tribe, with a population of over 22,000. They live mainly on fish, coconuts and pigs and are organised into villages controlled by village headmen. The last group, the Shompens, are found on Great Nicobar. So far, they have resisted integration into Indian society and tend to shy away from areas occupied by Indian immigrants from the mainland, preferring to live according to their own traditions.

The Indian government is fond of eulogising its efforts to bring 'civilisation' to these islands but, reading between the lines, it obviously regards the indigenous tribes here as stone-age people, and its attitude towards them is condescending. In an effort to develop the islands economically, the Indian government has completely disregarded the needs and land rights of the tribes and has encouraged massive transmigration from the mainland – mainly of Tamils who were expelled from Sri Lanka – which has pushed the population from 50,000 to 180,000 in just 15 years. The original islanders' culture is being swamped.

In the early 18th century, the Andaman and Nicobar islands were the base of the Maratha admiral, Kanhoji Angre, whose navy harassed and frequently captured British, Dutch and Portuguese merchant vessels. In 1713, Angre even managed to

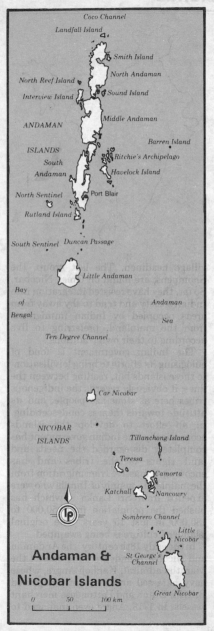

Coco Channel
Landfall Island
Smith Island
North Andaman
North Reef Island
Sound Island
Interview Island
ANDAMAN
Middle Andaman
Barren Island
ISLANDS
Ritchie's Archipelago
South
Andaman
Havelock Island
North Sentinel
Port Blair
Rutland Island
South Sentinel
Duncan Passage
Little Andaman
Bay
of
Andaman
Bengal
Sea
Ten Degree Channel
Car Nicobar
NICOBAR
ISLANDS
Tillanchong Island
Teressa
Camorta
Katchall
Nancowry
Sombrero Channel
Little
Nicobar
Andaman &
St George's
Channel
Nicobar Islands
Great Nicobar
0   50   100 km

capture the yacht of the British governor of Bombay, releasing it only after delivery of a ransom of powder and shot. Though attacked by the British, and later, by a combined British-Portuguese naval task force, Angre remained undefeated right up to his death in 1729.

The islands were finally annexed by the British in the 19th century and used as a penal colony for Indian freedom fighters.

In the notorious 'cellular jail', one of the 'tourist attractions' of Port Blair, many of the inmates were executed, either judicially or clandestinely. Building started in the last decade of the 19th century and the jail was finished in 1908. During WW II, the islands were occupied for a time by the Japanese, but they were not welcomed as liberators and the local tribes took up guerrilla activities against them. The islands were incorporated into the Indian Union when independence came to India in 1947.

A big effort is currently being made to develop the islands and, although vast tracts of forest were felled in the '60s and '70s, a more responsible approach has been adopted in recent times. There has been some replanting of the land with 'economic' timber like teak, but much of it has been turned over to rubber plantations.

Climate

There is little seasonal variation in climate. Continuous sea breezes keep temperatures within the 23°C to 31°C range and the humidity at around 80% all year. The south-west monsoons come to the islands between mid-May and October and the north-east monsoons between November and January. The best time to visit is between mid-November and April.

Permits

Foreigners need a permit to visit the Andaman Islands. (The Nicobar Islands are completely off limits to tourists.) It is valid for 15 days and can usually be extended for a further 15 days. The

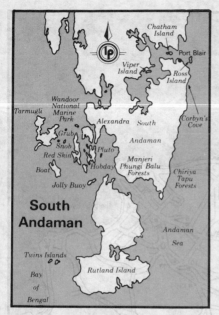

South Andaman

Andamans' permits are issued to visitors, without fuss, on arrival in Port Blair by air. Those arriving by ship need to get their permit in advance from the Foreigners' Registration Office in either Madras or Calcutta. The Shipping Corporation won't issue a ticket to anyone without a permit. In Madras, the permit takes 48 hours to issue.

The permit only allows tourists to visit South Andaman Island. Certain other islands can be visited with an additional permit, obtainable from the District Commissioner of Police in Port Blair, but the Nicobar and other southern islands are out of bounds to foreign visitors.

Having gone through the rigmarole of getting the permit, you have to be stamped out of the place when you leave as well. Indian red tape is alive and well in the Andamans!

PORT BLAIR
Port Blair, the administrative capital and only town of any size on the islands, has the lively air of any Indian market town. It is pleasantly situated on the main harbour and, as it's a hilly town, there are good views from quite a few vantage points.

Even though the Andamans are not far from mainland Burma, they still run on Indian time, which means that it is dark by 6 pm and light by 4 am.

At 5.30 pm each Monday, Wednesday and Friday, the Tourist Home has a free screening of a couple of documentary films about the islands. One is dreadful but the other is well worth seeing. The library on the same road as the post office is also a good place to find information about the islands.

Orientation
The town is spread out over a few hills, but most of the hotels, as well as the bus station, passenger dock, and Shipping Corporation of India office, are in the main bazaar area, known as Aberdeen Bazaar. The airport is a few km south of town over at least one steep hill.

Information
Tourist Offices The Government of India tourist office (tel 21006) is in a crazy location, halfway between the airport and the Secretariat building and at least 20 minutes walk from the centre so, as they have nothing of interest, don't waste your time.

There is a regional tourist office at the Tourist Home (tel 20380) in Haddo, about 20 minutes walk from the centre. This is the place to ask about boats to other islands and what permits are needed, but, unfortunately, the office hours are rather irregular. Then there's the Port Blair tourist office at the gate to the Secretariat, which is at the top of the hill overlooking the town. There is also a railways out-station booking office and a Shipping Corporation of India office here.

Post & Telephone The post office is not far

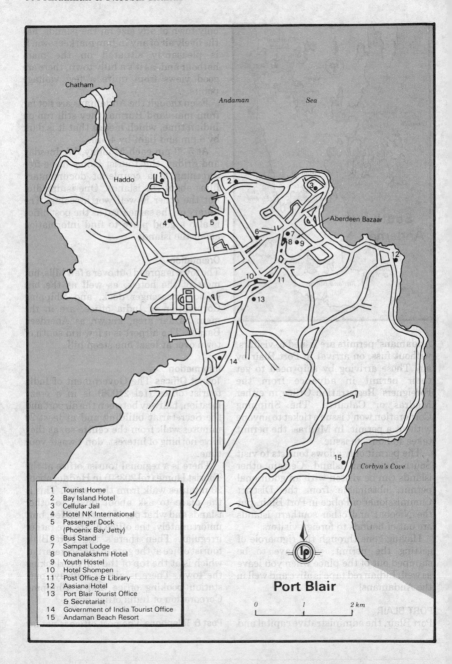

1. Tourist Home
2. Bay Island Hotel
3. Cellular Jail
4. Hotel NK International
5. Passenger Dock
   (Phoenix Bay Jetty)
6. Bus Stand
7. Sampat Lodge
8. Dhanalakshmi Hotel
9. Youth Hostel
10. Hotel Shompen
11. Post Office & Library
12. Aasiana Hotel
13. Port Blair Tourist Office
    & Secretariat
14. Government of India Tourist Office
15. Andaman Beach Resort

Port Blair

0   1   2 km

from the centre, with the telegraph office in a wooden shack next door, but links to the mainland are unreliable. It is open from 7 am to 10 pm weekdays, 8 am to 6 pm weekends.

Banks Foreign exchange facilities are available at banks and at the larger hotels.

Other Offices The Shipping Corporation of India office is right opposite the Dhanalakshmi Hotel in Aberdeen Bazaar. Buying a ticket to Madras or Calcutta can be a real circus. First, you go to the SCI office in Aberdeen Bazaar and get a piece of paper confirming that you have booked a ticket. From there, you trudge up the hill to the SCI office at the Secretariat, where you pay half the fare and get another piece of paper confirming this. Then you go back to the first office in the bazaar and

pay the balance. After all this, you might reasonably think that you would get your ticket. No, come back the next morning and it will be issued!

The Indian Airlines office is behind the post office. Flights are heavily booked and you need to have a confirmed ticket to be sure of a seat. Wait-listed passengers usually miss out.

Cellular Jail
The main point of interest is the huge Cellular Jail, built by the British at the beginning of this century. It originally consisted of six wings radiating out from a central tower, but only three remain today. It still gives a fair impression of the terrible conditions under which the detainees were incarcerated.

There is a booklet on sale titled *The Cellular Jail, the National Monument* by Gauri Shanker Pandey, which was no doubt written to explain the history of the

Cellular Jail

jail. Unfortunately, it is full of barely comprehensible nonsense and is a waste of Rs 12. This is a short extract:

Every silent bricks of this Jail is a mute witness of the various dramas of horror and cruelties enacted in this Jail by the British and Japs alien rulers and every brick here has several hundred such horror tales buried in them. Perhaps the burden of human sufferings witnesses by these bricks and mortar have made each of them silent for ever. The history of human race will be further blackened by its own misdeeds if only these bricks and mortars of the Andaman Cellular Jail starts speaking about what they saw during the past so many years.

Harbour Cruise

Every afternoon at 3 pm, a 1½-hour harbour cruise leaves from the Phoenix Bay Jetty. The trip on the old boat, the MV *Dugung*, costs a hefty Rs 26. To get there, walk in through the blue steel gates with the sign 'Pass Holders Only'. There is no English-speaking guide on the cruise, and the main point of 'interest' is the huge, floating dry-dock facility. The tour stops briefly at tiny Viper Island where the remains of the gallows tower built by the British still stand.

There are various other scheduled cruises and tours, but these seem to be a figment of someone's imagination and are always cancelled.

Corbyn's Cove

Corbyn's Cove is the nearest beach to Port Blair, 10 km from the town and four km beyond the airport. The easiest way to get there is to hire a bicycle in Aberdeen Bazaar and cycle out for the day. It's not a bad beach and you can slip into the Andaman Beach Resort for a beer if your wallet is not too thin. Taxis from Aberdeen Bazaar cost about Rs 20 each way.

Places to Stay

The islands are mainly a tourist resort and the accommodation is geared to this. Prices are generally higher than on the mainland although, even in the season, it is possible to bargain prices down quite a bit.

Places to Stay – bottom end

There are a few cheap places in Aberdeen Bazaar. The *Sampat Lodge* is about as basic as you can get. Hardboard-partitioned rooms without windows go for Rs 30. Not much better is the friendly *KK Guest House* which has tiny rooms for Rs 20/40 with common bath, although this price is definitely negotiable.

The *Central Lodge*, out past the Hotel Shompen at Middle Point, is a wooden lodge with a verandah, friendly management and rooms from Rs 60.

There is quite a bit of government accommodation around, but it is so bound up by complicated booking procedures and inconvenient locations that it hardly warrants the effort. The *Tourist Home* at Haddo is perhaps the only one in Port Blair worth bothering with. It is a solid 20 minutes walk from the bazaar, and rooms cost Rs 25/50. Food is available but the menu is limited and unexciting.

There is also a government-run *Guest House* out at Corbyn's Cove, just past the Andaman Beach Resort. It's a good place to stay, but you need to check with the tourist office at the Tourist Home in Haddo to see if it's full. Rooms cost Rs 40 for a double.

Places to Stay – middle

The new *Hotel Dhanalakshmi* (tel 21306) in Aberdeen Bazaar has good rooms for Rs 95/125 with attached bath although, once again, you can get the price down if things are quiet. Air-con rooms cost Rs 170/200.

Another new place is the *Hotel Shompen* (tel 2948) near the Indian Airlines office. Room rates are set at Rs 125/190, or Rs 190/200 with air-con. The front rooms have a balcony and views of the harbour. Bargaining is also possible here, and rates of Rs 30/50 have been reported out of season. They have a free bus which meets all incoming flights.

Around towards the Tourist Home, the *Hotel NK International* (tel 21066) has double rooms for Rs 125, or Rs 200 with air-con.

Places to Stay - top end

Perched on a cliff overlooking the harbour, the *Welcomgroup Bay Island Hotel* has rooms for Rs 490/610, rising to Rs 660/785 with air-con. The hotel has a beautiful open-air bar with great views – good for a quiet beer, although the wind usually gets up in the late afternoon.

Out at Corbyn's Cove, the *Andaman Beach Resort* (tel 2599) is in a very quiet and peaceful part of the island. The off-season (May to September) rates are Rs 320/380, rising to Rs 480/570 (from mid-December to mid-February) for rooms without air-con. Meals are available at Rs 45 for breakfast, Rs 80 for lunch and Rs 90 for dinner, but the food is reportedly not all that great. There is also the new *Aasiana Hotel* on the waterfront road to Corbyn's Cove.

Places to Eat

The best restaurant in Port Blair is in the *Dhanalakshmi Hotel* in Aberdeen Bazaar. The food is good, the place is clean and the young owners have a good collection of tapes. This is the place to meet other travellers in the evenings. It's open until 11 pm, which is late by Port Blair standards – the streets here are deserted by 9.30 each night.

After the Dhanalakshmi, everything else looks extremely basic. On the ground floor of the same building, the tiny *Kattappamman Hotel* has plain banana-leaf thalis for Rs 5. You pay extra for meat (Rs 4) and an omelette (Rs 2.50), and have to clean your own leaf away.

Further up the same road, the friendly *Annapurna Cafe* serves good vegetarian and non-vegetarian meals, and even has a visitors' book which you'll be asked to sign!

Getting There & Away

Air Indian Airlines has three-times-weekly flights between Port Blair and Madras (Rs 1255), or Calcutta (Rs 1245). The flights take two hours.

Boat There are regular sailings between Port Blair and Madras, and Port Blair and Calcutta. The Shipping Corporation of India operates these vessels and puts out a schedule roughly every three months, so it's possible to plan ahead. Foreigners have to travel 1st or 2nd class. The food is usually nonstop thalis for breakfast, lunch and dinner, so you need to bring something to supplement this boring diet.

Visitors travelling to the islands by boat need to get their permit in either Madras or Calcutta before buying the boat ticket.

The Port Blair SCI office in the Secretariat is open for Madras bookings from 10 to 11 am and 2 to 3 pm, and for Calcutta bookings from 10 am to 12 noon and 2 to 4 pm.

The ships MV *Nejd II* and MV *Nejd III* operate an approximately twice-weekly service between Madras and Port Blair. The journey is supposed to take about 56 hours, but is often longer due to rough seas. The boats are air-conditioned. Fares are Rs 583/375 in 1st/2nd class, and a daily charge of Rs 40 is made for food.

The MV *Andamans* connects Port Blair with Calcutta, making about two journeys per month. In Port Blair, bookings close four days before the scheduled departure date. The fares are Rs 583 in 'C' class and food is an extra Rs 38 per day.

Getting Around

There are taxis buzzing around Port Blair, and the drivers charge what they feel you'll pay. From the airport, the trip to Aberdeen Bazaar costs Rs 25; it's about Rs 20 to Corbyn's Cove.

The best way to explore, however, is to hire a bicycle in Aberdeen Bazaar for Rs 1 per hour and pedal yourself around. There's only one shop in the bazaar which rents them – it's on the left-hand side as you head down towards the bus station.

Glossary

Indian English is full of interesting little everyday expressions. Where in New York you might get robbed by a mugger, in India it will be a *dacoit* who relieves you of your goods. Politicians may employ strong-arm heavies known in India as *goondas*. There is a plethora of Indian terms for strikes, lock-outs and sit-ins – Indians can have *hartals, bhands* and *gheraos* for example. And then there are all those Indian servants – children get looked after by *ayahs*, your house (and your *godown* if you have one) is guarded by a *chowkidah* (but they're reputed to be a lazy bunch much given to lying around on *charpois*), and when the toilet needs cleaning there is no way your *bearer* is going to do it, that requires calling in a *sweeper*.

Then there are all the religious terms, the numerous Hindu gods, their attendants, consorts, vehicles and symbols. The multiplicity of religions in India also provides a whole series of terms for temples, shrines, tombs or memorials. It's surprising how many Indian terms have crept into everyday English usage. We can sit out on a *verandah*, wear *pyjamas* or *sandals* and *dungarees* (which may well be *khaki*), *shampoo* our hair, visit the *jungle*, worry about protecting our *loot* – they're all Indian words.

The glossary that follows is just a sample of words you may come across during your Indian wanderings.

Acha – OK.

Acharya – revered teacher, originally a spiritual guide or preceptor.

Agarbathi – incense.

Anikut – weir or dam.

Anna – one sixteenth of a rupee, now extinct but still used in marketplace conversation, ie eight annas are Rs 0.50, four annas are Rs 0.25.

Arrack – spirit drink made from coconut sap or rice wine.

Ashram – spiritual college cum retreat.

Astrology – far more than just a newspaper space filler; marriages are not arranged, flights not taken, elections not called without checking the astrological charts.

Avalokitesvara – one of the Buddha's most important disciples.

Ayah – children's nurse or nanny.

Ayurvedic – Indian natural and herbal medicine.

Baba – religious master, father, and a term of respect.

Babu – lower-level clerical worker.

Bagh – garden.

Bahadur – brave or chivalrous, honorific title.

Baksheesh – tip, bribe or donation.

Bandar – monkey.

Bandh – general strike.

Banain – T-shirt or undervest.

Baniya – moneylender.

Banyan – Indian fig tree.

Baoli – well, particularly a step well with landings and galleries.

Baradari – summer house.

Bazaar – market area. A market town is called a bazaar.

Bearer – rather like a butler.

Begum – Muslim woman of high rank.

Betel – nut of the betel tree, chewed as a mild intoxicant.

Bhagvadgita – Krishna's lessons to Arjuna, part of the *Mahabharata*.

Bhang – dried leaves and flowering shoots of the marijuana plant.

Bhang lassi – a blend of lassi with bhang, a drink with a kick.

Bhisti (bheesti) – water carrier.

Bidis (beedis) – small, hand-rolled cigarettes – really just a rolled-up tobacco leaf.

Black money – undeclared, untaxed money. There's lots of it in India.

Bodhisattva – near Buddha, follower of Buddha.

Bo tree – *ficus religiosa*, the tree under which the Buddha attained enlightenment.

Brahmin – a member of the priest caste, the highest Indian caste.

Bund – embankment or dyke.

Bugyal – meadow.

Burkha – one-piece garment which totally covers Muslim women.

Bustee – slum areas of Calcutta.

Cantonment – administrative and military area of a British Raj-era town.

Caste – one's station in life.

Chaitya – Buddhist temple.

Chakra – focus of one's spiritual power, disc-like weapon of Vishnu.

Chalo, chalo, chalo – 'let's go, let's go, let's go'.

Chance List – the wait list on Indian Airline flights.

Chang – Tibetan rice beer.

Choultries – dharamsalas in the south.

Chappals – sandals.

Chappati – unleavened Indian bread.

Charas – resinous exudate of the marijuana plant, hashish.

Charpoi – Indian rope bed.

Chat – general term for small snacks, papris, etc.

Chatri – tomb or mausoleum.

Chauri – fly whisk.

Chela – pupil or follower, as George Harrison was to Ravi Shankar.

Chikan – embroidered cloth.

Chillum – pipe part of a hookah, commonly used to describe the small pipes for smoking ganja.

Chinkara – gazelle.

Choli – sari blouse.

Chorten – Tibetan word for stupa.

Choultry – pilgrim accommodation.

Chowk – courtyard or marketplace.

Chowkidah – nightwatchman.

Cong (I) – Congress Party of India.

Country Liquor – locally produced liquor.

CPI – Communist Party of India.

CPI (M) – the Communist Party of India (Marxist). It's the bigger, more powerful party and is currently in power in West Bengal (Calcutta).

Crore – 10 million.

Curd – yoghurt.

Cutchery – office or building for public business.

Dacoit – robber, particularly armed robber.

Dargah – shrine or place of burial of a Muslim saint.

Darshan – offering or audience with someone, usually a guru.

Darwaza – gateway or door.

Devadasi – temple dancer.

Dhaba – hole-in-the-wall restaurant or snack bar.

Dhal – lentil soup, what most of India lives on.

Dharamsala – religious guest house.

Dharma – Hindu-Buddhist moral code of behaviour.

Dhobi – person who washes clothes.

Dhobi ghat – the place where the clothes are washed.

Dhoti – like a lunghi, but the cloth is then pulled up between the legs.

Digambara – 'sky-clad' Jain sect followers who extend their disdain for worldly goods to include not wearing clothes.

Diwan – principal officer in a princely state, royal court or council.

Diwan-i-Am – Hall of Public Audience.

Diwan-i-Khas – Hall of Private Audience.

Dooli – covered litter or stretcher. You may still see elderly tourists being carried around in a dooli.

Dowry – it's illegal but no arranged marriage (and most marriages are arranged) can be made without it.

Dravidian – a member of one of the aboriginal races of India, pushed south by the Indo-Europeans and now mixed with them. The Dravidian languages include Tamil, Malayalam, Telugu and Kannada.

Dupatta – scarf worn by Punjabi women.

Durbar – royal court, also used to describe a government.

Durga – same as Kali, terrible manifestation of Parvati.

Durrie – rug.

Dwarpal – doorkeeper, sculpture beside the doorways to Hindu or Buddhist shrines.

Election symbols – identifying symbols for the various political parties, since so many voters are illiterate.

Emergency – the period during which Indira Gandhi suspended many rights and many observers assumed she was intent on establishing a dictatorship.

Eve-teasing – the Indian equivalent of Italian bottom pinching.

Export gurus – gurus whose following is principally from the west.

Fakir – accurately a Muslim who has taken a vow of poverty, but also applied to Hindu ascetics such as sadhus.

Feni – spirit drink made from cashews, found in Goa.

Firman – a royal order or grant.

Freaks – westerners wandering India. The '60s live!

Gaddi – throne of a Hindu prince.
Ganesh – god of wisdom and prosperity, elephant-headed son of Shiva and Parvati, probably the most popular god in the whole Hindu pantheon.
Ganga – Ganges River.
Ganja – dried flowering tips of marijuana plant.
Gari – vehicle; motor gari is a car and rail gari is a train.
Garuda – man-bird vehicle of Vishnu.
Ghat – steps or landing on a river, place where corpses are cremated.
Ghazal – Urdu songs derived from poetry, sad love themes.
Ghee – clarified butter.
Gherao – lock-in, where the workers lock the management in!
Godmen – commercial-minded gurus, see export gurus.
Godown – warehouse.
Gompa – Tibetan-Buddhist monastery.
Gonds – aboriginal Indian race, now mainly found in the jungles in central India.
Goondas – ruffians or toughs. Political parties often have gangs of goondas.
Gopis – cowherd girls. Krishna was very fond of them.
Gopuram – soaring pyramidal gateway tower of a Dravidian temple.
Gurdwara – Sikh temple.
Guru – teacher or holy person.

Haji – a Muslim who has made the pilgrimage (haj) to Mecca.
Hammam – Turkish bath.
Hanuman – monkey god.
Harijan – literally 'Children of God', the name Mahatma Gandhi gave to the untouchables.
Hartal – strike.
Haveli – traditional mansions with interior courtyards, particularly in Rajasthan and Gujarat.
Hindol – swing.
Hookah – water pipe for smoking tobacco.
Howdah – framework for carrying people on an elephant's back.
Hypothecated – Indian equivalent of leased or mortgaged. You often see small signs on taxis or auto-rickshaws stating that the vehicle is 'hypothecated' to some bank or other.

Idgah – open enclosure to the west of a town where prayers are offered during the Muslim festival of Id-ul-Zuhara.
Imam – Muslim religious leader.

Imambara – tomb of a Shi'ite Muslim holy man.
IMFL – Indian Made Foreign Liquor – beer or spirits produced in India.
Indra – king of the Vedic gods.

Jaggery – hard, brown sugar-like sweetener made from kitul palm sap.
Janata – people, thus the Janata Party is the People's Party.
Jatakas – tales from the Buddha's various lives.
Jauhar – ritual mass suicide by immolation, traditionally performed by Rajput women at times of military defeat to avoid being dishonoured by their captors.
Jheels – swampy areas.
Ji – honorific title that can be added to the end of almost anything – thus Babaji, Gandhiji.
Juggernauts – huge, extravagantly decorated temple 'cars' dragged through the streets during Hindu festivals.
Jumkahs – earrings.
Jyotorlinga – 12 holy Shiva shrines in India are known as the 12 Jyotorlingas.

Kachahri – see Cutchery.
Kali – Parvati's terrible side.
Karma – fate.
Karmachario – workers.
Kartikiya – god of war, Shiva's son.
Kata – Tibetan prayer shawl, traditionally given to a lama when one is brought into his presence.
Khadi – homespun cloth. Mahatma Gandhi spent much energy in encouraging people to spin their own khadi cloth rather than buy imported English material.
Khalistan – Sikh movement for an independent Punjab.
Khan – Muslim honorific title.
Kibla – niche in the wall to which Muslims look when praying in order to face Mecca.
Kot – fort.
Kothi – residence, house or mansion.
Kotwali – police station.
Krishna – Vishnu's eighth incarnation, often coloured blue.
Kumbh – pitcher.
Kundalini – coiled serpent, the manifestation of Kali, the place at the base of your spine where your shakti resides.
Kurta – shirt.

Lakh – 100,000.

Lama – Tibetan-Buddhist priest or holy man.

Lassi – very refreshing sweet yoghurt and iced-water drink.

Lathi – baton, what Indian police hit you with if you get in the way of a lathi charge.

Laxmi (or Lakshmi) – Vishnu's consort, goddess of wealth, very popular in Bombay.

Lenga – baggy cotton pants.

Lingam – phallic symbol, symbol of Shiva.

Lok – people.

Lok Dal – political party, one of the components of the Janata party.

Lok Sabha – lower house in the Indian parliament, comparable to the House of Representatives or House of Commons.

Lungi – like a sarong.

Mahabharata – Vedic epics, one of the two major Hindu epics.

Mahal – house or palace.

Maharaja – Hindu king.

Mahatma – literally 'great soul'.

Mahayana – large-vehicle Buddhism.

Mahout – elephant rider/master.

Maidan – open place or square.

Makara – crocodile.

Mali – gardener.

Mandala – Tibetan geometrical and astrological representation of the world.

Mandapam – pillared pavilion in front of a temple.

Mandir – temple.

Mani stone – stone carved with the Tibetan-Buddhist chant 'Om mani padme hum' or 'Hail to the jewel in the lotus'.

Mantra – prayer formula or chant.

Mantra-shakti – priest power.

Mara – Buddhist god of death, has three eyes and holds the wheel of life.

Maratha (Mahratta) – war-like central Indian race who often controlled much of India and gave the Moghuls a lot of trouble.

Masjid – mosque. Jami Masjid is the Friday Mosque or main mosque.

Math – monastery.

Maund – now largely superseded unit of weight.

Mela – a fair.

Memsahib – European married lady, from 'madam-sahib', still more widely used than you'd think.

Mendi – ornate patterns painted on women's hands and feet for important festivals, particularly in Rajasthan. Beauty parlours and bazaar stalls will do it for you.

Mihrab – see Kibla.

Moghul – the Muslim dynasty of Indian emperors; from Babur to Aurangzeb.

Moksha – salvation.

Monsoon – rainy season from around June to October, when it rains virtually every day.

Moorcha – mob march or protest march.

Mughal – same as Moghul.

Muezzin – one who calls Muslims to prayer from the minaret.

Mullah – Muslim scholar, teacher or religious leader.

Munshi – writer, secretary or teacher of languages.

Naga – snake or a person from Nagaland.

Nandi – bull, vehicle of Shiva and usually found at Shiva temples.

Narayan – an incarnation of Vishnu.

Narsimha (Narsingh) – man-lion incarnation of Vishnu.

Nautch Girls – dancing girls, a nautch is a dance.

Nawab – Muslim ruling prince or powerful landowner.

Naxalites – ultra-leftist political movement, started in northern part of West Bengal where it appeared as a rebellion against landlords by peasants. Characterised by extreme violence, it originated in the village of Naxal and is now fairly subdued in West Bengal, but still exists in Uttar Pradesh.

Nilakantha – form of Shiva with blue throat from swallowing poison that would have destroyed the world.

Nilgai – antelope.

Nirvana – the ultimate aim of Buddhist existence, a state where one leaves the cycle of existence and does not have to suffer further rebirths.

Nizam – hereditary title of the rulers of Hyderabad.

Nullah – ditch or small stream.

Numda – Rajasthani rug.

Padyatra – 'foot journey' made by politicians to raise support at the village level.

Pagoda – Buddhist religious monument composed of a solid hemisphere containing relics of the Buddha – also known as a dagoba, stupa or chedi.

Palanquin – box-like enclosure carried on poles on four men's shoulders; the occupant sits inside on a seat.

Pali – the original language in which the Buddhist scriptures were recorded. Scholars still look to the original Pali texts for the true interpretations.

Palia – memorial stone.

Pan – betel nut plus the chewing additives.

Pandit – teacher or wise man. The word is often used in Kashmir where there are many of these. Sometimes used to mean a bookworm.

Peepul – fig tree, especially a bo tree.

Peon – lowest grade clerical worker.

Pice – a quarter of an anna.

Pinjrapol – animal hospital maintained by Jains.

Pranayama – study of breath control.

Prasad – food offering, something you can eat.

Pukkah – proper, very much a Raj-era term.

Puja – offering or prayers.

Punkah – cloth fan, swung by pulling a cord.

Puranas – the ancient Hindu scriptures.

Purdah – isolation in which Muslim women are kept.

Raga – any of several conventional patterns of melody and rhythm that form the basis for freely interpreted compositions.

Railhead – station or town at the end of a railway line, termination point.

Rakhi – amulet.

Raj – rule or sovereignty, but specifically applied to the period of British rule in India.

Raja – king.

Rajput – Hindu warrior caste, royal rulers of Rajasthan.

Ramayana – the story of Rama and Sita and their conflict with Rawana, one of India's most well-known legends and retold in various forms throughout almost all South-East Asia.

Rangoli – design (chalk).

Rani – wife of a princely ruler or a ruler in her own right.

Rasta roko – road block for protest purposes.

Rath – temple chariot or car used in religious festivals.

Raths – rock-cut Dravidian temples at Mahabalipuram.

Rickshaw – two-wheeled vehicle in which one or two passengers are pulled. Only in Calcutta and one or two hill stations do the old man-powered rickshaws still exist. In towns they are now generally bicycle-rickshaws.

Rishis – great sages of old, nowadays applied to any distinguished poet, philosopher or spiritual personality.

Road – railway town which serves as a communication point to a larger town off the line, ie Mt Abu and Abu Road.

Sadhu – ascetic, holy person, one who is trying to achieve enlightenment. They will usually be addressed as 'swamiji' or 'babaji.

Sahib – 'lord', title applied to any gentleman and most Europeans.

Saivaite – (or Shaivaite) follower of Lord Shiva.

Salwar – trousers worn by Punjabi women.

Samadhi – an ecstatic state, sometimes defined as 'ecstasy, trance, communion with God' or 'ecstatic state of mystic consciousness'. Another definition is the place where a holy man was cremated, usually venerated as a shrine.

Sangam – meeting of two rivers.

Sati – 'honourable woman', what a woman becomes if she throws herself on her husband's funeral pyre. Although banned a century or so ago, occasionally satis are still performed.

Satsang – discourse by a swami.

Satyagraha – nonviolent protest involving a fast, popularised by Gandhi. From Sanskrit, literally 'insistence on truth'.

Sepoy – private in the infantry.

Serai – place for accommodation of travellers, specifically a caravanserai where camel caravans once stopped.

Shakti – spiritual energy, life force or strength.

Shikar – hunting expedition, now virtually extinct.

Shikara – gondola-like boat used on Dal Lake in Kashmir.

Shirting – material shirts are made out of.

Sikhara – Hindu temple spire or temple.

Sirdar – leader or commander.

Sitar – Indian stringed instrument.

Sof – aniseed seeds, comes with the bill after a meal and you chew a pinch of it as a digestive.

Sonam – karma built up in successive reincarnations.

Sufi – ascetic Muslim mystic.

Suiting – material suits are made out of.

Swami – title given to initiated monks, means 'lord of the self'.

Sweeper – lowest caste servant, who performs the most menial of tasks.

Syce – groom.

Tabla – a pair of kettle drums which are played with the fingers.

Tank – artificial water-storage lake.

Tantric Buddhism – Tibetan Buddhism with strong sexual and occult overtones.

Tatty – woven grass screen which is wetted and hung outside windows in the hot season to provide a remarkably effective system of air-cooling.

Tempo – noisy three-wheeler public transport vehicle.

Thali – traditional south Indian 'all-you-can-eat' vegetarian meal, very widespread and an excellent, tasty meal – the name derives from the 'thali' plate the food is served on.

Thanka – rectangular Tibetan painting on cloth.

Theravada – small-vehicle Buddhism.

Thirathyatara – sort of pilgrimage.

Thug – follower of thuggee, religious-inspired ritual murderers in the last century.

Tiffin – snack, particularly around lunchtime.

Tirthankars – the 24 great Jain teachers.

Toddy – alcoholic drink, tapped from the palm tree.

Tonga – two-wheeled horse or pony carriage.

Tope – grove of trees, usually mangoes.

Topi – hat, much used by the British in the Raj era.

Torana – architrave over temple entrance.

Trimurti – three-faced Shiva image.

Tripitaka – the classical Theravada Buddhist scriptures, which are divided into three categories, hence its name the 'three baskets'. The Mahayanists have other scriptures in addition.

Tripolia – triple gateway.

Untouchable – lowest caste for whom the most menial tasks are reserved. The name derives from the belief that higher castes risk defilement if they touch one.

Upanishads – ancient Vedic scripts, the last part of the Vedas.

Varuna – supreme Vedic god.

Vedas – ancient spiritual texts, the orthodox Hindu scriptures.

Vihar – monastery.

Vimana – principle part of a Hindu temple.

Wallah – person involved with a specific thing. Can be added onto almost anything – thus dhobi-wallah (clothes washer), taxi-wallah (taxi driver).

Wazir – prime minister.

Yagna – religious self-mortification, such as a snake-yagna where you sit in a cage full of snakes trying to get yourself in the Guinness Book of Records. Being interred alive is another popular yagna feat.

Yakshi – maiden.

Yatra – pilgrimage.

Yoni – vagina, female fertility symbol.

Zamindar – landowner.

Zenana – area of a high-class Muslim household where the women are secluded.

Index

MAPS

THANKS

Writers (apologies if we've misspelt your names) to whom thanks must go include:

Healey & Daisy Abbott (UK), Gianni Acquistapace (It), Mr & Mrs Adams (UK), Scott Adams (Aus), Jennifer Adamson (Aus), Sunil Adesare (I), Indresh Advani, Dev Raj Agarwal (I), Mari-Luise Agius (Aus), Luciano Agresti (It), Bill Aitken (I), Marinus Albers (Nl), JJ Sesma Albizu (Sp), Ilene Aleshive (USA), Ivan D Alexander (USA), H Allan (Om), Tony Allen, Robert Alvis (USA), Martin Ambrose (UK), Nigel Amies (UK), Kamlesh Amin (I), P Anand (I), Robert Andechsbeager, Hans-Erik Andersen (Dk), Lars Anderson (UK), A J Anderson (UK), K Anderson (UK), Patrick Andersson, Kay Andrews (UK), Grant Andrews (NZ), Rick Andriesian, Mr & Mrs Angell (UK), Angus (NZ), Muntajib Ansari (USA), Stan Anson, Renmans Antoon (B), Anz & Judd (C), Helen Apouchtine (A), Mary Archer, Dr John Arlinstall (Aus), Maureen Armstrong (Aus), Chris Armstrong (C), Robert Arnett (USA), Kenneth Ashby (UK), T & M Askham, A Atherton (Aus), Peter Atkin, John Atkinson (UK), Adam Austerfield (UK), David Averbuch, Christian Awuy (In), Louise Aylmer (UK), Anne Bach (Dk), Catherine Baddid (CH), Raja Birendra Bahadur Singh (I), Jody Bailey, Anil Bajaj (I), W B Baker (UK), Garth Baker (NZ), Ruth Baks (Isr), Peter J Balfry (UK), Michael Ball (UK), Patricia Ball, Sanjai Banerji (I), Villa Barbosa (I), Ron Barcikowski (USA), Cecile Baril (USA), Francois Barker (UK), Caroline Barker (UK), Jeffrey Barnes (USA), Chris Barnes (Aus), Dr Gene Barnett (USA), S & S Barratt (Aus), Debbie Barris (CAN), Maes Bart (B), John Bartholomew (UK), David Barton (USA), J & T Bartow (UK), Ira Bashkow (USA), Bonnie Baskin (USA), Arjun Basu (C), Carl Bater (UK), Sergio Battaglia (It), Stephen Beale (UK), Chris Beale (Aus), Teddy Bear (Aus), Dr K G Beauchamp (UK), Alexandre Beaudet (C), Claus Becker (Dk), Rahul Bedi (C), Daphne Bell (NZ), George Bell (USA), Roy Bell (UK), Claire Bendall (UK), Kristina Bengtsson (Sw), Jannine Bennett, Sally Bennett (UK), B & T Berezan (C), David Berg (Aus), Chloe Berman (UK), Sarah Berry (UK), Mark Beshara (Aus), James Best (USA), Bestebreurtje, John Betts (UK), Kees Beukelman (Nl), Catherine Beurle (Aus), Charlene Bevens (USA), S S Bhatia (I), Vijay Bhatia, Jagmohan Bhatia (Aus), H Bhatt (Aus), Anjana Bhattacharya (I), Shyam Bhurke (I), Virat Bhushan (I), Roger Biefer (CH), Gerry Bill (Aus), Raunder Sharma Bindle (I), Via Binnjenbruck (D), D Biran (UK), Jim Bird, Liz & Mike Bissett (UK), Per Bjorkman (Sw), Fiona Black (UK), Dr R Lester Black (UK), Ms Deborah Blackie (I), Sue & Barry Blain (UK), Bill Blair (C), G E Bleasdale (Aus), C Blewett (C), Machiel Blok (Nl), Francis Blondel (B), Ms S J Bloomfield (UK), Kathy & Andrew Bluefield (I), R F de Bode (Nl), Christopher Boenke (D), Paul Boers (Aus), P M Boers (Aus), J & M Dufty Boes (Sw), Odd Bolin (Sw), Andrew Bolton (Aus), Michael Bonin (UK), W E Booth (UK), Ulrike Born (D), Dorus Borst (UK), Marten Bottcher (Dk), Simon Bourke (UK), Chris Bourne (Aus), Ju Bouven (Nl), Myriam Bouverat (CH), Steven Bower (USA), David Bowles (UK), Michael Bowman, Susan Boyce (Aus), Caroline Boyd (UK), Hannah Bradby (UK), Mark Braddock (NZ), Chris Bradshaw (USA), Grandhi Brahmaji (I), Sheila Brandon (USA), Mariet Brannuijh, Arthur Braun (Aust), Sheila Braun (USA), Suzan Luna Braun (USA), Carlos Catala Bravo (Sp), Judy Brenchley (UK), Cathy Brenchley (UK), Sarah Brennan (UK), David Bressoud (USA), Chris Brewer (UK), Sue Brierly (UK), K Briggs (UK), Frank Briscoe (I), F Briscoe, Kate Broadbent (UK), Eric Bronson (USA), Douglas Brooks (UK), Andrea Broughton (UK), Kenneth Brown (UK), Carolyn Brown (UK), David Brownscombe (Aus), M H Bruce (Aus), Valerie Bruister, Lone Brun-Jensen (Dk), H Asokananda Brust (D), Lorrie Buchanan (USA), Jim Buck (UK), Greg Buckman, Lybb Budi, Bulolo (In), Glen Buras (M), Sylvie Burgener (Sw), Michele Burke (In), Lana Burnstad (C), D Andrew Burr (UK), Serge Burri (Aus), S P Burrows (UK), P Butler (UK), John Butler (UK), Jane Butterfield, Sophie & David Button (UK), Rhian Cadvan-Jones (UK), Sarah Cairns (Aus), Graeme Cairns (NZ), Antonio Calderisi (It), C Callanan (C), Mary Cameron, Patricia Campbell (USA), Clair Canning (UK), Lena & Tony Cansdale (Aus), Diane Caulbett (UK), Jennifer Canvin (UK), Kate & Eric Cape (Aus), M & C Caprio (J), Ralph Carabetta (USA), Jesus Cardenas, Scott Carlsson (USA), Paul & Leslie Carr (UK), Richard Carroll (Ire), Peter Carter (Aus), M Carter (USA), Lee Cass (Aus), Mrs Diane Caulbelt (UK), C Andrew Causey (USA), Catherine Cawood (Aus), Sonja

Ceulemans (B), Thomas Chacko (I), Jonathan Chapman (Aus), Jill Chapman (UK), Keith Charge (UK), Dudley Chignall (Ken), Hong Kuen Chiu (HK), Paula Chivers (USA), Richard Chorley (USA), Herbert Chouinard, Glen Christian (Nl), George Chryssides (UK), Robert Churchill (USA), Adam Chyer (Aus), Charlie Cicerale (USA), Rosa Maria Cimino (It), Ian Clark (UK), Campbell Clarke (Aus), Sue Clarke (UK), Paul Clarke, Leanne & Susan Clarke (NZ), E A M W de Clercq (Nl), David Clilverd (UK), Natalie Coburn (I), Leon Cohen (Aus), Ezra Cohen-Yashar, Don J Cohn (HK), Bruce Coker (UK), Kate Colchongh (UK), Carolyn Cole (Aus), R Collins (Aus), C Collins (UK), Heather Collins (UK), P Collins (UK), Gary Collinson (Aus), Alix Collison (USA), Steven Connell (Aus), Giles Constable, Carol Cooke (UK), Alan & Dinah Cooke (UK), H Coolidge (CH), Stephen Coombs (Aus), Teresa Cooney (Ban), M J Cooper (UK), Ilay A Cooper (UK), Mrs E Cooper, C & I Copper, Annabel Core, Justin Corrfield (UK), Donna Costin (UK), Barry Cottee (UK), Geoff Coulthard (UK), Simon Cowell-Parker (UK), William Cox (USA), Maria & Lars Cranlund (Sw), Mark Crapelle (C), Alan Crawford (UK), Mark Crean (UK), Ineke Crezee (NZ), Maria & Lars Cronlund (Sw), Peter Croome, Justin Cumberlege (UK), Ian Cunningham (In), J Curran (Ire), Anthony Curran (Aus), Robert Curtis (USA), Suzy Curtis (UK), William Curtis (UK), Paul Cusack (Aus), Helen Cushing (Aus), Bruce Cuthbertson (USA), Lucy Cuzneil (UK), Michael D'Sauza (Aus), Cathrine Dahlberg (Sw), Glenn Dais (USA), Erin Ann Daly (USA), Marco Dandola, N Arden Danekas (USA), Achyutagraja Das (I), Thomas Davenport, Mrs A Davidson (UK), Jane Davidson (C), Charlotte Davies (UK), Darlene Davis (Aus), Andy & Alison Dawson (UK), Jaap De Graaf (Nl), Guy De La Rupelle (USA), Roger Deacon (UK), M Dedicoat (UK), Desk Deepak (I), P Dekkers (Nl), Paula Delaney (UK), George Delegas (USA), Marc Denys (B), Steve Derne (I), Rona Dexter (C), G S Dhar (Aus), S S Dhillon (I), C M Dhoot (I), Aires Dias (It), Babette Dibber (I), Alison Dickson (Aus), Prakash Dikshit (I), Tamas Dilian (Isr), Guy Dimond (UK), Susan Disman (USA), Mohan Divakaran (I), Achmad Djimar (In), Tjeerd Djkstra (Nl), Jeremy Dobbs (UK), Jose Dominic (It), H Donkers (Nl), Peter Dooley (Aus), Yatin Dossa (I), Larry Dougherty (USA), Catherine Douxchamps (B), Nat Dovell (USA), Guido Doyer (UK), Sean oyle (Aus), Eli Dresner (Isr), Bill Driedger, Cathy Driver (UK), Robert Drzisnik (Y), David Du Bois (C), Dusko Dudic (Yog), Jerry & Elspeth Dugdale (UK), Willy Dumoulin (FRA), D B Duncan (Aus), Nicky Dunnington-Jeff (Aus), Gregory Durell (USA), Luca Dussi (It), Cindy Dyball (Aus), Roman Dyer, Lis Dyke (Aus), Gwendoline Grey Eagle (USA), R W Earl (Aus), Christof Ebenig (D), Monica Echaves (I), Stephen Van Eck (USA), O Eck (Thai), Edwin Ederle (D), D W Edgerley (Aus), Julian Edgoose (UK), Louise Edwards (USA), Tony Edwards (UK), Alan Ehnich, Alan Ehrlich (USA), Hans Eijpe (Nl), Serena Eisenberg (USA), Nienlie Eising (Nl), Clare Eisner (UK), R M Eke, Melanie Ellicot (UK), Philip Elliott (Aus), Jell Ellis, Richard Ellis (I), F L & M A Ellis (Aus), E & H van der Elsen (Nl), Emily Engel (UK), Nicola Howson (UK), Aidan English (UK), Eldad Eran (Isr), Mark Errett (C), Victor Esbensen (S), Soren Eskildsen (Dk), Michael & Sandy Essex (In), Steve Estvanik (USA), Tim Evans (Aus), John Everard, Rein Everard (Nl), Sybil Faigin (C), Brian Faithfull (Aus), Carol Falconer (Aus), Leon Falk (USA), Jerry Fardell (Aus), S M Farrington (UK), Marsena Farris (USA), Michael Fasman (USA), Peter Fay, Sabine Feldwieser (D), Ferdinand Fellinger (A), Clint & Ina Ferguson (Nl), Jakes Ferguson (UK), R A Fernandes (I), Patrick Fernandes (I), Keith Fernandez (I), Nerissa Fields (UK), Chloe Fiering (USA), Chris & Julia Finill (UK), Tim Fisher (Aus), Susan Flatau (Dk), T Flemming (USA), K Fletcher (UK), Effie Fletcher (USA), Stuart Flinders (UK), J Flint (UK), Clementel Fobrisic (I), Robert Fogelnest (USA), Marianne Fonseca (I), R Fox (USA), Julie Fox (UK), Ilana & Raffi Frank (Isr), L Miller & J Franklin (USA), Maria Frasse, Frederick (B), Patrick Freeline (USA), Jennifer Freeman (Aus), Marcos Freire (Chi), A Frezmanis (Sw), Solomon Friedburg (USA), Friedrich (D), Andrew Fries (Aus), Gloria Frydman (Aus), Des Fryer (USA), Julien Fudge (UK), John & Shirley Fulan (USA), Alan Furnell, Brian Furze (Aus), Michael Fysh QC (UK), Brian Gabriel (USA), Ann Gallagher (UK), Phil Game (Aus), Kathryn Game (Aus), Rustom Gandhi (I), Sharon Ganton (C), Andy Gardener, Donna Gardiner (USA), Richard Garneau (C), Dale Garton (NZ), Ben Durand-Gasselin (I), Kristin Gaughan (USA), G Gautier, Ian Gay (Aus), Lex Geers, Anne Geib (USA),

Sarah Geiger (Thai), Harry de Gelder (Nl), Anna Gelzer (CH), Ia Genberg (Sw), E G George (I), Mohan Gera (I), Rebecca German (USA), Gloria Germani (It), Marian Gersen (Nl), J Ghosh, Arabella Gibbs (UK), Carol Giddings (UK), Roel Gieler (Nl), Anne Gilbert (UK), Andy Gilbert (UK), Anna Gleeson (UK), Danielle Godfrey (UK), Karen Godley (USA), Marilyn Godmaire (C), Marina Goeman (B), Ellen S Goldberg (I), Luke Golobitsh (D), Patricia Gomes (I), Snowkon W M Gonsalves (I), Yoga Gontama, Susan Goodwin (UK), H Goossens (Nl), Barbara Gordon (C), P Gordon (Aus), Mary Gorman (B), Peter Gorman, Jonathon Gorty, Diana et al Granes (Sp), Catherine Granger (F), Evelyn Greeley (USA), Les Green (Om), Mitch Greenhill (USA), Stephen Greig (Aus), Emyr Griffiths (UK), D C Griffiths (Aus), Kingsley Grimble (UK), Susanne Groble (CH), S Groenewold (Nl), C Luke & R Groom, Olan Grotenhuis (Nl), Gisela Groticke (D), B Grunbauer (Nl), Sumangal Guha (I), D Gullison (C), Bunny Gupta (I), A K Das Gupta (I), Jan Gustafsson (Sw), Gote Gustafsson (Sw), Reinhold Haar (D), E P van Haarst (Nl), Ruth Hackh (D), Tom Hails (USA), Michael Haines (HK), Kathy Haire (Aus), Diane Hall, Andrew Hall (UK), Nigel Hall (UK), J R Hallam (Aus), Sylvie Hamelle (F), Annette Hames (UK), Jan Hamilton (Aus), Doug Hamilton (USA), Steve Hammonan (UK), Soren Hansen (Dk), Fiona Hardy (Aus), Peter & Georgia Harper (Aus), R I Harries, Chris Hart (UK), M Hart (USA), Danny Harty (Ire), Ms Leigh Haskett (UK), John Hatt (UK), Jackie Hawker (UK), Philip Hawks (UK), John Hay, David Hayano (USA), Mike Haylor, Andy Hazell (UK), Corinne Heber (USA), Peter Hedges (UK), Ann Hedreen (USA), Carl J Hefner (USA), C Heij (Nl), Mark Helfer (UK), S C Hellier (UK), Mac vd Helm (Nl), Ian Henderson (UK), Nick Henderson (UK), Arvid Henriksen (Dk), Klaus Hensler (D), Margit Herman (CH), Hans Hermans (USA), Yves Heroux (C), Jeff Herrick (USA), Bernd Herrmann (D), T E Hesse (D), Jane Heyer (C), Kim & Rob Heyman (I), Roger Hickman-Barnes (Aus), C P Hicks (USA), L Higgins (USA), Darrell High (UK), Keith Hill (UK), Myra Hill McLeod (I), Lynda Hillyu (UK), Ulf Hjalmarsson (Sw), Camilla Hjalsted (DK), Mrs D H Hobson (UK), Ellen Hochman (USA), Liz Hodgkinson (UK), Joost Hoeties (Nl), Lauren Hoffman, H Hoffmann (UK), Nils Hogberg (Sw), Bridget & Mike Hogg (Aus), R Holdsworth (Aus), John Hollam (Aus), Miel Hollander (Nl), JC & M Holtes (Nl), Barry Holzman (USA), E vom Hon (Nl), Louise Hope (USA), Ruth Hopf (USA), Floris Hoppener (Nl), Ursula Horn (GER), Jeremy Horner (UK), Scott Horton (USA), James & Debra House (Aus), Mrs M Howarth (UK), Belinda Howell (UK), Aviva S Hoyer (USA), Hoppener, C J L Huculak (C), Janet Huddleston (NZ), Mr Hughes (I), W Hughes (UK), Paul Hughes-Smith (UK), Ross Hume (Aus), Greg Hunt (NZ), Drew Hunton (USA), Abdullah Husin (In), Mark Hutchinson (UK), Pippa Hyde (UK), Lene Illum (Den), Giorgio Ingrami (It), V K Isaac (I), Muhammad Nur Isnaeni (In), Paul Jacoby, Joe James, Lorna James (Aus), Arnold Jamie (Aus), Ronald Jannes (B), Nel Jans (Nl), Tom Janssen (Nl), Hakan Jarskog (Sw), Javier (Sp), V Jeet (I), Genefer Jeffers (UK), Julia Jeffree (UK), Helen Jeffs, Henrik Jensen (Dk), P Jensen (Dk), Soren Jeppesen (DK), PJ Jethi (I), RJ Jethi (I), Jo & Diddy (UK), Sam Joffe (USA), Christian Johannisson (S), Stephen Johansen (Aus), Graeme John (Aus), Murray & Susan Johnson (C), Andy Johnson (UK), Ian Johnston (Aus), R Carlisle & S Johnstone (UK), Malcolm Jones (Aus), Julia Jones, Hazel Jones (Sau), H B Jones (Sau), Gary Jones (UK), Denise Jones (UK), Mohan Joshi (USA), Rosa Jou (Sp), Valerie Joy (Aus), Jan Junge (D), Jan Justesen (USA), Bruno Kahn (F), V S Kane, Karen & Tim (NZ), Gerhard Karl (Aus), Paul Karp (Aus), Nico Karsdorp (Nl), Kryss Katsiavriades (UK), Nathan Katz (USA), Kavido (UK), Ma Dhyan Kavita (I), Stuart Kay (Aus), Sara Kaye (Aus), Michael Keith (USA), Sue Kelly, Richard Kelly, Greg Kempton (Aus), Michael Kerrisb (I), T D Khandelwal (I), Ritu Khanna (Tur), Gopal & Shashi Khattri (UK), L M Khungar (I), Tom Kidman, Andrew Kiefer (Aus), Janice Killen (Aus), Carina Killick (A), Brett King (USA), Nancy King (USA), John King (UK), Jay Kinn (I), Stephanie Kip (USA), Reinhard Kirchof (D), Ray Kitson (Aus), Jan Kleinman (USA), Peter Klesius (D), Richard Knights (Aus), Lousie E Knowles (UK), Katherine Knox (Aus), Michael Koch (USA), Ben Koster (Nl), Suzanne Krakover-Nickel (USA), Klaas Kramer (Nl), Annie Kramer (Nl), Taco Kramer (Nl), Ralph Kramer (UK), Stefan Kressler (Aus), Lars Kristionsson (Sw), Kromann (Dk), E J A Kselik (Nl), Victor Kuijper (Nl), J Kuitse (Nl), J Kullmann (D), Saji Kumar (I), Saji Kumard (I),

Apurba Kundu (UK), M Yunnus Kunju (I), Keith Kurz (USA), Ronen Kuznik (Isr), Mr Samir Kyas (I), P H La Mare (UK), Jan Lampaert (B), B Lanafield (USA), Henrik Lanfeldt (N), Ian Lange (Aus), Tim Langer (UK), Lee Langley (UK), Petra Langwald (D), Fran Lantz (USA), Pete Larrett (USA), Claire Larrivee (Aus), Sheena Latham (Aus), Emile Laumans (I), Martyn Lavender (UK), Susan Lawrence (USA), Dave Lawson (UK), Veronique Le Nalbaut (F), & Foder Leach (Aus), Genevieve Leblanc, Robert Lebovic (Aus), Hanka & Michael Lee (I), Paul Leete (Aus), Henning Lege (D), Markus Lehtipuu (Fin), Jan Lensing (Nl), John M Leo (USA), Grace & John Lerner (C), Patrice Leroy (F), Jacques, Andrew Levin (USA), Mark Lewis (Aus), Adrian Lewis (C), Phoebe Liebig (USA), M & C Linard (F), Dick Lincoln (USA), Dirch Lind (Dk), Linda (USA), Tara de Linde (F), N Z van der Linde-Pulk (Nl), Joan Lindeman (UK), Karen Linden (Sw), David Lindup (Aus), Mary Lingham (Aus), Margit Linnebjerg (Dk), Marie Lippens (B), R Lipsey (UK), Laurie Living (Aus), Richard Livingstone (Aus), Lizzy, C Llewelyn (Aus), Dee Loader-Oliver (UK), Mrs L Alexine Loane (UK), Dr J Lobstein (F), Ruth Lockwood (I), Susan Loochin (I), Michelle Loretz (Aus), Deborah Love (UK), Rowena Love (UK), Rod Lovell (Aus), Adrian Lucas (UK), H Luethe (Nl), Richard Luff (UK), Poul Lundby (Dk), Hilde Lundgaard (N), Steen Lundoer (Dk), Laurie Lunn (USA), Jenny Lunnon (UK), Rosemary Lyndall (Aus), Janice E Lynn (USA), Mrs B MacClement, T Macdonald (USA), Sue Macgregor (Aus), Rachael MacHeese (UK), Niall Mackay (UK), Ross Mackintosh (UK), Ian G Mackley (UK), R H Maclachlan (USA), Mary Kay Macnaughton (USA), Darren Madigan (UK), Jesper M Madsen, Marc Maes (B), Jan Magnasson, Jacqueline Mahieu (Nl), G Maldlakis (Aus), Hakan Mannerskog (Sw), Iain Manson (UK), Beatrice Mantel (CH), Fiona Marchbanks (UK), Lex Marinos (Aus), Ros Markby (I), Paul Marks (Aus), Lee Marks (USA), Arthur Marris (UK), D J Marshall (SL), Leigh Martin (Aus), Richard Martin, Robert A Martin (USA), Katherine Martin (Aus), Debbie Martyr (UK), N Massouridis (G), S Master (I), Philip Mathew (I), H Mathias (It), Pierre Mathieu (J), Peter Mattersdorff (J), Mari Mattheeliwse (Nl), Veronica Matthew (UK), Herdis Matthewman, Sharon & Brian Matthews (Aus), Liz Maudslay (UK), Nicola Mauger (UK), Brent Maupin (USA), Brigette May, George Mayo (C), Kate McCafferty (USA), Dan & Ali McClosky (Aus), Damian J McColl (Aus), Roslyn McConaghy (Aus), Boo McConnell (I), Bridget McCoy (I), Margaret McCulloch (C), Paul & Margo McCuteheon (USA), Steven McDaniel (USA), G McDermott (UK), Joann McDonald (USA), Brenda McDonald (Aus), Rory McDonough (USA), Joce McDowell (Aus), Greg McFetridge (NZ), Helen McGregor, Stephen McIntyre (Bhu), Alex McLean (Aus), Gary McMahon (C), Jill McMurray (Aus), Adrian McNeil (Aus), Kathy McPherrin (C), Trish McPherson (UK), Baul & Barbara Meertens (A), Lynda J Mekkelholt (Aus), Professor I A Melcuk (C), Caron Menashe (Isr), Elaine Mendes (USA), Aury C Mendes (It), Steven Mendoza (Aus), G Mercer (Tan), Stephen Meredith (In), Dino Ferrero Meriino (It), Mohan Gera, Michael (USA), Jaffe Michal (Isr), Erik Michels (Hol), Asne Midtgarden (N), Elva & George Miksevicius (Aus), Stephen Miles (UK), Tom & Geri Millard (C), Robin Miller (UK), Amanda Miller, Grant Miller, Sheila Miller (UK), Christopher G Miller (UK), Warren Mills (Aus), Lorna Milne, Gali Mindel, Jorgen Minster (Sw), A Mirhadi (USA), Pichow Misrachi (Isr), Joanna Mitchell (UK), J & G P Moelder (Nl), J Moelker (Nl), Kristin Moen (N), J Molenaar (Nl), Emmanuel Monjaras (Mex), Simon Monkhouse (UK), Michael Monroe (USA), Louise Montgomery (UK), Giovanni Monti (It), Yubandran Moodley (UK), Kelvin Moody (NZ), Lee Yew Moon, Anthony Moore (UK), Paul F Moose (USA), Iddo Morag (Isr), Mary Anne Morel (C), Kevin & Betta Morgan (Aus), R Allan & G Morgan (UK), Rebecca Morgan (UK), Margaret Morgan (Aus), David & Fiona Morgan (UK), Debra Morris (UK), Gisele Morrissette (C), John Morrow (NZ), Vincenzo Moschini (It), Michael Moss (USA), Prem Motta (I), Jeremy Mottershead (A), Rusty Muchfree (In), James Muffy (UK), Steve Muir (Aus), Arundhati Mukheruee (I), Berthy Muller, June Mullette (Aus), K B Mullins (USA), Mary Munro (NZ), Mary Murphy (Aus), Jon Murray (Aus), Susan Murray (UK), Krishna Murthy (I), Robert Musgrove (USA), Nicola Mussett (UK), Helen Mutch, Bhaskar Muthuswamy (I), Debbie Myers (UK), John Myers (USA), M K B Nagar (I), Wilfried Nagengrast (D), J Nagy (USA), Seema P Nair (I), Sanat Nanavati (I), Nancy & Rob (USA), Saddia Naizal Narewan, Rachma

Natawijaya (INDO), R Z Rachma Natawijaya (In), V Natrajan, L Naylor (UK), Mike Naylor (Aus), Vivian Barslund Nebel (Dk), L Neilson (Aus), Richard Nemeth (USA), Patricia Nessmann (Aus), Lynette Newby (UK), Bob Newman (I), Linda Nichols (USA), Heather Nicholson (Aus), B Andersson Nick Quantock (Dk), Tine Nielsen (Dk), Henrik Hjortshj Nielsen, Rina Nissih (CH), Roberto Nocchieri (It), Patrick Nolan (UK), Patrick Nolan (Aus), Edith Nlot (F), Hellmuth Nordwig (D), Norvin Aus (A), Sue Nuttall (Aus), Tom Nuttjens (UK), Susannah O'Ferrall (UK), Eileen O'Leary (Aus), John O'Neill (Aus), Peter O'Rourke, P O'Sullivan (UK), Brian Oakes (Aus), Paul O'Brien (Aus), S Oelnes (N), Sonja Ohlsson (Sw), Jordi Olle (Sp), Margaret Olmstead, Cael Olsen, Peter Ons (B), Karlien van Oostea (Nl), S Ormiston (Aus), Marc Osborne (Pak), John Osman (Aus), Henry Osmaston (UK), John Oswald (UK), Emily Owen, Malcolm Paes (UK), Shoba Pais (I), Angela Palmer (NZ), Ian C Palmer (USA), Stephen Palmers (UK), Bob Paquin (C), R Park (UK), Russell Parker (Aus), Graham Parker (Aus), Michael Parker (Aus), Carolyn Parkinson (UK), Eliza Parkinson (C), Emma Parsons (UK), Arnold Parzer (F), Christian Paschen (D), Anrea Fratta Pasini (It), Surendra Patel (I), Heather Paterson (Aus), James Paterson (Aus), Rakesh Patial (I), Susan Paton (Aus), T Banambar Patra (I), Ian Patrick (Aus), Patrick & Kaye (Aus), Pam & Derek Patterson (UK), Leni Paul, Nick Peacock (UK), Judy Pearse (UK), Harry Pearson (NZ), Whitney Peckman, Ann Peers (UK), Joanna Pegum (UK), Ev Pejovic (Aus), Euto Pelli, Fernando B Pena (Sp), Ian Percy (Aus), A J Perkins (UK), Harry Peronius (Sw), D V Perry, Deborah Perry (UK), Gronlands Peter Appel (Dk), Th Peters (Nl), Ann Peters (UK), Pernille Petersen (DK), Leonie Petersen (UK), M & P Phelan (Aus), Susan Philipps (USA), Guy & Brigitt Philips, Frederic Pichor (F), Willems Pierre (B), Jan Piesse (Aus), M Pillon (It), Derek Pinchbeck (Aus), Gordon Pincott (UK), Daniel H Pink (USA), Leona & Max Pinsky (C), Assy Pipecidou (G), Eliza Poklewsikoziel (UK), Alberto Poli (It), Jan Pollak (C), Ignace Pollet (B), Mrs Poluan-Lasut (In), Adam Pope (UK), Charles Porter (UK), Diane Porter (Ir), George Porter (UK), Clive Porter (UK), J Posnett, Russell Potter, Dianne Powell (Aus), Varsha Pradip Patel (I), Rajiv Prakash (I), Alan Preston (Aus), Larry Price (Aus), Carol Price-Santo (USA), Rebecca Pride (UK), Masry Prince (USA), Willem Proos (Nl), Robert Pryor (USA), S M T Puister, Professor G Puri (UK), Elaine Purnell (B), Jim Quinn, Feddy von Rabenau (Aus), T Rabern (USA), Suzanne Racunica (Aus), Radiah (In), Andrea Radic (It), P Rae (Aus), I Raeside (UK), Maggie Railton (Aus), Andreas Rametsteiner (A), Ramu (I), Hema Raney (I), John Rath (USA), Michael L Ratner (USA), Helmut Raumann (D), Julie Read (Aus), Lesley Reader (Bhu), C J Reag (I), Hans en Agnes Recourt (Nl), Jeremy Redfern (F), Barbara Reeve (USA), S J Reeve-Tucker (UK), H Refshammer (Dk), Tirtza Regev (Isr), G R Regi (Aus), Gonvant Reissig (I), J L Reissig (USA), Garry Renshaw (Aus), Vera & Reto (CH), Yvonne Rich (USA), Elizabeth Richards (Aus), John Richards (I), Prentis Riddle (USA), Steve Ridgeway (UK), Reinhard Rieger (D), A Rijsdijk (Nl), Sheila Ringqvist (Sw), Mary Dawn Rippell (C), Stefan Rischer (UK), Ian & Andrew Riseley (Aus), Adam Robertson (Aus), Sue Roberts (PNG), Peter Roberts (Aus), Mike & Denise Roberts (UK), Guy Roberts-Holmes (UK), Peter & Susan Robinson (UK), Simon Robinson (Pak), Cristina Rodes (Sp), Sten Rodhe (Sw), M Rodrigues (UK), L Mort & P Rolph (UK), R Ronkin (Aus), S Roper (Kuw), Eitel Rosa (D), Stanley F Rose (USA), Laura Rosenfeld (In), Julian Ross (UK), Morey Rossman, Cristina & Luca Rosso (D), Rebecca Rottberg (USA), Zoe Rowe (UK), Clare Rowntree (UK), Pamela Royle, Hugo Rusbridge (NZ), Bridie Russell (UK), Julia Rux (USA), Paul Ryan (Aus), Harmen Rypkema (Nl), Kirsten Sonderby (Dk), Lorna Sadler-Akhil (USA), Amiruddin Saharuna (In), Kai Sairanen (F), Clive Salmon (UK), James Salmon (UK), B J Salmon (Aus), E Sammer (Nl), Tim Sandberg (C), Shell Sanders (USA), William Sanders (USA), Robert J Sandy (USA), Indra Saputra (In), Jeremy de Sausmarez (Thai), Kamal Saxena (I), Mehleoob Sayed, A Scarpelli (It), Peter Schatz (Aus), John Schaumburg (USA), M Schawlann (N), A L Scheepers (I), Reimer Schefold, Birgit Schindler (D), Barbara Schirmer (CH), L Schmidbauer (Aus), Peter Schmidt, David & Diane Schofield (Aus), George E Scholz, Vivienne Schroder (Aus), Aleida Schudde (Nl), Mike Schwab (D), Doris Schwartz (USA), Gitte Schwartz (Dk), Sandy Scott (UK), Carol & Chris Seamons, T C Sebastian (USA), Tania Seibelman, Tamsyn Seimon (USA), Josef Seitz (D), Debbi

928

Peter Wilkins, Richard Williams (UK), Shorty
Williams (USA), Brian Williams (J), Tim
Willing (Aus), A V Willis (UK), Jean-Philipe
Wilmshurst (C), Ian Wilson (Aus), Robert
F Winans (USA), Fiona Wingett (UK), R Rosner
(USA), K Winicov (USA), P M Wink (Nl),
John & Susan Winter (C), Georgia Wisbey
(UK), Henrik Wisborg (Dk), Irene Wolf (D),
Maurice Wolfberg (USA), Vivien Wolff (Aus),
James Wolford (USA), Thomas Wolinski
(USA), Andreej Wolski (UK), Jos Lun Hing
Wong (Nl), Alyson & Nicky Wood (UK),
Marianne Woodward (UK), Andrew Wooster
(UK), Jane Worth (UK), Gary Worthington
(USA), Joyce Wouters (Nl), David Wright
(UK), J W Wright (UK), E S Wrigley (Aus),
Chris Wroe (UK), Arthur Wurgler (CH), Chris
Wynant (I), Johansyah Yasin (In), Yaz (UK),
C Y Yong (HK), Richard Young (UK), The
Yowie (Aus), E Ypsilanti, M Yusof (I), Stephan
Zajac (USA), Dr R A Zambardino (UK), Maria

Zanoni, M Zarky (USA), Dick Zegezs (Nl),
Claudia Zeiler (USA), Eileen Zimdahl (Aus),
Rena Ziolkowski (Aus), Paanan Zour (Isr),
C Zuidema (Nl), Marek Zyromski (P).

A – Austria, Aus – Australia, B – Belgium,
Ban – Bangladesh, Bhu – Bhutan, Bra – Brazil,
C – Canada, CH – Switzerland, Chi – China,
Cy – Cyprus, D – West Germany, Dk – Denmark,
F – France, Fin – Finland, G – Greece, HK – Hong
Kong, I – India, In – Indonesia, Ir – Ireland,
Isr – Israel, It – Italy, J – Japan, Ken – Kenya,
Kuw – Kuwait, Mex – Mexico, N – Norway,
Nl – Netherlands, NZ – New Zealand,
Om – Oman, P – Poland, Pak – Pakistan,
Phil – Philippines, PNG – Papua New Guinea,
S – Singapore, SL – Sri Lanka, Sp – Spain,
Sw – Sweden, Tan – Tanzania, Thai – Thailand,
Tur – Turkey, UAE – United Arab Emirates,
UK – United Kingdom, USA – United States of
America

Temperature

To convert °C to °F multiply by 1.8 and add 32

To convert °F to °C subtract 32 and multiply by ·55

Length, Distance & Area

	multiply by
inches to centimetres	2.54
centimetres to inches	0.39
feet to metres	0.30
metres to feet	3.28
yards to metres	0.91
metres to yards	1.09
miles to kilometres	1.61
kilometres to miles	0.62
acres to hectares	0.40
hectares to acres	2.47

Weight

	multiply by
ounces to grams	28.35
grams to ounces	0.035
pounds to kilograms	0.45
kilograms to pounds	2.21
British tons to kilograms	1016
US tons to kilograms	907

A British ton is 2240 lbs, a US ton is 2000 lbs

Volume

	multiply by
Imperial gallons to litres	4.55
litres to imperial gallons	0.22
US gallons to litres	3.79
litres to US gallons	0.26

5 imperial gallons equals 6 US gallons
a litre is slightly more than a US quart, slightly less
than a British one

°C	°F
50	122
45	113
40	104
35	95
30	86
25	75
20	68
15	59
10	50
5	41
0	32

Guides to the Indian Subcontinent

Bangladesh – a travel survival kit
Travel is easy in Bangladesh, with only short distances
between markedly different environments – tropical
forests and beaches, wooded marshlands and jungles,
ancient ruins of temples and palaces, and fascinating
remnants of colonial cultures.

Karakoram Highway, the high road to China – a travel survival kit
Travel in the footsteps of Alexander the Great and Marco
Polo on the Karakoram Highway, following the ancient
and fabled Silk Road. This comprehensive guide also
covers treks and villages away from the highway.

Kashmir, Ladakh & Zanskar – a travel survival kit
Detailed information on three contrasting Himalayan
regions in the Indian state of Jammu and Kashmir – the
narrow valley of Zanskar, the isolated *little Tibet* of
Ladakh, and the stunningly beautiful Vale of Kashmir.

Kathmandu & the Kingdom of Nepal – a travel survival kit
Few travellers can resist the lure of magical Kathmandu
and its surrounding mountains. This guidebook has all
the facts, including information on trekking.

Pakistan – a travel survival kit
Discover 'the unknown land of the Indus' with this
informative guidebook – from bustling Karachi to ancient
cities and tranquil mountain valleys.

Sri Lanka - a travel survival kit
This guidebook uses the restrictions placed on travelling in some parts of Sri Lanka as an incentive to explore other areas more closely – making the most of friendly people, good food and pleasant places to stay – all at reasonable cost.

Trekking in the Indian Himalaya
All the advice you'll need for planning and equipping a trek, including detailed route descriptions for some of the world's most exciting treks.

Trekking in the Nepal Himalaya
Complete trekking information for Nepal, including day-by-day route descriptions and detailed maps – a wealth of advice for both independent and group trekkers.

Also available:
Hindi/Urdu phrasebook, **Nepali** phrasebook, and **Sri Lanka** phrasebook.

Lonely Planet Guidebooks

Lonely Planet guidebooks cover virtually every accessible part of Asia as well as Australia, the Pacific, Central and South America, Africa, the Middle East and parts of North America. There are four main series: 'travel survival kits', covering a single country for a range of budgets; 'shoestring' guides with compact information for low-budget travel in a major region; trekking guides; and 'phrasebooks'.

Australia & the Pacific
Australia
Bushwalking in Australia
Papua New Guinea
Papua New Guinea phrasebook
New Zealand
Tramping in New Zealand
Rarotonga & the Cook Islands
Solomon Islands
Tahiti & French Polynesia
Fiji
Micronesia
Tonga
Samoa

South-East Asia
South-East Asia on a shoestring
Malaysia, Singapore & Brunei
Indonesia
Bali & Lombok
Indonesia phrasebook
Burma
Burmese phrasebook
Thailand
Thai phrasebook
Philippines
Pilipino phrasebook

North-East Asia
North-East Asia on a shoestring
China
China phrasebook
Tibet
Tibet phrasebook
Japan
Japanese phrasebook
Korea
Korean phrasebook
Hong Kong, Macau & Canton
Taiwan

West Asia
West Asia on a shoestring
Trekking in Turkey
Turkey
Turkish phrasebook .

Indian Ocean
Madagascar & Comoros
Maldives & Islands of the East Indian Ocean
Mauritius, Réunion & Seychelles

Mail Order

Lonely Planet guidebooks are distributed worldwide and are sold by good bookshops everywhere. They are also available by mail order from Lonely Planet, so if you have difficulty finding a title please write to us. US and Canadian residents should write to Embarcadero West, 112 Linden St, Oakland CA 94607, USA and residents of other countries to PO Box 617, Hawthorn, Victoria 3122, Australia.

Eastern Europe
Eastern Europe

Indian Subcontinent
India
Hindi/Urdu phrasebook
Kashmir, Ladakh & Zanskar
Trekking in the Indian Himalaya
Pakistan
Kathmandu & the Kingdom of Nepal
Trekking in the Nepal Himalaya
Nepal phrasebook
Sri Lanka
Sri Lanka phrasebook
Bangladesh
Karakoram Highway

Africa
Africa on a shoestring
East Africa
Swahili phrasebook
West Africa
Central Africa
Morocco, Algeria & Tunisia

North America
Canada
Alaska

Mexico
Mexico
Baja California

South America
South America on a shoestring
Ecuador & the Galapagos Islands
Colombia
Chile & Easter Island
Bolivia
Brazil
Brazilian phrasebook
Peru
Argentina
Quechua phrasebook

Middle East
Israel
Egypt & the Sudan
Jordan & Syria
Yemen

Lonely Planet

Lonely Planet published its first book in 1973. Tony and Maureen Wheeler had made a lengthy overland trip from England to Australia and, in response to numerous 'how do you do it?' questions, Tony wrote and they published *Across Asia on the Cheap*. It became an instant local best-seller and inspired thoughts of a second travel guide. A year and a half in South-East Asia resulted in their second book, *South-East Asia on a Shoestring*, which they put together in a backstreet Chinese hotel in Singapore in 1975. The 'yellow book', as it quickly became known, soon became *the* guide to the region and has gone through five editions, always with its familiar yellow cover.

Soon other writers came to them with ideas for similar books – books that went off the beaten track with an adventurous approach to travel, books that 'assumed you knew how to get your luggage off the carousel,' as one reviewer put it. Lonely Planet grew from a kitchen table operation to a spare room and then to its own office. Its international reputation began to grow as the Lonely Planet logo began to appear in more and more countries. In 1982 *India – a travel survival kit* won the Thomas Cook award for the best guidebook of the year.

These days there are over 70 Lonely Planet titles. Over 40 people work at our office in Melbourne, Australia and another half dozen at our US office in Oakland, California.

At first Lonely Planet specialised in the Asia region but these days we are also developing major ranges of guidebooks to the Pacific region, to South America and to Africa. The list of walking guides is growing and Lonely Planet now has a unique series of phrasebooks to 'unusual' languages. The emphasis continues to be on travel for travellers and Tony and Maureen still manage to fit in a number of trips each year and play a very active part in the writing and updating of Lonely Planet's guides.

Keeping guidebooks up to date is a constant battle which requires an ear to the ground and lots of walking, but technology also plays its part. All Lonely Planet guidebooks are now stored and updated on computer, and some authors even take lap-top computers into the field. Lonely Planet is also using computers to draw maps and eventually many of the maps will be stored on disk.

The people at Lonely Planet strongly feel that travellers can make a positive contribution to the countries they visit both by better appreciation of cultures and by the money they spend. In addition the company tries to make a direct contribution to the countries and regions it covers. Since 1986 a percentage of the income from each book has gone to aid groups and associations. This has included donations to famine relief in Africa, to aid projects in India, to agricultural projects in Central America, to Greenpeace's efforts to halt French nuclear testing in the Pacific and to Amnesty International. In 1989 $41,000 was donated by Lonely Planet to these projects.